SAMPSON & TINDALL'S

TEXAS
FAMILY CODE ANNOTATED

WITH RELATED STATE AND FEDERAL STATUTES

ANNOTATIONS BY

JOHN J. SAMPSON
HARRY L. TINDALL
ROBERT O. DAWSON

AUGUST 2004 EDITION

THOMSON
WEST

Mat #: 40187218

West has created this publication to provide you with accurate and authoritative information concerning the subject matter covered. However, this publication was not necessarily prepared by persons licensed to practice law in a particular jurisdiction. West is not engaged in rendering legal or other professional advice, and this publication is not a substitute for the advice of an attorney. If you require legal or other expert advice, you should seek the services of a competent attorney or other professional.

ISBN: 0–314–11094–1

ISSN: 1092–6119

Dedication for the 14th Edition

The 2004 Edition of *Sampson & Tindall's Texas Family Code Annotated* is dedicated to:

Charles G. Childress
Austin, Texas

for his years of dedicated service to improving the practice of family law in Texas.

Co-Director, Children's Rights Clinic
University of Texas School of Law (2001–Present)

Chief Attorney, Field Operations, Legal Division, Texas Department of Protective and Regulatory Services (1997–2001)

Assistant Attorney General, Child Support Division (1987–1995)
IV–D Director (1995–1996)

*

The Authors

John J. Sampson is the William Benjamin Wynne Professor of Law at the University of Texas School of Law, where he has taught since 1970. He has been the editor of the *State Bar Family Law Section Report* since 1976, and a legislative advisor to both Legislative Committees and the Family Law Council since 1975. In 1996, he received the Dan Price Award for his contributions to Texas family law. Professor Sampson served as co-reporter or reporter for the Uniform Interstate Family Support Act, National Conference of Commissioners on Uniform State Laws, from 1990 to the present. In 1993 Texas was the second state to enact UIFSA. Subsequently, the U.S. Congress mandated that 1996 amendments be enacted by all states. Most recently, he completed the comments to additional amendments to UIFSA promulgated in 2001. In 1997, he was appointed to be the reporter for the redraft of the Uniform Parentage Act. The revised act was approved in July, 2000 and enacted by the Texas Legislature in 2001. In Spring 2003 and 2004 he was a member of the U.S. State Dept. Delegation to The Hague, Netherlands, for multilateral negotiations to draft new maintenance convention for international support enforcement. He also was a member of the State Dept. delegation to Costa Rica, Honduras, and El Salvador for bilateral negotiations of support enforcement agreements in Summer, 2002.

Harry L. Tindall is a family law attorney in Houston, Texas, where he has practiced in the firm of Tindall & Foster, P.C. since 1973. He currently serves as Chair of the Joint Editorial Board—Family Law, a joint project of the American Bar Association, American Academy of Matrimonial Lawyers, and the National Conference of Commissioners on Uniform State Laws. He is also a Texas Commissioner, National Conference of Commissioners on Uniform State Laws (1995–2005), where he served as Chair of the drafting committee for the Uniform Parentage Act (2000). He is currently a member of the Board of Trustees, Collaborative Law Institute of Texas.

Robert O. Dawson, the Bryant Smith Chair in Law at the University of Texas School of Law, is the Editor of the *State Bar Juvenile Law Section Report.* He was the principal draftsman of the original Texas Family Code Title 3, enacted in 1973, and of the Texas Determinate Sentencing Act for juveniles. Since 1995, Professor Dawson has been a primary draftsman of the amendments to Title 3, the Juvenile Justice Code.

Angela G. Pence, is a board certified family law attorney in Houston, Texas, where she is a shareholder with the firm of Tindall & Foster, P.C. She currently serves as Immediate Past Chair of the Family Law Section of the Houston Bar Association and is a member of the Texas Family Law Practice Committee for the family law section of the State Bar of Texas.

Guest Commentators

Howard G. Baldwin, Jr., Former First Assistant, Office of the Attorney General of Texas.

Cynthia Bryant, Former Deputy Attorney General for Child Support Enforcement.

Bree Buchanan, Co-Director, Children's Rights Clinic, University of Texas School of Law.

Charles G. Childress, Co-Director, Children's Rights Clinic, University of Texas School of Law.

Honorable David Farr, Associate Judge, 257th District Court, Houston, Texas.

Honorable Toby Goodman, State Representative and Past-Chair, Juvenile Justice and Family Issues Committee.

Honorable J. Andrew Hathcock, Associate Judge, Travis County; Former Associate Judge, Child Protection Court of Central Texas.

Bernard E. Jones, Attorney at Law, Houston, Texas.

Alicia Gray Key, Administrative Director, Texas Office of Court Administration; Former General Counsel for Child Support Enforcement, Office of the Deputy Attorney General.

John V. McShane, Partner, McShane & Davis, L.L.P., Dallas, Texas.

Donald R. Royall, Partner, The Royalls, Houston, Texas.

H. Patrick Sullivan, Director for Judicial Information, Office of Court Administration; Former Director of Federal Policy Analysis, Child Support Enforcement, Office of the Attorney General.

Preface By The Authors

The August 2004 Edition of *Sampson & Tindall's Texas Family Code Annotated*, our 14th annual edition, reports the actions of the 78th Legislature, through the Fourth Called Session.

2003 legislative changes that are prospective in application are maintained in this edition and noted in the legislative history so that the user of the publication is alerted that the former law may apply to an existing case.

As in previous editions, new case citations have been added this year, along with an update of yearly CLE and law review articles.

New with this edition, we have included the Servicemembers Civil Relief Act enacted by the U.S. Congress and approved by the President on December 19, 2003. The act replaces the former Soldiers and Sailors Civil Relief Act.

We are especially grateful to Joyce Sampson and Debbie Steed of Austin for their continued dedication to helping produce this book in record time. Finally, we acknowledge the great assistance of our Attorney Editor, Alex Medrano of Thomson West.

John J. Sampson
University of Texas School of Law
727 Dean Keeton Street
Austin, Texas 78705
Telephone: (512) 232–1267
Fax: (512) 471–6988
E-mail: jsampson@mail.law.utexas.edu

Harry L. Tindall
Tindall & Foster, P.C.
1300 Post Oak Blvd., Suite 1550
Houston, Texas 77056–3081
Telephone: (713) 622–8733
Fax: (713) 622–8744
E-mail: htindall@tindallfoster.com

*

All statutory references, author commentary, legal articles, case citations and other references in this publication are through:

—Legislation—

78th Texas Legislature, Fourth Called Session (2004)

108th Congress, Second Session, Public Law 108–261 (June 25, 2004)

—CLE Materials—

2004 Adv. Fam. L. (San Antonio)

2004 Marriage Dissolution (Fort Worth)

2004 U. Tex. Fam. L. Front Lines (Galveston)

2004 U. Tex. Fam. L. On the Border (El Paso)

—Cases—

132 S.W.3d (June 2004)

www.supremecourts.state.tx.us (June 2004)

*

RELATED PRODUCTS FROM WEST

TEXAS PRACTICE SERIES

Guide to the Texas Rules of Evidence: Civil and Criminal
Steven Goode, Olin Guy Wellborn III, and M. Michael Sharlot

Courtroom Handbook on Texas Evidence
Steven Goode, Olin Guy Wellborn III, and M. Michael Sharlot

Texas Land Titles and Title Examination
Fred A. Lange and Aloysius A. Leopold

Texas Criminal Law
Michael B. Charlton

Texas Criminal Forms and Trial Manual
Michael J. McCormick, Thomas D. Blackwell and Betty Blackwell

Texas Wills
Aloysius A. Leopold and Gerry W. Beyer

Texas Methods of Practice
Frank W. Elliott, John E. Krahmer, Hal M. Bateman, and Nancy Saint–Paul

Texas Foreclosure: Law and Practice
Mike Baggett

Texas Probate and Decedents' Estates
M.K. Woodward and Ernest E. Smith III

Texas Business Organizations
Robert W. Hamilton

Texas Property Taxes
Jay D. Howell, Jr.

Texas Municipal Law and Practice
David B. Brooks

Texas Consumer Rights and Remedies
Stephen G. Cochran

Texas Consumer Law Handbook
Stephen G. Cochran

Texas Juvenile Law and Practice
Thomas S. Morgan and Harold C. Gaither, Jr.

Handbook of Texas Family Law
Don Koons

The Jury Charge in Texas Civil Litigation
Gus M. Hodges and T. Ray Guy

Texas County and Special District Law
David B. Brooks

Texas Workers' Compensation Law and Practice
Karen A. Lerner

Texas Marital Property and Homesteads
Aloysius A. Leopold

Texas Criminal Practice and Procedure
George E. Dix and Robert O. Dawson

Texas Medical Malpractice
Michael P. Penick

Texas Environmental Law
Jeff Civins, Jimmy Alan Hall and Mark K. Sahs

Handbook on Texas Discovery Practice
Alex W. Albright, Charles Herring, Jr. and Robert H. Pemberton

---

WEST'S TEXAS FORMS

Texas Creditors' Remedies and Debtors' Rights—Forms
Allen E. Smith

Texas Administrative Practice—Forms
Steven L. Martin

Texas Business Litigation—Forms and Commentary
Glidden Partners

Texas Minerals, Oil and Gas—Forms
John S. Lowe

Texas Business Enterprises—Forms
Hal M. Bateman

Texas Civil Trial and Appellate Practice—Forms
Frank W. Elliott

Texas Estate Planning—Forms
Donald J. Malouf and Henry J. Lischer

Administration of Decedents' Estates and Guardianships—Forms
Aloysius A. Leopold and Gerry W. Beyer

Texas Real Property—Forms
Gerry W. Beyer

Texas Family Law—Forms
John F. Elder

STATUTES AND CODES

Vernon's Annotated Texas Statutes and Codes

Vernon's Texas Rules Annotated—Civil Procedure, Evidence and Appellate Procedure

Texas Administrative Code

Anderson, Bartlett & East's Texas Uniform Commercial Code Annotated

Carlson's Texas Employment Laws Annotated

Cooper, Hensley & Marshall's Texas Rules of Civil Procedure Annotated

Elliott & Morris' Texas Tax Code Annotated

Gaba's Texas Environmental Laws Annotated

Hampton, Schick & McGehee's Texas Civil Practice and Remedies Code Annotated

Hanby's Texas Rules of Appellate Procedure Annotated

Johanson's Texas Probate Code Annotated

Kinkeade & McColloch's Texas Penal Code Annotated

Roach's Texas Rules of Evidence Annotated

Sampson & Tindall's Texas Family Code Annotated

Texas Business Statutes Annotated

Texas Civil Practice Statutes and Rules Annotated

West's Texas Statutes and Codes

Texas Business and Commerce Code
Texas Civil Practice and Remedies Code
Texas Corporation and Partnership Laws
Texas Criminal and Motor Vehicle Code
Texas Criminal Procedure—Code and Rules
Texas Environmental Laws
Texas Family Code
Texas Insurance Code
Texas Local Government Code
Texas Penal Code
Texas Probate Code
Texas Property Code

CASES

Texas Cases: Covering Southwestern 1st

Texas Cases: Covering Southwestern 2d

Texas Cases: Covering Southwestern 3d

FORMS

Vernon's Texas Code Forms Annotated–UCC Forms

Texas Forms: Legal and Business

Texas Jurisprudence Pleading and Practice Forms 2d

West's Texas Forms

Texas Legal Practice Forms 2d

DIGEST & ENCYCLOPEDIAS

Texas Jurisprudence 3d

West's Texas Digest (1840–1934)

West's Texas Digest 2d (1935–date)

Texas Encyclopedia of Criminal Law

OTHER RESEARCH TOOLS FOR TEXAS

Texas Practice Guide

Texas Family Law Service

West's Complete Texas Family Law (CD–ROM)

Texas Lawdesk Library (CD–ROM)

Texas Litigation Library (CD–ROM)

Texas Practice Series

McDonald & Carlson Texas Civil Practice 2d

Westlaw & KeyCite

Texas Court Rules—State, Federal and Local

Texas Digest

Texas Law Finder

Westlaw

WIN®

WESTCheck® and WESTMATE®

WEST*fax*®

West CD–ROM Libraries™

WESTLAW AND WEST BOOKS
The Ultimate Research System

Many of these products are also available on CD–ROM and online via Westlaw.

To order any of these Texas practice tools, call your West Representative or **1–800–328–9352**.

NEED RESEARCH HELP?

You can get quality research results with free help—call the West Reference Attorney when you have questions concerning Westlaw or West Publications at 1–800–733–2889.

NEED A NEW CASE TODAY?

You can get copies of new court cases faxed to you today—office, courthouse or hotel, anywhere a fax machine is available. Call West*fax* at 1–800–562–2329.

INTERNET ACCESS

Contact the West Editorial Department directly with your questions and suggestions by email at west.editor@thomson.com. Visit West's home page on the World Wide Web at http://west.thomson.com

*

Table of Contents

TEXAS FAMILY CODE

TITLE 1: The Marriage Relationship

Subtitle A: Marriage

Subtitle B: Property Rights and Liabilities

Subtitle C: Dissolution of Marriage

Page

TITLE 3: Juvenile Justice Code

TITLE 4: Protection of the Family

Subtitle A. General Provisions

Subtitle B. Protective Orders

Page

Subtitle E. Protection of the Child

★★★

TEXAS CONSTITUTION AND RELATED TEXAS LAW

Texas Constitution of 1876

Texas Civil Practice and Remedies Code

Texas Code of Criminal Procedure

Texas Government Code

Texas Penal Code

Texas Property Code

★★★

RELATED FEDERAL LAW

Federal Criminal Law

Indian Child Welfare Act of 1978

Federal Income Tax

Full Faith and Credit

International Child Abduction Remedies Act

Servicemembers Civil Relief Act

★★★

TITLE 1
The Marriage Relationship

As amended through the 78th Legislature, Fourth Called Session (2004)

Subtitle A. Marriage.

Subtitle B. Property Rights and Liabilities.

Subtitle C. Dissolution of Marriage.

★★★

Subtitle A. Marriage.

★★★

Chapter 1. General Provisions.

Subchapter A. Definitions

§ 1.001. Applicability of Definitions.

(a) The definitions in this subchapter apply to this title.

(b) Except as provided by this subchapter, the definitions in Chapter 101 apply to terms used in this title.

(c) If, in another part of this title, a term defined by this subchapter has a meaning different from the meaning provided by this subchapter, the meaning of that other provision prevails.

§ 1.002. Court.

"Court" means the district court, juvenile court having the jurisdiction of a district court, or other court expressly given jurisdiction of a suit under this title.

§ 1.003. Suit for Dissolution of Marriage.

"Suit for dissolution of a marriage" includes a suit for divorce or annulment or to declare a marriage void.

Subchapter B. Public Policy

Introductory Comment

Sections 1.101–.103 declare that a marriage is valid unless made void by Chapter 6 *[Suit for Dissolution of Marriage]*. This reflects a long standing rule in American law. More importantly, when there are two or more marriages alleged, the most recent marriage is presumed valid unless the person challenging validity proves the continued existence of a prior marriage.

CLE/Other Legal Publication

Proof and validity of foreign marriage and foreign divorce. Cynthia Rucker Allen, 2002 ADV. FAM. L.

Leading Cases

Rogers v. Office of Personnel Management, 87 F.3d 471 (Fed. Cir. 1996) (first wife's unreasonable delay [35 years] in challenging her husband's purported marriage to second wife is barred by laches)

Davis v. Davis, 521 S.W.2d 603 (Tex. 1975) (landmark case affirming presumption that last marriage is presumed valid)

Texas Employers' Ins. Ass'n v. Elder, 282 S.W.2d 371 (Tex. 1955) (common law marriage upheld in absence of evidence upholding earlier common law marriage)

Bailey-Mason v. Mason, 122 S.W.3d 894 (Tex. App.—Dallas 2003, pet. denied) (although docket sheet says "divorce granted," no judgment ever presented or signed; undissolved first marriage renders subsequent marriage void)

Jordan v. Jordan, 938 S.W.2d 177 (Tex. App.—Houston [1st Dist.] 1997, no writ) (most recent marriage presumed valid, but fact issue of existence and validity of decedent's second marriage precludes directed verdict for third wife)

Loera v. Loera, 815 S.W.2d 910 (Tex. App.—Corpus Christi 1991, no writ) (presumption of validity of latest marriage, plus 7–year absence, overcomes proof of undissolved first marriage)

Franklin v. Smalldridge, 616 S.W.2d 655 (Tex. Civ. App.—Corpus Christi 1981, no writ) (prior undissolved Mexican marriage bars claim of common law marriage)

Caruso v. Lucius, 448 S.W.2d 711 (Tex. Civ. App.—Austin 1969, writ ref'd n.r.e.) (second marriage void because earlier marriage shown to be undissolved)

---

§ 1.101. Every Marriage Presumed Valid.

In order to promote the public health and welfare and to provide the necessary records, this code specifies detailed rules to be followed in establishing the marriage relationship. However, in order to provide stability for those entering into the marriage relationship in good faith and to provide for an orderly determination of parentage and security for the children of the relationship, it is the policy of this state to preserve and uphold each marriage against claims of invalidity unless a strong reason exists for holding the marriage void or voidable. Therefore, every marriage entered into in this state is presumed to be valid unless expressly made void by Chapter 6 *[Suit for Dissolution of Marriage]* or unless expressly made voidable by Chapter 6 and annulled as provided by that chapter.

§ 1.102. Most Recent Marriage Presumed Valid.

When two or more marriages of a person to different spouses are alleged, the most recent marriage is presumed to be valid as against each marriage that precedes the most recent marriage until one who asserts the validity of a prior marriage proves the validity of the prior marriage.

§ 1.103. Persons Married Elsewhere.

The law of this state applies to persons married elsewhere who are domiciled in this state.

§ 1.104. Capacity of Spouse.

Except as expressly provided by statute or by the constitution, a person, regardless of age, who has been married in accordance with the law of this state has the capacity and power of an adult, including the capacity to contract.

Comment

This section and the following section make clear that a person, without joinder of his or her spouse, has the full power to act independently of the other spouse, including the right to contract. This freedom, however, does not give a spouse the right to sell jointly managed or titled property, § 3.102, or the homestead, § 5.001 *et seq.*, without joinder of the other spouse.

Leading Case

Husband v. Pierce, 800 S.W.2d 661 (Tex. App.—Tyler 1990, no writ) (underage wife had valid common law and Mexican marriages)

---

§ 1.105. Joinder in Civil Suits.

(a) A spouse may sue and be sued without the joinder of the other spouse.

(b) When claims or liabilities are joint and several, the spouses may be joined under the rules relating to joinder of parties generally.

Comment

Historically, a married woman could not sue or be sued without joinder of her husband. This section overturns that antiquated practice and makes clear that a wife may be sued in her individual capacity.

Leading Cases

Cooper v. Texas Gulf Industries, Inc., 513 S.W.2d 200 (Tex. 1974) (a suit naming only the husband is not binding on the wife; doctrine of virtual representation repudiated)

Few v. Charter Oak Fire Insurance Co., 463 S.W.2d 424 (Tex. 1971) (joinder of spouse not required in lawsuit)

---

§ 1.106. Criminal Conversation Not Authorized.

A right of action by one spouse against a third party for criminal conversation is not authorized in this state.

§ 1.107. Alienation of Affection Not Authorized.

A right of action by one spouse against a third party for alienation of affection is not authorized in this state.

Comment

Abolition of the torts of criminal conversation and alienation of affection is consistent with the law of the vast majority of American jurisdictions.

Leading Cases

Smith v. Smith, 126 S.W.3d 660 (Tex. App.—Houston [14th Dist.] 2004) (constitutional for legislature to abolish torts of criminal conversation and alienation of affection)

Helena Laboratories Corp. v. Snyder, 886 S.W.2d 767 (Tex. 1994) (no independent cause of action exists in Texas for negligent interference with the familial relationship)

Stites v. Gillum, 872 S.W.2d 786 (Tex. App.—Fort Worth 1994, writ denied) (suit for interference with familial relationship held to be the same as a suit for alienation of affections)

---

§ 1.108. Promise or Agreement Must be in Writing.

A promise or agreement made on consideration of marriage or nonmarital conjugal cohabitation is not enforceable unless the promise or agreement or a memorandum of the promise or agreement is in writing and signed by the person obligated by the promise or agreement.

Comment

During the 1997 recodification of Title 1, this section was moved from the Business & Commerce Code, where undoubtedly it was often overlooked.

Leading Cases

Braddock v. Braddock, 64 S.W.3d 581 (Tex. App.—Texarkana 2001, no pet.) (divorced couple resumed cohabitation but did not remarry, creating a confidential relationship which was sufficient for the court to impose a constructive trust when a dispute arose over property purchased during the cohabitation)

Littleton v. Prange, 9 S.W.3d 223 (Tex. App.—San Antonio 1999, pet. denied), *cert. denied,* 121 S.Ct. 174 (2000) (transsexual born male cannot become legal spouse of male)

O'Farrill v. Gonzalez, 974 S.W.2d 237 (Tex. App.—San Antonio 1998, pet. denied) (court enforces written contract between unmarried parents for monthly support and oral agreement to pay mortgage)

Zaremba v. Cliburn, 949 S.W.2d 822 (Tex. App.—Fort Worth 1997, writ denied) (no same-sex palimony without written agreement)

CLE/Other Legal Publication

Same sex divorce: where are we now and where are we going? Jennifer Tull, 2003 ADV. FAM. L.

Texas Family Law Practice Manual

Chapter 48. Property Agreements: I. Nonmarital Cohabitation Agreements

---

Chapter 2. The Marriage Relationship.

Subchapter A. Application for Marriage License

Subchapter B. Underage Applicants

Subchapter C. Ceremony and Return of License

Subchapter D. Validity of Marriage

Subchapter E. Marriage Without Formalities

Subchapter F. Rights and Duties of Spouses

Subchapter A. Application for Marriage License

§ 2.001. Marriage License.

(a) A man and a woman desiring to enter into a ceremonial marriage must obtain a marriage license from the county clerk of any county of this state.

(b) A license may not be issued for the marriage of persons of the same sex.

Comment

As originally enacted in 1969, this section referred to "persons desiring to enter into a ceremonial marriage." Because it was believed such language could be read to imply authorization of marriage of persons of the same sex, it was amended in 1973 to make clear that only persons of the opposite sex can marry. Obviously the proponents of the amendment were well ahead of their time to anticipate that same-sex marriages would someday become a matter of public controversy. In response to debate over the validity of such marriages in 1996, the U.S. Congress enacted the Defense of Marriage Act (a.k.a. DOMA), 28 U.S.C.A. § 1738C, *infra*. In 2003 Texas joined almost 40 other states to enact our own version of DOMA, § 6.204. Recognition of Same-Sex Marriage or Civil Union, *infra*.

CLE/Other Legal Publications

Same sex divorce: where are we now and where are we going? Jennifer Tull, 2003 ADV. FAM. L.

Same-sex marriage, choice of law, and public policy. Andrew Koppelman, 76 TEX. L. REV. 921 (1998)

Leading Case

Littleton v. Prange, 9 S.W.3d 223 (Tex. App.—San Antonio 1999, pet. denied), *cert. denied,* 121 S.Ct. 174 (2000) (transsexual born male cannot be spouse of male; marriage limited to man and woman)

Cross Reference

TEX. FAM. CODE ANN. § 2.401. Proof of informal marriage, *infra*

---

§ 2.002. Application for License.

Except as provided by Section 2.006, each person applying for a license must:

(1) appear before the county clerk;

(2) submit the person's proof of identity and age as provided by this subchapter;

(3) provide the information applicable to that person for which spaces are provided in the application for a marriage license;

(4) mark the appropriate boxes provided in the application; and

(5) take the oath printed on the application and sign the application before the county clerk.

§ 2.003. Application for License by Minor.

In addition to the other requirements provided by this chapter, a person under 18 years of age applying for a license must provide to the county clerk:

(1) documents establishing, as provided by Section 2.102, parental consent for the person to the marriage;

(2) documents establishing that a prior marriage of the person has been dissolved; or

(3) a court order granted under Section 2.103 authorizing the marriage of the person.

§ 2.004. Application Form.

(a) The county clerk shall furnish the application form as prescribed by the bureau of vital statistics.

(b) The application form must contain:

(1) a heading entitled "Application for Marriage License, ____________ County, Texas";

(2) spaces for each applicant's full name, including the woman's maiden surname, address, social security number, if any, date of birth, and place of birth, including city, county, and state;

(3) a space for indicating the document tendered by each applicant as proof of identity and age;

(4) spaces for indicating whether each applicant has been divorced within the last 30 days;

(5) printed boxes for each applicant to check "true" or "false" in response to the following statement: "I am not presently married.";

(6) printed boxes for each applicant to check "true" or "false" in response to the following statement: "The other applicant is not related to me as:

(A) an ancestor or descendant, by blood or adoption;

(B) a brother or sister, of the whole or half blood or by adoption;

(C) a parent's brother or sister, of the whole or half blood or by adoption; or

(D) a son or daughter of a brother or sister, of the whole or half blood or by adoption.";

(7) printed boxes for each applicant to check "true" or "false" in response to the following statement: "I am not presently delinquent in the payment of court-ordered child support.";

(8) a printed oath reading: "I SOLEMNLY SWEAR (OR AFFIRM) THAT THE INFORMATION I HAVE GIVEN IN THIS APPLICATION IS CORRECT.";

(9) spaces immediately below the printed oath for the applicants' signatures;

(10) a certificate of the county clerk that:

(A) each applicant made the oath and the date and place that it was made; or

(B) an applicant did not appear personally but the prerequisites for the license have been fulfilled as provided by this chapter;

(11) spaces for indicating the date of the marriage and the county in which the marriage is performed; and

(12) a space for the address to which the applicants desire the completed license to be mailed.

Comment

Largely a statutory directive for clerks, this section provides answers to two questions that sometimes arise. First, an applicant for a marriage license must furnish his or her social security number, if any, which may later prove important for parent locator services. Secondly, while it is unlawful to marry an aunt, uncle, nephew or niece, Texas law does not prohibit marriage of first cousins as some states do.

---

§ 2.005. Proof of Identity and Age.

(a) The county clerk shall require proof of the identity and age of each applicant.

(b) The proof must be established by a certified copy of the applicant's birth certificate or by some certificate, license, or document issued by this state or another state, the United States, or a foreign government.

§ 2.006. Absent Applicant.

(a) If an applicant is unable to appear personally before the county clerk to apply for a marriage license, any adult person or the other applicant may apply on behalf of the absent applicant.

(b) The person applying on behalf of an absent applicant shall provide to the clerk:

(1) the affidavit of the absent applicant as provided by this subchapter;

(2) proof of the identity and age of the absent applicant as provided by this subchapter; and

(3) if required because the absent applicant is a person under 18 years of age, the documents establishing parental consent, documents establishing that a prior marriage has been dissolved, or a court order authorizing the marriage of the absent, underage applicant.

§ 2.007. Affidavit of Absent Applicant.

The affidavit of an absent applicant must include:

(1) the absent applicant's full name, including the maiden surname of a female applicant, address, date of birth, place of birth, including city, county, and state, citizenship, and social security number, if any;

(2) a declaration that the absent applicant has not been divorced within the last 30 days;

(3) a declaration that the absent applicant is:

(A) not presently married; or

(B) married to the other applicant and they wish to marry again;

(4) a declaration that the other applicant is not related to the absent applicant as:

(A) an ancestor or descendant, by blood or adoption;

(B) a brother or sister, of the whole or half blood or by adoption;

(C) a parent's brother or sister, of the whole or half blood or by adoption; or

(D) a son or daughter of a brother or sister, of the whole or half blood or by adoption;

(5) a declaration that the absent applicant desires to marry and the name, age, and address of the person to whom the absent applicant desires to be married;

(6) the approximate date on which the marriage is to occur;

(7) the reason the absent applicant is unable to appear personally before the county clerk for the issuance of the license; and

(8) if the absent applicant will be unable to attend the ceremony, the appointment of any adult, other than the other applicant, to act as proxy for the purpose of participating in the ceremony.

Comment

Sections 2.006 and 2.007, along with § 2.203(b), authorize proxy marriage, largely to accommodate members of the armed services.

---

§ 2.008. Execution of Application by Clerk.

(a) The county clerk shall:

(1) determine that all necessary information, other than the date of the marriage ceremony, the county in which the ceremony is conducted, and the name of the person who performs the ceremony, is recorded on the application and that all necessary documents are submitted;

(2) administer the oath to each applicant appearing before the clerk;

(3) have each applicant appearing before the clerk sign the application in the clerk's presence; and

(4) execute the clerk's certificate on the application.

(b) A person appearing before the clerk on behalf of an absent applicant is not required to take the oath on behalf of the absent applicant.

§ 2.009. Issuance of License.

(a) Except as provided by Subsections (b) and (d), the county clerk may not issue a license if either applicant:

(1) fails to provide the information required by this subchapter;

(2) fails to submit proof of age and identity;

(3) is under 14 years of age and has not been granted a court order as provided by Section 2.103;

(4) is 14 years of age or older but under 18 years of age and has not presented at least one of the following:

(A) parental consent as provided by Section 2.102;

(B) documents establishing that a prior marriage of the applicant has been dissolved; or

(C) a court order as provided by Section 2.103;

(5) checks "false" in response to a statement in the application, except as provided by Subsection (b) or (d), or fails to make a required declaration in an affidavit required of an absent applicant; or

(6) indicates that the applicant has been divorced by a decree of a court of this state within the last 30 days, unless:

(A) the applicants were divorced from each other; or

(B) the prohibition against remarriage is waived as provided by Section 6.802.

(b) If an applicant checks "false" in response to the statement "I am not presently married," the county clerk shall inquire as to whether the applicant is presently married to the other applicant. If the applicant states that the applicant is currently married to the other applicant, the county clerk shall record that statement on the license before the administration of the oath. The county clerk may not refuse to issue a license on the ground that the applicants are already married to each other.

(c) On the proper execution of the application, the clerk shall:

(1) prepare the license;

(2) enter on the license the names of the licensees, the date that the license is issued, and, if applicable, the name of the person appointed to act as proxy for an absent applicant, if any;

(3) record the time at which the license was issued;

(4) distribute to each applicant printed materials about acquired immune deficiency syndrome (AIDS) and human immunodeficiency virus (HIV) and note on the license that the distribution was made; and

(5) distribute to each applicant a premarital education handbook provided by the attorney general under Section 2.014.

(d) The county clerk may not refuse to issue a license to an applicant on the ground that the applicant checked "false" in response to the statement "I am not presently delinquent in the payment of court-ordered child support."

Comment

The clerk must time-stamp the license at the time of issuance to facilitate enforcing the 72–hour waiting period required by § 2.204. Sections 2.009(c)(4) and 2.010 were added in 1989 as public health concerns developed about AIDS.

---

§ 2.010. AIDS Information.

Materials providing information about acquired immune deficiency syndrome (AIDS) and human immunodeficiency virus (HIV) shall be prepared and provided to the clerk by the Texas Department of Health and shall be designed to inform the applicants about:

(1) the incidence and mode of transmission of AIDS and HIV;

(2) the local availability of medical procedures, including voluntary testing, designed to show or help show whether a person has AIDS or HIV infection, antibodies to HIV, or infection with any other probable causative agent of AIDS; and

(3) available and appropriate counseling services regarding AIDS and HIV infection.

§ 2.011. Recording.

The county clerk shall record all licenses issued by the clerk and all documents submitted with an application for a license or note a summary of the documents on the application.

§ 2.012. Violation by County Clerk; Penalty.

A county clerk or deputy county clerk who violates or fails to comply with this subchapter commits an offense. An offense under this section is a misdemeanor punishable by a fine of not less than $200 and not more than $500.

§ 2.013. Premarital Education Requirements; Waiver.

(a) Each person applying for a marriage license is encouraged to attend a premarital education course of at least four hours during the year preceding the date of the application for the license.

(b) The course under Subsection (a) may be completed by:

(1) personal instruction;

(2) videotape instruction;

(3) instruction through an electronic medium; or

(4) a combination of these methods.

(c) A premarital education course should include instruction in:

(1) conflict management;

(2) communication skills;

(3) children and parenting responsibilities; and

(4) financial responsibilities.

(d) A course under this section should be offered by:

(1) a mental health professional who holds at least a master's degree with a background in family therapy; or

(2) a religious practitioner who performs counseling consistent with the laws of this state or another person designated as a program counselor by a church or religious institution.

(e) Each county clerk may maintain a roster of area course providers who meet the requirements of this section, including providers who offer the course on a sliding scale or without charge. The clerk may provide a copy of the roster on request to an applicant for a marriage license.

(f) An applicant for a marriage license who takes a course under this section shall pay any fee charged for the course.

(g) A person who seeks to be listed as a course provider on a list maintained under Subsection (e) shall notify the county clerk of the county in which the person intends to offer a course. The notification must include the applicant's professional license number or evidence of the person's position or affiliation with a church or religious institution, as appropriate, and an address at which the course provider may be contacted.

§ 2.014. Family Trust Fund.

(a) The family trust fund is created as a trust fund with the state comptroller and shall be administered by the attorney general for the beneficiaries of the fund.

(b) Money in the trust fund is derived from depositing $3 of each marriage license fee as authorized under Section 118.018(c), Local Government Code, and may be used only for:

(1) the development and distribution of a premarital education handbook;

(2) grants to institutions of higher education having academic departments that are capable of research on marriage and divorce that will assist in determining programs, courses, and policies to help strengthen families and assist children whose parents are divorcing;

(3) support for counties to create or administer free or low-cost premarital education courses;

(4) programs intended to reduce the amount of delinquent child support; and

(5) other programs the attorney general determines will assist families in this state.

(c) The premarital education handbook under Subsection (b)(1) shall be distributed to each applicant for a marriage license as provided by Section 2.009(c)(5) and shall contain information on:

(1) conflict management;
(2) communication skills;
(3) children and parenting responsibilities; and
(4) financial responsibilities.

(d) The attorney general shall appoint an advisory committee to assist in the development of the premarital education handbook. The advisory committee shall consist of nine members, including at least three members who are eligible under Section 2.013(d) to provide a premarital education course. A member of the advisory committee is not entitled to reimbursement of the member's expenses.

Subchapter B. Underage Applicants

§ 2.101. General Age Requirement.

Except as otherwise provided by this subchapter or on a showing that a prior marriage has been dissolved, a county clerk may not issue a marriage license if either applicant is under 18 years of age.

Comment

This section establishes the basic rule that the minimum age of marriage without parental or judicial consent is 18 years. This section was amended in 1987 to permit an underage applicant to remarry without parental consent, thereby recognizing that the first marriage emancipated the minor under § 1.104.

§ 2.102. Parental Consent for Underage Applicant.

(a) If an applicant is 14 years of age or older but under 18 years of age, the county clerk shall issue the license if parental consent is given as provided by this section.

(b) Parental consent must be evidenced by a written declaration on a form supplied by the county clerk in which the person consents to the marriage and swears that the person is a parent (if there is no judicially designated managing conservator or guardian of the applicant's person) or a judicially designated managing conservator or guardian (whether an individual, authorized agency, or court) of the applicant's person.

(c) Except as otherwise provided by this section, consent must be acknowledged before a county clerk.

(d) If the person giving parental consent resides in another state, the consent may be acknowledged before an officer authorized to issue marriage licenses in that state.

(e) If the person giving parental consent is unable because of illness or incapacity to comply with the provisions of Subsection (c) or (d), the consent may be acknowledged before any officer authorized to take acknowledgments. A consent under this subsection must be accompanied by a physician's affidavit stating that the person giving parental consent is unable to comply because of illness or incapacity.

(f) Parental consent must be given at the time the application for the marriage license is made or not earlier than the 30th day preceding the date the application is made.

Comment

This section is something of a relic, authorizing as it does an applicant for a marriage license between the ages of 14 and 18 to marry ceremonially with parental consent. Since enactment of Title 1 in 1969, the average age for first marriages has steadily increased, leaving teenage marriages of today as almost an anomaly.

---

§ 2.103. Court Order for Underage Applicant.

(a) A minor may petition the court in the minor's own name for an order granting permission to marry. In a suit under this section, the trial judge may advance the suit if the best interest of the applicant would be served by an early hearing.

(b) The petition must be filed in the county where a parent resides if a managing conservator or a guardian of the person has not been appointed. If a managing conservator or a guardian of the person has been appointed, the petition must be filed in the county where the managing conservator or the guardian of the person resides. If no person authorized to consent to marriage for the minor resides in this state, the petition must be filed in the county where the minor lives.

(c) The petition must include:

(1) a statement of the reasons the minor desires to marry;

(2) a statement of whether each parent is living or is dead;

(3) the name and residence address of each living parent; and

(4) a statement of whether a managing conservator or a guardian of the person has been appointed for the minor.

(d) Process shall be served as in other civil cases on each living parent of the minor or, if a managing conservator or a guardian of the person has been appointed, on the managing conservator or guardian of the person. Citation may be given by publication as in other civil cases, except that notice shall be published one time only.

(e) The court shall appoint a guardian ad litem to represent the minor in the proceeding and to speak for or against the petition in the manner the guardian ad litem believes to be in the best interest of the minor. The court shall specify a fee to be paid by the minor for the services of the guardian ad litem. The fee shall be collected in the same manner as other costs of the proceeding.

(f) If after a hearing the court, sitting without a jury, believes marriage to be in the best interest of the minor, the court, by order, shall grant the minor permission to marry.

Comment

With a court order, there is no minimum age for a ceremonial marriage in Texas—that is, the 14 years minimum for parental consent does not apply. Parents or managing conservators must be served with process if marriage authorization for a child under 18 is sought. Pregnancy is the usual, and as a practical matter probably the only, reason to justify court approval of an underage marriage over the objection of the parents. Approval of underage marriage is left entirely to the court's discretion, to be exercised on a "best interest" basis.

Subchapter C. Ceremony and Return of License

§ 2.201. Expiration of License.

If a marriage ceremony has not been conducted before the 31st day after the date the license is issued, the marriage license expires.

Comment

A marriage license is valid for 30 days. However, because of the 72–hour waiting period required by § 2.204, there is only a 27–day "window" for the marriage ceremony to take place before the license expires. However, the window to seek an annulment of a marriage performed during the 72 hour waiting period is almost as narrow, *i.e.*, 30 days after the ceremony, *see* § 6.110, *infra*.

---

§ 2.202. Persons Authorized to Conduct Ceremony.

(a) The following persons are authorized to conduct a marriage ceremony:

(1) a licensed or ordained Christian minister or priest;

(2) a Jewish rabbi;

(3) a person who is an officer of a religious organization and who is authorized by the organization to conduct a marriage ceremony; and

(4) a justice of the supreme court, judge of the court of criminal appeals, justice of the courts of appeals, judge of the district, county, and probate courts, judge of the county courts at law, judge of the courts of domestic relations, judge of the juvenile courts, retired justice or judge of those courts, justice of the peace, retired justice of the peace, or judge or magistrate of a federal court of this state.

(b) For the purposes of this section, a retired judge or justice is a former judge or justice who is vested in the Judicial Retirement System of Texas Plan One or the Judicial Retirement System of Texas Plan Two or who has an aggregate of at least 12 years of service as judge or justice of any type listed in Subsection (a)(4).

Comment

This section prescribes who may perform marriages, which has often been the subject of legislative maneuvering. Just about the only judicial officers left off the list are former judges (not retired) and municipal court judges.

---

§ 2.203. Ceremony.

(a) On receiving an unexpired marriage license, an authorized person may conduct the marriage ceremony as provided by this subchapter.

(b) A person unable to appear for the ceremony may assent to marriage by the appearance of a proxy appointed in the affidavit authorized by Subchapter A.

§ 2.204. 72-Hour Waiting Period; Exceptions.

(a) Except as provided by this section, a marriage ceremony may not take place during the 72-hour period immediately following the issuance of the marriage license.

(b) The 72-hour waiting period after issuance of a marriage license does not apply to an applicant who:

(1) is a member of the armed forces of the United States and on active duty; or

(2) obtains a written waiver under Subsection (c).

(c) An applicant may request a judge of a court with jurisdiction in family law cases, a justice of the supreme court, a judge of the court of criminal appeals, a county judge, or a judge of a court of appeals for a written waiver permitting the marriage ceremony to take place during the 72-hour period immediately following the issuance of the marriage license. If the judge finds that there is good cause for the marriage to take place during the period, the judge shall sign the waiver. Notwithstanding any other provision of law, a judge under this section has the authority to sign a waiver under this section.

Comment

The 72–hour waiting period after obtaining a license was enacted in 1987. Ostensibly the basis for the law was the argument that applicants were marrying in haste without time for proper reflection. The truth is that suburban justices of the peace lobbied for the change because courthouse J.P.'s were taking the lion's share of the lucrative business of performing marriages. Requiring couples to wait 72 hours makes it unlikely that they will return downtown to get married. In 1995, the statute was amended to permit a "waiver" of the waiting period. Presumably this is less difficult than securing an "order."

---

§ 2.205. Discrimination in Conducting Marriage Prohibited.

(a) A person authorized to conduct a marriage ceremony by this subchapter is prohibited from discriminating on the basis of race, religion, or national origin against an applicant who is otherwise competent to be married.

(b) On a finding by the State Commission on Judicial Conduct that a person has intentionally violated Subsection (a), the commission may recommend to the supreme court that the person be removed from office.

Comment

This section makes clear that discrimination in conducting the ceremony based on race, religion, or national origin is prohibited. Notably missing from the anti-discrimination list is discrimination based on sex. In 2003 the legislature confirmed that the omission was not accidental by enacting § 6.204. Recognition of Same-Sex Marriage or Civil Union, *infra*.

---

§ 2.206. Return of License; Penalty.

(a) The person who conducts a marriage ceremony shall record on the license the date on which and the county in which the ceremony is performed and the person's name, subscribe the license, and return the license to the county clerk who issued it not later than the 30th day after the date the ceremony is conducted.

(b) A person who fails to comply with this section commits an offense. An offense under this section is a misdemeanor punishable by a fine of not less than $200 and not more than $500.

§ 2.207. Marriage Conducted After License Expired; Penalty.

(a) A person who is to conduct a marriage ceremony shall determine whether the license has expired from the county clerk's endorsement on the license.

(b) A person who conducts a marriage ceremony after the marriage license has expired commits an offense. An offense under this section is a misdemeanor punishable by a fine of not less than $200 and not more than $500.

Comment

A marriage license is valid for 30 days. However, because of the 72–hour waiting period required by § 2.204, absent a waiver there is only a 27–day "window" for the marriage ceremony to take place. Note the marriage is valid and that the penalty for engaging in a ceremony based on an expired license may be assessed only against the person who conducted the festivities (this has almost certainly never occurred since the enactment of the Family Code and predictably never will).

---

§ 2.208. Recording and Delivery of License.

(a) The county clerk shall record a returned marriage license and mail the license to the address indicated on the application.

(b) On the application form the county clerk shall record:

(1) the date of the marriage ceremony;

(2) the county in which the ceremony was conducted; and

(3) the name of the person who conducted the ceremony.

§ 2.209. Duplicate License.

(a) On the application and proof of identity of a person whose marriage is recorded in the records of the county clerk, the county clerk shall issue a duplicate marriage license completed with information as contained in the records.

(b) On the application and proof of identity of both persons to whom a marriage license was issued but not recorded as required by Section 2.208, the county clerk shall issue a duplicate license if each person applying submits to the clerk an affidavit stating:

(1) that the persons to whom the original license was issued were married to each other before the expiration date of the original license by a person authorized to conduct a marriage ceremony;

(2) the name of the person who conducted the ceremony; and

(3) the date of the ceremony.

Subchapter D. Validity of Marriage

§ 2.301. Fraud, Mistake, or Illegality in Obtaining License.

Except as otherwise provided by this chapter, the validity of a marriage is not affected by any fraud, mistake, or illegality that occurred in obtaining the marriage license.

Comment

Buttressing the presumption that every marriage is valid, even the very serious defects identified in obtaining the marriage license do not affect the validity of the marriage.

---

§ 2.302. Ceremony Conducted by Unauthorized Person.

The validity of a marriage is not affected by the lack of authority of the person conducting the marriage ceremony if:

(1) there was a reasonable appearance of authority by that person; and

(2) at least one party to the marriage participated in the ceremony in good faith and that party treats the marriage as valid.

Comment

Again, because of the presumption that every marriage is valid, a lack of authority to marry the couple does not affect the marriage if at least one of the parties acted in good faith.

Subchapter E. Marriage Without Formalities

§ 2.401. Proof of Informal Marriage.

(a) In a judicial, administrative, or other proceeding, the marriage of a man and woman may be proved by evidence that:

(1) a declaration of their marriage has been signed as provided by this subchapter; or

(2) the man and woman agreed to be married and after the agreement they lived together in this state as husband and wife and there represented to others that they were married.

(b) If a proceeding in which a marriage is to be proved as provided by Subsection (a)(2) is not commenced before the second anniversary of the date on which the parties separated and ceased living together, it is rebuttably presumed that the parties did not enter into an agreement to be married.

(c) A person under 18 years of age may not:

(1) be a party to an informal marriage; or

(2) execute a declaration of informal marriage under Section 2.402.

Comment

This section sets forth two methods of establishing a common law marriage, either by:

(1) execution of a declaration under § 2.402; or

(2) a "three-prong test," requiring evidence showing:

(i) an "agreement" to be married;

(ii) "cohabitation" in this state; and,

(iii) "holding out" to others that the parties are married.

Although the caption of the subchapter calls it one thing and the caption of the section calls it another, everyone else calls the relationship created by this statute a "common law marriage." Until 1989, "cohabitation" and "holding out" constituted a basis for inferring an agreement—in reality basically creating a two-prong test. In 1995, subsection (b) was amended to provide an evidentiary presumption of no marriage if a suit for proof of marriage was not filed within two years of the parties having "separated and ceased living together." In 1997, subsection (c) was added based on the perception that minors were circumventing the minimum age of 18 by means of an informal marriage.

CLE/Other Legal Publications

Informal marriages and marriages in other states. Laura D. Dale, Susan Myres & Ellen A. Yarrell, 2004 Marriage Dissolution

Common law marriage and rights of putative spouses. Katherine A. Kinser & Julie P. Crawford, 2001 Adv. Fam. L.

Leading Cases

Russell v. Russell, 865 S.W.2d 929 (Tex. 1993) (proof of informal marriage may be established by direct or circumstantial evidence)

Mossler v. Shields, 818 S.W.2d 752 (Tex. 1991) (prior dismissal of suit with prejudice precludes later claim of common law marriage)

Estate of Claveria v. Claveria, 615 S.W.2d 164 (Tex. 1981) (effort to challenge a second marriage by claiming a prior undissolved common law marriage rejected)

Collora v. Navarro, 574 S.W.2d 65 (Tex. 1978) (upholding a directed verdict finding a common law marriage based on uncorroborated testimony of a surviving spouse)

Wilson ex rel. C.M.W. v. Estate of Williams, 99 S.W.3d 640 (Tex. App.—Waco 2003, no pet.) (mother #2 proved common law marriage, thereby obtaining heirship for herself and child presumed to be his child)

Ganesan v. Vallabhaneni, 96 S.W.3d 345 (Tex. App.—Austin 2002, no pet.) (jury had sufficient instructions and evidence to support its finding of common law marriage)

Mills v. Mest, 94 S.W.3d 72 (Tex. App.—Houston [14th Dist.] 2002, no pet.) (cohabitation for over a decade does nothing to prove common law marriage in absence of proof of agreement and holding out)

Reynolds v. Reynolds, 86 S.W.3d 272 (Tex. App.—Austin 2002, no pet.) (no justiciable issue for declaratory judgment on whether Virginia couple have Texas common law marriage)

Amayé v. Oravetz, 57 S.W.3d 581 (Tex. App.—Houston [14th Dist.] 2001, pet. denied) (woman claiming common-law marriage in suit filed more than two years after couple separated bore burden of rebutting presumption of no marriage)

Lee v. Lee, 44 S.W.3d 151 (Tex. App.—Houston [1st Dist.] 2001, pet. denied) (appellate court found no common law marriage—on remand that is law of case)

Eris v. Phares, 39 S.W.3d 708 (Tex. App.—Houston [1st Dist.] 2001, pet. denied) (insufficient evidence on holding out common law marriage by the woman although the man represented marital status to others because she never held herself out as married)

Osteen v. Osteen, 38 S.W.3d 809 (Tex. App.—Houston [14th Dist.] 2001, no pet.) (default divorce defective; claimed "wife" presented no evidence of common law marriage)

In re Osteen, 999 S.W.2d 28 (Tex. App.—Houston [14th Dist.] 1999, no pet.) (error to dismiss second divorce suit alleging new common law marriage because parties previously had divorced)

Nava v. Reddy Partnership/Quail Chase, 988 S.W.2d 346 (Tex. App.—Houston [1st Dist.] 1999, no pet.) (application for widow's social security benefits was requisite proceeding to prove common law marriage)

Ballesteros v. Jones, 985 S.W.2d 485 (Tex. App.—San Antonio 1998, no pet.) (contingent fee in dispute over existence of common law marriage approved)

Lee v. Lee, 981 S.W.2d 903 (Tex. App.—Houston [1st Dist.] 1998, no pet.) ("holding out" requirement is more than isolated introductions)

Allen v. Allen, 966 S.W.2d 658 (Tex. App.—San Antonio 1998, pet. denied) (misleading definition of "cohabitation" submitted to jury—irregular shack-up doesn't qualify)

Jordan v. Jordan, 938 S.W.2d 177 (Tex. App.—Houston [1st Dist.] 1997, no writ) (common law marriage is jury issue)

Dalworth Trucking Co. v. Bulen, 924 S.W.2d 728 (Tex. App.—Texarkana 1996, no writ) (elements of common law marriage may be established by circumstantial evidence)

Welch v. State, 908 S.W.2d 258 (Tex. App.—El Paso 1995, no writ) (common law marriage not established—alleged wife compelled to testify against murderous non-husband)

State v. Mireles, 904 S.W.2d 385 (Tex. App.—Corpus Christi 1995, no writ) (common law marriage prevents wife's testimony about murderous husband's crime)

Georgiades v. DiFerrante, 871 S.W.2d 878 (Tex. App.—Houston [14th Dist.] 1994, writ denied) (marital status may be determined by declaratory judgment)

Collins v. Collins, 870 S.W.2d 682 (Tex. App.—Amarillo 1994, no writ) (then applicable one year limitation to establish common law marriage is an affirmative defense which must be pled)

Flores v. Flores, 847 S.W.2d 648 (Tex. App.—Waco 1993, writ denied) (ex-spouses living together after divorce not enough to prove common law marriage)

Bradley v. Robertson, 832 S.W.2d 199 (Tex. App.—Houston [14th Dist.] 1992, writ dismissed) (death of putative husband does not affect viability of litigation over existence of common law marriage)

Dannelley v. Almond, 827 S.W.2d 582 (Tex. App.—Houston [14th Dist.] 1992, no writ) (then applicable one-year statute of limitations to assert common law marriage is constitutional)

Winfield v. Renfro, 821 S.W.2d 640 (Tex. App.—Houston [1st Dist.] 1991, writ denied) ("holding out in Texas" element not proven to sustain jury finding of common law marriage—jury instruction erroneous)

Husband v. Pierce, 800 S.W.2d 661 (Tex. App.—Tyler 1990, no writ) (underage wife had valid common law and Mexican marriages)

Garduno v. Garduno, 760 S.W.2d 735 (Tex. App.—Corpus Christi 1988, no writ) (common law marriage created when impediment removed)

Cross References

Tex. Fam. Code Ann. § 2.001. Marriage license, *supra*

Tex. Fam. Code Ann. § 6.204. Recognition of Same-Sex Marriage or Civil Union, *infra*

Defense of Marriage Act, 28 U.S.C.A. § 1738C, *infra*

Texas Pattern Jury Charges: Family

PJC 201.4. Existence of Informal Marriage.

---

§ 2.402. Declaration and Registration of Informal Marriage.

(a) A declaration of informal marriage must be signed on a form prescribed by the bureau of vital statistics and provided by the county clerk. Each party to the declaration shall provide the information required in the form.

(b) The declaration form must contain:

(1) a heading entitled "Declaration and Registration of Informal Marriage, ___________ County, Texas";

(2) spaces for each party's full name, including the woman's maiden surname, address, date of birth, place of birth, including city, county, and state, and social security number, if any;

(3) a space for indicating the type of document tendered by each party as proof of age and identity;

(4) printed boxes for each party to check "true" or "false" in response to the following statement: "The other party is not related to me as:

(A) an ancestor or descendant, by blood or adoption;

(B) a brother or sister, of the whole or half blood or by adoption;

(C) a parent's brother or sister, of the whole or half blood or by adoption; or

(D) a son or daughter of a brother or sister, of the whole or half blood or by adoption.";

(5) a printed declaration and oath reading: "I SOLEMNLY SWEAR (OR AFFIRM) THAT WE, THE UNDERSIGNED, ARE MARRIED TO EACH OTHER BY VIRTUE OF THE FOLLOWING FACTS: ON OR ABOUT (DATE) WE AGREED TO BE MARRIED, AND AFTER THAT DATE WE LIVED TOGETHER AS HUSBAND AND WIFE AND IN THIS STATE WE REPRESENTED TO OTHERS THAT WE WERE MARRIED. SINCE THE DATE OF MARRIAGE TO THE OTHER PARTY I HAVE NOT BEEN MARRIED TO ANY OTHER PERSON. THIS DECLARATION IS TRUE AND THE INFORMATION IN IT WHICH I HAVE GIVEN IS CORRECT.";

(6) spaces immediately below the printed declaration and oath for the parties' signatures; and

(7) a certificate of the county clerk that the parties made the declaration and oath and the place and date it was made.

§ 2.403. Proof of Identity and Age.

The county clerk shall require proof of the identity and age of each party to the declaration of informal marriage to be established by a certified copy of the party's birth certificate or by some certificate, license, or document issued by this state or another state, the United States, or a foreign government.

§ 2.404. Recording of Declaration of Informal Marriage.

(a) The county clerk shall:

(1) determine that all necessary information is recorded on the declaration of informal marriage form and that all necessary documents are submitted to the clerk;

(2) administer the oath to each party to the declaration;

(3) have each party sign the declaration in the clerk's presence; and

(4) execute the clerk's certificate to the declaration.

(b) The county clerk may not certify or record the declaration if:

(1) either party fails to supply any information or provide any document required by this subchapter;

(2) either party is under 18 years of age; or

(3) either party checks "false" in response to the statement of relationship to the other party.

(c) On execution of the declaration, the county clerk shall record the declaration and all documents submitted with the declaration or note a summary of them on the declaration form, deliver the original of the declaration to the parties, and send a copy to the bureau of vital statistics.

(d) A declaration recorded as provided in this section is prima facie evidence of the marriage of the parties.

(e) At the time the parties sign the declaration, the clerk shall distribute to each party printed materials about acquired immune deficiency syndrome (AIDS) and human immunodeficiency virus (HIV). The clerk shall note on the declaration that the distribution was made. The materials shall be prepared and provided to the clerk by the Texas Department of Health and shall be designed to inform the parties about:

(1) the incidence and mode of transmission of AIDS and HIV;

(2) the local availability of medical procedures, including voluntary testing, designed to show or help show whether a person has AIDS or HIV infection, antibodies to HIV, or infection with any other probable causative agent of AIDS; and

(3) available and appropriate counseling services regarding AIDS and HIV infection.

§ 2.405. Violation by County Clerk; Penalty.

A county clerk or deputy county clerk who violates this subchapter commits an offense. An offense under this section is a misdemeanor punishable by a fine of not less than $200 and not more than $500.

Subchapter F. Rights and Duties of Spouses

§ 2.501. Duty to Support.

(a) Each spouse has the duty to support the other spouse.

(b) A spouse who fails to discharge the duty of support is liable to any person who provides necessaries to the spouse to whom support is owed.

Comment

This section states the basic rule that spouses have a mutual duty to support each other. The liability of a spouse to a third party who furnished necessaries to a spouse codifies Texas case law. Despite the publicity often given to this provision, it seems to be a dead-letter in today's society. Note that the most recent case cited below is over thirty years old.

Leading Cases

Gabel v. Blackburn Operating Corp., 442 S.W.2d 818 (Tex. Civ. App.—Amarillo 1969, no writ) (husband liable to department store for purchases of necessities by wife)

Jarvis v. Jenkins, 417 S.W.2d 383 (Tex. Civ. App.—Waco 1967, no writ) (airplane ticket held to be a necessary)

Daggett v. Neiman–Marcus Co., 348 S.W.2d 796 (Tex. Civ. App.—Houston [1st Dist.] 1961, no writ) (husband found liable for wife's purchases of clothing consistent with her station in life)

Subtitle B. Property Rights and Liabilities.

★★★

Chapter 3. Marital Property Rights and Liabilities.

Subchapter A. General Rules for Separate and Community Property

Subchapter B. Management, Control, and Disposition of Marital Property

Subchapter C. Marital Property Liabilities

Subchapter D. Management, Control, and Disposition of Marital Property Under Unusual Circumstances

Subchapter E. Claims for Economic Contribution and Reimbursement

---

Subchapter A. General Rules for Separate and Community Property

§ 3.001. Separate Property.

A spouse's separate property consists of:

(1) the property owned or claimed by the spouse before marriage;

(2) the property acquired by the spouse during marriage by gift, devise, or descent; and

(3) the recovery for personal injuries sustained by the spouse during marriage, except any recovery for loss of earning capacity during marriage.

§ 3.002. Community Property.

Community property consists of the property, other than separate property, acquired by either spouse during marriage.

Comment

Texas has operated under a community property system since 1840, although the present marital property regime is substantially different from the original form. Simply stated, property owned before marriage and property acquired during the marriage by gift, devise or descent is a spouse's separate property. Separate property gives the owner exclusive rights of management, is not subject to divestiture at time of divorce, and is solely under the testamentary power of the owner. In 1913, the Legislature initiated a series of laws which ultimately culminated in 1967 in the current system of divided management and control of community property. Essentially, each spouse is free to control, manage and dispose of that community property the spouse would control if single. Absent fraudulent conduct, a spouse is free to spend his or her income, sell or exchange property, and give away property as that spouse sees fit. There may be property that requires joinder of the spouse, such as an account with a financial institution requiring the signature of both parties.

The Matrimonial Property Act of 1967 also gave women for the first time equality of management in their solely managed community property and an equal voice in the management of jointly controlled community property. A significant change instituted by the Act provided that any recovery from personal injury claims remains separate property. This change abolished the community property defense by which the negligence of one spouse would be imputed to the other.

Section 3.002 provides that if property is not shown to be within the definition of separate property, the property is community property. This rule, coupled with the presumption that all property on hand at the time of dissolution of the marriage by death, divorce, or annulment is community property, § 3.003, form the fundamentals of our marital property system.

During the 150 years under the community property system, Texas courts have engrafted a number of rules with which a practitioner must be familiar in order to fathom the complexities of the community property system, to wit:

1. ***Commingling:*** the separate assets of a spouse have been so hopelessly mixed or combined with community assets that they can no longer be traced.

2. ***Inception of title:*** the character of property is determined at the earliest moment to which the claimant can claim title. With regard to real estate, this is generally the signing of the purchase contract, not necessarily the date of the deed.

3. ***Increases:*** the natural increase or decrease in the value of a separate asset. This fluctuation does not affect character.

4. ***Jury:*** Texas, with its unique jury system in family law cases, allows the jury to determine the character of property. However, the judge determines the division of the marital estate; *see* annotations to § 6.703 and §§ 7.001–7.004, *infra*.

5. ***Mutation:*** An asset of a specific character, whether separate or community, retains that character after undergoing a change in form and now exists in the form of another asset. For example, a certificate of deposit owned by a spouse before marriage may be used to purchase an automobile or real estate during marriage. The resulting asset is separate property.

6. ***Non-marital property:*** a potpourri of items, including professional goodwill, certain governmental benefits (usually arising from physical disability), college education, and the specific assets of an organized business entity in which the spouse has an ownership interest.

7. ***Property of mixed character:*** An asset is not necessarily entirely community property or entirely separate property. Because the source of funds used to purchase an asset may come from different marital estates, the resulting asset may be owned in differing percentage interests by the marital estates. A typical example is where one spouse uses separate funds as the down payment on the purchase of a residence, but the general credit of the spouses (*i.e.*, community) is used to secure the balance of the purchase price. An asset acquired in this fashion has mixed character.

8. ***Reimbursement:*** expenditure of the funds from one estate used to benefit another estate giving rise to a claim for equitable reimbursement. The most typical example is the spending of community funds to discharge the mortgage on separately owned real estate. This gives rise to a claim for reimbursement. Reimbursement claims may also be made where community time, toil and effort or community funds are used to enhance a spouse's separate estate. These rules were changed in 1999 and 2001 with the addition of a claim for economic contribution against another marital estate, *see* §§ 3.401–.410, *infra*.

9. ***Retirement benefits:*** Retirement benefits are among the most difficult assets to allocate between separate property and community claims. Determining the separate claim for employment before marriage and its proper allocation for service during marriage can give rise to a number of complexities. Case law is extensive on the subject; the rules are discussed at length in the annotations to § 7.003, *infra*.

10. ***Tracing:*** the documentary evidence necessary to show that an existing asset can be traced back to an asset in another form which was of a particular character—usually separate property. If property of a specified character has been sold, a variety of methods to trace the funds into another asset through the process of mutation have been developed, including:

(a) **Community First-out Method:** If funds from different estates are deposited into a bank account, the first funds withdrawn are presumed to be community property.

(b) **Clearinghouse/Identical Sum Inference Method:** there is a pattern of identifiable deposits and withdrawals of separate funds to and from an account.

(c) **Minimum Sum Balance Method:** the lowest subsequent amount in an account originally containing only separate funds.

(d) **Pro Rata Method:** apportions ownership of an asset purchased with mixed funds in the ratio of the amount of separate and community funds in an account.

11. ***Transfers between spouses:*** Texas has developed an extensive body of case law dealing with transfers of property between spouses and the doctrine of significant recitals. These rules are quite numerous and are discussed in more detail in the articles cited below.

12. ***Trust distributions:*** Depending on the terms of the trust instrument, distributions from a separate property trust may be community or separate.

CLE/Other Legal Publications

Characterization and Tracing

Characterization and tracing. Cheryl L. Wilson, 2004 Adv. Fam. L.

Retirement characterization—preserving separate property. Dawn E. Fowler, 2003 Adv. Fam. L.

Stock options: valuation, characterization and division. Randall B. Wilhite, 2003 Adv. Fam. L.

Marital property and estate planning issues: characterization and attacking trusts, family limited partnerships (FLPs), etc. Michael P. Geary, Gary Stolbach, Diana S. Friedman & David Carlock, 2003 Adv. Fam. L.

Characterization and tracing workshop. Janice L. Green, Thomas L. Ausley, James D. Stewart & J. Kenneth Huff, 2003 Adv. Fam. L.

Marital property and estate planning issues: characterization and attacking trusts, family limited partnerships (FLPs), etc. Michael P. Geary & Gary Stolbach, 2003 Adv. Fam. L.

Characterization and tracing on a budget. Gary L. Nickelson, 2003 Marriage Dissolution

Economic contribution. Thomas A. Greenwald & Bryan C. Rice, 2004 U. Tex. Fam. L. Front Lines

Bank accounts, brokerage accounts, what did I really sign and what does that mean? Wendy S. Burgower, 2003 New Frontiers

Reimbursement

Equitable reimbursement claims without an expert. Cheryl L. Wilson, 2004 Marriage Dissolution

Economic contribution/reimbursement. (Workshop) 2003, 2002 Adv. Fam. L.

Statutory and common law reimbursement. Stewart W. Gagnon & Sonya C. Garza, 2002 Adv. Fam. L.

Miscellaneous Issues

Tort litigation in the family law arena. Wendy S. Burgower, 2004 U. Tex. Fam. L. Front Lines

Torts: economic torts, constructive and actual fraud/fraudulent transfers, excessive gifts, waste, conspiracy and 3rd parties, breach of fiduciary duty, community opportunity doctrine. Wendy S. Burgower & Tommy Fibich, 2003 Adv. Fam. L.

Tort litigation: fiduciary duties of spouses and non-physical torts. Edwin J. Ted Terry, Karl E. Hays, & Andrea Foltz, 2003 U. Tex. Fam. L. Front Lines

Leading Cases

Characterization—Community Property

Douglas v. Delp, 987 S.W.2d 879 (Tex. 1999) (spouse's earning capacity and credit reputation are sole management community property)

Lewis v. Lewis, 944 S.W.2d 630 (Tex. 1997) (worker's compensation benefits for loss of earning capacity are characterized as community)

Broussard v. Tian, 156 Tex. 371, 295 S.W.2d 405 (1956) (payment of community debt with separate property funds does not alter character)

Madrigal v. Madrigal, 115 S.W.3d 32 (Tex. App.—San Antonio 2003, no pet.) (deceased named Wife #1 beneficiary of life insurance proceeds purchased during marriage to Wife #2-absent evidence that gift by deceased was fair, Wife #2 awarded 50% of proceeds)

Alsenz v. Alsenz, 101 S.W.3d 648 (Tex. App.—Houston 1st Dist. 2003, pet. denied) (royalty income from separate property patents received during marriage is community property)

Charriere v. Charriere, 7 S.W.3d 217 (Tex. App.—Dallas 1999, no pet.) (stock options received during marriage but not exercised are community property—whether continued employment is requirement doesn't affect character)

Osborn v. Osborn, 961 S.W.2d 408 (Tex. App.—Houston [1st Dist.] 1997, writ denied) (lost wages, medical costs, and other expenses are community property)

Ridgell v. Ridgell, 960 S.W.2d 144 (Tex. App.—Corpus Christi 1997, no writ) (income earned during marriage by testamentary trust for benefit of wife is community property)

Bodin v. Bodin, 955 S.W.2d 380 (Tex. App.—San Antonio 1997, no writ) (unvested stock options are community property if earned during marriage)

McElwee v. McElwee, 911 S.W.2d 182 (Tex. App.—Houston [1st Dist.] 1995, no writ) (community property mischaracterized as separate property)

Jones v. Jones, 890 S.W.2d 471 (Tex. App.—Corpus Christi 1994, no writ) (no evidence creditor agreed to look only to separate estate of borrower, loan proceeds are community property)

Harris v. Harris, 765 S.W.2d 798 (Tex. App.—Houston [14th Dist.] 1988, writ denied) (only partner's rights are subject to characterization—not individual partnership assets)

Duke v. Duke, 605 S.W.2d 408 (Tex. Civ. App.—El Paso 1980, writ dism'd w.o.j.) (property titled in joint names is prima facie community property)

Characterization—Inception of Title

Welder v. Lambert, 44 S.W. 281 (Tex. 1898) (origin of title determines character of property, not acquisition of final title)

Camp v. Camp, 972 S.W.2d 906 (Tex. App.—Corpus Christi 1998, pet. denied) (inception of title applies to term life insurance)

Winkle v. Winkle, 951 S.W.2d 80 (Tex. App.—Corpus Christi 1997, writ denied) (character determined by small downpayment of community funds—only reimbursement claim for separate property payment of balance of purchase price and construction costs)

Characterization—Mixed

Gleich v. Bongio, 99 S.W.2d 881 (Tex. 1937) (ratio of ownership of property is in proportion to the consideration supplied by the separate and community estates)

Murray v. Murray, 15 S.W.3d 202 (Tex. App.—Texarkana 2000, no pet.) (spouses own real property purchased by them before marriage in proportional percentage contributed by each to the total purchase price)

Characterization—Separate Property

Tarver v. Tarver, 394 S.W.2d 780 (Tex. 1965) (burden of proof on party asserting separate property claim)

Norris v. Vaughan, 260 S.W.2d 676 (Tex. 1953) (royalty payments for oil and gas production held to be separate property)

Arnold v. Leonard, 273 S.W. 799 (Tex. 1925) (Tex. Const. defines separate property, cannot be altered by statute)

In re Marriage of Royal, 107 S.W.3d 846 (Tex. App.—Amarillo 2003, no pet.) (testimony of donor-grandparents regarding gift to husband rebutted by contrary evidence of forgiven loan as gift to couple)

Lee v. Lee, 43 S.W.3d 636 (Tex. App.—Fort Worth 2001, no pet.) (judicial admission that gifts were community property binds donees)

Case v. Case, 28 S.W.3d 154 (Tex. App.—Texarkana 2000, no pet.) (trial court error in characterizing husband's separate property as community requires reversal—character proven by wife's testimony regarding husband's inheritance)

Smith v. Smith, 22 S.W.3d 140 (Tex. App.—Houston [14th Dist.] 1999, no pet.)(tort damages received during marriage for pre-marriage claims are separate property)

Morris v. Morris, 12 S.W.3d 877 (Tex. App.—Texarkana 2000, no pet.) (taking title to husband's separate realty in names of both spouses makes gift to wife of one-half interest)

Licata v. Licata, 11 S.W.3d 269 (Tex. App.—Houston [14th Dist.] 1999, pet. denied) (pain and suffering payments in settlement of personal injury are wife's separate property)

In re Taylor, 992 S.W.2d 616 (Tex. App.—Texarkana 1999, no pet.) (lesson in basic marital property; award of land in first divorce is separate property in second divorce)

Slaton v. Slaton, 987 S.W.2d 180 (Tex. App.—Houston [14th Dist.] 1999, pet. denied) (medical malpractice recovery for injuries to the wife proven to be over 90% her separate property)

Osborn v. Osborn, 961 S.W.2d 408 (Tex. App.—Houston [1st Dist.] 1997, writ denied) (damages for personal injury and loss of consortium are separate property)

Cleaver v. Cleaver, 935 S.W.2d 492 (Tex. App.—Tyler 1996, no writ) (wife's interest in trust was separate property since acquired before marriage)

Lemke v. Lemke, 929 S.W.2d 662 (Tex. App.—Fort Worth 1996, writ denied) (undistributed income from discretionary trust is trust property not community property)

Leighton v. Leighton, 921 S.W.2d 365 (Tex. App.—Houston [1st Dist.] 1996, no writ) (borrowing funds to improve separate property via deed of trust does not alter character of property)

Morrison v. Morrison, 913 S.W.2d 689 (Tex. App.—Texarkana 1995, writ denied) (husband gave wife gift of his share of community realty—continued maintenance by community irrelevant to character of property)

Siefkas v. Siefkas, 902 S.W.2d 72 (Tex. App.—El Paso 1995, no writ) (separate property incorrectly characterized as community)

Burgess v. Easley, 893 S.W.2d 87 (Tex. App.—Dallas 1995, no writ) (deed containing gift of real property signed by grantor during marriage not delivered until after divorce—separate property results)

Walton v. Johnson, 879 S.W.2d 942 (Tex. App.—Tyler 1994, writ denied) (mineral estates inherited by former wife from her father were her separate property)

Celso v. Celso, 864 S.W.2d. 652 (Tex. App.—Tyler 1993, no writ) (jointly titled property shown to be one spouse's separate property)

Pankhurst v. Wertinger & Tucker, 850 S.W.2d 726 (Tex. App.—Corpus Christi 1993, writ denied) (interspousal gift upheld; partition is not the exclusive method of converting community property into separate property)

Johnson v. Holly Farms of Texas, Inc., 731 S.W.2d 641 (Tex. App.—Amarillo 1987, no writ) (damages from wrongful death claim held to be separate property)

Reimbursement

Heggen v. Pemelton, 836 S.W.2d 145 (Tex. 1992) (lien on homestead for reimbursement claim restricted to purchase money, taxes, and mutually agreed upon home improvement)

Penick v. Penick, 783 S.W.2d 194 (Tex. 1988) (reimbursement for debts, taxes, interest or insurance is measured by amount paid less any benefit received)

Anderson v. Gilliland, 684 S.W.2d 673 (Tex. 1985) (reimbursement for improvements to real estate is enhancement in value less any benefit received)

Jensen v. Jensen, 665 S.W.2d 107 (Tex. 1984) (reimbursement for community time, toil and effort allowed less any benefits received)

Vallone v. Vallone, 644 S.W.2d 455 (Tex. 1982) (party seeking reimbursement has burden of proof)

Zeptner v. Zeptner, 111 S.W.3d 727 (Tex. App.—Fort Worth 2003, pet. granted) (trial court's errors on reimbursement issues and characterization sufficiently serious to warrant remand of division of property)

Langston v. Langston, 82 S.W.3d 686 (Tex. App.—Eastland 2002, no pet.) (husband's separate property home cannot be awarded to wife even though community claim for economic contribution may impose lien on property)

Loftis v. Loftis, 40 S.W.3d 160 (Tex. App.—Texarkana 2001, no pet.) (no reimbursement allowed for payments made before marriage)

Case v. Case, 28 S.W.3d 154 (Tex. App.—Texarkana 2001, no pet.) (separate funds used to purchase community property creates prima facie right of reimbursement)

McCann v. McCann, 22 S.W.3d 21 (Tex. App.—Houston [14th Dist.] 2000, pet. denied) (no reimbursement for community funds enhancing separate property without evidence as to enhancement value attributable to community expenditures)

Morris v. Morris, 12 S.W.3d 877 (Tex. App.—Texarkana 2000, no pet.) (trial court failure to identify reimbursement award attributable to reimbursement claims reversible error)

Hilton v. Hilton, 678 S.W.2d 645 (Tex. App.—Houston [14th Dist.] 1984, no writ) (separate estate allowed reimbursement for payment of community obligations)

Tracing

Estate of Hanau v. Hanau, 730 S.W.2d 664 (Tex. 1987) (clearinghouse method: identifiable sums of separate funds deposited, identifiable withdrawals made that clearly identify character of transaction)

Sibley v. Sibley, 286 S.W.2d 658 (Tex. 1955), Welder v. Welder, 794 S.W.2d 420 (Tex. App.—Corpus Christi 1990, no writ) ("community out first"; withdrawals from mixed fund presumed to be community, withdrawals presumed separate only when community funds exhausted)

Osorno v. Osorno, 76 S.W.3d 509 (Tex. App.—Houston [14th Dist.] 2002, no pet.) (husband's testimony regarding financial accounts not enough to trace his separate property claim even given premarital agreement)

Celso v. Celso, 864 S.W.2d 652, 654 (Tex. App.—Tyler 1993, no writ) (separate property retains character through series of exchanges to overcome presumption of community property)

Texas Pattern Jury Charges: Family

PJC 202.1. Separate and Community Property; PJC 202.2. Inception of Title; PJC 202.3. Gift, Devise, and Descent; PJC 202.4. Tracing; PJC 202.5. Property Acquired on Credit; PJC 202.6. Property with Mixed Characterization; PJC 202.11. Separate Property–One Party Claiming Separate Interest; PJC 202.12. Separate Property–Both Parties Claiming Separate Interests; PJC 204.1. Economic Contribution; PJC 204.2. Reimbursement; PJC 204.3. Reimbursement–Advisory Questions.

Cross Reference

Tex. Const., art. XVI, § 15. Separate and Community Property of Husband and Wife.

---

§ 3.003. Presumption of Community Property.

(a) Property possessed by either spouse during or on dissolution of marriage is presumed to be community property.

(b) The degree of proof necessary to establish that property is separate property is clear and convincing evidence.

Comment

The presumption that all property owned by one or both spouses is community property has been part of Texas law since 1840. In 1987, this section was amended to clarify that the burden of proof to establish an item of property as separate is by "clear and convincing evidence."

Leading Cases

Zagorski v. Zagorski, 116 S.W.3d 309 (Tex. App.—Houston [14th] 2003, pet. denied) (testimony and circumstantial documentary evidence rebutted community presumption)

Faram v. Gervitz-Faram, 895 S.W.2d 839 (Tex. App.—Fort Worth 1995, no writ) (tracing separate property overcomes community property presumption)

Walton v. Johnson, 879 S.W.2d 942 (Tex. App.—Tyler 1994, writ denied) (judicial divestiture of one-half of spouse's separate property creates separate property by a means not embraced within the Constitution)

Yaklin v. Glusing, Sharpe & Krueger, 875 S.W.2d 380 (Tex. App.—Corpus Christi 1994, no writ) (husband's stipulation that notes receivable were community property resulted in entire proceeds of notes being community)

Kyles v. Kyles, 832 S.W.2d 194 (Tex. App.—Beaumont 1992, no writ) (presumption of community overcome regarding realty deeded to wife by her family, but not with respect to husband's personal injury settlement)

Welder v. Welder, 794 S.W.2d 420, (Tex. App.—Corpus Christi 1990, no writ) (if community property and separate property are commingled and cannot be resegregated, community property presumption prevails)

Gutierrez v. Gutierrez, 791 S.W.2d 659 (Tex. App.—San Antonio 1990, no writ) (separate property cattle herd commingled with calves, resulting herd is community property)

Allen v. Allen, 704 S.W.2d 600 (Tex. App.—Fort Worth 1986, no writ) (corporation organized during marriage shown to be separate property, funds used to create corporation shown to be separate property)

Whorrall v. Whorrall, 691 S.W.2d 32 (Tex. App.—Austin 1985, writ dism'd w.o.j.) (wife overcame presumption of community property by showing payment came from her separate property)

Roach v. Roach, 672 S.W.2d 524 (Tex. App.—Amarillo 1984, no writ) (inception of title begins with origin of title, not when the title finally vests)

§ 3.004. Recordation of Separate Property.

(a) A subscribed and acknowledged schedule of a spouse's separate property may be recorded in the deed records of the county in which the parties, or one of them, reside and in the county or counties in which the real property is located.

(b) A schedule of a spouse's separate real property is not constructive notice to a good faith purchaser for value or a creditor without actual notice unless the instrument is acknowledged and recorded in the deed records of the county in which the real property is located.

Comment

This section allows for recordation of separate property in the deed records of the county where the property is located. Arguably the section is working quite well because there have been no reported cases since its enactment in 1973; or perhaps very few, if any, people take advantage of this statute.

Cross Reference

TEX. PROP. CODE ANN. § 112.001. Instruments Concerning Property.

§ 3.005. Gifts Between Spouses.

If one spouse makes a gift of property to the other spouse, the gift is presumed to include all the income and property that may arise from that property.

Comment

In 1980, the Texas Constitution was amended to provide that a gift by one spouse to the other is presumed to include all income or property that might arise from the gift. In 1981, the legislature enacted this section to codify the constitutional mandate.

Leading Case

McClure v. McClure, 870 S.W.2d 358 (Tex. App.—Fort Worth 1994, no writ) (conditional spousal gift—donee spouse partially complied with conditions, entitled to opportunity to complete performance of conditions)

Texas Pattern Jury Charges: Family

PJC 202.3. Gift, Devise, and Descent.

---

§ 3.006. Proportional Ownership of Property by Marital Estates.

If the community estate of the spouses and the separate estate of a spouse have an ownership interest in property, the respective ownership interests of the marital estates are determined by the rule of inception of title.

Comment

This relatively innocuous provision establishes the rule for determining the relative ownership interests of the three marital estates in a "mixed title" case. The husband's separate property estate, the wife's separate property estate, and the community estate may jointly own an asset in any of four combinations (H&W; H,W&C: H&C; or W&C).

Subchapter B. Management, Control, and Disposition of Marital Property.

§ 3.101. Managing Separate Property.

Each spouse has the sole management, control, and disposition of that spouse's separate property.

Comment

From 1840 to 1913, the husband managed the separate estates of both spouses. From 1913 to 1967, there was a gradual expansion to ratify a woman's right to manage her own separate estate. Since 1967, both spouses have had equal rights to manage their own separate estates, with one major exception: joinder of both spouses is necessary to convey the family homestead, even if it is the separate property of one spouse. For annotations regarding characterization of property, *see* §§ 3.001–.002, *supra*; for annotations regarding management and liability of property, *see* §§ 3.201–.202, *infra*.

---

§ 3.102. Managing Community Property.

(a) During marriage, each spouse has the sole management, control, and disposition of the community property that the spouse would have owned if single, including:

(1) personal earnings;

(2) revenue from separate property;

(3) recoveries for personal injuries; and

(4) the increase and mutations of, and the revenue from, all property subject to the spouse's sole management, control, and disposition.

(b) If community property subject to the sole management, control, and disposition of one spouse is mixed or combined with community property subject to the sole management, control, and disposition of the other spouse, then the mixed or combined community property is subject to the joint management, control, and disposition of the spouses, unless the spouses provide otherwise by power of attorney in writing or other agreement.

(c) Except as provided by Subsection (a), community property is subject to the joint management, control, and disposition of the spouses unless the spouses provide otherwise by power of attorney in writing or other agreement.

Comment

This section provides for the Texas system of divided management and control of community property. Each spouse is entitled to control that portion of the community property as "if single"; those assets consist of that spouse's earnings, revenues from separate property, recoveries for personal injuries, and the increase and mutations of the first three elements. Solely managed community property that is "mixed or combined" with solely managed community property of the other spouse becomes subject to "joint management" unless the parties otherwise agree. Subsection (c) provides that all other community property will be subject to joint management unless the parties otherwise agree. Courts have struggled to determine whether property is "mixed or combined" and subject to "joint" control.

Leading Cases

Vallone v. Vallone, 644 S.W.2d 455 (Tex. 1982) (discharge of debts by one spouse through bankruptcy does not relieve other spouse of liability to the extent of community property set aside to that spouse in divorce)

Stewart Title Co. v. Huddleston, 608 S.W.2d 611 (Tex. 1980) (wife not personally liable for husband's judgment debt, creditor did not pursue former community property held by her)

Cockerham v. Cockerham, 527 S.W.2d 162 (Tex. 1975) (most often cited as "community debt" case, but actually involves joint action of both spouses)

Cooper v. Texas Gulf Industries, Inc., 513 S.W.2d 200 (Tex. 1974) (suit against a spouse does not bind other spouse under discredited doctrine of virtual representation)

Osuna v. Quintana, 993 S.W.2d 201 (Tex. App.—Corpus Christi 1999, no pet.) (mistress should beware of husband bearing gifts; wife can recover community property conveyed by him)

Owen v. Porter, 796 S.W.2d 265 (Tex. App.—San Antonio 1990, no writ) (creditor successfully attached property of ex-wife where debtor could not demonstrate sole management of community property)

Le Blanc v. Waller, 603 S.W.2d 265 (Tex. Civ. App.—Houston [14th Dist.] 1980, no writ) (guidelines prescribed for "other agreements" allowing for sole management of community property)

Carnes v. Meador, 533 S.W.2d 365 (Tex. Civ. App.—Dallas 1975, writ ref'd n.r.e.) (gift of community property by a spouse to 3rd party will be upheld if there is other community property to reimburse other spouse)

Horlock v. Horlock, 533 S.W.2d 52 (Tex. Civ. App.—Houston [14th Dist.] 1975, writ dism'd w.o.j.) (gift of solely managed community property does not require approval by other spouse)

Texas Pattern Jury Charges: Family

PJC 202.14. Management, Control, and Disposition of Marital Property.

§ 3.103. Managing Earnings of Minor.

Except as provided by Section 264.0111, during the marriage of the parents of an unemancipated minor for whom a managing conservator has not been appointed, the earnings of the minor are subject to the joint management, control, and disposition of the parents of the minor, unless otherwise provided by agreement of the parents or by judicial order.

Comment

This section provides for parental control of a child's earnings, which probably does not reflect reality in the typical family. No doubt most children with jobs manage to exert control over their earnings. No cases have cited this section in more than 25 years.

The cross-reference to § 264.0111 is to a 2001 addition that eliminates the ownership and managerial rights of parents to the accumulated earnings of a child who has been returned home after earning money and establishing a bank account while in state custody. Residential treatment centers commonly encourage such children to earn and manage their own money to improve self-esteem and responsibility.

Cross Reference

TEX. PROB. CODE ANN. § 901. Contracts in Arts, Entertainment, Advertisement and Sports.

§ 3.104. Protection of Third Persons.

(a) During marriage, property is presumed to be subject to the sole management, control, and disposition of a spouse if it is held in that spouse's name, as shown by muniment, contract, deposit of funds, or other evidence of ownership, or if it is in that spouse's possession and is not subject to such evidence of ownership.

(b) A third person dealing with a spouse is entitled to rely, as against the other spouse or anyone claiming from that spouse, on that spouse's authority to deal with the property if:

(1) the property is presumed to be subject to the sole management, control, and disposition of the spouse; and

(2) the person dealing with the spouse:

(A) is not a party to a fraud on the other spouse or another person; and

(B) does not have actual or constructive notice of the spouse's lack of authority.

Comment

This section protects innocent third parties dealing with one spouse in a business transaction, absent fraud or notice of the spouse's lack of authority to deal with the property in question. Millions of transactions occur every day involving Texas community property being bought, sold or transferred by one spouse. The cashing of checks, the use of credit cards, and the purchase of consumer goods ranging from groceries to automobiles are most often done by just one spouse. Whether one spouse can sell his or her interest in jointly titled property without joinder of the spouse has not been definitively resolved.

Leading Cases

Fajkus v. First Nat'l Bank, 735 S.W.2d 882 (Tex. App.—Austin 1987, writ denied) (participation by a spouse in other transactions relating to the property did not overcome presumption of sole managed community property where property was titled in other spouse)

Dalton v. Don J. Jackson, Inc., 691 S.W.2d 765 (Tex. App.—Austin 1985, no writ) (unless both spouses join in sale of jointly titled property there can be no conveyance of any interest)

Subchapter C. Marital Property Liabilities

§ 3.201. Spousal Liability.

(a) A person is personally liable for the acts of the person's spouse only if:

(1) the spouse acts as an agent for the person; or

(2) the spouse incurs a debt for necessaries as provided by Subchapter F, Chapter 2 *[The Marriage Relationship]*.

(b) Except as provided by this subchapter, community property is not subject to a liability that arises from an act of a spouse.

(c) A spouse does not act as an agent for the other spouse solely because of the marriage relationship.

Comment

This section attempts to clarify the ambiguous and amorphous notion of "community liability" or "community debt." Since the Matrimonial Property Act of 1967, it has been the intent of Texas law to mandate that one spouse is not personally liable for the debts of the other spouse, except when the other spouse was acting as an agent for the first spouse or incurring a debt for necessaries. The concept of personal liability of a spouse must be distinguished from the liability imposed on property, both community and separate, which may be subject to execution depending upon the type of obligation. This section attempts to clearly delineate these principles of liability and non-liability of the spouses, and expressly provides that the marriage relationship alone does not create a basis for personal liability. This statute is specifically intended to clarify the misleading and confusing discussion in *Cockerham v. Cockerham*, 527 S.W.2d 162 (Tex. 1975) which actually held that both spouses were personally liable for the debts created by a business primarily, but not exclusively, managed by one of them.

CLE/Other Legal Publication

She got the goldmine, I got the shaft: marital liability between spouses, including responsibility for child's liability. Sondra Kaighen, 2001 Adv. Fam. L.

Leading Cases

Nelson v. Citizens Bank & Trust Co., 881 S.W.2d 128 (Tex. App.—Houston [14th Dist.] 1994, no writ) (wife not personally liable for husband's separate property debt despite signing deed of trust as security)

Carr v. Houston Business Forms, Inc., 794 S.W.2d 849 (Tex. App.—Houston [14th Dist.] 1990, no writ) (the jury must be instructed on relevant factors to determine joint liability of spouses)

Latimer v. City Nat'l Bank, 715 S.W.2d 825 (Tex. App.—Eastland 1986, no writ) (wife has no personal liability for husband's notes)

Humphrey v. Taylor, 673 S.W.2d 954 (Tex. App.—Tyler 1984, no writ) (where wife took no action to ratify debt of husband, there is no joint liability on note)

Miller v. City Nat'l Bank, 594 S.W.2d 823 (Tex. Civ. App.—Waco 1980, no writ) (wife not liable for debts of husband where she has no knowledge of debts)

Texas Pattern Jury Charges: Family

PJC 202.5. Property Acquired on Credit; PJC 202.15. Personal and Marital Property Liability.

---

§ 3.202. Rules of Marital Property Liability.

(a) A spouse's separate property is not subject to liabilities of the other spouse unless both spouses are liable by other rules of law.

(b) Unless both spouses are personally liable as provided by this subchapter, the community property subject to a spouse's sole management, control, and disposition is not subject to:

(1) any liabilities that the other spouse incurred before marriage; or

(2) any nontortious liabilities that the other spouse incurs during marriage.

(c) The community property subject to a spouse's sole or joint management, control, and disposition is subject to the liabilities incurred by the spouse before or during marriage.

(d) All community property is subject to tortious liability of either spouse incurred during marriage.

Comment

As with the Texas system of divided management of community property, a complementary system exists for divided liability of community property. Essentially, each spouse's solely managed community property is liable for that spouse's own obligations, but it is not liable for the other spouse's non-tortious liabilities (almost always meaning contractual liabilities). All community property is liable for tortious conduct of either spouse. This section deals only with liability of property and not with the personal liability of each spouse; that is covered by § 3.201 (*Spousal Liability*).

CLE/Other Legal Publications

In debt up to their ears! Marital liabilities and bankruptcy. Joseph D. Martinec, 2004 ADV. FAM. L.

Bankruptcy. Joseph A. Friedman, 2003 ADV. FAM. L.

Bankruptcy—affirmative use of the Code. Richard T. Chapman, 2002 ADV. FAM. L.

She got the goldmine, I got the shaft: marital liability between spouses, including responsibility for child's liability. Sondra Kaighen, 2001 ADV. FAM. L.

Leading Cases

Carlton v. *Estate of* Estes, 664 S.W.2d 322 (Tex. 1983) (jointly managed community property subject to other spouse's individually incurred debt)

Stewart Title Co. v. Huddleston, 608 S.W.2d 611 (Tex. 1980) (wife not joined in creditors' action against ex-husband, property awarded to her in divorce may be subject to debts incurred during marriage)

Cockerham v. Cockerham, 527 S.W.2d 162 (Tex. 1975) (personal liability of husband for wife's operation of business founded upon doctrine of "implied assent")

Wilkinson v. Stevison, 514 S.W.2d 895 (Tex. 1974) (marital status alone does not impose liability or imputed negligence)

Blake v. Amoco Federal Credit Union, 900 S.W.2d 108 (Tex. App.—Houston [14th Dist.] 1995, no writ) (divorce court cannot alter ex-spouse's liability on joint debt)

Nelson v. Citizens Bank & Trust Co., 881 S.W.2d 128 (Tex. App.—Houston [14th Dist.] 1994, no writ) (wife not personally liable for husband's separate property debt despite signing deed of trust as security)

State Farm Lloyds, Inc. v. Williams, 791 S.W.2d 542 (Tex. App.—Dallas 1990, writ denied) (liability of property is "in rem" judgment, not "personal" judgment against spouse holding property)

Miller v. City Nat'l Bank, 594 S.W.2d 823 (Tex. Civ. App.—Waco 1980, no writ) (ex-wife held not liable for ex-husband's debts incurred during marriage)

Lawrence v. Hardy, 583 S.W.2d 795 (Tex. Civ. App.—San Antonio 1978, writ ref'd n.r.e.) (liability of all community property for tort damages does not make the other spouse "individually" or "personally" liable)

De Anda v. Blake, 562 S.W.2d 497 (Tex. Civ. App.—San Antonio 1978, no writ) (liability of community property for tort liability does not require joinder of spouse)

Pope Photo Records, Inc. v. Malone, 539 S.W.2d 224 (Tex. Civ. App.—Amarillo 1976, no writ) (in absence of evidence demonstrating any knowledge of debt, wife held not liable for late husband's debts)

Texas Pattern Jury Charges: Family

PJC 202.5. Property Acquired on Credit; PJC 202.15. Personal and Marital Property Liability.

---

§ 3.203. Order in Which Property is Subject to Execution.

(a) A judge may determine, as deemed just and equitable, the order in which particular separate or community property is subject to execution and sale to satisfy a judgment, if the property subject to liability for a judgment includes any combination of:

(1) a spouse's separate property;

(2) community property subject to a spouse's sole management, control, and disposition;

(3) community property subject to the other spouse's sole management, control, and disposition; and

(4) community property subject to the spouses' joint management, control, and disposition.

(b) In determining the order in which particular property is subject to execution and sale, the judge shall consider the facts surrounding the transaction or occurrence on which the suit is based.

Comment

This section is commonly called the "marshalling statute." It permits a court to establish a rank order of liability to satisfy any judgment against a spouse. There are no reported cases citing this section since its enactment in 1970.

Subchapter D. Management, Control, and Disposition of Marital Property Under Unusual Circumstances

Introductory Comment

The sections in this subchapter deal with seldom encountered situations in which an unimpaired spouse, not otherwise authorized to manage certain community property, may manage property if the other spouse has become unable to do so for one or more of the specified reasons. In each circumstance, the spouse may petition the court for control and management of the property. If a spouse is judicially declared to be incapacitated, the management of a community estate is governed by Tex. Probate Code §§ 883–884A, Incapacitated Spouse and Community Property. Amendments in 2001 deleted all references to incapacitated spouses in the Family Code, leaving the provisions in the Guardianship chapter of the Probate Code as the sole source of rules governing the management of community property in such fact situations.

---

§ 3.301. Missing, Abandoned, or Separated Spouse.

(a) A spouse may file a sworn petition stating the facts that make it desirable for the petitioning spouse to manage, control, and dispose of community property described or defined in the petition that would otherwise be subject to the sole or joint management, control, and disposition of the other spouse if:

(1) the other spouse has disappeared and that spouse's location remains unknown to the petitioning spouse, unless the spouse is reported to be a prisoner of war or missing on public service;

(2) the other spouse has permanently abandoned the petitioning spouse; or

(3) the spouses are permanently separated.

(b) The petition may be filed in a court in the county in which the petitioner resided at the time the separation began, or the abandonment or disappearance occurred, not earlier than the 60th day after the date of the occurrence of the event. If both spouses are nonresidents of this state at the time the petition is filed, the petition may be filed in a court in a county in which any part of the described or defined community property is located.

§ 3.302. Spouse Missing on Public Service.

(a) If a spouse is reported by an executive department of the United States to be a prisoner of war or missing on the public service of the United States, the spouse of the prisoner of war or missing person may file a sworn petition stating the facts that make it desirable for the petitioner to manage, control, and dispose of the community property described or defined in the petition that would otherwise be subject to the sole or joint management, control, and disposition of the imprisoned or missing spouse.

(b) The petition may be filed in a court in the county in which the petitioner resided at the time the report was made not earlier than six months after the date of the notice that a spouse is reported to be a prisoner of war or missing on public service. If both spouses were nonresidents of this state at the time the report was made, the petition shall be filed in a court in a county in which any part of the described or defined property is located.

§ 3.303. Appointment of Attorney.

(a) Except as provided by Subsection (b), the court may appoint an attorney in a suit filed under this subchapter for the respondent.

(b) The court shall appoint an attorney in a suit filed under this subchapter for a respondent reported to be a prisoner of war or missing on public service.

(c) The court shall allow a reasonable fee for an appointed attorney's services as a part of the costs of the suit.

§ 3.304. Notice of Hearing; Citation.

(a) Notice of the hearing, accompanied by a copy of the petition, shall be issued and served on the attorney representing the respondent, if an attorney has been appointed.

(b) If an attorney has not been appointed for the respondent, citation shall be issued and served on the respondent as in other civil cases.

§ 3.305. Citation by Publication.

(a) If the residence of the respondent, other than a respondent reported to be a prisoner of war or missing on public service, is unknown, citation shall be published in a newspaper of general circulation published in the county in which the petition was filed. If that county has no newspaper of general circulation, citation shall be published in a newspaper of general circulation in an adjacent county or in the nearest county in which a newspaper of general circulation is published.

(b) The notice shall be published once a week for two consecutive weeks before the hearing, but the first notice may not be published after the 20th day before the date set for the hearing.

§ 3.306. Court Order for Management, Control, and Disposition of Community Property.

(a) After hearing the evidence in a suit under this subchapter, the court, on terms the court considers just and equitable, shall render an order describing or defining the community property at issue that will be subject to the management, control, and disposition of each spouse during marriage.

(b) The court may:

(1) impose any condition and restriction the court deems necessary to protect the rights of the respondent;

(2) require a bond conditioned on the faithful administration of the property; and

(3) require payment to the registry of the court of all or a portion of the proceeds of the sale of the property, to be disbursed in accordance with the court's further directions.

§ 3.307. Continuing Jurisdiction of Court; Vacating Original Order.

(a) The court has continuing jurisdiction over the court's order rendered under this subchapter.

(b) On the motion of either spouse, the court shall amend or vacate the original order after notice and hearing if:

(1) the spouse who disappeared reappears;

(2) the abandonment or permanent separation ends; or

(3) the spouse who was reported to be a prisoner of war or missing on public service returns.

§ 3.308. Recording Order to Affect Real Property.

An order authorized by this subchapter affecting real property is not constructive notice to a good faith purchaser for value or to a creditor without actual notice unless the order is recorded in the deed records of the county in which the real property is located.

§ 3.309. Remedies Cumulative.

The remedies provided in this subchapter are cumulative of other rights, powers, and remedies afforded spouses by law.

Subchapter E. Claims for Economic Contribution and Reimbursement

Guest Commentary

State Representative Toby Goodman

Juvenile Justice and Family Issues Committee

Arlington, Texas

Beginning in 1999 and continuing in 2001 and 2003, the legislature addressed the issue of adjusting the claims of a contributing marital estate against a benefited marital estate. The results of these efforts go far to address the inequities of the Texas case law that did not fairly recognize the claims of one marital estate for making an economic contribution to another marital estate.

These amendments make several important changes to the methodology of adjusting the financial equities between marital estates, namely:

- Contribution to the value of a benefited estate is clearly defined to refer to the equity in the property.
- The triggering date for measuring the economic contribution is dependent upon the first date a contributing marital estate makes an economic contribution for the benefit of another marital estate. For example, suppose a residence is owned as separate property by one spouse at time of marriage, and monthly mortgage payments are made during the marriage by the community estate. The triggering date for measurement of the contribution will be the date of the marriage. However, if the property is fully owned before marriage and no mortgage payments are made during the marriage, it may be several years before the community estate advances funds for improvements to the separate property. The economic contribution to value would then be measured from that time forward. A typical example of this is a situation in which one spouse owns unimproved real estate at the time of marriage and later the couple uses community funds and credit to build a home on the property. Note that the payment of the property taxes on the unimproved real estate by community property funds prior to the home construction does not affect the equity of the separate estate, nor is it an improvement to the property. Therefore, the claim of the contributing estate for taxes paid is for reimbursement, not for economic improvement.
- Claims for economic contribution apply equally to both separate property and community property, and the claims apply to all forms of property, not just real property.
- The claim for payment of a debt must be for a specific lien on the benefited property. If the payment is of an unsecured debt, the principles established for the "economic contribution" established by this subchapter are inapplicable. The claim is for common law reimbursement.
- Section 3.406 enumerates the types of payments that give rise to an economic contribution (mortgage reduction, home equity loan reduction, separate property loan reductions, refinancing payments, and capital improvements). Furthermore,

the statute disallows economic contribution claims for payments of maintenance, taxes, interest, and insurance.

- While the formula for measuring the economic contributions may appear at first glance to be quite complicated, in fact its application is relatively simple and straightforward, especially when contrasted with the complexity of the doctrine of reimbursement.
- Basically, the amount of the claim is calculated by dividing the total economic contribution by the total equity in the property and multiplying that percentage by the equity at time of divorce or death. Amendments in 2003 make clear there is no double crediting for contributions.
- There is an express prohibition against offsetting benefits for use and enjoyment of property.
- Liens may be imposed to secure the economic contribution with the recognition that there may be offsetting liens.
- Other forms of reimbursement not specifically covered by Subchapter E are also recognized. One likely example of this is a fact situation in which one spouse brings a significant unsecured debt to the marriage, which subsequently is paid off by community funds. The equitable nature of the reimbursement claim by the community estate may be affected by whether the debt was for a credit card obligation for premarital living expenses or for loans that contributed to the community finances through a premarital business venture.

Below are some examples of how these provisions apply:

Hypothetical fact situation No. 1

Purchase price of residence: $80,000

Down Payment: $15,000

Original Mortgage balance: $65,000

Mortgage reduction before marriage: $15,000

Value of residence on date of marriage: $100,000

Mortgage balance on date of marriage: $50,000

Equity in property on date of marriage: $50,000

Mortgage reduction during marriage: $30,000

Value of residence on date of divorce: $200,000

Mortgage balance on day of divorce: $20,000

Net equity on day of divorce: $180,000

The Formula Is: $30,000 [community payments] divided by the sum of $30,000 [community payments] plus $50,000 [equity on date of marriage] [$30,000/$80,000 equals 37.5%]

This percentage is multiplied times the current equity of $180,000.

The community estate has an economic contribution claim of [37.5% X $180,000] $67,500 in favor of the community.

The separate property interest is $112,500 [$180,000 minus $67,500 or 62.5% of $180,000].

Hypothetical fact situation No. 2

Same as above, but property has not appreciated in value; FMV is still $100,000.

Purchase price of residence: $80,000

Down Payment: $15,000

Original Mortgage balance: $65,000

Mortgage reduction before marriage: $15,000

Value of residence on date of marriage: $100,000

Mortgage balance on date of marriage: $50,000

Equity in property on date of marriage: $50,000

Mortgage reduction during marriage: $30,000

Value of residence on date of divorce: $100,000

Mortgage balance on day of divorce: $20,000

Net equity on day of divorce: $80,000

The Formula Is: $30,000 [community payments] divided by the sum of $30,000 [community payments] plus $50,000 [equity on date of marriage] [$30,000/$80,000 equals 37.5%].

37.5% times current equity $80,000 [FMV $100,000 less current mortgage balance of $20,000] or community claim of $30,000 and separate property share of $50,000.

Hypothetical fact situation No. 3

Same as above, but property has declined in value to $80,000.

Purchase price of residence: $80,000

Down Payment $15,000

Original Mortgage balance $65,000

Mortgage reduction before marriage $15,000

Value of residence on date of marriage $100,000

Mortgage balance on date of marriage $50,000

Equity in property on date of marriage $50,000

Mortgage reduction during marriage $30,000

Value of residence on date of divorce $80,000

Mortgage balance on day of divorce $20,000

Net equity on day of divorce: $60,000

The Formula Is: $30,000 [community payments] divided by the sum of $30,000 [community payments] plus $50,000 [equity on date of marriage] [$30,000/$80,000 equals 37.5%]

37.5% times current equity $60,000 [$80,000 value less current mortgage balance of $20,000 = $60,000]

Community property estate economic contribution of $22,500 of FMV [paid $30,000; Community property estate takes a loss of $7,500].

Separate property interest is $37,500 [contributed $50,000 equity at time of marriage, although actual out-of-pocket cost was $30,000 (15,000 + 15,000)]; Separate property estate lost $12,500 of paper capital gain, but still has residual gain over actual basis

Hypothetical fact situation No. 4

Same as hypothetical fact situation No 1, but property was fully paid for at time of marriage.

Ten years later, one spouse inherits some money and spends $50,000 improving the property (pool, deck, new bathrooms and kitchen). When the improvements begin, the residence had a value of $140,000.

Purchase price of residence: N/A

Value of residence on date of marriage N/A

Equity on date of improvements: $140,000

Cost of improvements: $50,000

Value of residence on date of divorce: $250,000

Net enhancement in value: $60,000

The Formula Is: $50,000 [other spouse's separate estate payments for improvements] divided by the sum of $50,000 [separate estate payments] plus $140,000 [equity on date of improvements] [$50,000/$190,000 equals 26.3%]

$50,000 [other spouse's separate property contribution] divided by the sum of $50,000 [other spouse's separate property contribution] plus $140,000 value of property when improvements began [$50,000/$190,000 equals 26.3%]

If property is now worth $250,000 the other spouse's separate estate claim for economic contribution is $65,789 [26.3% times $250,000 equals $65,789]

Editors' Note: *Ch. 838, 77th Legis., Reg. Sess. (2001) amended Subchapter E, and contains the following uncodified prefatory provision:*

PUBLIC POLICY. In accordance with the duty of the legislature under Section 15, Article XVI, Texas Constitution, to pass laws more clearly defining the rights of spouses in relation to separate and community property, the legislature declares that, under certain circumstances, the economic contributions to the value of property during the marriage made by one marital estate for the benefit of another marital estate create a claim for economic contribution for the contributing marital estate in the property of the benefited estate as provided by Subchapter E, Chapter 3, Family Code.

CLE/Other Legal Publications

Economic contribution. Thomas A. Greenwald & Bryan C. Rice, 2004 U. TEX. FAM. L. FRONT LINES

An overview of economic contribution. Randall B. Wilhite & Kyle W. Sanders, 2003 U. HOUSTON FAM. L. PRACTICE SEM. (MARCH)

Economic contribution and reimbursement. Warren Cole, Stewart W. Gagnon, Chris Wrampelmeier & Janice Pardue, 2003 ADV. FAM. L.

Demystifying economic contribution. Warren Cole, 2003 MARRIAGE DISSOLUTION

Economic contribution and reimbursement: so you won, what happens now? Warren Cole, 2003 U. TEX. FAM. L. FRONT LINES

Economic contribution claims. Jim Penn & Sara Hartley, 2003 U. HOUSTON FAM. L. PRACTICE SEM. (OCT.)

Leading Cases

Langston v. Langston, 82 S.W.3d 686 (Tex. App.—Eastland 2002, no pet.) (husband's separate property home cannot be awarded to wife even though community claim for economic contribution may impose lien on property)

Gill v. Gill, 41 S.W.3d 255 (Tex. App.—Waco 2000, no pet.) ("net enhanced value" under previous statute means increase in the market value of the property)

Texas Pattern Jury Charges: Family

PJC 204.1. Economic Contribution.

---

§ 3.401. Definitions.

In this subchapter:

(1) "Claim for economic contribution" means a claim made under this subchapter.

(2) "Economic contribution" means the contribution to a marital estate described by Section 3.402.

(3) "Equity" means, with respect to specific property owned by one or more marital estates, the amount computed by subtracting from the fair market value of the property as of a specific date the amount of a lawful lien specific to the property on that same date.

(4) "Marital estate" means one of three estates:

(A) the community property owned by the spouses together and referred to as the community marital estate;

(B) the separate property owned individually by the husband and referred to as a separate marital estate; or

(C) the separate property owned individually by the wife, also referred to as a separate marital estate.

(5) "Spouse" means a husband, who is a man, or a wife, who is a woman. A member of a civil union or similar relationship entered into in another state between persons of the same sex is not a spouse.

§ 3.402. Economic Contribution.

(a) For purposes of this subchapter, "economic contribution" is the dollar amount of:

(1) the reduction of the principal amount of a debt secured by a lien on property owned before marriage, to the extent the debt existed at the time of marriage;

(2) the reduction of the principal amount of a debt secured by a lien on property received by a spouse by gift, devise, or descent during a marriage, to the extent the debt existed at the time the property was received;

(3) the reduction of the principal amount of that part of a debt, including a home equity loan:

(A) incurred during a marriage;

(B) secured by a lien on property; and

(C) incurred for the acquisition of, or for capital improvements to, property;

(4) the reduction of the principal amount of that part of a debt:

(A) incurred during a marriage;

(B) secured by a lien on property owned by a spouse;

(C) for which the creditor agreed to look for repayment solely to the separate marital estate of the spouse on whose property the lien attached; and

(D) incurred for the acquisition of, or for capital improvements to, property;

(5) the refinancing of the principal amount described by Subdivisions (1)–(4), to the extent the refinancing reduces that principal amount in a manner described by the appropriate subdivision; and

(6) capital improvements to property other than by incurring debt.

(b) "Economic contribution" does not include the dollar amount of:

(1) expenditures for ordinary maintenance and repair or for taxes, interest, or insurance; or

(2) the contribution by a spouse of time, toil, talent, or effort during the marriage.

§ 3.403. Claim Based on Economic Contribution.

(a) A marital estate that makes an economic contribution to property owned by another marital estate has a claim for economic contribution with respect to the benefited estate.

(b) The amount of the claim under this section is equal to the product of:

(1) the equity in the benefited property on the date of dissolution of the marriage, the death of a spouse, or disposition of the property; multiplied by

(2) a fraction of which:

(A) the numerator is the economic contribution to the property owned by the benefited marital estate by the contributing marital estate; and

(B) the denominator is an amount equal to the sum of:

(i) the economic contribution to the property owned by the benefited marital estate by the contributing marital estate; and

(ii) the contribution by the benefited estate to the equity in the property owned by the benefited estate.

(b–1) The amount of the contribution by the benefited marital estate under Subsection (b)(2)(B)(ii) is measured by determining:

(1) if the benefited estate is the community property estate:

(A) the net equity of the community property estate in the property owned by the community property estate as of the date of the first economic contribution to that property by the contributing separate property estate; and

(B) any additional economic contribution to the equity in the property owned by the community property estate made by the benefited community property estate after the date described by Subdivision (A); or

(2) if the benefited estate is the separate property estate of a spouse:

(A) the net equity of the separate property estate in the property owned by the separate property estate as of the date of the first economic contribution to that property by the contributing community property estate or the separate property estate of the other spouse; and

(B) any additional contribution to the equity in the property owned by the separate property estate made by the benefited separate property estate after the date described by Subdivision (A).

(c) The amount of a claim under this section may be less than the total of the economic contributions made by the contributing estate, but may not cause the contributing estate to owe funds to the benefited estate.

(d) The amount of a claim under this section may not exceed the equity in the property on the date of dissolution of the marriage, the death of a spouse, or disposition of the property.

(e) The use and enjoyment of property during a marriage for which a claim for economic contribution to the property exists does not create a claim of an offsetting benefit against the claim.

§ 3.404. Application of Inception of Title Rule; Ownership Interest Not Created.

(a) This subchapter does not affect the rule of inception of title under which the character of property is determined at the time the right to own or claim the property arises.

(b) The claim for economic contribution created under this subchapter does not create an ownership interest in property, but does create a claim against the property of the benefited estate by the contributing estate. The claim matures on dissolution of the marriage or the death of either spouse.

§ 3.405. Management Rights.

This subchapter does not affect the right to manage, control, or dispose of marital property as provided by this chapter.

§ 3.406. Equitable Lien.

(a) On dissolution of a marriage, the court shall impose an equitable lien on property of a marital estate to secure a claim for economic contribution in that property by another marital estate.

(b) On the death of a spouse, a court shall, on application for a claim of economic contribution brought by the surviving spouse, the personal representative of the estate of the deceased spouse, or any other person interested in the estate, as defined by Section 3, Texas Probate Code, impose an equitable lien on the property of a benefited marital estate to secure a claim for economic contribution by a contributing marital estate.

(c) Subject to homestead restrictions, an equitable lien under this section may be imposed on the entirety of a spouse's property in the marital estate and is not limited to the item of property that benefited from an economic contribution.

§ 3.407. Offsetting Claims.

The court shall offset a claim for one marital estate's economic contribution in a specific asset of a second marital estate against the second marital estate's claim for economic contribution in a specific asset of the first marital estate.

§ 3.408. Claim for Reimbursement.

(a) A claim for economic contribution does not abrogate another claim for reimbursement in a factual circumstance not covered by this subchapter. In the case of a conflict between a claim for economic contribution under this subchapter and a claim for reimbursement, the claim for economic contribution, if proven, prevails.

(b) A claim for reimbursement includes:

(1) payment by one marital estate of the unsecured liabilities of another marital estate; and

(2) inadequate compensation for the time, toil, talent, and effort of a spouse by a business entity under the control and direction of that spouse.

(c) The court shall resolve a claim for reimbursement by using equitable principles, including the principle that claims for reimbursement may be offset against each other if the court determines it to be appropriate.

(d) Benefits for the use and enjoyment of property may be offset against a claim for reimbursement for expenditures to benefit a marital estate on property that does not involve a claim for economic contribution to the property.

§ 3.409. Nonreimbursable Claims.

The court may not recognize a marital estate's claim for reimbursement for:

(1) the payment of child support, alimony, or spousal maintenance;

(2) the living expenses of a spouse or child of a spouse;

(3) contributions of property of a nominal value;

(4) the payment of a liability of a nominal amount; or

(5) a student loan owed by a spouse.

§ 3.410. Effect of Marital Property Agreements.

A premarital or marital property agreement, whether executed before, on, or after September 1, 1999, that satisfies the requirements of Chapter 4 is effective to waive, release, assign, or partition a claim for economic contribution under this subchapter to the same extent the agreement would have been effective to waive, release, assign, or partition a claim for reimbursement under the law as it existed immediately before September 1, 1999, unless the agreement provides otherwise.

Chapter 4. Premarital and Marital Property Agreements.

Subchapter A. Uniform Premarital Agreement Act

Subchapter B. Marital Property Agreement

Subchapter C. Agreement To Convert Separate Property to Community Property

---

CLE/Other Legal Publications

Hoping for the best and planning for the worst: creative pre- and post-marital agreements. Diana S. Friedman, 2004 Adv. Fam. L.

The price of love: negotiating the pre-nuptial agreement. Jack W. Marr, 2004 Marriage Dissolution

Marital agreements—representing the monied vs. non-monied spouse. Richard R. Orsinger & Ike Vanden Eykel, 2003 Adv. Fam. L.

Top ten ways to screw up a premarital agreement. R. Scott Downing & Richard R. Orsinger, 2003 Adv. Fam. L. Drafting & Advocacy

Did your client "get hitched" without a hitch? Defending and attacking premarital and post-marital agreements. Carson P. Epes & Mary Johanna McCurley, 2003 New Frontiers

Premarital and marital agreements. Alvin L. Zimmerman & Gary J. Zimmerman, 2003 U. Houston Fam. L. Practice Sem. (Oct.)

Pre-marital and marital agreements and handling litigation about them: a practicing lawyer's outline. Philip C. Friday, 2003 U. Houston Fam. L. Practice Sem. (March)

Pre-marital planning without a pre-marital agreement. Mario A. Mata, 2003 U. HOUSTON FAM. L. PRACTICE SEM. (OCT.)

Texas Family Law Practice Manual

Forms 48–2. Waiver of Disclosure of Financial Information [Premarital Agreement]; *48–3.* Premarital Agreement

Texas Pattern Jury Charges: Family

PJC 202.7. Premarital Agreement; PJC 202.9. Agreement Concerning Income or Property Derived from Separate Property; PJC 207.1. Enforceability of Property Agreements; PJC 207.2. Enforceability of Premarital Agreement; PJC 207.4. Enforceability of Agreement Concerning Income or Property Derived from Separate Property.

Subchapter A. Uniform Premarital Agreement Act

> ***Editors' Note:*** *Previous editions of this publication contained the Official Commentary to the Uniform Premarital Act. That commentary has been omitted because sufficient case law has developed in Texas to render that commentary either redundant or perhaps even misleading. The entire act, with the Official Commentary, is found at the National Conference of Commissioners on Uniform State Laws' website: www.nccusl.org*

§ 4.001. Definitions.

In this subchapter:

(1) "Premarital agreement" means an agreement between prospective spouses made in contemplation of marriage and to be effective on marriage.

(2) "Property" means an interest, present or future, legal or equitable, vested or contingent, in real or personal property, including income and earnings.

Comment

This subchapter adopts the Uniform Premarital Agreement Act promulgated by the National Conference of Commissioners on Uniform State Laws. The Act is in effect in twenty-six (26) jurisdictions as of the date of publication, to wit: Arizona, Arkansas, California, Connecticut, Delaware, District of Columbia, Hawaii, Idaho, Illinois, Indiana, Iowa, Kansas, Maine, Montana, Nebraska, Nevada, New Jersey, New Mexico, North Carolina, North Dakota, Oregon, Rhode Island, South Dakota, Texas, Utah, and Virginia. 9B U.L.A. 75 (1997 Supp.).

Leading Case

Beck v. Beck, 814 S.W.2d 745 (Tex. 1991) (pre–1980 agreement impliedly validated by passage of constitutional amendment), *cert. denied,* 112 S.Ct. 1266 (1992)

Cross Reference

TEX. CONST., art. XVI, § 15. Separate and Community Property of Husband and Wife.

---

§ 4.002. Formalities.

A premarital agreement must be in writing and signed by both parties. The agreement is enforceable without consideration.

Comment

The section requires the premarital agreement to be in writing and signed by the parties. This requirement is consistent with Tex. Const. art. 16, § 15 mandating a "written instrument." Note that consideration is explicitly not required in order for a premarital contract to be valid and enforceable.

---

§ 4.003. Content.

(a) The parties to a premarital agreement may contract with respect to:

(1) the rights and obligations of each of the parties in any of the property of either or both of them whenever and wherever acquired or located;

(2) the right to buy, sell, use, transfer, exchange, abandon, lease, consume, expend, assign, create a security interest in, mortgage, encumber, dispose of, or otherwise manage and control property;

(3) the disposition of property on separation, marital dissolution, death, or the occurrence or nonoccurrence of any other event;

(4) the modification or elimination of spousal support;

(5) the making of a will, trust, or other arrangement to carry out the provisions of the agreement;

(6) the ownership rights in and disposition of the death benefit from a life insurance policy;

(7) the choice of law governing the construction of the agreement; and

(8) any other matter, including their personal rights and obligations, not in violation of public policy or a statute imposing a criminal penalty.

(b) The right of a child to support may not be adversely affected by a premarital agreement.

Comment

Subject to limits of public policy and criminal laws, this section allows parties to a premarital agreement the broadest possible freedom to arrange their marital property rights as they desire. The most important limitation is that child support may not be "adversely affected" by the premarital agreement.

Leading Cases

Manning v. Hayes, 212 F.3d 866 (5th Cir. 2000) (Tex.), *cert. denied,* 121 S.Ct. 1401 (2001) (employer provided life insurance benefits can not be waived by spouse in a premarital agreement)

Calmes v. United States, 926 F.Supp. 582 (N.D. Tex. 1996) (premarital agreement found not to be executed with intent to defraud I.R.S.)

Fanning v. Fanning, 847 S.W.2d 225 (Tex. 1993) (prenuptial agreement effective on passage of 1980 constitutional amendment—duress and unconscionability separate issues)

Williams v. Williams, 569 S.W.2d 867 (Tex. 1978) (homestead rights may be waived in a premarital agreement)

McClary v. Thompson, 65 S.W.3d 829 (Tex. App.—Fort Worth 2002, pet. denied) (parties' premarital agreement identified the separate property existing at the time of marriage but did not provide basis to assert that future additions to defined retirement benefit would be husband's separate property)

Koch v. Koch, 27 S.W.3d 93 (Tex. App.—San Antonio 2000, no pet.) (provision to arbitrate any future disputes over premarital agreement binding on divorce court)

Dokmanovic v. Schwarz, 880 S.W.2d 272 (Tex. App.—Houston [14th Dist.] 1994, no writ) (premarital agreement which provided income from all separate property to remain separate property precluded creation of any community property during marriage)

Winger v. Pianka, 831 S.W.2d 853 (Tex. App.—Austin 1992, writ denied) (prenuptial agreement may partition future earnings of persons about to marry)

Scott v. Scott, 805 S.W.2d 835 (Tex. App.—Waco 1991, writ denied) (premarital agreement may provide for "excess" income to be separate property)

Dewey v. Dewey, 745 S.W.2d 514 (Tex. App.—Corpus Christi 1988, writ denied) (premarital agreement did not provide for personal earnings to be separate property even though earnings from separate property were to be separate property)

Cross Reference

TEX. PROB. CODE ANN. § 59A. Contracts Concerning Succession.

---

§ 4.004. Effect of Marriage.

A premarital agreement becomes effective on marriage.

Comment

A premarital agreement is not effective until marriage. An agreement not conditioned on marriage would need to comply with § 1.108, *supra,* which requires an agreement arising out of "nonmarital conjugal cohabitation" be in writing and signed by the party charged with the obligation.

Leading Case

Marshall v. Marshall, 735 S.W.2d 587 (Tex. App.—Dallas 1987, writ ref'd n.r.e.) (premarital agreement of first marriage held inapplicable to parties' remarriage to each other)

Cross Reference

TEX. FAM. CODE ANN. § 1.108. Promise or Agreement Must Be in Writing.

---

§ 4.005. Amendment or Revocation.

After marriage, a premarital agreement may be amended or revoked only by a written agreement signed by the parties. The amended agreement or the revocation is enforceable without consideration.

Comment

Tales abound of spouses "tearing up" the premarital agreement or "burning it" in the fireplace. Beware of such practices; this section requires that revocation must be in writing and signed by the parties. Moreover, attorneys who draft such an agreement typically retain a duplicate original.

---

§ 4.006. Enforcement.

(a) A premarital agreement is not enforceable if the party against whom enforcement is requested proves that:

(1) the party did not sign the agreement voluntarily; or

(2) the agreement was unconscionable when it was signed and, before signing the agreement, that party:

(A) was not provided a fair and reasonable disclosure of the property or financial obligations of the other party;

(B) did not voluntarily and expressly waive, in writing, any right to disclosure of the property or financial obligations of the other party beyond the disclosure provided; and

(C) did not have, or reasonably could not have had, adequate knowledge of the property or financial obligations of the other party.

(b) An issue of unconscionability of a premarital agreement shall be decided by the court as a matter of law.

(c) The remedies and defenses in this section are the exclusive remedies or defenses, including common law remedies or defenses.

Comment

The burden of proof is placed on the party challenging the premarital agreement. Unless the agreement was involuntarily signed (usually very difficult to establish), the opponent must show the premarital agreement was unconscionable at time of signing and that there was improper disclosure of the identity and extent of the other spouse's property. Unconscionability standing alone is not enough.

Subsection (c) was added in 1993 and is intended to overrule those cases suggesting other defenses to premarital agreements.

Leading Cases

Fanning v. Fanning, 847 S.W.2d 225 (Tex. 1993) (prenuptial agreement effective on passage of 1980 constitutional amendment—duress and unconscionability separate issues)

Beck v. Beck, 814 S.W.2d 745 (Tex. 1991) (under doctrine of implied ratification, a premarital agreement signed in 1978 was made valid by the 1980 amendment to the Texas Constitution), *cert. denied,* 117 L.Ed.2d 494, 112 S.Ct. 1266 (1992)

Sadler v. Sadler, 769 S.W.2d 886 (Tex. 1989) (the law to apply to a premarital agreement is the applicable law at time of divorce)

Osorno v. Osorno, 76 S.W.3d 509 (Tex. App.—Houston [14th Dist.] 2002, no pet.) (wife signed premarital agreement voluntarily and not under duress—"sign or no marriage" may present tough choice to pregnant woman, but man has prerogative not to marry)

Morris v. Morris, 12 S.W.3d 877 (Tex. App.—Texarkana 1999, no pet.) (premarital agreement to keep separate property segregated impaired by marital gifts)

Pletcher v. Goetz, 9 S.W.3d 442 (Tex. App.—Fort Worth 1999, pet. denied) (professional businesswoman's attack on allegedly unconscionable premarital agreement fails)

Fazakerly v. Fazakerly, 996 S.W.2d 260 (Tex. App.—Eastland 1999, pet. denied) (statute of limitations and laches bar attack on stepmother's prenuptial agreement by decedent's daughter)

Marsh v. Marsh, 949 S.W.2d 734 (Tex. App.—Houston [14th Dist.] 1997, no writ) (one-sided premarital contract signed by 78 year old favoring 58 year old does not meet standard of unconscionability)

Dokmanovic v. Schwarz, 880 S.W.2d 272 (Tex. App.—Houston [14th Dist.] 1994, no writ) (premarital agreement which provided income from all separate property to remain separate property precluded creation of any community property during marriage)

Winger v. Pianka, 831 S.W.2d 853 (Tex. App.—Austin 1992, writ denied) (prenuptial agreement may partition future earnings of persons about to marry)

Grossman v. Grossman, 799 S.W.2d 511 (Tex. App.—Corpus Christi 1990, no writ) (summary judgment was proper in upholding a premarital agreement)

Chiles v. Chiles, 779 S.W.2d 127 (Tex. App.—Houston [14th Dist.] 1989, writ denied) (whether a premarital agreement is unfair is immaterial; unconscionability is the legal standard)

Williams v. Williams, 720 S.W.2d 246 (Tex. App.—Houston [14th Dist.] 1986, no writ) (signing premarital agreement one day before wedding did not invalidate agreement)

---

§ 4.007. Enforcement: Void Marriage.

If a marriage is determined to be void, an agreement that would otherwise have been a premarital agreement is enforceable only to the extent necessary to avoid an inequitable result.

Comment

This section is consistent with long-standing Texas law for putative spouses.

Leading Case

Davis v. Davis, 521 S.W.2d 603 (Tex. 1975) (good faith putative spouse entitled to same property rights as legal spouse)

---

§ 4.008. Limitation of Actions.

A statute of limitations applicable to an action asserting a claim for relief under a premarital agreement is tolled during the marriage of the parties to the agreement. However, equitable defenses limiting the time for enforcement, including laches and estoppel, are available to either party.

Comment

In order to avoid the potentially disruptive effect of compelling litigation between the spouses in order to escape the running of an applicable statute of limitations, this section tolls any applicable statute during the marriage of the parties.

---

§ 4.009. Application and Construction.

This subchapter shall be applied and construed to effect its general purpose to make uniform the law with respect to the subject of this subchapter among states enacting these provisions.

§ 4.010. Short Title.

This subchapter may be cited as the Uniform Premarital Agreement Act.

Subchapter B. Marital Property Agreement

Introductory Comment

Until 1948, Texas residents had no method of changing the character of community property into separate property. By constitutional amendment that year, spouses were permitted to partition or exchange community property and thus convert community property into separate property. The original motivation was to lessen the impact of federal estate taxes (no longer a problem), but after 40 years this method of marital property planning is thoroughly engrafted in Texas jurisprudence.

In 1980, a constitutional amendment allowed Texas domiciliaries to agree that income from separate property would be separate property. This provision is now common in premarital agreements and postmarital agreements.

In 1999, Texas voters dropped the other shoe. By an overwhelming majority, conversion of separate property into community property was authorized by constitutional amendment; *see* §§ 4.201–.206, *infra*.

CLE/Other Legal Publications

See annotations to Subchapter A. UNIFORM PREMARITAL AGREEMENT ACT, *supra.*

Leading Cases

In re Hinsley, 201 F.3d 638 (5th Cir. Tex. 2000) (partition agreement found to be invalid transfer of property as an attempt to impair rights of creditors)

In re Marriage of Smith, 115 S.W.3d 126 (Tex. App.—Texarkana 2003, pet. denied) (residuary clause in agreement covered pension; 1982 divorce suit never finalized, property division governed by "separation and partition agreement")

Nesmith v. Berger, 64 S.W.3d 110 (Tex. App.—Austin 2001, pet. denied) (couple's post-marital agreement maintained separate estates of both spouses; cash buy-out of wife's separate property share in jointly owned home was appropriate partition between co-tenants)

Byrnes v. Byrnes, 19 S.W.3d 556 (Tex. App.—Fort Worth 2000, no pet.) (agreement incident to divorce not considered a partition agreement unless specifically stated to be the same)

Blonstein v. Blonstein, 831 S.W.2d 468 (Tex. App.—Houston [14th Dist.] 1992, writ denied) (shift of burden of proof to person attacking post-nuptial agreement procedural—statute applies to agreements signed before effective date of amendment)

Pearce v. Pearce, 824 S.W.2d 195 (Tex. App.—El Paso 1991, writ denied) (pre–1987 postnuptial agreement enforceable under 1987 amendment regarding enforceability)

Bradley v. Bradley, 725 S.W.2d 503 (Tex. App.—Corpus Christi 1987, no writ) (premarital agreement contemplated future partitions as written, property not partitioned)

Texas Family Law Practice Manual

Chapter 48. Property Agreements: II. Marital Property Agreements

Texas Pattern Jury Charges: Family

PJC 202.8. Partition or Exchange Agreement; PJC 202.9. Agreement Concerning Income or Property Derived from Separate Property; PJC 207.1. Enforceability of Property Agreements–Separate Trials; PJC 207.3. Enforceability of Partition or Exchange Agreement; PJC 207.4. Enforceability of Agreement Concerning Income or Property Derived from Separate Property.

---

§ 4.101. Definition.

In this subchapter, "property" has the meaning assigned by Section 4.001.

§ 4.102. Partition or Exchange of Community Property.

At any time, the spouses may partition or exchange between themselves **all or** [~~any~~] part of their community property, then existing or to be acquired, as the spouses may desire. Property or a property interest transferred to a spouse by a partition or exchange agreement becomes that spouse's separate property. **The partition or exchange of property includes future earnings and income arising from the property as the separate property of the owning spouse unless the spouses agree in a record that the future earnings and income will be community property after the partition or exchange.**

History: Amended by 78th Legis., Reg. Sess. (2003), H.B. 885, eff. Sept. 1, 2003, and "applies only to an agreement to partition or exchange property made on or after the effective date of this Act. An agreement made before the effective date of this Act is governed by the law in effect on the date the agreement was made, and the former law is continued in effect for that purpose."

Comment

The 2003 amendment provides that partitioned property includes the future income from the partitioned property. This is probably the expected result in nearly all cases. A gift between spouses already carries with it a presumption that the gifted property includes future income from that property.

Cross Reference

Tex. Const., art. XVI, § 15. Separate and Community Property of Husband and Wife.

---

§ 4.103. Agreement Between Spouses Concerning Income or Property From Separate Property.

At any time, the spouses may agree that the income or property arising from the separate property that is then owned by one of them, or that may thereafter be acquired, shall be the separate property of the owner.

Leading Case

Beck v. Beck, 814 S.W.2d 745 (Tex. 1991) (an agreement for income from separate property to be separate property signed before the 1980 amendment is valid under the doctrine of "implied ratification"), *cert. denied,* 117 L.Ed.2d 494, 112 S.Ct. 1266 (1992)

Cross Reference

Tex. Const., art. XVI, § 15. Separate and Community Property of Husband and Wife.

---

§ 4.104. Formalities.

A partition or exchange agreement must be in writing and signed by both parties.

Comment

Marital agreements must be in writing and signed by the parties. This requirement is consistent with the mandate of Tex. Const., art. XVI, § 15 for a "written instrument."

Leading Cases

Collins v. Collins, 752 S.W.2d 636 (Tex. App.—Fort Worth 1988, writ ref'd) (listing of property as separate property in a joint tax return was not sufficient to be a partition agreement)

Patino v. Patino, 687 S.W.2d 799 (Tex. App.—San Antonio 1985, no writ) (partition or exchange agreement does not require judicial approval)

---

§ 4.105. Enforcement.

(a) A partition or exchange agreement is not enforceable if the party against whom enforcement is requested proves that:

(1) the party did not sign the agreement voluntarily; or

(2) the agreement was unconscionable when it was signed and, before execution of the agreement, that party:

(A) was not provided a fair and reasonable disclosure of the property or financial obligations of the other party;

(B) did not voluntarily and expressly waive, in writing, any right to disclosure of the property or financial obligations of the other party beyond the disclosure provided; and

(C) did not have, or reasonably could not have had, adequate knowledge of the property or financial obligations of the other party.

(b) An issue of unconscionability of a partition or exchange agreement shall be decided by the court as a matter of law.

(c) The remedies and defenses in this section are the exclusive remedies or defenses, including common law remedies or defenses.

Comment

The same standard of enforcement exists for a marital agreement as for a premarital agreement, § 4.006, *supra*. Although the section specifically refers only to "partition or exchange" agreements, the court in *Daniel, infra*, held the section generally applicable to "income from separate property" agreements. The 1993 amendment, sponsored by the Family Law Section, was intended to overrule those cases suggesting other defenses to marital agreements such as in *Fanning* and *Daniel, infra*.

Leading Cases

Fanning v. Fanning, 847 S.W.2d 225 (Tex. 1993) (prenuptial agreement effective on passage of 1980 constitutional amendment—duress and unconscionability separate issues—apparently overruled by later enactment of subsection (c))

Marsh v. Marsh, 949 S.W.2d 734 (Tex. App.—Houston [14th Dist.] 1997, no writ) (one-sided premarital contract signed by 78 year old favoring 58 year old does not meet standard of unconscionability)

Blonstein v. Blonstein, 831 S.W.2d 468 (Tex. App.—Houston [14th Dist.] 1992, writ denied) (shift of burden of proof to person attacking post-nuptial agreement procedural—statute applies to agreements signed before effective date of amendment)

Daniel v. Daniel, 779 S.W.2d 110 (Tex. App.—Houston [1st Dist.] 1989, no writ) (standard of enforcement is that in effect at time of divorce; and although common law defenses are available to enforcement of a marital agreement, directed verdict upheld on appeal—apparently overruled by later enactment of subsection (c))

Matthews v. Matthews, 725 S.W.2d 275 (Tex. App.—Houston [1st Dist.] 1986, writ ref'd n.r.e.) (evidence that husband was hiding parties' child established that wife did not voluntarily sign marital agreement)

---

§ 4.106. Rights of Creditors and Recordation Under Partition or Exchange Agreement.

(a) A provision of a partition or exchange agreement made under this subchapter is void with respect to the rights of a preexisting creditor whose rights are intended to be defrauded by it.

(b) A partition or exchange agreement made under this subchapter may be recorded in the deed records of the county in which a party resides and in the county in which the real property affected is located. An agreement made under this subchapter is constructive notice to a good faith purchaser for value or a creditor without actual notice only if the instrument is acknowledged and recorded in the county in which the real property is located.

Comment

Recordation of marital agreements is permitted, but not required, as a means of notice to third parties. In reality, very few agreements are recorded because of the privacy concerns of the parties.

Cross Reference

TEX. PROP. CODE ANN. § 12.001. Instruments Concerning Property.

Subchapter C. Agreement To Convert Separate Property to Community Property

Guest Commentary

Bernard E. Jones, Davis, Ridout, Jones & Gerstner, LLP Houston

> ***Editors' Note:*** *Barney Jones is a Houston attorney, board certified in Estate Planning and Probate Law, and was a chief draftsman of the statute.*

Summary. Subchapter C, § 4.201 *et seq.*, allows married persons to convert separate property of either spouse into community property. Prior to this section's enactment in 1999, spouses could partition or exchange community property into separate property but there was no direct means of converting separate into community. Thus, spouses could "opt out" of the community property system but could not "opt in." Subchapter C became law on January 1, 2000, after Texas voters approved an amendment to Article 16, Section 15 of the Texas Constitution, *infra*, authorizing conversions of separate property to community property.

Technical requirements. The statute sets out several technical requirements and limitations. A conversion to community must be by written agreement signed by both spouses; the unilateral action of one spouse is not sufficient. Only existing property may be converted; spouses cannot, for instance, agree that all future gifts and inheritances will be community property when received. The spouses must execute the agreement voluntarily and must receive a fair and reasonable disclosure of the effect of the agreement. Although the disclosure may not be waived, the statute provides a suggested disclosure statement which, if conspicuously included in the agreement, establishes a rebuttable presumption that the proper disclosure was made.

Tax planning benefit: basis "step up." Because community property enjoys several tax planning advantages over separate property, conversions to community will be especially useful for estate planning purposes. For example, when an individual dies, his or her property receives a so-called "step up" in basis. (See Internal Revenue Code § 1014.) The step up adjusts the cost basis of the decedent's property up (or down) to the value of the property as of the date of death, thus effectively forgiving the capital gains tax on all pre-death gains. And since virtually all persons face the prospect of capital gains taxes, this is a benefit to both wealthy and modest couples.

As a general rule, the step up only applies to the decedent's interest in property as of the date of death. Thus, when a married individual dies owning only separate property, the deceased spouse's property receives a step up but the surviving spouse's property does not. The result is the same even if the property is jointly owned. For example, assume that a husband and wife jointly purchased a beach house for $100,000 cash ($50,000 each) prior to their marriage. As a result, they jointly own the beach house as tenants in common. If the husband dies when the house is worth $300,000, his one-half of the house gets a basis step up from $50,000 to $150,000; however, the wife's one-half retains its original $50,000 cost basis. The total basis in the beach house is $200,000. If the wife sells it for its market value, she will realize a $100,000 capital gain.

There is, however, a special rule for community property: both halves of the community property receive a "step up" when either spouse dies. Thus, if the husband and wife in the preceding example convert their jointly owned beach house to community property prior to the husband's death, there will be a total basis step up of $200,000 (from $100,000 to $300,000). Now, if the wife sells the house for market value, her capital gain is reduced from $100,000 to zero. The result is the same even if the beach house starts out as the wife's separate property: she and her husband could convert it to their community property and on his death all of her built in capital gains would be forgiven. Of course, in this case the conversion would also give the husband the ability to devise his newly acquired one-half community interest to someone other than his surviving wife. That is, conversions to community are not merely tax schemes; they can cause fundamental changes in property rights.

Tax planning benefit: preservation of both spouses' $1,500,000 tax-free amount. Currently every American citizen is entitled to leave up to $1,500,000 at death without incurring any estate tax; a married couple can generally leave an aggregate of up to $3,000,000 tax-free. However, if one spouse has all the wealth and the other spouse dies first, the deceased spouse's $1,500,000 amount is wasted. Under prior Texas law, the only solution was for the rich spouse to give property to the less wealthy spouse to bring his or her net worth up to $1,500,000. Allowing conversions to community enables both spouses' $1,500,000 tax-free amounts to be utilized without the donor spouse being forced to lose management authority over the property at issue. Further, by holding their property as community instead of as separate, the basis step up is captured for all of the property on the death of the first spouse: If property is simply given to the poorer spouse as his or her separate property and the wealthier spouse dies first, the basis step up for the gifted property is lost. *Note:* The $1,500,000 tax free amount is scheduled to increase to $2,000,000 in 2005 ($4,000,000 per couple) and $3,500,000 in 2009 ($7,000,000 per couple). The estate tax is scheduled to be repealed for all of 2010. On January 1, 2011, the estate tax is scheduled to be reinstated and the tax free amount returned to $1,000,000 per individual. Whether and to what extent these changes actually will take place is a matter of speculation.

Other benefits. Perhaps more important to most married couples are the non-tax applications of conversions to community. For example, for the first time in Texas: (1)

Marital property agreements can effectively provide that one or more properties are community. Under prior law, such agreements might evidence intent but only the utter inability to trace would result in separate becoming community. (2) Previously executed marital partition agreements can be effectively reversed. Under prior law, a partition of community property—even an inadvertent one resulting from signature card language for a joint brokerage account—was irreversible (save by convoluted means unavailable to all but the most sophisticated individuals). (3) Migrant couples who have settled in Texas can eliminate the uncertain character of their property once and for all. Under prior law, the dissolution of a migrant couple's marriage by death or divorce frequently entailed substantial tracing and conflicts of law issues.

Disadvantages. There are also clear disadvantages to conversions to community. In the event of death, one-half of the property will be subject to disposition by the deceased spouse's will; if the property had remained the separate property of the surviving spouse this would not be the case. In the event of divorce, the converted property will be subject to division by the court; separate property is generally not divisible on divorce, *but see* the "Economic Contribution" provisions of Texas Family Code §§ 3.401–3.410, *supra*, creating statutory authority to award claims payable out of—and secured by a lien on—a spouse's separate property. A spouse's interest in community property is often subject to the other spouse's debts; separate property is not. If the conversion agreement is poorly prepared, the owner of the separate property may lose his or her sole management rights and the property may become subject to joint management. Conceivably, an unscrupulous individual might use the lure of tax benefits to beguile his or her spouse into converting separate property into community property for ulterior motives. For example, a spouse might extract a conversion to community as a way to make property available to provide for his or her own creditors. Nevertheless, conversions to community should not result in significant increase in inter-spousal fraud inasmuch there are other, superior techniques available to those who are willing to defraud their spouses. For example, an individual could obtain his or her spouse's power of attorney upon the accurate representation that no ownership rights were being transferred. The individual could then dispose of his or her spouse's property freely.

Practical considerations. Conversions to community should be treated the same as marital property partition agreements and inter-spousal gifts: Whenever substantial property is involved, detailed disclosures and separate representation may be advisable. However, the issues seem less significant for conversions of separate to community than for partitions of community into separate: Partition agreements can place one spouse's future wages and income forever out of the reach of the other spouse. By comparison, a conversion to community can only subject separate property to the rules of community property, under which the original spouse retains ownership—albeit jointly with his or her spouse—and because only currently existing property may be converted, the risk of unforeseen, long term inequities appears to be substantially less.

Constitutional issues. The legislature passed as amendment to Article 16, Section 15 of the constitution to facilitate conversions to community. The amendment is necessary because the Texas rules of marital property are spelled out in—and thus cannot be inconsistent with—the Texas Constitution. The constitutional amendment adds a brief sentence to Section 16 that authorizes spouses to agree that any separate property currently owned by either of them will be their community property.

Texas Family Law Practice Manual

Form 48–9. Agreement To Convert Separate Property to Community Property

Texas Pattern Jury Charges: Family

PJC 202.10. Agreement To Convert Separate Property to Community Property; PJC 207.1. Enforceability of Property Agreements–Separate Trials; PJC 207.5. Enforceability of Agreement To Convert Separate Property to Community Property.

---

§ 4.201. Definition.

In this subchapter, "property" has the meaning assigned by Section 4.001.

§ 4.202. Agreement to Convert to Community Property.

At any time, spouses may agree that all or part of the separate property owned by either or both spouses is converted to community property.

§ 4.203. Formalities of Agreement.

(a) An agreement to convert separate property to community property:

(1) must be in writing and:

(A) be signed by the spouses;

(B) identify the property being converted; and

(C) specify that the property is being converted to the spouses' community property; and

(2) is enforceable without consideration.

(b) The mere transfer of a spouse's separate property to the name of the other spouse or to the name of both spouses is not sufficient to convert the property to community property under this subchapter.

§ 4.204. Management of Converted Property.

Except as specified in the agreement to convert the property and as provided by Subchapter B, Chapter 3 *[Marital Property Rights and Liabilities]*, and other law, property converted to community property under this subchapter is subject to:

(1) the sole management, control, and disposition of the spouse in whose name the property is held;

(2) the sole management, control, and disposition of the spouse who transferred the property if the property is not subject to evidence of ownership;

(3) the joint management, control, and disposition of the spouses if the property is held in the name of both spouses; or

(4) the joint management, control, and disposition of the spouses if the property is not subject to evidence of ownership and was owned by both spouses before the property was converted to community property.

§ 4.205. Enforcement.

(a) An agreement to convert property to community property under this subchapter is not enforceable if the spouse against whom enforcement is sought proves that the spouse did not:

(1) execute the agreement voluntarily; or

(2) receive a fair and reasonable disclosure of the legal effect of converting the property to community property.

(b) An agreement that contains the following statement, or substantially similar words, prominently displayed in bold-faced type, capital letters, or underlined, is rebuttably presumed to provide a fair and reasonable disclosure of the legal effect of converting property to community property:

"THIS INSTRUMENT CHANGES SEPARATE PROPERTY TO COMMUNITY PROPERTY. THIS MAY HAVE ADVERSE CONSEQUENCES DURING MARRIAGE AND ON TERMINATION OF THE MARRIAGE BY DEATH OR DIVORCE. FOR EXAMPLE:

"EXPOSURE TO CREDITORS. IF YOU SIGN THIS AGREEMENT, ALL OR PART OF THE SEPARATE PROPERTY BEING CONVERTED TO COMMUNITY PROPERTY MAY BECOME SUBJECT TO THE LIABILITIES OF YOUR SPOUSE. IF YOU DO NOT SIGN THIS AGREEMENT, YOUR SEPARATE PROPERTY IS GENERALLY NOT SUBJECT TO THE LIABILITIES OF YOUR SPOUSE UNLESS YOU ARE PERSONALLY LIABLE UNDER ANOTHER RULE OF LAW.

"LOSS OF MANAGEMENT RIGHTS. IF YOU SIGN THIS AGREEMENT, ALL OR PART OF THE SEPARATE PROPERTY BEING CONVERTED TO COMMUNITY PROPERTY MAY BECOME SUBJECT TO EITHER THE JOINT MANAGEMENT, CONTROL, AND DISPOSITION OF YOU AND YOUR SPOUSE OR THE SOLE MANAGEMENT, CONTROL, AND DISPOSITION OF YOUR SPOUSE ALONE. IN THAT EVENT, YOU WILL LOSE YOUR MANAGEMENT RIGHTS OVER THE PROPERTY. IF YOU DO NOT SIGN THIS AGREEMENT, YOU WILL GENERALLY RETAIN THOSE RIGHTS."

"LOSS OF PROPERTY OWNERSHIP. IF YOU SIGN THIS AGREEMENT AND YOUR MARRIAGE IS SUBSEQUENTLY TERMINATED BY THE DEATH OF EITHER SPOUSE OR BY DIVORCE, ALL OR PART OF THE SEPARATE PROPERTY BEING CONVERTED TO COMMUNITY PROPERTY MAY BECOME THE SOLE PROPERTY OF YOUR SPOUSE OR YOUR SPOUSE'S HEIRS. IF YOU DO NOT SIGN THIS AGREEMENT, YOU GENERALLY CANNOT BE DEPRIVED OF OWNERSHIP OF YOUR SEPARATE PROPERTY ON TERMINATION OF YOUR MARRIAGE, WHETHER BY DEATH OR DIVORCE."

(c) If a proceeding regarding enforcement of an agreement under this subchapter occurs after the death of the spouse against whom enforcement is sought, the proof required by Subsection (a) may be made by an heir of the spouse or the personal representative of the estate of that spouse.

§ 4.206. Rights of Creditors; Recording.

(a) A conversion of separate property to community property does not affect the rights of a preexisting creditor of the spouse whose separate property is being converted.

(b) A conversion of separate property to community property may be recorded in the deed records of the county in which a spouse resides and of the county in which any real property is located.

(c) A conversion of real property from separate property to community property is constructive notice to a good faith purchaser for value or a creditor without actual notice only if the agreement to convert the property is acknowledged and recorded in the deed records of the county in which the real property is located.

Chapter 5. Homestead Rights.

Subchapter A. Sale of Homestead; General Rule

Subchapter B. Sale of Homestead Under Unusual Circumstances

Subchapter A. Sale of Homestead; General Rule

§ 5.001. Sale, Conveyance, or Encumbrance of Homestead.

Whether the homestead is the separate property of either spouse or community property, neither spouse may sell, convey, or encumber the homestead without the joinder of the other spouse except as provided in this chapter or by other rules of law.

Comment

In 1997, after many years of discussion the Texas Constitution was amended to permit home equity loans and reverse mortgages on the homestead of an individual or family, *see* Tex. Const. Art. XVI, § 50, *infra*. Obviously this has been a very difficult concept to draft correctly. Every two years the legislature has gone back to the drawing board for further amendments to the constitution, the last being in 2003.

CLE/Other Legal Publication

Homestead—what you need to know in the 21st century. Barbara D. Nunneley, 2003 MARRIAGE DISSOLUTION

Leading Cases

Farrey v. Sanderfoot, 500 U.S. 291, L.Ed.2d 337, 111 S.Ct. 1825 (1991) (ex-wife's judicial lien on homestead awarded to ex-husband on divorce not discharged by his bankruptcy)

Benchmark Bank v. Crowder, 919 S.W.2d 657 (Tex. 1996) (bank loan made to pay off tax lien, bank subrogated to IRS lien against homestead—wife entitled to compensation for loss of homestead)

Heggen v. Pemelton, 836 S.W.2d 145 (Tex. 1992) (equitable lien may be imposed on separate property homestead only to secure right of reimbursement for community improvements, not to insure just and right division of community property)

Laster v. First Huntsville Properties Co., 826 S.W.2d 125 (Tex. 1991) (ex-spouse could validly convey his interest in family homestead to third party—ex-wife lost homestead protection when child turned 18 by terms of decree)

Caulley v. Caulley, 806 S.W.2d 795 (Tex. 1991) (once homestead rights are shown to exist, they are presumed to continue, and anyone asserting abandonment has burden of proof)

Lot 39, Section C, Northern Hills v. State, 85 S.W.3d 429 (Tex. App.—Eastland 2002, pet. filed) (homestead exemption inapplicable to forfeiture for criminal conduct on premises)

Estate of Montague, 70 S.W.3d 242 (Tex. App.—San Antonio 2002, pet. denied) (parties not estopped from asserting homestead exemption for actual property they lived on despite designation of another property as their homestead)

Skelton v. Washington Mut. Bank, F.A., 61 S.W.3d 56 (Tex. App.—Amarillo 2001, no pet.) (only husband signed vendor's lien for community homestead—after his death bank may foreclose notwithstanding absence of wife's signature on lien documents)

Lawrence v. Lawrence, 911 S.W.2d 450 (Tex. App.—Texarkana 1995, writ denied) (ex-husband lacks present possessory interest in separate property necessary for homestead protection)

Magallanez v. Magallanez, 911 S.W.2d 91 (Tex. App.—El Paso 1995, no writ) (ex-husband entitled to foreclose vendor's lien on homestead awarded to ex-wife)

Copeland v. Tarrant Appraisal District, 906 S.W.2d 148 (Tex. App.—Fort Worth 1995, writ denied) (surviving spouse entitled to homestead exemption—paid taxes and maintenance on deceased husband's separate realty)

Svacina v. Gardner, 905 S.W.2d 780 (Tex. App.—Texarkana 1995, no writ) (summary judgment to foreclose owelty lien appropriate; homestead defense not asserted)

Cole v. Cole, 880 S.W.2d 477 (Tex. App.—Fort Worth 1994, no writ) (amount secured by lien to secure payment of amount awarded to other spouse is limited to the homestead interest awarded to the other spouse)

Kurtz v. Jackson, 859 S.W.2d 609 (Tex. App.—Houston [1st Dist.] 1993, no writ) (court property placed lien on homestead, lien triggered when ex-spouse remarried)

Gregory v. Sunbelt Savings, 835 S.W.2d 155 (Tex. App.—Dallas 1992, writ denied) (the house was not a homestead when the note was signed)

Cross Reference

TEX. CONST. art. XVI, § 50. Homestead; Protection from Forced Sale; Mortgages, Trust Deeds, and Liens.

---

§ 5.002. Sale of Separate Homestead After Spouse Judicially Declared Incapacitated.

If the homestead is the separate property of a spouse and the other spouse has been judicially declared incapacitated by a court exercising original jurisdiction over guardianship and other matters under Chapter XIII, Texas Probate Code, the owner may sell, convey, or encumber the homestead without the joinder of the other spouse.

Comment

If a spouse has been declared incompetent by a court decree, the other spouse is authorized to act alone to deal with the homestead. Probably an implicit fiduciary duty to act fairly with regard to the interest of the incompetent spouse is presumed, but it is not explicitly stated.

---

§ 5.003. Sale of Community Homestead after Spouse Judicially Declared Incapacitated.

If the homestead is the community property of the spouses and one spouse has been judicially declared incapacitated by a court exercising original jurisdiction over guardianship and other matters under Chapter XIII, Texas Probate Code, the competent spouse may sell, convey, or encumber the homestead without the joinder of the other spouse.

Subchapter B. Sale of Homestead Under Unusual Circumstances

Introductory Comment

Sections 5.101–.108 deal with unusual situations in which a spouse: (1) is incompetent; (2) has disappeared; (3) has abandoned the homestead; or (4) is missing on public service. These sections prescribe procedures for the sale of the homestead which vary depending on whether the property is separate or community. No cases have cited these sections since enactment in 1970.

§ 5.101. Sale of Separate Homestead Under Unusual Circumstances.

If the homestead is the separate property of a spouse, that spouse may file a sworn petition that gives a description of the property, states the facts that make it desirable for the spouse to sell, convey, or encumber the homestead without the joinder of the other spouse, and alleges that the other spouse:

(1) has disappeared and that the location of the spouse remains unknown to the petitioning spouse;

(2) has permanently abandoned the homestead and the petitioning spouse;

(3) has permanently abandoned the homestead and the spouses are permanently separated; or

(4) has been reported by an executive department of the United States to be a prisoner of war or missing on public service of the United States.

§ 5.102. Sale of Community Homestead Under Unusual Circumstances.

If the homestead is the community property of the spouses, one spouse may file a sworn petition that gives a description of the property, states the facts that make it desirable for the petitioning spouse to sell, convey, or encumber the homestead without the joinder of the other spouse, and alleges that the other spouse:

(1) has disappeared and that the location of the spouse remains unknown to the petitioning spouse;

(2) has permanently abandoned the homestead and the petitioning spouse;

(3) has permanently abandoned the homestead and the spouses are permanently separated; or

(4) has been reported by an executive department of the United States to be a prisoner of war or missing on public service of the United States.

§ 5.103. Time for Filing Petition.

The petitioning spouse may file the petition in a court of the county in which any portion of the property is located not earlier than the 60th day after the date of the occurrence of an event described by Sections 5.101(1)–(3) and 5.102(1)–(3) or not less than six months after the date the other spouse has been reported to be a prisoner of war or missing on public service.

§ 5.104. Appointment of Attorney.

(a) Except as provided by Subsection (b), the court may appoint an attorney in a suit filed under this subchapter for the respondent.

(b) The court shall appoint an attorney in a suit filed under this subchapter for a respondent reported to be a prisoner of war or missing on public service.

(c) The court shall allow a reasonable fee for the appointed attorney's services as a part of the costs of the suit.

§ 5.105. Citation; Notice of Hearing.

Citation and notice of hearing for a suit filed as provided by this subchapter shall be issued and served in the manner provided in Subchapter D, Chapter 3 *[Marital Property Rights and Liabilities]*.

§ 5.106. Court Order.

(a) After notice and hearing, the court shall render an order the court deems just and equitable with respect to the sale, conveyance, or encumbrance of a separate property homestead.

(b) After hearing the evidence, the court, on terms the court deems just and equitable, shall render an order describing or defining the community property at issue that will be subject to the management, control, and disposition of each spouse during marriage.

(c) The court may:

(1) impose any conditions and restrictions the court deems necessary to protect the rights of the respondent;

(2) require a bond conditioned on the faithful administration of the property; and

(3) require payment to the registry of the court of all or a portion of the proceeds of the sale of the property to be disbursed in accordance with the court's further directions.

§ 5.107. [renumbered as § 5.003.]

§ 5.108. Remedies and Powers Cumulative.

The remedies and the powers of a spouse provided by this subchapter are cumulative of the other rights, powers, and remedies afforded the spouses by law.

Subtitle C. Dissolution of Marriage.

★★★

Chapter 6. Suit for Dissolution of Marriage.

Subchapter A. Grounds for Divorce and Defenses

Subchapter B. Grounds for Annulment

Subchapter C. Declaring a Marriage Void

Subchapter D. Jurisdiction, Venue, and Residence Qualifications

§ 6.304. Armed Forces Personnel Not Previously Residents.
§ 6.305. Acquiring Jurisdiction Over Nonresident Respondent.
§ 6.306. Jurisdiction To Annul Marriage.
§ 6.307. Jurisdiction To Declare Marriage Void.
§ 6.308. Exercising Partial Jurisdiction.

Subchapter E. Filing Suit

§ 6.401. Caption.
§ 6.402. Pleadings.
§ 6.403. Answer.
§ 6.4035. Waiver of Service.
§ 6.404. Statement on Alternate Dispute Resolution. **[repealed]**
§ 6.405. Protective Order.
§ 6.406. Mandatory Joinder of Suit Affecting Parent–Child Relationship.
§ 6.407. Suit Affecting Parent–Child Relationship To Be Transferred to Divorce Court.
§ 6.408. Service of Citation.
§ 6.409. Citation by Publication.
§ 6.410. Report to Accompany Petition. *[first of two]*
§ 6.410. Confidentiality of Pleadings. *[second of two]*

Subchapter F. Temporary Orders

§ 6.501. Temporary Restraining Order.
§ 6.502. Temporary Injunction and Other Temporary Orders.
§ 6.503. Affidavit, Verified Pleading, and Bond Not Required.
§ 6.504. Protective Orders.
§ 6.505. Counseling.
§ 6.506. Contempt.
§ 6.507. Interlocutory Appeal.

Subchapter G. Alternative Dispute Resolution

§ 6.601. Arbitration Procedures.
§ 6.602. Mediation Procedures.
§ 6.603. Collaborative Law.

Subchapter H. Trial and Appeal

§ 6.701. Failure To Answer.
§ 6.702. Waiting Period.
§ 6.703. Jury.
§ 6.704. Testimony of Husband or Wife.
§ 6.705. Testimony by Marriage Counselor.
§ 6.706. Change of Name.
§ 6.707. Transfers and Debts Pending Decree.
§ 6.708. Costs.
§ 6.709. Temporary Orders During Appeal.
§ 6.710. Copy of Decree.
§ 6.711. Findings of Fact and Conclusions of Law.

Subchapter I. Remarriage

Subchapter A. Grounds for Divorce and Defenses

§ 6.001. Insupportability.

On the petition of either party to a marriage, the court may grant a divorce without regard to fault if the marriage has become insupportable because of discord or conflict of personalities that destroys the legitimate ends of the marital relationship and prevents any reasonable expectation of reconciliation.

Comment

Insupportability as a ground for divorce was introduced to Texas law on January 1, 1970. More commonly known as "no fault" divorce, insupportability provides the basis for granting nearly all divorces in Texas. Recently, some social conservatives have advocated repeal of "no fault" divorce when there are children of the marriage. Legislation to this effect has been introduced in every session since 1997 but has not been enacted to date.

Leading Cases

Waite v. Waite, 64 S.W.3d 217 (Tex. App.—Houston [14th Dist.] 2001, pet. denied) (no fault divorce held constitutional on several grounds)

Richards v. Richards, 991 S.W.2d 32 (Tex. App.—Amarillo 1999, no pet.) (wife doesn't want the divorce, but "no fault" prevails)

Saltarelli v. Saltarelli, 670 S.W.2d 785 (Tex. App.—Fort Worth 1984, no writ) (discretion of court in granting a divorce will not be disturbed on appeal)

Trickey v. Trickey, 642 S.W.2d 47 (Tex. App.—Fort Worth 1982, writ dism'd w.o.j.) (right to divorce for insupportability unaffected by whether marriage performed in church)

Cusack v. Cusack, 491 S.W.2d 714 (Tex. App.—Corpus Christi 1973, writ dism'd w.o.j.) (classic case of no-fault means "no-fault")

Texas Family Law Practice Manual

Chapter 3. Divorce Pleadings: I. The Suit; II. Dissolution of the Marriage; III. Division of the Property; IV. The Parent–Child Relationship; V. Additional Causes of Action; VI. Intervenor's Pleadings

Texas Pattern Jury Charges: Family

PJC 201.1. Divorce.

---

§ 6.002. Cruelty.

The court may grant a divorce in favor of one spouse if the other spouse is guilty of cruel treatment toward the complaining spouse of a nature that renders further living together insupportable.

Comment

Until the introduction of no fault divorce in 1970, cruelty was the most common ground for divorce. Cruelty is still occasionally pled, most often as an alternative, and generally to serve as a basis for justifying an unequal division of property or tactically to assist in a dispute over the conservatorship of a child.

Leading Cases

McCaskill v. McCaskill, 761 S.W.2d 470 (Tex. App.—Corpus Christi 1988, writ denied) (wife's pleading constituted a judicial admission as to grounds for divorce which could not be challenged on insufficiency of evidence grounds)

Clay v. Clay, 550 S.W.2d 730 (Tex. Civ. App.—Houston [1st Dist.] 1977, no writ) (notwithstanding a jury finding of cruel treatment, the trial court was authorized to enter a divorce under no fault provisions)

§ 6.003. Adultery.

The court may grant a divorce in favor of one spouse if the other spouse has committed adultery.

Comment

Not uncommonly, adultery is pled as an alternative ground for divorce, and more rarely as the sole ground. From the lawyer's perspective, most often the allegation is made to gain a tactical advantage to support an unequal division of property or to assist with a contest over conservatorship of a child. From the petitioner's perspective, the allegation may be made to seek vindication.

Leading Case

Bell v. Bell, 540 S.W.2d 432 (Tex. Civ. App.—Houston [1st Dist.] 1976, no writ) (acts of adultery are not limited to adultery committed before separation)

§ 6.004. Conviction of Felony.

(a) The court may grant a divorce in favor of one spouse if during the marriage the other spouse:

(1) has been convicted of a felony;

(2) has been imprisoned for at least one year in the state penitentiary, a federal penitentiary, or the penitentiary of another state; and

(3) has not been pardoned.

(b) The court may not grant a divorce under this section against a spouse who was convicted on the testimony of the other spouse.

§ 6.005. Abandonment.

The court may grant a divorce in favor of one spouse if the other spouse:

(1) left the complaining spouse with the intention of abandonment; and

(2) remained away for at least one year.

§ 6.006. Living Apart.

The court may grant a divorce in favor of either spouse if the spouses have lived apart without cohabitation for at least three years.

§ 6.007. Confinement in Mental Hospital.

The court may grant a divorce in favor of one spouse if at the time the suit is filed:

(1) the other spouse has been confined in a state mental hospital or private mental hospital, as defined in Section 571.003, Health and Safety Code, in this state or another state for at least three years; and

(2) it appears that the hospitalized spouse's mental disorder is of such a degree and nature that adjustment is unlikely or that, if adjustment occurs, a relapse is probable.

Leading Case

Saldarriaga v. Saldarriaga, 121 S.W.3d 493 (Tex. App.—Austin 2003, no pet.) (allegedly incompetent spouse entitled to guardian in Probate Court, not just next friend in divorce court)

---

§ 6.008. Defenses.

(a) The defenses to a suit for divorce of recrimination and adultery are abolished.

(b) Condonation is a defense to a suit for divorce only if the court finds that there is a reasonable expectation of reconciliation.

Comment

This section has little relevance in the 21st century. Recrimination and condonation as defenses to a suit for divorce were vestiges of family law as it existed before the official implementation of "no fault" divorce on January 1, 1970, the effective date of Title 1, Tex. Fam. Code Ann. The defense of adultery precluded one party from alleging adultery against his or her spouse if that party was also guilty of adultery.

Subchapter B. Grounds for Annulment

Introductory Comment

Sections 6.101–.104 provide very limited standing for an aggrieved parent to seek an annulment of the marriage of his or her underage child. Sections 6.105–.109 all relate to alleged defects in the voluntary consent to the marriage; each expiring when the ability to consent is restored. Section 6.110 has a unique basis for being, and § 6.111 common sensibly ends the possibility of annulment on the death of a spouse.

Texas Family Law Practice Manual

Chapter 47. Annulment and Suit to Declare Marriage Void: I. General Considerations; II. Annulment

Texas Pattern Jury Charges: Family

PJC 201.2. Annulment.

---

§ 6.101. Annulment of Marriage of Person Under Age 14.

(a) The court may grant an annulment of a licensed marriage of a person under 14 years of age unless a court order has been obtained as provided in Subchapter B, Chapter 2 *[The Marriage Relationship]*.

(b) A petition for annulment under this section may be filed by a next friend for the benefit of a person under 14 years of age or on the petition of the parent or the judicially designated managing conservator or guardian, whether an individual, authorized agency, or court, of the person.

(c) A suit by a parent, managing conservator, or guardian of the person may be brought at any time before the person is 14 years of age.

(d) A suit under this section to annul the marriage of a person 14 years of age or older that was entered into before the person was 14 years of age is barred unless the suit is filed within the later of:

(1) 90 days after the date the petitioner knew or should have known of the marriage; or

(2) 90 days after the date of the 14th birthday of the underage party.

§ 6.102. Annulment of Marriage of Person Under Age 18.

(a) The court may grant an annulment of a licensed or informal marriage of a person 14 years of age or older but under 18 years of age that occurred without parental consent or without a court order as provided by Subchapters B and E, Chapter 2 *[The Marriage Relationship]*.

(b) A petition for annulment under this section may be filed by:

(1) a next friend for the benefit of the underage party;

(2) a parent; or

(3) the judicially designated managing conservator or guardian of the person of the underage party, whether an individual, authorized agency, or court.

(c) A suit filed under this subsection by a next friend is barred unless it is filed within 90 days after the date of the marriage.

Leading Case

Husband v. Pierce, 800 S.W.2d 661 (Tex. App.—Tyler 1990, no writ) (underage wife had valid common law and Mexican marriages)

---

§ 6.103. Underage Annulment Barred by Adulthood.

A suit to annul a marriage may not be filed under Section 6.101 or 6.102 by a parent, managing conservator, or guardian of a person after the 18th birthday of the person.

§ 6.104. Discretionary Annulment of Underage Marriage.

(a) An annulment under Section 6.101 or 6.102 of a marriage may be granted at the discretion of the court sitting without a jury.

(b) In exercising its discretion, the court shall consider the pertinent facts concerning the welfare of the parties to the marriage, including whether the female is pregnant.

§ 6.105. Under Influence of Alcohol or Narcotics.

The court may grant an annulment of a marriage to a party to the marriage if:

(1) at the time of the marriage the petitioner was under the influence of alcoholic beverages or narcotics and as a result did not have the capacity to consent to the marriage; and

(2) the petitioner has not voluntarily cohabited with the other party to the marriage since the effects of the alcoholic beverages or narcotics ended.

Comment

A person claiming intoxication at time of marriage may seek an annulment provided there has been no cohabitation after becoming sober. It appears that the "window of opportunity" presented to a claimant for such an annulment may be open no longer than the morning after.

---

§ 6.106. Impotency.

The court may grant an annulment of a marriage to a party to the marriage if:

(1) either party, for physical or mental reasons, was permanently impotent at the time of the marriage;

(2) the petitioner did not know of the impotency at the time of the marriage; and

(3) the petitioner has not voluntarily cohabited with the other party since learning of the impotency.

Comment

Inability to have sexual intercourse by either a man or a woman can be grounds for an annulment. Frigidity and infertility are not covered by this section.

---

§ 6.107. Fraud, Duress, or Force.

The court may grant an annulment of a marriage to a party to the marriage if:

(1) the other party used fraud, duress, or force to induce the petitioner to enter into the marriage; and

(2) the petitioner has not voluntarily cohabited with the other party since learning of the fraud or since being released from the duress or force.

Comment

Fraud is probably the most common ground used for an annulment. The section is rather narrowly drawn; fraud must be part of the inducement for marriage and cohabitation must cease after the defrauded party learns of the fraud.

---

§ 6.108. Mental Incapacity.

(a) The court may grant an annulment of a marriage to a party to the marriage on the suit of the party or the party's guardian or next friend, if the court finds it to be in the party's best interest to be represented by a guardian or next friend, if:

(1) at the time of the marriage the petitioner did not have the mental capacity to consent to marriage or to understand the nature of the marriage ceremony because of a mental disease or defect; and

(2) since the marriage ceremony, the petitioner has not voluntarily cohabited with the other party during a period when the petitioner possessed the mental capacity to recognize the marriage relationship.

(b) The court may grant an annulment of a marriage to a party to the marriage if:

(1) at the time of the marriage the other party did not have the mental capacity to consent to marriage or to understand the nature of the marriage ceremony because of a mental disease or defect;

(2) at the time of the marriage the petitioner neither knew nor reasonably should have known of the mental disease or defect; and

(3) since the date the petitioner discovered or reasonably should have discovered the mental disease or defect, the petitioner has not voluntarily cohabited with the other party.

Comment

Although seldom used, in theory this section provides a significant no-fault basis for annulling a marriage.

§ 6.109. Concealed Divorce.

(a) The court may grant an annulment of a marriage to a party to the marriage if:

(1) the other party was divorced from a third party within the 30-day period preceding the date of the marriage ceremony;

(2) at the time of the marriage ceremony the petitioner did not know, and a reasonably prudent person would not have known, of the divorce; and

(3) since the petitioner discovered or a reasonably prudent person would have discovered the fact of the divorce, the petitioner has not voluntarily cohabited with the other party.

(b) A suit may not be brought under this section after the first anniversary of the date of the marriage.

Comment

This is a limited heartbalm remedy for the aggrieved party who unexpectedly learns that the other party had not divulged that he or she had been divorced within 30 days preceding the marriage. If knowledge of the divorce is delayed for one year or more, the annulment ground disappears. (It is never too late for divorce, however.)

§ 6.110. Marriage Less Than 72 Hours After Issuance of License.

(a) The court may grant an annulment of a marriage to a party to the marriage if the marriage ceremony took place in violation of Section 2.204 during the 72-hour period immediately following the issuance of the marriage license.

(b) A suit may not be brought under this section after the 30th day after the date of the marriage.

Comment

This section was added in conjunction with the enactment of the 72–hour waiting period between issuance of a license and the marriage ceremony provided in § 2.204, *supra*. A challenge to void the marriage is restricted to a short time after the "offense" occurs, *i.e.*, 30 days.

§ 6.111. Death of Party to Voidable Marriage.

A marriage subject to annulment may not be challenged in a proceeding instituted after the death of either party to the marriage.

Subchapter C. Declaring a Marriage Void

§ 6.201. Consanguinity.

A marriage is void if one party to the marriage is related to the other as:

(1) an ancestor or descendant, by blood or adoption;

(2) a brother or sister, of the whole or half blood or by adoption;

(3) a parent's brother or sister, of the whole or half blood or by adoption; or

(4) a son or daughter of a brother or sister, of the whole or half blood or by adoption.

Comment

The prohibition set forth in this section corresponds with the incest prohibition in the Penal Code. Although it is unlawful to marry an aunt, uncle, nephew or niece, Texas law does not prohibit marriage of first cousins as some states do.

Texas Family Law Practice Manual

Chapter 47. Annulment and Suit To Declare Marriage Void: I. General Considerations; III. Suit To Declare Marriage Void

Texas Pattern Jury Charges: Family

PJC 201.3. Void Marriage.

Cross Reference

TEX. PEN. CODE ANN. § 25.02. Prohibited Sexual Conduct.

---

§ 6.202. Marriage During Existence of Prior Marriage.

(a) A marriage is void if entered into when either party has an existing marriage to another person that has not been dissolved by legal action or terminated by the death of the other spouse.

(b) The later marriage that is void under this section becomes valid when the prior marriage is dissolved if, after the date of the dissolution, the parties have lived together as husband and wife and represented themselves to others as being married.

Leading Cases

Loera v. Loera, 815 S.W.2d 910 (Tex. App.—Corpus Christi 1991, no writ) (burden of proof on party claiming prior undissolved marriage)

Rodriguez v. Avalos, 567 S.W.2d 85 (Tex. Civ. App.—El Paso 1978, no writ) (finding of prior undissolved common law marriage upheld)

Caddel v. Caddel, 486 S.W.2d 141 (Tex. Civ. App.—Amarillo 1972, no writ) (subsequent marriage found to exist when prior impediment removed)

Cross Reference

TEX. PEN. CODE ANN. § 25.01. Bigamy.

---

§ 6.203. Certain Void Marriages Validated.

Except for a marriage that would have been void under Section 6.201, a marriage that was entered into before January 1, 1970, in violation of the prohibitions of Article 496,

Penal Code of Texas, 1925, is validated from the date the marriage commenced if the parties continued until January 1, 1970, to live together as husband and wife and to represent themselves to others as being married.

§ 6.204. Recognition of Same–Sex Marriage or Civil Union.

(a) In this section, "civil union" means any relationship status other than marriage that:

(1) is intended as an alternative to marriage or applies primarily to cohabitating persons; and

(2) grants to the parties of the relationship legal protections, benefits, or responsibilities granted to the spouses of a marriage.

(b) A marriage between persons of the same sex or a civil union is contrary to the public policy of this state and is void in this state.

(c) The state or an agency or political subdivision of the state may not give effect to a:

(1) public act, record, or judicial proceeding that creates, recognizes, or validates a marriage between persons of the same sex or a civil union in this state or in any other jurisdiction; or

(2) right or claim to any legal protection, benefit, or responsibility asserted as a result of a marriage between persons of the same sex or a civil union in this state or in any other jurisdiction.

History: Enacted by 78th Legis., Reg. Sess. (2003), S.B. 7, eff. Sept. 1, 2003, and "applies to a same-sex marriage or a civil union regardless of whether the marriage or civil union was entered into before, on or after the effective date of this Act."

Editors' Note: *S.B. 7, 78th Legis., Reg. Sess. (2003) amended Subchapter C by adding Section 6.204, and contains the following uncodified provision:*

The legislature finds that through the designation of guardians, the appointment of agents, and the use of private contracts persons may adequately and properly appoint guardians and arrange rights relating to hospital visitation, property, and the entitlement to proceeds of life insurance policies without the existence of any legally recognized familial relationship between the persons.

Comment

With the enactment of this section, Texas joins approximately 40 other states that forbid recognition of same-sex marriages or civil unions in accordance with the Defense of Marriage Act, 28 U.S.C.A. § 1738c, *infra.*

Cross Reference

Tex. Fam. Code Ann. § 2.001. Marriage license, *supra*

Tex. Fam. Code Ann. § 2.401. Proof of informal marriage, *supra*

Defense of Marriage Act, 28 U.S.C.A. § 1738C, *infra*

Subchapter D. Jurisdiction, Venue, and Residence Qualifications

Introductory Comment

In order to maintain an action for divorce, all states, including Texas, have traditionally imposed durational state domiciliary and county residency requirements; six months and one-year are most typical. However, historically some states have enacted very short durational residency requirements designed to encourage interstate forum shopping by litigants, *e.g.*, six weeks in Nevada. To counter the image of being a "divorce mill," most states have clearly constitutional laws regarding durational residency. *Sosna v. Iowa*, 419 U.S. 394 (1975). In Texas, a county durational residency requirement is added because of the size of the state. Often overlooked is the correlative proviso in § 6.302 that a nonresident petitioner may bring suit if the respondent has been domiciled in Texas for six months without regard to the respondent's length of county residency.

In some divorce suits involving two Texans, the petitioner has a choice of venue if the parties have separated; the action may be filed in the county of residence of either party so long as the durational county residency of 90 days is met.

CLE/Other Legal Publications

Jurisdiction, special appearance, and conflicts of law. Donn C. Fullenweider, 2004 ADV. FAM. L.

Jurisdiction, venue, transfers and standing. Brian L. Webb, Miriam L. Ackels & Ashlie L. Thomas, 2003 ADV. FAM. L.

Conflicts of law—Texas law and the Restatement. Joan F. Jenkins, 2003 NEW FRONTIERS

Thoughts in general and in particular regarding Texas personal jurisdiction, special appearance and other interstate jurisdictional issues. James E. Farris, 2003 NEW FRONTIERS

Venue and special appearance. James E. Farris, 2002 ADV. FAM. L.

Leading Cases

McAlister v. McAlister, 75 S.W.3d 981 (Tex. App.—San Antonio 2002, pet. denied) (first-filed divorce by wife in her dual residence county has dominant jurisdiction over husband's later suit)

Jones v. Jones, 64 S.W.3d 206 (Tex. App.—El Paso 2001, no pet.) (incarcerated husband denied continuance for 2 months until scheduled release constitutes an abuse of discretion)

Johnson v. Johnson, 37 S.W.3d 523 (Tex. App.—El Paso 2001, no pet.) (Full Faith and Credit due to N.C. separation decree)

Boots v. Lopez, 6 S.W.3d 292 (Tex. App.—Houston [14th Dist.] 1999, pet. denied) (dismissal of Texas divorce affirmed as Arizona more convenient forum)

Clawson v. Millard, 934 S.W.2d 899 (Tex. App.—Houston [1st Dist.] 1996, no writ) (ordinarily "first-filed" divorce establishes dominant jurisdiction, but "second-filed" court may find an estoppel on facts demonstrating unreasonable delay in service of citation)

Cook v. Mayfield, 886 S.W.2d 840 (Tex. App.—Waco 1994, no writ) (plea in abatement and dismissal mandatory when divorce petitioner has not met durational county residency) (residency requires actual, physical, continuous living in the county of suit by one of the parties for the period specified, along with a good-faith intent to make that county home)

Dokmanovic v. Schwarz, 880 S.W.2d 272 (Tex. App.—Houston [14th Dist.] 1994, no writ) (inclusion in pleadings that residency requirements have been met requires no further proof of that admitted fact)

Harmon v. Harmon, 879 S.W.2d 213 (Tex. App.—Houston [14th Dist.] 1994, writ denied) (residency requirements not jurisdictional; judgment based on false testimony of residency not void, but voidable by direct appeal or equitable proceeding)

McCaskill v. McCaskill, 761 S.W.2d 470 (Tex. App.—Corpus Christi 1988, writ denied) (residence requirements are not jurisdictional, but must be met before rendition of divorce)

Allen v. Allen, 593 S.W.2d 133 (Tex. Civ. App.—Amarillo 1979, no writ) (filing in one county does not preclude other spouse from filing and obtaining a divorce in second county)

Posey v. Posey, 561 S.W.2d 602 (Tex. Civ. App.—Waco 1978, writ dism'd w.o.j.) (temporary absence from county does not affect right to maintain suit)

§ 6.301. General Residency Rule for Divorce Suit.

A suit for divorce may not be maintained in this state unless at the time the suit is filed either the petitioner or the respondent has been:

(1) a domiciliary of this state for the preceding six-month period; and

(2) a resident of the county in which the suit is filed for the preceding 90-day period.

§ 6.302. Suit for Divorce by Nonresident Spouse.

If one spouse has been a domiciliary of this state for at least the last six months, a spouse domiciled in another state or nation may file a suit for divorce in the county in which the domiciliary spouse resides at the time the petition is filed.

Comment

This section, along with § 6.301, allows a non-resident to maintain a suit for divorce in Texas if the other party is properly domiciled in Texas. Venue is fixed in the county in which the Texan "is domiciled," but there is no durational county residency requirement of 90 days as mandated in § 6.301, *supra*.

§ 6.303. Absence on Public Service.

Time spent by a Texas domiciliary outside this state or outside the county of residence of the domiciliary while in the service of the armed forces or other service of the United States or of this state is considered residence in this state and in that county.

Comment

This curative statute is designed to assist Texans to obtain a divorce when they are members of the Armed Forces or "other service of the United States or of this state" stationed or working outside the state.

Cross Reference

Servicemembers Civil Relief Act of 2004, 50 App. U.S.C. 501 *et seq.*, *infra*.

§ 6.304. Armed Forces Personnel Not Previously Residents.

A person not previously a resident of this state who is serving in the armed forces of the United States and has been stationed at one or more military installations in this state for at least the last six months and at a military installation in a county of this state for at least the last 90 days is considered to be a Texas domiciliary and a resident of that county for those periods for the purpose of filing suit for dissolution of a marriage.

Comment

The corollary to § 6.303, this section allows armed services personnel stationed in Texas to file for divorce even though they may intend to return to another state of their domicile on discharge.

Leading Cases

Skubal v. Skubal, 584 S.W.2d 45 (Tex. Civ. App.—San Antonio 1979, writ dism'd w.o.j.) (soldier may maintain suit for divorce even though intending to establish domicile outside Texas)

Fox v. Fox, 559 S.W.2d 407 (Tex. Civ. App.—Austin 1977, no writ) (court may grant in rem divorce to soldier stationed in Texas even though spouse a non-resident)

Cross Reference

Servicemembers Civil Relief Act of 2004, 50 App. U.S.C. 501 *et seq.*, *infra*.

---

§ 6.305. Acquiring Jurisdiction Over Nonresident Respondent.

(a) If the petitioner in a suit for dissolution of a marriage is a resident or a domiciliary of this state at the time the suit for dissolution is filed, the court may exercise personal jurisdiction over the respondent or over the respondent's personal representative although the respondent is not a resident of this state if:

(1) this state is the last marital residence of the petitioner and the respondent and the suit is filed before the second anniversary of the date on which marital residence ended; or

(2) there is any basis consistent with the constitutions of this state and the United States for the exercise of the personal jurisdiction.

(b) A court acquiring jurisdiction under this section also acquires jurisdiction over the respondent in a suit affecting the parent-child relationship.

Comment

A Texas court may grant a divorce to a Texas resident even if there is no personal jurisdiction over the nonresident spouse—such a decree is known as a "status adjudication." Such proceeding may not provide wholly adequate relief for a Texas spouse, however, in the absence of personal jurisdiction over the nonresident spouse. This section provides for "long-arm" jurisdiction over the nonresident spouse if the parties had lived in Texas as their last marital residence within the last two years, or if there is any other basis under the state and federal constitution for exercising jurisdiction.

In the absence of personal jurisdiction over an absent respondent, a Texas divorce court is not authorized to render an order that requires such jurisdiction, such as payment of spousal maintenance or attorney's fees, or division of marital property not subject to the court's adjudicative power, *e.g.*, real property in another state.

CLE/Other Legal Publications

Jurisdiction, special appearance, and conflicts of law. Donn C. Fullenweider, 2004 ADV. FAM. L.

Jurisdiction, venue, transfers and standing. Brian L. Webb, Miriam L. Ackels & Ashlie L. Thomas, 2003 ADV. FAM. L.

Conflicts of law-Texas law and the Restatement. Joan F. Jenkins, 2003 NEW FRONTIERS

Thoughts in general and in particular regarding Texas personal jurisdiction, special appearance and other interstate jurisdictional issues. James E. Farris, 2003 NEW FRONTIERS

Jurisdiction over foreign litigants: dissolution, property division, spousal support, child support. Bill De La Garza & Jo Ann Carter, 2002 ADV. FAM. L.

Personal jurisdiction in Texas divorce practice and special appearance proceedings. James E. Farris, 2002 ADV. FAM. L.

Leading U.S. Supreme Court Cases

Burnham v. Superior Court of California, 495 U.S. 604, 109 L.Ed.2d 631, 110 S.Ct. 2105 (1990) (in personam jurisdiction obtained by service of citation in forum state on transient respondent)

Vanderbilt v. Vanderbilt, 354 U.S. 416, 1 L.Ed.2d 1456, 77 S.Ct. 1360 (1957) (Nevada court has jurisdiction to grant divorce but did not have jurisdiction to extinguish wife's right to support from her husband as provided by New York law)

Estin v. Estin, 334 U.S. 541, 92 L.Ed. 1561, 68 S.Ct. 1213 (1948) (service by publication sufficient to satisfy procedural due process for granting of divorce only)

Williams v. North Carolina, 325 U.S. 226, 89 L.Ed. 1577, 65 S.Ct. 1092 (1945) (North Carolina court not required to recognize Nevada divorce where Nevada lacked jurisdiction)

Williams v. North Carolina, 317 U.S. 287, 87 L.Ed. 279, 63 S.Ct. 207 (1942) (domicile of a spouse is a sufficient basis for divorce jurisdiction)

Leading Texas Cases

Dawson–Austin v. Austin, 968 S.W.2d 319 (Tex. 1998) (nonresident wife made valid special appearance—no minimum contacts, so no jurisdiction to divide marital estate)

Mitchim v. Mitchim, 518 S.W.2d 362 (Tex. 1975) (Arizona assertion of long-arm jurisdiction over Texas resident entitled to Full Faith and Credit)

Goodenbour v. Goodenbour, 64 S.W.3d 69 (Tex. App.—Austin 2001, no pet.) (as last marital residence, Texas has long-arm personal jurisdiction over husband/father for divorce/SAPCR)

Reynolds v. Reynolds, 2 S.W.3d 429 (Tex. App.—Houston [1st Dist.] 1999, no pet.) (husband left Texas significantly more than two years ago—long arm jurisdiction for divorce still applies based on sufficient "minimum contacts")

Hoffman v. Hoffman, 821 S.W.2d 3 (Tex. App.—Fort Worth 1992, no writ) (divorce court's subject matter jurisdiction does not supply personal jurisdiction over nonresident spouse or property outside Texas)

Letersky v. Letersky, 820 S.W.2d 12 (Tex. App.—Eastland 1991, no writ) (120a motion by wife residing in Scotland not compromised by accompanying letter of explanation)

Cossey v. Cossey, 602 S.W.2d 591 (Tex. Civ. App.—Waco 1980, no writ) (marital residence means more than occasional visits)

Cross References

TEX. FAM. CODE ANN. § 102.011. Acquiring Jurisdiction Over Nonresident; § 102.012. Exercising Partial Jurisdiction; ch. 152, subch. C. Jurisdiction [UCCJEA §§ 152.201–.210]; ch. 159, subch. C. Jurisdiction [UIFSA §§ 159.201–.211]; § 160.604. Personal Jurisdiction [Uniform Parentage Act].

---

§ 6.306. Jurisdiction to Annul Marriage.

(a) A suit for annulment of a marriage may be maintained in this state only if the parties were married in this state or if either party is domiciled in this state.

(b) A suit for annulment is a suit in rem, affecting the status of the parties to the marriage.

Comment

A suit for an annulment or an action to declare a marriage void, § 6.307, *infra*, is declared to be an in rem proceeding dissolving the marriage without further elaboration. The statute states that suit may be maintained in Texas only if the marriage took place in this state or if one of the parties is domiciled in this state. Importantly, there are no prescribed periods of durational residency or a requirement of domicile such as those established in § 6.301 for maintaining a divorce. Rather obviously, the statute has a potential for unconstitutional application if literally applied under certain fact circumstances. For example, suppose that an out-of-state couple marries while on vacation on South Padre Island and returns forthwith to their home state where they reside for a number of years. If one of the spouses returns to Texas for an annulment, it seems rather clear that a decree of annulment granted by a Texas court will exceed the bounds of constitutional due process. This conclusion is purely speculative; apparently no one has attempted this particular course of action—at least no one with a reported case.

There is a common misconception that once a marriage is annulled, it is considered to have never existed. Texas law clearly holds to the contrary. Property acquired and children born during an annulled marriage receive the same treatment as if the marriage is dissolved by divorce.

§ 6.307. Jurisdiction to Declare Marriage Void.

(a) Either party to a marriage made void by this chapter may sue to have the marriage declared void, or the court may declare the marriage void in a collateral proceeding.

(b) The court may declare a marriage void only if:

(1) the purported marriage was contracted in this state; or

(2) either party is domiciled in this state.

(c) A suit to have a marriage declared void is a suit in rem, affecting the status of the parties to the purported marriage.

Comment

A void marriage can be attacked in a collateral proceeding. Such a procedure is not permitted for an attack on a voidable marriage, which may be dissolved by annulment (or divorce).

§ 6.308. Exercising Partial Jurisdiction.

(a) A court in which a suit for dissolution of a marriage is filed may exercise its jurisdiction over those portions of the suit for which it has authority.

(b) The court's authority to resolve the issues in controversy between the parties may be restricted because the court lacks:

(1) the required personal jurisdiction over a nonresident party in a suit for dissolution of the marriage;

(2) the required jurisdiction under Chapter 152 *[UCCJEA]*; or

(3) the required jurisdiction under Chapter 159 *[UIFSA]*.

Comment

See comment and citations to § 6.305. Acquiring Jurisdiction Over Nonresident Respondent, *supra*.

Subchapter E. Filing Suit

§ 6.401. Caption.

(a) Pleadings in a suit for divorce or annulment shall be styled "In the Matter of the Marriage of __________ and __________."

(b) Pleadings in a suit to declare a marriage void shall be styled "A Suit To Declare Void the Marriage of __________ and __________."

§ 6.402. Pleadings.

(a) A petition in a suit for dissolution of a marriage is sufficient without the necessity of specifying the underlying evidentiary facts if the petition alleges the grounds relied on substantially in the language of the statute.

(b) Allegations of grounds for relief, matters of defense, or facts relied on for a temporary order that are stated in short and plain terms are not subject to special exceptions because of form or sufficiency.

(c) The court shall strike an allegation of evidentiary fact from the pleadings on the motion of a party or on the court's own motion.

Comment

This section is designed to purge divorce pleadings of detailed, often inflammatory, allegations of marital misbehavior. Before its enactment, Texas practitioners were quite vivid in their pleadings when describing the allegations of marital misconduct against the opposing party. The statute does not deal with ancillary litigation, such as issues of alter ego, wasting of marital assets, or third-party claims.

Leading Cases

Wahlenmaier v. Wahlenmaier, 762 S.W.2d 575 (Tex. 1988) (next friend may obtain divorce on behalf of mentally incompetent individual)

Bahr v. Kohr, 980 S.W.2d 723 (Tex. App.—San Antonio 1998, no pet.) (issue of separate property can be raised by a general denial)

Stubbs v. Ortega, 977 S.W.2d 718 (Tex. App.—Fort Worth 1998, pet. denied) (court approval for filing divorce by guardian affirmed)

Morgan v. Morgan, 657 S.W.2d 484 (Tex. App.—Houston [1st Dist.] 1983, writ dism'd w.o.j.) (divorce pleadings are construed more liberally than in other civil cases)

§ 6.403. Answer.

The respondent in a suit for dissolution of a marriage is not required to answer on oath or affirmation.

Comment

As in other civil cases, a respondent in a divorce case must file a written answer to the petition for divorce or face the consequences of a default judgment. In a default judgment proceeding, the petitioner must still put on evidence sufficient for the court to grant a divorce and for other appropriate relief, such as the division of property and orders regarding conservatorship of any children of the marriage. The degree of proof necessarily depends upon the particular case and the practice of the local court, but rather obviously a sworn statement of "insupportability" is universally sufficient to prove a no fault ground.

Leading Cases

McAlister v. McAlister, 75 S.W.3d 481 (Tex. App.—San Antonio 2002, pet. denied) (first-filed Bexar County divorce suit established dominant jurisdiction—mailing petition and waiver and attempting negotiations excuses failure to serve citation promptly)

Ratisseau v. Ratisseau, 44 S.W.3d 695 (Tex. App.—Houston [14th Dist.] 2001, no pet.) (divorce petition must be supported by evidence at trial—default judgments in divorce differ from other civil suits)

In re Daugherty, 42 S.W.3d 331 (Tex. App.—Texarkana 2001, no pet.) (an incarcerated spouse has right to participate in divorce trial; accommodation must be made for him to put forward his case, even if it is only by telephone)

Zuniga v. Zuniga, 13 S.W.3d 798 (Tex. App.—San Antonio 1999, no pet.); Dodd v. Dodd, 17 S.W.3d 714 (Tex. App.—Houston [1st Dist.] 2000, no pet.) (incarcerated husband's right to respond to divorce petition should trigger balancing test by trial court to protect access to the courts)

Gone v. Gone, 993 S.W.2d 845 (Tex. App.—Houston [14th Dist.] 1999, pet. denied) (ignore divorce papers at your own peril)

Harris v. Harris, 850 S.W.2d 241 (Tex. App.—Houston [1st Dist.] 1993, no writ) (default disallowed, respondent's letter to court constitutes pro se answer)

Avila v. Avila, 843 S.W.2d 280 (Tex. App.—El Paso 1992, no writ) (default divorce reversed, TRCP require strict compliance for service of citation)

Considine v. Considine, 726 S.W.2d 253 (Tex. App.—Austin 1987, no writ) (in default case, petitioner must still prove grounds for divorce)

---

§ 6.4035. Waiver of Service.

(a) A party to a suit for the dissolution of a marriage may waive the issuance or service of process after the suit is filed by filing with the clerk of the court in which the suit is filed the waiver of the party acknowledging receipt of a copy of the filed petition.

(b) The waiver must contain the mailing address of the party who executed the waiver.

(c) The waiver must be sworn but may not be sworn before an attorney in the suit.

(d) The Texas Rules of Civil Procedure do not apply to a waiver executed under this section.

§ 6.404. [repealed]

Comment

In the mid–1990's ADR was seen as a means to discourage contested trials. This now-repealed statute was designed to ensure that the parties to a lawsuit were informed about the existence and utility of ADR. Obviously, the legislature did not want to rely on a directive to attorneys to communicate such information orally to their clients because the statute mandated that a positive statement about ADR be included in the "first pleading filed by a party," which included petitions and general denials. Moreover, the statement had to be signed by the individual party, not by the attorney.

The statute had unintended consequences which redounded to the detriment of individual litigants. The client "signing requirement" meant that either at least two trips to the attorney's office were necessary or an exchange of documents by mail was needed. In either event, increased costs and delays were endemic. Further, the ever-increasing popularity of ADR with both attorneys and judges has reached such heights that a formal emphasis on the ADR process seems redundant. Accordingly, in 2003 the Council of the Family Law Section sought and obtained repeal of the ADR notification-statute.

Texas Family Law Practice Manual

Chapter 15. Alternative Dispute Resolution

---

§ 6.405. Protective Order.

(a) The petition in a suit for dissolution of a marriage must state whether a protective order under Title 4 is in effect or if an application for a protective order is pending with regard to the parties to the suit.

(b) The petitioner shall attach to the petition a copy of each protective order issued under Title 4 in which one of the parties to the suit was the applicant and the other party was the respondent without regard to the date of the order. If a copy of the protective order is not available at the time of filing, the petition must state that a copy of the order will be filed with the court before any hearing.

CLE/Other Legal Publications

See *CLE/Other Legal Publications* following *Prefatory Note* to Chapter 71, *infra*.

Texas Family Law Practice Manual

Chapter 14. Protective Orders

---

§ 6.406. Mandatory Joinder of Suit Affecting Parent-Child Relationship.

(a) The petition in a suit for dissolution of a marriage shall state whether there are children born or adopted of the marriage who are under 18 years of age or who are otherwise entitled to support as provided by Chapter 154 *[Child Support]*.

(b) If the parties are parents of a child, as defined by Section 101.003, and the child is not under the continuing jurisdiction of another court as provided by Chapter 155 *[Continuing, Exclusive Jurisdiction; Transfer]*, the suit for dissolution of a marriage must include a suit affecting the parent-child relationship under Title 5.

Leading Case

Diaz v. Diaz, 126 S.W.3d 406 (Tex. App.—Corpus Christi 2004, no pet.) (default divorce void for failure to include SAPCR in pleading; merely mentioning children in petition not enough)

---

§ 6.407. Transfer of Suit Affecting Parent-Child Relationship to Divorce Court.

(a) If a suit affecting the parent-child relationship is pending at the time the suit for dissolution of a marriage is filed, the suit affecting the parent-child relationship shall be transferred as provided by Section 103.002 to the court in which the suit for dissolution is filed.

(b) If the parties are parents of a child, as defined by Section 101.003, and the child is under the continuing jurisdiction of another court under Chapter 155 *[Continuing, Exclusive Jurisdiction; Transfer]*, either party to the suit for dissolution of a marriage may move that court for transfer of the suit affecting the parent-child relationship to the court having jurisdiction of the suit for dissolution. The court with continuing jurisdiction shall transfer the proceeding as provided by Chapter 155. On the transfer of the proceedings, the court with jurisdiction of the suit for dissolution of a marriage shall consolidate the two causes of action.

(c) After transfer of a suit affecting the parent-child relationship as provided in Chapter 155, the court with jurisdiction of the suit for dissolution of a marriage has jurisdiction to render an order in the suit affecting the parent-child relationship as provided by Title 5.

Comment

The TEX. FAM. CODE ANN. authorizes distinct actions under Title 1 (*The Marriage Relationship*), Title 4 (*Protective Orders and Family Violence*), and Title 5 (*Parent and Child*), all of which may be joined in one suit. Indeed, if minor children were born to the wife during the marriage, a SAPCR must be joined with a suit for dissolution of marriage. Texas lawyers and judges are now accustomed to this conceptual arrangement of Texas family law. This section provides the critical bridge between Title 1 and Title 5 actions.

Leading Case

Neal v. Avey, 853 S.W.2d 707 (Tex. App.—Houston [14th Dist.] 1993, writ denied) (filing divorce mandates transfer of termination action)

Texas Family Law Practice Manual

Chapter 33. Transfer

---

§ 6.408. Service of Citation.

Citation on the filing of an original petition in a suit for dissolution of a marriage shall be issued and served as in other civil cases. Citation may also be served on any other person who has or who may assert an interest in the suit for dissolution of the marriage.

Leading Cases

In re Marriage of Seals, 83 S.W.3d 870 (Tex. App.—Texarkana 2002, no pet.) (DWOP of inmate's divorce petition for "failure to appear" reversed)

McAlister v. McAlister, 75 S.W.3d 481 (Tex. App.—San Antonio 2002, pet. denied) (wife's attorney did not unreasonably delay procuring citation such that she was stopped from asserting dominant jurisdiction)

---

§ 6.409. Citation by Publication.

(a) Citation in a suit for dissolution of a marriage may be by publication as in other civil cases, except that notice shall be published one time only.

(b) The notice shall be sufficient if given in substantially the following form:

To (name of person to be served with citation), and to all whom it may concern (if the name of any person to be served with citation is unknown), Respondent(s),

"STATE OF TEXAS

"You have been sued. You may employ an attorney. If you or your attorney do not file a written answer with the clerk who issued this citation by 10 a.m. on the Monday next following the expiration of 20 days after you were served this citation and petition, a default judgment may be taken against you. The petition of ________, Petitioner, was filed in the Court of ________ County, Texas, on the ______ day of ________, against ________, Respondent(s), numbered ______, and entitled 'In the Matter of

Marriage of ________ and ________. The suit requests ________ (statement of relief sought).'

"The Court has authority in this suit to enter any judgment or decree dissolving the marriage and providing for the division of property that will be binding on you.

"Issued and given under my hand and seal of said Court at ________, Texas, this the ___ day of ____, ____.

"________________
Clerk of the ________ Court of
________ County, Texas
By ________, Deputy."

(c) The form authorized in this section and the form authorized by Section 102.010 may be combined in appropriate situations.

(d) If the citation is for a suit in which a parent-child relationship does not exist, service by publication may be completed by posting the citation at the courthouse door for seven days in the county in which the suit is filed.

(e) If the petitioner or the petitioner's attorney of record makes an oath that no child presently under 18 years of age was born or adopted by the spouses and that no appreciable amount of property was accumulated by the spouses during the marriage, the court may dispense with the appointment of an attorney ad litem. In a case in which citation was by publication, a statement of the evidence, approved and signed by the judge, shall be filed with the papers of the suit as a part of the record.

Comment

This section prescribes the contents of citation by publication in a suit to dissolve a marriage. The statute authorizes a procedure dramatically different from that prescribed for other civil lawsuits. The notice need appear only once in a legal newspaper, not four times, and the time for the respondent to answer is shorter (the usual time after regular personal service of citation). If there are no children, the citation may be posted in the courthouse for seven days. The court, under limited circumstances, may waive the appointment of an attorney ad litem.

Leading Case

In re A.Y., 16 S.W.3d 387 (Tex. App.—El Paso 2000, no pet.) (rejection of argument that publication should be in county of last known residence of respondent rather than county in which suit is pending)

Cross References

TEX. FAM. CODE ANN. § 102.010. Service of Citation by Publication.

TEX. R. CIV. P. 109. Citation by Publication; 114. Citation by Publication—Requisites; 116. Service of Citation by Publication; 117. Return of Citation by Publication.

§ 6.410. Report to Accompany Petition [first of two].

At the time a petition for divorce or annulment of a marriage is filed, the petitioner shall also file a completed report that may be used by the district clerk, at the time the petition is granted, to comply with Section 194.002, Health and Safety Code.

History: Amended by 78th Legis., Reg. Sess. (2003), H.B. 2886, eff. Sept. 1, 2003, and "applies only to a certificate or report that the bureau of vital statistics of the Texas Department of Health determines requires correction on or after that date."

§ 6.410. Confidentiality of Pleadings [second of two].

(a) This section applies only in a county with a population of 3.4 million or more.

(b) Except as otherwise provided by law, all pleadings and other documents filed with the court in a suit for dissolution of a marriage are confidential, are excepted from required public disclosure under Chapter 552, Government Code, and may not be released to a person who is not a party to the suit until after the date of service of citation or the 31st day after the date of filing the suit, whichever date is sooner.

History: Amended by 78th Legis., Reg. Sess. (2003), H.B. 1391, eff. Sept. 1, 2003, and "applies only to a suit for dissolution of a marriage filed on or after the effective date of this Act. A suit for dissolution of a marriage filed before the effective date of this Act is governed by the law in effect on the date the suit was filed, and the former law is continued in effect for that purpose."

Comment

In an effort to regulate solicitation of business by family law attorneys in Harris County, the legislature recognized a need to prevent notification of the filing of a filing of a lawsuit to a respondent in the context of divorce, SAPCR, or a protective order prior to service of citation. In these types of cases there is the potential of violence or destruction of assets before a restraining order can be served. On the other hand, arguably solicitation of legal representation in family law cases is protected under the U.S. Constitution. Therefore, the legislature created confidentiality requirements in an attempt to balance the competing interests of safety and free speech.

For Harris County only, there is a statutorily mandated delay of public disclosure of the filing of this type of litigation. If the Houston practice of this particular version of legal advertising spreads to other counties, it seems likely that the application of the statute solely to Harris County may be expanded.

Subchapter F. Temporary Orders

Introductory Comment

The authorization of temporary orders attempts to balance the rights of the parties with respect to temporary restraining orders, temporary injunctions, and other orders. A trial court may not issue a temporary restraining order that excludes a spouse from the family home, prohibits reasonable and necessary spending of funds for living expenses, or forbids reasonable and necessary conduct of a party's usual business. At the hearing for the temporary injunction where both parties have been given notice and opportunity to be heard, the court may enter more extensive orders, including temporary injunctions, orders for support of a spouse, and interim attorney's fees, as well as for temporary exclusive use of marital property.

CLE/Other Legal Publications

Receiverships in family law cases. John T. Eck, 2003 U. Tex. Fam. L. Front Lines

Temporary orders: how to look prepared, even if you just met your client yesterday. Eric Robertson, 2003 U. Tex. Fam. L. Front Lines

Preserving and protecting assets during the divorce proceeding and what to do when they disappear. Ellen Elkins Grimes, 2003 U. Houston Fam. L. Practice Sem. (Oct.)

Temporary hearings, temporary orders, and other pre-trial matters. Heather M. Hughes, 2003 U. Houston Fam. L. Practice Sem. (March)

Puttin' on the writs: mandamus, prohibition and habeas. John Christopher Nickelson & Linda B. Thomas, 2002 ADV. FAM. L.

Temporary and protective order traps. James M. Loveless, 2002 ADV. FAM. L.

Temporary hearings: family violence, guns, and related issues. Rhonda F. Hunter, 2002 MARRIAGE DISSOLUTION

Leading Cases

Ex parte Hall, 854 S.W.2d 656 (Tex. 1993) (temporary support order requires evidence, cannot be based on premarital agreement)

Walker v. Towslee, 677 S.W.2d 502 (Tex. 1984) (interim fees cannot be granted as part of motion for new trial)

Norem v. Norem, 105 S.W.3d 213 (Tex. App.—Dallas 2003, no pet.) (receiver's appointment approved, but receiver given too much power to control corporations run by husband)

Johnston v. Crook, 93 S.W.3d 263 (Tex. App.—Houston [14th Dist.] 2002, no pet.) (receiver's pursuit of property allegedly fraudulently transferred by husband to Wife #2 wrongly dismissed by summary judgment)

In re Marriage of Edwards, 79 S.W.3d 88 (Tex. App.—Texarkana 2002, no pet.) (trial court's practice of appointing receiver when parties can't agree abuse of discretion, but moot in this case because everything was sold and proceeds were divided)

Rusk v. Rusk, 5 S.W.3d 299 (Tex. App.—Houston [14th Dist.] 1999, pet. denied) (courts particularly loathe to appoint receiver which is extraordinarily harsh remedy)

Herschberg v. Herschberg, 994 S.W.2d 273 (Tex. App.—Corpus Christi 1999, pet. denied) (temporary support due to wife while property division on remand—but amount subject to abuse of discretion)

Walston v. Walston, 971 S.W.2d 687 (Tex. App.—Waco 1998, pet. denied) (if property not subject to partition in kind trial court may appoint a receiver and order property incapable of partition to be sold and the proceeds divided between the parties in just and right manner)

Collins v. State, 955 S.W.2d 464 (Tex. App.—Fort Worth 1997, no pet.) (protective order criminally enforceable although lack of specificity would not sustain contempt for disobedience of court order)

Ruiz v. Ruiz, 946 S.W.2d 124 (Tex. App.—Waco 1997, no writ) (protective order granted while divorce pending which didn't dispose of all issues is non-appealable interlocutory order)

Rider v. Rider, 887 S.W.2d 255 (Tex. App.—Beaumont 1994, no writ) (wife's transfer of quitclaim deeds to father violated orders restraining her from selling, transferring, assigning, mortgaging, or otherwise alienating her interest in real property)

Cook v. Cook, 886 S.W.2d 838 (Tex. App.—Waco 1994, no writ) (temporary orders are not subject to interlocutory appeal)

Tschirhart v. Tschirhart, 876 S.W.2d 507 (Tex. App.—Austin 1994, no writ) (unless formally admitted into evidence at trial, sworn inventory and appraisement may not be relied upon on appeal)

Post v. Garza, 867 S.W.2d 88 (Tex. App.—Corpus Christi 1993, no writ) (award of interim fees must be based on notice and opportunity to be heard)

Chiles v. Schuble, 788 S.W.2d 205 (Tex. App.—Houston [14th Dist.] 1990, no writ) (refusal of trial court to enforce temporary orders is abuse of discretion)

Eikenhorst v. Eikenhorst, 746 S.W.2d 882 (Tex. App.—Houston [1st Dist.] 1988, no writ) (court has authority to order temporary support pending appeal of its ruling)

Readhimer v. Readhimer, 728 S.W.2d 872 (Tex. App.—Houston [1st Dist.] 1987, no writ) (there must be some evidence justifying the appointment of a receiver)

Ismail v. Ismail, 702 S.W.2d 216 (Tex. App.—Houston [1st Dist.] 1985, writ ref'd n.r.e.) (an order for an inventory is a type of discovery allowed under this section)

Querner v. Querner, 668 S.W.2d 801 (Tex. App.—San Antonio 1984, writ ref'd n.r.e.) (temporary orders not appealable except appointment of receiver and injunctive relief)

Texas Family Law Practice Manual

Chapter 4. Divorce—Temporary Orders
Chapter 7. Inventory and Appraisement

---

§ 6.501. Temporary Restraining Order.

(a) After the filing of a suit for dissolution of a marriage, on the motion of a party or on the court's own motion, the court may grant a temporary restraining order without notice to the adverse party for the preservation of the property and for the protection of the parties as necessary, including an order prohibiting one or both parties from:

(1) intentionally communicating by telephone or in writing with the other party by use of vulgar, profane, obscene, or indecent language or in a coarse or offensive manner, with intent to annoy or alarm the other;

(2) threatening the other, by telephone or in writing, to take unlawful action against any person, intending by this action to annoy or alarm the other;

(3) placing a telephone call, anonymously, at an unreasonable hour, in an offensive and repetitious manner, or without a legitimate purpose of communication with the intent to annoy or alarm the other;

(4) intentionally, knowingly, or recklessly causing bodily injury to the other or to a child of either party;

(5) threatening the other or a child of either party with imminent bodily injury;

(6) intentionally, knowingly, or recklessly destroying, removing, concealing, encumbering, transferring, or otherwise harming or reducing the value of the property of the parties or either party with intent to obstruct the authority of the court to order a division of the estate of the parties in a manner that the court deems just and right, having due regard for the rights of each party and any children of the marriage;

(7) intentionally falsifying a writing or record relating to the property of either party;

(8) intentionally misrepresenting or refusing to disclose to the other party or to the court, on proper request, the existence, amount, or location of any property of the parties or either party;

(9) intentionally or knowingly damaging or destroying the tangible property of the parties or either party; or

(10) intentionally or knowingly tampering with the tangible property of the parties or either party and causing pecuniary loss or substantial inconvenience to the other.

(b) A temporary restraining order under this subchapter may not include a provision:

(1) the subject of which is a requirement, appointment, award, or other order listed in Section 64.104, Civil Practice and Remedies Code; or

(2) that:

(A) excludes a spouse from occupancy of the residence where that spouse is living except as provided in a protective order made in accordance with Title 4;

(B) prohibits a party from spending funds for reasonable and necessary living expenses; or

(C) prohibits a party from engaging in acts reasonable and necessary to conduct that party's usual business and occupation.

§ 6.502. Temporary Injunction and Other Temporary Orders.

(a) While a suit for dissolution of a marriage is pending and on the motion of a party or on the court's own motion after notice and hearing, the court may render an appropriate order, including the granting of a temporary injunction for the preservation of the property and protection of the parties as deemed necessary and equitable and including an order directed to one or both parties:

(1) requiring a sworn inventory and appraisement of the real and personal property owned or claimed by the parties and specifying the form, manner, and substance of the inventory and appraisal and list of debts and liabilities;

(2) requiring payments to be made for the support of either spouse;

(3) requiring the production of books, papers, documents, and tangible things by a party;

(4) ordering payment of reasonable attorney's fees and expenses;

(5) appointing a receiver for the preservation and protection of the property of the parties;

(6) awarding one spouse exclusive occupancy of the residence during the pendency of the case;

(7) prohibiting the parties, or either party, from spending funds beyond an amount the court determines to be for reasonable and necessary living expenses;

(8) awarding one spouse exclusive control of a party's usual business or occupation; or

(9) prohibiting an act described by Section 6.501(a).

(b) Not later than the 30th day after the date a receiver is appointed under Subsection (a)(5), the receiver shall give notice of the appointment to each lienholder of any property under the receiver's control.

§ 6.503. Affidavit, Verified Pleading, and Bond Not Required.

(a) A temporary restraining order or temporary injunction under this subchapter:

(1) may be granted without an affidavit or a verified pleading stating specific facts showing that immediate and irreparable injury, loss, or damage will result before notice can be served and a hearing can be held; and

(2) need not:

(A) define the injury or state why it is irreparable;

(B) state why the order was granted without notice; or

(C) include an order setting the suit for trial on the merits with respect to the ultimate relief sought.

(b) In a suit for dissolution of a marriage, the court may dispense with the issuance of a bond between the spouses in connection with temporary orders for the protection of the parties and their property.

§ 6.504. Protective Orders.

On the motion of a party to a suit for dissolution of a marriage, the court may render a protective order as provided by Subtitle B, Title 4.

Comment

This section must be read in conjunction with the protective order statutes in Title 4, TEX. FAM. CODE ANN. An order under that title must be in a separate document so that it will not be confused with the temporary order issued in a divorce case. *See* the extensive annotations to Title 4, *infra.*

Texas Family Law Practice Manual

Chapter 14. Protective Orders

Cross References

TEX. FAM. CODE ANN. Title 4. Protective Orders and Family Violence.

TEX. PEN. CODE ANN. § 25.07. Violation of Protective Order or Magistrate's Order; § 42.07. Harassment; § 42.072. Stalking.

---

§ 6.505. Counseling.

(a) While a divorce suit is pending, the court may direct the parties to counsel with a person named by the court.

(b) The person named by the court to counsel the parties shall submit a written report to the court and to the parties before the final hearing. In the report, the counselor shall give only an opinion as to whether there exists a reasonable expectation of reconciliation of the parties and, if so, whether further counseling would be beneficial. The sole purpose of the report is to aid the court in determining whether the suit for divorce should be continued pending further counseling.

(c) A copy of the report shall be furnished to each party.

(d) If the court believes that there is a reasonable expectation of the parties' reconciliation, the court may by written order continue the proceedings and direct the parties to a person named by the court for further counseling for a period fixed by the court not to exceed 60 days, subject to any terms, conditions, and limitations the court considers desirable. In ordering counseling, the court shall consider the circumstances of the parties, including the needs of the parties' family and the availability of counseling services. At the expiration of the period specified by the court, the counselor to whom the parties were directed shall report to the court whether the parties have complied with the court's order. Thereafter, the court shall proceed as in a divorce suit generally.

(e) If the court orders counseling under this section and the parties to the marriage are the parents of a child under 18 years of age born or adopted during the marriage, the counseling shall include counseling on issues that confront children who are the subject of a suit affecting the parent-child relationship.

Leading Cases

Baxla v. Baxla, 522 S.W.2d 736 (Tex. Civ. App.—Dallas 1975), *appeal after remand*, 623 S.W.2d 462 (Tex. App.—Waco 1981, writ dism'd w.o.j.) (if there is hesitancy about divorce, court may refer parties to marriage counseling)

Philp v. Philp, 516 S.W.2d 294 (Tex. Civ. App.—Waco 1974, no writ) (there is no abuse of court's discretion in not ordering parties to counseling)

---

§ 6.506. Contempt.

The violation of a temporary restraining order, temporary injunction, or other temporary order issued under this subchapter is punishable as contempt.

Comment

Most of the caselaw relating to contempt has been developed in SAPCRs rather than in the divorce cause of action. The due process restrictions on incarceration are identical, however. This subject is annotated extensively in Chapter 157 *[Enforcement]*, *infra*.

Leading Cases

In re Gabbai, 968 S.W.2d 929 (Tex. 1998) (trial court lacks jurisdiction to enforce by contempt an order of appellate court)

Collins v. State, 955 S.W.2d 464 (Tex. App.—Fort Worth 1997, no pet.) (protective order is criminally enforceable even if lack of details would not sustain contempt judgment)

---

§ 6.507. Interlocutory Appeal.

An order under this subchapter, except an order appointing a receiver, is not subject to interlocutory appeal.

Leading Cases

Ruiz v. Ruiz, 946 S.W.2d 124 (Tex. App.—Waco 1997, no writ) (protective order granted while divorce pending which didn't dispose of all issues is non-appealable interlocutory order)

Cook v. Cook, 886 S.W.2d 838 (Tex. App.—Waco 1994, no writ) (temporary orders are not subject to interlocutory appeal)

Eikenhorst v. Eikenhorst, 746 S.W.2d 882 (Tex. App.—Houston [1st Dist.] 1988, no writ) (court has authority to order temporary support pending appeal of its ruling)

Querner v. Querner, 668 S.W.2d 801 (Tex. App.—San Antonio 1984, writ ref'd n.r.e.) (temporary orders not appealable except appointment of receiver and injunctive relief)

Subchapter G. Alternative Dispute Resolution

Introductory Comment

No innovation of recent years has had a greater impact on the practice of family law than the advent of "court-ordered ADR" (as a practical matter, it is virtually mandatory in many cases). Notwithstanding more than a little grumbling in courthouse halls, the fact remains that in many counties docket congestion has been significantly reduced, largely thanks to this process. Yes, ADR is here to stay—get used to it.

Texas Family Law Practice Manual

Chapter 15. Alternative Dispute Resolution

---

§ 6.601. Arbitration Procedures.

(a) On written agreement of the parties, the court may refer a suit for dissolution of a marriage to arbitration. The agreement must state whether the arbitration is binding or nonbinding.

(b) If the parties agree to binding arbitration, the court shall render an order reflecting the arbitrator's award.

CLE/Other Legal Publication

Arbitration and other alternative dispute resolution methods. John E. Van Ness, 2003 So. Tex. Fam. L. Gen. Practice Ch. K

Leading Case

Goetz v. Goetz, 130 S.W.3d 359 (Tex. App.—Houston [14th Dist.] 2004, no pet. hist.) (court may appoint arbitrator when agreement does not specify method for appointment)

Jabri v. Qaddura, 108 S.W.3d 404 (Tex. App.—Fort Worth 2003, no pet.) (parties agreed to resolve marital disputes by religious arbitration; trial court erred in not compelling them to do so)

Koch v. Koch, 27 S.W.3d 93 (Tex. App.—San Antonio 2000, no pet.) (provision to arbitrate disputes over prenuptial agreement binding on divorce court)

§ 6.602. Mediation Procedures.

(a) On the written agreement of the parties or on the court's own motion, the court may refer a suit for dissolution of a marriage to mediation.

(b) A mediated settlement agreement is binding on the parties if the agreement:

(1) provides, in a prominently displayed statement that is in boldfaced type or capital letters or underlined, that THE AGREEMENT IS NOT SUBJECT TO REVOCATION;

(2) is signed by each party to the agreement; and

(3) is signed by the party's attorney, if any, who is present at the time the agreement is signed.

(c) If a mediated settlement agreement meets the requirements of this section, a party is entitled to judgment on the mediated settlement agreement notwithstanding Rule 11, Texas Rules of Civil Procedure, or another rule of law.

(d) A party may at any time prior to the final mediation order file a written objection to the referral of a suit for dissolution of a marriage to mediation on the basis of family violence having been committed against the objecting party by the other party. After an objection is filed, the suit may not be referred to mediation unless, on the request of the other party, a hearing is held and the court finds that a preponderance of the evidence does not support the objection. If the suit is referred to mediation, the court shall order appropriate measures be taken to ensure the physical and emotional safety of the party who filed the objection. The order shall provide that the parties not be required to have face-to-face contact and that the parties be placed in separate rooms during mediation.

Comment

Alternative dispute resolution procedures have been part of Texas law since 1987. In 1995, Title 5 (*Parent and Child*) was amended to formally recognize these procedures in Tex. Fam. Code Ann. and to address issues of enforceability. Similar rules, though not quite identical due to the children's issues in Title 5, are now formally recognized in Title 1.

CLE/Other Legal Publications

Collaboration, mediation and settlement: ethical and malpractice considerations. Alison H. Moore, 2004 Adv. Fam. L.

Drafting a mediation notebook and position statement. Norma Levine Trusch, 2003 Adv. Fam. L. Drafting & Advocacy

Family law ADR: mediation and beyond. John Compere, 2003 U. Tex. Fam. L. Front Lines

Creative solutions to property issues. Brenda Keen, Judy L. Warne & Beth Dickson, 2003 So. Tex. Fam. L. Mediation

Effective communication skills for mediators: getting to a better "yes." Richard H. Lucas, 2003 So. Tex. Fam. L. Mediation

The opening statement: use it or lose it. Trey Bergman, 2003 So. Tex. Fam. L. Mediation

Mediators: what to look for, and how you can help them help you. Danielle L. Hargrove, San Antonio Lawyer 5 (Jan./Feb. 2004)

Leading Cases

Boyd v. Boyd, 67 S.W.3d 398 (Tex. App.—Fort Worth 2002, no pet.) (mediated settlement agreement not enforced because of failure to disclose existence of bonus)

Cayan v. Cayan, 38 S.W.3d 161 (Tex. App.—Houston [14th Dist.] 2000, pet. denied) (mediated settlement binding on parties means "you can't take it back"; judgment properly entered based on mediated settlement agreement despite husband's repudiation)

In re Kasschau, 11 S.W.3d 305 (Tex. App.—Houston [14th Dist.] 1999, no pet.) (mediated settlement requiring destruction of illegal tape recordings is void and unenforceable)

Alvarez v. Reiser, 958 S.W.2d 232 (Tex. App.—Eastland 1997, writ denied) (attempted revocation of mediated settlement agreement ineffective, statement prohibiting revocation enforced)

Cross Reference

Tex. Civ. Prac. & Rem. Code Ann. ch. 154. Alternative Dispute Resolution Procedures.

---

§ 6.603. Collaborative Law.

(a) On a written agreement of the parties and their attorneys, a dissolution of marriage proceeding may be conducted under collaborative law procedures.

(b) Collaborative law is a procedure in which the parties and their counsel agree in writing to use their best efforts and make a good faith attempt to resolve their dissolution of marriage dispute on an agreed basis without resorting to judicial intervention except to have the court approve the settlement agreement, make the legal pronouncements, and sign the orders required by law to effectuate the agreement of the parties as the court determines appropriate. The parties' counsel may not serve as litigation counsel except to ask the court to approve the settlement agreement.

(c) A collaborative law agreement must include provisions for:

(1) full and candid exchange of information between the parties and their attorneys as necessary to make a proper evaluation of the case;

(2) suspending court intervention in the dispute while the parties are using collaborative law procedures;

(3) hiring experts, as jointly agreed, to be used in the procedure;

(4) withdrawal of all counsel involved in the collaborative law procedure if the collaborative law procedure does not result in settlement of the dispute; and

(5) other provisions as agreed to by the parties consistent with a good faith effort to collaboratively settle the matter.

(d) Notwithstanding Rule 11, Texas Rules of Civil Procedure, or another rule or law, a party is entitled to judgment on a collaborative law settlement agreement if the agreement:

(1) provides, in a prominently displayed statement that is boldfaced, capitalized, or underlined, that the agreement is not subject to revocation; and

(2) is signed by each party to the agreement and the attorney of each party.

(e) Subject to Subsection (g), a court that is notified 30 days before trial that the parties are using collaborative law procedures to attempt to settle a dispute may not, until a party notifies the court that the collaborative law procedures did not result in a settlement:

(1) set a hearing or trial in the case;

(2) impose discovery deadlines;

(3) require compliance with scheduling orders; or

(4) dismiss the case.

(f) The parties shall notify the court if the collaborative law procedures result in a settlement. If they do not, the parties shall file:

(1) a status report with the court not later than the 180th day after the date of the written agreement to use the procedures; and

(2) a status report on or before the first anniversary of the date of the written agreement to use the procedures, accompanied by a motion for continuance that the court shall grant if the status report indicates the desire of the parties to continue to use collaborative law procedures.

(g) If the collaborative law procedures do not result in a settlement on or before the second anniversary of the date that the suit was filed, the court may:

(1) set the suit for trial on the regular docket; or

(2) dismiss the suit without prejudice.

Guest Commentary

Donald R. Royall and John V. McShane

> ***Editors' Note:*** *Don Royall, Houston, and John McShane, Dallas, are leaders of collaborative law in Texas.*

This is a rapidly growing model of alternative dispute resolution in Texas. The last 17 years have seen a growing body of evidence suggesting that, given a safe legal environment, more and more married couples want to avoid as of much the stress integral to the resolution of divorce and custody issues as possible. In this decision, they are uniquely qualified to fashion their own solutions to the issues of the break-up without judicial intervention. This awareness has, in turn, produced increasing statutory encouragement and implementation of alternative dispute resolution procedures for resolving family law disputes.

In 1987, the Texas Legislature enacted legislation outlining alternative dispute resolution procedures generally, and placing special emphasis on the applicability of these procedures in family law, as a matter of state policy. TEX. CIV. PRAC. & REM. CODE ANN. ch. 154. In 1995, the Legislature explicitly incorporated mediation and arbitration procedures into the Family Code, provided means for enforcement of the resulting agreement or award, and instituted the requirement that each parties' first pleading contain a signed statement acknowledging awareness of the existence of such procedures and pledging to make a good faith effort to utilize alternative dispute resolution before resorting to trial. TEX. FAM. CODE ANN. §§ 6.404, 102.0085, 153.0071. This requirement was equally applicable to suits for dissolution of a marriage and suits affecting the parent-child relationship. This statute was repealed in 2003 because ADR has become such an integral part of the day-to-day practice of family law that a formal acknowledgement of this fact was more of a burden on clients than a benefit.

In 1997, the applicability of arbitration and mediation to suits for dissolution of a marriage was moved from the indirect references in § 153.0071(f), to the explicit provisions in §§ 6.601 and 6.602. Aside from that, while the ADR provisions of the Texas Family

Code were tweaked in 1999, the basic statutory ADR landscape remained virtually unchanged until the collaborative law legislation was enacted.

Collaborative law seeks to create an environment in which the parties, with the aid of their attorneys, can address the issues presented as problems to be solved, rather than contests to be won. Essential to that process is elimination of the threat, spoken or unspoken, that "if you don't agree with my position on the matter, we can just let the Judge decide." This is accomplished by a written "four way" agreement, binding the parties and their attorneys to the proposition that the consequence of failure to reach some solution to all issues presented is the abandonment of the process, and the attendant withdrawal of the attorneys from any further involvement beyond an orderly transition of the matter to new counsel, who will presumably, then prepare the case for trial in the conventional adversarial manner. The resulting atmosphere is one in which the parties and their attorneys have the same conscious and subconscious incentives to reach a negotiated settlement as well as the same disincentives for failure.

Sections 6.603(a),(b), and (c) are largely descriptive of the process. Section 6.603(d) seeks to accord the same finality to an agreement reached through collaborative law as is accorded a Mediated Settlement Agreement that meets the statutory requirements of § 6.602(b). Section 6.603(e) seeks to free the collaborative law case from the scheduling orders and procedural deadlines so necessary to the orderly progress of a case through the adversarial system. Sections 6.603(f) and (g) address the judiciary's concern that it should nevertheless have some supervisory authority, since in the final analysis, the court has ultimate responsibility for the disposition of all cases on its docket.

Collaborative law procedures have also been made equally applicable in suits affecting the parent-child relationship. *See* § 153.0072, *infra*.

CLE/Other Legal Publications

Collaborative law: what is it? Why do it? Kevin R. Fuller, 2004 Adv. Fam. L.

Collaboration, mediation and settlement: ethical and malpractice considerations. Alison H. Moore, 2004 Adv. Fam. L.

Collaborative law: if I can't go to court, what do I do? Thomas L. Ausley & Larry Hance, 2004 U. Tex. Fam. L. Front Lines

Client centered collaborative law—a human bridge to serendipity. C. Mike McCurley, Robert Gordon & Carson P. Epes, 2004 Marriage Dissolution

Collaborative law. Harry L. Tindall, 2003 Adv. Fam. L.

Collaborative law training: materials and forms. Leota H. Alexander, Larry Hance, John V. McShane, Donald R. Royall, Harry L. Tindall & Norma Levine Trusch, 2003 Adv. Fam. L.

Subchapter H. Trial and Appeal

Introductory Comment

Although some might argue that family law is merely a subset of general civil litigation, the CLE publications listed below contradict such an assertion. Indeed existence of separate subchapters in this chapter establishing special rules for venue, jurisdiction, trial and appeal also indicate otherwise.

CLE/Other Legal Publications

Appeals

Anticipating an appeal: the ultimate C.Y.A. Pamela E. George, 2004 Adv. Fam. L.

Avoiding a permanent 'waive': preservation of error. Ann C. McClure, 2004 MARRIAGE DISSOLUTION

Appeals and mandamus: how to repair your case and prevent the need for repairs. Jimmy Vaught, 2003 ADV. FAM. L.

Appeals and mandamus-how to repair your case and prevent the need for repairs (or what to do when your case is in the ditch). Georganna L. Simpson, 2003 ADV. FAM. L.

Relief is just an appeal way: drafting with appeal. Gary L. Nickelson, 2003 ADV. FAM. L. DRAFTING & ADVOCACY

Trying case with appeal—preserving error. Alene Ross Levy & Lori Massey Cliffe, 2002 ADV. FAM. L.

Activities in the trial court during appeal and after remand. Richard R. Orsinger, 2002 MARRIAGE DISSOLUTION

Take me higher: preparing the appeal, including findings of fact and conclusions of law. Georganna L. Simpson, 2002 MARRIAGE DISSOLUTION

Discovery

Basic discovery. Bruce L. Beverly, 2004 ADV. FAM. L.; 2003 ADV. FAM. L.

Discovery points. Joan F. Jenkins, Sallee S. Smyth & Lauren Fornea, 2004 MARRIAGE DISSOLUTION

Electronic evidence. Randall B. Wilhite & Karl Hays, 2004 MARRIAGE DISSOLUTION

Information sources in the 21st century: big brother is watching. Sydney A. Beckman, 2004 U. TEX. FAM. L. FRONT LINES

Discovery procedures and objections. Kevin R. Fuller, 2003 ADV. FAM. L.

Electronic discovery: finding the cyber-skeletons in the closet. Edwin J. (Ted) Terry, Jr., Karl E. Hays, & Andrea Foltz, 2003 MARRIAGE DISSOLUTION

Creative discovery. Douglas R. Woodburn & Michele Kindle, 2002 ADV. FAM. L. DRAFTING

Creative discovery techniques. David Carlock, 2002 ADV. FAM. L. DRAFTING

Using a private investigator—who hires, privileges, problems. Marilea Whatley Lewis, 2002 ADV. FAM. L.

Conducting discovery in foreign lands. Richard R. Orsinger, 2002 ADV. FAM. L.

Teaching old dogs old tricks: discovery 2002. Ike Vanden Eykel, Christopher M. Lake & Amy J. Nisbet, 2002 ADV. FAM. L.

Evidence

Effective evidence: what works, what doesn't work, and how to get it in! Sydney Aaron Beckman, 2004 ADV. FAM. L.

High tech evidence and internet research. Richard L. Robertson, 2004 ADV. FAM. L.

Revisiting the rules of evidence. Warren Cole, 2004 U. TEX. FAM. L. FRONT LINES

A walkthrough the TRE: your top ten problems. Frank W. Sullivan III, 2004 MARRIAGE DISSOLUTION

Proving it up and getting it in: foreign law and foreign evidence. Ann Crawford McClure & Richard R. Orsinger, 2004 U. TEX. FAM. L. ON THE BORDER

Illegally obtained evidence. Warren Cole, 2003 ADV. FAM. L.

High tech evidence. Richard L. Robertson, 2003 ADV. FAM. L.

Difficult evidence issues: children and property. Coye Conner, Jr., Robert Hughes Wilson, Don Emerson, J. Lindsey Short & J. Steven King, 2003 ADV. FAM. L.

Trails from the Aether: cyber-evidence. Karl E. Hays, 2003 ADV. FAM. L. DRAFTING & ADVOCACY

Common evidentiary issues in family law cases. Robinson C. Ramsey, 2003 U. HOUSTON FAM. L. PRACTICE SEM. (MARCH)

Jury

See annotations to § 6.703, *infra.*

Trial Techniques

Fundamental litigation techniques. J. Steven King & Kyle A. Whitaker, 2004 ADV. FAM. L.

Litigation outside the box. Lisa Kaye Hoppes, 2004 ADV. FAM. L.

Preparing witnesses and clients for trial. Sydney Aaron Beckman, 2003 ADV. FAM. L.

Leading Cases

Daubert v. Merrill Dow Pharmaceuticals, Inc., 113 S.Ct. 2786 (1993) (landmark case excluding "junk science")

Gammill v. Jack Williams Chevrolet, Inc., 972 S.W.2d 713 (Tex. 1998) (*Daubert* standards apply to all experts, not just novel scientific techniques)

E.I. Dupont de Nemours and Co., Inc. v. Robinson, 923 S.W.2d 549 (Tex. 1995) (landmark Texas case excluding "junk" science)

Ham v. Ham, 59 S.W.3d 326 (Tex. App.—Texarkana 2001, no pet.) (whether fraud procured wife's signature on divorce decree question of material fact precluding summary judgment)

Daugherty v. Daugherty, 42 S.W.3d 331 (Tex. App.—Texarkana 2001, no pet.) (prisoner deprived of right to participate in divorce to present evidence on property issues)

Palomino v. Palomino, 960 S.W.2d 899 (Tex. App.—El Paso 1997, writ denied) (chronology of "divorce hearing, husband died, divorce decree rendered" is error—abate and dismiss the correct procedure)

Dearing v. Johnson, 947 S.W.2d 641 (Tex. App.—Texarkana 1997, no writ) (divorce final on oral rendition—fact decree signed after husband died does not void judgment)

America West Airlines, Inc. v. Tope, 935 S.W.2d 908 (Tex. App.—El Paso 1996, no writ) (*Robinson* standard as applied to mental health expert)

§ 6.701. Failure to Answer.

In a suit for divorce, the petition may not be taken as confessed if the respondent does not file an answer.

Comment

As in other civil cases, a respondent in a divorce case must file a written answer to the petition for divorce or face the consequences of a default judgment. Individuals unfamiliar with the process might be surprised to learn that a large number of divorces are granted by default. In any event, the petitioner must put on evidence sufficient for the court to grant a divorce and other appropriate relief, such as the division of property and orders regarding conservatorship of children of the marriage. The degree of proof necessary depends upon the particular case and the practice of the local court. No doubt due to the no-fault aspect of Texas divorce practice, summary testimony of "insupportability" is universally sufficient to prove grounds for divorce.

Leading Cases

O'Neal v. O'Neal, 69 S.W.3d 347 (Tex. App.—Eastland 2002, no pet.) (husband's conclusory testimony in default divorce is no evidence regarding just and right division)

Gone v. Gone, 993 S.W.2d 845 (Tex. App.—Houston [14th Dist.] 1999, pet. denied) (ignore divorce papers at your own peril)

Harris v. Harris, 850 S.W.2d 241 (Tex. App.—Houston [1st Dist.] 1993, no writ) (default disallowed, respondent's letter to court constitutes pro se answer)

Avila v. Avila, 843 S.W.2d 280 (Tex. App.—El Paso 1992, no writ) (default divorce reversed, TRCP require strict compliance for service of citation)

Considine v. Considine, 726 S.W.2d 253 (Tex. App.—Austin 1987, no writ) (in default case, petitioner must still prove grounds for divorce)

§ 6.702. Waiting Period.

(a) The court may not grant a divorce before the 60th day after the date the suit was filed. A decree rendered in violation of this subsection is not subject to collateral attack.

(b) A waiting period is not required before a court may grant an annulment or declare a marriage void other than as required in civil cases generally.

Comment

The 60–day waiting period required before a divorce may be granted is based on the rationale that parties ought not rush into divorce when there might still be a genuine prospect for reconciliation. Whether this comports with modern-day realities of marriage and divorce is debated by some, but the fact remains that a significant percentage of divorce suits are filed and not finalized by way of nonsuit or dismissal for want of prosecution

Leading Case

Whiteman v. Whiteman, 682 S.W.2d 357 (Tex. App.—Dallas 1984, no writ) (divorce granted 38 days after filing an amended petition held to be reversible error)

---

§ 6.703. Jury.

In a suit for dissolution of a marriage, either party may demand a jury trial unless the action is a suit to annul an underage marriage under Section 6.101 or 6.102.

Comment

Texas has always accorded divorce litigants the right to a trial by jury. This is almost unique in American jurisprudence, but is a time-tested Texas institution widely supported by the practicing bar. However, even their strongest advocates must admit that jury trials are more talked-about than practiced. Nonetheless, threat of a jury trial remains a favorite tactical weapon in the litigator's bag of persuasive arguments. Although the Texas Constitution grants the right to trial by jury in civil cases, that right is conditioned by the fact that the legislature may prescribe the circumstances of its exercise.

CLE/Other Legal Publications

Pattern jury charges are for more than jury trials. John F. Nichols, 2004 ADV. FAM. L.

Effectively trying property issues to a jury. C. Mike McCurley, 2002 ADV. FAM. L.

Voir dire and opening statements. James E. Monnig, 2002 ADV. FAM. L.

Leading Cases

Texas Dept. of Human Services v. E.B., 802 S.W.2d 647 (Tex. 1990) (broad form submission explained in termination of parental rights case)

Crittenden v. Crittenden, 52 S.W.3d 768 (Tex. App.—San Antonio 2001, pet. denied) (presumptively valid jury demand denied on showing it is only attempt to delay divorce)

Minnich v. Jones, 799 S.W.2d 327 (Tex. App.—Texarkana 1990, no writ) (appointment of a master in chancery does not deprive a party of a jury trial)

Cross References

TEX. CONST., art. I, § 15. Right of Trial by Jury; art. V, § 10. Trial by Jury.

---

§ 6.704. Testimony of Husband or Wife.

(a) In a suit for dissolution of a marriage, the husband and wife are competent witnesses for and against each other. A spouse may not be compelled to testify as to a matter that will incriminate the spouse.

(b) If the husband or wife testifies, the court or jury trying the case shall determine the credibility of the witness and the weight to be given the witness's testimony.

Comment

This section codifies long-standing Texas case law that husband and wife are competent to testify against each other in civil matters, but may not be required to testify about matters that may tend to incriminate the person so testifying.

---

§ 6.705. Testimony by Marriage Counselor.

(a) The report by the person named by the court to counsel the parties to a suit for divorce may not be admitted as evidence in the suit.

(b) The person named by the court to counsel the parties is not competent to testify in any suit involving the parties or their children.

(c) The files, records, and other work products of the counselor are privileged and confidential for all purposes and may not be admitted as evidence in any suit involving the parties or their children.

§ 6.706. Change of Name.

(a) In a decree of divorce or annulment, the court shall change the name of a party specifically requesting the change to a name previously used by the party unless the court states in the decree a reason for denying the change of name.

(b) The court may not deny a change of name solely to keep the last name of family members the same.

(c) A change of name does not release a person from liability incurred by the person under a previous name or defeat a right the person held under a previous name.

(d) A person whose name is changed under this section may apply for a change of name certificate from the clerk of the court as provided by Section 45.106.

Comment

Texas has long allowed a party (read almost exclusively "the wife") to change his or her name at the time of divorce. This statute is not restricted to a woman desiring to return to her maiden name, but it is restricted to a name "previously used." In 1995, reports reached the legislature that some courts were still denying women name changes if the order would result in the mother and her child having different last names. The statute was amended to make certain that a woman would properly be accorded the right to choose her surname without regard to the gender bias of some judges.

Leading Cases

Fly v. Fly, 590 S.W.2d 179 (Tex. Civ. App.—Corpus Christi 1979, no writ) (trial court erred in changing wife's name without her consent)

Lindsey v. Lindsey, 564 S.W.2d 143 (Tex. Civ. App.—Austin 1978, no writ) (court acted properly in granting the wife a change of name over objection of husband)

Cross Reference

TEX. FAM. CODE ANN. ch. 45. Change of Name.

---

§ 6.707. Transfers and Debts Pending Decree.

(a) A transfer of real or personal community property or a debt incurred by a spouse while a suit for divorce or annulment is pending that subjects the other spouse or the community property to liability is void with respect to the other spouse if the transfer was made or the debt incurred with the intent to injure the rights of the other spouse.

(b) A transfer or debt is not void if the person dealing with the transferor or debtor spouse did not have notice of the intent to injure the rights of the other spouse.

(c) The spouse seeking to void a transfer or debt incurred while a suit for divorce or annulment is pending has the burden of proving that the person dealing with the transferor or debtor spouse had notice of the intent to injure the rights of the spouse seeking to void the transaction.

Comment

This section provides limited protection to the innocent spouse if during the pendency of a divorce a culpable spouse attempts to transfer property or incur debt for the purpose of injuring the property rights of the innocent spouse. A transfer of the economic interest in the property or the incurring of a debt is void if a third party had notice of the spouse's intent to injure the innocent spouse. Without such notice, however, the transfer is valid; the burden of proof rests with the complaining spouse. While this section seeks to serve an important social purpose, its application to ordinary consumer debt is problematic. With respect to insider transactions, such as those between family members or with business associates, the burden of proof may not be as onerous as in most other scenarios involving the concept.

Leading Case

Thomas v. Casale, 924 S.W.2d 433 (Tex. App.—Fort Worth 1996, writ denied) (wife failed to prove paramour knew about transfer of community assets)

Texas Pattern Jury Charges: Family

PJC 206.2. Actual Fraud by Spouse against Community Estate; PJC 206.3. Actual Fraud by Spouse against Separate Estate; PJC 206.4. Constructive Fraud by Spouse against Community Estate; PJC 206.5. Fraud Action against Nonspouse Party.

Cross Reference

TEX. BUS. & COM. CODE ANN. ch. 24. Uniform Fraudulent Transfer Act.

---

§ 6.708. Costs.

(a) In a suit for dissolution of a marriage, the court as it considers reasonable may award costs to a party. Costs may not be adjudged against a party against whom a divorce is granted for confinement in a mental hospital under Section 6.007.

(b) The expenses of counseling may be taxed as costs against either or both parties.

Comment

This section refers to fees and expenses collected by the clerk of the court, court reporters, and other related charges typically included in a costs bill. Costs ordinarily do not include attorney's fees, *see* annotations to §§ 7.001–.002, *infra*.

Leading Case

Currie v. Currie, 518 S.W.2d 386 (Tex. Civ. App.—San Antonio 1974, writ dism'd w.o.j.) (there is no statutory authority for taxing witness fees as costs)

§ 6.709. Temporary Orders During Appeal.

(a) Not later than the 30th day after the date an appeal is perfected, on the motion of a party or on the court's own motion, after notice and hearing, the trial court may render a temporary order necessary for the preservation of the property and for the protection of the parties during the appeal, including an order to:

(1) require the support of either spouse;

(2) require the payment of reasonable attorney's fees and expenses;

(3) appoint a receiver for the preservation and protection of the property of the parties; or

(4) award one spouse exclusive occupancy of the parties' residence pending the appeal.

(b) The trial court retains jurisdiction to enforce a temporary order under this section unless the appellate court, on a proper showing, supersedes the trial court's order.

Leading Cases

In re Gabbai, 968 S.W.2d 929 (Tex. 1998) (trial court lacks jurisdiction to enforce by contempt an order of appellate court)

In re Boyd, 34 S.W.3d 708 (Tex. App.—Fort Worth 2000, no pet.) (temporary orders to preserve litigant's property rights on appeal of divorce decree must be timely or they are void)

Richards v. Richards, 991 S.W.2d 30 (Tex. App.—Amarillo 1998, no pet.) (no cost bond in appeal of divorce decree—Rule 24 inapplicable, spouses not in debtor-creditor relationship)

Grossnickle v. Grossnickle, 935 S.W.2d 830 (Tex. App.—Texarkana 1996, writ denied) (temporary spousal support pending appeal was proper)

Texas Family Law Practice Manual

Chapter 20. Post-trial Proceedings and Appeal

§ 6.710. Copy of Decree.

The clerk of the court shall mail a copy of the final decree of dissolution of a marriage to the party who waived service of process under Section 6.4035 by mailing the copy of the decree to the party at the mailing address contained in the waiver or to the office of the party's attorney of record.

Comment

This section incorporates Tex. R. Civ. P. 119a into the Tex. Fam. Code Ann.

Texas Family Law Practice Manual

Chapter 17. Divorce—Decrees and Agreements Incident to Divorce: I. Decrees

§ 6.711. Findings of Fact and Conclusions of Law.

(a) In a suit for dissolution of a marriage in which the court has rendered a judgment dividing the estate of the parties, on request by a party, the court shall state in writing its findings of fact and conclusions of law concerning:

(1) the characterization of each party's assets, liabilities, claims, and offsets on which disputed evidence has been presented; and

(2) the value or amount of the community estate's assets, liabilities, claims, and offsets on which disputed evidence has been presented.

(b) A request for findings of fact and conclusions of law under this section must conform to the Texas Rules of Civil Procedure.

CLE/Other Legal Publications

Findings of fact and conclusions of law: the rhyme and reason of the ruling. Sallee S. Smyth, 2001 Adv. Fam. L. Drafting

A blind hog in search of an acorn—what findings of fact do you need? Ann C. McClure, 2001 Adv. Fam. L.

Subchapter I. Remarriage

§ 6.801. Remarriage.

(a) Except as otherwise provided by this subchapter, neither party to a divorce may marry a third party before the 31st day after the date the divorce is decreed.

(b) The former spouses may marry each other at any time.

§ 6.802. Waiver of Prohibition Against Remarriage.

For good cause shown the court may waive the prohibition against remarriage provided by this subchapter as to either or both spouses if a record of the proceedings is made and preserved or if findings of fact and conclusions of law are filed by the court.

Comment

The prohibition on remarriage for 30 days prescribed by § 6.801 is akin to the 60–day waiting period for divorce prescribed in § 6.702—an attempt by the legislature to stop an impulsive remarriage. This section has no application to divorced parties wishing to remarry each other.

Section 6.802 provides the court may waive the restriction on remarriage for good cause. Neither § 6.801 or this section have out-of-state application. It is common knowledge that a recently divorced party may immediately drive to a neighboring state for a quick marriage following a Texas divorce.

Leading Case

Galbraith v. Galbraith, 619 S.W.2d 238 (Tex. Civ. App.—Texarkana 1981, no writ) (remarriage within 30 days does not render a marriage voidable where parties continue to cohabit thereafter)

Chapter 7. Award of Marital Property.

§ 7.001. General Rule of Property Division.

In a decree of divorce or annulment, the court shall order a division of the estate of the parties in a manner that the court deems just and right, having due regard for the rights of each party and any children of the marriage.

§ 7.002. Division and Disposition of Certain Property Under Special Circumstances.

(a) In addition to the division of the estate of the parties required by Section 7.001, in a decree of divorce or annulment the court shall order a division of the following real and personal property, wherever situated, in a manner that the court deems just and right, having due regard for the rights of each party and any children of the marriage:

(1) property that was acquired by either spouse while domiciled in another state and that would have been community property if the spouse who acquired the property had been domiciled in this state at the time of the acquisition; or

(2) property that was acquired by either spouse in exchange for real or personal property and that would have been community property if the spouse who acquired the property so exchanged had been domiciled in this state at the time of its acquisition.

(b) In a decree of divorce or annulment, the court shall award to a spouse the following real and personal property, wherever situated, as the separate property of the spouse:

(1) property that was acquired by the spouse while domiciled in another state and that would have been the spouse's separate property if the spouse had been domiciled in this state at the time of acquisition; or

(2) property that was acquired by the spouse in exchange for real or personal property and that would have been the spouse's separate property if the spouse had been domiciled in this state at the time of acquisition.

(c) In a decree of divorce or annulment, the court shall confirm the following as the separate property of a spouse if partitioned or exchanged by written agreement of the spouses:

(1) income and earnings from the spouses' property, wages, salaries, and other forms of compensation received on or after January 1 of the year in which the suit for dissolution of marriage was filed; or

(2) income and earnings from the spouses' property, wages, salaries, and other forms of compensation received in another year during which the spouses were married for any part of the year.

Comment (§§ 7.001–.002)

Sections 7.001 and 7.002 are the most important sections in Title 1. The origins of these statutes date from 1841; the mandate consistently has been for the courts to divide the property in a manner that the judge deems "just and right," not "50/50" or "equally" as many people seem to think. The Supreme Court of Texas has held that these sections apply only to community property and that they do not authorize the divesting or division of a spouse's separate property.

While the statutory mandate to divide the property in a "just and right" manner may seem simple, its application is fraught with complexity. The valuation of the marital assets, factors to be considered in making a just and right division of the property, and the technique for dividing the marital assets can be very complicated. Issues regarding disposition of the homestead, division of retirement benefits, as well as payment of attorney's fees, further compound the problems. Decrees of divorce, often exceeding 50 to 75 pages, are necessary in order to properly divide and dispose of property.

Always looming in the background is the specter that a spouse may abscond with property, waste assets, fail to disclose important assets, or in the event of an undesired ruling, seek protection of the United States Bankruptcy Court. Finally, an aggrieved spouse may appeal the case seeking a reversal of the division of property and seek a new trial for a re-division of the assets.

Texas lawyers and judges appeared to be quite content with our system of community property for the years between 1988 and 1998. Until the 1999 legislative session, the Texas Legislature enacted relatively few amendments to the TEX. FAM. CODE ANN. affecting the substantive rules of marital property rights and liabilities. That year and the following sessions in 2001 and 2003 saw the apparent equilibrium in this quiet corner of family law came to an end, and the great social forces of the 1960s through the 1980s which wrought so much change in the remainder of the Family Code reappeared in connection with "conversion of separate property to community," see §§ 4.201–.206, and economic contribution, see §§ 3.401–.410 and § 7.007.

Subsection (b) was added in 2003 to provide for the same treatment of out of state property, regardless of whether it is claimed to be separate or community. Logically, because property acquired in another jurisdiction that would have been community property if acquired in Texas is treated in the same manner as community, property acquired in another jurisdiction that would have been separate property if acquired in Texas requires identical treatment.

Subsection (c) was added in 2003 to allow spouses to partition earnings and wages in the year of separation or any other year. This will give statutory sanction to the practice of divorcing spouses filing separate tax returns and reporting their individual earnings at the end of the year of divorce, thus avoiding the need to suffer the complication of reporting one half of each other's income up to the day of divorce.

CLE/Other Legal Publications

Alimony

See annotations to § 8.001 *et seq.*, *infra.*

Appeals

See annotations to subch. H, ch. 6, *supra.*

Attorney's Fees

Earning what you are worth: an ethical perspective on assessing your own value and collecting fees. Larry H. Schwartz, 2004 Adv. Fam. L.

Attorneys' fees: setting and collecting. Larry H. Schwartz, 2003 Adv. Fam. L.

Setting and collecting fees. G. Thomas Vick, Jr., 2003 Marriage Dissolution

Attorney's fees: so you want to be paid? Barbara D. Nunneley, 2003 U. Tex. Fam. L. Front Lines

Bankruptcy

In debt up to their ears! Marital liabilities and bankruptcy. Joseph D. Martinec, 2004 Adv. Fam. L.

Bankruptcy. Joseph A. Friedman, 2003 Adv. Fam. L.

Bankruptcy—affirmative use of the Code. Richard T. Chapman, 2002 Adv. Fam. L.

Characterization, Reimbursement, and Tracing

See annotations to §§ 3.001–.002, *supra*.

Dividing Community Property

Dividing the marital estate. Grady W. James, Jr., 2004 Adv. Fam. L.

Getting what you got! Enforcing the property division—including judgment collection. J. Lindsey Short, Jr., 2004 Adv. Fam. L.

Dividing intellectual property. Janice L. Green, 2003 Adv. Fam. L.

Property division—handling the odd ball asset. Brenda Keen, 2003 Adv. Fam. L.

Drafting Techniques

Drafting 101. Heather L. King, 2004 Adv. Fam. L.

Relief is just an appeal way: drafting with appeal. Gary L. Nickelson, 2003 Adv. Fam. L. Drafting & Advocacy

Drafting third party actions: three's a crowd—drafting third party actions. Susan Myres & Tara Luedke-Mora, 2002 Adv. Fam. L. Drafting

Drafting trial documents with an eye toward winning. J. Steven King & Heather L. King, 2002 Adv. Fam. L. Drafting

Economic Contribution

See annotations to §§ 3.401–.410, *supra*.

Marital Property Liabilities

See annotations to § 3.202, *supra*.

Pension Plans

See annotations to § 7.003, *infra*.

Property Subject to Division

Closely held corporations. Bruce Beverly, 2004 U. Tex. Fam. L. Front Lines

Handling an American divorce when the assets are in Mexico. C. Jeff Minor, 2004 U. Tex. Fam. L. on the Border

Getting $ from FLPs and trusts. Gary Stolbach, 2004 Adv. Fam. L.

Banking relationships. James M. Loveless, 2003 Marriage Dissolution

Insurance. Tim McClendon & Gus Bates III, 2003 Marriage Dissolution

Horses and divorces. Barbara D. Nunneley, 2003 Adv. Fam. L.

Property division—stock options. (Workshop) 2003 Adv. Fam. L.

Complex trust issues. (Workshop) 2003 Adv. Fam. L.

Top ten things you need to know about handling property cases. Douglas R. Woodburn, 2003 Marriage Dissolution

Asserting CP claims/complex trust issues. Paula Larsen & Gary Stolback, 2002 Adv. Fam. L.

Dividing stock options on divorce. Warren Cole, 2002 Adv. Fam. L.

Texas real estate law issues and the family lawyer. James L. Gosdin, 2002 ADV. FAM. L.

Sports and entertainment—representing big hitters. Katherine Anne Kinser, 2002 ADV. FAM. L.

Reimbursement

See annotations to §§ 3.001–.002, *supra*.

Retirement Benefits

See annotations to § 7.003, *infra*.

Taxation Issues

Top 10 tax issues everyone should understand. Geoffrey S. Poll, 2004 ADV. FAM. L.

Alimony and maintenance: enforceability, contractual agreements, creative uses and new tax traps. Patricia A. Wicoff, 2004 ADV. FAM. L.

Dissecting the complex tax return. Randall B. Wilhite, 2004 ADV. FAM. L.

Divorce and taxes. Geoffrey Poll, 2004 U. TEX. FAM. L. FRONT LINES

Tax issues: significant income tax developments. Patrice L. Ferguson, 2003 ADV. FAM. L.

Who gets custody of Uncle Sam? Edwin W. Davis, 2003 ADV. FAM. L.

Drafting for tax issues. Patrice L. Ferguson, 2003 ADV. FAM. L. DRAFTING & ADVOCACY

Demystifying tax returns. Patrice L. Ferguson, 2003 MARRIAGE DISSOLUTION

What every family lawyer should know about tax. Elizabeth Copeland, 2003 U. TEX. FAM. L. FRONT LINES

Negatives of the big estate: tax, bankruptcy, debt-tax tips (Brian Rice) the billionaire in trouble, fraud sow's ear to silk purse. 2003 NEW FRONTIERS

Torts

Tort litigation in the family law arena. Wendy S. Burgower, 2004 U. TEX. FAM. L. FRONT LINES

Torts: economic torts, constructive and actual fraud, excessive gifts, waste, conspiracy and 3rd parties. Wendy S. Burgower and Tommy Fibich, 2003 ADV. FAM. L.

Tort litigation: fiduciary duties of spouses and non-physical torts. Edwin J. Ted Terry, Karl E. Hays, & Andrea Foltz, 2003 U. TEX. FAM. L. FRONT LINES

Economic and physical torts—what's left after Schlueter? John F. Nichols, 2001 ADV. FAM. L.

Trial Techniques

See annotations to ch. 6, Subchapter H. Trial and Appeal, *supra*.

Valuation

The art of evaluating your property case. Warren Cole, 2004 ADV. FAM. L.

Valuing the small business on a budget. Bill De La Garza, 2004 ADV. FAM. L.

Top ten accounting tips for family lawyers. Robert D. Cocanower, Jr. & Robert C. Cocanower, 2004 MARRIAGE DISSOLUTION

Internet investigation of personal information and assets. Heather L. King & Bruce L. Beverly, 2004 MARRIAGE DISSOLUTION

Ethics and financial experts. Robert D. Cocanower & Diana S. Friedman, 2004 U. TEX. FAM. L. FRONT LINES

Valuation of property in divorce. Randall B. Wilhite, 2004 U. TEX. FAM. L. FRONT LINES

Valuation of professional practices: medical and legal. Edwin J. Ted Terry, Karl E. Hays, Andrea Foltz, James W. LaRue & J. Kenneth Huff, 2003 ADV. FAM. L.

Stock options: valuing, characterizing, and dividing. Randall B. Wilhite, 2003 ADV. FAM. L.

Real estate appraisals and receivers—how to use and abuse. Joseph Indelicato, 2003 MARRIAGE DISSOLUTION

Experts: where are we now? Diana S. Friedman, 2003 MARRIAGE DISSOLUTION

Valuing the pots and pans. Jack W. Marr, 2003 MARRIAGE DISSOLUTION

Hiring experts: practical tips based on Daubert/Robinson knowledge and case law. Jan Marie DeLipsey, 2003 U. Tex. Fam. L. Front Lines

Valuations for dummies. Robert A. Hancock, 2003 U. Tex. Fam. L. Front Lines

Employee benefits: identify, value, divide and award. Randall B. Wilhite, 2003 U. Tex. Fam. L. Front Lines

Leading Cases

Alimony

See annotations to Chapter 8, *infra*.

Attorney's Fees

Brown v. Fullenweider, 52 S.W.3d 169 (Tex. 2001) (attorney's fees not subject to post divorce clarification and enforcement provisions)

Carle v. Carle, 149 Tex. 469, 234 S.W.2d 1002 (1950) (attorney's fees are a factor in making a just and right division)

Gutierrez v. Gutierrez, 86 S.W.3d 729 (Tex. App.—El Paso 2002, no pet.) (second—wife's attorney can testify regarding attorney's fees under new rules)

In re Striegler, 915 S.W.2d 629 (Tex. App.—Amarillo 1996, writ denied) (attorney's testimony on fees allowed despite not being listed as witness)

Roever v. Roever, 824 S.W.2d 674 (Tex. App.—Dallas 1992, no writ) (award of attorney's fees sustained by nominal community estate)

Powell v. Powell, 822 S.W.2d 181 (Tex. App.—Houston [1st Dist.] 1991, writ denied) (attorney's fees awarded to wife notwithstanding fact community estate contains negative balance)

Bankruptcy

Farrey v. Sanderfoot, 500 U.S. 291, L.Ed.2d 337, 111 S.Ct. 1825 (1991) (ex-wife's judicial lien on homestead awarded to ex-husband on divorce not discharged by his bankruptcy)

In re Davidson, 947 F.2d 1294 (5th Cir. 1991) (quasi-estoppel precludes discharge of alimony obligations)

In re Badgett, 647 F.2d 550 (5th Cir. 1981); *In re* Nunnally, 506 F.2d 1024 (5th Cir. 1975) (Texas-style contractual alimony not dischargeable)

In re Finch 130 B.R. 753 (S.D. Tex. 1991) (judicial lien imposed for "just and right" division not dischargeable in bankruptcy)

Douglas v. Delp, 987 S.W.2d 879 (Tex. 1999) (malpractice suit as an asset of the community swept into husband's bankruptcy)

Ruhe v. Rowland, 706 S.W.2d 709 (Tex. App.—Dallas 1986, no writ) (judgment for arrearages based on contractual child support not dischargeable)

Characterization, Reimbursement, and Tracing

See annotations to §§ 3.001–3.002, *supra*.

Dividing Community Property

Boggs v. Boggs, 520 U.S. 833, 117 S.Ct. 1754, 138 L.Ed.2d 49 (1997) (ERISA preempts LA community property law—first wife's attempt to leave "her share" of husband's retirement plan to her heirs ineffective; second wife takes as surviving spouse)

Keen v. Weaver, 46 Tex. Sup. Ct. J. 804 (2003) (decree is sufficient to waive a nonemployee's interest in retirement, QDRO not required)

Schlueter v. Schlueter, 975 S.W.2d 584 (Tex. 1998) (fraud on the community factor for division but not separate tort)

Dawson–Austin v. Austin, 968 S.W.2d 319 (Tex. 1998) (Texas divorce law governs separate property acquired in Minnesota because Texas has most significant relationship to the action)

Wilde v. Murchie, 949 S.W.2d 331 (Tex. 1997) (words of divestiture not required to convey interest in homestead)

Tenery v. Tenery, 932 S.W.2d 29 (Tex. 1996) (failure of trial court to file findings of fact and conclusions of law not reversible error)

Heggen v. Pemelton, 836 S.W.2d 145 (Tex. 1992) (equitable lien may be imposed on separate property homestead only to secure right of reimbursement for community improvements, not to insure just and right division of community property)

Jacobs v. Jacobs, 687 S.W.2d 731 (Tex. 1985) (appellate court cannot substitute its judgment for trial court's division of property; remand required)

McGoodwin v. McGoodwin, 671 S.W.2d 880 (Tex. 1984) (purchase money lien arises in favor of ex-spouse to secure divorce division of homestead)

Cameron v. Cameron, 641 S.W.2d 210 (Tex. 1982) (court may not divest spouse of separate personalty)

Murff v. Murff, 615 S.W.2d 696 (Tex. 1981) (list of factors court may consider in making division, including earning disparity)

Young v. Young, 609 S.W.2d 758 (Tex. 1980) (fault in breakup of marriage may be considered in division)

Mann v. Mann, 607 S.W.2d 243 (Tex. 1980) (division of property will not be reversed unless manifestly unfair)

Eggemeyer v. Eggemeyer, 554 S.W.2d 137 (Tex. 1977) (court may not divest spouse of his or her separate realty)

McKnight v. McKnight, 543 S.W.2d 863 (Tex. 1976) (appellate court can reverse trial court's division, but cannot divide property itself)

Nail v. Nail, 486 S.W.2d 761 (Tex. 1972) (professional goodwill not to be valued in dividing marital estate)

Hailey v. Hailey, 331 S.W.2d 299 (Tex. 1960) (to make just and right division the trial court should first decide whether the community estate is subject to partition in kind)

Sandone v. Miller-Sandone, 116 S.W.3d 204 (Tex. App.—El Paso 2003, no pet.) (default divorce containing property division based on zero evidence reversed; no property division without valuation evidence)

Rice v. Rice, 96 S.W.3d 642 (Tex. App.—Texarkana 2003, no pet.) (income-producing properties awarded to wife)

Zorilla v. Wahid, 83 S.W.3d 247 (Tex. App.—Corpus Christi 2002, no pet.) (children's "educational fund" quasi-community property subject to 60–40 split)

Edwards v. Edwards, 79 S.W.3d 88 (Tex. App.—Texarkana 2002, no pet.) (ordering all community property sold and proceeds divided in lieu of in-kind property division a mind-blowing abuse of discretion-but affirmed)

Osorno v. Osorno, 76 S.W.3d 509 (Tex. App.—Houston [14th Dist.] 2002, no pet.) (award of 75% of marital property to husband found to be unreasonable without findings or conclusions)

Phillips v. Phillips, 75 S.W.3d 564 (Tex. App.—Beaumont 2002, no pet.) (fault as a property division factor in an insupportability-only divorce called into question)

O'Neal v. O'Neal, 69 S.W.3d 347 (Tex. App.—Eastland 2002, pet. denied) (error for trial court in default divorce to take the husband's word for the fact that the property division was fair and equitable; evidence of values a necessary to support the judgment)

Wright v. Wright, 65 S.W.3d 715 (Tex. App.—Eastland 2001, no pet.) (88–12% division favoring wife justified on facts)

Nolder v. Nolder, 48 S.W.3d 432 (Tex. App.—Texarkana 2001, no pet.) (constructive trust follows property awarded to ex-wife into successful investments)

Wilson v. Wilson, 44 S.W.3d 597 (Tex. App.—Fort Worth 2001, no pet.) (wife reaps toward 50% share of husband's property 10 years after leaving him and their child to fend for themselves)

Daugherty v. Daugherty, 42 S.W.3d 331 (Tex. App.—Texarkana 2001, no pet.) (prisoner deprived of right to participate in divorce to present evidence on property issues)

Alford v. Alford, 40 S.W.3d 187 (Tex. App.—Texarkana 2001, no pet.) (award of 200,000 flier miles to be enforced by the court to insure that she is given her free tickets as a community asset)

Southwest Texas Pathology v. Roosth, 27 S.W.3d 204 (Tex. App.—San Antonio 2000, pet. dism. w.o.j.) (wife joined doctor/husband's partnership as respondent in divorce claiming conspiracy to deprive her community rights—terms of partnership don't bind her)

Wilburn v. Wilburn, 18 S.W.3d 837 (Tex. App.—Tyler 1999, pet. denied) (divorce pronounced orally and then husband dies; new trial permitted on property division, but divorce stands)

Kline v. Kline, 17 S.W.3d 445 (Tex. App.—Houston [1st Dist.] 1999, pet. denied) (unvested stock options awarded for past services are divisible community property)

Vandiver v. Vandiver, 4 S.W.3d 300 (Tex. App.—Corpus Christi 1999, pet. denied) (award of all disputed "wife's separate property" to her as just and right; although she failed to trace, trial court's award made irrespective of character excuses any mischaracterization)

Roberts v. Roberts, 999 S.W.2d 424 (Tex. App.—El Paso 1999, no pet.) (valuation of assets required to enable appellate court to determine whether trial court abused discretion)

Hill v. Hill, 971 S.W.2d 153 (Tex. App.—Amarillo 1998, no pet.) (findings of fact not required as to personalty)

Walston v. Walston, 955 S.W.2d 677 (Tex. App.—Waco 1997, no writ) (divorce award to parties of undivided 50–50 joint ownership interests is error, division must be in kind)

Wilson v. Uzzel, 953 S.W.2d 384 (Tex. App.—El Paso 1997, no writ) (*Taggart* formula, not *Berry* formula, applied to 1977 divorce division of retirement benefits—*Berry* formula not retroactively applied)

Grossnickle v. Grossnickle, 935 S.W.2d 830 (Tex. App.—Texarkana 1996, writ denied) (3% error in division of the estate not reversible)

Zieba v. Martin, 928 S.W.2d 782 (Tex. App.—Houston [14th Dist.] 1996, no writ) (trial court does not have unlimited discretion in dividing property)

Dankowski v. Dankowski, 922 S.W.2d 298 (Tex. App.—Fort Worth 1996, writ denied) (trial court has wide discretion in dividing property)

Forgason v. Forgason, 911 S.W.2d 893 (Tex. App.—Amarillo 1995, writ denied) (wife not entitled as matter of law to certain percentage of undivided marital assets in post-divorce litigation)

Panozzo v. Panozzo, 904 S.W.2d 780 (Tex. App.—Corpus Christi 1995, no writ) (award of corporate equipment reversed pending evidence of ownership)

Siefkas v. Siefkas, 902 S.W.2d 72 (Tex. App.—El Paso 1995, no writ) (alleged inequitable division can't be analyzed without valuations—remand of entire matter triggered by relatively insignificant award of H's separate property to W)

Faram v. Gervitz-Faram, 895 S.W.2d 839 (Tex. App.—Fort Worth 1995, no writ) (disproportionate division upheld, 72.9% vs. 27.1%)

Biaza v. Biaza, 879 S.W.2d 349 (Tex. App.—Houston [14th Dist.] 1994, writ denied) (severance of property division from the divorce action to create final judgment is not permitted)

Ramirez v. Ramirez, 873 S.W.2d 735 (Tex. App.—El Paso 1994, no writ) (wife can't recover both lump sum payment for her community interest and specific pieces of the community estate)

Harris v. Holland, 867 S.W.2d 86 (Tex. App.—Texarkana 1993, no writ) (trial court improperly considered potential tax consequences inherent in assets divided on divorce)

Golias v. Golias, 861 S.W.2d 401 (Tex. App.—Beaumont 1993, no writ) (79% division in favor of wife upheld)

Vannerson v. Vannerson, 857 S.W.2d 659 (Tex. App.—Houston [1st Dist.] 1993, writ denied) (even in default decree court has discretion to make unequal division)

Hopf v. Hopf, 841 S.W.2d 898 (Tex. App.—Houston [14th Dist.] 1992, no writ) (mischaracterization of homestead as community led to erroneous division on divorce)

Demler v. Demler, 836 S.W.2d 696 (Tex. App.—Dallas 1992, no writ) (failure to divide stock options constitutes reversible error)

Finch v. Finch, 825 S.W.2d 218 (Tex. App.—Houston [1st Dist.] 1992, no writ) (65–35 division of community upheld)

Thomas v. Thomas, 738 S.W.2d 342 (Tex. App.—Houston [1st Dist.] 1987, writ denied) (retained earnings in a Subchapter S corporation not marital property)

Marshall v. Marshall, 735 S.W.2d 587 (Tex. App.—Dallas 1987, writ ref'd n.r.e.) (partnership property is not divisible, only community's partnership interest)

Rathmell v. Morrison, 732 S.W.2d 6 (Tex. App.—Houston [14th Dist.] 1987, no writ) (divisible property includes business good will, excluding value of husband's personal good will, but not his right to compete and earnings following divorce)

Finn v. Finn, 658 S.W.2d 735 (Tex. App.—Dallas 1983, writ ref'd n.r.e.) (value of attorney's interest in good will of law firm is divisible, as distinguished from personal good will)

Robbins v. Robbins, 601 S.W.2d 90 (Tex. Civ. App.—Houston [1st Dist.] 1980, no writ) (trial court properly considered tax liability in dividing estate)

Economic Contribution

Langston v. Langston, 82 S.W.3d 686 (Tex. App.—Eastland 2002, no pet.) (husband's separate property home cannot be awarded to wife even though community claim for economic contribution may impose lien on property)

Quasi-Community Property

Estate of Hanau v. Hanau, 730 S.W.2d 663 (Tex. 1987) (quasi-community property inapplicable in probate proceedings)

Cameron v. Cameron, 641 S.W.2d 210 (Tex. 1982) (common law application of statutory rule for quasi-community property before statute effective)

Zorilla v. Wahid, 83 S.W.3d 247 (Tex. App.—Corpus Christi 2002, no pet.) (children's "educational fund" quasi-community property subject to 60–40 split)

Ismail v. Ismail, 702 S.W.2d 216 (Tex. App.—Houston [1st Dist.] 1985, no writ) (Texas quasi-community property rules apply to non-resident)

Reimbursement

See also annotations to Characterization, Reimbursement, and Tracing, §§ 3.001–.002, *supra*.

Heggen v. Pemelton, 836 S.W.2d 145 (Tex. 1992) (equitable lien may be imposed on separate property homestead only to secure right of reimbursement for community improvements, not to insure just and right division of community property)

Penick v. Penick, 783 S.W.2d 194 (Tex. 1988) (enhancement of separate estate offset by benefit to community estate)

Anderson v. Gilliland, 684 S.W.2d 673 (Tex. 1985) (reimbursement measured by enhancement)

Jensen v. Jensen, 665 S.W.2d 107 (Tex. 1984) (community time, toil, and effort contributed towards value of separate estate)

Gill v. Gill, 41 S.W.3d 255 (Tex. App.—Waco 2001, no pet.) (insufficient evidence to sustain husband's assertion of community estate reimbursement claim)

In re Marriage of Loftis, 40 S.W.3d 160 (Tex. App.—Texarkana 2001, pet. denied) (wife to be paid off mortgage on property of husband-to-be; no remedy available for recovery of her money on divorce)

Farrish v. Farrish, 982 S.W.2d 623 (Tex. App.—Houston [1st Dist.] 1998, no pet.) (child support for children of prior marriage not reimbursable)

Kimsey v. Kimsey, 965 S.W.2d 690 (Tex. App.—El Paso 1998, pet. denied) (major money judgment to reimburse wife for community improvement of husband's separate real property)

Winkle v. Winkle, 951 S.W.2d 80 (Tex. App.—Corpus Christi 1997, writ denied) (reversible error to place lien on separate property and not reimburse separate estate for building community home)

Hunt v. Hunt, 952 S.W.2d 564 (Tex. App.—Eastland 1997, no writ), Pelzig v. Berkebile, 931 S.W.2d 398 (Tex. App.—Corpus Christi 1996, no writ) (community estate has no right of reimbursement for payment of husband's legal obligations to pay alimony and child support to first family)

Zieba v. Martin, 928 S.W.2d 782 (Tex. App.—Houston [14th Dist.] 1996, no writ) (community estate not entitled to reimbursement for court-ordered expenses arising from a husband's prior marriage)

Thurmond v. Thurmond, 888 S.W.2d 269 (Tex. App.—Amarillo 1994, writ denied) (equitable title is a property right greater than the right of reimbursement)

Rider v. Rider, 887 S.W.2d 255 (Tex. App.—Beaumont 1994, no writ) (because the right of reimbursement is in equity, mathematical certainty is not required)

Golias v. Golias, 861 S.W.2d 401 (Tex. App.—Beaumont 1993, no writ) (trial court's discretion regarding reimbursement as broad as that for dividing property)

Graham v. Graham, 836 S.W.2d 308 (Tex. App.—Texarkana 1992, no writ) (reimbursement due for husband's separate property, i.e., proceeds from sale of house used to pay for purchase of new home)

Halbert v. Halbert, 794 S.W.2d 535 (Tex. App.—Tyler 1990, no writ) (expenses of spouse's education not reimbursable)

Separate Property

Langston v. Langston, 82 S.W.3d 686 (Tex. App.—Eastland 2002, no pet.) (husband's separate property home cannot be awarded to wife even though community claim for economic contribution may impose lien on property)

Osorno v. Osorno, 76 S.W.3d 509 (Tex. App.—Houston [14th Dist.] 2002, no pet.) (husband's testimony regarding financial accounts not enough to trace his separate property claim, even with premarital agreement)

McClary v. Thompson, 65 S.W.3d 829 (Tex. App.—Fort Worth 2002, pet. denied) (parties' premarital agreement identified the separate property existence at the time of the marriage but did not provide a basis to assert that future additions to a defined retirement benefit would be the husband's separate property)

Nesmith v. Berger, 64 S.W.3d 110 (Tex. App.—Austin 2001, pet. denied) (wife has no separate interest in marital residence; postnuptial agreement maintained status of husband's separate property)

Loftis v. Loftis, 40 S.W.3d 160 (Tex. App.—Texarkana 2001, no pet.) (no resulting trust for wife who paid off mortgage on husband's property before marriage—without a wrong, there is no right)

Schlafly v. Schlafly, 33 S.W.3d 863 (Tex. App.—Houston [14th Dist.] 2000, no pet.) (trial court's award of husband's separate interest in homestead triggers reversal—but misconduct requires him to pay all appellate costs)

Taxation Issues

United States v. Mitchell, 403 U.S. 190, 29 L.Ed.2d 406, 91 S.Ct. 1763 (1971) (state law controls whether income is separate or community)

Francis v. Francis, 412 S.W.2d 29 (Tex. 1967) (contractual alimony enforceable under Texas law of contracts)

Brooks v. Brooks, 515 S.W.2d 730 (Tex. Civ. App.—Eastland 1974, writ ref'd n.r.e.) (order to pay "community debts" does not include obligation to pay taxes)

Torts

Vickery v. Vickery, 999 S.W.2d 342 (Tex. 1999) (*Schlueter* still the law, notwithstanding unpublished opinion complicating the picture)

Schlueter v. Schlueter, 975 S.W.2d 584 (Tex. 1998) (fraud on the community factor for division but not separate tort)

Oliver v. Oliver, 889 S.W.2d 271 (Tex. 1994) (counterclaim for fraud after final divorce decree rendered was timely under Civil Practice and Remedies Code)

Twyman v. Twyman, 855 S.W.2d 619 (Tex. 1993) (Texas recognizes tort of intentional infliction of emotional distress, which may be joined in divorce if "double-counting" eliminated)

Bounds v. Caudle, 560 S.W.2d 925 (Tex. 1977) (no spousal immunity for intentional tort)

Alford v. Thornburg, 113 S.W.3d 575 (Tex. App.—Texarkana 2003, no pet.) (divorce agreement for wife to receive funds from husband's trust ran afoul of term in trust—she has tort suit against ex-husband and trustee)

Clayton v. Richards, 47 S.W.3d 149 (Tex. App.—Texarkana 2001, pet. denied) (private investigator who assisted in wiring the wife's bedroom in order to spy on the husband while wife took a trip was potentially liable to the husband for tortious conduct. Let the trial go forward)

Mayes v. Stewart, 11 S.W.3d 440 (Tex. App.—Houston [14th Dist.] 2000, pet. denied) (fraudulent concealment of lottery winnings leads to tort damages against ex-spouse and co-conspirator)

Harper v. Harper, 8 S.W.3d 782 (Tex. App.—Fort Worth 1999, pet. denied) (decedent's estate has no cause of action against surviving spouse's third party for fraud on the community)

Brinkman v. Brinkman, 966 S.W.2d 780 (Tex. App.—San Antonio 1998, no writ) (divorce serves as res judicata barring post-divorce tort lawsuit)

Moore v. Moore, 890 S.W.2d 821 (Tex. App.—Amarillo 1994, no writ) (fraud on the community or breach of fiduciary duty not separate causes of action in divorce—that's double recovery)

Behringer v. Behringer, 884 S.W.2d 839 (Tex. App.—Fort Worth 1994, no writ) (husband victimized by intentional infliction of emotional distress)

DeVine v. DeVine, 869 S.W.2d 415 (Tex. App.—Amarillo 1993, no writ) (evidence supports finding of constructive fraud)

Valuation

Morris v. Morris, 12 S.W.3d 877 (Tex. App.—Texarkana 2000, no pet.) (valuation of items of property acquired when it is component of cash award controlling issue)

Roberts v. Roberts, 999 S.W.2d 424 (Tex. App.—El Paso 1999, no pet.) (valuation of assets required in order for appellate court to determine whether trial court abused its discretion)

Baw v. Baw, 949 S.W.2d 764 (Tex. App.—Dallas 1997, no pet.), Iglinsky v. Iglinsky, 735 S.W.2d 536 (Tex. App.—Tyler 1987, no writ) (to measure increase in value of defined contribution plan during marriage, simply subtract balance at beginning from balance on divorce)

Pelzig v. Berkebile, 931 S.W.2d 398 (Tex. App.—Corpus Christi 1996, no writ) (court has discretion in choosing value assigned to property)

Collins v. Collins, 904 S.W.2d (Tex. App.—Houston [1st Dist.] 1995, writ denied per curiam, 923 S.W.2d 569 (Tex. 1996)) (husband not listed as witness on value of his corporations—supreme court takes narrow view)

Siefkas v. Siefkas, 902 S.W.2d 72 (Tex. App.—El Paso 1995, no writ) (alleged inequitable division can't be analyzed without valuations)

Turner v. Montgomery, 836 S.W.2d 848 (Tex. App.—Houston [1st Dist.] 1992, mand. mot. overruled) (wife has right to discover value of husband's law practice—attorney-client privilege may be protected by in camera inspection of documents)

Smith v. Smith, 836 S.W.2d 688 (Tex. App.—Houston [1st Dist.] 1992, no writ) (if business wholly dependent on spouse's continued personal services, good will must be excluded from valuation)

Texas Family Law Practice Manual

Chapter 17. Divorce—Decrees and Agreements Incident to Divorce: I. Decrees; II. Agreements Incident to Divorce; III. Tax Considerations

Texas Pattern Jury Charges: Family

PJC 202.13. Property Division–Advisory Questions; PJC 203.1. Value; PJC 203.2. Factors to Be Excluded for Valuation of Business; PJC 203.3. Value of Property; PJC 204.1. Economic Contribution; PJC 204.2. Reimbursement; PJC 204.3. Reimbursement–Advisory Questions; PJC

205.1. Alter Ego; PJC 205.2. Unfair Device; PJC 205.3. Disregarding Corporate Identity of Corporation Owned Entirely by Spouses; PJC 205.4. Disregarding Corporate Identity of Corporation Additional Instructions and Questions; PJC 206.1. Confidence and Trust Relationship between Spouses.

Cross References

TEX. CIV. PRAC. & REM. CODE § 31.001. Passage of Title; ch. 64. Receivership.

---

§ 7.003. Disposition of Retirement and Employment Benefits and Other Plans.

In a decree of divorce or annulment, the court shall determine the rights of both spouses in a pension, retirement plan, annuity, individual retirement account, employee stock option plan, stock option, or other form of savings, bonus, profit-sharing, or other employer plan or financial plan of an employee or a participant, regardless of whether the person is self-employed, in the nature of compensation or savings.

CLE/Other Legal Publications

Retirement: QDROs for qualified plans under ERISA (including using QDROs for child support). Charla Bradshaw Conner, 2003 ADV. FAM. L.; 2003 U. HOUSTON FAM. L. PRACTICE SEM. (OCTOBER)

Retirement. Jack W. Marr, 2003 ADV. FAM. L.

Retirement characterization-preserving separate property. Dawn E. Fowler, 2003 ADV. FAM. L.

Employee benefits: identify, value, divide and award. Randall B. Wilhite, 2003 U. TEX. FAM. L. FRONT LINES

ERISA retirement plans: an analysis of the new Texas Family Law Practice Manual QDRO forms and QDRO drafting tips. Charla Bradshaw Conner, 2002 ADV. FAM. L.

Community property and ERISA five years after Boggs*—are things any clearer?* John L. Hopwood, 2002 ADV. FAM. L.

Federal retirement plans. David R. McClure, 2002 ADV. FAM. L.

Unusual uses of QDROs: using the QDRO to collect child support and spousal maintenance. John T. Eck, 2002 MARRIAGE DISSOLUTION

What's on the menu? Cafeteria plans and other employee benefits. Jack W. Marr, 2002 MARRIAGE DISSOLUTION

Handling the state retirement plans: teacher retirement, county and district retirement, and state employment retirement, including survivor benefits. Curtis M. Loveless, 2001 ADV. FAM. L.

Leading Cases

Formula for Division

Grier v. Grier, 731 S.W.2d 931 (Tex. 1987) (division of community interest in military retirement pay based on the rank held by service member on day of divorce)

Berry v. Berry, 647 S.W.2d 945 (Tex. 1983) (defined benefit retirement payments to be apportioned based on community's interest at time of divorce)

Taggart v. Taggart, 552 S.W.2d 422 (Tex. 1977) (community interest in retirement benefit is the fraction of number of months married divided by the number of months employed)

Cearley v. Cearley, 544 S.W.2d 661 (Tex. 1976) (nonvested retirement benefits divisible on divorce)

Boyd v. Boyd, 67 S.W.3d 398 (Tex. App.—Fort Worth 2002, no pet.) (spouse is not entitled to an award of any interest in retirement benefits arising from other spouse's post-divorce employment)

McClary v. Thompson, 65 S.W.3d 829 (Tex. App.—Fort Worth 2002, pet. denied) (division of defined contribution retirement plan remanded; contributions and interest earned in plan during marriage are community property)

Smith v. Smith, 22 S.W.3d 140 (Tex. App.—Houston [14th Dist.] 1999, no pet) (community share of defined contribution plan calculated by subtracting value at marriage from value at divorce)

Kline v. Kline, 17 S.W.3d 445 (Tex. App.—Houston [1st Dist.] 1999, pet. denied) (unvested stock options awarded for past services are divisible community property)

Lipsey v. Lipsey, 983 S.W.2d 345 (Tex. App.—Fort Worth 1999, no pet.) (income accumulated in premarital 401(k) are trust assets if not distributed or distributable during marriage)

Albrecht v. Albrecht, 974 S.W.2d 262 (Tex. App.—San Antonio 1998, no pet.) (pension value is as of date of divorce)

Wade v. Wade, 923 S.W.2d 735 (Tex. App.—Texarkana 1996, writ denied) (termination benefits are not earned on day of vesting but rather over a period of time during spouse's employment)

Hatteberg v. Hatteberg, 933 S.W.2d 522 (Tex. App.—Houston [1st Dist.] 1994, no writ) (spouse's separate property interest in defined contribution plan is account balance on date of marriage)

Barnard v. Barnard, 863 S.W.2d. 770 (Tex. App.—Fort Worth 1993, no writ) (trial court correctly divided retirement, no second guessing at time payments due)

Parliament v. Parliament, 860 S.W.2d 144 (Tex. App.—San Antonio 1993, writ denied) (*Taggart* formula for dividing retirement benefits reaffirmed)

Humble v. Humble, 805 S.W.2d 558 (Tex. App.—Beaumont 1991, writ denied) (proper to apportion the benefit by the number of years second spouse married to employee, not by increase in benefits)

Iglinsky v. Iglinsky, 735 S.W.2d 536 (Tex. App.—Tyler 1987, no writ) (apportionment formula does not apply to defined contribution retirement plan)

Enforcement

Reiss v. Reiss, 118 S.W.3d 439 (Tex. 2003) (division of retirement benefits enforced as res judicata—error in applying law not appealed cannot be collaterally corrected)

Shanks v. Treadway, 110 S.W.3d 444 (Tex. 2003) (1981 prospective division of retirement benefits enforced as decreed—remedy for division contrary to current law was not appealed, so ex-wife takes 25% of 1998 retirement benefits)

Keen v. Weaver, 121 S.W.3d 721 (Tex. 2003) (ex-wife's interest in ERISA plan enforceable under federal common law)

Baxter v. Ruddle, 794 S.W.2d 761 (Tex. 1990) (unambiguous decree awarding fixed % of military benefits is res judicata and must be enforced as written)

Stubbe v. Stubbe, 733 S.W.2d 132 (Tex. 1987) (alimony agreement enforced against military retirement pay)

Charriere v. Charriere, 7 S.W.3d 217 (Tex. App.—Dallas 1999, no pet.) (stock options received during marriage but not exercised are community property—whether continued employment is requirement doesn't affect character)

Chandler v. Chandler, 991 S.W.2d 367 (Tex. App.—El Paso 1999, pet. denied) (ex-husband enjoined from relitigating military retirement issues over and over—enough's enough)

Harvey v. Harvey, 905 S.W.2d 760 (Tex. App.—Austin 1995, no writ) (survivor benefits awarded to ex-spouse in clarifying order)

Acosta v. Acosta, 836 S.W.2d 652 (Tex. App.—El Paso 1992, writ denied) (stock purchase plan included in "any retirement benefits" awarded to employee spouse on divorce)

Arena v. Arena, 822 S.W.2d 645 (Tex. App.—Fort Worth 1991, no writ) (QDRO permissible even though judgment rendered before enactment of Retirement Equity Act)

Governmental Benefits

Mansell v. Mansell, 490 U.S. 581, 104 L.Ed.2d 675, 109 S.Ct. 2023 (1989) (VA disability benefits are not divisible community property)

Kunin v. Feofanov, 69 F.3d 58 (5th Cir. 1995) (termination of nonemployee spouse's interest in public pension plan upheld—Tex. Gov't Code doesn't violate state constitution)

Havlen v. McDougall, 22 S.W.3d 343 (Tex. 2000) (pre–1981 divorce decree silent about partition of military retirement, USFSPA amendments prohibit post-divorce partition)

Veterans Administration v. Kee, 706 S.W.2d 101 (Tex. 1986) (VA disability benefits not subject to garnishment)

Ex parte Burson, 615 S.W.2d 192 (Tex. 1981) (divorce decree cannot prevent husband from electing disability pay in lieu of retirement pay)

Ex parte Johnson, 591 S.W.2d 453 (Tex. 1979) (VA disability benefits not divisible as community property)

Perez v. Perez, 587 S.W.2d 671 (Tex. 1979) (military readjustment allowance is not divisible as community property)

Valdez v. Ramirez, 574 S.W.2d 748 (Tex. 1978) (civil service retirement benefits do not pass to heirs of deceased spouse)

Limbaugh v. Limbaugh, 71 S.W.3d 1 (Tex. App.—Waco 2002, no pet.) (reversible error for trial court to order increased direct payments to ex-spouse contingent on military member decreasing Navy retirement pay by substituting VA disability pay)

Wright v. Eckhardt, 32 S.W.3d 891 (Tex. App.—Corpus Christi 2000, no pet.) (divorce division included ex-husband's navy fleet reserve pay)

Sanderlin v. Sanderlin, 929 S.W.2d 121 (Tex. App.—San Antonio 1996, writ denied) (teacher retirement account balance earned before marriage is separate property)

Bloomer v. Bloomer, 927 S.W.2d 118 (Tex. App.—Houston [1st Dist.] 1996, writ denied) (community portion of reserve military retirement to be measured by "points earned" during marriage, not months served)

Marsh v. Wallace, 924 S.W.2d 203 (Tex. App.—Austin 1996, no writ) (military Special Separation Benefit payment is retirement pay in which ex-wife entitled to share under divorce decree)

Jones v. Jones, 900 S.W.2d 786 (Tex. App.—San Antonio 1995, writ denied) (service member opted for 40% disability pay—res judicata bars his attack on final decree awarding ex-wife fixed at 25% of "major's retirement pay")

Trahan v. Trahan, 894 S.W.2d 113 (Tex. App.—Austin 1995, writ denied) (res judicata precludes application of 1990 USFSPA amendment to restrict post hoc partition)

Walton v. Lee, 888 S.W.2d 604 (Tex. App.—Beaumont 1994, writ denied) (partition suit for share of military retired pay not divided in 1976 allowed—tenancy in common created)

Sutherland v. Cobern, 843 S.W.2d 127 (Tex. App.—Texarkana 1992, no writ) (military retired pay COLA's are community property)

Duckett v. Board of Trustees, City of Houston Fireman's Relief & Retirement Fund, 832 S.W.2d 438 (Tex. App.—Houston [1st Dist.] 1992, writ denied) (percentage of fireman's retirement benefits awarded on divorce is irrelevant when death benefits due—ex-wife doesn't fit definition of widow)

Rucker v. Rucker, 810 S.W.2d 793 (Tex. App.—Houston [14th Dist.] 1991, writ denied) (policeman's disability pension is community property)

Undivided Retirement Benefits Subject to Partition

Buys v. Buys, 924 S.W.2d 369 (Tex. 1996) (residuary clause unambiguously awarded retirement benefits to nonemployee spouse although benefits not expressly mentioned)

Koepke v. Koepke, 732 S.W.2d 299 (Tex. 1987) (partition mandated of undivided retirement benefits that were not expressly awarded in divorce decree)

Allison v. Allison, 700 S.W.2d 914 (Tex. 1985) and Constance v. Constance, 544 S.W.2d 659 (Tex. 1976) (express award of retirement benefits bars subsequent partition)

Berry v. Berry, 647 S.W.2d 945 (Tex. 1983) (defined benefit retirement payments to be apportioned based on the community's interest at time of divorce)

Taggart v. Taggart, 552 S.W.2d 422 (Tex. 1977) *and* Cearley v. Cearley, 544 S.W.2d 661 (Tex. 1976) (spouse has community property interest in nonvested, nonmatured retirement benefits not divided on divorce)

Phillips v. Parrish, 814 S.W.2d 501 (Tex. App.—Houston [1st Dist.] 1991, writ denied) (retirement benefits not "in possession" for purposes of applying residuary clause)

Texas Family Law Practice Manual

Chapter 19. Retirement Benefits: I. Introduction; II. Retirement Benefits Divisible on Divorce; III. General Definitions; IV. Amendment of Order Dividing Plan; V. Private Retirement Plans; VI. Texas Public Retirement System; VII. Uniformed Services Former Spouses' Protection Act; VIII. Civil Service and Federal Employees' Retirement Systems; IX. Railroad Retirement

Cross References

TEX. FAM. CODE ANN. ch. 9, Post–Decree Proceedings; § 9.302. Pre–Decree Designation of Ex–Spouse as Beneficiary in Retirement Benefits and Other Financial Plans

TEX. GOV'T CODE ch. 804, Domestic Relations Orders and Spousal Consent

Civil Service Retirement Benefits. 5 U.S.C.A. §§ 2105, 8331 *et seq.*

Uniformed Services Former Spouses Protection Act. 10 U.S.C.A. § 1072 *et seq.*, § 1408 *et seq.*

Retirement Equity Act. 26 U.S.C.A. §§ 401, 402, 414.

Employee Retirement Income Security Act of 1974. 29 U.S.C.A. § 1055 *et seq.*

---

§ 7.004. Disposition of Rights in Insurance.

In a decree of divorce or annulment, the court shall specifically divide or award the rights of each spouse in an insurance policy.

CLE/Other Legal Publications

Health issues in family law: health insurance, COBRA, life insurance. William F. Neal & Janette L. Baldwin, 2003 ADV. FAM. L.

Insurance. Tim McClendon & Gus Bates III, 2003 MARRIAGE DISSOLUTION

Ensuring insurance coverage for your client (COBRA, Qualified Medical Support Orders and finding, using and characterizing insurance coverage). Susan Myres, 2001 ADV. FAM. L.

Cross Reference

TEX. FAM. CODE ANN. ch. 9, Post–Decree Proceedings; § 9.301. Pre–Decree Designation of Ex–Spouse as Beneficiary of Life Insurance.

Leading Cases

Egelhoff v. Egelhoff, 532 U.S. 141, 121 S.Ct. 1322 (2001) (ERISA preempts state statute voiding pre-divorce designation of spouse as beneficiary of employee's life insurance and pension)

Barnett v. Barnett, 67 S.W.3d 107 (Tex. 2001), *reversing pet. granted in part,* 985 S.W.2d 520 (federal ERISA preempts Texas Family Code regarding life insurance obtained through employment)

J.C. Penney Life Ins. Co. v. Heinrich, 32 S.W.3d 280 (Tex. App.—San Antonio 2000, pet. denied) (woman #2 paid life insurance proceeds; woman #1 as surviving common-law spouse takes umbrage and the cash from insurer)

---

§ 7.005. Insurance Coverage Not Specifically Awarded.

(a) If in a decree of divorce or annulment the court does not specifically award all of the rights of the spouses in an insurance policy other than life insurance in effect at the time the decree is rendered, the policy remains in effect until the policy expires according to the policy's own terms.

(b) The proceeds of a valid claim under the policy are payable as follows:

(1) if the interest in the property insured was awarded solely to one former spouse by the decree, to that former spouse;

(2) if an interest in the property insured was awarded to each former spouse, to those former spouses in proportion to the interests awarded; or

(3) if the insurance coverage is directly related to the person of one of the former spouses, to that former spouse.

(c) The failure of either former spouse to change the endorsement on the policy to reflect the distribution of proceeds established by this section does not relieve the insurer of liability to pay the proceeds or any other obligation on the policy.

(d) This section does not affect the right of a former spouse to assert an ownership interest in an undivided life insurance policy, as provided by Subchapter D, Chapter 9 *[Post–Decree Proceedings]*.

Leading Cases

Brandon v. Travelers Insurance Co., 18 F.3d 1321 (5th Cir. 1994) (Texas statute requiring redesignation of ex-spouse as beneficiary on life insurance policy preempted by ERISA), *cert. denied,* 115 S.Ct. 732 (1995)

Hunt v. Jefferson–Pilot Life Insurance Co., 900 S.W.2d 453 (Tex. App.—Fort Worth 1995, writ denied) (life insurance proceeds properly paid to ex-wife)

In re Group Life Insurance Proceeds of Mallory, 872 S.W.2d 800 (Tex. App.—Amarillo 1994, no writ) (naming stepchildren beneficiaries remains valid despite subsequent divorce of stepfather and mother)

Cross Reference

TEX. FAM. CODE ANN. ch. 9, Post–Decree Proceedings; § 9.201. Procedure for Division of Certain Property Not Divided on Divorce or Annulment, *et seq.*

TEX. PROB. CODE ANN. § 69. Voidness Arising from Divorce.

§ 7.006. Agreement Incident to Divorce or Annulment.

(a) To promote amicable settlement of disputes in a suit for divorce or annulment, the spouses may enter into a written agreement concerning the division of the property and the liabilities of the spouses and maintenance of either spouse. The agreement may be revised or repudiated before rendition of the divorce or annulment unless the agreement is binding under another rule of law.

(b) If the court finds that the terms of the written agreement in a divorce or annulment are just and right, those terms are binding on the court. If the court approves the agreement, the court may set forth the agreement in full or incorporate the agreement by reference in the final decree.

(c) If the court finds that the terms of the written agreement in a divorce or annulment are not just and right, the court may request the spouses to submit a revised agreement or may set the case for a contested hearing.

Comment

This section attempts to reflect the reality of Texas family law practice wherein ordinarily parties enter into settlement agreements. Whether these agreements are incorporated into the final decree of divorce varies widely around Texas. Some lawyers prefer to embody all terms of the settlement in the agreement and file a very short decree of divorce that merely refers to the agreement, which most often is not filed of record. Other lawyers prefer a single document, the final decree of divorce, which embodies the agreement as evidenced by signing. The decree may or may not itself be a contract. A settlement that also constitutes a contract may contain additional provisions that ordinarily could not be included in a decree, *e.g.,* contractual remedies, fixing of venue, and college education for the children.

Undoubtedly, by far the most significant impact on day-to-day practice involving agreements incident to divorce (AID, a.k.a. property settlement agreements, PSA) are the statutory rules applicable to mediated agreements and those resulting from collaborative law, *see* §§ 6.602–.603, and annotations, *supra*. Settlement agreements reached through those procedures are binding on the court because "a party is entitled to judgment" on such agreements.

CLE/Other Legal Publications

Enforceability of marital property agreements in the community property states. Douglas R. Woodburn, 2002 ADV. FAM. L.

Structured settlement. William W. Morris, 2001 ADV. FAM. L. DRAFTING

Leading Cases

Buys v. Buys, 924 S.W.2d 369 (Tex. 1996) (ex-wife owns military retirement benefits covered by property settlement residuary clause incorporated into divorce decree)

Padilla v. LaFrance, 907 S.W.2d 454 (Tex. 1995) (series of letters between the parties constitutes Rule 11 Settlement Agreement, enforceable by the court as a binding contract)

Phillips v. Phillips, 820 S.W.2d 785 (Tex. 1991) (settlement agreement providing penalty of ten times actual damages unenforceable)

Allen v. Allen, 717 S.W.2d 311 (Tex. 1986) (settlement agreement reformed to correct mutual mistake)

McCray v. McCray, 584 S.W.2d 279 (Tex. 1979) (alimony agreement approved by court is enforceable)

O'Carolan v. Hopper, 71 S.W.3d 529 (Tex. App.—Austin 2002, no pet.) (disproportionate property settlement busted; 100% of property to high earning, healthy husband and two-years alimony to incapacitated wife suggests abuse of discretion)

Welkener v. Welkener, 71 S.W.3d 364 (Tex. App.—Corpus Christi 2001, no pet.) (wife's unilateral "mistake" in agreeing to consent decree not a justification for remanding final decree)

Stewart v. Stine, 57 S.W.3d 94 (Tex. App.—Fort Worth 2001, no pet.) (mother who loaned substantial funds to daughter and son-in-law not a beneficiary of AID)

Byrnes v. Byrnes, 19 S.W.3d 556 (Tex. App.—Fort Worth 2000, no pet.) (agreement incident to divorce not considered a partition agreement unless specifically stated to be the same)

Guyot v. Guyot, 3 S.W.3d 243 (Tex. App.—Fort Worth 1999, no pet.) (attempted last-minute withdrawal of consent to agreement incident to divorce came too late) (docket sheet entry insufficient to preserve error)

Keim v. Anderson, 943 S.W.2d 938 (Tex. App.—El Paso 1997, no writ) (Rule 11 stipulation treated same as AID after rendition of divorce—trial court lacks jurisdiction to modify terms)

Cavazos v. Cavazos, 942 S.W.2d 211 (Tex. App.—Corpus Christi 1997, writ denied) ("exhibit" to settlement agreement not attached or incorporated is unenforceable)

McMann v. McMann, 942 S.W.2d 94 (Tex. App.—Houston [1st Dist.] 1997, no writ) (settlement agreement precluded attorney's fees)

Fryman v. Fryman, 926 S.W.2d 602 (Tex. App.—Fort Worth 1996, writ denied) (provision incorporated into an AID providing for automatic termination of contractual alimony if modification of support, conservatorship or visitation sought void as against public policy)

Clanin v. Clanin, 918 S.W.2d 673 (Tex. App.—Fort Worth 1996, no writ) (Rule 11 agreement made under oath and recorded by court reporter sufficient to be "in writing" requirement)

Delaup v. Delaup, 917 S.W.2d 411 (Tex. App.—Houston [14th Dist.] 1996, no writ) (testimony in open court reduced to writing sufficient to meet agreement in writing requirement)

Sohocki v. Sohocki, 897 S.W.2d 422 (Tex. App.—Corpus Christi 1995, no writ) (revocation of consent by wife voids agreed divorce decree)

Banks v. Banks, 887 S.W.2d 160 (Tex. App.—Texarkana 1994, no writ) (parties required to honor settlement agreement entered into pursuant to court-ordered mediation under the Civil Practice & Remedies Code)

DeVine v. DeVine, 869 S.W.2d 415 (Tex. App.—Amarillo 1993, no writ) (evidence supports finding of constructive fraud)

Ames v. Ames, 860 S.W.2d 590 (Tex. App.—Amarillo 1993, no writ) (settlement reached through mediation process binding; consent cannot be revoked)

McLendon v. McLendon, 847 S.W.2d 601 (Tex. App.—Dallas 1992, writ denied) (agreed order dictated into court record satisfies "written agreement" requirement)

McCubbin v. McCubbin, 844 S.W.2d 913 (Tex. App.—Tyler 1992, no writ) (mutual mistake in agreement can be corrected by reformation, partition inapplicable)

Rousseau v. Sprecher, 843 S.W.2d 300 (Tex. App.—Houston [14th Dist.] 1992, no writ) ("approved" divorce decree sufficient to support agreement to pay contractual alimony)

Trison Invest. Co. v. Woodard, 838 S.W.2d 790 (Tex. App.—Dallas 1992, writ denied) (implied vendor's lien not applicable to specific property because settlement agreement provided for unsecured payments)

Bakali v. Bakali, 830 S.W.2d 251 (Tex. App.—Dallas 1992, no writ) (trial court had jurisdiction over divorce even though decree did not reflect that settlement was approved in open court)

Giles v. Giles, 830 S.W.2d 232 (Tex. App.—Fort Worth 1992, no writ) (settlement agreement providing for alimony can be made part of court's order)

Baccus v. Baccus, 808 S.W.2d 694 (Tex. App.—Beaumont 1991, no writ) (verbal settlement agreement not enforceable)

Rogers v. Rogers, 806 S.W.2d 886 (Tex. App.—Corpus Christi 1991, no writ) (trial court cannot supply missing terms to agreement)

Traylor v. Traylor, 789 S.W.2d 701 (Tex. App.—Texarkana 1990, no writ) (agreements incident to divorce are contracts and may be enforced as such)

Pettitt v. Pettitt, 704 S.W.2d 921 (Tex. App.—Houston [14th Dist.] 1986, writ ref'd n.r.e.) (enforcement of an agreement is governed by ten year statute of limitations)

Texas Family Law Practice Manual

Chapter 17. Divorce—Decrees and Agreements Incident to Divorce: II. Agreements Incident to Divorce

Cross References

TEX. CIV. PRAC. & REM. CODE ANN. ch. 154. Alternative Dispute Resolution Procedures.

TEX. FAM. CODE ANN. § 153.007. Agreement Concerning Conservatorship; § 153.0071. Alternative Dispute Resolution Procedures; § 154.124. Agreement Concerning Support.

§ 7.007. Disposition of Claim for Economic Contribution or Claim for Reimbursement.

(a) In a decree of divorce or annulment, the court shall determine the rights of both spouses in a claim for economic contribution as provided by Subchapter E, Chapter 3, and in a manner that the court considers just and right, having due regard for the rights of each party and any children of the marriage, shall:

(1) order a division of a claim for economic contribution of the community marital estate to the separate marital estate of one of the spouses;

(2) order that a claim for an economic contribution by one separate marital estate of a spouse to the community marital estate of the spouses be awarded to the owner of the contributing separate marital estate; and

(3) order that a claim for economic contribution of one separate marital estate in the separate marital estate of the other spouse be awarded to the owner of the contributing marital estate.

(b) In a decree of divorce or annulment, the court shall determine the rights of both spouses in a claim for reimbursement as provided by Subchapter E, Chapter 3, and shall apply equitable principles to:

(1) determine whether to recognize the claim after taking into account all the relative circumstances of the spouses; and

(2) order a division of the claim for reimbursement, if appropriate, in a manner that the court considers just and right, having due regard for the rights of each party and any children of the marriage.

Leading Case

Langston v. Langston, 82 S.W.3d 686 (Tex. App.—Eastland 2002, no pet.) (husband's separate property home cannot be awarded to wife even though community claim for economic contribution may impose lien on property)

Chapter 8. Maintenance.

Subchapter A. General Provisions

Subchapter B. Court–Ordered Maintenance

Subchapter C. Income Withholding

Subchapter D. Procedure

Subchapter E. Rights and Duties of Employer

Subchapter F. Writ of Withholding Issued by Clerk

Subchapter G. Modification, Reduction, or Termination of Withholding

---

Introductory Comment

This chapter authorizing post-divorce alimony in Texas clearly marks a significant change in Texas family law, albeit somewhat more symbolic than practical. For many years Texas was the only state without any form of post-divorce court-ordered alimony. The passage of this law in 1995 resulted from the wave of "welfare reform" sweeping the country. Alimony was enacted, at least in part, as a measure to prevent an economically displaced spouse from going on welfare.

The statutes are carefully drafted to eliminate the legendary abuses surrounding Hollywood-style alimony. With some minor exceptions, the basic requirements are that the party seeking alimony must have been married ten years and be unable to be self-supporting. The monthly payment is limited to no more than $2,500.00 or 20% of the payor's income, whichever is less. Alimony generally is limited to no more than three years. However, if the former spouse is physically or mentally disabled, payments may be extended indefinitely. In the wake of a constitutional amendment, the provisions authorizing wage-withholding orders for the collection of spousal maintenance were enacted in 1999 and further clarified in 2001.

CLE/Other Legal Publications

Alimony and maintenance: enforceability, contractual agreements, creative uses and new tax traps. Patricia A. Wicoff, 2004 ADV. FAM. L.

Spousal maintenance-not an illusion in Texas. Julie Pruett Crawford & Ellen A. Yarrell, 2003 MARRIAGE DISSOLUTION

Maintenance is alive and well in Texas. Jim Penn & Mary Johanna McCurley, 2002 ADV. FAM. L.

Enforcement: new tools for enforcing spousal maintenance and visitation rights. Charles E. Miller, Jr., 2001 ADV. FAM. L. DRAFTING

Maintenance–"the price he has to pay for telling me that we're through" (including proving or disproving "minimum reasonable needs" and the (in)ability to provide for them). Rhonda F. Hunter, 2001 ADV. FAM. L.

Leading Cases

Francis v. Francis, 412 S.W.2d 29 (Tex. 1967) (pre-statute seminal case; agreed payment of contractual alimony enforceable by law of contracts, not by law of judgments)

In re Davidson, 947 F.2d 1294 (5th Cir. 1991) (Tex.) (parties' conduct precludes claim that contractual alimony not agreed upon)

In re Dupree, 118 S.W.3d 911 (Tex. App.—Dallas 2003, orig. proceeding) (contractual alimony not enforceable by contempt; court did not order payment)

Smith v. Smith, 115 S.W.3d 303 (Tex. App.—Corpus Christi-Edinburg 2003, no pet.) (disabled husband awarded nine years of spousal maintenance, after which he will receive Social Security retirement)

Cardwell v. Sicola-Cardwell, 978 S.W.2d 722 (Tex. App.—Austin 1998, pet. denied) (contractual alimony enforceable against payor's estate)

Carlin v. Carlin, 92 S.W.3d 902 (Tex. App.—Beaumont 2002, no pet.) (ex-wife failed to prove her physical disability was incapacitating to warrant continued spousal maintenance beyond three years)

Amos v. Amos, 79 S.W.3d 747 (Tex. App.—Corpus Christi 2002, no pet.) (alimony award upheld for maximum amount (20%) and maximum time (three years))

Limbaugh v. Limbaugh, 71 S.W.3d 1 (Tex. App.—Waco 2002, no pet.) (trial court's findings of statutory elements for award of maintenance are the only findings necessary but order to pay spousal support if husband trades in military retirement pay for VA disability benefits went too far)

Mastin v. Mastin, 70 S.W.3d 148 (Tex. App.—San Antonio 2001, no pet.) (ex-wife entitled to contractual alimony arrears but unequivocal notice of intent to accelerate contractual alimony after breach not provided, so no acceleration)

Pickens v. Pickens, 62 S.W.3d 212 (Tex. App.—Dallas 2001, pet. denied) (incapacitating disability and inability to meet minimum reasonable needs calls for spousal maintenance order for indefinite time)

Woolam v. Tussing, 54 S.W.3d 442 (Tex. App.—Corpus Christi 2001, no pet.) (ex-wife has valid claim for breach of contractual alimony—but not for contempt for deal made before 1995 enactment of Ch. 8)

Jenkins v. Jenkins, 991 S.W.2d 440 (Tex. App.—Fort Worth 1999, pet. denied) (wife's trustee in bankruptcy collects her contractual alimony)

Alexander v. Alexander, 982 S.W.2d 116 (Tex. App.—Houston [1st Dist.] 1998, no pet.) (order for post divorce "spousal support" to allow wife time to finish college was proper)

Butler v. Butler, 975 S.W.2d 765 (Tex. App.—Corpus Christi 1998, no pet.) (award of future earnings of spouse not allowed)

In re Hale, 975 S.W.2d 694 (Tex. App.—Texarkana 1998, no pet.) (award of alimony is within discretion of court)

O'Farrill v. Gonzalez, 974 S.W.2d 237 (Tex. App.—San Antonio 1998, pet. denied) (court enforces written contract between unmarried parents for monthly support and oral agreement to pay mortgage)

Crenshaw v. Crenshaw, 957 S.W.2d 171 (Tex. App.—San Antonio 1997, no writ) (no spousal maintenance if divorce filed [by husband] before 9/1/95, even though wife filed counter-petition after that date)

DuBois v. DuBois, 956 S.W.2d 607 (Tex. App.—Tyler 1997, no writ) (amount of property awarded plus wife's employable skills, justifies trial court's discretionary denial of alimony)

Bergman v. Bergman, 888 S.W.2d 580 (Tex. App.—El Paso 1994, no writ) (money judgment for alimony entitled to full faith, but Texas law exempting retirement payments from turnover prevails regarding enforcement remedy)

Subchapter A. General Provisions.

§ 8.001. Definitions.

In this chapter:

(1) "Maintenance" means an award in a suit for dissolution of a marriage of periodic payments from the future income of one spouse for the support of the other spouse.

(2) "Notice of application for a writ of withholding" means the document delivered to an obligor and filed with the court as required by this chapter for the nonjudicial determination of arrears and initiation of withholding for spousal maintenance.

(3) "Obligee" means a person entitled to receive payments under the terms of an order for spousal maintenance.

(4) "Obligor" means a person required to make periodic payments under the terms of an order for spousal maintenance.

(5) "Writ of withholding" means the document issued by the clerk of a court and delivered to an employer, directing that earnings be withheld for payment of spousal maintenance as provided by this chapter.

Subchapter B. Court-Ordered Maintenance

§ 8.051. Eligibility for Maintenance; Court Order.

In a suit for dissolution of a marriage or in a proceeding for maintenance in a court with personal jurisdiction over both former spouses following the dissolution of their marriage by a court that lacked personal jurisdiction over an absent spouse, the court may order maintenance for either spouse only if:

(1) the spouse from whom maintenance is requested was convicted of or received deferred adjudication for a criminal offense that also constitutes an act of family violence under Title 4 and the offense occurred:

(A) within two years before the date on which a suit for dissolution of the marriage is filed; or

(B) while the suit is pending; or

(2) the duration of the marriage was 10 years or longer, the spouse seeking maintenance lacks sufficient property, including property distributed to the spouse under this code, to provide for the spouse's minimum reasonable needs, as limited by Section 8.054, and the spouse seeking maintenance:

(A) is unable to support himself or herself through appropriate employment because of an incapacitating physical or mental disability;

(B) is the custodian of a child who requires substantial care and personal supervision because a physical or mental disability makes it necessary, taking into consideration the needs of the child, that the spouse not be employed outside the home; or

(C) clearly lacks earning ability in the labor market adequate to provide support for the spouse's minimum reasonable needs, as limited by Section 8.054.

Leading Cases

Smith v. Smith, 115 S.W.3d 303 (Tex. App.—Corpus Christi-Edinburg 2003, no pet.) (disabled husband awarded nine years of spousal maintenance, after which he will receive Social Security retirement)

Carlin v. Carlin, 92 S.W.3d 902 (Tex. App.—Beaumont 2002, no pet.) (ex wife failed to prove her physical disability was incapacitating to warrant continued spousal maintenance beyond three years)

Pickens v. Pickens, 62 S.W.3d 212 (Tex. App.—Dallas 2001, pet. denied) (finding an incapacitating disability and an inability to meet minimum reasonable needs mandates an order for spousal maintenance for an indefinite time)

DuBois v. DuBois, 956 S.W.2d 607 (Tex. App.—Tyler 1997, no writ) (amount of property awarded plus wife's employable skills, justifies trial court's discretionary denial of alimony)

---

§ 8.052. Factors in Determining Maintenance.

A court that determines that a spouse is eligible to receive maintenance under this chapter shall determine the nature, amount, duration, and manner of periodic payments by considering all relevant factors, including:

(1) the financial resources of the spouse seeking maintenance, including the community and separate property and liabilities apportioned to that spouse in the dissolution proceeding, and that spouse's ability to meet the spouse's needs independently;

(2) the education and employment skills of the spouses, the time necessary to acquire sufficient education or training to enable the spouse seeking maintenance to find appropriate employment, the availability of that education or training, and the feasibility of that education or training;

(3) the duration of the marriage;

(4) the age, employment history, earning ability, and physical and emotional condition of the spouse seeking maintenance;

(5) the ability of the spouse from whom maintenance is requested to meet that spouse's personal needs and to provide periodic child support payments, if applicable, while meeting the personal needs of the spouse seeking maintenance;

(6) acts by either spouse resulting in excessive or abnormal expenditures or destruction, concealment, or fraudulent disposition of community property, joint tenancy, or other property held in common;

(7) the comparative financial resources of the spouses, including medical, retirement, insurance, or other benefits, and the separate property of each spouse;

(8) the contribution by one spouse to the education, training, or increased earning power of the other spouse;

(9) the property brought to the marriage by either spouse;

(10) the contribution of a spouse as homemaker;

(11) marital misconduct of the spouse seeking maintenance; and

(12) the efforts of the spouse seeking maintenance to pursue available employment counseling as provided by Chapter 304, Labor Code.

§ 8.053. Presumption.

(a) Except as provided by Subsection (b), it is presumed that maintenance is not warranted unless the spouse seeking maintenance has exercised diligence in:

(1) seeking suitable employment; or

(2) developing the necessary skills to become self-supporting during a period of separation and during the time the suit for dissolution of the marriage is pending.

(b) This section does not apply to a spouse who is not able to satisfy the presumption in Subsection (a) because of an incapacitating physical or mental disability.

§ 8.054. Duration of Maintenance Order.

(a) Except as provided by Subsection (b), a court:

(1) may not order maintenance that remains in effect for more than three years after the date of the order; and

(2) shall limit the duration of a maintenance order to the shortest reasonable period that allows the spouse seeking maintenance to meet the spouse's minimum reasonable needs by obtaining appropriate employment or developing an appropriate skill, unless the ability of the spouse to provide for the spouse's minimum reasonable needs through employment is substantially or totally diminished because of:

(A) physical or mental disability;

(B) duties as the custodian of an infant or young child; or

(C) another compelling impediment to gainful employment.

(b) If a spouse seeking maintenance is unable to support himself or herself through appropriate employment because of an incapacitating physical or mental disability, the court may order maintenance for an indefinite period for as long as the disability continues. The court may order periodic review of its order, on the request of either party or on its own motion, to determine whether the disability is continuing. The continuation of spousal maintenance under these circumstances is subject to a motion to modify as provided by Section 8.057.

Leading Case

Pickens v. Pickens, 62 S.W.3d 212 (Tex. App.—Dallas 2001, pet. denied) (proof of inability for self-support that will continue for indefinite time provided by layperson testimony without supporting medical evidence regarding the condition or its prognosis)

---

§ 8.055. Amount of Maintenance.

(a) A court may not order maintenance that requires an obligor to pay monthly more than the lesser of:

(1) $2,500; or

(2) 20 percent of the spouse's average monthly gross income.

(b) The court shall set the amount that an obligor is required to pay in a maintenance order to provide for the minimum reasonable needs of the obligee, considering employment or property received in the dissolution of the marriage or otherwise owned by the obligee that contributes to the minimum reasonable needs of the obligee.

(c) Department of Veterans Affairs service-connected disability compensation, social security benefits and disability benefits, and workers' compensation benefits are excluded from maintenance.

(d) For purposes of this chapter, "gross income" means resources as defined in Sections 154.062(b) and (c), disregarding any deductions listed in Section 154.062(d) and disregarding those benefits excluded under Subsection (c) of this section.

§ 8.056. Termination.

(a) The obligation to pay future maintenance terminates on the death of either party or on the remarriage of the obligee.

(b) After a hearing, the court shall terminate the maintenance order if the obligee cohabits with another person in a permanent place of abode on a continuing, conjugal basis.

§ 8.057. Modification of Maintenance Order.

(a) The amount of maintenance specified in a court order or the portion of a decree that provides for the support of a former spouse may be reduced by the filing of a motion in the court that originally rendered the order. A party affected by the order or the portion of the decree to be modified may file the motion.

(b) Notice of a motion to modify maintenance and the response, if any, are governed by the Texas Rules of Civil Procedure applicable to the filing of an original lawsuit. Notice must be given by service of citation, and a response must be in the form of an answer due on or before 10 a.m. of the first Monday after 20 days after the date of service. A court shall set a hearing on the motion in the manner provided by Rule 245, Texas Rules of Civil Procedure.

(c) After a hearing, the court may modify an original or modified order or portion of a decree providing for maintenance on a proper showing of a material and substantial change in circumstances of either party. The court shall apply the modification only to payment accruing after the filing of the motion to modify.

(d) A loss of employment or circumstances that render a former spouse unable to support himself or herself through appropriate employment by reason of incapacitating physical or mental disability that occur after the divorce or annulment are not grounds for the institution of spousal maintenance for the benefit of the former spouse.

§ 8.058. Maintenance Arrearages.

A spousal maintenance payment not timely made constitutes an arrearage.

§ 8.059. Enforcement of Maintenance Order.

(a) The court may enforce by contempt the court's maintenance order or an agreement for the payment of maintenance voluntarily entered into between the parties and approved by the court.

(b) On the suit to enforce by an obligee, the court may render judgment against a defaulting party for the amount of arrearages after notice by service of citation, answer, if any, and a hearing finding that the defaulting party has failed or refused to carry out the terms of the order. The judgment may be enforced by any means available for the enforcement of judgment for debts.

(c) It is an affirmative defense to an allegation of contempt of court or the violation of a condition of probation requiring payment of court-ordered maintenance that the obligor:

(1) lacked the ability to provide maintenance in the amount ordered;

(2) lacked property that could be sold, mortgaged, or otherwise pledged to raise the funds needed;

(3) attempted unsuccessfully to borrow the needed funds; and

(4) did not know of a source from which the money could have been borrowed or otherwise legally obtained.

(d) The issue of the existence of an affirmative defense does not arise unless evidence is admitted supporting the defense. If the issue of the existence of an affirmative defense arises, an obligor must prove the affirmative defense by a preponderance of the evidence.

(e) A court may enforce an order for spousal maintenance under this chapter by ordering garnishment of the obligor's wages or by any other means available under this section.

Texas Family Law Practice Manual

Chapter 23. Enforcement—Spousal Maintenance: I. Enforcement Procedures

---

§ 8.060. Putative Spouse.

In a suit to declare a marriage void, a putative spouse who did not have knowledge of an existing impediment to a valid marriage may be awarded maintenance if otherwise qualified to receive maintenance under this chapter.

§ 8.061. Unmarried Cohabitants.

An order for maintenance is not authorized between unmarried cohabitants under any circumstances.

Subchapter C. Income Withholding

Introductory Comment

This subchapter, along with subchapters D, E, and F, set forth the procedures for payment of spousal maintenance through income withholding. Based largely on the procedures for child support, these provisions resemble those found in Chapter 158 *[Withholding from Earnings for Child Support].* Texas voters approved the amendment in November 1999 which allowed for the garnishment of wages to enforce spousal maintenance, however, there was no statutory guidance as to the proper procedures. Furthermore, there was confusion as to whether or not income withholding could be ordered only in the event of enforcement for non-payment.

Effective September 2001, any court ordered spousal maintenance payments, along with certain contractual payments, may be subject to income withholding. However, current child support obligations take precedence over spousal maintenance withholding.

---

§ 8.101. Income Withholding; General Rule.

(a) In a proceeding in which periodic payments of spousal maintenance are ordered, modified, or enforced, the court may order that income be withheld from the disposable earnings of the obligor as provided by this chapter.

(b) This subchapter does not apply to contractual alimony or spousal maintenance, regardless of whether the alimony or maintenance is taxable, unless:

(1) the contract specifically permits income withholding; or

(2) the alimony or maintenance payments are not timely made under the terms of the contract.

(c) An order or writ of withholding for spousal maintenance may be combined with an order or writ of withholding for child support only if the obligee has been appointed managing conservator of the child for whom the child support is owed and is the conservator with whom the child primarily resides.

(d) An order or writ of withholding that combines withholding for spousal maintenance and child support must:

(1) require that the withheld amounts be paid to the appropriate place of payment under Section 154.004;

(2) be in the form prescribed by the Title IV-D agency under Section 158.106;

(3) clearly indicate the amounts withheld that are to be applied to current spousal maintenance and to any maintenance arrearages; and

(4) subject to the maximum withholding allowed under Section 8.106, order that withheld income be applied in the following order of priority:

(A) current child support;

(B) current spousal maintenance;

(C) child support arrearages; and

(D) spousal maintenance arrearages.

(e) Garnishment for the purposes of spousal maintenance does not apply to unemployment insurance benefit payments.

§ 8.102. Withholding for Arrearages in Addition to Current Spousal Maintenance.

(a) The court may order that, in addition to income withheld for current spousal maintenance, income be withheld from the disposable earnings of the obligor to be applied toward the liquidation of any arrearages.

(b) The additional amount withheld to be applied toward arrearages must be whichever of the following amounts will discharge the arrearages in the least amount of time:

(1) an amount sufficient to discharge the arrearages in not more than two years; or

(2) 20 percent of the amount withheld for current maintenance.

§ 8.103. Withholding for Arrearages When Current Maintenance is Not Due.

A court may order income withholding to be applied toward arrearages in an amount sufficient to discharge those arrearages in not more than two years if current spousal maintenance is no longer owed.

§ 8.104. Withholding to Satisfy Judgment for Arrearages.

The court, in rendering a cumulative judgment for arrearages, may order that a reasonable amount of income be withheld from the disposable earnings of the obligor to be applied toward the satisfaction of the judgment.

§ 8.105. Priority of Withholding.

An order or writ of withholding under this chapter has priority over any garnishment, attachment, execution, or other order affecting disposable earnings, except for an order or writ of withholding for child support under Chapter 158.

§ 8.106. Maximum Amount Withheld From Earnings.

An order or writ of withholding must direct that an obligor's employer withhold from the obligor's disposable earnings the lesser of:

(1) the amount specified in the order or writ; or

(2) an amount that, when added to the amount of income being withheld by the employer for child support, is equal to 50 percent of the obligor's disposable earnings.

§ 8.107. Order or Writ Binding on Employer Doing Business in This State.

An order or writ of withholding issued under this chapter and delivered to an employer doing business in this state is binding on the employer without regard to whether the obligor resides or works outside this state.

§ 8.108. Voluntary Writ of Withholding by Obligor.

(a) An obligor may file with the clerk of the court a notarized or acknowledged request signed by the obligor and the obligee for the issuance and delivery to the obligor's employer of a writ of withholding. The obligor may file the request under this section regardless of whether a writ or order has been served on any party or whether the obligor owes arrearages.

(b) On receipt of a request under this section, the clerk shall issue and deliver a writ of withholding in the manner provided by this subchapter.

(c) An employer who receives a writ of withholding issued under this section may request a hearing in the same manner and according to the same terms provided by Section 8.205.

(d) An obligor whose employer receives a writ of withholding issued under this section may request a hearing in the manner provided by Section 8.258.

(e) An obligee may contest a writ of income withholding issued under this section by requesting, not later than the 180th day after the date on which the obligee discovers that the writ was issued, a hearing to be conducted in the manner provided by Section 8.258 for a hearing on a motion to stay.

(f) A writ of withholding under this section may not reduce the total amount of spousal maintenance, including arrearages, owed by the obligor.

Subchapter D. Procedure

§ 8.151. Time Limit.

The court may issue an order or writ for withholding under this chapter at any time before all spousal maintenance and arrearages are paid.

§ 8.152. Contents of Order of Withholding.

(a) An order of withholding must state:

(1) the style, cause number, and court having jurisdiction to enforce the order;

(2) the name, address, and, if available, the social security number of the obligor;

(3) the amount and duration of the spousal maintenance payments, including the amount and duration of withholding for arrearages, if any; and

(4) the name, address, and, if available, the social security number of the obligee.

(b) The order for withholding must require the obligor to notify the court promptly of any material change affecting the order, including a change of employer.

(c) On request by an obligee, the court may exclude from an order of withholding the obligee's address and social security number if the obligee or a member of the obligee's family or household is a victim of family violence and is the subject of a protective order to which the obligor is also subject. On granting a request under this subsection, the court shall order the clerk to:

(1) strike the address and social security number required by Subsection (a) from the order or writ of withholding; and

(2) maintain a confidential record of the obligee's address and social security number to be used only by the court.

§ 8.153. Request for Issuance of Order or Writ of Withholding.

An obligor or obligee may file with the clerk of the court a request for issuance of an order or writ of withholding.

§ 8.154. Issuance and Delivery of Order or Writ of Withholding.

(a) On receipt of a request for issuance of an order or writ of withholding, the clerk of the court shall deliver a certified copy of the order or writ to the obligor's current employer or to any subsequent employer of the obligor. The clerk shall attach a copy of Subchapter E to the order or writ.

(b) Not later than the fourth working day after the date the order is signed or the request is filed, whichever is later, the clerk shall issue and deliver the certified copy of the order or writ by:

(1) certified or registered mail, return receipt requested, to the employer; or

(2) service of citation to:

(A) the person authorized to receive service of process for the employer in civil cases generally; or

(B) a person designated by the employer by written notice to the clerk to receive orders or notices of income withholding.

Subchapter E. Rights and Duties of Employer

§ 8.201. Order or Writ Binding on Employer.

(a) An employer required to withhold income from earnings under this chapter is not entitled to notice of the proceedings before the order of withholding is rendered or writ of withholding is issued.

(b) An order or writ of withholding is binding on an employer regardless of whether the employer is specifically named in the order or writ.

§ 8.202. Effective Date and Duration of Income Withholding.

An employer shall begin to withhold income in accordance with an order or writ of withholding not later than the first pay period after the date the order or writ was delivered to the employer. The employer shall continue to withhold income as required by the order or writ as long as the obligor is employed by the employer.

§ 8.203. Remitting Withheld Payments.

(a) The employer shall remit to the person or office named in the order or writ of withholding the amount of income withheld from an obligor on each pay date. The remittance must include the date on which the income withholding occurred.

(b) The employer shall include with each remittance:

(1) the cause number of the suit under which income withholding is required;

(2) the payor's name; and

(3) the payee's name, unless the remittance is made by electronic funds transfer.

§ 8.204. Employer May Deduct Fee From Earnings.

An employer may deduct an administrative fee of not more than $5 each month from the obligor's disposable earnings in addition to the amount withheld as spousal maintenance.

§ 8.205. Hearing Requested by Employer.

(a) Not later than the 20th day after the date an order or writ of withholding is delivered to an employer, the employer may file with the court a motion for a hearing on the applicability of the order or writ to the employer.

(b) The hearing under this section must be held on or before the 15th day after the date the motion is made.

(c) An order or writ of withholding is binding and the employer shall continue to withhold income and remit the amount withheld pending further order of the court.

§ 8.206. Liability and Obligation of Employer for Payments.

(a) An employer who complies with an order or writ of withholding under this chapter is not liable to the obligor for the amount of income withheld and remitted as required by the order or writ.

(b) An employer who receives, but does not comply with, an order or writ of withholding is liable to:

(1) the obligee for any amount of spousal maintenance not paid in compliance with the order or writ;

(2) the obligor for any amount withheld from the obligor's disposable earnings, but not remitted to the obligee; and

(3) the obligee or obligor for reasonable attorney's fees and court costs incurred in recovering an amount described by Subdivision (1) or (2).

(c) An employer shall comply with an order of withholding for spousal maintenance or alimony issued in another state that appears regular on its face in the same manner as an order issued by a tribunal of this state. The employer shall notify the employee of the order and comply with the order in the manner provided by Subchapter F, Chapter 159*[UIFSA]*, with respect to an order of withholding for child support issued by another state. The employer may contest the order of withholding in the manner provided by that subchapter with respect to an order of withholding for child support issued by another state.

§ 8.207. Employer Receiving Multiple Orders or Writs.

(a) An employer who receives more than one order or writ of withholding to withhold income from the same obligor shall withhold the combined amounts due under each order or writ unless the combined amounts due exceed the maximum total amount of allowed income withholding under Section 8.106.

(b) If the combined amounts to be withheld under multiple orders or writs for the same obligor exceed the maximum total amount of allowed income withholding under Section 8.106, the employer shall pay, until that maximum is reached, in the following order of priority:

(1) an equal amount toward current child support owed by the obligor in each order or writ until the employer has complied fully with each current child support obligation;

(2) an equal amount toward current maintenance owed by the obligor in each order or writ until the employer has complied fully with each current maintenance obligation;

(3) an equal amount toward child support arrearages owed by the obligor in each order or writ until the employer has complied fully with each order or writ for child support arrearages; and

(4) an equal amount toward maintenance arrearages owed by the obligor in each order or writ until the employer has complied fully with each order or writ for spousal maintenance arrearages.

§ 8.208. Employer's Liability for Discriminatory Hiring or Discharge.

(a) An employer may not use an order or writ of withholding as grounds in whole or part for the termination of employment of, or for any other disciplinary action against, an employee.

(b) An employer may not refuse to hire an employee because of an order or writ of withholding.

(c) An employer who intentionally discharges an employee in violation of this section is liable to that employee for current wages, other employment benefits, and reasonable attorney's fees and court costs incurred in enforcing the employee's rights.

(d) In addition to liability imposed under Subsection (c), the court shall order with respect to an employee whose employment was suspended or terminated in violation of this section appropriate injunctive relief, including reinstatement of:

(1) the employee's position with the employer; and

(2) fringe benefits or seniority lost as a result of the suspension or termination.

(e) An employee may bring an action to enforce the employee's rights under this section.

§ 8.209. Penalty for Noncompliance.

(a) In addition to the civil remedies provided by this subchapter or any other remedy provided by law, an employer who knowingly violates this chapter by failing to withhold income for spousal maintenance or to remit withheld income in accordance with an order or writ of withholding issued under this chapter commits an offense.

(b) An offense under this section is punishable by a fine not to exceed $200 for each violation.

§ 8.210. Notice of Termination of Employment and of New Employment.

(a) An obligor who terminates employment with an employer who has been withholding income and the obligor's employer shall each notify the court and the obligee of:

(1) the termination of employment not later than the seventh day after the date of termination;

(2) the obligor's last known address; and

(3) the name and address of the obligor's new employer, if known.

(b) The obligor shall inform a subsequent employer of the order or writ of withholding after obtaining employment.

Subchapter F. Writ of Withholding Issued by Clerk

§ 8.251. Notice of Application for Writ of Withholding; Filing.

(a) An obligor or obligee may file a notice of application for a writ of withholding if income withholding was not ordered at the time spousal maintenance was ordered.

(b) The obligor or obligee may file the notice of application for a writ of withholding in the court that ordered the spousal maintenance under Subchapter B.

§ 8.252. Contents of Notice of Application for Writ of Withholding.

The notice of application for a writ of withholding must be verified and:

(1) state the amount of monthly maintenance due, including the amount of arrearages or anticipated arrearages, and the amount of disposable earnings to be withheld under a writ of withholding;

(2) state that the withholding applies to each current or subsequent employer or period of employment;

(3) state that the obligor's employer will be notified to begin the withholding if the obligor does not contest the withholding on or before the 10th day after the date the obligor receives the notice;

(4) describe the procedures for contesting the issuance and delivery of a writ of withholding;

(5) state that the obligor will be provided an opportunity for a hearing not later than the 30th day after the date of receipt of the notice of contest if the obligor contests the withholding;

(6) state that the sole ground for successfully contesting the issuance of a writ of withholding is a dispute concerning the identity of the obligor or the existence or amount of the arrearages;

(7) describe the actions that may be taken if the obligor contests the notice of application for a writ of withholding, including the procedures for suspending issuance of a writ of withholding; and

(8) include with the notice a suggested form for the motion to stay issuance and delivery of the writ of withholding that the obligor may file with the clerk of the appropriate court.

§ 8.253. Interstate Request for Withholding.

(a) The registration of a foreign order that provides for spousal maintenance or alimony as provided in Chapter 159 *[UIFSA]* is sufficient for filing a notice of application for a writ of withholding.

(b) The notice must be filed with the clerk of the court having venue as provided in Chapter 159.

(c) The notice of application for a writ of withholding may be delivered to the obligor at the same time that an order is filed for registration under Chapter 159.

§ 8.254. Additional Arrearages.

If the notice of application for a writ of withholding states that the obligor has failed to pay more than one spousal maintenance payment according to the terms of the spousal maintenance order, the writ of withholding may include withholding for arrearages that accrue between the filing of the notice and the date of the hearing or the issuance of the writ.

§ 8.255. Delivery of Notice of Application for Writ of Withholding; Time of Delivery.

(a) The party who files a notice of application for a writ of withholding shall deliver the notice to the obligor by:

(1) first-class or certified mail, return receipt requested, addressed to the obligor's last known address or place of employment; or

(2) service of citation as in civil cases generally.

(b) If the notice is delivered by mail, the party who filed the notice shall file with the court a certificate stating the name, address, and date the party mailed the notice.

(c) The notice is considered to have been received by the obligor:

(1) on the date of receipt, if the notice was mailed by certified mail;

(2) on the 10th day after the date the notice was mailed, if the notice was mailed by first-class mail; or

(3) on the date of service, if the notice was delivered by service of citation.

§ 8.256. Motion to Stay Issuance of Writ of Withholding.

(a) The obligor may stay issuance of a writ of withholding by filing a motion to stay with the clerk of the court not later than the 10th day after the date the notice of application for a writ of withholding was received.

(b) The grounds for filing a motion to stay issuance are limited to a dispute concerning the identity of the obligor or the existence or the amount of the arrearages.

(c) The obligor shall verify that the statements of fact in the motion to stay issuance of the writ are correct.

§ 8.257. Effect of Filing Motion to Stay.

If the obligor files a motion to stay as provided by Section 8.256, the clerk of the court may not deliver the writ of withholding to the obligor's employer before a hearing is held.

§ 8.258. Hearing on Motion to Stay.

(a) If the obligor files a motion to stay as provided by Section 8.256, the court shall set a hearing on the motion and the clerk of the court shall notify the obligor and obligee of the date, time, and place of the hearing.

(b) The court shall hold a hearing on the motion to stay not later than the 30th day after the date the motion was filed unless the obligor and obligee agree and waive the right to have the motion heard within 30 days.

(c) After the hearing, the court shall:

(1) render an order for income withholding that includes a determination of any amount of arrearages; or

(2) grant the motion to stay.

§ 8.259. Special Exceptions.

(a) A defect in a notice of application for a writ of withholding is waived unless the respondent specially excepts in writing and cites with particularity the alleged defect, obscurity, or other ambiguity in the notice.

(b) A special exception under this section must be heard by the court before hearing the motion to stay issuance.

(c) If the court sustains an exception, the court shall provide the party filing the notice an opportunity to refile and shall continue the hearing to a specified date without requiring additional service.

§ 8.260. Writ of Withholding After Arrearages Are Paid.

(a) The court may not refuse to order withholding solely on the basis that the obligor paid the arrearages after the obligor received the notice of application for a writ of withholding.

(b) The court shall order that a reasonable amount of income be withheld and applied toward the liquidation of arrearages, even though a judgment confirming arrearages was rendered against the obligor.

§ 8.261. Request for Issuance and Delivery of Writ of Withholding.

(a) If a notice of application for a writ of withholding is delivered and the obligor does not file a motion to stay within the time provided by Section 8.256, the party who filed the notice shall file with the clerk of the court a request for issuance of the writ of withholding stating the amount of current spousal maintenance, the amount of arrearages, and the amount to be withheld from the obligor's income.

(b) The party who filed the notice may not file a request for issuance before the 11th day after the date the obligor received the notice of application for a writ of withholding.

§ 8.262. Issuance and Delivery of Writ of Withholding.

The clerk of the court shall, on the filing of a request for issuance of a writ of withholding, issue and deliver the writ as provided by Subchapter D not later than the second working day after the date the request is filed. The clerk shall charge a fee in the amount of $15 for issuing the writ of withholding.

§ 8.263. Contents of Writ of Withholding.

A writ of withholding must direct that an obligor's employer or a subsequent employer withhold from the obligor's disposable earnings an amount for current spousal maintenance and arrearages consistent with this chapter.

§ 8.264. Extension of Repayment Schedule by Party; Unreasonable Hardship.

A party who files a notice of application for a writ of withholding and who determines that the schedule for repaying arrearages would cause unreasonable hardship to the obligor or the obligor's family may extend the payment period in the writ.

§ 8.265. Remittance of Amount to be Withheld.

The obligor's employer shall remit the amount withheld to the person or office named in the writ on each pay date and shall include with the remittance the date on which the withholding occurred.

§ 8.266. Failure to Receive Notice of Application for Writ of Withholding.

(a) Not later than the 30th day after the date of the first pay period after the date the obligor's employer receives a writ of withholding, the obligor may file an affidavit with the court stating that:

(1) the obligor did not timely file a motion to stay because the obligor did not receive the notice of application for a writ of withholding; and

(2) grounds exist for a motion to stay.

(b) The obligor may:

(1) file with the affidavit a motion to withdraw the writ of withholding; and

(2) request a hearing on the applicability of the writ.

(c) Income withholding may not be interrupted until after the hearing at which the court renders an order denying or modifying withholding.

§ 8.267. Issuance and Delivery of Writ of Withholding to Subsequent Employer.

(a) After the clerk of the court issues a writ of withholding, a party authorized to file a notice of application for a writ of withholding under this subchapter may deliver a copy of the writ to a subsequent employer of the obligor by certified mail.

(b) Except as provided by an order under Section 8.152, the writ of withholding must include the name, address, and signature of the party and clearly indicate that the writ is being issued to a subsequent employer.

(c) The party shall file:

(1) a copy of the writ of withholding with the clerk not later than the third working day after the date of delivery of the writ to the subsequent employer; and

(2) the postal return receipt from the delivery to the subsequent employer not later than the third working day after the date the party receives the receipt.

(d) The party shall pay the clerk a fee in the amount of $15 for filing the copy of the writ.

Subchapter G. Modification, Reduction, or Termination of Withholding

§ 8.301. Agreement by Parties Regarding Amount or Duration of Withholding.

(a) An obligor and obligee may agree to reduce or terminate income withholding for spousal maintenance on the occurrence of any contingency stated in the order.

(b) The obligor and obligee may file a notarized or acknowledged request with the clerk of the court under Section 8.108 for a revised writ of withholding or notice of termination of withholding.

(c) The clerk shall issue and deliver to the obligor's employer a writ of withholding that reflects the agreed revision or a notice of termination of withholding.

(d) An agreement by the parties under this section does not modify the terms of an order for spousal maintenance.

§ 8.302. Modifications to or Termination of Withholding in Voluntary Withholding Cases.

(a) If an obligor initiates voluntary withholding under Section 8.108, the obligee may file with the clerk of the court a notarized request signed by the obligor and the obligee for the issuance and delivery to the obligor of:

(1) a modified writ of withholding that reduces the amount of withholding; or

(2) a notice of termination of withholding.

(b) On receipt of a request under this section, the clerk shall issue and deliver a modified writ of withholding or notice of termination in the manner provided by Section 8.301.

(c) The clerk may charge a fee in the amount of $15 for issuing and delivering the modified writ of withholding or notice of termination.

(d) An obligee may contest a modified writ of withholding or notice of termination issued under this section by requesting a hearing in the manner provided by Section 8.258 not later than the 180th day after the date the obligee discovers that the writ or notice was issued.

§ 8.303. Termination of Withholding in Mandatory Withholding Cases.

(a) An obligor for whom withholding for maintenance owed or withholding for maintenance and child support owed is mandatory may file a motion to terminate withholding. On a showing by the obligor that the obligor has complied fully with the terms of the maintenance or child support order, as applicable, the court shall render an order for the issuance and delivery to the obligor of a notice of termination of withholding.

(b) The clerk shall issue and deliver the notice of termination ordered under this section to the obligor.

(c) The clerk may charge a fee in the amount of $15 for issuing and delivering the notice.

§ 8.304. Delivery of Order of Reduction or Termination of Withholding.

Any person may deliver to the obligor's employer a certified copy of an order that reduces the amount of spousal maintenance to be withheld or terminates the withholding.

§ 8.305. Liability of Employers.

The provisions of this chapter regarding the liability of employers for withholding apply to an order that reduces or terminates withholding.

Chapter 9. Post–Decree Proceedings.

Subchapter A. Suit To Enforce Decree

Subchapter B. Post–Decree Qualified Domestic Relations Order

Subchapter C. Post–Decree Division of Property

Subchapter D. Disposition of Undivided Beneficial Interest

Subchapter A. Suit To Enforce Decree

Introductory Comment

TEX. FAM. CODE ANN. §§ 7.001-.007, *supra*, authorizing a division of the marital estate do not automatically result in the property awarded to a spouse being delivered promptly and intact. This subchapter was enacted to grant a trial court wide-ranging enforcement powers to carry out the terms of its decree. Although trial court is not authorized to modify its decree, it is authorized to issue clarifying and enforcing orders. This subchapter does not apply to property previously undivided; that is covered by Tex. Fam. Code Ann. § 9.201 *et seq.*

CLE/Other Legal Publications

Getting what you got! Enforcing the property division—including judgment collection. J. Lindsey Short, Jr., 2004 Adv. Fam. L.

Enforcement of Texas matrimonial judgments, decrees, and orders in Mexico. Eva M. Guzman, 2002 Adv. Fam. L.

Recognition and enforcement of matrimonial judgments, decrees, and orders in the United States and foreign countries. Pamela K. Pergman & John F. Nichols, 2002 Adv. Fam. L.

Judgment recovery. Rhett Hoestenbach, 2002 Adv. Fam. L. Drafting

Enforcing the property division. H. E. Mendez, 2002 Marriage Dissolution

Avoiding the thorns while picking the roses: enforcing, securing and clarifying property divisions. Mike Gregory, 2001 Adv. Fam. L.

Leading Cases

Farrey v. Sanderfoot, 500 U.S. 291, 114 L.Ed.2d 337, 111 S.Ct. 1825 (1991) (lien on homestead awarded ex-wife by divorce not discharged in ex-husband's bankruptcy)

In re Finch, 130 B.R. 753 (S.D. Tex. 1991) (ex-wife's equitable lien on homestead awarded to ex-husband survives his bankruptcy)

Brown v. Fullenweider, 52 S.W.3d 169 (Tex. 2001) (attorney's fees not subject to post divorce clarification and enforcement provisions)

Schwartz v. Jefferson, 520 S.W.2d 881 (Tex. 1975) (court could properly enter orders to enforce its decree)

McKnight v. Trogdon-McKnight, 132 S.W.3d 126 (Tex. App.—Houston [14th Dist.] 2004, no pet. hist.) (clarifying orders for sale of house, new QDRO, and judgment for attorney's fees change terms of divorce decree); *accord*, *In re* Marriage of McDonald, 118 S.W.3d 829 (Tex. App.—Texarkana 2003, pet. denied)

In re Goodson, 110 S.W.3d 81 (Tex. App.—Houston [1st] 2003, orig. proceeding) (divorce decree awarding spouse 50% of proceeds of sale of home clarified and then subsequently enforced by contempt)

Marshall v. Priess, 99 S.W.3d 150 (Tex. App.—Houston [14th Dist.] 2002, no pet.) (trial court exceeded its authority to clarify division of spouse's retirement plans by making substantive changes to divorce decree)

Preston v. Burmeister, 52 S.W.3d 386 (Tex. App.—Fort Worth 2001, no pet.) (Texas court has no business awarding retirement benefits not addressed in 1979 Florida divorce—that's Florida's territory)

Zeolla v. Zeolla, 15 S.W.3d 239 (Tex. App.—Houston [14th Dist.] 2000, pet. denied) (original decree had latent ambiguity when husband retired early—cured by proportional adjustment to reflect early retirement plus payback of benefits already received within trial court's power)

Ackerly v. Ackerly, 13 S.W.3d 454 (Tex. App.—Corpus Christi 2000, no pet.) (motion for money judgment to enforce divorce award improper; separate lawsuit with citation required)

Chavez v. Chavez, 12 S.W.3d 563 (Tex. App.—San Antonio 1999, no pet.) (ex-wife's enforcement for proceeds of future sale of stock filed within two years of discovery of sale)

Arnold v. Eaton, 910 S.W.2d 181 (Tex. App.—Eastland 1995, no writ) (intervening foreclosure extinguished ex-wife's equitable lien on former homestead awarded to ex-husband)

Dechon v. Dechon, 909 S.W.2d 950 (Tex. App.—El Paso 1995, no writ) (ex-husband's special appearance inadequate to prevent clarification and enforcement)

Bina v. Bina, 908 S.W.2d 595 (Tex. App.—Fort Worth 1995, no writ) (clarification order does not modify original decree)

Day v. Day, 896 S.W.2d 373 (Tex. App.—Amarillo 1995, no writ) (statute of limitations for right to enforce wife's chose in action began when right accrued, not at date of divorce decree)

Bryant v. Flint, 894 S.W.2d 397 (Tex. App.—Houston [1st Dist.] 1994, no writ) (IRS innocent spouse finding doesn't release wife from contractual obligation to pay her share of taxes)

Bergman v. Bergman, 888 S.W.2d 580 (Tex. App.—El Paso 1994, no writ) (money judgment for alimony entitled to full faith, but Texas law exempting retirement payments from turnover prevails regarding enforcement remedy)

Conti v. Conti, 866 S.W.2d 671 (Tex. App.—Houston [14th Dist.] 1993, writ denied) (Govt. Code permits issuance of valid QDRO for public retirement system without regard to statute of limitations under Tex. Fam. Code Ann.)

Young v. Young, 765 S.W.2d 440 (Tex. App.—Dallas 1988), *later proceeding*, 810 S.W.2d 850 (Tex. App.—Dallas 1991, writ denied) (trial court's enforcement order determining that "furniture" includes china, silverware, crystal, etc. valid enforcement)

Bowden v. Knowlton, 734 S.W.2d 206 (Tex. App.—Houston [1st Dist.] 1987, no writ) (trial court properly imposed lien on husband's separate property to enforce decree)

Pettitt v. Pettitt, 704 S.W.2d 921 (Tex. App.—Houston [14th Dist.] 1986, writ ref'd n.r.e.) (two year limitation inapplicable to action to enforce division of property secured by settlement agreement)

Texas Family Law Practice Manual

Chapter 22. Enforcement—Property: I. Enforcement Procedures; II. Enforcement Remedies; III. Uniform Enforcement of Foreign Judgments Act

§ 9.001. Enforcement of Decree.

(a) A party affected by a decree of divorce or annulment providing for a division of property as provided by Chapter 7 *[Award of Marital Property]* may request enforcement of that decree by filing a suit to enforce as provided by this chapter in the court that rendered the decree.

(b) Except as otherwise provided in this chapter, a suit to enforce shall be governed by the Texas Rules of Civil Procedure applicable to the filing of an original lawsuit.

(c) A party whose rights, duties, powers, or liabilities may be affected by the suit to enforce is entitled to receive notice by citation and shall be commanded to appear by filing a written answer. Thereafter, the proceedings shall be as in civil cases generally.

Leading Case

Ackerly v. Ackerly, 13 S.W.3d 454 (Tex. App.—Corpus Christi 2000, no pet.) (motion for money judgment to enforce divorce award improper; separate lawsuit with citation required)

§ 9.002. Continuing Authority to Enforce Decree.

The court that rendered the decree of divorce or annulment retains the power to enforce the property division as provided by Chapter 7 *[Award of Marital Property]*.

§ 9.003. Filing Deadlines.

(a) A suit to enforce the division of tangible personal property in existence at the time of the decree of divorce or annulment must be filed before the second anniversary of the date the decree was signed or becomes final after appeal, whichever date is later, or the suit is barred.

(b) A suit to enforce the division of future property not in existence at the time of the original decree must be filed before the second anniversary of the date the right to the property matures or accrues or the decree becomes final, whichever date is later, or the suit is barred.

Leading Case

Chavez v. Chavez, 12 S.W.3d 563 (Tex. App.—San Antonio 1999, no pet.) (ex-wife's enforcement for proceeds of future sale of stock filed within two years of discovery of sale)

§ 9.004. Applicability to Undivided Property.

The procedures and limitations of this subchapter do not apply to existing property not divided on divorce, which are governed by Subchapter C and by the rules applicable to civil cases generally.

§ 9.005. No Jury.

A party may not demand a jury trial if the procedures to enforce a decree of divorce or annulment provided by this subchapter are invoked.

§ 9.006. Enforcement of Division of Property.

(a) Except as provided by this subchapter and by the Texas Rules of Civil Procedure, the court may render further orders to enforce the division of property made in the decree of divorce or annulment to assist in the implementation of or to clarify the prior order.

(b) The court may specify more precisely the manner of effecting the property division previously made if the substantive division of property is not altered or changed.

(c) An order of enforcement does not alter or affect the finality of the decree of divorce or annulment being enforced.

§ 9.007. Limitation on Power of Court to Enforce.

(a) A court may not amend, modify, alter, or change the division of property made or approved in the decree of divorce or annulment. An order to enforce the division is limited to an order to assist in the implementation of or to clarify the prior order and may not alter or change the substantive division of property.

(b) An order under this section that amends, modifies, alters, or changes the actual, substantive division of property made or approved in a final decree of divorce or annulment is beyond the power of the divorce court and is unenforceable.

(c) The power of the court to render further orders to assist in the implementation of or to clarify the property division is abated while an appellate proceeding is pending.

Comment

As a counterpart to § 9.001, this section prohibits the trial court from attempting to substantively redivide the property of the parties. The duty of the trial court is simply to enforce its original order; it may only issue implementing orders to enforce or clarify its earlier ruling. As the cases cited below indicate, this mandate is somewhat easier to state categorically than to execute in practice (a.k.a., easier said than done).

Leading Cases

Contreras v. Contreras, 974 S.W.2d 155 (Tex. App.—San Antonio 1998, no pet.) (trial court impermissibly made substantive changes to QDRO)

McLaurin v. McLaurin, 968 S.W.2d 947 (Tex. App.—Texarkana 1998, no pet.) (trial court properly clarified earlier QDRO)

Pate v. Pate, 874 S.W.2d 186 (Tex. App.—Houston [14th Dist.] 1994, writ denied) (trial court improperly changed final decree to alter the division of retirement benefits)

Whittington v. Whittington, 853 S.W.2d 193 (Tex. App.—Beaumont 1993, no writ) (trial court had duty to require ex-husband to sign note)

Pierce v. Pierce, 850 S.W.2d 675 (Tex. App.—El Paso 1993, writ denied) (when divorce decree is unambiguous, trial court cannot alter or modify original property division)

Sharman v. Schuble, 846 S.W.2d 574 (Tex. App.—Houston [14th Dist.] 1993, no writ) (house ordered sold and proceeds divided 50–50; trial court cannot amend that provision to redress noncompliance with other aspects of final order)

Elliott v. Elliott, 797 S.W.2d 388 (Tex. App.—Austin 1990, no writ) (trial court could not adjust division of retirement pay to deduct disability benefits)

Haworth v. Haworth, 795 S.W.2d 296 (Tex. App.—Houston [14th Dist.] 1990, no writ) (trial court acted improperly in attempting to modify division of pension benefits to give ex-spouse a share of post-divorce adjustments)

Reiter v. Reiter, 788 S.W.2d 201 (Tex. App.—Fort Worth 1990, writ denied) (ordering ex-spouse to sign note and impressing lien on real estate was permissible clarification of earlier order)

Spradley v. Hutchison, 787 S.W.2d 214 (Tex. App.—Fort Worth 1990, writ denied) (trial court's allowance of offset on monetary judgment not an impermissible modification of original order)

Cain v. Cain, 746 S.W.2d 861 (Tex. App.—El Paso 1988, writ denied) (turnover order is not an impermissible modification of decree)

Able v. Able, 725 S.W.2d 778 (Tex. App.—Houston [14th Dist.] 1987, writ ref'd n.r.e.) (court acted properly in requiring husband to pay taxes to reimburse wife for taxes in year of divorce)

McDowell v. McDowell, 705 S.W.2d 345 (Tex. App.—Dallas 1986, no writ) (appointment of receiver to sell property impermissibly modified terms of decree)

Griffith v. Griffith, 698 S.W.2d 729 (Tex. App.—El Paso 1985, no writ) (trial court acted properly in requiring ex-husband to designate ex-wife for military survivors benefit plan)

---

§ 9.008. Clarification Order.

(a) On the request of a party or on the court's own motion, the court may render a clarifying order before a motion for contempt is made or heard, in conjunction with a motion for contempt or on denial of a motion for contempt.

(b) On a finding by the court that the original form of the division of property is not specific enough to be enforceable by contempt, the court may render a clarifying order setting forth specific terms to enforce compliance with the original division of property.

(c) The court may not give retroactive effect to a clarifying order.

(d) The court shall provide a reasonable time for compliance before enforcing a clarifying order by contempt or in another manner.

Comment

This section provides the trial court with an important enforcement tool to secure compliance with its orders. Subsection (a) authorizes the court to issue its own clarifying order in conjunction with a contempt motion. A court determining that its order might be unenforceable by that ultimate remedy may issue a clarifying order to make its order truly effective.

Leading Cases

Appleton v. Appleton, 76 S.W.3d 78 (Tex. App.—Houston [14th Dist.] 2002, no pet.) (post-divorce attack on unambiguous award of community property elicits Rule 13 sanctions for attorney's fees)

Bishop v. Bishop, 74 S.W.3d 877 (Tex. App.—San Antonio 2002, no pet.) (divorce awarded wife the home and husband the mortgage—her rental of house doesn't create ambiguity in decree)

Lundy v. Lundy, 973 S.W.2d 687 (Tex. App.—Tyler 1998, pet. denied) (alleged clarifying order in fact was impermissible substantive change of unambiguous child support order)

Pearcy v. Pearcy, 884 S.W.2d 512 (Tex. App.—San Antonio 1994, no writ) (clarification order proper where original property division is ambiguous or not specific enough to enforce)

Traylor v. Traylor, 789 S.W.2d 701 (Tex. App.—Texarkana 1990, no writ) (this section does not authorize clarification of provisions in settlement agreement which the court could not have originally rendered)

Tyler v. Tyler, 742 S.W.2d 740 (Tex. App.—Houston [14th Dist.] 1987, writ denied) (trial court's attempt to make husband reimburse wife for payments following divorce an impermissible modification of final property division)

---

§ 9.009. Delivery of Property.

To enforce the division of property made in a decree of divorce or annulment, the court may make an order to deliver the specific existing property awarded, without regard to whether the property is of especial value, including an award of an existing sum of money or its equivalent.

Comment

Before 1983 Texas appellate courts had held that a trial court could not order a party to deliver any specific item of property unless it was "of especial value." This section reverses those cases and specifically authorizes the court to require delivery of property that may not be of especial value, such as stock certificates, certificates of deposit, ordinary automobiles, and the like.

---

§ 9.010. Reduction to Money Judgment.

(a) If a party fails to comply with a decree of divorce or annulment and delivery of property awarded in the decree is no longer an adequate remedy, the court may render a money judgment for the damages caused by that failure to comply.

(b) If a party did not receive payments of money as awarded in the decree of divorce or annulment, the court may render judgment against a defaulting party for the amount of unpaid payments to which the party is entitled.

(c) The remedy of a reduction to money judgment is in addition to the other remedies provided by law.

(d) A money judgment rendered under this section may be enforced by any means available for the enforcement of judgment for debt.

Comment

If all else fails and the property is not (or cannot be) delivered as ordered, the court is authorized to render a money judgment against a recalcitrant party.

Cross References

Tex. Civ. Prac. & Rem. Code Ann. § 31.002. Collection of Judgment Through Court Proceeding; § 31.0025. Authority of Court To Order Turnover of Wages.

---

§ 9.011. Right to Future Property.

(a) The court may, by any remedy provided by this chapter, enforce an award of the right to receive installment payments or a lump-sum payment due on the maturation of an existing vested or nonvested right to be paid in the future.

(b) The subsequent actual receipt by the non-owning party of property awarded to the owner in a decree of divorce or annulment creates a fiduciary obligation in favor of the owner and imposes a constructive trust on the property for the benefit of the owner.

Comment

This section is designed primarily for the division of pension and annuity benefits. Its passage predated the enactment of the federal Retirement Equity Act, which authorizes direct payment from pension trusts and annuities. See ERISA, 29 U.S.C.A. § 1055, *et seq.*

Leading Case

Zeolla v. Zeolla, 15 S.W.3d 239 (Tex. App.—Houston [14th Dist.] 2000, pet. denied) (original decree had latent ambiguity when husband retired early—cured by proportional adjustment to reflect early retirement plus payback of benefits already received within trial court's power)

Texas Family Law Practice Manual

Chapter 19. Retirement Benefits: I. Introduction; II. Retirement Benefits Divisible on Divorce; III. General Definitions; IV. Amendment of Order Dividing Plan; V. Private Retirement Plans; VI. Texas Public Retirement System; VII. Uniformed Services Former Spouses' Protection Act; VIII. Civil Service and Federal Employees' Retirement Systems; IX. Railroad Retirement

---

§ 9.012. Contempt.

(a) The court may enforce by contempt an order requiring delivery of specific property or an award of a right to future property.

(b) The court may not enforce by contempt an award in a decree of divorce or annulment of a sum of money payable in a lump sum or in future installment payments in the nature of debt, except for:

(1) a sum of money in existence at the time the decree was rendered; or

(2) a matured right to future payments as provided by Section 9.011.

(c) This subchapter does not detract from or limit the general power of a court to enforce an order of the court by appropriate means.

Comment

This section makes clear that an order of the court to deliver specific property is enforceable by contempt.

---

§ 9.013. Costs.

The court may award costs in a proceeding to enforce a property division under this subchapter as in other civil cases.

---

§ 9.014. Attorney's Fees.

The court may award reasonable attorney's fees as costs in a proceeding under this subchapter. The court may order the attorney's fees to be paid directly to the attorney, who may enforce the order for fees in the attorney's own name by any means available for the enforcement of a judgment for debt.

Comment

Before passage of this section there was no provision for the recovery of attorney's fees against an uncooperative party after a divorce. Thwarting the order of the court elicited no punitive consequences, even when a party was found to be the wrongdoer. This section now makes clear that the award of attorney's fees is appropriate in such a fact situation.

CLE/Other Legal Publications

See annotations to §§ 7.001–.002, *supra.*

Leading Cases

Mullins v. Mullins, 785 S.W.2d 5 (Tex. App.—Fort Worth 1990, no writ) ($3,500 awarded as attorney's fees for enforcement of court order)

McEntire v. McEntire, 706 S.W.2d 347 (Tex. App.—San Antonio 1986, writ dism'd w.o.j.) (attorney's fees awarded to enforce and clarify agreed decree of divorce)

Subchapter B. Post–Decree Qualified Domestic Relations Order

Introductory Comment

This subchapter authorizes a court to issue a new, corrective and amended domestic relations order for direct payment of retirement benefits. Somewhat akin to the concept of continuing, exclusive jurisdiction in Title 5 cases, the court that first attempts to divide retirement benefits retains continuing jurisdiction to render a new order to provide direct payment of retirement benefits. This remedial statute is to be liberally construed to effect its purpose.

CLE/Other Legal Publications

See annotations to §§ 7.003, *supra*.

Leading Cases

Harvey v. Harvey, 905 S.W.2d 760 (Tex. App.—Austin 1995, no writ) (survivor benefits awarded to ex-spouse in clarifying order)

Cook v. Cook, 888 S.W.2d 130 (Tex. App.—Corpus Christi 1994, no writ) (trial court allowed to modify divorce decree and QDRO after oral rendition but before final judgment had been signed)

Pate v. Pate, 874 S.W.2d 186 (Tex. App.—Houston [14th Dist.] 1994, writ denied) (QDRO issued by the trial court must be consistent with agreed divorce decree)

Conti v. Conti, 866 S.W.2d 671 (Tex. App.—Houston [14th Dist.] 1993, writ denied) (referring to the Government Code to allow the court that would otherwise have had jurisdiction to resolve any dispute as to domestic relations orders)

Arena v. Arena, 822 S.W.2d 645 (Tex. App.—Fort Worth 1991, no writ) (divorce decree deemed a QDRO because it contained all required information)

Texas Family Law Practice Manual

Chapter 19. Retirement Benefits: I. Introduction; II. Retirement Benefits Divisible on Divorce; III. General Definitions; IV. Amendment of Order Dividing Plan; V. Private Retirement Plans; VI. Texas Public Retirement System; VII. Uniformed Services Former Spouses' Protection Act; VIII. Civil Service and Federal Employees' Retirement Systems; IX. Railroad Retirement

Chapter 22. Enforcement—Property: I. Enforcement Procedures; II. Enforcement Remedies; III. Uniform Enforcement of Foreign Judgments Act

---

§ 9.101. Jurisdiction for Qualified Domestic Relations Order.

(a) Notwithstanding any other provision of this chapter, the court that rendered a final decree of divorce or annulment or another final order dividing property under this title retains continuing, exclusive jurisdiction to render an enforceable qualified domestic relations order or similar order permitting payment of pension, retirement plan, or other employee benefits divisible under the law of this state or of the United States to an alternate payee or other lawful payee.

(b) Unless prohibited by federal law, a suit seeking a qualified domestic relations order or similar order under this section applies to a previously divided pension, retirement plan, or other employee benefit divisible under the law of this state or of the United States, whether the plan or benefit is private, state, or federal.

§ 9.102. Procedure.

(a) A party to a decree of divorce or annulment may petition the court for a qualified domestic relations order or similar order.

(b) Except as otherwise provided by this code, a petition under this subchapter is governed by the Texas Rules of Civil Procedure that apply to the filing of an original lawsuit.

(c) Each party whose rights may be affected by the petition is entitled to receive notice by citation and shall be commanded to appear by filing a written answer.

(d) The proceedings shall be conducted in the same manner as civil cases generally.

§ 9.103. Prior Failure to Render Qualified Domestic Relations Order.

A party may petition a court to render a qualified domestic relations order or similar order if the court that rendered a final decree of divorce or annulment or another final order dividing property under this chapter did not provide a qualified domestic relations order or similar order permitting payment of benefits to an alternate payee or other lawful payee.

§ 9.104. Defective Prior Domestic Relations Order.

If a plan administrator or other person acting in an equivalent capacity determines that a domestic relations order does not satisfy the requirements of a qualified domestic relations order or similar order, the court retains continuing, exclusive jurisdiction over the parties and their property to the extent necessary to render a qualified domestic relations order.

§ 9.105. Liberal Construction.

The court shall liberally construe this subchapter to effect payment of retirement benefits that were divided by a previous decree that failed to contain a qualified domestic relations order or similar order or that contained an order that failed to meet the requirements of a qualified domestic relations order or similar order.

Subchapter C. Post–Decree Division of Property

§ 9.201. Procedure for Division of Certain Property Not Divided on Divorce or Annulment.

(a) Either former spouse may file a suit as provided by this subchapter to divide property not divided or awarded to a spouse in a final decree of divorce or annulment.

(b) Except as otherwise provided by this subchapter, the suit is governed by the Texas Rules of Civil Procedure applicable to the filing of an original lawsuit.

Leading Cases

Wilde v. Murchie, 949 S.W.2d 331 (Tex. 1997) (surrounding circumstances of divorce and post-divorce actions compel conclusion marital home awarded to ex-husband)

Preston v. Burmeister, 52 S.W.3d 386 (Tex. App.—Fort Worth 2001, no pet.) (error for a Texas court to award retirement benefits not addressed in a 1979 Florida divorce; issue of marital property not divided on divorce is for Florida law to determine)

Mayes v. Stewart, 11 S.W.2d 440 (Tex. App.—Houston [14th Dist.] 1999, pet. denied) (ex-wife proves lottery winnings were community property for division)

McPherren v. McPherren, 967 S.W.2d 485 (Tex. App.—El Paso 1998, no pet.) (partition suit fails because "Mother Hubbard" clause awarded benefits)

Ballesteros v. Jones, 985 S.W.2d 485 (Tex. App.—San Antonio 1998, no writ) (evidence supports jury's finding of lawyer's negligence in not discovering assets held in husband's name)

Burgess v. Easley, 893 S.W.2d 87 (Tex. App.—Dallas 1995, no writ) (divorced parties became "co-tenants or joint owners" of overlooked community property which is subject to division when discovered)

---

§ 9.202. Limitations.

(a) A suit under this subchapter must be filed before the second anniversary of the date a former spouse unequivocally repudiates the existence of the ownership interest of the other former spouse and communicates that repudiation to the other former spouse.

(b) The two-year limitations period is tolled for the period that a court of this state does not have jurisdiction over the former spouses or over the property.

Leading Cases

Sagester v. Waltrip, 970 S.W.2d 767 (Tex. App.—Austin 1998, pet. denied) (general denial and failure to pay did not constitute "unequivocal repudiation")

Phillips v. Phillips, 951 S.W.2d 955 (Tex. App.—Waco 1997, writ denied) (material issue of fact re post-divorce partition of undivided community property subject to limitations—Property Code § 21.001 may provide additional remedy)

Jenkins v. Jenkins, 856 S.W.2d 820 (Tex. App.—Beaumont 1993, no writ) (partition of retirement benefits denied; ex-spouse knew about benefits, kept silent, and received majority of marital property)

Carter v. Charles, 853 S.W.2d 667 (Tex. App.—Houston [14th Dist.] 1993, no writ) (partition suit unaffected by two year statute of limitations)

---

§ 9.203. Division of Undivided Assets When Prior Court Had Jurisdiction.

(a) If a court of this state failed to dispose of property subject to division in a final decree of divorce or annulment even though the court had jurisdiction over the spouses or over the property, the court shall divide the property in a manner that the court deems just and right, having due regard for the rights of each party and any children of the marriage.

(b) If a final decree of divorce or annulment rendered by a court in another state failed to dispose of property subject to division under the law of that state even though the court had jurisdiction to do so, a court of this state shall apply the law of the other state regarding undivided property as required by Section 1, Article IV, United States Constitution (the full faith and credit clause), and enabling federal statutes.

Leading Cases

Forgason v. Forgason, 911 S.W.2d 893 (Tex. App.—Amarillo 1995, no writ) (first wife's just and right share of undivided retirement benefits was to take nothing)

Walton v. Lee, 888 S.W.2d 604 (Tex. App.—Beaumont 1994, writ denied) (trial court allowed to divide previously undivided retirement benefits in partition suit)

Haynes v. McIntosh, 776 S.W.2d 784 (Tex. App.—Corpus Christi 1989, writ denied) (in a post-divorce division suit, trial court properly refused to divide husband's military retirement)

Rathmell v. Morrison, 732 S.W.2d 6 (Tex. App.—Houston [14th Dist.] 1987, no writ) (husband's extrinsic fraud permits wife to collaterally attack divorce division by bill of review)

Miller v. Miller, 700 S.W.2d 941 (Tex. App.—Dallas 1985, writ ref'd n.r.e.) (husband's breach of fiduciary duty to wife permits rescission of agreement made incident to divorce)

Dessommes v. Dessommes, 505 S.W.2d (Tex. Civ. App.—Dallas 1973, writ ref'd n.r.e.) (award of "property now in possession" did not include interest in husband's retirement benefits)

---

§ 9.204. Division of Undivided Assets When Prior Court Lacked Jurisdiction.

(a) If a court of this state failed to dispose of property subject to division in a final decree of divorce or annulment because the court lacked jurisdiction over a spouse or the property, and if that court subsequently acquires the requisite jurisdiction, that court may divide the property in a manner that the court deems just and right, having due regard for the rights of each party and any children of the marriage.

(b) If a final decree of divorce or annulment rendered by a court in another state failed to dispose of property subject to division under the law of that state because the court lacked jurisdiction over a spouse or the property, and if a court of this state subsequently acquires the requisite jurisdiction over the former spouses or over the property, the court in this state may divide the property in a manner that the court deems just and right, having due regard for the rights of each party and any children of the marriage.

§ 9.205. Attorney's Fees.

In a proceeding to divide property previously undivided in a decree of divorce or annulment as provided by this subchapter, the court may award reasonable attorney's fees as costs. The court may order the attorney's fees to be paid directly to the attorney, who may enforce the order in the attorney's own name by any means available for the enforcement of a judgment for debt.

CLE/Other Legal Publications

See annotations to §§ 7.001–.002, *supra*.

Subchapter D. Disposition of Undivided Beneficial Interest

§ 9.301. Pre-Decree Designation of Ex-Spouse as Beneficiary of Life Insurance.

(a) If a decree of divorce or annulment is rendered after an insured has designated the insured's spouse as a beneficiary under a life insurance policy in force at the time of rendition, a provision in the policy in favor of the insured's former spouse is not effective unless:

(1) the decree designates the insured's former spouse as the beneficiary;

(2) the insured redesignates the former spouse as the beneficiary after rendition of the decree; or

(3) the former spouse is designated to receive the proceeds in trust for, on behalf of, or for the benefit of a child or a dependent of either former spouse.

(b) If a designation is not effective under Subsection (a), the proceeds of the policy are payable to the named alternative beneficiary or, if there is not a named alternative beneficiary, to the estate of the insured.

(c) An insurer who pays the proceeds of a life insurance policy issued by the insurer to the beneficiary under a designation that is not effective under Subsection (a) is liable for payment of the proceeds to the person or estate provided by Subsection (b) only if:

(1) before payment of the proceeds to the designated beneficiary, the insurer receives written notice at the home office of the insurer from an interested person that the designation is not effective under Subsection (a); and

(2) the insurer has not interpleaded the proceeds into the registry of a court of competent jurisdiction in accordance with the Texas Rules of Civil Procedure.

Comment

This section attempted to correct an anomaly in Texas law regarding disposition of certain property rights in insurance policies. For example, formerly if a party was awarded an interest in a life insurance policy but did not change the designation of the ex-spouse as the beneficiary following the parties' divorce, the policy benefits would be paid to the ex-spouse on death of the insured. This was inconsistent with the Texas Probate Code rule that a beneficial designation of an ex-spouse in a will was voided by an intervening divorce. Except in rare cases, the former rule would result in an unintended disposition of benefits from a life insurance policy (a non-probate asset).

This section also deals with other forms of insurance to provide that the insurance protection is awarded to the party receiving the property unless the court otherwise expressly provides.

Unfortunately, the attempt at reform was only partially successful. The federal ERISA preempts state law governing insurance plans directly related to the employment of the insured. As the cases cited below demonstrate, the exact extent of preemption is a work in progress. Fortunately, a very substantial portion of insurance is not derived from employment, *e.g.*, perhaps most life insurance and virtually all automobile and homeowners policies. In those instances the federal intervention into regulation of family law is inapplicable. Moreover, questions remain unanswered, such as whether a life insurance policy derived from employment may be awarded to the nonemployee spouse in the division of community property on divorce.

Of course, the employee ex-spouse may redesignate the former spouse as the beneficiary of life insurance following divorce, or the court may require the party to name the former spouse as a beneficiary or as trustee of the proceeds. The latter is often ordered to protect the interest of the children in their continued support.

CLE/Other Legal Publications

See annotations, § 7.004, *supra*.

Leading Cases

Egelhoff v. Egelhoff, 532 U.S. 141, 121 S.Ct. 1322 (2001) (ERISA preempts state statute voiding pre-divorce designation of spouse as beneficiary of employee's life insurance and pension)

Barnett v. Barnett, 67 S.W.3d 107 (Tex. 2001) (federal ERISA preempts Texas Family Code regarding life insurance obtained through employment)

Clift v. Clift, 210 F.3d 268 (5th Cir. 2000) (Tex.) (award to husband of "any and all insurance policies insuring the life of Husband" sufficient to prevent wife from collecting proceeds under policy; language is valid waiver under ERISA)

Brandon v. Travelers Insurance Co., 18 F.3d 1321 (5th Cir. 1994) (although Texas statute requiring redesignation of ex-spouse as beneficiary on life insurance policy preempted by ERISA, divorce decree language was bona fide waiver of former wife's rights to proceeds), *cert. denied,* 115 S.Ct. 732 (1995)

Barnett v. Barnett, 67 S.W.3d 107 (Tex. 2001) (federal ERISA preempts Texas Family Code regarding beneficiary designation of life insurance obtained through employment; employee has absolute right to designate the beneficiary, notwithstanding fact that life insurance policy is community property)

Sever v. Massachusetts Mutual Life Insurance Co., 944 S.W.2d 486 (Tex. App.—Amarillo 1997, writ denied) (oral statements declining to change beneficiary does not overcome statute voiding ex-wife as beneficiary after divorce)

Hunt v. Jefferson–Pilot Life Insurance Co., 900 S.W.2d 453 (Tex. App.—Fort Worth 1995, writ denied) (life insurance proceeds properly paid to ex-wife)

In re Group Life Insurance Proceeds of Mallory, 872 S.W.2d 800 (Tex. App.—Amarillo 1994, no writ) (naming stepchildren beneficiaries remains valid despite subsequent divorce of stepfather and mother)

Cross Reference

TEX.PROB.CODE ANN. § 69. Voidness Arising from Divorce.

---

§ 9.302. Pre-Decree Designation of Ex-Spouse as Beneficiary in Retirement Benefits and Other Financial Plans.

(a) If a decree of divorce or annulment is rendered after a spouse, acting in the capacity of a participant, annuitant, or account holder, has designated the other spouse as a beneficiary under an individual retirement account, employee stock option plan, stock option, or other form of savings, bonus, profit-sharing, or other employer plan or financial plan of an employee or a participant in force at the time of rendition, the designating provision in the plan in favor of the other former spouse is not effective unless:

(1) the decree designates the other former spouse as the beneficiary;

(2) the designating former spouse redesignates the other former spouse as the beneficiary after rendition of the decree; or

(3) the other former spouse is designated to receive the proceeds or benefits in trust for, on behalf of, or for the benefit of a child or dependent of either former spouse.

(b) If a designation is not effective under Subsection (a), the benefits or proceeds are payable to the named alternative beneficiary or, if there is not a named alternative beneficiary, to the designating former spouse.

(c) A business entity, employer, pension trust, insurer, financial institution, or other person obligated to pay retirement benefits or proceeds of a financial plan covered by this section who pays the benefits or proceeds to the beneficiary under a designation of the other former spouse that is not effective under Subsection (a) is liable for payment of the benefits or proceeds to the person provided by Subsection (b) only if:

(1) before payment of the benefits or proceeds to the designated beneficiary, the payor receives written notice at the home office or principal office of the payor from an interested person that the designation of the beneficiary or fiduciary is not effective under Subsection (a); and

(2) the payor has not interpleaded the benefits or proceeds into the registry of a court of competent jurisdiction in accordance with the Texas Rules of Civil Procedure.

(d) This section does not affect the right of a former spouse to assert an ownership interest in an undivided pension, retirement, annuity, or other financial plan described by this section as provided by this subchapter.

(e) This section does not apply to the disposition of a beneficial interest in a retirement benefit or other financial plan of a public retirement system as defined by Section 802.001, Government Code.

Comment

This companion measure to the preceding section was an attempt to deal with the disposition of the beneficial interest in retirement benefits after a divorce. A non-employee ex-spouse could make claims on the retirement benefits of a deceased ex-spouse if the deceased had not taken action following their divorce to change the designation of the non-employee ex-spouse as a beneficiary of the retirement plan. Unfortunately, the attempt at reform was only partially successful and, to a large extent, the anomaly persists. The federal ERISA preempts state law governing retirement plans directly related to employment. No doubt the vast majority of retirement plans are directly derived from employment, so perhaps only some individual retirement plans (IRA's) are not subject to ERISA coverage. Fortunately, every competent Texas lawyer is fully aware of the necessity to award separate ownership interests in retirement plans to the spouses on divorce. With that knowledge should come legal advice to arrange the beneficial interest to conform to the client's intent.

Of course, the employee ex-spouse may redesignate the former spouse as the beneficiary of retirement benefits following divorce, or the court may require the party to name the former spouse as a beneficiary.

CLE/Other Legal Publications

See annotations to § 7.003, *supra*.

Leading Cases

Egelhoff v. Egelhoff, 532 U.S. 141, 121 S.Ct. 1322 (2001) (ERISA preempts state statute voiding pre-divorce designation of spouse as beneficiary of employee's life insurance and pension)

Keen v. Weaver, 121 S.W.3d 721 (Tex. 2003) (ex-wife's interest in ERISA plan enforceable under federal common law)

Reiss v. Reiss, 118 S.W.3d 439 (Tex. 2003) (division of retirement benefits enforced as res judicata—error in applying law not appealed cannot be collaterally corrected)

Sanderlin v. Sanderlin, 929 S.W.2d 121 (Tex. App.—San Antonio 1996, writ denied) (divorce decree entered after the husband signed the beneficiary form for his retirement benefits extinguishes any rights ex-wife may have had as beneficiary)

Texas Family Law Practice Manual

Chapter 19. Retirement Benefits: I. Introduction; II. Retirement Benefits Divisible on Divorce; III. General Definitions; IV. Amendment of Order Dividing Plan; V. Private Retirement Plans; VI. Texas Public Retirement System; VII. Uniformed Services Former Spouses' Protection Act; VIII. Civil Service and Federal Employees' Retirement Systems; IX. Railroad Retirement

Cross References

TEX. GOV'T CODE ch. 804, Domestic Relations Orders and Spousal Consent.

Civil Service Retirement Benefits. 5 U.S.C.A. §§ 2105, 8331 *et seq.*

Uniformed Services Former Spouses Protection Act. 10 U.S.C.A. § 1072 *et seq.*, § 1408 *et seq.*

Retirement Equity Act. 26 U.S.C.A. §§ 401, 402, 414.

Employee Retirement Income Security Act of 1974. 29 U.S.C.A. § 1055 *et seq.*

TITLE 2
Child in Relation to the Family

As amended through the 78th Legislature, Fourth Called Session (2004)

★★★

Subtitle A. Limitations of Minority.

Chapter

31. Removal of Disabilities of Minority.
32. Consent to Treatment of Child by Non–Parent or Child.
33. Notice of Abortion.

★★★

Chapter 31. Removal of Disabilities of Minority.

Introductory Comment

Lowering the age of majority from 21 to 18 in 1973 largely eliminated the utility of this chapter. On rare occasions, a 17–year-old, or even a 16–year-old, may be sufficiently independent and self-supporting to be eligible for the limited removal of disabilities permitted by this chapter. Although the general rule is that the minor will then have the power and capacity of an adult, a wide variety of specific constitutional and statutory restrictions based on age will remain in place, *e.g.*, no voting, no drinking, etc.

Cross References

TEX. EDUC. CODE ANN. § 21.032. Compulsory Attendance.

TEX. FAM. CODE ANN. § 1.104. Capacity of Spouses; ch. 101. Definitions.

TEX. PRAC. & REM. CODE ANN. ch. 129. Age of Minority.

TEX. R. CIV. P. 44. May Appear by Next Friend; Rule 173. Guardian Ad Litem.

---

§ 31.001. Requirements.

(a) A minor may petition to have the disabilities of minority removed for limited or general purposes if the minor is:

(1) a resident of this state;

(2) 17 years of age, or at least 16 years of age and living separate and apart from the minor's parents, managing conservator, or guardian; and

(3) self-supporting and managing the minor's own financial affairs.

(b) A minor may file suit under this chapter in the minor's own name. The minor need not be represented by next friend.

§ 31.002. Requisites of Petition; Verification.

(a) The petition for removal of disabilities of minority must state:

(1) the name, age, and place of residence of the petitioner;

(2) the name and place of residence of each living parent;

(3) the name and place of residence of the guardian of the person and the guardian of the estate, if any;

(4) the name and place of residence of the managing conservator, if any;

(5) the reasons why removal would be in the best interest of the minor; and

(6) the purposes for which removal is requested.

(b) A parent of the petitioner must verify the petition, except that if a managing conservator or guardian of the person has been appointed, the petition must be verified by that person. If the person who is to verify the petition is unavailable or that person's whereabouts are unknown, the guardian ad litem shall verify the petition.

§ 31.003. Venue.

The petitioner shall file the petition in the county in which the petitioner resides.

§ 31.004. Guardian Ad Litem.

The court shall appoint a guardian ad litem to represent the interest of the petitioner at the hearing.

§ 31.005. Order.

The court by order, or the Texas Supreme Court by rule or order, may remove the disabilities of minority of a minor, including any restriction imposed by Chapter 32 *[Consent to Treatment of Child by Non-parent or Child]*, if the court or the Texas Supreme Court finds the removal to be in the best interest of the petitioner. The order or rule must state the limited or general purposes for which disabilities are removed.

§ 31.006. Effect of General Removal.

Except for specific constitutional and statutory age requirements, a minor whose disabilities are removed for general purposes has the capacity of an adult, including the capacity to contract. Except as provided by federal law, all educational rights accorded to the parent of a student, including the right to make education decisions under Section 151.003(a)(10), transfer to the minor whose disabilities are removed for general purposes.

§ 31.007. Registration of Order of Another State or Nation.

(a) A nonresident minor who has had the disabilities of minority removed in the state of the minor's residence may file a certified copy of the order removing disabilities in the deed records of any county in this state.

(b) When a certified copy of the order of a court of another state or nation is filed, the minor has the capacity of an adult, except as provided by Section 31.006 and by the terms of the order.

Chapter 32. Consent to Treatment of Child by Non–Parent or Child.

Subchapter A. Consent to Medical, Dental, Psychological, and Surgical Treatment

Subchapter B. Immunization

Subchapter C. Miscellaneous Provisions

Subchapter A. Consent to Medical, Dental, Psychological, and Surgical Treatment

Introductory Comment

If the person ordinarily empowered to consent to medical treatment of a child is unavailable, this chapter provides for backup consent in an emergency.

Leading Case

Miller ex rel. Miller v. HCA, Inc., 118 S.W.3d 758 (Tex. 2003) (exigent circumstances create exception to parental consent to treatment of child)

Little v. Little, 576 S.W.2d 493 (Tex. Civ. App.—San Antonio 1979, no writ) (general rule is that a minor cannot consent to medical or surgical treatment)

Cross Reference

Tex. Hum. Res. Code Ann. ch. 42. Child Care Facilities.

---

§ 32.001. Consent by Non-Parent.

(a) The following persons may consent to medical, dental, psychological, and surgical treatment of a child when the person having the right to consent as otherwise provided by law cannot be contacted and that person has not given actual notice to the contrary:

(1) a grandparent of the child;

(2) an adult brother or sister of the child;

(3) an adult aunt or uncle of the child;

(4) an educational institution in which the child is enrolled that has received written authorization to consent from a person having the right to consent;

(5) an adult who has actual care, control, and possession of the child and has written authorization to consent from a person having the right to consent;

(6) a court having jurisdiction over a suit affecting the parent-child relationship of which the child is the subject;

(7) an adult responsible for the actual care, control, and possession of a child under the jurisdiction of a juvenile court or committed by a juvenile court to the care of an agency of the state or county; or

(8) a peace officer who has lawfully taken custody of a minor, if the peace officer has reasonable grounds to believe the minor is in need of immediate medical treatment.

(b) The Texas Youth Commission may consent to the medical, dental, psychological, and surgical treatment of a child committed to it under Title 3 when the person having the right to consent has been contacted and that person has not given actual notice to the contrary.

(c) This section does not apply to consent for the immunization of a child.

(d) A person who consents to the medical treatment of a minor under Subsection (a)(7) or (8) is immune from liability for damages resulting from the examination or treatment of the minor, except to the extent of the person's own acts of negligence. A physician or dentist licensed to practice in this state, or a hospital or medical facility at which a minor is treated is immune from liability for damages resulting from the examination or treatment of a minor under this section, except to the extent of the person's own acts of negligence.

§ 32.002. Consent Form.

(a) Consent to medical treatment under this subchapter must be in writing, signed by the person giving consent, and given to the doctor, hospital, or other medical facility that administers the treatment.

(b) The consent must include:

(1) the name of the child;

(2) the name of one or both parents, if known, and the name of any managing conservator or guardian of the child;

(3) the name of the person giving consent and the person's relationship to the child;

(4) a statement of the nature of the medical treatment to be given; and

(5) the date the treatment is to begin.

§ 32.003. Consent to Treatment by Child.

(a) A child may consent to medical, dental, psychological, and surgical treatment for the child by a licensed physician or dentist if the child:

(1) is on active duty with the armed services of the United States of America;

(2) is:

(A) 16 years of age or older and resides separate and apart from the child's parents, managing conservator, or guardian, with or without the consent of the parents, managing conservator, or guardian and regardless of the duration of the residence; and

(B) managing the child's own financial affairs, regardless of the source of the income;

(3) consents to the diagnosis and treatment of an infectious, contagious, or communicable disease that is required by law or a rule to be reported by the licensed physician or dentist to a local health officer or the Texas Department of Health, including all diseases within the scope of Section 81.041, Health and Safety Code;

(4) is unmarried and pregnant and consents to hospital, medical, or surgical treatment, other than abortion, related to the pregnancy;

(5) consents to examination and treatment for drug or chemical addiction, drug or chemical dependency, or any other condition directly related to drug or chemical use; or

(6) is unmarried, is the parent of a child, and has actual custody of his or her child and consents to medical, dental, psychological, or surgical treatment for the child.

(b) Consent by a child to medical, dental, psychological, and surgical treatment under this section is not subject to disaffirmance because of minority.

(c) Consent of the parents, managing conservator, or guardian of a child is not necessary in order to authorize hospital, medical, surgical, or dental care under this section.

(d) A licensed physician, dentist, or psychologist may, with or without the consent of a child who is a patient, advise the parents, managing conservator, or guardian of the child of the treatment given to or needed by the child.

(e) A physician, dentist, psychologist, hospital, or medical facility is not liable for the examination and treatment of a child under this section except for the provider's or the facility's own acts of negligence.

(f) A physician, dentist, psychologist, hospital, or medical facility may rely on the written statement of the child containing the grounds on which the child has capacity to consent to the child's medical treatment.

§ 32.004. Consent to Counseling.

(a) A child may consent to counseling for:

(1) suicide prevention;

(2) chemical addiction or dependency; or

(3) sexual, physical, or emotional abuse.

(b) A licensed or certified physician, psychologist, counselor, or social worker having reasonable grounds to believe that a child has been sexually, physically, or emotionally abused, is contemplating suicide, or is suffering from a chemical or drug addiction or dependency may:

(1) counsel the child without the consent of the child's parents or, if applicable, managing conservator or guardian;

(2) with or without the consent of the child who is a client, advise the child's parents or, if applicable, managing conservator or guardian of the treatment given to or needed by the child; and

(3) rely on the written statement of the child containing the grounds on which the child has capacity to consent to the child's own treatment under this section.

(c) Unless consent is obtained as otherwise allowed by law, a physician, psychologist, counselor, or social worker may not counsel a child if consent is prohibited by a court order.

(d) A physician, psychologist, counselor, or social worker counseling a child under this section is not liable for damages except for damages resulting from the person's negligence or wilful misconduct.

(e) A parent, or, if applicable, managing conservator or guardian, who has not consented to counseling treatment of the child is not obligated to compensate a physician, psychologist, counselor, or social worker for counseling services rendered under this section.

§ 32.005. Examination Without Consent of Abuse or Neglect of Child.

(a) Except as provided by Subsection (c), a physician, dentist, or psychologist having reasonable grounds to believe that a child's physical or mental condition has been adversely affected by abuse or neglect may examine the child without the consent of the child, the child's parents, or other person authorized to consent to treatment under this subchapter.

(b) An examination under this section may include X-rays, blood tests, photographs, and penetration of tissue necessary to accomplish those tests.

(c) Unless consent is obtained as otherwise allowed by law, a physician, dentist, or psychologist may not examine a child:

(1) 16 years of age or older who refuses to consent; or

(2) for whom consent is prohibited by a court order.

(d) A physician, dentist, or psychologist examining a child under this section is not liable for damages except for damages resulting from the physician's or dentist's negligence.

Subchapter B. Immunization

§ 32.101. Who May Consent to Immunization of Child.

(a) In addition to persons authorized to consent to immunization under Chapter 151 *[The Parent–Child Relationship]* and Chapter 153 *[Conservatorship, Possession, and Access]*, the following persons may consent to the immunization of a child:

(1) a guardian of the child; and

(2) a person authorized under the law of another state or a court order to consent for the child.

(b) If the persons listed in Subsection (a) are not available and the authority to consent is not denied under Subsection (c), consent to the immunization of a child may be given by:

(1) a grandparent of the child;

(2) an adult brother or sister of the child;

(3) an adult aunt or uncle of the child;

(4) a stepparent of the child;

(5) an educational institution in which the child is enrolled that has written authorization to consent for the child from a parent, managing conservator, guardian, or other person who under the law of another state or a court order may consent for the child;

(6) another adult who has actual care, control, and possession of the child and has written authorization to consent for the child from a parent, managing conservator, guardian, or other person who, under the law of another state or a court order, may consent for the child;

(7) a court having jurisdiction of a suit affecting the parent-child relationship of which the minor is the subject;

(8) an adult having actual care, control, and possession of the child under an order of a juvenile court or by commitment by a juvenile court to the care of an agency of the state or county; or

(9) an adult having actual care, control, and possession of the child as the child's primary caregiver.

(c) A person otherwise authorized to consent under Subsection (a) may not consent for the child if the person has actual knowledge that a parent, managing conservator, guardian of the child, or other person who under the law of another state or a court order may consent for the child:

(1) has expressly refused to give consent to the immunization;

(2) has been told not to consent for the child; or

(3) has withdrawn a prior written authorization for the person to consent.

(d) The Texas Youth Commission may consent to the immunization of a child committed to it if a parent, managing conservator, or guardian of the minor or other person who, under the law of another state or court order, may consent for the minor has been contacted and:

(1) refuses to consent; and

(2) does not expressly deny to the Texas Youth Commission the authority to consent for the child.

(e) A person who consents under this section shall provide the health care provider with sufficient and accurate health history and other information about the minor for whom the consent is given and, if necessary, sufficient and accurate health history and information about the minor's family to enable the person who may consent to the minor's immunization and the health care provider to determine adequately the risks and benefits inherent in the proposed immunization and to determine whether immunization is advisable.

(f) Consent to immunization must meet the requirements of Section 32.002(a).

§ 32.102. Informed Consent to Immunization.

(a) A person authorized to consent to the immunization of a child has the responsibility to ensure that the consent, if given, is an informed consent. The person authorized to consent is not required to be present when the immunization of the child is requested if a consent form that meets the requirements of Section 32.002 has been given to the health care provider.

(b) The responsibility of a health care provider to provide information to a person consenting to immunization is the same as the provider's responsibility to a parent.

(c) As part of the information given in the counseling for informed consent, the health care provider shall provide information to inform the person authorized to consent to immunization of the procedures available under the National Childhood Vaccine Injury Act of 1986 (42 U.S.C. Section 300aa–1 *et seq.*) to seek possible recovery for unreimbursed expenses for certain injuries arising out of the administration of certain vaccines.

§ 32.103. Limited Liability for Immunization.

(a) In the absence of wilful misconduct or gross negligence, a health care provider who accepts the health history and other information given by a person who is delegated the authority to consent to the immunization of a child during the informed consent counseling is not liable for an adverse reaction to an immunization or for other injuries to the child resulting from factual errors in the health history or information given by the person to the health care provider.

(b) A person consenting to immunization of a child, a physician, nurse, or other health care provider, or a public health clinic, hospital, or other medical facility is not liable for damages arising from an immunization administered to a child authorized under this subchapter except for injuries resulting from the person's or facility's own acts of negligence.

Subchapter C. Miscellaneous Provisions

§ 32.201. Emergency Shelter or Care for Minors.

(a) An emergency shelter facility may provide shelter and care to a minor and the minor's child or children, if any.

(b) An emergency shelter facility may provide shelter or care only during an emergency constituting an immediate danger to the physical health or safety of the minor or the minor's child or children.

(c) Shelter or care provided under this section may not be provided after the 15th day after the date the shelter or care is commenced unless:

(1) the facility receives consent to continue services from the minor in accordance with Section 32.202; or

(2) the minor has qualified for financial assistance under Chapter 31, Human Resources Code, and is on the waiting list for housing assistance.

§ 32.202. Consent to Emergency Shelter or Care by Minor.

(a) A minor may consent to emergency shelter or care to be provided to the minor or the minor's child or children, if any, under Section 32.201(c) if the minor is:

(1) 16 years of age or older and:

(A) resides separate and apart from the minor's parent, managing conservator, or guardian, regardless of whether the parent, managing conservator, or guardian consents to the residence and regardless of the duration of the residence; and

(B) manages the minor's own financial affairs, regardless of the source of income; or

(2) unmarried and is pregnant or is the parent of a child.

(b) Consent by a minor to emergency shelter or care under this section is not subject to disaffirmance because of minority.

(c) An emergency shelter facility may, with or without the consent of the minor's parent, managing conservator, or guardian, provide emergency shelter or care to the minor or the minor's child or children under Section 32.201(c).

(d) An emergency shelter facility is not liable for providing emergency shelter or care to the minor or the minor's child or children if the minor consents as provided by this section, except that the facility is liable for the facility's own acts of negligence.

(e) An emergency shelter facility may rely on the minor's written statement containing the grounds on which the minor has capacity to consent to emergency shelter or care.

(f) To the extent of any conflict between this section and Section 32.003, Section 32.003 prevails.

Chapter 33. Notice of Abortion.

Introductory Comment

Chapter 33 was the first legislation to be enacted in Texas affecting reproductive rights since the landmark decision of *Roe v. Wade*, 410 U.S. 113 (1973). Approximately 35 other states have similar parental involvement laws. In 2003, Texas legislation was passed entitled "Woman's Right To Know Act" imposing a 24 hour waiting period before an abortion may be performed.

Requiring parental notification or judicial approval before a minor can have an abortion has been addressed in a number of cases. In *Bellotti v. Baird (Bellotti II)*, 443 U.S. 622 (1979), the Supreme Court held that a judicial bypass for a parental consent must satisfy four criteria: the court hearing the young woman's request must authorize the abortion if she possesses the maturity to make her decision, regardless of her best interest; her abortion must be permitted if it is in her best interest, regardless of her maturity; the court proceedings must be confidential; and, the proceedings must be expedient. In *Ohio v. Akron Center for Reproductive Health (Akron II)*, 497 U.S. 502 (1990), the Court upheld Ohio's one-parent notification law, which included judicial bypass. In *Hodgson v. Minnesota,* 490 U.S. 417 (1990), the Court upheld only the section of that state's two-parent notification law that provided for judicial bypass. Lastly, in *Lambert v. Wicklund,* 520 U.S. 592 (1997), the Court upheld Montana's one-parent notification statute, including a judicial bypass in which the court must decide whether parental notification, rather than the abortion itself, is or is not in the minor's best interest. However the Supreme Court specifically declined to decide whether parental notification statutes must include some sort of judicial bypass to be constitutional. It is safe to predict that further litigation on this subject will cause additional decisions to be forthcoming in the years ahead.

CLE/Other Legal Publications

Parental notification. Sherri L. Cothrun, 2002 Adv. Fam. L.

Parental Notification Act Chapter 33, Texas Family Code: representing Jane Doe. Sherri L. Cothrun, 2001 Adv. Fam. L. Drafting

Leading Cases

In re Jane Doe 11, 92 S.W.3d 511 (Tex. 2002) (district court's failure to follow statute again results in minor's application for judicial bypass of parental notification of minor's abortion to be deemed granted)

In re Jane Doe 10, 78 S.W.3d 338 (Tex. 2002) (trial court's failure to issue findings of fact and conclusions of law on asserted ground of potential physical or emotional abuse required Supreme Court to deem application granted)

In re Jane Doe 4 (II), 19 S.W.3d 337 (Tex. 2000), *In re* Doe 4 (I) 19 S.W.3d 322 (Tex. 2000); *In re* Jane Doe 3, 19 S.W.3d 300 (Tex. 2000) (minor failed to prove she is mature and sufficiently well informed to have an abortion without notifying her parents)

In re Jane Doe, 19 S.W.3d 249 (Tex. 2000); *In re* Jane Doe (II) 19 S.W.3d 346 (Tex. 2000); *In re* Jane Doe 2, 19 S.W.3d 278 (Tex. 2000) (clarification of the "mature and sufficiently well informed" and "best interest" requirements)

Cross Reference

TEX. HEALTH AND SAFETY CODE ANN. ch. 171. Woman's Right To Know Act.

---

§ 33.001. Definitions.

In this chapter:

(1) "Abortion" means the use of any means to terminate the pregnancy of a female known by the attending physician to be pregnant, with the intention that the termination of the pregnancy by those means will with reasonable likelihood cause the death of the fetus. This definition, as applied in this chapter, applies only to an unemancipated minor known by the attending physician to be pregnant and may not be construed to limit a minor's access to contraceptives.

(2) "Fetus" means an individual human organism from fertilization until birth.

(3) "Guardian" means a court-appointed guardian of the person of the minor.

(4) "Physician" means an individual licensed to practice medicine in this state.

(5) "Unemancipated minor" includes a minor who:

(A) is unmarried; and

(B) has not had the disabilities of minority removed under Chapter 31.

§ 33.002. Parental Notice.

(a) A physician may not perform an abortion on a pregnant unemancipated minor unless:

(1) the physician performing the abortion gives at least 48 hours actual notice, in person or by telephone, of the physician's intent to perform the abortion to:

(A) a parent of the minor, if the minor has no managing conservator or guardian; or

(B) a court-appointed managing conservator or guardian;

(2) the judge of a court having probate jurisdiction, the judge of a county court at law, the judge of a district court, including a family district court, or a court of appellate jurisdiction issues an order authorizing the minor to consent to the abortion as provided by Section 33.003 or 33.004;

(3) a probate court, county court at law, district court, including a family district court, or court of appeals, by its inaction, constructively authorizes the minor to consent to the abortion as provided by Section 33.003 or 33.004; or

(4) the physician performing the abortion:

(A) concludes that on the basis of the physician's good faith clinical judgment, a condition exists that complicates the medical condition of the pregnant minor and necessitates the immediate abortion of her pregnancy to avert her death or to avoid a serious risk of substantial and irreversible impairment of a major bodily function; and

(B) certifies in writing to the Texas Department of Health and in the patient's medical record the medical indications supporting the physician's judgment that the circumstances described by Paragraph (A) exist.

(b) If a person to whom notice may be given under Subsection (a)(1) cannot be notified after a reasonable effort, a physician may perform an abortion if the physician gives 48 hours constructive notice, by certified mail, restricted delivery, sent to the last known address, to the person to whom notice may be given under Subsection (a)(1). The period under this subsection begins when the notice is mailed. If the person required to be notified is not notified within the 48-hour period, the abortion may proceed even if the notice by mail is not received.

(c) The requirement that 48 hours actual notice be provided under this section may be waived by an affidavit of:

(1) a parent of the minor, if the minor has no managing conservator or guardian; or

(2) a court-appointed managing conservator or guardian.

(d) A physician may execute for inclusion in the minor's medical record an affidavit stating that, according to the best information and belief of the physician, notice or constructive notice has been provided as required by this section. Execution of an affidavit under this subsection creates a presumption that the requirements of this section have been satisfied.

(e) The Texas Department of Health shall prepare a form to be used for making the certification required by Subsection (a)(4).

(f) A certification required by Subsection (a)(4) is confidential and privileged and is not subject to disclosure under Chapter 552, Government Code, or to discovery, subpoena, or other legal process. Personal or identifying information about the minor, including her name, address, or social security number, may not be included in a certification under Subsection (a)(4). The physician must keep the medical records on the minor in compliance with the rules adopted by the Texas State Board of Medical Examiners under Section 153.003, Occupations Code.

(g) A physician who intentionally performs an abortion on a pregnant unemancipated minor in violation of this section commits an offense. An offense under this subsection is punishable by a fine not to exceed $10,000. In this subsection, "intentionally" has the meaning assigned by Section 6.03(a), Penal Code.

(h) It is a defense to prosecution under this section that the minor falsely represented her age or identity to the physician to be at least 18 years of age by displaying an apparently valid governmental record of identification such that a reasonable person under similar circumstances would have relied on the representation. The defense does not apply if the physician is shown to have had independent knowledge of the minor's actual age or identity or failed to use due diligence in determining the minor's age or identity. In this subsection, "defense" has the meaning and application assigned by Section 2.03, Penal Code.

(i) In relation to the trial of an offense under this section in which the conduct charged involves a conclusion made by the physician under Subsection (a)(4), the defendant may seek a hearing before the Texas State Board of Medical Examiners on whether the physician's conduct was necessary to avert the death of the minor or to avoid a serious risk of substantial and irreversible impairment of a major bodily function. The findings of the Texas State Board of Medical Examiners under this subsection are admissible on that issue in the trial of the defendant. Notwithstanding any other reason for a continuance provided under the Code of Criminal Procedure or other law, on motion of the defendant, the court shall delay the beginning of the trial for not more than 30 days to permit a hearing under this subsection to take place.

§ 33.003. Judicial Approval.

(a) A pregnant minor who wishes to have an abortion without notification to one of her parents, her managing conservator, or her guardian may file an application for a court order authorizing the minor to consent to the performance of an abortion without notification to either of her parents or a managing conservator or guardian.

(b) The application may be filed in any county court at law, court having probate jurisdiction, or district court, including a family district court, in this state.

(c) The application must be made under oath and include:

(1) a statement that the minor is pregnant;

(2) a statement that the minor is unmarried, is under 18 years of age, and has not had her disabilities removed under Chapter 31;

(3) a statement that the minor wishes to have an abortion without the notification of either of her parents or a managing conservator or guardian; and

(4) a statement as to whether the minor has retained an attorney and, if she has retained an attorney, the name, address, and telephone number of her attorney.

(d) The clerk of the court shall deliver a courtesy copy of the application made under this section to the judge who is to hear the application.

(e) The court shall appoint a guardian ad litem for the minor. If the minor has not retained an attorney, the court shall appoint an attorney to represent the minor. If the guardian ad litem is an attorney admitted to the practice of law in this state, the court may appoint the guardian ad litem to serve as the minor's attorney.

(f) The court may appoint to serve as guardian ad litem:

(1) a person who may consent to treatment for the minor under Sections 32.001(a)(1)–(3);

(2) a psychiatrist or an individual licensed or certified as a psychologist under Chapter 501, Occupations Code;

(3) an appropriate employee of the Department of Protective and Regulatory Services;

(4) a member of the clergy; or

(5) another appropriate person selected by the court.

(g) The court shall fix a time for a hearing on an application filed under Subsection (a) and shall keep a record of all testimony and other oral proceedings in the action. The court shall enter judgment on the application immediately after the hearing is concluded.

(h) The court shall rule on an application submitted under this section and shall issue written findings of fact and conclusions of law not later than 5 p.m. on the second business day after the date the application is filed with the court. On request by the minor, the court shall grant an extension of the period specified by this subsection. If a request for an extension is made, the court shall rule on an application and shall issue written findings of fact and conclusions of law not later than 5 p.m. on the second business day after the date the minor states she is ready to proceed to hearing. If the court fails to rule on the application and issue written findings of fact and conclusions of law within the period specified by this subsection, the application is deemed to be granted and the physician may perform the abortion as if the court had issued an order authorizing the minor to consent to the performance of the abortion without notification under Section 33.002. Proceedings under this section shall be given precedence over other pending matters to the extent necessary to assure that the court reaches a decision promptly.

(i) The court shall determine by a preponderance of the evidence whether the minor is mature and sufficiently well informed to make the decision to have an abortion performed without notification to either of her parents or a managing conservator or guardian, whether notification would not be in the best interest of the minor, or whether notification may lead to physical, sexual, or emotional abuse of the minor. If the court finds that the minor is mature and sufficiently well informed, that notification would not be in the minor's best interest, or that notification may lead to physical, sexual, or emotional abuse of the minor, the court shall enter an order authorizing the minor to consent to the performance of the abortion without notification to either of her parents or a managing conservator or guardian and shall execute the required forms.

(j) If the court finds that the minor does not meet the requirements of Subsection (i), the court may not authorize the minor to consent to an abortion without the notification authorized under Section 33.002(a)(1).

(k) The court may not notify a parent, managing conservator, or guardian that the minor is pregnant or that the minor wants to have an abortion. The court proceedings shall be conducted in a manner that protects the anonymity of the minor. The application and all other court documents pertaining to the proceedings are confidential and privileged and are not subject to disclosure under Chapter 552, Government Code, or to discovery, subpoena, or other legal process. The minor may file the application using a pseudonym or using only her initials.

(l) An order of the court issued under this section is confidential and privileged and is not subject to disclosure under Chapter 552, Government Code, or discovery, subpoena, or other legal process. The order may not be released to any person but the pregnant minor, the pregnant minor's guardian ad litem, the pregnant minor's attorney, another person designated to receive the order by the minor, or a governmental agency or attorney in a criminal or administrative action seeking to assert or protect the interest of the minor. The supreme court may adopt rules to permit confidential docketing of an application under this section.

(m) The clerk of the supreme court shall prescribe the application form to be used by the minor filing an application under this section.

(n) A filing fee is not required of and court costs may not be assessed against a minor filing an application under this section.

§ 33.004. Appeal.

(a) A minor whose application under Section 33.003 is denied may appeal to the court of appeals having jurisdiction over civil matters in the county in which the application was filed. On receipt of a notice of appeal, the clerk of the court that denied the application shall deliver a copy of the notice of appeal and record on appeal to the clerk of the court of appeals. On receipt of the notice and record, the clerk of the court of appeals shall place the appeal on the docket of the court.

(b) The court of appeals shall rule on an appeal under this section not later than 5 p.m. on the second business day after the date the notice of appeal is filed with the court that denied the application. On request by the minor, the court shall grant an extension of the period specified by this subsection. If a request for an extension is made, the court shall rule on the appeal not later than 5 p.m. on the second business day after the date the minor states she is ready to proceed. If the court of appeals fails to rule on the appeal within the period specified by this subsection, the appeal is deemed to be granted and the physician may perform the abortion as if the court had issued an order authorizing the minor to consent to the performance of the abortion without notification under Section 33.002. Proceedings under this section shall be given precedence over other pending matters to the extent necessary to assure that the court reaches a decision promptly.

(c) A ruling of the court of appeals issued under this section is confidential and privileged and is not subject to disclosure under Chapter 552, Government Code, or discovery, subpoena, or other legal process. The ruling may not be released to any person but the pregnant minor, the pregnant minor's guardian ad litem, the pregnant minor's attorney, another person designated to receive the ruling by the minor, or a governmental agency or attorney in a criminal or administrative action seeking to assert or protect the interest of the minor. The supreme court may adopt rules to permit confidential docketing of an appeal under this section.

(d) The clerk of the supreme court shall prescribe the notice of appeal form to be used by the minor appealing a judgment under this section.

(e) A filing fee is not required of and court costs may not be assessed against a minor filing an appeal under this section.

(f) An expedited confidential appeal shall be available to any pregnant minor to whom a court of appeals denies an order authorizing the minor to consent to the performance of an abortion without notification to either of her parents or a managing conservator or guardian.

Leading Case

In re Jane Doe 11, 92 S.W.3d 511 (Tex. 2002) (order not appealable because district court failed to deny minor's application—thereby abortion deemed granted)

§ 33.005. Affidavit of Physician.

(a) A physician may execute for inclusion in the minor's medical record an affidavit stating that, after reasonable inquiry, it is the belief of the physician that:

(1) the minor has made an application or filed a notice of an appeal with a court under this chapter;

(2) the deadline for court action imposed by this chapter has passed; and

(3) the physician has been notified that the court has not denied the application or appeal.

(b) A physician who in good faith has executed an affidavit under Subsection (a) may rely on the affidavit and may perform the abortion as if the court had issued an order granting the application or appeal.

§ 33.006. Guardian ad Litem Immunity.

A guardian ad litem appointed under this chapter and acting in the course and scope of the appointment is not liable for damages arising from an act or omission of the guardian ad litem committed in good faith. The immunity granted by this section does not apply if the conduct of the guardian ad litem is committed in a manner described by Sections 107.003(b)(1)–(4).

§ 33.007. Costs Paid by State.

(a) A court acting under Section 33.003 or 33.004 may issue an order requiring the state to pay:

(1) the cost of any attorney ad litem and any guardian ad litem appointed for the minor;

(2) notwithstanding Sections 33.003(n) and 33.004(e), the costs of court associated with the application or appeal; and

(3) any court reporter's fees incurred.

(b) An order issued under Subsection (a) must be directed to the comptroller, who shall pay the amount ordered from funds appropriated to the Texas Department of Health.

§ 33.008. Physician's Duty to Report Abuse of a Minor; Investigation and Assistance.

(a) A physician who has reason to believe that a minor has been or may be physically or sexually abused by a person responsible for the minor's care, custody, or welfare, as that term is defined by Section 261.001, shall immediately report the suspected abuse to the Department of Protective and Regulatory Services and shall refer the minor to the department for services or intervention that may be in the best interest of the minor.

(b) The Department of Protective and Regulatory Services shall investigate suspected abuse reported under this section and, if appropriate, shall assist the minor in making an application with a court under Section 33.003.

§ 33.009. Other Reports of Sexual Abuse of a Minor.

A court or the guardian ad litem or attorney ad litem for the minor shall report conduct reasonably believed to violate Section 22.011, 22.021, or 25.02, Penal Code, based on information obtained during a confidential court proceeding held under this chapter to:

(1) any local or state law enforcement agency;

(2) the Department of Protective and Regulatory Services, if the alleged conduct involves a person responsible for the care, custody, or welfare of the child;

(3) the state agency that operates, licenses, certifies, or registers the facility in which the alleged conduct occurred, if the alleged conduct occurred in a facility operated, licensed, certified, or registered by a state agency; or

(4) an appropriate agency designated by the court.

§ 33.010. Confidentiality.

Notwithstanding any other law, information obtained by the Department of Protective and Regulatory Services or another entity under Section 33.008 or 33.009 is confidential except to the extent necessary to prove a violation of Section 22.011, 22.021, or 25.02, Penal Code.

§ 33.011. Information Relating to Judicial Bypass.

The Texas Department of Health shall produce and distribute informational materials that explain the rights of a minor under this chapter. The materials must explain the procedures established by Sections 33.003 and 33.004 and must be made available in English and in Spanish. The material provided by the department shall also provide information relating to alternatives to abortion and health risks associated with abortion.

Subtitle B. Parental Liability.

★★★

Chapter 41. Liability of Parents for Conduct of Child.

Introductory Comment

The liability of a parent for a child's tortious conduct that injures property is more theoretical than real. While a parent can be held liable for up to $25,000 in damages for negligent or malicious acts of the child, very few instances of a court actually holding parents liable have been reported. Undoubtedly the relatively low limit on recoverable damages severely limits the availability of legal representation, whether by hourly employment or contingent fee.

CLE/Other Legal Publications

Increasing the price of parenthood: when should parents be held civilly liable for the torts of their children? Andrew C. Gratz, 39 HOUSTON L. REV. 169 (2002)

Paying For The Sins of Another in Texas for the Torts of Children. David F. Johnson, 8 TEX. WESLEYAN L. REV. 359 (2002)

She got the goldmine, I got the shaft: marital liability between spouses, including responsibility for child's liability. Sondra Kaighen, 2001 ADV. FAM. L.

Leading Cases

Rodriguez v. Spencer, 902 S.W.2d 37 (Tex. App.—Houston [1st Dist.] 1995, no writ) (parent not responsible for violent tort committed by minor son)

Williams v. Lavender, 797 S.W.2d 410 (Tex. App.—Fort Worth 1990, writ denied) (exemplary damages against malicious 14–year old)

Buie v. Longspaugh, 598 S.W.2d 673 (Tex. Civ. App.—Fort Worth 1980, writ ref'd n.r.e.) (constitutionality of statute upheld—parental liability limited to recovery of statutory maximum per act as opposed to limiting liability for several malicious acts in one episode)

Cross References

TEX. FAM. CODE ANN. § 151.003. Rights and Duties of Parent; ch. 153. Conservatorship, Possession and Access.

---

§ 41.001. Liability.

A parent or other person who has the duty of control and reasonable discipline of a child is liable for any property damage proximately caused by:

(1) the negligent conduct of the child if the conduct is reasonably attributable to the negligent failure of the parent or other person to exercise that duty; or

(2) the wilful and malicious conduct of a child who is at least 10 years of age but under 18 years of age.

§ 41.002. Limit of Damages.

Recovery for damage caused by wilful and malicious conduct is limited to actual damages, not to exceed $25,000 per occurrence, plus court costs and reasonable attorney's fees.

§ 41.0025. Liability for Property Damage to an Inn or Hotel.

(a) Notwithstanding Section 41.002, recovery of damages by an inn or hotel for wilful and malicious conduct is limited to actual damages, not to exceed $25,000 per occurrence, plus court costs and reasonable attorney's fees.

(b) In this section "occurrence" means one incident on a single day in one hotel room. The term does not include incidents in separate rooms or incidents that occur on different days.

Comment

Reports of prom night bashes that got out of hand led to this legislative response. The 1997 addition of this section was strongly supported by the hotel industry.

§ 41.003. Venue.

A suit as provided by this chapter may be filed in the county in which the conduct of the child occurred or in the county in which the defendant resides.

Chapter 42. Civil Liability for Interference with Possessory Interest in Child.

Introductory Comment

This chapter is intended to be a "comprehensive attack on parental kidnapping," but it has been little used to date. Although a broad range of individuals who assist a child-snatching parent may be held liable for their actions, obviously a statute permitting money damages will have a significant deterrent effect only on middle class and wealthy parents. Deterrence to encourage poor folks from engaging in the prohibited conduct will have to come from the Penal Code, see below.

CLE/Other Legal Publications

Symposium. Increasing the price of parenthood: when should parents be held civilly liable for the torts of their children? Andrew C. Gratz, 39 HOUSTON L. REV. 169 (2002)

She got the goldmine, I got the shaft: marital liability between spouses, including responsibility for child's liability. Sondra Kaighen, 2001 ADV. FAM. L.

Liability of parents for conduct of their child under Section 33.01 of the Texas Family Code: defining the requisite standards of "culpability." L. Wayne Scott, 20 ST. MARY'S L.J. 69 (1988)

Leading Cases

Lozano v. Lozano, 52 S.W.3d 141 (Tex. 2001) (mother has cause of action against father's siblings who assisted him in snatching and concealing child)

Ex parte Rhodes, 974 S.W.2d 735 (Tex. Crim. App. 1998) (prior criminal contempt conviction bars prosecution for interference with child custody based on double jeopardy)

Weirich v. Weirich, 833 S.W.2d 942 (Tex. 1992) (whether grandmother entitled to notice of suit filed under provisions of earlier version of this chapter depends on whether she aided and assisted the father's interference with child custody)

Silcott v. Oglesby, 721 S.W.2d 290 (Tex. 1986) (Texas recognized the common law tort of child abduction before enactment of *[now Chapter 42]*)

Eberle v. Adams, 73 S.W.3d 322 (Tex. App.—Houston [1st Dist.] 2001, pet. denied) (jury verdict of almost $1.4 million affirmed against father's ex-parents-in-law and mother's boyfriend—only uncle and aunt escape liability)

A.H. Belo Corp. v. Corcoran, 52 S.W.3d 375 (Tex. App.—Houston [1st Dist.] 2001, pet. denied) (TV interview did not interfere with possessory interests of father; no duty owed to father to reveal location of child)

Cross Reference

TEX. PEN. CODE ANN. § 25.03. Interference with Child Custody; § 25.031. Agreement To Abduct from Custody; § 25.04. Enticing a Child.

---

§ 42.001. Definitions.

In this chapter:

(1) "Order" means a temporary or final order of a court of this state or another state or nation.

(2) "Possessory right" means a court-ordered right of possession of or access to a child, including conservatorship, custody, and visitation.

§ 42.002. Liability for Interference with Possessory Right.

(a) A person who takes or retains possession of a child or who conceals the whereabouts of a child in violation of a possessory right of another person may be liable for damages to that person.

(b) A possessory right is violated by the taking, retention, or concealment of a child at a time when another person is entitled to possession of or access to the child.

§ 42.003. Aiding or Assisting Interference with Possessory Right.

(a) A person who aids or assists in conduct for which a cause of action is authorized by this chapter is jointly and severally liable for damages.

(b) A person who was not a party to the suit in which an order was rendered providing for a possessory right is not liable unless the person at the time of the violation:

(1) had actual notice of the existence and contents of the order; or

(2) had reasonable cause to believe that the child was the subject of an order and that the person's actions were likely to violate the order.

§ 42.004. [repealed]

§ 42.005. Venue.

A suit may be filed in a county in which:

(1) the plaintiff resides;

(2) the defendant resides;

(3) a suit affecting the parent-child relationship as provided by Chapter 102 *[Filing Suit]* may be brought, concerning the child who is the subject of the court order; or

(4) a court has continuing, exclusive jurisdiction as provided by Chapter 155 *[Continuing, Exclusive Jurisdiction; Transfer]*.

§ 42.006. Damages.

(a) Damages may include:

(1) the actual costs and expenses incurred, including attorney's fees, in:

(A) locating a child who is the subject of the order;

(B) recovering possession of the child if the petitioner is entitled to possession; and

(C) enforcing the order and prosecuting the suit; and

(2) mental suffering and anguish incurred by the plaintiff because of a violation of the order.

(b) A person liable for damages who acted with malice or with an intent to cause harm to the plaintiff may be liable for exemplary damages.

Leading Case

Smith v. Smith, 720 S.W.2d 586 (Tex. App.—Houston [1st Dist.] 1986, no writ) (actual costs and expenses include prospective damages; future damages and attorney's fees tried by consent, so pleadings not necessary)

§ 42.007. Affirmative Defense.

The defendant may plead as an affirmative defense that the defendant acted in violation of the order with the express consent of the plaintiff.

§ 42.008. Remedies Not Affected.

This chapter does not affect any other civil or criminal remedy available to any person, including the child, for interference with a possessory right, nor does it affect the power of a parent to represent the interest of a child in a suit filed on behalf of the child.

§ 42.009. Frivolous Suit.

A person sued for damages as provided by this chapter is entitled to recover attorney's fees and court costs if:

(1) the claim for damages is dismissed or judgment is awarded to the defendant; and

(2) the court or jury finds that the claim for damages is frivolous, unreasonable, or without foundation.

Subtitle C. Change of Name.

★★★

Chapter 45. Change of Name.

Subchapter A. Change of Name of Child

Subchapter B. Change of Name of Adult

Subchapter A. Change of Name of Child

Introductory Comment

Most often this chapter is used to change the name of a minor to conform the child's "legal name" to the name by which the child is known. Occasionally, however, litigation has resulted when one parent sought to change the name of a child allegedly in derogation of the rights of the other parent or of the child.

Leading Cases

In re M.C.F., 121 S.W.3d 891 (Tex. App.—Fort Worth 2003, no pet. hist.) (trial court abused discretion by ordering child's name changed to surname of putative father—not in child's best interest)

In re Guthrie, 45 S.W.3d 719 (Tex. App.—Dallas 2001, pet. denied) (Texas ERA mandates parents of child-without-presumed-father have equal right to choose surname—best interests test yields surname of biological father here)

In re C.B.M., 14 S.W.3d 855 (Tex. App.—Beaumont 2000, no pet.) (no abuse of discretion in refusing to change child's name to father's after paternity established)

In re Hathcock, 981 S.W.2d 422 (Tex. App.—Texarkana 1998, no pet.) (father has no say in surname change sought by 18–year old)

In re C.C.N.S., 955 S.W.2d 448 (Tex. App.—Fort Worth 1997, no writ) (bio-dad established his paternity, child's last name changed—mother failed to object to insufficiency of his pleadings)

G.K. v. K.A., 936 S.W.2d 70 (Tex. App.—Austin 1996, writ denied) (trial court's denial of change of name to father's surname upheld in paternity action)

In re J.K., 922 S.W.2d 220 (Tex. App.—San Antonio 1996, no writ) (mother gave child father's surname—father fails to show change to mother's surname is appropriate)

In re Griffiths, 780 S.W.2d 899 (Tex. App.—Amarillo 1989, no writ) (mother had no right to unilaterally change child's name; ordered to refer to child by father's surname)

In re Baird, 610 S.W.2d 252 (Tex. Civ. App.—Fort Worth 1980, no writ) (father has protectable interest in child bearing his surname)

---

§ 45.001. Who May File; Venue.

A parent, managing conservator, or guardian of a child may file a petition requesting a change of name of the child in the county where the child resides.

§ 45.002. Requirements of Petition.

(a) A petition to change the name of a child must be verified and include:

(1) the present name and place of residence of the child;

(2) the reason a change of name is requested;

(3) the full name requested for the child; [~~and~~]

(4) whether the child is subject to the continuing exclusive jurisdiction of a court under Chapter 155 *[Continuing, Exclusive Jurisdiction; Transfer]*; **and**

(5) whether the child is subject to the registration requirements of Chapter 62, Code of Criminal Procedure.

(b) If the child is 10 years of age or older, the child's written consent to the change of name must be attached to the petition.

History: Amended by 78th Legis., Reg. Sess. (2003), S.B. 146, eff. Sept. 1, 2003, and "applies only to a petition for a change of name of a child or adult that is filed on or after the effective date of this Act. A petition filed before the effective date of this Act is governed by the law in effect on the date the petition was filed, and the former law is continued in effect for that purpose."

§ 45.003. Citation.

(a) The following persons are entitled to citation in a suit under this subchapter:

(1) a parent of the child whose parental rights have not been terminated;

(2) any managing conservator of the child; and

(3) any guardian of the child.

(b) Citation must be issued and served in the same manner as under Chapter 102 *[Filing Suit]*.

§ 45.004. Order.

(a) The court may order the name of a child changed if:

(1) the change is in the best interest of the child; **and**

(2) for a child subject to the registration requirements of Chapter 62, Code of Criminal Procedure:

(A) the change is in the interest of the public; and

(B) the person petitioning on behalf of the child provides the court with proof that the child has notified the appropriate local law enforcement authority of the proposed name change.

(b) If the child is subject to the continuing jurisdiction of a court under Chapter 155 *[Continuing, Exclusive Jurisdiction; Transfer]*, the court shall send a copy of the order to the central record file as provided in Chapter 108 *[Central Record File; Vital Statistics]*.

(c) In this section, "local law enforcement authority" has the meaning assigned by Article 62.01, Code of Criminal Procedure.

History: Amended by 78th Legis., Reg. Sess. (2003), S.B. 146, eff. Sept. 1, 2003, and "applies only to a petition for a change of name of a child or adult that is filed on or after the effective date of this Act. A petition filed before the effective date of this Act is governed by the law in effect on the date the petition was filed, and the former law is continued in effect for that purpose."

§ 45.005. Liabilities and Rights Unaffected.

A change of name does not:

(1) release a child from any liability incurred in the child's previous name; or

(2) defeat any right the child had in the child's previous name.

Subchapter B. Change of Name of Adult

Introductory Comment

Women now routinely choose to resume a maiden name or a prior married name on divorce. This chapter provides that such name change may also be accomplished in an independent action.

Leading Cases

In re Dickey, 919 S.W.2d 798 (Tex. App.—Texarkana 1996, writ denied) (felon in federal prison in Texas not permitted name change)

Lindsey v. Lindsey, 564 S.W.2d 143 (Tex. Civ. App.—Austin 1978, no writ) (name change granted although no evidence offered to support request)

In re Erickson, 547 S.W.2d 357 (Tex. Civ. App.—Houston [14th Dist.] 1977, no writ) (request for name change should be granted unless for a wrongful, fraudulent or capricious purpose)

Cross Reference

TEX. FAM. CODE ANN. § 6.706. Change of Name.

---

§ 45.101. Who May File; Venue.

An adult may file a petition requesting a change of name in the county of the adult's place of residence.

§ 45.102. Requirements of Petition.

(a) A petition to change the name of an adult must be verified and include:

(1) the present name and place of residence of the petitioner;

(2) the full name requested for the petitioner;

(3) the reason the change in name is requested; [~~and~~]

(4) whether the petitioner has been the subject of a final felony conviction; **and**

(5) *[first of two]* **whether the petitioner is subject to the registration requirements of Chapter 62, Code of Criminal Procedure.**

(5) *[second of two]* **a legible and complete set of the petitioner's fingerprints on a fingerprint card format acceptable to the Department of Public Safety and the Federal Bureau of Investigation.**

(b) The petition must include each of the following or a reasonable explanation why the required information is not included:

(1) the petitioner's:

(A) full name;

(B) sex;

(C) race;

(D) date of birth;

(E) driver's license number for any driver's license issued in the 10 years preceding the date of the petition;

(F) social security number; and

(G) assigned FBI number, state identification number, if known, or any other reference number in a criminal history record system that identifies the petitioner;

(2) any offense above the grade of Class C misdemeanor for which the petitioner has been charged; and

(3) the case number and the court if a warrant was issued or a charging instrument was filed or presented for an offense listed in Subsection (b)(2).

History: Amended by 78th Legis., Reg. Sess. (2003), S.B. 146, and H.B. 162, eff. Sept. 1, 2003, and "applies only to a petition for a change of name of a child or adult that is filed on or after the effective date of this Act. A petition filed before the effective date of this Act is governed by the law in effect on the date the petition was filed, and the former law is continued in effect for that purpose."

§ 45.103. Order.

(a) The court shall order a change of name under this subchapter for a person other than a person with a final felony conviction **or a person subject to the registration requirements of Chapter 62, Code of Criminal Procedure,** if the change is in the interest or to the benefit of the petitioner and in the interest of the public.

(b) A court may order a change of name under this subchapter for a person with a final felony conviction if, in addition to the requirements of Subsection (a), the person has:

(1) received a certificate of discharge by the pardons and paroles division of the Texas Department of Criminal Justice or completed a period of probation ordered by a court and not less than two years have passed from the date of the receipt of discharge or completion of probation; or

(2) been pardoned.

(c) A court may order a change of name under this subchapter for a person subject to the registration requirements of Chapter 62, Code of Criminal Procedure, if, in addition to the requirements of Subsection (a), the person provides the court with proof that the person has notified the appropriate local law enforcement authority of the proposed name change. In this subsection, "local law enforcement authority" has the meaning assigned by Article 62.01, Code of Criminal Procedure.

History: Amended by 78th Legis., Reg. Sess. (2003), S.B. 146, eff. Sept. 1, 2003, and "applies only to a petition for a change of name of a child or adult that is filed on or after the effective date of this Act. A petition filed before the effective date of this Act is governed by the law in effect on the date the petition was filed, and the former law is continued in effect for that purpose."

§ 45.104. Liabilities and Rights Unaffected.

A change of name under this subchapter does not release a person from liability incurred in that person's previous name or defeat any right the person had in the person's previous name.

§ 45.105. Change of Name in Divorce Suit.

(a) On the final disposition of a suit for divorce, for annulment, or to declare a marriage void, the court shall enter a decree changing the name of a party specially praying for the change to a prior used name unless the court states in the decree a reason for denying the change of name. The court may not deny a change of name solely to keep last names of family members the same.

(b) A person whose name is changed under this section may apply for a change of name certificate from the clerk of the court as provided by Section 45.106.

§ 45.106. Change of Name Certificate.

(a) A person whose name is changed under Section 6.706 or 45.105 may apply to the clerk of the court ordering the name change for a change of name certificate.

(b) A certificate under this section is a one-page document that includes:

(1) the name of the person before the change of name was ordered;

(2) the name to which the person's name was changed by the court;

(3) the date on which the name change was made;

(4) the person's social security number and driver's license number, if any;

(5) the name of the court in which the name change was ordered; and

(6) the signature of the clerk of the court that issued the certificate.

(c) An applicant for a certificate under this section shall pay a $10 fee to the clerk of the court for issuance of the certificate.

(d) A certificate under this section constitutes proof of the change of name of the person named in the certificate.

TITLE 3

Juvenile Justice Code

As amended through the 78th Legislature, Fourth Called Session (2004)

Title 3 Annotated by

ROBERT O. DAWSON

Bryant Smith Chair in Law

University of Texas School of Law

Chapter

Introductory Comment

Title 3, consisting of Chapters 51 through 61, is the juvenile justice code for Texas. It deals with adolescent misconduct in the form of delinquent conduct and conduct indicating a need for supervision and prescribes the procedural framework for responding to that misconduct. Other aspects of children and the law, such as child abuse and neglect, child support, paternity and adoption, appear in Title 5 of the Family Code.

Chapter 51 states most of the general principles that guide the juvenile justice system. Chapters 52 through 56 are procedural, each dealing with a different segment of the process. Chapter 57 deals with rights of victims of juvenile offenses. Chapter 58 creates a state-wide juvenile justice information system. Chapter 59 creates a system of progressive sanctions guidelines for the juvenile system. Chapter 60 is the Uniform Interstate Compact on Juveniles. Chapter 61, enacted in 2003, deals with the rights and responsibilities of the parents of children in the juvenile justice process.

The 1995 amendments to Title 3 made the most important changes in juvenile law since the Title was enacted in 1973.

CLE/Other Legal Publications

The State Bar of Texas Family Law Section Report provided commentaries on amendments to Title 3 following the 1977, 1979, 1981, 1983 and 1985 legislative sessions: Vols. 77–2 (June 1977); 79–2 (June 1979); 81–2 (Summer 1981); 83–2 (Summer 1983); 85–2 (Special Legis. 1985).

Thereafter, commentaries on amendments to Title 3 following the 1987, 1989, 1991, 1993, 1995, 1997, 1999, 2001, and 2003 legislative sessions appeared in the State Bar of Texas Juvenile Law Section Report: Vols. 1–3 (Sept. 1987); 3–3 (Sept. 1989); 5–3 (Sept. 1991); 7–3 (Sept. 1993), 9–3 (Special Legis. 1995), 11–3 (Special Legis. 1997), 13–3 (Special Legis. 1999), 15–3 (Special Legis. 2001), and 17–3 (Special Legis. 2003).

There are two treatises on Texas Juvenile Law:

R. Dawson, *Texas Juvenile Law (Texas Juvenile Probation Commission*, 5th Ed. 2000) and Statutory Supplement to Texas Juvenile Law (5th Ed. 2000). 2001 Supplement to Texas Juvenile Law (5th Ed.) and to Statutory Supplement to Texas Juvenile Law (2001).

T. Morgan and H. Gaither, *Juvenile Law and Practice* (Texas Practice 1999).

Cross References

Tex. Hum. Res. Code Ann. ch. 61: Texas Youth Commission; ch. 141: Texas Juvenile Probation Commission; ch. 142: Juvenile Probation Departments; ch. 152: Juvenile Boards.

Tex. Gov't Code Ann. ch. 54: Juvenile Law Referees and Family Law Masters.

★★★

Chapter 51. General Provisions.

Introductory Comment

Chapter 51 states the general principles of law that govern the juvenile justice system. Chapters 52 through 61 deal with specific procedural steps or functions of the juvenile system.

---

§ 51.01. Purpose and Interpretation.

This title shall be construed to effectuate the following public purposes:

(1) to provide for the protection of the public and public safety;

(2) consistent with the protection of the public and public safety:

(A) to promote the concept of punishment for criminal acts;

(B) to remove, where appropriate, the taint of criminality from children committing certain unlawful acts; and

(C) to provide treatment, training, and rehabilitation that emphasizes the accountability and responsibility of both the parent and the child for the child's conduct;

(3) to provide for the care, the protection, and the wholesome moral, mental, and physical development of children coming within its provisions;

(4) to protect the welfare of the community and to control the commission of unlawful acts by children;

(5) to achieve the foregoing purposes in a family environment whenever possible, separating the child from the child's parents only when necessary for the child's welfare or in the interest of public safety and when a child is removed from the child's family, to give the child the care that should be provided by parents; and

(6) to provide a simple judicial procedure through which the provisions of this title are executed and enforced and in which the parties are assured a fair hearing and their constitutional and other legal rights recognized and enforced.

§ 51.02. Definitions.

In this title:

(1) "Aggravated controlled substance felony" means an offense under Subchapter D, Chapter 481, Health and Safety Code, that is punishable by:

(A) a minimum term of confinement that is longer than the minimum term of confinement for a felony of the first degree; or

(B) a maximum fine that is greater than the maximum fine for a felony of the first degree.

(2) "Child" means a person who is:

(A) ten years of age or older and under 17 years of age; or

(B) seventeen years of age or older and under 18 years of age who is alleged or found to have engaged in delinquent conduct or conduct indicating a need for supervision as a result of acts committed before becoming 17 years of age.

(3) "Custodian" means the adult with whom the child resides.

(4) "Guardian" means the person who, under court order, is the guardian of the person of the child or the public or private agency with whom the child has been placed by a court.

(5) "Judge" or "juvenile court judge" means the judge of a juvenile court.

(6) "Juvenile court" means a court designated under Section 51.04 of this code to exercise jurisdiction over proceedings under this title.

(7) "Law-enforcement officer" means a peace officer as defined by Article 2.12, Code of Criminal Procedure.

(8) "Nonoffender" means a child who:

(A) is subject to jurisdiction of a court under abuse, dependency, or neglect statutes under Title 5 for reasons other than legally prohibited conduct of the child; or

(B) has been taken into custody and is being held solely for deportation out of the United States.

(9) "Parent" means the mother or the father of a child, but does not include a parent whose parental rights have been terminated.

(10) "Party" means the state, a child who is the subject of proceedings under this subtitle, or the child's parent, spouse, guardian, or guardian ad litem.

(11) "Prosecuting attorney" means the county attorney, district attorney, or other attorney who regularly serves in a prosecutory capacity in a juvenile court.

(12) "Referral to juvenile court" means the referral of a child or a child's case to the office or official, including an intake officer or probation officer, designated by the juvenile board to process children within the juvenile justice system.

(13) "Secure correctional facility" means any public or private residential facility, including an alcohol or other drug treatment facility, that:

(A) includes construction fixtures designed to physically restrict the movements and activities of juveniles or other individuals held in lawful custody in the facility; and

(B) is used for the placement of any juvenile who has been adjudicated as having committed an offense, any nonoffender, or any other individual convicted of a criminal offense.

(14) "Secure detention facility" means any public or private residential facility that:

(A) includes construction fixtures designed to physically restrict the movements and activities of juveniles or other individuals held in lawful custody in the facility; and

(B) is used for the temporary placement of any juvenile who is accused of having committed an offense, any nonoffender, or any other individual accused of having committed a criminal offense.

(15) "Status offender" means a child who is accused, adjudicated, or convicted for conduct that would not, under state law, be a crime if committed by an adult, including:

(A) truancy under Section 51.03(b)(2);

(B) running away from home under Section 51.03(b)(3);

(C) a fineable only offense under Section 51.03(b)(1) transferred to the juvenile court under Section 51.08(b), but only if the conduct constituting the offense would not have been criminal if engaged in by an adult;

(D) failure to attend school under Section 25.094, Education Code;

(E) a violation of standards of student conduct as described by Section 51.03(b)(5);

(F) a violation of a juvenile curfew ordinance or order;

(G) a violation of a provision of the Alcoholic Beverage Code applicable to minors only; or

(H) a violation of any other fineable only offense under Section 8.07(a)(4) or (5), Penal Code, but only if the conduct constituting the offense would not have been criminal if engaged in by an adult.

(16) "Traffic offense" means:

(A) a violation of a penal statute cognizable under Chapter 729, Transportation Code, except for:

(i) conduct constituting an offense under Section 521.457, Transportation Code;

(ii) conduct constituting an offense under Section 550.021, Transportation Code;

(iii) [~~(ii)~~]conduct constituting an offense punishable as a Class B misdemeanor under Section 550.022, Transportation Code; [~~or~~]

(iv) [~~(iii)~~]conduct constituting an offense punishable as a Class B misdemeanor under Section 550.024, Transportation Code; or

(v) conduct constituting an offense punishable as a Class B misdemeanor under Section 550.025, Transportation Code; or

(B) a violation of a motor vehicle traffic ordinance of an incorporated city or town in this state.

(17) "Valid court order" means a court order entered under Section 54.04 concerning a child adjudicated to have engaged in conduct indicating a need for supervision as a status offender.

History: Amended by 78th Legis., Reg. Sess. (2003), H.B. 2319, eff. Sept. 1, 2003. Applies only to conduct occurring on or after effective date.

Comment

The most important definition is that of "child." The conduct must have been engaged in when the person was 10 years of age but under 17 years of age for the juvenile court to have jurisdiction. The juvenile court has jurisdiction over a 17 year old for an offense committed before his or her 17th birthday.

The "aggravated controlled substance felony" defined by subsection (1) is included as a covered offense in the determinate sentence provisions. *See* § 53.045.

The definition of "referral to juvenile court" in subsection (12) is used to define when the right to send a juvenile record to the state-wide system is triggered in Chapter 58.

The definitions of "nonoffender" in subsection (8), "secure correctional facility" in subsection (13), "secure detention facility" in subsection (14), "status offender" in subsection (15) and "valid court order" in subsection (17) are all related to various provisions dealing with conforming Texas law to federal requirements respecting the detention of status offenders and nonoffenders in any facilities and the detention of juvenile offenders in adult facilities. *See* §§ 51.12, 52.027, 52.028, 54.011, 54.022, and 54.04.

The definition of traffic offense in subsection (16) excludes from that definition failure to stop and render aid punishable as a Class B misdemeanor or higher. This has the effect of making those offenses delinquent conduct when committed by a juvenile. In 2003, the definition of traffic offense was contracted to exclude leaving the scene after colliding with a stationary object and driving while license invalid.

CLE/Other Legal Publication

Responding to misrepresentations, nondisclosures and incorrect assumptions about the age of the accused: the jurisdictional boundary between juvenile and criminal courts in Texas. Robert O. Dawson, 18 St. Mary's L.J. 1117 (1987)

Leading Cases

Ex parte Mercado, 590 S.W.2d 464 (Tex. Crim. App. 1979) (§ 51.02(1) (B) does not exempt child from criminal liability for offense committed while 17)

Adair v. Kupper, Judge, 890 S.W.2d 216 (Tex. App.—Amarillo 1994, leave denied) (parents have right to participate in proceedings in which state seeks to hold them liable for money)

In re A.S., 875 S.W.2d 402 (Tex. App.—Corpus Christi 1994, no writ) (proof of age jurisdictional)

In re S.E.C., 605 S.W.2d 955 (Tex. Civ. App.—Houston [1st Dist.] 1980, no writ) (proof of age by respondent's out-of-court statement)

---

§ 51.03. Delinquent Conduct; Conduct Indicating a Need for Supervision.

(a) Delinquent conduct is:

(1) conduct, other than a traffic offense, that violates a penal law of this state or of the United States punishable by imprisonment or by confinement in jail;

(2) conduct that violates a lawful order of a [~~municipal~~] court [~~or justice court~~] under circumstances that would constitute contempt of that court in:

(A) a justice or municipal court; or.

(B) a county court for conduct punishable only by a fine;

(3) conduct that violates Section 49.04, 49.05, 49.06, 49.07, or 49.08, Penal Code; or

(4) conduct that violates Section 106.041, Alcoholic Beverage Code, relating to driving under the influence of alcohol by a minor (third or subsequent offense).

(b) Conduct indicating a need for supervision is:

(1) subject to Subsection (f), conduct, other than a traffic offense, that violates:

(A) the penal laws of this state of the grade of misdemeanor that are punishable by fine only; or

(B) the penal ordinances of any political subdivision of this state;

(2) the absence of a child on 10 or more days or parts of days within a six-month period in the same school year or on three or more days or parts of days within a four-week period from school;

(3) the voluntary absence of a child from the child's home without the consent of the child's parent or guardian for a substantial length of time or without intent to return;

(4) conduct prohibited by city ordinance or by state law involving the inhalation of the fumes or vapors of paint and other protective coatings or glue and other adhesives and the volatile chemicals itemized in Section 484.002, Health and Safety Code;

(5) an act that violates a school district's previously communicated written standards of student conduct for which the child has been expelled under Section 37.007(c), Education Code; or

(6) conduct that violates a reasonable and lawful order of a court entered under Section 264.305.

(c) Nothing in this title prevents criminal proceedings against a child for perjury.

(d) It is an affirmative defense to an allegation of conduct under Subsection (b)(2) that one or more of the absences required to be proven under that subsection have been excused by a school official or should be excused by the court or that one of the absences was involuntary. The burden is on the respondent to show by a preponderance of the evidence that the absence has been or should be excused or that the absence was involuntary. A decision by the court to excuse an absence for purposes of this subsection does not affect the ability of the school district to determine whether to excuse the absence for another purpose.

(e) For the purposes of Subsection (b)(3), "child" does not include a person who is married, divorced, or widowed.

(f) Except as provided by Subsection (g), conduct described under Subsection (b)(1), other than conduct that violates Section 49.02, Penal Code, prohibiting public intoxication, does not constitute conduct indicating a need for supervision unless the child has been referred to the juvenile court under Section 51.08(b).

(g) In a county with a population of less than 100,000, conduct described by Subsection (b)(1)(A) that violates Section 25.094, Education Code, is conduct indicating a need for supervision.

History: Amended by 78th Legis., Reg. Sess. (2003), S.B. 358, eff. Sept. 1, 2003. Applies only to conduct occurring on or after effective date.

Comment

Two types of juvenile misconduct are defined by this section: delinquent conduct and conduct indicating a need for supervision. The principal difference is that a child adjudicated of delinquent conduct can be placed on probation or, under restrictions enacted in 1999, be committed to the TYC, while a child adjudicated for conduct indicating a need for supervision cannot be committed to the TYC.

As a result of 2001 amendments, there are four types of delinquent conduct: violation of a felony or jailable misdemeanor statute, contempt of a justice or municipal court, D.W.I. and related offenses, and third offense driving by a minor while under the influence of alcohol. In 2001, the legislature eliminated subsection (a)(2) [violation of a reasonable and lawful court order] because restrictions in § 54.04 on TYC commitments made it obsolete.

The 2003 amendments in subsection (a)(2) are part of a bill that gives the constitutional county courts of Dallas and Harris Counties (acting through magistrates) jurisdiction over failure to attend school cases.

There are seven types of conduct indicating a need for supervision: public intoxication, other fineable only offense that has been transferred to a juvenile court from a municipal or justice court, truancy, running away from home, violation of an inhalant abuse statute or ordinance, an act that violated a school disciplinary code resulting in expulsion, and violation of a court order under the Services to At–Risk Youth program in Chapter 264 of Title 5.

Legislation in 2001 re-wrote truancy laws, making excused absences an affirmative defense rather than an element of the State's prima facie case. This definition of truancy is identical to the fineable offense of Failure to Attend School in § 25.094 of the Education Code. The addition of subsection (g) in 2001 makes no substantive change in which court has jurisdiction over conduct constituting truancy and should be ignored.

A 2001 amendment in subsection (e) eliminates the "marriage defense" in truancy cases, but not in running away from home cases.

CLE/Other Legal Publications

Assault and Family Violence. Sarah M. Buel, 17TH ANN. JUVE. L. CONF. (Feb. 2004)

Redefining the Objectively Reasonable Person in Texas: A Case for Battered Child Syndrome as Pure Self-Defense for Parricide. Rebecca A. Olla, 17 JUVE. L. SECT. RPT. (Sep. 2003)

Forcing Kids to Behave: Contempt of Court Enforcement in Justice and Municipal Courts. Caj Boatright, 16 JUVE. L. SECT. RPT. (Dec. 2002)

Guarding the Gateway: Truancy Law Enforcement in Texas. Robert Greenlaw, 16 JUVE. L. SECT. RPT. (Dec. 2002)

Contempt Proceedings. Sharon Pruitt, 15TH ANN. JUVE. L. CONF. (Feb. 2002)

Females in the Texas Juvenile Justice System. Vanessa P. Bailey, 13 JUVE. L. SECT. RPT. (March 1999)

The Overrepresentation of Minority Youth in the Texas Juvenile Justice System. Vanessa Pogue, 12 JUVE. L. SECT. RPT. (March 1998)

Juvenile Jurisdiction in Federal Enclaves. Jonathan Paul Harmon, 9 JUVE. L. SECT. RPT. (March 1995)

Leading Cases/Att'y Gen. Op.

Qutb v. Strauss, 11 F.3d 488 (5th Cir. 1993) (constitutionality of Dallas juvenile curfew ordinance upheld)

Urbanski v. State, 993 S.W.2d 789 (Tex. App.—Dallas 1999, no pet.) (absence for less than 24 hours still substantial under definition of running away)

Ponce v. State, 985 S.W.2d 594 (Tex. App.—Houston [1st Dist.] 1999, no pet.) (13–year-old may be convicted of aggravated perjury without juvenile court certification)

In re M.E., 982 S.W.2d 528 (Tex. App.—San Antonio 1998, no writ) (marriage does not preclude juvenile court jurisdiction)

Op. Tex. Att'y Gen. No. GA–0125 (2003) (unemancipated 17 year old who voluntarily leaves home is not a missing child if parents know of child's whereabouts)

Op. Tex. Att'y Gen. No. GA–0131 (2003) (child referred for contempt of JP court may be detained if criteria warrant but may not be placed in secure post-adjudication facility)

Op. Tex. Att'y Gen. No. JC–0454 (2002) (J.P. cannot order confinement in juvenile detention facility for contempt)

Op. Tex. Att'y Gen. No. LO–98–027 (1998) (new offense of driving under the influence by a minor doesn't prevent prosecuting minor for DWI)

---

§ 51.031. Habitual Felony Conduct.

(a) Habitual felony conduct is conduct violating a penal law of the grade of felony, other than a state jail felony, if:

(1) the child who engaged in the conduct has at least two previous final adjudications as having engaged in delinquent conduct violating a penal law of the grade of felony;

(2) the second previous final adjudication is for conduct that occurred after the date the first previous adjudication became final; and

(3) all appeals relating to the previous adjudications considered under Subdivisions (1) and (2) have been exhausted.

(b) For purposes of this section, an adjudication is final if the child is placed on probation or committed to the Texas Youth Commission.

(c) An adjudication based on conduct that occurred before January 1, 1996, may not be considered in a disposition made under this section.

Comment

Habitual felony conduct, as defined by this section, is part of the determinate sentence act. It is patterned after § 12.42 of the Texas Penal Code.

This section was clarified by a 1997 amendment that provides that an adjudication counts whether it resulted in probation or a TYC commitment, but not if it is still pending on appeal. The conduct upon which an adjudication is based must have occurred on or after January 1, 1996, the effective date of the act that added § 51.031.

---

§ 51.04. Jurisdiction.

(a) This title covers the proceedings in all cases involving the delinquent conduct or conduct indicating a need for supervision engaged in by a person who was a child within the meaning of this title at the time the person engaged in the conduct, and, except as provided by Subsection (h), the juvenile court has exclusive original jurisdiction over proceedings under this title.

(b) In each county, the county's juvenile board shall designate one or more district, criminal district, domestic relations, juvenile, or county courts or county courts at law as the juvenile court, subject to Subsections (c) and (d) of this section.

(c) If the county court is designated as a juvenile court, at least one other court shall be designated as the juvenile court. A county court does not have jurisdiction of a proceeding involving a petition approved by a grand jury under Section 53.045 of this code.

(d) If the judge of a court designated in Subsection (b) or (c) of this section is not an attorney licensed in this state, there shall also be designated an alternate court, the judge of which is an attorney licensed in this state.

(e) A designation made under Subsection (b) or (c) of this section may be changed from time to time by the authorized boards or judges for the convenience of the people and the welfare of children. However, there must be at all times a juvenile court designated for each county. It is the intent of the legislature that in selecting a court to be the juvenile court of each county, the selection shall be made as far as practicable so that the court designated as the juvenile court will be one which is presided over by a judge who has a sympathetic understanding of the problems of child welfare and that changes in the designation of juvenile courts be made only when the best interest of the public requires it.

(f) If the judge of the juvenile court or any alternate judge named under Subsection (b) or (c) is not in the county or is otherwise unavailable, any magistrate may make a determination under Section 53.02(f) or may conduct the detention hearing provided for in Section 54.01.

(g) The juvenile board may appoint a referee to make determinations under Section 53.02(f) or to conduct hearings under this title. The referee shall be an attorney licensed to practice law in this state and shall comply with Section 54.10. Payment of any referee services shall be provided from county funds.

(h) In a county with a population of less than 100,000, the juvenile court has concurrent jurisdiction with the justice and municipal courts over conduct engaged in by a child that violates Section 25.094, Education Code.

Comment

This section gives juvenile courts exclusive, original jurisdiction over proceedings under Title 3. There are no courts in Texas that have been created as juvenile courts. However, any district level or county level court can be designated by the county juvenile board to exercise juvenile jurisdiction. More than one court may and usually is designated to exercise juvenile jurisdiction. A court must be currently designated as a juvenile court to have juvenile jurisdiction. If the constitutional county court is designated to exercise juvenile jurisdiction, the juvenile board must also designate an alternate juvenile court. The constitutional county court does not have jurisdiction over determinate sentence proceedings.

A 2001 amendment in (g) replaces the juvenile court with the juvenile board as the authority to appoint a referee. The addition of (h) makes no substantive change in the law and should be ignored.

CLE/Other Legal Publication

Texas Family Code Designations—A Primer. Darlene A. Whitten, 8TH ANN. JUVE. L. CONF. (Feb. 1995)

Leading Cases/Att'y Gen. Op.

Contreras v. State, 998 S.W.2d 656 (Tex. App.—Amarillo 1999, no pet.) (burden on respondent to show that court had not been designated as a juvenile court)

R.X.F. v. State, 921 S.W.2d 888 (Tex. App.—Waco 1996, no writ) (county court at law has jurisdiction under the determinate sentence act)

G.C.D. v. State, 577 S.W.2d 302 (Tex. Civ. App.—Beaumont 1978, no writ) (court with jurisdiction must be designated juvenile court to have power to hear juvenile case)

Op. Tex. Att'y Gen. No. H–1301 (1978) (non-lawyer judge can serve as detention magistrate)

---

§ 51.041. Jurisdiction After Appeal.

(a) The court retains jurisdiction over a person, without regard to the age of the person, for conduct engaged in by the person before becoming 17 years of age if, as a result of an appeal by the person **or the state** under Chapter 56 or **by the person** under Article 44.47, Code of Criminal Procedure, of an order of the court, the order is reversed or modified and the case remanded to the court by the appellate court.

(b) If the respondent is at least 18 years of age when the order of remand from the appellate court is received by the juvenile court, the juvenile court shall proceed as provided by Sections 54.02(*o*)–(r) for the detention of a person at least 18 years of age in discretionary transfer proceedings. Pending retrial of the adjudication or transfer proceeding, the juvenile court may:

(1) order the respondent released from custody;

(2) order the respondent detained in a juvenile detention facility; or

(3) set bond and order the respondent detained in a county adult facility if bond is not made.

History: Amended by 78th Legis., Reg. Sess. (2003), H.B. 2319, eff. Sept. 1, 2003. Applies only to conduct occurring on or after effective date.

Comment

Under this section, the fact that the respondent has turned 18 years of age during the pendency of an appeal does not prevent the juvenile court from continuing with the case following appellate reversal and remand. It thus creates an exception to the rule that the jurisdiction of the juvenile court ends at the person's 18th birthday. A 2001 amendment in subsection (a), by referring to the Code of Criminal Procedure, makes it clear that this rule also applies to reversed certifications to criminal court.

Subsection (b) provides for detention of the now-adult respondent in a juvenile detention facility or the county jail pending re-hearing by the juvenile court. The procedures enacted in 1999 for detention of 18 year or older respondents in certification proceedings are to be used.

The 2003 amendment in subsection (a) reflects the addition of 56.03 which enables the State to appeal in certain determinate sentence act cases from the juvenile court to the court of appeals. The addition of "by the person" is intended to restrict appeals from certification proceedings to the person who is the subject to the proceedings and to continue the policy to exclude the State from taking such appeals.

---

§ 51.0411. Jurisdiction for Transfer or Release Hearing.

The court retains jurisdiction over a person, without regard to the age of the person, who is referred to the court under Section 54.11 for transfer to the Texas Department of Criminal Justice or release under supervision.

Comment

The juvenile court has jurisdiction in a release/transfer hearing under the determinate sentence act even if the subject person is 18 years of age or older at the time of the proceedings.

---

§ 51.0412. Jurisdiction Over Incomplete Proceedings.

The court retains jurisdiction over a person, without regard to the age of the person, who is a respondent in an adjudication proceeding, a disposition proceeding, or a proceeding to modify disposition if:

(1) the petition or motion to modify was filed while the respondent was younger than 18 years of age;

(2) the proceeding is not complete before the respondent becomes 18 years of age; and

(3) the court enters a finding in the proceeding that the prosecuting attorney exercised due diligence in an attempt to complete the proceeding before the respondent became 18 years of age.

Comment

This section abrogates the rule of *In re* N.J.A. 997 S.W.2d 554 (Tex. 1999), in which the Texas Supreme Court held that the juvenile court loses jurisdiction over proceedings when the child becomes 18. This section extends that jurisdiction to enable completion of the proceedings if the adjudication petition or motion or petition to modify was filed before age 18 and the State proceeds with diligence.

Leading Case

In re D.C., 49 S.W.3d 26 (Tex. App.—San Antonio 2001, no pet.) (under prior law, court loses jurisdiction to revoke when respondent becomes 18)

---

§ 51.042. Objection to Jurisdiction Because of Age of the Child.

(a) A child who objects to the jurisdiction of the court over the child because of the age of the child must raise the objection at the adjudication hearing or discretionary transfer hearing, if any.

(b) A child who does not object as provided by Subsection (a) waives any right to object to the jurisdiction of the court because of the age of the child at a later hearing or on appeal.

Comment

Age of the respondent is an element of the State's proof in a juvenile proceeding. This section provides that the respondent must make an age objection to juvenile proceedings at the adjudication or transfer hearing or he or she waives the right to complain on appeal or habeas that the State has failed to prove age.

---

§ 51.045. Juries in County Courts at Law.

If a provision of this title requires a jury of 12 persons, that provision prevails over any other law that limits the number of members of a jury in a particular county court at law. The state and the defense are entitled to the same number of peremptory challenges allowed in a district court.

Comment

This section applies only to determinate sentence cases filed in a juvenile court presided over by a county court-at-law judge.

---

§ 51.05. Court Sessions and Facilities.

(a) The juvenile court shall be deemed in session at all times. Suitable quarters shall be provided by the commissioners court of each county for the hearing of cases and for the use of the judge, the probation officer, and other employees of the court.

(b) The juvenile court and the juvenile board shall report annually to the commissioners court on the suitability of the quarters and facilities of the juvenile court and may make recommendations for their improvement.

§ 51.06. Venue.

(a) A proceeding under this title shall be commenced in

(1) the county in which the alleged delinquent conduct or conduct indicating a need for supervision occurred; or

(2) the county in which the child resides at the time the petition is filed, but only if:

(A) the child was under probation supervision in that county at the time of the commission of the delinquent conduct or conduct indicating a need for supervision;

(B) it cannot be determined in which county the delinquent conduct or conduct indicating a need for supervision occurred; or

(C) the county in which the child resides agrees to accept the case for prosecution, in writing, prior to the case being sent to the county of residence for prosecution.

(b) An application for a writ of habeas corpus brought by or on behalf of a person who has been committed to an institution under the jurisdiction of the Texas Youth Commission and which attacks the validity of the judgment of commitment shall be brought in the county in which the court that entered the judgment of commitment is located.

Comment

A 1999 amendment to (a) restricts residence venue in order to prevent the "dumping" of juvenile cases into the county of residence from the county in which the offense was committed.

---

§ 51.07. Transfer to Another County.

(a) When a child has been found to have engaged in delinquent conduct or conduct indicating a need for supervision under Section 54.03 of this code, the juvenile court, with the consent of the child and appropriate adult given in accordance with Section 51.09 of this code, may transfer the case and transcripts of records and documents to the juvenile court of the county where the child resides for disposition of the case under Section 54.04 of this code.

(b) When a child who is on probation moves with his family from one county to another, the juvenile court may transfer the case to the juvenile court in the county of the child's new residence if the transfer is in the best interest of the child. In all other cases of transfer, consent of the receiving court is required. The transferring court shall forward transcripts of records and documents in the case to the judge of the receiving court.

Comment

Subsection (a) deals with the situation in which the offense was committed in one county but the child resides in another. It permits the adjudication hearing to be held in the county where the offense was committed but the disposition hearing to be held in the county in which the child resides. Subsection (b) deals with the transfer of a child on probation to a different county for supervision. This is different than "courtesy supervision" in that full power to adjudicate the matter of revocation is transferred under this subsection.

Leading Att'y Gen. Op.

Op. Tex. Att'y Gen. Letter No. 95–030 (1995) (consent of receiving court not required for transfer for disposition under § 51.07(a))

---

§ 51.08. Transfer from Criminal Court.

(a) If the defendant in a criminal proceeding is a child who is charged with an offense other than perjury, a traffic offense, a misdemeanor punishable by fine only other than public intoxication, or a violation of a penal ordinance of a political subdivision, unless he has been transferred to criminal court under Section 54.02 of this code, the court exercising criminal jurisdiction shall transfer the case to the juvenile court, together with a copy of the accusatory pleading and other papers, documents, and transcripts of testimony relating to the case, and shall order that the child be taken to the place of detention designated by the juvenile court, or shall release him to the custody of his parent, guardian, or custodian, to be brought before the juvenile court at a time designated by that court.

(b) A court in which there is pending a complaint against a child alleging a violation of a misdemeanor offense punishable by fine only other than a traffic offense or public intoxication or a violation of a penal ordinance of a political subdivision other than a traffic offense:

(1) except as provided by Subsection (d), shall waive its original jurisdiction and refer a child to juvenile court if the child has previously been convicted of:

(A) two or more misdemeanors punishable by fine only other than a traffic offense or public intoxication;

(B) two or more violations of a penal ordinance of a political subdivision other than a traffic offense; or

(C) one or more of each of the types of misdemeanors described in Paragraph (A) or (B) of this subdivision; and

(2) may waive its original jurisdiction and refer a child to juvenile court if the child:

(A) has not previously been convicted of a misdemeanor punishable by fine only other than a traffic offense or public intoxication or a violation of a penal ordinance of a political subdivision other than a traffic offense; or

(B) has previously been convicted of fewer than two misdemeanors punishable by fine only other than a traffic offense or public intoxication or two violations of a penal ordinance of a political subdivision other than a traffic offense.

(c) A court in which there is pending a complaint against a child alleging a violation of a misdemeanor offense punishable by fine only other than a traffic offense or public intoxication or a violation of a penal ordinance of a political subdivision other than a traffic offense shall notify the juvenile court of the county in which the court is located of the pending complaint and shall furnish to the juvenile court a copy of the final disposition of any matter for which the court does not waive its original jurisdiction under Subsection (b) of this section.

(d) A court that has implemented a juvenile case manager program under Article **45.056** [~~45.054~~], Code of Criminal Procedure, may, but is not required to, waive its original jurisdiction under Subsection (b)(1).

History: Amended by 78th Legis., Reg. Sess. (2003), H.B. 2319, eff. Sept. 1, 2003. Applies only to conduct occurring on or after effective date.

Comment

Subsection (a) requires a criminal court to transfer a case to juvenile court upon discovery that the child is underage. Subsection (b) establishes the system for criminal prosecution of children who are believed to have committed fineable only offenses other than traffic offenses. The criminal court may transfer any such case to juvenile court, but is required to transfer a case if the child has two prior convictions of fineable only offenses. Subsection (c) makes the juvenile court the county-wide depository of records concerning these cases. Subsection (d) creates an exception to the mandatory transfer rule if the justice or municipal court has a juvenile case manager available to aid it in handling cases of persistent juvenile misconduct. The Code of Criminal Procedure reference was changed in 2003 to reflect a change in the case manager Code article.

CLE/Other Legal Publications

Juvenile Case Managers in Justice and Municipal Courts. Mark Curley, 16 JUVE. L. SECT. RPT. (Dec. 2002)

Responding to Misrepresentations, Nondisclosures and Incorrect Assumptions About the Age of the Accused: The Jurisdictional Boundary Between Juvenile and Criminal Courts in Texas. Robert O. Dawson, 18 ST. MARY'S L.J. 1117 (1987)

Cross References

TEX. CODE CRIM. PROC. ANN. art. 45.051: Suspension of Sentence and Deferral of Final Disposition; art. 45.052: Dismissal of Misdemeanor Charge on Completion of Teen Court; art. 45.0216: Expunction of Certain Conviction Records of Children.

§ 51.09. Waiver of Rights.

Unless a contrary intent clearly appears elsewhere in this title, any right granted to a child by this title or by the constitution or laws of this state or the United States may be waived in proceedings under this title if:

(1) the waiver is made by the child and the attorney for the child;

(2) the child and the attorney waiving the right are informed of and understand the right and the possible consequences of waiving it;

(3) the waiver is voluntary; and

(4) the waiver is made in writing or in court proceedings that are recorded.

Comment

This section sets the requirements for waiver of rights except in the context of custodial interrogation, which is dealt with by § 51.095.

Leading Cases

R.X.F. v. State, 921 S.W.2d 888 (Tex. App.—Waco, 1996, no writ) (by taking stand, child waives self-incrimination privilege under 51.09)

R.A.M. v. State, 599 S.W.2d 841 (Tex. Civ. App.—San Antonio 1980, no writ) (no waiver by failure to object)

In re K.W.S., 521 S.W.2d 890 (Tex. Civ. App.—Beaumont 1975, no writ) (attorney cannot waive rights without juvenile's concurrence)

§ 51.095. Admissibility of a Statement of a Child.

(a) Notwithstanding Section 51.09, the statement of a child is admissible in evidence in any future proceeding concerning the matter about which the statement was given if:

(1) the statement is made in writing under a circumstance described by Subsection (d) and:

(A) the statement shows that the child has at some time before the making of the statement received from a magistrate a warning that:

(i) the child may remain silent and not make any statement at all and that any statement that the child makes may be used in evidence against the child;

(ii) the child has the right to have an attorney present to advise the child either prior to any questioning or during the questioning;

(iii) if the child is unable to employ an attorney, the child has the right to have an attorney appointed to counsel with the child before or during any interviews with peace officers or attorneys representing the state; and

(iv) the child has the right to terminate the interview at any time;

(B) and:

(i) the statement must be signed in the presence of a magistrate by the child with no law enforcement officer or prosecuting attorney present, except that a magistrate may require a bailiff or a law enforcement officer if a bailiff is not available to be present if the magistrate determines that the presence of the bailiff or law enforcement officer is necessary for the personal safety of the magistrate or other court personnel, provided that the bailiff or law enforcement officer may not carry a weapon in the presence of the child; and

(ii) the magistrate must be fully convinced that the child understands the nature and contents of the statement and that the child is signing the same voluntarily, and if a statement is taken, the magistrate must sign a written statement verifying the foregoing requisites have been met;

(C) the child knowingly, intelligently, and voluntarily waives these rights before and during the making of the statement and signs the statement in the presence of a magistrate; and

(D) the magistrate certifies that the magistrate has examined the child independent of any law enforcement officer or prosecuting attorney, except as required to ensure the personal safety of the magistrate or other court personnel, and has determined that the child understands the nature and contents of the statement and has knowingly, intelligently, and voluntarily waived these rights;

(2) the statement is made orally and the child makes a statement of facts or circumstances that are found to be true and tend to establish the child's guilt, such as the finding of secreted or stolen property, or the instrument with which the child states the offense was committed;

(3) the statement was res gestae of the delinquent conduct or the conduct indicating a need for supervision or of the arrest;

(4) the statement is made:

(A) in open court at the child's adjudication hearing;

(B) before a grand jury considering a petition, under Section 53.045, that the child engaged in delinquent conduct; or

(C) at a preliminary hearing concerning the child held in compliance with this code, other than at a detention hearing under Section 54.01; or

(5) the statement is made orally under a circumstance described by Subsection (d) and the statement is recorded by an electronic recording device, including a device that records images, and:

(A) before making the statement, the child is given the warning described by Subdivision (1)(A) by a magistrate, the warning is a part of the recording, and the child knowingly, intelligently, and voluntarily waives each right stated in the warning;

(B) the recording device is capable of making an accurate recording, the operator of the device is competent to use the device, the recording is accurate, and the recording has not been altered;

(C) each voice on the recording is identified; and

(D) not later than the 20th day before the date of the proceeding, the attorney representing the child is given a complete and accurate copy of each recording of the child made under this subdivision.

(b) This section and Section 51.09 do not preclude the admission of a statement made by the child if:

(1) the statement does not stem from interrogation of the child under a circumstance described by Subsection (d); or

(2) without regard to whether the statement stems from interrogation of the child under a circumstance described by Subsection (d), the statement is voluntary and has a bearing on the credibility of the child as a witness.

(c) An electronic recording of a child's statement made under Subsection (a)(5) shall be preserved until all juvenile or criminal matters relating to any conduct referred to in the statement are final, including the exhaustion of all appeals, or barred from prosecution.

(d) Subsections (a)(1) and (a)(5) apply to the statement of a child made:

(1) while the child is in a detention facility or other place of confinement;

(2) while the child is in the custody of an officer; or

(3) during or after the interrogation of the child by an officer if the child is in the possession of the Department of Protective and Regulatory Services and is suspected to have engaged in conduct that violates a penal law of this state.

(e) A juvenile law referee or master may perform the duties imposed on a magistrate under this section without the approval of the juvenile court if the juvenile board of the county in which the statement of the child is made has authorized a referee or master to perform the duties of a magistrate under this section.

Comment

Under current law, a magistrate is required to warn a juvenile of his Miranda rights. Legislation in 1997 authorized tape recorded oral statements to be admitted into evidence, as they have been for a number of years under Tex. Code Crim. Proc. Ann. art. 38.22. There is one difference in that the warnings must be given by a magistrate in this section but may be given by a peace officer or magistrate under art. 38.22.

In 1999, subsection (d) was added to make it clear that a child who is in the custody of the Texas Department of Protective and Regulatory Services is per se in police custody when being questioned as a suspect and is therefore entitled to the protections afforded to a child in custody by this Section.

Subsection (e) was added in 1999 to authorize a referee or master to perform the magistrate duties under this section without requiring juvenile court ratification of those acts.

CLE/Other Legal Publication

Police Interactions with Juveniles and Their Effect on Juvenile Confessions. Pat Garza, 16 Juve. L. Sect. Rpt. (Jun. 2002)

Confessions and the Juvenile Processing Office. Patrick Garza, 15th Ann. Juve. L. Conf. (Feb. 2002)

The Texas "Custody" Determination: Does It Protect Juveniles from the Dangers of Custodial Interrogation? Sean Ryan Buckley, 13 Juve. L. Sect. Rpt. (Dec. 1999)

Leading Cases/Att'y Gen. Op.

Yarborough v. Alvarado, 124 S.Ct. 2140 (2004) (age and lack of experience with law enforcement not factors in determining whether suspect was in custody during interrogation)

Fare v. C., 442 U.S. 707, 61 L.Ed.2d 197, 99 S.Ct. 2560 (1979) (juvenile's request to speak to probation officer not invocation of right to counsel; voluntariness determined by totality of circumstances)

Vega v. State, 84 S.W.3d 613 (Tex.Crim.App. 2002) (Court of Criminal Appeals remands question of admissibility of statement taken out-of-state to Court of Appeals)

Griffin v. State, 765 S.W.2d 422 (Tex. Crim. App. 1989) (written statement as fruit of prior, inadmissible oral statement)

Meza v. State, 577 S.W.2d 705 (Tex. Crim. App. 1979) (custodial oral statement must be preceded by Miranda warning to be admissible)

Lovell v. State, 525 S.W.2d 511 (Tex. Crim. App. 1975) (confession of juvenile must conform to this section to be admissible in criminal trial)

Martinez v. State, 131 S.W.3d 22 (Tex. App.—San Antonio 2003, no pet.) (capital murder statement admissible because juvenile not in custody)

Horton v. State, 78 S.W.3d 701 (Tex.App.—Austin 2002, pet. refused) (written statement not proved to be a product of earlier, inadmissible oral statement)

In re D.A.R., 73 S.W.3d 505 (Tex.App.—El Paso 2002, no pet.) (statement excluded because questioning by police officer in school was custodial)

Diaz v. State, 61 S.W.3d 525 (Tex. App.—San Antonio 2001, no pet.) (statement involuntary because magistrate made error in advising as to punishment range for offense)

Rushing v. State, 50 S.W.3d 715 (Tex. App.—Waco 2001, pet. denied) (oral statements made to probation officer in detention admissible because no interrogation)

In re V.P., 55 S.W.3d 25 (Tex. App.—Austin 2001, pet. denied) (questioning by assistant principal about handgun on campus not custodial)

Childs v. State, 21 S.W.3d 631 (Tex. App.—Houston [14th Dist.] 2000, pet. refused) (claim by juvenile that he is 17 waived Family Code interrogation protections)

In re M.R.R., 2 S.W.3d 319 (Tex. App.—San Antonio 1999, no pet.) (questioning not custodial so warnings not required)

In re L.M., 993 S.W.2d 276 (Tex. App.—Austin 1999, pet. denied) (young child in DPRS custody is in police custody for questioning)

Op. Tex. Att'y Gen. No. DM–476 (1998) (school may not block DPRS child abuse interview or insist that school official be present)

Kendrick v. State, 942 S.W.2d 120 (Tex. App.—Beaumont 1997, no writ) (oral custodial statement leading to tangible evidence admissible in criminal trial)

In re T.R.S., 931 S.W.2d 756 (Tex. App.—Waco 1996, no writ) (admissibility of statement given in Oklahoma determined by applying Texas law)

Laird v. State, 933 S.W.2d 707 (Tex. App.—Houston [14th Dist.] 1996, writ ref'd) (custodial statement given in Pennsylvania admissible although not given in juvenile processing office)

Melendez v. State, 873 S.W.2d 723 (Tex. App.—San Antonio 1994, no writ) (oral statement from juvenile not in custody and not being interrogated admissible)

In re R.D., 627 S.W.2d 803 (Tex. App.—Tyler 1982, no writ) (request to speak to mother not invocation of right to counsel)

E.A.W. v. State, 547 S.W.2d 63 (Tex. Civ. App.—Waco 1977, no writ) (11 year old did not voluntarily confess despite procedural compliance with the confession statute)

---

§ 51.10. Right to Assistance of Attorney; Compensation.

(a) A child may be represented by an attorney at every stage of proceedings under this title, including:

(1) the detention hearing required by Section 54.01 of this code;

(2) the hearing to consider transfer to criminal court required by Section 54.02 of this code;

(3) the adjudication hearing required by Section 54.03 of this code;

(4) the disposition hearing required by Section 54.04 of this code;

(5) the hearing to modify disposition required by Section 54.05 of this code;

(6) hearings required by Chapter 55 of this code;

(7) habeas corpus proceedings challenging the legality of detention resulting from action under this title; and

(8) proceedings in a court of civil appeals or the Texas Supreme Court reviewing proceedings under this title.

(b) The child's right to representation by an attorney shall not be waived in:

(1) a hearing to consider transfer to criminal court as required by Section 54.02 of this code;

(2) an adjudication hearing as required by Section 54.03 of this code;

(3) a disposition hearing as required by Section 54.04 of this code;

(4) a hearing prior to commitment to the Texas Youth Commission as a modified disposition in accordance with Section 54.05(f) of this code; or

(5) hearings required by Chapter 55 of this code.

(c) If the child was not represented by an attorney at the detention hearing required by Section 54.01 of this code and a determination was made to detain the child, the child shall immediately be entitled to representation by an attorney. The court shall order the retention of an attorney according to Subsection (d) or appoint an attorney according to Subsection (f).

(d) The court shall order a child's parent or other person responsible for support of the child to employ an attorney to represent the child, if:

(1) the child is not represented by an attorney;

(2) after giving the appropriate parties an opportunity to be heard, the court determines that the parent or other person responsible for support of the child is financially able to employ an attorney to represent the child; and

(3) the child's right to representation by an attorney:

(A) has not been waived under Section 51.09 of this code; or

(B) may not be waived under Subsection (b) of this section.

(e) The court may enforce orders under Subsection (d) by proceedings under Section 54.07 or by appointing counsel and ordering the parent or other person responsible for support of the child to pay a reasonable attorney's fee set by the court. The order may be enforced under Section 54.07.

(f) The court shall appoint an attorney to represent the interest of a child entitled to representation by an attorney, if:

(1) the child is not represented by an attorney;

(2) the court determines that the child's parent or other person responsible for support of the child is financially unable to employ an attorney to represent the child; and

(3) the child's right to representation by an attorney:

(A) has not been waived under Section 51.09 of this code; or

(B) may not be waived under Subsection (b) of this section.

(g) The juvenile court may appoint an attorney in any case in which it deems representation necessary to protect the interests of the child.

(h) Any attorney representing a child in proceedings under this title is entitled to 10 days to prepare for any adjudication or transfer hearing under this title.

(i) Except as provided in Subsection (d) of this section, an attorney appointed under this section to represent the interests of a child shall be paid from the general fund of the county in which the proceedings were instituted according to the schedule in Article 26.05 of the Texas Code of Criminal Procedure, 1965. For this purpose, a bona fide appeal to a court of civil appeals or proceedings on the merits in the Texas Supreme Court are considered the equivalent of a bona fide appeal to the Texas Court of Criminal Appeals.

(j) The juvenile board of a county may make available to the public the list of attorneys eligible for appointment to represent children in proceedings under this title as provided in the plan adopted under Section 51.102. The list of attorneys must indicate the level of case for which each attorney is eligible for appointment under Section 51.102(b)(2).

(k) Subject to Chapter 61, the juvenile court may order the parent or other person responsible for support of the child to reimburse the county for payments the county made to counsel appointed to represent the child under Subsection (f) or (g). The court may:

(1) order payment for each attorney who has represented the child at any hearing, including a detention hearing, discretionary transfer hearing, adjudication hearing, disposition hearing, or modification of disposition hearing;

(2) include amounts paid to or on behalf of the attorney by the county for preparation time and investigative and expert witness costs; and

(3) require full or partial reimbursement to the county.

(l) The court may not order payments under Subsection (k) that exceed the financial ability of the parent or other person responsible for support of the child to meet the payment schedule ordered by the court.

History: Amended by 78th Legis., Reg. Sess. (2003), H.B. 2319, eff. Sept. 1, 2003. Applies only to conduct occurring on or after effective date.

Comment

A juvenile has a right to counsel at all stages of Title 3 proceedings. That right cannot be waived in a transfer, adjudication, disposition, probation revocation, or Chapter 55 proceeding. Counsel, appointed or retained, is entitled to 10 days to prepare for an adjudication or transfer hearing.

As a result of the Fair Defense Act, enacted in 2001, each juvenile board must maintain a list of attorneys eligible for appointment to juvenile cases. The addition in 2003 of subsection (j) permits the board to make that list available to the public to aid parents and others to choose an attorney to retain for a juvenile case.

Subsections (k) and (l) recognize the power of the juvenile court to order parents and others to reimburse the county for its expenditures to and on behalf of appointed counsel. Enforcement of such orders is governed by Chapter 61, which was added in 2003.

CLE/Other Legal Publications

Pre-trial Proceedings in Juvenile Court. Bill Patillo, 17TH ANN. JUVE. L. CONF. (Feb. 2004)

Ethics: Duty to Report Child Abuse. Camile DuBose & Cathy Morris, 17TH ANN. JUVE. L. CONF. (Feb. 2004)

Defense 101. Kameron Johnson, 16TH ANN. JUVE. L. CONF. (Feb. 2003)

Defense Ethics. Sylvia Andrews, 16TH ANN. JUVE. L. CONF. (Feb. 2003)

Guardian and Attorney Ad Litem: an Ethical Dilemma. Kelly Clark, 14TH ANN. JUVE. L. CONF. (Feb. 2001)

Prosecutor Tips to the Defense. Kris Moore, 14TH ANN. JUVE. L. CONF. (Feb. 2001)

My Child (Ethics). Arthur C. Washington, 13TH ANN. JUVE. L. CONF. (Feb. 2000)

Are We Doing This in the Best Interest of the Child or the Best Interest of Society According to Society's Norms? Earlean Cobbin Murphy, 13TH ANN. JUVE. L. CONF. (Feb. 2000)

Attorney-Client and Work Product Privileges. A. Michelle May, 13TH ANN. JUVE. L. CONF. (Feb. 2000)

Leading Cases/Att'y Gen. Op.

In re Gault, 387 U.S. 1, 18 L.Ed.2d 527, 87 S.Ct. 1428 (1967) (juvenile has right to counsel under 14th Amendment)

In re I.R., 124 S.W.3d 294 (Tex. App.—El Paso 2003, no pet.) (failure to subpoena alibi witness was ineffective assistance of counsel)

Op. Tex. Att'y Gen. LO–97–063 (1997) (county must pay fee of appointed counsel even when there is a public defender office in the county)

R.X.F. v. State, 921 S.W.2d 888 (Tex. App.—Waco 1996, no writ) (attorney without consent of child has power to waive 10–day-preparation time)

Cross Reference

TEX. CODE CRIM. PROC. ANN. art. 26.05. Compensation of Counsel Appointed To Defend.

§ 51.101. Appointment of Attorney and Continuation of Representation.

(a) If an attorney is appointed at the initial detention hearing and the child is detained, the attorney shall continue to represent the child until the case is terminated, the family retains an attorney, or a new attorney is appointed by the juvenile court. Release of the child from detention does not terminate the attorney's representation.

(b) If there is an initial detention hearing without an attorney and the child is detained, the attorney appointed under Section 51.10(c) shall continue to represent the child until the case is terminated, the family retains an attorney, or a new attorney is appointed by the juvenile court. Release of the child from detention does not terminate the attorney's representation.

(c) The juvenile court shall determine, on the filing of a petition, whether the child's family is indigent if:

(1) the child is released by intake;

(2) the child is released at the initial detention hearing; or

(3) the case was referred to the court without the child in custody.

(d) A juvenile court that makes a finding of indigence under Subsection (c) shall appoint an attorney to represent the child on or before the fifth working day after the date the petition for adjudication or discretionary transfer hearing was served on the child. An attorney appointed under this subsection shall continue to represent the child until the case is terminated, the family retains an attorney, or a new attorney is appointed by the juvenile court.

(e) The juvenile court shall determine whether the child's family is indigent if a motion or petition is filed under Section 54.05 seeking to modify disposition by committing the child to the Texas Youth Commission or placing the child in a secure correctional facility. A court that makes a finding of indigence shall appoint an attorney to represent the child on or before the fifth working day after the date the petition or motion has been filed. An attorney appointed under this subsection shall continue to represent the child until the court rules on the motion or petition, the family retains an attorney, or a new attorney is appointed.

Comment

This section seeks to assure that an appointed attorney is provided early enough in the process to benefit the respondent. In some counties, an attorney appointed for a detention hearing represents the child only for that hearing. If the child is detained, he or she may be without counsel until the State files a petition. This section provides that if the child is detained, that same attorney becomes the attorney for the merits of the case until the case is terminated or other counsel is provided.

There is an exception for a child who is released by police, intake, or at the initial detention hearings. Because many such children will be handled nonjudicially and without prejudicing their rights, providing counsel for them would be expensive and not particularly productive. Children in such cases must have counsel appointed if their families are indigent when a petition is filed; counties are free to provide counsel in such cases earlier in the process.

---

§ 51.102. Appointment of Counsel Plan.

(a) The juvenile board in each county shall adopt a plan that:

(1) specifies the qualifications necessary for an attorney to be included on an appointment list from which attorneys are appointed to represent children in proceedings under this title; and

(2) establishes **the** procedures for:

(A) including attorneys on the appointment list and removing attorneys from the list; and

(B) appointing attorneys from the appointment list to individual cases.

(b) A plan adopted under Subsection (a) must:

(1) to the extent practicable, comply with the requirements of Article 26.04, Code of Criminal Procedure, except that:

(A) the income and assets of the child's parent or other person responsible for the child's support must be used in determining whether the child is indigent; and

(B) any alternative plan for appointing counsel is established by the juvenile board in the county; and

(2) recognize the differences in qualifications and experience necessary for appointments to cases in which:

(A) the allegation is:

(i) conduct indicating a need for supervision **or** [~~; (ii)~~] delinquent conduct, and commitment to the Texas Youth Commission is not an authorized disposition; or

(ii) delinquent conduct, and commitment to the Texas Youth Commission without a determinate sentence is an authorized disposition; **or**

(B) determinate sentence proceedings have been initiated or [~~(c)~~] proceedings for discretionary transfer to criminal court have been initiated.

History: Amended by 78th Legis., Reg. Sess. (2003), H.B. 2319, eff. Sept. 1, 2003. Applies only to conduct occurring on or after effective date.

Comment

This section implements the Texas Fair Defense Act by requiring the juvenile board to devise and make public a plan for the qualifications of and appointment of attorneys to represent indigent juveniles. Originally, it was required that the plan must recognize the five different levels of seriousness of juvenile charges: CINS, delinquency cases with no TYC commitment possible, delinquency cases with TYC commitment possible, determinate sentence act cases, and certification cases. In 2003, that scheme was simplified to only three types of cases.

The Fair Defense Act provides for a state-wide standard setting and monitoring agency in the Office of Court Administration to implement the legislation and for an estimated 12 million dollars per year in state aid to counties to aid in paying for attorneys, investigative expenses and the fees of expert witnesses.

CLE/Other Legal Publications

Juvenile Board Plans for Appointment of Counsel. Robert Dawson, 15 Juve. L. Sect. Rpt. (Sept. 2001)

---

§ 51.11. Guardian Ad Litem.

(a) If a child appears before the juvenile court without a parent or guardian, the court shall appoint a guardian ad litem to protect the interests of the child. The juvenile court need not appoint a guardian ad litem if a parent or guardian appears with the child.

(b) In any case in which it appears to the juvenile court that the child's parent or guardian is incapable or unwilling to make decisions in the best interest of the child with respect to proceedings under this title, the court may appoint a guardian ad litem to protect the interests of the child in the proceedings.

(c) An attorney for a child may also be his guardian ad litem. A law-enforcement officer, probation officer, or other employee of the juvenile court may not be appointed guardian ad litem.

Comment

A guardian ad litem must be appointed where there is no parent or guardian in court with the child. The defense attorney may be appointed guardian ad litem.

CLE/Other Legal Publications

The Guardian ad Litem Dilemma. M. Kelly Clark & Caroline A. Clark, 13th Ann. Juve. L. Conf. (Feb. 2000)

Leading Cases

Flynn v. State, 707 S.W.2d 87 (Tex. Crim. App. 1986) (error but harmless not to appoint guardian ad litem when respondent's aunt was in court)

In re P.S.G., 942 S.W.2d 227 (Tex. App.—Beaumont 1997, no writ) (refusal to appoint GAL when same person was victim and respondent's mother OK)

---

§ 51.115. Attendance at Hearing: Parent or Other Guardian.

(a) Each parent of a child, each managing and possessory conservator of a child, each court-appointed custodian of a child, and a guardian of the person of the child shall attend each hearing affecting the child held under:

(1) Section 54.02 (waiver of jurisdiction and discretionary transfer to criminal court);

(2) Section 54.03 (adjudication hearing);

(3) Section 54.04 (disposition hearing);

(4) Section 54.05 (hearing to modify disposition); and

(5) Section 54.11 (release or transfer hearing).

(b) Subsection (a) does not apply to:

(1) a person for whom, for good cause shown, the court waives attendance;

(2) a person who is not a resident of this state; or

(3) a parent of a child for whom a managing conservator has been appointed and the parent is not a conservator of the child.

(c) A person required under this section to attend a hearing is entitled to reasonable written or oral notice that includes a statement of the place, date, and time of the hearing and that the attendance of the person is required. The notice may be included with or attached to any other notice required by this chapter to be given the person. Separate notice is not required for a disposition hearing that convenes on the adjournment of an adjudication hearing. If a person required under this section fails to attend a hearing, the juvenile court may proceed with the hearing.

(d) A person who is required by Subsection (a) to attend a hearing, who receives the notice of the hearing, and who fails to attend the hearing may be punished by the court for contempt by a fine of not less than $100 and not more than $1,000. In addition to or in lieu of contempt, the court may order the person to receive counseling or to attend an educational course on the duties and responsibilities of parents and skills and techniques in raising children.

Comment

This provision is intended to induce greater parental responsibility in the juvenile process. Parents and others can be ordered to attend juvenile court hearings and fined for contempt of court for failure to attend.

---

§ 51.116. Right to Reemployment.

(a) An employer may not terminate the employment of a permanent employee because the employee is required under Section 51.115 to attend a hearing.

(b) An employee whose employment is terminated in violation of this section is entitled to return to the same employment that the employee held when notified of the hearing if the employee, as soon as practical after the hearing, gives the employer actual notice that the employee intends to return.

(c) A person who is injured because of a violation of this section is entitled to reinstatement to the person's former position and to damages, but the damages may not exceed an amount equal to six months' compensation at the rate at which the person was compensated when required to attend the hearing.

(d) The injured person is also entitled to reasonable attorney's fees in an amount approved by the court.

(e) It is a defense to an action brought under this section that the employer's circumstances changed while the employee attended the hearing so that reemployment was impossible or unreasonable. To establish a defense under this subsection, an employer must prove that the termination of employment was because of circumstances other than the employee's attendance at the hearing.

Comment

This section, a companion to § 51.115, is intended to facilitate the attendance of parents and other adults at juvenile court hearings by prohibiting employers from firing an employee for attending a hearing in response to a juvenile court order. This section is modeled on a similar provision to protect jurors from being fired for responding to a jury summons. *See* Tex. Civ. Prac. & Rem. Code § 122.001.

§ 51.12. Place and Conditions of Detention.

(a) Except as provided by Subsection (h), a child may be detained only in a:

(1) juvenile processing office in compliance with Section 52.025;

(2) place of nonsecure custody in compliance with Article 45.058, Code of Criminal Procedure;

(3) certified juvenile detention facility that complies with the requirements of Subsection (f);

(4) secure detention facility as provided by Subsection (j); or

(5) county jail or other facility as provided by Subsection (*l*).

(b) The proper authorities in each county shall provide a suitable place of detention for children who are parties to proceedings under this title, but the juvenile board shall control the conditions and terms of detention and detention supervision and shall permit visitation with the child at all reasonable times.

(c) In each county, each judge of the juvenile court and a majority of the members of the juvenile board shall personally inspect the juvenile pre-adjudication secure detention facilities and any public or private juvenile secure correctional facilities used for post-adjudication confinement that are located in the county and operated under authority of the juvenile board at least annually and shall certify in writing to the authorities responsible for operating and giving financial support to the facilities and to the Texas Juvenile Probation Commission that they are suitable or unsuitable for the detention of children in accordance with:

(1) the requirements of Subsections (a), (f), and (g); and

(2) minimum professional standards for the detention of children in pre-adjudication or post-adjudication secure confinement promulgated by the Texas Juvenile Probation Commission or, at the election of the juvenile board, the current standards promulgated by the American Correctional Association.

(d) Except as provided by Subsections (j) and (*l*), a child may not be placed in a facility that has not been certified under Subsection (c) as suitable for the detention of children and registered under Subsection (i). Except as provided by Subsections (j) and (*l*), a child detained in a facility that has not been certified under Subsection (c) as suitable for the detention of children or that has not been registered under Subsection (i) shall be entitled to immediate release from custody in that facility.

(e) If there is no certified place of detention in the county in which the petition is filed, the designated place of detention may be in another county.

(f) A child detained in a building that contains a jail, lockup, or other place of secure confinement, including an alcohol or other drug treatment facility, shall be separated by sight and sound from adults detained in the same building. Children and adults are separated by sight and sound only if they are unable to see each other and conversation between them is not possible. The separation must extend to all areas of the facility, including sally ports and passageways, and those areas used for admission, counseling, sleeping, toileting, showering, dining, recreational, educational, or vocational activities, and health care. The separation may be accomplished through architectural design.

(g) Except for a child detained in a juvenile processing office, a place of nonsecure custody, a secure detention facility as provided by Subsection (j), or a facility as provided by Subsection (*l*), a child detained in a building that contains a jail or lockup may not have any contact with:

(1) part-time or full-time security staff, including management, who have contact with adults detained in the same building; or

(2) direct-care staff who have contact with adults detained in the same building.

(h) This section does not apply to a person:

(1) after transfer to criminal court for prosecution under Section 54.02; or

(2) who is at least 17 years of age and who has been taken into custody after having:

(A) escaped from a juvenile facility operated by or under contract with the Texas Youth Commission; or

(B) violated a condition of release under supervision of the Texas Youth Commission.

(i) Except for a facility operated or certified by the Texas Youth Commission or a facility as provided by Subsection (*l*), a governmental unit or private entity that operates or contracts for the operation of a juvenile pre-adjudication secure detention facility or a juvenile post-adjudication secure correctional facility in this state shall:

(1) register the facility annually with the Texas Juvenile Probation Commission; and

(2) adhere to all applicable minimum standards for the facility.

(j) After being taken into custody, a child may be detained in a secure detention facility until the child is released under Section 53.01, 53.012, or 53.02 or until a detention hearing is held under Section 54.01(a), regardless of whether the facility has been certified under Subsection (c), if:

(1) a certified juvenile detention facility is not available in the county in which the child is taken into custody;

(2) the detention facility complies with:

(A) the short-term detention standards adopted by the Texas Juvenile Probation Commission; and

(B) the requirements of Subsection (f); and

(3) the detention facility has been designated by the county juvenile board for the county in which the facility is located.

(k) If a child who is detained under Subsection (j) or (*l*) is not released from detention at the conclusion of the detention hearing for a reason stated in Section 54.01(e), the child may be detained after the hearing only in a certified juvenile detention facility.

(l) A child who is taken into custody and required to be detained under Section 53.02(f) may be detained in a county jail or other facility until the child is released under Section 53.02(f) or until a detention hearing is held as required by Section 54.01(p), regardless of whether the facility complies with the requirements of this section, if:

(1) a certified juvenile detention facility or a secure detention facility described by Subsection (j) is not available in the county in which the child is taken into custody or in an adjacent county;

(2) the facility has been designated by the county juvenile board for the county in which the facility is located;

(3) the child is separated by sight and sound from adults detained in the same facility through architectural design or time-phasing;

(4) the child does not have any contact with management or direct-care staff that has contact with adults detained in the same facility on the same work shift;

(5) the county in which the child is taken into custody is not located in a metropolitan statistical area as designated by the United States Bureau of the Census; and

(6) each judge of the juvenile court and a majority of the members of the juvenile board of the county in which the child is taken into custody have personally inspected the facility at least annually and have certified in writing to the Texas Juvenile Probation Commission that the facility complies with the requirements of Subdivisions (3) and (4).

Comment

Currently, no juveniles in Texas are detained in jail except for very brief periods awaiting transport elsewhere. Detention occurs in over 60 regional juvenile detention facilities located throughout the state. A child may be detained in an approved facility located outside the county where the offense is believed to have been committed.

Subsection (j) permits juveniles taken into custody in a county without a certified juvenile detention facility to be temporarily detained in an adult detention facility that complies with statutory requirements on sight and sound separation, that meets TJPC standards for temporary detention and that has been designated by the local juvenile board. Detention in such a facility is authorized only until the initial detention hearing is conducted. The maximum period of detention in such a facility would therefore be four nights. The purpose of the provision is to reduce travel to and from out-of-county detention facilities.

A 1999 amendment in subsection (h) lowers from 18 to 17 the age at which a person can be detained in a county jail after escaping from a TYC facility or for violation of TYC parole. It excludes probation violations from the authority to detain in the county jail. Of course, if a 17 year old on juvenile probation violates it by committing a new offense, he or she can be detained in the county jail for the new offense or in the juvenile detention facility for the probation violation.

Subsection (l) is part of the 1999 carry-a-firearm-go-to-detention bill. It permits detention under very limited circumstances in a sight-and-sound separated part of the county jail when juvenile detention facilities are not available in the county or an adjacent county.

CLE/Other Legal Publication

Exploring the Pros and Cons of Texas Juvenile Hold Over Facilities. Rachel Bergstrom, 12 Juve. L. Sect. Rpt. (Dec. 1998)

Leading Cases/Att'y Gen. Op.

In re M.C., 915 S.W.2d 118 (Tex. App.—San Antonio 1996, no writ) (certification of detention facility by juvenile board requires majority, not unanimous, action by board members)

Op. Tex. Att'y Gen. No. DM–439 (1997) (juvenile court's control over detention overrides contract between county and private provider)

Op. Tex. Att'y Gen. No. DM–38 (1991) (arrested person 18 or older cannot be detained in same compartment of detention facility as juvenile)

---

§ 51.13. Effect of Adjudication or Disposition.

(a) Except as provided by Subsection (d), an order of adjudication or disposition in a proceeding under this title is not a conviction of crime. Except as provided by Chapter 841, Health and Safety Code, an order of adjudication or disposition does not impose any civil disability ordinarily resulting from a conviction or operate to disqualify the child in any civil service application or appointment.

(b) The adjudication or disposition of a child or evidence adduced in a hearing under this title may be used only in subsequent:

(1) proceedings under this title in which the child is a party;

(2) sentencing proceedings in criminal court against the child to the extent permitted by the Texas Code of Criminal Procedure, 1965; or

(3) civil commitment proceedings under Chapter 841, Health and Safety Code.

(c) A child may not be committed or transferred to a penal institution or other facility used primarily for the execution of sentences of persons convicted of crime, except:

(1) for temporary detention in a jail or lockup pending juvenile court hearing or disposition under conditions meeting the requirements of Section 51.12 of this code;

(2) after transfer for prosecution in criminal court under Section 54.02 of this code; or

(3) after transfer from the Texas Youth Commission under Section 61.084, Human Resources Code.

(d) An adjudication under Section 54.03 that a child engaged in conduct that occurred on or after January 1, 1996, and that constitutes a felony offense resulting in commitment to the Texas Youth Commission under Section 54.04(d)(2), (d)(3), or (m) or 54.05(f) is a final felony conviction only for the purposes of Sections **12.42(a), (b), (c)(1),** [~~12.42(a)-(c)~~] and (e), Penal Code.

History: Amended by 78th Legis., Reg. Sess. (2003), H.B. 2319, eff. Sept. 1, 2003. Applies only to conduct occurring on or after effective date.

Comment

This section establishes that an adjudication in juvenile court is not a criminal conviction and imposes none of the legal disabilities of a criminal conviction. It also establishes the basic confidentiality rule for evidence and rulings of the juvenile court.

Subsection (d) provides that a felony adjudication with a TYC commitment constitutes a prior felony conviction under Tex. Penal Code Ann. § 12.42 should the respondent later be charged with a felony as an adult in criminal court. Only enhancement of punishment, not habitual offender treatment, is affected by this provision. A 1997 amendment specifies that to count under this provision the offense must have been committed on or after January 1, 1996, which was the effective date of the 1995 amendment that added this provision. A 2003 amendment provides that a prior juvenile adjudication does not count as a felony conviction for mandatory life imprisonment upon second conviction of a sex crime under Section 12.42.

The amendments in (a) and (b) referring to the Health and Safety Code were made in 1999. The legislature in 1999 established a system of super intensive post-incarceration supervision for certain released inmates classified as "sexual predators." To be eligible for intensive supervision, a person must have two criminal convictions or juvenile adjudications for a sexually violent offense. To qualify, a juvenile adjudication for a sexually violent offense must have been under the determinate sentence act and must have led to a TYC commitment. If after the first conviction or adjudication, the person commits a new sexually violent offense, is convicted for it and receives a prison sentence to TDCJ, he or she becomes eligible for consideration as a sexually violent predator upon release. The offenses that qualify as sexually violent offenses are indecency with a child by contact, sexual assault, aggravated sexual assault, aggravated kidnapping for a sexual purpose, burglary for a sexual purpose, or an attempt, conspiracy or solicitation to commit any of those offenses. Therefore, an adjudication for one of those offenses under the determinate sentence act resulting in a TYC commitment can be the first step toward sexual predator status.

Leading Cases

Davis v. Alaska, 415 U.S. 308, 39 L.Ed.2d 347, 94 S.Ct. 1105 (1974) (defendant may cross-examine witness for bias and show he is on juvenile probation)

Goodman v. State, 701 S.W.2d 850 (Tex. Crim. App. 1985) (juvenile adjudication admissible before jury in penalty phase of capital case)

Love v. State, 533 S.W.2d 6 (Tex. Crim. App. 1976) (may cross-examine character witness about juvenile record with "have you heard" questions)

Ruth v. State, 522 S.W.2d 517 (Tex. Crim. App. 1975) (juvenile adjudication not admissible to impeach)

Walker v. State, 493 S.W.2d 239 (Tex. Crim. App. 1973) (juvenile record admissible before judge in non-capital penalty proceedings)

Garner v. State, 957 S.W.2d 112 (Tex. App.—Amarillo 1997, no writ) (juvenile court packet admissible at penalty when limited to adjudications)

Zepeda v. State, 797 S.W.2d 258 (Tex. App.—Corpus Christi 1990, pet. ref'd) (juvenile proceedings may be used as deposition if witness becomes unavailable)

Cross References

TEX. R. EVID. 609(d). Juvenile Adjudication Not Admissible to Impeach in Civil or Criminal Proceedings.

TEX. CODE CRIM. PROC. ANN. art. 37.07. Admissibility of Juvenile Felony and Jailable Misdemeanor Adjudications in the Penalty Phase of Criminal Proceedings.

---

§ 51.14. [repealed]

§ 51.15. [repealed]

---

§ 51.151. Polygraph Examination.

If a child is taken into custody under Section 52.01 of this code, a person may not administer a polygraph examination to the child without the consent of the child's attorney or the juvenile court unless the child is transferred to criminal court for prosecution under Section 54.02 of this code.

Leading Cases/Att'y Gen. Op.

Romero v. State, 493 S.W.2d 206 (Tex. Crim. App. 1973) (polygraph results not admissible in criminal proceedings)

Op. Tex. Att'y Gen. No. JM–1141 (1990) (§ 51.151 does not apply to child witnesses not in custody under Title 3)

---

§ 51.16. [repealed]

§ 51.17. Procedure and Evidence.

(a) Except for the burden of proof to be borne by the state in adjudicating a child to be delinquent or in need of supervision under Section 54.03(f) or otherwise when in conflict with a provision of this title, the Texas Rules of Civil Procedure govern proceedings under this title.

(b) Discovery in a proceeding under this title is governed by the Code of Criminal Procedure and by case decisions in criminal cases.

(c) Except as otherwise provided by this title, the Texas Rules of Evidence applicable to criminal cases and Chapter 38, Code of Criminal Procedure, apply in a judicial proceeding under this title.

(d) When on the motion for appointment of an interpreter by a party or on the motion of the juvenile court, in any proceeding under this title, the court determines that the child, the child's parent or guardian, or a witness does not understand and speak English, an interpreter must be sworn to interpret for the person as provided by Article 38.30, Code of Criminal Procedure.

(e) In any proceeding under this title, if a party notifies the court that the child, the child's parent or guardian, or a witness is deaf, the court shall appoint a qualified interpreter to interpret the proceedings in any language, including sign language, that the deaf person can understand, as provided by Article 38.31, Code of Criminal Procedure.

(f) Any requirement under this title that a document contain a person's signature, including the signature of a judge or a clerk of the court, is satisfied if the document contains the signature of the person as captured on an electronic device or as a digital signature. Article 2.26, Code of Criminal Procedure, applies in a proceeding held under this title.

History: Amended by 78th Legis., Reg. Sess. (2003), H.B. 2319, eff. Sept. 1, 2003. Applies only to conduct occurring on or after effective date.

Comment

The legislature in 1995 changed the discovery rules from civil to criminal. Thus, the primary sources of discovery law in juvenile cases is chapter 39 of the Tex. Code Crim. Proc. Ann. and the caselaw dealing with the prosecutor's obligations under due process of law to disclose exculpatory and mitigatory material to the defense, rather than the Rules of Civil Procedure.

The legislature in 1995 also changed the source of evidence law from the Rules of Evidence to the Rules of Criminal Evidence, now the integrated Texas Rules of Evidence. If there is a difference between civil and criminal rules under the integrated Rules, the criminal version controls.

With those two exceptions, the Rules of Civil Procedure govern procedure in the absence of a specific provision in the Family Code.

The additions of subsections (d) and (e) in 2003 require the appointment of language interpreters and interpreters for the deaf under the same circumstances as in criminal cases. The addition of subsection (f) permits digital signatures to be employed to the same extent they can be used in criminal cases.

CLE/Other Legal Publications

What Is So Special About Juvenile Law? Scott K. Stevens, 13TH ANN. JUVE. L. CONF. (Feb. 2000)

Evidence Issues in Juvenile Hearings. Mike Coulson & Rebecca Coulson, 13TH ANN. JUVE. L. CONF. (Feb. 2000)

Leading Case

S.D.G. v. State, 936 S.W.2d 371 (Tex. App.—Houston [14th Dist.] 1996, writ denied) (civil discovery rules are incompatible with juvenile proceedings)

---

§ 51.18. Election Between Juvenile Court and Alternate Juvenile Court.

(a) This section applies only to a child who has a right to a trial before a juvenile court the judge of which is not an attorney licensed in this state.

(b) On any matter that may lead to an order appealable under Section 56.01 of this code, a child may be tried before either the juvenile court or the alternate juvenile court.

(c) The child may elect to be tried before the alternate juvenile court only if the child files a written notice with that court not later than 10 days before the date of the trial. After the notice is filed, the child may be tried only in the alternate juvenile court. If the child does not file a notice as provided by this subsection, the child may be tried only in the juvenile court.

(d) If the child is tried before the juvenile court, the child is not entitled to a trial de novo before the alternate juvenile court.

(e) The child may appeal any order of the juvenile court or alternate juvenile court only as provided by Section 56.01 of this code.

§ 51.19. Limitation Periods.

(a) The limitation periods and the procedures for applying the limitation periods under Chapter 12, Code of Criminal Procedure, and other statutory law apply to proceedings under this title.

(b) For purposes of computing a limitation period, a petition filed in juvenile court for a transfer or an adjudication hearing is equivalent to an indictment or information and is treated as presented when the petition is filed in the proper court.

(c) The limitation period is two years for an offense or conduct that is not given a specific limitation period under Chapter 12, Code of Criminal Procedure, or other statutory law.

Comment

This section specifies that criminal statutes of limitation, as provided by Chapter 12 of the TEX. CODE CRIM. PROC. ANN. or elsewhere in connection with the statutory definition of the offense, apply to juvenile proceedings despite their legal character as civil proceedings. The residuary limitations period is 2 years.

---

§ 51.20. Physical or Mental Examination.

(a) At any stage of the proceedings under this title, the juvenile court may order a child who is referred to the juvenile court or who is alleged by a petition or found to have engaged in delinquent conduct or conduct indicating a need for supervision to be examined by **a disinterested** [~~the local mental health or mental retardation authority or another appropriate~~] expert, including a physician, psychiatrist, or psychologist**, qualified by education and clinical training in mental health or mental retardation and experienced in forensic evaluation, to determine whether the child has a mental illness as defined by Section 571.003, Health and Safety Code, or is a person with mental retardation as defined by Section 591.003, Health and Safety Code. If the examination is to include a determination of the child's fitness to proceed, an expert may be appointed to conduct the examination only if the expert is qualified under Subchapter B, Chapter 46B, Code of Criminal Procedure, to examine a defendant in a criminal case, and the examination and the report resulting from an examination under this subsection must comply with the requirements under Subchapter B, Chapter 46B, Code of Criminal Procedure, for the examination and resulting report of a defendant in a criminal case**.

(b) If, after conducting an examination of a child ordered under Subsection (a) and reviewing any other relevant information, there is reason to believe that the child has a mental illness or mental retardation, the probation department shall refer the child to the local mental health or mental retardation authority for evaluation and services, unless the prosecuting attorney has filed a petition under Section 53.04.

History: Amended by 78th Legis., Reg. Sess. (2003), S.B. 1057, eff. Jan. 1, 2004. Applies only to competency proceedings not initiated before the effective date.

Comment

This section authorizes a judge to order an appropriate physical or mental examination of any child who is in the juvenile system. The section is placed here because it is of general applicability and is not limited to Chapter 55 proceedings. Thus, for example, this section would authorize a judge to require a physical examination prior to a child being admitted to a boot camp. Subsection (a) also makes it clear that the authority to order an examination is not dependent upon whether a petition has been filed.

The 2003 amendments to subsection (a) were made by the bill that re-wrote the criminal provisions dealing with competency to stand trial. These amendments establish standards for mental health or retardation examiners and for fitness to stand trial examinations.

Subsection (b) addresses the situation in which a child referred to the juvenile court may be mentally ill or retarded. It places on the probation department the responsibility to refer such a child for services if the case is in a pre-petition status. This provision furthers the overall Family Code policy to facilitate treatment for mental illness or mental retardation of children in the juvenile justice system.

CLE/Other Legal Publications

Mental Illness Screening at Juvenile Court Intake. Marilee Manning & Lorie Smith, 16 Juve. L. Sect. Rpt. (Jun. 2002)

Texas Special Needs Diversionary Programs: A Team Approach to Contending With Mental Illness in Juvenile Offenders. Stephanie Dreyer, 16 Juve. L. Sect. Rpt. (Jun. 2002)

Chapter 52. Proceedings Before and Including Referral to Juvenile Court.

Introductory Comment

Chapter 52 deals with police work with juveniles, including the circumstances under which police may take juveniles into custody and what may be done with juveniles taken into custody.

---

§ 52.01. Taking into Custody; Issuance of Warning Notice.

(a) A child may be taken into custody:

(1) pursuant to an order of the juvenile court under the provisions of this subtitle;

(2) pursuant to the laws of arrest;

(3) by a law-enforcement officer, including a school district peace officer commissioned under Section 37.081, Education Code, if there is probable cause to believe that the child has engaged in:

(A) conduct that violates a penal law of this state or a penal ordinance of any political subdivision of this state; [~~or~~]

(B) delinquent conduct or conduct indicating a need for supervision; **or**

(C) conduct that violates a condition of probation imposed by the juvenile court;

(4) by a probation officer if there is probable cause to believe that the child has violated a condition of probation imposed by the juvenile court; or

(5) pursuant to a directive to apprehend issued as provided by Section 52.015.

(b) The taking of a child into custody is not an arrest except for the purpose of determining the validity of taking him into custody or the validity of a search under the laws and constitution of this state or of the United States.

(c) A law-enforcement officer authorized to take a child into custody under Subdivisions (2) and (3) of Subsection (a) of this section may issue a warning notice to the child in lieu of taking the child into custody if:

(1) guidelines for warning disposition have been issued by the law-enforcement agency in which the officer works;

(2) the guidelines have been approved by the juvenile **board** [~~court~~] of the county in which the disposition is made;

(3) the disposition is authorized by the guidelines;

(4) the warning notice identifies the child and describes the child's alleged conduct;

(5) a copy of the warning notice is sent to the child's parent, guardian, or custodian as soon as practicable after disposition; and

(6) a copy of the warning notice is filed with the law-enforcement agency and the office or official designated by the juvenile board.

(d) A warning notice filed with the office or official designated by the juvenile board may be used as the basis of further action if necessary.

History: Amended by 78th Legis., Reg. Sess. (2003), H.B. 2319, eff. Sept. 1, 2003. Applies only to conduct occurring on or after effective date.

Comment

Subsection (a) permits a juvenile to be taken into custody under five circumstances: (1) when the juvenile court has endorsed a custody order on the summons that accompanies a juvenile petition, (2) pursuant to the laws of arrest for adults, (3) if there is probable cause to believe the child engaged in delinquent conduct or conduct indicating a need for supervision, (4) by a probation officer if there is probable cause to believe that probation has been violated, or (5) pursuant to a juvenile court's directive to apprehend (juvenile arrest warrant). A 2003 amendment added a sixth circumstance: a law enforcement officer may take a child into custody without a warrant for a violation of judicial probation.

Subsections (c) and (d) permit law enforcement officers to issue warning notices (like traffic citations) in lieu of taking the child into custody.

CLE/Other Legal Publications

School Related Issues. Chris Hubner, 17TH ANN. JUVE. L. CONF. (Feb. 2004)

Search and Seizure. Pat Garza, 16TH ANN. JUVE. L. CONF. (Feb. 2003)

The Juvenile Arrest Process. Pat Garza, 14TH ANN. JUVE. L. CONF. (Feb. 2001)

Arrest, Search and Seizure. Pat Garza, 13TH ANN. JUVE. L. CONF. (Feb. 2000)

School Search and Seizure. Pat Garza, 13 JUVE. L. SECT. RPT. (June 1999)

Leading Cases/Att'y Gen. Op.

Cornealius v. State, 900 S.W.2d 731 (Tex. Crim. App. 1995) (juvenile arrest without warrant valid under Family Code; warrant not required for arrest on front porch)

Coronado v. State, 835 S.W.2d 636 (Tex. Crim. App. 1992) (school search unconstitutional)

Lanes v. State, 767 S.W.2d 789 (Tex. Crim. App. 1989) (juvenile arrest requires probable cause)

Vasquez v. State, 739 S.W.2d 37 (Tex. Crim. App. 1987), *reh'g denied*, 816 S.W.2d 750 (Tex. Crim. App. 1991) (arrest of juvenile governed by Family Code, not Code of Criminal Procedure.)

Russell v. State, 74 S.W.3d 887 (Tex.App.—Waco, pet. refused) (search of pocket of baggy trousers worn on school campus lawful without probable cause or a warrant)

In re D.G., 96 S.W.3d 465 (Tex.App.—Austin 2002, no pet.) (talking to juvenile was voluntary encounter, not stop, and search that uncovered crack was consensual)

In re J.D., 68 S.W.3d 775 (Tex. App.—San Antonio 2001, rev. denied) (warrantless search of juvenile's home justified as an emergency)

Wilcher v. State, 876 S.W.2d 466 (Tex. App.—El Paso 1994, no writ) (school search based on weapon report valid)

Garcia v. State, 661 S.W.2d 754 (Tex. App.—Beaumont 1983, no writ) (Family Code authorization to arrest without a warrant does not violate equal protection)

Op. Tex. Att'y Gen. No. DM–294 (1994) (scope of school notification requirements)

Op. Tex. Att'y Gen. LO–94–058 (1994) (authority to arrest for truancy)

Cross References

TEX. CODE CRIM. PROC. ANN. ch. 14 and art. 18.16. Laws governing arrests of adults.

Education Code § 37.081. School district peace officers.

§ 52.015. Directive to Apprehend.

(a) On the request of a law-enforcement or probation officer, a juvenile court may issue a directive to apprehend a child if the court finds there is probable cause to take the child into custody under the provisions of this title.

(b) On the issuance of a directive to apprehend, any law-enforcement or probation officer shall take the child into custody.

(c) An order under this section is not subject to appeal.

Comment

A directive to apprehend is an arrest warrant issued by a juvenile court to take a child into custody for a criminal offense or for non-criminal prohibited conduct, such as running away from home or a technical violation of probation. Of course, if otherwise authorized by law, an arrest warrant can also be issued for a juvenile.

§ 52.02. Release or Delivery to Court.

(a) Except as provided by Subsection (c), a person taking a child into custody, without unnecessary delay and without first taking the child to any place other than a juvenile processing office designated under Section 52.025, shall do one of the following:

(1) release the child to a parent, guardian, custodian of the child, or other responsible adult upon that person's promise to bring the child before the juvenile court as requested by the court;

(2) bring the child before the office or official designated by the juvenile board if there is probable cause to believe that the child engaged in delinquent conduct, [~~or~~] conduct indicating a need for supervision, **or conduct that violates a condition of probation imposed by the juvenile court**;

(3) bring the child to a detention facility designated by the juvenile board;

(4) bring the child to a secure detention facility as provided by Section 51.12(j);

(5) bring the child to a medical facility if the child is believed to suffer from a serious physical condition or illness that requires prompt treatment; or

(6) dispose of the case under Section 52.03.

(b) A person taking a child into custody shall promptly give notice of the person's action and a statement of the reason for taking the child into custody, to:

(1) the child's parent, guardian, or custodian; and

(2) the office or official designated by the juvenile board.

(c) A person who takes a child into custody and who has reasonable grounds to believe that the child has been operating a motor vehicle in a public place while having any detectable amount of alcohol in the child's system may, before complying with Subsection (a):

(1) take the child to a place to obtain a specimen of the child's breath or blood as provided by Chapter 724, Transportation Code; and

(2) perform intoxilyzer processing and videotaping of the child in an adult processing office of a law enforcement agency.

(d) Notwithstanding Section 51.09(a), a child taken into custody as provided by Subsection (c) may submit to the taking of a breath specimen or refuse to submit to the taking of a breath specimen without the concurrence of an attorney, but only if the request made of the child to give the specimen and the child's response to that request is videotaped. A videotape made under this subsection must be maintained until the disposition of any proceeding against the child relating to the arrest is final and be made available to an attorney representing the child during that period.

History: Amended by 78th Legis., Reg. Sess. (2003), H.B. 2319, eff. Sept. 1, 2003. Applies only to conduct occurring on or after effective date.

Comment

Subsection (a) requires a law enforcement officer who has taken a child into custody immediately to dispose of the case in one of six different ways: (1) take the child to the juvenile processing office designated by the juvenile board, (2) release the child to a parent or other responsible adult, (3) bring the child to the office or official designated by the juvenile board, (4) bring the child to the designated detention facility, (5) bring the child to a medical facility for treatment of physical condition or illness, or (6) dispose of the case without referral to the juvenile court as authorized by § 52.03.

Subsection (b) requires notice to the child's parent and to the office designated by the juvenile board that the child has been taken into custody.

Subsections (c) and (d) authorize bringing a child who has been taken into custody for driving under the influence of alcohol to an adult processing facility but only for the purpose of taking a blood sample, administering an intoxilyzer test or being videotaped. The child is permitted to waive or assert his or her rights regarding taking an intoxilyzer without the concurrence of an attorney, but the offering of the intoxilyzer and the child's response must be videotaped.

CLE/Other Legal Publications

Notification to Parents of Juveniles—New Law Gives Parents the Right to be Informed and the Right to Access to the Juvenile—And the Results of Gonzales v. State. Ellen Hamilton Baugh, 17 Juve. L. Sect. Rpt. (Dec. 2003)

Leading Cases

Hampton v. State, 86 S.W.3d 603 (Tex. Crim. App. 2002) (requiring parental notice of reason for taking into custody doesn't require notice of interrogation purpose)

Gonzales v. State, 67 S.W.3d 910 (Tex. Crim. App. 2002) (failure to notify parents of arrest doesn't require exclusion absent proof of a causal connection)

Roquemore v. State, 60 S.W.3d 862 (Tex. Crim. App. 2001) (detour to recover stolen property on way to processing office violates Family Code)

Contreras v. State, 67 S.W.3d 181 (Tex. Crim. App. 2001) (50 minute delay to secure murder scene not unnecessary)

Le v. State, 993 S.W.2d 650 (Tex. Crim. App. 1999) (failure to take juvenile from processing office to approved place invalidates confession)

Comer v. State, 776 S.W.2d 191 (Tex. Crim. App. 1989) (taking child to Justice of the Peace, who had not been designated, made confession inadmissible; consent of juvenile court to interrogation required)

Pham v. State, 125 S.W.3d 622 (Tex.App.—Houston [1st Dist.] 2003, no pet.) (burden to show causal connection between failure to notify parents and confession is on juvenile respondent)

State v. Simpson, 105 S.W.3d 238 (Tex.App.—Tyler, 2003, no pet.) (delay in notifying parents of arrest invalidated confession under causal connection rule of *Gonzales*)

Dang v. State, 99 S.W.3d 172 (Tex.App.—Houston [14th Dist.] 2002, no pet.) (three hour delay before transporting detained juvenile to station OK because he was not in custody until transported)

In re J.B.J., 86 S.W.3d 810 (Tex.App.—Beaumont 2002, no pet.) (parental notification one and one-half hours after taking into custody prompt when prior efforts failed)

Vann v. State, 93 S.W.3d 182 (Tex.App.—Houston [14th Dist.] 2002, pet. refused) (arrest notice can be given to adult cousin as custodian; two and one-half hour delay OK)

In re J.D., 68 S.W.3d 775 (Tex. App.—San Antonio 2001, rev. denied) (delay in taking juvenile to processing office justified by need to secure the scene of the arrest)

In re E.M.R., 55 S.W.3d 712 (Tex. App.—Corpus Christi 2001, no pet.) (parental notification requirement doesn't apply to juvenile questioned when not in custody)

State v. Langley, 852 S.W.2d 708 (Tex. App.—Corpus Christi 1993, pet. ref'd) (telephone conversation with juvenile probation officer does not comply with *Comer*)

---

§ 52.025. Designation of Juvenile Processing Office.

(a) The juvenile board may designate an office or a room, which may be located in a police facility or sheriff's offices, as the juvenile processing office for the temporary detention of a child taken into custody under Section 52.01. The office may not be a cell or holding facility used for detentions other than detentions under this section. The juvenile board by written order may prescribe the conditions of the designation and limit the activities that may occur in the office during the temporary detention.

(b) A child may be detained in a juvenile processing office only for:

(1) the return of the child to the custody of a person under Section 52.02(a)(1);

(2) the completion of essential forms and records required by the juvenile court or this title;

(3) the photographing and fingerprinting of the child if otherwise authorized at the time of temporary detention by this title;

(4) the issuance of warnings to the child as required or permitted by this title; or

(5) the receipt of a statement by the child under Section 51.095(a)(1), (2), (3), or (5).

(c) A child may not be left unattended in a juvenile processing office and is entitled to be accompanied by the child's parent, guardian, or other custodian or by the child's attorney.

(d) A child may not be detained in a juvenile processing office for longer than six hours.

Comment

This section, added in 1991, is intended to deal with *Comer v. State*, 776 S.W.2d 191 (Tex. Crim. App. 1989), in which a conviction of capital murder was reversed because a confession had been admitted into evidence that had been taken in violation of § 52.02. A statement of a child taken in a juvenile processing office designated by a juvenile board will not be excluded from evidence because of a § 52.02 violation. The child can be detained in such an office only for a maximum period of six hours, reflecting federal limitations on the time a juvenile can be detained in a secure adult detention facility.

CLE/Other Legal Publications

The Role of the Juvenile Probation Officer Under Comer. Dan Quinn, 10 Juve. L. Sect. Rpt. (March 1996)

The Designation and Use of Juvenile Processing Offices. Quyen H. Khuong, 6 Juve. L. Sect. Rpt. (June 1992)

Leading Cases/Att'y Gen. Op.

Anthony v. State, 954 S.W.2d 132 (Tex. App.—San Antonio 1997, no writ) (order designating entire police station not specific enough to be valid)

Wilson v. State, 948 S.W.2d 21 (Tex. App.—Eastland 1997, pet. ref'd) (permission of probation department for interrogation in processing office not required)

In re R.R., 931 S.W.2d 11 (Tex. App.—Corpus Christi 1996, no writ) (confession excluded because police did not use juvenile processing office)

Smith v. State, 881 S.W.2d 727 (Tex. App.—Houston [1st Dist.] 1994, no writ) (confession admissible because police station designated as processing office)

Op. Tex. Att'y Gen. LO–93–38 (1993) (juvenile court may designate multiple juvenile processing offices in a county)

---

§ 52.026. Responsibility for Transporting Juvenile Offenders.

(a) It shall be the duty of the law enforcement officer who has taken a child into custody to transport the child to the appropriate detention facility if the child is not released to the parent, guardian, or custodian of the child.

(b) If the juvenile detention facility is located outside the county in which the child is taken into custody, it shall be the duty of the law enforcement officer who has taken the child into custody or, if authorized by the commissioners court of the county, the sheriff of that county to transport the child to the appropriate juvenile detention facility unless the child is:

(1) detained in a secure detention facility under Section 51.12(j); or

(2) released to the parent, guardian, or custodian of the child.

(c) On adoption of an order by the juvenile board and approval of the juvenile board's order by record vote of the commissioners court, it shall be the duty of the sheriff of the county in which the child is taken into custody to transport the child to and from all scheduled juvenile court proceedings and appearances and other activities ordered by the juvenile court.

Comment

This section places responsibility for transporting juveniles primarily in the hands of law-enforcement officers. It abrogates Op. Tex. Att'y Gen. No. DM–87 (1992) that opined law enforcement could not be required to provide such transportation service to the juvenile court. A 1999 amendment to subsection (b) places primary responsibility on the law enforcement officer who took the child into custody to transport the child to an out-of-county juvenile detention facility.

Leading Att'y Gen. Op.

Op. Tex. Att'y Gen. LO–94–065 (1994) (sheriff is required to transport juveniles only upon juvenile court order and commissioner's court approval)

---

§ 52.027. [~~Children Taken into Custody for Traffic Offenses, Other Fineable Only Offenses, of as a Status Offender.~~] [repealed]

History: Repealed by 78th Legis., Reg. Sess. (2003), H.B. 2319 and H.B. 3507, eff. Sept. 1, 2003. Applies only to conduct occurring on or after effective date.

Comment

Section 52.027 is repealed by HB 2319, Section 61(l). In 2001, SB 1432, which re-wrote the laws regarding justice and municipal court proceedings involving juveniles, repealed this section, revised it somewhat, and re-enacted it as article 45.058 of the Code of Criminal Procedure. However, the same language was enacted as this section by another bill. The result of the 2001 legislation was to make 52.027 redundant to article 45.058, which is why it was repealed in 2003.

Cross Reference

Code of Criminal Procedure art. 45.058.

CLE/Other Legal Publication

Places of Nonsecure Custody for the Processing of Juveniles Taken Into Custody for Fineable Only Misdemeanors. Celeste May, 12 JUVE. L. SECT. RPT. (Dec. 1998)

---

§ 52.028. [repealed]

Comment

This section provided a place of non-secure custody for juvenile curfew violators. The head of a law enforcement agency was permitted to designate the same places as both curfew processing offices and places of non-secure custody, or could designate separate places for those two purposes.

In 2001, this section was repealed, revised slightly, and re-enacted as article 45.059 of the Code of Criminal Procedure by SB 1432.

CLE/Other Legal Publication

Day-Time Curfews and Truancy Programs in Texas. David Lauritzen, 9 JUVE. L. SECT. RPT. (June 1995)

Cross References

TEX. LOCAL GOV'T CODE ANN. § 341.904. General Law Municipality May Adopt Curfew Ordinance; § 351.903. County May Adopt Curfew Order for Unincorporated Areas; § 370.002. Curfew Ordinance or Order Must Be Reviewed and Re-enacted Each 3 Years.

---

§ 52.03. Disposition Without Referral to Court.

(a) A law-enforcement officer authorized by this title to take a child into custody may dispose of the case of a child taken into custody without referral to juvenile court, if:

(1) guidelines for such disposition have been adopted by the juvenile board of the county in which the disposition is made as required by Section 52.032;

(2) the disposition is authorized by the guidelines; and

(3) the officer makes a written report of the officer's disposition to the law-enforcement agency, identifying the child and specifying the grounds for believing that the taking into custody was authorized.

(b) No disposition authorized by this section may involve:

(1) keeping the child in law-enforcement custody; or

(2) requiring periodic reporting of the child to a law-enforcement officer, law-enforcement agency, or other agency.

(c) A disposition authorized by this section may involve:

(1) referral of the child to an agency other than the juvenile court;

(2) a brief conference with the child and his parent, guardian, or custodian; or

(3) referral of the child and the child's parent, guardian, or custodian for services under Section 264.302.

(d) Statistics indicating the number and kind of dispositions made by a law-enforcement agency under the authority of this section shall be reported at least annually to the office or official designated by the juvenile board, as ordered by the **board** [~~court~~].

History: Amended by 78th Legis., Reg. Sess. (2003), H.B. 2319, eff. Sept. 1, 2003. Applies only to conduct occurring on or after effective date.

Comment

About one-quarter of all juveniles taken into custody by police are not referred to the juvenile courts. These cases, usually very minor in seriousness, are disposed of under this section or the next.

A 1999 amendment requires juvenile boards to promulgate guidelines for informal disposition. *See* § 52.032.

Cross Reference

TEX. FAM. CODE § 264.302. Early Youth Intervention Services of Texas Department of Protective and Regulatory Services.

---

§ 52.031. First Offender Program.

(a) A juvenile board may establish a first offender program under this section for the referral and disposition of children taken into custody for:

(1) conduct indicating a need for supervision; or

(2) delinquent conduct other than conduct that constitutes:

(A) a felony of the first, second, or third degree, an aggravated controlled substance felony, or a capital felony; or

(B) a state jail felony or misdemeanor involving violence to a person or the use or possession of a firearm, illegal knife, or club, as those terms are defined by Section 46.01, Penal Code, or a prohibited weapon, as described by Section 46.05, Penal Code.

(b) Each juvenile board in the county in which a first offender program is established shall designate one or more law enforcement officers and agencies, which may be law enforcement agencies, to process a child under the first offender program.

(c) The disposition of a child under the first offender program may not take place until guidelines for the disposition have been adopted by the juvenile board of the county in which the disposition is made as required by Section 52.032.

(d) A law enforcement officer taking a child into custody may refer the child to the law enforcement officer or agency designated under Subsection (b) for disposition under the first offender program and not refer the child to juvenile court only if:

(1) the child has not previously been adjudicated as having engaged in delinquent conduct;

(2) the referral complies with guidelines for disposition under Subsection (c); and

(3) the officer reports in writing the referral to the agency, identifying the child and specifying the grounds for taking the child into custody.

(e) A child referred for disposition under the first offender program may not be detained in law enforcement custody.

(f) The parent, guardian, or other custodian of the child must receive notice that the child has been referred for disposition under the first offender program. The notice must:

(1) state the grounds for taking the child into custody;

(2) identify the law enforcement officer or agency to which the child was referred;

(3) briefly describe the nature of the program; and

(4) state that the child's failure to complete the program will result in the child being referred to the juvenile court.

(g) The child and the parent, guardian, or other custodian of the child must consent to participation by the child in the first offender program.

(h) Disposition under a first offender program may include:

(1) voluntary restitution by the child or the parent, guardian, or other custodian of the child to the victim of the conduct of the child;

(2) voluntary community service restitution by the child;

(3) educational, vocational training, counseling, or other rehabilitative services; and

(4) periodic reporting by the child to the law enforcement officer or agency to which the child has been referred.

(i) The case of a child who successfully completes the first offender program is closed and may not be referred to juvenile court, unless the child is taken into custody under circumstances described by Subsection (j)(3).

(j) The case of a child referred for disposition under the first offender program shall be referred to juvenile court if:

(1) the child fails to complete the program;

(2) the child or the parent, guardian, or other custodian of the child terminates the child's participation in the program before the child completes it; or

(3) the child completes the program but is taken into custody under Section 52.01 before the 90th day after the date the child completes the program for conduct other than the conduct for which the child was referred to the first offender program.

(k) A statement made by a child to a person giving advice or supervision or participating in the first offender program may not be used against the child in any proceeding under this title or any criminal proceeding.

(l) The law enforcement agency must report to the juvenile board in December of each year the following:

(1) the last known address of the child, including the census tract;

(2) the gender and ethnicity of the child referred to the program; and

(3) the offense committed by the child.

Comment

The first offender program described by this section is a particular version of the more general program authorized by § 52.03. This section was enacted in 1995.

A 1999 amendment reflects the shift in responsibility to promulgate guidelines from the law enforcement agency to the juvenile board. *See* § 52.032.

CLE/Other Legal Publication

First Offender Programs: Working to Remove the Criminal Tendency from Juveniles. Susan Frances Hatcher, 12 Juve. L. Sect. Rpt. (June 1998)

---

§ 52.032. Informal Disposition Guidelines.

The juvenile board of each county, in cooperation with each law enforcement agency in the county, shall adopt guidelines for the disposition of a child under Section 52.03 or 52.031. The guidelines adopted under this section shall not be considered mandatory.

Comment

This 1999 section requires juvenile boards to promulgate non-binding guidelines for informal disposition or first offender programs. The purpose of the section is to encourage more law enforcement agencies to use such programs.

---

§ 52.04. Referral to Juvenile Court; Notice to Parents.

(a) The following shall accompany referral of a child or a child's case to the office or official designated by the juvenile board or be provided as quickly as possible after referral:

(1) all information in the possession of the person or agency making the referral pertaining to the identity of the child and the child's address, the name and address of the child's parent, guardian, or custodian, the names and addresses of any witnesses, and the child's present whereabouts;

(2) a complete statement of the circumstances of the alleged delinquent conduct or conduct indicating a need for supervision;

(3) when applicable, a complete statement of the circumstances of taking the child into custody; and

(4) when referral is by an officer of a law-enforcement agency, a complete statement of all prior contacts with the child by officers of that law-enforcement agency.

(b) The office or official designated by the juvenile board may refer the case to a law-enforcement agency for the purpose of conducting an investigation to obtain necessary information.

(c) If the office of the prosecuting attorney is designated by the juvenile court to conduct the preliminary investigation under Section 53.01, the referring entity shall first transfer the child's case to the juvenile probation department for statistical reporting purposes only. On the creation of a statistical record or file for the case, the probation department shall within three business days forward the case to the prosecuting attorney for review under Section 53.01.

(d) On referral of the case of a child who has not been taken into custody to the office or official designated by the juvenile **board** [~~court~~], the office or official designated by the juvenile **board** [~~court~~] shall promptly give notice of the referral and a statement of the reason for the referral to the child's parent, guardian, or custodian.

History: Amended by 78th Legis., Reg. Sess. (2003), H.B. 2319, eff. Sept. 1, 2003. Applies only to conduct occurring on or after effective date.

Comment

Subsection (a) specifies the information that must accompany the referral of a case to the juvenile court. Subsection (b) permits court intake to return a case to law enforcement for further investigation, which may include interrogation of the juvenile under specified procedures.

Subsection (c) requires that all referrals be made to the juvenile probation department for statistics-gathering purposes even if the prosecutor exercises the intake function in the county.

Subsection (d), added in 2001, requires that intake notify parents when a child has been referred to the court without being in custody.

---

§ 52.041. Referral of Child to Juvenile Court After Expulsion.

(a) A school district that expels a child shall refer the child to juvenile court in the county in which the child resides.

(b) The board of the school district or a person designated by the board shall deliver a copy of the order expelling the student and any other information required by Section 52.04 on or before the second working day after the date of the expulsion hearing to the authorized officer of the juvenile court.

(c) Within five working days of receipt of an expulsion notice under this section by the office or official designated by the juvenile board, a preliminary investigation and determination shall be conducted as required by Section 53.01.

(d) The office or official designated by the juvenile board shall within two working days notify the school district that expelled the child if:

(1) a determination was made under Section 53.01 that the person referred to juvenile court was not a child within the meaning of this title;

(2) a determination was made that no probable cause existed to believe the child engaged in delinquent conduct or conduct indicating a need for supervision;

(3) no deferred prosecution or formal court proceedings have been or will be initiated involving the child;

(4) the court or jury finds that the child did not engage in delinquent conduct or conduct indicating a need for supervision and the case has been dismissed with prejudice; or

(5) the child was adjudicated but no disposition was or will be ordered by the court.

(e) In any county where a juvenile justice alternative education program is operated, no student shall be expelled without written notification by the board of the school district or its designated agent to the juvenile board's designated representative. The notification shall be made not later than two business days following the board's determination that the student is to be expelled. Failure to timely notify the designated representative of the juvenile board shall result in the child's duty to continue attending the school district's educational program, which shall be provided to that child until such time as the notification to the juvenile board's designated representative is properly made.

Comment

This section enacts the principle that each child expelled from school must be referred to the juvenile court to determine whether juvenile court action is needed. Education Code § 37.010 contains a similar provision.

Subsection (c) requires the juvenile court to complete its investigation of the case within five working days of receiving the referral and expulsion notice. Subsection (d) requires the juvenile court to notify the school district within two working days if the case on which the expulsion was based terminated without an adjudication and disposition. Subsection (e) provides that in a county with a juvenile justice alternative education program an expulsion is not legally effective until the juvenile system is notified of the expulsion.

CLE/Other Legal Publication

Implementation of SB 1 Juvenile Justice Alternative Education Programs. Cheryl Holder, 11 Juve. L. Sect. Rpt. (No. 4, Dec. 1997)

Chapter 53. Proceedings Prior to Judicial Proceedings.

Introductory Comment

Chapter 53 deals with that phase of the juvenile system beginning with referral to the court and ending with judicial proceedings. The scope of the determinate sentence act is in this chapter, as are the requirements of the petition and summons.

---

§ 53.01. Preliminary Investigation and Determinations; Notice to Parents.

(a) On referral of a person believed to be a child or on referral of the person's case to the office or official designated by the juvenile board, the intake officer, probation officer, or other person authorized by the **board** [~~court~~] shall conduct a preliminary investigation to determine whether:

(1) the person referred to juvenile court is a child within the meaning of this title; and

(2) there is probable cause to believe the person:

(A) engaged in delinquent conduct or conduct indicating a need for supervision; **or**

(B) is a nonoffender who has been taken into custody and is being held solely for deportation out of the United States.

(b) If it is determined that the person is not a child or there is no probable cause, the person shall immediately be released.

(c) When custody of a child is given to the office or official designated by the juvenile board, the intake officer, probation officer, or other person authorized by the **board** [~~court~~] shall promptly give notice of the whereabouts of the child and a statement of the reason the child was taken into custody to the child's parent, guardian, or custodian unless the notice given under Section 52.02(b) provided fair notice of the child's present whereabouts.

(d) Unless the juvenile board approves a written procedure proposed by the office of prosecuting attorney and chief juvenile probation officer which provides otherwise, if it is determined that the person is a child and, regardless of a finding of probable cause, or a lack thereof, there is an allegation that the child engaged in delinquent conduct of the grade of felony, or conduct constituting a misdemeanor offense involving violence to a person or the use or possession of a firearm, illegal knife, or club, as those terms are defined by Section 46.01, Penal Code, or prohibited weapon, as described by Section

46.05, Penal Code, the case shall be promptly forwarded to the office of the prosecuting attorney, accompanied by:

(1) all documents that accompanied the current referral; and

(2) a summary of all prior referrals of the child to the juvenile court, juvenile probation department, or a detention facility.

(e) If a juvenile board adopts an alternative referral plan under Subsection (d), the board shall register the plan with the Texas Juvenile Probation Commission.

(f) A juvenile board may not adopt an alternate referral plan that does not require the forwarding of a child's case to the prosecuting attorney as provided by Subsection (d) if probable cause exists to believe that the child engaged in delinquent conduct that violates Section 19.03, Penal Code (capital murder), or Section 19.02, Penal Code (murder).

History: Amended by 78th Legis., Reg. Sess. (2003), H.B. 2319, eff. Sept. 1, 2003. Applies only to conduct occurring on or after effective date.

Comment

This is the "gatekeeping" requirement. A case referred to the juvenile court must be subjected to an intake inquiry. There, the intake worker must determine that the person referred is a child as defined in Title 3 and that there is probable cause to believe he or she committed delinquent conduct or conduct indicating a need for supervision. Unless these findings are made, the child must be immediately released from custody and all proceedings terminated.

Unless a local agreement provides otherwise, if the referral is for a felony, an offense involving violence, or a weapon offense, the case must be referred with proper documentation to the prosecutor for a decision whether to file a petition or to handle the matter nonjudicially. Referral to the prosecutor is required even if the intake officer has made a finding of no probable case. Cases that fall outside the scope of mandatory prosecutorial referral may continue to be handled nonjudicially by intake as before the 1995 enactment of intake power-sharing.

The 2003 amendment to subsection (a) is intended to make unlawful the confinement of alien juveniles for the sole purpose of facilitating their deportation. It should be read in conjunction with Section 54.011(f).

CLE/Other Legal Publications

A Change in Juvenile Intake Law: Shouldn't Juvenile Prosecution Mean Prosecution? Leslie Webb, 12 Juve. L. Sect. Rpt. (March 1998)

H.B. 327 and the STAR Programs: A Reprieve from the Get Tough Policy in Texas. Ellen Yeager, 10 Juve. L. Sect. Rpt. (June 1996)

---

§ 53.012. Review by Prosecutor.

(a) The prosecuting attorney shall promptly review the circumstances and allegations of a referral made under Section 53.01 for legal sufficiency and the desirability of prosecution and may file a petition without regard to whether probable cause was found under Section 53.01.

(b) If the prosecuting attorney does not file a petition requesting the adjudication of the child referred to the prosecuting attorney, the prosecuting attorney shall:

(1) terminate all proceedings, if the reason is for lack of probable cause; or

(2) return the referral to the juvenile probation department for further proceedings.

(c) The juvenile probation department shall promptly refer a child who has been returned to the department under Subsection (b)(2) and who fails or refuses to participate in a program of the department to the prosecuting attorney for review of the child's case and determination of whether to file a petition.

Comment

The decision whether to file a petition rests exclusively with the prosecutor. If the prosecutor declines prosecution, the case is to be returned to probation for nonjudicial handling, unless the reason for declining to prosecute is lack of probable cause as determined by the prosecutor.

---

§ 53.013. Progressive Sanctions Program.

[~~(a)~~] Each juvenile board may adopt a progressive sanctions program using the **model** [~~guidelines~~] for progressive sanctions in Chapter 59.

[~~(b) A juvenile court or probation department that deviates from the guidelines under Section 59.003 shall state in writing the reasons for the deviation and submit the statement to the juvenile board regardless of whether the juvenile board has adopted a progressive sanctions program.~~]

History: Amended by 78th Legis., Reg. Sess. (2003), H.B. 888, eff. Sept. 1, 2003. Applies only to conduct occurring on or after effective date.

Comment

Chapter 59 establishes a set of progressive guidelines for the disposition of juvenile cases. Departure from the guidelines is permitted upon documentation as to the reason for the deviation.

A 2003 amendment relieves local authorities from the burdens of filing a deviation report because normal case documentation provides state officials with access to the same information. See Chapter 59 for more of this set of amendments.

---

§ 53.02. Release from Detention.

(a) If a child is brought before the court or delivered to a detention facility as authorized by Sections 51.12(a)(3) and (4), the intake or other authorized officer of the court shall immediately make an investigation and shall release the child unless it appears that his detention is warranted under Subsection (b). The release may be conditioned upon requirements reasonably necessary to insure the child's appearance at later proceedings, but the conditions of the release must be in writing and filed with the office or official designated by the court and a copy furnished to the child.

(b) A child taken into custody may be detained prior to hearing on the petition only if:

(1) the child is likely to abscond or be removed from the jurisdiction of the court;

(2) suitable supervision, care, or protection for the child is not being provided by a parent, guardian, custodian, or other person;

(3) the child has no parent, guardian, custodian, or other person able to return the child to the court when required;

(4) the child may be dangerous to himself or herself or the child may threaten the safety of the public if released;

(5) the child has previously been found to be a delinquent child or has previously been convicted of a penal offense punishable by a term in jail or prison and is likely to commit an offense if released; or

(6) the child's detention is required under Subsection (f).

(c) If the child is not released, a request for detention hearing shall be made and promptly presented to the court, and an informal detention hearing as provided in Section 54.01 of this code shall be held promptly, but not later than the time required by Section 54.01 of this code.

(d) A release of a child to an adult under Subsection (a) must be conditioned on the agreement of the adult to be subject to the jurisdiction of the juvenile court and to an order of contempt by the court if the adult, after notification, is unable to produce the child at later proceedings.

(e) Unless otherwise agreed in the memorandum of understanding under Section 37.011, Education Code, in a county with a population greater than 125,000, if a child being released under this section is expelled under Section 37.007, Education Code, the release shall be conditioned on the child's attending a juvenile justice alternative education program pending a deferred prosecution or formal court disposition of the child's case.

(f) A child who is alleged to have engaged in delinquent conduct and to have used, possessed, or exhibited a firearm, as defined by Section 46.01, Penal Code, in the commission of the offense shall be detained until the child is released at the direction of the judge of the juvenile court, a substitute judge authorized by Section 51.04(f), or a referee appointed under Section 51.04(g), including an oral direction by telephone, or until a detention hearing is held as required by Section 54.01.

Comment

This section authorizes intake workers to release a child from detention without the necessity of a detention hearing. The release must be conditioned on an adult agreeing to be responsible for producing the child in court when required upon pain of contempt.

Subsection (e) requires that a release from detention be accompanied by an order requiring a child to attend the JJAEP pending court hearing in a county of more than 125,000 people.

Subsection (f) requires detention for a firearms offense in a secure juvenile detention facility, or a secure adult facility under § 51.12, until the initial detention hearing or until released by order of a judge, referee, or magistrate. Offenses covered include all offenses committed with a firearm as well as illegal carrying or possessing a firearm.

§ 53.03. Deferred Prosecution.

(a) Subject to Subsections (e) and (g), if the preliminary investigation required by Section 53.01 of this code results in a determination that further proceedings in the case are authorized, the probation officer or other designated officer of the court, subject to the direction of the juvenile court, may advise the parties for a reasonable period of time not to exceed six months concerning deferred prosecution and rehabilitation of a child if:

(1) deferred prosecution would be in the interest of the public and the child;

(2) the child and his parent, guardian, or custodian consent with knowledge that consent is not obligatory; and

(3) the child and his parent, guardian, or custodian are informed that they may terminate the deferred prosecution at any point and petition the court for a court hearing in the case.

(b) Except as otherwise permitted by this title, the child may not be detained during or as a result of the deferred prosecution process.

(c) An incriminating statement made by a participant to the person giving advice and in the discussions or conferences incident thereto may not be used against the declarant in any court hearing.

(d) The **juvenile board** [~~court~~] may adopt a fee schedule for deferred prosecution services and rules for the waiver of a fee for financial hardship in accordance with guidelines that the Texas Juvenile Probation Commission shall provide. The maximum fee is $15 a month. If the **board** [~~court~~] adopts a schedule and rules for waiver, the probation officer or other designated officer of the court shall collect the fee authorized by the schedule from the parent, guardian, or custodian of a child for whom a deferred prosecution is authorized under this section or waive the fee in accordance with the rules adopted by the **board** [~~court~~]. The officer shall deposit the fees received under this section in the county treasury to the credit of a special fund that may be used only for juvenile probation or community-based juvenile corrections services or facilities in which a juvenile may be required to live while under court supervision. If the **board** [~~court~~] does not adopt a schedule and rules for waiver, a fee for deferred prosecution services may not be imposed.

(e) A prosecuting attorney may defer prosecution for any child. A probation officer or other designated officer of the court:

(1) may not defer prosecution for a child for a case that is required to be forwarded to the prosecuting attorney under Section 53.01(d); and

(2) may defer prosecution for a child who has previously been adjudicated for conduct that constitutes a felony only if the prosecuting attorney consents in writing.

(f) The probation officer or other officer designated by the court supervising a program of deferred prosecution for a child under this section shall report to the juvenile court any violation by the child of the program.

(g) Prosecution may not be deferred for a child alleged to have engaged in conduct that:

(1) is an offense under Section 49.04, 49.05, 49.06, 49.07, or 49.08, Penal Code; or

(2) is a third or subsequent offense under Section 106.04 or 106.041, Alcoholic Beverage Code.

(h) If the child is alleged to have engaged in delinquent conduct or conduct indicating a need for supervision that violates Section 28.08, Penal Code, deferred prosecution under this section may include:

(1) voluntary attendance in a class with instruction in self-responsibility and empathy for a victim of an offense conducted by a local juvenile probation department, if the class is available; and

(2) voluntary restoration of the property damaged by the child by removing or painting over any markings made by the child, if the owner of the property consents to the restoration.

(i) The court may defer prosecution for a child at any time:

(1) for an adjudication that is to be decided by a jury trial, before the jury is sworn;

(2) for an adjudication before the court, before the first witness is sworn; or

(3) for an uncontested adjudication, before the child pleads to the petition or agrees to a stipulation of evidence.

(j) The court may add the period of deferred prosecution under Subsection (i) to a previous order of deferred prosecution, except that the court may not place the child on deferred prosecution for a combined period longer than one year.

History: Amended by 78th Legis., Reg. Sess. (2003), H.B. 2319, eff. Sept. 1, 2003. Applies only to conduct occurring on or after effective date.

Comment

This section authorizes use of a 6–month period of voluntary (informal) probation, thereby permitting many cases to be disposed of without a formal court petition, hearing and disposition.

Subject to subsection (i), consent of the prosecutor is required to employ this disposition in any case within the scope of mandatory prosecutorial referral under § 53.01(d). Prosecutorial consent is also required for use of this disposition in any case when the juvenile has a prior felony adjudication.

Subsection (g) prohibits deferred prosecution for DWI and related offenses, third-offense consumption of alcohol by a minor, or third-offense driving by minor under the influence of alcohol.

Subsections (i) and (j), added in 2003, permit the juvenile court to place a child on deferred prosecution without consent of or over objection of the prosecutor. Under (j), this may be done even if the child has already experienced deferred prosecution for that same offense. The court, like probation and the prosecutor, is subject to the prohibition of (g) not to grant deferred prosecution for one of the enumerated alcohol-related offenses.

Leading Att'y Gen. Op.

Op. Tex. Att'y Gen. Letter No. 98–069 (1998) (deferred prosecution not violated by offense committed after it has expired)

---

§ 53.035. Grand Jury Referral.

(a) The prosecuting attorney may, before filing a petition under Section 53.04, refer an offense to a grand jury in the county in which the offense is alleged to have been committed.

(b) The grand jury has the same jurisdiction and powers to investigate the facts and circumstances concerning an offense referred to the grand jury under this section as it has to investigate other criminal activity.

(c) If the grand jury votes to take no action on an offense referred to the grand jury under this section, the prosecuting attorney may not file a petition under Section 53.04 concerning the offense unless the same or a successor grand jury approves the filing of the petition.

(d) If the grand jury votes for approval of the prosecution of an offense referred to the grand jury under this section, the prosecuting attorney may file a petition under Section 53.04.

(e) The approval of the prosecution of an offense by a grand jury under this section does not constitute approval of a petition by a grand jury for purposes of Section 53.045.

Comment

This 1999 section authorizes a prosecutor to refer any juvenile case for a grand jury "advisory opinion" as to whether prosecution should occur. This is the same power the prosecutor has to refer sensitive adult cases to the grand jury. Approval by the grand jury is not an indictment, but merely authorizes the prosecutor who has elected this procedure to file a juvenile court petition. This procedure is entirely separate from the determinate sentence act grand jury function under § 53.045.

---

§ 53.04. Court Petition; Answer.

(a) If the preliminary investigation, required by Section 53.01 of this code results in a determination that further proceedings are authorized and warranted, a petition for an adjudication or transfer hearing of a child alleged to have engaged in delinquent conduct or conduct indicating a need for supervision may be made as promptly as practicable by a prosecuting attorney who has knowledge of the facts alleged or is informed and believes that they are true.

(b) The proceedings shall be styled "In the matter of ______________."

(c) The petition may be on information and belief.

(d) The petition must state:

(1) with reasonable particularity the time, place, and manner of the acts alleged and the penal law or standard of conduct allegedly violated by the acts;

(2) the name, age, and residence address, if known, of the child who is the subject of the petition;

(3) the names and residence addresses, if known, of the parent, guardian, or custodian of the child and of the child's spouse, if any;

(4) if the child's parent, guardian, or custodian does not reside or cannot be found in the state, or if their places of residence are unknown, the name and residence address of any known adult relative residing in the county or, if there is none, the name and residence address of the known adult relative residing nearest to the location of the court; and

(5) if the child is alleged to have engaged in habitual felony conduct, the previous adjudications in which the child was found to have engaged in conduct violating penal laws of the grade of felony.

(e) An oral or written answer to the petition may be made at or before the commencement of the hearing. If there is no answer, a general denial of the alleged conduct is assumed.

Comment

The requirements of the juvenile petition are specified in this section. The meat of the section is subsection (d) (1) requiring the petition to state "with reasonable particularity the time, place, and manner of the acts alleged."

When habitual felony conduct is charged to invoke determinate sentence proceedings, the State is required to allege in the petition the prior felony adjudications upon which it intends to rely.

CLE/Other Legal Publications

Prosecutor Ethics. Kris Moore, 16TH ANN. JUVE. L. CONF. (Feb. 2003)

Ethics from a Prosecutor's Point of View. Kris Moore, 13TH ANN. JUVE. L. CONF. (Feb. 2000)

Use of Gang Membership as a Processing Criterion in the Juvenile Justice System. Catherine Robb, 11 JUVE. L. SECT. RPT. (Sept. 1997)

Leading Cases

In re J.K.R., 986 S.W.2d 278 (Tex. App.—Eastland 1998, pet. denied) (consolidation of charges proper under civil standards)

In re S.D.W., 811 S.W.2d 739 (Tex. App.—Houston [1st Dist.] 1991, no writ) (law of parties need not be plead)

In re H.R.A., 790 S.W.2d 102 (Tex. App.—Beaumont 1990, no writ) (Penal Code section violated need not be plead)

T.R.S. v. State, 663 S.W.2d 920 (Tex. App.—Fort Worth 1984, no writ) (criminal procedure property description requirements do not apply to juvenile petitions)

In re M.H., 662 S.W.2d 764 (Tex. App.—Corpus Christi 1983, no writ) (specific prayer for restitution not required)

In re W.H.C., 580 S.W.2d 606 (Tex. Civ. App.—Amarillo 1979, no writ) (all elements of offense must be plead)

In re H.S., 564 S.W.2d 446 (Tex. Civ. App.—Amarillo 1978, no writ) (petition must allege county in which acts occurred)

---

§ 53.045. Violent or Habitual Offenders.

(a) Except as provided by Subsection (e), the prosecuting attorney may refer the petition to the grand jury of the county in which the court in which the petition is filed presides if the petition alleges that the child engaged in delinquent conduct that constitutes habitual felony conduct as described by Section 51.031 or that included the violation of any of the following provisions:

(1) Section 19.02, Penal Code (murder);

(2) Section 19.03, Penal Code (capital murder);

(3) Section 19.04, Penal Code (manslaughter);

(4) Section 20.04, Penal Code (aggravated kidnapping);

(5) Section 22.011, Penal Code (sexual assault) or Section 22.021, Penal Code (aggravated sexual assault);

(6) Section 22.02, Penal Code (aggravated assault);

(7) Section 29.03, Penal Code (aggravated robbery);

(8) Section 22.04, Penal Code (injury to a child, elderly individual, or disabled individual), if the offense is punishable as a felony, other than a state jail felony;

(9) Section 22.05(b), Penal Code (felony deadly conduct involving discharging a firearm);

(10) Subchapter D, Chapter 481, Health and Safety Code, if the conduct constitutes a felony of the first degree or an aggravated controlled substance felony (certain offenses involving controlled substances);

(11) Section 15.03, Penal Code (criminal solicitation);

(12) Section 21.11(a)(1), Penal Code (indecency with a child);

(13) Section 15.031, Penal Code (criminal solicitation of a minor);

(14) Section 15.01, Penal Code (criminal attempt), if the offense attempted was an offense under Section 19.02, Penal Code (murder), or Section 19.03, Penal Code (capital murder), or an offense listed by Section 3g(a)(1), Article 42.12, Code of Criminal Procedure;

(15) Section 28.02, Penal Code (arson), if bodily injury or death is suffered by any person by reason of the commission of the conduct; or

(16) Section 49.08, Penal Code (intoxication manslaughter).

(b) A grand jury may approve a petition submitted to it under this section by a vote of nine members of the grand jury in the same manner that the grand jury votes on the presentment of an indictment.

(c) The grand jury has all the powers to investigate the facts and circumstances relating to a petition submitted under this section as it has to investigate other criminal activity but may not issue an indictment unless the child is transferred to a criminal court as provided by Section 54.02 of this code.

(d) If the grand jury approves of the petition, the fact of approval shall be certified to the juvenile court, and the certification shall be entered in the record of the case. For the purpose of the transfer of a child to the Texas Department of Corrections as provided by Section 61.084(c), Human Resources Code, a juvenile court petition approved by a grand jury under this section is an indictment presented by the grand jury.

(e) The prosecuting attorney may not refer a petition that alleges the child engaged in conduct that violated Section 22.011(a)(2), Penal Code, or Sections 22.021(a)(1)(B) and (2)(B), Penal Code, unless the child is more than three years older than the victim of the conduct.

Comment

This section defines the scope of the Texas determinate sentence act for juveniles. Under it, a juvenile court judge or jury can sentence a respondent adjudicated to have committed one of the covered felonies to probation or a sentence of incarceration. Initially, the sentence is served in the TYC.

Amendments made in 1995 greatly expanded the offenses covered by the legislation from the original six to over thirty. A capital or first degree felony carries a term of up to 40 years; a second degree felony carries up to 20 years; and a third degree felony up to 10 years. *See* § 54.04.

Under 1995 amendments, the TYC can administratively parole a juvenile without a court hearing who has served a statutory minimum length of stay—10 years for capital murder, 3 years for a first degree felony, 2 years for a second degree felony and 1 year for a third degree felony. If the juvenile is paroled by TYC before he or she becomes 19, he or she remains on TYC parole until age 21, when he or she is administratively transferred to adult parole for the balance of the sentence. If TYC parole is granted on or after the youth's 19th birthday, he or she goes directly to adult parole supervision. Upon revocation of adult parole, the youth can be committed directly to the institutional division of TDCJ.

TYC can petition the juvenile court for parole before the statutory minimum length of stay has been served. It can also petition the juvenile court to transfer any determinate sentenced youth 16 or older to the institutional division of TDCJ. A youth who violates TYC parole must be revoked before the TYC can petition the juvenile court to transfer him or her to the institutional division.

In 2001, manslaughter and intoxication manslaughter, both second degree felonies, were added to the list of covered offenses.

CLE/Other Legal Publications

Determinate Sentencing Proceedings for the Violent or Habitual Offender. Jean Boyd, 17TH ANN. JUVE. L. CONF. (Feb. 2004)

Determinate Sentencing. Jean Boyd, 15TH ANN. JUVE. L. CONF. (Feb. 2002)

Determinate Sentence and Certifications. Brian Fischer, 14TH ANN. JUVE. L. CONF. (Feb. 2001)

Determinate Sentencing. Jean Boyd, 13TH ANN. JUVE. L. CONF. (Feb. 2000)

Texas Juvenile Blended Sentencing: An Empirical Study of the Uses of Determinate Sentencing. Robert O. Dawson, 17 JUVE. L. SECT. RPT. (June 2003)

The Violent Juvenile Offender: An Empirical Study of Juvenile Determinate Sentencing Proceedings as an Alternative to Criminal Prosecution. Robert O. Dawson, 21 TEX. TECH L. REV. 1897 (1990)

The Third Justice System: The New Juvenile–Criminal System of Determinate Sentencing for the Youthful Violent Offender in Texas. Robert O. Dawson, 19 ST. MARY'S L.J. 943 (1988)

Leading Cases

In re G.A.T., 16 S.W.3d 818 (Tex. App.—Houston [14th Dist.] 2000, pet. denied) (failure to serve amended petition approved by grand jury on juvenile not jurisdictional defect)

In re S.J., 977 S.W.2d 147 (Tex. App.—San Antonio 1998, no writ) (mistakes in grand jury approval certification not fatal)

In re A.R.A., 898 S.W.2d 14 (Tex. App.—Austin 1995, no writ) (juvenile and lawyer have capacity to waive grand jury approval if § 51.09 complied with)

In re A.G.G., 860 S.W.2d 160 (Tex. App.—Dallas 1993, no writ) (State's waiver of right to proceed under DSA precludes determinate sentence)

In re S.D.W., 811 S.W.2d 739 (Tex. App.—Houston [1st Dist.] 1991, no writ) (written grand jury certificate of approval required; amendments in petition; lesser included offenses)

In re S.C., 790 S.W.2d 766 (Tex. App.—Austin 1990, writ denied) (prohibition on involuntary servitude not violated; adult parole rules apply after transfer to prison)

In re J.T.H., 779 S.W.2d 954 (Tex. App.—Austin 1989, no writ) (right to grand jury indictment not violated; statute not vague; no equal protection violation)

In re R.L.H., 771 S.W.2d 697 (Tex. App.—Austin 1989, writ denied) (act does not violate equal protection of the laws; no violation of right to grand jury indictment)

Cross References

TEX. FAM. CODE ANN. § 54.04. Disposition Hearing; § 54.11. Release or Transfer Hearing.

TEX. HUM. RES. CODE ANN. § 61.079. Referral for Transfer; § 61.081. Minimum lengths of stay; § 61.084. Parole and Administrative Transfer.

TEX. GOV'T CODE ANN. § 499.053. Transfers from Texas Youth Commission; § 508.156. Determinate Sentence Parole.

---

§ 53.05. Time Set for Hearing.

(a) After the petition has been filed, the juvenile court shall set a time for the hearing.

(b) The time set for the hearing shall not be later than 10 working days after the day the petition was filed if:

(1) the child is in detention; or

(2) the child will be taken into custody under Section 53.06(d) of this code.

Leading Cases

Grayless v. State, 567 S.W.2d 216 (Tex. Crim. App. 1978) (juvenile's constitutional right to speedy trial not violated by 2 year 9 month delay)

In re J.W.G., 988 S.W.2d 318 (Tex. App.—Houston [1st Dist.] 1999, no pet.) (one year delay not a denial of speedy trial)

In re S.D.W., 811 S.W.2d 739 (Tex. App.—Houston [1st Dist.] 1991, no writ) (Texas Supreme Court's guidelines for prompt disposition are not binding on juvenile court)

In re D.M., 611 S.W.2d 880 (Tex. Civ. App.—Amarillo 1980, no writ) (13 month delay not a violation of constitutional right to speedy trial)

L.L.S. v. State, 565 S.W.2d 252 (Tex. Civ. App.—Dallas 1978, writ ref'd n.r.e.) (failure to hold hearing within 10 days doesn't invalidate court's decision)

---

§ 53.06. Summons.

(a) The juvenile court shall direct issuance of a summons to:

(1) the child named in the petition;

(2) the child's parent, guardian, or custodian;

(3) the child's guardian ad litem; and

(4) any other person who appears to the court to be a proper or necessary party to the proceeding.

(b) The summons must require the persons served to appear before the court at the time set to answer the allegations of the petition. A copy of the petition must accompany the summons.

(c) The court may endorse on the summons an order directing the person having the physical custody or control of the child to bring the child to the hearing. A person who violates an order entered under this subsection may be proceeded against under Section 53.08 or 54.07 of this code.

(d) If it appears from an affidavit filed or from sworn testimony before the court that immediate detention of the child is warranted under Section 53.02(b) of this code, the court may endorse on the summons an order that a law-enforcement officer shall serve the summons and shall immediately take the child into custody and bring him before the court.

(e) A party, other than the child, may waive service of summons by written stipulation or by voluntary appearance at the hearing.

Comment

Service of summons may be waived by voluntary appearance by any person except the juvenile respondent. Personal service on the juvenile respondent is required to give the juvenile court jurisdiction over the case.

Leading Cases

Carner v. State, 592 S.W.2d 618 (Tex. Crim. App. 1980) (juvenile court may proceed with hearing in absence of parent who was summoned)

Grayless v. State, 567 S.W.2d 216 (Tex. Crim. App. 1978) (failure to serve transfer motion on respondent deprives criminal court of jurisdiction)

In re D.W.M., 562 S.W.2d 851 (Tex. 1978) (failure of juvenile to object to absence of personal service does not waive defect)

In re W.L.C., 562 S.W.2d 454 (Tex. 1978) (burden on State to show that respondent was personally served)

Johnson v. State, 551 S.W.2d 379 (Tex. Crim. App. 1977) (failure to make personal service on child deprives criminal court of jurisdiction after transfer)

In re A.B., 938 S.W.2d 537 (Tex. App.—Texarkana 1997, writ denied) (failure to serve juvenile requires reversal; service on juvenile's attorney not sufficient)

In re P.C., 858 S.W.2d 6 (Tex. App.—Houston [1st Dist.] 1993, no writ) (directing service of summons on only one parent sufficient)

In re K.P.S., 840 S.W.2d 706 (Tex. App.—Corpus Christi 1992, no writ) (oral notice of hearing date by judge in court sufficient notice)

§ 53.07. Service of Summons.

(a) If a person to be served with a summons is in this state and can be found, the summons shall be served upon him personally at least two days before the day of the adjudication hearing. If he is in this state and cannot be found, but his address is known or can with reasonable diligence be ascertained, the summons may be served on him by mailing a copy by registered or certified mail, return receipt requested, at least five days before the day of the hearing. If he is outside this state but he can be found or his address is known, or his whereabouts or address can with reasonable diligence be ascertained, service of the summons may be made either by delivering a copy to him personally or mailing a copy to him by registered or certified mail, return receipt requested, at least five days before the day of the hearing.

(b) The juvenile court has jurisdiction of the case if after reasonable effort a person other than the child cannot be found nor his post-office address ascertained, whether he is in or outside this state.

(c) Service of the summons may be made by any suitable person under the direction of the court.

(d) The court may authorize payment from the general funds of the county of the costs of service and of necessary travel expenses incurred by persons summoned or otherwise required to appear at the hearing.

(e) Witnesses may be subpoenaed in accordance with the Texas Code of Criminal Procedure, 1965.

Leading Cases/Att'y Gen. Op.

In re D.W.L., 828 S.W.2d 520 (Tex. App.—Houston [14th Dist.] 1992, no writ) (State used reasonable effort to serve parents)

In re D.B.C, 695 S.W.2d 248 (Tex. App.—Austin 1985, no writ) (court order authorizing probation officer to serve summons not required)

P.G. v. State, 616 S.W.2d 635 (Tex. Civ. App.—San Antonio 1981, writ ref'd n.r.e.) (juvenile probation officer may serve summons)

Op. Tex. Att'y Gen. No. GA–0017 (2003) (juvenile court may order child or parent to reimburse county for cost of service of summons if child is adjudicated)

§ 53.08. Writ of Attachment.

(a) The juvenile court may issue a writ of attachment for a person who violates an order entered under Section 53.06(c).

(b) A writ of attachment issued under this section is executed in the same manner as in a criminal proceeding as provided by Chapter 24, Code of Criminal Procedure.

Comment

If the juvenile court has required a person served to bring the respondent to the court and that person fails to do so, this section authorizes the issuance of an attachment to take the adult into custody and bring him or her before the court. Previously, the sole remedy was contempt of court proceedings under § 54.07.

Chapter 54. Judicial Proceedings.

Introductory Comment

Chapter 54 deals with six different kinds of judicial hearings: detention; discretionary transfer (certification); adjudication, disposition; modification of disposition hearings; and release/transfer hearings under the determinate sentence act.

---

§ 54.01. Detention Hearing.

(a) Except as provided by Subsection (p), if the child is not released under Section 53.02, a detention hearing without a jury shall be held promptly, but not later than the second working day after the child is taken into custody; provided, however, that when a child is detained on a Friday or Saturday, then such detention hearing shall be held on the first working day after the child is taken into custody.

(b) Reasonable notice of the detention hearing, either oral or written, shall be given, stating the time, place, and purpose of the hearing. Notice shall be given to the child and, if they can be found, to his parents, guardian, or custodian. Prior to the commencement of the hearing, the court shall inform the parties of the child's right to counsel and to appointed counsel if they are indigent and of the child's right to remain silent with respect to any allegations of delinquent conduct, [~~or~~] conduct indicating a need for supervision**, or conduct that violates an order of probation imposed by a juvenile court**.

(c) At the detention hearing, the court may consider written reports from probation officers, professional court employees, or professional consultants in addition to the testimony of witnesses. Prior to the detention hearing, the court shall provide the attorney for the child with access to all written matter to be considered by the court in making the detention decision. The court may order counsel not to reveal items to the child or his parent, guardian, or guardian ad litem if such disclosure would materially harm the treatment and rehabilitation of the child or would substantially decrease the likelihood of receiving information from the same or similar sources in the future.

(d) A detention hearing may be held without the presence of the child's parents if the court has been unable to locate them. If no parent or guardian is present, the court shall appoint counsel or a guardian ad litem for the child.

(e) At the conclusion of the hearing, the court shall order the child released from detention unless it finds that:

(1) he is likely to abscond or be removed from the jurisdiction of the court;

(2) suitable supervision, care, or protection for him is not being provided by a parent, guardian, custodian, or other person;

(3) he has no parent, guardian, custodian, or other person able to return him to the court when required;

(4) he may be dangerous to himself or may threaten the safety of the public if released; or

(5) he has previously been found to be a delinquent child or has previously been convicted of a penal offense punishable by a term in jail or prison and is likely to commit an offense if released.

(f) Unless otherwise agreed in the memorandum of understanding under Section 37.011, Education Code, a release may be conditioned on requirements reasonably necessary to insure the child's appearance at later proceedings, but the conditions of the release must be in writing and a copy furnished to the child. In a county with a population greater than 125,000, if a child being released under this section is expelled under Section 37.007, Education Code, the release shall be conditioned on the child's attending a juvenile justice alternative education program pending a deferred prosecution or formal court disposition of the child's case.

(g) No statement made by the child at the detention hearing shall be admissible against the child at any other hearing.

(h) A detention order extends to the conclusion of the disposition hearing, if there is one, but in no event for more than 10 working days. Further detention orders may be made following subsequent detention hearings. The initial detention hearing may not be waived but subsequent detention hearings may be waived in accordance with the requirements of Section 51.09. Each subsequent detention order shall extend for no more than 10 working days, except that in a county that does not have a certified juvenile detention facility, as described by Section 51.12(a)(3), each subsequent detention order shall extend for no more than 15 working days.

(i) A child in custody may be detained for as long as 10 days without the hearing described in Subsection (a) of this section if:

(1) a written request for shelter in detention facilities pending arrangement of transportation to his place of residence in another state or country or another county of this state is voluntarily executed by the child not later than the next working day after he was taken into custody;

(2) the request for shelter contains:

(A) a statement by the child that he voluntarily agrees to submit himself to custody and detention for a period of not longer than 10 days without a detention hearing;

(B) an allegation by the person detaining the child that the child has left his place of residence in another state or country or another county of this state, that he is in need of shelter, and that an effort is being made to arrange transportation to his place of residence; and

(C) a statement by the person detaining the child that he has advised the child of his right to demand a detention hearing under Subsection (a) of this section; and

(3) the request is signed by the juvenile court judge to evidence his knowledge of the fact that the child is being held in detention.

(j) The request for shelter may be revoked by the child at any time, and on such revocation, if further detention is necessary, a detention hearing shall be held not later than the next working day in accordance with Subsections (a) through (g) of this section.

(k) Notwithstanding anything in this title to the contrary, the child may sign a request for shelter without the concurrence of an adult specified in Section 51.09 of this code.

(l) The juvenile board may appoint a referee to conduct the detention hearing. The referee shall be an attorney licensed to practice law in this state. Such payment or additional payment as may be warranted for referee services shall be provided from county funds. Before commencing the detention hearing, the referee shall inform the parties who have appeared that they are entitled to have the hearing before the juvenile court judge or a substitute judge authorized by Section 51.04(f). If a party objects to the referee conducting the detention hearing, an authorized judge shall conduct the hearing within 24 hours. At the conclusion of the hearing, the referee shall transmit written findings and recommendations to the juvenile court judge or substitute judge. The juvenile court judge or substitute judge shall adopt, modify, or reject the referee's recommendations not later than the next working day after the day that the judge receives the recommendations. Failure to act within that time results in release of the child by operation of law. A recommendation that the child be released operates to secure the child's immediate release, subject to the power of the juvenile court judge or substitute judge to reject or modify that recommendation. The effect of an order detaining a child shall be computed from the time of the hearing before the referee.

(m) The detention hearing required in this section may be held in the county of the designated place of detention where the child is being held even though the designated place of detention is outside the county of residence of the child or the county in which the alleged delinquent conduct, [~~or~~] conduct indicating a need for supervision, **or probation violation** occurred.

(n) An attorney appointed by the court under Section 51.10(c) because a determination was made under this section to detain a child who was not represented by an attorney may request on behalf of the child and is entitled to a de novo detention hearing under this section. The attorney must make the request not later than the 10th working day after the date the attorney is appointed. The hearing must take place not later than the second working day after the date the attorney filed a formal request with the court for a hearing.

(o) The court or referee shall find whether there is probable cause to believe that a child taken into custody without an arrest warrant or a directive to apprehend has engaged in delinquent conduct, [~~or~~] conduct indicating a need for supervision**, or conduct that violates an order of probation imposed by a juvenile court**. The court or referee must make the finding within 48 hours, including weekends and holidays, of the time the child was taken into custody. The court or referee may make the finding on any reasonably reliable information without regard to admissibility of that information under the Texas Rules of [~~Criminal~~] Evidence. A finding of probable cause is required to detain a child after the 48th hour after the time the child was taken into custody. If a court or referee finds probable cause, additional findings of probable cause are not required in the same cause to authorize further detention.

(p) If a child is detained in a county jail or other facility as provided by Section 51.12(*l*) and the child is not released under Section 53.02(f), a detention hearing without a jury shall be held promptly, but not later than the 24th hour, excluding weekends and holidays, after the time the child is taken into custody.

(q) If a child has not been released under Section 53.02 or this section and a petition has not been filed under Section 53.04 **or 54.05** concerning the child, the court shall order the child released from detention not later than:

(1) the 30th working day after the date the initial detention hearing is held, if the child is alleged to have engaged in conduct constituting a capital felony, an aggravated controlled substance felony, or a felony of the first degree; or

(2) the 15th working day after the date the initial detention hearing is held, if the child is alleged to have engaged in conduct constituting an offense other than an offense listed in Subdivision (1) **or conduct that violates an order of probation imposed by a juvenile court**.

(r) On the conditional release of a child from detention by judicial order under Subsection (f), the court, referee, or detention magistrate may order that the child's parent, guardian, or custodian present in court at the detention hearing engage in acts or omissions specified by the court, referee, or detention magistrate that will assist the child in complying with the conditions of release. The order must be in writing and a copy furnished to the parent, guardian, or custodian. An order entered under this subsection may be enforced as provided by Chapter 61.

History: Amended by 78th Legis., Reg. Sess. (2003), H.B. 2319, eff. Sept. 1, 2003. Applies only to conduct occurring on or after effective date.

Comment

If a child is not released from detention administratively, a detention hearing before a judge, referee or master must be conducted within the second working day after the child was taken into custody. The hearing may be informal and the child may be, but need not be, represented by counsel. This section requires release from detention unless one or more of five specified grounds justifying detention is found to exist.

Amendments made in 1995 expanded the length of a detention order from 10 days to 10 working days and expanded the time within which a judge must approve a referee's recommendations from 24 hours to the conclusion of the next working day. They also provide that the initial detention hearing cannot be waived. In addition, the 1995 amendments codified the constitutional requirement of a judicial determination of probable cause within 48 hours of the juvenile being taken into custody.

Changes made in 1997 in subsection (h) extend the life of a second and subsequent detention order to 15 working days in counties without certified juvenile detention facilities.

Subsection (f) requires that in a county of 125,000 or more a child who has been expelled must, if released from detention, be released on condition that he attend the county JJAEP pending handling of the case.

In 1999, subsection (q) was added to require the filing of a petition within 30 or 15 working days, depending upon the offense, after the initial detention hearing if the child is detained. The remedy for violation of this requirement is release of the child from detention, not dismissal of the case.

The 2003 amendments in subsections (b), (o), and (q) make it clear that a child being detained for violation of probation is entitled to detention hearings on the same basis as a child being held on new charges.

Subsection (r), added in 2003, authorizes the court or referee to place a parent of a released child under an order of cooperation that can be enforced by contempt proceedings under new Chapter 61.

CLE/Other Legal Publications

Detention and Pleas. Carlos R. Garcia, 17th Ann. Juve. L. Conf. (FEB. 2004)

Detention Hearings. William D. King, 13TH ANN. JUVE. L. CONF. (Feb. 2000)

Leading Cases/Att'y Gen. Op.

County of Riverside v. McLaughlin, 500 U.S. 44, 114 L.Ed.2d 49, 111 S.Ct. 1661 (1991) ("prompt" under *Gerstein v. Pugh* means within 48 hours)

Schall v. Martin, 467 U.S. 253, 81 L.Ed.2d 207, 104 S.Ct. 2403 (1984) (preventive detention of juveniles constitutional under some circumstances)

Gerstein v. Pugh, 420 U.S. 103, 43 L.Ed.2d 54, 95 S.Ct. 854 (1975) (4th Amendment requires prompt judicial finding of probable cause to detain arrestee)

Moss v. Weaver, 525 F.2d 1258 (5th Cir. 1976) (*Gerstein v. Pugh* applies to juvenile proceedings)

Ex parte D.W.C., 1 S.W.3d 396 (Tex. App.—Beaumont 1999, no pet.) (juvenile has no constitutional right to bail)

Op. Tex. Att'y Gen. No. DM–411 (1996) (hearing-impaired party to juvenile detention hearing entitled to interpreter, but custodian is not)

In re G.B.B., 572 S.W.2d 751 (Tex. Civ. App.—El Paso 1978, writ ref'd n.r.e.) (no requirement that petition be filed before detention hearing)

D.B. v. State, 556 S.W.2d 845 (Tex. Civ. App.—Houston [14th Dist.] 1977, no writ) (failure to hold detention hearing does not invalidate adjudication)

In re G.T.H., 541 S.W.2d 527 (Tex. Civ. App.—Eastland 1976, no writ) (holding child in uncertified detention facility requires immediate release on habeas)

---

§ 54.011. Detention Hearings for Status Offenders and Nonoffenders; Penalty.

(a) The detention hearing for a status offender or nonoffender who has not been released administratively under Section 53.02 shall be held before the 24th hour after the time the child arrived at a detention facility, excluding hours of a weekend or a holiday. Except as otherwise provided by this section, the judge or referee conducting the detention hearing shall release the status offender or nonoffender from secure detention.

(b) The judge or referee may order a child in detention accused of the violation of a valid court order as defined by Section 51.02 detained not longer than 72 hours after the time the detention order was entered, excluding weekends and holidays, if:

(1) the judge or referee finds at the detention hearing that there is probable cause to believe the child violated the valid court order; and

(2) the detention of the child is justified under Section 54.01(e)(1), (2), or (3).

(c) Except as provided by Subsection (d), a detention order entered under Subsection (b) may be extended for one additional 72-hour period, excluding weekends and holidays, only on a finding of good cause by the juvenile court.

(d) A detention order for a child under this section may be extended on the demand of the child's attorney only to allow the time that is necessary to comply with the requirements of Section 51.10(h), entitling the attorney to 10 days to prepare for an adjudication hearing.

(e) A status offender may be detained for a necessary period, not to exceed five days, to enable the child's return to the child's home in another state under Chapter 60.

(f) Except as provided by Subsection (a), a nonoffender, including a person who has been taken into custody and is being held solely for deportation out of the United States, may not be detained for any period of time in a secure detention facility or secure correctional facility, regardless of whether the facility is publicly or privately operated. A nonoffender who is detained in violation of this subsection is entitled to immediate release from the facility and may bring a civil action for compensation for the illegal detention against any person responsible for the detention. A person commits an offense if the person knowingly detains or assists in detaining a nonoffender in a secure detention facility or secure correctional facility in violation of this subsection. An offense under this subsection is a Class B misdemeanor.

History: Amended by 78th Legis., Reg. Sess. (2003), H.B. 2319, eff. Sept. 1, 2003. Applies only to a nonoffender who is detained in a secure detention facility or in a secure correctional facility on or after the effective date. A nonoffender who is detained in a secure detention facility or secure correctional facility before the effective date is not entitled to bring a civil action.

Comment

This section enacts federal restrictions on the detention of status offenders into Texas law. *See* § 51.02(15) for the definition of status offender. A status offender can be kept in a secure detention facility for a maximum of 24 hours, not counting weekend and holiday hours, unless he or she is charged with violation of a valid court order from a previous case.

Subsection (f), added in 2003, makes confinement of an alien juvenile for the purpose of deportation illegal after 24 hours. A civil lawsuit and criminal prosecution for a B misdemeanor are authorized by this amendment.

---

§ 54.012. Interactive Video Recording of Detention Hearing.

(a) A detention hearing under Section 54.01, other than the first detention hearing, may be held using interactive video equipment if:

(1) the child and the child's attorney agree to the video hearing; and

(2) the parties to the proceeding have the opportunity to cross-examine witnesses.

(b) A detention hearing may not be held using video equipment unless the video equipment for the hearing provides for a two-way communication of image and sound among the child, the court, and other parties at the hearing.

(c) A recording of the communications shall be made. The recording shall be preserved until the earlier of:

(1) the 91st day after the date on which the recording is made if the child is alleged to have engaged in conduct constituting a misdemeanor;

(2) the 120th day after the date on which the recording is made if the child is alleged to have engaged in conduct constituting a felony; or

(3) the date on which the adjudication hearing ends.

(d) An attorney for the child may obtain a copy of the recording on payment of the reasonable costs of reproducing the copy.

Comment

This section authorizes subsequent, but not initial, detention hearings to be conducted by two-way television, much like criminal court arraignments are conducted in some cities.

§ 54.02. Waiver of Jurisdiction and Discretionary Transfer to Criminal Court.

(a) The juvenile court may waive its exclusive original jurisdiction and transfer a child to the appropriate district court or criminal district court for criminal proceedings if:

(1) the child is alleged to have violated a penal law of the grade of felony;

(2) the child was:

(A) 14 years of age or older at the time he is alleged to have committed the offense, if the offense is a capital felony, an aggravated controlled substance felony, or a felony of the first degree, and no adjudication hearing has been conducted concerning that offense; or

(B) 15 years of age or older at the time the child is alleged to have committed the offense, if the offense is a felony of the second or third degree or a state jail felony, and no adjudication hearing has been conducted concerning that offense; and

(3) after a full investigation and a hearing, the juvenile court determines that there is probable cause to believe that the child before the court committed the offense alleged and that because of the seriousness of the offense alleged or the background of the child the welfare of the community requires criminal proceedings.

(b) The petition and notice requirements of Sections 53.04, 53.05, 53.06, and 53.07 of this code must be satisfied, and the summons must state that the hearing is for the purpose of considering discretionary transfer to criminal court.

(c) The juvenile court shall conduct a hearing without a jury to consider transfer of the child for criminal proceedings.

(d) Prior to the hearing, the juvenile court shall order and obtain a complete diagnostic study, social evaluation, and full investigation of the child, his circumstances, and the circumstances of the alleged offense.

(e) At the transfer hearing the court may consider written reports from probation officers, professional court employees, or professional consultants in addition to the testimony of witnesses. At least one day prior to the transfer hearing, the court shall provide the attorney for the child with access to all written matter to be considered by the court in making the transfer decision. The court may order counsel not to reveal items to the child or his parent, guardian, or guardian ad litem if such disclosure would materially harm the treatment and rehabilitation of the child or would substantially decrease the likelihood of receiving information from the same or similar sources in the future.

(f) In making the determination required by Subsection (a) of this section, the court shall consider, among other matters:

(1) whether the alleged offense was against person or property, with greater weight in favor of transfer given to offenses against the person;

(2) the sophistication and maturity of the child;

(3) the record and previous history of the child; and

(4) the prospects of adequate protection of the public and the likelihood of the rehabilitation of the child by use of procedures, services, and facilities currently available to the juvenile court.

(g) If the petition alleges multiple offenses that constitute more than one criminal transaction, the juvenile court shall either retain or transfer all offenses relating to a single transaction. A child is not subject to criminal prosecution at any time for any offense arising out of a criminal transaction for which the juvenile court retains jurisdiction.

(h) If the juvenile court waives jurisdiction, it shall state specifically in the order its reasons for waiver and certify its action, including the written order and findings of the court, and shall transfer the person to the appropriate court for criminal proceedings and cause the results of the diagnostic study of the person ordered under Subsection (d), including psychological information, to be transferred to the appropriate criminal prosecutor. On transfer of the person for criminal proceedings, the person shall be dealt with as an adult and in accordance with the Code of Criminal Procedure. The transfer of custody is an arrest.

(i) A waiver under this section is a waiver of jurisdiction over the child and the criminal court may not remand the child to the jurisdiction of the juvenile court.

(j) The juvenile court may waive its exclusive original jurisdiction and transfer a person to the appropriate district court or criminal district court for criminal proceedings if:

(1) the person is 18 years of age or older;

(2) the person was:

(A) 10 years of age or older and under 17 years of age at the time the person is alleged to have committed a capital felony or an offense under Section 19.02, Penal Code;

(B) 14 years of age or older and under 17 years of age at the time the person is alleged to have committed an aggravated controlled substance felony or a felony of the first degree other than an offense under Section 19.02, Penal Code; or

(C) 15 years of age or older and under 17 years of age at the time the person is alleged to have committed a felony of the second or third degree or a state jail felony;

(3) no adjudication concerning the alleged offense has been made or no adjudication hearing concerning the offense has been conducted;

(4) the juvenile court finds from a preponderance of the evidence that:

(A) for a reason beyond the control of the state it was not practicable to proceed in juvenile court before the 18th birthday of the person; or

(B) after due diligence of the state it was not practicable to proceed in juvenile court before the 18th birthday of the person because:

(i) the state did not have probable cause to proceed in juvenile court and new evidence has been found since the 18th birthday of the person;

(ii) the person could not be found; or

(iii) a previous transfer order was reversed by an appellate court or set aside by a district court; and

(5) the juvenile court determines that there is probable cause to believe that the child before the court committed the offense alleged.

(k) The petition and notice requirements of Sections 53.04, 53.05, 53.06, and 53.07 of this code must be satisfied, and the summons must state that the hearing is for the purpose of considering waiver of jurisdiction under Subsection (j) of this section.

(l) The juvenile court shall conduct a hearing without a jury to consider waiver of jurisdiction under Subsection (j) of this section.

(m) Notwithstanding any other provision of this section, the juvenile court shall waive its exclusive original jurisdiction and transfer a child to the appropriate district court or criminal court for criminal proceedings if:

(1) the child has previously been transferred to a district court or criminal district court for criminal proceedings under this section, unless:

(A) the child was not indicted in the matter transferred by the grand jury;

(B) the child was found not guilty in the matter transferred;

(C) the matter transferred was dismissed with prejudice; or

(D) the child was convicted in the matter transferred, the conviction was reversed on appeal, and the appeal is final; and

(2) the child is alleged to have violated a penal law of the grade of felony.

(n) A mandatory transfer under Subsection (m) may be made without conducting the study required in discretionary transfer proceedings by Subsection (d). The requirements of Subsection (b) that the summons state that the purpose of the hearing is to consider discretionary transfer to criminal court does not apply to a transfer proceeding under Subsection (m). In a proceeding under Subsection (m), it is sufficient that the summons provide fair notice that the purpose of the hearing is to consider mandatory transfer to criminal court.

(o) If a respondent is taken into custody for possible discretionary transfer proceedings under Subsection (j), the juvenile court shall hold a detention hearing in the same manner as provided by Section 54.01, except that the court shall order the respondent released unless it finds that the respondent:

(1) is likely to abscond or be removed from the jurisdiction of the court;

(2) may be dangerous to himself or herself or may threaten the safety of the public if released; or

(3) has previously been found to be a delinquent child or has previously been convicted of a penal offense punishable by a term of jail or prison and is likely to commit an offense if released.

(p) If the juvenile court does not order a respondent released under Subsection *(o)*, the court shall, pending the conclusion of the discretionary transfer hearing, order that the respondent be detained in:

(1) a certified juvenile detention facility as provided by Subsection (q); or

(2) an appropriate county facility for the detention of adults accused of criminal offenses.

(q) The detention of a respondent in a certified juvenile detention facility must comply with the detention requirements under this title, except that, to the extent practicable, the person shall be kept separate from children detained in the same facility.

(r) If the juvenile court orders a respondent detained in a county facility under Subsection (p), the county sheriff shall take custody of the respondent under the juvenile court's order. The juvenile court shall set or deny bond for the respondent as required by the Code of Criminal Procedure and other law applicable to the pretrial detention of adults accused of criminal offenses.

Comment

A juvenile court in its discretion may waive its exclusive jurisdiction and transfer a child to criminal court for prosecution as an adult if certain conditions exist. The certification hearing is without a jury and the mandatory investigative/diagnostic report is admissible in evidence. The court is directed to consider four factors in making the transfer decision, but need not make any particular factual findings on any of the factors.

By 1995 amendment, the minimum certification age was lowered from 15 to 14, but only for capital, first degree, and aggravated controlled substance felonies.

Amendments in 1995 enacted subsections (m) and (n) to establish a rule that once a juvenile is certified, he is certified for subsequent felonies committed before age 17. A hearing in juvenile court is required to establish the predicate facts for mandatory certification in this circumstance.

A 1999 amendment to subsection (h) requires that the criminal court prosecutor be provided with a copy of the diagnostic study when a child is transferred to criminal court.

The post–18 year old certification provision in subsection (j) was expanded in 1995 to encompass any circumstance beyond the control of the state which precluded proceeding before the respondent became 18 and reversals of previous certification orders by a district court or on appeal.

A 1999 amendment to subsection (j) permits certification of a person who is 18 who is alleged to have committed murder or capital murder between the ages of 10 and 14 if the State could not have proceeded earlier. Such cases are now likely to arise as a result of solving cold cases through DNA testing.

The 1999 additions of subsections (o) through (r) give the juvenile court judge discretion to detain a person 18 or older being held for a certification hearing either in the juvenile detention facility or in the county jail. A detention hearing must be held using detention criteria, excluding those applicable only to children. If the juvenile court orders the person detained in a county jail, the juvenile court must set or deny bail as provided by law for adults.

CLE/Other Legal Publications

Certification. Ellen Smith, 17TH ANN. JUVE. L. CONF. (Feb. 2004)

Who Gets Certified? An Empirical Study of Discretionary Transfers from Juvenile to Criminal Court. Robert O. Dawson, 16 JUVE. L. SECT. RPT. (Dec. 2002)

Certification v. Determinate Sentence. Jean Boyd, Roseanna Salinas and Tiffany Burks, 16TH ANN. JUVE. L. CONF. (Feb. 2003)

Certification. Ellen Smith, 15TH ANN. JUVE. L. CONF. (Feb. 2002)

Determinate Sentence and Certifications. Brian Fischer, 14TH ANN. JUVE. L. CONF. (Feb. 2001)

Waiver of Jurisdiction Certification Hearings. Brian J. Fischer, 13TH ANN. JUVE. L. CONF. (Feb. 2000)

Procedural Aspects of the Mandatory Transfer Provision in Accordance with Title III, § 54.02 of the Texas Family Code—"Once Certified, Always Certified." David M. Kleckner & Rebecca A. Erb, 10 JUVE. L. SECT. RPT. (Dec. 1996)

An Empirical Study of Kent Style Juvenile Transfers to Criminal Court. Robert O. Dawson, 23 ST. MARY'S L.J. 975 (1992)

Responding to Misrepresentations, Nondisclosures and Incorrect Assumptions About the Age of the Accused: The Jurisdictional Boundary Between Juvenile and Criminal Courts in Texas. Robert O. Dawson, 18 ST. MARY'S L.J. 1117 (1987)

An Analysis of the Juvenile Court's Discretionary Power in Waiver of Jurisdiction Hearings. Jo Ann Ottis, 21 SO. TEX. L.J. 80 (1980)

Psychological Evaluation in Certification of Juveniles for Trial as Adults. J. Rays Hays & Kenneth S. Solway, 9 HOUSTON L. REV. 709 (1972)

Leading Cases

Breed v. Jones, 421 U.S. 519, 44 L.Ed.2d 346, 95 S.Ct. 1779 (1975) (double jeopardy requirements in transfer proceedings)

Kent v. United States, 383 U.S. 541, 16 L.Ed.2d 84, 86 S.Ct. 1045 (1966) (due process requirements in transfer proceedings)

Faisst v. State, 98 S.W.3d 226 (Tex. Crim. App. 2002) (certified juvenile may challenge juvenile court transfer after open plea in criminal court)

Rushing v. State, 85 S.W.3d 283 (Tex. Crim. App. 2002) (statute requiring pre-trial objection for failure to certify from juvenile court is constitutional)

Ex parte Gomez, 15 S.W.3d 103 (Tex. Crim. App. 2000) (juvenile entitled to good conduct credit on criminal sentence for time in juvenile detention before certification)

Hidalgo v. State, 983 S.W.2d 746 (Tex. Crim. App. 1999) (juvenile not entitled to have counsel notified of court order for diagnostic study interview)

Coffin v. State, 885 S.W.2d 140 (Tex. Crim. App. 1994) (testimony of deceased witness at transfer hearing admissible at criminal penalty phase)

In re R.A.G., 866 S.W.2d 199 (Tex. 1993) (probable cause for each offense transferred required to be shown at certification hearing)

Hardesty v. State, 659 S.W.2d 823 (Tex. Crim. App. 1983) (requirement that summons state purpose of hearing can be satisfied by summons' reference to petition)

Ex parte Allen, 618 S.W.2d 357 (Tex. Crim. App. 1981) (respondent can be prosecuted only for conduct for which juvenile court ordered transfer)

Ex parte Redmond, 605 S.W.2d 600 (Tex. Crim. App. 1980) (age of respondent at time of offense controls)

Faisst v. State, 105 S.W.3d 8 (Tex. App.—Tyler 2003, no pet.) (evidence sufficient to support certification for intoxication manslaughter because inadequate juvenile probation time)

In re M.A.V., 40 S.W.3d 581 (Tex. App.—San Antonio 2001, no pet.) (visiting judge should have recused himself on respondent's demand)

Melendez v. State, 4 S.W.3d 437 (Tex. App.—Houston [1st Dist.] 1999, no pet.) (failure to notify consular officer that national arrested not a jurisdictional defect in certification proceedings)

In re N.M.P., 969 S.W.2d 95 (Tex. App.—Amarillo 1999, no pet.) (novelty of DNA testing in 1988 justified delay in certification proceedings)

In re D.L.J., 981 S.W.2d 815 (Tex. App.—Houston [1st Dist.] 1998, no writ) (conducting hearing without counsel reversible)

In re J.C.C., 952 S.W.2d 47 (Tex. App.—San Antonio 1997, no writ) (due diligence not shown for post–18 year old certification proceedings)

In re T.L.C., 948 S.W.2d 41 (Tex. App.—Houston [14th Dist.] 1997, no writ) (S.A.R. not followed)

In re S.A.R., 931 S.W.2d 585 (Tex. App.—San Antonio 1996, writ denied) (confession not admissible at transfer hearing unless § 51.09(b) complied with)

In re B.N.E., 927 S.W.2d 271 (Tex. App.—Houston [1st Dist.] 1996, no writ) (court not required to hear alibi evidence once probable cause is shown)

In re S.J.M, 922 S.W.2d 241 (Tex. App.—Houston [14th Dist.] 1996, no writ) (no constitutional right to confrontation of witnesses at transfer hearing)

Brosky v. State, 915 S.W.2d 120 (Tex. App.—Fort Worth 1996, review ref'd) (prosecuting for different overt act but same conspiracy as alleged in certification petition OK)

In re J.C.J., 900 S.W.2d 753 (Tex. App.—Tyler 1995, no writ) (diagnostic interview warnings not required; appointment of psychiatrist not required)

In re Joseph, 864 S.W.2d 737 (Tex. App.—Houston [1st Dist.] 1993, no writ) (failure to transfer uncharged offense does not preclude transfer of charged offense)

L.M.C. v. State, 861 S.W.2d 541 (Tex. App.—Houston [14th Dist.] 1993, no writ) (confession and autopsy report admissible without regard to rules of evidence)

Turner v. State, 796 S.W.2d 492 (Tex. App.—Dallas 1990, no writ) (State may nonsuit unproved charges to permit transfer of all remaining charges)

A.T.S. v. State, 694 S.W.2d 252 (Tex. App.—Fort Worth 1985, writ dism'd w.o.j.) (insufficient evidence to support need for transfer to criminal court)

C.J.P. v. State, 650 S.W.2d 465 (Tex. App.—Houston [14th Dist.] 1983, no writ) (no mental health privilege regarding psychiatric examination)

In re I.B., 619 S.W.2d 584 (Tex. Civ. App.—Amarillo 1981, no writ) (full investigation does not require field investigation that resolves conflicting stories)

K.W.M. v. State, 598 S.W.2d 660 (Tex. Civ. App.—Houston [14th Dist.] 1980, no writ) (no Fifth Amendment claim regarding psychiatric examination)

R.S. v. State, 575 S.W.2d 641 (Tex. Civ. App.—Austin 1978, no writ) (court's refusal to disclose written material to defense attorney reversible error)

In re J.R.C., 551 S.W.2d 748 (Tex. Civ. App.—Texarkana 1977, writ ref'd n.r.e.) (reports admissible over hearsay objections; court not required to make affirmative findings on all statutory transfer factors)

R.E.M. v. State, 541 S.W.2d 841 (Tex. Civ. App.—San Antonio 1976, writ ref'd n.r.e.) (failure to do a complete study not fatal when respondent refused to cooperate)

R.E.M. v. State, 532 S.W.2d 645 (Tex. Civ. App.—San Antonio 1975, no writ) (requirement of diagnostic study is mandatory)

---

§ 54.021. County, Justice, or Municipal Court: Truancy.

(a) The juvenile court may waive its exclusive original jurisdiction and transfer a child to **the constitutional county court, if the county has a population of two million or more, or to** an appropriate justice or municipal court, with the permission of the county, justice, or municipal court, for disposition in the manner provided by Subsection (b) [~~of this section~~] if the child is alleged to have engaged in conduct described in Section 51.03(b)(2)[~~of this code~~]. A waiver of jurisdiction under this subsection may be for an individual case or for all cases in which a child is alleged to have engaged in conduct described in Section 51.03(b)(2) [~~of this code~~]. The waiver of a juvenile court's exclusive original jurisdiction for all cases in which a child is alleged to have engaged in conduct described in Section 51.03(b)(2) [~~of this code~~] is effective for a period of one year.

(b) A **county,** justice, or municipal court may exercise jurisdiction over a person alleged to have engaged in conduct indicating a need for supervision by engaging in conduct described in Section 51.03(b)(2) in a case where:

(1) the juvenile court has waived its original jurisdiction under this section; and

(2) a complaint is filed by the appropriate authority in the **county,** justice, or municipal court charging an offense under Section 25.094, Education Code.

(c) A proceeding in a **county,** justice, or municipal court on a complaint charging an offense under Section 25.094, Education Code, is governed by Chapter 45, Code of Criminal Procedure.

(d) Notwithstanding any other law, the costs assessed in a case filed in or transferred to a constitutional county court for an offense under Section 25.093 or 25.094, Education Code, must be the same as the costs assessed for a case filed in a justice court for an offense under Section 25. 093 or 25.094, Education Code.

(e) The proceedings before a constitutional county court related to an offense under Section 25.093 or 25.094, Education Code, may be recorded in any manner provided by Section 30.00010, Government Code, for recording proceedings in a municipal court of record.

History: Amended by 78th Legis., Reg. Sess. (2003), S.B. 358, eff. Sept. 1, 2003. Applies only to conduct occurring on or after effective date.

Comment

This section authorizes the juvenile court judge to transfer any conduct indicating a need for supervision case based on truancy to a justice or municipal court for adjudication and disposition proceedings. Consent of the justice court is required for waiver. Further, waiver of only one truancy case or of all cases by all juveniles for one year is authorized.

Amendments in 2001 make it clear that when a juvenile court sends a truancy case to a justice or municipal court, that court may exercise jurisdiction over the case as Failure to Attend School under the Education Code, not as an agent of the juvenile court, which was the case under prior law.

Old subsections (c) through (h) were repealed, revised, and re-enacted as article 45.054 of the Code of Criminal Procedure.

In 2003, amendments in (a), (b), (c) and new subsections (d) and (e) were enacted as part of a bill permitting the constitutional county judge in Dallas and Harris Counties to conduct, through magistrates, proceedings in failure to attend school cases or parental contributing to failure to attend school. It is expected only Dallas County will use this new authorization.

Leading Cases/Att'y Gen. Op.

In re B.A.M., 980 S.W.2d 788 (Tex. App.—San Antonio 1998, pet. denied) (juvenile has no right to appointed counsel when charged in justice court with failure to attend school)

Op. Tex. Att'y Gen. No. JC–0110 (1999) (JP or MC may compel custodian to attend court in truancy or failure to attend school case)

Op. Tex. Att'y Gen. No. LO–94–058 (1994) (community service as punishment; duty of schools to readmit)

Op. Tex. Att'y Gen. No. DM–200 (1993) (hearing not required before transfer to J.P.; juvenile entitled to counsel in J.P. court)

Cross Reference

Education Code § 7.111. High School Equivalency Examinations.

§ 54.022. [repealed]

§ 54.023. [~~Justice or Municipal Court: Enforcement.~~] [repealed]

History: Repealed by 78th Legis., Reg. Sess. (2003), H.B. 2319 and H.B. 3507, eff. Sept. 1, 2003. Applies only to conduct occurring on or after effective date.

Comment

This section in 2001 set out the enforcement powers of a justice or municipal court over juveniles who have been adjudicated for fineable offenses. Also in 2001, another bill, SB 1432, enacted substantially the same provisions as Tex. Code Crim. Proc. art. 45.050.

Since the provisions of this section are duplicated in the Code of Criminal Procedure, this section is repealed by HB 2319, Section 61(1).

§ 54.03. Adjudication Hearing.

(a) A child may be found to have engaged in delinquent conduct or conduct indicating a need for supervision only after an adjudication hearing conducted in accordance with the provisions of this section.

(b) At the beginning of the adjudication hearing, the juvenile court judge shall explain to the child and his parent, guardian, or guardian ad litem:

(1) the allegations made against the child;

(2) the nature and possible consequences of the proceedings, including the law relating to the admissibility of the record of a juvenile court adjudication in a criminal proceeding;

(3) the child's privilege against self-incrimination;

(4) the child's right to trial and to confrontation of witnesses;

(5) the child's right to representation by an attorney if he is not already represented; and

(6) the child's right to trial by jury.

(c) Trial shall be by jury unless jury is waived in accordance with Section 51.09. If the hearing is on a petition that has been approved by the grand jury under Section 53.045, the jury must consist of 12 persons and be selected in accordance with the requirements in criminal cases. Jury verdicts under this title must be unanimous.

(d) Except as provided by Section 54.031, only material, relevant, and competent evidence in accordance with the Texas Rules of Evidence applicable to criminal cases and Chapter 38, Code of Criminal Procedure, may be considered in the adjudication hearing. Except in a detention or discretionary transfer hearing, a social history report or social service file shall not be viewed by the court before the adjudication decision and shall not be viewed by the jury at any time.

(e) A child alleged to have engaged in delinquent conduct or conduct indicating a need for supervision need not be a witness against nor otherwise incriminate himself. An extrajudicial statement which was obtained without fulfilling the requirements of this title or of the constitution of this state or the United States, may not be used in an adjudication hearing. A statement made by the child out of court is insufficient to support a finding of delinquent conduct or conduct indicating a need for supervision unless it is corroborated in whole or in part by other evidence. An adjudication of delinquent conduct or conduct indicating a need for supervision cannot be had upon the testimony of an accomplice unless corroborated by other evidence tending to connect the child with the alleged delinquent conduct or conduct indicating a need for supervision; and the corroboration is not sufficient if it merely shows the commission of the alleged conduct. Evidence illegally seized or obtained is inadmissible in an adjudication hearing.

(f) At the conclusion of the adjudication hearing, the court or jury shall find whether or not the child has engaged in delinquent conduct or conduct indicating a need for supervision. The finding must be based on competent evidence admitted at the hearing. The child shall be presumed to be innocent of the charges against the child and no finding that a child has engaged in delinquent conduct or conduct indicating a need for supervision may be returned unless the state has proved such beyond a reasonable doubt. In all jury cases the jury will be instructed that the burden is on the state to prove that a child has engaged in delinquent conduct or is in need of supervision beyond a reasonable doubt. A child may be adjudicated as having engaged in conduct constituting a lesser included offense as provided by Articles 37.08 and 37.09, Code of Criminal Procedure.

(g) If the court or jury finds that the child did not engage in delinquent conduct or conduct indicating a need for supervision, the court shall dismiss the case with prejudice.

(h) If the finding is that the child did engage in delinquent conduct or conduct indicating a need for supervision, the court or jury shall state which of the allegations in the petition were found to be established by the evidence. The court shall also set a date and time for the disposition hearing.

(i) In order to preserve for appellate or collateral review the failure of the court to provide the child the explanation required by Subsection (b), the attorney for the child must comply with Rule **33.1** [~~52(a)~~], Texas Rules of Appellate Procedure, before testimony begins or, if the adjudication is uncontested, before the child pleads to the petition or agrees to a stipulation of evidence.

(j) When the state and the child agree to the disposition of the case, in whole or in part, the prosecuting attorney shall inform the court of the agreement between the state and the child. The court shall inform the child that the court is not required to accept the agreement. The court may delay a decision on whether to accept the agreement until after reviewing a report filed under Section 54.04(b). If the court decides not to accept the agreement, the court shall inform the child of the court's decision and give the child an opportunity to withdraw the plea or stipulation of evidence. If the court rejects the agreement, no document, testimony, or other evidence placed before the court that relates to the rejected agreement may be considered by the court in a subsequent hearing in the case. A statement made by the child before the court's rejection of the agreement to a person writing a report to be filed under Section 54.04(b) may not be admitted into evidence in a subsequent hearing in the case. If the court accepts the agreement, the court shall make a disposition in accordance with the terms of the agreement between the state and the child.

History: Amended by 78th Legis., Reg. Sess. (2003), H.B. 2319, eff. Sept. 1, 2003. Applies only to conduct occurring on or after effective date.

Comment

This section specifies the procedures to be used in adjudication hearings. The hearing must be separate from the disposition hearing. The child has a right to a trial by jury. The State must prove the allegations of its petition beyond a reasonable doubt. Illegally-seized evidence or an unlawfully-obtained confession is inadmissible. The testimony of an accomplice must be corroborated.

Amendments made in 1995 provided that the Rules of Criminal Evidence control in adjudication proceedings, not the Rules of Evidence, which was formerly the case. Amendments in 1999 change the reference from Rules of Criminal Evidence to Rules of Evidence applicable in criminal cases to reflect the integration of the rules into one set in 1998.

Subsection (i), added in 1997, requires a contemporaneous trial objection to preserve a failure to admonish claim for appellate or collateral review. Subsection (j), provides safeguards for the juvenile in plea bargaining by requiring that if the juvenile court judge refuses to honor the agreement, he or she must give the juvenile the opportunity to withdraw the plea.

The amendment in subsection (f) made in 1999 makes clear what was always the law: a court or jury may adjudicate for any lesser included offense raised by the evidence, even if the original charge was brought under the determinate sentence act.

The 2001 amendment in subsection (c) provides that jury selection in determinate sentence trials is governed by the Code of Criminal Procedure. Among other matters, that means that each party is entitled to 10 strikes, not six.

CLE/Other Legal Publications

Domestic Violence in Juvenile Court. Sarah Buel, 16TH ANN. JUVE. L. CONF. (Feb. 2003)

The Art of the Deal. Larry Gist, 16TH ANN. JUVE. L. CONF. (Feb. 2003)

Voir Dire and Jury Trials. Scott Stevens, 16TH ANN. JUVE. L. CONF. (Feb. 2003)

Advice to Prosecutors, Defense Attorneys and Judges (Ethics). Robert Riley & Dave Contreras, 15TH ANN. JUVE. L. CONF. (Feb. 2002)

Motions. Brian Fischer, 15TH ANN. JUVE. L. CONF. (Feb. 2002)

Detention, Adjudication and Modification of Disposition. Nydia Thomas, 15TH ANN. JUVE. L. CONF. (Feb. 2002)

Admonishments in Juvenile Adjudications. Floyd T. Getz, 13TH ANN. JUVE. L. CONF. (Feb. 2000)

Fairness First, Therapy Second: Charging a Jury in Juvenile Proceedings. Larry Wagenbach, 13TH ANN. JUVE. L. CONF. (Feb. 2000)

Jury Trials. Kent Ellis, 13TH ANN. JUVE. L. CONF. (Feb. 2000)

Child Witness Testimony. Bobby Dale Barina & A. Michelle May, 13TH ANN. JUVE. L. CONF. (Feb. 2000)

Leading Cases/Att'y Gen. Op.

Edmonson v. Leesville Concrete Co., 500 U.S. 614, 114 L.Ed.2d 660, 111 S.Ct. 2077 (1991) (*Batson* applies to strikes by private parties in civil litigation)

Powers v. Ohio, 499 U.S. 400, 113 L.Ed.2d 411, 111 S.Ct. 1364 (1991) (defendant and person struck from panel need not be of same race)

Batson v. Kentucky, 476 U.S. 79, 90 L.Ed.2d 69, 106 S.Ct. 1712 (1986) (State's use of peremptory strikes to eliminate racial group from jury violates equal protection)

McKeiver v. Pennsylvania, 403 U.S. 528, 29 L.Ed.2d 647, 91 S.Ct. 1976 (1971) (due process does not require right to jury trial in adjudication hearing)

In re Winship, 397 U.S. 358, 25 L.Ed.2d 368, 90 S.Ct. 1068 (1970) (due process requires State to prove charges beyond a reasonable doubt in juvenile adjudication proceedings)

In re Gault, 387 U.S. 1, 18 L.Ed.2d 527, 87 S.Ct. 1428 (1967) (due process requires notice, counsel, confrontation and privilege against self-incrimination in adjudication hearing)

In re D.I.B., 988 S.W.2d 753 (Tex. 1999) (defect in probation eligibility admonition harmful error)

In re K.L.C., 990 S.W.2d 242 (Tex. 1999) (prosecutor reading petition error but harmless)

In re J.R.R., 696 S.W.2d 382 (Tex. 1985) (failure to corroborate accomplice requires acquittal of respondent)

In re M.P., 126 S.W.3d 228 (Tex. App.—San Antonio 2003, no pet.) (error not to require unanimous verdict on at least one of four theories of aggravated sexual assault alleged)

In re D.D., 101 S.W.3d 695 (Tex. App.—Austin 2003, no pet.) (no jurisdiction to adjudicate for an offense not alleged in the petition or included in what was alleged)

In re J.W., 57 S.W.3d 446 (Tex. App.—Houston [14th Dist.] 2001, no pet.) (admonition as to adult record erroneous, but harmless)

In re M.A.V., 40 S.W.3d 581 (Tex. App.—San Antonio 2001, no pet.) (visiting judge should have recused himself on respondent's demand)

Atty. Gen. Opinion No. JC–0242, (2000) (state has no right to jury trial in juvenile proceedings)

In re E.J.G.P., 5 S.W.3d 868 (Tex. App.—El Paso 1999, no pet.) (no duty to admonish as to immigration consequences of a juvenile adjudication)

In re C.T.C., 2 S.W.3d 407 (Tex. App.—San Antonio 1999, no pet.) (OK to proceed with trial when juvenile fled after jury selected)

In re C.P., 998 S.W.2d 703 (Tex. App.—Waco 1999, no pet.) (error, but harmless, not to sever two counts of unauthorized use of motor vehicle)

In re B.G.M., 929 S.W.2d 604 (Tex. App.—Texarkana 1996, no writ) (court not required to admonish as to sex offender registration requirements)

In re J.M., 930 S.W.2d 820 (Tex. App.—Corpus Christi 1996, no writ) (juvenile waived under § 51.09(a) his right to admonitions under § 54.03(b))

In re C.L., 930 S.W.2d 935 (Tex. App.—Houston [14th Dist.] 1996, no writ) (error for prosecutor to argue that jury should find delinquent conduct to remove juvenile from abusive home)

In re K.B.H., 913 S.W.2d 684 (Tex. App.—Texarkana 1995, no writ) (failure to list witness does not preclude testimony of that witness)

In re G.M.P., 909 S.W.2d 198 (Tex. App.—Houston [14th Dist.] 1995, no writ) (juvenile court has no power to adjudicate when respondent is 18 or older at time of appellate reversal and remand)

In re A.S., 875 S.W.2d 402 (Tex. App.—Corpus Christi 1994, no writ) (proof of age jurisdictional requirement)

In re A.G.G., 860 S.W.2d 160 (Tex. App.—Dallas 1993, no writ) (failure to appoint guardian ad litem reversible error)

In re C.D.F., 852 S.W.2d 281 (Tex. App.—Dallas 1993, no writ) (jury waiver requires concurrence of attorney on record)

In re E.Q., 839 S.W.2d 144 (Tex. App.—Austin 1992, no writ) (plea of true involuntary because based on erroneous advice of counsel)

C.E.J. v. State, 788 S.W.2d 849 (Tex. App.—Dallas 1990, writ denied) (State's striking panel members on account of race violated equal protection in juvenile case)

In re D.L.K., 690 S.W.2d 654 (Tex. App.—Eastland 1985, no writ) (court not required to admonish regarding lesser included offenses)

V.C.H. v. State, 630 S.W.2d 787 (Tex. App.—Houston [1st Dist.] 1982, no writ) (jury waiver requires assent by child as well as attorney)

W.J.M.A. v. State, 602 S.W.2d 397 (Tex. Civ. App.—Beaumont 1980, no writ) (admonitions must be directed at child, not attorney)

R.E.M. v. State, 569 S.W.2d 613 (Tex. Civ. App.—Waco 1978, writ ref'd n.r.e.) (hearing prerequisite to order of adjudication)

State v. L.J.B., 561 S.W.2d 547 (Tex. Civ. App.—Dallas 1977), *rev'd*, 567 S.W.2d 795 (Tex. 1978) (summary judgment procedure inappropriate)

In re N.S.D., 555 S.W.2d 807 (Tex. Civ. App.—El Paso 1977, no writ) (adjudication hearing cannot be waived)

A.E.M. v. State, 552 S.W.2d 952 (Tex. Civ. App.—San Antonio 1977, no writ) (court required to admonish regarding lesser included offenses)

In re A.N.M., 542 S.W.2d 916 (Tex. Civ. App.—Dallas 1976, no writ) (six-person jury in county level court acceptable in non-determinate sentence case)

Op. Tex. Att'y. Gen. No. JC–0103 (1999) (juvenile court lacks jurisdiction over truancy by 17 year old)

§ 54.031. Hearsay Statement of Child Abuse Victim.

(a) This section applies to a hearing under this title in which a child is alleged to be a delinquent child on the basis of a violation of any of the following provisions of the Penal Code, if a child 12 years of age or younger is the alleged victim of the violation:

(1) Chapter 21 (Sexual Offenses) or 22 (Assaultive Offenses);

(2) Section 25.02 (Prohibited Sexual Conduct); or

(3) Section 43.25 (Sexual Performance by a Child).

(b) This section applies only to statements that describe the alleged violation that:

(1) were made by the child who is the alleged victim of the violation; and

(2) were made to the first person, 18 years of age or older, to whom the child made a statement about the violation.

(c) A statement that meets the requirements of Subsection (b) of this section is not inadmissible because of the hearsay rule if:

(1) on or before the 14th day before the date the hearing begins, the party intending to offer the statement:

(A) notifies each other party of its intention to do so;

(B) provides each other party with the name of the witness through whom it intends to offer the statement; and

(C) provides each other party with a written summary of the statement;

(2) the juvenile court finds, in a hearing conducted outside the presence of the jury, that the statement is reliable based on the time, content, and circumstances of the statement; and

(3) the child who is the alleged victim testifies or is available to testify at the hearing in court or in any other manner provided by law.

Comment

This section, patterned after Tex. Code Crim. Proc. Ann. art. 38.072, authorizes under limited circumstances "outcry" statements of a child to be admitted into evidence against a claim of hearsay.

Leading Cases/Att'y Gen. Op.

In re Z.L.B., 102 S.W.3d 120 (Tex. 2003) (respondent must prove outcry witness was not the first told about the sexual offense)

In re Z.L.B., 56 S.W.3d 818 (Tex. App.—Dallas 2001, pet. filed) (hearsay erroneously admitted as outcry testimony)

§ 54.032. Deferral of Adjudication and Dismissal of Certain Cases on Completion of Teen Court Program.

(a) A juvenile court may defer adjudication proceedings under Section 54.03 for not more than 180 days if the child:

(1) is alleged to have engaged in conduct indicating a need for supervision that violated a penal law of this state of the grade of misdemeanor that is punishable by fine only or a penal ordinance of a political subdivision of this state;

(2) waives, under Section 51.09, the privilege against self-incrimination and testifies under oath that the allegations are true;

(3) presents to the court an oral or written request to attend a teen court program; and

(4) has not successfully completed a teen court program [~~for the violation of the same penal law or ordinance~~] in the two years preceding the date that the alleged conduct occurred.

(b) The teen court program must be approved by the court.

(c) A child for whom adjudication proceedings are deferred under Subsection (a) shall complete the teen court program not later than the 90th day after the date the teen court hearing to determine punishment is held or the last day of the deferral period, whichever date is earlier. The court shall dismiss the case with prejudice at the time the child presents satisfactory evidence that the child has successfully completed the teen court program.

(d) A case dismissed under this section may not be part of the child's records for any purpose.

(e) The court may require a child who requests a teen court program to pay a fee not to exceed $10 that is set by the court to cover the costs of administering this section. The court shall deposit the fee in the county treasury of the county in which the court is located. A child who requests a teen court program and does not complete the program is not entitled to a refund of the fee.

(f) A court may transfer a case in which proceedings have been deferred as provided by this section to a court in **another** [~~a contiguous~~] county if the court to which the case is transferred consents. A case may not be transferred unless it is within the jurisdiction of the court to which it is transferred.

(g) In addition to the fee authorized by Subsection (e), the court may require a child who requests a teen court program to pay a $10 fee to cover the cost to the teen court for performing its duties under this section. The court shall pay the fee to the teen court program, and the teen court program must account to the court for the receipt and disbursal of the fee. A child who pays a fee under this subsection is not entitled to a refund of the fee, regardless of whether the child successfully completes the teen court program.

History: Amended by 78th Legis., Reg. Sess. (2003), H.B. 2319, eff. Sept. 1, 2003. Applies only to conduct occurring on or after effective date.

CLE/Other Legal Publication

The Teen Court Program in Texas: Where Texas Teenagers Can Find True Juries of Their Peers. Jill Juncker, 11 JUVE. L. SECT. RPT. (March 1997)

Cross Reference

TEX. CODE CRIM. PROC. ANN. art. 45.052. Dismissal of Misdemeanor Charge on Completion of Teen Court Program.

§ 54.033. Sexually Transmitted Disease, AIDS, and HIV Testing.

(a) A child found at the conclusion of an adjudication hearing under Section 54.03 of this code to have engaged in delinquent conduct that included a violation of Sections

21.11(a)(1), 22.011, or 22.021, Penal Code, shall undergo a medical procedure or test at the direction of the juvenile court designed to show or help show whether the child has a sexually transmitted disease, acquired immune deficiency syndrome (AIDS), human immunodeficiency virus (HIV) infection, antibodies to HIV, or infection with any other probable causative agent of AIDS. The court may direct the child to undergo the procedure or test on the court's own motion or on the request of the victim of the delinquent conduct.

(b) If the child or another person who has the power to consent to medical treatment for the child refuses to submit voluntarily or consent to the procedure or test, the court shall require the child to submit to the procedure or test.

(c) The person performing the procedure or test shall make the test results available to the local health authority. The local health authority shall be required to notify the victim of the delinquent conduct and the person found to have engaged in the delinquent conduct of the test result.

(d) The state may not use the fact that a medical procedure or test was performed on a child under this section or use the results of the procedure or test in any proceeding arising out of the delinquent conduct.

(e) Testing under this section shall be conducted in accordance with written infectious disease control protocols adopted by the Texas Board of Health that clearly establish procedural guidelines that provide criteria for testing and that respect the rights of the child and the victim of the delinquent conduct.

(f) Nothing in this section allows a court to release a test result to anyone other than a person specifically authorized under this section. Section 81.103(d), Health and Safety Code, may not be construed to allow the disclosure of test results under this section except as provided by this section.

Comment

This section is similar to Article 21.31 of the TEX. CODE CRIM. PROC. ANN. in that it authorizes a court to order tests for HIV of a respondent adjudicated for sexual assault, aggravated sexual assault or indecency with a child.

Cross Reference

TEX. HEALTH & SAFETY CODE ANN. § 81.103. Confidentiality; Criminal Penalty.

§ 54.034. Limited Right to Appeal: Warning.

Before the court may accept a child's plea or stipulation of evidence in a proceeding held under this title, the court shall inform the child that if the court accepts the plea or stipulation and the court makes a disposition in accordance with the agreement between the state and the child regarding the disposition of the case, the child may not appeal an order of the court entered under Section 54.03, 54.04, or 54.05, unless:

(1) the court gives the child permission to appeal; or

(2) the appeal is based on a matter raised by written motion filed before the proceeding in which the child entered the plea or agreed to the stipulation of evidence.

Comment

This provision requires the court to warn the child about the restrictions on appeal in a plea-bargained case that are imposed by § 56.01(n).

§ 54.04. Disposition Hearing.

(a) The disposition hearing shall be separate, distinct, and subsequent to the adjudication hearing. There is no right to a jury at the disposition hearing unless the child is in jeopardy of a determinate sentence under Subsection (d)(3) or (m), in which case, the child is entitled to a jury of 12 persons to determine the sentence.

(b) At the disposition hearing, the juvenile court may consider written reports from probation officers, professional court employees, or professional consultants in addition to the testimony of witnesses. Prior to the disposition hearing, the court shall provide the attorney for the child with access to all written matter to be considered in disposition. The court may order counsel not to reveal items to the child or the child's parent, guardian, or guardian ad litem if such disclosure would materially harm the treatment and rehabilitation of the child or would substantially decrease the likelihood of receiving information from the same or similar sources in the future.

(c) No disposition may be made under this section unless the child is in need of rehabilitation or the protection of the public or the child requires that disposition be made. If the court or jury does not so find, the court shall dismiss the child and enter a final judgment without any disposition. No disposition placing the child on probation outside the child's home may be made under this section unless the court or jury finds that the child, in the child's home, cannot be provided the quality of care and level of support and supervision that the child needs to meet the conditions of the probation.

(d) If the court or jury makes the finding specified in Subsection (c) allowing the court to make a disposition in the case:

(1) the court or jury may, in addition to any order required or authorized under Section 54.041 or 54.042, place the child on probation on such reasonable and lawful terms as the court may determine:

(A) in the child's own home or in the custody of a relative or other fit person; or

(B) subject to the finding under Subsection (c) on the placement of the child outside the child's home, in:

(i) a suitable foster home; or

(ii) a suitable public or private institution or agency, except the Texas Youth Commission;

(2) if the court or jury found at the conclusion of the adjudication hearing that the child engaged in delinquent conduct that violates a penal law of this state or the United States of the grade of felony or, if the requirements of Subsection (s) or (t) are met, of the grade of misdemeanor, and if the petition was not approved by the grand jury under Section 53.045, the court may commit the child to the Texas Youth Commission without a determinate sentence;

(3) if the court or jury found at the conclusion of the adjudication hearing that the child engaged in delinquent conduct that included a violation of a penal law listed in Section 53.045(a) and if the petition was approved by the grand jury under Section 53.045, the court or jury may sentence the child to commitment in the Texas Youth Commission with a possible transfer to the institutional division or the pardons and paroles division of the Texas Department of Criminal Justice for a term of:

(A) not more than 40 years if the conduct constitutes:

(i) a capital felony;

(ii) a felony of the first degree; or

(iii) an aggravated controlled substance felony;

(B) not more than 20 years if the conduct constitutes a felony of the second degree; or

(C) not more than 10 years if the conduct constitutes a felony of the third degree;

(4) the court may assign the child an appropriate sanction level and sanctions as provided by the assignment guidelines in Section 59.003; or

(5) if applicable, the court or jury may make a disposition under Subsection (m).

(e) The Texas Youth Commission shall accept a person properly committed to it by a juvenile court even though the person may be 17 years of age or older at the time of commitment.

(f) The court shall state specifically in the order its reasons for the disposition and shall furnish a copy of the order to the child. If the child is placed on probation, the terms of probation shall be written in the order.

(g) If the court orders a disposition under Subsection (d)(3) or (m) and there is an affirmative finding that the defendant used or exhibited a deadly weapon during the commission of the conduct or during immediate flight from commission of the conduct, the court shall enter the finding in the order. If there is an affirmative finding that the deadly weapon was a firearm, the court shall enter that finding in the order.

(h) At the conclusion of the dispositional hearing, the court shall inform the child of:

(1) the child's right to appeal, as required by Section 56.01; and

(2) the procedures for the sealing of the child's records under Section 58.003.

(i) If the court places the child on probation outside the child's home or commits the child to the Texas Youth Commission, the court:

(1) shall include in its order its determination that:

(A) it is in the child's best interests to be placed outside the child's home;

(B) reasonable efforts were made to prevent or eliminate the need for the child's removal from the home and to make it possible for the child to return to the child's home; and

(C) the child, in the child's home, cannot be provided the quality of care and level of support and supervision that the child needs to meet the conditions of probation; and

(2) may approve an administrative body to conduct permanency hearings pursuant to 42 U.S.C. Section 675 if required during the placement or commitment of the child.

(j) If the court or jury found that the child engaged in delinquent conduct that included a violation of a penal law of the grade of felony or jailable misdemeanor, the court:

(1) shall require that the child's thumbprint be affixed to the order; and

(2) may require that a photograph of the child be attached to the order.

(k) Except as provided by Subsection (m), the period to which a court or jury may sentence a person to commitment to the Texas Youth Commission with a transfer to the Texas Department of Criminal Justice under Subsection (d)(3) applies without regard to whether the person has previously been adjudicated as having engaged in delinquent conduct.

(l) Except as provided by Subsection (q), a court or jury may place a child on probation under Subsection (d)(1) for any period, except that probation may not continue on or after the child's 18th birthday. Except as provided by Subsection (q), the court may, before the period of probation ends, extend the probation for any period, except that the probation may not extend to or after the child's 18th birthday.

(m) The court or jury may sentence a child adjudicated for habitual felony conduct as described by Section 51.031 to a term prescribed by Subsection (d)(3) and applicable to the conduct adjudicated in the pending case if:

(1) a petition was filed and approved by a grand jury under Section 53.045 alleging that the child engaged in habitual felony conduct; and

(2) the court or jury finds beyond a reasonable doubt that the allegation described by Subdivision (1) in the grand jury petition is true.

(n) A court may order a disposition of secure confinement of a status offender adjudicated for violating a valid court order only if:

(1) before the order is issued, the child received the full due process rights guaranteed by the Constitution of the United States or the Texas Constitution; and

(2) the juvenile probation department in a report authorized by Subsection (b):

(A) reviewed the behavior of the child and the circumstances under which the child was brought before the court;

(B) determined the reasons for the behavior that caused the child to be brought before the court; and

(C) determined that all dispositions, including treatment, other than placement in a secure detention facility or secure correctional facility, have been exhausted or are clearly inappropriate.

(o) In a disposition under this title:

(1) a status offender may not, under any circumstances, be committed to the Texas Youth Commission for engaging in conduct that would not, under state or local law, be a crime if committed by an adult;

(2) a status offender may not, under any circumstances other than as provided under Subsection (n), be placed in a post-adjudication secure correctional facility; and

(3) a child adjudicated for contempt of a **county,** justice, or municipal court order may not, under any circumstances, be placed in a post-adjudication secure correctional facility or committed to the Texas Youth Commission for that conduct.

(p) Except as provided by Subsection (*l*), a court that places a child on probation under Subsection (d)(1) for conduct described by Section 54.0405(b) and punishable as a felony shall specify a minimum probation period of two years.

(q) If a court or jury sentences a child to commitment in the Texas Youth Commission under Subsection (d)(3) for a term of not more than 10 years, the court or jury may place the child on probation under Subsection (d)(1) as an alternative to making the disposition under Subsection (d)(3). The court shall prescribe the period of probation ordered under this subsection for a term of not more than 10 years. The court may, before the sentence of probation expires, extend the probationary period under Section 54.05, except that the sentence of probation and any extension may not exceed 10 years. The court may, before the child's 18th birthday, discharge the child from the sentence of probation. If a sentence of probation ordered under this subsection and any extension of probation ordered under Section 54.05 will continue after the child's 18th birthday, the court shall discharge the child from the sentence of probation on the child's 18th birthday unless the court transfers the child to an appropriate district court under Section 54.051.

(r) If the judge orders a disposition under this section and there is an affirmative finding that the victim or intended victim was younger than 17 years of age at the time of the conduct, the judge shall enter the finding in the order.

(s) The court may make a disposition under Subsection (d)(2) for delinquent conduct that violates a penal law of the grade of misdemeanor if:

(1) the child has been adjudicated as having engaged in delinquent conduct violating a penal law of the grade of misdemeanor on at least two previous occasions;

(2) of the previous adjudications, the conduct that was the basis for one of the adjudications occurred after the date of another previous adjudication; and

(3) the conduct that is the basis of the current adjudication occurred after the date of at least two previous adjudications.

(t) The court may make a disposition under Subsection (d)(2) for delinquent conduct that violates a penal law of the grade of misdemeanor if:

(1) the child has been adjudicated as having engaged in delinquent conduct violating a penal law of the grade of felony on at least one previous occasion; and

(2) the conduct that is the basis of the current adjudication occurred after the date of that previous adjudication.

(u) For the purposes of disposition under Subsection (d)(2), delinquent conduct that violates a penal law of this state of the grade of felony or misdemeanor does not include conduct that violates a lawful order of a **county,** municipal, justice, or juvenile court under circumstances that would constitute contempt of that court.

History: Amended by 78th Legis., Reg. Sess. (2003), S.B. 358, eff. Sept. 1, 2003. Applies only to conduct occurring on or after effective date.

Comment

This section establishes the procedures for the disposition hearing. Except in a determinate sentence case, there is no right to a jury at the disposition hearing. A social history report is admissible in evidence with prior disclosure to the parties. A child adjudicated for conduct indicating a need for supervision may not be committed to the Texas Youth Commission and there are restrictions on the commitment of a child adjudicated of a misdemeanor. A child adjudicated under the determinate sentence act may be given probation for up to 10 years or a sentence of up to 40 years for a capital or first degree felony, 20 years for a second degree felony and 10 years for a third degree felony.

The court or jury must find that the child is in need of rehabilitation or that the protection of the public requires disposition or else dismiss the case.

In 2001, the legislature prohibited the placement of a status offender in a secure correctional facility except as authorized by (n). It also prohibited the placement of a child adjudicated for contempt of a justice or municipal court in a secure facility or commitment to the TYC.

Added in 1999, subsection (q) authorizes up to 10 years probation in a determinate sentence act case. Probation is granted by the judge or jury as the case may be, but the length of the probation term is set by the court. Provisions under § 54.051 permit transfer of supervision to criminal court at age 18. This change is intended to make probation a more realistic possibility in some determinate sentence act cases.

Subsection (s) prohibits an indeterminate commitment to the TYC unless the respondent is adjudicated for a felony or, if for a misdemeanor, he has two previous adjudications for delinquent conduct in violation of a penal law. Each new offense must have occurred after adjudication of the previous offense. *See* also § 54.05(k).

In 2001, subsection (t) was added to permit commitment of one adjudicated for a misdemeanor to the TYC upon proof of one prior felony adjudication. Subsection (u) was added in 2001 to make it clear that an adjudication for contempt of a justice or municipal court does not count as a misdemeanor adjudication for TYC commitment.

CLE/Other Legal Publications

Disposition and Modification. Art Provenghi, 17TH ANN. JUVE. L. CONF. (Feb. 2004)

TYC Overview. Ross Robinson, 17TH ANN. JUVE. L. CONF. (Feb. 2004)

Female Juvenile Probation Programming in Texas. Melissa Jacobs, 18 JUVE. L. SECT. RPT. (Mar. 2004)

Shades of Gray: A Look at the Probation Disposition and Its Role within the Determinate Sentencing Act. Sue Beckage, 17 JUVE. L. SECT. RPT. (Dec. 2003)

Juvenile Sex Offender Un–Registration: An Analysis of the Application of Article 62.13(a)-(k) and the Evolution Towards Discretion in Juvenile Sex Offender Registration. John Zepeda, 16 JUVE. L. SECT. RPT. (Sep. 2002)

Juvenile Sex Offender Treatment Programs. Katheryn Kelly Graul, 16 JUVE. L. SECT. RPT. (Sep. 2002)

Drugs and the Adolescent Brain. Michael Nerney, 16TH ANN. JUVE. L. CONF. (Feb. 2003)

Sex Offender De–Registration. Kevin Collins, 16TH ANN. JUVE. L. CONF. (Feb. 2003)

Sex Offender Assessment Tools and Registration. David Montague, 16TH ANN. JUVE. L. CONF. (Feb. 2003)

The Adolescent Brain. Daniel T. Matthews, 15TH ANN. JUVE. L. CONF. (Feb. 2002)

TYC Resocialization and Specialized Treatment Programs. Linda Reyes, 15TH ANN. JUVE. L. CONF. (Feb. 2002)

Sex Offender Registration. David Montague, 15TH ANN. JUVE. L. CONF. (Feb. 2002)

Successful Probation Programs: An Overview of Available Research Tools. Carey Cockerell, 15TH ANN. JUVE. L. CONF. (Feb. 2002)

Sex Offender Un-registration and De-registration. Robert O. Dawson, 15 JUVE. L. SECT. RPT. (June 2001)

Sex Offender De-registration. Robert O. Dawson, 15 JUVE. L. SECT. RPT. (Sept. 2001)

Drugs and the Adolescent Brain. Michael Nerney, 14TH ANN. JUVE. L. CONF. (Feb. 2001)

TYC Commitment Criteria. Neil Nichols, 14TH ANN. JUVE. L. CONF. (Feb. 2001)

Critical Analysis of Psychological Reports. F. Gary Mears, 14TH ANN. JUVE. L. CONF. (Feb. 2001)

Sex Offender Registration. David Montague, 14TH ANN. JUVE. L. CONF. (Feb. 2001)

The Problems with Commitment Orders to the Texas Youth Commission. Stacie Henderson, 14 JUVE. L. SECT. RPT. (March 2000)

TYC Commitment Criteria. Neil Nichols, 13TH ANN. JUVE. L. CONF. (Feb. 2000)

Sex Offender Risk Assessment Tool. Melinda Bozarth & Ana Aguirre, 13TH ANN. JUVE. L. CONF. (Feb. 2000)

Sex Offender Registration. Paul Jordon, 13TH ANN. JUVE. L. CONF. (Feb. 2000)

About Face! Are Juvenile Boot Camps on the Right Track? Michael P. Cooley, 12 JUVE. L. SECT. RPT. (Sept. 1998)

Marlin Reception Center: What Can a Juvenile Expect? Kim Osburn, 12 JUVE. L. SECT. RPT. (June 1998)

The Change in Philosophy and Operation of the Texas Youth Commission. Jody Roberts, 12 JUVE. L. SECT. RPT. (March 1998)

Leading Cases/Att'y Gen. Op.

Texas Home Management v. Peavy, 89 S.W.3d 30 (Tex. 2002) (intermediate care facility owed duty to public to control violent retarded juvenile)

In re K.T., 107 S.W.3d 65 (Tex. App.—San Antonio 2003, no pet.) (en banc) (abuse of discretion, not evidence sufficiency, standard applied to removal from home disposition)

In re C.J.H., 79 S.W.3d 698 (Tex. App.—Fort Worth 2002, no pet.) (TYC commitment OK when placements rejected respondent because of his sexual orientation)

In re J.S.S., 20 S.W.3d 837 (Tex. App.—El Paso 2000, pet. denied) (privilege against self-incrimination applies to interview for social history report)

In re M.A.C., 999 S.W.2d 442 (Tex. App.—El Paso, 1999, no pet.) (no equal pro violation to commit Mexican national to TYC because of probation limitations)

In re J.S., 993 S.W.2d 370 (Tex. App.—San Antonio 1999, no pet.) (abuse of discretion in TYC commitment for sexual assault)

In re K.L.C., 972 S.W.2d 203 (Tex. App.—Beaumont 1998, no pet.) (factual insufficiency to support efforts to keep child at home requires commitment reversal)

In re A.S., 954 S.W.2d 855 (Tex. App.—El Paso 1997, no writ) (TYC commitment set aside as abuse of discretion)

Tex. Att'y Gen. Open Records Decision 645 (1996) (sex offender registration records are public)

In re J.R., 907 S.W.2d 107 (Tex. App.—Austin 1995, no writ) (no requirement of findings of fact in addition to statement of reasons for disposition)

In re A.F., 895 S.W.2d 481 (Tex. App.—Austin 1995, no writ) (social history report need not comply with rules of evidence; deadly weapon finding requires proof respondent personally used weapon)

K.K.B. v. State, 609 S.W.2d 824 (Tex. Civ. App.—Texarkana 1980, no writ) (court did not unlawfully delegate to foster parents power to fix conditions)

In re D.H, 556 S.W.2d 628 (Tex. Civ. App.—Waco 1977, writ ref'd n.r.e.) (court cannot order DHS to pay for treatment of DHS child in residential facility)

In re N.S.D., 555 S.W.2d 807 (Tex. Civ. App.—El Paso 1977, no writ) (insufficient evidence to support disposition selected)

In re A.N.M, 542 S.W.2d 916 (Tex. Civ. App.—Dallas 1976, no writ) (court may consider evidence admitted at adjudication hearing in selecting disposition; except under determinate sentence act, court cannot commit to TYC for a fixed term)

In re T.R.W, 533 S.W.2d 139 (Tex. Civ. App.—Dallas 1976, no writ) (requirement of a specific statement of reasons for disposition selected)

Op. Tex. Att'y Gen. No. LO 93–95 (1993) (dress and hair probation conditions may violate juvenile's free expression rights)

---

§ 54.0405. Child Placed on Probation for Conduct Constituting Sexual Offense.

(a) If a court or jury makes a disposition under Section 54.04 in which a child described by Subsection (b) is placed on probation, the court:

(1) may require as a condition of probation that the child:

(A) attend psychological counseling sessions for sex offenders as provided by Subsection (e); and

(B) submit to a polygraph examination as provided by Subsection (f) for purposes of evaluating the child's treatment progress; and

(2) shall require as a condition of probation that the child:

(A) register under Chapter 62, Code of Criminal Procedure; and

(B) submit a blood sample or other specimen to the Department of Public Safety under Subchapter G, Chapter 411, Government Code, for the purpose of creating a DNA record of the child, unless the child has already submitted the required specimen under other state law.

(b) This section applies to a child placed on probation for conduct constituting an offense for which the child is required to register as a sex offender under Chapter 62, Code of Criminal Procedure.

(c) Psychological counseling required as a condition of probation under Subsection (a) must be with an individual or organization that:

(1) provides sex offender treatment or counseling;

(2) is specified by the local juvenile probation department supervising the child; and

(3) meets minimum standards of counseling established by the local juvenile probation department.

(d) A polygraph examination required as a condition of probation under Subsection (a) must be administered by an individual who is:

(1) specified by the local juvenile probation department supervising the child; and

(2) licensed as a polygraph examiner under Chapter 1703, Occupations Code.

(e) A local juvenile probation department that specifies a sex offender treatment provider under Subsection (c) to provide counseling to a child shall:

(1) establish with the cooperation of the treatment provider the date, time, and place of the first counseling session between the child and the treatment provider;

(2) notify the child and the treatment provider, not later than the 21st day after the date the order making the disposition placing the child on probation under Section 54.04 becomes final, of the date, time, and place of the first counseling session between the child and the treatment provider; and

(3) require the treatment provider to notify the department immediately if the child fails to attend any scheduled counseling session.

(f) A local juvenile probation department that specifies a polygraph examiner under Subsection (d) to administer a polygraph examination to a child shall arrange for a polygraph examination to be administered to the child:

(1) not later than the 60th day after the date the child attends the first counseling session established under Subsection (e); and

(2) after the initial polygraph examination, as required by Subdivision (1), on the request of the treatment provider specified under Subsection (c).

(g) A court that requires as a condition of probation that a child attend psychological counseling under Subsection (a) may order the parent or guardian of the child to:

(1) attend four sessions of instruction with an individual or organization specified by the court relating to:

(A) sexual offenses;

(B) family communication skills;

(C) sex offender treatment;

(D) victims' rights;

(E) parental supervision; and

(F) appropriate sexual behavior; and

(2) during the period the child attends psychological counseling, participate in monthly treatment groups conducted by the child's treatment provider relating to the child's psychological counseling.

(h) A court that orders a parent or guardian of a child to attend instructional sessions and participate in treatment groups under Subsection (g) shall require:

(1) the individual or organization specified by the court under Subsection (g) to notify the court immediately if the parent or guardian fails to attend any scheduled instructional session; and

(2) the child's treatment provider specified under Subsection (c) to notify the court immediately if the parent or guardian fails to attend a session in which the parent or guardian is required to participate in a scheduled treatment group.

(i) A court that requires as a condition of probation that a child attend psychological counseling under Subsection (a) may, before the date the probation period ends, extend the probation for any additional period necessary to complete the required counseling as determined by the treatment provider, except that the probation may not be extended to a date after the date of the child's 18th birthday.

Comment

This section prescribes a particular form of sex offender treatment involving counseling and regular polygraph examinations and authorizes, but does not require, that the juvenile court make participation in that therapy a condition of probation. The entire section applies only to cases involving the commission of sex offenses against children under the age of 17. Similar provisions authorize making participation in counseling/polygraphing a condition of TYC parole. See Tex. Hum. Res. Code Ann. § 61.0813.

Leading Att'y Gen. Op.

In re D.L.C., 124 S.W.3d 354 (Tex. App.—Fort Worth 2003, no pet.) (requirement of DNA sample is constitutional and applies to probationers with excused registration)

Op. Tex. Att'y Gen. No. JC–0070 (1999) (probationer has 5th but not 6th Amendment rights in sex treatment program)

Op. Tex. Att'y Gen. No. DM–458 (1997) (registered sex offender treatment provider must report all information, even if dated or incomplete, regarding child abuse)

§ 54.0406. Child Placed on Probation for Conduct Involving a Handgun.

(a) If a court or jury places a child on probation under Section 54.04(d) for conduct that violates a penal law that includes as an element of the offense the possession, carrying, using, or exhibiting of a handgun, as defined by Section 46.01, Penal Code, and if at the adjudication hearing the court or jury affirmatively finds that the child personally possessed, carried, used, or exhibited the handgun, the court shall require as a condition of probation that the child, not later than the 30th day after the date the court places the child on probation, notify the juvenile probation officer who is supervising the child of the manner in which the child acquired the handgun, including the date and place of and any person involved in the acquisition.

(b) On receipt of information described by Subsection (a), a juvenile probation officer shall promptly notify the appropriate local law enforcement agency of the information.

(c) Information provided by a child to a juvenile probation officer as required by Subsection (a) and any other information derived from that information may not be used as evidence against the child in any juvenile or criminal proceeding.

Comment

This section requires a child placed on probation for an offense involving a handgun to inform his or her probation officer of how he or she acquired the handgun. Subsection (c) insures that anything said by the child in conformity to the requirements of this section cannot be used against the child in later judicial proceedings.

§ 54.0407. Cruelty to Animals: Counseling Required.

If a child is found to have engaged in delinquent conduct constituting an offense under Section 42.09, Penal Code, the juvenile court shall order the child to participate in psychological counseling for a period to be determined by the court.

§ 54.041. Orders Affecting Parents and Others.

(a) When a child has been found to have engaged in delinquent conduct or conduct indicating a need for supervision and the juvenile court has made a finding that the child is in need of rehabilitation or that the protection of the public or the child requires that disposition be made, the juvenile court, on notice by any reasonable method to all persons affected, may:

(1) order any person found by the juvenile court to have, by a wilful act or omission, contributed to, caused, or encouraged the child's delinquent conduct or conduct indicating a need for supervision to do any act that the juvenile court determines to be reasonable and necessary for the welfare of the child or to refrain from doing any act that the juvenile court determines to be injurious to the welfare of the child;

(2) enjoin all contact between the child and a person who is found to be a contributing cause of the child's delinquent conduct or conduct indicating a need for supervision; [~~or~~]

(3) after notice and a hearing of all persons affected order any person living in the same household with the child to participate in social or psychological counseling to assist in the rehabilitation of the child and to strengthen the child's family environment**; or**

(4) after notice and a hearing of all persons affected order the child's parent or other person responsible for the child's support to pay all or part of the reasonable costs of treatment programs in which the child is required to participate during the period of probation if the court finds the child's parent or person responsible for the child's support is able to pay the costs.

(b) If a child is found to have engaged in delinquent conduct or conduct indicating a need for supervision arising from the commission of an offense in which property damage or loss or personal injury occurred, the juvenile court, on notice to all persons affected and on hearing, may order the child or a parent to make full or partial restitution to the victim of the offense. The program of restitution must promote the rehabilitation of the child, be appropriate to the age and physical, emotional, and mental abilities of the child, and not conflict with the child's schooling. When practicable and subject to court supervision, the court may approve a restitution program based on a settlement between the child and the victim of the offense. An order under this subsection may provide for periodic payments by the child or a parent of the child for the period specified in the order but except as provided by Subsection (h), that period may not extend past the date of the 18th birthday of the child or past the date the child is no longer enrolled in an accredited secondary school in a program leading toward a high school diploma, whichever date is later.

(c) Restitution under this section is cumulative of any other remedy allowed by law and may be used in addition to other remedies; except that a victim of an offense is not entitled to receive more than actual damages under a juvenile court order.

(d) A person subject to an order proposed under Subsection (a) of this section is entitled to a hearing on the order before the order is entered by the court.

(e) An order made under this section may be enforced as provided by Section 54.07 of this code.

(f) If a child is found to have engaged in conduct indicating a need for supervision described under Section 51.03(b)(2) or (g), the court may order the child's parents or guardians to attend a program described by Section 25.093(f), Education Code, if a program is available.

(g) On a finding by the court that a child's parents or guardians have made a reasonable good faith effort to prevent the child from engaging in delinquent conduct or engaging in conduct indicating a need for supervision and that, despite the parents' or guardians' efforts, the child continues to engage in such conduct, the court shall waive any requirement for restitution that may be imposed on a parent under this section.

(h) If the juvenile court places the child on probation in a determinate sentence proceeding initiated under Section 53.045 and transfers supervision on the child's 18th birthday to a district court for placement on community supervision, the district court shall require the payment of any unpaid restitution as a condition of the community supervision. The liability of the child's parent for restitution may not be extended by transfer to a district court for supervision.

History: Amended by 78th Legis., Reg. Sess. (2003), H.B. 2319, eff. Sept. 1, 2003. Applies only to conduct occurring on or after effective date.

Comment

This section authorizes and limits the orders that may be placed by the juvenile court on the parents or other persons associated with a juvenile who has been adjudicated under Title 3.

The addition of (h) in 2001 authorizes extension of the child's but not a parent's obligations to make restitution beyond age 18 when the child is placed on determinate sentence probation.

Subsection (a)(4), added in 2003, authorizes a parental order to pay for treatment of the child while on probation.

CLE/Other Legal Publications

Juvenile Court Orders Affecting Parents and Others. Tracy Sneed, 7 Juve. L. Sect. Rpt. (Dec. 1993)

The Use of Restitution in Juvenile Dispositions. John Dahill, 4 Juve. L. Sect. Rpt. (Sept. 1990)

Leading Cases

In re C.T., 43 S.W.3d 600 (Tex. App.—Corpus Christi 2001, no pet.) (restitution may be ordered for vehicle damage from accident when adjudication is for leaving the scene)

In re M.S., 985 S.W.2d 278 (Tex. App.—Corpus Christi 1999, no pet.) (child and parent can be ordered to make restitution to victim's insurance company)

In re D.S., 921 S.W.2d 860 (Tex. App.—San Antonio 1996, no writ) (cannot order restitution in criminal trespass case because loss not caused by offense)

In re J.R., 907 S.W.2d 107 (Tex. App.—Austin 1995, no writ) (restitution—no requirement that State show that medical bills were reasonable charges)

---

§ 54.0411. Juvenile Probation Diversion Fund.

(a) If a disposition hearing is held under Section 54.04 of this code, the juvenile court, after giving the child, parent, or other person responsible for the child's support a reasonable opportunity to be heard, shall order the child, parent, or other person, if financially able to do so, to pay a fee as costs of court of $20.

(b) Orders for the payment of fees under this section may be enforced as provided by Section 54.07 of this code.

(c) An officer collecting costs under this section shall keep separate records of the funds collected as costs under this section and shall deposit the funds in the county treasury.

(d) Each officer collecting court costs under this section shall file the reports required under Article 103.005, Code of Criminal Procedure. If no funds due as costs under this section have been collected in any quarter, the report required for each quarter shall be filed in the regular manner, and the report must state that no funds due under this section were collected.

(e) The custodian of the county treasury may deposit the funds collected under this section in interest-bearing accounts. The custodian shall keep records of the amount of funds on deposit collected under this section and not later than the last day of the month following each calendar quarter shall send to the comptroller of public accounts the funds collected under this section during the preceding quarter. A county may retain 10 percent of the funds as a service fee and may retain the interest accrued on the funds if the custodian of a county treasury keeps records of the amount of funds on deposit collected under this section and remits the funds to the comptroller within the period prescribed under this subsection.

(f) Funds collected are subject to audit by the comptroller and funds expended are subject to audit by the State Auditor.

(g) The comptroller shall deposit the funds in a special fund to be known as the juvenile probation diversion fund.

(h) The legislature shall determine and appropriate the necessary amount from the juvenile probation diversion fund to the Texas Juvenile Probation Commission for the purchase of services the commission considers necessary for the diversion of any juvenile who is at risk of commitment to the Texas Youth Commission. The Texas Juvenile Probation Commission shall develop guidelines for the use of the fund. The commission may not purchase the services if a person responsible for the child's support or a local juvenile probation department is financially able to provide the services.

§ 54.042. License Suspension.

(a) A juvenile court, in a disposition hearing under Section 54.04, shall:

(1) order the Department of Public Safety to suspend a child's driver's license or permit, or if the child does not have a license or permit, to deny the issuance of a license or permit to the child if the court finds that the child has engaged in conduct that violates a law of this state enumerated in Section 521.342(a), Transportation Code; or

(2) notify the Department of Public Safety of the adjudication, if the court finds that the child has engaged in conduct that violates a law of this state enumerated in Section 521.372(a), Transportation Code.

(b) A juvenile court, in a disposition hearing under Section 54.04, may order the Department of Public Safety to suspend a child's driver's license or permit or, if the child does not have a license or permit, to deny the issuance of a license or permit to the child, if the court finds that the child has engaged in conduct that violates Section 28.08, Penal Code.

(c) The order under Subsection (a)(1) shall specify a period of suspension or denial [~~that is until the child reaches the age of 19 or for a period~~] of 365 days [~~, whichever is longer~~].

(d) The order under Subsection (b) shall specify a period of suspension or denial [~~that is~~]:

(1) [~~for a period~~] not to exceed 365 days; or

(2) **of 365 days** if the court finds the child has been previously adjudicated as having engaged in conduct violating Section 28.08, Penal Code[~~, until the child reaches the age of 19 or for a period not to exceed 365 days, whichever is longer~~].

(e) A child whose driver's license or permit has been suspended or denied pursuant to this section may, if the child is otherwise eligible for, and fulfills the requirements for issuance of, a provisional driver's license or permit under Chapter 521, Transportation Code, apply for and receive an occupational license in accordance with the provisions of Subchapter L of that chapter.

(f) A juvenile court, in a disposition hearing under Section 54.04, may order the Department of Public Safety to suspend a child's driver's license or permit or, if the child does not have a license or permit, to deny the issuance of a license or permit to the child for a period not to exceed 12 months if the court finds that the child has engaged in conduct in need of supervision or delinquent conduct other than the conduct described by Subsection (a).

(g) A juvenile court that places a child on probation under Section 54.04 may require as a reasonable condition of the probation that if the child violates the probation, the court may order the Department of Public Safety to suspend the child's driver's license or permit or, if the child does not have a license or permit, to deny the issuance of a license or permit to the child for a period not to exceed 12 months. The court may make this order if a child that is on probation under this condition violates the probation. A suspension under this subsection is cumulative of any other suspension under this section.

(h) If a child is adjudicated for conduct that violates Section 49.04, 49.07, or 49.08, Penal Code, and if any conduct on which that adjudication is based is a ground for a driver's license suspension under Chapter 524 or 724, Transportation Code, each of the suspensions shall be imposed. The court imposing a driver's license suspension under this section shall credit a period of suspension imposed under Chapter 524 or 724, Transportation Code, toward the period of suspension required under this section, except that if the child was previously adjudicated for conduct that violates Section 49.04, 49.07, or 49.08, Penal Code, credit may not be given.

History: Amended by 78th Legis., Reg. Sess. (2003), H.B. 2319, eff. Sept. 1, 2003. Applies only to conduct occurring on or after effective date.

Comment

The juvenile court is required to order the suspension of the driver's license of a juvenile who has been adjudicated for DWI or a controlled substance violation. The juvenile court may order the suspension of the juvenile's driving license for any other offense or as part of the revocation of probation.

Subsection (b) authorizes, but does not require, a juvenile court to order suspension or denial of driver's license upon adjudication of the offense of graffiti writing. Subsection (f) deals with the relationship of a license suspension for DWI and administrative license suspension.

In 2003, amendments in (c) and (d) conform the duration of suspensions for children to those authorized by other laws in cases of adults.

CLE/Other Legal Publication

The Discretionary Suspension of Juvenile's Driver's Licenses. Elizabeth M. Galaway, 7 JUVE. L. SECT. RPT. (Dec. 1993)

Leading Cases

In re R.S.J., 998 S.W.2d 871 (Tex. App.—Tyler 1999, no pet.) (misdemeanor POM does not authorize license denial until age 19; automatic provisions apply)

In re C.E.M., 981 S.W.2d 771 (Tex. App.—Houston [1st Dist.] 1998, no pet.) (no authority to suspend driver's license until age 19 for felony controlled substance violation)

Cross References

TEX. TRANSP. CODE ANN. ch. 521, subchapter L, Occupational Driver's License; § 521.342, Suspension of License for Person Under 21; § 521.372, Automatic Suspension of License on Conviction of Certain Felony Drug Violations.

---

§ 54.043. Monitoring School Attendance.

If the court places a child on probation under Section 54.04(d) and requires as a condition of probation that the child attend school, the probation officer charged with supervising the child shall monitor the child's school attendance and report to the court if the child is voluntarily absent from school.

§ 54.044. Community Service.

(a) If the court places a child on probation under Section 54.04(d), the court shall require as a condition of probation that the child work a specified number of hours at a community service project approved by the court and designated by the juvenile probation department as provided by Subsection (e), unless the court determines and enters a finding on the order placing the child on probation that:

(1) the child is physically or mentally incapable of participating in the project;

(2) participating in the project will be a hardship on the child or the family of the child; or

(3) the child has shown good cause that community service should not be required.

(b) The court may also order under this section that the child's parent perform community service with the child.

(c) The court shall order that the child and the child's parent perform a total of not more than 500 hours of community service under this section.

(d) A municipality or county that establishes a program to assist children and their parents in rendering community service under this section may purchase insurance policies protecting the municipality or county against claims brought by a person other than the child or the child's parent for a cause of action that arises from an act of the child or parent while rendering community service. The municipality or county is not liable under this section to the extent that damages are recoverable under a contract of insurance or under a plan of self-insurance authorized by statute. The liability of the municipality or county for a cause of action that arises from an action of the child or the child's parent while rendering community service may not exceed $100,000 to a single person and $300,000 for a single occurrence in the case of personal injury or death, and $10,000 for a single occurrence of property damage. Liability may not extend to punitive or exemplary damages. This subsection does not waive a defense, immunity, or jurisdictional bar available to the municipality or county or its officers or employees, nor shall this section be construed to waive, repeal, or modify any provision of Chapter 101, Civil Practice and Remedies Code.

(e) For the purposes of this section, a court may submit to the juvenile probation department a list of organizations or projects approved by the court for community service. The juvenile probation department may:

(1) designate an organization or project for community service only from the list submitted by the court; and

(2) reassign or transfer a child to a different organization or project on the list submitted by the court under this subsection without court approval.

(f) A person subject to an order proposed under Subsection (a) or (b) is entitled to a hearing on the order before the order is entered by the court.

(g) On a finding by the court that a child's parents or guardians have made a reasonable good faith effort to prevent the child from engaging in delinquent conduct or engaging in conduct indicating a need for supervision and that, despite the parents' or guardians' efforts, the child continues to engage in such conduct, the court shall waive any requirement for community service that may be imposed on a parent under this section.

(h) An order made under this section may be enforced as provided by Section 54.07.

(i) In a disposition hearing under Section 54.04 in which the court finds that a child engaged in conduct violating Section 521.453, Transportation Code, the court, in addition to any other order authorized under this title and if the court is located in a municipality or county that has established a community service program, may order the child to perform eight hours of community service as a condition of probation under Section 54.04(d) unless the child is shown to have previously engaged in conduct violating Section 521.453, Transportation Code, in which case the court may order the child to perform 12 hours of community service.

Comment

This section makes community service a mandatory condition of all juvenile probation orders. It also authorizes the juvenile court to order parents to perform community service with the child.

Subsection (i) authorizes but does not require community service of 8 hours for first offense and 12 hours for subsequent offense of possessing a fictitious driver's license or certificate.

---

§ 54.045. Admission of Unadjudicated Conduct.

(a) During a disposition hearing under Section 54.04, a child may:

(1) admit having engaged in delinquent conduct or conduct indicating a need for supervision for which the child has not been adjudicated; and

(2) request the court to take the admitted conduct into account in the disposition of the child.

(b) If the prosecuting attorney agrees in writing, the court may take the admitted conduct into account in the disposition of the child.

(c) A court may take into account admitted conduct over which exclusive venue lies in another county only if the court obtains the written permission of the prosecuting attorney for that county.

(d) A child may not be adjudicated by any court for having engaged in conduct taken into account under this section, except that, if the conduct taken into account included conduct over which exclusive venue lies in another county and the written permission of the prosecuting attorney of that county was not obtained, the child may be adjudicated for that conduct, but the child's admission under this section may not be used against the child in the adjudication.

Comment

This section tracks TEX. PEN. CODE ANN. § 12.45.

---

§ 54.046. Conditions of Probation for Damaging Property With Graffiti.

(a) If a juvenile court places on probation under Section 54.04(d) a child adjudicated as having engaged in conduct in violation of Section 28.08, Penal Code, in addition to other conditions of probation, the court may, with consent of the owner of the property, order the child as a condition of probation to restore the property by removing or painting over any markings made by the child on the property.

(b) In addition to a condition imposed under Subsection (a), the court may require the child as a condition of probation to attend a class with instruction in self-responsibility and empathy for a victim of an offense conducted by a local juvenile probation department.

Comment

In 1997, a separate offense of graffiti writing was created in § 28.08 of the Penal Code. This section authorizes but does not require the juvenile court to order restorative measures and/or educational classes as conditions of probation for that offense.

---

§ 54.0461. Payment of Juvenile Delinquency Prevention [~~Graffiti Eradication~~] Fees.

(a) If a child is adjudicated as having engaged in delinquent conduct that violates Section 28.08, Penal Code, the juvenile court shall order the child, parent, or other person responsible for the child's support to pay to the court a $5 **juvenile delinquency prevention** [~~graffiti eradication~~] fee as a cost of court.

(b) The court shall deposit fees received under this section to the credit of the county **juvenile delinquency prevention** [~~graffiti eradication~~] fund provided for under Article 102.0171, Code of Criminal Procedure.

(c) If the court finds that a child, parent, or other person responsible for the child's support is unable to pay the **juvenile delinquency prevention** [~~graffiti eradication~~] fee required under Subsection (a), the court shall enter into the child's case records a statement of that finding. The court may waive a fee under this section only if the court makes the finding under this subsection.

History: Amended by 78th Legis., Reg. Sess. (2003), H.B. 1828, eff. Sept. 1, 2003. Applies only to conduct occurring on or after effective date.

§ 54.047. Alcohol Related Offense.

If the court or jury finds at an adjudication hearing for a child that the child engaged in conduct indicating a need for supervision or delinquent conduct that violates the alcohol-related offenses in Section 106.02, 106.025, 106.04, 106.05, or 106.07, Alcoholic Beverage Code, or Section 49.02, Penal Code, the court shall, subject to a finding under Section 54.04(c), order, in addition to any other order authorized by this title, that, in the manner provided by Section 106.071(d), Alcoholic Beverage Code:

(1) the child perform community service; and

(2) the child's driver's license or permit be suspended or that the child be denied issuance of a driver's license or permit.

Comment

By reference to § 106.071(d), Alcoholic Beverage Code, this section requires the court to impose 8 to 12 hours of community service for the first offense and 20 to 40 hours for subsequent offenses and requires the court to order driver's license suspension for 30 days for a first offender, 60 days for a second-time offender and 180 for a third time offender.

§ 54.048. Restitution.

(a) A juvenile court, in a disposition hearing under Section 54.04, may order restitution to be made by the child and the child's parents.

(b) This section applies without regard to whether the petition in the case contains a plea for restitution.

§ 54.05. Hearing to Modify Disposition.

(a) Any disposition, except a commitment to the Texas Youth Commission, may be modified by the juvenile court as provided in this section until:

(1) the child reaches his 18th birthday; or

(2) the child is earlier discharged by the court or operation of law.

(b) Except for a commitment to the Texas Youth Commission, all dispositions automatically terminate when the child reaches his 18th birthday.

(c) There is no right to a jury at a hearing to modify disposition.

(d) A hearing to modify disposition shall be held on the petition of the child and his parent, guardian, guardian ad litem, or attorney, or on the petition of the state, a probation officer, or the court itself. Reasonable notice of a hearing to modify disposition shall be given to all parties.

(e) After the hearing on the merits or facts, the court may consider written reports from probation officers, professional court employees, or professional consultants in addition to the testimony of other witnesses. Prior to the hearing to modify disposition, the court shall provide the attorney for the child with access to all written matter to be considered by the court in deciding whether to modify disposition. The court may order counsel not to reveal items to the child or his parent, guardian, or guardian ad litem if such disclosure would materially harm the treatment and rehabilitation of the child or would substantially decrease the likelihood of receiving information from the same or similar sources in the future.

(f) Except as provided by Subsection (j), a disposition based on a finding that the child engaged in delinquent conduct that violates a penal law of this state or the United States of the grade of felony or, if the requirements of Subsection (k) are met, of the grade of misdemeanor, may be modified so as to commit the child to the Texas Youth Commission if the court after a hearing to modify disposition finds by a preponderance of the evidence that the child violated a reasonable and lawful order of the court. A disposition based on a finding that the child engaged in habitual felony conduct as described by Section 51.031 or in delinquent conduct that included a violation of a penal law listed in Section 53.045(a) may be modified to commit the child to the Texas Youth Commission with a possible transfer to the institutional division or the pardons and paroles division of the Texas Department of Criminal Justice for a definite term prescribed by Section 54.04(d)(3) if the original petition was approved by the grand jury under Section 53.045 and if after a hearing to modify the disposition the court finds that the child violated a reasonable and lawful order of the court.

(g) Except as provided by Subsection (j), a disposition based solely on a finding that the child engaged in conduct indicating a need for supervision may not be modified to commit the child to the Texas Youth Commission. A new finding in compliance with Section 54.03 must be made that the child engaged in delinquent conduct that meets the requirements for commitment under Section 54.04.

(h) A hearing shall be held prior to placement in a post-adjudication secure correctional facility for a period longer than 30 days or commitment to the Texas Youth Commission as a modified disposition. In other disposition modifications, the child and the child's parent, guardian, guardian ad litem, or attorney may waive hearing in accordance with Section 51.09.

(i) The court shall specifically state in the order its reasons for modifying the disposition and shall furnish a copy of the order to the child.

(j) If, after conducting a hearing to modify disposition without a jury, the court finds by a preponderance of the evidence that a child violated a reasonable and lawful condition of probation ordered under Section 54.04(q), the court may modify the disposition to commit the child to the Texas Youth Commission under Section 54.04(d)(3) for a term that does not exceed the original sentence assessed by the court or jury.

(k) The court may modify a disposition under Subsection (f) that is based on **an adjudication** [~~a finding~~] that the child engaged in delinquent conduct that violates a penal law of the grade of misdemeanor if:

(1) the child has been adjudicated as having engaged in delinquent conduct violating a penal law of the grade of felony or misdemeanor on at least **one** [~~two~~] previous **occasion before the adjudication that prompted the disposition that is being modified** [~~occasions~~]; and

(2) [~~of the previous adjudications,~~] the conduct that was the basis [~~for one~~] of the **adjudication that prompted the disposition that is being modified** [~~adjudications~~] occurred after the date of **the** [~~another~~] previous adjudication.

(l) The court may extend a period of probation under this section at any time during the period of probation or, if a motion for revocation or modification of probation is filed before the period of supervision ends, before the first anniversary of the date on which the period of probation expires.

History: Amended by 78th Legis., Reg. Sess. (2003), H.B. 2319, eff. Sept. 1, 2003. Applies only to conduct occurring on or after effective date.

Comment

This section specifies the procedures for a wide range of modifications of dispositional orders, from early termination of probation through its revocation and commitment to the Texas Youth Commission.

The 2001 amendment in (d) eliminates reference to the procedure for "revoking" CINS probation that was made obsolete by changes in 1999 in TYC commitment requirements. *See* § 51.03.

Subsection (j) authorizes the revocation of determinate sentence act probation and the imposition of any sentence up to the sentence that was originally assessed by the judge or jury. Because determinate sentence act probation now has a ceiling of 10 years upon revocation, the right to a jury at the revocation hearing has been eliminated.

Subsection (k) restricts TYC commitments to revocation of felony probation or revocation of misdemeanor probation if the child has two previous misdemeanor adjudications. 2003 amendments in (k) make it clear that a child who violates misdemeanor probation can be committed to TYC if the State proves at least one felony or misdemeanor adjudication prior to the adjudication that resulted in placing the child on probation. A total of two, not three, adjudications is required.

The 2001 amendment in subsection (h) requires that a modification hearing be held for a modification that results in a term of longer than 30 days in a local secure correctional facility, just as in the case of commitment to the TYC. Waiver of the hearing is not permitted.

Subsection (l), added in 2003, permits the court to extend the probation term at any time up to one year after it expired. It is modeled on a provision in the Code of Criminal Procedure applicable to criminal cases.

Leading Cases

In re E.D., 127 S.W.3d 860 (Tex. App.—Austin 2004, no pet.) (probation report authorized court to place runaway in secure confinement)

In re B.J., 100 S.W.3d 448 (Tex.App.—Texarkana 2003, no pet.) (non-association violation requires proof juvenile knew of other's probation status)

In re S.B., 94 S.W.3d 717 (Tex.App.—San Antonio 2002, no pet.) (three adjudications required for revocation of misdemeanor probation under prior law)

In re J.L.D., 74 S.W.3d 166 (Tex.App.—Texarkana 2002, no pet.) (violates due process to revoke probation for same offense for which the probation term had earlier been extended)

In re D.S.S., 72 S.W.3d 725 (Tex.App.—Waco 2002, no pet.) (written matter disclosure requirement applies only to penalty phase of modification hearing)

In re L.R., 67 S.W.3d 332 (Tex. App.—El Paso 2001, no pet.) (removal from home findings required for probation revocation)

In re M.A.W., 55 S.W.3d 101 (Tex. App.—Amarillo 2001, no pet.) (for 30 days court has plenary power to change probation term previously set by it)

In re D.R.A., 47 S.W.3d 813 (Tex. App.—Fort Worth 2001, no pet.) (removal from home findings not required for probation revocation)

In re J.A.D., 31 S.W.3d 668 (Tex. App.—Waco 2000, no pet.) (cannot revoke probation based on motion filed after probation expired)

In re S.H., 846 S.W.2d 103 (Tex. App.—Corpus Christi 1992, no writ) (no right to jury trial at modification hearing)

In re R.G., 687 S.W.2d 774 (Tex. App.—Amarillo 1985, no writ) (probation may be revoked after it has expired)

In re A.M.B., 676 S.W.2d 448 (Tex. App.—Houston [1st Dist.] 1984, no writ) (denial of jury at revocation hearing valid under Texas Constitution)

In re M.H., 662 S.W.2d 764 (Tex. App.—Corpus Christi 1983, no writ) (probation revoked for failure to pay restitution)

In re A.B.R., 596 S.W.2d 615 (Tex. Civ. App.—Corpus Christi 1980, writ ref'd n.r.e.) (statutory revocation procedures must be followed for suspended commitments)

In re M.L.S., 590 S.W.2d 626 (Tex. Civ. App.—San Antonio 1979, no writ) (10 days' notice of revocation required)

In re S.C., 556 S.W.2d 119 (Tex. Civ. App.—Waco 1977, no writ) (no requirement of 10 days' notice of revocation hearing)

A.Y. v. State, 554 S.W.2d 805 (Tex. Civ. App.—San Antonio 1977, no writ) (requirement of a specific statement of reasons for revoking probation)

In re R.A.B., 525 S.W.2d 892 (Tex. Civ. App.—Corpus Christi 1975, no writ) (illegally seized evidence inadmissible in probation revocation hearing)

In re E.B., 525 S.W.2d 543 (Tex. Civ. App.—Amarillo 1975, writ ref'd n.r.e.) (Chapter 55 applies to modification proceedings)

In re D.E.P., 512 S.W.2d 789 (Tex. Civ. App.—Houston [14th Dist.] 1974, no writ) (probation condition violated must have been a reasonable one)

---

§ 54.051. Transfer of Determinate Sentence Probation to Appropriate District Court.

(a) On motion of the state concerning a child who is placed on probation under Section 54.04(q) for a period, including any extension ordered under Section 54.05, that will continue after the child's 18th birthday, the juvenile court shall hold a hearing to determine whether to transfer the child to an appropriate district court or discharge the child from the sentence of probation.

(b) The hearing must be conducted before the child's 18th birthday and in the same manner as a hearing to modify disposition under Section 54.05.

(c) If, after a hearing, the court determines to discharge the child, the court shall specify a date on or before the child's 18th birthday to discharge the child from the sentence of probation.

(d) If, after a hearing, the court determines to transfer the child, the court shall transfer the child to an appropriate district court on the child's 18th birthday.

(e) A district court that exercises jurisdiction over a child transferred under Subsection (d) shall place the child on community supervision under Article 42.12, Code of Criminal Procedure, for the remainder of the child's probationary period and under conditions consistent with those ordered by the juvenile court.

(e–1) The restrictions on a judge placing a defendant on community supervision imposed by Section 3g, Article 42.12, Code of Criminal Procedure, do not apply to a case transferred from the juvenile court. The minimum period of community supervision imposed by Section 3(b), Article 42.12, Code of Criminal Procedure, does not apply to a case transferred from the juvenile court.

(e–2) If a child who is placed on community supervision under this **section** [~~subsection~~] violates a condition of that supervision or if the child violated a condition of probation ordered under Section 54.04(q) and that probation violation was not discovered by the state before the child's 18th birthday, the district court shall dispose of the violation of community supervision or probation, as appropriate, in the same manner as if the court had originally exercised jurisdiction over the case. **If the judge revokes community supervision, the judge may reduce the prison sentence to any length without regard to the minimum term imposed by Section 23(a), Article 42.12, Code of Criminal Procedure.**

(e–3) The time that a child serves on probation ordered under Section 54.04(q) is the same as time served on community supervision ordered under this **section** [~~subsection~~] for purposes of determining the child's eligibility for early discharge from community supervision under Section 20, Article 42.12, Code of Criminal Procedure.

(f) The juvenile court may transfer a child to an appropriate district court as provided by this section without a showing that the child violated a condition of probation ordered under Section 54.04(q).

(g) If the juvenile court places the child on probation for an offense for which registration as a sex offender is required by Chapter 62, Code of Criminal Procedure, and defers the registration requirement until completion of treatment for the sex offense under Article 62.13, Code of Criminal Procedure, the authority under that article to reexamine the need for registration on completion of treatment is transferred to the court to which probation is transferred.

(h) If the juvenile court places the child on probation for an offense for which registration as a sex offender is required by Chapter 62, Code of Criminal Procedure, and the child registers, the authority of the court to excuse further compliance with the registration requirement under Articles 62.13(*l*)–(r), Code of Criminal Procedure, is transferred to the court to which probation is transferred.

(i) If the juvenile court exercises jurisdiction over a person who is 18 years of age or older under Section 51.041 or 51.0412, the court or jury may, if the person is otherwise eligible, place the person on probation under Section 54.04(q). The juvenile court shall set the conditions of probation and immediately transfer supervision of the person to the appropriate court exercising criminal jurisdiction under Subsection (e).

History: Amended by 78th Legis., Reg. Sess. (2003), H.B. 2319, eff. Sept. 1, 2003. Applies to all cases without regard to whether the conduct or proceedings occur before, on, or after the effective date.

Comment

This section deals with the mechanics of administering the 1999 ten year determinate sentence act probation provision of section 54.04(q). If the juvenile court has imposed a probation term that extends beyond the child's 18 birthday, the State may file a motion for transfer before that date. If no such motion is filed probation terminates automatically upon the child's 18th birthday. After hearing, the juvenile court may discharge the child or order supervision to be transferred to district court. If the child is transferred, he or she is placed on adult community supervision on substantially the same terms as were provided for juvenile probation. A revocation after transfer or discovered after transfer is handled in the criminal courts; a pre-age 18 revocation is handled in the juvenile court.

In 2003, subsection (e–1) was added to make it clear that when a juvenile court transfers probation to criminal court, the criminal court is not prohibited by so-called 3g offense restrictions (aggravated offenses or deadly weapon findings) from placing the child on adult probation. It also makes it clear that minimum probation terms of adult law—2 years for second or third degree felony and 5 years for a first degree felony—do not apply. Subsection (e–2) relieves the criminal court judge of the minimum prison sentence restrictions upon revocation—2 years for a second or third degree felony and 5 years for a first degree felony.

Subsection (g), added in 2003, makes it clear that the authority to re-examine the need for sex offender registration in cases of registration deferral is transferred to the criminal court if probation supervision is transferred to criminal court. Under (h), authority to grant de-registration of a registered juvenile probationer is transferred to criminal court if probation supervision is transferred.

Subsection (i), added in 2003, permits a juvenile court to place a person 18 or older properly adjudicated under the determinate sentence act on probation and immediately transfer supervision to adult court. This means that a child does not lose probation eligibility just because disposition of his or her case is delayed until after the 18th birthday.

---

§ 54.06. Judgments for Support.

(a) At any stage of the proceeding, when a child has been placed outside the child's home, the juvenile court, after giving the parent or other person responsible for the child's support a reasonable opportunity to be heard, shall order the parent or other person to pay in a manner directed by the court a reasonable sum for the support in whole or in part of the child or the court shall waive the payment by order. The court shall order that the payment for support be made to the local juvenile probation department to be used only for residential care and other support for the child unless the child has been committed to the Texas Youth Commission, in which case the court shall order that the payment be made to the Texas Youth Commission for deposit in a special account in the general revenue fund that may be appropriated only for the care of children committed to the commission.

(b) At any stage of the proceeding, when a child has been placed outside the child's home and the parent of the child is obligated to pay support for the child under a court order under Title 5, the juvenile court shall order that the person entitled to receive the support assign the person's right to support for the child placed outside the child's home to the local juvenile probation department to be used for residential care and other support for the child unless the child has been committed to the Texas Youth Commission, in which event the court shall order that the assignment be made to the Texas Youth Commission.

(c) A court may enforce an order for support under this section by ordering garnishment of the wages of the person ordered to pay support or by any other means available to enforce a child support order under Title 5.

(d) Repealed by Acts 2003, 78th Leg., ch. 283, § 61(1).

(e) The court shall apply the child support guidelines under Subchapter C, Chapter 154, in an order requiring the payment of child support under this section. The court shall also require in an order to pay child support under this section that health insurance be provided for the child. Subchapter D, Chapter 154, applies to an order requiring health insurance for a child under this section.

(f) An order under this section prevails over any previous child support order issued with regard to the child to the extent of any conflict between the orders.

History: Amended by 78th Legis., Reg. Sess. (2003), H.B. 2319, eff. Sept. 1, 2003. Applies only to conduct occurring on or after effective date.

Comment

Subsection (d) was repealed in 2003 by HB 2319, Section 61(1) because Section 54.07, to which it refers, was modified to speak only to court orders other than child support. Subsection (c) accesses all Title 5 remedies for child support orders entered under this section.

§ 54.061. Payment of Probation Fees.

(a) If a child is placed on probation under Section 54.04(d)(1) of this code, the juvenile court, after giving the child, parent, or other person responsible for the child's support a reasonable opportunity to be heard, shall order the child, parent, or other person, if financially able to do so, to pay to the court a fee of not more than $15 a month during the period that the child continues on probation.

(b) Orders for the payment of fees under this section may be enforced as provided by Section 54.07 of this code.

(c) The court shall deposit the fees received under this section in the county treasury to the credit of a special fund that may be used only for juvenile probation or community-based juvenile corrections services or facilities in which a juvenile may be required to live while under court supervision.

(d) If the court finds that a child, parent, or other person responsible for the child's support is financially unable to pay the probation fee required under Subsection (a), the court shall enter into the records of the child's case a statement of that finding. The court may waive a fee under this section only if the court makes the finding under this subsection.

§ 54.07. Enforcement of Order.

(a) **Except as provided by Subsection (b) or a juvenile court child support order, any** [~~Any~~] order of the juvenile court may be enforced **as provided by Chapter 61** [~~by contempt~~].

(b) **A violation of any of the following orders of the** [~~The~~] juvenile court may **not be enforced by contempt of court proceedings against the child:**

(1) an order setting conditions of probation;

(2) an order setting conditions of deferred prosecution; and

(3) an order setting conditions of release from detention [~~enforce its order for support or for the payment of restitution or probation fees by civil contempt proceedings after 10 days' notice to the defaulting person of his failure or refusal to carry out the terms of the order~~].

(c) **This section and Chapter 61 do not preclude a** [~~On the motion of the~~] juvenile court **from summarily finding** [~~or any person or agency entitled to receive restitution or probation payments or payments for the benefit of~~] a child **or other** [~~, the juvenile court may render judgment against a defaulting~~] person **in direct contempt of the juvenile court for conduct occurring in the presence of the judge of the court. Direct contempt of the juvenile court by a child is punishable by a maximum of** [~~for any amount unpaid and owing after~~] 10 days' **confinement in a secure juvenile detention facility or by a maximum of 40 hours of community service, or both. The juvenile court may not impose a fine on a child for direct contempt** [~~notice to the defaulting person of his failure or refusal to carry out the terms of the order. The judgment may be enforced by any means available for the enforcement of judgments for other debts~~].

(d) This section and Chapter 61 do not preclude a juvenile court in an appropriate case from using a civil or coercive contempt proceeding to enforce an order.

History: Amended by 78th Legis., Reg. Sess. (2003), H.B. 2319, eff. Sept. 1, 2003. Applies only to conduct occurring on or after effective date.

Comment

2003 amendments to this section conform to the enactment of Chapter 61 dealing with parental rights and responsibilities. The amendment to (a) excepts child support orders from Title 3 enforcement of parental orders because 54.06 accesses the full range of Title

5 enforcement remedies for such orders. 2003 amendments in (b) prohibit using contempt of court proceedings to enforce violations of probation, deferred prosecution or conditional release from detention, since specific remedies for such violations are provided elsewhere. 2003 amendments in (c) save direct contempt from procedural complexities of Chapter 61 and restrict the penalties that may be imposed for direct contempt by juveniles. Subsection (d), added in 2003, saves civil or coercive contempt—confinement until the subject complies with a court order—from the requirements of Chapter 61.

§ 54.08. Public Access to Court Hearings.

(a) Except as provided by this section, the court shall open hearings under this title to the public unless the court, for good cause shown, determines that the public should be excluded.

(b) The court may not prohibit a person who is a victim of the conduct of a child, or the person's family, from personally attending a hearing under this title relating to the conduct by the child unless the victim or member of the victim's family is to testify in the hearing or any subsequent hearing relating to the conduct and the court determines that the victim's or family member's testimony would be materially affected if the victim or member of the victim's family hears other testimony at trial.

(c) If a child is under the age of 14 at the time of the hearing, the court shall close the hearing to the public unless the court finds that the interests of the child or the interests of the public would be better served by opening the hearing to the public.

(d) In this section, "family" has the meaning assigned by Section 71.003.

Comment

Subsection (b) expands the victim's right to attend a juvenile hearing to include members of the victim's family. Subsection (c) provides that if the respondent is under the age of 14 at the time of the hearing, the hearing is presumed to be closed, but may be opened by the judge upon a finding that the interests of the child or the public would be better served by an open hearing. If the child is 14 years of age or older, the hearing is presumptively open but the court can for good cause shown close the hearing.

CLE/Other Legal Publication

A Media Policy for Juvenile Offenders: Does the Publication Fit the Crime? Michelle Cawley, 11 Juve. L. Sect. Rpt. (Sept. 1997)

§ 54.09. Recording of Proceedings.

All judicial proceedings under this chapter except detention hearings shall be recorded by stenographic notes or by electronic, mechanical, or other appropriate means. Upon request of any party, a detention hearing shall be recorded.

Leading Cases

In re S.J., 940 S.W.2d 332 (Tex. App.—San Antonio 1997, no writ) (juvenile waived under § 51.09 right to have proceedings recorded)

S.S. v. State, 879 S.W.2d 395 (Tex. App.—Eastland 1994, no writ) (failure to record jury argument reversible error)

§ 54.10. Hearings Before Referee.

(a) Except as provided by Subsection (e), a hearing under Section 54.03, 54.04, or 54.05, including a jury trial, a hearing under Chapter 55, including a jury trial, or a hearing under Article IV, Article V, and Article VI of the Uniform Interstate Compact on Juveniles (Chapter 60) may be held by a referee appointed in accordance with Section 51.04(g) or a master appointed under Chapter 54, Government Code, provided:

(1) the parties have been informed by the referee or master that they are entitled to have the hearing before the juvenile court judge; and

(2) after each party is given an opportunity to object, no party objects to holding the hearing before the referee or master.

(b) The determination under Section 53.02(f) whether to release a child may be made by a referee appointed in accordance with Section 51.04(g) if:

(1) the child has been informed by the referee that the child is entitled to have the determination made by the juvenile court judge or a substitute judge authorized by Section 51.04(f); or

(2) the child and the attorney for the child have in accordance with Section 51.09 waived the right to have the determination made by the juvenile court judge or a substitute judge.

(c) If a child objects to a referee making the determination under Section 53.02(f), the juvenile court judge or a substitute judge authorized by Section 51.04(f) shall make the determination.

(d) At the conclusion of the hearing or immediately after making the determination, the referee shall transmit written findings and recommendations to the juvenile court judge. The juvenile court judge shall adopt, modify, or reject the referee's recommendations not later than the next working day after the day that the judge receives the recommendations. Failure to act within that time results in release of the child by operation of law and a recommendation that the child be released operates to secure the child's immediate release subject to the power of the juvenile court judge to modify or reject that recommendation.

(e) The hearings provided by Sections 54.03, 54.04, and 54.05 may not be held before a referee if the grand jury has approved of the petition and the child is subject to a determinate sentence.

Comment

A referee or master may conduct a detention hearing, an adjudication hearing, a disposition hearing or a modification of disposition hearing. He or she may not conduct a transfer (certification) hearing but under a 1999 amendment may conduct a chapter 55 (mental illness or retardation) hearing and may conduct a jury trial if otherwise authorized to conduct that type of hearing. A referee or master may not conduct an adjudication, disposition or modification hearing under the determinate sentence act.

Subsections (b) and (c) were added in 1999 by the carry-a-firearm-go-to-detention bill to address the situation in which a referee or master releases the child from detention.

CLE/Other Legal Publication

The Texas Juvenile Referee and Master System. Lisa Crosswell, 5 JUVE. L. SECT. RPT. (Dec. 1991)

Leading Cases

Swisher v. Brady, 438 U.S. 204, 57 L.Ed.2d 705, 98 S.Ct. 2699 (1978) (double jeopardy not violated by judge's overruling referee's recommendation that respondent be acquitted)

In re D.L.M., 982 S.W.2d 146 (Tex. App.—Houston [1st Dist.] 1998, no writ) (Harris County juvenile law master must obtain waiver from juvenile to hear case)

In re E.B.S., 756 S.W.2d 852 (Tex. App.—Austin 1988, no writ) (failure of referee to inform parties of right to hearing before judge voids proceedings)

A.R. v. State, 678 S.W.2d 177 (Tex. App.—Tyler 1984, no writ) (judge's granting new trial on evidence sufficiency grounds precludes re-trial)

§ 54.11. Release or Transfer Hearing.

(a) On receipt of a referral under Section 61.079(a), Human Resources Code, for the transfer to the institutional division of the Texas Department of Criminal Justice of a person committed to the Texas Youth Commission under Section 54.04(d)(3), 54.04(m), or 54.05(f), or on receipt of a request by the commission under Section 61.081(g), Human Resources Code, for approval of the release under supervision of a person committed to the commission under Section 54.04(d)(3), 54.04(m), or 54.05(f), the court shall set a time and place for a hearing on the release of the person.

(b) The court shall notify the following of the time and place of the hearing:

(1) the person to be transferred or released under supervision;

(2) the parents of the person;

(3) any legal custodian of the person, including the Texas Youth Commission;

(4) the office of the prosecuting attorney that represented the state in the juvenile delinquency proceedings;

(5) the victim of the offense that was included in the delinquent conduct that was a ground for the disposition, or a member of the victim's family; and

(6) any other person who has filed a written request with the court to be notified of a release hearing with respect to the person to be transferred or released under supervision.

(c) Except for the person to be transferred or released under supervision and the prosecuting attorney, the failure to notify a person listed in Subsection (b) of this section does not affect the validity of a hearing conducted or determination made under this section if the record in the case reflects that the whereabouts of the persons who did not receive notice were unknown to the court and a reasonable effort was made by the court to locate those persons.

(d) At a hearing under this section the court may consider written reports from probation officers, professional court employees, professional consultants, or employees of the Texas Youth Commission, in addition to the testimony of witnesses. At least one day before the hearing, the court shall provide the attorney for the person to be transferred or released under supervision with access to all written matter to be considered by the court.

(e) At the hearing, the person to be transferred or released under supervision is entitled to an attorney, to examine all witnesses against him, to present evidence and oral argument, and to previous examination of all reports on and evaluations and examinations of or relating to him that may be used in the hearing.

(f) A hearing under this section is open to the public unless the person to be transferred or released under supervision waives a public hearing with the consent of his attorney and the court.

(g) A hearing under this section must be recorded by a court reporter or by audio or video tape recording, and the record of the hearing must be retained by the court for at least two years after the date of the final determination on the transfer or release of the person by the court.

(h) The hearing on a person who is referred for transfer under Section 61.079(a), Human Resources Code, shall be held not later than the 60th day after the date the court receives the referral.

(i) On conclusion of the hearing on a person who is referred for transfer under Section 61.079(a), Human Resources Code, the court may order:

(1) the return of the person to the Texas Youth Commission; or

(2) the transfer of the person to the custody of the institutional division of the Texas Department of Criminal Justice for the completion of the person's sentence.

(j) On conclusion of the hearing on a person who is referred for release under supervision under Section 61.081(f), Human Resources Code, the court may order the return of the person to the Texas Youth Commission:

(1) with approval for the release of the person under supervision; or

(2) without approval for the release of the person under supervision.

(k) In making a determination under this section, the court may consider the experiences and character of the person before and after commitment to the youth commission, the nature of the penal offense that the person was found to have committed and the manner in which the offense was committed, the abilities of the person to contribute to society, the protection of the victim of the offense or any member of the victim's family, the recommendations of the youth commission and prosecuting attorney, the best interests of the person, and any other factor relevant to the issue to be decided.

(l) Pending the conclusion of a transfer hearing, the juvenile court shall order that the person who is referred for transfer be detained in a certified juvenile detention facility as provided by Subsection (m). If the person is at least 17 years of age, the juvenile court may order that the person be detained without bond in an appropriate county facility for the detention of adults accused of criminal offenses.

(m) The detention of a person in a certified juvenile detention facility must comply with the detention requirements under this title, except that, to the extent practicable, the person must be kept separate from children detained in the same facility.

(n) If the juvenile court orders that a person who is referred for transfer be detained in a county facility under Subsection (*l*), the county sheriff shall take custody of the person under the juvenile court's order.

History: Amended by 78th Legis., Reg. Sess. (2003), H.B. 2319, eff. Sept. 1, 2003. Applies only to conduct occurring on or after effective date.

Comment

Amendments made in 1995 abolished the requirement of a release/transfer hearing in each determinate sentence case. Under the amendments, a hearing is required only upon discretionary request of the TYC to release a youth before the statutory minimum length of stay has been served or to transfer a youth 16 years or older to TDCJ.

Subsections (l) through (n), added in 2003, authorize a juvenile court, pending a transfer/release hearing, to confine a person 17 or older in a certified juvenile detention facility or without bond in the county jail.

CLE/Other Legal Publications

Juvenile Transfer from TYC to TDCJ: TYC Screening and Judicial Response. Zach Redington, 17 Juve. L. Sect. Rpt. (Mar. 2003)

Determinate Sentence Transfers. Sharon Pruitt, 16th Ann. Juve. L. Conf. (Feb. 2003)

Release/Transfer Hearings Under the Determinate Sentence Act. Beth Weinmann, 9 Juve. L. Sect. Rpt. (Sept. 1995)

Parole Supervision and Revocation Under the Determinate Sentence Act. Gillian Galbraith, 8 JUVE. L. SECT. RPT. (March 1994)

Leading Cases

In re C.D.T., III, 98 S.W.3d 280 (Tex.App.—Houston [1st Dist.] 2003, rev. denied) (OK for TYC to give judge letters from juvenile; gatekeeper finding not required for experts)

In re J.L.S., 47 S.W.3d 128 (Tex. App.—Waco 2001, no pet.) (notice in court of time and place of hearing to consider transfer to TDCJ complies with statute)

In re R.D.B., 20 S.W.3d 255 (Tex. App.—Texarkana 2000, no pet.) (ineffective assistance of counsel in failure to seek appointment of mental health expert for transfer hearing)

In re B.D., 16 S.W.3d 77 (Tex. App.—Houston [1st Dist.] 2000, pet. denied) (Chapter 55 does not apply to release/transfer hearing when respondent is 18 or older)

In re M.R., 5 S.W.3d 879 (Tex. App.—San Antonio 1999, no pet.) (failure to grant continuance in hearing denied confrontation right)

In re R.G., 994 S.W.2d 309 (Tex. App.—Houston [1st Dist.] 1999, no pet.) (no discretion abuse in transfer contrary to expert recommendation)

In re J.M.O., 980 S.W.2d 811 (Tex. App.—San Antonio 1998, pet. denied) (confrontation right not violated by hearsay testimony at hearing)

In re J.E.H., 972 S.W.2d 928 (Tex. App.—Beaumont 1998, no writ) (error not to appoint mental health expert for child at hearing)

In re T.C.K., 877 S.W.2d 43 (Tex. App.—Beaumont 1994, no writ) (hearsay testimony of TYC employee admissible at hearing)

In re C.D.R., 827 S.W.2d 589 (Tex. App.—Houston [1st Dist.] 1992, no writ) (TYC report admissible at release/transfer hearing)

Chapter 55. Proceedings Concerning Children With Mental Illness or Mental Retardation.

Subchapter A. General Provisions

§ 55.01. Meaning of "Having a Mental Illness."
§ 55.02. Mental Health and Mental Retardation Jurisdiction.
§ 55.03. Standards of Care.

Subchapter B. Child with Mental Illness.

§ 55.11. Mental Illness Determination; Examination.
§ 55.12. Initiation Of Commitment Proceedings.
§ 55.13. Commitment Proceedings in Juvenile Court.
§ 55.14. Referral for Commitment Proceedings.
§ 55.15. Standards of Care; Expiration of Court Order for Mental Health Services.
§ 55.16. Order for Mental Health Services; Stay of Proceedings.
§ 55.17. Mental Health Services Not Ordered; Dissolution of Stay.
§ 55.18. Discharge from Mental Health Facility Before Reaching 18 Years of Age.
§ 55.19. Transfer to Criminal Court on 18th Birthday. **[amended]**

Subchapter C. Child Unfit to Proceed as a Result of Mental Illness or Mental Retardation

§ 55.31. Unfitness to Proceed Determination; Examination.
§ 55.32. Hearing on Issue of Fitness To Proceed.
§ 55.33. Proceedings Following Finding of Unfitness To Proceed.
§ 55.34. Transportation to and from Facility.
§ 55.35. Information Required To Be to Facility; Report to Court.
§ 55.36. Report that Child Is Fit To Proceed; Hearing on Objection.
§ 55.37. Report that Child Is Unfit To Proceed as a Result of Mental Illness; Initiation of Commitment Proceedings.
§ 55.38. Commitment Proceedings in Juvenile Court for Mental Illness.
§ 55.39. Referral for Commitment Proceedings for Mental Illness.
§ 55.40. Report That Child Is Unfit To Proceed as a Result of Mental Retardation.
§ 55.41. Commitment Proceedings in Juvenile Court for Mental Retardation.
§ 55.42. Referral for Commitment Proceedings for Mental Retardation.
§ 55.43. Restoration Hearing.
§ 55.44. Transfer to Criminal Court on 18th Birthday of Child. **[amended]**
§ 55.45. Standards of Care; Notice of Release or Furlough.

Subchapter D. Lack of Responsibility for Conduct as a Result of Mental Illness or Mental Retardation

§ 55.51. Lack of Responsibility for Conduct Determination; Examination.
§ 55.52. Proceedings Following Finding of Lack of Responsibility for Conduct.
§ 55.53. Transportation To and From Facility.
§ 55.54. Information Required To Be Sent to Facility; Report to Court.
§ 55.55. Report That Child is Not Mentally Ill or Mentally Retarded; Hearing on Objection.
§ 55.56. Report That Child Has Mental Illness; Initiation of Commitment Proceedings.

Introductory Comment

Chapter 55 deals with children who are before the juvenile court for delinquent conduct or conduct indicating a need for supervision and who are believed to be suffering from some form of mental illness or mental retardation.

The chapter was totally re-written and re-enacted in 1999 (1) to spell out in more detail the procedures to be used, (2) to give juvenile courts the option of conducting commitment proceedings themselves or referring such cases to county courts to conduct proceedings, and (3) to provide for a brief evaluation period in the care of Texas Department of Mental Health and Mental Retardation before actual commitment proceedings are initiated following a finding of unfitness to proceed or non-responsibility.

The new Chapter 55, like the one it replaces, deals with three different situations. (1) The child who is before the juvenile court and is believed to be mentally ill is covered by Subchapter B. (2) The child who is believed to be unfit (incompetent) to proceed because of mental illness or mental retardation is covered by Subchapter C. (3) The child who is believed to be not responsible for his conduct because of mental illness or mental retardation is covered by Subchapter D.

Subchapter A. General Provisions

§ 55.01. Meaning of "Having a Mental Illness."

For purposes of this chapter, a child who is described as having a mental illness means a child who suffers from mental illness as defined by Section 571.003, Health and Safety Code.

Comment

Section 571.003(14) of the Health and Safety Code defines mental illness as "an illness, disease, or condition, other than epilepsy, senility, alcoholism, or mental deficiency, that: (A) substantially impairs a person's thought, perception of reality, emotional process, or judgment; or (B) grossly impairs behavior as demonstrated by recent disturbed behavior."

The provision authorizing the juvenile court to order a physical or mental examination is § 51.20.

CLE/Other Legal Publications

Chapter 55 Proceedings. Harold Gaither, 15TH ANN. JUVE. L. CONF. (Feb. 2002)

Juveniles and Mental Health Issues: Recent Revisions and a Review of Chapter 55. Guy Herman, 13TH ANN. JUVE. L. CONF. (Feb. 2000)

Overview of the Texas Youth Commission's Corsicana Residential Treatment Center for Emotionally Disturbed Juvenile Offenders. Cheri A. Abbage, 11 JUVE. L. SECT. RPT. (March 1997)

Leading Cases

S.D.J. v. State, 879 S.W.2d 370 (Tex. App.—Eastland 1994, writ denied) (insufficient evidence to require hearing on motion suggesting mental illness)

In re M.D.B., 757 S.W.2d 415 (Tex. App.—Houston [14th Dist.] 1988, no writ) (child committed under § 55.02 [now Subchapter B] can be placed in any TDMHMR facility)

T.P.S. v. State, 590 S.W.2d 946 (Tex. Civ. App.—Dallas 1979, writ ref'd n.r.e.) (§ 55.02 [now Subchapter B] is applicable in transfer proceedings)

R.K.A. v. State, 553 S.W.2d 781 (Tex. Civ. App.—Fort Worth 1977, no writ) (§ 55.02 [now Subchapter B] is not applicable in transfer proceedings)

§ 55.02. Mental Health and Mental Retardation Jurisdiction.

For the purpose of initiating proceedings to order mental health or mental retardation services for a child or for commitment of a child as provided by this chapter, the juvenile court has jurisdiction of proceedings under Subtitle C or D, Title 7, Health and Safety Code.

Comment

TEX. HEALTH & SAFETY CODE ANN. subtitle C deals with persons with mental illness and subtitle D with persons with mental retardation.

§ 55.03. Standards of Care.

(a) Except as provided by this chapter, a child for whom inpatient mental health services is ordered by a court under this chapter shall be cared for as provided by Subtitle C, Title 7, Health and Safety Code.

(b) Except as provided by this chapter, a child who is committed by a court to a residential care facility for mental retardation shall be cared for as provided by Subtitle D, Title 7, Health and Safety Code.

Subchapter B. Child With Mental Illness

Introductory Comment

Subchapter B deals with children who are believed to be mentally ill but who are not necessarily also unfit to proceed because of mental illness or not responsible for their conduct because of mental illness.

§ 55.11. Mental Illness Determination; Examination.

(a) On a motion by a party, the juvenile court shall determine whether probable cause exists to believe that a child who is alleged by petition or found to have engaged in delinquent conduct or conduct indicating a need for supervision has a mental illness. In making its determination, the court may:

(1) consider the motion, supporting documents, professional statements of counsel, and witness testimony; and

(2) make its own observation of the child.

(b) If the court determines that probable cause exists to believe that the child has a mental illness, the court shall temporarily stay the juvenile court proceedings and immediately order the child to be examined under Section 51.20. The information obtained from the examination must include expert opinion as to whether the child has a mental illness and whether the child meets the commitment criteria under Subtitle C,

Title 7, Health and Safety Code. If ordered by the court, the information must also include expert opinion as to whether the child is unfit to proceed with the juvenile court proceedings.

(c) After considering all relevant information, including information obtained from an examination under Section 51.20, the court shall:

(1) if the court determines that evidence exists to support a finding that the child has a mental illness and that the child meets the commitment criteria under Subtitle C, Title 7, Health and Safety Code, proceed under Section 55.12; or

(2) if the court determines that evidence does not exist to support a finding that the child has a mental illness or that the child meets the commitment criteria under Subtitle C, Title 7, Health and Safety Code, dissolve the stay and continue the juvenile court proceedings.

Comment

If the juvenile court from any source has probable cause to believe that a child before it may be mentally ill, it is required to stay juvenile proceedings temporarily and to order an appropriate examination. If from that examination, the court determines there is evidence to support a finding that the child is mentally ill and committable, it proceeds under the next section; otherwise, it dissolves the stay and proceeds with the juvenile case.

§ 55.12. Initiation of Commitment Proceedings.

If, after considering all relevant information, the juvenile court determines that evidence exists to support a finding that a child has a mental illness and that the child meets the commitment criteria under Subtitle C, Title 7, Health and Safety Code, the court shall:

(1) initiate proceedings as provided by Section 55.13 to order temporary or extended mental health services, as provided in Subchapter C, Chapter 574, Health and Safety Code; or

(2) refer the child's case as provided by Section 55.14 to the appropriate court for the initiation of proceedings in that court for commitment of the child under Subchapter C, Chapter 574, Health and Safety Code.

Comment

If there is evidence to support a finding the child is mentally ill and committable, the juvenile court has an option: it may conduct commitment proceedings itself or it may refer the case to the appropriate court (ordinarily the county court) for it to conduct commitment proceedings. The referral option is new and is intended to relieve juvenile courts that are not comfortable with conducting commitment proceedings (because they are called upon to do so infrequently) of the responsibility for doing so.

§ 55.13. Commitment Proceedings in Juvenile Court.

(a) If the juvenile court initiates proceedings for temporary or extended mental health services under Section 55.12(1), the prosecuting attorney or the attorney for the child may file with the juvenile court an application for court-ordered mental health services under Section 574.001, Health and Safety Code. The juvenile court shall:

(1) set a date for a hearing and provide notice as required by Sections 574.005 and 574.006, Health and Safety Code; and

(2) conduct the hearing in accordance with Subchapter C, Chapter 574, Health and Safety Code.

(b) The burden of proof at the hearing is on the party who filed the application.

(c) The juvenile court shall appoint the number of physicians necessary to examine the child and to complete the certificates of medical examination for mental illness required under Section 574.009, Health and Safety Code.

(d) After conducting a hearing on an application under this section, the juvenile court shall:

(1) if the criteria under Section 574.034, Health and Safety Code, are satisfied, order temporary mental health services for the child; or

(2) if the criteria under Section 574.035, Health and Safety Code, are satisfied, order extended mental health services for the child.

Comment

At this stage, juvenile proceedings are stayed pending outcome of the commitment proceedings. This section spells out the procedures when the juvenile court elects to conduct the commitment proceedings itself. The prosecutor or the juvenile's attorney has discretion to file an application for commitment or not. Juvenile proceedings cannot be resumed until the commitment issue is resolved by application and hearing. The burden of proof at the commitment hearing is upon the party who filed the application.

The juvenile court decides the case according to the commitment criteria for temporary or extended mental health services that are in the Health and Safety Code.

§ 55.14. Referral for Commitment Proceedings.

(a) If the juvenile court refers the child's case to the appropriate court for the initiation of commitment proceedings under Section 55.12(2), the juvenile court shall:

(1) send all papers relating to the child's mental illness to the clerk of the court to which the case is referred;

(2) send to the office of the appropriate county attorney or, if a county attorney is not available, to the office of the appropriate district attorney, copies of all papers sent to the clerk of the court under Subdivision (1); and

(3) if the child is in detention:

(A) order the child released from detention to the child's home or another appropriate place;

(B) order the child detained in an appropriate place other than a juvenile detention facility; or

(C) if an appropriate place to release or detain the child as described by Paragraph (A) or (B) is not available, order the child to remain in the juvenile detention facility subject to further detention orders of the court.

(b) The papers sent to the clerk of a court under Subsection (a)(1) constitute an application for mental health services under Section 574.001, Health and Safety Code.

Comment

If the juvenile court elects the referral option, the papers are sent to the appropriate court and prosecuting authority. If the child is in detention, he or she may be released or detained in the juvenile detention facility pending outcome of the commitment proceedings. If detained, the requirements of § 54.01 respecting the duration of detention orders and subsequent detention hearings must be met.

§ 55.15. Standards of Care; Expiration of Court Order for Mental Health Services.

If the juvenile court or a court to which the child's case is referred under Section 55.12(2) orders mental health services for the child, the child shall be cared for, treated, and released in conformity to Subtitle C, Title 7, Health and Safety Code, except:

(1) a court order for mental health services for a child automatically expires on the 120th day after the date the child becomes 18 years of age; and

(2) the administrator of a mental health facility shall notify, in writing, by certified mail, return receipt requested, the juvenile court that ordered mental health services or the juvenile court that referred the case to a court that ordered the mental health services of the intent to discharge the child at least 10 days prior to discharge.

Comment

Unlike commitments of adults, a commitment of a child from a juvenile court or juvenile court referral automatically expires 120 days after the child's 18th birthday. Under some circumstances, § 55.19 provides for transfer of such cases to criminal court on the child's 18th birthday. If the care provider intends to discharge the child, it is required to give certified mail notice to the juvenile court in order to permit the court to resume custody of the child for possible further proceedings in juvenile court.

---

§ 55.16. Order for Mental Health Services; Stay of Proceedings.

(a) If the court to which the child's case is referred under Section 55.12(2) orders temporary or extended inpatient mental health services for the child, the court shall immediately notify in writing the referring juvenile court of the court's order for mental health services.

(b) If the juvenile court orders temporary or extended inpatient mental health services for the child or if the juvenile court receives notice under Subsection (a) from the court to which the child's case is referred, the proceedings under this title then pending in juvenile court shall be stayed.

Comment

If the child is committed, juvenile proceedings must be stayed for the duration of the commitment.

---

§ 55.17. Mental Health Services Not Ordered; Dissolution of Stay.

(a) If the court to which a child's case is referred under Section 55.12(2) does not order temporary or extended inpatient mental health services for the child, the court shall immediately notify in writing the referring juvenile court of the court's decision.

(b) If the juvenile court does not order temporary or extended inpatient mental health services for the child or if the juvenile court receives notice under Subsection (a) from the court to which the child's case is referred, the juvenile court shall dissolve the stay and continue the juvenile court proceedings.

Comment

If the child is not committed following a hearing, the stay of juvenile proceedings must be dissolved so the proceedings can be resumed.

---

§ 55.18. Discharge From Mental Health Facility Before Reaching 18 Years of Age.

If the child is discharged from the mental health facility before reaching 18 years of age, the juvenile court may:

(1) dismiss the juvenile court proceedings with prejudice; or

(2) continue with proceedings under this title as though no order of mental health services had been made.

Comment

If the child is discharged before age 18, the juvenile court has discretion, in the interest of justice, either to dismiss the juvenile proceedings or permit them to continue.

---

§ 55.19. Transfer to Criminal Court on 18th Birthday.

(a) The juvenile court shall transfer all pending proceedings from the juvenile court to a criminal court on the 18th birthday of a child for whom the juvenile court or a court to which the child's case is referred under Section 55.12(2) has ordered inpatient mental health services if:

(1) the child is not discharged or furloughed from the inpatient mental health facility before reaching 18 years of age; and

(2) the child is alleged to have engaged in delinquent conduct that included a violation of a penal law listed in Section 53.045 and no adjudication concerning the alleged conduct has been made.

(b) The juvenile court shall send notification of the transfer of a child under Subsection (a) to the inpatient mental health facility. The criminal court shall, within 90 days of the transfer, institute proceedings under **Chapter 46B** [~~Article 46.02~~], Code of Criminal Procedure. If those or any subsequent proceedings result in a determination that the defendant is competent to stand trial, the defendant may not receive a punishment for the delinquent conduct described by Subsection (a)(2) that results in confinement for a period longer than the maximum period of confinement the defendant could have received if the defendant had been adjudicated for the delinquent conduct while still a child and within the jurisdiction of the juvenile court.

History: Amended by 78th Legis., Reg. Sess. (2003), S.B. 1057, eff. Jan. 1, 2004. Applies only to competency proceedings not initiated before effective date.

Comment

This section mandates the transfer to the criminal justice system of a child charged with a determinate sentence offense who is confined under a juvenile court mental health commitment when he becomes 18 years of age. The criminal court is to conduct a competency examination and proceed appropriately with the case depending upon the results of the examination.

Subchapter C. Child Unfit to Proceed as a Result of Mental Illness or Mental Retardation

Introductory Comment

Section 55.03, dealing with children with mental retardation, is repealed. The criteria and procedures for proceedings involving mental retardation are distributed in this and the next subchapter.

This subchapter deals with children who are or may be unfit to proceed in juvenile court because of either mental illness or mental retardation.

CLE/Other Legal Publication

Residential Treatment for Mentally Retarded Juvenile Offenders. Kimberly Pack, 9 JUVE. L. SECT. RPT. (Dec. 1995)

Leading Cases

In re E.M.R., 55 S.W.3d 712 (Tex. App.—Corpus Christi 2001, no pet.) (juvenile court has no duty to order fitness hearing without motion for hearing)

Pratt v. State, 907 S.W.2d 38 (Tex. App.—Dallas 1995, error denied) (burden of proof beyond a reasonable doubt on juvenile who files application for mental retardation commitment)

---

§ 55.31. Unfitness to Proceed Determination; Examination.

(a) A child alleged by petition or found to have engaged in delinquent conduct or conduct indicating a need for supervision who as a result of mental illness or mental retardation lacks capacity to understand the proceedings in juvenile court or to assist in the child's own defense is unfit to proceed and shall not be subjected to discretionary transfer to criminal court, adjudication, disposition, or modification of disposition as long as such incapacity endures.

(b) On a motion by a party, the juvenile court shall determine whether probable cause exists to believe that a child who is alleged by petition or who is found to have engaged in delinquent conduct or conduct indicating a need for supervision is unfit to proceed as a result of mental illness or mental retardation. In making its determination, the court may:

(1) consider the motion, supporting documents, professional statements of counsel, and witness testimony; and

(2) make its own observation of the child.

(c) If the court determines that probable cause exists to believe that the child is unfit to proceed, the court shall temporarily stay the juvenile court proceedings and immediately order the child to be examined under Section 51.20. The information obtained from the examination must include expert opinion as to whether the child is unfit to proceed as a result of mental illness or mental retardation.

(d) After considering all relevant information, including information obtained from an examination under Section 51.20, the court shall:

(1) if the court determines that evidence exists to support a finding that the child is unfit to proceed, proceed under Section 55.32; or

(2) if the court determines that evidence does not exist to support a finding that the child is unfit to proceed, dissolve the stay and continue the juvenile court proceedings.

Comment

Due process of law prohibits placing a person on trial who because of mental illness or retardation cannot comprehend the nature of the proceedings or assist in his or her own defense. This section defines the fitness standard and specifies the procedures to initiate a fitness inquiry.

This section is on a parallel with § 55.11 dealing with initiating an inquiry into whether a child before the juvenile court is mentally ill.

Leading Cases

Dusky v. United States, 362 U.S. 402, 4 L.Ed.2d 824, 80 S.Ct. 788 (1960) (constitutional requirement for competency to stand trial)

In re J.K.N., 115 S.W.3d 166 (Tex. App.—Fort Worth 2003, no pet.) (fitness inquiry not required without motion from party)

M.A.V. v. Webb County Court at Law, 842 S.W.2d 739 (Tex. App.—San Antonio 1992, writ denied) (jury trial required upon request)

In re K.A.H., 700 S.W.2d 782 (Tex. App.—Fort Worth 1985, no writ) (raising the issue of fitness to proceed)

V.C.H. v. State, 630 S.W.2d 787 (Tex. App.—Houston [1st Dist.] 1982, no writ) (jury waiver for fitness to proceed hearing must be by both child and attorney)

In re V.C.H., 605 S.W.2d 643 (Tex. Civ. App.—Houston [1st Dist.] 1980, no writ) (fitness to proceed must be tried in a separate proceeding from adjudication)

H.L.H. v. State, 560 S.W.2d 536 (Tex. Civ. App.—Austin 1978, no writ) (sufficiency of evidence to support finding of fitness to proceed)

Dominguez v. State, 546 S.W.2d 398 (Tex. Civ. App.—Austin 1977, no writ) (finding of unfitness persists until changed by juvenile court)

§ 55.32. Hearing on Issue of Fitness to Proceed.

(a) If the juvenile court determines that evidence exists to support a finding that a child is unfit to proceed as a result of mental illness or mental retardation, the court shall set the case for a hearing on that issue.

(b) The issue of whether the child is unfit to proceed as a result of mental illness or mental retardation shall be determined at a hearing separate from any other hearing.

(c) The court shall determine the issue of whether the child is unfit to proceed unless the child or the attorney for the child demands a jury before the 10th day before the date of the hearing.

(d) Unfitness to proceed as a result of mental illness or mental retardation must be proved by a preponderance of the evidence.

(e) If the court or jury determines that the child is fit to proceed, the juvenile court shall continue with proceedings under this title as though no question of fitness to proceed had been raised.

(f) If the court or jury determines that the child is unfit to proceed as a result of mental illness or mental retardation, the court shall:

(1) stay the juvenile court proceedings for as long as that incapacity endures; and

(2) proceed under Section 55.33.

(g) The fact that the child is unfit to proceed as a result of mental illness or mental retardation does not preclude any legal objection to the juvenile court proceedings which is susceptible of fair determination prior to the adjudication hearing and without the personal participation of the child.

Comment

A fitness hearing is required if there is evidence to support a finding of unfitness to proceed. The hearing is to be before the judge, unless the defense demands a jury. If the child is found to be unfit to proceed, juvenile proceedings are stayed pending the outcome of commitment proceedings.

§ 55.33. Proceedings Following Finding of Unfitness to Proceed.

(a) If the juvenile court or jury determines under Section 55.32 that a child is unfit to proceed with the juvenile court proceedings for delinquent conduct, the court shall:

(1) if the unfitness to proceed is a result of mental illness or mental retardation:

(A) provided that the child meets the commitment criteria under Subtitle C or D, Title 7, Health and Safety Code, order the child placed with the Texas Department of Mental Health and Mental Retardation for a period of not more than 90 days, which order may not specify a shorter period, for placement in a facility designated by the department; or

(B) on application by the child's parent, guardian, or guardian ad litem, order the child placed in a private psychiatric inpatient facility for a period of not more than 90 days, which order may not specify a shorter period, but only if the placement is agreed to in writing by the administrator of the facility; or

(2) if the unfitness to proceed is a result of mental illness and the court determines that the child may be adequately treated in an alternative setting, order the child to receive treatment for mental illness on an outpatient basis for a period of not more than 90 days, which order may not specify a shorter period.

(b) If the court orders a child placed in a private psychiatric inpatient facility under Subsection (a)(1)(B), the state or a political subdivision of the state may be ordered to pay any costs associated with the child's placement, subject to an express appropriation of funds for the purpose.

Comment

If there is a finding that the juvenile is unfit to proceed, the court has three alternatives: order a placement with MHMR for 90 days, order a placement in a private facility for 90 days, or if the cause is mental illness, order outpatient evaluation for 90 days. The court must find that the child meets commitment criteria to order MHMR placement, but that finding is based on the evidence already heard by the court and does not require a separate commitment hearing since the purpose of the placement is to obtain an evaluation to be used in a later commitment hearing. Under subsection (b), the court can order the government to pay for placement in a private psychiatric inpatient facility only if there are funds expressly made available for that purpose.

---

§ 55.34. Transportation to and From Facility.

(a) If the court issues a placement order under Section 55.33(a)(1), the court shall order the probation department or sheriff's department to transport the child to the designated facility.

(b) On receipt of a report from a facility to which a child has been transported under Subsection (a), the court shall order the probation department or sheriff's department to transport the child from the facility to the court. If the child is not transported to the court before the 11th day after the date of the court's order, an authorized representative of the facility shall transport the child from the facility to the court.

(c) The county in which the juvenile court is located shall reimburse the facility for the costs incurred in transporting the child to the juvenile court as required by Subsection (b).

Comment

The court is responsible for ordering transportation to and from the placement facility. If the court does not have the child transported back to the county upon notice of discharge, MHMR may do so and the county is responsible for the transportation cost.

---

§ 55.35. Information Required to be Sent to Facility; Report to Court.

(a) If the juvenile court issues a placement order under Section 55.33(a), the court shall order the probation department to send copies of any information in the possession of the department and relevant to the issue of the child's mental illness or mental retardation to the public or private facility or outpatient center, as appropriate.

(b) Not later than the 75th day after the date the court issues a placement order under Section 55.33(a), the public or private facility or outpatient center, as appropriate, shall submit to the court a report that:

(1) describes the treatment of the child provided by the facility or center; and

(2) states the opinion of the director of the facility or center as to whether the child is fit or unfit to proceed.

(c) The court shall provide a copy of the report submitted under Subsection (b) to the prosecuting attorney and the attorney for the child.

Comment

The juvenile court must order all relevant information, including information in the possession of the probation department, to be sent to the evaluation facility. Not later than 75 days after placement, the facility is required to report to the court on the mental condition of the child.

---

§ 55.36. Report That Child is Fit to Proceed; Hearing on Objection.

(a) If a report submitted under Section 55.35(b) states that a child is fit to proceed, the juvenile court shall find that the child is fit to proceed unless the child's attorney objects in writing or in open court not later than the second day after the date the attorney receives a copy of the report under Section 55.35(c).

(b) On objection by the child's attorney under Subsection (a), the juvenile court shall promptly hold a hearing to determine whether the child is fit to proceed, except that the hearing may be held after the date that the placement order issued under Section 55.33(a) expires. At the hearing, the court shall determine the issue of the fitness of the child to proceed unless the child or the child's attorney demands in writing a jury before the 10th day before the date of the hearing.

(c) If, after a hearing, the court or jury finds that the child is fit to proceed, the court shall dissolve the stay and continue the juvenile court proceedings as though a question of fitness to proceed had not been raised.

(d) If, after a hearing, the court or jury finds that the child is unfit to proceed, the court shall proceed under Section 55.37.

Comment

The 90 day evaluation placement gives MHMR the opportunity, in the case of mental illness, to stabilize the child on medication in order to make the child fit to proceed. If the report states the child is fit to proceed, the court may dissolve the stay and proceed with juvenile proceedings unless the defense objects, in which event a hearing, which may be with a jury, must be held on the question of fitness to proceed.

§ 55.37. Report That Child is Unfit to Proceed as a Result of Mental Illness; Initiation of Commitment Proceedings.

If a report submitted under Section 55.35(b) states that a child is unfit to proceed as a result of mental illness and that the child meets the commitment criteria for civil commitment under Subtitle C, Title 7, Health and Safety Code, the director of the public or private facility or outpatient center, as appropriate, shall submit to the court two certificates of medical examination for mental illness. On receipt of the certificates, the court shall:

(1) initiate proceedings as provided by Section 55.38 in the juvenile court for commitment of the child under Subtitle C, Title 7, Health and Safety Code; or

(2) refer the child's case as provided by Section 55.39 to the appropriate court for the initiation of proceedings in that court for commitment of the child under Subtitle C, Title 7, Health and Safety Code.

Comment

If the report states the child is unfit to proceed because of mental illness, the juvenile court must either initiate commitment proceedings or refer those proceedings to the appropriate court. The two medical certificates are required by the Health and Safety Code to initiate mental health commitment proceedings.

§ 55.38. Commitment Proceedings in Juvenile Court for Mental Illness.

(a) If the juvenile court initiates commitment proceedings under Section 55.37(1), the prosecuting attorney may file with the juvenile court an application for court-ordered mental health services under Section 574.001, Health and Safety Code. The juvenile court shall:

(1) set a date for a hearing and provide notice as required by Sections 574.005 and 574.006, Health and Safety Code; and

(2) conduct the hearing in accordance with Subchapter C, Chapter 574, Health and Safety Code.

(b) After conducting a hearing under Subsection (a)(2), the juvenile court shall:

(1) if the criteria under Section 574.034, Health and Safety Code, are satisfied, order temporary mental health services; or

(2) if the criteria under Section 574.035, Health and Safety Code, are satisfied, order extended mental health services.

Comment

If the juvenile court elects to initiate commitment proceedings, the prosecutor must file the application, if one is to be filed. After hearing, the juvenile court orders temporary or extended mental health services based upon the evidence and the commitment criteria.

§ 55.39. Referral for Commitment Proceedings for Mental Illness.

(a) If the juvenile court refers the child's case to an appropriate court for the initiation of commitment proceedings under Section 55.37(2), the juvenile court shall:

(1) send all papers relating to the child's unfitness to proceed, including the verdict and judgment of the juvenile court finding the child unfit to proceed, to the clerk of the court to which the case is referred;

(2) send to the office of the appropriate county attorney or, if a county attorney is not available, to the office of the appropriate district attorney, copies of all papers sent to the clerk of the court under Subdivision (1); and

(3) if the child is in detention:

(A) order the child released from detention to the child's home or another appropriate place;

(B) order the child detained in an appropriate place other than a juvenile detention facility; or

(C) if an appropriate place to release or detain the child as described by Paragraph (A) or (B) is not available, order the child to remain in the juvenile detention facility subject to further detention orders of the court.

(b) The papers sent to a court under Subsection (a)(1) constitute an application for mental health services under Section 574.001, Health and Safety Code.

Comment

If the juvenile court elects to refer commitment proceedings to the county court, the papers go to that court and to the appropriate prosecutor's office. If the child is in detention, the court may release the child or detain the child under detention orders as specified in § 54.01.

§ 55.40. Report That Child is Unfit to Proceed as a Result of Mental Retardation.

If a report submitted under Section 55.35(b) states that a child is unfit to proceed as a result of mental retardation and that the child meets the commitment criteria for civil commitment under Subtitle D, Title 7, Health and Safety Code, the director of the residential care facility shall submit to the court an affidavit stating the conclusions reached as a result of the diagnosis. On receipt of the affidavit, the court shall:

(1) initiate proceedings as provided by Section 55.41 in the juvenile court for commitment of the child under Subtitle D, Title 7, Health and Safety Code; or

(2) refer the child's case as provided by Section 55.42 to the appropriate court for the initiation of proceedings in that court for commitment of the child under Subtitle D, Title 7, Health and Safety Code.

Comment

If the evaluative report states the child is unfit to proceed because of mental retardation, the juvenile court must either initiate commitment proceedings or refer those proceedings to the appropriate county court.

§ 55.41. Commitment Proceedings in Juvenile Court for Mental Retardation.

(a) If the juvenile court initiates commitment proceedings under Section 55.40(1), the prosecuting attorney may file with the juvenile court an application for placement under Section 593.041, Health and Safety Code. The juvenile court shall:

(1) set a date for a hearing and provide notice as required by Sections 593.047 and 593.048, Health and Safety Code; and

(2) conduct the hearing in accordance with Sections 593.049–593.056, Health and Safety Code.

(b) After conducting a hearing under Subsection (a)(2), the juvenile court may order commitment of the child to a residential care facility if the commitment criteria under Section 593.052, Health and Safety Code, are satisfied.

(c) On receipt of the court's order, the Texas Department of Mental Health and Mental Retardation or the appropriate community center shall admit the child to a residential care facility.

Comment

If the juvenile court elects to conduct the proceedings, the prosecutor must file the application if one is to be filed. If after hearing it is shown that the commitment criteria of the Health and Safety Code are met, the court commits the child to a residential care facility.

The 2001 addition of (c) requires MHMR or a community center to accept a child committed under this section.

---

§ 55.42. Referral for Commitment Proceedings for Mental Retardation.

(a) If the juvenile court refers the child's case to an appropriate court for the initiation of commitment proceedings under Section 55.40(2), the juvenile court shall:

(1) send all papers relating to the child's mental retardation to the clerk of the court to which the case is referred;

(2) send to the office of the appropriate county attorney or, if a county attorney is not available, to the office of the appropriate district attorney, copies of all papers sent to the clerk of the court under Subdivision (1); and

(3) if the child is in detention:

(A) order the child released from detention to the child's home or another appropriate place;

(B) order the child detained in an appropriate place other than a juvenile detention facility; or

(C) if an appropriate place to release or detain the child as described by Paragraph (A) or (B) is not available, order the child to remain in the juvenile detention facility subject to further detention orders of the court.

(b) The papers sent to a court under Subsection (a)(1) constitute an application for placement under Section 593.041, Health and Safety Code.

Comment

If the juvenile court elects to refer mental retardation commitment proceedings to the county court, the juvenile court sends the papers to the appropriate court and prosecutor's office. The matter of detention is dealt with in the same manner as for mental health proceedings under § 55.39.

---

§ 55.43. Restoration Hearing.

(a) The prosecuting attorney may file with the juvenile court a motion for a restoration hearing concerning a child if:

(1) the child is found unfit to proceed as a result of mental illness or mental retardation; and

(2) the child:

(A) is not:

(i) ordered by a court to receive inpatient mental health services;

(ii) committed by a court to a residential care facility; or

(iii) ordered by a court to receive treatment on an outpatient basis; or

(B) is discharged or furloughed from a mental health facility or outpatient center before the child reaches 18 years of age.

(b) At the restoration hearing, the court shall determine the issue of whether the child is fit to proceed.

(c) The restoration hearing shall be conducted without a jury.

(d) The issue of fitness to proceed must be proved by a preponderance of the evidence.

(e) If, after a hearing, the court finds that the child is fit to proceed, the court shall continue the juvenile court proceedings.

(f) If, after a hearing, the court finds that the child is unfit to proceed, the court shall dismiss the motion for restoration.

Comment

This section gives the State the right to demand a restoration hearing if the child was found unfit to proceed but was not committed for treatment or was discharged from treatment before becoming 18. If after a hearing without a jury the court finds the child is fit to proceed, then juvenile proceedings can resume.

---

§ 55.44. Transfer to Criminal Court on 18th Birthday of Child.

(a) The juvenile court shall transfer all pending proceedings from the juvenile court to a criminal court on the 18th birthday of a child for whom the juvenile court or a court to which the child's case is referred has ordered inpatient mental health services or residential care for persons with mental retardation if:

(1) the child is not discharged or furloughed from the facility before reaching 18 years of age; and

(2) the child is alleged to have engaged in delinquent conduct that included a violation of a penal law listed in Section 53.045 and no adjudication concerning the alleged conduct has been made.

(b) The juvenile court shall send notification of the transfer of a child under Subsection (a) to the facility. The criminal court shall, before the 91st day after the date of the transfer, institute proceedings under **Chapter 46B** [~~Article 46.02~~], Code of Criminal Procedure. If those or any subsequent proceedings result in a determination that the defendant is competent to stand trial, the defendant may not receive a punishment for the delinquent conduct described by Subsection (a)(2) that results in confinement for a period longer than the maximum period of confinement the defendant could have received if the defendant had been adjudicated for the delinquent conduct while still a child and within the jurisdiction of the juvenile court.

History: Amended by 78th Legis., Reg. Sess. (2003), S.B. 1057, eff. Jan. 1, 2004. Applies only to competency proceedings not initiated before effective date.

Comment

This section is parallel to § 55.19. It requires transfer of the juvenile case to criminal court if the child is charged with a determinate sentence offense and is still committed for treatment at age 18.

---

§ 55.45. Standards of Care; Notice of Release or Furlough.

(a) If the juvenile court or a court to which the child's case is referred under Section 55.37(2) orders mental health services for the child, the child shall be cared for, treated, and released in accordance with Subtitle C, Title 7, Health and Safety Code, except that the administrator of a mental health facility shall notify, in writing, by certified mail, return receipt requested, the juvenile court that ordered mental health services or that referred the case to a court that ordered mental health services of the intent to discharge the child on or before the 10th day before the date of discharge.

(b) If the juvenile court or a court to which the child's case is referred under Section 55.40(2) orders the commitment of the child to a residential care facility, the child shall be cared for, treated, and released in accordance with Subtitle D, Title 7, Health and Safety Code, except that the administrator of the residential care facility shall notify, in writing, by certified mail, return receipt requested, the juvenile court that ordered commitment of the child or that referred the case to a court that ordered commitment of the child of the intent to discharge or furlough the child on or before the 20th day before the date of discharge or furlough.

Subchapter D. Lack of Responsibility for Conduct as a Result of Mental Illness or Mental Retardation

Introductory Comment

Subchapter D deals with non-responsibility for conduct as a result of mental illness or mental retardation, what in criminal law is called legal insanity.

---

§ 55.51. Lack of Responsibility for Conduct Determination; Examination.

(a) A child alleged by petition to have engaged in delinquent conduct or conduct indicating a need for supervision is not responsible for the conduct if at the time of the conduct, as a result of mental illness or mental retardation, the child lacks substantial capacity either to appreciate the wrongfulness of the child's conduct or to conform the child's conduct to the requirements of law.

(b) On a motion by a party in which it is alleged that a child may not be responsible as a result of mental illness or mental retardation for the child's conduct, the court shall order the child to be examined under Section 51.20. The information obtained from the examinations must include expert opinion as to whether the child is not responsible for the child's conduct as a result of mental illness or mental retardation.

(c) The issue of whether the child is not responsible for the child's conduct as a result of mental illness or mental retardation shall be tried to the court or jury in the adjudication hearing.

(d) Lack of responsibility for conduct as a result of mental illness or mental retardation must be proved by a preponderance of the evidence.

(e) In its findings or verdict the court or jury must state whether the child is not responsible for the child's conduct as a result of mental illness or mental retardation.

(f) If the court or jury finds the child is not responsible for the child's conduct as a result of mental illness or mental retardation, the court shall proceed under Section 55.52.

(g) A child found to be not responsible for the child's conduct as a result of mental illness or mental retardation shall not be subject to proceedings under this title with respect to such conduct, other than proceedings under Section 55.52.

Comment

This section is the same in substance as the prior law. If a question of lack of responsibility is raised, an examination must be ordered. The question of lack of responsibility is litigated before the judge or jury in the adjudication hearing with any other adjudication issues that may be present.

Leading Cases

W.D.A. v. State, 835 S.W.2d 227 (Tex. App.—Waco 1992, no writ) (Family Code, not Penal Code, definition of legal insanity controls)

T.P.S. v. State, 620 S.W.2d 728 (Tex. Civ. App.—Dallas 1981, no writ) (§ 55.05 does not apply to transfer proceedings)

In re A.N.M., 542 S.W.2d 916 (Tex. Civ. App.—Dallas 1976, no writ) (raising issue of insanity)

In re E.B., 525 S.W.2d 543 (Tex. Civ. App.—Amarillo 1975, writ ref'd n.r.e.) (insanity defense applies at probation revocation proceedings)

---

§ 55.52. Proceedings Following Finding of Lack of Responsibility for Conduct.

(a) If the court or jury finds that a child is not responsible for the child's conduct under Section 55.51, the court shall:

(1) if the lack of responsibility is a result of mental illness or mental retardation:

(A) provided that the child meets the commitment criteria under Subtitle C or D, Title 7, Health and Safety Code, order the child placed with the Texas Department of Mental Health and Mental Retardation for a period of not more than 90 days, which order may not specify a shorter period, for placement in a facility designated by the department; or

(B) on application by the child's parent, guardian, or guardian ad litem, order the child placed in a private psychiatric inpatient facility for a period of not more than 90 days, which order may not specify a shorter period, but only if the placement is agreed to in writing by the administrator of the facility; or

(2) if the child's lack of responsibility is a result of mental illness and the court determines that the child may be adequately treated in an alternative setting, order the child to receive treatment on an outpatient basis for a period of not more than 90 days, which order may not specify a shorter period.

(b) If the court orders a child placed in a private psychiatric inpatient facility under Subsection (a)(1)(B), the state or a political subdivision of the state may be ordered to pay any costs associated with the child's placement, subject to an express appropriation of funds for the purpose.

Comment

If the child is found not responsible because of mental illness or mental retardation, a 90 day evaluative placement must be ordered. The requirement that the child must meet the commitment criteria of the Health and Safety Code is met by a finding by the court based on the evidence already before it; a commitment hearing is not required since the purpose of the 90 day placement is to obtain expert assistance in determining whether the child is committable under those same criteria.

§ 55.53. Transportation to and From Facility.

(a) If the court issues a placement order under Section 55.52(a)(1), the court shall order the probation department or sheriff's department to transport the child to the designated facility.

(b) On receipt of a report from a facility to which a child has been transported under Subsection (a), the court shall order the probation department or sheriff's department to transport the child from the facility to the court. If the child is not transported to the court before the 11th day after the date of the court's order, an authorized representative of the facility shall transport the child from the facility to the court.

(c) The county in which the juvenile court is located shall reimburse the facility for the costs incurred in transporting the child to the juvenile court as required by Subsection (b).

Comment

This section deals with transportation when the child has been found unfit to proceed.

§ 55.54. Information Required to be Sent to Facility; Report to Court.

(a) If the juvenile court issues a placement order under Section 55.52(a), the court shall order the probation department to send copies of any information in the possession of the department and relevant to the issue of the child's mental illness or mental retardation to the public or private facility or outpatient center, as appropriate.

(b) Not later than the 75th day after the date the court issues a placement order under Section 55.52(a), the public or private facility or outpatient center, as appropriate, shall submit to the court a report that:

(1) describes the treatment of the child provided by the facility or center; and

(2) states the opinion of the director of the facility or center as to whether the child is mentally ill or mentally retarded.

(c) The court shall send a copy of the report submitted under Subsection (b) to the prosecuting attorney and the attorney for the child.

Comment

This section parallels § 55.35, dealing with a child found unfit to proceed.

§ 55.55. Report That Child is Not Mentally Ill or Mentally Retarded; Hearing on Objection.

(a) If a report submitted under Section 55.54(b) states that a child does not have a mental illness or mental retardation, the juvenile court shall discharge the child unless:

(1) an adjudication hearing was conducted concerning conduct that included a violation of a penal law listed in Section 53.045(a) and a petition was approved by a grand jury under Section 53.045; and

(2) the prosecuting attorney objects in writing not later than the second day after the date the attorney receives a copy of the report under Section 55.54(c).

(b) On objection by the prosecuting attorney under Subsection (a), the juvenile court shall hold a hearing without a jury to determine whether the child has a mental illness or mental retardation and whether the child meets the commitment criteria for civil commitment under Subtitle C or D, Title 7, Health and Safety Code.

(c) At the hearing, the burden is on the state to prove by clear and convincing evidence that the child has a mental illness or mental retardation and that the child meets the commitment criteria for civil commitment under Subtitle C or D, Title 7, Health and Safety Code.

(d) If, after a hearing, the court finds that the child does not have a mental illness or mental retardation and that the child does not meet the commitment criteria under Subtitle C or D, Title 7, Health and Safety Code, the court shall discharge the child.

(e) If, after a hearing, the court finds that the child has a mental illness or mental retardation and that the child meets the commitment criteria under Subtitle C or D, Title 7, Health and Safety Code, the court shall issue an appropriate commitment order.

Comment

If the report states the child is not mentally ill or mentally retarded, the court is required to discharge the child unless in a determinate sentence case the State objects. In that event, a hearing is held in which the State is given the opportunity to prove by clear and convincing evidence that the child is mentally ill or mentally retarded. The juvenile court is empowered to commit the child contrary to the evaluation of MHMR if that burden is carried by the State at the hearing.

---

§ 55.56. Report That Child Has Mental Illness; Initiation of Commitment Proceedings.

If a report submitted under Section 55.54(b) states that a child has a mental illness and that the child meets the commitment criteria for civil commitment under Subtitle C, Title 7, Health and Safety Code, the director of the public or private facility or outpatient center, as appropriate, shall submit to the court two certificates of medical examination for mental illness. On receipt of the certificates, the court shall:

(1) initiate proceedings as provided by Section 55.57 in the juvenile court for commitment of the child under Subtitle C, Title 7, Health and Safety Code; or

(2) refer the child's case as provided by Section 55.58 to the appropriate court for the initiation of proceedings in that court for commitment of the child under Subtitle C, Title 7, Health and Safety Code.

Comment

If the report states the child is mentally ill, then the juvenile court either initiates commitment proceedings or refers those proceedings to the appropriate county court.

---

§ 55.57. Commitment Proceedings in Juvenile Court for Mental Illness.

(a) If the juvenile court initiates commitment proceedings under Section 55.56(1), the prosecuting attorney may file with the juvenile court an application for court-ordered mental health services under Section 574.001, Health and Safety Code. The juvenile court shall:

(1) set a date for a hearing and provide notice as required by Sections 574.005 and 574.006, Health and Safety Code; and

(2) conduct the hearing in accordance with Subchapter C, Chapter 574, Health and Safety Code.

(b) After conducting a hearing under Subsection (a)(2), the juvenile court shall:

(1) if the criteria under Section 574.034, Health and Safety Code, are satisfied, order temporary mental health services; or

(2) if the criteria under Section 574.035, Health and Safety Code, are satisfied, order extended mental health services.

Comment

If the juvenile court elects to conduct commitment proceedings itself, the application must be filed by the prosecutor, if one is to be filed. Appropriate commitment orders are to be entered depending upon the evidence at the hearing.

§ 55.58. Referral for Commitment Proceedings for Mental Illness.

(a) If the juvenile court refers the child's case to an appropriate court for the initiation of commitment proceedings under Section 55.56(2), the juvenile court shall:

(1) send all papers relating to the child's mental illness, including the verdict and judgment of the juvenile court finding that the child was not responsible for the child's conduct, to the clerk of the court to which the case is referred;

(2) send to the office of the appropriate county attorney or, if a county attorney is not available, to the office of the district attorney, copies of all papers sent to the clerk of the court under Subdivision (1); and

(3) if the child is in detention:

(A) order the child released from detention to the child's home or another appropriate place;

(B) order the child detained in an appropriate place other than a juvenile detention facility; or

(C) if an appropriate place to release or detain the child as described by Paragraph (A) or (B) is not available, order the child to remain in the juvenile detention facility subject to further detention orders of the court.

(b) The papers sent to a court under Subsection (a)(1) constitute an application for mental health services under Section 574.001, Health and Safety Code.

Comment

This section parallels § 55.39, dealing with unfitness to proceed. It sets out the procedures when the juvenile court elects to refer commitment proceedings to the county court.

§ 55.59. Report That Child Has Mental Retardation; Initiation of Commitment Proceedings.

If a report submitted under Section 55.54(b) states that a child has mental retardation and that the child meets the commitment criteria for civil commitment under Subtitle

D, Title 7, Health and Safety Code, the director of the residential care facility shall submit to the court an affidavit stating the conclusions reached as a result of the diagnosis. On receipt of an affidavit, the juvenile court shall:

(1) initiate proceedings in the juvenile court as provided by Section 55.60 for commitment of the child under Subtitle D, Title 7, Health and Safety Code; or

(2) refer the child's case to the appropriate court as provided by Section 55.61 for the initiation of proceedings in that court for commitment of the child under Subtitle D, Title 7, Health and Safety Code.

Comment

This section is parallel to § 55.40, dealing with unfitness to proceed. If the report states the child is mentally retarded, the juvenile court must either initiate commitment proceedings or refer them to the appropriate county court.

---

§ 55.60. Commitment Proceedings in Juvenile Court for Mental Retardation.

(a) If the juvenile court initiates commitment proceedings under Section 55.59(1), the prosecuting attorney may file with the juvenile court an application for placement under Section 593.041, Health and Safety Code. The juvenile court shall:

(1) set a date for a hearing and provide notice as required by Sections 593.047 and 593.048, Health and Safety Code; and

(2) conduct the hearing in accordance with Sections 593.049–593.056, Health and Safety Code.

(b) After conducting a hearing under Subsection (a)(2), the juvenile court may order commitment of the child to a residential care facility only if the commitment criteria under Section 593.052, Health and Safety Code, are satisfied.

(c) On receipt of the court's order, the Texas Department of Mental Health and Mental Retardation or the appropriate community center shall admit the child to a residential care facility.

Comment

This section parallels § 55.41, dealing with unfitness to proceed. It sets out the procedures when the juvenile court elects to conduct commitment proceedings for mental retardation itself.

Subsection (c), added in 2001, requires MHMR or a community center to admit a child committed by a juvenile court under this section.

---

§ 55.61. Referral for Commitment Proceedings for Mental Retardation.

(a) If the juvenile court refers the child's case to an appropriate court for the initiation of commitment proceedings under Section 55.59(2), the juvenile court shall:

(1) send all papers relating to the child's mental retardation to the clerk of the court to which the case is referred;

(2) send to the office of the appropriate county attorney or, if a county attorney is not available, to the office of the appropriate district attorney, copies of all papers sent to the clerk of the court under Subdivision (1); and

(3) if the child is in detention:

(A) order the child released from detention to the child's home or another appropriate place;

(B) order the child detained in an appropriate place other than a juvenile detention facility; or

(C) if an appropriate place to release or detain the child as described by Paragraph (A) or (B) is not available, order the child to remain in the juvenile detention facility subject to further detention orders of the court.

(b) The papers sent to a court under Subsection (a)(1) constitute an application for placement under Section 593.041, Health and Safety Code.

Comment

This section parallels § 55.42, dealing with unfitness to proceed. It sets out the procedures when the juvenile court elects to refer mental retardation commitment proceedings to the county court.

Chapter 56. Appeal.

Introductory Comment

This chapter deals with the child's rights of appeal and with providing the appellate court with a record of the trial proceedings. It also grants the State a limited right of appeal from certain rulings in determinate sentence proceedings.

---

§ 56.01. Right to Appeal.

(a) An appeal from an order of a juvenile court is to a court of appeals and the case may be carried to the Texas Supreme Court by writ of error or upon certificate, as in civil cases generally.

(b) The requirements governing an appeal are as in civil cases generally. When an appeal is sought by filing a notice of appeal, security for costs of appeal, or an affidavit of inability to pay the costs of appeal, and the filing is made in a timely fashion after the date the disposition order is signed, the appeal must include the juvenile court adjudication and all rulings contributing to that adjudication. An appeal of the adjudication may be sought notwithstanding that the adjudication order was signed more than 30 days before the date the notice of appeal, security for costs of appeal, or affidavit of inability to pay the costs of appeal was filed. A motion for new trial seeking to vacate an adjudication is timely if the motion is filed not later than the 30th day after the date on which the disposition order is signed.

(c) An appeal may be taken:

(1) except as provided by Subsection (n), by or on behalf of a child from an order entered under:

(A) Section 54.03 with regard to delinquent conduct or conduct indicating a need for supervision;

(B) Section 54.04 disposing of the case;

(C) Section 54.05 respecting modification of a previous juvenile court disposition; or

(D) Chapter 55 by a juvenile court committing a child to a facility for the mentally ill or mentally retarded; or

(2) by a person from an order entered under Section 54.11(i)(2) transferring the person to the custody of the institutional division of the Texas Department of Criminal Justice.

(d) A child has the right to:

(1) appeal, as provided by this subchapter;

(2) representation by counsel on appeal; and

(3) appointment of an attorney for the appeal if an attorney cannot be obtained because of indigency.

(e) On entering an order that is appealable under this section, the court shall advise the child and the child's parent, guardian, or guardian ad litem of the child's rights listed under Subsection (d) of this section.

(f) If the child and his parent, guardian, or guardian ad litem express a desire to appeal, the attorney who represented the child before the juvenile court shall file a notice of appeal with the juvenile court and inform the court whether that attorney will handle the appeal. Counsel shall be appointed under the standards provided in Section 51.10 of this code unless the right to appeal is waived in accordance with Section 51.09 of this code.

(g) An appeal does not suspend the order of the juvenile court, nor does it release the child from the custody of that court or of the person, institution, or agency to whose care the child is committed, unless the juvenile court so orders. However, the appellate court may provide for a personal bond.

(h) If the order appealed from takes custody of the child from his parent, guardian, or custodian, the appeal has precedence over all other cases.

(i) The appellate court may affirm, reverse, or modify the judgment or order, including an order of disposition or modified disposition, from which appeal was taken. It may reverse or modify an order of disposition or modified order of disposition while affirming the juvenile court adjudication that the child engaged in delinquent conduct or conduct indicating a need for supervision. It may remand an order that it reverses or modifies for further proceedings by the juvenile court.

(j) Neither the child nor his family shall be identified in an appellate opinion rendered in an appeal or habeas corpus proceedings related to juvenile court proceedings under this title. The appellate opinion shall be styled, "In the matter of ....," identifying the child by his initials only.

(k) The appellate court shall dismiss an appeal on the state's motion, supported by affidavit showing that the appellant has escaped from custody pending the appeal and, to the affiant's knowledge, has not voluntarily returned to the state's custody on or before the 10th day after the date of the escape. The court may not dismiss an appeal, or if the appeal has been dismissed, shall reinstate the appeal, on the filing of an affidavit of an officer or other credible person showing that the appellant voluntarily returned to custody on or before the 10th day after the date of the escape.

(l) The court may order the child, the child's parent, or other person responsible for support of the child to pay the child's costs of appeal, including the costs of representation by an attorney, unless the court determines the person to be ordered to pay the costs is indigent.

(m) For purposes of determining indigency of the child under this section, the court shall consider the assets and income of the child, the child's parent, and any other person responsible for the support of the child.

(n) A child who enters a plea or agrees to a stipulation of evidence in a proceeding held under this title may not appeal an order of the juvenile court entered under Section 54.03, 54.04, or 54.05 if the court makes a disposition in accordance with the agreement between the state and the child regarding the disposition of the case, unless:

(1) the court gives the child permission to appeal; or

(2) the appeal is based on a matter raised by written motion filed before the proceeding in which the child entered the plea or agreed to the stipulation of evidence.

(o) This section does not limit a child's right to obtain a writ of habeas corpus.

Comment

Except as provided by § 56.03, only the child or the child's representative may appeal from the juvenile court to the Court of Appeals. The appeal is governed by civil, not criminal, rules. The child is entitled to be represented by counsel, including appointed counsel if his or her family is indigent. The juvenile court must inform the child of his or her right to appeal at all appropriate stages of the proceedings.

Under 1995 amendments it is no longer possible to appeal directly from the entry of a certification order. The issues that formerly could be raised in such a direct appeal can now be raised but only in an appeal from a criminal conviction as provided by art. 44.47 of the Code of Criminal Procedure.

The provision concerning dismissing an appeal when the juvenile escapes from custody tracks the language in Rule 42.4 of the Rules of Appellate Procedure.

In 1997 subsection (b) was amended to abrogate caselaw and to provide that timely initiating an appeal following a disposition decision is also an appeal of adjudication issues even if no separate notice of appeal is filed for adjudication and even if the disposition decision occurred more than 30 days after the adjudication decision.

The amendment to subsection (c) in 1999 reflects the option given juvenile courts to conduct commitment proceedings themselves or refer them to county courts. If referral is elected, appeal rights are determined by the Health and Safety Code.

The addition of subsection (n) restricts the right of appeal when the child received a plea-bargained disposition to those cases in which the juvenile court grants permission or in which issues are raised by written pretrial motion, such as a motion to suppress evidence. This is similar to the adult provision in the Texas Rules of Appellate Procedure, but with the difference that, unlike under criminal practice, in juvenile practice it is not necessary to state the basis of appeal in the notice of appeal.

Subsection (o) states the obvious principle that in creating a right of appeal this section does not restrict the constitutional right of the juvenile to petition for release on habeas corpus.

CLE/Other Legal Publications

Juvenile Appeals. Bill Connolly, 15TH ANN. JUVE. L. CONF. (Feb. 2002)

Juvenile Appeals. Eric Andell, 14TH ANN. JUVE. L. CONF. (Feb. 2001)

Leading Cases

Ex parte Valle, 104 S.W.3d 888 (Tex. Crim. App. 2003) (constitutional habeas, not CCP 11.07, is appropriate to challenge confinement in TDCJ under determinate sentence act)

Woods v. State, 68 S.W.3d 667 (Tex. Crim. App. 2002) (special notice of appeal required to challenge certification rulings in appeal from plea bargained criminal conviction)

In re D.A.S., 973 S.W.2d 296 (Tex. 1998) (*Anders* frivolous appeal procedures apply to juvenile cases)

In re M.R., 858 S.W.2d 365 (Tex. 1993) (motion for new trial required to preserve for appeal factual sufficiency claim)

L.L.S. v. State, 569 S.W.2d 495 (Tex. 1978) (notice of appeal must be given within 30 days of order appealed from)

C.L.B. v. State, 567 S.W.2d 795 (Tex. 1978) (State has no right to appeal from juvenile court ruling)

In re S.N., 95 S.W.3d 535 (Tex.App.—Houston [1st Dist.] 2002, pet. filed) (State has no right to appeal from dismissal resulting from pre-trial suppression order)

In re A.E.E., 89 S.W.3d 250 (Tex.App.—Texarkana 2002, no pet.) (juvenile's father lacks standing to appeal a plea bargained disposition)

In re J.C.H., 12 S.W.3d 561 (Tex. App.—San Antonio 1999, no pet.) (notice of appeal must be filed not later than 30 days following disposition)

In re D.W.R., 990 S.W.2d 446 (Tex. App.—San Antonio 1999, no pet.) (court of appeals sets conditions for appeal bond)

In re J.A.H., 986 S.W.2d 39 (Tex. App.—Waco 1998, no pet.) (*Anders* brief must be served on parent or guardian as well as child)

In re J.V., 944 S.W.2d 15 (Tex. App.—El Paso 1997, no writ) (Court of Appeal details factors in discretionary denial of personal bond on appeal)

In re D.V., 955 S.W.2d 379 (Tex. App.—San Antonio 1997, no writ) (civil harmless error rule used in indeterminate commitment cases; criminal used in determinate sentence cases)

In re A.S., 954 S.W.2d 835 (Tex. App.—El Paso 1997, no writ) (criminal standard of evidence sufficiency review applied)

In re S.A.M., 933 S.W.2d 744 (Tex. App.—San Antonio 1996, no writ) (cannot review evidence to support disposition without adjudication hearing statement of facts)

In re C.F., 897 S.W.2d 464 (Tex. App.—El Paso 1995, no writ) (good faith filing of notice of appeal sufficient to perfect appeal)

M.B. v. State, 905 S.W.2d 344 (Tex. App.—El Paso 1995, no writ) (juvenile may not challenge adjudication by habeas while direct appeal is still pending)

In re D.Z., 869 S.W.2d 561 (Tex. App.—Corpus Christi 1993, writ denied) (criminal harmless error standard applies in appeal of determinate sentence act case)

In re L.G., 728 S.W.2d 939 (Tex. App.—Austin 1987, writ ref'd) (court of appeals may affirm adjudication but set aside TYC commitment)

In re J.L.D., 704 S.W.2d 395 (Tex. App.—Corpus Christi 1985, no writ) (respondent cannot appeal from order of detention)

§ 56.02. Transcript on Appeal.

(a) An attorney retained to represent a child on appeal who desires to have included in the record on appeal a transcription of notes of the reporter has the responsibility of obtaining and paying for the transcription and furnishing it to the clerk in duplicate in time for inclusion in the record.

(b) The juvenile court shall order the reporter to furnish a transcription without charge to the attorney if the court finds, after hearing or on an affidavit filed by the child's parent or other person responsible for support of the child that the parent or other responsible person is unable to pay or to give security therefor.

(c) On certificate of the court that a transcription has been provided without charge, payment therefor shall be made from the general funds of the county in which the proceedings appealed from occurred.

(d) The court reporter shall report any portion of the proceedings requested by either party or directed by the court and shall report the proceedings in question and answer form unless a narrative transcript is requested.

Comment

This section deals with responsibility for providing the appellate court with a record of the trial proceedings, including payment for the record when the child's family is indigent.

Leading Cases

B.J.M. v. State, 997 S.W.2d 626 (Tex. App.—Dallas 1999, no pet.) (failure of court to enter written order sustaining indigency contest results in free transcript)

In re M.S., 940 S.W.2d 789 (Tex. App.—Austin 1997, no writ) (criminal rules permitting late filing of record applied to juvenile case)

In re L.B., 936 S.W.2d 335 (Tex. App.—El Paso 1996, no writ) (procedures for producing statement of facts from audio-tape record established)

In re M.R.R., Jr., 903 S.W.2d 49 (Tex. App.—San Antonio 1995, no writ) (applying deadline for filing statement of facts would deny juvenile effective assistance of counsel)

J.W.D. v. State, 903 S.W.2d 44 (Tex. App.—Houston [14th Dist.] 1995, error den.) (failure to file timely transcript requires dismissal of appeal)

In re M.B., 894 S.W.2d 82 (Tex. App.—El Paso 1995, no writ) (court of appeals has no authority to extend time to file a transcript)

E.T.J. v. State, 766 S.W.2d 871 (Tex. App.—Dallas 1989, no writ) (statement of facts must be filed within 60 days after judgment is signed)

Mitchell v. Baum, 668 S.W.2d 757 (Tex. App.—Houston [14th Dist.] 1984, no writ) (standard of indigency for free transcript)

---

§ 56.03. Appeal by State in Cases of Violent or Habitual Offender.

(a) In this section, "prosecuting attorney" means the county attorney, district attorney, or criminal district attorney who has the primary responsibility of presenting cases in the juvenile court. The term does not include an assistant prosecuting attorney.

(b) The state is entitled to appeal an order of a court in a juvenile case in which the grand jury has approved of the petition under Section 53.045 if the order:

(1) dismisses a petition or any portion of a petition;

(2) arrests or modifies a judgment;

(3) grants a new trial;

(4) sustains a claim of former jeopardy; or

(5) grants a motion to suppress evidence, a confession, or an admission and if:

(A) jeopardy has not attached in the case;

(B) the prosecuting attorney certifies to the trial court that the appeal is not taken for the purpose of delay; and

(C) the evidence, confession, or admission is of substantial importance in the case.

(c) The prosecuting attorney may not bring an appeal under Subsection (b) later than the 15th day after the date on which the order or ruling to be appealed is entered by the court.

(d) The state is entitled to a stay in the proceedings pending the disposition of an appeal under Subsection (b).

(e) The court of appeals shall give preference in its docket to an appeal filed under Subsection (b).

(f) The state shall pay all costs of appeal under Subsection (b), other than the cost of attorney's fees for the respondent.

(g) If the respondent is represented by appointed counsel, the counsel shall continue to represent the respondent as appointed counsel on the appeal. If the respondent is not represented by appointed counsel, the respondent may seek the appointment of counsel to represent the respondent on appeal. The juvenile court shall determine whether the parent or other person responsible for support of the child is financially able to obtain an attorney to represent the respondent on appeal. If the court determines that the parent or other

person is financially unable to obtain counsel for the appeal, the court shall appoint counsel to represent the respondent on appeal.

(h) If the state appeals under this section and the respondent is not detained, the court shall permit the respondent to remain at large subject only to the condition that the respondent appear in court for further proceedings when required by the court. If the respondent is detained, on the state's filing of notice of appeal under this section, the respondent is entitled to immediate release from detention on the allegation that is the subject of the appeal. The court shall permit the respondent to remain at large regarding that allegation subject only to the condition that the respondent appear in court for further proceedings when required by the court.

(i) The Texas Rules of Appellate Procedure apply to a petition by the state to the supreme court for review of a decision of a court of appeals in a juvenile case.

History: Enacted by 78th Legis., Reg. Sess. (2003), H.B. 2319, eff. Sept. 1, 2003. Applies only to an appeal by the State of an order rendered by a juvenile court on or after the effective date

Comment

This section, enacted in 2003, is modeled after Code of Criminal Procedure article 44.01. It permits the State to appeal in determinate sentence proceedings under circumstances in which conducting further proceedings following appellate reversal is not precluded by double jeopardy.

Chapter 57. Rights of Victims.

Introductory Comment

This chapter deals with victims of juvenile offenses and defines their rights in the juvenile process.

CLE/Other Legal Publications

Victim Impact Panels: Empowering Victims to Impact Juvenile Offenders. Jennifer Britton, 12 JUVE. L. SECT. RPT. (Sept. 1998)

The Implementation of the Rights of Victims Act: Chapter 57 of the Texas Family Code. Amy Hutson, 6 JUVE. L. SECT. RPT. (June 1992)

---

§ 57.001. Definitions.

In this chapter:

(1) "Close relative of a deceased victim" means a person who was the spouse of a deceased victim at the time of the victim's death or who is a parent or adult brother, sister, or child of the deceased victim.

(2) "Guardian of a victim" means a person who is the legal guardian of the victim, whether or not the legal relationship between the guardian and victim exists because of the age of the victim or the physical or mental incompetency of the victim.

(3) "Victim" means a person who as the result of the delinquent conduct of a child suffers a pecuniary loss or personal injury or harm.

Comment

By 1995 amendment the scope of this chapter was greatly expanded to include property offenses committed by juveniles.

In 1997 the definition of victim was expanded to its broadest logical definition to mean anyone injured in any fashion by delinquent conduct.

---

§ 57.002. Victim's Rights.

(a) A victim, guardian of a victim, or close relative of a deceased victim is entitled to the following rights within the juvenile justice system:

(1) the right to receive from law enforcement agencies adequate protection from harm and threats of harm arising from cooperation with prosecution efforts;

(2) the right to have the court or person appointed by the court take the safety of the victim or the victim's family into consideration as an element in determining whether the child should be detained before the child's conduct is adjudicated;

(3) the right, if requested, to be informed of relevant court proceedings, including appellate proceedings, and to be informed in a timely manner if those court proceedings have been canceled or rescheduled;

(4) the right to be informed, when requested, by the court or a person appointed by the court concerning the procedures in the juvenile justice system, including general procedures relating to:

(A) the preliminary investigation and deferred prosecution of a case; and

(B) the appeal of the case;

(5) the right to provide pertinent information to a juvenile court conducting a disposition hearing concerning the impact of the offense on the victim and the victim's family by testimony, written statement, or any other manner before the court renders its disposition;

(6) the right to receive information regarding compensation to victims as provided by Subchapter B, Chapter 56, Code of Criminal Procedure, including information related to the costs that may be compensated under that subchapter and the amount of compensation, eligibility for compensation, and procedures for application for compensation under that subchapter, the payment of medical expenses under Section 56.06, Code of Criminal Procedure, for a victim of a sexual assault, and when requested, to referral to available social service agencies that may offer additional assistance;

(7) the right to be informed, upon request, of procedures for release under supervision or transfer of the person to the custody of the pardons and paroles division of the Texas Department of Criminal Justice for parole, to participate in the release or transfer for parole process, to be notified, if requested, of the person's release, escape, or transfer for parole proceedings concerning the person, to provide to the Texas Youth Commission for inclusion in the person's file information to be considered by the commission before the release under supervision or transfer for parole of the person, and to be notified, if requested, of the person's release or transfer for parole;

(8) the right to be provided with a waiting area, separate or secure from other witnesses, including the child alleged to have committed the conduct and relatives of the child, before testifying in any proceeding concerning the child, or, if a separate waiting area is not available, other safeguards should be taken to minimize the victim's contact with the child and the child's relatives and witnesses, before and during court proceedings;

(9) the right to prompt return of any property of the victim that is held by a law enforcement agency or the attorney for the state as evidence when the property is no longer required for that purpose;

(10) the right to have the attorney for the state notify the employer of the victim, if requested, of the necessity of the victim's cooperation and testimony in a proceeding that may necessitate the absence of the victim from work for good cause;

(11) the right to be present at all public court proceedings related to the conduct of the child as provided by Section 54.08, subject to that section; and

(12) any other right appropriate to the victim that a victim of criminal conduct has under Article 56.02, Code of Criminal Procedure.

(b) In notifying a victim of the release or escape of a person, the Texas Youth Commission shall use the same procedure established for the notification of the release or escape of an adult offender under Article 56.11, Code of Criminal Procedure.

§ 57.003. Duty of Juvenile Board.

(a) The juvenile board shall ensure to the extent practicable that a victim, guardian of a victim, or close relative of a deceased victim is afforded the rights granted by Section 57.002 and, on request, an explanation of those rights.

(b) The juvenile board may designate a person to serve as victim assistance coordinator in the juvenile board's jurisdiction for victims of juvenile offenders.

(c) The victim assistance coordinator shall ensure that a victim, or close relative of a deceased victim, is afforded the rights granted victims, guardians, and relatives by Section 57.002 and, on request, an explanation of those rights. The victim assistance coordinator shall work closely with appropriate law enforcement agencies, prosecuting attorneys, the Texas Juvenile Probation Commission, and the Texas Youth Commission in carrying out that duty.

(d) The victim assistance coordinator shall ensure that at a minimum, a victim, guardian of a victim, or close relative of a deceased victim receives:

(1) a written notice of the rights outlined in Section 57.002;

(2) an application for compensation under the Crime Victims' Compensation Act (Subchapter B, Chapter 56, Code of Criminal Procedure); and

(3) a victim impact statement with information explaining the possible use and consideration of the victim impact statement at detention, adjudication, and release proceedings involving the juvenile.

(e) The victim assistance coordinator shall, on request, offer to assist a person receiving a form under Subsection (d) to complete the form.

(f) The victim assistance coordinator shall send a copy of the victim impact statement to the court conducting a disposition hearing involving the juvenile.

§ 57.0031. Notification of Rights of Victims of Juveniles.

At the initial contact or at the earliest possible time after the initial contact between the victim of a reported crime and the juvenile probation office having the responsibility for the disposition of the juvenile, the office shall provide the victim a written notice:

(1) containing information about the availability of emergency and medical services, if applicable;

(2) stating that the victim has the right to receive information regarding compensation to victims of crime as provided by the Crime Victims' Compensation Act (Subchapter B, Chapter 56, Code of Criminal Procedure), including information about:

(A) the costs that may be compensated and the amount of compensation, eligibility for compensation, and procedures for application for compensation;

(B) the payment for a medical examination for a victim of a sexual assault; and

(C) referral to available social service agencies that may offer additional assistance;

(3) stating the name, address, and phone number of the victim assistance coordinator for victims of juveniles;

(4) containing the following statement: "You may call the crime victim assistance coordinator for the status of the case and information about victims' rights.";

(5) stating the rights of victims of crime under Section 57.002;

(6) summarizing each procedural stage in the processing of a juvenile case, including preliminary investigation, detention, informal adjustment of a case, disposition hearings, release proceedings, restitution, and appeals;

(7) suggesting steps the victim may take if the victim is subjected to threats or intimidation;

(8) stating the case number and assigned court for the case; and

(9) stating that the victim has the right to file a victim impact statement and to have it considered in juvenile proceedings.

§ 57.004. Notification.

A court, a person appointed by the court, or the Texas Youth Commission is responsible for notifying a victim, guardian of a victim, or close relative of a deceased victim of a proceeding under this chapter only if the victim, guardian of a victim, or close relative of a deceased victim requests the notification in writing and provides a current address to which the notification is to be sent.

§ 57.005. Liability.

The Texas Youth Commission, a juvenile board, a court, a person appointed by a court, an attorney for the state, a peace officer, or a law enforcement agency is not liable for a failure or inability to provide a right listed under Section 57.002 of this code.

§ 57.006. Appeal.

The failure or inability of any person to provide a right or service listed under Section 57.002 of this code may not be used by a child as a ground for appeal or for a post conviction writ of habeas corpus.

§ 57.007. Standing.

A victim, guardian of a victim, or close relative of a victim does not have standing to participate as a party in a juvenile proceeding or to contest the disposition of any case.

§ 57.008. Court Order for Protection From Juveniles.

(a) A court may issue an order for protection from juveniles directed against a child to protect a victim of the child's conduct who, because of the victim's participation in the juvenile justice system, risks further harm by the child.

(b) In the order, the court may prohibit the child from doing specified acts or require the child to do specified acts necessary or appropriate to prevent or reduce the likelihood of further harm to the victim by the child.

Chapter 58. Records; Juvenile Justice Information System.

Subchapter A. Records

Subchapter B. Juvenile Justice Information System

Subchapter C. Automatic Restriction of Access to Records

Subchapter D. Local Juvenile Justice Information System

Introductory Comment

Chapter 58, added in 1995, is a comprehensive regulation of juvenile records. It creates a state-wide computerized juvenile records system operated by the DPS as part of the adult system created by Chapter 60 of the TEX. CODE CRIM. PROC. ANN.

Subchapter A deals with local records and with sealing of records. Subchapter B deals with the state-wide system. Subchapter C, added in 2001, deals with a new method of automatic restriction of access to records and Subchapter D deals with local juvenile justice information systems.

CLE/Other Legal Publications

Juvenile Records as Adult Punishment Evidence—"I Will Follow You." Catherine Greene Burnett, 13TH ANN. JUVE. L. CONF. (Feb. 2000)

Texas's Centralized Juvenile Justice Information System. Olga Seelig Sanchez, 10 JUVE. L. SECT. RPT. (Sept. 1996)

Texas's Computerized Criminal History Record System: A Profile for the Juvenile Bar. Brian Stettin, 9 JUVE. L. SECT. RPT. (June 1995)

Leading Att'y Gen. Op.

Op. Tex. Att'y Gen. ORD 655 (1997) (housing authority can obtain juvenile records from DPS)

Subchapter A. Records

§ 58.001. Collection of Records of Children.

(a) Law enforcement officers and other juvenile justice personnel shall collect information described by Section 58.104 as a part of the juvenile justice information system created under Subchapter B.

(b) The information is available as provided by Subchapter B.

(c) A law enforcement agency shall forward information, including fingerprints, relating to a child who has been taken into custody under Section 52.01 by the agency to the Department of Public Safety for inclusion in the juvenile justice information system created under Subchapter B, but only if the child is referred to juvenile court on or before the 10th day after the date the child is taken into custody under Section 52.01. If the child is not referred to juvenile court within that time, the law enforcement agency shall destroy all information, including photographs and fingerprints, relating to the child unless the child is placed in a first offender program under Section 52.031 or on informal disposition under Section 52.03. The law enforcement agency may not forward any information to the Department of Public Safety relating to the child while the child is in a first offender program under Section 52.031, or during the 90 days following successful completion of the program or while the child is on informal disposition under Section 52.03. Except as provided by Subsection (f), after the date the child completes an informal disposition under Section 52.03 or after the 90th day after the date the child successfully completes a first offender program under Section 52.031, the law enforcement agency shall destroy all information, including photographs and fingerprints, relating to the child.

(d) If information relating to a child is contained in a document that also contains information relating to an adult and a law enforcement agency is required to destroy all information relating to the child under this section, the agency shall alter the document so that the information relating to the child is destroyed and the information relating to the adult is preserved.

(e) The deletion of a computer entry constitutes destruction of the information contained in the entry.

(f) A law enforcement agency may maintain information relating to a child after the 90th day after the date the child successfully completes a first offender program under Section 52.031 only to determine the child's eligibility to participate in a first offender program.

Comment

A law enforcement agency may photograph and fingerprint any child taken into custody for a criminal offense of the grade of B misdemeanor or higher under § 58.002, *infra*. However, it may send those documents and other information to the state-wide system only if it makes a referral to the juvenile court system within 10 days of arrest. If it chooses not to make a referral, the records must be destroyed, unless the child is placed on informal disposition or in a first offender program.

Subsection (c) prohibits law enforcement from sending juvenile records to DPS for ninety days after successful completion of a first offender program and, subject to (f), requires records destruction at that time. Subsection (d) makes it clear that when law enforcement is required to destroy juvenile records, it can do so by eliminating any reference to the identity of the juvenile and need not also destroy those parts of the record that are needed for successful prosecution of a criminal case. Subsection (e) states that deletion of a computer entry is destruction of that record even though the record could possibly be re-constructed by a computer expert. Subsection (f) permits law enforcement to keep a record beyond the 90 day destruction deadline for the sole purpose of determining future ineligibility for a first offender program.

Amendments in 1999 make it clear that a law enforcement agency is required to submit information to the DPS relating to any child it takes into custody if a referral to the juvenile court is made within 10 days. This requirement applies only to children taken into full custody, not just temporarily detained in a public place.

CLE/Other Legal Publication

Confidentiality of Juvenile Information since the Public Information Act. Jennifer L.C. Stack, 17 JUVE. L. SECT. RPT. (June 2003)

Leading Att'y Gen. Op.

Op. Tex. Att'y Gen. No. DM–435 (1997) (obligation under § 58.001 to destroy law enforcement information explained)

---

§ 58.002. Photographs and Fingerprints of Children.

(a) Except as provided by Chapter 63, Code of Criminal Procedure, a child may not be photographed or fingerprinted without the consent of the juvenile court unless the child is taken into custody or referred to the juvenile court for conduct that constitutes a felony or a misdemeanor punishable by confinement in jail.

(b) On or before December 31 of each year, the head of each municipal or county law enforcement agency located in a county shall certify to the juvenile board for that county that the photographs and fingerprints required to be destroyed under Section 58.001 have been destroyed. The juvenile board shall conduct or cause to be conducted an audit of the records of the law enforcement agency to verify the destruction of the photographs and fingerprints and the law enforcement agency shall make its records available for this purpose. If the audit shows that the certification provided by the head of the law enforcement agency is false, that person is subject to prosecution for perjury under Chapter 37, Penal Code.

(c) This section does not prohibit a law enforcement officer from photographing or fingerprinting a child who is not in custody if the child's parent or guardian voluntarily consents in writing to the photographing or fingerprinting of the child.

(d) This section does not apply to fingerprints that are required or authorized to be submitted or obtained for an application for a driver's license or personal identification card.

(e) This section does not prohibit a law enforcement officer from fingerprinting or photographing a child as provided by Section 58.0021.

Comment

Only children arrested for B misdemeanors or above may be fingerprinted and photographed without the consent of the juvenile court. The juvenile board has the duty to determine by audit of law enforcement records that those records that should be destroyed are destroyed.

Subsection (c) provides that a law enforcement officer may fingerprint or photograph a child not in custody but only with written parental consent.

Language added to subsection (a) in 1999 is intended to authorize juvenile intake and probation officials to fingerprint and photograph children who are referred to the juvenile court without being taken into custody.

Leading Cases

Hayes v. Florida, 470 U.S. 811, 84 L.Ed.2d 705, 105 S.Ct. 1643 (1985) (taking fingerprints from arrestee without consent requires probable cause)

Lanes v. State, 767 S.W.2d 789 (Tex. Crim. App. 1989) (probable cause as well as juvenile court's consent required to take fingerprints from arrestee)

In re Franklin, 699 S.W.2d 689 (Tex. App.—Texarkana 1985, no writ) (failure to send juvenile photograph to court does not preclude in-court identification)

§ 58.0021. Fingerprints or Photographs for Comparison in Investigation.

(a) A law enforcement officer may take temporary custody of a child to take the child's fingerprints if:

(1) the officer has probable cause to believe that the child has engaged in delinquent conduct;

(2) the officer has investigated that conduct and has found other fingerprints during the investigation; and

(3) the officer has probable cause to believe that the child's fingerprints will match the other fingerprints.

(b) A law enforcement officer may take temporary custody of a child to take the child's photograph if:

(1) the officer has probable cause to believe that the child has engaged in delinquent conduct; and

(2) the officer has probable cause to believe that the child's photograph will be of material assistance in the investigation of that conduct.

(c) Temporary custody for the purpose described by Subsection (a) or (b):

(1) is not a taking into custody under Section 52.01; and

(2) may not be reported to the juvenile justice information system under Subchapter B.

(d) If a law enforcement officer does not take the child into custody under Section 52.01, the child shall be released from temporary custody authorized under this section as soon as the fingerprints or photographs are obtained.

(e) A law enforcement officer who under this section obtains fingerprints or photographs from a child shall:

(1) immediately destroy them if they do not lead to a positive comparison or identification; and

(2) make a reasonable effort to notify the child's parent, guardian, or custodian of the action taken.

(f) A law enforcement officer may under this section obtain fingerprints or photographs from a child at:

(1) a juvenile processing office; or

(2) a location that affords reasonable privacy to the child.

Comment

Under prior law, if a law enforcement officer had probable cause and wished to fingerprint or photograph a child to confirm or dispel suspicion, the officer, absent consent by the juvenile, was required to take the juvenile into custody to enable fingerprinting and photographing as part of the booking process. That action creates statewide and nationwide records of the event. This section affords a less intrusive alternative when the officer has probable cause. It enables the information to be obtained without creating a record.

§ 58.0022. Fingerprints or Photographs to Identify Runaways.

A law enforcement officer who takes a child into custody with probable cause to believe that the child has engaged in conduct indicating a need for supervision as described by Section 51.03(b)(3) and who after reasonable effort is unable to determine the identity of the child, may fingerprint or photograph the child to establish the child's identity. On determination of the child's identity or that the child cannot be identified by the fingerprints or photographs, the law enforcement officer shall immediately destroy all copies of the fingerprint records or photographs of the child.

Comment

This section permits an officer who has taken a runaway into custody to fingerprint and photograph the person if necessary to identify the person.

§ 58.003. Sealing of Records.

(a) Except as provided by Subsections (b) and (c), on the application of a person who has been found to have engaged in delinquent conduct or conduct indicating a need for supervision, or a person taken into custody to determine whether the person engaged in delinquent conduct or conduct indicating a need for supervision, on the juvenile court's own motion or on receipt of a certification from the Department of Public Safety of the State of Texas that the records of a person are eligible for sealing under this section, the court shall order the sealing of the records in the case if the court finds that:

(1) two years have elapsed since final discharge of the person or since the last official action in the person's case if there was no adjudication; and

(2) since the time specified in Subdivision (1), the person has not been convicted of a felony or a misdemeanor involving moral turpitude or found to have engaged in delinquent conduct or conduct indicating a need for supervision and no proceeding is pending seeking conviction or adjudication.

(b) A court may not order the sealing of the records of a person who has received a determinate sentence for engaging in delinquent conduct that violated a penal law listed in Section 53.045 or engaging in habitual felony conduct as described by Section 51.031.

(c) Subject to Subsection (b), a court may order the sealing of records concerning a person adjudicated as having engaged in delinquent conduct that violated a penal law of the grade of felony only if:

(1) the person is 21 years of age or older;

(2) the person was not transferred by a juvenile court under Section 54.02 to a criminal court for prosecution;

(3) the records have not been used as evidence in the punishment phase of a criminal proceeding under Section 3(a), Article 37.07, Code of Criminal Procedure; and

(4) the person has not been convicted of a penal law of the grade of felony after becoming age 17.

(d) The court may grant the relief authorized in Subsection (a) at any time after final discharge of the person or after the last official action in the case if there was no adjudication. If the child is referred to the juvenile court for conduct constituting any offense and at the adjudication hearing the child is found to be not guilty of each offense alleged, the court shall immediately order the sealing of all files and records relating to the case.

(e) Reasonable notice of the hearing shall be given to:

(1) the person who made the application or who is the subject of the records named in the motion;

(2) the prosecuting attorney for the juvenile court;

(3) the authority granting the discharge if the final discharge was from an institution or from parole;

(4) the public or private agency or institution having custody of records named in the application or motion; and

(5) the law enforcement agency having custody of files or records named in the application or motion.

(f) A copy of the sealing order shall be sent to each agency or official named in the order.

(g) On entry of the order:

(1) all law enforcement, prosecuting attorney, clerk of court, and juvenile court records ordered sealed shall be sent before the 61st day after the date the order is received to the court issuing the order;

(2) all records of a public or private agency or institution ordered sealed shall be sent before the 61st day after the date the order is received to the court issuing the order;

(3) all index references to the records ordered sealed shall be deleted before the 61st day after the date the order is received, and verification of the deletion shall be sent before the 61st day after the date of the deletion to the court issuing the order;

(4) the juvenile court, clerk of court, prosecuting attorney, public or private agency or institution, and law enforcement officers and agencies shall properly reply that no record exists with respect to the person on inquiry in any matter; and

(5) the adjudication shall be vacated and the proceeding dismissed and treated for all purposes other than a subsequent capital prosecution, including the purpose of showing a prior finding of delinquent conduct, as if it had never occurred.

(h) Inspection of the sealed records may be permitted by an order of the juvenile court on the petition of the person who is the subject of the records and only by those persons named in the order.

(i) On the final discharge of a child or on the last official action in the case if there is no adjudication, the child shall be given a written explanation of the child's rights under this section and a copy of the provisions of this section.

(j) A person whose records have been sealed under this section is not required in any proceeding or in any application for employment, information, or licensing to state that the person has been the subject of a proceeding under this title and any statement that the person has never been found to be a delinquent child shall never be held against the person in any criminal or civil proceeding.

(k) A prosecuting attorney may, on application to the juvenile court, reopen at any time the files and records of a person adjudicated as having engaged in delinquent conduct that violated a penal law of the grade of felony sealed by the court under this section for the purposes of Sections 12.42(a)–(c) and (e), Penal Code.

(l) On the motion of a person in whose name records are kept or on the court's own motion, the court may order the destruction of records that have been sealed under this section if:

(1) the records relate to conduct that did not violate a penal law of the grade of felony or a misdemeanor punishable by confinement in jail;

(2) five years have elapsed since the person's 16th birthday; and

(3) the person has not been convicted of a felony.

(m) On request of the Department of Public Safety, a juvenile court shall reopen and allow the department to inspect the files and records of the juvenile court relating to an applicant for a license to carry a concealed handgun under Subchapter H, Chapter 411, Government Code.

(n) A record created or maintained under **Chapter 62, Code of Criminal Procedure** [~~Article 6252–13c.1, Revised Statutes~~], may not be sealed under this section if the person who is the subject of the record has a continuing obligation to register under that **chapter** [~~article~~].

(o) An agency or official named in the order that cannot seal the records because there is incorrect or insufficient information in the order shall notify the court issuing the order before the 61st day after the date the agency or official receives the order. The court shall notify the person who made the application or who is the subject of the records named in the motion, or the attorney for that person, before the 61st day after the date the court receives the notice that the agency or official cannot seal the records because there is incorrect or insufficient information in the order.

History: Amended by 78th Legis., Reg. Sess. (2003), H.B. 2319, eff. Sept. 1, 2003. Applies only to conduct occurring on or after effective date.

Comment

This section establishes five different categories relating to the sealing of a juvenile's records: (1) If the juvenile has received a determinate sentence, the records can never be sealed; (2) If the juvenile has been adjudicated for any other felony, the sealing applicant must wait until he becomes 21 years of age; (3) The right to seal any non-felony adjudication records arises two years after the juvenile exits the system; (4) The juvenile court has discretion to order sealing for non-felony adjudication records anytime after the juvenile exits the system; (5) Finally, if the juvenile is found not guilty of all offenses, no matter what the charges, the records must immediately be ordered sealed by the juvenile court.

Subsection (m) prohibits the sealing of sex offender registration records so long as there is a continuing duty to register. All other juvenile records can be sealed as provided by this section. Sex offender registration records can be sealed once the juvenile no longer has an obligation to register.

1999 amendments to subsection (g) require that agencies holding records comply with a sealing order within 60 days of receiving the order. If the order is insufficient, the agency under subsection (o) must report that back to the court within 60 days.

CLE/Other Legal Publications

Files and Records: Sealing the Juvenile Record. Kris Moore, 14TH ANN. JUVE. L. CONF. (Feb. 2001)

What's All the Fuss About? A License to Lie—The Sealing of Juvenile Records. Courtney Hamilton, 8 JUVE. L. SECT. RPT. (Dec. 1994)

Leading Att'y Gen. Op.

Op. Tex. Att'y Gen. No. DM–9 (1991) (unless record sealed, juvenile must report adjudication on employment application)

---

§ 58.004. [repealed]

§ 58.005. Confidentiality of Records.

(a) **Records and files concerning a child, including personally identifiable information, and information** [~~Information~~] obtained for the purpose of diagnosis, examination, evaluation, or treatment or for making a referral for treatment of a child by a public or private agency or institution providing supervision of a child by arrangement of the juvenile court or having custody of the child under order of the juvenile court may be disclosed only to:

(1) the professional staff or consultants of the agency or institution;

(2) the judge, probation officers, and professional staff or consultants of the juvenile court;

(3) an attorney for the child;

(4) a governmental agency if the disclosure is required or authorized by law;

(5) a person or entity to whom the child is referred for treatment or services if the agency or institution disclosing the information has entered into a written confiden-

tiality agreement with the person or entity regarding the protection of the disclosed information;

(6) the Texas Department of Criminal Justice and the Texas Juvenile Probation Commission for the purpose of maintaining statistical records of recidivism and for diagnosis and classification; or

(7) with leave of the juvenile court, any other person, agency, or institution having a legitimate interest in the proceeding or in the work of the court.

(b) This section does not apply to information collected under Section 58.104.

History: Amended by 78th Legis., Reg. Sess. (2003), H.B. 2319, eff. Sept. 1, 2003. Applies only to conduct occurring on or after effective date.

Comment

This section is restricted to treatment and social information and other personally-identifiable information. It covers information in the possession of local probation departments, the TYC, public and private placement facilities, court consultants and treatment personnel. The reference to § 58.104 is to information that is sent to the Juvenile Justice Information System.

Leading Att'y Gen. Op.

Op. Tex. Att'y Gen. No. DM–334 (1995) (victim of juvenile's offense may have legitimate interest in juvenile court records)

---

§ 58.0051. Interagency Sharing of Records.

(a) Within each county, a district school superintendent and the juvenile probation department may enter into a written interagency agreement to share information about juvenile offenders. The agreement must specify the conditions under which summary criminal history information is to be made available to appropriate school personnel and the conditions under which school records are to be made available to appropriate juvenile justice agencies.

(b) Information disclosed under this section by a school district must relate to the juvenile system's ability to serve, before adjudication, the student whose records are being released.

(c) A juvenile justice agency official who receives educational information under this section shall certify in writing that the institution or individual receiving the personally identifiable information has agreed not to disclose it to a third party, other than another juvenile justice agency.

(d) A juvenile justice agency that receives educational information under this section shall destroy all information when the child is no longer under the jurisdiction of a juvenile court.

Comment

This section implements the federal FERPA provisions authorizing the sharing of otherwise confidential educational records with juvenile justice officials. There is also a provision in Education Code § 37.084 that is reciprocal to this provision. The educational information must be provided to assist only in pre-adjudication decisions in the juvenile process. A juvenile justice agency is authorized to disclose criminal history information to schools under a local agreement.

---

§ 58.006. Destruction of Certain Records.

The court shall order the destruction of the records relating to the conduct for which a child is taken into custody, including records contained in the juvenile justice information system, if:

(1) a determination that no probable cause exists to believe the child engaged in the conduct is made under Section 53.01 and the case is not referred to a prosecutor for review under Section 53.012; or

(2) a determination that no probable cause exists to believe the child engaged in the conduct is made by a prosecutor under Section 53.012.

Comment

This section requires the automatic destruction, not just sealing, of records when a determination of no probable cause is made by intake or by the prosecutor.

---

§ 58.007. Physical Records or Files.

(a) This section applies only to the inspection and maintenance of a physical record or file concerning a child and the storage of information, by electronic means or otherwise, concerning the child from which a physical record or file could be generated and does not affect the collection, dissemination, or maintenance of information as provided by Subchapter B. This section does not apply to a record or file relating to a child that is:

(1) required or authorized to be maintained under the laws regulating the operation of motor vehicles in this state;

(2) maintained by a municipal or justice court; or

(3) subject to disclosure under Chapter 62, Code of Criminal Procedure, as added by Chapter 668, Acts of the 75th Legislature, Regular Session, 1997.

(b) Except as provided by Article 15.27, Code of Criminal Procedure, the records and files of a juvenile court, a clerk of court, a juvenile probation department, or a prosecuting attorney relating to a child who is a party to a proceeding under this title are open to inspection only by:

(1) the judge, probation officers, and professional staff or consultants of the juvenile court;

(2) a juvenile justice agency as that term is defined by Section 58.101;

(3) an attorney for a party to the proceeding;

(4) a public or private agency or institution providing supervision of the child by arrangement of the juvenile court, or having custody of the child under juvenile court order; or

(5) with leave of the juvenile court, any other person, agency, or institution having a legitimate interest in the proceeding or in the work of the court.

(c) Except as provided by Subsection (d), law enforcement records and files concerning a child and information stored, by electronic means or otherwise, concerning the child from which a record or file could be generated may not be disclosed to the public and shall be:

(1) if maintained on paper or microfilm, kept separate from adult files and records;

(2) if maintained electronically in the same computer system as records or files relating to adults, be accessible under controls that are separate and distinct from controls to access electronic data concerning adults; and

(3) maintained on a local basis only and not sent to a central state or federal depository, except as provided by Subchapter B.

(d) The law enforcement files and records of a person who is transferred from the Texas Youth Commission to the institutional division or the pardons and paroles division of the Texas Department of Criminal Justice may be transferred to a central state or federal depository for adult records on or after the date of transfer.

(e) Law enforcement records and files concerning a child may be inspected by a juvenile justice agency as that term is defined by Section 58.101 and a criminal justice agency as that term is defined by Section 411.082, Government Code.

(f) If a child has been reported missing by a parent, guardian, or conservator of that child, information about the child may be forwarded to and disseminated by the Texas Crime Information Center and the National Crime Information Center.

(g) For the purpose of offering a record as evidence in the punishment phase of a criminal proceeding, a prosecuting attorney may obtain the record of a defendant's adjudication that is admissible under Section 3(a), Article 37.07, Code of Criminal Procedure, by submitting a request for the record to the juvenile court that made the adjudication. If a court receives a request from a prosecuting attorney under this subsection, the court shall, if the court possesses the requested record of adjudication, certify and provide the prosecuting attorney with a copy of the record.

(h) The juvenile court may disseminate to the public the following information relating to a child who is the subject of a directive to apprehend or a warrant of arrest and who cannot be located for the purpose of apprehension:

(1) the child's name, including other names by which the child is known;

(2) the child's physical description, including sex, weight, height, race, ethnicity, eye color, hair color, scars, marks, and tattoos;

(3) a photograph of the child; and

(4) a description of the conduct the child is alleged to have committed, including the level and degree of the alleged offense.

(i) In addition to the authority to release information under Subsection (b)(5), a juvenile probation department may release information contained in its records without leave of the juvenile court pursuant to guidelines adopted by the juvenile board.

Comment

This section deals with physical records other than the information contained in the statewide Juvenile Justice Information System. Examples would be offense or incident reports, a witness statement, and laboratory reports. Those records must be maintained on a local basis and are subject to confidentiality restrictions similar to those that apply to treatment records.

Subsection (a) restates the rule that municipal or justice court records of criminal cases involving juveniles are not subject to the confidentiality requirements of this section. A 1997 amendment to Subsection (c) is intended to abrogate Open Records Decision 644 (1996) that the Family Code does not make law enforcement physical records of juvenile cases confidential. Subsections (a) and (c) specify confidentiality rules for electronic data maintained locally. Subsection (a)(3) provides that sex offender registration information is not subject to the confidentiality provisions of this section. Subsection (h) permits public disclosure by a juvenile court of information that may be helpful to apprehend a child who is the subject of an arrest warrant or directive to apprehend and who cannot be located by law enforcement.

Subsection (i), permits juvenile probation departments to release information under juvenile board guidelines without having to obtain juvenile court permission in every case.

CLE/Other Legal Publications

Sharing Information from Juvenile Records: Consistently Inconsistent. Jessica Bolger, 6 JUVE. L. SECT. RPT. (Sept. 1992)

Leading Cases/Att'y Gen. Op.

Op. Tex. Att'y Gen. No. DM–334 (1995) (victim has legitimate interest in juvenile records to authorize disclosure, which is in discretion of juvenile court)

In re W.R.M., 534 S.W.2d 178 (Tex. Civ. App.—Eastland 1976, no writ) (§ 51.14 does not grant discovery rights to respondent)

---

§ 58.0071. Destruction of Certain Physical Records and Files.

(a) In this section:

(1) "Juvenile case" means:

(A) a referral for conduct indicating a need for supervision or delinquent conduct; or

(B) if a petition was filed, all charges made in the petition.

(2) "Physical records and files" include entries in a computer file or information on microfilm, microfiche, or any other electronic storage media.

(b) The custodian of physical records and files in a juvenile case may destroy the records and files if the custodian duplicates the information in the records and files in a computer file or information on microfilm, microfiche, or any other electronic storage media.

(c) The following persons may authorize, subject to Subsections (d) and (e) and any other restriction the person may impose, the destruction of the physical records and files relating to a closed juvenile case:

(1) a juvenile board in relation to the records and files in the possession of the juvenile probation department;

(2) the head of a law enforcement agency in relation to the records and files in the possession of the agency; and

(3) a prosecuting attorney in relation to the records and files in the possession of the prosecuting attorney's office.

(d) The physical records and files of a juvenile case may only be destroyed if the child who is the respondent in the case:

(1) is at least 18 years of age and:

(A) the most serious allegation adjudicated was conduct indicating a need for supervision;

(B) the most serious allegation was conduct indicating a need for supervision and there was not an adjudication; or

(C) the referral or information did not relate to conduct indicating a need for supervision or delinquent conduct and the juvenile court or the court's staff did not take action on the referral or information for that reason;

(2) is at least 21 years of age and:

(A) the most serious allegation adjudicated was delinquent conduct that violated a penal law of the grade of misdemeanor; or

(B) the most serious allegation was delinquent conduct that violated a penal law of the grade of misdemeanor or felony and there was not an adjudication; or

(3) is at least 31 years of age and the most serious allegation adjudicated was delinquent conduct that violated a penal law of the grade of felony.

(e) If a record or file contains information relating to more than one juvenile case, information relating to each case may only be destroyed if:

(1) the destruction of the information is authorized under this section; and

(2) the information can be separated from information that is not authorized to be destroyed under this section.

(f) This section does not affect the destruction of physical records and files authorized by the Texas State Library Records Retention Schedule.

Comment

This is a "spring cleaning" provision, enacted in 2001, that enables juvenile justice agencies to clean out old, unnecessary files that are expensive to maintain. Destruction of clerk of court files is not authorized unless they are duplicated and put into electronic form. This section is not a sealing provision, but is intended to benefit those records custodians who wish to take advantage of it.

Subchapter B. Juvenile Justice Information System

Introductory Comment

This subchapter establishes a state-wide computerized database for juvenile justice information, which is maintained by the Texas Department of Public Safety as part of its adult records system. The information is subject to the Automatic Fingerprint Identification System, which permits computer-matching of latent fingerprints with those in the database, as in the case of adults.

Information relating to juvenile arrests, prosecutions, adjudications and dispositions are sent to the DPS.

This information is subject to sealing of the records in accordance with § 58.003.

Unlike records of adult cases in the DPS system, juvenile case records are not public but may be accessed only by criminal justice agencies and other agencies identified by statute.

CLE/Other Legal Publication

The New Juvenile Justice Information System. Charles R. Mattox, 9TH ANN. JUVE. L. CONF. (Feb. 1996)

---

§ 58.101. Definitions.

In this subchapter:

(1) "Criminal justice agency" has the meaning assigned by Section 411.082, Government Code.

(2) "Department" means the Department of Public Safety of the State of Texas.

(3) "Disposition" means an action that results in the termination, transfer of jurisdiction, or indeterminate suspension of the prosecution of a juvenile offender.

(4) "Incident number" means a unique number assigned to a child during a specific custodial or detention period or for a specific referral to the office or official designated

by the juvenile board, if the juvenile offender was not taken into custody before the referral.

(5) "Juvenile justice agency" means an agency that has custody or control over juvenile offenders.

(6) "Juvenile offender" means a child who has been assigned an incident number.

(7) "State identification number" means a unique number assigned by the department to a child in the juvenile justice information system.

(8) "Uniform incident fingerprint card" means a multiple-part form containing a unique incident number with space for information relating to the conduct for which a child has been taken into custody, detained, or referred, the child's fingerprints, and other relevant information.

§ 58.102. Juvenile Justice Information System.

(a) The department is responsible for recording data and maintaining a database for a computerized juvenile justice information system that serves:

(1) as the record creation point for the juvenile justice information system maintained by the state; and

(2) as the control terminal for entry of records, in accordance with federal law, rule, and policy, into the federal records system maintained by the Federal Bureau of Investigation.

(b) The department shall develop and maintain the system with the cooperation and advice of the:

(1) Texas Youth Commission;

(2) Texas Juvenile Probation Commission;

(3) Criminal Justice Policy Council; and

(4) juvenile courts and clerks of juvenile courts.

(c) The department may not collect or retain information relating to a juvenile if this chapter prohibits or restricts the collection or retention of the information.

(d) The database must contain the information required by this subchapter.

(e) The department shall designate the offense codes and has the sole responsibility for designating the state identification number for each juvenile whose name appears in the juvenile justice system.

§ 58.103. Purpose of System.

The purpose of the juvenile justice information system is to:

(1) provide agencies and personnel within the juvenile justice system accurate information relating to children who come into contact with the juvenile justice system of this state;

(2) provide, where allowed by law, adult criminal justice agencies accurate and easily accessible information relating to children who come into contact with the juvenile justice system;

(3) provide an efficient conversion, where appropriate, of juvenile records to adult criminal records;

(4) improve the quality of data used to conduct impact analyses of proposed legislative changes in the juvenile justice system; and

(5) improve the ability of interested parties to analyze the functioning of the juvenile justice system.

§ 58.104. Types of Information Collected.

(a) Subject to Subsection (f), the juvenile justice information system shall consist of information relating to delinquent conduct committed by a juvenile offender that, if the conduct had been committed by an adult, would constitute a criminal offense other than an offense punishable by a fine only, including information relating to:

(1) the juvenile offender;

(2) the intake or referral of the juvenile offender into the juvenile justice system;

(3) the detention of the juvenile offender;

(4) the prosecution of the juvenile offender;

(5) the disposition of the juvenile offender's case, including the name and description of any program to which the juvenile offender is referred; and

(6) the probation or commitment of the juvenile offender.

(b) To the extent possible and subject to Subsection (a), the department shall include in the juvenile justice information system the following information for each juvenile offender taken into custody, detained, or referred under this title for delinquent conduct:

(1) the juvenile offender's name, including other names by which the juvenile offender is known;

(2) the juvenile offender's date and place of birth;

(3) the juvenile offender's physical description, including sex, weight, height, race, ethnicity, eye color, hair color, scars, marks, and tattoos;

(4) the juvenile offender's state identification number, and other identifying information, as determined by the department;

(5) the juvenile offender's fingerprints;

(6) the juvenile offender's last known residential address, including the census tract number designation for the address;

(7) the name and identifying number of the agency that took into custody or detained the juvenile offender;

(8) the date of detention or custody;

(9) the conduct for which the juvenile offender was taken into custody, detained, or referred, including level and degree of the alleged offense;

(10) the name and identifying number of the juvenile intake agency or juvenile probation office;

(11) each disposition by the juvenile intake agency or juvenile probation office;

(12) the date of disposition by the juvenile intake agency or juvenile probation office;

(13) the name and identifying number of the prosecutor's office;

(14) each disposition by the prosecutor;

(15) the date of disposition by the prosecutor;

(16) the name and identifying number of the court;

(17) each disposition by the court, including information concerning custody of a juvenile offender by a juvenile justice agency or probation;

(18) the date of disposition by the court;

(19) any commitment or release under supervision by the Texas Youth Commission;

(20) the date of any commitment or release under supervision by the Texas Youth Commission; and

(21) a description of each appellate proceeding.

(c) The department may designate codes relating to the information described by Subsection (b).

(d) The department shall designate a state identification number for each juvenile offender.

(e) This subchapter does not apply to a disposition that represents an administrative status notice of an agency described by Section 58.102(b).

(f) Records maintained by the department in the depository are subject to being sealed under Section 58.003. The department shall send to the appropriate juvenile court its certification of records that the department determines, according to the department's records, are eligible for sealing under Section 58.003(a).

Comment

Under subsection (a) only Class B misdemeanors and above are part of the Juvenile Justice Information System. Class C cases and status offender cases, such as truancy and running away, are not part of the system

A 1997 amendment to subsection (f) is intended to make it clear that the obligation upon DPS is only to search its own records and to certify that in accordance with those records eligibility for sealing exists. From that point on, the obligation is upon local officials.

---

§ 58.105. Duties of Juvenile Board.

Each juvenile board shall provide for:

(1) the compilation and maintenance of records and information needed for reporting information to the department under this subchapter;

(2) the transmittal to the department, in the manner provided by the department, of all records and information required by the department under this subchapter; and

(3) access by the department to inspect records and information to determine the completeness and accuracy of information reported.

§ 58.106. Confidentiality.

(a) Except as otherwise provided by this section, information contained in the juvenile justice information system is confidential information for the use of the department and may not be disseminated by the department except:

(1) with the permission of the juvenile offender, to military personnel of this state or the United States;

(2) to a person or entity to which the department may grant access to adult criminal history records as provided by Section 411.083, Government Code;

(3) to a juvenile justice agency; and

(4) to the Criminal Justice Policy Council, the Texas Youth Commission, and the Texas Juvenile Probation Commission for analytical purposes.

(b) Subsection (a) does not apply to a document maintained by a juvenile justice agency that is the source of information collected by the department.

(c) The department may, if necessary to protect the welfare of the community, disseminate to the public the following information relating to a juvenile who has escaped from the custody of the Texas Youth Commission or from another secure detention or correctional facility:

(1) the juvenile's name, including other names by which the juvenile is known;

(2) the juvenile's physical description, including sex, weight, height, race, ethnicity, eye color, hair color, scars, marks, and tattoos;

(3) a photograph of the juvenile; and

(4) a description of the conduct for which the juvenile was committed to the Texas Youth Commission or detained in the secure detention or correctional facility, including the level and degree of the alleged offense.

(d) The department may, if necessary to protect the welfare of the community, disseminate to the public the information listed under Subsection (c) relating to a juvenile offender when notified by a law enforcement agency of this state that the law enforcement agency has been issued a directive to apprehend the offender or an arrest warrant for the offender or that the law enforcement agency is otherwise authorized to arrest the offender and that the offender is suspected of having:

(1) committed a felony offense under the following provisions of the Penal Code:

(A) Title 5;

(B) Section 29.02; or

(C) Section 29.03; and

(2) fled from arrest or apprehension for commission of the offense.

Comment

The information in the Juvenile Justice Information System is not open to public inspection. It is available only to juvenile justice, criminal justice or certain other agencies and organizations authorized by statute. As to most of those agencies, the information will be available by computer search, as in the case of information in the criminal history system. Numerous public and private organizations are given access to information under Chapter 411 of the Government Code. Virtually all occupational licensing agencies have such access. Examples are the Board of Law Examiners and the Central Education Agency.

---

§ 58.107. Compatibility of Data.

Data supplied to the juvenile justice information system must be compatible with the system and must contain both incident numbers and state identification numbers.

§ 58.108. Duties of Agencies and Courts.

(a) A juvenile justice agency and a clerk of a juvenile court shall:

(1) compile and maintain records needed for reporting data required by the department;

(2) transmit to the department in the manner provided by the department data required by the department;

(3) give the department or its accredited agents access to the agency or court for the purpose of inspection to determine the completeness and accuracy of data reported; and

(4) cooperate with the department to enable the department to perform its duties under this chapter.

(b) A juvenile justice agency and clerk of a court shall retain documents described by this section.

§ 58.109. Uniform Incident Fingerprint Card.

(a) The department may provide for the use of a uniform incident fingerprint card in the maintenance of the juvenile justice information system.

(b) The department shall design, print, and distribute to each law enforcement agency and juvenile intake agency uniform incident fingerprint cards.

(c) The incident cards must:

(1) be serially numbered with an incident number in a manner that allows each incident of referral of a juvenile offender who is the subject of the incident fingerprint card to be readily ascertained; and

(2) be multiple-part forms that can be transmitted with the juvenile offender through the juvenile justice process and that allow each agency to report required data to the department.

(d) Subject to available telecommunications capacity, the department shall develop the capability to receive by electronic means from a law enforcement agency the information on the uniform incident fingerprint card. The information must be in a form that is compatible to the form required of data supplied to the juvenile justice information system.

§ 58.110. Reporting.

(a) The department by rule shall develop reporting procedures that ensure that the juvenile offender processing data is reported from the time a juvenile offender is initially taken into custody, detained, or referred until the time a juvenile offender is released from the jurisdiction of the juvenile justice system.

(b) The law enforcement agency or the juvenile intake agency that initiates the entry of the juvenile offender into the juvenile justice information system for a specific incident shall prepare a uniform incident fingerprint card and initiate the reporting process for each incident reportable under this subchapter.

(c) The clerk of the court exercising jurisdiction over a juvenile offender's case shall report the disposition of the case to the department. A clerk of the court who violates this subsection commits an offense. An offense under this subsection is a Class C misdemeanor.

(d) In each county, the reporting agencies may make alternative arrangements for reporting the required information, including combined reporting or electronic reporting, if the alternative reporting is approved by the juvenile board and the department.

(e) Except as otherwise required by applicable state laws or regulations, information required by this chapter to be reported to the department shall be reported promptly. The information shall be reported not later than the 30th day after the date the information is received by the agency responsible for reporting the information, except that a juvenile offender's custody, detention, or referral without previous custody shall be reported to the department not later than the seventh day after the date of the custody, detention, or referral.

(f) Subject to available telecommunications capacity, the department shall develop the capability to receive by electronic means the information required under this section to be reported to the department. The information must be in a form that is compatible to the form required of data to be reported under this section.

Comment

The central idea of this section is that as a case is initiated and passes through the juvenile justice system, the agency responsible for the case adds information to the system as to the status of the case, resulting in a complete step-by-step record of the case.

---

§ 58.111. Local Data Advisory Boards.

The commissioners court of each county may create a local data advisory board to perform the same duties relating to the juvenile justice information system as the duties performed by a local data advisory board in relation to the criminal history record system under Article 60.09, Code of Criminal Procedure.

§ 58.112. Report to Legislature.

Not later than August 15 of each year, the Texas Juvenile Probation Commission shall submit to the lieutenant governor, the speaker of the house of representatives, and the governor a report that contains the following statistical information relating to children referred to a juvenile court during the preceding year:

(1) the ages, races, and counties of residence of the children transferred to a district court or criminal district court for criminal proceedings; and

(2) the ages, races, and counties of residence of the children committed to the Texas Youth Commission, placed on probation, or discharged without any disposition.

§ 58.113. Warrants.

The department shall maintain in a computerized database that is accessible by the same entities that may access the juvenile justice information system information relating to a warrant of arrest, as that term is defined by Article 15.01, Code of Criminal Procedure, or a directive to apprehend under Section 52.015 for any child, without regard to whether the child has been taken into custody.

Comment

Warrants are kept in a separate database from criminal history information. This section allows warrant information on juveniles to be maintained by DPS in that database and restricts access to those agencies that may access criminal history information.

Subchapter C. Automatic Restriction of Access to Records

Introductory Comment

This subchapter introduces a new concept to Texas juvenile law: automatic restriction of access to records. When a record is placed on restricted access, it is not destroyed, nor is it sealed. It remains in place but access is thereafter restricted to criminal justice agencies for a criminal justice purpose. For collateral purposes—employers, the military, occupational licensing agencies, educational institutions—the record ceases to exist and the subject is authorized to deny the occurrence of the events that gave rise to the creation of the record. This restriction occurs automatically by action of the DPS and local juvenile justice agencies; unlike sealing, it does not require the juvenile's family to employ an attorney to draft, file and present a petition to the juvenile court. Therefore, unlike sealing, restriction of access should be available regardless of the economic status of the subject or the subject's family.

---

§ 58.201. Definition.

In this subchapter, "department" means the Department of Public Safety of the State of Texas.

§ 58.202. Exempted Records.

The following records are exempt from this subchapter:

(1) sex offender registration records maintained by the department or a local law enforcement agency under Chapter 62, Code of Criminal Procedure; and

(2) records relating to a criminal combination or criminal street gang maintained by the department or a local law enforcement agency under Chapter 61, Code of Criminal Procedure.

§ 58.203. Certification.

The department shall certify to the juvenile court or the juvenile probation department to which a referral was made that resulted in information being submitted to the juvenile justice information system that the records relating to a person's juvenile case are subject to automatic restriction of access if:

(1) the person is at least 21 years of age;

(2) the juvenile case did not include violent or habitual felony conduct resulting in proceedings in the juvenile court under Section 53.045;

(3) the juvenile case was not certified for trial in criminal court under Section 54.02; and

(4) the department has not received a report in its criminal history system that the person was granted deferred adjudication for or convicted of a felony or a misdemeanor punishable by confinement in jail for an offense committed after the person became 17 years of age.

Comment

To be eligible for restricted access, the subject must be 21, must not have been adjudicated under the determinate sentence act or have been certified to criminal court, and must not have been convicted of or received deferred adjudication for a felony or jailable misdemeanor committed after reaching the age of 17.

CLE/Other Legal Publication

Memorandum and Brochure on Automatic Restriction of Access to Juvenile Records. 15 JUVE. L. SECT. RPT. (Dec. 2001)

---

§ 58.204. Restricted Access on Certification.

(a) On certification of records in a case under Section 58.203, the department, except as provided by Subsection (b):

(1) may not disclose the existence of the records or any information from the records in response to an inquiry from:

(A) a law enforcement agency;

(B) a criminal or juvenile justice agency;

(C) a governmental or other agency given access to information under Chapter 411, Government Code; or

(D) any other person, agency, organization, or entity; and

(2) shall respond to a request for information about the records by stating that the records do not exist.

(b) On certification of records in a case under Section 58.203, the department may permit access to the information in the juvenile justice information system relating to the case of an individual only:

(1) by a criminal justice agency for a criminal justice purpose, as those terms are defined by Section 411.082, Government Code; or

(2) for research purposes, by the Texas Juvenile Probation Commission, the Texas Youth Commission, or the Criminal Justice Policy Council.

Comment

Once access to a record is restricted, it can thereafter be accessed only by a criminal justice agency for a criminal justice purpose. Under the Government Code definition, criminal justice purpose includes employment screening for employment by a criminal justice agency.

---

§ 58.205. Request to the Federal Bureau of Investigation on Certification.

On certification of records in a case under Section 58.203, the department shall request the Federal Bureau of Investigation to:

(1) place the information in its files on restricted status, with access only by a criminal justice agency for a criminal justice purpose, as those terms are defined by Section 411.082, Government Code; or

(2) if the action described in Subdivision (1) is not feasible, delete all information in its database concerning the case.

Comment

Since nobody is certain how the FBI will regard restricted access, the alternatives are to first request the FBI to honor the restrictions and, failing that, to request that it delete the record totally, which the FBI says it will do upon DPS request. Upon implementation of restricted access in March 2003, the FBI informed DPS that it cannot impose restricted access on the records, so will delete them, when time and resources permit.

---

§ 58.206. Effect of Certification in Relation to the Protected Person.

(a) On certification of records in a case under Section 58.203:

(1) the person who is the subject of the records is not required to state in any proceeding, except as otherwise authorized by law in a criminal proceeding in which the person is testifying as a defendant, or in any application for employment, licensing, or other public or private benefit that the person has been a respondent in a case under this title and may not be punished, by perjury prosecution or otherwise, for denying:

(A) the existence of the records; or

(B) the person's participation in a juvenile proceeding related to the records; and

(2) information from the records may not be admitted against the person who is the subject of the records in a civil or criminal proceeding except a proceeding in which a juvenile adjudication was admitted under:

(A) Section 12.42, Penal Code;

(B) Article 37.07, Code of Criminal Procedure; or

(C) as otherwise authorized by criminal procedural law.

(b) A person who is the subject of records certified under this subchapter may not waive the restricted status of the records or the consequences of the restricted status.

§ 58.207. Juvenile Court Orders on Certification.

(a) On certification of records in a case under Section 58.203, the juvenile court shall order:

(1) that the following records relating to the case may be accessed only as provided by Section 58.204(b):

(A) if the respondent was committed to the Texas Youth Commission, records maintained by the commission;

(B) records maintained by the juvenile probation department and by any agency that provided care or custody of the child under order or arrangement of the juvenile court;

(C) records maintained by the clerk of the court;

(D) records maintained by the prosecutor's office; and

(E) records maintained by a law enforcement agency; and

(2) the juvenile probation department to make a reasonable effort to notify the person who is the subject of records for which access has been restricted of the action restricting access and the legal significance of the action for the person.

(b) On receipt of an order under Subsection (a)(1), the agency maintaining the records:

(1) may allow access only as provided by Section 58.204(b); and

(2) shall respond to a request for information about the records by stating that the records do not exist.

§ 58.208. Information to Child on Discharge.

On the final discharge of a child from the juvenile system or on the last official action in the case, if there is no adjudication, the appropriate juvenile justice official shall provide to the child:

(1) a written explanation of how automatic restricted access under this subchapter works; and

(2) a copy of this subchapter.

§ 58.209. Information to Child by Probation Officer or Texas Youth Commission.

(a) When a child is placed on probation for an offense that may be eligible for automatic restricted access at age 21 or when a child is received by the Texas Youth Commission on an indeterminate commitment, a probation officer or an official at the Texas Youth Commission reception center, as soon as practicable, shall explain the substance of the following information to the child:

(1) if the child was adjudicated as having committed delinquent conduct for a felony or jailable misdemeanor, that the child probably has a juvenile record with the department and the Federal Bureau of Investigation;

(2) that the child's juvenile record is a permanent record that is not destroyed or erased unless the record is eligible for sealing and the child or the child's family hires a lawyer and files a petition in court to have the record sealed;

(3) that the child's juvenile record, other than treatment records made confidential by law, can be accessed by police, sheriff's officers, prosecutors, probation officers, correctional officers, and other criminal and juvenile justice officials in this state and elsewhere;

(4) that the child's juvenile record, other than treatment records made confidential by law, can be accessed by employers, educational institutions, licensing agencies, and other organizations when the child applies for employment or educational programs;

(5) if the child's juvenile record is placed on restricted access when the child becomes 21 years of age, that access will be denied to employers, educational institutions, and others except for criminal justice agencies;

(6) that to have the child's juvenile record placed on restricted access at age 21, the child must not:

(A) commit a felony or jailable misdemeanor; and

(B) receive deferred adjudication for or be convicted in adult court of a felony or jailable misdemeanor; and

(7) that restricted access does not require any action by the child or the child's family, including the filing of a petition or hiring of a lawyer, but occurs automatically at age 21 if the child does not commit a criminal offense in the future.

(b) The probation officer or Texas Youth Commission official shall:

(1) give the child a written copy of the explanation provided; and

(2) communicate the same information to at least one of the child's parents or, if none can be found, to the child's guardian or custodian.

(c) The Texas Juvenile Probation Commission and the Texas Youth Commission shall adopt rules to implement this section and to facilitate the effective explanation of the information required to be communicated by this section.

§ 58.210. Sealing or Destruction of Records Not Affected.

(a) This subchapter does not prevent or restrict the sealing or destruction of juvenile records as authorized by law.

(b) Restricted access provided under this subchapter is in addition to sealing or destruction of juvenile records.

(c) A person who is the subject of records certified under this subchapter is entitled to access to the records for the purpose of preparing and presenting a motion to seal or destroy the records.

Subchapter D. Local Juvenile Justice Information System

Introductory Comment

This subchapter sets out in detail how a computerized juvenile records system that is being constructed in Dallas County is intended to operate. It was enacted to present a model of an integrated local juvenile justice information system for other counties to copy. The model is only a model; it is not mandatory. No county is required to have such a system and if it chooses to have a local juvenile justice information system, it is not required to follow the Dallas model.

The system seeks to integrate information about juveniles from the police, schools, justice and municipal courts, prosecutor's office, juvenile court and probation departments in the county, while protecting confidentiality of such information and restricting access on a need to know basis.

---

§ 58.301. Definitions.

In this subchapter:

(1) "County juvenile board" means a juvenile board created under Chapter 152, Human Resources Code.

(2) "Governmental placement facility" means a juvenile residential placement facility operated by a unit of government.

(3) "Governmental service provider" means a juvenile justice service provider operated by a unit of government.

(4) "Local juvenile justice information system" means a county or multicounty computerized database of information concerning children, with data entry and access by the partner agencies that are members of the system.

(5) "Partner agency" means a governmental service provider or governmental placement facility that is required by this subchapter to be a member of a local juvenile justice information system or that has applied to be a member of a local juvenile justice information system and has been approved by the county juvenile board or regional juvenile board committee as a member of the system.

(6) "Regional juvenile board committee" means a committee that is composed of two members from each county juvenile board in a region that comprises a multicounty local juvenile information system.

§ 58.302. Purposes of System.

The purposes of a local juvenile justice information system are to:

(1) provide accurate information at the county or regional level relating to children who come into contact with the juvenile justice system;

(2) assist in the development and delivery of services to children in the juvenile justice system;

(3) assist in the development and delivery of services to children:

(A) who school officials have reasonable cause to believe have committed an offense for which a report is required under Section 37.015, Education Code; or

(B) who have been expelled, the expulsion of which school officials are required to report under Section 52.041;

(4) provide for an efficient transmission of juvenile records from justice and municipal courts to county juvenile probation departments and the juvenile court and from county juvenile probation departments and juvenile court to the state juvenile justice information system created by Subchapter B;

(5) provide efficient computerized case management resources to juvenile courts, county juvenile probation departments, and partner agencies authorized by this subchapter;

(6) provide a directory of services available to children to the partner agencies to facilitate the delivery of services to children;

(7) provide an efficient means for municipal and justice courts to report filing of charges, adjudications, and dispositions of juveniles to the juvenile court as required by Section 51.08; and

(8) provide a method for agencies to fulfill their duties under Section 58.108, including the electronic transmission of information required to be sent to the Department of Public Safety by Section 58.110(f).

§ 58.303. Local Juvenile Justice Information System.

(a) Juvenile justice agencies in a county or region of this state may jointly create and maintain a local juvenile justice information system to aid in processing the cases of children under this code, to facilitate the delivery of services to children in the juvenile justice system, and to aid in the early identification of at-risk and delinquent children.

(b) A local juvenile justice information system must contain the following components:

(1) case management resources for juvenile courts, prosecuting attorneys, and county juvenile probation departments;

(2) reporting systems to fulfill statutory requirements for reporting in the juvenile justice system;

(3) service provider directories and indexes of agencies providing services to children; and

(4) victim-witness notices required under Chapter 57.

(c) A local juvenile justice information system may contain the following components:

(1) electronic filing of complaints or petitions;

(2) electronic offense and intake processing;

(3) case docket management and calendaring;

(4) communications by email or other electronic communications between partner agencies;

(5) reporting of charges filed, adjudications and dispositions of juveniles by municipal and justice courts and the juvenile court, and transfers of cases to the juvenile court as authorized or required by Section 51.08;

(6) reporting to schools under Article 15.27, Code of Criminal Procedure, by law enforcement agencies, prosecuting attorneys, and juvenile courts;

(7) records of adjudications and dispositions, including probation conditions ordered by the juvenile court; and

(8) warrant management and confirmation capabilities.

(d) Membership in a local juvenile justice information system is determined by this subchapter. Membership in a regional juvenile justice information system is determined by the regional juvenile board committee from among partner agencies that have applied for membership.

§ 58.304. Types of Information Contained in a Local Juvenile Information System.

(a) Subject to Subsection (d), a local juvenile justice information system must consist of:

(1) information relating to all referrals to the juvenile court of any type, including referrals for conduct indicating a need for supervision and delinquent conduct; and

(2) information relating to:

(A) the juvenile;

(B) the intake or referral of the juvenile into the juvenile justice system for any offense or conduct;

(C) the detention of the juvenile;

(D) the prosecution of the juvenile;

(E) the disposition of the juvenile's case, including the name and description of any program to which the juvenile is referred; and

(F) the probation, placement, or commitment of the juvenile.

(b) To the extent possible and subject to Subsections (a) and (d), the local juvenile justice information system may include the following information for each juvenile taken into custody, detained, or referred under this title:

(1) the juvenile's name, including other names by which the juvenile is known;

(2) the juvenile's date and place of birth;

(3) the juvenile's physical description, including sex, weight, height, race, ethnicity, eye color, hair color, scars, marks, and tattoos;

(4) the juvenile's state identification number and other identifying information;

(5) the juvenile's fingerprints and photograph;

(6) the juvenile's last known residential address, including the census tract number designation for the address;

(7) the name, address, and phone number of the juvenile's parent, guardian, or custodian;

(8) the name and identifying number of the agency that took into custody or detained the juvenile;

(9) each date of custody or detention;

(10) a detailed description of the conduct for which the juvenile was taken into custody, detained, or referred, including the level and degree of the alleged offense;

(11) the name and identifying number of the juvenile intake agency or juvenile probation office;

(12) each disposition by the juvenile intake agency or juvenile probation office;

(13) the date of disposition by the juvenile intake agency or juvenile probation office;

(14) the name and identifying number of the prosecutor's office;

(15) each disposition by the prosecutor;

(16) the date of disposition by the prosecutor;

(17) the name and identifying number of the court;

(18) each disposition by the court, including information concerning custody of a juvenile by a juvenile justice agency or county juvenile probation department;

(19) the date of disposition by the court;

(20) any commitment or release under supervision by the Texas Youth Commission, including the date of the commitment or release; and

(21) information concerning each appellate proceeding.

(c) If the Department of Public Safety assigns a state identification number for the juvenile, the identification number shall be entered in the local juvenile information system.

(d) Information obtained for the purpose of diagnosis, examination, evaluation, or treatment or for making a referral for treatment of a child by a public or private agency or institution providing supervision of a child by arrangement of the juvenile court or having custody of the child under order of the juvenile court may not be collected under Subsection (a) or (b).

§ 58.305. Partner Agencies.

(a) A local juvenile justice information system for a single county shall include the following partner agencies within that county:

(1) the juvenile court;

(2) justice of the peace and municipal courts;

(3) the county juvenile probation department;

(4) the prosecuting attorneys who prosecute juvenile cases in juvenile court, municipal court, or justice court;

(5) law enforcement agencies;

(6) each public school district in the county;

(7) governmental service providers approved by the county juvenile board; and

(8) governmental placement facilities approved by the county juvenile board.

(b) A local juvenile justice information system for a multicounty region shall include the partner agencies listed in Subsections (a)(1)–(6) for each county in the region and the following partner agencies from within the multicounty region that have applied for membership in the system and have been approved by the regional juvenile board committee:

(1) governmental service providers; and

(2) governmental placement facilities.

§ 58.306. Access to Information; Levels.

(a) This section describes the level of access to information to which each partner agency in a local juvenile justice information system is entitled.

(b) Information is at Access Level 1 if the information relates to a child:

(1) who:

(A) a school official has reasonable grounds to believe has committed an offense for which a report is required under Section 37.015, Education Code; or

(B) has been expelled, the expulsion of which is required to be reported under Section 52.041; and

(2) who has not been charged with a fineable only offense, a status offense, or delinquent conduct.

(c) Information is at Access Level 2 if the information relates to a child who:

(1) is alleged in a justice or municipal court to have committed a fineable only offense, municipal ordinance violation, or status offense; and

(2) has not been charged with delinquent conduct or conduct indicating a need for supervision.

(d) Information is at Access Level 3 if the information relates to a child who is alleged to have engaged in delinquent conduct or conduct indicating a need for supervision.

(e) Level 1 Access is by public school districts in the county or region served by the local juvenile justice information system.

(f) Level 2 Access is by:

(1) justice of the peace courts that process juvenile cases; and

(2) municipal courts that process juvenile cases.

(g) Level 3 Access is by:

(1) the juvenile court;

(2) the prosecuting attorney;

(3) the county juvenile probation department;

(4) law enforcement agencies;

(5) governmental service providers that are partner agencies; and

(6) governmental placement facilities that are partner agencies.

(h) Access for Level 1 agencies is only to information at Level 1. Access for Level 2 agencies is only to information at Levels 1 and 2. Access for Level 3 agencies is to information at Levels 1, 2, and 3.

§ 58.307. Confidentiality of Information.

(a) Information that is part of a local juvenile justice system is not public information and may not be released to the public, except as authorized by law.

(b) Information that is part of a local juvenile justice information system is for the professional use of the partner agencies that are members of the system and may be used only by authorized employees of those agencies to discharge duties of those agencies.

(c) Information from a local juvenile justice information system may not be disclosed to persons, agencies, or organizations that are not members of the system except to the extent disclosure is authorized or mandated by this title.

(d) Information in a local juvenile justice information system is subject to destruction, sealing, or restricted access as provided by this title.

(e) Information in a local juvenile justice information system shall be protected from unauthorized access by a system of access security and any access to information in a local juvenile information system performed by browser software shall be at the level of at least 128-bit encryption. A juvenile board or a regional juvenile board committee shall require all partner agencies to maintain security and restrict access in accordance with the requirements of this title.

Chapter 59. Progressive Sanctions Model [~~Guidelines~~].

---

§ 59.001. Purposes.

The purposes of the progressive sanctions **model** [~~guidelines~~] are to:

(1) ensure that juvenile offenders face uniform and consistent consequences and punishments that correspond to the seriousness of each offender's current offense, prior delinquent history, special treatment or training needs, and effectiveness of prior interventions;

(2) balance public protection and rehabilitation while holding juvenile offenders accountable;

(3) permit flexibility in the decisions made in relation to the juvenile offender to the extent allowed by law;

(4) consider the juvenile offender's circumstances; [~~and~~]

(5) **recognize that departure of a disposition from this model is not necessarily undesirable and in some cases is highly desirable; and**

(6) improve juvenile justice planning and resource allocation by ensuring uniform and consistent reporting of disposition decisions at all levels.

History: Amended by 78th Legis., Reg. Sess. (2003), H.B. 888, eff. Sept. 1, 2003. Applies only to conduct occurring on or after effective date.

Comment

Chapter 59 was re-evaluated by the legislature in 2003. The legislature came to realize that departures from the progressive sanctions model were more often desirable than undesirable and should not be treated as dispositional failures.

CLE/Other Legal Publications

Progressive Sanctions. Wesley Shackelford, 13TH ANN. JUVE. L. CONF. (Feb. 2000)

Progressive Sanction Guidelines. Pat Garza, 11TH ANN. JUVE. L. CONF. (Feb. 1998)

The Implementation of the Progressive Sanctions Guidelines for Juveniles in Texas: The First Year. Jennifer Alyn Munzel, 11 JUVE. L. SECT. RPT. (June 1997)

§ 59.002. Sanction Level Assignment by Probation Department.

(a) The probation department may assign a sanction level of one to a child referred to the probation department under Section 53.012.

(b) The probation department may assign a sanction level of two to a child for whom deferred prosecution is authorized under Section 53.03.

Comment

Of the seven sanction levels, a juvenile probation department may make assignment without court order only to levels one and two.

---

§ 59.003. Sanction Level Assignment Model [~~Guidelines~~].

(a) Subject to Subsection (e), after a child's first commission of delinquent conduct or conduct indicating a need for supervision, the probation department or prosecuting attorney may, or the juvenile court may, in a disposition hearing under Section 54.04 or a modification hearing under Section 54.05, assign a child one of the following sanction levels according to the child's conduct:

(1) for conduct indicating a need for supervision, other than conduct described in Section 51.03(b)(5) or a Class A or B misdemeanor, the sanction level is one;

(2) for conduct indicating a need for supervision under Section 51.03(b)(5) or a Class A or B misdemeanor, other than a misdemeanor involving the use or possession of a firearm, or for delinquent conduct under Section 51.03(a)(2), the sanction level is two;

(3) for a misdemeanor involving the use or possession of a firearm or for a state jail felony or a felony of the third degree, the sanction level is three;

(4) for a felony of the second degree, the sanction level is four;

(5) for a felony of the first degree, other than a felony involving the use of a deadly weapon or causing serious bodily injury, the sanction level is five;

(6) for a felony of the first degree involving the use of a deadly weapon or causing serious bodily injury, for an aggravated controlled substance felony, or for a capital felony, the sanction level is six; or

(7) for a felony of the first degree involving the use of a deadly weapon or causing serious bodily injury, for an aggravated controlled substance felony, or for a capital felony, if the petition has been approved by a grand jury under Section 53.045, or if a petition to transfer the child to criminal court has been filed under Section 54.02, the sanction level is seven.

(b) Subject to Subsection (e), if the child subsequently is found to have engaged in delinquent conduct in an adjudication hearing under Section 54.03 or a hearing to modify a disposition under Section 54.05 on two separate occasions and each involves a violation of a penal law of a classification that is less than the classification of the child's previous conduct, the juvenile court may assign the child a sanction level that is one level higher than the previously assigned sanction level, unless the child's previously assigned sanction level is six.

(c) Subject to Subsection (e), if the child's subsequent commission of delinquent conduct or conduct indicating a need for supervision involves a violation of a penal law of a classification that is the same as or greater than the classification of the child's previous conduct, the juvenile court may assign the child a sanction level authorized by law that is one level higher than the previously assigned sanction level.

(d) Subject to Subsection (e), if the child's previously assigned sanction level is four or five and the child's subsequent commission of delinquent conduct is of the grade of felony, the juvenile court may assign the child a sanction level that is one level higher than the previously assigned sanction level.

(e) [~~Except as otherwise provided by this subsection, a juvenile court or probation department that deviates from the guidelines under this section shall state in writing its reasons for the deviation and submit the statement to the juvenile board regardless of whether a progressive sanctions program has been adopted by the juvenile board. Nothing in this chapter prohibits the imposition of appropriate sanctions that are different from those provided at any sanction level. A juvenile court that makes a disposition required by this title that deviates from the guidelines under this section is not required to report the disposition as a deviation.~~

[~~(f)~~]The probation department may, in accordance with Section 54.05, request the extension of a period of probation specified under sanction levels one through five if the circumstances of the child warrant the extension.

(f) [~~(g)~~] Before the court assigns the child a sanction level that involves the revocation of the child's probation and the commitment of the child to the Texas Youth Commission, the court shall hold a hearing to modify the disposition as required by Section 54.05.

History: Amended by 78th Legis., Reg. Sess. (2003), H.B. 888, eff. Sept. 1, 2003. Applies only to conduct occurring on or after effective date.

Comment

Each offense is assigned to one of the seven sanction levels. That sanction level is the presumptive disposition for that offense. However, it is not mandatory that the sanction level disposition match the assignment guidelines. It is required that departures must be documented.

The disposition of juvenile cases must conform to the dispositional authorizations in the Family Code. Because the entire progressive sanctions program is discretionary with respect to each case, if there is a conflict between the progressive sanctions guidelines and the dispositional authorization elsewhere in the Family Code, the dispositional authorization must control.

Subsection (e), requiring written reports of departures from the guidelines, was repealed in 2003. The legislature came to realize that full information about departures was available to state agencies from cases documentation sources so that the written reports served no additional purposes.

---

§ 59.004. Sanction Level One.

(a) For a child at sanction level one, the juvenile court or probation department may:

(1) require counseling for the child regarding the child's conduct;

(2) inform the child of the progressive sanctions that may be imposed on the child if the child continues to engage in delinquent conduct or conduct indicating a need for supervision;

(3) inform the child's parents or guardians of the parents' or guardians' responsibility to impose reasonable restrictions on the child to prevent the conduct from recurring;

(4) provide information or other assistance to the child or the child's parents or guardians in securing needed social services;

(5) require the child or the child's parents or guardians to participate in a program for services under Section 264.302, if a program under Section 264.302 is available to the child or the child's parents or guardians;

(6) refer the child to a community-based citizen intervention program approved by the juvenile court; and

(7) release the child to the child's parents or guardians.

(b) The probation department shall discharge the child from the custody of the probation department after the provisions of this section are met.

Comment

Sanction level one is customarily called supervisory caution.

The reference to § 264.302 (in Title 5 of the Family Code) is a reference to the Early Youth Intervention Services program operated by the Texas Department of Regulatory and Protective Services for youth as young as seven years of age.

CLE/Other Legal Publication

Neighborhood Conference Committee. David T. Chang, 11 JUVE. L. SECT. RPT. (Dec. 1997)

Juvenile Offender and Victim Mediation in Texas: An Overview. Clare Carpenter, 8 JUVE. L. SECT. RPT. (March 1994)

---

§ 59.005. Sanction Level Two.

(a) For a child at sanction level two, the juvenile court, the prosecuting attorney, or the probation department may, as provided by Section 53.03:

(1) place the child on deferred prosecution for not less than three months or more than six months;

(2) require the child to make restitution to the victim of the child's conduct or perform community service restitution appropriate to the nature and degree of harm caused and according to the child's ability;

(3) require the child's parents or guardians to identify restrictions the parents or guardians will impose on the child's activities and requirements the parents or guardians will set for the child's behavior;

(4) provide the information required under Sections 59.004(a)(2) and (4);

(5) require the child or the child's parents or guardians to participate in a program for services under Section 264.302, if a program under Section 264.302 is available to the child or the child's parents or guardians;

(6) refer the child to a community-based citizen intervention program approved by the juvenile court; and

(7) if appropriate, impose additional conditions of probation.

(b) The juvenile court or the probation department shall discharge the child from the custody of the probation department on the date the provisions of this section are met or on the child's 18th birthday, whichever is earlier.

Comment

Sanction level two describes what is called Deferred Prosecution. It is a period of pre-adjudication probation that may extend for up to six months in length.

---

§ 59.006. Sanction Level Three.

(a) For a child at sanction level three, the juvenile court may:

(1) place the child on probation for not less than six months [~~or more than 12 months~~];

(2) require the child to make restitution to the victim of the child's conduct or perform community service restitution appropriate to the nature and degree of harm caused and according to the child's ability;

(3) impose specific restrictions on the child's activities and requirements for the child's behavior as conditions of probation;

(4) require a probation officer to closely monitor the child's activities and behavior;

(5) require the child or the child's parents or guardians to participate in programs or services designated by the court or probation officer; and

(6) if appropriate, impose additional conditions of probation.

(b) The juvenile court shall discharge the child from the custody of the probation department on the date the provisions of this section are met or on the child's 18th birthday, whichever is earlier.

History: Amended by 78th Legis., Reg. Sess. (2003), H.B. 888, eff. Sept. 1, 2003. Applies only to conduct occurring on or after effective date.

Comment

This sanction level describes judicial probation.

---

§ 59.007. Sanction Level Four.

(a) For a child at sanction level four, the juvenile court may:

(1) require the child to participate as a condition of probation for not less than three months or more than 12 months in an intensive services probation program that emphasizes frequent contact and reporting with a probation officer, discipline, intensive supervision services, social responsibility, and productive work;

(2) after release from the program described by Subdivision (1), continue the child on probation supervision [~~for not less than six months or more than 12 months~~];

(3) require the child to make restitution to the victim of the child's conduct or perform community service restitution appropriate to the nature and degree of harm caused and according to the child's ability;

(4) impose highly structured restrictions on the child's activities and requirements for behavior of the child as conditions of probation;

(5) require a probation officer to closely monitor the child;

(6) require the child or the child's parents or guardians to participate in programs or services designed to address their particular needs and circumstances; and

(7) if appropriate, impose additional sanctions.

(b) The juvenile court shall discharge the child from the custody of the probation department on the date the provisions of this section are met or on the child's 18th birthday, whichever is earlier.

History: Amended by 78th Legis., Reg. Sess. (2003), H.B. 888, eff. Sept. 1, 2003. Applies only to conduct occurring on or after effective date.

Comment

Sanction level four can be viewed as intensive probation supervision for a period of at least 3 months, to be followed by normal supervision. A 2001 amendment makes it clear that the program need not follow the boot camp model.

---

§ 59.008. Sanction Level Five.

(a) For a child at sanction level five, the juvenile court may:

(1) as a condition of probation, place the child for not less than six months or more than 12 months in a post-adjudication secure correctional facility;

(2) after release from the program described by Subdivision (1), continue the child on probation supervision [~~for not less than six months or more than 12 months~~];

(3) require the child to make restitution to the victim of the child's conduct or perform community service restitution appropriate to the nature and degree of harm caused and according to the child's ability;

(4) impose highly structured restrictions on the child's activities and requirements for behavior of the child as conditions of probation;

(5) require a probation officer to closely monitor the child;

(6) require the child or the child's parents or guardians to participate in programs or services designed to address their particular needs and circumstances; and

(7) if appropriate, impose additional sanctions.

(b) The juvenile court shall discharge the child from the custody of the probation department on the date the provisions of this section are met or on the child's 18th birthday, whichever is earlier.

History: Amended by 78th Legis., Reg. Sess. (2003), H.B. 888, eff. Sept. 1, 2003. Applies only to conduct occurring on or after effective date.

Comment

Sanction level five is probation with secure residential placement outside the home.

---

§ 59.009. Sanction Level Six.

(a) For a child at sanction level six, the juvenile court may commit the child to the custody of the Texas Youth Commission. The commission may:

(1) require the child to participate in a highly structured residential program that emphasizes discipline, accountability, fitness, training, and productive work for not less than nine months or more than 24 months unless the commission extends the period and the reason for an extension is documented;

(2) require the child to make restitution to the victim of the child's conduct or perform community service restitution appropriate to the nature and degree of the harm caused and according to the child's ability, if there is a victim of the child's conduct;

(3) require the child and the child's parents or guardians to participate in programs and services for their particular needs and circumstances; and

(4) if appropriate, impose additional sanctions.

(b) On release of the child under supervision, the Texas Youth Commission parole programs may:

(1) impose highly structured restrictions on the child's activities and requirements for behavior of the child as conditions of release under supervision;

(2) require a parole officer to closely monitor the child for not less than six months; and

(3) if appropriate, impose any other conditions of supervision.

(c) The Texas Youth Commission may discharge the child from the commission's custody on the date the provisions of this section are met or on the child's 19th birthday, whichever is earlier.

Comment

Sanction level six is indeterminate commitment to the TYC, authorizing that agency to maintain custody of the youth until age 21.

---

§ 59.010. Sanction Level Seven.

(a) For a child at sanction level seven, the juvenile court may certify and transfer the child under Section 54.02 or sentence the child to commitment to the Texas Youth Commission under Section 54.04(d)(3), 54.04(m), or 54.05(f). The commission may:

(1) require the child to participate in a highly structured residential program that emphasizes discipline, accountability, fitness, training, and productive work for not less than 12 months or more than 10 years unless the commission extends the period and the reason for the extension is documented;

(2) require the child to make restitution to the victim of the child's conduct or perform community service restitution appropriate to the nature and degree of harm caused and according to the child's ability, if there is a victim of the child's conduct;

(3) require the child and the child's parents or guardians to participate in programs and services for their particular needs and circumstances; and

(4) impose any other appropriate sanction.

(b) On release of the child under supervision, the Texas Youth Commission parole programs may:

(1) impose highly structured restrictions on the child's activities and requirements for behavior of the child as conditions of release under supervision;

(2) require a parole officer to monitor the child closely for not less than 12 months; and

(3) impose any other appropriate condition of supervision.

Comment

Sanction level seven is determinate sentencing and certification to criminal court. Obviously, how long the TYC keeps the juvenile depends on the sentence given by the judge or jury, not the guidelines in this sanction level description.

---

§ 59.011. Duty of Juvenile Board.

A juvenile board shall require the juvenile probation department to report progressive sanction data electronically to the Texas Juvenile Probation Commission in the format and time frames specified by the commission.

§ 59.012. Reports by Criminal Justice Policy Council.

(a) The Criminal Justice Policy Council shall analyze trends related to juvenile referrals [~~, compliance with the progressive sanctions guidelines,~~] and the impact of [~~the~~

~~guidelines and related~~] reforms on recidivism rates using standard scientific sampling or appropriate scientific methodologies to represent statewide patterns. The council shall compile other policy studies as determined by the executive director of the council or as requested by the governor, lieutenant governor, or speaker of the house of representatives to assist in policy development.

(b) The Criminal Justice Policy Council shall report its findings and related recommendations to improve juvenile justice policies to the governor and the members of the legislature on or before January 15 of each odd-numbered year.

(c) The Criminal Justice Policy Council may incorporate its findings and recommendations under this section into its report required under Section 413.013, Government Code.

History: Amended by 78th Legis., Reg. Sess. (2003), H.B. 888, eff. Sept. 1, 2003. Applies only to conduct occurring on or after effective date.

Comment

One of the purposes of creating sanction level guidelines was to gather data on the dispositions employed by the juvenile justice system using a uniform terminology. Nevertheless, it is a mistake to focus on departures from guidelines at the expense of other features of juvenile justice decision-making. 2003 amendments to this section direct the Criminal Justice Policy Council to study all juvenile justice reforms, not just departures from guidelines, in its evaluative reports on juvenile justice.

§ 59.013. Liability.

The Texas Youth Commission, a juvenile board, a court, a person appointed by a court, an attorney for the state, a peace officer, or a law enforcement agency is not liable for a failure or inability to provide a service listed under Sections 59.004–59.010.

§ 59.014. Appeal.

A child may not bring an appeal or a postconviction writ of habeas corpus based on:

(1) the failure or inability of any person to provide a service listed under Sections 59.004–59.010;

(2) the failure of a court or of any person to make a sanction level assignment as provided in Section 59.002 or 59.003; [~~or~~]

(3) a **departure** [~~deviation~~] from the sanction level assignment **model** [~~guidelines~~] provided by this chapter; or

(4) the failure of a juvenile court or probation department to report a **departure** [~~deviation~~] from the **model** [~~guidelines as required by Section 59.003(e)~~].

History: Amended by 78th Legis., Reg. Sess. (2003), H.B. 888, eff. Sept. 1, 2003. Applies only to conduct occurring on or after effective date.

Comment

Failure to report a departure from the guidelines is not grounds for appeal. Subsection (3) in the second provision makes it abundantly clear that a deviation from the guidelines is not grounds for appeal.

§ 59.015. Waiver of Sanctions on Parents or Guardians.

On a finding by the juvenile court or probation department that a child's parents or guardians have made a reasonable good faith effort to prevent the child from engaging in delinquent conduct or engaging in conduct indicating a need for supervision and that, despite the parents' or guardians' efforts, the child continues to engage in such conduct, the court or probation department shall waive any sanction that may be imposed on the parents or guardians at any sanction level.

Chapter 60. Uniform Interstate Compact on Juveniles.

Introductory Comment

This chapter consists of the Uniform Interstate Compact on Juveniles and supplementary enactments. The Interstate Compact deals with many of the same issues as the Uniform Criminal Extradition Act in article 51.13 of the Code of Criminal Procedure

In 1965, the legislature enacted what is now Chapter 60, which required the Texas Governor to enter into the Interstate Compact with other American states. All fifty states and the District of Columbia have now joined the Compact.

The Compact deals with four distinct interstate proceedings: (1) the out-of-state placement of children on juvenile probation or parole; (2) the return of juveniles who have absconded from probation, parole, or an institution to another state; (3) the return from another state of a juvenile to the state where an act of delinquency is believed to have occurred; and (4) the return of a runaway from another state to the state of residency.

---

§ 60.001. Short Title.

This chapter may be cited as the Uniform Interstate Compact on Juveniles.

§ 60.002. Execution of Interstate Compact.

The governor shall execute a compact on behalf of the state with any other state or states legally joining in it in substantially the following form:

INTERSTATE COMPACT ON JUVENILES

The contracting states solemnly agree:

Article I

Findings and Purpose

That juveniles who are not under proper supervision and control, or who have absconded, escaped, or run away are likely to endanger their own health, morals, and welfare, and the health, morals, and welfare of others. The cooperation of the states party to this compact is therefore necessary to provide for the welfare and protection of juveniles and of the public with respect to (1) cooperative supervision of delinquent juveniles on probation or parole; (2) the return, from one state to another, of delinquent juveniles who have escaped or absconded; (3) the return, from one state to another, of nondelinquent juveniles who have run away from home; and (4) additional measures for the protection of juveniles and of the public, which any two or more of the party states may find desirable to undertake cooperatively. In carrying out the provisions of this compact the party states shall be guided by the noncriminal, reformative, and protective policies which guide their laws concerning delinquent, neglected, or dependent juveniles generally. It shall be the policy of the states party to this compact to cooperate and observe their respective responsibilities for the prompt return and acceptance of juveniles and delinquent juveniles who become subject to the provisions of this compact. The provisions of this compact shall be reasonably and liberally construed to accomplish the foregoing purposes.

Article II

Existing Rights and Remedies

That all remedies and procedures provided by this compact shall be in addition to and not in substitution for other rights, remedies, and procedures, and shall not be in derogation of parental rights and responsibilities.

Article III

Definitions

That, for the purpose of this compact, "delinquent juvenile" means any juvenile who has been adjudged delinquent and who, at the time the provisions of this compact are invoked, is still subject to the jurisdiction of the court that has made such adjudication or to the jurisdiction or supervision of an agency or institution pursuant to an order of such court; "probation or parole" means any kind of conditional release of juveniles authorized under the laws of the states party hereto; "court" means any court having jurisdiction over delinquent, neglected, or dependent children; "state" means any state, territory, or possessions of the United States, the District of Columbia, and the Commonwealth of Puerto Rico; and "residence" or any variant thereof means a place at which a home or regular place of abode is maintained.

Article IV

Return of Runaways

(a) That the parent, guardian, person, or agency entitled to legal custody of a juvenile who has not been adjudged delinquent but who has run away without the consent of such parent, guardian, person, or agency may petition the appropriate court in the demanding state for the issuance of a requisition for his return. The petition shall state the name and age of the juvenile, the name of the petitioner, and the basis of entitlement to the juvenile's custody, the circumstances of his running away, his location if known at the time application is made, and such other facts as may tend to show that the juvenile who has run away is endangering his own welfare or the welfare of others and is not an emancipated minor. The petition shall be verified by affidavit, shall be executed in duplicate, and shall be accompanied by two certified copies of the document or documents on which the petitioner's entitlement to the juvenile's custody is based, such as birth certificates, letters of guardianship, or custody decrees. Such further affidavits and other documents as may be deemed proper may be submitted with such petition. The judge of the court to which this application is made may hold a hearing thereon to determine whether for the purposes of this compact the petitioner is entitled to the legal custody of the juvenile, whether or not it appears that the juvenile has in fact run away without consent, whether or not he is an emancipated minor, and whether or not it is in the best interest of the juvenile to compel his return to the state. If the judge determines, either with or without a hearing, that the juvenile should be returned, he shall present to the appropriate court or to the executive authority of the state where the juvenile is alleged to be located a written requisition for the return of such juvenile.

Such requisition shall set forth the name and age of the juvenile, the determination of the court that the juvenile has run away without the consent of a parent, guardian, person, or agency entitled to his legal custody, and that it is in the best interest and for the protection of such juvenile that he be returned. In the event that a proceeding for the adjudication of the juvenile as a delinquent, neglected, or dependent juvenile is pending in the court at the time when such juvenile runs away, the court may issue a requisition for the return of such juvenile upon its own motion, regardless of the consent of the parent, guardian, person, or agency entitled to legal custody, reciting therein the nature and circumstances of the pending proceeding. The requisition shall in every case be executed in duplicate and shall be signed by the judge. One copy of the requisition shall be filed with the compact administrator of the demanding state, there to remain on file subject to the provisions of law governing records of such court. Upon the receipt of a requisition demanding the return of a juvenile who has run away, the court or the executive authority to whom the requisition is addressed shall issue an order to any peace officer or other appropriate person directing him to take into custody and detain such juvenile. Such detention order must substantially recite the facts necessary to the validity of its issuance hereunder. No juvenile detained upon such order shall be delivered over to the officer whom the court demanding him shall have appointed to receive him unless he shall first be taken forthwith before a judge of a court in the state, who shall inform him of the demand made for his return, and who may appoint counsel or guardian ad litem for him. If the judge of such court shall find that the requisition is in order, he shall deliver such juvenile over to the officer whom the court demanding him shall have appointed to receive him. The judge, however, may fix a reasonable time to be allowed for the purpose of testing the legality of the proceeding.

Upon reasonable information that a person is a juvenile who has run away from another state party to this compact without the consent of a parent, guardian, person, or agency entitled to his legal custody, such juvenile may be taken into custody without a requisition and brought forthwith before a judge of the appropriate court who may appoint counsel or guardian ad litem for such juvenile and who shall determine after a hearing whether sufficient cause exists to hold the person, subject to the order of the court, for his own protection and welfare, for such a time not exceeding 90 days as will enable his return to another state party to this compact pursuant to a requisition for his return from a court of that state. If, at the time when a state seeks the return of a juvenile who has run away, there is pending in the state wherein he is found any criminal charge, or any proceeding to have him adjudicated a delinquent juvenile for an act committed in such state, or if he is suspected of having committed within such state a criminal offense or an act of juvenile delinquency, he shall not be returned without the consent of such state until discharged from prosecution or other form of proceeding, imprisonment, detention, or supervision for such offense of juvenile delinquency. The duly accredited officers of any state party to this compact, upon the establishment of their authority and the identity of the juvenile being returned, shall be permitted to transport such juvenile through any and all states party to this compact, without interference. Upon his return to the state from which he ran away, the juvenile shall be subject to such further proceedings as may be appropriate under the laws of that state.

(b) That the state to which a juvenile is returned under this article shall be responsible for payment of the transportation costs of such return.

(c) That "juvenile" as used in this article means any person who is a minor under the law of the state of residence of the parent, guardian, person, or agency entitled to the legal custody of such minor.

Article V

Return of Escapees and Absconders

(a) That the appropriate person or authority from whose probation or parole supervision a delinquent juvenile has absconded or from whose institutional custody he has escaped shall present to the appropriate court or to the executive authority of the state where the delinquent juvenile is alleged to be located a written requisition for the return of such delinquent juvenile. Such requisition shall state the name and age of the delinquent juvenile, the particulars of his adjudication as a delinquent juvenile, the circumstances of the breach of the terms of his probation or parole or of his escape from an institution or agency vested with his legal custody or supervision, and the location of such delinquent juvenile, if known, at the time the requisition is made. The requisition shall be verified by affidavit, shall be executed in duplicate, and shall be accompanied by two certified copies of the judgment, formal adjudication, or order of commitment which subjects such delinquent juvenile to probation or parole or to the legal custody of the institution or agency concerned. Such further affidavits and other documents as may be deemed proper may be submitted with such requisition. One copy of the requisition shall be filed with the compact administrator of the demanding state, there to remain on file subject to the provisions of law governing records of the appropriate court. Upon the receipt of a requisition demanding the return of a delinquent juvenile who has absconded or escaped, the court or the executive authority to whom the requisition is addressed shall issue an order to any peace officer or other appropriate person directing him to take into custody and detain such delinquent juvenile. Such detention order must substantially recite the facts necessary to the validity of its issuance hereunder. No delinquent juvenile detained upon such order shall be delivered over to the officer whom the appropriate person or authority demanding him shall have appointed to receive him unless he shall first be taken forthwith before a judge of an appropriate court in the state, who shall inform him of the demand made for his return and who may appoint counsel or guardian ad litem for him. If the judge of such court shall find that the requisition is in order, he shall deliver such delinquent juvenile over to the officer whom the appropriate person or authority demanding him shall have appointed to receive him. The judge, however, may fix a reasonable time to be allowed for the purpose of testing the legality of the proceeding.

Upon reasonable information that a person is a delinquent juvenile who has absconded while on probation or parole, or escaped from an institution or agency vested with this legal custody or supervision in any state party to this compact, such person may be taken into custody in any other state party to this compact without a requisition. But in such event, he must be taken forthwith before a judge of the appropriate court, who may appoint counsel or guardian ad litem for such person and who shall determine, after a hearing, whether sufficient cause exists to hold the person subject to the order of the court for such a time, not exceeding 90 days, as will enable his detention under a detention order issued on a requisition pursuant to this article. If, at the time when a state seeks the return of a delinquent juvenile who has either absconded while on probation or parole or escaped from an institution or agency vested with his legal custody or supervision, there is pending in the state wherein he is detained any criminal charge or any proceeding to have him adjudicated a delinquent juvenile for an act committed in such state, or if he is suspected of having committed within such state a criminal offense or an act of juvenile delinquency, he shall not be returned without the consent of such state until discharged from prosecution or other form of proceeding, imprisonment, detention, or supervision for such offense of juvenile delinquency. The duly accredited officers of any state party to this compact, upon the establishment of their authority and the identity of the delinquent juvenile being returned, shall be permitted to transport such delinquent juvenile through any and all states party to this compact, without interference. Upon his return to the state from which he escaped or absconded, the delinquent juvenile shall be subject to such further proceedings as may be appropriate under the laws of that state.

(b) That the state to which a delinquent juvenile is returned under this article shall be responsible for the payment of the transportation costs of such return.

Article VI
Voluntary Return Procedure

That any delinquent juvenile who has absconded while on probation or parole, or escaped from an institution or agency vested with his legal custody or supervision in any state party to this compact, and any juvenile who has run away from any state party to this compact, who is taken into custody without a requisition in another state party to this compact under the provisions of Article IV(a) or of Article V(a), may consent to his immediate return to the state from which he absconded, escaped, or ran away. Such consent shall be given by the juvenile or delinquent juvenile and his counsel or guardian ad litem, if any, by executing or subscribing in writing, in the presence of a judge of the appropriate court, which states that the juvenile or delinquent juvenile and his counsel or guardian ad litem, if any, consent to his return to the demanding state. Before such consent shall be executed or subscribed, however, the judge, in the presence of counsel or guardian ad litem, if any, shall inform the juvenile or delinquent juvenile of his rights under this compact. When the consent has been duly executed, it shall be forwarded to and filed with the compact administrator of the state in which the court is located and the judge shall direct the officer having the juvenile or delinquent juvenile in custody to deliver him to the duly accredited officer or officers of the state demanding his return, and shall cause to be delivered to such officer or officers a copy of the consent. The court may, however, upon the request of the state to which the juvenile or delinquent juvenile is being returned, order him to return unaccompanied to such state and shall provide him with a copy of such court order; in such event a copy of the consent shall be forwarded to the compact administrator of the state to which said juvenile or delinquent juvenile is ordered to return.

Article VII
Cooperative Supervision of Probationers and Parolees

(a) That the duly constituted judicial and administrative authorities of a state party to this compact (herein called "sending state") may permit any delinquent juvenile within such state, placed on probation or parole, to reside in any other state party to this compact (herein called "receiving state") while on probation or parole, and the receiving state shall accept such delinquent juvenile, if the parent, guardian, or person entitled to the legal custody of such delinquent juvenile is residing or undertakes to reside within the receiving state. Before granting such permission, opportunity shall be given to the receiving state to make such investigations as it deems necessary. The authorities of the sending state shall send to the authorities of the receiving state copies of pertinent court orders, social case studies, and all other available information which may be of value to and assist the receiving state in supervising a probationer or parolee under this compact. A receiving state, in its discretion, may agree to accept supervision of a probationer or parolee in cases where the parent, guardian, or person entitled to the legal custody of the delinquent juvenile is not a resident of the receiving state, and if so accepted the sending state may transfer supervision accordingly.

(b) That each receiving state will assume the duties of visitation and of supervision over any such delinquent juvenile and in the exercise of those duties will be governed by the same standards of visitation and supervision that prevail for its own delinquent juveniles released on probation or parole.

(c) That, after consultation between the appropriate authorities of the sending state and of the receiving state as to the desirability and necessity of returning such a delinquent juvenile, the duly accredited officers of a sending state may enter a receiving state and there apprehend and retake any such delinquent juvenile on probation or parole. For that purpose, no formalities will be required, other than establishing the authority of the officer and the identity of the delinquent juvenile to be retaken and returned. The decision of the sending state to retake a delinquent juvenile on probation or parole shall be conclusive upon and not reviewable within the receiving state, but if, at the time the sending state seeks to retake a delinquent juvenile on probation or parole, there is pending against him within the receiving state any criminal charge or any proceedings to have him adjudicated a delinquent juvenile for any act committed in such state or if he is suspected of having committed within such state a criminal offense or an act of juvenile delinquency, he shall not be returned without the consent of the receiving state until discharged from prosecution or other form of proceeding, imprisonment, detention, or supervision for such offense of juvenile delinquency. The duly accredited officers of the sending state shall be permitted to transport delinquent juveniles being so returned through any and all states party to this compact, without interference.

(d) That the sending state shall be responsible under this article for paying the costs of transporting any delinquent juvenile to the receiving state or of returning any delinquent juvenile to the sending state.

Article VIII

Responsibility for Costs

(a) That the provisions of Articles IV(b), V(b), and VII(d) of this compact shall not be construed to alter or affect any internal relationship among the departments, agencies, and officers of and in the government of a party state, or between a party state and its subdivisions, as to the payment of costs, or responsibilities therefor.

(b) That nothing in this compact shall be construed to prevent any party state or subdivision thereof from asserting any right against any person, agency, or other entity in regard to costs for which such party state or subdivision thereof may be responsible pursuant to Articles IV(b), V(b), or VII(d) of this compact.

Article IX

Detention Practices

That, to every extent possible, it shall be the policy of states party to this compact that no juvenile or delinquent juvenile shall be placed or detained in any prison, jail, or lockup nor be detained or transported in association with criminal, vicious, or dissolute persons.

Article X

Supplementary Agreements

That the duly constituted administrative authorities of a state party to this compact may enter into supplementary agreements with any other state or states party hereto for the cooperative care, treatment, and rehabilitation of delinquent juveniles whenever they shall find that such agreements will improve the facilities or programs available for such care, treatment, and rehabilitation. Such care, treatment, and rehabilitation may be provided in an institution located within any state entering into such supplementary agreement. Such supplementary agreements shall (1) provide the rates to be paid for the care, treatment, and custody of such delinquent juveniles, taking into consideration the character of facilities, services, and subsistence furnished; (2) provide that the delinquent juvenile shall be given a court hearing prior to his being sent to another state for care, treatment, and custody; (3) provide that the state receiving such a delinquent juvenile in one of its institutions shall act solely as agent for the state sending such delinquent juvenile; (4) provide that the sending state shall at all times retain jurisdiction over delinquent juveniles sent to an institution in another state; (5) provide for reasonable inspection of such institutions by the sending state; (6) provide that the consent of the parent, guardian, person, or agency entitled to the legal custody of said delinquent juvenile shall be secured prior to his being sent to another state; and (7) make provision for such other matters and details as shall be necessary to protect the rights and equities of such delinquent juveniles and of the cooperating states.

Article XI

Acceptance of Federal and Other Aid

That any state party to this compact may accept any and all donations, gifts, and grants of money, equipment, and services from the federal or any local government, or any agency thereof and from any person, firm, or corporation, for any of the purposes and functions of this compact, and may receive and utilize the same, subject to the terms, conditions, and regulations governing such donations, gifts, and grants.

Article XII

Compact Administrators

That the governor of each state party to this compact shall designate an officer who, acting jointly with like officers of other party states, shall promulgate rules and regulations to carry out more effectively the terms and provisions of this compact.

Comment

The Governor of Texas has appointed the Executive Director of the Texas Youth Commission as the Texas Interstate Compact Administrator. The primary responsibility of the Administrator is to receive and keep records of actions under the Compact and to communicate case information to Texas officials and Interstate Compact Administrators in other states. The Texas Administrator has promulgated regulations and forms, to be found in 37 Texas Administrative Code ch. 101.

Article XIII

Execution of Compact

That this compact shall become operative immediately upon its execution by any state as between it and any other state or states so executing. When executed it shall have the full force and effect of law within such state, the form or execution to be in accordance with the laws of the executing state.

Article XIV

Renunciation

That this compact shall continue in force and remain binding upon each executing state until renounced by it. Renunciation of this compact shall be by the same authority which executed it, by sending six months notice in writing of its intention to withdraw from the compact to the other states party hereto. The duties and obligations of a renouncing state under Article VII hereof shall continue as to parolees and probationers residing therein at the time of withdrawal until retaken or finally discharged. Supplementary agreements entered into under Article X hereof shall be subject to renunciation as provided by such supplementary agreements, and shall not be subject to the six months renunciation notice of the present article.

Article XV

Severability

That the provisions of this compact shall be severable and if any phrase, clause, sentence, or provision of this compact is declared to be contrary to the constitution of any participating state or of the United States or the applicability thereof to any government, agency, person, or circumstance is held invalid, the validity of the remainder of this compact and the applicability thereof to any government, agency, person, or circumstances shall not be affected thereby. If this compact shall be held contrary to the constitution of any state participating therein, the compact shall remain in full force and effect as to the remaining states and in full force and effect as to the state affected as to all severable matters.

§ 60.003. Execution of Additional Article.

The governor shall also execute on the behalf of the state with any other state or states legally joining in it, an additional article to the Interstate Compact on Juveniles in substantially the following form:

Article XVI

Additional Article

That this article shall provide additional remedies, and shall be binding only as among and between those party states which specifically execute the same.

For the purposes of this article, "child," as used herein, means any minor within the jurisdictional age limits of any court in the home state.

When any child is brought before a court of a state of which such child is not a resident, and such state is willing to permit such child's return to the home state of such child, such home state, upon being so advised by the state in which such proceeding is pending, shall immediately institute proceedings to determine the residence and jurisdictional facts as to such child in such home state, and upon finding that such child is in fact a resident of said state and subject to the jurisdiction of the court thereof shall within five days authorize the return of such child to the home state, and to the parent or custodial agency legally authorized to accept such custody in such home state, and at the expense of such home state, to be paid from such funds as such home state may procure, designate, or provide, prompt action being of the essence.

§ 60.004. Execution of Amendment.

The governor shall also execute on the behalf of the state with any other state or states legally joining in it, an amendment to the Interstate Compact on Juveniles in substantially the following form:

RENDITION AMENDMENT

(a) This amendment shall provide additional remedies, and shall be binding only as among and between those party states which specifically execute the same.

(b) All provisions and procedures of Articles V and VI of the Interstate Compact on Juveniles shall be construed to apply to any juvenile charged with being a delinquent by reason of a violation of any criminal law. Any juvenile charged with being a delinquent by reason of violating any criminal law shall be returned to the requesting state upon a requisition to the state where the juvenile may be found. A petition in such case shall be filed in a court of competent jurisdiction in the requesting state where the violation of criminal law is alleged to have been committed. The petition may be filed regardless of whether the juvenile has left the state before or after the filing of the petition. The requisition described in Article V of the compact shall be forwarded by the judge of the court in which the petition has been filed.

§ 60.005. Juvenile Compact Administrator.

Under the compact, the governor may designate an officer as the compact administrator. The administrator, acting jointly with like officers of other party states, shall adopt regulations to carry out more effectively the terms of the compact. The compact administrator serves at the pleasure of the governor. The compact administrator shall cooperate with all departments, agencies, and officers of and in the government of this state and its subdivisions in facilitating the proper administration of the compact or of a supplementary agreement entered into by this state.

§ 60.006. Supplementary Agreements.

A compact administrator may make supplementary agreements with appropriate officials of other states pursuant to the compact. If a supplementary agreement requires or contemplates the use of an institution or facility of this state or requires or contemplates the provision of a service of this state, the supplementary agreement has no force or effect until approved by the head of the department or agency under whose jurisdiction the institution is operated, or whose department or agency is charged with performing the service.

§ 60.007. Financial Arrangements.

The compact administrator may make or arrange for the payments necessary to discharge the financial obligations imposed upon this state by the compact or by a supplementary agreement made under the compact, subject to legislative appropriations.

§ 60.008. Enforcement.

The courts, departments, agencies, and officers of this state and its subdivisions shall enforce this compact and shall do all things appropriate to effectuate its purposes and intent which are within their respective jurisdictions.

§ 60.009. Additional Procedures Not Precluded.

In addition to the procedures provided in Articles IV and VI of the compact for the return of a runaway juvenile, the particular states, the juvenile, or his parents, the courts, or other legal custodian involved may agree upon and adopt any plan or procedure legally authorized under the laws of this state and the other respective party states for the return of the runaway juvenile.

Leading Case

In re: The State of Texas, Relator, 97 S.W.3d 746 (Tex.App.—El Paso 2003, no pet.) (Texas judge under duty to honor Arizona request for return of a runaway)

Chapter 61. Rights and Responsibilities of Parents and Other Eligible Persons [NEW]

> ***Editors' Note:*** *All of the provisions in this new chapter have the following legislative history:*
>
> *History: Enacted by 78th Legis., Reg. Sess. (2003), H.B. 2319, eff. Sept. 1, 2003. Applies only to conduct occurring on or after effective date.*

Subchapter A. Entry of Orders Against Parents and Other Eligible Persons

Subchapter B. Enforcement of Order Against Parent or Other Eligible Person

Subchapter C. Rights of Parents

Introductory Comment

Chapter 61 attempts to bring the strengths and resources of parents to the juvenile justice system to assist the child in making life-altering efforts at change. Subchapter A deals with entering juvenile court orders requiring parents to take actions or refrain from taking actions to benefit their child. Subchapter B deals with the judicial process by which those orders are enforced. Subchapter C deals with parental rights to know about their child's case and to participate in its handling.

CLE/Other Legal Publications

Parental Rights and the Juvenile Justice System. Keiko Huey, 17 JUVE. L. SECT. RPT. (Mar. 2003)

Subchapter A. Entry of Orders Against Parents and Other Eligible Persons

§ 61.001. Definitions.

In this chapter:

(1) "Juvenile court order" means an order by a juvenile court in a proceeding to which this chapter applies requiring a parent or other eligible person to act or refrain from acting.

(2) "Other eligible person" means the respondent's guardian, the respondent's custodian, or any other person described in a provision under this title authorizing the court order.

Comment

This chapter is directed primarily at parents, but also includes other persons who under Title 3 substantive provisions are eligible to have the juvenile court order them to take or refrain from action.

---

§ 61.002. Applicability.

(a) Except as provided by Subsection (b), this chapter applies to a proceeding to enter a juvenile court order:

(1) for payment of probation fees under Section 54.061;

(2) for restitution under Sections 54.041(b) and 54.048;

(3) for payment of graffiti eradication fees under Section 54.0461;

(4) for community service under Section 54.044(b);

(5) for payment of costs of court under Section 54.0411 or other provisions of law;

(6) requiring the person to refrain from doing any act injurious to the welfare of the child under Section 54.041(a)(1);

(7) enjoining contact between the person and the child who is the subject of a proceeding under Section 54.041(a)(2);

(8) ordering a person living in the same household with the child to participate in counseling under Section 54.041(a)(3);

(9) requiring a parent or guardian of a child found to be truant to participate in an available program addressing truancy under Section 54.041(f);

(10) requiring a parent or other eligible person to pay reasonable attorney's fees for representing the child under Section 51.10(e);

(11) requiring the parent or other eligible person to reimburse the county for payments the county has made to an attorney appointed to represent the child under Section 51.10(j);

(12) requiring payment of deferred prosecution supervision fees under Section 53.03(d);

(13) requiring a parent or other eligible person to attend a court hearing under Section 51.115;

(14) requiring a parent or other eligible person to act or refrain from acting to aid the child in complying with conditions of release from detention under Section 54.01(r); or

(15) requiring a parent or other eligible person to act or refrain from acting under any law imposing an obligation of action or omission on a parent or other eligible person because of the parent's or person's relation to the child who is the subject of a proceeding under this title.

(b) This subchapter does not apply to the entry and enforcement of a child support order under Section 54.06.

Comment

Subsection (a) lists each instance in Title 3 in which a juvenile court is authorized to enter an order against a parent or other eligible adult. Subsection (a)(15) is an open-ended clause intended to catch any provisions omitted from the list or that may be enacted by later legislatures. It is important to note that a Chapter 61 order can be imposed only if a substantive basis elsewhere in Title 3 can be found authorizing the order. Subsection (b) excludes child support orders because their enforcement is dealt with by the comprehensive tools available to the court under Title 5.

§ 61.003. Entry of Juvenile Court Order Against Parent or Other Eligible Person.

(a) To comply with the requirements of due process of law, the juvenile court shall:

(1) provide sufficient notice in writing or orally in a recorded court hearing of a proposed juvenile court order; and

(2) provide a sufficient opportunity for the parent or other eligible person to be heard regarding the proposed order.

(b) A juvenile court order must be in writing and a copy promptly furnished to the parent or other eligible person.

(c) The juvenile court may require the parent or other eligible person to provide suitable identification to be included in the court's file. Suitable identification includes fingerprints, a driver's license number, a social security number, or similar indicia of identity.

Comment

Subsection (a) sets out the basics of procedural due process—adequate notice and sufficient opportunity to be heard. Subchapter B makes it a defense to enforcement efforts that due process was not afforded when the order was entered. Subsection (c) requires documentation of identification to facilitate any enforcement efforts that may later become necessary.

§ 61.004. Appeal.

(a) The parent or other eligible person against whom a final juvenile court order has been entered may appeal as provided by law from judgments entered in civil cases.

(b) The movant may appeal from a judgment denying requested relief regarding a juvenile court order as provided by law from judgments entered in civil cases.

(c) The pendency of an appeal initiated under this section does not abate or otherwise affect the proceedings in juvenile court involving the child.

Comment

Both the parent and the state may appeal an order or denial of order as in other civil cases. Subsection (c) makes it clear that the appeal is between the parent and the state and does not affect the handling of the child's case.

Subchapter B. Enforcement of Order Against Parent or Other Eligible Person

§ 61.051. Motion for Enforcement.

(a) A party initiates enforcement of a juvenile court order by filing a written motion. In ordinary and concise language, the motion must:

(1) identify the provision of the order allegedly violated and sought to be enforced;

(2) state specifically and factually the manner of the person's alleged noncompliance;

(3) state the relief requested; and

(4) contain the signature of the party filing the motion.

(b) The movant must allege in the same motion for enforcement each violation by the person of the juvenile court orders described by Section 61. 002(a) that the movant had a reasonable basis for believing the person was violating when the motion was filed.

(c) The juvenile court retains jurisdiction to enter a contempt order if the motion for enforcement is filed not later than six months after the child's 18th birthday.

Comment

Subsection (a) sets out the requirements of the written motion for enforcement. Subsection (b) mandates joinder of all claims the party filing the motion has a reasonable basis for believing exist; the person filing the motion for enforcement cannot hold back claims for later proceedings. Subsection (c) permits a motion for enforcement to be filed up to six months after the child becomes 18 since some violations will not be discovered until after the child is discharged from the system at age 18.

§ 61.052. Notice and Appearance.

(a) On the filing of a motion for enforcement, the court shall by written notice set the date, time, and place of the hearing and order the person against whom enforcement is sought to appear and respond to the motion.

(b) The notice must be given by personal service or by certified mail, return receipt requested, on or before the 10th day before the date of the hearing on the motion. The notice must include a copy of the motion for enforcement. Personal service must comply with the Code of Criminal Procedure.

(c) If a person moves to strike or specially excepts to the motion for enforcement, the court shall rule on the exception or motion to strike before

the court hears evidence on the motion for enforcement. If an exception is sustained, the court shall give the movant an opportunity to replead and continue the hearing to a designated date and time without the requirement of additional service.

(d) If a person who has been personally served with notice to appear at the hearing does not appear, the juvenile court may not hold the person in contempt, but may issue a capias for the arrest of the person. The court shall set and enforce bond as provided by Subchapter C, Chapter 157. If a person served by certified mail, return receipt requested, with notice to appear at the hearing does not appear, the juvenile court may require immediate personal service of notice.

Comment

Subsection (b) permits either personal or certified mail service of the motion for enforcement and notice of hearing. Subsection (d) permits a capias to be issued when a person personally served fails to appear, but requires personal service if the non-appearing person was only originally served by certified mail.

---

§ 61.053. Attorney for the Person.

(a) In a proceeding on a motion for enforcement where incarceration is a possible punishment against a person who is not represented by an attorney, the court shall inform the person of the right to be represented by an attorney and, if the person is indigent, of the right to the appointment of an attorney.

(b) If the person claims indigency and requests the appointment of an attorney, the juvenile court may require the person to file an affidavit of indigency. The court may hear evidence to determine the issue of indigency.

(c) The court shall appoint an attorney to represent the person if the court determines that the person is indigent.

(d) The court shall allow an appointed or retained attorney at least 10 days after the date of the attorney's appointment or retention to respond to the movant's pleadings and to prepare for the hearing. The attorney may waive the preparation time or agree to a shorter period for preparation.

Comment

Subsection (a) was amended in the Senate to add the words "where incarceration is a possible punishment." Since under Section 61.057(a) incarceration is always a possible punishment, the Senate language added nothing to the subsection. Subsections (b) and (c) codify federal constitutional mandates by requiring the court to appoint counsel for an indigent parent to represent that person in enforcement proceedings.

---

§ 61.054. Compensation of Appointed Attorney.

(a) An attorney appointed to represent an indigent person is entitled to a reasonable fee for services to be paid from the general fund of the county according to the schedule for compensation adopted by the county juvenile board. The attorney must meet the qualifications required of attorneys for appointment to Class B misdemeanor cases in juvenile court.

(b) For purposes of compensation, a proceeding in the supreme court is the equivalent of a proceeding in the court of criminal appeals.

(c) The juvenile court may order the parent or other eligible person for whom it has appointed counsel to reimburse the county for the fees the county pays to appointed counsel.

Comment

Subsection (a) requires that an attorney appointed to represent a parent must meet the qualifications for handing Class B misdemeanor juvenile cases. That qualification was chosen since it most closely approximates the punishment authorized for contempt of court.

---

§ 61.055. Conduct of Enforcement Hearing.

(a) The juvenile court shall require that the enforcement hearing be recorded as provided by Section 54.09.

(b) The movant must prove beyond a reasonable doubt that the person against whom enforcement is sought engaged in conduct constituting contempt of a reasonable and lawful court order as alleged in the motion for enforcement.

(c) The person against whom enforcement is sought has a privilege not to be called as a witness or otherwise to incriminate himself or herself.

(d) The juvenile court shall conduct the enforcement hearing without a jury.

(e) The juvenile court shall include in its judgment findings as to each violation alleged in the motion for enforcement and the punishment, if any, to be imposed.

(f) If the person against whom enforcement is sought was not represented by counsel during any previous court proceeding involving a motion for enforcement, the person may through counsel raise any defense or affirmative defense to the proceeding that could have been lodged in the previous court proceeding but was not because the person was not represented by counsel.

(g) It is an affirmative defense to enforcement of a juvenile court order that the juvenile court did not provide the parent or other eligible person with due process of law in the proceeding in which the court entered the order.

Comment

Subsection (f) makes available to the parent in enforcement proceedings any defense that could have been presented in previous court proceedings but was not because the parent was unrepresented. Subsection (g) makes failure to provide due process as provided in § 61.003(a) an affirmative defense to enforcement proceedings.

---

§ 61.056. Affirmative Defense of Inability to Pay.

(a) In an enforcement hearing in which the motion for enforcement alleges that the person against whom enforcement is sought failed to pay restitution, court costs, supervision fees, or any other payment ordered by the court, it is an affirmative defense that the person was financially unable to pay.

(b) The burden of proof to establish the affirmative defense of inability to pay is on the person asserting it.

(c) In order to prevail on the affirmative defense of inability to pay, the person asserting it must show that the person could not have reasonably paid the court-ordered obligation after the person discharged the person's other important financial obligations, including payments for housing, food, utilities, necessary clothing, education, and preexisting debts.

Comment

This section makes inability to pay court-ordered money an affirmative defense to enforcement proceedings. It is modeled on article 42.12, Sec. 21(c) of the Code of Criminal Procedure. Subsection (c) defines inability to pay in terms of whether the defendant could have paid the court-ordered money in light of the defendant's legal duties to pay pre-existing obligations.

---

§ 61.057. Punishment for Contempt.

(a) On a finding of contempt, the juvenile court may commit the person to the county jail for a term not to exceed six months or may impose a fine in an amount not to exceed $500, or both.

(b) The court may impose only a single jail sentence not to exceed six months or a single fine not to exceed $500, or both, during an enforcement proceeding, without regard to whether the court has entered multiple findings of contempt.

(c) On a finding of contempt in an enforcement proceeding, the juvenile court may, instead of issuing a commitment to jail, enter an order requiring the person's future conduct to comply with the court's previous orders.

(d) Violation of an order entered under Subsection (c) may be the basis of a new enforcement proceeding.

(e) The juvenile court may assign a juvenile probation officer to assist a person in complying with a court order issued under Subsection (c).

(f) A juvenile court may reduce a term of incarceration or reduce payment of all or part of a fine at any time before the sentence is fully served or the fine fully paid.

(g) A juvenile court may reduce the burden of complying with a court order issued under Subsection (c) at any time before the order is fully satisfied, but may not increase the burden except following a new finding of contempt in a new enforcement proceeding.

Comment

Subsection (a) makes contempt punishable to the same extent of contempt of court under the Government Code for any other order of a district or county level court. Subsection (b) restricts the court to one finding of contempt per enforcement proceeding and prohibits the imposition of multiple sentences. Section 61.051(b) required the state to join all reasonably knowable violations in a single enforcement proceeding. Instead of imposing a fine and/or incarceration, the court is authorized by subsection (c) to enter a further court order as a sanction for contempt, a violation of which may later become the basis of fresh enforcement proceedings. Under Subsection (e) the court may assign a juvenile probation officer to assist the defendant in complying with a newly-entered court order. Subsection (f) permits the court to reduce a term of incarceration or remit a fine before it has been fully served or paid.

Subchapter C. Rights of Parents

§ 61.101. Definition.

In this subchapter, "parent" includes the guardian or custodian of a child.

---

§ 61.102. Right to be Informed of Proceeding.

(a) The parent of a child referred to a juvenile court is entitled as soon as practicable after the referral to be informed by staff designated by the juvenile board, based on the information accompanying the referral to the juvenile court, of:

(1) the date and time of the offense;

(2) the date and time the child was taken into custody;

(3) the name of the offense and its penal category;

(4) the type of weapon, if any, that was used;

(5) the type of property taken or damaged and the extent of damage, if any;

(6) the physical injuries, if any, to the victim of the offense;

(7) whether there is reason to believe that the offense was gang-related;

(8) whether there is reason to believe that the offense was related to consumption of alcohol or use of an illegal controlled substance;

(9) if the child was taken into custody with adults or other juveniles, the names of those persons;

(10) the aspects of the juvenile court process that apply to the child;

(11) if the child is in detention, the visitation policy of the detention facility that applies to the child;

(12) the child's right to be represented by an attorney and the local standards and procedures for determining whether the parent qualifies for appointment of counsel to represent the child; and

(13) the methods by which the parent can assist the child with the legal process.

(b) If the child was released on field release citation, or from the law enforcement station by the police, by intake, or by the judge or associate judge at the initial detention hearing, the information required by Subsection (a) may be communicated to the parent in person, by telephone, or in writing.

(c) If the child is not released before or at the initial detention hearing, the information required by Subsection (a) shall be communicated in person to the parent unless that is not feasible, in which event it may be communicated by telephone or in writing.

(d) Information disclosed to a parent under Subsection (a) is not admissible in a judicial proceeding under this title as substantive evidence or as evidence to impeach the testimony of a witness for the state.

Comment

This section gives the parent the right to be informed of certain facts about the arrest of his or her child. Those facts that a parent would reasonably be expected to want to know are included, but not included is a general narrative of the offense as it would appear in an offense report. Duty to inform the parent is placed on probation staff. All of the information can be obtained from the law enforcement incident report that accompanied the referral. Subsection (d) provides that this information disclosed to the parent is for the benefit of the parent and may not be admitted in proceedings in juvenile court involving the child.

---

§ 61.103. Right of Access to Child.

(a) The parent of a child taken into custody for delinquent conduct, conduct indicating a need for supervision, or conduct that violates a condition of probation imposed by the juvenile court has the right to communicate in person privately with the child for reasonable periods of time while the child is in:

(1) a juvenile processing office;

(2) a secure detention facility;

(3) a secure correctional facility;

(4) a court-ordered placement facility; or

(5) the custody of the Texas Youth Commission.

(b) The time, place, and conditions of the private, in-person communication may be regulated to prevent disruption of scheduled activities and to maintain the safety and security of the facility.

Comment

This section gives parents a right of access to their children at all times, subject to reasonable regulation by the custodian.

---

§ 61.104. Parental Written Statement.

(a) When a petition for adjudication, a motion or petition to modify disposition, or a motion or petition for discretionary transfer to criminal court is served on a parent of the child, the parent must be provided with a form prescribed by the Texas Juvenile Probation Commission on which the parent can make a written statement about the needs of the child or family or any other matter relevant to disposition of the case.

(b) The parent shall return the statement to the juvenile probation department, which shall transmit the statement to the court along with the discretionary transfer report authorized by Section 54.02(e), the disposition report authorized by Section 54.04(b), or the modification of disposition report authorized by Section 54.05(e), as applicable. The statement shall be disclosed to the parties as appropriate and may be considered by the court at the disposition, modification, or discretionary transfer hearing.

Comment

This section creates the opportunity for a parent to communicate relevant dispositional information to the juvenile court as part of the social history report. It is modeled on victim's impact statement procedures used in both criminal and juvenile cases.

---

§ 61.105. Parental Oral Statement.

(a) After all the evidence has been received but before the arguments of counsel at a hearing for discretionary transfer to criminal court, a disposition

hearing without a jury, or a modification of disposition hearing, the court shall give a parent who is present in court a reasonable opportunity to address the court about the needs or strengths of the child or family or any other matter relevant to disposition of the case.

(b) The parent may not be required to make the statement under oath and may not be subject to cross-examination, but the court may seek clarification or expansion of the statement from the person giving the statement.

(c) The court may consider and act on the statement as the court considers appropriate.

Comment

This section gives the parent the right to make an unsworn oral statement to the juvenile court regarding disposition of his or her child's case and for the court to give such a statement whatever weight it believes appropriate. To encourage parents to provide such an oral statement, cross-examination by either state or child's attorney is prohibited. The court may ask clarifying questions only.

---

§ 61.106. Appeal or Collateral Challenge.

The failure or inability of a person to perform an act or to provide a right or service listed under this subchapter may not be used by the child or any party as a ground for:

(1) appeal;

(2) an application for a post-adjudication writ of habeas corpus; or

(3) exclusion of evidence against the child in any proceeding or forum.

Comment

The rights provided by this subchapter belong to the parent, not the child. This section precludes using failure to provide parental rights as a defense in the trial, appeal or collateral attack in the child's case. A similar provision appears in the victim's rights chapter, for similar reasons. See § 57.006.

---

§ 61.107. Liability.

The Texas Youth Commission, a juvenile board, a court, a person appointed by the court, an employee of a juvenile probation department, an attorney for the state, a peace officer, or a law enforcement agency is not liable for a failure or inability to provide a right listed in this chapter.

Comment

This provision protects public officials from civil liability for failure to provide a right defined by this subchapter. A similar provision appears in the victim's rights chapter. See § 57.005.

TITLE 4

Protective Orders and Family Violence

As amended through the 78th Legislature, Fourth Called Session (2004)

Subtitle A. General Provisions.

Subtitle B. Protective Orders.

Subtitle C. Reporting Family Violence.

★★★

***Editors' Note:** Title 4 contains guest commentary throughout by Bree Buchanan, Children's Rights Clinic, University of Texas School of Law, and former Public Policy Director, Texas Council on Family Violence, 1998–2002, identified as (B.B.).*

Introductory Comment

Prevalence of Family Violence. Family violence has reached epidemic proportions in Texas and in the nation as a whole. One out of every four American women report that they have been physically or sexually assaulted by a husband or boyfriend at some point in their lives. PREVALENCE, INCIDENCE, AND CONSEQUENCES OF VIOLENCE AGAINST WOMEN: FINDINGS FROM THE NATIONAL VIOLENCE AGAINST WOMEN SURVEY, NATIONAL INSTITUTE OF JUSTICE AND CENTERS FOR DISEASE CONTROL AND PREVENTION, November 1998. In 2001, almost 700,000 incidents of intimate partner violence occurred, 85% of which were against women. INTIMATE PARTNER VIOLENCE, 1993–2001, BUREAU OF JUSTICE STATISTICS, February 2003. Health-related costs alone exceed $5.8 billion each year. COSTS OF INTIMATE PARTNER VIOLENCE, CENTER FOR DISEASE CONTROL, 2003. Recent studies also reveal that domestic violence is experienced by young women at disproportionate rates. Specifically, women between 16 and 24 are nearly three times more vulnerable to intimate partner violence than women in other age groups. INTIMATE PARTNER VIOLENCE AND AGE OF VICTIM, BUREAU OF JUSTICE STATISTICS, October 2001.

In Texas, intimate partner homicide occurs at one of the highest rates in the country. SURVEILLANCE FOR HOMICIDE AMONG INTIMATE PARTNERS, CENTER FOR DISEASE CONTROL, October 2001. A statewide poll conducted in 2002 found that 74% of all Texans responding stated that either a family member, a friend, or themselves personally had experienced some form of domestic violence. PREVALENCE, PERCEPTIONS AND AWARENESS OF DOMESTIC VIOLENCE IN TEXAS, TEXAS COUNCIL ON FAMILY VIOLENCE, 2003. Concerning nonfatal incidents, Texas law enforcement agencies received 183,440 reports of family violence in 2002, an increase of almost 50% from 1991. 2002 CRIME IN TEXAS, TEXAS DEPARTMENT OF PUBLIC SAFETY. While this number may seem staggering, studies show that only one-half of all family violence incidents are actually reported to the police. INTIMATE PARTNER VIOLENCE, BUREAU OF JUSTICE STATISTICS, May 2000. Of those reports received in 2002, the age group with the highest number of victims was the 20 to 24 year old bracket. 2002 CRIME IN TEXAS, TEXAS DEPARTMENT OF PUBLIC SAFETY. In the same year, the Texas Department of Human Services reported that 28,886 adult victims and their children were forced to seek refuge at family violence shelters across the state.

History of Protective Orders in Texas. Since 1979, protective orders have existed as the primary civil legal remedy for victims of family violence in Texas. As society's tolerance for family violence has decreased over the past two decades, the protections afforded under this title have consistently increased. In 1989, the definition of "family violence" was amended to include threats of violence, in addition to violent acts. Two years later, mutual protective orders were prohibited. In 1995, the 74th Legislature created the magistrate's order of emergency protection by amendment to the Code of Criminal Procedure. art. 17.292, TEX. CRIM. PROC. CODE ANN. During the same session, a centralized protective order registry was established as part of the Texas Crime Information Center (TCIC), now linked with its federal counterpart at the Federal Bureau of Investigation (NCIC).

Other recent significant improvements include doubling the maximum duration of protective orders from one to two years and extending protection to victims of dating violence. In 2003, conflicts between magistrate's orders of emergency protection and subsequent Title 4 protective orders were addressed. *See* TEX. CODE CRIM. PROC. art. 17.292 (f–2) (as amended by H.B. 297, 78th Legis., Reg. Sess. (2003)). The 78th Legislature also authorized the entry of a Title 4–style protective order for victims of sexual assault. *See* TEX. CODE CRIM. PROC. ch. 7A (as amended by S.B. 433, 78th Legis., Reg. Sess. (2003)).

Effectiveness of Protective Orders. Many believe that a victim will be safe once separated from the abuser. To the contrary, statistics have shown the risk of violent assault increases whenever a victim takes action that challenges the abuser's control (making plans to separate, filing for divorce, calling the police). WILSON AND DALY, SPOUSAL HOMICIDE RISK AND ESTRANGEMENT: VIOLENCE AND VICTIMS, 1993. Over half of the murders of women by an intimate partner in Texas in 1998 occurred after separation or while she was attempting to leave, GRIM TALLY, TEXAS COUNCIL ON FAMILY VIOLENCE, 1998.

Protective orders can be an effective method for intervening in the often escalating violence that occurs at separation, particularly when orders are crafted with specificity and the relief granted addresses the particular needs of the applicant (including orders regarding children and property). Abuse victims who obtain a protective order are 60% less likely to have further contact with the perpetrator and 70% less likely to suffer further injury than victims who only made a report to the police. AM. J. PREVENTIVE MEDICINE, January 2003.

The power of protective orders lies in their quasi-criminal nature. Violation of one of the criminally enforceable provisions of TEX. FAM. CODE ANN. § 85.022(b) is a Class A misdemeanor, punishable by confinement up to one year and/or a fine up to $4,000. TEX. PENAL CODE ANN. § 25.07. The response of law enforcement to family violence offenses committed subsequent to the entry of a protective order is often enhanced. In fact, peace officers are required to arrest a person whom the officer has probable cause to believe has violated a protective order. TEX. CODE CRIM. PROC. art. 14.03.

For information regarding local family violence services, contact the National Domestic Violence Hotline at 1–800–799–7233. (B.B.)

CLE/Other Legal Publications

Domestic violence: including protective orders and the psychology of abuse. Judy L. Warne, 2004 ADV. FAM. L.

What's love got to do with it? How a finding of family violence directly affects your family law case. Kathleen A. Hamilton, 2004 MARRIAGE DISSOLUTION

Protective orders: taking it to the next level. Jeana L. Lungwitz & Amy C. Wright, 2004 U. TEX. FAM. L. FRONT LINES

When domestic violence and child abuse collide: tension within the family violence field. Bree Buchanan, 2003 ADV. FAM. L.

Prosecuting and defending protective orders. Patricia J. Lasher, 2003 ADV. FAM. L.

Taking domestic violence seriously: the role of lawyers, judges and probation officers. Sarah M. Buel, 2003 U. TEX. FAM. L. FRONT LINES

Understanding the connection between domestic violence, crime, and poverty: how welfare reform may keep battered women from leaving abusive relationships. Shelby A.D. Moore, 12 TEX. J. WOMEN & LAW 451 (2003)

Violence Against Women Act: protections for victims of abuse. Teresa Coles-Davila, 66 TEX. B.J. 890 (2003)

Online Resources: Domestic and Sexual Violence

National Center for Victims of Crime http://www.ncvc.org

National Domestic Violence Hotline http://www.ndvh.org

National Sexual Violence Resource Center http://www.nsvrc.org

Texas Association Against Sexual Assault http://www.taasa.org

Texas Council on Family Violence http://www.tcfv.org

Texas Office of Attorney General Sexual Assault Prevention and Crisis Services http://www.oag.state.tx.us/victims/sapcs

U.S. Department of Justice Office on Violence Against Women http://www.ojp.usdoj.gov/ovc

Violence Against Women Online http://www.vaw.umn.edu

Women's Advocacy Project http://www.women-law.org

Leading Cases

In General

U.S. v. Morrison, 529 U.S. 598, 120 S.Ct. 1740, 146 L.Ed.2d 658 (2000) (VAWA's federal civil remedy for victims of gender-motivated violence, 42 U.S.C.A. § 13981, exceeds Congress' constitutional authority)

Pena v. Pena, 8 S.W.3d 639 (Tex. 1999) (appellate court statement that provocation might be relevant in determining existence of "pattern of abuse" disapproved)

Taherzadeh v. Ghaleh-Assadi, 108 S.W.3d 927 (Tex. App.—Dallas 2003, pet. denied) (husband failed to show hearing for protective order should be continued)

Martinez v. Martinez, 52 S.W.3d 429 (Tex. App.—Fort Worth 2001, pet. denied) (discovery may not impede protective order process; trial court lacks authority to order husband's attorney to pay for and report to court on batterer's program)

James v. Hubbard, 21 S.W.3d 558 (Tex. App.—San Antonio 1998, no pet.) (divorce ends "family relationship," therefore, applicant not entitled to protective order from daughter's husband)

Collins v. State, 955 S.W.2d 464 (Tex. App.—Fort Worth 1997, no pet.) (protective order is criminally enforceable even if lack of details would not sustain contempt judgment)

Moreno v. Moore, 897 S.W.2d 439 (Tex. App.—Corpus Christi 1995, no writ) (mutual protective order void; requirements of §§ 71.12–.121 not complied with)

White v. Blake, 859 S.W.2d 551 (Tex. App.—Tyler 1993, no writ) (Texas has jurisdiction to issue protective order for child even though another state has custody jurisdiction)

Appeal of Protective Order

Vongontard v. Tippit, No. 01–03–00814–CV (Tex. App.—Houston [1st Dist.] 2004) (protective order is akin to a permanent injunction and is, therefore, appealable if it disposes of all parties and issues) (former boyfriend's actions justified dating violence protective order)

Ulmer v. Ulmer, 130 S.W.3d 294 (Tex. App.—Houston [14th Dist.] 2004) (protective order providing injunctive relief and disposing of all issues and parties is final, appealable order)

In re Compton, 117 S.W.3d 548 (Tex. App.—Texarkana 2003, no pet.) (possibility district court would issue SAPCR order conflicting with prior protective order not sufficient basis for mandamus)

B.C. v. Rhodes, 116 S.W.3d 878 (Tex. App.—Austin 2003, no pet.) (protective order that disposes of all the parties and issues can be appealed despite the continuing jurisdiction of the trial court)

In re K.S.L.-C., 109 S.W.3d 577 (Tex. App.—Tyler 2003, no pet.) (protective order rendered during pendency of divorce is not final and appealable order)

Bilyeu v. Bilyeu, 86 S.W.3d 278 (Tex. App.—Austin 2002, no pet.) (protective order rendered during pendency of divorce not appealable—it's not a final order)

Kelt v. Kelt, 67 S.W.3d 364 (Tex. App.—Waco 2001, no pet.) (protective order is appealable, reversing earlier position in Normand v. Fox, 940 S.W.2d 401 no pet.), *accord* Cooke v. Cooke, 65 S.W.3d 785 (Tex. App.—Dallas 2001, no pet.); Pena v. Garza, 61 S.W.3d 529 (Tex. App.—San Antonio 2001, no pet.)

In re Salgado, 53 S.W.3d 752 (Tex. App.—El Paso 2001, no pet.) (protective order validly issued by court other than the CEJ court—mandamus can substitute for appeal in Title 4 cases)

Striedel v. Striedel, 15 S.W.3d 163 (Tex. App.—Corpus Christi 2000, no pet.) (protective order appealable; error to refuse to allow respondent to testify or present evidence)

In re Cummings, 13 S.W.3d 472 (Tex. App.—Corpus Christi 2000, no pet.) (protective order appealable; expiration of one year term of order does not moot appeal)

Winsett v. Edgar, 22 S.W.3d 509 (Tex. App.—Fort Worth 1999), *opinion after grant of appeal*, 22 S.W.3d 510 (Tex. App.—Fort Worth 2000, pet. denied) (protective order found to be final, appealable order; protective order to be determined by court, not jury)

Ruiz v. Ruiz, 946 S.W.2d 124 (Tex. App.—Waco 1997, no writ) (protective order granted while divorce pending which did not dispose of all issues is non-appealable interlocutory order)

Texas Family Law Practice Manual

Chapter 14. Protective Orders

Cross References

TEX. CRIM. PROC. CODE ANN. ch. 5. Family Violence Prevention; art. 17.292. Magistrate's Order for Emergency Protection; art. 42.141. *et seq.* Battering Intervention and Prevention Program; ch. 7A. Protective Order for Victim of Sexual Assault; ch. 56. Rights of Crime Victims; art. 56.31 *et seq.* Crime Victim Compensation.

TEX. FAM. CODE ANN. §§ 6.501–.502. Temporary Orders; § 6.504. Protective Orders; § 8.002. Eligibility for Maintenance; § 105.001. Temporary Orders; § 153.004. History of Domestic Violence; § 153.010. Order for Family Counseling; § 153.131. Presumption that Parent To Be Appointed Managing Conservator; §§ 153.501–.503; Prevention of International Parental Child Abduction; § 159.312. Nondisclosure of Information in Exceptional Circumstances; § 233.015. Issuance of Child Support Review Order; § 262.102. Emergency Order Authorizing Possession of Child; § 262.201. Full Adversary Hearing.

TEX. HEALTH & SAFETY CODE ANN. ch. 672. Adult Fatality Review & Investigations.

TEX. PEN. CODE ANN. § 22.01. Assault; § 22.07. Terroristic Threat; § 25.07. Violation of Protective Order and Magistrate's Order; § 42.062. Interference with Emergency Telephone Call; § 42.07. Harassment; § 42.072. Stalking.

VIOLENCE AGAINST WOMEN ACT, 18 U.S.C.A. § 2265 *et seq.*; 42 U.S.C.A. § 13931, *et seq.*

Subtitle A. General Provisions

Chapter 71. Definitions.

---

§ 71.001. Applicability of Definitions.

(a) Definitions in this chapter apply to this title.

(b) If, in another part of this title, a term defined by this chapter has a meaning different from the meaning provided by this chapter, the meaning of that other provision prevails.

(c) Except as provided by this chapter, the definitions in Chapter 101 *[Definitions]* apply to terms used in this title.

§ 71.002. Court.

"Court" means the district court, court of domestic relations, juvenile court having the jurisdiction of a district court, statutory county court, constitutional county court, or other court expressly given jurisdiction under this title.

Leading Case

Williams v. Williams, 19 S.W.3d 544 (Tex. App.—Fort Worth 2000, pet. denied) (respondent not entitled to jury trial; court decides whether to render protective order)

---

§ 71.0021. Dating Violence.

(a) "Dating violence" means an act by an individual that is against another individual with whom that person has or has had a dating relationship and that is intended to result in physical harm, bodily injury, assault, or sexual assault or that is a threat that reasonably places the individual in fear of imminent physical harm, bodily injury, assault, or sexual assault, but does not include defensive measures to protect oneself.

(b) For purposes of this title, "dating relationship" means a relationship between individuals who have or have had a continuing relationship of a romantic or intimate nature. The existence of such a relationship shall be determined based on consideration of:

(1) the length of the relationship;

(2) the nature of the relationship; and

(3) the frequency and type of interaction between the persons involved in the relationship.

(c) A casual acquaintanceship or ordinary fraternization in a business or so(context does not constitute a "dating relationship" under Subsection (b).

Comment

Prior to September 1, 2001, victims of intimate partner violence who had never been married, lived together, nor had a child together were ineligible to apply for a protective order even if the dynamics of violence in their relationships were the same as for those who were otherwise eligible to apply. Ironically, research has found that young adults ages 16 to 24 experience the highest rate of intimate partner violence, and yet, this is the age group least likely to meet the eligibility criteria. *Intimate Partner Violence*, Bureau of Justice Statistics, May 2000.

In 2001, following the lead of 32 other states that offer protection for victims of dating violence, Texas extended the relief afforded under this title to victims who have a "continuing relationship of a romantic or intimate nature" with an abusive individual. The definition of "dating relationship" mirrors the federal definition found in the Violence Against Women Act of 2000 (42 U.S.C.A. 3796), as well as the definitions found in many other state statutes. The factors listed for consideration by the court also track those of other states. *(B.B.)*

Leading Case

Vongontard v. Tippit, ___ S.W.3d ___, 2004 WL 440438 (Tex. App.—Houston [1st Dist.] 2004, no pet. hist.) (three incidents of pushing while dating and continued threatening behavior after break up were legally and factually sufficient to support finding that dating violence had occurred)

---

§ 71.003. Family.

"Family" includes individuals related by consanguinity or affinity, as determined under Sections 573.022 and 573.024, Government Code, individuals who are former spouses of each other, individuals who are the parents of the same child, without regard to marriage, and a foster child and foster parent, without regard to whether those individuals reside together.

Comment

The definition of "family" is very broad in order to maximize protection and to minimize domestic violence.

---

§ 71.004. Family Violence.

"Family violence" means:

(1) an act by a member of a family or household against another member of the family or household that is intended to result in physical harm, bodily injury, assault, or sexual assault or that is a threat that reasonably places the member in fear of imminent physical harm, bodily injury, assault, or sexual assault, but does not include defensive measures to protect oneself;

(2) abuse, as that term is defined by Sections 261.001(1)(C), (E), and (G), by a member of a family or household toward a child of the family or household; or

(3) dating violence, as that term is defined by Section 71.0021.

Comment

By including "dating violence" in the definition of family violence, the legislature has ensured that dating violence protective orders are subject to the same procedures and penalties as all other family violence protective orders. Because magistrate's orders for emergency protection are authorized "after arrest for an offense involving family violence," victims of dating violence are also eligible for these 31 to 61 day protective orders. *See* TEX. CODE CRIM. PROC. art. 17.292. *(B.B.)*

---

§ 71.005. Household.

"Household" means a unit composed of persons living together in the same dwelling, without regard to whether they are related to each other.

§ 71.006. Member of a Household.

"Member of a household" includes a person who previously lived in a household.

§ 71.007. Prosecuting Attorney.

"Prosecuting attorney" means the attorney, determined as provided in this title, who represents the state in a district or statutory county court in the county in which venue of the application for a protective order is proper.

Subtitle B. Protective Orders

Chapter

★★★

Chapter 81. General Provisions.

Editors' Note: *See Introductory Comment at beginning of Title 4, supra.*

§ 81.001. Entitlement to Protective Order.

A court shall render a protective order as provided by Section 85.001(b) if the court finds that family violence has occurred and is likely to occur in the future.

Comment

A 2001 amendment to the Code of Criminal Procedure provides for an application for a protective order by a victim of sexual assault without regard to the relationship between the applicant and the alleged offender. *See* Tex. Crim. Proc. Code Ann. ch. 7A, *infra. (B.B.)*

---

§ 81.002. No Fee for Applicant.

An applicant for a protective order or an attorney representing an applicant may not be assessed a fee, cost, charge, or expense by a district or county clerk of the court or a sheriff, constable, or other public official or employee in connection with the filing, serving, or entering of a protective order or for any other service described by this subsection, including:

(1) a fee to dismiss, modify, or withdraw a protective order;

(2) a fee for certifying copies;

(3) a fee for comparing copies to originals;

(4) a court reporter fee;

(5) a judicial fund fee;

(6) a fee for any other service related to a protective order; or

(7) a fee to transfer a protective order.

§ 81.003. Fees and Costs Paid by Party Found to Have Committed Family Violence.

(a) Except on a showing of good cause or of the indigence of a party found to have committed family violence, the court shall require in a protective order that the party against whom the order is rendered pay the $16 protective order fee, the standard fees charged by the clerk of the court in a general civil proceeding for the cost of serving the order, the costs of court, and all other fees, charges, or expenses incurred in connection with the protective order.

(b) The court may order a party against whom an agreed protective order is rendered under Section 85.005 to pay the fees required in Subsection (a).

§ 81.004. Contempt for Nonpayment of Fee.

(a) A party who is ordered to pay fees and costs and who does not pay before the date specified by the order may be punished for contempt of court as provided by Section 21.002, Government Code.

(b) If a date is not specified by the court under Subsection (a), payment of costs is required before the 60th day after the date the order was rendered.

§ 81.005. Attorney's Fees.

(a) The court may assess reasonable attorney's fees against the party found to have committed family violence or a party against whom an agreed protective order is rendered under Section 85.005 as compensation for the services of a private or prosecuting attorney or an attorney employed by the Department of Protective and Regulatory Services.

(b) In setting the amount of attorney's fees, the court shall consider the income and ability to pay of the person against whom the fee is assessed.

§ 81.006. Payment of Attorney's Fees.

The amount of fees collected under this chapter as compensation for the fees:

(1) of a private attorney shall be paid to the private attorney who may enforce the order for fees in the attorney's own name;

(2) of a prosecuting attorney shall be paid to the credit of the county fund from which the salaries of the employees of the prosecuting attorney are paid or supplemented; and

(3) of an attorney employed by the Department of Protective and Regulatory Services shall be deposited in the general revenue fund to the credit of the Department of Protective and Regulatory Services.

§ 81.007. Prosecuting Attorney.

(a) The county attorney or the criminal district attorney is the prosecuting attorney responsible for filing applications under this subtitle unless the district attorney assumes the responsibility by giving notice of that assumption to the county attorney.

(b) The prosecuting attorney responsible for filing an application under this subtitle shall provide notice of that responsibility to all law enforcement agencies in the jurisdiction of the prosecuting attorney.

(c) The prosecuting attorney shall comply with Article 5.06, Code of Criminal Procedure, in filing an application under this subtitle.

§ 81.0075. Representation by Prosecuting Attorney in Certain Subsequent Actions.

A prosecuting attorney who represents a party in a proceeding under this subtitle is not precluded from representing the Department of Protective and Regulatory Services in a subsequent action involving the party.

§ 81.008. Relief Cumulative.

Except as provided by this subtitle, the relief and remedies provided by this subtitle are cumulative of other relief and remedies provided by law.

Chapter 82. Applying For Protective Order.

Subchapter A. Application for Protective Order

Subchapter B. Pleadings by Respondent

Subchapter C. Notice of Application for Protective Order

Editors' Note: *See Introductory Comment at beginning of Title 4, supra.*

Texas Family Law Practice Manual

Chapter 14. Protective Orders

Subchapter A. Application for Protective Order

§ 82.001. Application.

A proceeding under this subtitle is begun by filing "An Application for a Protective Order" with the clerk of the court.

§ 82.002. Who May File Application.

(a) With regard to family violence under Section 71.004(1) or (2), an adult member of the family or household may file an application for a protective order to protect the applicant or any other member of the applicant's family or household

(b) With regard to family violence under Section 71.004(3), an application for a protective order to protect the applicant may be filed by an adult member of the dating relationship.

(c) Any adult may apply for a protective order to protect a child from family violence.

(d) In addition, an application may be filed for the protection of any person alleged to be a victim of family violence by:

(1) a prosecuting attorney; or

(2) the Department of Protective and Regulatory Services.

(e) The person alleged to be the victim of family violence in an application filed under Subsection (c) or (d) is considered to be the applicant for a protective order under this subtitle.

Comment

Beginning in 2001, an adult in a dating relationship may file an application for a protective order. Further, any adult may apply for a protective order for the benefit of a child, including a child who is a victim of dating violence. *(B.B.)*

Leading Case

B.C. v. Rhodes, 116 S.W.3d 878 (Tex. App.—Austin 2003, no pet.) (because "dating violence" is expressly defined as a type of "family violence," any adult may apply for a protective order to protect a child from dating violence)

§ 82.003. Venue.

An application may be filed in:

(1) the county in which the applicant resides; or

(2) the county in which the respondent resides.

Comment

The ability of the applicant to file in his or her own county of residence is a significant departure from TEX. PRAC. & REM. CODE ANN. § 15.002, but certainly not without precedent in the Texas Family Code.

Leading Case

Magill v. Sheffield, 612 S.W.2d 677 (Tex. Civ. App.—Dallas 1981, no writ) (venue for protective order governed by Title 4; continuing jurisdiction of SAPCR court not relevant)

§ 82.004. Contents of Application.

An application must state:

(1) the name and county of residence of each applicant;

(2) the name and county of residence of each individual alleged to have committed family violence;

(3) the relationships between the applicants and the individual alleged to have committed family violence; and

(4) a request for one or more protective orders.

§ 82.005. Application Filed During Suit for Dissolution of Marriage or Suit Affecting Parent–Child Relationship.

A person who wishes to apply for a protective order with respect to the person's spouse and who is a party to a suit for the dissolution of a marriage or a suit affecting the parent-child relationship that is pending in a court must file the application as required by Subchapter D, Chapter 85 *[Issuance of Protective Order]*.

§ 82.006. Application Filed After Dissolution of Marriage.

If an applicant for a protective order is a former spouse of the individual alleged to have committed family violence, the application must include:

(1) a copy of the decree dissolving the marriage; or

(2) a statement that the decree is unavailable to the applicant and that a copy of the decree will be filed with the court before the hearing on the application.

§ 82.007. Application Filed for Child Subject to Continuing Jurisdiction.

An application that requests a protective order for a child who is subject to the continuing exclusive jurisdiction of a court under Title 5 or alleges that a child who is subject to the continuing exclusive jurisdiction of a court under Title 5 has committed family violence must include:

(1) a copy of each court order affecting the conservatorship, support, and possession of or access to the child; or

(2) a statement that the orders affecting the child are unavailable to the applicant and that a copy of the orders will be filed with the court before the hearing on the application.

§ 82.008. Application Filed After Expiration of Former Protective Order.

(a) An application for a protective order that is filed after a previously rendered protective order has expired must include:

(1) a copy of the expired protective order attached to the application or, if a copy of the expired protective order is unavailable, a statement that the order is unavailable to the applicant and that a copy of the order will be filed with the court before the hearing on the application;

(2) a description of either:

(A) the violation of the expired protective order, if the application alleges that the respondent violated the expired protective order by committing an act prohibited by that order before the order expired; or

(B) the threatened harm that reasonably places the applicant in fear of imminent physical harm, bodily injury, assault, or sexual assault; and

(3) if a violation of the expired order is alleged, a statement that the violation of the expired order has not been grounds for any other order protecting the applicant that has been issued or requested under this subtitle.

(b) The procedural requirements for an original application for a protective order apply to a protective order requested under this section.

§ 82.0085. Application Filed Before Expiration of Previously Rendered Protective Order.

(a) If an application for a protective order alleges that an unexpired protective order applicable to the respondent is due to expire not later than the 30th day after the date the application was filed, the application for the subsequent protective order must include:

(1) a copy of the previously rendered protective order attached to the application or, if a copy of the previously rendered protective order is unavailable, a statement that

the order is unavailable to the applicant and that a copy of the order will be filed with the court before the hearing on the application; and

(2) a description of the threatened harm that reasonably places the applicant in fear of imminent physical harm, bodily injury, assault, or sexual assault.

(b) The procedural requirements for an original application for a protective order apply to a protective order requested under this section.

Comment

Prior to 1999 an applicant who continued to be endangered by the respondent was required to wait until the protective order expired before application could be made for a subsequent order. This section allows an applicant to file for a new protective order within 30 days prior to expiration so that a lapse in protection can be avoided. The subsequent application may be based on a reasonable fear of imminent physical harm rather than requiring proof of a violation of the original order. *(B.B.)*

---

§ 82.009. Application for Temporary ex Parte Order.

An application that requests the issuance of a temporary ex parte order under Chapter 83 *[Temporary Ex Parte Orders]* must:

(1) contain a detailed description of the facts and circumstances concerning the alleged family violence and the need for the immediate protective order; and

(2) be signed by each applicant under an oath that the facts and circumstances contained in the application are true to the best knowledge and belief of each applicant.

§ 82.010. Confidentiality of Application.

(a) This section applies only in a county with a population of 3.4 million or more.

(b) Except as otherwise provided by law, an application for a protective order is confidential, is excepted from required public disclosure under Chapter 552, Government Code, and may not be released to a person who is not a respondent to the application until after the date of service of notice of the application or the date of the hearing on the application, whichever date is sooner.

(c) Except as otherwise provided by law, an application requesting the issuance of a temporary ex parte order under Chapter 83 is confidential, is excepted from required public disclosure under Chapter 552, Government Code, and may not be released to a person who is not a respondent to the application until after the date that the court or law enforcement informs the respondent of the court's order.

Comment

For some time family law attorneys in Harris County have complained about a local practice that arguably created an unreasonable risk of harm for applicants for protective orders, to wit: notification of a respondent regarding the filing of an application for protective order before the respondent was served notice of the application as a method of solicitation for legal services by an enterprising attorney. Particularly in the protective order context, such early notification of the respondent might facilitate additional domestic violence.

For Harris County only, a delay in full public disclosure at the time of filing is statutorily mandated for three types of suits: divorce, SAPCRs, and protective order applications. If the Houston practice of early notice of filed family law litigation spreads to other counties, the limitation of the statute to Harris County may be expanded to apply statewide.

Subchapter B. Pleadings by Respondent

§ 82.021. Answer.

A respondent to an application for a protective order who is served with notice of an application for a protective order may file an answer at any time before the hearing. A respondent is not required to file an answer to the application.

§ 82.022. Request by Respondent for Protective Order.

To apply for a protective order, a respondent to an application for a protective order must file a separate application.

Subchapter C. Notice of Application for Protective Order

§ 82.041. Contents of Notice of Application.

(a) A notice of an application for a protective order must:

(1) be styled "The State of Texas";

(2) be signed by the clerk of the court under the court's seal;

(3) contain the name and location of the court;

(4) show the date the application was filed;

(5) show the date notice of the application for a protective order was issued;

(6) show the date, time, and place of the hearing;

(7) show the file number;

(8) show the name of each applicant and each person alleged to have committed family violence;

(9) be directed to each person alleged to have committed family violence;

(10) show the name and address of the attorney for the applicant or the mailing address of the applicant, if the applicant is not represented by an attorney; and

(11) contain the address of the clerk of the court.

(b) The notice of an application for a protective order must state: "An application for a protective order has been filed in the court stated in this notice alleging that you have committed family violence. You may employ an attorney to defend you against this allegation. You or your attorney may, but are not required to, file a written answer to the application. Any answer must be filed before the hearing on the application. If you receive this notice within 48 hours before the time set for the hearing, you may request the court to reschedule the hearing not later than 14 days after the date set for the hearing. If you do not attend the hearing, a default judgment may be taken and a protective order may be issued against you."

§ 82.042. Issuance of Notice of Application.

(a) On the filing of an application, the clerk of the court shall issue a notice of an application for a protective order and deliver the notice as directed by the applicant.

(b) On request by the applicant, the clerk of the court shall issue a separate or additional notice of an application for a protective order.

§ 82.043. Service of Notice of Application.

(a) Each respondent to an application for a protective order is entitled to service of notice of an application for a protective order.

(b) An applicant for a protective order shall furnish the clerk with a sufficient number of copies of the application for service on each respondent.

(c) Notice of an application for a protective order must be served in the same manner as citation under the Texas Rules of Civil Procedure, except that service by publication is not authorized.

(d) Service of notice of an application for a protective order is not required before the issuance of a temporary ex parte order under Chapter 83 *[Temporary Ex Parte Orders]*.

(e) The requirements of service of notice under this subchapter do not apply if the application is filed as a motion in a suit for dissolution of a marriage. Notice for the motion is given in the same manner as any other motion in a suit for dissolution of a marriage.

Chapter 83. Temporary Ex Parte Orders.

***Editors' Note:** See Introductory Comment at beginning of Title 4, supra.*

---

§ 83.001. Requirements for Temporary ex Parte Order.

(a) If the court finds from the information contained in an application for a protective order that there is a clear and present danger of family violence, the court, without further notice to the individual alleged to have committed family violence and without a hearing, may enter a temporary ex parte order for the protection of the applicant or any other member of the family or household of the applicant.

(b) In a temporary ex parte order, the court may direct a respondent to do or refrain from doing specified acts.

§ 83.002. Duration of Order; Extension.

(a) A temporary ex parte order is valid for the period specified in the order, not to exceed 20 days.

(b) On the request of an applicant or on the court's own motion, a temporary ex parte order may be extended for additional 20-day periods.

§ 83.003. Bond Not Required.

The court, at the court's discretion, may dispense with the necessity of a bond for a temporary ex parte order.

§ 83.004. Motion to Vacate.

Any individual affected by a temporary ex parte order may file a motion at any time to vacate the order. On the filing of the motion to vacate, the court shall set a date for hearing the motion as soon as possible.

§ 83.005. Conflicting Orders.

During the time the order is valid, a temporary ex parte order prevails over any other court order made under Title 5 to the extent of any conflict between the orders.

Comment

In 2003, the legislature addressed the confusion caused by the entry of a temporary ex parte order under Title 4 after the entry of a magistrate's order of emergency protection under Tex. Crim. Proc. Code. art. 17.292. That statute provides that the terms and conditions imposed by the magistrate's order prevail unless the court issuing the subsequent temporary ex parte order is informed of the existence of the magistrate's order, and makes a finding that the court is superseding the magistrate's order. The terms of a final protective order always prevail over a magistrate's order of emergency protection. *(B.B.)*

---

§ 83.006. Exclusion of Party From Residence.

(a) Subject to the limitations of Section 85.021(2), a person may only be excluded from the occupancy of the person's residence by a temporary ex parte order under this chapter if the applicant:

(1) files a sworn affidavit that provides a detailed description of the facts and circumstances requiring the exclusion of the person from the residence; and

(2) appears in person to testify at a temporary ex parte hearing to justify the issuance of the order without notice.

(b) Before the court may render a temporary ex parte order excluding a person from the person's residence, the court must find from the required affidavit and testimony that:

(1) the applicant requesting the excluding order either resides on the premises or has resided there within 30 days before the date the application was filed;

(2) the person to be excluded has within the 30 days before the date the application was filed committed family violence against a member of the household; and

(3) there is a clear and present danger that the person to be excluded is likely to commit family violence against a member of the household.

§ 83.007. Recess of Hearing To Contact Respondent.

The court may recess the hearing on a temporary ex parte order to contact the respondent by telephone and provide the respondent the opportunity to be present when the court resumes the hearing. Without regard to whether the respondent is able to be present at the hearing, the court shall resume the hearing before the end of the working day.

Chapter 84. Hearing.

Editors' Note: *See Introductory Comment at beginning of Title 4, supra.*

---

§ 84.001. Time Set for Hearing.

(a) On the filing of an application for a protective order, the court shall set a date and time for the hearing unless a later date is requested by the applicant. Except as provided by Section 84.002, the court may not set a date later than the 14th day after the date the application is filed.

(b) The court may not delay a hearing on an application in order to consolidate it with a hearing on a subsequently filed application.

§ 84.002. Extended Time for Hearing in District Court In Certain Counties.

(a) On the request of the prosecuting attorney in a county with a population of more than 1.5 million or in a county in a judicial district that is composed of more than one county, the district court shall set the hearing on a date and time not later than 20 days after the date the application is filed or 20 days after the date a request is made to reschedule a hearing under Section 84.003.

(b) The district court shall grant the request of the prosecuting attorney for an extended time in which to hold a hearing on a protective order either on a case-by-case basis or for all cases filed under this subtitle.

§ 84.003. Hearing Rescheduled for Failure of Service.

(a) If a hearing set under this chapter is not held because of the failure of a respondent to receive service of notice of an application for a protective order, the applicant may request the court to reschedule the hearing.

(b) Except as provided by Section 84.002, the date for a rescheduled hearing shall be not later than 14 days after the date the request is made.

§ 84.004. Hearing Rescheduled for Insufficient Notice.

(a) If a respondent receives service of notice of an application for a protective order within 48 hours before the time set for the hearing, on request by the respondent, the court shall reschedule the hearing for a date not later than 14 days after the date set for the hearing.

(b) The respondent is not entitled to additional service for a hearing rescheduled under this section.

§ 84.005. Legislative Continuance.

If a proceeding for which a legislative continuance is sought under Section 30.003, Civil Practice and Remedies Code, includes an application for a protective order, the continuance is discretionary with the court.

Chapter 85. Issuance of Protective Order.

Subchapter A. Findings and Orders

Subchapter B. Contents of Protective Order

Subchapter C. Delivery of Protective Order

Subchapter D. Relationship Between Protective Order and Suit for Dissolution of Marriage and Suit Affecting the Parent–Child Relationship.

Editors' Note: *See Introductory Comment at beginning of Title 4, supra.*

Comment

In 1999 the legislature significantly enhanced the effectiveness of protective orders by extending their duration from a maximum of one year to two years. In some cases respondents continued to harass, threaten and endanger applicants up to the one-year expiration date and beyond. Giving courts the discretion to enter orders up to two years allows more time for victims of the most severe abuse to relocate or establish support systems for their protection and for abusers to separate themselves psychologically from their victim. *(B.B.)*

Leading Cases

In re Compton, 117 S.W.3d 548 (Tex. App.—Texarkana 2003, no pet.) (transfer protective order action to court in which divorce or custody suit is pending discretionary; statutory scheme recognizes two actions might proceed simultaneously); accord Bilyeu v. Bilyeu, 86 S.W.3d 278 (Tex. App.—Austin 2002)

In re Marriage of Edwards, 79 S.W.3d 88 (Tex. App.—Texarkana 2002, no. pet.) (protective order against husband issued in conjunction with divorce must be in separate document)

Sisk v. State, 74 S.W.3d 893 (Tex. App.—Fort Worth 2002, no pet.) (defendant more than once intentionally followed alleged victim knowing she would regard his conduct as threatening bodily injury)

Ex parte Pool, 71 S.W.3d 462 (Tex. App.—Tyler 2002, no pet.) (defendant pled guilty to violation of a protective order to escape burglary charge stemming from the same incident—not double jeopardy)

Williams v. Williams, 19 S.W.3d 544 (Tex. App.—Fort Worth 2000, pet. denied) (denial of in court request for a jury trial at time of hearing not abuse of discretion—husband not entitled to jury determination of whether family violence occurred or likely to occur in future)

Poteet v. State, 957 S.W.2d 165 (Tex. App.—Fort Worth 1997, no writ) (respondent who appeared at hearing on protective order cannot collaterally attack its validity by alleging failure of service)

Collins v. State, 955 S.W.2d 464 (Tex. App.—Fort Worth 1997, no writ) (protective order criminally enforceable even if lack of details would not support judgment of contempt)

Subchapter A. Findings and Orders

§ 85.001. Required Findings and Orders.

(a) At the close of a hearing on an application for a protective order, the court shall find whether:

(1) family violence has occurred; and

(2) family violence is likely to occur in the future.

(b) If the court finds that family violence has occurred and that family violence is likely to occur in the future, the court:

(1) shall render a protective order as provided by Section 85.022 applying only to a person found to have committed family violence; and

(2) may render a protective order as provided by Section 85.021 applying to both parties that is in the best interest of the person protected by the order or member of the family or household of the person protected by the order.

(c) A protective order that requires the first applicant to do or refrain from doing an act under Section 85.022 shall include a finding that the first applicant has committed family violence and is likely to commit family violence in the future.

§ 85.002. Exception for Violation of Expired Protective Order.

If the court finds that a respondent violated a protective order by committing an act prohibited by the order as provided by Section 85.022, that the order was in effect at the time of the violation, and that the order has expired after the date that the violation occurred, the court, without the necessity of making the findings described by Section 85.001(a), shall render a protective order as provided by Section 85.022 applying only to the respondent and may render a protective order as provided by Section 85.021.

§ 85.003. Separate Protective Orders Required.

(a) A court that renders separate protective orders that apply to both parties and require both parties to do or refrain from doing acts under Section 85.022 shall render two distinct and separate protective orders in two separate documents that reflect the appropriate conditions for each party.

(b) A court that renders protective orders that apply to both parties and require both parties to do or refrain from doing acts under Section 85.022 shall render the protective orders in two separate documents. The court shall provide one of the documents to the applicant and the other document to the respondent.

(c) A court may not render one protective order under Section 85.022 that applies to both parties.

Leading Case

Moreno v. Moore, 897 S.W.2d 439 (Tex. App.—Corpus Christi 1995, no writ) (mutual protective order void; requirements of the source statute prior to the 1997 recodification not complied with)

§ 85.004. Protective Order in Suit for Dissolution of Marriage.

A protective order in a suit for dissolution of a marriage must be in a separate document entitled "PROTECTIVE ORDER."

§ 85.005. Agreed Order.

(a) To facilitate settlement, the parties to a proceeding may agree in writing to the terms of a protective order as provided by Section 85.021. An agreement under this subsection is subject to the approval of the court.

(b) To facilitate settlement, a respondent may agree in writing to the terms of a protective order as provided by Section 85.022, subject to the approval of the court. The court may not approve an agreement that requires the applicant to do or refrain from doing an act under Section 85.022.

(c) If the court approves an agreement between the parties, the court shall render an agreed protective order that is in the best interest of the applicant, the family or household, or a member of the family or household.

(d) An agreed protective order is not enforceable as a contract.

(e) An agreed protective order expires on the date the court order expires.

Leading Case

U.S. v. Spruill, 292 F.3d 207 (5th Cir. Tex. 2002) ("agreed" protective order issued without hearing failed to satisfy criminal statute's "after a hearing" requirement)

§ 85.006. Default Order.

(a) A court may render a protective order that is binding on a respondent who does not attend a hearing if the respondent received service of the application and notice of the hearing.

(b) If the court reschedules the hearing under Chapter 84 *[Hearing]*, a protective order may be rendered if the respondent does not attend the rescheduled hearing.

§ 85.007. Confidentiality of Certain Information.

(a) On request by a person protected by an order or member of the family or household of a person protected by an order, the court may exclude from a protective order the address and telephone number of:

(1) a person protected by the order, in which case the order shall state the county in which the person resides;

(2) the place of employment or business of a person protected by the order; or

(3) the child-care facility or school a child protected by the order attends or in which the child resides.

(b) On granting a request for confidentiality under this section, the court shall order the clerk to:

(1) strike the information described by Subsection (a) from the public records of the court; and

(2) maintain a confidential record of the information for use only by the court.

§ 85.008. [repealed]

§ 85.009. Order Valid Until Superseded.

A protective order rendered under this chapter is valid and enforceable pending further action by the court that rendered the order until the order is properly superseded by another court with jurisdiction over the order.

Subchapter B. Contents of Protective Order

§ 85.021. Requirements of Order Applying to Any Party.

In a protective order, the court may:

(1) prohibit a party from:

(A) removing a child who is a member of the family or household from:

(i) the possession of a person named in the order; or

(ii) the jurisdiction of the court; or

(B) transferring, encumbering, or otherwise disposing of property, other than in the ordinary course of business, that is mutually owned or leased by the parties;

(2) grant exclusive possession of a residence to a party and, if appropriate, direct one or more parties to vacate the residence if the residence:

(A) is jointly owned or leased by the party receiving exclusive possession and a party being denied possession;

(B) is owned or leased by the party retaining possession; or

(C) is owned or leased by the party being denied possession and that party has an obligation to support the party or a child of the party granted possession of the residence;

(3) provide for the possession of and access to a child of a party if the person receiving possession of or access to the child is a parent of the child;

(4) require the payment of support for a party or for a child of a party if the person required to make the payment has an obligation to support the other party or the child; or

(5) award to a party the use and possession of specified property that is community property or jointly owned or leased property.

§ 85.022. Requirements of Order Applying to Person Who Committed Family Violence.

(a) In a protective order, the court may order the person found to have committed family violence to:

(1) complete a battering intervention and prevention program as provided by Article 42.141, Code of Criminal Procedure, and that meets the guidelines adopted by the community justice assistance division of the Texas Department of Criminal Justice if a program is available;

(2) counsel with a social worker, family service agency, physician, psychologist, licensed therapist, or licensed professional counselor if a program under Subdivision (1) is not available; or

(3) perform acts specified by the court that the court determines are necessary or appropriate to prevent or reduce the likelihood of family violence.

(b) In a protective order, the court may prohibit the person found to have committed family violence from:

(1) committing family violence;

(2) communicating:

(A) directly with a person protected by an order or a member of the family or household of a person protected by an order, in a threatening or harassing manner;

(B) a threat through any person to a person protected by an order or a member of the family or household of a person protected by an order; and

(C) if the court finds good cause, in any manner with a person protected by an order or a member of the family or household of a person protected by an order, except through the party's attorney or a person appointed by the court;

(3) going to or near the residence or place of employment or business of a person protected by an order or a member of the family or household of a person protected by an order;

(4) going to or near the residence, child-care facility, or school a child protected under the order normally attends or in which the child normally resides; and

(5) engaging in conduct directed specifically toward a person who is a person protected by an order or a member of the family or household of a person protected by an order, including following the person, that is reasonably likely to harass, annoy, alarm, abuse, torment, or embarrass the person.

(6) possessing a firearm, unless the person is a peace officer, as defined by Section 1.07, Penal Code, actively engaged in employment as a sworn, full-time paid employee of a state agency or political subdivision.

(c) In an order under Subsection (b)(3) or (4), the court shall specifically describe each prohibited location and the minimum distances from the location, if any, that the party must maintain. This subsection does not apply to an order in which Section 85.007 applies.

(d) In a protective order, the court may suspend a license to carry a concealed handgun issued under Section 411.177, Government Code, that is held by a person found to have committed family violence.

(e) In this section, "firearm" has the meaning assigned by Section 46.01, Penal Code.

Comment

Subsection (b)(6) authorizes the court to prohibit a person from possessing a firearm for the duration of a protective order. This subsection conforms to 2001 amendments to the Penal Code that created an offense for possession of a firearm while subject to an active protective order. The same legislation made it illegal to possess a firearm for five years following conviction of a family violence assault punishable as a Class A misdemeanor, TEX. PENAL CODE ANN. § 46.04. This legislation was enacted to give local law enforcement agencies authority to take action against weapons declared illegal by federal law (albeit rarely enforced in that context), *see* 18 U.S.C.A. 922(g)(8), (9). The "official use exemption" for on-duty peace officers mirrors language in the corresponding federal statute. 18 U.S.C.A. 922(a). *(B.B.)*

§ 85.023. Effect on Property Rights.

A protective order or an agreement approved by the court under this subtitle does not affect the title to real property.

§ 85.024. Enforcement of Counseling Requirement.

(a) A person found to have engaged in family violence who is ordered to attend a program or counseling under Section 85.022(a)(1) or (2) shall file with the court an affidavit before the 60th day after the date the order was rendered stating either that the person has begun the program or counseling or that a program or counseling is not available within a reasonable distance from the person's residence. A person who files an affidavit that the person has begun the program or counseling shall file with the court before the date the protective order expires a statement that the person completed the program or counseling not later than the 30th day before the expiration date of the protective order. An affidavit under this subsection must be accompanied by a letter, notice, or certificate from the program or counselor that verifies the person's completion of the program or counseling. A person who fails to comply with this subsection may be punished for contempt of court under Section 21.002, Government Code.

(b) A protective order under Section 85.022 must specifically advise the person subject to the order of the requirement of this section and the possible punishment if the person fails to comply with the requirement.

§ 85.025. Duration of Protective Order.

(a) Except as provided by Subsection (b) or (c), an order under this subtitle is effective:

(1) for the period stated in the order, not to exceed two years; or

(2) if a period is not stated in the order, until the second anniversary of the date the order was issued.

(b) A person who is the subject of a protective order may file a motion not earlier than the first anniversary of the date on which the order was rendered requesting that the court review the protective order and determine whether there is a continuing need for the order. After a hearing on the motion, if the court finds there is a continuing need for the protective order, the protective order remains in effect until the date the order expires under this section. If the court finds there is no continuing need for the protective order, the court shall order that the protective order expires on a date set by the court.

(c) If a person who is the subject of a protective order is confined or imprisoned on the date the protective order would expire under Subsection (a), the period for which the order is effective is extended, and the order expires on the first anniversary of the date the person is released from confinement or imprisonment.

Leading Case

B.C. v. Rhodes, 116 S.W.3d 878 (Tex. App.—Austin 2003, no pet.) (protective orders generally in effect for the period stated, not to exceed two years or until modified by issuing court)

§ 85.026. Warning on Protective Order.

(a) Each protective order issued under this subtitle, including a temporary ex parte order, must contain the following prominently displayed statements in boldfaced type, capital letters, or underlined:

"A PERSON WHO VIOLATES THIS ORDER MAY BE PUNISHED FOR CONTEMPT OF COURT BY A FINE OF AS MUCH AS $500 OR BY CONFINEMENT IN JAIL FOR AS LONG AS SIX MONTHS, OR BOTH."

"NO PERSON, INCLUDING A PERSON WHO IS PROTECTED BY THIS ORDER, MAY GIVE PERMISSION TO ANYONE TO IGNORE OR VIOLATE ANY PROVISION OF THIS ORDER. DURING THE TIME IN WHICH THIS ORDER IS VALID, EVERY PROVISION OF THIS ORDER IS IN FULL FORCE AND EFFECT UNLESS A COURT CHANGES THE ORDER."

"IT IS UNLAWFUL FOR ANY PERSON, OTHER THAN A PEACE OFFICER, AS DEFINED BY SECTION 1.07, PENAL CODE, ACTIVELY ENGAGED IN EMPLOYMENT AS A SWORN, FULL-TIME PAID EMPLOYEE OF A STATE AGENCY OR POLITICAL SUBDIVISION, WHO IS SUBJECT TO A PROTECTIVE ORDER TO POSSESS A FIREARM OR AMMUNITION."

(b) Each protective order issued under this subtitle, except for a temporary ex parte order, must contain the following prominently displayed statement in boldfaced type, capital letters, or underlined:

"A VIOLATION OF THIS ORDER BY COMMISSION OF AN ACT PROHIBITED BY THE ORDER MAY BE PUNISHABLE BY A FINE OF AS MUCH AS $4,000 OR BY CONFINEMENT IN JAIL FOR AS LONG AS ONE YEAR, OR BOTH. AN ACT THAT RESULTS IN FAMILY VIOLENCE MAY BE PROSECUTED AS A SEPARATE MISDEMEANOR OR FELONY OFFENSE. IF THE ACT IS PROSECUTED AS A SEPARATE FELONY OFFENSE, IT IS PUNISHABLE BY CONFINEMENT IN PRISON FOR AT LEAST TWO YEARS."

(c) Each protective order issued under this subtitle, including a temporary ex parte order, must contain the following prominently displayed statement in boldfaced type, capital letters, or underlined:

"NO PERSON, INCLUDING A PERSON WHO IS PROTECTED BY THIS ORDER, MAY GIVE PERMISSION TO ANYONE TO IGNORE OR VIOLATE ANY PROVISION OF THIS ORDER. DURING THE TIME IN WHICH THIS ORDER IS VALID, EVERY PROVISION OF THIS ORDER IS IN FULL FORCE AND EFFECT UNLESS A COURT CHANGES THE ORDER."

Subchapter C. Delivery of Protective Order

§ 85.041. Delivery to Respondent.

(a) A protective order rendered under this subtitle shall be:

(1) delivered to the respondent as provided by Rule 21a, Texas Rules of Civil Procedure;

(2) served in the same manner as a writ of injunction; or

(3) served in open court at the close of the hearing as provided by this section.

(b) The court shall serve an order in open court to a respondent who is present at the hearing by giving to the respondent a copy of the order, reduced to writing and signed by the judge or master. A certified copy of the signed order shall be given to the applicant at the time the order is given to the respondent. If the applicant is not in court at the conclusion of the hearing, the clerk of the court shall mail a certified copy of the order to the applicant not later than the third business day after the date the hearing is concluded.

(c) If the order has not been reduced to writing, the court shall give notice orally to a respondent who is present at the hearing of the part of the order that contains prohibitions under Section 85.022 or any other part of the order that contains provisions necessary to prevent further family violence. The clerk of the court shall mail a copy of the order to the respondent and a certified copy of the order to the applicant not later than the third business day after the date the hearing is concluded.

(d) If the respondent is not present at the hearing and the order has been reduced to writing at the conclusion of the hearing, the clerk of the court shall immediately provide a certified copy of the order to the applicant and mail a copy of the order to the respondent not later than the third business day after the date the hearing is concluded.

§ 85.042. Delivery of Order to Other Persons.

(a) The clerk of the court issuing an original or modified protective order under this subtitle shall send a copy of the order, along with the information provided by the applicant or the applicant's attorney that is required under Section 411.042(b)(6), Government Code, to the chief of police of the municipality in which the person protected by the order resides, if the person resides in a municipality, or to the appropriate constable and the sheriff of the county in which the person resides, if the person does not reside in a municipality.

(b) If a protective order made under this chapter prohibits a respondent from going to or near a child-care facility or school, the clerk of the court shall send a copy of the order to the child-care facility or school.

(c) The clerk of a court that vacates an original or modified protective order under this subtitle shall notify the chief of police or constable and sheriff who received a copy of the original or modified order that the order is vacated.

(d) The applicant or the applicant's attorney shall provide to the clerk of the court:

(1) the name and address of each law enforcement agency, child-care facility, and school to which the clerk is required to mail a copy of the order under this section; and

(2) any other information required under Section 411.042(b)(6), Government Code.

(e) The clerk of the court issuing an original or modified protective order under Section 85.022 that suspends a license to carry a concealed handgun shall send a copy of the order to the appropriate division of the Department of Public Safety at its Austin headquarters. On receipt of the order suspending the license, the department shall:

(1) record the suspension of the license in the records of the department;

(2) report the suspension to local law enforcement agencies, as appropriate; and

(3) demand surrender of the suspended license from the license holder.

Subchapter D. Relationship Between Protective Order and Suit for Dissolution of Marriage and Suit Affecting the Parent–Child Relationship

Introductory Comment

This subchapter attempts to harmonize two conflicting policies: first, the need of a victim of family violence to have convenient access to court; and second, deciding which court order should prevail in the event of conflicting orders. As enacted, the protective order prevails even when there is a pending suit for dissolution of marriage or a SAPCR. The subchapter, however, does provide for a method to transfer protective orders back to the original court under § 85.064. The tension between these two conflicting legal policies will doubtless continue.

Leading Cases

In re M.R., 975 S.W.2d 51 (Tex. App.—San Antonio 1998, no writ) (trial court mandated to consider evidence of domestic violence in making conservatorship decision)

Ruiz v. Ruiz, 946 S.W.2d 124 (Tex. App.—Waco 1997, no writ) (protective order granted while divorce pending which did not dispose of all issues is non-appealable interlocutory order)

---

§ 85.061. Dismissal of Application Prohibited; Subsequently Filed Suit for Dissolution of Marriage or Suit Affecting Parent–Child Relationship.

If an application for a protective order is pending, a court may not dismiss the application or delay a hearing on the application on the grounds that a suit for dissolution of marriage or suit affecting the parent-child relationship is filed after the date the application was filed.

§ 85.062. Application Filed While Suit for Dissolution of Marriage or Suit Affecting Parent–Child Relationship Pending.

(a) If a suit for dissolution of a marriage or suit affecting the parent-child relationship is pending, a party to the suit may apply for a protective order against another party to the suit by filing an application:

(1) in the court in which the suit is pending; or

(2) in a court in the county in which the applicant resides if the applicant resides outside the jurisdiction of the court in which the suit is pending.

(b) An applicant subject to this section shall inform the clerk of the court that renders a protective order that a suit for dissolution of a marriage or a suit affecting the parent-child relationship is pending in which the applicant is party.

(c) If a final protective order is rendered by a court other than the court in which a suit for dissolution of a marriage or a suit affecting the parent-child relationship is pending, the clerk of the court that rendered the protective order shall:

(1) inform the clerk of the court in which the suit is pending that a final protective order has been rendered; and

(2) forward a copy of the final protective order to the court in which the suit is pending.

(d) A protective order rendered by a court in which an application is filed under Subsection (a)(2) is subject to transfer under Section 85.064.

§ 85.063. Application Filed After Final Order Rendered in Suit for Dissolution of Marriage or Suit Affecting Parent–Child Relationship.

(a) If a final order has been rendered in a suit for dissolution of marriage or suit affecting the parent-child relationship, an application for a protective order by a party to the suit against another party to the suit filed after the date the final order was rendered, and that is:

(1) filed in the county in which the final order was rendered, shall be filed in the court that rendered the final order; and

(2) filed in another county, shall be filed in a court having jurisdiction to render a protective order under this subtitle.

(b) A protective order rendered by a court in which an application is filed under Subsection (a)(2) is subject to transfer under Section 85.064.

Leading Case

Cooke v. Cooke, 65 S.W.3d 785 (Tex. App.—Dallas 2001, no pet.) (statutory requirements for filing protective order application in court that rendered divorce decree)

§ 85.064. Transfer of Protective Order.

(a) If a protective order was rendered before the filing of a suit for dissolution of marriage or suit affecting the parent-child relationship or while the suit is pending as provided by Section 85.062, the court that rendered the order may, on the motion of a party or on the court's own motion, transfer the protective order to the court having jurisdiction of the suit if the court makes the finding prescribed by Subsection (c).

(b) If a protective order that affects a party's right to possession of or access to a child is rendered after the date a final order was rendered in a suit affecting the parent-child relationship, on the motion of a party or on the court's own motion, the court may transfer the protective order to the court of continuing, exclusive jurisdiction if the court makes the finding prescribed by Subsection (c).

(c) A court may transfer a protective order under this section if the court finds that the transfer is:

(1) in the interest of justice; or

(2) for the safety or convenience of a party or a witness.

(d) The transfer of a protective order under this section shall be conducted according to the procedures provided by Section 155.207.

(e) Except as provided by Section 81.002, the fees or costs associated with the transfer of a protective order shall be paid by the movant.

§ 85.065. Effect of Transfer.

(a) A protective order transferred under Section 85.064 has the same effect as if the order remained in the court that rendered the order. The protective order may be enforced by the court that receives the order in the same manner as if the court originally rendered the order.

(b) A protective order that is transferred is enforceable by contempt or by any other means by which the court that rendered the order could enforce the order. The court that receives the protective order may punish a violation of the order regardless of whether the violation occurred before or after the date of the transfer.

(c) A protective order that is transferred is subject to modification by the court that receives the order to the same extent modification is permitted under Chapter 87 *[Modification of Protective Orders]* by a court that rendered the order.

Chapter 86. Law Enforcement Duties Relating to Protective Orders.

Editors' Note: *See Introductory Comment at beginning of Title 4, supra.*

---

§ 86.001. Adoption of Procedures by Law Enforcement Agency.

(a) To ensure that law enforcement officers responding to calls are aware of the existence and terms of protective orders issued under this subtitle, each law enforcement agency shall establish procedures in the agency to provide adequate information or access to information for law enforcement officers of the names of each person protected by an order issued under this subtitle and of each person against whom protective orders are directed.

(b) A law enforcement agency may enter a protective order in the agency's computer records of outstanding warrants as notice that the order has been issued and is currently in effect. On receipt of notification by a clerk of court that the court has vacated or dismissed an order, the law enforcement agency shall remove the order from the agency's computer record of outstanding warrants.

§ 86.0011. Duty To Enter Information Into Statewide Law Enforcement Information System.

On receipt of an original or modified protective order from the clerk of the issuing court, a law enforcement agency shall immediately, but not later than the 10th day after the date the order is received, enter the information required by Section 411.042(b)(6), Government Code, into the statewide law enforcement information system maintained by the Department of Public Safety.

Comment

In 1995 the legislature directed the Department of Public Safety to establish a centralized protective order database that would promote statewide and national enforcement of protective orders granted by Texas courts. The registry of protective orders is maintained as part of the Texas Crime Information Center (TCIC), and is linked with the F.B.I.'s National Crime Information Center (NCIC). The law enforcement agency with jurisdiction over the protected person is charged with the duty of registering the order with T.C.I.C. *See* § 85.042(a), *supra*.

More than five years after its creation, forty percent of counties in Texas had wholly failed to comply with the registration mandate (note that is about 100 counties). Because the original statute did not provide a timeframe for registration, many orders were not entered until weeks or even months after receipt. Thus, in 2001 the legislature sought to remedy this situation by describing with specificity the duty of a law enforcement agency in this stand alone section, requiring entry "immediately, but not later than the 10th day" after the order is received. As of June 1, 2003, eighteen months following enactment of this legislation, 28% of Texas counties still had failed to register any protective orders with TCIC. Enhancing Legal Safety: An Evaluation of the Texas Protective Order Database, Women's Advocacy Project, 2004. *(B.B.)*

---

§ 86.002. Duty To Provide Information to Firearms Dealers.

(a) On receipt of a request for a law enforcement information system record check of a prospective transferee by a licensed firearms dealer under the Brady Handgun Violence Prevention Act, 18 U.S.C. Section 922, the chief law enforcement officer shall determine whether the Department of Public Safety has in the department's law enforcement information system a record indicating the existence of an active protective order directed to the prospective transferee.

(b) If the department's law enforcement information system indicates the existence of an active protective order directed to the prospective transferee, the chief law enforcement officer shall immediately advise the dealer that the transfer is prohibited.

§ 86.003. Court Order for Law Enforcement Assistance Under Temporary Order.

On request by an applicant obtaining a temporary ex parte protective order that excludes the respondent from the respondent's residence, the court granting the temporary order shall render a written order to the sheriff, constable, or chief of police to provide a law enforcement officer from the department of the chief of police, constable, or sheriff to:

(1) accompany the applicant to the residence covered by the order;

(2) inform the respondent that the court has ordered that the respondent be excluded from the residence;

(3) protect the applicant while the applicant takes possession of the residence; and

(4) protect the applicant if the respondent refuses to vacate the residence while the applicant takes possession of the applicant's necessary personal property.

§ 86.004. Court Order for Law Enforcement Assistance Under Final Order.

On request by an applicant obtaining a final protective order that excludes the respondent from the respondent's residence, the court granting the final order shall render a written order to the sheriff, constable, or chief of police to provide a law enforcement officer from the department of the chief of police, constable, or sheriff to:

(1) accompany the applicant to the residence covered by the order;

(2) inform the respondent that the court has ordered that the respondent be excluded from the residence;

(3) protect the applicant while the applicant takes possession of the residence and the respondent takes possession of the respondent's necessary personal property; and

(4) if the respondent refuses to vacate the residence:

(A) remove the respondent from the residence; and

(B) arrest the respondent for violating the court order.

§ 86.005. Protective Order from Another Jurisdiction.

To ensure that law enforcement officers responding to calls are aware of the existence and terms of a protective order from another jurisdiction, each law enforcement agency shall establish procedures in the agency to provide adequate information or access to information for law enforcement officers regarding the name of each person protected by an order rendered in another jurisdiction and of each person against whom the protective order is directed.

Chapter 87. Modification of Protective Orders.

Editors' Note: *See Introductory Comment at beginning of Title 4, supra.*

Leading Cases

B.C. v. Rhodes, 116 S.W.3d 878 (Tex. App.—Austin 2003, no pet.) (trial court's jurisdiction during first year of protective order limited to modification)

Bilyeu v. Bilyeu, 86 S.W.3d 278 (Tex. App.—Austin 2002, no pet.) (transferred protective order subject to modification by court receiving order to same extent as original issuing court)

---

§ 87.001. Modification of Protective Order.

On the motion of any party, the court, after notice and hearing, may modify an existing protective order to:

(1) exclude any item included in the order; or

(2) include any item that could have been included in the order.

§ 87.002. Modification May Not Extend Duration of Order.

A protective order may not be modified to extend the period of the order's validity beyond the second anniversary of the date the original order was rendered or beyond the date the order expires under Section 85.025(c), whichever date occurs later.

§ 87.003. Notification of Motion To Modify.

Notice of a motion to modify a protective order is sufficient if delivery of the motion is attempted on the respondent at the respondent's last known address by registered or certified mail as provided by Rule 21a, Texas Rules of Civil Procedure.

§ 87.004. Change of Address or Telephone Number.

(a) If a protective order contains the address or telephone number of a person protected by the order, of the place of employment or business of the person, or of the child-care facility or school of a child protected by the order and that information is not confidential under Section 85.007, the person protected by the order may file a notification of change of address or telephone number with the court that rendered the order to modify the information contained in the order.

(b) The clerk of the court shall attach the notification of change to the protective order and shall deliver a copy of the notification to the respondent by registered or certified mail as provided by Rule 21a, Texas Rules of Civil Procedure.

(c) The filing of a notification of change of address or telephone number and the attachment of the notification to a protective order does not affect the validity of the order.

Chapter 88. Uniform Interstate Enforcement of Protective Orders Act.

Editors' Introductory Comment

The Violence Against Women Act, 18 U.S.C.A. § 2265 *et seq.*; 42 U.S.C.A. § 13931, *et seq.*, requires that states give full faith and credit to protective orders from other states. Because ordinarily full faith and credit is granted only to "final" orders, a number of states, including Texas, had held that protective orders were "temporary orders" not entitled to such respect. *See Normand v. Fox*, 940 S.W.2d 401 (Tex. App.—Waco 1997, no writ). The former version of this chapter was added in 1997 to conform Texas law to the federal mandate. In 2000 the National Conference of Commissioners on Uniform State Laws promulgated a new uniform act and urged enactment by all states to facilitate nationwide uniform treatment of protective orders across state lines. The Texas Legislature responded favorably to this recommendation in 2001 and replaced the 1997 statute with the Uniform Act. At the time of publication, four other states have adopted the Act—California, Idaho, Indiana, Montana—and legislation is currently pending in at least four additional states, as well as in the District of Columbia.

CLE/Leading Publications

Uniform Interstate Enforcement of Domestic–Violence Protection Orders Act (with Prefatory Note and Comments). Andrew Spiropoulos, 35 Fam. L. Q. 205 (Spring 2001)

COMMISSIONERS' OFFICIAL PREFATORY NOTE TO THE UNIFORM INTERSTATE ENFORCEMENT OF DOMESTIC–VIOLENCE PROTECTION ORDERS ACT

I. Introduction

The Uniform Interstate Enforcement of Domestic–Violence Protection Orders Act ("the Act") provides a uniform mechanism for the interstate enforcement of domestic-violence protective orders. The need for such a mechanism is founded on the widespread understanding that states have not consistently or effectively enforced domestic-violence protective orders issued by other states. The Act, therefore, has two main purposes. First, it defines the meaning of interstate enforcement in the context of the enforcement of domestic-violence protective orders. Second, it establishes uniform procedures for the effective interstate enforcement of domestic-violence protective orders.

Many states, recognizing the severity of the problems regarding the interstate enforcement of domestic-violence protective orders, have enacted legislation requiring their courts to enforce the domestic-violence protective orders of other states. Many of these statutes, however, while mandating enforcement, are either silent or ambiguous regarding several important questions that must be answered in order to establish an effective system for the interstate enforcement of these orders. The Congress of the United States, as well, has enacted legislation requiring interstate enforcement of domestic-violence protective orders, but this legislation is also silent or ambiguous regarding these important questions.

First, many of the existing statutes do not sufficiently explain the core requirements of interstate enforcement of protective orders. For example, many of the state statutes, and the federal legislation, require courts and law enforcement officers to enforce the orders of other states as if they were the protective orders of the enforcing state. This provision, however, does not answer the question of whether state courts and officers are required to enforce provisions of foreign protective orders that would not be authorized by the law of the enforcing state. This question, and others, must be answered if there is to be effective uniform enforcement of protective orders. Second, many of the existing statutes do not specify the procedures state courts and officers must follow in enforcing foreign protective orders. For example, many of the statutes are silent on whether individuals seeking the enforcement of a protective order must register or file the order with the enforcing state before action can be taken on their behalf. This Act resolves the issues left unanswered in existing legislation and provides a uniform scheme for enforcement of these orders.

II. The Requirements of Interstate Enforcement

The Act first defines what it means to accord interstate enforcement to domestic-violence protective orders. These orders must be enforced if the issuing tribunals had jurisdiction over both the parties and the matter under the law of the issuing state and if the individuals against whom the order is enforced were given reasonable notice and had an opportunity to be heard consistent with the right to due process. If the order was obtained ex parte, this notice and opportunity to be heard must be provided within a reasonable time.

The Act makes it clear that all the terms of the orders of the issuing states must be enforced, including terms that provide relief that the courts of the enforcing state would lack power to provide. The Act also provides that all protective orders that both recognize the standing of the protected individual to seek enforcement of the order and satisfy the criteria of validity established by the Act must be enforced. In addition, provisions of protective orders governing custody and visitation matters are enforceable under this Act. Terms that concern support are not. The terms of mutual protective orders which favor of a respondent are also not enforceable if they were not issued in response to a written pleading filed by the respondent and if the issuing tribunal did not make specific findings in favor of the respondent.

> ***Editors' Note:*** *The Texas enactment allows for enforcement of support.*

III. Enforcement Procedures

The Act also provides uniform procedures for the interstate enforcement of domestic-violence protective orders. The Act envisions that the enforcement of foreign protective orders will require law enforcement officers of enforcing states to rely on probable cause judgments that a valid order exists and has been violated. The Act, however, provides that if a protected individual can provide direct proof of the existence of a facially valid order, by, for example, presenting a paper copy or through an electronic registry, probable cause is conclusively established. If no such proof is forthcoming, the Act provides that if officers, relying on the totality of the circumstances, determine that there is probable cause to believe that a valid protective order exists and has been violated, the order will be enforced. The individual against whom the order is enforced will have sufficient opportunity to demonstrate that the order is invalid when the case is brought before the enforcing tribunal. Law enforcement officers, as well as other government agents, will be encouraged to rely on probable cause judgments by the Act's inclusion of an immunity provision, protecting agents of the government acting in good faith.

The Act does not require individuals seeking the enforcement of a protective order to register or file the order with the enforcing state. The Act does, however, include an optional registration process. This process permits individuals to register a protective order by presenting a copy of the order to a responsible state agency or any state officer or agency. The copy presented must be certified by the issuing state. The purpose of these procedures is to make it as easy as possible for the protected individual to register the protective order and thus facilitate its enforcement.

***Editors' Note:** Texas has traditionally used the term "protective order," not "protection order" as is used in federal law and in this uniform act. The drafters decided to retain the term "protective order" except in the title of the Act. The editors have taken the liberty of making a similar change in the official commentary for ease of reading. The Texas enactment departs from the uniform version in a few sections; the commentary has been edited to reflect those changes. The full act, with unedited commentary, is found at the National Conference of Commissioners on Uniform State Laws' website: www.nccusl.org.*

§ 88.001. Short Title.

This chapter may be cited as the Uniform Interstate Enforcement of Domestic Violence Protection Orders Act.

§ 88.002. Definitions.

In this chapter:

(1) "Foreign protective order" means a protective order issued by a tribunal of another state.

(2) "Issuing state" means the state in which a tribunal issues a protective order.

(3) "Mutual foreign protective order" means a foreign protective order that includes provisions issued in favor of both the protected individual seeking enforcement of the order and the respondent.

(4) "Protected individual" means an individual protected by a protective order.

(5) "Protective order" means an injunction or other order, issued by a tribunal under the domestic violence or family violence laws or another law of the issuing state, to prevent an individual from engaging in violent or threatening acts against, harassing, contacting or communicating with, or being in physical proximity to another individual.

(6) "Respondent" means the individual against whom enforcement of a protective order is sought.

(7) "State" means a state of the United States, the District of Columbia, the Commonwealth of Puerto Rico, the United States Virgin Islands, or a territory or insular possession subject to the jurisdiction of the United States. The term includes

a military tribunal of the United States, an Indian tribe or band, and an Alaskan native village that has jurisdiction to issue protective orders.

(8) "Tribunal" means a court, agency, or other entity authorized by law to issue or modify a protective order.

Commissioners' Comment to Section 88.002

The term "protective order" includes those orders issued under the domestic-violence, family-violence laws or other law of the issuing state. The scope of enforceable protective orders is limited by the provisions of Section 88.003 (d). In addition, the term "protective order" includes an order modifying a previous order. Thus, a modified order, is enforceable, under the Act, in the same manner as a newly issued order. The terms "protected individual" and "respondent" refer to the relief sought by the parties in the action brought in the enforcing state. The Act recognizes that neither the protected individual nor the respondent may have been a named party in the action brought in the issuing state; the Act applies to individuals meeting the definition of protected individual or respondent whether they were named in the caption or the body of the protective order. The Act also recognizes that the parties may have been called by different terms, *e.g.* plaintiff, defendant, petitioner, in the issuing state.

The term "mutual protective orders" refers to protective orders in which an issuing state includes provisions protecting both parties. Enforcement of these foreign protective orders is governed by Section 88.003(g).

The Violence Against Women Act, 18 U.S.C.A. Sec. 2265, requires that states accord full faith and credit to tribal protective orders. Like state orders, tribal orders must satisfy the criteria for validity, as defined in Section 88.003 (e), in order to qualify for interstate enforcement across state or tribal lines.

The Act uses the term "tribunal", rather than "court", in order to accommodate states that rely upon administrative or other entities to issue or modify protective orders.

§ 88.003. Judicial Enforcement of Order.

(a) A tribunal of this state shall enforce the terms of a foreign protective order, including a term that provides relief that a tribunal of this state would not have power to provide but for this section. The tribunal shall enforce the order regardless of whether the order was obtained by independent action or in another proceeding, if the order is an order issued in response to a complaint, petition, or motion filed by or on behalf of an individual seeking protection. In a proceeding to enforce a foreign protective order, the tribunal shall follow the procedures of this state for the enforcement of protective orders.

(b) A tribunal of this state shall enforce the provisions of the foreign protective order that govern the possession of and access to a child if the provisions were issued in accordance with the jurisdictional requirements governing the issuance of possession and access orders in the issuing state.

(c) A tribunal of this state may enforce a provision of the foreign protective order relating to child support if the order was issued in accordance with the jurisdictional requirements of Chapter 159 *[UIFSA]* and the federal Full Faith and Credit for Child Support Orders Act, 28 U.S.C. Section 1738B, as amended.

(d) A foreign protective order is valid if the order:

(1) names the protected individual and the respondent;

(2) is currently in effect;

(3) was rendered by a tribunal that had jurisdiction over the parties and the subject matter under the law of the issuing state; and

(4) was rendered after the respondent was given reasonable notice and an opportunity to be heard consistent with the right to due process, either:

(A) before the tribunal issued the order; or

(B) in the case of an ex parte order, within a reasonable time after the order was rendered.

(e) A protected individual seeking enforcement of a foreign protective order establishes a prima facie case for its validity by presenting an order that is valid on its face.

(f) It is an affirmative defense in an action seeking enforcement of a foreign protective order that the order does not meet the requirements for a valid order under Subsection (d).

(g) A tribunal of this state may enforce the provisions of a mutual foreign protective order that favor a respondent only if:

(1) the respondent filed a written pleading seeking a protective order from the tribunal of the issuing state; and

(2) the tribunal of the issuing state made specific findings in favor of the respondent.

Commissioners' Comment to Section 88.003

Subsection (a) implements the core purpose of the Act. Effective interstate enforcement of protective orders is founded on the principle that enforcing states must enforce all the substantive terms of a foreign protective order, including terms that provide relief that a tribunal of the enforcing state would lack power to provide, but for this Act. This provision means that the tribunals of enforcing states must enforce the specific terms of a foreign protective order even if their state law would not allow the relief in question. For example, if the law of the issuing state provides that a court may issue a protective order including terms that concern the possession of property, *e.g.*, an order giving the protected individual possession of the family automobile, but the law of the enforcing state does not authorize such substantive relief, the tribunal of the enforcing state must enforce the order in its entirety. To give another example, if the law of the issuing state allows protective orders to remain effective for a longer period than is allowed by the enforcing state, the tribunal of the enforcing state should enforce the order for the time specified in the order of the issuing state. In a proceeding to enforce the substantive terms of the foreign protective order, however, the court of the enforcing state shall follow its own procedures.

Subsection (a) provides that any person authorized by the law of the enforcing state to seek enforcement of a protective order may seek enforcement of valid foreign protective order in the enforcing state. This provision recognizes that states frequently authorize public agencies and officers, such as a local prosecutor, to bring enforcement actions on behalf of a protected individual. The Act, however, in recognizing the importance of these agencies and officers, should not be interpreted to mean that states, and their agencies and officers, are required to bring these actions when possible. This subsection further provides that only protective orders that were issued in response to a complaint, petition, or motion filed by or on behalf of an individual seeking protection can be enforced under this Act; orders issued sua sponte are not enforceable under this Act.

Subsections (b) and (c) further define the scope of enforceable protective orders under the Act. Subsection (b) provides that the provisions of protective orders that govern custody and visitation rights must be enforced. Enforcement of these provisions is essential because, first, the award of custody is often essential for the protection of children from potential violence, and, second, because the protected individual will not seek a safe distance from a threatening individual if custody of a child is jeopardized. These provisions may only be enforced, however, if they were issued in accordance with the jurisdictional requirements for the issuance of all custody and visitation orders, contained, depending on the state, either in the Uniform Child Custody Jurisdiction Act or the Uniform Child Custody Jurisdiction and Enforcement Act, and the federal Parental Kidnapping Prevention Act. This Act, however, does not provide for the enforcement of orders governing custody and visitation rights that are not included in a protective order.

Under subsection (c) support orders are enforceable if issued consistent with the jurisdictional standards of Uniform Interstate Family Support Act and federal law.

Subsection (d) requires that, to be valid for the purpose of enforcement under this Act, a foreign protective order must be "currently in effect." This provision includes orders that have been modified; the modified order is the one currently in effect. While the Act requires that a foreign protective order, to be valid, identify the protected individual and respondent, merely technical errors, such as an incorrect spelling of a name, should not preclude enforcement of the order. The question of the validity of an order is a question of law for the court of the enforcing state. Once an order is adjudged valid, the proceeding shall be governed by the established procedures of the enforcing state.

The respondent's constitutional right to due process is protected by the opportunity to raise defenses in the enforcement proceeding, as provided in subsection (f). If, for example, the respondent was not provided with reasonable notice and opportunity to be heard by the tribunal of the state issuing the protective order, the enforcing tribunal may not enforce the order. Thus, the interstate enforcement of a valid foreign protective order, even without a prior hearing, does not deprive the respondent of any rights to due process because the respondent was provided with reasonable notice and opportunity to be heard when the order was issued.

The enforcement mechanisms established by the Act do not require the presentation by the protected individual of an authenticated copy of the foreign protective order. While states, as required by the Constitution and federal statutes that articulate authentication requirements, including 28 U.S.C.A. Sec. 1738, must accord properly authenticated foreign judgments full faith and credit enforcement, they may choose to enforce foreign orders they would not be required to enforce under the provisions of the Constitution or other federal law. By adopting this Act, states have chosen to give that extra measure of full faith and credit to foreign protective orders.

In addition, in recent years, particularly with regard to the enforcement of domestic relations orders, the federal government has employed the power granted to it by Article IV, Sec. 1 of the Constitution of the United States to prescribe the manner in which states give full faith and credit to the acts, records, and proceedings of other states to require states to enforce foreign orders in circumstances in which states have traditionally been reluctant to render such enforcement. For example, the federal Parental Kidnapping Prevention Act, 28 U.S.C.A. Sec. 1738A, requires greater interstate enforcement of child custody orders and the federal Personal Responsibility and Work Opportunity Reconciliation Act, 110 Stat. 2105 (1996), requires that states, in order to facilitate the enforcement of support orders, adopt the provisions of the Uniform Interstate Family Support Act. The Violence Against Women Act extends the principle of these laws to the subject of the interstate enforcement of domestic-violence protective orders.

Subsection (g), adapted from the federal Violence Against Women Act, 18 U.S.C.A. Sec. 2265(c), addresses the enforcement of mutual foreign protective orders, which contain provisions protecting both the protected individual and the respondent. Provisions of a mutual foreign protective order issued in favor of the respondent will not be enforced without proof that the respondent filed a written pleading seeking a protective order. If a respondent can prove that he or she made a specific request for relief and that the issuing tribunal made specific findings that the respondent was entitled to the requested relief, the protective orders will be enforced against the protected individual.

In order to facilitate the interstate enforcement of foreign protective orders, states should strongly consider requiring tribunals that issue protective orders to state clearly that these orders are entitled to interstate enforcement under both federal and state law. Such enforcement would also be greatly facilitated if issuing states provided each protected individual with a certified copy of the protective order. In addition, states should consider adopting a standard certification or confirmation form stating the protective order issued by their tribunals satisfies the criteria of validity articulated in subsection (d), thus qualifying the protective order for interstate enforcement. Use of the following certification form is recommended.

(Name),	)	**IN THE COURT OF**
Plaintiff	)	**(County/Judicial District)**
	)	**(State/Territory)**
vs.	)	**CIVIL ACTION–LAW**
	)	**PROTECTIVE/RESTRAINING**
(Name),	)	**ORDER**
Defendant	)	**Docket No.__________, 200__**

Certification of Protective/Restraining Order

It is hereby certified that the attached is a true and correct copy of the order entered in the above-captioned action on ______(date) and that the original of the attached order was duly executed by the judicial authority whose signature appears thereon. The order expires on ______ (date).

The order is: [ ] a civil protective/restraining order

OR [ ] a criminal protective/restraining order, that recognizes the standing of the plaintiff to seek enforcement of the order

It is further certified that:

(a) the issuing court determined that it had jurisdiction over the parties and the subject matter under the laws of ____________________ (state or Indian tribe).

(b) the defendant was given reasonable notice and had opportunity to be heard before this order was issued; or if the order was issued ex parte, the defendant was given notice and had opportunity to be heard after the order was issued, consistent with the rights of the defendant to due process.

(c) the order was otherwise issued in accordance with the requirements of the Uniform Interstate Enforcement of Domestic–Violence Protection Orders Act, and the Violence Against Women Act, 18 U.S.C. § 2265.

For custody and visitation orders:

The order was issued in accordance with the requirements of the Uniform Child Custody Jurisdiction Act or the Uniform Child Custody Jurisdiction and Enforcement Act of this state/territory and is consistent with the provisions of the Parental Kidnapping Prevention Act. 28 U.S.C. § 1738A.

The attached order shall be presumed to be valid and enforceable in this and other jurisdictions.

Signature of Clerk of Court or other authorized official:____________________

Judicial District:____________________

Address:____________________ Phone:____________________

Fax:____________________ Date:____________________

Seal:

§ 88.004. Nonjudicial Enforcement of Order.

(a) A law enforcement officer of this state, on determining that there is probable cause to believe that a valid foreign protective order exists and that the order has been violated, shall enforce the foreign protective order as if it were an order of a tribunal of this state. A law enforcement officer has probable cause to believe that a foreign protective order exists if the protected individual presents a foreign protective order that identifies both the protected individual and the respondent and on its face, is currently in effect.

(b) For the purposes of this section, a foreign protective order may be inscribed on a tangible medium or may be stored in an electronic or other medium if it is retrievable in a perceivable form. Presentation of a certified copy of a protective order is not required for enforcement.

(c) If a protected individual does not present a foreign protective order, a law enforcement officer may determine that there is probable cause to believe that a valid foreign protective order exists by relying on any relevant information.

(d) A law enforcement officer of this state who determines that an otherwise valid foreign protective order cannot be enforced because the respondent has not been notified or served with the order shall inform the respondent of the order and make a reasonable effort to serve the order on the respondent. After informing the respondent and attempting to serve the order, the officer shall allow the respondent a reasonable opportunity to comply with the order before enforcing the order.

(e) The registration or filing of an order in this state is not required for the enforcement of a valid foreign protective order under this chapter.

Commissioners' Comment to Section 88.004

The enforcement procedures in subsections (a) and (b) rely on the sound exercise of the judgment of law enforcement officers to determine whether there exists probable cause to believe that a valid foreign protective order exists and has been violated. These procedures anticipate that there will be many instances in which the protected individual does not have, or cannot, under the circumstances, produce a paper copy of the foreign protective order. Subsections (a) and (b) establish a per se rule for determining probable cause of the existence of an order. If the protected individual presents, whether by providing a paper copy (which need not be certified) of a protective order or through an electronic medium, such as access to a state registry of orders, proof of a facially valid order, the order should be enforced. In determining whether there is proof of a facially valid order, a law enforcement officer, where possible, may, and, indeed, should, search, using an electronic or other medium, a state or federal registry of orders.

Subsection (c) concerns the circumstance in which the protected individual cannot present direct proof of the protective order. In this situation, law enforcement officers are expected to obtain information from all available sources, including interviewing the parties and contacting other law enforcement agencies, to determine whether there is a valid protective order in effect. If the officer finds, after considering the totality of the circumstances, that there is probable cause to believe that a valid foreign protective order exists and has been violated, he or she should enforce the order. This probable cause determination must meet the constitutional standards for determining probable cause. If it is later determined that no such order was in place or the order was otherwise unenforceable, law enforcement agencies, officers, or other state officials will be protected by the immunity provision of Section 88.006 for actions taken in good faith.

Subsection (d) provides that if a law enforcement officer discovers in the course of a probable cause investigation that the respondent has not been notified of the issuance of or served with an otherwise valid foreign protective order, the officer must then inform the respondent of the terms and conditions of the protective order and make a reasonable effort to serve the order upon the respondent. The respondent must be allowed a reasonable opportunity to comply with the order before the order is enforced.

Subsection (e) makes clear that, if a state either adopts its own process for the registration or filing of foreign protective orders or adopts the process provided in Section 5, the state shall not require the registration or filing of a foreign protective order for enforcement.

---

§ 88.005. Registration of Order.

(a) An individual may register a foreign protective order in this state. To register a foreign protective order, an individual shall:

(1) present a certified copy of the order to a sheriff, constable, or chief of police responsible for the registration of orders in the local computer records and in the statewide law enforcement system maintained by the Texas Department of Public Safety; or

(2) present a certified copy of the order to the Department of Public Safety and request that the order be registered in the statewide law enforcement system maintained by the Department of Public Safety.

(b) On receipt of a foreign protective order, the agency responsible for the registration of protective orders shall register the order in accordance with this section and furnish to the individual registering the order a certified copy of the registered order.

(c) The agency responsible for the registration of protective orders shall register a foreign protective order on presentation of a copy of a protective order that has been certified by the issuing state. A registered foreign protective order that is inaccurate or not currently in effect shall be corrected or removed from the registry in accordance with the law of this state.

(d) An individual registering a foreign protective order shall file an affidavit made by the protected individual that, to the best of the protected individual's knowledge, the order is in effect.

(e) A foreign protective order registered under this section may be entered in any existing state or federal registry of protective orders, in accordance with state or federal law.

(f) A fee may not be charged for the registration of a foreign protective order.

Commissioners' Comment to Section 88.005

While a protected individual is not required to register a valid foreign protective order in order for it be enforced, it is highly desirable that states provide an optional registration process. A registration system supplies law enforcement officers and agencies more accurate information, more quickly, about both the existence and status of foreign protective orders and their terms and conditions. An enforcing state may facilitate the collection and dissemination of this information either by establishing a central registry or by providing a process by which information regarding registered orders is distributed to law enforcement officers and agencies across the state.

While the management of state registries is purely governed by state law, in implementing a registration system, however, enforcing states should strongly consider keeping these protective orders under seal. The purpose of more effectively protecting victims of domestic violence will be undermined if respondents can use the process of registration to locate the very people who are trying to escape from them. In addition, the federal Violence Against Women Act, as amended by the Violence Against Women Act of 2000 (Pub. L No.106–386), prohibits states that provide for the registration or filing of orders from, without the permission of the individual registering or filing the order, notifying other states of the registration or filing of the order.

Subsection (a) provides that any person, including a potential respondent, may register foreign protective orders. This reason behind this provision is to ensure that all parties have the opportunity to provide relevant information to the state. Orders, for example, may be modified with custody arrangements. Subsection (a) also requires that a person seeking to register a foreign protective order must present a certified copy of that order. The copy must be a writing on paper, thus exempting this requirement from the provisions of the Uniform Electronic Transactions Act.

Subsection (c) provides that if the state has registered orders that are no longer in effect or are inaccurate, these orders must be removed from the registry or, in the case of error, corrected. The precise method of how state and federal registries manage their registries, including the deletion of inaccurate information, is governed by each government's law regarding the management of records.

If an order is registered under this Section, the individual who registered the order is expected to inform the enforcing state of any modifications to the registered protective order.

§ 88.006. Immunity.

A state or local governmental agency, law enforcement officer, prosecuting attorney, clerk of court, or any state or local governmental official acting in an official capacity is immune from civil and criminal liability for an act or omission arising from the registration or enforcement of a foreign protective order or the detention or arrest of a person alleged to have violated a foreign protective order if the act or omission was done in good faith in an effort to comply with this chapter.

Commissioners' Comment to Section 88.006

This immunity provision includes States, state and local governmental agencies, and all state and local government officials acting in their official capacity in order to prevent those seeking the imposition of criminal and civil liability for acts or omissions done in good faith in an effort to comply with the provisions of this Act from circumventing this immunity provision. The necessity for a generous immunity provision for the enforcement of foreign protection orders does not preclude state and local governments from using personnel and other internal sanctions in order to prevent and punish actions that, in the absence of this immunity provision, would have rendered the government agencies, officers, or officials civilly or criminally liable.

§ 88.007. Other Remedies.

A protected individual who pursues a remedy under this chapter is not precluded from pursuing other legal or equitable remedies against the respondent.

Commissioners' Comment to Section 88.007

This section clarifies that the protective orders enforced under the Act are not the only means of protection available to victims of domestic violence. Other legal remedies, such as tort actions and criminal prosecution, are left undisturbed by this Act.

§ 88.008. Uniformity of Application and Construction.

In applying and construing this chapter, consideration shall be given to the need to promote uniformity of the law with respect to its subject matter among the states that enact the Uniform Interstate Enforcement of Domestic Violence Protection Orders Act.

Editors' Note: The Official Commentary regarding application of the Act to foreign protective orders issued before the effective date states:

"The provisions of this Act apply to all requests for enforcement of foreign protective orders, both continuing and newly filed, made on or after its effective date. In addition, the provisions of this Act apply to the enforcement of foreign protective orders issued before the effective date of this Act and to requests for enforcement of foreign protective orders in which the alleged violation took place before the effective date of the Act. Application of the Act in these circumstances does not constitute an unconstitutional ex post facto law because, under the principles of the Full Faith and Credit Clause of the Constitution of the United States, valid foreign protective orders should have always been entitled to interstate enforcement. As stated by the Supreme Court of the United States in *Weaver v. Graham*, 450 U.S. 24, 28 (1981), an ex post facto law is a law that imposes a punishment for an act that was not punishable at the time the act was committed or imposes additional punishment to that originally prescribed. Enforcement, under the Act, of a preexisting order does not punish acts that were not punishable at the time the acts were committed; the order, as soon as it was entered, subjected the respondent to punishment upon its violation. The laws of the enforcing states also prescribed, before enforcement under this Act, the amount of punishment imposed for the violation of protective orders. The Act, therefore, does not effect a substantive change in the law regarding the enforcement of foreign protective orders; respondents should have always been aware that protective orders issued by states are subject to interstate enforcement. This Act only ensures that states carry out their constitutional responsibility to enforce these orders."

Subtitle C. Reporting Family Violence

★★★

Chapter 91. Reporting Family Violence.

---

§ 91.001. Definitions.

In this subtitle:

(1) "Family violence" has the meaning assigned by Section 71.004.

(2) "Medical professional" means a licensed doctor, nurse, physician assistant, or emergency medical technician.

§ 91.002. Reporting by Witnesses Encouraged.

A person who witnesses family violence is encouraged to report the family violence to a local law enforcement agency.

§ 91.003. Information Provided by Medical Professionals.

A medical professional who treats a person for injuries that the medical professional has reason to believe were caused by family violence shall:

(1) immediately provide the person with information regarding the nearest family violence shelter center;

(2) document in the person's medical file:

(A) the fact that the person has received the information provided under Subdivision (1); and

(B) the reasons for the medical professional's belief that the person's injuries were caused by family violence; and

(3) give the person a written notice in substantially the following form, completed with the required information, in both English and Spanish:

"It is a crime for any person to cause you any physical injury or harm even if that person is a member or former member of your family or household.

"NOTICE TO ADULT VICTIMS OF FAMILY VIOLENCE

"It is a crime for any person to cause you any physical injury or harm even if that person is a member or former member of your family or household.

"You may report family violence to a law enforcement officer by calling the following telephone numbers: ______________________________.

"If you, your child, or any other household resident has been injured or if you feel you are going to be in danger after a law enforcement officer investigating family violence leaves your residence or at a later time, you have the right to:

"Ask the local prosecutor to file a criminal complaint against the person committing family violence; and

"Apply to a court for an order to protect you. You may want to consult with a legal aid office, a prosecuting attorney, or a private attorney. A court can enter an order that:

"(1) prohibits the abuser from committing further acts of violence;

"(2) prohibits the abuser from threatening, harassing, or contacting you at home;

"(3) directs the abuser to leave your household; and

"(4) establishes temporary custody of the children or any property.

"A VIOLATION OF CERTAIN PROVISIONS OF COURT-ORDERED PROTECTION MAY BE A FELONY.

"CALL THE FOLLOWING VIOLENCE SHELTERS OR SOCIAL ORGANIZATIONS IF YOU NEED PROTECTION: ____________________________."

Comment

Despite widespread confusion, this section only mandates that medical professionals provide patients whom they believe to have been victims of family violence with information regarding the local shelter and document their injuries. Medical professionals are not required to report family violence injuries to law enforcement, unless the victim is a child (Tex. Fam. Code Ann. § 261.101), elderly or disabled person (Tex. Hum. Res. Code Ann. § 48.051(d)) or the injury involves a gunshot wound (Tex. Health & Safety Code Ann. § 161.041). *(B.B.)*.

§ 91.004. Application of Subtitle.

This subtitle does not affect a duty to report child abuse under Chapter 261 *[Investigation of Report of Child Abuse or Neglect]*.

Chapter 92. Immunity.

5h§ 92.001. Immunity.

(a) Except as provided by Subsection (b), a person who reports family violence under Section 91.002 or provides information under Section 91.003 is immune from civil liability that might otherwise be incurred or imposed.

(b) A person who reports the person's own conduct or who otherwise reports family violence in bad faith is not protected from liability under this section.

TITLE 5

The Parent–Child Relationship and the Suit Affecting the Parent–Child Relationship

As amended through the 78th Legislature, Fourth Called Session (2004)

Subtitle A. General Provisions

Chapter

Subtitle B. Suits Affecting the Parent–Child Relationship

Subtitle C. Judicial Resources and Services

Subtitle D. Administrative Services

Subtitle E. Protection of the Child

★★★

Subtitle A. General Provisions

Introductory Comment to Subtitle A

Subtitle A contains eleven short chapters that establish general provisions intended to govern all of the wide variety of suits affecting the parent-child relationship (commonly known as SAPCR's). Unless otherwise specified, the general provisions apply whether the action is between parents for conservatorship and support, between parents and relatives for conservatorship or visitation, and perhaps for support, for termination and adoption, or between the state and the parents for any of these aspects of the relief available in a SAPCR. On occasion this creates a certain awkwardness because the issues involved in such different types of litigation vary considerably, especially given the constitutional dimensions of the parent-child relationship when the state intervenes in the family.

★★★

Chapter 101. Definitions.

Introductory Comment

As the size of this book indicates, the Texas Family Code is both comprehensive and complex. This beginning chapter defines 44 terms found throughout the next several hundred pages. Note, however, that the definitions in this chapter are applicable only if a more specific definition is not provided in a particular chapter or title. The most prominent chapters in which definitions are provided that may differ from the definitions in this chapter are the uniform acts which include the Uniform Child Custody and Jurisdiction and Enforcement Act (Chapter 152), the Uniform Interstate Family Support Act (Chapter 159), and the Uniform Parentage Act (Chapter 160). No caselaw has developed in which a conflict has arisen between the specific definitions and the various chapters and these general definitions which are applicable throughout Title 5 unless superceded by a more specific definition in a chapter.

An amendment in a non-Family Code bill dealing with reorganization of the Health and Human Services Agencies of Texas may initially cause some confusion. That amendment which will affect the definitions and text throughout the Family Code. The name of the agency mandated to protect abused and neglected children has been changed, yet again, to "Department of Family and Protective Services." For newcomers who know only of DPRS or TDPRS, be advised that old-timers remember DPW, DHR, and DHS as predecessors to that agency. Further, H.B. 2292, eff. Sept. 1, 2003, § 1.27 states: "A reference in law to the Department of Protective and Regulatory Services means the Department of Family and Protective Services."

§ 101.001. Applicability of Definitions.

(a) Definitions in this subchapter apply to this title.

(b) If, in another part of this title, a term defined by this chapter has a meaning different from the meaning provided by this chapter, the meaning of that other provision prevails.

§ 101.0010. Acknowledged Father.

"Acknowledged father" means a man who has established a father-child relationship under Chapter 160 [*Uniform Parentage Act*].

§ 101.0011. Administrative Writ of Withholding.

"Administrative writ of withholding" means the document issued by the Title IV-D agency and delivered to an employer directing that earnings be withheld for payment of child support as provided by Chapter 158 [*Withholding from Earnings for Child Support*].

§ 101.0015. Alleged Father.

(a) "Alleged father" means a man who alleges himself to be, or is alleged to be, the genetic father or a possible genetic father of a child, but whose paternity has not been determined.

(b) The term does not include:

(1) a presumed father;

(2) a man whose parental rights have been terminated or declared to not exist; or

(3) a male donor.

§ 101.002. Authorized Agency.

"Authorized agency" means a public social agency authorized to care for children, including the Texas Department of Protective and Regulatory Services.

§ 101.0021. Bureau of Vital Statistics.

"Bureau of vital statistics" means the bureau of vital statistics of the Texas Department of Health.

§ 101.003. Child or Minor; Adult.

(a) "Child" or "minor" means a person under 18 years of age who is not and has not been married or who has not had the disabilities of minority removed for general purposes.

(b) In the context of child support, "child" includes a person over 18 years of age for whom a person may be obligated to pay child support.

(c) "Adult" means a person who is not a child.

§ 101.004. Child Support Agency.

"Child support agency" means:

(1) the Title IV–D agency;

(2) a county or district attorney or any other county officer or county agency that executes a cooperative agreement with the Title IV–D agency to provide child support services under Part D of Title IV of the federal Social Security Act (42 U.S.C. Section 651 et seq.) and Chapter 231 [*Title IV–D Services*]; or

(3) a domestic relations office.

§ 101.005. Child Support Review Officer.

"Child support review officer" means an individual designated and trained by a child support agency to conduct reviews under this title.

§ 101.006. Child Support Services.

"Child support services" means administrative or court actions to:

(1) establish paternity;

(2) establish, modify, or enforce child support or medical support obligations;

(3) locate absent parents; or

(4) cooperate with other states in these actions and any other action authorized or required under Part D of Title IV of the federal Social Security Act (42 U.S.C. Section 651 et seq.) or Chapter 231 [*Title IV–D Services*].

§ 101.007. Clear and Convincing Evidence.

"Clear and convincing evidence" means the measure or degree of proof that will produce in the mind of the trier of fact a firm belief or conviction as to the truth of the allegations sought to be established.

§ 101.008. Court.

"Court" means the district court, juvenile court having the same jurisdiction as a district court, or other court expressly given jurisdiction of a suit affecting the parent-child relationship.

§ 101.009. Danger to Physical Health or Safety of Child.

"Danger to the physical health or safety of a child" includes exposure of the child to loss or injury that jeopardizes the physical health or safety of the child without regard to whether there has been an actual prior injury to the child.

§ 101.010. Disposable Earnings.

"Disposable earnings" means the part of the earnings of an individual remaining after the deduction from those earnings of any amount required by law to be withheld, union dues, nondiscretionary retirement contributions, and medical, hospitalization, and disability insurance coverage for the obligor and the obligor's children.

§ 101.011. Earnings.

"Earnings" means a payment to or due an individual, regardless of source and how denominated. The term includes a periodic or lump-sum payment for:

(1) wages, salary, compensation received as an independent contractor, overtime pay, severance pay, commission, bonus, and interest income;

(2) payments made under a pension, an annuity, workers' compensation, and a disability or retirement program; and

(3) unemployment benefits.

§ 101.012. Employer.

"Employer" means a person, corporation, partnership, workers' compensation insurance carrier, governmental entity, the United States, or any other entity that pays or owes earnings to an individual. The term includes, for the purposes of enrolling dependents in a group health insurance plan, a union, trade association, or other similar organization.

§ 101.0125. Family Violence.

"Family violence" has the meaning assigned by Section 71.004.

§ 101.013. Filed.

"Filed" means officially filed with the clerk of the court.

§ 101.014. Governmental Entity.

"Governmental entity" means the state, a political subdivision of the state, or an agency of the state.

§ 101.015. Health Insurance.

"Health insurance" means insurance coverage that provides basic health care services, including usual physician services, office visits, hospitalization, and laboratory, X-ray, and emergency services, that may be provided through a health maintenance organization or other private or public organization, other than medical assistance under Chapter 32, Human Resources Code.

§ 101.016. Joint Managing Conservatorship.

"Joint managing conservatorship" means the sharing of the rights and duties of a parent by two parties, ordinarily the parents, even if the exclusive right to make certain decisions may be awarded to one party.

§ 101.0161. Judicial Writ of Withholding.

"Judicial writ of withholding" means the document issued by the clerk of a court and delivered to an employer directing that earnings be withheld for payment of child support as provided by Chapter 158 [*Withholding from Earnings for Child Support*].

§ 101.017. Licensed Child Placing Agency.

"Licensed child placing agency" means a person, private association, or corporation approved by the Department of Protective and Regulatory Services to place children for adoption through a license, certification, or other means.

§ 101.018. Local Registry.

"Local registry" means an agency or entity operated under the authority of a district clerk, county government, juvenile board, juvenile probation office, domestic relations office, or other county agency or entity that serves a county or a court that has jurisdiction under this title and that:

(1) receives child support payments;

(2) maintains records of child support payments;

(3) distributes child support payments as required by law; and

(4) maintains custody of official child support payment records.

§ 101.019. Managing Conservatorship.

"Managing conservatorship" means the relationship between a child and a managing conservator appointed by court order.

§ 101.020. Medical Support.

"Medical support" means periodic payments or a lump-sum payment made under an order to cover medical expenses, including health insurance coverage, incurred for the benefit of a child.

§ 101.0201. Notice of Application for Judicial Writ of Withholding.

"Notice of application for judicial writ of withholding" means the document delivered to an obligor and filed with the court as required by Chapter 158 [*Withholding from Earnings for Child Support*] for the nonjudicial determination of arrears and initiation of withholding.

§ 101.021. Obligee.

"Obligee" means a person or entity entitled to receive payments of child support, including an agency of this state or of another jurisdiction to which a person has assigned the person's right to support.

§ 101.022. Obligor.

"Obligor" means a person required to make payments under the terms of a support order for a child.

§ 101.023. Order.

"Order" means a final order unless identified as a temporary order or the context clearly requires a different meaning. The term includes a decree and a judgment.

§ 101.024. Parent.

"Parent" means the mother, a man presumed to be the father, a man legally determined to be the father, a man who has been adjudicated to be the father by a court of competent jurisdiction, a man who has acknowledged his paternity under applicable law, or an adoptive mother or father. The term does not include a parent as to whom the parent-child relationship has been terminated.

§ 101.025. Parent-Child Relationship.

"Parent-child relationship" means the legal relationship between a child and the child's parents as provided by Chapter 160 *[Uniform Parentage Act]*. The term includes the mother and child relationship and the father and child relationship.

§ 101.026. Render.

"Render" means the pronouncement by a judge of the court's ruling on a matter. The pronouncement may be made orally in the presence of the court reporter or in writing, including on the court's docket sheet or by a separate written instrument.

§ 101.027. Parent Locator Service.

"Parent locator service" means the service established under 42 U.S.C. Section 653.

§ 101.028. School.

"School" means a primary or secondary school in which a child is enrolled or, if the child is not enrolled in a primary or secondary school, the public school district in which the child primarily resides.

§ 101.029. Standard Possession Order.

"Standard possession order" means an order that provides a parent with rights of possession of a child in accordance with the terms and conditions of Subchapter F, Chapter 153 [*Conservatorship, Possession, and Access*].

§ 101.030. State.

"State" means a state of the United States, the District of Columbia, the Commonwealth of Puerto Rico, or a territory or insular possession subject to the jurisdiction of the United States. The term includes an Indian tribe and a foreign jurisdiction that has established procedures for rendition and enforcement of an order that are substantially similar to the procedures of this title.

§ 101.0301. State Case Registry.

"State case registry" means the registry established and operated by the Title IV-D agency under 42 U.S.C. Section 654a that has responsibility for maintaining records with respect to child support orders in all Title IV-D cases and in all other cases in which a support order is rendered or modified under this title on or after October 1, 1998.

§ 101.0302. State Disbursement Unit.

"State disbursement unit" means the unit established and operated by the Title IV–D agency under 42 U.S.C. Section 654b that has responsibility for receiving, distributing, maintaining, and furnishing child support payments and records on or after October 1, 1999.

§ 101.031. Suit.

"Suit" means a suit affecting the parent-child relationship.

§ 101.032. Suit Affecting the Parent-Child Relationship.

(a) "Suit affecting the parent-child relationship" means a suit filed as provided by this title in which the appointment of a managing conservator or a possessory conservator, access to or support of a child, or establishment or termination of the parent-child relationship is requested.

(b) The following are not suits affecting the parent-child relationship:

(1) a habeas corpus proceeding under Chapter 157 [*Enforcement*];

(2) a proceeding filed under Chapter 159 [*UIFSA*] to determine parentage or to establish, enforce, or modify child support, whether this state is acting as the initiating or responding state; and

(3) a proceeding under Title 2.

§ 101.033. Title IV–D Agency.

"Title IV–D agency" means the state agency designated under Chapter 231 [*Title IV–D Services*] to provide services under Part D of Title IV of the federal Social Security Act (42 U.S.C. Section 651 et seq.).

§ 101.034. Title IV-D Case.

"Title IV-D case" means an action in which services are provided by the Title IV-D agency under Part D, Title IV, of the federal Social Security Act (42 U.S.C. Section 651 et seq.), relating to the location of an absent parent, determination of parentage, or establishment, modification, or enforcement of a child support or medical support obligation.

§ 101.035. Tribunal.

"Tribunal" means a court, administrative agency, or quasi-judicial entity of a state authorized to establish, enforce, or modify support orders or to determine parentage.

Chapter 102. Filing Suit.

Editors' Note: *This chapter contains guest comments by Alicia Gray Key, Executive Director, Office of Court Administration; and H. Patrick Sullivan, Director of Federal Policy Analysis, Child Support, Office of the Attorney General, identified as (A.G.K. & H.P.S.).*

---

§ 102.001. Suit Authorized; Scope of Suit.

(a) A suit may be filed as provided in this title.

(b) One or more matters covered by this title may be determined in the suit. The court, on its own motion, may require the parties to replead in order that any issue affecting the parent-child relationship may be determined in the suit.

§ 102.002. Commencement of Suit.

An original suit begins by the filing of a petition as provided by this chapter.

§ 102.003. General Standing to File Suit.

(a) An original suit may be filed at any time by:

(1) a parent of the child;

(2) the child through a representative authorized by the court;

(3) a custodian or person having the right of visitation with or access to the child appointed by an order of a court of another state or country;

(4) a guardian of the person or of the estate of the child;

(5) a governmental entity;

(6) an authorized agency;

(7) a licensed child placing agency;

(8) a man alleging himself to be the father of a child filing in accordance with Chapter 160, subject to the limitations of that chapter, but not otherwise;

(9) a person, other than a foster parent, who has had actual care, control, and possession of the child for at least six months ending not more than 90 days preceding the date of the filing of the petition;

(10) a person designated as the managing conservator in a revoked or unrevoked affidavit of relinquishment under Chapter 161 or to whom consent to adoption has been given in writing under Chapter 162;

(11) a person with whom the child and the child's guardian, managing conservator, or parent have resided for at least six months ending not more than 90 days preceding the date of the filing of the petition if the child's guardian, managing conservator, or parent is deceased at the time of the filing of the petition;

(12) a person who is the foster parent of a child placed by the Department of Protective and Regulatory Services in the person's home for at least 12 months ending not more than 90 days preceding the date of the filing of the petition; [~~or~~]

(13) a person who is a relative of the child within the third degree by consanguinity, as determined by Chapter 573, Government Code, if the child's parents are deceased at the time of the filing of the petition; or

(14) a person who has been named as a prospective adoptive parent of a child by a pregnant woman or the parent of the child, in a verified written statement to confer standing executed under Section 102.0035, regardless of whether the child has been born.

(b) In computing the time necessary for standing under Subsections (a)(9), (11), and (12), the court may not require that the time be continuous and uninterrupted but shall consider the child's principal residence during the relevant time preceding the date of commencement of the suit.

(c) Notwithstanding the time requirements of Subsection (a)(12), a person who is the foster parent of a child may file a suit to adopt a child for whom the person is providing foster care at any time after the person has been approved to adopt the child. The standing to file suit under this subsection applies only to the adoption of a child who is eligible to be adopted.

History: Amended by 78th Legis., Reg. Sess. (2003), H.B. 1648, eff. Sept. 1, 2003, and "applies only to a suit affecting the parent-child relationship filed on or after the effective date of this Act. A suit affecting the parent-child relationship filed before that date is governed by the law in effect on the date the suit was filed, and the former law is continued in effect for that purpose."

Comment

As originally enacted in 1973, the standing to sue provision was extremely short, allowing "any person with an interest in the child" to bring a SAPCR. Hard as it is to believe, this formulation was more restrictive than the prior statute, at least in an abuse or neglect situation which had granted "any adult" the authority to bring a suit. Unfortunately, that code provision was sometimes tightly construed with regard to exactly who "had an interest" in the child. Some decisions had the effect of unduly restricting access to the courts, at lest in the retrospective judgment of the legislature. As a result, over time the legislature has defined a wide variety of specific fact situations for which standing to sue is granted. Considerably more predictability is brought to the subject, with the result that there has been a marked fall-off in litigation over questions of standing.

For years, controversy has raged over the standing of foster parents to seek an independent remedy apart from that sought by DPRS when a child has lived in the foster parents' home for a considerable period of time. In 1997 the legislature attempted to resolve the controversy by providing that if a child has resided in a foster home for 18 months, the foster parents have standing to seek general relief in a SAPCR. The question of whether this narrowed the standing for foster parents by eliminating their claim under subsection (a)(9) was not resolved until 1999. Then the legislature limited application of the "actual care, control and possession of a child" grounds for standing to a person "other than a foster parent." Foster parents continue to have their own provision; the amendment to subsection (a)(12) reduces the time for foster parents to acquire standing to sue based on their actual custody of the child from 18 months to 12 months. This may not be much of a concession, given the one-year deadline for temporary foster care for cases filed by DPRS established in § 262.401, *infra*.

Subsection (a)(13) adds an extremely narrow provision applicable only if the child's parents are deceased at the time of the filing of the petition. In that case, a person "within the third degree by consanguinity" has standing. Third degree of consanguinity of an individual includes parents, grandparents, and great-grandparents, paternal and maternal uncles and aunts, siblings, and nephews and nieces.

The newest designation of standing is provided by Subsection (14), which provides that a pregnant woman or a parent of a child be conferred standing to a prospective adoptive parent. Section 102.0035, *infra*, provides specific details that must contained in a statement to confer standing on a prospective adoptive parent.

Subsection (c) adds yet another more particularized standing provision, which applies to a narrow range of foster parents who have been approved to adopt a child eligible for adoption.

CLE/Other Legal Publications

Standing after Troxel*: grandparents, step-parents and other interlopers.* Linda S. Good, 2004 ADV. FAM. L.

Third party standing. Miriam L. Ackels, 2004 U. TEX. FAM. L. FRONT LINES

The death of abuelita: Troxel's *implications for the border.* Paula L. Thomas, 2004 U. TEX. FAM. L. ON THE BORDERS

Jurisdiction, venue, transfers and standing of SAPCRs. Brian L. Webb, 2003 ADV. FAM. L.

Nuts and bolts of third party practice: grandparent and non-parent standing. Brian L. Webb & Miriam L. Ackels, 2003 MARRIAGE DISSOLUTION

O Brother (or Sister), Where Art Thou: Sibling Standing in Texas, 55 BAYLOR L. REV. 749 (2003)

Texas grandparents: 2002 update. (Workshop) 2002 ADV. FAM. L.

Who's left standing? Third party standing after Troxel, Aubin *and* Lilley. Linda Sue Good, 2002 MARRIAGE DISSOLUTION

*All those with standing, step forward . . . not so fast, grandma! Post-*Troxel *third-party standing to bring SAPCRs and representing extended family and non-family members*. Brian L. Webb, Miriam L. Ackels & Lorna M. Burton, 2001 ADV. FAM. L.

Leading Cases

In re C.T.H., 112 S.W.3d 262 (Tex. App.—Beaumont 2003, no pet.) (grandparents have justiciable interest in custody modification after caring for child for over six months)

In re A.J.L., 108 S.W.3d 414 (Tex. App.—Fort Worth 2003, pet. denied) (ex-stepfather lacks standing to obtain visitation with stepkids by modifying his divorce decree of the prior SAPCR order between his ex and kids' father)

Coons-Andersen v. Andersen, 104 S.W.3d 630 (Tex. App.—Dallas 2003, no pet.) (mother's ex-partner lacked standing to seek conservatorship of child born while the two women were still living together)

Doncer v. Dickerson, 81 S.W.3d 349 (Tex. App.—El Paso 2002, no pet.) (step-mother has standing to seek possessory conservatorship of step-child after her husband dies under facts of case)

Jones v. Fowler, 969 S.W.2d 429 (Tex. 1998) (omission of "immediately" before "proceeding" in recodification of statute was not a substantive change in law)

In re J.W.T., 872 S.W.2d 189 (Tex. 1994) (under certain factual circumstances, biological father has Tex. Const. right to establish his paternity over objections of mother and her husband)

Davis v. Guerrero, 64 S.W.3d 685 (Tex. App.—Austin 2001, no pet.) (court should not entertain motions to alter SAPCR provisions relating to issues covered by an existing guardianship until the guardianship is revoked)

Morales v. Morales, 968 S.W.2d 508 (Tex. App.—Corpus Christi 1998, no pet.) (husband excluded as biological father has no standing re child)

Segovia–Slape v. Paxson, 893 S.W.2d 694 (Tex. App.—El Paso 1995, no writ) (aunt with limited past contact with children lacks standing to intervene to seek conservatorship)

Attorney General of Texas v. Allred, 871 S.W.2d 298 (Tex. App.—Fort Worth 1994, no writ) (prior dismissal of paternity suit with prejudice does not affect A.G.'s independent right to bring suit)

In re Pringle, 862 S.W.2d 722 (Tex. App.—Tyler 1993, no writ) (grandparents lack standing to seek further remedy to contest mother's MC absent serious situation)

Williams v. Anderson, 850 S.W.2d 281 (Tex. App.—Austin 1993, writ denied) (family friend lacks standing absent six consecutive months of actual possession and control of child; distinguished from constructive or cumulative possession)

Landry v. Nauls, 831 S.W.2d 603 (Tex. App.—Houston [14th Dist.] 1992, no writ) (grandma cannot be named MC unless she is a party in the SAPCR and rebuts parental preference)

T.W.E. v. K.M.E., 828 S.W.2d 806 (Tex. App.—San Antonio 1992, no writ) (rebuttal of husband's paternity does not deprive him of standing to seek conservatorship)

Rodarte v. Cox, 828 S.W.2d 65 (Tex. App.—Tyler 1991, writ denied) (long-term foster parents have standing to seek termination over objection of TDHS)

Von Behren v. Von Behren, 800 S.W.2d 919 (Tex. App.—San Antonio 1990, writ denied) (grandmother does not have standing for managing conservatorship of grandchildren despite allegation of sexual abuse)

McCord v. Watts, 777 S.W.2d 809 (Tex. App.—Austin 1989, no writ) (intervention measured by different principles than standing to sue)

Jasso v. Robertson, 771 S.W.2d 231 (Tex. App.—Houston [1st Dist.] 1989, no writ) (alleged father has standing)

Jacobs v. Balew, 765 S.W.2d 532 (Tex. App.—Beaumont 1989, no writ) (absent abuse, former stepfather lacks standing to seek conservatorship—managing conservatorship or possessory conservatorship)

Espree v. Guillory, 753 S.W.2d 722 (Tex. App.—Houston [1st Dist.] 1988, no writ) (third party man claiming paternity has no standing after final SAPCR decree)

Harrison v. Harrison, 734 S.W.2d 737 (Tex. App.—Eastland 1987, no writ) (intervening grandparents need not show mother endangered child)

---

§ 102.0035. Statement to Confer Standing.

(a) A pregnant woman or a parent of a child may execute a statement to confer standing to a prospective adoptive parent as provided by this section to assert standing under Section 102.003(a)(14). A statement to confer standing under this section may not be executed in a suit brought by a governmental entity under Chapter 262 or 263.

(b) A statement to confer standing must contain:

(1) the signature, name, age, and address of the person named as a prospective adoptive parent;

(2) the signature, name, age, and address of the pregnant woman or of the parent of the child who is consenting to the filing of a petition for adoption or to terminate the parent-child relationship as described by Subsection (a);

(3) the birth date of the child or the anticipated birth date if the child has not been born; and

(4) the name of the county in which the suit will be filed.

(c) The statement to confer standing must be attached to the petition in a suit affecting the parent-child relationship. The statement may not be used for any purpose other than to confer standing in a proceeding for adoption or to terminate the parent-child relationship.

(d) A statement to confer standing may be signed at any time during the pregnancy of the mother of the unborn child whose parental rights are to be terminated.

(e) A statement to confer standing is not required in a suit brought by a person who has standing to file a suit affecting the parent-child relationship under Sections 102.003(a)(1)–(13) or any other law under which the person has standing to file a suit.

(f) A person who executes a statement to confer standing may revoke the statement at any time before the person executes an affidavit for voluntary relinquishment of parental rights. The revocation of the statement must be in writing and must be sent by certified mail, return receipt requested, to the prospective adoptive parent.

(g) On filing with the court proof of the delivery of the revocation of a statement to confer standing under Subsection (f), the court shall dismiss any suit affecting the parent-child relationship filed by the prospective adoptive parent named in the statement.

§ 102.004. Standing for Grandparent.

(a) In addition to the general standing to file suit provided by Section 102.003(13), a grandparent may file an original suit requesting managing conservatorship if there is satisfactory proof to the court that:

(1) the order requested is necessary because the child's present environment presents a serious question concerning the child's physical health or welfare; or

(2) both parents, the surviving parent, or the managing conservator or custodian either filed the petition or consented to the suit.

(b) An original suit requesting possessory conservatorship may not be filed by a grandparent or other person. However, the court may grant a grandparent or other person deemed by the court to have had substantial past contact with the child leave to intervene in a pending suit filed by a person authorized to do so under this subchapter.

(c) Access to a child by a grandparent is governed by the standards established by Chapter 153 *[Conservatorship, Possession, and Access]*.

Leading Cases

In re Pensom, 126 S.W.3d 251 (Tex. App.—San Antonio 2003, orig. proceeding) (grandparent access statute facially constitutional)

In re A.M., 60 S.W.3d 166 (Tex. App.—Houston [1st Dist.] 2001, no pet.) (foster parents have standing to intervene in termination suit based on substantial past contact with child)

In re M.A.M., 35 S.W.3d 788 (Tex. App.—Beaumont 2001, no pet.) (undisputed biological maternal grandmother of the child satisfied standing requirements to intervene in SAPCR without a finding of substantial past contact with the child)

Smelscer v. Smelscer, 901 S.W.2d 708 (Tex. App.—El Paso 1995, no writ) (grandparents' intervention in divorce does not survive dismissal after death of father)

CLE/Other Legal Publications

Standing after Troxel*: grandparents, step-parents and other interlopers.* Linda S. Good, 2004 ADV. FAM. L.

Third party standing. Miriam L. Ackels, 2004 U. TEX. FAM. L. FRONT LINES

The death of abuelita: Troxel's *implications for the border.* Paula L. Thomas, 2004 U. TEX. FAM. L. ON THE BORDER

Jurisdiction, venue, transfers and standing of SAPCRs. Brian L. Webb, 2003 ADV. FAM. L.

Nuts and bolts of third party practice: grandparent and non-parent standing. Brian L. Webb & Miriam L. Ackels, 2003 MARRIAGE DISSOLUTION

Texas grandparents: 2002 update. (Workshop) 2002 ADV. FAM. L.

Who's left standing? Third party standing after Troxel, Aubin *and* Lilley. Linda Sue Good, 2002 MARRIAGE DISSOLUTION

*All those with standing, step forward . . . not so fast, grandma! Post-*Troxel *third-party standing to bring SAPCRs . . . .* Brian L. Webb, Miriam L. Ackels & Lorna M. Burton, 2001 ADV. FAM. L.

---

§ 102.005. Standing to Request Termination and Adoption.

An original suit requesting only an adoption or for termination of the parent-child relationship joined with a petition for adoption may be filed by:

(1) a stepparent of the child;

(2) an adult who, as the result of a placement for adoption, has had actual possession and control of the child at any time during the 30–day period preceding the filing of the petition;

(3) an adult who has had actual possession and control of the child for not less than two months during the three-month period preceding the filing of the petition; or

(4) another adult whom the court determines to have had substantial past contact with the child sufficient to warrant standing to do so.

§ 102.006. Limitations on Standing.

(a) Except as provided by Subsection (b), if the parent-child relationship between the child and every living parent of the child has been terminated, an original suit may not be filed by:

(1) a former parent whose parent-child relationship with the child has been terminated by court order;

(2) the father of the child; or

(3) a family member or relative by blood, adoption, or marriage of either a former parent whose parent-child relationship has been terminated or of the father of the child.

(b) The limitations on filing suit imposed by this section do not apply to a person who:

(1) has a continuing right to possession of or access to the child under an existing court order; or

(2) has the consent of the child's managing conservator, guardian, or legal custodian to bring the suit.

§ 102.007. Standing of Title IV–D Agency.

In providing services authorized by Chapter 231 *[Title IV–D Services]*, the Title IV–D agency or a political subdivision contracting with the attorney general to provide Title

IV–D services under this title may file a child support action authorized under this title, including a suit for modification or a motion for enforcement.

§ 102.008. Contents of Petition.

(a) The petition and all other documents in a proceeding filed under this title, except a suit for adoption of an adult, shall be entitled "In the interest of ________, a child." In a suit in which adoption of a child is requested, the style shall be "In the interest of a child."

(b) The petition must include:

(1) a statement that the court in which the petition is filed has continuing, exclusive jurisdiction or that no court has continuing jurisdiction of the suit;

(2) the name and date of birth of the child, except that if adoption of a child is requested, the name of the child may be omitted;

(3) the full name of the petitioner and the petitioner's relationship to the child or the fact that no relationship exists;

(4) the names of the parents, except in a suit in which adoption is requested;

(5) the name of the managing conservator, if any, or the child's custodian, if any, appointed by order of a court of another state or country;

(6) the names of the guardians of the person and estate of the child, if any;

(7) the names of possessory conservators or other persons, if any, having possession of or access to the child under an order of the court;

(8) the name of an alleged father of the child or a statement that the identity of the father of the child is unknown;

(9) a full description and statement of value of all property owned or possessed by the child;

(10) a statement describing what action the court is requested to take concerning the child and the statutory grounds on which the request is made; and

(11) any other information required by this title.

Comment

Prior to September 1, 2001, certain identification information was required in an application for a protective order, the registration for enforcement of a support order, and a petition in a SAPCR, *see* §§ 82.004 and 159.602. In some counties, a few attorneys searched the public records in order to notify respondents of the existence of proceedings under the Family Code before service could be effected. The Family Law Council expressed concern that some of the information required, especially the petitioner's address, could provide a method for an abusive spouse to locate the abused spouse. In response, the 2001 amendment to this section (and the others cited above) removes the requirement that certain information be included in the specified applications and petitions in order to protect the location of a party until the court can make a determination of whether that location should be revealed. The information deleted from the filed documents includes the address requirement for an application for a protective order and registration for enforcement of a support order, and the sex, age, place of birth, and place of residence of a child in a SAPCR petition.

Leading Case

Rodriguez v. Lutheran Social Services, Inc., 814 S.W.2d 153 (Tex. App.—San Antonio 1991, writ denied) (adoption pleadings must comply with requirements of interstate compact)

CLE/Other Legal Publications

Family Law Practice Manual: changes/new forms. Norma Levine Trusch, 2002 ADV. FAM. L.

Cross Reference

TEX. FAM. CODE ANN. § 6.406. Mandatory Joinder of SAPCR; § 6.407. SAPCR To Be Transferred to Divorce Court.

Texas Family Law Practice Manual

Chapter 31. Original Suit Affecting the Parent–Child Relationship

---

§ 102.0085. [~~Statement on Alternative Dispute Resolution.~~] [repealed]

History: Repealed by 78th Legis., Reg. Sess. (2003), H.B. 884, eff. Sept. 1, 2003, and "applies to a suit for dissolution of a marriage or a suit affecting the parent-child relationship filed before, on, or after that date."

Comment

In the mid–1990's ADR was seen as a means to discourage contested trials. This now-repealed statute was designed to ensure that the parties to a lawsuit were informed about the existence and utility of ADR. Obviously, the legislature did not want to rely on a directive to attorneys to communicate such information orally to their clients because the statute mandated that a positive statement about ADR be included in the "first pleading filed by a party," which included petitions and general denials. Moreover, the statement had to be signed by the individual party, not by the attorney.

The statute had unintended consequences which redounded to the detriment of individual litigants. The client "signing requirement" meant that either at least two trips to the attorney's office were necessary or an exchange of documents by mail was needed. In either event, increased costs and delays were endemic. Further, the ever-increasing popularity of ADR with both attorneys and judges has reached such heights that a formal emphasis on the ADR process seems redundant. Accordingly, in 2003 the Council of the Family Law Section sought and obtained repeal of the ADR notification-statute.

Cross Reference

TEX. CIV. PRAC. & REM. CODE ANN. ch. 154. Alternative Dispute Resolution Procedures, *infra*

Texas Family Law Practice Manual

Form 2–1. Statement on Alternate Dispute Resolution [not required after Sept. 1, 2003]

Chapter 15. Alternative Dispute Resolution

---

§ 102.0086. Confidentiality of Pleadings.

(a) This section applies only in a county with a population of 3.4 million or more.

(b) Except as otherwise provided by law, all pleadings and other documents filed with the court in a suit affecting the parent-child relationship are confidential, are excepted from required public disclosure under Chapter 552, Government Code, and may not be released to a person who is not a party to

the suit until after the date of service of citation or the 31st day after the date of filing the suit, whichever date is sooner.

History: Enacted by 78th Legis., Reg. Sess. (2003), H.B. 1391, eff. Sept. 1, 2003, and "applies only to a suit affecting the parent-child relationship filed on or after the effective date of this Act. A suit affecting the parent-child relationship filed before the effective date of this Act is governed by the law in effect on the date the suit was filed, and the former law is continued in effect for that purpose."

Comment

This is the latest installment in the struggle to regulate solicitation of business by family law attorneys in Harris County. The legislature previously noted and attempted to prevent notification of respondents in a divorce, SAPCR, or protective order context prior to service of citation. Particularly in the protective order context, notification of an application for a protective order was thought to have a potential for facilitating additional domestic violence. Notwithstanding this argument, the federal Fifth Circuit has ruled that solicitation of business and family law cases is legal under the U.S. Constitution. Confidentiality requirements in this new section are deemed by the legislature not to be inconsistent with that decision. For Harris County only there is a delay in full public disclosure at the time of filing for three types of suits: divorce, SAPCRs, and protective order applications. If the Houston practice spreads to other counties, it seems likely that the limitation of the statute to Harris County may be altered.

§ 102.009. Service of Citation.

(a) Except as provided by Subsection (b), the following are entitled to service of citation on the filing of a petition in an original suit:

(1) a managing conservator;

(2) a possessory conservator;

(3) a person having possession of or access to the child under an order;

(4) a person required by law or by order to provide for the support of the child;

(5) a guardian of the person of the child;

(6) a guardian of the estate of the child;

(7) each parent as to whom the parent-child relationship has not been terminated or process has not been waived under Chapter 161 *[Termination of the Parent-Child Relationship]*;

(8) an alleged father, unless there is attached to the petition an affidavit of waiver of interest in a child executed by the alleged father as provided by Chapter 161 or unless the petitioner has complied with the provisions of Section 161.002(b)(2) or (b)(3);

(9) a man who has filed a notice of intent to claim paternity as provided by Chapter 160 *[Uniform Parentage Act]*;

(10) the Department of Protective and Regulatory Services, if the petition requests that the department be appointed as managing conservator of the child; and

(11) the Title IV-D agency, if the petition requests the termination of the parent-child relationship and support rights have been assigned to the Title IV-D agency under Chapter 231 *[Title IV-D Services]*.

(b) Citation may be served on any other person who has or who may assert an interest in the child.

(c) Citation on the filing of an original petition in a suit shall be issued and served as in other civil cases.

(d) If the petition requests the establishment, modification, or enforcement of a support right assigned to the Title IV–D agency under Chapter 231 or the rescission of a voluntary acknowledgment of paternity under Chapter 160, notice shall be given to the Title IV–D agency in a manner provided by Rule 21a, Texas Rules of Civil Procedure.

Leading Cases

Griggs v. Latham, 98 S.W.3d 382 (Tex. App.—Corpus Christi 2003, pet. denied) (father JMC necessary party in maternal grandparent's access suit; nonsuiting him and continuing to seek access reversible error)

Roberson v. Pickett, 900 S.W.2d 112 (Tex. App.—Houston [14th Dist.] 1995, no writ) (orphan's grandmother seeking guardianship entitled to notice of SAPCR)

Texas Family Law Practice Manual

Forms 8–18. Motion for Alternative Service [Rule 106]; *8–19.* Affidavit of Attempted Personal Service; *8–20.* Affidavit in Support of Method of Alternative Service [Rule 106]; *8–21.* Order on Motion for Alternative Service; *8–22.* Motion for Other Substituted Service; *8–23.* Affidavit in Support of Motion for Other Substituted Service; *8–24.* Order on Motion for Other Substituted Service [Rule 109a]; *8–25.* Order Authorizing Service of Process [Rule 103]

---

§ 102.010. Service of Citation by Publication.

(a) Citation may be served by publication as in other civil cases to persons entitled to service of citation who cannot be notified by personal service or registered or certified mail and to persons whose names are unknown.

(b) Citation by publication shall be published one time. If the name of a person entitled to service of citation is unknown, the notice to be published shall be addressed to "All Whom It May Concern." One or more causes to be heard on a certain day may be included in one notice and hearings may be continued from time to time without further notice.

(c) Citation by publication shall be sufficient if given in substantially the following form:

To (names of persons to be served with citation) and to all whom it may concern (if the name of any person to be served with citation is unknown), Respondent(s),

"STATE OF TEXAS

"You have been sued. You may employ an attorney. If you or your attorney do (does) not file a written answer with the clerk who issued this citation by 10 a.m. on the Monday next following the expiration of 20 days after you were served this citation and petition, a default judgment may be taken against you. The petition of _______, Petitioner, was filed in the Court of _______ County, Texas, on the ___ day of _______, _____, against _______, Respondent(s), numbered _______, and entitled 'In the interest of _______, a child (or children).' The suit requests (statement of relief requested, e.g., 'terminate the parent-child relationship'). The date and place of birth of the child (children) who is (are) the subject of the suit: _______.

"The court has authority in this suit to render an order in the child's (children's) interest that will be binding on you, including the termination of the parent-child relationship, the determination of paternity, and the appointment of a conservator with authority to consent to the child's (children's) adoption.

"Issued and given under my hand and seal of the Court at ________, Texas, this the ___ day of _______, ____.

". . . . .

Clerk of the District Court of
_______________ County, Texas.

By ______________, Deputy."

(d) In any suit in which service of citation is by publication, a statement of the evidence of service, approved and signed by the court, must be filed with the papers of the suit as a part of the record.

(e) In a suit filed under Chapter 161 or 262 in which the last name of the respondent is unknown, the court may order substituted service of citation by publication, including publication by posting the citation at the courthouse door for a specified time, if the court finds and states in its order that the method of substituted service is as likely as citation by publication in a newspaper in the manner described by Subsection (b) to give the respondent actual notice of the suit. If the court orders that citation by publication shall be completed by posting the citation at the courthouse door for a specified time, service must be completed on, and the answer date is computed from, the expiration date of the posting period. If the court orders another method of substituted service of citation by publication, service shall be completed as directed by the court.

History: Amended by 78th Legis., Reg. Sess. (2003), H.B. 518, eff. Sept. 1, 2003, and "applies only to a suit affecting the parent-child relationship filed on or after that date. A suit affecting the parent-child relationship filed before the effective date of this Act is governed by the law in effect on the date that the suit was filed, and the former law is continued in effect for that purpose."

Comment

Generally, in civil cases a court may order citation by publication through posting notice at the courthouse door, provided the court finds this method will give respondent actual notice of the proceeding. Heretofore, there has been some question as to whether this method of service is applicable in a SAPCR. Henceforth, posting at the courthouse door is an acceptable method of citation by publication if the court deems it to be appropriate.

Leading Case

Rider v. Farris, 718 S.W.2d 883 (Tex. App.—Beaumont 1986, writ dism'd w.o.j.) (inadequate citation by publication)

Texas Family Law Practice Manual

Forms 10–1. Appointment of Attorney Ad Litem after Publication; *10–2*. Original Answer Filed by Attorney Ad Litem for Respondent Cited by Publication; *39–8*. Affidavit for Citation by Publication; *39–9*. Affidavit in Support of Citation by Publication by Birth Mother; *39–10*. Notice by Publication; *39–11*. Appointment of Attorney Ad Litem after Publication; *39–12*. Original Answer Filed by Attorney Ad Litem for Respondent Cited by Publication

---

§ 102.011. Acquiring Jurisdiction over Nonresident.

(a) The court may exercise status or subject matter jurisdiction over the suit as provided by Chapter 152 *[UCCJEA]*.

(b) The court may also exercise personal jurisdiction over a person on whom service of citation is required or over the person's personal representative, although the person is not a resident or domiciliary of this state, if:

(1) the person is personally served with citation in this state;

(2) the person submits to the jurisdiction of this state by consent, by entering a general appearance, or by filing a responsive document having the effect of waiving any contest to personal jurisdiction;

(3) the child resides in this state as a result of the acts or directives of the person;

(4) the person resided with the child in this state;

(5) the person resided in this state and provided prenatal expenses or support for the child;

(6) the person engaged in sexual intercourse in this state and the child may have been conceived by that act of intercourse;

(7) the person registered with the paternity registry maintained by the bureau of vital statistics as provided by Chapter 160 *[Uniform Parentage Act]*; or

(8) there is any basis consistent with the constitutions of this state and the United States for the exercise of the personal jurisdiction.

Comment

Following the enactment of the UCCJA in 1983, coupled with the federal enactment of the PKPA in 1980, any possible argument that personal jurisdiction is required to adjudicate managing conservatorship or custody has been definitively repudiated and replaced with the concept that a determination of conservatorship or visitation is a "status adjudication." Thus, conservatorship issues may be decided by a court with SAPCR jurisdiction even if there is no personal jurisdiction over an absent parent. If the court has jurisdiction over the custody status, a valid assertion of long-arm personal jurisdiction over an absent respondent will enable a Texas court to settle all issues in a SAPCR, including child support.

Amendments in 1993 and 1997 conformed this long-arm statute, which is applicable to conservatorship, to be consistent with the long-arm statute applicable to child support, as provided in the Uniform Interstate Family Support Act, § 159.201, *infra*.

The establishment of a paternity registry, § 160.251 *et seq.*, triggered a 1997 amendment extending long arm jurisdiction over a man who has registered his claim of paternity.

CLE/Other Legal Publications

Jurisdiction, special appearance, and conflicts of law. Donn C. Fullenweider, 2004 Adv. Fam. L.

Jurisdiction, venue, plea in abatement and the UCCJEA. Douglas R. Woodburn, 2004 Marriage Dissolution

Jurisdiction and enforcement of custody and possession. Brian L. Webb, 2004 U. Tex. Fam. L. on the Border

The ABCs of interstate family support jurisdiction. Angela G. Pence, 2003 Adv. Fam. L.

Jurisdiction over foreign litigants: dissolution, property division, spousal support, child support. Bill De La Garza & Jo Ann Carter, 2002 Adv. Fam. L.

Venue and special appearance. James E. Farris, 2002 Adv. Fam. L.

Interstate alphabet soup. Sally H. Emerson, 2002 Adv. Fam. L.

International and cross border issues. (Workshop) 2002 Adv. Fam. L.

Extraterritorial custody issues: the UCCJEA, PKPA, and the Hague Convention. Lynn Kamin, 2001 Adv. Fam. L.

Leading Cases

In re McCormick, 87 S.W.3d 746 (Tex. App.—Amarillo 2002, no pet.) (Texas retains UCCJEA modification jurisdiction over father and son now living in Kansas)

In re Calderon-Garza, 81 S.W.3d 899 (Tex. App.—El Paso 2002, no pet.) (Texas was two-month-old infant's home state under UCCJEA when alleged father filed paternity suit)

Burnham v. Superior Court of California, 495 U.S. 604, 109 L.Ed.2d 631, 110 S.Ct. 2105 (1990) (in personam jurisdiction obtained by service of citation in forum state on transient respondent)

Kulko v. Superior Court of California, 436 U.S. 84, 56 L.Ed.2d 132, 98 S.Ct. 1690 (1978) (application of California long-arm statute did not conform to constitutional requirements)

May v. Anderson, 345 U.S. 528, 97 L.Ed. 1221, 73 S.Ct. 840 (1953) (leading pre-UCCJA case on custody jurisdiction)

In re S.A.V., 837 S.W.2d 80 (Tex. 1992) (Texas and Minnesota had concurrent custody jurisdiction under UCCJA, Minnesota declined to exercise its continuing jurisdiction under PKPA)

Cotton v. Cotton, 57 S.W.3d 506 (Tex. App.—Waco 2001, no pet.) (without personal jurisdiction over parent, court may not order child support payments; where there is no basis for in personam jurisdiction of a parent, a trial court lacks the authority to render judgment against the parent)

Phillips v. Phillips, 826 S.W.2d 746 (Tex. App.—Houston [14th Dist.] 1992, no writ) (father, living in Kenya, subject to personal jurisdiction; minimum contacts in Texas exceed those of any other U.S. forum)

Creavin v. Moloney, 773 S.W.2d 698 (Tex. App.—Corpus Christi 1989, writ denied) (nonresident submits to jurisdiction by suing Texan)

Williams v. Knott, 690 S.W.2d 605 (Tex. App.—Austin 1985, no writ) (termination of parental rights does not require personal jurisdiction [dicta])

Cross Reference

Parental Kidnapping Prevention Act (PKPA) 28 U.S.C.A. § 1738A

---

§ 102.012. Exercising Partial Jurisdiction.

(a) A court in which a suit is filed may exercise its jurisdiction over those portions of the suit for which it has authority.

(b) The court's authority to resolve all issues in controversy between the parties may be restricted because the court lacks:

(1) the required personal jurisdiction over a nonresident party;

(2) the required jurisdiction under Chapter 152 *[UCCJEA]*; or

(3) the required jurisdiction under Chapter 159 *[UIFSA]*.

(c) If a provision of Chapter 152 or Chapter 159 expressly conflicts with another provision of this title and the conflict cannot be reconciled, the provision of Chapter 152 or Chapter 159 prevails.

(d) In exercising jurisdiction, the court shall seek to harmonize the provisions of this code, the federal Parental Kidnapping Prevention Act (28 U.S.C. Section 1738A), and the federal Full Faith and Credit for Child Support Order Act (28 U.S.C. Section 1738B).

§ 102.013. Docketing Requirements.

(a) In a suit for modification or a motion for enforcement, the clerk shall file the petition or motion and all related papers under the same docket number as the prior proceeding without additional letters, digits, or special designations.

(b) If a suit requests the adoption of a child, the clerk shall file the suit and all other papers relating to the suit in a new file having a new docket number.

(c) In a suit to determine parentage under this title in which the court has rendered an order relating to an earlier born child of the same parents, the clerk shall file the suit and all other papers relating to the suit under the same docket number as the prior parentage action. For all other purposes, including the assessment of fees and other costs, the suit is a separate suit.

Comment

Subsection (c) is intended to promote judicial economy by reducing the number of motions to transfer and consolidate actions. It should also make it easier to track and distribute child support payments for multiple children of the same parents, although the ease and the accuracy of that process really rests more with the effectiveness of automated disbursement systems than with the nimbleness of the human mind. No other savings, however, are contemplated by the subsection inasmuch as the amount of filing fees and costs remains unaffected by the use of the same docket number for more than one suit. (*A.G.K. & H.P.S.*)

Chapter 103. Venue and Transfer of Original Proceedings.

Introductory Comment

The basic venue rule for an original SAPCR is to file where the child resides. The numerous exceptions to the general rule have not resulted in much reported litigation. Further, SAPCR venue applies only in a case in which a divorce suit is not pending, because divorce venue controls if there is conflict between divorce venue and SAPCR venue, § 6.407, *supra*, § 103.002, *infra*. Even in the event that an action for divorce is filed later than the SAPCR, the SAPCR court is required to transfer the action to the divorce county. However, there is a special exception to the rule of divorce-venue dominance in instances in which DPRS files a SAPCR alleging abuse or neglect, *see* § 6.407, *supra*, and § 262.203, *infra*.

CLE/Other Legal Publications

Jurisdiction, venue, plea in abatement and the UCCJEA. Douglas R. Woodburn, 2004 Marriage Dissolution

Jurisdiction, venue, transfers and standing of SAPCRs. Brian L. Webb, 2003 Adv. Fam. L.

Venue and special appearance. James E. Farris, 2002 Adv. Fam. L.

Leading Cases

Chalu v. Shamala, 125 S.W.3d 737 (Tex. App.—Houston [1st Dist.] 2003, no pet.) (no interlocutory appeal from transfer orders)

Scanio v. McFall, 877 S.W.2d 888 (Tex. App.—Amarillo 1994, no writ) (father's tort suit against mother and her attorney for actions in SAPCR is not governed by Family Code venue)

Matter of Marriage of Allen, 593 S.W.2d 133 (Tex. Civ. App.—Amarillo 1980, no writ) (divorce venue controls over SAPCR venue)

Cross References

Tex. Fam. Code Ann. ch. 155. Continuing, Exclusive Jurisdiction: Transfer; subch. C. Transfer of Continuing, Exclusive Jurisdiction

Texas Family Law Practice Manual

Forms 8–34. Motion for Change of Venue; *8–35*. Order for Change of Venue

---

§ 103.001. Venue for Original Suit.

(a) Except as otherwise provided by this title, an original suit shall be filed in the county where the child resides, unless:

(1) another court has continuing exclusive jurisdiction under Chapter 155 *[Continuing, Exclusive Jurisdiction; Transfer]*; or

(2) venue is fixed in a suit for dissolution of a marriage under Subchapter D, Chapter 6 *[Suit for Dissolution of Marriage]*.

(b) A suit in which adoption is requested may be filed in the county where the child resides or in the county where the petitioners reside.

(c) A child resides in the county where the child's parents reside or the child's parent resides, if only one parent is living, except that:

(1) if a guardian of the person has been appointed by order of a county or probate court and a managing conservator has not been appointed, the child resides in the county where the guardian of the person resides;

(2) if the parents of the child do not reside in the same county and if a managing conservator, custodian, or guardian of the person has not been appointed, the child resides in the county where the parent having actual care, control, and possession of the child resides;

(3) if the child is in the care and control of an adult other than a parent and a managing conservator, custodian, or guardian of the person has not been appointed, the child resides where the adult having actual care, control, and possession of the child resides;

(4) if the child is in the actual care, control, and possession of an adult other than a parent and the whereabouts of the parent and the guardian of the person is unknown, the child resides where the adult having actual possession, care, and control of the child resides;

(5) if the person whose residence would otherwise determine venue has left the child in the care and control of the adult, the child resides where that adult resides;

(6) if a guardian or custodian of the child has been appointed by order of a court of another state or country, the child resides in the county where the guardian or custodian resides if that person resides in this state; or

(7) if it appears that the child is not under the actual care, control, and possession of an adult, the child resides where the child is found.

§ 103.002. Transfer of Original Proceedings Within State.

(a) If venue of a suit is improper in the court in which an original suit is filed and no other court has continuing, exclusive jurisdiction of the suit, on the timely motion of a party other than the petitioner, the court shall transfer the proceeding to the county where venue is proper.

(b) On a showing that a suit for dissolution of the marriage of the child's parents has been filed in another court, a court in which a suit is pending shall transfer the proceedings to the court where the dissolution of the marriage is pending.

(c) The procedures in Chapter 155 *[Continuing, Exclusive Jurisdiction; Transfer]* apply to a transfer of:

(1) an original suit under this section; or

(2) a suit for modification or a motion for enforcement under this title.

§ 103.003. Transfer of Original Suit Within State when Party or Child Resides Outside State.

(a) A court of this state in which an original suit is filed or in which a suit for child support is filed under Chapter 159 *[UIFSA]* shall transfer the suit to the county of residence of the party who is a resident of this state if all other parties and children affected by the proceedings reside outside this state.

(b) If one or more of the parties affected by the suit reside outside this state and if more than one party or one or more children affected by the proceeding reside in this state in different counties, the court shall transfer the suit according to the following priorities:

(1) to the court of continuing, exclusive jurisdiction, if any;

(2) to the county of residence of the child, if applicable, provided that:

(A) there is no court of continuing, exclusive jurisdiction; or

(B) the court of continuing, exclusive jurisdiction finds that neither a party nor a child affected by the proceeding resides in the county of the court of continuing jurisdiction; or

(3) if Subdivisions (1) and (2) are inapplicable, to the county most appropriate to serve the convenience of the resident parties, the witnesses, and the interest of justice.

(c) If a transfer of an original suit or suit for child support under Chapter 159 is sought under this section, Chapter 155 *[Continuing, Exclusive Jurisdiction; Transfer]* applies to the procedures for transfer of the suit.

Chapter 104. Evidence.

Introductory Comment

Several very dissimilar procedures regarding testimony of a child in a SAPCR are established by this Chapter. The first is designed to facilitate the testimony of a child given at trial, either by remote live broadcast or by prerecorded tape. The second procedure deals with a wholly unrelated matter, *i.e.*, the videotape pre-trial recording of the "first outcry" of an allegedly abused or neglected child. If the methodology described is followed carefully, the resulting videotape may be introduced into evidence at trial as yet another exception to the hearsay rule. Third, procedures are detailed for remote broadcast of a child's testimony at trial. Finally, provisions are made for a variety of other methods to put the child's statements in the record. The last of these was added in 2003, when expert testimony could be given through video conference.

CLE/Other Legal Publications

High tech evidence and internet research. Richard L. Robertson, 2004 Adv. Fam. L.

Effective evidence: what works, what doesn't work, and how to get it in! Sydney Aaron Beckman, 2004 Adv. Fam. L.

A walkthrough the TRE: your top ten problems. Frank W. Sullivan III, 2004 Marriage Dissolution

Electronic evidence. Randall B. Wilhite & Karl Hays, 2004 Marriage Dissolution

Revisiting the rules of evidence. Warren Cole, 2004 U. Tex. Fam. L. Front Lines

Proving it up and getting it in: foreign law and foreign evidence. Ann Crawford McClure & Richard R. Orsinger, 2004 U. Tex. Fam. L. on the Border

Difficult evidence questions. Coye Conner, 2003 Adv. Fam. L.

Keeping private stuff private. Katherine A. Kinser, 2003 Adv. Fam. L.

Tracking the cyber-predator—electronic evidence in child abuse cases. E. Hays, Edwin (Ted) Terry, Andrea Foltz, 2003 Adv. Fam. L.

Illegally obtained evidence. Warren Cole, 2003 Adv. Fam. L.

High tech evidence: how to find it, retrieve it, and get it in. Edwin J. (Ted) Terry, Karl E. Hays, James A. Vaught & James LaRue, 2002 Adv. Fam. L.

Use and abuse of mental health professionals after Daubert. Keith M. Nelson & Jan Marie DeLipsey, 2002 Adv. Fam. L.

Evidence law update. Frank W. Sullivan III, 2002 Adv. Fam. L.

Persuasive evidence in custody cases. Kevin R. Fuller, 2002 Adv. Fam. L.

Child's voice in custody litigation. (Workshop) 2002 Adv. Fam. L.

Look who's talking now: hearsay and its exceptions, including child's state of mind. Sally H. Emerson, 2001 Adv. Fam. L.

A blind hog in search of an acorn—what findings of fact do you need? Ann C. McClure, 2001 Adv. Fam. L.

Leading Cases

In re Kuntz, 124 S.W.3d 179 (Tex. 2003) (defining what is required regarding discovery or documents in person's "possession, custody, or control")

Kumho Tire Company, Ltd. v. Carmichael, 526 U.S. 137, 119 S.Ct. 1167 (1999) (*Daubert* factors apply to scientific testimony not just to "scientific" testimony)

Thompson v. Davis, 901 S.W.2d 939 (Tex. 1995) (court abused discretion by extending discovery sanction in child support action to custody case)

Richardson v. Green, 677 S.W.2d 497 (Tex. 1984) (termination reversed, videotape of child replete with leading questions by caseworker)

In re C.D.K., 64 S.W.3d 679 (Tex. App.—Amarillo 2002, no pet.) (admission of expert witness testimony that father had propensity for sexual deviancy without showing of reliability and validity of testing is abuse of discretion)

James v. Texas Dept. of Human Services, 836 S.W.2d 236 (Tex. App.—Texarkana 1992, no writ) (termination justified despite erroneously admitted videotape of child being asked leading questions)

Ochs v. Martinez, 789 S.W.2d 949 (Tex. App.—San Antonio 1990, writ denied) (caseworker's questions on alleged sex abuse too leading)

---

§ 104.001. Rules of Evidence.

Except as otherwise provided, the Texas Rules of Civil Evidence apply as in other civil cases.

Comment

Although effective March 1, 1998, the Supreme Court of Texas renamed the "Texas Rules of Civil Evidence" as the Texas Rules of Evidence, there has been no corrective amendment to the Family Code.

Leading Cases

Daubert v. Merrill Dow Pharmaceuticals, Inc. 113 S.Ct. 2786 (1993) (landmark case excluding "junk" science)

Moore v. Ashland Chemical, Inc., 151 F.3d 269 (5th Cir. 1997), *cert. denied*, 119 S.Ct. 1454 (1999) (*Daubert* standard inapplicable to clinical medical testimony)

Gammill v. Jack Williams Chevrolet, Inc., 972 S.W.2d 713 (Tex. 1998) (*Daubert* standards apply to all experts, not just novel scientific techniques)

E.I. Dupont de Nemours and Co., Inc. v. Robinson, 923 S.W.2d 549 (Tex. 1995) (landmark Texas case excluding "junk "science)

America West Airlines, Inc. v. Tope, 935 S.W.2d 908 (Tex. App.—El Paso 1996, no writ) (*Dupont* standard applied to mental health expert)

Wolfe v. Wolfe, 918 S.W.2d 533 (Tex. App.—El Paso 1996, writ denied) (demonstrative evidence of father's sexual practices properly excluded)

---

§ 104.002. Prerecorded Statement of Child.

If a child 12 years of age or younger is alleged in a suit under this title to have been abused, the recording of an oral statement of the child recorded prior to the proceeding is admissible into evidence if:

(1) no attorney for a party was present when the statement was made;

(2) the recording is both visual and aural and is recorded on film or videotape or by other electronic means;

(3) the recording equipment was capable of making an accurate recording, the operator was competent, and the recording is accurate and has not been altered;

(4) the statement was not made in response to questioning calculated to lead the child to make a particular statement;

(5) each voice on the recording is identified;

(6) the person conducting the interview of the child in the recording is present at the proceeding and available to testify or be cross-examined by either party; and

(7) each party is afforded an opportunity to view the recording before it is offered into evidence.

CLE/Other Legal Publications

The child as a witness. Jan Marie Delipsey & Paula Larsen, 2000 ADV. FAM. L.

---

§ 104.003. Prerecorded Videotaped Testimony of Child.

(a) The court may, on the motion of a party to the proceeding, order that the testimony of the child be taken outside the courtroom and be recorded for showing in the courtroom before the court, the finder of fact, and the parties to the proceeding.

(b) Only an attorney for each party, an attorney ad litem for the child or other person whose presence would contribute to the welfare and well-being of the child, and persons necessary to operate the equipment may be present in the room with the child during the child's testimony.

(c) Only the attorneys for the parties may question the child.

(d) The persons operating the equipment shall be placed in a manner that prevents the child from seeing or hearing them.

(e) The court shall ensure that:

(1) the recording is both visual and aural and is recorded on film or videotape or by other electronic means;

(2) the recording equipment was capable of making an accurate recording, the operator was competent, and the recording is accurate and is not altered;

(3) each voice on the recording is identified; and

(4) each party to the proceeding is afforded an opportunity to view the recording before it is shown in the courtroom.

§ 104.004. Remote Televised Broadcast of Testimony of Child.

(a) If in a suit a child 12 years of age or younger is alleged to have been abused, the court may, on the motion of a party to the proceeding, order that the testimony of the child be taken in a room other than the courtroom and be televised by closed-circuit equipment in the courtroom to be viewed by the court and the parties.

(b) The procedures that apply to prerecorded videotaped testimony of a child apply to the remote broadcast of testimony of a child.

Leading Cases

Maryland v. Craig, 497 U.S. 836, 111 L.Ed.2d 666, 110 S.Ct. 3157 (1990) (closed circuit TV testimony by child victim of criminal sexual abuse does not violate confrontation clause)

In re R.V., 977 S.W.2d 777 (Tex. App.—Fort Worth 1998, no pet.) (court to authorize child's testimony by remote TV on case-by-case basis as required to mitigate negative effect on child)

---

§ 104.005. Substitution for In-Court Testimony of Child.

(a) If the testimony of a child is taken as provided by this chapter, the child may not be compelled to testify in court during the proceeding.

(b) The court may allow the testimony of a child of any age to be taken in any manner provided by this chapter if the child, because of a medical condition, is incapable of testifying in open court.

Comment

The special rules for testimony of a child 12 or younger are extended to older children if the court finds that a child is incapable of testifying in open court. The literal language seems to limit this exception to a medical condition, and not to a psychological or emotional condition. This, of course, leads to the option of "medical treatment" by a psychiatrist, thereby opening the door for the argument that psychiatric difficulties are a medical condition.

---

§ 104.006. Hearsay Statement of Child Abuse Victim.

In a suit affecting the parent-child relationship, a statement made by a child 12 years of age or younger that describes alleged abuse against the child, without regard to whether the statement is otherwise inadmissible as hearsay, is admissible as evidence if, in a hearing conducted outside the presence of the jury, the court finds that the time, content, and circumstances of the statement provide sufficient indications of the statement's reliability and:

(1) the child testifies or is available to testify at the proceeding in court or in any other manner provided for by law; or

(2) the court determines that the use of the statement in lieu of the child's testimony is necessary to protect the welfare of the child.

Comment

Prosecutors representing DPRS, or other litigants alleging child abuse, may find this section extremely useful. Third parties may testify as to hearsay statements by a child about abuse. Several requirements are imposed. Either the child must be available to testify, or actually does testify. More importantly, the court may determine that the introduction of the statement is an appropriate substitute for the child's testimony if necessary to protect the child's welfare. Of course, the court must also find the statement to be reliable. A young child whose memory is of the short term variety thus may have the original outcry reproduced in court by a substitute witness.

Leading Cases

In re P.E.W., 105 S.W.3d 771 (Tex. App.—Amarillo 2003, no pet.) (child's abuse statements deemed reliable)

---

§ 104.007. Video Testimony of Certain Professionals.

(a) In this section, "professional" has the meaning assigned by Section 261.101(b).

(b) In a proceeding brought by the Department of Protective and Regulatory Services concerning a child who is alleged in a suit to have been abused or

neglected, the court may order, with the agreement of the state's counsel and the defendant's counsel, that the testimony of a professional be taken outside the courtroom by videoconference.

(c) In ordering testimony to be taken as provided by Subsection (b), the court shall ensure that the videoconference testimony allows:

(1) the parties and attorneys involved in the proceeding to be able to see and hear the professional as the professional testifies; and

(2) the professional to be able to see and hear the parties and attorneys examining the professional while the professional is testifying.

(d) If the court permits the testimony of a professional by videoconference as provided by this section to be admitted during the proceeding, the professional may not be compelled to be physically present in court during the same proceeding to provide the same testimony unless ordered by the court.

History: Enacted by 78th Legis., Reg. Sess. (2003), H.B. 1869, eff. Sept. 1, 2003, and "applies to testimony taken on or after the effective date of this Act in a proceeding in a suit affecting the parent-child relationship involving an allegation of the abuse or neglect of a child regardless of whether: (1) the allegation was made before, on, or after the effective date of this Act; or (2) the suit commenced before, on, or after the effective date of this Act."

Comment

Over the years, the courts have become accustomed to the relatively rare situation in which a child is permitted to testify either by pre-recorded videotape or by remote live televised broadcast. The extension of this privilege to professionals to accept video conference testimony regarding alleged abuse or neglect of a child is obviously based on quite different philosophy. That is, the child's testimony through video means is to protect the child, while this extension will be necessary only for the convenience of the professional and perhaps the attorneys.

Chapter 105. Settings, Hearings, and Orders.

---

§ 105.001. Temporary Orders Before Final Order.

(a) In a suit, the court may make a temporary order, including the modification of a prior temporary order, for the safety and welfare of the child, including an order:

(1) for the temporary conservatorship of the child;

(2) for the temporary support of the child;

(3) restraining a party from [~~molesting or~~] disturbing the peace of the child or another party;

(4) prohibiting a person from removing the child beyond a geographical area identified by the court; or

(5) for payment of reasonable attorney's fees and expenses.

(b) Except as provided by Subsection (c), temporary restraining orders and temporary injunctions under this section shall be granted without the necessity of an affidavit or verified pleading stating specific facts showing that immediate and irreparable injury, loss, or damage will result before notice can be served and a hearing can be held. Except as provided by Subsection (h), an order may not be rendered under Subsection (a)(1), (2), or (5) except after notice and a hearing. A temporary restraining order or temporary injunction granted under this section need not:

(1) define the injury or state why it is irreparable;

(2) state why the order was granted without notice; or

(3) include an order setting the cause for trial on the merits with respect to the ultimate relief requested.

(c) Except on a verified pleading or an affidavit in accordance with the Texas Rules of Civil Procedure, an order may not be rendered:

(1) attaching the body of the child;

(2) taking the child into the possession of the court or of a **person** [~~parent~~] designated by the court; or

(3) excluding a parent from possession of or access to a child.

(d) In a suit, the court may dispense with the necessity of a bond in connection with temporary orders on behalf of the child.

(e) Temporary orders rendered under this section are not subject to interlocutory appeal.

(f) The violation of a temporary restraining order, temporary injunction, or other temporary order rendered under this section is punishable by contempt and the order is subject to and enforceable under Chapter 157 *[Enforcement]*.

(g) The rebuttable presumptions established in favor of the application of the guidelines for a child support order and for the standard possession order under Chapters 153 *[Conservatorship, Possession, and Access]* and 154 *[Child Support]* apply to temporary orders. The presumptions do not limit the authority of the court to render other temporary orders.

(h) An order under Subsection (a)(1) may be rendered without notice and an adversary hearing if the order is an emergency order sought by a governmental entity under Chapter 262 *[Procedures in Suit by Governmental Unit]*.

History: Amended by 78th Legis., Reg. Sess. (2003), H.B. 913, eff. Sept. 1, 2003. "The changes in law made by this Act to Sections 105.001(a) and (c), Family Code, apply only to an order rendered in a suit affecting the parent-child relationship on or after the effective date of this Act. An order rendered in a suit affecting the parent-child relationship before the effective date of this Act is governed by the law in effect on the date the order was rendered, and the former law is continued in effect for that purpose."

Comment

A trial court has great discretion in rendering temporary orders, particularly because those orders are nonappealable. Temporary orders for custody and child support may be entered only after a hearing, although the status quo may be maintained by an *ex parte* court order pending a hearing. The legislature has decided that an *ex parte* order awarding use of the family home may be rendered in situations involving domestic violence. The broad power of a trial court permits modification of temporary orders at any time. The test for rendition of a new temporary order in a SAPCR is identical to that for the original order, *i.e.*, "for the safety and welfare of the child."

Chapter 262 provides that a court has the power to enter a temporary order when the DPRS seeks an emergency order to authorize a rescue of an allegedly abused or neglected child or to approve a prior rescue of a child from an emergency situation. Subsection (h) recognizes that authority and declares that the temporary order statute is consistent with such emergency orders.

CLE/Other Legal Publications

Temporary and protective order traps. James M. Loveless, 2002 Adv. Fam. L.

Trying the complicated TRO in two hours. Susan A. Rankin, 2002 Adv. Fam. L.

Temporary hearings: family violence, guns, and related issues. Rhonda F. Hunter, 2002 Marriage Dissolution

Preparing the trial notebook for the temporary orders hearing. Sheri Cothrun, 2001 Adv. Fam. L.

Temporary orders. Wendy S. Burgower, 2001 Marriage Dissolution

Leading Cases

Baltimore City Dept. Social Services v. Bouknight, 493 U.S. 549, 107 L.Ed.2d 992, 110 S.Ct. 900 (1990) (mother may be ordered to produce suspected abused child; contempt upheld, 5th amendment does not apply)

Grigsby v. Coker, 904 S.W.2d 619 (Tex. 1995) ("gag order" only valid in civil proceeding under strict conditions not present in this case)

Ex parte Slavin, 412 S.W.2d 43 (Tex. 1967) (specificity required for contempt enforcement)

In re Aubin, 29 S.W.3d 199 (Tex. App.—Beaumont 2000, no pet.) (Texas court cannot issue writ of attachment for possession of child residing in another state)

Ex parte Hughey, 932 S.W.2d 308 (Tex. App.—Tyler 1996, no writ) (no habeas—order that obligor comply with temporary orders, pay support and attorney fee arrearages, is not restraint of liberty)

In re Shaftner, 900 S.W.2d 439 (Tex. App.—Texarkana 1995, no writ) (father seeking access to child entitled to jury)

Saxton v. Daggett, 864 S.W.2d 729 (Tex. App.—Houston [1st Dist.] 1993, no writ) (failure to pay attorney's fees doesn't justify suspending visitation or striking pleadings)

Ex parte Wessell, 807 S.W.2d 17 (Tex. App.—Houston [14th Dist.] 1991, no writ) (receiver authorized to take paychecks to enforce child support and attorney's fees)

O.G. v. Baum, 790 S.W.2d 839 (Tex. App.—Houston [1st Dist.] 1990, no writ) (temporary orders in a medical emergency/blood transfusion)

Cross References

Tex. Fam. Code Ann. §§ 6.501–.502. Temporary Orders; § 6.504. Protective Orders.

Tex. R. Civ. P. 171. Master in Chancery; 680. Temporary Restraining Order.

Texas Family Law Practice Manual

Forms 31–2. Petitioner's Supporting Affidavit; *31–3.* Temporary Restraining Order and Order Setting Hearing for Temporary Orders; *31–4.* Notice of Hearing for Temporary Orders; *31–5.* Temporary Orders in Suit Affecting Parent–Child Relationship

---

§ 105.002. Jury.

(a) Except as provided by Subsection (b), a party may demand a jury trial.

(b) A party may not demand a jury trial in:

(1) a suit in which adoption is sought, including a trial on the issue of denial or revocation of consent to the adoption by the managing conservator; or

(2) a suit to adjudicate parentage under Chapter 160 *[Uniform Parentage Act]*.

(c) In a jury trial:

(1) a party is entitled to a verdict by the jury **and the court may not contravene a jury verdict** on the issues of:

(A) the appointment of a **sole** managing conservator;

(B) the appointment of joint managing conservators;

(C) the appointment of a possessory conservator; [~~and~~]

(D) the determination of **which joint managing conservator has the exclusive right to designate** the primary residence of the child;

(E) the determination of whether to impose a restriction on the geographic area in which a joint managing conservator may designate the child's primary residence; and

(F) if a restriction described by Paragraph (E) is imposed, the determination of the geographic area within which the joint managing conservator must designate the child's primary residence; and

(2) **the court may not submit** [~~a party is not entitled~~] to **the** [~~a~~] jury **questions** [~~verdict~~] on the issues of:

(A) [~~child~~] support **under Chapter 154 or Chapter 159**;

(B) a specific term or condition of possession of or access to the child; or

(C) any right or duty of a [~~possessory or managing~~] conservator, other than the **determination of which joint managing conservator has the exclusive**

right to designate the [~~issue of~~] primary residence **of the child** [~~determined~~] under Subdivision (1)(D)[~~; and~~

[~~(3) the court may submit to the jury an issue described by Subdivision (2)~~].

(C) any right or duty of a [~~possessory or managing~~] conservator, other than the **determination of which joint managing conservator has the exclusive right to designate the** [~~issue of~~] primary residence **of the child** [~~determined~~] under Subdivision (1)(D)[~~; and~~

(d) [~~The court may not contravene a jury verdict on an issue submitted under Subsection (c)(1). A jury verdict on an issue submitted under Subsection (c)(3) is advisory only.~~] Repealed by Acts 2003, 78th Leg., ch. 1036, § 22.

History: Amended by 78th Legis., Reg. Sess. (2003), H.B. 913, eff. Sept. 1, 2003. "The changes in law made by this Act to Sections 105.002(c) and 153.008, Family Code, apply only to a suit affecting the parent-child relationship filed on or after the effective date of this Act. A suit affecting the parent-child relationship filed before the effective date of this Act is governed by the law in effect on the date that the suit was filed, and the former law is continued in effect for that purpose."

Comment

Lawyers in other states regard Texas with a mixture of wonderment, awe and distaste because of our wide-ranging availability of jury trials in SAPCRs as stated in subsection (a). Texas lawyers not only are accustomed to the practice, but swear by it. In truth, jury trials are more talked and written about than actually conducted because of the time and cost involved. For example, for the fiscal year ending August 31, 2002, the Office of Court Administration produced some startling statistics. There were 628,786 family law cases (divorce, UIFSA, and other) on the docket, and 327,214 dispositions. Of these, there were 164 jury verdicts and 112 directed verdicts. In sum, .0008% of all family law dispositions were resolved through a jury trial.

There are limits to jury trials in SAPCR's; the prohibition of a jury in an adoption case long-predates the Family Code. In 1999, the legislature conformed to the demands of the U.S. Congress prohibiting a jury trial in a parentage action. The 1996 Welfare Reform Act, commonly known as PRWORA, tied the federal child support subsidy to such a prohibition. 42 U.S.C.A. § 666(a)(5)(I).

For over 25 years the rule has been that when a trial court disagrees with a jury verdict on custody, the court cannot enter a judgment N.O.V. Rather, the court's power is limited to ordering a new trial.

In 1995, the restriction prohibiting rendition of a judgment that contravenes the jury's determination of custody was potentially undercut by the enactment of a presumptive award of joint managing conservatorship. Award of a JMC "ordinarily should involve the designation of a primary residence for the child." A real question arose regarding whether the designation of the primary residence is to be left to the discretion of the trial court on the principle that terms of a JMC are reserved to the court. In the opinion of many, including the Family Law Council, such a statutory construction would virtually eliminate the utility of a custody jury trial. A 1997 amendment attempted to settle this issue by declaring that the primary residence of the child is for the jury to decide, which decision of the jury may not be contravened by the trial court. The issue probably is best viewed as a recognition that the ultimate issue is no longer "which party should be sole MC?" Rather, it is "which JMC should provide the child's principal residence?" From that perspective, the amendment continues broad form submission and does not herald a return to special issues practice.

Notwithstanding the revised language of 1997, the balance between the determination of a jury for the fundamental issues of custody and the details left to the court as terms of conservatorship remained in an uneasy balance. This was exemplified by the extended litigation and final resolution of the case of *Lenz v. Lenz*, 79 S.W.3d 10 (Tex. 2002), which held that the trial court had improperly contravened the jury's verdict when it ruled that the mother's right to establish the primary residence of the child could be restricted by the court to Bexar County. The operative language was:

> [A]lthough the trial court ordered modification 'pursuant to the jury's verdict,' it imposed its own primary residence restriction. By doing this, the trial court rejected the jury's verdict giving [the mother] the exclusive right to decide her sons' primary residence and granted their alternative remedy [the father] sought in his motion, which was to restrict the children's primary residence to Bexar County. In this way, the trial court implicitly disposed of the motion for judgment notwithstanding the verdict. ... [The mother] is correct that the statute's plain language means that she was entitled to a jury verdict in this case, and the trial court was not authorized to contravene that verdict by imposing an additional geographical restriction. *Id*. at 13, 20.

In 2003 the legislature, spurred on by the Family Law Council, again sought to settle the issue and resolve the balance in favor of the jury. If the issue is relocation, the issue is primary residence, and not just title of joint managing conservator, but rather the primary conservator versus the JMC who in other states would be called the noncustodial parent. The legislature has come down on the side of a jury verdict on this issue. Other issues, such as child support and other terms of conservatorship, are left for the judge to decide.

CLE/Other Legal Publications

Developing and preparing witnesses in custody cases. Jo Chris G. Lopez, 2004 Adv. Fam. L.

Deposition strategies for kids and cash. Thomas Albert Greenwald, 2004 Adv. Fam. L.

The art of evaluating a custody case. Keith M. Nelson, 2004 Adv. Fam. L.

Fundamental litigation techniques. J. Steven King & Kyle A. Whitaker, 2004 Adv. Fam. L.

Litigation outside the box. Lisa Kaye Hoppes, 2004 Adv. Fam. L.

Handling a custody case on a shoe string. Glenn David Villafranca, 2003 Adv. Fam. L.

Preparing witnesses and clients for trial. Sydney A. Beckman, 2003 Adv. Fam. L.

Creative trial presentation. Sydney A. Beckman, 2002 Marriage Dissolution

So you've paid a jury fee—now what are you going to ask them? Binding and non-binding jury issues in family law. Wendy S. Burgower, 2001 Adv. Fam. L.

Voir dire on the hard issues. (Panel) 2001 Adv. Fam. L.

Leading Cases

J.E.B. v. T.B., 511 U.S. 127, 128 L.Ed.2d 89, 114 S.Ct. 1419 (1994) (U.S. Const. prohibits discrimination in jury selection on basis of sex)

Ex parte Sproull, 815 S.W.2d 250 (Tex. 1991) (alleged contemnor has right to jury trial, contempt yields sentence longer than six months)

Texas Dept. of Human Services v. E.B., 802 S.W.2d 647 (Tex. 1990) (controlling question in termination of parental rights case; PJC–5 approved)

Martin v. Martin, 776 S.W.2d 572 (Tex. 1989) (no absolute right to jury when issue is terms and conditions of conservatorship; answers would not bind court)

In re Hill, 893 S.W.2d 753 (Tex. App.—Amarillo 1995, writ denied) (jury charge setting forth alternative grounds for termination of parental rights acceptable)

In re A.D.E., 880 S.W.2d 241 (Tex. App.—Corpus Christi 1994, no writ) (mother's *Batson* challenge fails; jury strikes adequately explained)

Grossnickel v. Grossnickel, 865 S.W.2d. 211 (Tex. App.—Texarkana 1993, no writ) (denial of jury trial held reversible error)

Ex parte Howell, 843 S.W.2d 241 (Tex. App.—Houston [1st Dist.] 1993, no writ) (no jury trial for contempt if sentence not more than six months)

Cross References

Tex. Const. art. I, § 15. Right of Trial by Jury; art. V, § 10. Trial by Jury.

Texas Family Law Practice Manual

Forms 16–9. Request for Jury Trial; *16–10*. Motion To Equalize Peremptory Challenges; *16–11*. Motion for Separate Peremptory Challenges; *16–14*. Motion for Special Instructions to Jury Panel; *16–16*. Requested Special Charge; *16–17*. Objections to Jury Charge.

Texas Pattern Jury Charges: Family

PJC ch. 215. Definitions and Instructions—Suits Affecting the Parent–Child Relationship.

PJC ch. 216. Conservatorship and Support—Original Suits.

PJC ch. 217. Modification of Conservatorship and Support.

PJC ch. 218. Termination of Parent–Child Relationship.

---

§ 105.003. Procedure for Contested Hearing.

(a) Except as otherwise provided by this title, proceedings shall be as in civil cases generally.

(b) On the agreement of all parties to the suit, the court may limit attendance at the hearing to only those persons who have a direct interest in the suit or in the work of the court.

(c) A record shall be made as in civil cases generally unless waived by the parties with the consent of the court.

(d) When information contained in a report, study, or examination is before the court, the person making the report, study, or examination is subject to both direct examination and cross-examination as in civil cases generally.

(e) The hearing may be adjourned from time to time.

Comment

Although this section states that rules of evidence and procedure are to be applied as in other civil cases, the trial of a SAPCR is likely to be technically less scrupulous because of the overriding interests of the child. Indeed, authority abounds for the proposition that "the paramount concern is the best interest of the children and the technical rules of pleading and practice are not of controlling importance." *Barrow v. Durham*, 574 S.W.2d 857 (Tex. Civ. App.—Corpus Christi 1978), *affirmed*, 600 S.W.2d 756 (Tex. 1980); *see* latest restatement of this principle.

CLE/Other Legal Publications

All together now! Uniform practices and procedures. Doretha Henderson & Diane Dockery, 2001 Adv. Fam. L.

Leading Cases

Rogers v. Rogers, 561 S.W.2d 172 (Tex. 1978) (inability to obtain statement of facts constitutes reversible error)

In re Vega, 10 S.W.3d 720 (Tex. App.—Amarillo 1999, no pet.) (trial court can not consent to waive making of record in parentage action when alleged father not present or represented by attorney)

G.S.K. v. T.K.N., 940 S.W.2d 797 (Tex. App.—El Paso 1997, no writ) (in termination proceeding, absent party did not waive record)

Henning v. Henning, 889 S.W.2d 611 (Tex. App.—Houston [14th Dist.] 1994, writ denied) (party waives right to record if fails to exercise diligence in seeking record)

§ 105.004. Preferential Setting.

After a hearing, the court may:

(1) grant a motion filed by a party or the attorney or guardian ad litem for the child for a preferential setting for a trial on the merits; and

(2) give precedence to that hearing over other civil cases if the court finds that the delay created by ordinary scheduling practices will unreasonably affect the best interest of the child.

Texas Family Law Practice Manual

Form 16–3. Motion for Preferential Setting

§ 105.005. Findings.

Except as otherwise provided by this title, the court's findings shall be based on a preponderance of the evidence.

Comment

Issues in a SAPCR are always serious, but an enhanced burden of proof is accorded explicit recognition in the statute only when the state seeks to terminate parental rights, *see* §§ 161.001, *et. seq.*, *infra*. But, because the parental preference is based on constitutional considerations, *see* § 153.131, *infra*, the state's burden when litigating against parents very well may be enhanced despite the fact that the statute nominally provides that a preponderance of the evidence is all that is ordinarily required in a SAPCR.

Leading Case

Lewelling v. Lewelling, 796 S.W.2d 164 (Tex. 1990) (parental preference creates very strong presumption)

§ 105.006. Contents of Final Order.

(a) A final order, other than in a proceeding under Chapter 161 *[Termination of the Parent–Child Relationship]* or 162 *[Adoption]*, must contain:

(1) the social security number and driver's license number of each party to the suit, including the child, except that the child's social security number or driver's license number is not required if the child has not been assigned a social security number or driver's license number; and

(2) each party's current residence address, mailing address, home telephone number, name of employer, address of employment, and work telephone number, except as provided by Subsection (c).

(b) Except as provided by Subsection (c), the court shall order each party to inform each other party, the court that rendered the order, and the state case registry under Chapter 234 *[State Case Registry]* of an intended change in any of the information required by this section as long as any person, as a result of the order, is under an obligation to pay child support or is entitled to possession of or access to a child. The court shall order that notice of the intended change be given at the earlier of:

(1) the 60th day before the date the party intends to make the change; or

(2) the fifth day after the date that the party knew of the change, if the party did not know or could not have known of the change in sufficient time to comply with Subdivision (1).

(c) If a court finds after notice and hearing that requiring a party to provide the information required by this section to another party is likely to cause the child or a conservator harassment, abuse, serious harm, or injury, the court may:

(1) order the information not to be disclosed to another party; or

(2) render any other order the court considers necessary.

(d) An order in a suit that orders child support or possession of or access to a child must contain the following prominently displayed statement in boldfaced type, capital letters, or underlined:

"FAILURE TO OBEY A COURT ORDER FOR CHILD SUPPORT OR FOR POSSESSION OF OR ACCESS TO A CHILD MAY RESULT IN FURTHER LITIGATION TO ENFORCE THE ORDER, INCLUDING CONTEMPT OF COURT. A FINDING OF CONTEMPT MAY BE PUNISHED BY CONFINEMENT IN JAIL FOR UP TO SIX MONTHS, A FINE OF UP TO $500 FOR EACH VIOLATION, AND A MONEY JUDGMENT FOR PAYMENT OF ATTORNEY'S FEES AND COURT COSTS."

"FAILURE OF A PARTY TO MAKE A CHILD SUPPORT PAYMENT TO THE PLACE AND IN THE MANNER REQUIRED BY A COURT ORDER MAY RESULT IN THE PARTY NOT RECEIVING CREDIT FOR MAKING THE PAYMENT."

"FAILURE OF A PARTY TO PAY CHILD SUPPORT DOES NOT JUSTIFY DENYING THAT PARTY COURT-ORDERED POSSESSION OF OR ACCESS TO A CHILD. REFUSAL BY A PARTY TO ALLOW POSSESSION OF OR ACCESS TO A CHILD DOES NOT JUSTIFY FAILURE TO PAY COURT-ORDERED CHILD SUPPORT TO THAT PARTY."

(e) Except as provided by Subsection (c), an order in a suit that orders child support or possession of or access to a child must also contain the following prominently displayed statement in boldfaced type, capital letters, or underlined:

"EACH PERSON WHO IS A PARTY TO THIS ORDER IS ORDERED TO NOTIFY EACH OTHER PARTY, THE COURT, AND THE STATE CASE REGISTRY OF ANY CHANGE IN THE PARTY'S CURRENT RESIDENCE ADDRESS, MAILING ADDRESS, HOME TELEPHONE NUMBER, NAME OF EMPLOYER, ADDRESS OF EMPLOYMENT, DRIVER'S LICENSE NUMBER, AND WORK TELEPHONE NUMBER. THE PARTY IS ORDERED TO GIVE NOTICE OF AN INTENDED CHANGE IN ANY OF THE REQUIRED INFORMATION TO EACH OTHER PARTY, THE COURT, AND THE STATE CASE REGISTRY ON OR BEFORE THE 60TH DAY BEFORE THE INTENDED CHANGE. IF THE PARTY DOES NOT KNOW OR COULD NOT HAVE KNOWN OF THE CHANGE IN SUFFICIENT TIME TO PROVIDE 60-DAY NOTICE, THE PARTY IS ORDERED TO GIVE NOTICE OF THE CHANGE ON OR BEFORE

THE FIFTH DAY AFTER THE DATE THAT THE PARTY KNOWS OF THE CHANGE."

"THE DUTY TO FURNISH THIS INFORMATION TO EACH OTHER PARTY, THE COURT, AND THE STATE CASE REGISTRY CONTINUES AS LONG AS ANY PERSON, BY VIRTUE OF THIS ORDER, IS UNDER AN OBLIGATION TO PAY CHILD SUPPORT OR ENTITLED TO POSSESSION OF OR ACCESS TO A CHILD."

"FAILURE BY A PARTY TO OBEY THE ORDER OF THIS COURT TO PROVIDE EACH OTHER PARTY, THE COURT, AND THE STATE CASE REGISTRY WITH THE CHANGE IN THE REQUIRED INFORMATION MAY RESULT IN FURTHER LITIGATION TO ENFORCE THE ORDER, INCLUDING CONTEMPT OF COURT. A FINDING OF CONTEMPT MAY BE PUNISHED BY CONFINEMENT IN JAIL FOR UP TO SIX MONTHS, A FINE OF UP TO $500 FOR EACH VIOLATION, AND A MONEY JUDGMENT FOR PAYMENT OF ATTORNEY'S FEES AND COURT COSTS."

(e–1) An order in a suit that provides for the possession of or access to a child must contain the following prominently displayed statement in boldfaced type, in capital letters, or underlined:

"NOTICE TO ANY PEACE OFFICER OF THE STATE OF TEXAS: YOU MAY USE REASONABLE EFFORTS TO ENFORCE THE TERMS OF CHILD CUSTODY SPECIFIED IN THIS ORDER. A PEACE OFFICER WHO RELIES ON THE TERMS OF A COURT ORDER AND THE OFFICER'S AGENCY ARE ENTITLED TO THE APPLICABLE IMMUNITY AGAINST ANY CLAIM, CIVIL OR OTHERWISE, REGARDING THE OFFICER'S GOOD FAITH ACTS PERFORMED IN THE SCOPE OF THE OFFICER'S DUTIES IN ENFORCING THE TERMS OF THE ORDER THAT RELATE TO CHILD CUSTODY. ANY PERSON WHO KNOWINGLY PRESENTS FOR ENFORCEMENT AN ORDER THAT IS INVALID OR NO LONGER IN EFFECT COMMITS AN OFFENSE THAT MAY BE PUNISHABLE BY CONFINEMENT IN JAIL FOR AS LONG AS TWO YEARS AND A FINE OF AS MUCH AS $10,000."

(f) Except for an action in which contempt is sought, in any subsequent child support enforcement action, the court may, on a showing that diligent effort has been made to determine the location of a party, consider due process requirements for notice and service of process to be met with respect to that party on delivery of written notice to the most recent residential or employer address filed by that party with the court and the state case registry.

(g) The Title IV-D agency shall promulgate and provide forms for a party to use in reporting to the court and, when established, to the state case registry under Chapter 234 the information required under this section.

(h) The court may include in a final order in a suit in which a party to the suit makes an allegation of child abuse or neglect a finding on whether the party who made the allegation knew that the allegation was false. This finding shall not constitute collateral estoppel for any criminal proceeding. The court may impose on a party found to have made a false allegation of child abuse or neglect any civil sanction permitted under law, including attorney's fees, costs of experts, and any other costs.

History: Amended by 78th Legis., Reg. Sess. (2003), H.B. 227, eff. Sept. 1, 2003, and "applies only to a court order providing for the possession of or access to a child that is rendered on or after the effective date of this Act. A court order providing for the possession of or access to a child that is rendered before the effective date of this Act is governed by the law in effect immediately before the effective date of this Act, and the former law is continued in effect for that purpose."

Comment

As complexity in SAPCR litigation has grown, so has the length of this section detailing what must be contained a final order. Yet, this is but a pale reflection of the extraordinary length of SAPCR decrees currently in vogue. The advent of statutory support guidelines and, more importantly, statutory visitation guidelines, significantly increased the length of the documentation thought to be necessary to regulate the behavior of the parties after a final SAPCR decree.

First, note that the Legislative Council has come up with a new way of relettering subsections. Subsection (e–1) gives Texas peace officers reasonable authority and responsibility to enforce terms of child custody orders in good faith. Exactly what "reasonable efforts to enforce" may ultimately be decided by court decisions at a later time. If the statute actually assists in keeping the peace and facilitates visitation, it will have fulfilled its purpose. The likelihood of unfortunate consequences seems relatively minor so long as the peace officers use good judgment, but there is always the chance of "things getting out of hand." But that is true with or without the statute.

CLE/Other Legal Publications

Drafting 101. Heather L. King, 2004 Adv. Fam. L.

Everyday orders—"to do or not to do": a dozen practical forms which didn't merit individual topic assignment. William A. Dudley, 2002 Adv. Fam. L. Drafting

Drafting the perfect decree. Doug Woodburn, 1999 Adv. Fam. L.

Parent-child related forms you never knew were in the family practice manual. Christopher K. Wrampelmeier, 1999 Adv. Fam. L. Drafting

Texas Family Law Practice Manual

Form 31–6. Order in Suit Affecting Parent–Child Relationship

---

§ 105.007. Compliance With Order Requiring Notice of Change of Required Information.

(a) A party shall comply with the order by giving written notice to each other party of an intended change in the party's current residence address, mailing address, home telephone number, name of employer, address of employment, and work telephone number.

(b) The party must give written notice by registered or certified mail of an intended change in the required information to each other party on or before the 60th day before the change is made. If the party does not know or could not have known of the change in sufficient time to provide 60-day notice, the party shall provide the written notice of the change on or before the fifth day after the date that the party knew of the change.

(c) The court may waive the notice required by this section on motion by a party if it finds that the giving of notice of a change of the required information would be likely to expose the child or the party to harassment, abuse, serious harm, or injury.

Comment

If possession of a child is to have meaning, the physical location of the child must be known. This section requires parties to keep each other informed of the child's current address. However, the mandate for conservators to notify each other of a pending move does not include a penalty for its violation.

Texas Family Law Practice Manual

Form 18–26. Change of Address

§ 105.008. Record of Support Order for State Case Registry.

(a) The clerk of the court shall provide the state case registry with a record of a court order for child support as required by procedures adopted under Section 234.003. The record of an order shall include information provided by the parties on a form developed by the Title IV-D agency. The form shall be completed by the petitioner and submitted to the clerk at the time the order is filed for record.

(b) To the extent federal funds are available, the Title IV-D agency shall reimburse the clerk of the court for the costs incurred in providing the record of support order required under this section.

§ 105.009. Parent Education and Family Stabilization Course.

(a) In a suit affecting the parent-child relationship, including an action to modify an order in a suit affecting the parent-child relationship providing for possession of or access to a child, the court may order the parties to the suit to attend a parent education and family stabilization course if the court determines that the order is in the best interest of the child.

(b) The parties to the suit may not be required to attend the course together. The court, on its own motion or the motion of either party, may prohibit the parties from taking the course together if there is a history of family violence in the marriage.

(c) A course under this section must be at least four hours, but not more than 12 hours, in length and be designed to educate and assist parents with regard to the consequences of divorce on parents and children. The course must include information on the following issues:

(1) the emotional effects of divorce on parents;

(2) the emotional and behavioral reactions to divorce by young children and adolescents;

(3) parenting issues relating to the concerns and needs of children at different development stages;

(4) stress indicators in young children and adolescents;

(5) conflict management;

(6) family stabilization through development of a coparenting relationship;

(7) the financial responsibilities of parenting;

(8) family violence, spousal abuse, and child abuse and neglect; and

(9) the availability of community services and resources.

(d) A course may not be designed to provide individual mental health therapy or individual legal advice.

(e) A course satisfies the requirements of this section if it is offered by:

(1) a mental health professional who has at least a master's degree with a background in family therapy or parent education; or

(2) a religious practitioner who performs counseling consistent with the laws of this state or another person designated as a program counselor by a church or religious institution if the litigant so chooses.

(f) Information obtained in a course or a statement made by a participant to a suit during a course may not be considered in the adjudication of the suit or in any subsequent legal proceeding. Any report that results from participation in the course may not become a record in the suit unless the parties stipulate to the record in writing.

(g) The court may take appropriate action with regard to a party who fails to attend or complete a course ordered by the court under this section, including holding the party in contempt of court, striking pleadings, or invoking any sanction provided by Rule 215, Texas Rules of Civil Procedure. The failure or refusal by a party to attend or complete a course required by this section may not delay the court from rendering a judgment in a suit affecting the parent-child relationship.

(h) The course required under this section may be completed by:

(1) personal instruction;

(2) videotape instruction;

(3) instruction through an electronic medium; or

(4) a combination of those methods.

(i) On completion of the course, the course provider shall issue a certificate of completion to each participant. The certificate must state:

(1) the name of the participant;

(2) the name of the course provider;

(3) the date the course was completed; and

(4) whether the course was provided by:

(A) personal instruction;

(B) videotape instruction;

(C) instruction through an electronic medium; or

(D) a combination of those methods.

(j) The county clerk in each county may establish a registry of course providers in the county and a list of locations at which courses are provided. The clerk shall include information in the registry identifying courses that are offered on a sliding fee scale or without charge.

(k) The court may not order the parties to a suit to attend a course under this section if the parties cannot afford to take the course. If the parties cannot afford to take a course, the court may direct the parties to a course that is offered on a sliding fee scale or without charge, if a course of that type is available. A party to a suit may not be required to pay more than $100 to attend a course ordered under this section.

(l) A person who has attended a course under this section may not be required to attend the course more than twice before the fifth anniversary of the date the person completes the course for the first time.

Chapter 106. Costs and Attorney's Fees.

CLE/Other Legal Publications

Earning what you are worth: an ethical perspective on assessing your own value and collecting fees. Larry H. Schwartz, 2004 ADV. FAM. L.

Attorney's fees—setting and collecting. Larry H. Schwartz, 2003 ADV. FAM. L.

Setting and getting fees. G. Thomas Vick, 2003 MARRIAGE DISSOLUTION

Convincing the court to award attorney fees. Dean Rucker, 2002 ADV. FAM. L.

Collecting your fees: judgments, turnovers, traps and tricks. (Workshop) 2002 ADV. FAM. L.

Billing & collecting your fees. Bruce Beverly, 2001 ADV. FAM. L.

Avoiding involuntary pro bono: setting and collecting interim and final fees and the specter of fee forfeiture. Larry H. Schwartz, 2001 ADV. FAM. L.

Leading Cases

Black v. Dallas County Child Welfare Unit, 835 S.W.2d 626 (Tex. 1992) (unreasonable persistence by Dallas CPS after trial court rejected its allegations of abuse, substantial attorney's fees awarded to harassed parent)

In re B.A.B., 124 S.W.3d 417 (Tex. App.—Dallas 2004, no pet.) (attorney's fees awarded to father after he successfully moved to enforce and modify)

Attorney General v. O'Quinn, 938 S.W.2d 542 (Tex. App.—Beaumont 1997, no writ) (attorney's fees and court costs may not be assessed against attorney general in IV-D case)

Ex parte Wagner, 905 S.W.2d 799 (Tex. App.—Houston [14th Dist.] 1995, no writ) (habeas denied, attorney's fees in paternity suit enforceable by contempt)

D.R. v. J.A.R., 894 S.W.2d 91 (Tex. App.—Fort Worth 1994, writ denied) (frivolous and harassing modification motion and attempt to terminate Dad's rights yields major award of attorney's fees)

McDuffie v. Blassingame, 883 S.W.2d 329 (Tex. App.—Amarillo 1994, writ denied) (after SAPCR modification, father's suit against mother and her attorney groundless; warrants payment of attorney's fees)

Roosth v. Daggett, 869 S.W.2d 634 (Tex. App.—Houston [14th Dist.] 1994, no writ) (attorney's fees cannot be enforced pending appeal)

Marachal v. Marachal, 832 S.W.2d 797 (Tex. App.—Houston [14th Dist.] 1992, no writ) (attorney's fees may be awarded to unsuccessful party if expended for benefit of child)

Cross References

TEX. FAM. CODE ANN. § 6.708. Costs; §§ 9.013–.014. Costs; Attorney's Fees.

TEX. CIV. PRAC. & REM. CODE ANN. ch. 38. Attorney's Fee.

Texas Pattern Jury Charges: Family

PJC 225.1. Attorney's Fees.

PJC 225.2. Attorney's Fees—Advisory Questions (Comment).

---

§ 106.001. Costs.

The court may award costs in a suit or motion under this title and in a habeas corpus proceeding.

§ 106.002. Attorney's Fees and Expenses.

(a) In a suit under this title, the court may render judgment for reasonable attorney's fees and expenses and order the judgment and postjudgment interest to be paid directly to an attorney.

(b) A judgment for attorney's fees and expenses may be enforced in the attorney's name by any means available for the enforcement of a judgment for debt.

Chapter 107. Special Appointments and Social Studies.

***Editors' Note:** The new statutory text enacted in this chapter will be shown in bold typeface as is the case throughout this book. However, because the amendments are so extensive, most of the struck-through text will not be shown to make for easier reading than would be the case for a reader of H.B. 1815, as signed by Governor Perry.*

All of the amendments to this subchapter were made as follows:

History: Amended by 78th Legis., Reg. Sess. (2003), H.B. 1815, eff. Sept. 1, 2003. The changes in law made by this Act apply only to a suit affecting the parent-child relationship filed on or after the effective date of this Act. A suit filed before the effective date of this Act is governed by the law in effect on the date the suit was filed, and the former law is continued in effect for that purpose.

Subchapter A. Court-Ordered Representation In Suits Affecting The Parent–Child Relationship

Subchapter B. Appointments in Certain Suits

Part 1. Appointments in Suits by Governmental Entity

Part 2. Appointments in Suits Other than Suits by Governmental Entity

Subchapter C. Appointment of Volunteer Advocates

Subchapter D. Social Study

Editors' Note: *In 2003 this chapter was completely revised. The amendments were the result of a year-long project initiated by Chairman Toby Goodman after the 2001 session when he appointed an ad hoc committee to study ad litem appointments and make a recommendation to the House Juvenile Justice and Family Issues Committee regarding appropriate legislation.*

The committee was composed of Professor John J. Sampson, University of Texas School of Law, Chair; three district court judges, Debra Lehrmann, Tarrant County, Tom Stansbury, Fort Bend County, and Scott McCown, Travis County; three practicing lawyers with extensive experience in representing children in custody cases, Steve Bavousett and Imogen Papadopoulos, Houston, and Rhonda Hunter, Dallas; two legal ethics experts, Dawn Miller, Chief Disciplinary Counsel, State Bar of Texas, and Professor John Dzienkowski, University of Texas School of Law; a member of the ABA committee on the subject, Professor Jeff Atkinson, DePaul University College of Law; Megan Ferland, Director, Texas CASA; Lynelle Yingling, Ph.D. psychologist, Rockwall; and Chris Young, Counsel, House Juvenile Justice and Family Issues Committee.

In addition, another dozen interested persons were sent emails of each draft of the proposed recommendations to elicit comments as the committee proceeded.

Editors' Note: *The Comments in this chapter contain significant editorial contributions from Judge Debra H. Lehrmann, 360th District Court, Tarrant County.*

Introductory Comment

Ever since the enactment of the Family Code in 1973, Texas courts have had discretionary authority to appoint a guardian ad litem [GAL] in any suit affecting the parent-child relationship (SAPCR). Following a federal court decision in 1979 holding the then-Texas law unconstitutional, Texas courts have been required to appoint an attorney ad litem [AAL] "to represent the interests of a child" in a suit filed by the agency now to be known as the Department of Family and Protective Services [formerly DPRS], a.k.a. on the local level as Children's Protective Services [CPS]. This rule applies whether the state is seeking conservatorship or termination of parental rights based on alleged child abuse or neglect. Further, since 1997 the court must also appoint a GAL as well as an AAL for an allegedly abused or neglected child. This change resulted from the mandates of the federal Adoption Assistance Act. An attorney may be appointed to serve both roles [AAL/GAL], or an attorney may be appointed to serve as AAL and a volunteer advocate (a.k.a., CASA) may be appointed as the GAL.

During this time, lawyers were required to intuit exactly what they were supposed to do from study of a very few cases and the disciplinary rules. Apparently many lawyers found their appointed role mystifying. A major source of the confusion surrounding this area of the law stemmed from the debate about whether a court-appointed attorney for a child should advocate according to the child's directions or whether the lawyer should determine the goal of representation and advocate what is in the child's best interests. Prior to 1984, it was generally believed that an attorney appointed to represent a child in a family law case should be best-interest directed. The passage of the Child Abuse Prevention and Treatment Act (CAPTA) in 1974 seemed to codify this widely held view by requiring states to appoint a "guardian ad litem" in order to receive federal funding, 42 U.S.C. § 5101 *et seq.* By 1984, however, a paradigm shift began to appear in the legal literature written by attorneys and law professors with experience in representing allegedly abused or neglected children in CPS cases. They argued that the function of an attorney, based upon ethical mandates, was to pursue legal objectives chosen by the child. Thus, the tone was set for a divisive debate, often pitting advocates dealing with CPS cases against those familiar with private custody cases.

Beginning in 1995, the legislature (read Rep. Toby Goodman, R–Arlington) responded to complaints about the performance of the child's appointed legal representatives in abuse and neglect cases heard on the civil side of the docket. Major reform occurred in 1997 when, at the urging of the state office of CASA, the legislature sought to clarify the responsibilities of AALs and GALs for children, focusing on CPS cases. The roles and duties of the ad litems were spelled out in detail, volunteer advocates (CASAs) were authorized to serve as GALs, and the distinctions between the roles of GALs and AALs were clarified. On a parallel track, the American Bar Association was also in the process of attempting to improve and clarify the role of legal representatives of children. In 1996, the ABA adopted Standards of Practice for Attorneys Representing Children in Abuse and Neglect Cases, 29 Fam. L. Q. 375 (1995); the ABA Standards are readily available at *www.abanet.org/child*. Seizing this good idea, in 1997 the legislature required AALs to "become familiar with" the ABA standards. Interestingly, ever since 1994 the ABA Family Law Section has labored to draft comparable guidelines for private custody cases. As of June, 2003 the process seems to be nearing completion.

In the context of this history, the ad hoc committee described in the *Editors' Note*, *supra*, proceeded with the following major principles in mind:

- Appointment in CPS cases of CASA as guardian ad litem, and a lawyer as attorney ad litem, is working well throughout Texas. Only relatively minor clarifications are necessary to court appointments in abuse and neglect cases initiated by the state agency.

- Although the practice is not ideal, because of considerations of financial restraint and efficiency, in many CPS cases one lawyer is appointed to both the AAL and GAL roles. It is highly unusual for the lawyer to be conflicted in representing the child as a lawyer, and also in advocating for the child's best interests; these interests almost always are the same.

- If there is a problem, the lawyer must continue to represent the child as AAL and seek appointment of a GAL without revealing the conflict.

- Appointments of lawyers in private custody battles, on the other hand, suffer from inadequate statutory clarity. This has led to considerable confusion among both bench and bar.

The ad hoc committee's focus was almost exclusively on bringing order to the chaos of attorneys appointed as GAL in private custody cases. The committee recommended amendments to the Texas Family Code Chapter 107 to accomplish that goal, namely:

The ad hoc committee's focus was almost exclusively on bringing order to the chaos of attorneys appointed as GAL in private custody cases. The committee recommended amendments to the Texas Family Code Chapter 107 to accomplish that goal, namely:

- Eliminate appointment of a lawyers as "guardian ad litem" to serve in the ambiguous role of providing legal services without a clear directive as to the nature or beneficiary of those services.
- Create a new, statutorily-defined role for lawyers in private custody cases, *i.e.*, appointment as "amicus attorney." The provision of legal services by an amicus attorney in a private custody case is to be strictly designed to assist the court in making a decision in the best interest of the child. Such appointment should be made only when the fact circumstances are compelling, and when payment of the amicus attorney can be secured.
- Resolve the terminology problem. That is, a lawyer appointed in the capacity of attorney, and expected to act as an attorney in *most every* respect, normally is given the title of GAL. This is the same title that a layperson is given in an abuse and neglect case, or rarely, in a private custody case. This leads to confusion in roles because a lawyer is often unclear whether the role is to represent the child as a lawyer, or as a GAL seeking the child's best interest.
- The confusion is compounded by the fact that a child enmeshed in a custody battle is often confused as well. Even if the child is of a sufficient age to form an attorney-client relationship, the question of how to direct the lawyer's activities is not an easy one for a child torn between two parents.
- Clarify the potential roles for a lawyer in a custody battle by identifying two separate and distinct goals that a judge may have in appointing a lawyer in this context.
- If a judge appoints a lawyer to represent the child in the attorney-client relationship, the lawyer will be appointed AAL (same title as in abuse and neglect cases).
- If the judge has the goal of appointing a lawyer seeking to represent the best interests of the child, the lawyer is to be appointed as an amicus attorney—a new term designed to end the confusion.
- Further, a judge may wish to appoint a layperson GAL in a custody battle; of course, the layperson will perform no legal services.
- Only one person may be appointed to represent a child in a custody battle, either a GAL, an AAL, or an amicus attorney. A lawyer may not be appointed in the role of AAL/GAL as occurs in CPS cases.
- Appointment of a lawyer in a private custody matter is solely at the discretion of the judge. For the first time, the new statute attempts to provide guidance as to when that discretion should be exercised.
- Finally, the judge must give attention to the requirement that an attorney appointed in a private custody case is entitled to reasonable compensation.

CLE/Other Legal Publications

Who's your boss now? Amicus attorneys and ad litems under the new chapter 107. Steve A. Bavousett & Bree Buchanan, 2004 U. Tex. Fam. L. Front Lines

New ad litem legislation, Debra H. Lehrmann, 2003 Adv. Fam. L.

What to do when you're stuck with/as an ad litem. Steve A. Bavousett, Eva M. Guzman & Elizabeth Van Orman, 2001 So. Tex. Fam. L. Gen. Practice Ch. L.

Who are we protecting? An analysis of the law regarding the duties of attorneys and guardians ad litem. Debra H. Lehrmann, 63 Tex. B. J. 122 (2000)

The role of ad litems: duties and liabilities. John J. Sampson, 2001 Adv. Fam. L.

Leading Cases

Lassiter v. Department of Social Services, 452 U.S. 18, 68 L.Ed.2d 640, 101 S.Ct. 2153 (1981) (due process does not require appointment of ad litem for indigent parent in termination case)

Frank A. Smith Sales, Inc. v. Flores, 907 S.W.2d 487 (Tex. 1995) (award of future ad litem fees disallowed)

In re Moers, 104 S.W.3d 609 (Tex. App.—Houston [1st Dist.] 2003, no pet.) (ad litem fees incurred in conservatorship modification suit not related to, or enforceable as, child support)

In re N.R.C., 94 S.W.3d 799 (Tex. App.—Houston [14th Dist.] 2002, pet. denied) (sanctions against parent who fails to deposit funds to cover attorney ad litem's fees inappropriate in private termination suit)

In re Smith, 70 S.W.3d 167 (Tex. App.—San Antonio 2002, no pet. hist.) (although parent was appointed attorney ad litem for termination trial, appointment of appellate attorney ad litem denied on basis of non-indigency)

Samara v. Samara, 52 S.W.3d 455 (Tex. App.—Houston [1st Dist.] 2001, pet. denied) (trial judge lacks authority to appoint attorney to represent layperson GAL in private custody case—children already appointed AAL)

In re M.J.M.L., 31 S.W.3d 347 (Tex. App.—San Antonio 2000, pet. denied) (delay in appointing attorney for indigent mother not reversible error)

In re A.Y., 16 S.W.3d 387 (Tex. App.—El Paso 2000, no pet.) (attorney ad litem in citation by publication case presents zealous defense—publication denied for out-of-state newspaper where respondent known to have resided years ago)

In re M.D.S., 1 S.W.3d 190 (Tex. App.—Amarillo 1999, no pet.) (CAL or AAL not needed in termination suit when trial court specifically finds maternal grandmother's position consistent with child's interest)

Bott v. Bott, 962 S.W.2d 626 (Tex. App.—Houston [14th Dist.] 1997, no writ) (party waived error by court not appointing guardian ad litem)

In re C.D., 962 S.W.2d 145 (Tex. App.—Fort Worth 1998, no pet.) (attorney ad litem may call undisclosed witness absent discovery request)

In re D.L.B., 943 S.W.2d 175 (Tex. App.—San Antonio 1997, no writ) (AAL unable to determine child's wishes, took neutral advocacy position in jury trial)

Delcourt v. Silverman, 919 S.W.2d 777 (Tex. App.—Houston [14th Dist.] 1996, writ denied) (court appointed guardian ad litem and psychiatrist entitled to absolute derived judicial immunity).

Brownsville Valley Regional Medical Center, Inc. v. Gamez, 894 S.W.2d 753 (Tex. 1995) (guardian ad litem's role ends on rendition of judgment)

Hefley v. Hefley, 859 S.W.2d 120 (Tex. App.—Tyler 1993, no writ) (approval given to refusal to appoint second ad litem after first ad litem withdrew)

Chapman v. Chapman, 852 S.W.2d 101 (Tex. App.—Waco 1993, no writ) (failure to appoint ad litem in termination case is error)

Ray v. Burns, 832 S.W.2d 431 (Tex. App.—Waco 1992, no writ) (ad litem not required when termination not involved in SAPCR)

Odoms v. Batts, 791 S.W.2d 677 (Tex. App.—San Antonio 1990, no writ) (indigent father entitled to appointment of ad litem in private termination)

Pleasant Hills Children's Home v. Nida, 596 S.W. 2d 947 (Tex. App.—Ft. Worth 1980, no writ) (ad litem appointed only for specific purposes, powers limited to matters concerning that lawsuit)

Texas Family Law Practice Manual

Chapter 10. Ad Litems

Forms 10–1. Appointment of Attorney Ad Litem after Publication; *10–2.* Original Answer Filed by Attorney Ad Litem for Respondent Cited by Publication; *39–8.* Affidavit for Citation by Publication; *39–9.* Affidavit in Support of Citation by Publication by Birth Mother; *39–10.* Notice by Publication; *39–11.* Appointment of Attorney Ad Litem after Publication; *39–12.* Original Answer Filed by Attorney Ad Litem for Respondent Cited by Publication

---

Subchapter A. Court-Ordered Representation In Suits Affecting the Parent–Child Relationship

§ 107.001. Definitions.

In this chapter:

(1) "Amicus attorney" means an attorney appointed by the court in a suit, other than a suit filed by a governmental entity, whose role is to provide legal services necessary to assist the court in protecting a child's best interests rather than to provide legal services to the child.

(2) "Attorney ad litem" means an attorney who provides legal services to a person, including a child, and who owes to the person the duties of undivided loyalty, confidentiality, and competent representation.

(3) "Developmentally appropriate" means structured to account for a child's age, level of education, cultural background, and degree of language acquisition.

(4) "Dual role" means the role of an attorney who is appointed under Section 107.0125 to act as both guardian ad litem and attorney ad litem for a child in a suit filed by a governmental entity.

(5) "Guardian ad litem" means a person appointed to represent the best interests of a child. The term includes:

(A) a volunteer advocate appointed under Subchapter C;

(B) a professional, other than an attorney, who holds a relevant professional license and whose training relates to the determination of a child's best interests;

(C) an adult having the competence, training, and expertise determined by the court to be sufficient to represent the best interests of the child; or

(D) an attorney ad litem appointed to serve in the dual role.

Comment

"Amicus attorney" is a new role for attorneys appointed in private custody cases. Note that this appointment may not be made in a suit filed by a governmental entity, a.k.a. a CPS case involving alleged abuse or neglect.

The definitions of "attorney ad litem," "developmentally appropriate," and "dual role," confirm the understanding of those terms prior to the enactment of this thoroughly revised chapter.

A restricted definition is provided for "guardian ad litem" [GAL], who may be a qualified nonlawyer, either a volunteer advocate or another trained professional, a layperson who the court deems to be the equivalent of the foregoing, or an attorney who serves in a dual role in CPS cases as provided in § 107.0125, *infra*. Further, an individual who happens to be an attorney may serve as a volunteer CASA, so long as no "lawyering" is performed in that role.

---

§ 107.002. Powers and Duties of Guardian ad Litem for Child.

(a) A guardian ad litem appointed **for a child** under this **chapter** [~~subchapter~~] is not a party to the suit but may:

(1) conduct an investigation to the extent that the guardian ad litem considers necessary to determine the best **interests** [~~interest~~] of the child [~~for whom the guardian is appointed~~]; and

(2) obtain and review copies of the child's relevant medical, psychological, and school records as provided by Section 107.006.

(b) A guardian ad litem appointed for the child under this **chapter** [~~subchapter~~] shall:

(1) [~~,~~] within a reasonable time after the appointment, interview:

(A) [~~(1)~~] the child **in a developmentally appropriate manner**, if the child is four years of age or older; [~~and~~]

(B) [~~(2)~~] each **person who has** [~~individual that the guardian ad litem considers likely to have~~] significant knowledge of the child's history and condition**, including any foster parent of the child; and**

(C) the parties to the suit;

(2) seek to elicit in a developmentally appropriate manner the child's expressed objectives of representation;

(3) consider the child's expressed objectives of representation without being bound by those objectives;

(4) encourage settlement and the use of alternative forms of dispute resolution; and

(5) perform any specific task directed by the court.

(c) A guardian ad litem appointed for the child under this **chapter** [~~subchapter~~] is not a party to the suit but is entitled to:

(1) receive a copy of each pleading or other paper filed with the court in the case in which the guardian ad litem is appointed;

(2) receive notice of each hearing in the case;

(3) participate in case staffings by an authorized agency concerning the child;

(4) attend all legal proceedings in the case but may not call or question a witness **or otherwise provide legal services** unless the **guardian** ad litem is a licensed attorney **who has been appointed in the dual role**;

(5) review and sign, or decline to sign, **an** [~~any~~] agreed order affecting the child; and

(6) **explain the basis** [~~testify in court, except as provided by Subsection (d), regarding the recommendations concerning the actions that the guardian ad litem considers to be in the best interest of the child, including giving reasons~~] for the guardian ad litem's opposition **to the agreed order** if the guardian ad litem does not agree to the terms of a proposed order.

(d) **The court may compel the guardian ad litem to attend a trial or hearing and to testify as necessary for the proper disposition of the suit.** [~~An attorney~~

~~who is appointed as attorney ad litem and guardian ad litem for a child may not testify under Subsection (c)(6).~~]

(e) **Unless the guardian ad litem is an attorney who has been appointed in the dual role and subject to the Texas Rules of Evidence, the court shall ensure in a hearing or in a trial on the merits that a guardian ad litem has an opportunity to testify or submit a report regarding the guardian ad litem's recommendations regarding:**

(1) the best interests of the child; and

(2) the bases for the guardian ad litem's recommendations. [~~An attorney who is appointed as attorney ad litem and guardian ad litem for a child shall:~~

[~~(1) become familiar with the American Bar Association's standards of practice for lawyers who represent children in abuse and neglect cases; and~~

[~~(2) comply with the requirements of the Texas Disciplinary Rules of Professional Conduct.~~]

(f) **In a nonjury trial, a party may call the guardian ad litem as a witness for the purpose of cross-examination regarding the guardian's report without the guardian ad litem being listed as a witness by a party. If the guardian ad litem is not called as a witness, the court shall permit the guardian ad litem to testify in the narrative.**

(g) In a contested case, the guardian ad litem shall provide copies of the guardian ad litem's report, if any, to the attorneys for the parties as directed by the court, but not later than the earlier of:

(1) the date required by the scheduling order; or

(2) the 10th day before the date of the commencement of the trial.

(h) Disclosure to the jury of the contents of a guardian ad litem's report to the court is subject to the Texas Rules of Evidence.

Comment

Confusion about the powers and duties of a GAL for a child has been resolved by legislative mandate. Effective September 1, 2003, courts are no longer to appoint attorneys as GAL with the expectation that the attorney will serve a role as a lawyer in the case and as a guardian ad litem for the child.

Subsection (c)(4) states that the GAL may not call or question a witness or otherwise provide legal services, thereby disqualifying an attorney from performing any lawyer-like activities in the case. The right to testify of a GAL is confirmed under subsection (e). More than that, subsections (d) and (f) make it clear that the testimony of a GAL may be compelled, an action forbidden to a lawyer who may not be a witness and an attorney in the same proceeding.

The appointing judge decides who is qualified to serve as a GAL. A volunteer advocate CASA who is converted into a GAL by appointment faces additional responsibilities to serve as a substitute decision-maker for the child in the SAPCR. This section specifically states twice that a GAL is "not a party to the suit," and therefore is not entitled to service of citation, § 102.009. Nonetheless, the GAL is the representative of the real party in interest, *i.e.*, the child who is the subject of the suit.

This section identifies the actions necessary for a GAL to undertake. The duties of the GAL under subsections (a)-(c) parallel many of the activities and duties of the AAL or amicus attorney in §§ 107.003–.005, *infra*. Although GALs are not parties, some of the rights and duties described resemble the rights of a party, *e.g.* receiving copies of pleadings and notice of hearings. Other named rights do not go that far. For example, although a GAL is entitled to review an agreed order affecting the child and sign or refuse to sign the agreement, the statute does not authorize the GAL to veto an agreement of the actual parties to the litigation.

---

§ 107.003. Powers and Duties of Attorney ad Litem for Child and Amicus Attorney.

An attorney ad litem appointed to represent a child or an amicus attorney appointed to assist the court:

(1) shall:

(A) subject to Rule 4.04, Texas Disciplinary Rules of Professional Conduct, and within a reasonable time after the appointment, interview:

(i) the child in a developmentally appropriate manner, if the child is four years of age or older;

(ii) each person who has significant knowledge of the child's history and condition, including any foster parent of the child; and

(iii) the parties to the suit;

(B) investigate the facts of the case to the extent the attorney considers appropriate;

(C) obtain and review copies of relevant records relating to the child as provided by Section 107.006;

(D) participate in the conduct of the litigation to the same extent as an attorney for a party;

(E) take any action consistent with the child's interests that the attorney considers necessary to expedite the proceedings; and

(F) encourage settlement and the use of alternative forms of dispute resolution;

(2) must be trained in child advocacy or have experience determined by the court to be equivalent to that training; and

(3) is entitled to:

(A) receive a copy of each pleading or other paper filed with the court;

(B) receive notice of each hearing in the suit;

(C) participate in any case staffing concerning the child conducted by an authorized agency; and

(D) attend all legal proceedings in the suit.

Comment

This revised section dealing with the powers and duties of both an AAL and an amicus attorney sets forth the expectations that a court will have for lawyer-like services to be performed. The legislative determination of years-past that lawyers needed instructions in how to conduct their business in these cases after court appointment has not been withdrawn. Originally the legislature passed the major provisions regulating attorney conduct (formerly § 107.014) in response to complaints about the poor quality of AAL representation of allegedly abused and neglected children when the state, via DPRS, intervened in a family. These complaints included the fact that some lawyers never saw or talked to their child-clients, even when they were mature teenagers. Although children enmeshed in the CPS system have an automatic right to be represented by an attorney ad litem, testimony to the legislature alleged that the quality of representation varied significantly not only from county to county, but from lawyer to lawyer. Because the child-client has no choice in his representation, the legislature found it desirable to guarantee a minimum level of legal representation. Just to ensure that lawyers get the point, the legislature continues to remind attorneys that they must comply with the disciplinary rules (as if there ever is a time when that is not the case).

Over the years the legislature continued to tighten AAL discretion, changing "may" to "shall" with regard to crucial duties. Thus, the AAL is required to investigate (but only to the extent that the AAL determines is appropriate), and to perform other duties, such as obtaining the relevant records of the child and interviewing people who know facts about the child's situation. The amendments of 1999 included a specification that the AAL interview a child's foster parents. Most challenging was the requirement to "interview the parties to the suit." When counsel for the child's parents won't consent to the AAL interview, however, the requirement appears to mandate formal discovery to comply with the statute without violating the prohibition against communicating with represented parties in the Disciplinary Rules. *See* Art. 10 § 9 Texas Disciplinary Rule of Professional Conduct 4.02. These strictures are continued in the 2003 revision of the chapter.

This section applies equally to attorneys in CPS cases and private custody cases, notwithstanding the fact that the complaints voiced to the legislature only related to CPS cases.

§ 107.004. Additional Duties of Attorney ad Litem for Child.

Except as otherwise provided by this chapter, the attorney ad litem appointed for a child shall:

(1) seek to elicit in a developmentally appropriate manner the child's expressed objectives of representation;

(2) advise the child;

(3) provide guidance to the child;

(4) represent the child's expressed objectives of representation and follow the child's expressed objectives of representation during the course of litigation if the attorney ad litem determines that the child is competent to understand the nature of an attorney-client relationship and has formed that relationship with the attorney ad litem;

(5) consider the impact on the child in formulating the attorney ad litem's presentation of the child's expressed objectives of representation to the court; and

(6) become familiar with:

(A) the American Bar Association's standards of practice for attorneys who represent children in abuse and neglect cases; and

(B) the suggested amendments to those standards adopted by the National Association of Counsel for Children.

Comment

This new section and the next make distinctions between lawyering required of an AAL and the lawyering expected from an amicus attorney. The major difference is that the AAL has a client. Subsection (4) provides that an appointed lawyer "shall follow the child's expressed objectives of representation if the AAL determines that the child is competent" to provide such direction. This language was derived from the National Association of Counsel for Children (NACC) Revised ABA Abuse and Neglect Standards. In the event the AAL determines that the child lacks that competence, reference is to be made to § 107.008 (substituted judgment). Thus, whether a child-client can actually direct the activities of the AAL is to be decided on a case-by-case basis. As will be discussed *infra*, the amicus attorney does not have a client but rather functions as an independent counsel to elicit all appropriate evidence regarding best interest of the child.

Amended subsection (6) refers the AAL the ABA standards of practice for attorneys who represent children in abuse and neglect cases, 29 Fam. L.Q. 375 (1995), also available at *www.abanet.org/child.* At their core, these standards tell lawyers to be lawyers, giving a child-client the "same duties of undivided loyalty, confidentiality, and competent representation . . . as is due an adult client." *See* Art. 10, § 9 Texas Disciplinary Rules of Professional Conduct 4.02. The standards mandate that lawyers advise and guide their clients, eliciting "the child's preferences in a developmentally appropriate manner," representing "the child's expressed preferences," and following "the child's direction throughout the course of litigation." When a child cannot or will not express preferences, the lawyer may determine the child's legal interests and advocate that position. Lawyers are also referred to the ABA Standards as amended and adopted by the NACC in 1999. These standards recognize that children "are not simply small adults and it would be inappropriate to treat them as such. All of the components of representation of adults are not readily transferable to the representation of children. There must be exceptions made to the rules of lawyering where children are concerned." *See http://nacchildlaw.org/training/standards.html*

---

§ 107.005. Additional Duties of Amicus Attorney.

(a) Subject to any specific limitation in the order of appointment, an amicus attorney shall advocate the best interests of the child after reviewing the facts and circumstances of the case. Notwithstanding Subsection (b), in determining the best interests of the child, an amicus attorney is not bound by the child's expressed objectives of representation.

(b) An amicus attorney shall:

(1) seek to elicit in a developmentally appropriate manner the child's expressed objectives of representation;

(2) with the consent of the child, ensure that the child's expressed objectives of representation are made known to the court;

(3) consider the impact on the child in formulating the amicus attorney's presentation of the child's expressed objectives of representation to the court;

(4) review and sign, or decline to sign, an agreed order affecting the child;

(5) explain the basis for the amicus attorney's opposition to the agreed order if the amicus attorney does not agree to the terms of a proposed order;

(6) explain the role of the amicus attorney to the child; and

(7) inform the child that the amicus attorney may use information that the child provides in providing assistance to the court.

(c) An amicus attorney may not disclose confidential communications between the amicus attorney and the child unless the amicus attorney deter-

mines that disclosure is necessary to assist the court regarding the best interests of the child.

Editors' Comment

The confusion surrounding the duties of a court-appointed lawyer for a child has left many judges unclear about their ability to appoint a lawyer to ensure that sufficient evidence is presented to the court to enable it to render a decision that is in the child's best interest. This is particularly problematic in custody cases, where there is no guardian ad litem to act as a safety net. This section clarifies that, in a custody case, the court has the authority to appoint a lawyer to advocate per the best interests of the child, without being bound by the child's objectives of representation.

The new role, denominated as "amicus attorney," at least in part is a codification of the way that many experienced attorneys appointed in the ambiguous role of GAL have conducted their representation of children in custody disputes. The attorney is to advocate the best interest of the child, taking into account a wide variety of information, including the views of the child. However, it is clear that the child does not direct the activities of the amicus attorney, nor does the child have an attorney-client relationship with the amicus attorney. Subsection (b)(7) indicates that the amicus attorney may use information that the child provides, even if the child has not authorized the disclosure of that information, or even has requested nondisclosure.

Subsection (b)(6) directs the amicus attorney to explain his role to the child. Assuming that honesty is the hallmark, in the opinion of the editors this must include the fact that there is no assurance of confidential communications.

Subsection (c) indicates something of a conflicted position, but leaves it entirely to the discretion of the amicus attorney whether to reveal information that otherwise would be a "confidential communication" if an attorney-client relationship existed. *See also* § 107.007, which provides other certain protections for the relationship between the amicus attorney and the child.

---

§ 107.006. Access to Child and Information Relating to Child.

(a) Except as provided by Subsection (c), in conjunction with an appointment under this chapter, other than an appointment of an attorney ad litem for an adult or a parent, the court shall issue an order authorizing the attorney ad litem, guardian ad litem for the child, or amicus attorney to have immediate access to:

(1) the child; and

(2) any otherwise privileged or confidential information relating to the child.

(b) Without requiring a further order or release, the custodian of any relevant records relating to the child, including records regarding social services, drug and alcohol treatment, or medical or mental health evaluation or treatment of the child, law enforcement records, school records, records of a probate or court proceeding, and records of a trust or account for which the child is a beneficiary, shall provide access to a person authorized to access the records under Subsection (a).

(c) A mental health record of a child at least 12 years of age that is privileged or confidential under other law may be released to a person appointed under Subsection (a) only in accordance with the other law.

Comment

Note that all three roles, GAL, AAL, and amicus attorney, have basically the same access to information by court order.

§ 107.007. Attorney Work Product and Testimony.

(a) An attorney ad litem, an attorney serving in the dual role, or an amicus attorney may not:

(1) be compelled to produce attorney work product developed during the appointment as an attorney;

(2) be required to disclose the source of any information;

(3) submit a report into evidence; or

(4) testify in court except as authorized by Rule 3.08, Texas Disciplinary Rules of Professional Conduct.

(b) Subsection (a) does not apply to the duty of an attorney to report child abuse or neglect under Section 261.101.

Comment

An attorney ad litem, an attorney serving in the AAL/GAL role, and the amicus attorney all are protected by the work product privilege. Moreover, a lawyer serving in any of these roles may not testify in court except in the narrow fashion authorized by the disciplinary rules. Particularly relevant to the amicus attorney (who does not have a client) is the protection against being: compelled to produce work product; required to disclose the source of any information; submitting a report into evidence; or, testifying in court.

Subsection (b) makes it clear that attorneys who are required to report child abuse or neglect under § 261.101, *infra*, are not exempt from that duty after being appointed in either a CPS case or a private custody case.

§ 107.008. Substituted Judgment of Attorney for Child.

(a) An attorney ad litem appointed to represent a child or an attorney appointed in the dual role may determine that the child cannot meaningfully formulate the child's objectives of representation in a case because the child:

(1) lacks sufficient maturity to understand and form an attorney-client relationship with the attorney;

(2) despite appropriate legal counseling, continues to express objectives of representation that would be seriously injurious to the child; or

(3) for any other reason is incapable of making reasonable judgments and engaging in meaningful communication.

(b) Except as provided by Subsection (c), an attorney ad litem or an attorney appointed in the dual role who determines that the child cannot meaningfully formulate the child's expressed objectives of representation under Subsection (a) may present to the court a position that the attorney determines will serve the best interests of the child.

(c) An attorney ad litem or attorney appointed in the dual role who determines that the child cannot meaningfully formulate the child's expressed objectives of representation under Subsection (a) shall, if a guardian ad litem has been appointed for the child:

(1) consult with the guardian ad litem; and

(2) present the child's objectives of representation to the court based on the guardian ad litem's opinion regarding the best interests of the child.

Comment

This section discusses a fact situation that is far more discussed than it is actually encountered in practice by attorneys representing abused or neglected children (AAL or AAL/GAL). In point of fact, the "hypothetical abused or neglected child" virtually never directs an AAL's activities in a manner that would seriously endanger the child's physical or emotional health. The issue does not arise for an amicus attorney because that attorney does not have a child-client. But an AAL or an AAL/GAL does have a client who may be capable of forming an attorney-client relationship with the attorney and relies on the confidentiality privilege in attempting to direct the attorney to advocate a position that would be "seriously injurious" to the child-client. This section, based on the NACC amended ABA Standards, seeks to balance the obligation of a lawyer to represent a child-client with the obligation of the AAL to insure that serious injury to the child does not result from the legal representation. This is an expansion of the lawyer's traditional duty to take protective action for an incompetent client.

The ABA Standards and the NACC Revised Standards, *supra,* recognize that when a child cannot meaningfully participate in the formulation of a legal position (either because the child is preverbal, very young or for some other reason is incapable of judgment and meaningful communication), the AAL must provide substituted judgment in order to serve the child's interests. The AAL must apply objective criteria, rather than rely on life experience or instinct. Criteria to reach a decision include a full and efficient investigation, review of all the options, and consideration of the available evidence.

§ 107.009. Immunity.

(a) A guardian ad litem, an attorney ad litem, or an amicus attorney appointed under this chapter is not liable for civil damages arising from a recommendation made or an opinion given in the capacity of guardian ad litem, attorney ad litem, or amicus attorney.

(b) Subsection (a) does not apply to an action taken or a recommendation or opinion given:

(1) with conscious indifference or reckless disregard to the safety of another;

(2) in bad faith or with malice; or

(3) that is grossly negligent or wilfully wrongful.

Comment

Fear of liability has reportedly frightened off some potential volunteer advocates, and probably more than a few lawyers. The 2003 version of this section extends the immunity formerly provided only for the GAL to the AAL and amicus attorney as well. This is consistent with the spirit of *Delcourt v. Silverman*, 919 S.W.2d 777 (Tex. App.—Houston [14th Dist.] 1996, no writ), although the immunity language in the statute goes beyond the facts and language of the *Delcourt* decision. This expanded immunity for ad litems of any stripe may seem excessive to some, especially the AAL who does have a client, sometimes even a sentient one. However, since it is only opinions and recommendations that are immunized, the section is not a general license to fall asleep at trial or otherwise commit malpractice. There is good justification to immunize an amicus attorney who, after all, is appointed by the court to represent the best interests of the child and to provide legal services to that end rather than to the end of representing a client.

§ 107.010. Discretionary Appointment of Attorney ad Litem for Incapacitated Person.

The court may appoint an attorney to serve as an attorney ad litem for a person entitled to service of citation in a suit if the court finds that the person is incapacitated. The attorney ad litem shall follow the person's expressed objectives of representation and, if appropriate, refer the proceeding to the proper court for guardianship proceedings.

Comment

This is a re-write of former § 107.001 which provides for an appointment in a fact situation in which an adult is incapacitated and needs legal representation. The attorney ad litem appointed in that context is encouraged to seek guardianship proceedings, if the attorney deems that to be appropriate.

Subchapter B. Appointments in Certain Suits

Part 1. Appointments in Suits by Governmental Entity

§ 107.011. Mandatory Appointment of Guardian ad Litem.

(a) Except as otherwise provided by this subchapter, in a suit filed by a governmental entity seeking termination of the parent-child relationship or the appointment of a conservator for a child, the court shall appoint a guardian ad litem to represent the best interests of the child immediately after the filing of the petition but before the full adversary hearing.

(b) The guardian ad litem appointed for a child under this section may be:

(1) a charitable organization composed of volunteer advocates or an individual volunteer advocate appointed under Subchapter C;

(2) an adult having the competence, training, and expertise determined by the court to be sufficient to represent the best interests of the child; or

(3) an attorney appointed in the dual role.

(c) The court may not appoint a guardian ad litem in a suit filed by a governmental entity if an attorney is appointed in the dual role unless the court appoints another person to serve as guardian ad litem for the child and restricts the role of the attorney to acting as an attorney ad litem for the child.

(d) The court may appoint an attorney to serve as guardian ad litem for a child without appointing the attorney to serve in the dual role only if the attorney is specifically appointed to serve only in the role of guardian ad litem. An attorney appointed solely as a guardian ad litem:

(1) may take only those actions that may be taken by a nonattorney guardian ad litem; and

(2) may not:

(A) perform legal services in the case; or

(B) take any action that is restricted to a licensed attorney, including engaging in discovery other than as a witness, making opening and closing statements, or examining witnesses.

Comment

Subchapter B, Part 1, is limited to suits by governmental entities, a.k.a., CPS suits alleging abuse or neglect of a child.

Federal law enacted in 1974, CAPTA, *supra,* authorized grants to states as reimbursement for expenses involved in child abuse prevention and treatment programs. In order to ensure continued receipt of the federal subsidy, state law must require appointment of GAL for an abused or neglected child; the GAL may be, but is not required to be, a lawyer. A 1996 amendment directed that the GAL "make recommendations to the court concerning the best interests of the child." Further, Congress authorized CASA volunteers to serve as guardians ad litem in the CPS cases.

§ 107.012. Mandatory Appointment of Attorney ad Litem for Child.

In a suit filed by a governmental entity requesting termination of the parent-child relationship or to be named conservator of a child, the court shall appoint an attorney ad litem to represent the interests of the child immediately after the filing, but before the full adversary hearing, to ensure adequate representation of the child.

Comment

Since 1979 this chapter has required appointment of an attorney ad litem for a child subject of a CPS suit. This is the only provision regarding appointment of attorneys in this chapter that was not amended in 2003. in order to ensure continued receipt of the federal subsidy

§ 107.0125. Appointment of Attorney in Dual Role.

(a) In order to comply with the mandatory appointment of a guardian ad litem under Section 107.011 and the mandatory appointment of an attorney ad litem under Section 107.012, the court may appoint an attorney to serve in the dual role.

(b) If the court appoints an attorney to serve in the dual role under this section, the court may at any time during the pendency of the suit appoint another person to serve as guardian ad litem for the child and restrict the attorney to acting as an attorney ad litem for the child.

(c) An attorney appointed to serve in the dual role may request the court to appoint another person to serve as guardian ad litem for the child. If the court grants the attorney's request, the attorney shall serve only as the attorney ad litem for the child.

(d) Unless the court appoints another person as guardian ad litem in a suit filed by a governmental entity, an appointment of an attorney to serve as an attorney ad litem in a suit filed by a governmental entity is an appointment to serve in the dual role regardless of the terminology used in the appointing order.

Comment

Since 1997, under this chapter a child in a CPS case is entitled to appointment of both an AAL and a GAL. For reasons of efficiency and protection of the public fisc, in many counties it is common practice to appoint a lawyer in the dual role of AAL/GAL. A lawyer so appointed hypothetically may face ethical dilemmas inherent in the dual role, *see* commentary to § 107.008, *supra*. Even more troublesome is the fact that in some counties the common practice has been to appoint a lawyer with the title of "GAL," and to ignore the fact that Texas law requires that the child in a CPS case be appointed "an attorney ad litem." Of course, the lawyer appointed as "GAL" is expected to provide legal representation to the child in the CPS case.

New Subsection (b) provides the court with full discretion to place a lawyer serving in a dual role with a nonlawyer GAL, and further, a lawyer in the dual role may request to be relieved of the GAL role. Formerly, this was a specific directive if the lawyer found that the two roles were in conflict. The requirement to continue as AAL was, and is, mandated by the fact that the lawyer assuredly could come to that conclusion from a dispute over the child's decision about best interest which is based, at least in part, on information obtained in the role of attorney for the child.

Subsection (d) anticipates that lawyers may no longer be appointed solely as "guardian ad litem" in CPS cases. Because news of a change in the law historically has traveled slowly, lawyers are instructed that such an appointment is as AAL/GAL by operation of law. In fact, the law has required an AAL be appointed for the child since 1979 (yes, nearly 25 years have passed since the terminology was supposed to have changed). The legislature makes it clear that when an attorney appointed in a CPS case is expected to provide legal services, the appointment is as an AAL/GAL unless another individual has been appointed GAL.

The requirement formerly found in § 107.002(f) for an attorney appointed in a dual role to withdraw from the GAL role and to request appointment of a new guardian ad litem in the event of a conflict has been deleted by the 2003 revision to this chapter. Texas Disciplinary Rule of Professional Conduct 1.02(g) requires an attorney to "take reasonable action to secure the appointment of a guardian or other legal representative for, or seek other protective orders with respect to, a client whenever the lawyer reasonably believes that the client lacks legal competence and that such action should be taken to protect the client." This required protective action may be in the form of using substituted judgment in certain conflict situations, as set out in § 107.008, *supra*.

---

§ 107.013. Mandatory Appointment of Attorney Ad Litem for Parent.

(a) In a suit **filed by a governmental entity** in which termination of the parent-child relationship is requested, the court shall appoint an attorney ad litem to represent the interests of:

(1) an indigent parent of the child who responds in opposition to the termination;

(2) a parent served by citation by publication;

(3) an alleged father who failed to register with the registry under Chapter 160 [*Uniform Parentage Act*] and whose identity or location is unknown; and

(4) an alleged father who registered with the paternity registry under Chapter 160, but the petitioner's attempt to personally serve citation at the address provided to the registry and at any other address for the alleged father known by the petitioner has been unsuccessful.

(b) If both parents of the child are entitled to the appointment of an attorney ad litem under this section and the court finds that the interests of the parents are not in conflict, the court may appoint **an** [~~a single~~] attorney ad litem to represent the interests of both parents.

Comment

The amendment to subsection (a) appears to be minor, but in fact corrects a long-standing statutory glitch. The appointment of an attorney for an indigent parent in a CPS case is not constitutionally mandated but has been statutorily mandated since 1979. The new restriction regarding the fact that the suit must be filed by governmental entity is tied directly to the succeeding section dealing with attorney's fees.

---

§ 107.014. [omitted]

§ 107.015. Attorney Fees.

(a) An attorney appointed **under this chapter to serve as an attorney ad litem for a child, an attorney in the dual role,** [~~to represent a child~~] or **an attorney ad litem for a** parent [~~as authorized by this subchapter~~] is entitled to reasonable fees and expenses in the amount set by the court to be paid by the parents of the child unless the parents are indigent.

(b) If the court [~~or associate judge~~] determines that one or more of the parties are able to defray the [~~costs of an attorney ad litem's~~] fees and expenses **of an attorney ad litem or guardian ad litem for the child** as determined by the reasonable and customary fees for similar services in the county of jurisdiction, the fees and expenses may be ordered paid by one or more of those parties, or the court [~~or associate judge~~] may order one or more of those parties, prior to final hearing, to pay the sums into the registry of the court or into an account authorized by the court for the use and benefit of the **payee** [~~attorney ad litem~~] on order of the court. The sums may be taxed as costs to be assessed against one or more of the parties.

(c) If indigency of the parents is shown, an attorney **ad litem** appointed to represent a child or parent in a suit **filed by a governmental entity in which termination of** [~~to terminate~~] the parent-child relationship **is requested** shall be paid from the general funds of the county according to the fee schedule that applies to an attorney appointed to represent a child in a suit under Title 3 as provided by Chapter 51. The court may not award attorney ad litem fees under this chapter against the state, a state agency, or a political subdivision of the state except as provided by this subsection.

(d) A person appointed as a guardian ad litem or attorney ad litem shall complete and submit to the court a voucher or claim for payment that lists the fees charged and hours worked by the guardian ad litem or attorney ad litem. Information submitted under this section is subject to disclosure under Chapter 552, Government Code.

Comment

Fees paid to attorneys ad litem in CPS cases have been a controversial subject only to those who serve in that capacity. That is, when the legislature mandated attorney's fees for AALs in 1981, the pay scale was tied to the compensation for defense counsel in cases under the Juvenile Justice Code. Needless to say, that scale is well below market price for many lawyers.

Subsections (b) and (c) codify what most folks thought was the law already, namely, the parents pay, if able; if not, the county pays; note, the state doesn't pay, even though

DPRS, a state agency, has filed the SAPCR for conservatorship or termination that resulted in the AAL's appointment.

Leading Cases

Gonzales v. Gonzales, 26 S.W.3d 657 (Tex. App.—San Antonio 1999, no pet.) (attorney ad litem appointment doesn't require hearing—court, not jury, sets ad litem's fees)

Harris County Children Protective Services v. Richker, 2 S.W.3d 741 (Tex. App.—Houston [14th Dist.] 1999, no pet.) (county children protective services, as agency, had sovereign immunity from liability for payment of attorney ad litem fees)

---

§ 107.016. Continued Representation.

In a suit **filed** [~~brought~~] by a governmental entity **in which** [~~seeking~~] termination of the parent-child relationship or appointment of the entity as conservator of the child **is requested**, an order appointing the Department of Protective and Regulatory Services as the child's managing conservator may provide for the continuation of the **appointment of the guardian ad litem or** attorney ad litem [~~appointment~~] for the child for any period set by the court.

Comment

At the discretion of the court, the appointment of an attorney ad litem may be continued until the child ages out of the system at 18. Between the time DPRS is named permanent managing conservator and that birthday, the main effort is social work; usually very little lawyering is needed.

---

§ 107.017. Appointment of Amicus Attorney Prohibited.

The court may not appoint a person to serve as an amicus attorney in a suit filed by a governmental entity under this chapter.

Comment

Just in case it isn't crystal clear from what went before, the appointment of an amicus attorney in a CPS case is explicitly forbidden.

Part 2. Appointments in Suits Other than Suits by Governmental Entity

Comment

This entirely new part is directed at private custody cases. As such, it is intended to codify what the ad hoc committee described in the Editors' Note to this chapter regarded as "best practices."

---

§ 107.021. Discretionary Appointments.

(a) In a suit in which the best interests of a child are at issue, other than a suit filed by a governmental entity, the court may appoint:

(1) an amicus attorney;

(2) an attorney ad litem; or

(3) a guardian ad litem.

(b) In determining whether to make an appointment under this section, the court:

(1) shall:

(A) give due consideration to the ability of the parties to pay reasonable fees to the appointee; and

(B) balance the child's interests against the cost to the parties that would result from an appointment by taking into consideration the cost of available alternatives for resolving issues without making an appointment;

(2) may make an appointment only if the court finds that the appointment is necessary to ensure the determination of the best interests of the child; and

(3) may not require a person appointed under this section to serve without reasonable compensation for the services rendered by the person.

Comment

In private custody cases the court has a choice of appointing one, but only one, of the following to represent the child: amicus attorney, attorney ad litem, or guardian ad litem. Note that the choice is written in the disjunctive, which by statutory construction means that multiple appointments of lawyers and laypersons to represent a child are impermissible. In many counties, the third option of appointing a non-lawyer guardian ad litem is not practical, as § 107.022(2) prohibits the court from appointing a volunteer advocate (CASA volunteer) from serving as a guardian ad litem in a custody case unless the training of the volunteer is designed for participation in suits other than those filed by a governmental entity. Since such training is not available in many areas of the state, the resources from which such an appointment could be made are limited.

Thus, as a practical matter in a custody case the court has the option of designating a court-appointed lawyer for a child as either an amicus attorney or an attorney ad litem. There is an implicit presumption that multiple children in a family will not require multiple appointed attorneys. Indeed, given the fact that the amicus attorney is seeking best interest for children without being the lawyer for any, it is difficult to conceive a situation in which multiple legal appointments would be appropriate in that context. On the other hand, an attorney ad litem appointed in a custody case might conceivably decide that two or more children in a custody dispute have such irreconcilable differences that legal representation by one attorney ad litem is ethically precluded.

Subsection (b) gives guidance to the court for appointments in private custody disputes. The involved legislators specifically indicated through comments and actions that such appointments can, and probably sometimes are, being abused by courts. Part of that abuse is the fact that appointments in private custody cases often go unpaid, or are paid at far less than at market rate. Secondly, such appointments are sometimes inimical to the functioning of the adversary system. The section directs the court to take into account the financial impact of the appointment, and also to restrict appointments to situations in which the "appointment is necessary to insure the determination of best interests of the child." The application of that test, of course, is left to the discretion of the court.

---

§ 107.022. Certain Prohibited Appointments.

In a suit other than a suit filed by a governmental entity, the court may not appoint:

(1) an attorney to serve in the dual role; or

(2) a volunteer advocate to serve as guardian ad litem for a child unless the training of the volunteer advocate is designed for participation in suits other than suits filed by a governmental entity.

Comment

This section places two important restrictions on an appointment in a private custody case. First the lawyer will either be an AAL or an amicus attorney; there is no dual role. Secondly, CASA volunteers are not to be appointed in private custody cases because their training is not designed for participation in suits other than those filed by CPS. In the event that there is a voluntary advocate program that trains its volunteers to participate in private custody cases, those members are eligible for appointment as a GAL in such cases.

---

§ 107.023. Fees in Suits Other Than Suits by Governmental Entity.

(a) In a suit other than a suit filed by a governmental entity, in addition to the attorney's fees that may be awarded under Chapter 106, the following persons are entitled to reasonable fees and expenses in an amount set by the court and ordered to be paid by one or more parties to the suit:

(1) an attorney appointed as an amicus attorney or as an attorney ad litem for the child; and

(2) a professional who holds a relevant professional license and who is appointed as guardian ad litem for the child, other than a volunteer advocate.

(b) The court shall:

(1) determine the fees and expenses of an amicus attorney, an attorney ad litem, or a guardian ad litem by reference to the reasonable and customary fees for similar services in the county of jurisdiction;

(2) order a reasonable cost deposit to be made at the time the court makes the appointment; and

(3) before the final hearing, order an additional amount to be paid to the credit of a trust account for the use and benefit of the amicus attorney, attorney ad litem, or guardian ad litem.

(c) A court may not award costs, fees, or expenses to an amicus attorney, attorney ad litem, or guardian ad litem against the state, a state agency, or a political subdivision of the state under this part.

Comment

This section attempts to resolve issues regarding payment of professional fees, whether to an attorney or to another individual with a relevant professional license, *e.g.*, a GAL with a MSW or a doctorate in psychology or child development. Further, at one time an issue was raised regarding whether the court was authorized to award a reasonable fee to an attorney appointed as a "guardian ad litem." This section makes it clear that a lawyer appointed as either an amicus attorney or an attorney ad litem is entitled to a reasonable fee.

To help ensure that payments are made, subsection (b) directs that reasonable payment be made, plus reasonable cost deposits and partial payments as the case develops.

Subsection (c) immunizes governmental entities from attorneys fees in private custody matters.

Subchapter C. Appointment of Volunteer Advocates

§ 107.031. Volunteer Advocates.

(a) In a suit filed by a governmental entity, the court may appoint a **charitable organization composed of volunteer advocates whose charter mandates the provision of services to allegedly abused and neglected children or an individual** [~~person~~] who has received the court's approved training **regarding abused and neglected children** and who has been certified by the court to appear at court hearings as a **guardian ad litem for the child or as a** volunteer advocate **for** [~~on behalf of~~] the child.

(b) In **a suit other than a suit filed by a governmental entity, the court may appoint a charitable organization composed of volunteer advocates whose training provides for the provision of services in private custody disputes or a person who has received the court's approved training regarding the subject matter of the suit and who has been certified by the court to appear at court hearings as a guardian ad litem for the child or as a volunteer advocate for the child. A person appointed under this subsection is not entitled to fees under Section 107.023** [~~addition, the court may appoint a group of court-certified volunteers to serve as an administrative review board to advise the court as to the conservatorship appointment and the placement of the child by the Department of or authorized agency in substitute care~~].

[~~(c) A court-appointed volunteer, a board member or employee of a volunteer advocate charitable organization, or a member of an administrative review board is not liable for civil damages for a recommendation made or opinion rendered while serving or having served as a court-appointed volunteer, board member or employee of a volunteer advocate charitable organization, or member of an administrative review board under this section unless the act or failure to act is wilfully wrongful, committed with conscious indifference or reckless disregard for the safety of another, committed in bad faith or with malice, or is grossly negligent.~~

[~~(d) This section does not prohibit the court from appointing as a guardian ad litem for a child under Section 107.001 a court-certified volunteer advocate appointed for the child under this section.~~

[~~(e) A court-certified volunteer advocate appointed under this section for a child with a disability may be assigned to act as a surrogate parent for the child, as provided by 20 U.S.C. Section 1415(b) and its subsequent amendments, if:~~

[~~(1) the child is in the conservatorship of the Department of Protective and Regulatory Services;~~

[~~(2) the volunteer advocate is serving as guardian ad litem for the child; and~~

[~~(3) a foster parent of the child is not acting as the child's parent under Section 29.015, Education Code.~~]

Comment

Since the early 1990's, volunteer advocacy programs authorized by this subchapter have proliferated through the state. Usually known as CASAs (Court–Appointed Special Advocates), private individuals have been appointed as volunteer advocates for children in child protection litigation. Official recognition of the vital role played by CASAs came in 1997 when via amendments to § 107.001 the legislature authorized the court to appoint a volunteer advocate as the guardian ad litem for the child. This brought Texas into compliance with federal funding requirements, P.L. 104–235, 42 U.S.C. § 5106A (b)(2)(ix)

(1997), and transformed the volunteer advocate appointed as GAL into a substitute decision-maker on behalf of the child in litigation.

Subsection (a) provides that the appointment may be to the CASA organization itself and does not necessarily require the appointment of an identified single individual.

Subsection (b) opens the way for non-CASA organizations to provide volunteer advocates in private custody disputes if that is the choice of the entity.

Subchapter D. Social Study

Introductory Comment

Although a social study is not "evidence," it may have a significant impact on judicial decision making. A peculiar aspect of the statute is that DPRS sought and received a statutory exemption from making social studies except in cases in which the agency is a party-litigant. How the agency can be both a party and a neutral factfinder is left to the imagination (but this has been the case for decades).

CLE/Other Legal Publications

Dealing with social studies, ad litems and CASA volunteers: a curse or a blessing? Lynn Kamin & E. Lorraine Wilson, 1998 Adv. Fam. L.

Leading Cases

Green v. Remling, 608 S.W.2d 905 (Tex. 1980) (court properly considered social study; failure to call social worker as witness not reversible error)

Chacon v. Chacon, 978 S.W.2d 633 (Tex. App.—El Paso 1998, no pet.) (CASAs written observations submitted as "court report" do not constitute a social study)

Bingham v. Bingham, 811 S.W.2d 678 (Tex. App.—Fort Worth 1991, no writ) (social study admissible as a governmental report)

Rossen v. Rossen, 792 S.W.2d 277 (Tex. App.—Houston [1st Dist.] 1990, no writ) (social study is generally inadmissible hearsay; author of report testified about procedure used in making report and her conclusions)

Texas Family Law Practice Manual

Forms 4–9. Motion for Preparation of Social Study; *4–10*. Order on Motion for Preparation of Social Study

§ 107.051. Order for Social Study.

(a) The court may order the preparation of a social study into the circumstances and condition of the child and of the home of any person requesting managing conservatorship or possession of the child.

(b) The social study may be made by a private entity, a person appointed by the court, or a state agency, including the Department of Protective and Regulatory Services if the department is a party to the suit.

(c) In a suit in which adoption is requested or possession of or access to the child is an issue and in which the Department of Protective and Regulatory Services is not a party, the court shall appoint a private agency or another person, including a domestic relations office, to conduct the social study.

Comment

The CPS involvement with social studies continues to be one of the strangest sections in the Family Code, if not all of the statute books. Despite the fact that CPS is a party to a lawsuit espousing its own legal position, it is permissible for the department to be ordered to prepare a social study in that suit. However, if CPS is not a party, and thereby neutral on the subject by definition, the court is forbidden to appoint CPS to conduct a social study—a somewhat bizarre system from a due process perspective.

---

§ 107.0511. Pre–Adoptive Home Screening.

(a) In this section, " department" means the Department of Protective and Regulatory Services.

(b) A pre-adoptive home screening shall be conducted as provided by this section to evaluate each party in a proceeding described by Subsection (c) who requests termination of the parent-child relationship or an adoption.

(c) Except for a suit brought by a licensed child-placing agency or the department, the home screening under this section shall be filed in any suit for:

(1) termination of the parent-child relationship in which a person other than a parent may be appointed managing conservator of a child; or

(2) an adoption.

(d) Other than in a suit in which a licensed child-placing agency or the department is appointed managing conservator of the child, the home screening under this section must be filed with the court before the court may sign the final order for termination of the parent-child relationship.

(e) The costs of a home screening in a suit for adoption under this section shall be paid by the prospective adoptive parent.

(f) Unless otherwise agreed to by the court, the home screening under this section must comply with the minimum requirements for the screening under rules adopted by the Board of Protective and Regulatory Services.

(g) In a stepparent adoption, the pre-adoptive home screening under this section and the post-placement adoptive report under Section 107.052 may be combined.

§ 107.052. Post–Placement Adoptive Report.

(a) In a proceeding in which a pre-adoptive home screening is required by Section 107.0511 for an adoption, a post-placement adoptive report must be conducted and filed with the court before the court may render a final order in the adoption.

(b) Unless otherwise agreed to by the court, the post-placement adoptive report must comply with the minimum requirements for the report under rules adopted by the Board of Protective and Regulatory Services.

Comment

When a licensed child placing agency or adoptive parent files a suit for adoption, the court is required by statute to order a home screening prior to placement of the child and a follow up social study, relabeled "post-placement adoptive report." In some cases of private adoptions, judges have ordered a home screening but not a social study. To ensure the best interest of the child, both a home screening and the post-placement report are fundamental. To that end, there was a thorough reworking of this system, basically adding two new provisions and further modifications to establish pre-adoptive home screenings and post-placement adoptive reports in adoption cases in an effort to study the home environment of the adoptive parents.

A pre-adoptive home screening must be conducted to evaluate each party who requests termination of the parent-child relationship or an adoption. Except for a suit brought by a licensed child-placing agency or DPRS, prescribed suits include any such suit in which a person other than a parent is authorized to be appointed managing conservator of a child. The screening is to be paid for by the prospective adoptive parent, and, unless otherwise agreed to by the court, must comply with the rules promulgated by the Board of DPRS.

Former provisions relating to the standards for conducting a social study, an adoptive home screening, and the time for an adoption hearing have been repealed. The details are left to compliance with the requirements set forth by the rules of the DFRS Board. The documentation must be filed with the court before it may render a final order in the adoption. In a step-parent adoption, the screening and the report may be combined. A social study may be made by a private entity, a person appointed by the court, or a state agency, including the department if the department is a party to the suit.

Finally, the court is required to grant a motion for a preferential setting for a final hearing on certain merits and to give precedence to that hearing over other civil cases under prescribed conditions. The final order in a termination of the parent-child relationship or adoption proceeding is not required to contain certain information regarding each party in the suit.

---

§ 107.053. Prospective Adoptive Parents to Receive Copy.

In all adoptions a copy of the report shall be made available to the prospective adoptive parents prior to a final order of adoption.

§ 107.054. Report Filed With Court.

The agency or person making the social study shall file with the court on a date set by the court a report containing its findings and conclusions. The report shall be made a part of the record of the suit.

§ 107.055. Introduction of Report at Trial.

(a) Disclosure to the jury of the contents of a report to the court of a social study is subject to the rules of evidence.

(b) In a contested case, the agency or person making the social study shall furnish copies of the report to the attorneys for the parties before the earlier of:

(1) the seventh day after the date the social study is completed; or

(2) the fifth day before the date of commencement of the trial.

(c) The court may compel the attendance of witnesses necessary for the proper disposition of the suit, including a representative of the agency making the social study, who may be compelled to testify.

§ 107.056. Preparation Fee.

If the court orders a social study to be conducted and a report to be prepared, the court shall award the agency or other person a reasonable fee for the preparation of the study that shall be taxed as costs and paid directly to the agency or other person. The person or agency may enforce the order for the fee.

Chapter 108. Central Record File; Vital Statistics.

Introductory Comment

Since 1995, the Bureau of Vital Statistics has maintained the central record file that identifies courts of continuing, exclusive jurisdiction in SAPCR cases. This central record file is not related to CANRIS, the computerized records of reports of alleged child abuse and neglect, which is maintained by the Department of Protective and Regulatory Services, *see* § 261.002, *infra*.

---

§ 108.001. Transmittal of Records of Suit by Clerk.

(a) Except as provided by this chapter, the clerk of the court shall transmit to the bureau of vital statistics a certified record of the order rendered in a suit, together with the name and all prior names, birth date, and place of birth of the child prepared by the petitioner on a form provided by the bureau.

(b) The bureau of vital statistics shall maintain these records in a central file according to the name, birth date, and place of birth of the child, the court that rendered the order, and the docket number of the suit.

(c) Except as otherwise provided by law, the records required under this section to be maintained by the bureau of vital statistics are confidential.

§ 108.002. Dissolution of Marriage Records Maintained by Clerk.

A clerk may not transmit to the central record file the pleadings, papers, studies, and records relating to a suit for divorce or annulment or to declare a marriage void.

§ 108.003. Transmittal of Information Regarding Adoption.

(a) The clerk of a court that renders a decree of adoption shall, not later than the 10th day of the first month after the month in which the adoption is rendered, transmit to the central registry of the bureau of vital statistics certified report of adoption that includes:

(1) the name of the adopted child after adoption as shown in the adoption order;

(2) the birth date of the adopted child;

(3) the docket number of the adoption suit;

(4) the identity of the court rendering the adoption;

(5) the date of the adoption order;

(6) the name and address of each parent, guardian, managing conservator, or other person whose consent to adoption was required or waived under Chapter 162 *[Adoption]*, or whose parental rights were terminated in the adoption suit;

(7) the identity of the licensed child placing agency, if any, through which the adopted child was placed for adoption; and

(8) the identity, address, and telephone number of the registry through which the adopted child may register as an adoptee.

(b) Except as otherwise provided by law, for good cause shown, or on an order of the court that granted the adoption or terminated the proceedings under Section 155.001, the records concerning a child maintained by the district clerk after rendition of a decree of adoption, the records of a child-placing agency that has ceased operations, and the records required under this section to be maintained by the bureau of vital statistics are confidential, and no person is entitled to access to or information from these records.

(c) If the bureau of vital statistics determines that a report filed with the bureau under this section requires correction, the bureau shall mail the report directly to an attorney of record with respect to the adoption. The attorney shall return the corrected report to the bureau. If there is no attorney of record, the bureau shall mail the report to the clerk of the court for correction.

History: Amended by 78th Legis., Reg. Sess. (2003), H.B. 2886, eff. Sept. 1, 2003, and "applies only to a certificate or report that the bureau of vital statistics of the Texas Department of Health determines requires correction on or after that date."

§ 108.004. Transmittal of Files on Loss of Jurisdiction.

On the loss of jurisdiction of a court under Chapter 155 *[Continuing, Exclusive Jurisdiction; Transfer]*, the clerk of the court shall transmit to the central registry of the bureau of vital statistics a certified record, on a form provided by the bureau, stating that jurisdiction has been lost, the reason for the loss of jurisdiction, and the name and all previous names, date of birth, and place of birth of the child.

§ 108.005. Adoption Records Received by Bureau of Vital Statistics.

(a) When the bureau of vital statistics receives a record from the district clerk showing that continuing, exclusive jurisdiction of a child has been lost due to the adoption of the child, the bureau shall close the records concerning that child.

(b) An inquiry concerning a child who has been adopted shall be handled as though the child had not previously been the subject of a suit affecting the parent-child relationship.

§ 108.006. Fees.

(a) The bureau of vital statistics may charge a reasonable fee to cover the cost of determining and sending information concerning the identity of the court with continuing, exclusive jurisdiction.

(b) On the filing of a suit requesting the adoption of a child, the clerk of the court shall collect an additional fee of $15.

(c) The clerk shall send the fees collected under Subsection (b) to the bureau of vital statistics for deposit in a special fund in the state treasury from which the legislature may appropriate money only to operate and maintain the central file and central registry of the bureau.

(d) The receipts from the fees charged under Subsection (a) shall be deposited in a financial institution as determined by the director of the bureau of vital statistics and withdrawn as necessary for the sole purpose of operating and maintaining the central record file.

§ 108.007. Microfilm.

(a) The bureau of vital statistics may use microfilm or other suitable means for maintaining the central record file.

(b) A certified reproduction of a document maintained by the bureau of vital statistics is admissible in evidence as the original document.

§ 108.008. Filing Information After Determination of Paternity.

(a) On a determination of paternity, the petitioner shall provide the clerk of the court in which the order was rendered the information necessary to prepare the report of determination of paternity. The clerk shall:

(1) prepare the report on a form provided by the Bureau of Vital Statistics; and

(2) complete the report immediately after the order becomes final.

(b) On completion of the report, the clerk of the court shall forward to the state registrar a report for each order that became final in that court.

§ 108.009. Birth Certificate.

(a) The state registrar shall substitute a new birth certificate for the original based on the order in accordance with laws or rules that permit the correction or substitution of a birth certificate for an adopted child or a child whose parents marry each other subsequent to the birth of the child.

(b) The new certificate may not show that the father and child relationship was established after the child's birth but may show the child's actual place and date of birth.

§ 108.110. Release of Information by Bureau of Vital Statistics.

(a) The bureau of vital statistics shall provide to the Department of Protective and Regulatory Services:

(1) adoption information as necessary for the department to comply with federal law or regulations regarding the compilation or reporting of adoption information to federal officials; and

(2) other information as necessary for the department to administer its duties.

(b) The bureau may release otherwise confidential information from the bureau's central record files to another governmental entity that has a specific need for the information and maintains appropriate safeguards to prevent further dissemination of the information.

Cross Reference

TEX. HEALTH & SAFETY CODE ANN. ch. 192. Birth Records.

Chapter 109. Appeals.

Introductory Comment

The life of a child who is the subject of a SAPCR is often significantly affected by the appellate process. To mitigate the negative effect, the legislature has directed that expedited appeals occur if an adoption would be delayed.

CLE/Other Legal Publications

Anticipating an appeal: the ultimate C.Y.A. Pamela E. George, 2004 ADV. FAM. L.

Avoiding a permanent "waive": preservation of error. Ann C. McClure, 2004 MARRIAGE DISSOLUTION

Appeals. Georganna L. Simpson & James A. Vaught, 2003 ADV. FAM. L.

Trying case with appeal—preserving error. Lynne Liberato, 2002 ADV. FAM. L.

Take me higher: preparing the appeal, including findings of fact and conclusions of law. Georganna L. Simpson, 2002 MARRIAGE DISSOLUTION

Activities in the trial court during appeal and after remand. Richard R. Orsinger, 2002 MARRIAGE DISSOLUTION

A blind hog in search of an acorn—what findings of fact do you need? Ann C. McClure, 2001 ADV. FAM. L.

Appellate—mandamus. Georganna L. Simpson, 2001 ADV. FAM. L. DRAFTING

Leading Cases

In re M.S., 115 S.W.3d 534 (Tex. 2003) (attorney's failure to preserve factual sufficiency issue for appeal constitutes ineffective assistance of counsel)

Stubbs v. Stubbs, 685 S.W.2d 643 (Tex. 1985) (signing of waiver is not participation in trial precluding writ of error)

In re Gonzalez, 981 S.W.2d 313 (Tex. App.—San Antonio 1998, no pet.) (trial court may continue to enforce child support during appeal absent appellate court assuming jurisdiction)

In re Hall, 871 S.W.2d 251 (Tex. App.—Amarillo 1994, no writ) (SAPCR appeal requires security for costs)

---

§ 109.001. Temporary Orders During Pendency of Appeal.

(a) Not later than the 30th day after the date an appeal is perfected, on the motion of any party or on the court's own motion and after notice and hearing, the court may make any order necessary to preserve and protect the safety and welfare of the child during the pendency of the appeal as the court may deem necessary and equitable. In addition to other matters, an order may:

(1) appoint temporary conservators for the child and provide for possession of the child;

(2) require the temporary support of the child by a party;

(3) restrain a party from molesting or disturbing the peace of the child or another party;

(4) prohibit a person from removing the child beyond a geographical area identified by the court;

(5) require payment of reasonable attorney's fees and expenses; or

(6) suspend the operation of the order or judgment that is being appealed.

(b) A court retains jurisdiction to enforce its orders rendered under this section unless the appellate court, on a proper showing, supersedes the court's order.

(c) A temporary order rendered under this section is not subject to interlocutory appeal.

(d) The court may not suspend under Subsection (a)(6) the operation of an order or judgment terminating the parent-child relationship in a suit brought by the state or a political subdivision of the state permitted by law to bring the suit.

Comment

Until a 2001 amendment, trial and appellate courts were authorized to suspend the operation of a judgment in any case involving the parent-child relationship. Because there was no express limitation, these provisions appeared to authorize the suspension of such a judgment even in a suit brought by DPRS in an abuse or neglect case. Although there were several protections and procedures under pre–2001 law for the child's placement during the pendency of a suit to terminate parental rights, there were no express procedures in place in the event of a suspension of a judgment. Thus, the appeals process could conceivably last longer than the time period involved in the pendency of a suit for termination at trial. As a result, a final judgment suspended by a trial court could leave the parties in limbo without the protections afforded them before the appeal.

The 2001 addition of subsection (d) prohibits a trial or an appellate court from suspending a judgment that terminates the parent-child relationship in a suit brought by the state or an authorized political subdivision of the state. An appeal in a DPRS suit in which termination of the parent-child relationship is at issue must accelerated by the appellate courts in accordance with the procedures for an accelerated appeal under Tex. R. App. P.

Texas Family Law Practice Manual

Forms 20–5. Motion for Temporary Orders Pending Appeal; *20–6.* Order on Motion for Temporary Orders Pending Appeal.

---

§ 109.002. Appeal.

(a) An appeal from a final order rendered in a suit, when allowed under this section or under other provisions of law, shall be as in civil cases generally. An appeal in a suit in which termination of the parent-child relationship is in issue shall be given precedence over other civil cases and shall be accelerated by the appellate courts. The procedures for an accelerated appeal under the Texas Rules of Appellate Procedure apply to an appeal in which the termination of the parent-child relationship is in issue.

(b) An appeal may be taken by any party to a suit from a final order rendered under this title.

(c) An appeal from a final order, with or without a supersedeas bond, does not suspend the order unless suspension is ordered by the court rendering the order. The appellate court, on a proper showing, may permit the order to be suspended, unless the order provides for the termination of the parent-child relationship in a suit brought by the state or a political subdivision of the state permitted by law to bring the suit.

(d) On the motion of the parties or on the court's own motion, the appellate court in its opinion may identify the parties by fictitious names or by their initials only.

Comment

Delay in legal procedures related to the disposition of cases involving the termination of parental rights is not in the best interest of the children of this state. Although pre–2001 law required that an appeal in a parental rights termination suit be given precedence over other civil cases, it did not require the appellate courts to accelerate appeals. In an accelerated appeal, briefs and the notice of appeal must be filed within 20 days, instead of 30 days of the last action. The clerk and the reporter must file the record of the appeal within 10 days after the notice, rather than taking up to 120 days to file. If so requested, the appellate court is authorized to hear the appeal on original papers forwarded by the trial court, or on sworn and uncontroverted copies of the papers.

§ 109.003. Payment for Statement of Facts.

(a) If the party requesting a statement of facts in an appeal of a suit has filed an affidavit stating the party's inability to pay costs as provided by Rule 20, Texas Rules of Appellate Procedure, and the affidavit is approved by the trial court, the trial court may order the county in which the trial was held to pay the costs of preparing the statement of facts.

(b) Nothing in this section shall be construed to permit an official court reporter to be paid more than once for the preparation of the statement of facts.

Chapter 110. Court Fees.

§ 110.001. General Rule.

Except as provided by this chapter, fees in a matter covered by this title shall be as in civil cases generally.

§ 110.002. Filing Fees and Deposits.

(a) The clerk of the court may collect a filing fee of $15 in a suit for filing:

(1) a suit **or motion** for modification;

(2) a motion for enforcement;

(3) a notice of application for judicial writ of withholding;

(4) a motion to transfer**;**[~~,~~]

(5) a petition for license suspension; [~~or~~]

(6) a motion to revoke a stay of license suspension**; or**

(7) a motion for contempt.

(b) No other filing fee may be collected or required for an action described in this section.

(c) The clerk may collect a deposit as in other cases, in the amount set by the clerk for payment of expected costs and other expenses arising in the proceeding.

History: Amended by 78th Legis., Reg. Sess. (2003), H.B. 1885, eff. Sept. 1, 2003, and "applies only to a suit affecting the parent-child relationship or motion in a suit affecting the parent-child relationship filed on or after the effective date of this Act. A suit affecting the parent-child relationship or motion in a suit affecting the parent-child relationship filed before the effective date of this Act is governed by the law in effect on the date the suit or motion was filed, and the former law is continued in effect for that purpose."

Comment

The statute sets a relatively modest fee for filing a motion to modify or to enforce. The Texas Attorney General, as the IV–D agency, is required to pay a filing fee for various motions to enforce. This provision is intended to assist counties in meeting expenses and generate additional federal funding for child support enforcement.

§ 110.003. No Separate or Additional Filing Fee.

The clerk of the court may not require:

(1) a separate filing fee in a suit joined with a suit for dissolution of marriage under Title 1; or

(2) an additional filing fee if more than one form of relief is requested in a suit.

§ 110.004. Fee for Issuing and Delivering Withholding Order or Writ.

The clerk of the court may charge a reasonable fee, not to exceed $15, for each order or writ of income withholding issued by the clerk and delivered to an employer.

§ 110.005. Transfer Fee.

(a) The fee for filing a transferred case is $45 payable to the clerk of the court to which the case is transferred. No portion of this fee may be sent to the state.

(b) A party may not be assessed any other fee, cost, charge, or expense by the clerk of the court or other public official in connection with filing of the transferred case.

(c) The fee limitation in this section does not affect a fee payable to the court transferring the case.

§ 110.006. Domestic Relations Office Fees.

If an administering entity of a domestic relations office adopts an initial operations fee under Section 203.005(a)(1) or an initial child support service fee under Section 203.005(a)(2), the clerk of the court shall collect the fee at the time the suit is filed and send the fee to the domestic relations office.

Chapter 111. Guidelines for Possession and Child Support.

Introductory Comment

The caption of the chapter is somewhat misleading; this chapter merely provides general provisions for the promulgation and review of the child support and visitation guidelines, which are found in Chapters 153 and 154, *infra*. For more than a decade the Texas Supreme Court was charged with appointing a committee to assist the legislature in formulating and reviewing guidelines. Since 1999 that duty has been performed by legislative committees, as described in the next comment.

Beginning in 1985 with the initial promulgation guidelines for child support, and a later legislative mandate for visitation guidelines, an annual review was conducted by a committee appointed by the Texas Supreme Court. Review of the support guidelines is a requirement to retain the federal child support subsidy, and review of the visitation guidelines was viewed as a political necessity. Through the 1999 legislative session, the committee, composed of both legal and lay-person members, met two to four times between legislative sessions to agree to disagree over many issues. The committee invariably wound up making recommendations to the legislature, which were generally enacted into law.

The process broke down in 1999, and none of the committee's rather minimal child support and visitation recommendations were accepted by the legislature. Most notably, a dissident lay-person member filed lawsuit in federal court against the co-chairs of the committee and the chairs of the two subcommittees. That was the final straw for the advisory committee process. The legislature decided that enough was enough, and abolished the committee. Since 1999, the guidelines review has been conducted by legislative interim committees of the House or Senate.

---

§ 111.001. Review of Guidelines.

(a) Prior to each regular legislative session, the standing committees of each house of the legislature having jurisdiction over family law issues shall review and, if necessary, recommend revisions to the guidelines for possession of and access to a child under Chapter 153 *[Conservatorship, Possession, and Access]* and for support of a child under Chapter 154 *[Child Support]*. The committee shall report the results of the review and shall include any recommended revisions in the committee's report to the legislature.

(b) Not later than December 1 of each even-numbered year, the Title IV–D agency shall submit a report to the standing committees of each house of the legislature having jurisdiction over family law issues for use by the committee in conducting the review required by Subsection (a). The report must contain:

(1) economic data obtained from the United States Department of Agriculture on the cost of raising children;

(2) an analysis of case data on the application of and deviations from the child support guidelines; and

(3) a summary of any federal legislation enacted since the date of the last review.

§ 111.002. Guidelines Supersede Court Rules.

(a) The guidelines in this title supersede local court rules and rules of the supreme court that conflict with the guidelines.

(b) Notwithstanding other law, the guidelines may not be repealed or modified by a rule adopted by the supreme court.

§ 111.003. Posting Guidelines.

A copy of the guidelines for possession of and access to a child under Chapter 153 *[Conservatorship, Possession, and Access]* and a copy of the guidelines for the support of a child under Chapter 154 *[Child Support]* shall be prominently displayed at or near the entrance to the courtroom of every court having jurisdiction of a suit.

Subtitle B. Suits Affecting the Parent–Child Relationship

Chapter

★★★

Chapter 151. Rights and Duties In Parent–Child Relationship.

Introductory Comment

Originally, this chapter was intended to define the parent-child relationship, which included the presumption of paternity, the elimination of the concept of illegitimacy, and baby-steps towards the brave new world of science through recognition of the only method of assisted reproduction known to the world in 1973 when the Family Code was first enacted, so-called "artificial insemination." Several years later, oocyte and embryo donation were statutorily recognized as advancements in the medical possibilities of that process.

The enactment of the Uniform Parentage Act in 2001 involved moving all of the provisions related to parentage to Chapter 160, *infra*. The net effect is that this chapter contains virtually no substantive law. Specifically, the laundry list of parental rights in this chapter is hortatory only. But, the substantive rights of parents flow from the litany, as the remaining chapters in Title 5 amply demonstrate.

---

§ 151.001. Rights and Duties of Parent.

(a) A parent of a child has the following rights and duties:

(1) the right to have physical possession, to direct the moral and religious training, and to designate the residence of the child;

(2) the duty of care, control, protection, and reasonable discipline of the child;

(3) the duty to support the child, including providing the child with clothing, food, shelter, medical and dental care, and education;

(4) the duty, except when a guardian of the child's estate has been appointed, to manage the estate of the child, including the right as an agent of the child to act in relation to the child's estate if the child's action is required by a state, the United States, or a foreign government;

(5) except as provided by Section 264.0111, the right to the services and earnings of the child;

(6) the right to consent to the child's marriage, enlistment in the armed forces of the United States, medical and dental care, and psychiatric, psychological, and surgical treatment;

(7) the right to represent the child in legal action and to make other decisions of substantial legal significance concerning the child;

(8) the right to receive and give receipt for payments for the support of the child and to hold or disburse funds for the benefit of the child;

(9) the right to inherit from and through the child;

(10) the right to make decisions concerning the child's education; and

(11) any other right or duty existing between a parent and child by virtue of law.

(b) The duty of a parent to support his or her child exists while the child is an unemancipated minor and continues as long as the child is fully enrolled in an accredited secondary school in a program leading toward a high school diploma until the end of the school year in which the child graduates.

(c) A parent who fails to discharge the duty of support is liable to a person who provides necessaries to those to whom support is owed.

(d) The rights and duties of a parent are subject to:

(1) a court order affecting the rights and duties;

(2) an affidavit of relinquishment of parental rights; and

(3) an affidavit by the parent designating another person or agency to act as managing conservator.

Comment

This enumerated list of parental rights and duties constitutes a legislative codification of custom, practice, and social mores in statutory form. Interestingly, there is no comparable listing of the rights and duties of a child.

The cross-reference in subsection (a)(5) cites a provision new in 2001 which eliminates the ownership and managerial rights of parents to the accumulated earnings of a child who has been returned home after earning money and establishing a bank account while in state custody. Residential treatment centers commonly encourage such children to earn and manage their own money to improve self-esteem and responsibility.

CLE/Other Legal Publication

Dangerously giving up rights—to share or not to share. Wendy S. Burgower & Charlote D. Rainwater, 2003 MARRIAGE DISSOLUTION

Rights and duties of parents, grand parents and non-parents. Curtis M. Loveless, 2002 ADV. FAM. L.

Leading Cases

In re Lemons, 47 S.W.3d 202 (Tex. App.—Beaumont 2001, no pet.) (court must specify rights and duties and time periods for the noncustodial parent to have possession of and access to the child)

In re B.T., 954 S.W.2d 44 (Tex. App.—San Antonio 1997, writ denied) (duty to support child exists independent of court order)

Rodriguez v. Spencer, 902 S.W.2d 37 (Tex. App.—Houston [1st Dist.] 1995, no writ) (parent not responsible for violent tort committed by child)

Lawrence v. Cox, 464 S.W.2d 674 (Tex. Civ. App.—Waco 1971, writ dism'd w.o.j.) (father is liable for child's dental bills even without court order to pay for dentist's bills)

§ 151.002. Rights of a Living Child After an Abortion or Premature Birth.

(a) A living human child born alive after an abortion or premature birth is entitled to the same rights, powers, and privileges as are granted by the laws of this state to any other child born alive after the normal gestation period.

(b) In this code, "born alive" means the complete expulsion or extraction from its mother of a product of conception, irrespective of the duration of pregnancy, which, after such separation, breathes or shows any other evidence of life such as beating of the heart, pulsation of the umbilical cord, or definite movement of voluntary muscles, whether or not the umbilical cord has been cut or the placenta is attached. Each product of the birth is considered born alive.

§ 151.003. Limitation on State Agency Action.

A state agency may not adopt rules or policies or take any other action that violates the fundamental right and duty of a parent to direct the upbringing of the parent's child.

Chapter 152. Uniform Child Custody Jurisdiction and Enforcement Act.

Subchapter A. Application and Construction

Subchapter B. General Provisions

Subchapter C. Jurisdiction

Subchapter D. Enforcement

Introductory Comment

Effective September 1, 1999, Texas adopted the Uniform Child Custody Jurisdiction and Enforcement Act (1997) [UCCJEA], replacing the previous Uniform Child Custody Jurisdiction Act (1968) [UCCJA]. This new uniform act was adopted by the National Conference of Commissioners on Uniform State Law in 1997 and recommended for approval by all states by the American Bar Association in 1998. As this book goes to print, 34 jurisdictions have adopted the UCCJEA: Alabama, Alaska, Arizona, Arkansas, California, Colorado, Connecticut, Delaware, District of Columbia, Florida, Georgia, Hawaii, Idaho, Illinois, Iowa, Kansas, Maine, Michigan, Minnesota, Montana, Nebraska, Nevada, New Mexico, New York, North Carolina, North Dakota, Oklahoma, Oregon, Tennessee, Texas, Utah, Virginia, Washington, and West Virginia. Legislation is pending in seven other states.

The original jurisdictional standards will look familiar to Texas lawyers and judges. Continuing jurisdiction has been changed, ending the old dichotomy between custody and visitation. After September 1, 1999, a court of this state will either have exclusive, continuing jurisdiction over both custody (managing conservatorship) and visitation (possessory conservatorship, or possession of and access of a child) or neither. Thus, Texas joins the vast majority of American jurisdictions for dealing with continuing jurisdiction. Case law under the former Texas version of the Uniform Child Custody Jurisdiction Act regarding continuing jurisdiction over custody will have little, if any, precedent value under the new act. The enforcement provisions are entirely new, but largely track current Texas writ of habeas corpus practice. The act applies to any original SAPCR and any suit for modification filed on or after September 1, 1999.

CLE/Other Legal Publications

Jurisdiction, special appearance, and conflicts of law. Donn C. Fullenweider, 2004 ADV. FAM. L.

Immigration and its effect on relocation, jurisdiction and divorce. J. Joseph Reina, 2004 ADV. FAM. L.

Jurisdiction, venue, plea in abatement and the UCCJEA. Douglas R. Woodburn, 2004 MARRIAGE DISSOLUTION

Jurisdiction and enforcement of custody and possession. Brian L. Webb, 2004 U. TEX. FAM. L. ON THE BORDER

The ABCs of interstate family support jurisdiction. Angela G. Pence, 2003 ADV. FAM. L.

Jurisdiction over foreign litigants: dissolution, property division, spousal support, child support. Bill De La Garza & Jo Ann Carter, 2002 ADV. FAM. L.

UCCJEA and Foreign Judgments. Angela G. Pence, 2003 ADV. FAM. L.

Interstate alphabet soup. Sally H. Emerson, 2002 ADV. FAM. L.

International and cross border issues. (Workshop) 2002 ADV. FAM. L.

Extraterritorial custody issues: the UCCJEA, PKPA, and the Hague Convention. Lynn Kamin & Sharon D. Cammack, 2001 ADV. FAM. L.

Leading Case Decided Under the UCCJEA

In re B.A.B., 124 S.W.3d 417 (Tex. App.—Dallas 2004, no pet.) (date of modification motion determines UCCJEA jurisdiction)

In re S.L.P., 123 S.W.3d 685 (Tex. App.—Fort Worth 2003, no pet.) (Texas court must decline jurisdiction to modify Nevada order because of unjustifiable conduct)

In re Powell, 121 S.W.3d 846 (Tex. App.—Beaumont 2003, pet. filed) (temporary absence to Tennessee did not remove Texas as home state)

In re Y.M.A., 111 S.W.3d 790 (Tex. App.—Fort Worth 2003, no pet.) (first filed Egyptian custody suit rendered order that precludes Texas SAPCR)

In re K.L.V., 109 S.W.3d 61 (Tex. App.—Fort Worth 2003, pet. denied) (appeal of UCCJEA order must follow accelerated timetable)

In re Oates, 104 S.W.3d 571 (Tex. App.—El Paso, orig. proceeding) (temporary order and Texas custody jurisdiction ended when Texas father died; grandparents have no right to access here against a N.Y. mother)

Saavedra v. Schmidt, 96 S.W.3d 533 (Tex. App.—Austin 2002, no pet.) (Texas court without authority to modify California decree unless California declines jurisdiction)

In re McCormick, 87 S.W.3d 746 (Tex. App.—Amarillo 2002, no pet.) (Texas retains UCCJEA modification jurisdiction over father and son now living in Kansas)

In re Calderon–Garza, 81 S.W.3d 899 (Tex. App.—El Paso 2002, no pet.) (Texas was two-month-old infant's home state under UCCJEA when alleged father filed paternity suit)

In re Bellamy, 62 S.W.3d 482 (Tex. App.—Texarkana 2002, no pet.) (Texas retains custody-visitation jurisdiction under UCCJEA by virtue of significant connections; when a provision of Chapter 152 conflicts with another provision of the Family Code or another statute or rule of Texas and the conflict cannot be reconciled, Chapter 152 prevails)

In re McCoy, 52 S.W.3d 297 (Tex. App.—Corpus Christi 2001, no pet.) (under the UCCJEA, Texas must be the children's home state or the residence of one parent in order to have jurisdiction to make an initial child custody determination)

In re B.O.G., 48 S.W.3d 312 (Tex. App.—Waco 2001, pet. filed) (trial court lacked jurisdiction over father's motion to modify child support and grandparents' motion to modify their visitation where both were filed after the effective date of UCCJEA)

McGuire v. McGuire, 18 S.W.3d 801 (Tex. App.—El Paso 2000, no pet.) (case law under former UCCJA regarding continuing jurisdiction will have little precedent value under UCCJEA)

Leading Cases Decided Under the UCCJA

Burnham v. Superior Court of California, 495 U.S. 604, 109 L.Ed. 631, 110 S.Ct. 2105 (1990) (in personam jurisdiction obtained by service in forum state on transient respondent)

Thompson v. Thompson, 484 U.S. 174, 98 L.Ed.2d 512, 108 S.Ct. 513 (1988) (PKPA does not create federal court jurisdiction to resolve interstate custody disputes)

Phillips v. Beaber, 995 S.W.2d 655 (Tex. 1999) (modification of terms of JMC constitutes a suit to modify custody, which Texas UCCJA prohibits when child has new home state— ***Editors' note:*** in our opinion, this holding under the UCCJA is not opposite under the UCCJEA)

Geary v. Peavy, 878 S.W.2d 602 (Tex. 1994) (Texas trial court lacked custody jurisdiction over Minnesota orphans)

Little v. Daggett, 858 S.W.2d 368 (Tex. 1993) (court lacks original SAPCR jurisdiction after child acquires new home state, earlier dismissal of paternity suit irrelevant)

In re S.A.V., 837 S.W.2d 80 (Tex. 1992) (although Texas and Minnesota had concurrent custody jurisdiction under UCCJA, Minnesota declined to exercise its continuing jurisdiction under PKPA)

In re Aubin, 29 S.W.3d 199 (Tex. App.—Beaumont 2000, no pet.) (Texas court cannot issue writ of attachment for possession of child residing in another state)

In re E.K.N., 24 S.W.3d 586 (Tex. App.—Fort Worth 1999, no pet.) (UCCJA applied correctly in refusal to abate SAPCR in deference to earlier filed custody suit in California)

In re Alley, 1 S.W.2d 268 (Tex. App.—Texarkana 1999, no pet.) (writ of mandamus may issue to require a trial court to dismiss a proceeding over which it does not have subject matter jurisdiction under UCCJA)

In re Hattenbach, 999 S.W.2d 636 (Tex. App.—Waco 1999, no pet.) (trial court declined modification jurisdiction; standard of review is abuse of discretion)

In re Lambert, 993 S.W.2d 123 (Tex. App.—San Antonio 1999, no pet.) (jurisdiction challenged by writ of mandamus and prohibition)

Lemley v. Miller, 932 S.W.2d 284 (Tex. App.—Austin 1996, no writ) (Texas can modify Oklahoma custody order even with father in Oklahoma—overlooking PKPA prohibition)

Arteaga v. Texas Dept of Department of Protective and Regulatory Services, 924 S.W.2d 756 (Tex. App.—Austin 1996, writ denied) (UCCJA allows Mexican national's parental rights to be terminated)

Koester v. Montgomery, 886 S.W.2d 432 (Tex. App.—Houston [1st Dist.] 1994, no writ) (Texas may exercise significant connection jurisdiction over children after Venezuela lost "home state" status)

Green v. McCoy, 870 S.W.2d 616 (Tex. App.—El Paso 1994, no writ) (Texas not required to recognize California custody order entered when home state of child is Texas)

Welborn–Hosler v. Hosler, 870 S.W.2d 323 (Tex. App.—Houston [14th Dist.] 1994, no writ) (Texas properly retained jurisdiction to modify possession of and access to child even after child acquires new home state)

Hughes v. Black, 863 S.W.2d 559 (Tex. App.—Waco 1993, no writ) (UCCJA jurisdiction can be challenged by appeal, but not by mandamus)

White v. Blake, 859 S.W.2d 551 (Tex. App.—Tyler 1993, no writ) (Texas has jurisdiction over termination proceeding against non-resident parent, but UCCJA and PKPA dictate Alabama is primary forum)

Abderholden v. Morizot, 856 S.W.2d 829 (Tex. App.—Austin 1993, no writ) (when child has home state, Texas does not have jurisdiction to modify custody, notwithstanding its "emergency" jurisdiction to render temporary order)

In re Carpenter, 835 S.W.2d 760 (Tex. App.—Amarillo 1992, no writ) (parental kidnapper can't bootstrap into "home state" jurisdiction by wrongful conduct)

Reppond v. Blake, 822 S.W.2d 759 (Tex. App.—Tyler 1992, no writ) (Texas court loses subject matter jurisdiction to modify managing conservatorship after child establishes new home state; child support remains modifiable—NOTE: THIS HOLDING NO LONGER PROPER UNDER UCCJEA)

In re Wilson, 799 S.W.2d 773 (Tex. App.—Tyler 1990, no writ) (agreement by Okla. court to release continuing jurisdiction in telephone conversation with Texas judge violated litigant's due process rights)

Henry v. Rivera, 783 S.W.2d 766 (Tex. App.—San Antonio 1990, no writ) and Hemingway v. Robertson, 778 S.W.2d 199 (Tex. App.—Houston [1st Dist.] 1989, no writ) (court cannot modify managing conservator after child establishes new home state—NOTE: THESE HOLDINGS NO LONGER PROPER UNDER UCCJEA)

Texas Family Law Practice Manual

Chapter 34. Interstate Proceedings, Subchapter I. Uniform Child Custody Jurisdiction and Enforcement Act

---

COMMISSIONERS' OFFICIAL PREFATORY NOTE TO UCCJEA

This Act, the Uniform Child Custody Jurisdiction and Enforcement Act (UCCJEA), revisits the problem of the interstate child almost thirty years after the Conference promulgated the Uniform Child Custody Jurisdiction Act (UCCJA). The UCCJEA accomplishes two major purposes.

First, it revises the law on child custody jurisdiction in light of federal enactments and almost thirty years of inconsistent case law. Article 2 of this Act provides clearer standards for which states can exercise original jurisdiction over a child custody determination. It also, for the first time, enunciates a standard of continuing jurisdiction and clarifies modification jurisdiction. Other aspects of the article harmonize the law on simultaneous proceedings, clean hands, and forum non conveniens.

Second, this Act provides in Article 3 for a remedial process to enforce interstate child custody and visitation determinations. In doing so, it brings a uniform procedure to the law of interstate enforcement that is currently producing inconsistent results. In many respects, this Act accomplishes for custody and visitation determinations the same uniformity that has occurred in interstate child support with the promulgation of the Uniform Interstate Family Support Act (UIFSA).

Revision of Uniform Child Custody Jurisdiction Act

The UCCJA was adopted as law in all 50 states, the District of Columbia, and the Virgin Islands. A number of adoptions, however, significantly departed from the original text. In addition, almost thirty years of litigation since the promulgation of the UCCJA produced substantial inconsistency in interpretation by state courts. As a result, the goals of the UCCJA were rendered unobtainable in many cases.

In 1980, the federal government enacted the Parental Kidnapping Prevention Act (PKPA), 28 U.S.C. § 1738A, to address the interstate custody jurisdictional problems that continued to exist after the adoption of the UCCJA. The PKPA mandates that state authorities give full faith and credit to other states' custody determinations, so long as those determinations were made in conformity with the provisions of the PKPA. The PKPA provisions regarding bases for jurisdiction, restrictions on modifications, preclusion of simultaneous proceedings, and notice requirements are similar to those in the UCCJA. There are, however, some significant differences. For example, the PKPA authorizes continuing exclusive jurisdiction in the original decree state so long as one parent or the child remains there and that state has continuing jurisdiction under its own law. The UCCJA did not directly address this issue. To further complicate the process, the PKPA partially incorporates state UCCJA law in its language. The relationship between these two statutes became "technical enough to delight a medieval property lawyer." Homer H. Clark, *Domestic Relations* § 12.5 at 494 (2d ed. 1988).

As documented in an extensive study by the American Bar Association's Center on Children and the Law, *Obstacles to the Recovery and Return of Parentally Abducted Children* (1993) (*Obstacles Study*), inconsistency of interpretation of the UCCJA and the technicalities of applying the PKPA, resulted in a loss of uniformity among the states. The Obstacles Study suggested a number of amendments which would eliminate the inconsistent state interpretations and harmonize the UCCJA with the PKPA.

The revisions of the jurisdictional aspects of the UCCJA eliminate the inconsistent state interpretations and can be summarized as follows:

1. Home state priority. The PKPA prioritizes "home state" jurisdiction by requiring that full faith and credit cannot be given to a child custody determination by a state that exercises initial jurisdiction as a "significant connection state" when there is a "home state." Initial custody determinations based on "significant connections" are not entitled to PKPA enforcement unless there is no home state. The UCCJA, however, specifically authorizes four independent bases of jurisdiction without prioritization. Under the UCCJA, a significant connection custody determination may have to be enforced even it if it would be denied enforcement under the PKPA. The UCCJEA prioritizes home state jurisdiction in Section 201.

2. Clarification of emergency jurisdiction. There are several problems with the current emergency jurisdiction provision of the UCCJA § 3(a)(3). First, the language of the UCCJA does not specify that emergency jurisdiction may be exercised only to protect the child on a temporary basis until the court with appropriate jurisdiction issues a permanent order. Some courts have interpreted the UCCJA language to so provide. Other courts, however, have held that there is no time limit on a custody determination based on emergency jurisdiction. Simultaneous proceedings and conflicting custody orders have resulted from these different interpretations.

Second, the emergency jurisdiction provisions predated the widespread enactment of state domestic violence statutes. Those statutes are often invoked to keep one parent away from the other parent and the children when there is a threat of violence. Whether these situations are sufficient to invoke the emergency jurisdiction provision of the UCCJA has been the subject of some confusion since the emergency jurisdiction provision does not specifically refer to violence directed against the parent of the child or against a sibling of the child.

The UCCJEA contains a separate section on emergency jurisdiction at Section 204 which addresses these issues.

3. Exclusive continuing jurisdiction for the state that entered the decree. The failure of the UCCJA to clearly enunciate that the decree-granting state retains exclusive continuing jurisdiction to modify a decree has resulted in two major problems. First, different interpretations of the UCCJA on continuing jurisdiction have produced conflicting custody decrees. States also have different interpretations as to how long continuing jurisdiction lasts. Some courts have held that modification jurisdiction continues until the last contestant leaves the state, regardless of how many years the child has lived outside the state or how tenuous the child's connections to the state have become. Other courts have held that continuing modification jurisdiction ends as soon as the child has established a new home state, regardless of how significant the child's connections to the decree state remain. Still other states distinguish between custody orders and visitation orders. This divergence of views leads to simultaneous proceedings and conflicting custody orders.

The second problem arises when it is necessary to determine whether the state with continuing jurisdiction has relinquished it. There should be a clear basis to determine when that court has relinquished jurisdiction. The UCCJA provided no guidance on this issue. The ambiguity regarding whether a court has declined jurisdiction can result in one court improperly exercising jurisdiction because it erroneously believes that the other court has declined jurisdiction. This caused simultaneous proceedings and conflicting custody orders. In addition, some courts have declined jurisdiction after only informal contact between courts with no opportunity for the parties to be heard. This raised significant due process concerns. The UCCJEA addresses these issues in Section 110, 202, and 206.

4. Specification of what custody proceedings are covered. The definition of custody proceeding in the UCCJA is ambiguous. States have rendered conflicting decisions regarding certain types of proceedings. There is no general agreement on whether the UCCJA applies to neglect, abuse, dependency, wardship, guardianship, termination of parental rights, and protection from domestic violence proceedings. The UCCJEA includes a sweeping definition that, with the exception of adoption, includes virtually all cases that can involve custody of or visitation with a child as a "custody determination."

5. Role of "Best Interests." The jurisdictional scheme of the UCCJA was designed to promote the best interests of the children whose custody was at issue by discouraging parental abduction and providing that, in general, the state with the closest connections to, and the most evidence regarding a child should decide that child's custody. The "best interest" language in the jurisdictional sections of the UCCJA was not intended to be an invitation to address the merits of the custody dispute in the jurisdictional determination or to otherwise provide that "best interests" considerations should override jurisdictional determinations or provide an additional jurisdictional basis.

The UCCJEA eliminates the term "best interests" in order to clearly distinguish between the jurisdictional standards and the substantive standards relating to custody and visitation of children.

6. Other Changes. This draft also makes a number of additional amendments to the UCCJA. Many of these changes were made to harmonize the provisions of this Act with those of the Uniform Interstate Family Support Act. One of the policy bases underlying this Act is to make uniform the law of interstate family proceedings to the extent possible, given the very different jurisdictional foundations. It simplifies the life of the family law practitioner when the same or similar provisions are found in both Acts.

Enforcement Provisions

One of the major purposes of the revision of the UCCJA was to provide a remedy for interstate visitation and custody cases. As with child support, state borders have become one of the biggest obstacles to enforcement of custody and visitation orders. If either parent leave the state where the custody determination was made, the other parent faces considerable difficulty in enforcing the visitation and custody provisions of the decree. Locating the child, making service of process, and preventing adverse modification in a new forum all present problems.

There is currently no uniform method of enforcing custody and visitation orders validly entered in another state. As documented by the *Obstacles Study*, despite the fact that both the UCCJA and the PKPA direct the enforcement of visitation and custody orders entered in accordance with mandated jurisdictional prerequisites and due process, neither act provides enforcement procedures or remedies.

As the *Obstacles Study* pointed out, the lack of specificity in enforcement procedures has resulted in the law of enforcement evolving differently in different jurisdictions. In one state, it might be common practice to file a Motion to Enforce or a Motion to Grant Full Faith and Credit to initiate an enforcement proceeding. In another state, a Writ of Habeas Corpus or a Citation for Contempt might be commonly used. In some states, Mandamus and Prohibition also may be utilized. All of these enforcement procedures differ from jurisdiction to jurisdiction. While many states tend to limit considerations in enforcement proceedings to whether the court which issued the decree had jurisdiction to make the custody determination, others broaden the considerations to scrutiny of whether enforcement would be in the best interests of the child.

Lack of uniformity complicates the enforcement process in several ways: (1) It increases the costs of the enforcement action in part because the services of more than one lawyer may be required—one in the original forum and one in the state where enforcement is sought; (2) It decreases the certainty of outcome; (3) It can turn enforcement into a long and drawn out procedure. A parent opposed to the provisions of a visitation determination may be able to delay implementation for many months, possibly even years, thereby frustrating not only the other parent, but also the process that led to the issuance of the original court order.

The provisions of Article 3 provide several remedies for the enforcement of a custody determination. First, there is a simple procedure for registering a custody determination in another state. This will allow a party to know in advance whether that state will recognize the party's custody determination. This is extremely important in estimating the risk of the child's non-return when the child is sent on visitation. The provision should prove to be very useful in international custody cases.

Second, the Act provides a swift remedy along the lines of habeas corpus. Time is extremely important in visitation and custody cases. If visitation rights cannot be enforced quickly, they often cannot be enforced at all. This is particularly true if there is a limited time within which visitation can be exercised such as may be the case when one parent has been granted visitation during the winter or spring holiday period. Without speedy consideration and resolution of the enforcement of such visitation rights, the ability to visit may be lost entirely. Similarly, a custodial parent must be able to obtain prompt enforcement when the noncustodial parent visitation extension will infringe on the school year. A swift enforcement mechanism is desirable for violations of both custody and visitation provisions.

The scope of the enforcing court's inquiry is limited to the issue of whether the decree court had jurisdiction and complied with due process in rendering the original custody decree. No further inquiry is necessary because neither Article 2 nor the PKPA allows an enforcing court to modify a custody determination.

Third, the enforcing court will be able to utilize an extraordinary remedy. If the enforcing court is concerned that the parent, who has physical custody of the child, will flee or harm the child, a warrant to take physical possession of the child is available.

Finally, there is a role for public authorities, such as prosecutors, in the enforcement process. Their involvement will encourage the parties to abide by the terms of the custody determination. If the parties know that public authorities and law enforcement officers are available to help in securing compliance with custody determinations, the parties may be deterred from interfering with the exercise of rights established by court order.

The involvement of public authorities will also prove more effective in remedying violations of custody determinations. Most parties do not have the resources to enforce a custody determination in another jurisdiction. The availability of the public authorities as an enforcement agency will help ensure that this remedy can be made available regardless of income level. In addition, the public authorities may have resources to draw on that are available to the average litigant.

This Act does not authorize the public authorities to be involved in the action leading up to the making of the custody determination, except when requested by the court, when there is a violation of the Hague Convention on the Civil Aspects of International Child Abduction, or when the person holding the child has violated a criminal statute. The Act does not mandate that public authorities be involved in all cases. Not all states, or local authorities, have the funds necessary for an effective custody and visitation enforcement program.

Subchapter A. Application and Construction

§ 152.001. Application and Construction.

This chapter shall be applied and construed to promote the uniformity of the law among the states that enact it.

§ 152.002. Conflicts Between Provisions.

If a provision of this chapter conflicts with a provision of this title or another statute or rule of this state and the conflict cannot be reconciled, this chapter prevails.

Comment

This section is not found in the uniform version of the UCCJEA, but was added by the legislature to make certain that the terms of this chapter prevail over any inconsistency that may exist elsewhere in the Family Code.

Subchapter B. General Provisions

§ 152.101. Short Title.

This chapter may be cited as the Uniform Child Custody Jurisdiction and Enforcement Act.

Commissioners' Comment

Section 1 of the UCCJA was a statement of the purposes of the Act. Although extensively cited by courts, it was eliminated because Uniform Acts no longer contain such a section. Nonetheless, this Act should be interpreted according to its purposes which are to:

(1) Avoid jurisdictional competition and conflict with courts of other states in matters of child custody which have in the past resulted in the shifting of children from state to state with harmful effects on their well-being;

(2) Promote cooperation with the courts of other states to the end that a custody decree is rendered in that state which can best decide the case in the interest of the child;

(3) Discourage the use of the interstate system for continuing controversies over child custody;

(4) Deter abductions of children;

(5) Avoid relitigation of custody decisions of other states in this state; and

(6) Facilitate the enforcement of custody decrees of other states;

---

§ 152.102. Definitions.

In this chapter:

(1) "Abandoned" means left without provision for reasonable and necessary care or supervision.

(2) "Child" means an individual who has not attained 18 years of age.

(3) "Child custody determination" means a judgment, decree, or other order of a court providing for legal custody, physical custody, or visitation with respect to a child. The term includes permanent, temporary, initial, and modification orders. The term does not include an order relating to child support or another monetary obligation of an individual.

(4) "Child custody proceeding" means a proceeding in which legal custody, physical custody, or visitation with respect to a child is an issue. The term includes a proceeding for divorce, separation, neglect, abuse, dependency, guardianship, paternity, termination of parental rights, and protection from domestic violence in which the issue may appear. The term does not include a proceeding involving juvenile delinquency, contractual emancipation, or enforcement under Subchapter D.

(5) "Commencement" means the filing of the first pleading in a proceeding.

(6) "Court" means an entity authorized under the law of a state to establish, enforce, or modify a child custody determination.

(7) "Home state" means the state in which a child lived with a parent or a person acting as a parent for at least six consecutive months immediately before the commencement of a child custody proceeding. In the case of a child less than six months of age, the term means the state in which the child lived from birth with a parent or a person acting as a parent. A period of temporary absence of a parent or a person acting as a parent is part of the period.

(8) "Initial determination" means the first child custody determination concerning a particular child.

(9) "Issuing court" means the court that makes a child custody determination for which enforcement is sought under this chapter.

(10) "Issuing state" means the state in which a child custody determination is made.

(11) "Legal custody" means the managing conservatorship of a child.

(12) "Modification" means a child custody determination that changes, replaces, supersedes, or is otherwise made after a previous determination concerning the same child, whether or not it is made by the court that made the previous determination.

(13) "Person acting as a parent" means a person, other than a parent, who:

(A) has physical custody of the child or has had physical custody for a period of six consecutive months, including any temporary absence, within one year immediately before the commencement of a child custody proceeding; and

(B) has been awarded legal custody by a court or claims a right to legal custody under the law of this state.

(14) "Physical custody" means the physical care and supervision of a child.

(15) "Tribe" means an Indian tribe or band, or Alaskan Native village, that is recognized by federal law or formally acknowledged by a state.

(16) "Visitation" means the possession of or access to a child.

(17) "Warrant" means an order issued by a court authorizing law enforcement officers to take physical custody of a child.

Commissioners' Comment

The UCCJA did not contain a definition of "child." The definition here is taken from the PKPA.

The definition of "child-custody determination" now closely tracks the PKPA definition. It encompasses any judgment, decree or other order which provides for the custody of, or visitation with, a child, regardless of local terminology, including such labels as "managing conservatorship" or "parenting plan."

The definition of "child-custody proceeding" has been expanded from the comparable definition in the UCCJA. These listed proceedings have generally been determined to be the type of proceeding to which the UCCJA and PKPA are applicable. The list of examples removes any controversy about the types of proceedings where a custody determination can occur. Proceedings that affect access to the child are subject to this Act. The inclusion of proceedings related to protection from domestic violence is necessary because in some states domestic violence proceedings may affect custody of and visitation with a child. Juvenile delinquency or proceedings to confer contractual rights are not "custody proceedings" because they do not relate to civil aspects of access to a child. While a determination of paternity is covered under the Uniform Interstate Family Support Act, the custody and visitation aspects of paternity cases are custody proceedings. Cases involving the Hague Convention on the Civil Aspects of International Child Abduction have not been included at this point because custody of the child is not determined in a proceeding under the International Child Abductions Remedies Act. Those proceedings are specially included in the Article 3 enforcement process.

"Commencement" has been included in the definitions as a replacement for the term "pending" found in the UCCJA. Its inclusion simplifies some of the simultaneous proceedings provisions of this Act.

The definition of "home state" has been reworded slightly. No substantive change is intended from the UCCJA.

The term "issuing state" is borrowed from UIFSA. In UIFSA, it refers to the court that issued the support or parentage order. Here, it refers to the state, or the court, which made the custody determination that is sought to be enforced. It is used primarily in Article 3.

The term "person" has been added to ensure that the provisions of this Act apply when the state is the moving party in a custody proceeding or has legal custody of a child. The definition of "person" is the one that is mandated for all Uniform Acts.

The term "person acting as a parent" has been slightly redefined. It has been broadened from the definition in the UCCJA to include a person who has acted as a parent for a significant period of time prior to the filing of the custody proceeding as well as a person who currently has physical custody of the child. In addition, a person acting as a parent must either have legal custody or claim a right to legal custody under the law of this state. The reference to the law of this state means that a court determines the issue of whether someone is a "person acting as a parent" under its own law. This reaffirms the traditional view that a court in a child custody case applies its own substantive law. The court does not have to undertake a choice-of-law analysis to determine whether the individual who is claiming to be a person acting as a parent has standing to seek custody of the child.

The definition of "tribe" is the one mandated for use in Uniform Acts. Should a state choose to apply this Act to tribal adjudications, this definition should be enacted as well as the entirety of Section 104.

The term "contestant" has been omitted from this revision. It was defined in the UCCJA § 2(1) as "a person, including a parent, who claims a right to custody or visitation rights with respect to a child." It seems to have served little purpose over the years, and whatever function it once had has been subsumed by state laws on who has standing to seek custody of or visitation with a child. In addition UCCJA § 2(5), which defined "decree" and "custody decree," has been eliminated as duplicative of the definition of "custody determination."

§ 152.103. Proceedings Governed by Other Law.

This chapter does not govern an adoption proceeding or a proceeding pertaining to the authorization of emergency medical care for a child.

Commissioners' Comment

Two proceedings are governed by other acts. Adoption cases are excluded from this Act because adoption is a specialized area which is thoroughly covered by the Uniform Adoption Act (UAA) (1994). Most states either will adopt that Act or will adopt the jurisdictional provisions of that Act. Therefore the jurisdictional provisions governing adoption proceeding are generally found elsewhere.

However, there are likely to be a number of instances where it will be necessary to apply this Act in an adoption proceeding. For example, if a state adopts the UAA, then Section 3 § 101 of the Act specifically refers in places to the Uniform Child Custody Jurisdiction Act which will become a reference to this Act. Second, the UAA requires that if an adoption is denied or set aside, the court is to determine the child's custody. UAA § 3—704. Those custody proceedings would be subject to this Act. *See* Joan Heifetz Hollinger, *The Uniform Adoption Act: Reporter's Ruminations*, 30 Fam. L. Q. 345 (1996).

Children that are the subject of interstate placements for adoption or foster care are governed by the Interstate Compact on the Placement of Children (ICPC). The UAA § 2—107 provides that the provisions of the compact, although not jurisdictional, supply the governing rules for all children who are subject to it. As stated in the Comments to that section: "Once a court exercises jurisdiction, the ICPC helps determine the legality of an interstate placement." For a discussion of the relationship between the UCCJA and the ICPC *see J.D.S. v. Franks*, 893 P.2d 732 (Ariz. 1995).

Proceedings pertaining to the authorization of emergency medical care for children are outside the scope of this Act since they are not custody determinations. All states have procedures which allow the state to temporarily supersede parental authority for purposes of emergency medical procedures. Those provisions will govern without regard to this Act.

---

§ 152.104. Application to Indian Tribes.

(a) A child custody proceeding that pertains to an Indian child as defined in the Indian Child Welfare Act of 1978 (25 U.S.C. Section 1901 et seq.) is not subject to this chapter to the extent that it is governed by the Indian Child Welfare Act.

(b) A court of this state shall treat a tribe as if it were a state of the United States for the purpose of applying this subchapter and Subchapter C.

(c) A child custody determination made by a tribe under factual circumstances in substantial conformity with the jurisdictional standards of this chapter must be recognized and enforced under Subchapter D.

Commissioners' Comment

This section allows states the discretion to extend the terms of this Act to Indian tribes by removing the brackets. The definition of "tribe" is found at Section 102(16). This Act does not purport to legislate custody jurisdiction for tribal courts. However, a Tribe could adopt this Act as enabling legislation by simply replacing references to "this State" with "this Tribe."

Subsection (a) is not bracketed. If the Indian Child Welfare Act requires that a case be heard in tribal court, then its provisions determine jurisdiction.

---

§ 152.105. International Application of Chapter.

(a) A court of this state shall treat a foreign country as if it were a state of the United States for the purpose of applying this subchapter and Subchapter C.

(b) Except as otherwise provided in Subsection (c), a child custody determination made in a foreign country under factual circumstances in substantial conformity with the jurisdictional standards of this chapter must be recognized and enforced under Subchapter D.

(c) A court of this state need not apply this chapter if the child custody law of a foreign country violates fundamental principles of human rights.

Commissioners' Comment

The provisions of this Act have international application to child custody proceedings and determinations of other countries. Another country will be treated as if it were a state of the United States for purposes of applying Articles 1 and 2 of this Act. Custody determinations of other countries will be enforced if the facts of the case indicate that jurisdiction was in substantial compliance with the requirements of this Act.

In this section, the term "child-custody determination" should be interpreted to include proceedings relating to custody or analogous institutions of the other country. *See* generally, Article 3 of The Hague Convention on Jurisdiction, Applicable Law, Recognition, Enforcement and Co-operation in Respect of Parental Responsibility and Measures for the Protection of Children, 35 I.L.M. 1391 (1996).

A court of this state may refuse to apply this Act when the child custody law of the other country violates basic principles relating to the protection of human rights and fundamental freedoms. The same concept is found in Section 20 of the Hague Convention on the Civil Aspects of International Child Abduction (return of the child may be refused if this would not be permitted by the fundamental principles of the requested state relating to the protection of human rights and fundamental freedoms). In applying Subsection (c), the court's scrutiny should be on the child custody law of the foreign country and not on other aspects of the other legal system. This Act takes no position on what laws relating to child custody would violate fundamental freedoms. While the provision is a traditional one in international agreements, it is invoked only in the most egregious cases.

This section is derived from Section 23 of the UCCJA.

---

§ 152.106. Effect of Child Custody Determination.

A child custody determination made by a court of this state that had jurisdiction under this chapter binds all persons who have been served in accordance with the laws of this state or notified in accordance with Section 152.108 or who have submitted to the jurisdiction of the court and who have been given an opportunity to be heard. As to those persons, the determination is conclusive as to all decided issues of law and fact except to the extent the determination is modified.

Commissioners' Comment

No substantive changes have been made to this section which was Section 12 of the UCCJA.

---

§ 152.107. Priority.

If a question of existence or exercise of jurisdiction under this chapter is raised in a child custody proceeding, the question, upon request of a party, must be given priority on the calendar and handled expeditiously.

Commissioners' Comment

No substantive change was made to this section which was Section 24 of the UCCJA. The section is placed toward the beginning of Article 1 to emphasize its importance.

The language change from "case" to "question" is intended to clarify that it is the jurisdictional issue which must be expedited and not the entire custody case. Whether the entire custody case should be given priority is a matter of local law.

§ 152.108. Notice to Persons Outside State.

(a) Notice required for the exercise of jurisdiction when a person is outside this state may be given in a manner prescribed by the law of this state for service of process or by the law of the state in which the service is made. Notice must be given in a manner reasonably calculated to give actual notice but may be by publication if other means are not effective.

(b) Proof of service may be made in the manner prescribed by the law of this state or by the law of the state in which the service is made.

(c) Notice is not required for the exercise of jurisdiction with respect to a person who submits to the jurisdiction of the court.

Commissioners' Comment

This section authorizes notice and proof of service to be made by any method allowed by either the state which issues the notice or the state where the notice is received. This eliminates the need to specify the type of notice in the Act and therefore the provisions of Section 5 of the UCCJA which specified how notice was to be accomplished were eliminated. The change reflects an approach in this Act to use local law to determine many procedural issues. Thus, service by facsimile is permissible if allowed by local rule in either state. In addition, where special service or notice rules are available for some procedures, in either jurisdiction, they could be utilized under this Act. For example, if a case involves domestic violence and the statute of either state would authorize notice to be served by a peace officer, such service could be used under this Act.

Although Section 105 requires foreign countries to be treated as states for purposes of this Act, attorneys should be cautioned about service and notice in foreign countries. Countries have their own rules on service which must usually be followed. Attorneys should consult the Hague Convention on the Service Abroad of Judicial and Extrajudicial Documents in Civil or Commercial Matters, 20 U.S.T. 36, T.I.A.S. 6638 (1965).

§ 152.109. Appearance and Limited Immunity.

(a) A party to a child custody proceeding, including a modification proceeding, or a petitioner or respondent in a proceeding to enforce or register a child custody determination, is not subject to personal jurisdiction in this state for another proceeding or purpose solely by reason of having participated, or of having been physically present for the purpose of participating, in the proceeding.

(b) A person who is subject to personal jurisdiction in this state on a basis other than physical presence is not immune from service of process in this state. A party present in this state who is subject to the jurisdiction of another state is not immune from service of process allowed under the laws of that state.

(c) The immunity granted by Subsection (a) does not extend to civil litigation based on acts unrelated to the participation in a proceeding under this chapter committed by an individual while present in this state.

Commissioners' Comment

This section establishes a general principle that participation in a custody proceeding does not, by itself, give the court jurisdiction over any issue for which personal jurisdiction over the individual is required. The term "participate" should be read broadly. For example, if jurisdiction is proper under Article 2, a respondent in an original custody determination, or a party in a modification determination, should be able to request custody without this constituting the seeking of affirmative relief that would waive personal jurisdictional objections. Once jurisdiction is proper under Article 2, a party should not be placed in the dilemma of choosing between seeking custody or protecting a right not to be subject to a monetary judgment by a court with no other relationship to the party.

This section is comparable to the immunity provision of UIFSA § 314. A party who is otherwise not subject to personal jurisdiction can appear in a custody proceeding or an enforcement action without being subject to the general jurisdiction of the state by virtue of the appearance. However, if the petitioner would otherwise be subject to the jurisdiction of the state, appearing in a custody proceeding or filing an enforcement proceeding will not provide immunity. Thus, if the non-custodial parent moves from the state that decided the custody determination, that parent is still subject to the state's jurisdiction for enforcement of child support if the child or an individual obligee continues to reside there. *See* UIFSA § 205. If the non-custodial parent returns to enforce the visitation aspects of the custody determination, the state can utilize any appropriate means to collect the back-due child support. However, the situation is different if both parties move from State A after the determination, with the custodial parent and the child establishing a new home state in State B, and the non-custodial parent moving to State C. The non-custodial parent is not, at this point, subject to the jurisdiction of State B for monetary matters. *See Kulko v. Superior Court*, 436 U.S. 84 (1978). If the non-custodial parent comes into State B to enforce the visitation aspects of the determination, the non-custodial parent is not subject to the jurisdiction of State B for those proceedings and issues requiring personal jurisdiction by filing the enforcement action.

A party also is immune from service of process during the time in the state for an enforcement action except for those claims for which jurisdiction could be based on contacts other than mere physical presence. Thus, when the non-custodial parent comes into State B to enforce the visitation aspects of the decree, State B cannot acquire jurisdiction over the child support aspects of the decree by serving the non-custodial parent in the state. *Cf.* UIFSA § 611 (personally serving the obligor in the state of the residence of the obligee is not by itself a sufficient jurisdictional basis to authorize a modification of child support). However, a party who is in this state and subject to the jurisdiction of another state may be served with process to appear in that state, if allowable under the laws of that state.

As the Comments to UIFSA § 314 note, the immunity provided by this section is limited. It does not provide immunity for civil litigation unrelated to the enforcement action. For example, a party to an enforcement action is not immune from service regarding a claim that involves an automobile accident occurring while the party is in the state.

---

§ 152.110. Communication Between Courts.

(a) In this section, "record" means information that is inscribed on a tangible medium or that is stored in an electronic or other medium and is retrievable in perceivable form.

(b) A court of this state may communicate with a court in another state concerning a proceeding arising under this chapter.

(c) The court may allow the parties to participate in the communication. If the parties are not able to participate in the communication, they must be given the opportunity to present facts and legal arguments before a decision on jurisdiction is made.

(d) If proceedings involving the same parties are pending simultaneously in a court of this state and a court of another state, the court of this state shall inform the other court of the simultaneous proceedings. The court of this state shall request that the other court hold the proceeding in that court in abeyance until the court in this state conducts a hearing to determine whether the court has jurisdiction over the proceeding.

(e) Communication between courts on schedules, calendars, court records, and similar matters may occur without informing the parties. A record need not be made of the communication.

(f) Except as otherwise provided in Subsection (e), a record must be made of any communication under this section. The parties must be informed promptly of the communication and granted access to the record.

Commissioners' Comment

This section emphasizes the role of judicial communications. It authorizes a court to communicate concerning any proceeding arising under this Act. This includes communication with foreign tribunals and tribal courts. Communication can occur in many different ways such as by telephonic conference and by on-line or other electronic communication. The Act does not preclude any method of communication and recognizes that there will be increasing use of modern communication techniques.

Communication between courts is required under Sections 204, 206, and 306 and strongly suggested in applying Section 207. Apart from those sections, there may be less need under this Act for courts to communicate concerning jurisdiction due to the prioritization of home state jurisdiction. Communication is authorized, however, whenever the court finds it would be helpful. The court may authorize the parties to participate in the communication. However, the Act does not mandate participation. Communication between courts is often difficult to schedule and participation by the parties may be impractical. Phone calls often have to be made after-hours or whenever the schedules of judges allow.

This section does require that a record be made of the conversation and that the parties have access to that record in order to be informed of the content of the conversation. The only exception to this requirement is when the communication involves relatively inconsequential matters such as scheduling, calendars, and court records. Included within this latter type of communication would be matters of cooperation between courts under Section 112. A record includes notes or transcripts of a court reporter who listened to a conference call between the courts, an electronic recording of a telephone call, a memorandum or an electronic record of the communication between the courts, or a memorandum or an electronic record made by a court after the communication.

The second sentence of Subsection (b) protects the parties against unauthorized ex parte communications. The parties' participation in the communication may amount to a hearing if there is an opportunity to present facts and jurisdictional arguments. However, absent such an opportunity, the participation of the parties should not be considered a substitute for a hearing and the parties must be given an opportunity to fairly and fully present facts and arguments on the jurisdictional issue before a determination is made.

This may be done through a hearing or, if appropriate, by affidavit or memorandum. The court is expected to set forth the basis for its jurisdictional decision, including any court-to-court communication which may have been a factor in the decision.

§ 152.111. Taking Testimony in Another State.

(a) In addition to other procedures available to a party, a party to a child custody proceeding may offer testimony of witnesses who are located in another state, including testimony of the parties and the child, by deposition or other means allowed in this state for testimony taken in another state. The court on its own motion may order that the testimony of a person be taken in another state and may prescribe the manner in which and the terms upon which the testimony is taken.

(b) A court of this state may permit an individual residing in another state to be deposed or to testify by telephone, audiovisual means, or other electronic means before a designated court or at another location in that state. A court of this state shall cooperate with courts of other states in designating an appropriate location for the deposition or testimony.

(c) Documentary evidence transmitted from another state to a court of this state by technological means that do not produce an original writing may not be excluded from evidence on an objection based on the means of transmission.

Commissioners' Comment

No substantive changes have been made to Subsection (a) which was Section 18 of the UCCJA.

Subsections (b) and (c) merely provide that modern modes of communication are permissible in the taking of testimony and the transmittal of documents. *See* UIFSA § 316.

§ 152.112. Cooperation Between Courts; Preservation of Records.

(a) A court of this state may request the appropriate court of another state to:

(1) hold an evidentiary hearing;

(2) order a person to produce or give evidence pursuant to procedures of that state;

(3) order that an evaluation be made with respect to the custody of a child involved in a pending proceeding;

(4) forward to the court of this state a certified copy of the transcript of the record of the hearing, the evidence otherwise presented, and any evaluation prepared in compliance with the request; and

(5) order a party to a child custody proceeding or any person having physical custody of the child to appear in the proceeding with or without the child.

(b) Upon request of a court of another state, a court of this state may hold a hearing or enter an order described in Subsection (a).

(c) Travel and other necessary and reasonable expenses incurred under Subsections (a) and (b) may be assessed against the parties according to the law of this state.

(d) A court of this state shall preserve the pleadings, orders, decrees, records of hearings, evaluations, and other pertinent records with respect to a child custody proceeding until the child attains 18 years of age. Upon appropriate request by a court or law enforcement official of another state, the court shall forward a certified copy of those records.

Commissioners' Comment

This section is the heart of judicial cooperation provision of this Act. It provides mechanisms for courts to cooperate with each other in order to decide cases in an efficient manner without causing undue expense to the parties. Courts may request assistance from courts of other states and may assist courts of other states.

The provision on the assessment of costs for travel provided in the UCCJA § 19 has been changed. The UCCJA provided that the costs may be assessed against the parties or the state or county. Assessment of costs against a government entity in a case where the government is not involved is inappropriate and therefore that provision has been removed. In addition, if the state is involved as a party, assessment of costs and expenses against the state must be authorized by other law. It should be noted that the term "expenses" means out-of-pocket costs. Overhead costs should not be assessed as expenses.

No other substantive changes have been made. The term "social study" as used in the UCCJA was replaced with the modern term: "custody evaluation." The Act does not take a position on the admissibility of a custody evaluation that was conducted in another state. It merely authorizes a court to seek assistance of, or render assistance to, a court of another state.

This section combines the text of Sections 19–22 of the UCCJA.

Subchapter C. Jurisdiction.

§ 152.201. Initial Child Custody Jurisdiction.

(a) Except as otherwise provided in Section 152.204, a court of this state has jurisdiction to make an initial child custody determination only if:

(1) this state is the home state of the child on the date of the commencement of the proceeding, or was the home state of the child within six months before the commencement of the proceeding and the child is absent from this state but a parent or person acting as a parent continues to live in this state;

(2) a court of another state does not have jurisdiction under Subdivision (1), or a court of the home state of the child has declined to exercise jurisdiction on the ground that this state is the more appropriate forum under Section 152.207 or 152.208, and:

(A) the child and the child's parents, or the child and at least one parent or a person acting as a parent, have a significant connection with this state other than mere physical presence; and

(B) substantial evidence is available in this state concerning the child's care, protection, training, and personal relationships;

(3) all courts having jurisdiction under Subdivision (1) or (2) have declined to exercise jurisdiction on the ground that a court of this state is the more appropriate forum to determine the custody of the child under Section 152.207 or 152.208; or

(4) no court of any other state would have jurisdiction under the criteria specified in Subdivision (1), (2), or (3).

(b) Subsection (a) is the exclusive jurisdictional basis for making a child custody determination by a court of this state.

(c) Physical presence of, or personal jurisdiction over, a party or a child is not necessary or sufficient to make a child custody determination.

Commissioners' Comment

This section provides mandatory jurisdictional rules for the original child custody proceeding. It generally continues the provisions of the UCCJA § 3. However, there have been a number of changes to the jurisdictional bases.

1. Home State Jurisdiction. The jurisdiction of the home state has been prioritized over other jurisdictional bases. Section 3 of the UCCJA provided four independent and concurrent bases of jurisdiction. The PKPA provides that full faith and credit can only be given to an initial custody determination of a "significant connection" State when there is no home state. This Act prioritizes home state jurisdiction in the same manner as the PKPA thereby eliminating any potential conflict between the two acts.

The six-month extended home state provision of Subsection (a)(1) has been modified slightly from the UCCJA. The UCCJA provided that home state jurisdiction continued for six months when the child had been removed by a person seeking the child's custody or for other reasons and a parent or a person acting as a parent continues to reside in the home state. Under this Act, it is no longer necessary to determine why the child has been removed. The only inquiry relates to the status of the person left behind. This change provides a slightly more refined home state standard than the UCCJA or the PKPA, which also requires a determination that the child has been removed "by a contestant or for other reasons." The scope of the PKPA's provision is theoretically narrower than this Act. However, the phrase "or for other reasons" covers most fact situations where the child is not in the home state and, therefore, the difference has no substantive effect.

In another sense, the six-month extended home state jurisdiction provision in this Act is narrower than the comparable provision in the PKPA. The PKPA's definition of extended home state is more expansive because it applies whenever a "contestant" remains in the home state. That class of individuals has been eliminated in this Act. This Act retains the original UCCJA classification of "parent or person acting as parent" to define who must remain for a state to exercise the six-month extended home state jurisdiction. This eliminates the undesirable jurisdictional determinations which would occur as a result of differing state substantive laws on visitation involving grandparents and others. For example, if State A's law provided that grandparents could obtain visitation with a child after the death of one of the parents, then the grandparents, who would be considered "contestants" under the PKPA, could file a proceeding within six months after the remaining parent moved and have the case heard in State A. However, if State A did not provide that grandparents could seek visitation under such circumstances, the grandparents would not be considered "contestants" and State B where the child acquired a new home state would provide the only forum. This Act bases jurisdiction on the parent and child or person acting as a parent and child relationship without regard to grandparents or other potential seekers of custody or visitation. There is no conflict with the broader provision of the PKPA. The PKPA in § (c)(1) authorizes states to narrow the scope of their jurisdiction.

2. Significant connection jurisdiction. This jurisdictional basis has been amended in four particulars from the UCCJA. First, the "best interest" language of the UCCJA has been eliminated. This phrase tended to create confusion between the jurisdictional issue and the substantive custody determination. Since the language was not necessary for the jurisdictional issue, it has been removed.

Second, the UCCJA based jurisdiction on the presence of a significant connection between the child and the child's parents or the child and at least one contestant. This Act requires that the significant connections be between the child, the child's parents or the child and a person acting as a parent.

Third, a significant connection state may assume jurisdiction only when there is no home state or when the home state decides that the significant connection state would be a more appropriate forum under Section 207 or 208. Fourth, the determination of significant connections has been changed to eliminate the language of "present or future care." The jurisdictional determination should be made by determining whether there is sufficient evidence in the state for the court to make an informed custody determination. That evidence might relate to the past as well as to the "present or future."

Emergency jurisdiction has been moved to a separate section. This is to make it clear that the power to protect a child in crisis does not include the power to enter a permanent order for that child except as provided by that section.

Paragraph (a)(3) provides for jurisdiction when all states with jurisdiction under paragraphs (a)(1) and (2) determine that this state is a more appropriate forum. The determination would have to be made by all states with jurisdiction under Subsection (a)(1) and (2). Jurisdiction would not exist under this paragraph because the home state determined it is a more appropriate place to hear the case if there is another state that could exercise significant connection jurisdiction under Subsection (a)(2).

Paragraph (a)(4) retains the concept of jurisdiction by necessity as found in the UCCJA and in the PKPA. This default jurisdiction only occurs if no other state would have jurisdiction under subsections (a)(1) through (a)(3).

Subsections (b) and (c) clearly state the relationship between jurisdiction under this Act and other forms of jurisdiction. Personal jurisdiction over, or the physical presence of, a parent or the child is neither necessary nor required under this Act. In other words neither minimum contacts nor service within the state is required for the court to have jurisdiction to make a custody determination. Further, the presence of minimum contacts or service within the state does not confer jurisdiction to make a custody determination. Subject to Section 204, satisfaction of the requirements of Subsection (a) is mandatory.

The requirements of this section, plus the notice and hearing provisions of the Act, are all that is necessary to satisfy due process. This Act, like the UCCJA and the PKPA is based on Justice Frankfurter's concurrence in *May v. Anderson*, 345 U.S. 528 (1953). As pointed out by Professor Bodenheimer, the reporter for the UCCJA, no "workable interstate custody law could be built around [Justice] Burton's plurality opinion. . . ." Bridgette Bodenheimer, *The Uniform Child Custody Jurisdiction Act: A Legislative Remedy for Children Caught in the Conflict of Laws*, 22 Vand. L. Rev. 1207, 1233 (1969). It should also be noted that since jurisdiction to make a child custody determination is subject matter jurisdiction, an agreement of the parties to confer jurisdiction on a court that would not otherwise have jurisdiction under this Act is ineffective.

Leading Case

In re McCoy, 52 S.W.3d 297 (Tex. App.—Corpus Christi 2001, no pet.) (under the UCCJEA, Texas must be the children's home state or the residence of one parent in order to have jurisdiction to make an initial child custody determination)

---

§ 152.202. Exclusive Continuing Jurisdiction.

(a) Except as otherwise provided in Section 152.204, a court of this state which has made a child custody determination consistent with Section 152.201 or 152.203 has exclusive continuing jurisdiction over the determination until:

(1) a court of this state determines that neither the child, nor the child and one parent, nor the child and a person acting as a parent, have a significant connection

with this state and that substantial evidence is no longer available in this state concerning the child's care, protection, training, and personal relationships; or

(2) a court of this state or a court of another state determines that the child, the child's parents, and any person acting as a parent do not presently reside in this state.

(b) A court of this state which has made a child custody determination and does not have exclusive, continuing jurisdiction under this section may modify that determination only if it has jurisdiction to make an initial determination under Section 152.201.

Commissioners' Comment

This is a new section addressing continuing jurisdiction. Continuing jurisdiction was not specifically addressed in the UCCJA. Its absence caused considerable confusion, particularly because the PKPA, § 1738(d), requires other states to give Full Faith and Credit to custody determinations made by the original decree state pursuant to the decree state's continuing jurisdiction so long as that state has jurisdiction under its own law and remains the residence of the child or any contestant.

This section provides the rules of continuing jurisdiction and borrows from UIFSA as well as recent UCCJA case law. The continuing jurisdiction of the original decree state is exclusive. It continues until one of two events occurs:

1. If a parent or a person acting as a parent remains in the original decree state, continuing jurisdiction is lost when neither the child, the child and a parent, nor the child and a person acting as a parent continue to have a significant connection with the original decree state and there is no longer substantial evidence concerning the child's care, protection, training and personal relations in that state. In other words, even if the child has acquired a new home state, the original decree state retains exclusive, continuing jurisdiction, so long as the general requisites of the "substantial connection" jurisdiction provisions of Section 201 are met. If the relationship between the child and the person remaining in the state with exclusive, continuing jurisdiction becomes so attenuated that the court could no longer find significant connections and substantial evidence, jurisdiction would no longer exist.

The use of the phrase "a court of this State" under Subsection (a)(1) makes it clear that the original decree state is the sole determinant of whether jurisdiction continues. A party seeking to modify a custody determination must obtain an order from the original decree state stating that it no longer has jurisdiction.

2. Continuing jurisdiction is lost when the child, the child's parents, and any person acting as a parent no longer reside in the original decree state. The exact language of subparagraph (a)(2) was the subject of considerable debate. Ultimately the Conference settled on the phrase that "a court of this State or a court of another State determines that the child, the child's parents, and any person acting as a parent do not presently reside in this State" to determine when the exclusive, continuing jurisdiction of a state ended. The phrase is meant to be identical in meaning to the language of the PKPA which provides that full faith and credit is to be given to custody determinations made by a state in the exercise of its continuing jurisdiction when that "State remains the residence of. . . . "The phrase is also the equivalent of the language "continues to reside" which occurs in UIFSA § 205(a)(1) to determine the exclusive, continuing jurisdiction of the state that made a support order. The phrase "remains the residence of" in the PKPA has been the subject of conflicting case law. It is the intention of this Act that paragraph (a)(2) of this section means that the named persons no longer continue to actually live within the state. Thus, unless a modification proceeding has been commenced, when the child, the parents, and

all persons acting as parents physically leave the state to live elsewhere, the exclusive, continuing jurisdiction ceases.

The phrase "do not presently reside" is not used in the sense of a technical domicile. The fact that the original determination state still considers one parent a domiciliary does not prevent it from losing exclusive, continuing jurisdiction after the child, the parents, and all persons acting as parents have moved from the state.

If the child, the parents, and all persons acting as parents have all left the state which made the custody determination prior to the commencement of the modification proceeding, considerations of waste of resources dictate that a court in State B, as well as a court in State A, can decide that State A has lost exclusive, continuing jurisdiction.

The continuing jurisdiction provisions of this section are narrower than the comparable provisions of the PKPA. That statute authorizes continuing jurisdiction so long as any "contestant" remains in the original decree state and that state continues to have jurisdiction under its own law. This Act eliminates the contestant classification. The Conference decided that a remaining grandparent or other third party who claims a right to visitation, should not suffice to confer exclusive, continuing jurisdiction on the state that made the original custody determination after the departure of the child, the parents and any person acting as a parent. The significant connection to the original decree state must relate to the child, the child and a parent, or the child and a person acting as a parent. This revision does not present a conflict with the PKPA. The PKPA's reference in § 1738(d) to § 1738(c)(1) recognizes that states may narrow the class of cases that would be subject to exclusive, continuing jurisdiction. However, during the transition from the UCCJA to this Act, some states may continue to base continuing jurisdiction on the continued presence of a contestant, such as a grandparent. The PKPA will require that such decisions be enforced. The problem will disappear as states adopt this Act to replace the UCCJA.

Jurisdiction attaches at the commencement of a proceeding. If State A had jurisdiction under this section at the time a modification proceeding was commenced there, it would not be lost by all parties moving out of the state prior to the conclusion of the proceeding. State B would not have jurisdiction to hear a modification unless State A decided that State B was more appropriate under Section 207.

Exclusive, continuing jurisdiction is not reestablished if, after the child, the parents, and all persons acting as parents leave the state, the non-custodial parent returns. As Subsection (b) provides, once a state has lost exclusive, continuing jurisdiction, it can modify its own determination only if it has jurisdiction under the standards of Section 201. If another state acquires exclusive continuing jurisdiction under this section, then its orders cannot be modified even if this state has once again become the home state of the child.

In accordance with the majority of UCCJA case law, the state with exclusive, continuing jurisdiction may relinquish jurisdiction when it determines that another state would be a more convenient forum under the principles of Section 207.

---

§ 152.203. Jurisdiction to Modify Determination.

Except as otherwise provided in Section 152.204, a court of this state may not modify a child custody determination made by a court of another state unless a court of this state has jurisdiction to make an initial determination under Section 152.201(a)(1) or (2) and:

(1) the court of the other state determines it no longer has exclusive continuing jurisdiction under Section 152.202 or that a court of this state would be a more convenient forum under Section 152.207; or

(2) a court of this state or a court of the other state determines that the child, the child's parents, and any person acting as a parent do not presently reside in the other state.

Commissioners' Comment

This section complements Section 202 and is addressed to the court that is confronted with a proceeding to modify a custody determination of another state. It prohibits a court from modifying a custody determination made consistently with this Act by a court in another state unless a court of that state determines that it no longer has exclusive, continuing jurisdiction under Section 202 or that this state would be a more convenient forum under Section 207. The modification state is not authorized to determine that the original decree state has lost its jurisdiction. The only exception is when the child, the child's parents, and any person acting as a parent do not presently reside in the other state. In other words, a court of the modification state can determine that all parties have moved away from the original state. The court of the modification state must have jurisdiction under the standards of Section 201.

---

§ 152.204. Temporary Emergency Jurisdiction.

(a) A court of this state has temporary emergency jurisdiction if the child is present in this state and the child has been abandoned or it is necessary in an emergency to protect the child because the child, or a sibling or parent of the child, is subjected to or threatened with mistreatment or abuse.

(b) If there is no previous child custody determination that is entitled to be enforced under this chapter and a child custody proceeding has not been commenced in a court of a state having jurisdiction under Sections 152.201 through 152.203, a child custody determination made under this section remains in effect until an order is obtained from a court of a state having jurisdiction under Sections 152.201 through 152.203. If a child custody proceeding has not been or is not commenced in a court of a state having jurisdiction under Sections 152.201 through 152.203, a child custody determination made under this section becomes a final determination, if it so provides and this state becomes the home state of the child.

(c) If there is a previous child custody determination that is entitled to be enforced under this chapter, or a child custody proceeding has been commenced in a court of a state having jurisdiction under Sections 152.201 through 152.203, any order issued by a court of this state under this section must specify in the order a period that the court considers adequate to allow the person seeking an order to obtain an order from the state having jurisdiction under Sections 152.201 through 152.203. The order issued in this state remains in effect until an order is obtained from the other state within the period specified or the period expires.

(d) A court of this state which has been asked to make a child custody determination under this section, upon being informed that a child custody proceeding has been commenced in or a child custody determination has been made by a court of a state having jurisdiction under Sections 152.201 through 152.203, shall immediately communicate with the other court. A court of this state which is exercising jurisdiction pursuant to Sections 152.201 through 152.203, upon being informed that a child custody proceeding has been commenced in or a child custody determination has been made by a court of another state under a statute similar to this section shall immediately communicate with the court of that state to resolve the emergency, protect the safety of the parties and the child, and determine a period for the duration of the temporary order.

Commissioners' Comment

The provisions of this section are an elaboration of what was formerly Section 3(a)(3) of the UCCJA. It remains, as Professor Bodenheimer's comments to that section noted, "an extraordinary jurisdiction reserved for extraordinary circumstances."

This section codifies and clarifies several aspects of what has become common practice in emergency jurisdiction cases under the UCCJA and PKPA. First, a court may take jurisdiction to protect the child even though it can claim neither home state nor significant connection jurisdiction. Second, the duties of states to recognize, enforce and not modify a custody determination of another state do not take precedence over the need to enter a temporary emergency order to protect the child. Third, a custody determination made under the emergency jurisdiction provisions of this section is a temporary order. The purpose of the order is to protect the child until the state that has jurisdiction under Sections 201–203 enters an order.

Under certain circumstances, however, Subsection (b) provides that an emergency custody determination may become a final custody determination. If there is no existing custody determination, and no custody proceeding is filed in a state with jurisdiction under Sections 201–203, an emergency custody determination made under this section becomes a final determination, if it so provides, when the state that issues the order becomes the home state of the child.

Subsection (c) is concerned with the temporary nature of the order when there exists a prior custody order that is entitled to be enforced under this Act or when a subsequent custody proceeding is filed in a state with jurisdiction under Sections 201–203. Subsection (c) allows the temporary order to remain in effect only so long as is necessary for the person who obtained the determination under this section to present a case and obtain an order from the state with jurisdiction under Sections 201–203. That time period must be specified in the order. If there is an existing order by a state with jurisdiction under Sections 201–203, that order need not be reconfirmed. The temporary emergency determination would lapse by its own terms at the end of the specified period or when an order is obtained from the court with jurisdiction under Sections 202–203. The court with appropriate jurisdiction also may decide, under the provisions of 207, that the court that entered the emergency order is in a better position to address the safety of the person who obtained the emergency order, or the child, and decline jurisdiction under Section 207.

Any hearing in the state with jurisdiction under Sections 201–203 on the temporary emergency determination is subject to the provisions of Sections 111 and 112. These sections facilitate the presentation of testimony and evidence taken out of state. If there is a concern that the person obtaining the temporary emergency determination under this section would be in danger upon returning to the state with jurisdiction under Sections 201–203, these provisions should be used.

Subsection (d) requires communication between the court of the state that is exercising jurisdiction under this section and the court of another state that is exercising jurisdiction under Sections 201–203. The pleading rules of Section 209 apply fully to determinations made under this section. Therefore, a person seeking a temporary emergency custody determination is required to inform the court pursuant to Section 209(d) of any proceeding concerning the child that has been commenced elsewhere. The person commencing the custody proceeding under Sections 201–203 is required under Section 209(a) to inform the court about the temporary emergency proceeding. These pleading requirements are to be strictly followed so that the courts are able to resolve the emergency, protect the safety of the parties and the child, and determine a period for the duration of the temporary order.

Relationship to the PKPA. The definition of emergency has been modified to harmonize it with the PKPA. The PKPA's definition of emergency jurisdiction does not use the term "neglect." It defines an emergency as "mistreatment or abuse." Therefore "neglect" has been eliminated as a basis for the assumption of temporary emergency jurisdiction. Neglect is so elastic a concept that it could justify taking emergency jurisdiction in a wide variety of cases. Under the PKPA, if a state exercised temporary emergency jurisdiction based on a finding that the child was neglected without a finding of mistreatment or abuse, the order would not be entitled to federal enforcement in other states.

Relationship to Protective Order Proceedings. The UCCJA and the PKPA were enacted long before the advent of state procedures on the use of protective orders to alleviate problems of domestic violence. Issues of custody and visitation often arise within the context of protective order proceedings since the protective order is often invoked to keep one parent away from the other parent and the children when there is a threat of violence. This Act recognizes that a protective order proceeding will often be the procedural vehicle for invoking jurisdiction by authorizing a court to assume temporary emergency jurisdiction when the child's parent or sibling has been subjected to or threatened with mistreatment or abuse.

In order for a protective order that contains a custody determination to be enforceable in another state it must comply with the provisions of this Act and the PKPA. Although the Violence Against Women's Act (VAWA), 18 U.S.C. § 2265, does provide an independent basis for the granting of full faith and credit to protective orders, it expressly excludes "custody" orders from the definition of "protective order," 22 U.S.C. § 2266.

Many states authorize the issuance of protective orders in an emergency without notice and hearing. This Act does not address the propriety of that procedure. It is left to local law to determine the circumstances under which such an order could be issued, and the type of notice that is required, in a case without an interstate element. However, an order issued after the assumption of temporary emergency jurisdiction is entitled to interstate enforcement and nonmodification under this Act and the PKPA only if there has been notice and a reasonable opportunity to be heard as set out in Section 205. Although VAWA does require that full faith and credit be accorded to ex parte protective orders if notice will be given and there will be a reasonable opportunity to be heard, it does not include a "custody" order within the definition of "protective order."

VAWA does play an important role in determining whether an emergency exists. That Act requires a court to give full faith and credit to a protective order issued in another state if the order is made in accordance with the VAWA. This would include those findings of fact contained in the order. When a court is deciding whether an emergency exists under this section, it may not relitigate the existence of those factual findings.

---

§ 152.205. Notice; Opportunity to be Heard; Joinder.

(a) Before a child custody determination is made under this chapter, notice and an opportunity to be heard in accordance with the standards of Section 152.108 must be given to all persons entitled to notice under the law of this state as in child custody proceedings between residents of this state, any parent whose parental rights have not been previously terminated, and any person having physical custody of the child.

(b) This chapter does not govern the enforceability of a child custody determination made without notice or an opportunity to be heard.

(c) The obligation to join a party and the right to intervene as a party in a child custody proceeding under this chapter are governed by the law of this state as in child custody proceedings between residents of this state.

Commissioners' Comment

This section generally continues the notice provisions of the UCCJA. However, it does not attempt to dictate who is entitled to notice. Local rules vary with regard to persons entitled to seek custody of a child. Therefore, this section simply indicates that persons entitled to seek custody should receive notice but leaves the rest of the determination to local law. Parents whose parental rights have not been previously terminated and persons having physical custody of the child are specifically mentioned as persons who must be given notice. The PKPA, § 1738A(e), requires that they be given notice in order for the custody determination to be entitled to full faith and credit under that Act.

State laws also vary with regard to whether a court has the power to issue an enforceable temporary custody order without notice and hearing in a case without any interstate element. Such temporary orders may be enforceable, as against due process objections, for a short period of time if issued as a protective order or a temporary restraining order to protect a child from harm. Whether such orders are enforceable locally is beyond the scope of this Act. Subsection (b) clearly provides that the validity of such orders and the enforceability of such orders is governed by the law which authorizes them and not by this Act. An order is entitled to interstate enforcement and nonmodification under this Act only if there has been notice and an opportunity to be heard. The PKPA, § 1738A(e), also requires that a custody determination is entitled to full faith and credit only if there has been notice and an opportunity to be heard.

Rules requiring joinder of people with an interest in the custody of and visitation with a child also vary widely throughout the country. The UCCJA has a separate section on joinder of parties which has been eliminated. The issue of who is entitled to intervene and who must be joined in a custody proceeding is to be determined by local state law.

A sentence of the UCCJA § 4 which indicated that persons outside the state were to be given notice and an opportunity to be heard in accordance with the provision of that Act has been eliminated as redundant.

§ 152.206. Simultaneous Proceedings.

(a) Except as otherwise provided in Section 152.204, a court of this state may not exercise its jurisdiction under this subchapter if, at the time of the commencement of the proceeding, a proceeding concerning the custody of the child has been commenced in a court of another state having jurisdiction substantially in conformity with this chapter, unless the proceeding has been terminated or is stayed by the court of the other state because a court of this state is a more convenient forum under Section 152.207.

(b) Except as otherwise provided in Section 152.204, a court of this state, before hearing a child custody proceeding, shall examine the court documents and other information supplied by the parties pursuant to Section 152.209. If the court determines that a child custody proceeding has been commenced in a court in another state having jurisdiction substantially in accordance with this chapter, the court of this state shall stay its proceeding and communicate with the court of the other state. If the court of the state having jurisdiction substantially in accordance with this chapter does not determine that the court of this state is a more appropriate forum, the court of this state shall dismiss the proceeding.

(c) In a proceeding to modify a child custody determination, a court of this state shall determine whether a proceeding to enforce the determination has been commenced in another state. If a proceeding to enforce a child custody determination has been commenced in another state, the court may:

(1) stay the proceeding for modification pending the entry of an order of a court of the other state enforcing, staying, denying, or dismissing the proceeding for enforcement;

(2) enjoin the parties from continuing with the proceeding for enforcement; or

(3) proceed with the modification under conditions it considers appropriate.

Commissioners' Comment

This section represents the remnants of the simultaneous proceedings provision of the UCCJA § 6. The problem of simultaneous proceedings is no longer a significant issue. Most of the problems have been resolved by the prioritization of home state jurisdiction under Section 201; the exclusive, continuing jurisdiction provisions of Section 202; and the prohibitions on modification of Section 203. If there is a home state, there can be no exercise of significant connection jurisdiction in an initial child custody determination and, therefore, no simultaneous proceedings. If there is a state of exclusive, continuing jurisdiction, there cannot be another state with concurrent jurisdiction and, therefore, no simultaneous proceedings. Of course, the home state, as well as the state with exclusive, continuing jurisdiction, could defer to another state under Section 207. However, that decision is left entirely to the home state or the state with exclusive, continuing jurisdiction.

Under this Act, the simultaneous proceedings problem will arise only when there is no home state, no state with exclusive, continuing jurisdiction and more than one significant connection state. For those cases, this section retains the "first in time" rule of the UCCJA. Subsection (b) retains the UCCJA's policy favoring judicial communication. Communication between courts is required when it is determined that a proceeding has been commenced in another state.

Subsection (c) concerns the problem of simultaneous proceedings in the state with modification jurisdiction and enforcement proceedings under Article 3. This section authorizes the court with exclusive, continuing jurisdiction to stay the modification proceeding pending the outcome of the enforcement proceeding, to enjoin the parties from continuing with the enforcement proceeding, or to continue the modification proceeding under such conditions as it determines are appropriate. The court may wish to communicate with the enforcement court. However, communication is not mandatory. Although the enforcement state is required by the PKPA to enforce according to its terms a custody determination made consistently with the PKPA, that duty is subject to the decree being modified by a state with the power to do so under the PKPA. An order to enjoin the parties from enforcing the decree is the equivalent of a temporary modification by a state with the authority to do so. The concomitant provision addressed to the enforcement court is Section 306 of this Act. That section requires the enforcement court to communicate with the modification court in order to determine what action the modification court wishes the enforcement court to take.

The term "pending" that was utilized in the UCCJA section on simultaneous proceeding has been replaced. It has caused considerable confusion in the case law. It has been replaced with the term "commencement of the proceeding" as more accurately reflecting the policy behind this section. The latter term is defined in Section 102(5).

---

§ 152.207. Inconvenient Forum.

(a) A court of this state which has jurisdiction under this chapter to make a child custody determination may decline to exercise its jurisdiction at any time if it determines that it is an inconvenient forum under the circumstances and that a court of another state is a more appropriate forum. The issue of inconvenient forum may be raised upon motion of a party, the court's own motion, or request of another court.

(b) Before determining whether it is an inconvenient forum, a court of this state shall consider whether it is appropriate for a court of another state to exercise jurisdiction. For this purpose, the court shall allow the parties to submit information and shall consider all relevant factors, including:

(1) whether domestic violence has occurred and is likely to continue in the future and which state could best protect the parties and the child;

(2) the length of time the child has resided outside this state;

(3) the distance between the court in this state and the court in the state that would assume jurisdiction;

(4) the relative financial circumstances of the parties;

(5) any agreement of the parties as to which state should assume jurisdiction;

(6) the nature and location of the evidence required to resolve the pending litigation, including testimony of the child;

(7) the ability of the court of each state to decide the issue expeditiously and the procedures necessary to present the evidence; and

(8) the familiarity of the court of each state with the facts and issues in the pending litigation.

(c) If a court of this state determines that it is an inconvenient forum and that a court of another state is a more appropriate forum, the court shall stay the proceedings upon condition that a child custody proceeding be promptly commenced in another designated state and may impose any other condition the court considers just and proper.

(d) A court of this state may decline to exercise its jurisdiction under this chapter if a child custody determination is incidental to an action for divorce or another proceeding while still retaining jurisdiction over the divorce or other proceeding.

Commissioners' Comment

This section retains the focus of Section 7 of the UCCJA. It authorizes courts to decide that another state is in a better position to make the custody determination, taking into consideration the relative circumstances of the parties. If so, the court may defer to the other state.

The list of factors that the court may consider has been updated from the UCCJA. The list is not meant to be exclusive. Several provisions require comment. Subparagraph (1) is concerned specifically with domestic violence and other matters affecting the health and safety of the parties. For this purpose, the court should determine whether the parties are located in different states because one party is a victim of domestic violence or child abuse. If domestic violence or child abuse has occurred, this factor authorizes the court to consider which state can best protect the victim from further violence or abuse.

In applying subparagraph (3), courts should realize that distance concerns can be alleviated by applying the communication and cooperation provisions of Sections 111 and 112.

In applying Subsection (7) on expeditious resolution of the controversy, the court could consider the different procedural and evidentiary laws of the two states, as well as the flexibility of the court dockets. It also should consider the ability of a court to arrive at a solution to all the legal issues surrounding the family. If one state has jurisdiction to decide both the custody and support issues, it would be desirable to determine that state to be the most convenient forum. The same is true when children of the same family live in different states. It would be inappropriate to require parents to have custody proceedings in several states when one state could resolve the custody of all the children.

Before determining whether to decline or retain jurisdiction, the court of this state may communicate, in accordance with Section 110, with a court of another state and exchange information pertinent to the assumption of jurisdiction by either court.

There are two departures from Section 7 of the UCCJA. First, the court may not simply dismiss the action. To do so would leave the case in limbo. Rather the court shall stay the case and direct the parties to file in the state that has been found to be the more convenient forum. The court is also authorized to impose any other conditions it considers appropriate. This might include the issuance of temporary custody orders during the time necessary to commence a proceeding in the designated state, dismissing the case if the custody proceeding is not commenced in the other state or resuming jurisdiction if a court of the other state refuses to take the case.

Second, UCCJA, § 7(g) which allowed the court to assess fees and costs if it was a clearly inappropriate court, has been eliminated. If a court has jurisdiction under this Act, it could not be a clearly inappropriate court.

---

§ 152.208. Jurisdiction Declined by Reason of Conduct.

(a) Except as otherwise provided in Section 152.204 or other law of this state, if a court of this state has jurisdiction under this chapter because a person seeking to invoke its jurisdiction has engaged in unjustifiable conduct, the court shall decline to exercise its jurisdiction unless:

(1) the parents and all persons acting as parents have acquiesced in the exercise of jurisdiction;

(2) a court of the state otherwise having jurisdiction under Sections 152.201 through 152.203 determines that this state is a more appropriate forum under Section 152.207; or

(3) no court of any other state would have jurisdiction under the criteria specified in Sections 152.201 through 152.203.

(b) If a court of this state declines to exercise its jurisdiction pursuant to Subsection (a), it may fashion an appropriate remedy to ensure the safety of the child and prevent a repetition of the unjustifiable conduct, including staying the proceeding until a child custody proceeding is commenced in a court having jurisdiction under Sections 152.201 through 152.203.

(c) If a court dismisses a petition or stays a proceeding because it declines to exercise its jurisdiction pursuant to Subsection (a), it shall assess against the party seeking to invoke its jurisdiction necessary and reasonable expenses including costs, communication expenses, attorney's fees, investigative fees, expenses for witnesses, travel expenses, and child care during the course of the proceedings, unless the party from whom fees are sought establishes that the assessment would be clearly inappropriate. The court may not assess fees, costs, or expenses against this state unless authorized by law other than this chapter.

Commissioners' Comment

The "Clean Hands" section of the UCCJA has been truncated in this Act. Since there is no longer a multiplicity of jurisdictions which could take cognizance of a child-custody proceeding, there is less of a concern that one parent will take the child to another jurisdiction in an attempt to find a more favorable forum. Most of the jurisdictional problems generated by abducting parents should be solved by the prioritization of home state in Section 201; the exclusive, continuing jurisdiction provisions of Section 202; and the ban on modification in Section 203. For example, if a parent takes the child from the home state and seeks an original custody determination elsewhere, the stay-at-home parent has six months to file a custody petition under the extended home state jurisdictional provision of Section 201, which will ensure that the case is retained in the home state. If a petitioner for a modification determination takes the child from the state that issued the original custody determination, another state cannot assume jurisdiction as long at the first state exercises exclusive, continuing jurisdiction.

Nonetheless, there are still a number of cases where parents, or their surrogates, act in a reprehensible manner, such as removing, secreting, retaining, or restraining the child. This section ensures that abducting parents will not receive an advantage for their unjustifiable conduct. If the conduct that creates the jurisdiction is unjustified, courts must decline to exercise jurisdiction that is inappropriately invoked by one of the parties. For example, if one parent abducts the child pre-decree and establishes a new home state, that jurisdiction will decline to hear the case. There are exceptions. If the other party has acquiesced in the court's jurisdiction, the court may hear the case. Such acquiescence may occur by filing a pleading submitting to the jurisdiction, or by not filing in the court that would otherwise have jurisdiction under this Act. Similarly, if the court that would have jurisdiction finds that the court of this state is a more appropriate forum, the court may hear the case.

This section applies to those situations where jurisdiction exists because of the unjustified conduct of the person seeking to invoke it. If, for example, a parent in the state with exclusive, continuing jurisdiction under Section 202 has either restrained the child from visiting with the other parent, or has retained the child after visitation, and seeks to modify the decree, this section in inapplicable. The conduct of restraining or retaining the child did not create jurisdiction. Jurisdiction existed under this Act without regard to the parent's conduct. Whether a court should decline to hear the parent's request to modify is a matter of local law.

The focus in this section is on the unjustified conduct of the person who invokes the jurisdiction of the court. A technical illegality or wrong is insufficient to trigger the applicability of this section. This is particularly important in cases involving domestic violence and child abuse. Domestic violence victims should not be charged with unjustifiable conduct for conduct that occurred in the process of fleeing domestic violence, even if their conduct is technically illegal. Thus, if a parent flees with a child to escape domestic violence and in the process violates a joint custody decree, the case should not be automatically dismissed under this section. An inquiry must be made into whether the flight was justified under the circumstances of the case. However, an abusive parent who seizes the child and flees to another state to establish jurisdiction has engaged in unjustifiable conduct and the new state must decline to exercise jurisdiction under this section.

Subsection (b) authorizes the court to fashion an appropriate remedy for the safety of the child and to prevent a repetition of the unjustified conduct. Thus, it would be appropriate for the court to notify the other parent and to provide for foster care for the child until the child is returned to the other parent. The court could also stay the

...ng and require that a custody proceeding be instituted in another state that would ...sdiction under this Act. It should be noted that the court is not making a forum ...veniens analysis in this section. If the conduct is unjustifiable, it must decline jurisdiction. It may, however, retain jurisdiction until a custody proceeding is commenced in the appropriate tribunal if such retention is necessary to prevent a repetition of the wrongful conduct or to ensure the safety of the child.

The attorney's fee standard for this section is patterned after the International Child Abduction Remedies Act, 42 U.S.C. § 11607(b)(3). The assessed costs and fees are to be paid to the respondent who established that jurisdiction was based on unjustifiable conduct.

---

§ 152.209. Information to be Submitted to Court.

(a) Except as provided by Subsection (e) **or unless each party resides in this state**, in a child custody proceeding, each party, in its first pleading or in an attached affidavit, shall give information, if reasonably ascertainable, under oath as to the child's present address or whereabouts, the places where the child has lived during the last five years, and the names and present addresses of the persons with whom the child has lived during that period. The pleading or affidavit must state whether the party:

(1) has participated, as a party or witness or in any other capacity, in any other proceeding concerning the custody of or visitation with the child and, if so, identify the court, the case number, and the date of the child custody determination, if any;

(2) knows of any proceeding that could affect the current proceeding, including proceedings for enforcement and proceedings relating to domestic violence, protective orders, termination of parental rights, and adoptions and, if so, identify the court, the case number, and the nature of the proceeding; and

(3) knows the names and addresses of any person not a party to the proceeding who has physical custody of the child or claims rights of legal custody or physical custody of, or visitation with, the child and, if so, the names and addresses of those persons.

(b) If the information required by Subsection (a) is not furnished, the court, upon motion of a party or its own motion, may stay the proceeding until the information is furnished.

(c) If the declaration as to any of the items described in Subsections (a)(1) through (3) is in the affirmative, the declarant shall give additional information under oath as required by the court. The court may examine the parties under oath as to details of the information furnished and other matters pertinent to the court's jurisdiction and the disposition of the case.

(d) Each party has a continuing duty to inform the court of any proceeding in this or any other state that could affect the current proceeding.

(e) If a party alleges in an affidavit or a pleading under oath that the health, safety, or liberty of a party or child would be jeopardized by disclosure of identifying information, the information must be sealed and may not be disclosed to the other party or the public unless the court orders the disclosure to be made after a hearing in which the court takes into consideration the health, safety, or liberty of the party or child and determines that the disclosure is in the interest of justice.

History: Amended by 78th Legis., Reg. Sess. (2003), H.B. 913, eff. Sept. 1, 2003. The changes in law made by this Act to Sections 152.209(a) and 155.301(a), Family Code, apply only to a child custody proceeding under Chapter 152, Family Code, filed on or after the effective date of this Act. A child custody proceeding under Chapter 152, Family Code, filed before the effective date of this Act is governed by the law in effect on the date that the proceeding was filed, and the former law is continued in effect for that purpose.

Editor's Comment

The wealth of detailed information required by Subsection (a) is imminently reasonable if the parties are separated and lost track of one another. It may even be reasonable when the parties live in different states even if they haven't lost track of each other or of the child. On the other hand, if the parties have been living together throughout the period under focus (the last five years), detailing all this information well-known to the respondent or to the petitioner, whether in a pleading or by attached affidavit, is an exercise in make work. It may make the pleadings longer, but it doesn't provide any information that is not already known. The 2003 amendment to subsection (a) sweeps with a broad brush—obviously too broad if the parties have been living together in Texas, all well and good. But if they are separated and one is living in Texarkana and the other is in El Paso, the separation is 806 miles long.

Commissioners' Comment

The pleading requirements from Section 9 of the UCCJA are generally carried over into this Act. However, the information is made subject to local law on the protection of names and other identifying information in certain cases. A number of states have enacted laws relating to the protection of victims in domestic violence and child abuse cases which provide for the confidentiality of victims names, addresses, and other information. These procedures must be followed if the child-custody proceeding of the state requires their applicability. See, *e.g.*, California Family Law Code § 3409(a). If a state does not have local law that provides for protecting names and addresses, then Subsection (e) or a similar provision should be adopted. Subsection (e) is based on the National Council of Juvenile and Family Court Judge's, Model Code on Domestic and Family Violence § 304(c). There are other models to choose from, in particular UIFSA § 312.

In Subsection (a)(2), the term "proceedings" should be read broadly to include more than custody proceedings. Thus, if one parent was being criminally prosecuted for child abuse or custodial interference, those proceedings should be disclosed. If the child is subject to the Interstate Compact on the Placement of Children, facts relating to compliance with the Compact should be disclosed in the pleading or affidavit.

Subsection (b) has been added. It authorizes the court to stay the proceeding until the information required in Subsection (a) has been disclosed, although failure to provide the information does not deprive the court of jurisdiction to hear the case. This follows the majority of jurisdictions which held that failure to comply with the pleading requirements of the UCCJA did not deprive the court of jurisdiction to make a custody determination.

---

§ 152.210. Appearance of Parties and Child.

(a) In a child custody proceeding in this state, the court may order a party to the proceeding who is in this state to appear before the court in person with or without the child. The court may order any person who is in this state and who has physical custody or control of the child to appear in person with the child.

(b) If a party to a child custody proceeding whose presence is desired by the court is outside this state, the court may order that a notice given pursuant to Section 152.108 include a statement directing the party to appear in person with or without the child and informing the party that failure to appear may result in a decision adverse to the party.

(c) The court may enter any orders necessary to ensure the safety of the child and of any person ordered to appear under this section.

(d) If a party to a child custody proceeding who is outside this state is directed to appear under Subsection (b) or desires to appear personally before the court with or without the child, the court may require another party to pay reasonable and necessary travel and other expenses of the party so appearing and of the child.

Commissioners' Comment

No major changes have been made to this section which was Section 11 of the UCCJA. Language was added to Subsection (a) to authorize the court to require a non-party who has physical custody of the child to produce the child.

Subsection (c) authorizes the court to enter orders providing for the safety of the child and the person ordered to appear with the child. If safety is a major concern, the court, as an alternative to ordering a party to appear with the child, could order and arrange for the party's testimony to be taken in another state under Section 111. This alternative might be important when there are safety concerns regarding requiring victims of domestic violence or child abuse to travel to the jurisdiction where the abuser resides.

Subchapter D. Enforcement.

§ 152.301. Definitions.

In this subchapter:

(1) "Petitioner" means a person who seeks enforcement of an order for return of a child under the Hague Convention on the Civil Aspects of International Child Abduction or enforcement of a child custody determination.

(2) "Respondent" means a person against whom a proceeding has been commenced for enforcement of an order for return of a child under the Hague Convention on the Civil Aspects of International Child Abduction or enforcement of a child custody determination.

Commissioners' Comment

For purposes of this article, "petitioner" and "respondent" are defined. The definitions clarify certain aspects of the notice and hearing sections.

---

§ 152.302. Enforcement Under Hague Convention.

Under this subchapter a court of this state may enforce an order for the return of the child made under the Hague Convention on the Civil Aspects of International Child Abduction as if it were a child custody determination.

Commissioners' Comment

This section applies the enforcement remedies provided by this article to orders requiring the return of a child issued under the authority of the International Child Abduction Remedies Act (ICARA), 42 U.S.C. § 11601 *et seq.*, implementing the Hague Convention on the Civil Aspects of International Child Abduction. Specific mention of ICARA proceedings is necessary because they often occur prior to any formal custody determination. However, the need for a speedy enforcement remedy for an order to return the child is just as necessary.

---

§ 152.303. Duty to Enforce.

(a) A court of this state shall recognize and enforce a child custody determination of a court of another state if the latter court exercised jurisdiction in substantial conformity with this chapter or the determination was made under factual circumstances meeting the jurisdictional standards of this chapter and the determination has not been modified in accordance with this chapter.

(b) A court of this state may utilize any remedy available under other law of this state to enforce a child custody determination made by a court of another state. The remedies provided in this subchapter are cumulative and do not affect the availability of other remedies to enforce a child custody determination.

Commissioners' Comment

This section is based on Section 13 of the UCCJA which contained the basic duty to enforce. The language of the original section has been retained and the duty to enforce is generally the same.

Enforcement of custody determinations of issuing states is also required by federal law in the PKPA, 28 U.S.C. § 1738A(a). The changes made in Article 2 of this Act now make a state's duty to enforce and not modify a child custody determination of another state consistent with the enforcement and nonmodification provisions of the PKPA. Therefore custody determinations made by a state pursuant to the UCCJA that would be enforceable under the PKPA will generally be enforced under this Act. However, if a state custody determination made pursuant to the UCCJA would not be enforceable under the PKPA, it will also not be enforceable under this Act. Thus a custody determination made by a "significant connection" jurisdiction when there is a home state is not enforceable under the PKPA regardless of whether a proceeding was ever commenced in the home state. Even though such a determination would be enforceable under the UCCJA with its four concurrent bases of jurisdiction, it would not be enforceable under this Act. This carries out the policy of the PKPA of strongly discouraging a state from exercising its concurrent "significant connection" jurisdiction under the UCCJA when another state could exercise "home state" jurisdiction.

This section also incorporates the concept of Section 15 of the UCCJA to the effect that a custody determination of another state will be enforced in the same manner as a custody determination made by a court of this state. Whatever remedies are available to enforce a local determination can be utilized to enforce a custody determination of another state. However, it remains a custody determination of the state that issued it. A child-custody determination of another state is not subject to modification unless the state would have jurisdiction to modify the determination under Article 2.

The remedies provided by this article for the enforcement of a custody determination will normally be used. This article does not detract from other remedies available under other local law. There is often a need for a number of remedies to ensure that a child-custody determination is obeyed. If other remedies would easily facilitate enforcement, they are still available. The petitioner, for example, can still cite the respondent for contempt of court or file a tort claim for intentional interference with custodial relations if those remedies are available under local law.

---

§ 152.304. Temporary Visitation.

(a) A court of this state which does not have jurisdiction to modify a child custody determination may issue a temporary order enforcing:

(1) a visitation schedule made by a court of another state; or

(2) the visitation provisions of a child custody determination of another state that does not provide for a specific visitation schedule.

(b) If a court of this state makes an order under Subsection (a)(2), the court shall specify in the order a period that it considers adequate to allow the petitioner to obtain an order from a court having jurisdiction under the criteria specified in Subchapter C. The order remains in effect until an order is obtained from the other court or the period expires.

Commissioners' Comment

This section authorizes a court to issue a temporary order if it is necessary to enforce visitation rights without violating the rules on nonmodification contained in Section 303. Therefore, if there is a visitation schedule provided in the custody determination that was made in accordance with Article 2, a court can issue an order under this section implementing the schedule. An implementing order may include make-up or substitute visitation.

A court may also issue a temporary order providing for visitation if visitation was authorized in the custody determination, but no specific schedule was included in the custody determination. Such an order could include a substitution of a specific visitation schedule for "reasonable and seasonable."

However, a court may not, under Subsection (a)(2) provide for a permanent change in visitation. Therefore, requests for a permanent change in the visitation schedule must be addressed to the court with exclusive, continuing jurisdiction under Section 202 or modification jurisdiction under Section 203. As under Section 204, Subsection (b) of this section requires that the temporary visitation order stay in effect only long enough to allow the person who obtained the order to obtain a permanent modification in the state with appropriate jurisdiction under Article 2.

---

§ 152.305. Registration of Child Custody Determination.

(a) A child custody determination issued by a court of another state may be registered in this state, with or without a simultaneous request for enforcement, by sending to the appropriate court in this state:

(1) a letter or other document requesting registration;

(2) two copies, including one certified copy, of the determination sought to be registered and a statement under penalty of perjury that to the best of the knowledge and belief of the person seeking registration the order has not been modified; and

(3) except as otherwise provided in Section 152.209, the name and address of the person seeking registration and any parent or person acting as a parent who has been awarded custody or visitation in the child custody determination sought to be registered.

(b) On receipt of the documents required by Subsection (a), the registering court shall:

(1) cause the determination to be filed as a foreign judgment, together with one copy of any accompanying documents and information, regardless of their form; and

(2) serve notice upon the persons named pursuant to Subsection (a)(3) and provide them with an opportunity to contest the registration in accordance with this section.

(c) The notice required by Subsection (b)(2) must state that:

(1) a registered determination is enforceable as of the date of the registration in the same manner as a determination issued by a court of this state;

(2) a hearing to contest the validity of the registered determination must be requested within 20 days after service of notice; and

(3) failure to contest the registration will result in confirmation of the child custody determination and preclude further contest of that determination with respect to any matter that could have been asserted.

(d) A person seeking to contest the validity of a registered order must request a hearing within 20 days after service of the notice. At that hearing, the court shall confirm the registered order unless the person contesting registration establishes that:

(1) the issuing court did not have jurisdiction under Subchapter C;

(2) the child custody determination sought to be registered has been vacated, stayed, or modified by a court having jurisdiction to do so under Subchapter C; or

(3) the person contesting registration was entitled to notice, but notice was not given in accordance with the standards of Section 152.108, in the proceedings before the court that issued the order for which registration is sought.

(e) If a timely request for a hearing to contest the validity of the registration is not made, the registration is confirmed as a matter of law and the person requesting registration and all persons served must be notified of the confirmation.

(f) Confirmation of a registered order, whether by operation of law or after notice and hearing, precludes further contest of the order with respect to any matter that could have been asserted at the time of registration.

Commissioners' Comment

The remainder of this article provides enforcement mechanisms for interstate child custody determinations.

This section authorizes a simple registration procedure that can be used to predetermine the enforceability of a custody determination. It parallels the process in UIFSA for the registration of child support orders. It should be as much of an aid to pro se litigants as the registration procedure of UIFSA.

A custody determination can be registered without any accompanying request for enforcement. This may be of significant assistance in international cases. For example, the custodial parent under a foreign custody order can receive an advance determination of whether that order would be recognized and enforced before sending the child to the United States for visitation. Article 26 of the 1996 Hague Convention on Jurisdiction, Applicable Law, Recognition and Cooperation in Respect of Parental Responsibility and Measures for the Protection of Children, 35 I.L.M. 1391 (1996), requires those states which accede to the Convention to provide such a procedure.

---

§ 152.306. Enforcement of Registered Determination.

(a) A court of this state may grant any relief normally available under the law of this state to enforce a registered child custody determination made by a court of another state.

(b) A court of this state shall recognize and enforce, but may not modify, except in accordance with Subchapter C, a registered child custody determination of a court of another state.

Commissioners' Comment

A registered child-custody determination can be enforced as if it was a child-custody determination of this state. However, it remains a custody determination of the state that issued it. A registered custody order is not subject to modification unless the state would have jurisdiction to modify the order under Article 2.

§ 152.307. Simultaneous Proceedings.

If a proceeding for enforcement under this subchapter is commenced in a court of this state and the court determines that a proceeding to modify the determination is pending in a court of another state having jurisdiction to modify the determination under Subchapter C, the enforcing court shall immediately communicate with the modifying court. The proceeding for enforcement continues unless the enforcing court, after consultation with the modifying court, stays or dismisses the proceeding.

Commissioners' Comment

The pleading rules of Section 308, require the parties to disclose any pending proceedings. Normally, an enforcement proceeding will take precedence over a modification action since the PKPA requires enforcement of child custody determinations made in accordance with its terms. However, the enforcement court must communicate with the modification court in order to avoid duplicative litigation. The courts might decide that the court with jurisdiction under Article 2 shall continue with the modification action and stay the enforcement proceeding. Or they might decide that the enforcement proceeding shall go forward. The ultimate decision rests with the court having exclusive, continuing jurisdiction under Section 202, or if there is no state with exclusive, continuing jurisdiction, then the decision rests with the state that would have jurisdiction to modify under Section 203. Therefore, if that court determines that the enforcement proceeding should be stayed or dismissed, the enforcement court should stay or dismiss the proceeding. If the enforcement court does not do so, the court with exclusive, continuing jurisdiction under Section 202, or with modification jurisdiction under Section 203, could enjoin the parties from continuing with the enforcement proceeding.

§ 152.308. Expedited Enforcement of Child Custody Determination.

(a) A petition under this subchapter must be verified. Certified copies of all orders sought to be enforced and of any order confirming registration must be attached to the petition. A copy of a certified copy of an order may be attached instead of the original.

(b) A petition for enforcement of a child custody determination must state:

(1) whether the court that issued the determination identified the jurisdictional basis it relied upon in exercising jurisdiction and, if so, what the basis was;

(2) whether the determination for which enforcement is sought has been vacated, stayed, or modified by a court whose decision must be enforced under this chapter and, if so, identify the court, the case number, and the nature of the proceeding;

(3) whether any proceeding has been commenced that could affect the current proceeding, including proceedings relating to domestic violence, protective orders, termination of parental rights, and adoptions and, if so, identify the court, the case number, and the nature of the proceeding;

(4) the present physical address of the child and the respondent, if known;

(5) whether relief in addition to the immediate physical custody of the child and attorney's fees is sought, including a request for assistance from law enforcement officials and, if so, the relief sought; and

(6) if the child custody determination has been registered and confirmed under Section 152.305, the date and place of registration.

(c) Upon the filing of a petition, the court shall issue an order directing the respondent to appear in person with or without the child at a hearing and may enter any order necessary to ensure the safety of the parties and the child. The hearing must be held on the next judicial day after service of the order unless that date is impossible. In that event, the court shall hold the hearing on the first judicial day possible. The court may extend the date of hearing at the request of the petitioner.

(d) An order issued under Subsection (c) must state the time and place of the hearing and advise the respondent that at the hearing the court will award the petitioner immediate physical custody of the child and order the payment of fees, costs, and expenses under Section 152.312, and may schedule a hearing to determine whether further relief is appropriate, unless the respondent appears and establishes that:

(1) the child custody determination has not been registered and confirmed under Section 152.305 and that:

(A) the issuing court did not have jurisdiction under Subchapter C;

(B) the child custody determination for which enforcement is sought has been vacated, stayed, or modified by a court having jurisdiction to do so under Subchapter C; or

(C) the respondent was entitled to notice, but notice was not given in accordance with the standards of Section 152.108, in the proceedings before the court that issued the order for which enforcement is sought; or

(2) the child custody determination for which enforcement is sought was registered and confirmed under Section 152.305, but has been vacated, stayed, or modified by a court of a state having jurisdiction to do so under Subchapter C.

Commissioners' Comment

This section provides the normal remedy that will be used in interstate cases: the production of the child in a summary, remedial process based on habeas corpus.

The petition is intended to provide the court with as much information as possible. Attaching certified copies of all orders sought to be enforced allows the court to have the necessary information. Most of the information relates to the permissible scope of the court's inquiry. The petitioner has the responsibility to inform the court of all proceedings that would affect the current enforcement action. Specific mention is made of certain proceedings to ensure that they are disclosed. A "procedure relating to domestic violence" includes not only protective order proceedings but also criminal prosecutions for child abuse or domestic violence.

The order requires the respondent to appear at a hearing on the next judicial day. The term "next judicial day" in this section means the next day when a judge is at the courthouse. At the hearing, the court will order the child to be delivered to the petitioner unless the respondent is prepared to assert that the issuing state lacked jurisdiction, that notice was not given in accordance with Section 108, or that the order sought to be enforced has been vacated, modified, or stayed by a court with jurisdiction to do so under Article 2. The court is also to order payment of the fees and expenses set out in Section 312. The court may set another hearing to determine whether additional relief available under this state's law should be granted.

If the order has been registered and confirmed in accordance with Section 304, the only defense to enforcement is that the order has been vacated, stayed or modified since the registration proceeding by a court with jurisdiction to do so under Article 2.

§ 152.309. Service of Petition and Order.

Except as otherwise provided in Section 152.311, the petition and order must be served, by any method authorized by the law of this state, upon the respondent and any person who has physical custody of the child.

Commissioners' Comment

In keeping with other sections of this Act, the question of how the petition and order should be served is left to local law.

§ 152.310. Hearing and Order.

(a) Unless the court issues a temporary emergency order pursuant to Section 152.204, upon a finding that a petitioner is entitled to immediate physical custody of the child, the court shall order that the petitioner may take immediate physical custody of the child unless the respondent establishes that:

(1) the child custody determination has not been registered and confirmed under Section 152.305 and that:

(A) the issuing court did not have jurisdiction under Subchapter C;

(B) the child custody determination for which enforcement is sought has been vacated, stayed, or modified by a court of a state having jurisdiction to do so under Subchapter C; or

(C) the respondent was entitled to notice, but notice was not given in accordance with the standards of Section 152.108, in the proceedings before the court that issued the order for which enforcement is sought; or

(2) the child custody determination for which enforcement is sought was registered and confirmed under Section 152.305 but has been vacated, stayed, or modified by a court of a state having jurisdiction to do so under Subchapter C.

(b) The court shall award the fees, costs, and expenses authorized under Section 152.312 and may grant additional relief, including a request for the assistance of law enforcement officials, and set a further hearing to determine whether additional relief is appropriate.

(c) If a party called to testify refuses to answer on the ground that the testimony may be self-incriminating, the court may draw an adverse inference from the refusal.

(d) A privilege against disclosure of communications between spouses and a defense of immunity based on the relationship of husband and wife or parent and child may not be invoked in a proceeding under this subchapter.

Commissioners' Comment

The scope of inquiry for the enforcing court is quite limited. Federal law requires the court to enforce the custody determination if the issuing state's decree was rendered in compliance with the PKPA. 28 U.S.C. § 1738A(a). This Act requires enforcement of custody determinations that are made in conformity with Article 2's jurisdictional rules.

The certified copy, or a copy of the certified copy, of the custody determination entitling the petitioner to the child is prima facie evidence of the issuing court's jurisdiction to enter the order. If the order is one that is entitled to be enforced under Article 2 and if it has been violated, the burden shifts to the respondent to show that the custody determination is not entitled to enforcement.

It is a defense to enforcement that another jurisdiction has issued a custody determination that is required to be enforced under Article 2. An example is when one court has based its original custody determination on the UCCJA § 3(a)(2) (significant connections) and another jurisdiction has rendered an original custody determination based on the UCCJA § 3(a)(1) (home state). When this occurs, Article 2 of this Act, as well as the PKPA, mandate that the home state determination be enforced in all other states, including the state that rendered the significant connections determination.

Lack of notice in accordance with Section 108 by a person entitled to notice and opportunity to be heard at the original custody determination is a defense to enforcement of the custody determination. The scope of the defense under this Act is the same as the defense would be under the law of the state that issued the notice. Thus, if the defense of lack of notice would not be available under local law if the respondent purposely hid from the petitioner, took deliberate steps to avoid service of process or elected not to participate in the initial proceedings, the defense would also not be available under this Act.

There are no other defenses to an enforcement action. If the child would be endangered by the enforcement of a custody or visitation order, there may be a basis for the assumption of emergency jurisdiction under Section 204 of this Act. Upon the finding of an emergency, the court issues a temporary order and directs the parties to proceed either in the court that is exercising continuing jurisdiction over the custody proceeding under Section 202, or the court that would have jurisdiction to modify the custody determination under Section 203.

The court shall determine at the hearing whether fees should be awarded under Section 312. If so, it should order them paid. The court may determine if additional relief is appropriate, including requesting law enforcement officers to assist the petitioner in the enforcement of the order. The court may set a hearing to determine whether further relief should be granted.

The remainder of this section is derived from UIFSA § 316 with regard to the privilege of self-incrimination, spousal privileges, and immunities. It is included to keep parallel the procedures for child support and child custody proceedings to the extent possible.

---

§ 152.311. Warrant to Take Physical Custody of Child.

(a) Upon the filing of a petition seeking enforcement of a child custody determination, the petitioner may file a verified application for the issuance of a warrant to take physical custody of the child if the child is imminently likely to suffer serious physical harm or be removed from this state.

(b) If the court, upon the testimony of the petitioner or other witness, finds that the child is imminently likely to suffer serious physical harm or be removed from this state, it may issue a warrant to take physical custody of the child. The petition must be heard on the next judicial day after the warrant is executed unless that date is impossible. In that event, the court shall hold the hearing on the first judicial day possible. The application for the warrant must include the statements required by Section 152.308(b).

(c) A warrant to take physical custody of a child must:

(1) recite the facts upon which a conclusion of imminent serious physical harm or removal from the jurisdiction is based;

(2) direct law enforcement officers to take physical custody of the child immediately; and

(3) provide for the placement of the child pending final relief.

(d) The respondent must be served with the petition, warrant, and order immediately after the child is taken into physical custody.

(e) A warrant to take physical custody of a child is enforceable throughout this state. If the court finds on the basis of the testimony of the petitioner or other witness that a less intrusive remedy is not effective, it may authorize law enforcement officers to enter private property to take physical custody of the child. If required by exigent circumstances of the case, the court may authorize law enforcement officers to make a forcible entry at any hour.

(f) The court may impose conditions upon placement of a child to ensure the appearance of the child and the child's custodian.

Commissioners' Comment

The section provides a remedy for emergency situations where there is a reason to believe that the child will suffer imminent, serious physical harm or be removed from the jurisdiction once the respondent learns that the petitioner has filed an enforcement proceeding. If the court finds such harm exists, it should temporarily waive the notice requirements and issue a warrant to take physical custody of the child. Immediately after the warrant is executed, the respondent is to receive notice of the proceedings.

The term "harm" cannot be totally defined and, as in the issuance of temporary retraining orders, the appropriate issuance of a warrant is left to the circumstances of the case. Those circumstances include cases where the respondent is the subject of a criminal proceeding as well as situations where the respondent is secreting the child in violation of a court order, abusing the child, a flight risk and other circumstances that the court concludes make the issuance of notice a danger to the child. The court must hear the testimony of the petitioner or another witness prior to issuing the warrant. The testimony may be heard in person, via telephone, or by any other means acceptable under local law. The court must state the reasons for the issuance of the warrant. The warrant can be enforced by law enforcement officers wherever the child is found in the state. The warrant may authorize entry upon private property to pick up the child if no less intrusive means are possible. In extraordinary cases, the warrant may authorize law enforcement to make a forcible entry at any hour.

The warrant must provide for the placement of the child pending the determination of the enforcement proceeding. Since the issuance of the warrant would not occur absent a risk of serious harm to the child, placement cannot be with the respondent. Normally, the child would be placed with the petitioner. However, if placement with the petitioner is not indicated, the court can order any other appropriate placement authorized under the laws of the court's state. Placement with the petitioner may not be indicated if there is a likelihood that the petitioner also will flee the jurisdiction. Placement with the petitioner may not be practical if the petitioner is proceeding through an attorney and is not present before the court.

This section authorizes the court to utilize whatever means are available under local law to ensure the appearance of the petitioner and child at the enforcement hearing. Such means might include cash bonds, a surrender of a passport, or whatever the court determines is necessary.

§ 152.312. Costs, Fees, and Expenses.

(a) The court shall award the prevailing party, including a state, necessary and reasonable expenses incurred by or on behalf of the party, including costs, communication expenses, attorney's fees, investigative fees, expenses for witnesses, travel expenses, and child care during the course of the proceedings, unless the party from whom fees or expenses are sought establishes that the award would be clearly inappropriate.

(b) The court may not assess fees, costs, or expenses against a state unless authorized by law other than this chapter.

Commissioners' Comment

This section is derived from the International Child Abduction Remedies Act, 42 U.S.C. § 11607(b)(3). Normally the court will award fees and costs against the non-prevailing party. Included as expenses are the amount of investigation fees incurred by private persons or by public officials as well as the cost of child placement during the proceedings.

The non-prevailing party has the burden of showing that such an award would be clearly inappropriate. Fees and costs may be inappropriate if their payment would cause the parent and child to seek public assistance.

This section implements the policies of Section 8(c) of Pub. L. 96–611 (part of the PKPA) which provides that:

> In furtherance of the purposes of section 1738A of title 28, United States Code [this section], as added by Subsection (a) of this section, state courts are encouraged to— .
>
> (2) award to the person entitled to custody or visitation pursuant to a custody determination which is consistent with the provisions of such section 1738A [this section], necessary travel expenses, attorneys' fees, costs of private investigations, witness fees or expenses, and other expenses incurred in connection with such custody determination....

The term "prevailing party" is not given a special definition for this Act. Each state will apply its own standard.

Subsection (b) was added to ensure that this section would not apply to the state unless otherwise authorized. The language is taken from UIFSA § 313 (court may assess costs against obligee or support enforcement agency only if allowed by local law).

---

§ 152.313. Recognition and Enforcement.

A court of this state shall accord full faith and credit to an order issued by another state and consistent with this chapter which enforces a child custody determination by a court of another state unless the order has been vacated, stayed, or modified by a court having jurisdiction to do so under Subchapter C.

Commissioners' Comment

The enforcement order, to be effective, must also be enforced by other states. This section requires courts of this state to enforce and not modify enforcement orders issued by other states when made consistently with the provisions of this Act.

---

§ 152.314. Appeals.

An appeal may be taken from a final order in a proceeding under this subchapter in accordance with expedited appellate procedures in other civil cases. Unless the court enters a temporary emergency order under Section 152.204, the enforcing court may not stay an order enforcing a child custody determination pending appeal.

Commissioners' Comment

The order may be appealed as an expedited civil matter. An enforcement order should not be stayed by the court. Provisions for a stay would defeat the purpose of having a quick enforcement procedure. If there is a risk of serious mistreatment or abuse to the child, a petition to assume emergency jurisdiction must be filed under Section 204. This section leaves intact the possibility of obtaining an extraordinary remedy such as mandamus or prohibition from an appellate court to stay the court's enforcement action. In many states, it is not possible to limit the constitutional authority of appellate courts to issue a stay. However, unless the information before the appellate panel indicates that emergency jurisdiction would be assumed under Section 204, there is no reason to stay the enforcement of the order pending appeal.

---

§ 152.315. Role of Prosecutor or Public Official.

(a) In a case arising under this chapter or involving the Hague Convention on the Civil Aspects of International Child Abduction, the prosecutor or other appropriate public official may take any lawful action, including resorting to a proceeding under this subchapter or any other available civil proceeding to locate a child, obtain the return of a child, or enforce a child custody determination if there is:

(1) an existing child custody determination;

(2) a request to do so from a court in a pending child custody proceeding;

(3) a reasonable belief that a criminal statute has been violated; or

(4) a reasonable belief that the child has been wrongfully removed or retained in violation of the Hague Convention on the Civil Aspects of International Child Abduction.

(b) A prosecutor or appropriate public official acting under this section acts on behalf of the court and may not represent any party.

Commissioners' Comment

Sections 315–317 are derived from the recommendations of the *Obstacles Study* that urge a role for public authorities in civil enforcement of custody and visitation determinations. One of the basic policies behind this approach is that, as is the case with child support, the involvement of public authorities will encourage the parties to abide by the terms of the court order. The prosecutor usually would be the most appropriate public official to exercise authority under this section. However, states may locate the authority described in the section in the most appropriate public office for their governmental structure. The authority could be, for example, the Friend of the Court Office or the Attorney General. If the parties know that prosecutors and law enforcement officers are available to help secure the return of a child, the parties may be deterred from interfering with the exercise of rights established by court order.

The use of public authorities should provide a more effective method of remedying violations of the custody determination. Most parties do not have the resources to enforce a custody determination in another jurisdiction. The availability of the prosecutor or other government official as an enforcement agency will help ensure that remedies of this Act can be made available regardless of income level. In addition, the prosecutor may have resources to draw on that are unavailable to the average litigant.

The role of the public authorities should generally not begin until there is a custody determination that is sought to be enforced. The Act does not authorize the public authorities to be involved in the action leading up to the making of the custody determination, except when requested by the court, when there is a violation the Hague Convention on the Civil Aspects of International Child Abduction, or when the person holding the child has violated a criminal statute. This Act does not mandate that the public authorities be involved in all cases referred to it. There is only so much time and money available for enforcement proceedings. Therefore, the public authorities eventually will develop guidelines to determine which cases will receive priority.

The use of civil procedures instead of, or in addition to, filing and prosecuting criminal charges enlarges the prosecutor's options and may provide a more economical and less disruptive means of solving problems of criminal abduction and retention. With the use of criminal proceedings alone, the procedure may be inadequate to ensure the return of the child. The civil options would permit the prosecutor to resolve that recurring and often frustrating problem.

A concern was expressed about whether allowing the prosecutor to use civil means as a method of settling a child abduction violated either DR 7—105(A) of the Code of Professional Responsibility or Model Rule of Professional Responsibility 4.4. Both provisions either explicitly or implicitly disapprove of a lawyer threatening criminal action to gain an advantage in a civil case. However, the prohibition relates to threats that are solely to gain an advantage in a civil case. If the prosecutor has a good faith reason for pursuing the criminal action, there is no ethical violation. *See Committee on Legal Ethics v. Printz*, 416 S.E. 2d 720 (W.Va. 1992) (lawyer can threaten to press criminal charges against a client's former employee unless employee made restitution).

It must be emphasized that the public authorities do not become involved in the merits of the case. They are authorized only to locate the child and enforce the custody determination. The public authority is authorized by this section to utilize any civil proceeding to secure the enforcement of the custody determination. In most jurisdictions, that would be a proceeding under this Act. If the prosecutor proceeds pursuant to this Act, the prosecutor is subject to its provisions. There is nothing in this Act that would prevent a state from authorizing the prosecutor or other public official to use additional remedies beyond those provided in this Act.

The public authority does not represent any party to the custody determination. It acts as a "friend of the court." Its role is to ensure that the custody determination is enforced.

Sections 315–317 are limited to cases covered by this Act, i.e. interstate cases. However, states may, if they wish, extend this part of the Act to intrastate cases.

It should also be noted that the provisions of this section relate to the civil enforcement of child custody determinations. Nothing in this section is meant to detract from the ability of the prosecutor to use criminal provisions in child abduction cases.

---

§ 152.316. Role of Law Enforcement.

At the request of a prosecutor or other appropriate public official acting under Section 152.315, a law enforcement officer may take any lawful action reasonably necessary to locate a child or a party and assist a prosecutor or appropriate public official with responsibilities under Section 152.315.

Commissioners' Comment

This section authorizes law enforcement officials to assist in locating a child and enforcing a custody determination when requested to do so by the public authorities. It is to be read as an enabling provision. Whether law enforcement officials have discretion in responding to a request by the prosecutor or other public official is a matter of local law.

---

§ 152.317. Costs and Expenses.

If the respondent is not the prevailing party, the court may assess against the respondent all direct expenses and costs incurred by the prosecutor or other appropriate public official and law enforcement officers under Section 152.315 or 152.316.

Commissioners' Comment

One of the major problems of utilizing public officials to locate children and enforce custody and visitation determinations is cost. This section authorizes the prosecutor and law enforcement to recover costs against the non-prevailing party. The use of the term "direct" indicates that overhead is not a recoverable cost. This section cannot be used to recover the value of the time spent by the public authorities' attorneys.

Chapter 153. Conservatorship, Possession, and Access.

Subchapter A. General Provisions

Subchapter B. Parent Appointed as Conservator: In General

Subchapter C. Parent Appointed as Sole or Joint Managing Conservator

Subchapter D. Parent Appointed as Possessory Conservator

Subchapter E. Guidelines for the Possession of a Child by a Parent Named as Possessory Conservator

Subchapter F. Standard Possession Order

Subchapter G. Appointment of Nonparent as Conservator

Subchapter H. Rights of Grandparent

Subchapter I. Prevention of International Parental Child Abduction

---

Introductory Comment

Chapter 153 is one of the primary sources of substantive law for a SAPCR. Subchapter A provides the major guiding principles for the issues of joint and sole managing conservatorship, and possession of and access to a child, a.k.a. custody and visitation. In recent years there had been a massive expansion of detailed specificity on these matters, particularly regarding the exercise and enforcement of the rights of the noncustodial parent—whether denominated as the possessory conservator or as a joint managing conservator. In 2001 the new section on Collaborative Law, § 153.0072, has had a significant impact on the practice of Family Law. In 2003 the trend continues with amendments and a new Subchapter I enacted to prevent international parental child abduction.

CLE/Other Legal Publications

The art of evaluating a custody case. Keith M. Nelson, 2004 ADV. FAM. L.

Developing and preparing witnesses in custody cases. Jo Chris G. Lopez, 2004 ADV. FAM. L.

Overcoming presumption in SAPCRs, JMC, SPO and parental presumptions. Sally H. Emerson, 2004 ADV. FAM. L.

How to settle hard to settle cases involving children. Kevin R. Fuller, 2004 MARRIAGE DISSOLUTION

Children inside wedlock/outside wedlock parent issues. Janet McClullar, 2003 ADV. FAM. L.

Top ten things you should know about handling kid cases. Mary Jo McCurley & Laura M. Hilliard, 2003 MARRIAGE DISSOLUTION

Evaluating a custody case: the custody equation from a lawyer's perspective. J. Steven King & Heather L. King, 2003 MARRIAGE DISSOLUTION

Leading Cases

In re P.D.M., 117 S.W.3d 453 (Tex. App.—Fort Worth 2003, pet. denied) (grandmother's suit after death of managing conservator is not an original suit and therefore is not subject to father's parental presumption)

Lide v. Lide, 116 S.W.3d 147 (Tex. App.—El Paso 2003, no pet.) (JMC presumption rebutted affirming mom's appointment as SMC)

In re Ostrofsky, 112 S.W.3d 925 (Tex. App.—Houston [14th Dist.] 2003, no pet.) (temporary order sending children to boarding school deprived joint managing conservator of right to determine primary residence)

Coleman v. Coleman, 109 S.W.3d 108 (Tex. App.—Austin 2003, no pet.) (clear and compelling reasons must be articulated by trial court to affirm splitting custody of siblings)

In re S.W.H., 72 S.W.3d 772 (Tex. App.—Fort Worth 2002, no pet.) (parental presumption prevails; court improperly appointed nonparent as conservator)

Roby v. Adams, 68 S.W.3d 822 (Tex. App.—El Paso 2002, no pet.) (grandparent seeking visitation rights to grandchildren has the burden to overcome the presumption that a fit parent acts in the best interest of the children)

Lohmann v. Lohmann, 62 S.W.3d 875 (Tex. App.—El Paso 2001, no pet.) (court with jurisdiction over child has duty to exercise equitable powers to make proper disposition of all matters; therefore technical rules of pleading and practice of little importance in determining child custody issues)

In re C.R.T., 61 S.W.3d 62 (Tex. App.—Amarillo 2001, pet. denied) (aunt named PMC of three of her druggie-sister's children, thereby confirming placement of kids by mom with aunt)

Cross Reference

TEX. PENAL CODE ANN. § 25.03. Interference with Child Custody.

Texas Family Law Practice Manual

Chapter 31. Original Suit Affecting the Parent–Child Relationship

Texas Pattern Jury Charges: Family

Chapter 215. Definitions and Instructions—Suits Affecting the Parent–Child Relationship
Chapter 216. Conservatorship and Support—Original Suits

Subchapter A. General Provisions

§ 153.001. Public Policy.

(a) The public policy of this state is to:

(1) assure that children will have frequent and continuing contact with parents who have shown the ability to act in the best interest of the child;

(2) provide a safe, stable, and nonviolent environment for the child; and

(3) encourage parents to share in the rights and duties of raising their child after the parents have separated or dissolved their marriage.

(b) A court may not render an order that conditions the right of a conservator to possession of or access to a child on the payment of child support.

Comment

Subsection (b) codifies the court-originated rule that support and custody are independent rights and duties.

Leading Case

In re A.N.H., 70 S.W.3d 918 (Tex. App.—Amarillo 2002, no pet.) (support order conditioned on obligor's right to visitation violates public policy and is void)

---

§ 153.002. Best Interest of Child.

The best interest of the child shall always be the primary consideration of the court in determining the issues of conservatorship and possession of and access to the child.

Comment

This is the most quoted section in the Family Code. However, it does not provide much guidance to predict the outcome of a case. Discretion of the trial court is extraordinarily broad; "best interest" is usually in the eye of the beholder, the trier of fact, judge or jury.

Leading Cases

Holley v. Adams, 544 S.W.2d 367 (Tex. 1976) (factors in "best interest" listed in termination of parental rights case)

Edwards v. Edwards, 79 S.W.3d 88 (Tex. App.—Texarkana 2002, no pet.) (trial court directed to explain "best interest" finding to appellate court when naming father sole managing conservator)

Lohmann v. Lohmann, 62 S.W.3d 875 (Tex. App.—El Paso 2001, no pet.) (technical rules of pleading and practice are of little importance in determining child custody issues as compared to best interest)

Dennis v. Smith, 962 S.W.2d 67 (Tex. App.—Houston [1st Dist.] 1997, writ denied) (awarding father, who was not primary possessory parent, right to determine child's domicile and school not abuse of discretion)

Wolfe v. Wolfe, 918 S.W.2d 533 (Tex. App.—El Paso 1996, writ denied) (demonstrative evidence of father's sexual practices properly excluded)

Hirczy v. Hirczy, 838 S.W.2d 783 (Tex. App.—Corpus Christi 1992, writ denied) (wife rebuts husband's paternity of child; he's denied custody and visitation on best interest basis)

Wristen v. Kosel, 742 S.W.2d 868 (Tex. App.—Eastland 1987, writ denied) (only best interest of children born of marriage to be considered in SAPCR; child of another marriage not involved)

§ 153.003. No Discrimination Based on Sex or Marital Status.

The court shall consider the qualifications of the parties without regard to their marital status or to the sex of the party or the child in determining:

(1) which party to appoint as sole managing conservator;

(2) whether to appoint a party as joint managing conservator; and

(3) the terms and conditions of conservatorship and possession of and access to the child.

Comment

When the court or jury is called upon to decide issues of custody and visitation, *a.k.a.* conservatorship and possession of and access to a child, the legal equality of the parents, the child, and of any other party, with regard to their sex or marital status is a relatively modern innovation. Gone are the days when, under certain fact situations, either the mother or the father was presumed to best the best choice for custody. Decreeing that unmarried parents should also be treated equally in custody matters is of somewhat more recent vintage, i.e., that did not receive statutory recognition until 1995.

§ 153.004. History of Domestic Violence.

(a) In determining whether to appoint a party as a sole or joint managing conservator, the court shall consider evidence of the intentional use of abusive physical force by a party against the party's spouse, a parent of the child, or any person younger than 18 years of age committed within a two-year period preceding the filing of the suit or during the pendency of the suit.

(b) The court may not appoint joint managing conservators if credible evidence is presented of a history or pattern of past or present child neglect, or physical or sexual abuse by one parent directed against the other parent, a spouse, or a child, including a sexual assault in violation of Section 22.011 or 22.021, Penal Code, that results in the other parent becoming pregnant with the child. A history of sexual abuse includes a sexual assault that results in the other parent becoming pregnant with the child, regardless of the prior relationship of the parents. It is a rebuttable presumption that the appointment of a parent as the sole managing conservator of a child or as the conservator who has the exclusive right to determine the primary residence of a child is not in the best interest of the child if credible evidence is presented of a history or pattern of past or present child neglect, or physical or sexual abuse by that parent directed against the other parent, a spouse, or a child.

(c) The court shall consider the commission of family violence in determining whether to deny, restrict, or limit the possession of a child by a parent who is appointed as a possessory conservator.

(d) The court may not allow a parent to have access to a child for whom it is shown by a preponderance of the evidence that there is a history or pattern of committing family violence during the two years preceding the date of the filing of the suit or during the pendency of the suit, unless the court:

(1) finds that awarding the parent access to the child would not endanger the child's physical health or emotional welfare and would be in the best interest of the child; and

(2) renders a possession order that is designed to protect the safety and well-being of the child and any other person who has been a victim of family violence committed by the parent and that may include a requirement that:

(A) the periods of access be continuously supervised by an entity or person chosen by the court;

(B) the exchange of possession of the child occur in a protective setting;

(C) the parent abstain from the consumption of alcohol or a controlled substance, as defined by Chapter 481, Health and Safety Code, within 12 hours prior to or during the period of access to the child; or

(D) the parent attend and complete a battering intervention and prevention program as provided by Article 42.141, Code of Criminal Procedure, or, if such a program is not available, complete a course of treatment under Section 153.010.

(e) It is a rebuttable presumption that it is not in the best interest of a child for a parent to have unsupervised visitation with the child if credible evidence is presented of a history or pattern of past or present child neglect or physical or sexual abuse by that parent directed against the other parent, a spouse, or a child.

(f) In determining under this section whether there is credible evidence of a history or pattern of past or present child neglect or physical or sexual abuse by a parent directed against the other parent, a spouse, or a child, the court shall consider whether a protective order was rendered under Chapter 85, Title 4, against the parent during the two-year period preceding the filing of the suit or during the pendency of the suit.

History: Amended by 78th Legis., Reg. Sess. (2003), H.B. 2099, eff. Sept. 1, 2003, and "applies only to an order in a suit affecting the parent-child relationship rendered on or after that date, without regard to whether the suit was filed before, on, or after that date. The enactment of this Act does not by itself constitute a material and substantial change of circumstances sufficient to warrant modification of a court order or portion of a decree that provides for the possession of or access to a child rendered before the effective date of this Act."

Comment

The test for whether there is a "credible evidence of a history or pattern of past or present child neglect or physical or sexual abuse by a parent" previously has been left to a case-by-case determination by the court. The addition of subsection (f) provides a nonexclusive test regarding whether such a history exists. That is, whether a protective order was rendered against the respondent in the preceding two year period. Arguably, rendition of a single protective within the past two years is not necessarily proof of a "pattern," but it surely is a good start on proof of a "history."

CLE/Other Legal Publications

Domestic violence: including protective orders and the psychology of abuse. Judy L. Warne, 2004 ADV. FAM. L.

What's love got to do with it? how a finding of family violence directly affects your family law case. Kathleen A. Hamilton, 2004 MARRIAGE DISSOLUTION

Overview of abuse, neglect and intra-family violence. Oscar Gabaldon, 2004 U. TEX. FAM. L. ON THE BORDER

When child abuse and domestic violence collide: tension within the family violence field. Bree Buchanan, 2003 ADV. FAM. L.

Protective/restrictive possession: substance abuse, family violence and other perils. Sally H. Emerson, 2002 MARRIAGE DISSOLUTION

Family violence. A. Michelle May, 2001 ADV. FAM. L. DRAFTING

Leading Cases

Burns v. Burns, 116 S.W.3d 916 (Tex. App.—Dallas 2003, no pet.) (family violence rebuts joint managing conservatorship presumption)

In re J.R.P., 55 S.W.3d 147 (Tex. App.—Corpus Christi 2001, pet. denied) (in determining conservatorship, a trial court considers whether a potential family for placement has a history of physical and substance abuse, and whether others that have access to the home pose a physical threat to the children)

In re M.R., 975 S.W.2d 51 (Tex. App.—San Antonio 1998, pet. denied) (trial court improperly refused to admit evidence of domestic violence against unmarried mother in modification)

---

§ 153.005. Appointment of Sole or Joint Managing Conservator.

(a) In a suit, the court may appoint a sole managing conservator or may appoint joint managing conservators. If the parents are or will be separated, the court shall appoint at least one managing conservator.

(b) A managing conservator must be a parent, a competent adult, an authorized agency, or a licensed child-placing agency.

§ 153.006. Appointment of Possessory Conservator.

(a) If a managing conservator is appointed, the court may appoint one or more possessory conservators.

(b) The court shall specify the rights and duties of a person appointed possessory conservator.

(c) The court shall specify and expressly state in the order the times and conditions for possession of or access to the child, unless a party shows good cause why specific orders would not be in the best interest of the child.

§ 153.007. Agreement Concerning Conservatorship.

(a) To promote the amicable settlement of disputes between the parties to a suit, the parties may enter into a written agreement containing provisions for conservatorship and possession of the child and for modification of the agreement, including variations from the standard possession order.

(b) If the court finds that the agreement is in the child's best interest, the court shall render an order in accordance with the agreement.

(c) Terms of the agreement contained in the order or incorporated by reference regarding conservatorship or support of or access to a child in an order may be enforced by all remedies available for enforcement of a judgment, including contempt, but are not enforceable as a contract.

(d) If the court finds the agreement is not in the child's best interest, the court may request the parties to submit a revised agreement or the court may render an order for the conservatorship and possession of the child.

Comment

This section, originally derived from the Uniform Marriage and Divorce Act, long bedeviled Texas lawyers. Prior to September 1, 1995, the Law of Contracts applied to an agreement concerning conservatorship, while the Law of Judgments applied to a court decree. Remedial actions available to a dissatisfied party could vary, depending on whether a contract or a judgment was involved. Since that date, subsection (c) places all remedies under the aegis of the Law of Judgments. *See* comment to § 154.124, *infra*. Contracts entered into before September 1, 1995 remain enforceable on that basis.

CLE/Other Legal Publications

Parental alienation. Reginald A. Hirsch, 2002 ADV. FAM. L.

Parent alienations: war and peace. Jan Marie DeLipsey & Barbara D. Nunneley, 2001 MARRIAGE DISSOLUTION

Leading Cases

Elfeldt v. Elfeldt, 730 S.W.2d 657 (Tex. 1987) (agreement must specify terms to be enforceable as contract) (apparently overruled by statute)

Ex parte Gorena, 595 S.W.2d 841 (Tex. 1979) (agreement incorporated in decree enforceable as judgment)

In re Burtch, 972 S.W.2d 882 (Tex. App.—Austin 1998, no pet.) (agreement to pay college expenses enforceable as a contract, not to be confused with child support)

Stein v. Stein, 868 S.W.2d 902 (Tex. App.—Houston [14th Dist.] 1994, no writ) (wife timely withdrew consent to settlement agreement given to associate judge)

Hill v. Hill, 819 S.W.2d 570 (Tex. App.—Dallas 1991, writ denied) (public policy prohibits enforcement of contracts seeking to fix child support permanently); *see also* Hibler v. Hibler, 813 S.W.2d 524 (Tex. App.—San Antonio 1991, writ denied) *and* Leonard v. Lane, 821 S.W.2d 275 (Tex. App.—Houston [1st Dist.] 1991, writ denied)

Pettit v. Pettit, 818 S.W.2d 561 (Tex. App.—Beaumont 1991, no writ) (child support provision incorporated in consent decree subject to modification)

---

§ 153.0071. Alternate Dispute Resolution Procedures.

(a) On written agreement of the parties, the court may refer a suit affecting the parent-child relationship to arbitration. The agreement must state whether the arbitration is binding or non-binding.

(b) If the parties agree to binding arbitration, the court shall render an order reflecting the arbitrator's award unless the court determines at a non-jury hearing that the award is not in the best interest of the child. The burden of proof at a hearing under this subsection is on the party seeking to avoid rendition of an order based on the arbitrator's award.

(c) On the written agreement of the parties or on the court's own motion, the court may refer a suit affecting the parent-child relationship to mediation.

(d) A mediated settlement agreement is binding on the parties if the agreement:

(1) provides, in a prominently displayed statement that is in boldfaced type or capital letters or underlined, that the agreement is not subject to revocation;

(2) is signed by each party to the agreement; and

(3) is signed by the party's attorney, if any, who is present at the time the agreement is signed.

(e) If a mediated settlement agreement meets the requirements of Subsection (d), a party is entitled to judgment on the mediated settlement agreement notwithstanding Rule 11, Texas Rules of Civil Procedure, or another rule of law.

(f) A party may at any time prior to the final mediation order file a written objection to the referral of a suit affecting the parent-child relationship to mediation on the basis of family violence having been committed by another party against the objecting party or a child who is the subject of the suit. After an objection is filed, the suit may not be referred to mediation unless, on the request of a party, a hearing is held and the court finds that a preponderance of the evidence does not support the objection. If the suit is referred to mediation, the court shall order appropriate measures be taken to ensure the physical and emotional safety of the party who filed the objection. The order shall provide that the parties not be required to have face-to-face contact and that the parties be placed in separate rooms during mediation. This subsection does not apply to suits filed under Chapter 262 *[Emergency Procedures in Suit by Governmental Entity].*

Comment

Subsections (a) and (b) recognize the validity of arbitration in suits affecting the parent-child relationship. These provisions reflect the majority rule in American law—family law arbitration is valid, subject to court review. *Miller v. Miller,* 620 A.2d 1161 (Pa. Super. 1993); *Faherty v. Faherty*, 477 A.2d 1257 (N.J. 1984).

Subsections (c)-(e) adopt the majority rule in Texas law that mediated settlement agreements are binding and not subject to revocation.

Subsection (f) responds to complaints that mediation is inappropriate if the parent-child relationship, or the parent-parent relationship, has been scarred by domestic violence. If the court finds an allegation of violence to be true, mediation is not to be ordered. But if mediation is ordered after an objection is overruled, the court is directed to ensure the safety of the parties by ordering that face-to-face contact between the parties is prohibited. This restriction seem a bit strange given the fact that, by definition, mediation can be ordered only if the court has rejected an objection to mediation based on alleged violence—presumptively such an order is based on a finding that the movant did not produce a preponderance of the evidence that violence occurred. Finally, if an objection is made based on past family violence, the subsection excuses a CPS suit alleging child abuse and neglect from mediation. This too is strange, given the fact that much of Chapter 262–263 litigation is settled through mediation.

CLE/Other Legal Publications

Collaboration, mediation and settlement: ethical and malpractice considerations. Alison H. Moore, 2004 Adv. Fam. L.

Collaborative law: if i can't go to court, what do i do? Thomas L. Ausley & Larry Hance, 2004 U. Tex. Fam. L. Front Lines

Drafting before and after mediation. Kimberly M. Naylor, 2002 Adv. Fam. L. Drafting

Private justice: arbitration as an alternative to the courthouse? Richard R. Orsinger, 2002 Adv. Fam. L.

Mediation: when is it really over? Gary L. Nickelson, 2002 Adv. Fam. L.

Unorthodox mediation techniques. Guy N. Harrison, 2002 Adv. Fam. L.

"Slam dunk the mediation": winning strategies for preparing and executing effective mediations of property and custody issues in divorce. Jan Marie DeLipsey, Patrice L. Ferguson & Randall B. Wilhite, 2002 Marriage Dissolution

Leading Cases

Goetz v. Goetz, 130 S.W.3d 359 (Tex. App.—Houston [14th Dist.] 2004, pet. filed) (trial court may appoint arbitrator when arbitration agreement does not specify method for appointment)

In re A.H., 114 S.W.3d 750 (Tex. App.—Dallas 2003, no pet.) (mediated settlement agreement with notice as to irrevocability terminating parental rights binding on parent)

Jabri v. Qaddura, 108 S.W.3d 404 (Tex. App.—Fort Worth 2003, no pet.) (agreement to arbitrate all family law claims enforceable; trial court must defer to arbitrator)

In re Cartwright, 104 S.W.3d 706 (Tex. App.—Houston [1st Dist.] 2003, no pet.) (trial court abused its discretion in appointing mediator as arbitrator)

Stieren v. McBroom, 103 S.W.3d 602 (Tex. App.—San Antonio 2003, pet. denied) (arbitrator's validation of obligor's double-cross of a deal he made one year earlier reversed on best interest test—but case goes back to arbitration as trial court lacks authority to decide motion to modify)

In re Calderon, 96 S.W.3d 711 (Tex. App.—Tyler 2003, orig. proceeding) (mandatory transfer of SAPCR not trumped by mediated settlement agreement signed more than 18 months previously)

Cooper v. Bushong, 10 S.W.3d 20 (Tex. App.—Austin 1999, pet. denied) (termination of father's rights based on binding arbitration)

Alvarez v. Reiser, 958 S.W.2d 232 (Tex. App.—Eastland 1997, writ denied) (party entitled to judgment on mediated agreement)

Davis v. Wickham, 917 S.W.2d 414 (Tex. App.—Houston [14th Dist.] 1996, no writ) (mediated settlement agreement is binding; enforceable by summary judgment)

Matter of Marriage of Ames, 860 S.W.2d 590 (Tex. App.—Amarillo 1993, no writ); *Matter of Marriage of* Banks, 887 S.W.2d 160 (Tex. App.—Texarkana 1994, no writ) (mediated settlement agreement binding, irrevocable)

Cross References

TEX. FAM. CODE ANN. §§ 6.601–.602. Alternative Dispute Resolution Procedures.

TEX. CIV. PRAC. & REM. CODE ANN. ch. 154. Alternative Dispute Resolution Procedures, *infra;* ch. 171. General Arbitration Law.

---

§ 153.0072. Collaborative Law.

(a) On a written agreement of the parties and their attorneys, a suit affecting the parent-child relationship may be conducted under collaborative law procedures.

(b) Collaborative law is a procedure in which the parties and their counsel agree in writing to use their best efforts and make a good faith attempt to resolve the suit affecting the parent-child relationship on an agreed basis without resorting to judicial intervention except to have the court approve the settlement agreement, make the legal pronouncements, and sign the orders required by law to effectuate the agreement of the parties as the court determines appropriate. The parties' counsel may not serve as litigation counsel except to ask the court to approve the settlement agreement.

(c) A collaborative law agreement must include provisions for:

(1) full and candid exchange of information between the parties and their attorneys as necessary to make a proper evaluation of the case;

(2) suspending court intervention in the dispute while the parties are using collaborative law procedures;

(3) hiring experts, as jointly agreed, to be used in the procedure;

(4) withdrawal of all counsel involved in the collaborative law procedure if the collaborative law procedure does not result in settlement of the dispute; and

(5) other provisions as agreed to by the parties consistent with a good faith effort to collaboratively settle the matter.

(d) Notwithstanding Rule 11, Texas Rules of Civil Procedure, or another rule or law, a party is entitled to judgment on a collaborative law settlement agreement if the agreement:

(1) provides, in a prominently displayed statement that is boldfaced, capitalized, or underlined, that the agreement is not subject to revocation; and

(2) is signed by each party to the agreement and the attorney of each party.

(e) Subject to Subsection (g), a court that is notified 30 days before trial that the parties are using collaborative law procedures to attempt to settle a dispute may not, until a party notifies the court that the collaborative law procedures did not result in a settlement:

(1) set a hearing or trial in the case;

(2) impose discovery deadlines;

(3) require compliance with scheduling orders; or

(4) dismiss the case.

(f) The parties shall notify the court if the collaborative law procedures result in a settlement. If they do not, the parties shall file:

(1) a status report with the court not later than the 180th day after the date of the written agreement to use the procedures; and

(2) a status report on or before the first anniversary of the date of the written agreement to use the procedures, accompanied by a motion for continuance that the court shall grant if the status report indicates the desire of the parties to continue to use collaborative law procedures.

(g) If the collaborative law procedures do not result in a settlement on or before the second anniversary of the date that the suit was filed, the court may:

(1) set the suit for trial on the regular docket; or

(2) dismiss the suit without prejudice.

Guest Comment by Donald R. Royall and John V. McShane

Collaborative law is an entirely new model of alternative dispute resolution in Texas. The last 15 years have seen a growing body of evidence suggesting that more and more parents, given a safe legal environment within which to work, want, and are uniquely qualified to fashion their own solutions to the issues presented by a suit affecting the parent-child relationship, without judicial intervention. This awareness has in turn produced increasing statutory encouragement and implementation of alternative dispute resolution procedures for resolving Family Law disputes.

In enacting the Texas Civil Practice and Remedies Code outlining alternative dispute resolution procedures generally, the Texas Legislature placed special emphasis on the applicability of these procedures in Family Law as a matter of state policy. TEX. CIV. PRAC. & REM. CODE ANN. § 154.002 (1987). In 1995 the legislature explicitly incorporated mediation and arbitration procedures into the Texas Family Code, provided means for enforcement of the resulting agreement or award, and instituted the requirement that each parties' first pleading contain a signed statement acknowledging awareness of the existence of such procedures, and pledging to make a good faith effort to utilize alternative dispute resolution before resorting to trial. TEX. FAM. CODE ANN. §§ 6.404, 102.0085, 153.0071 (1995). This requirement was equally applicable to suits for dissolution of a marriage and suits affecting the parent-child relationship.

In 1997, the applicability of arbitration and mediation to suits for dissolution of a marriage was moved from the indirect references in § 153.0071(f), to the explicit provisions of new § 6.601 and § 6.602 (1997). But aside from that, while the ADR provisions of the Texas Family Code were tweaked in 1999, the basic statutory ADR landscape has remained virtually unchanged until now.

Collaborative Law seeks to create an environment in which the parties, with the aid of their attorneys, can address the issues presented as problems to be solved, rather than contests to be won. Essential to that process is elimination of the threat, spoken or unspoken, that "If you don't agree with my position on the matter, we can just let the Judge decide." This is accomplished by a written "four way" agreement, binding the parties and their attorneys to the proposition that the consequence of failure to reach some solution to all issues presented is the abandonment of the process, and the attendant withdrawal of the attorneys from any further involvement beyond an orderly transition of the matter to new counsel, who will presumably prepare the case for trial in the conventional adversarial manner. The resulting atmosphere is one in which the parties and their attorney have the same conscious and subconscious incentives to reach a negotiated settlement as well as the same disincentives to failure.

Sections 153.0072(a)-(c) are largely descriptive of the process. Section 153.0072(d) seeks to accord the same finality to an agreement reached through this process as is accorded a Mediated Settlement Agreement that meets the statutory requirements of § 153.0071(e). Section 153.0072 (e) seeks to free the case proceeding under Collaborative Law procedures, from the scheduling orders and procedural deadlines so necessary to the orderly progress of a case through the adversarial system. Sections 153.0072 (f), (g), address the judiciary's concern that it should nevertheless have some supervisory authority, since in the final analysis it has ultimate responsibility for the disposition of all cases on its docket.

Collaborative law procedures have also been made equally applicable in suits for dissolution of marriage. *See* § 6.603, *supra*.

CLE/Other Legal Publications

Collaborative law: what is it? Why do it? Kevin R. Fuller, 2004 Adv. Fam. L.

Collaboration, mediation and settlement: ethical and malpractice considerations. Alison H. Moore, 2004 Adv. Fam. L.

Client centered collaborative law—a human bridge to serendipity. C. Mike McCurley, Robert Gordon & Carson P. Epes, 2004 Marriage Dissolution

Collaborative law training. (Workshop) 2003, 2002, 2001 Adv. Fam. L.

Creating a collaborative law office. Dolly M. Garlo, 64 Tex. B. J. 904 (2001)

The anatomy of collaborative law: a Texas perspective. Donald R. Royall, 2001 Adv. Fam. L. Drafting

See also annotations to § 153.0071, *supra*.

---

§ 153.008. Child's Preference [~~Choice~~] of Person to Designate Residence [~~Managing Conservator~~].

A [~~If the~~] child [~~is~~] 12 years of age or older **may file** [~~, the child may, by writing filed~~] with the court **in writing** [~~, choose~~] the **name of the person who is the child's preference to have the exclusive right to designate the primary residence of the child** [~~managing conservator~~], subject to the approval of the court.

History: Amended by 78th Legis., Reg. Sess. (2003), H.B. 913, eff. Sept. 1, 2003. "The changes in law made by this Act to Sections 105.002(c) and 153.008, Family Code, apply only to a suit affecting the parent-child relationship filed on or after the effective date of this Act. A suit affecting the parent-child relationship filed before the effective date of this Act is governed by the law in effect on the date that the suit was filed, and the former law is continued in effect for that purpose."

Comment

Over the years, there had been a steady progression of reducing the age for a child to "express a preference regarding managing conservatorship" that culminated in 1999, when the age was reduced to 10. However, the age at which a child was deemed appropriate to be included in a SAPCR was not always consistent. For example, the age for a judge to interview a child in chambers was mandated at age 10, § 153.009, while a child's choice of a joint managing conservator was retained at age 12, § 153.134 (probably a drafting oversight).

Critics of the 1999 amendment (and there were plenty of them) vigorously asserted that a child 10 years of age would be subject to undue parental pressure if the child attempted to announce a choice of managing conservator. Whether the choice was freely given would always remain a question. The assumption that free-choice would be available to a 12 year-old, while unavailable to a 10 year-old, was implicit. It seems likely that the adjustments of the age standard has been resolved by 2001 amendments to the relevant sections. As of 2001, age 12 is established throughout Title 5 as the touchstone for children's autonomy.

As of 2003 these autonomous children may designate in writing their preference for which adult can designate their primary residence, subject to the approval of the court, of course.

CLE/Other Legal Publications

Overcoming presumption in SAPCRs, JMC, SPO and parental presumptions. Sally H. Emerson, 2004 Adv. Fam. L.

Rebutting the joint custody presumption—child preferences. Darcy E. Loveless, 2003 Adv. Fam. L.

Don't forget the child. James D. Stewart & Mary Jo McCurley, 2003 Adv. Fam. L.

Hearing children's voices: enlightenment and empowerment. Richard A. Warshak, 2002 Adv. Fam. L.

Who are we listening to? An analysis of currently accepted practice regarding the involvement of children in custody litigation. Debra H. Lehrmann, Janice E. Pardue, Steve A. Bavousett & Brenda Garrett Green, 2002 Adv. Fam. L.

Child's voice in custody litigation. (Workshop) 2002 Adv. Fam. L.

From the mouths of babes: the art of interviewing children in chambers. Judy Parker & Peter A. Sakai, 2001 Adv. Fam. L.

A child's preference v. the best interest standard. J. Lindsey Short, Jr., 2001 Adv. Fam. L.

Leading Cases

In re Moss, 887 S.W.2d 186 (Tex. App.—Texarkana 1994, no writ) (award of sole managing conservatorship to father at request of child found to be appropriate)

Cole v. Cole, 880 S.W.2d 477 (Tex. App.—Fort Worth 1994, no writ) (trial court overrules son's desire to live with father)

Boriack v. Boriack, 541 S.W.2d 237 (Tex. Civ. App.—Corpus Christi 1976, writ dism'd w.o.j.) (child's choice of conservator subject to court approval)

---

§ 153.009. Interview of Child in Chambers.

(a) In a nonjury trial the court may interview the child in chambers to determine the child's wishes as to conservatorship.

(b) When the issue of managing conservatorship is contested, on the application of a party, the court shall interview a child 12 years of age or older and may interview a child under 12 years of age. Interviewing a child does not diminish the discretion of the court.

(c) The court may permit the attorney for a party or the attorney ad litem for the child to be present at the interview.

(d) On the motion of a party or on the court's own motion, the court shall cause a record of the interview to be made when the child is 12 years of age or older. A record of the interview shall be part of the record in the case.

Comment

Mandatory interviewing of a child in chambers, on request from a party, is an important step in giving a child a voice in a lawsuit in which the child is "the real party in interest." Following 2001 amendments, age 12 is consistently identified as the appropriate age for a child's choice to be given special weight. *See also* § 153.008 *supra*, § 156.101, *infra*.

CLE/Legal Publications

Rebutting the joint custody presumption—child preferences. Darcy E. Loveless, 2003 ADV. FAM. L.

Don't forget the child. James D. Stewart & Mary Jo McCurley, 2003 ADV. FAM. L.

Dangerously giving up rights—to share or not to share. Wendy S. Burgower & Charlotte D. Rainwater, 2003 MARRIAGE DISSOLUTION

Hearing children's voices: enlightenment and empowerment. Richard A. Warshak, 2002 ADV. FAM. L.

Who are we listening to? An analysis of currently accepted practice regarding the involvement of children in custody litigation. Debra H. Lehrmann, Janice E. Pardue, Steve A. Bavousett & Brenda Garrett Green, 2002 ADV. FAM. L.

Child's voice in custody litigation. (Workshop) 2002 ADV. FAM. L.

From the mouths of babes: the art of interviewing children in chambers. Judy Parker & Peter A. Sakai, 2001 ADV. FAM. L.

A child's preference v. the best interest standard. J. Lindsey Short, Jr., 2001 ADV. FAM. L.

The child as a witness. Jan Marie Delipsey & Paula Larsen, 2000 ADV. FAM. L.

Texas Family Law Practice Manual

Forms 16–7. Motion for Judge To Confer with Child; *16–8*. Order on Motion for Judge To Confer with Child

---

§ 153.010. Order for Family Counseling.

(a) If the court finds at the time of a hearing that the parties have a history of conflict in resolving an issue of conservatorship or possession of or access to the child, the court may order a party to:

(1) participate in counseling with a mental health professional who:

(A) has a background in family therapy;

(B) has a mental health license that requires as a minimum a master's degree; and

(C) has training in domestic violence if the court determines that the training is relevant to the type of counseling needed; and

(2) pay the cost of counseling.

(b) If a person possessing the requirements of Subsection (a)(1) is not available in the county in which the court presides, the court may appoint a person the court believes is qualified to conduct the counseling ordered under Subsection (a).

§ 153.011. Security Bond.

If the court finds that a person who has a possessory interest in a child may violate the court order relating to the interest, the court may order the party to execute a bond or deposit security. The court shall set the amount and condition the bond or security on compliance with the order.

§ 153.012. Right to Privacy; Deletion of Personal Information in Records.

The court may order the custodian of records to delete all references in the records to the place of residence of either party appointed as a conservator of the child before the release of the records to another party appointed as a conservator.

§ 153.013. False Report of Child Abuse.

(a) If a party to a pending suit affecting the parent-child relationship makes a report alleging child abuse by another party to the suit that the reporting party knows lacks a factual foundation, the court shall deem the report to be a knowingly false report.

(b) Evidence of a false report of child abuse is admissible in a suit between the involved parties regarding the terms of conservatorship of a child.

(c) If the court makes a finding under Subsection (a), the court shall impose a civil penalty not to exceed $500.

§ 153.014. Visitation Centers and Visitation Exchange Facilities.

A county may establish a visitation center or a visitation exchange facility for the purpose of facilitating the terms of a court order providing for the possession of or access to a child.

Subchapter B. Parent Appointed as Conservator: In General

Introductory Comment

The Family Code originally allocated powers of conservators along the lines of managing and possessory conservators. The parent-managing conservator had "all the rights of a parent" to the exclusion of the parent-possessory conservator, except for those rights specifically allocated to the PC. Gradually, the lines became blurred with the rise, first of the ability of parents to agree to joint conservatorship, then of the power of a court to order joint conservatorship, and since 1995, the presumption of joint conservatorship. Accordingly, the various rights and duties of conservators must now be allocated to the parties as independent, joint, or exclusive rights. This subchapter defines certain rights to exist at all times and other rights that exist only when the child is with the conservator.

CLE/Other Legal Publications

Overcoming presumption in SAPCRs, JMC, SPO and parental presumptions. Sally H. Emerson, 2004 Adv. Fam. L.

Relocation debate. Kathryn J. Murphy & Mary Johanna McCurley, 2004 Adv. Fam. L.

Immigration and its effect on relocation, jurisdiction and divorce. J. Joseph Reina, 2004 Adv. Fam. L.

To move or not to move? That is the question! Barbara D. Nunnelly, 2004 Marriage Dissolution

Relocation. Jan Marie DeLipsey & Barbara D. Nunneley, 2004 U. Tex. Fam. L. Front Lines

Rebutting the joint custody presumption—child preferences. Darcy E. Loveless, 2003 Adv. Fam. L.

Dangerously giving up rights—to share or not to share. Wendy S. Burgower & Charlotte D. Rainwater, 2003 Marriage Dissolution

Rights and duties of parents, grandparents and non-parents. Curtis M. Loveless, 2002 Adv. Fam. L.

Parental alienation: syndrome or symptom. Reginald A. Hirsch, 2002 Adv. Fam. L.

Rebutting the JMC presumption. Coye Conner, Jr., 2001 Adv. Fam. L.

Dealing with mobile parents: domicile restrictions and relocation. Jennifer Tull, 2001 Adv. Fam. L.

Using MMPI (and other psychological tests) to establish character traits impacting parental abilities. Patricia A. Wicoff & Jeffrey Siegal, 2001 Adv. Fam. L.

Visitation: a psychological perspective. Jan Marie DeLipsey, 2001 Adv. Fam. L.

Sex, lies, and psychologists. Panel, 2001 Adv. Fam. L.

Parental alienation syndrome. Anne Turner Beletic & Richard Washak, 2000 Adv. Fam. L.

How to get even when you already are: equal evidence custody cases. Kevin R. Fuller, 2000 Marriage Dissolution

Leading Cases

Phillips v. Beaber, 995 S.W.2d 655 (Tex. 1999), *reversing*, 971 S.W.2d 127 (parent with right to establish principle residence is equivalent of sole MC, modification of terms of JMC constitutes a suit to modify custody)

Lewelling v. Lewelling, 796 S.W.2d 164 (Tex. 1990) (statutory parental preference creates strong presumption)

Urbish v. 127th Judicial District Court, 708 S.W.2d 429 (Tex. 1986) (noncustodial parent's right to maintain suit on behalf of minor child upheld when MC slow to object)

Ex parte Rhodes, 352 S.W.2d 249 (Tex. 1961) (restrictions on custodian's power to choose domicile of child upheld)

In re Ostrofsky, 112 S.W.3d 825 (Tex. App.—Houston [14th] 2003, orig. proceeding) (temporary order placing children in boarding school deprives mother of possession of children and her right to determine primary residence)

In re Z.B.P., 109 S.W.3d 772 (Tex. App.—Fort Worth 2003, no pet.) (traditional household in children's best interest)

In re K.R.P., 80 S.W.3d 669 (Tex. App.—Houston [1st Dist.] 2002, pet. denied) (step-parent named sole MC over wishes of unfit biological parents)

In re A.P.S., 54 S.W.3d 493 (Tex. App.—Texarkana 2001, no pet.) (in an order appointing a parent as possessory conservator, the trial court must specifically state the times and conditions for possession of or access to the children)

In re Lemons, 47 S.W.3d 202 (Tex. App.—Beaumont 2001, orig. proceeding) (trial court may not order "reasonable visitation;" court must specify rights and duties and time periods for noncustodial parent to have possession of and access to the child)

Enochs v. Brown, 872 S.W.2d 312 (Tex. App.—Austin 1994, no writ) (MC empowered to contract with lawyer to pursue child's tort claim—PC lacks standing to object)

---

§ 153.071. Court to Specify Rights and Duties of Parent Appointed a Conservator.

If both parents are appointed as conservators of the child, the court shall specify the rights and duties of a parent that are to be exercised:

(1) by each parent independently;

(2) by the joint agreement of the parents; and

(3) exclusively by one parent.

§ 153.072. Written Finding Required to Limit Parental Rights and Duties.

The court may limit the rights and duties of a parent appointed as a conservator if the court makes a written finding that the limitation is in the best interest of the child.

§ 153.073. Rights of Parent at All Times.

(a) Unless limited by court order, a parent appointed as a conservator of a child has at all times the right:

(1) to receive information from any other conservator of the child concerning the health, education, and welfare of the child;

(2) to confer with the other parent to the extent possible before making a decision concerning the health, education, and welfare of the child;

(3) of access to medical, dental, psychological, and educational records of the child;

(4) to consult with a physician, dentist, or psychologist of the child;

(5) to consult with school officials concerning the child's welfare and educational status, including school activities;

(6) to attend school activities;

(7) to be designated on the child's records as a person to be notified in case of an emergency;

(8) to consent to medical, dental, and surgical treatment during an emergency involving an immediate danger to the health and safety of the child; and

(9) to manage the estate of the child to the extent the estate has been created by the parent or the parent's family.

(b) The court shall specify in the order the rights that a parent retains at all times.

Leading Case

Abrams v. Jones, 35 S.W.3d 620 (Tex. 2000) (psychological records do not have to be revealed to parent when psychologist testifies conclusively that disclosure to parent would be harmful to child)

---

§ 153.074. Rights and Duties During Period of Possession.

Unless limited by court order, a parent appointed as a conservator of a child has the following rights and duties during the period that the parent has possession of the child:

(1) the duty of care, control, protection, and reasonable discipline of the child;

(2) the duty to support the child, including providing the child with clothing, food, shelter, and medical and dental care not involving an invasive procedure;

(3) the right to consent for the child to medical and dental care not involving an invasive procedure; and

(4) the right to direct the moral and religious training of the child.

Comment

Deleting former subdivision (4) cures a redundancy with § 153.073(a)(8), which gives a parent the right to consent to medical treatment in an emergency at all times.

---

§ 153.075. Duties of Parent Not Appointed Conservator.

The court may order a parent not appointed as a managing or a possessory conservator to perform other parental duties, including paying child support.

§ 153.076. Duty to Provide Information.

(a) **The** [~~If both parents are appointed as conservators of the child, the~~] court shall order that **each conservator of a child** [~~parent~~] has a duty to inform the other **conservator of the child** [~~parent~~] in a timely manner of significant information concerning the health, education, and welfare of the child.

(b) **The** [~~If both parents are appointed as conservators of a child, the~~] court shall order that **each conservator of a child** [~~parent~~] has the duty to inform the other **conservator of the child** [~~parent~~] if the **conservator** [~~parent~~] resides with for at least 30 days, marries, or intends to marry a person who the **conservator** [~~parent~~] knows:

(1) is registered as a sex offender under Chapter 62, Code of Criminal Procedure [~~, as added by Chapter 668, Acts of the 75th Legislature, Regular Session, 1997~~]; or

(2) is currently charged with an offense for which on conviction the person would be required to register under that chapter.

(c) The notice required to be made under Subsection (b) must be made as soon as practicable but not later than the 40th day after the date the **conservator of the child** [~~parent~~] begins to reside with the person or the 10th day after the date the marriage occurs, as appropriate. The notice must include a description of the offense that is the basis of the person's requirement to register as a sex offender or of the offense with which the person is charged.

(d) A **conservator** [~~person~~] commits an offense if the **conservator** [~~person~~] fails to provide notice in the manner required by Subsections (b) and (c). An offense under this subsection is a Class C misdemeanor.

History: Amended by 78th Legis., Reg. Sess. (2003), H.B. 913, eff. Sept. 1, 2003, and applies "only to a court order providing for possession of or access to a child rendered on or after that date. A court order rendered before the effective date of this Act is governed by the law in effect on the date the order was rendered, and the former law is continued in effect for that purpose."

Comment

From one perspective, subsection (a) is merely a statement of sound public policy directing civilized behavior between parents after their appointment as conservators. Often the legislature enacts such statements of public policy, even though enforceability may be questionable or impossible. This latter aspect led to some controversy over this particular provision because it appears that the failure to define "timely manner" and "significant information" probably renders the court order unenforceable by contempt.

Subsections (b)-(d), on the other hand, may be criticized because: (1) the behavior described does not sound particularly civilized; (2) the provisions were drafted for very rare instances; and (3) almost surely a parent covered by the statute will disobey it if and when such a fact situation does arise, either consciously or unknowingly.

Subchapter C. Parent Appointed as Sole or Joint Managing Conservator

Introductory Comment

Joint managing conservatorship was introduced to Texas law in 1979, when such arrangements were permitted by agreement only. In 1987, the legislature granted the trial court the authority to order a JMC. Theoretically, at least, such an arrangement may be imposed on two unwilling parents. A distinguishing feature of the Texas statute is the fact that, either by agreement or by court order, the process for reaching certain decisions must be included in the decree. Issues that have a heightened likelihood for future controversy must be resolved in advance, such as the method for determining the residence/domicile of the child and where the child will go to school. Either joint managing conservator may be awarded the authority to determine these issues, or the court itself may fix the outcome in advance, *e.g.,* the child resides in Travis County, Texas, and attends public school until further order of the court.

Successive amendments in 1987, 1991, 1993, 1995, and 1999 triggered dramatic changes in the appointment of a parent as a managing conservator since the Family Code was enacted.

Although there may be innumerable reasons why appointment of a parent is not in the best interest of a child, the statute provides that there is only one satisfactory reason to deny a parent's appointment as a managing conservator (either sole or joint). The "best interest test" is limited by the restriction that a parent should be denied managing conservatorship only if "appointment would significantly impair the child's physical health or emotional development." The fact that another contesting party, most typically a grandparent, would likely be a better custodian is not sufficient to rebut the parental preference. That presumption, however, remains fully rebuttable if the facts warrant a finding of future harm to the child.

The "winner-loser" aspect of custody litigation between parents came to an end with the deletion of the statement that "a parent appointed as sole managing conservator of the child retains all the rights, privileges, duties, and powers of a parent to the exclusion of the other parent, subject to the rights, privileges, duties, and powers of a possessory conservator ... and, to any limitation imposed by court order.... "To replace this relatively harsh statement, the legislature substituted lists of rights of parents at all times and during possession, *supra*, and those exclusive to the managing conservator, *infra*.

The 1995 addition creating a presumption of joint managing conservatorship is, in the opinion of the authors, far less revolutionary than might be supposed at first glance. The amendment, standing alone without amending the details of court-ordered JMC, does little more than change the title of the parents, who are presumptively appointed as JMCs. The relationships between the "custodial" and "noncustodial" parent JMCs remain basically unchanged as far as the balance of the relevant statutes are concerned. The effect on the psychology of the JMC parents may be more significant.

CLE/Other Legal Publications

Overcoming presumption in SAPCRs, JMC, SPO and parental presumptions. Sally H. Emerson, 2004 ADV. FAM. L.

The art of evaluating a custody case. Keith M. Nelson, 2004 ADV. FAM. L.

Developing and preparing witnesses in custody cases. Jo Chris G. Lopez, 2004 ADV. FAM. L.

Overcoming presumption in SAPCRs, JMC, SPO and parental presumptions. Sally H. Emerson, 2004 ADV. FAM. L.

How to settle hard to settle cases involving children. Kevin R. Fuller, 2004 MARRIAGE DISSOLUTION

Bad facts custody cases. JoAl Cannon–Sheridan, 2003 ADV. FAM. L.

Dangerously giving up rights—to share or not to share. Wendy S. Burgower & Charlotte D. Rainwater, 2003 MARRIAGE DISSOLUTION

Handling a custody case on a shoe string. Glenn David Villafranca, 2003 ADV. FAM. L.

Rebutting the joint custody presumption—child preferences. Darcy Elizabeth Loveless, 2003 ADV. FAM. L.

Myths and truths regarding the affect of divorce on children (and the role family law attorneys can play, morally and emotionally to alleviate their hurt and pain). E. Edward Reitman, 2003 ADV. FAM. L.

Representing extended family and non–family members (parental presumptions, post-Troxel grandparents). Stewart W. Gagnon, 2003 ADV. FAM. L.

Relocation—can you pass go? Douglas R. Woodburn, 2003 ADV. FAM. L.

Custody. (Workshop) 2003 ADV. FAM. L.

Psychological testing (a primer on psychological testing—what are they, how to interpret and use, validity and liability). Keith M. Nelson, 2003 ADV. FAM. L.

International—unusual child issues, Hague, Indian child welfare, UCCJEA, etc. (Workshop) 2003 ADV. FAM. L.

Rights and duties of parents, grandparents and non-parents. Curtis M. Loveless, 2002 ADV. FAM. L.

Relocation—where is anyone going? Joan F. Jenkins, 2002 ADV. FAM. L.

Leading Cases

Santosky v. Kramer, 455 U.S. 745, 71 L.Ed.2d 599, 102 S.Ct. 1388 (1982) (constitutional dimensions of parent-child relationship)

Phillips v. Beaber, 995 S.W.2d 655 (Tex. 1999) (JMC-parent's right to establish principle residence is equivalent of sole MC; modification of that term of JMC constitutes a suit to modify custody)

Brook v. Brook, 881 S.W.2d 297 (Tex. 1994) (parental preference not offended when one parent named JMC with a nonparent)

Lewelling v. Lewelling, 796 S.W.2d 164 (Tex. 1990) (statutory parental preference creates strong presumption)

Ex parte Rhodes, 352 S.W.2d 249 (Tex. 1961) (restrictions on custodian's power to choose domicile of child)

In re C.J.F., ___ S.W.3d ____ (Tex. App.—Amarillo 2003, pet. denied) (parental presumption rebutted)

In re P.D.M., 117 S.W.3d 453 (Tex. App.—Fort Worth 2003, pet. denied) (grandmother's suit after death of managing conservator is not original suit subject to father's parental presumption)

Lide v. Lide, 116 S.W.3d 147 (Tex. App.—E1 Paso 2003, no pet.) (JMC presumption rebutted)

In re Ostrofsky, 112 S.W.3d 925 (Tex. App.—Houston [14th Dist.] 2003, no pet.) (temporary order sending children to boarding school deprived joint managing conservator of right to determine primary residence)

Robinson v. Robinson, 16 S.W.3d 451 (Tex. App.—Waco 2000, no pet.) (JMC presumption rebutted by conflict and geographical distance between the parents)

Gray v. Gray, 971 S.W.2d 212 (Tex. App.—Beaumont 1998, no pet.) (modification awarding JMC 50/50 time split affirmed on appeal)

In re Rodriguez, 940 S.W.2d 265 (Tex. App.—San Antonio 1997, writ denied) (unrelated caretakers since birth of two-year-old prevail over biological father)

In re Ferguson, 927 S.W.2d 766 (Tex. App.—Texarkana 1996, no writ) (parental presumption doesn't apply when modification of grandparents' managing conservatorship sought by mother)

Bruneio v. Bruneio, 890 S.W.2d 150 (Tex. App.—Corpus Christi 1994, no writ) (father's special appearance and custody contest entitles him to notice of trial setting)

R.S. v. B.J.J., 883 S.W.2d 711 (Tex. App.—Dallas 1994, no writ) (nonparents prevail in custody battle with parents following lengthy voluntary relinquishment of possession)

Whitwell v. Whitwell, 878 S.W.2d 221 (Tex. App.—El Paso 1994, no writ) (Australian mother of disabled child prevails in custody battle with paternal grandparents)

Alaniz v. Alaniz, 867 S.W.2d 54 (Tex. App.—El Paso 1993, no writ) (state cannot prefer one religious belief over another)

Brigham v. Brigham, 863 S.W.2d 761 (Tex. App.—Dallas 1993, writ denied) (leaving town without disclosing whereabouts is not evidence that party will harm child)

Thomas v. Thomas, 852 S.W.2d 31 (Tex. App.—Waco 1993, no writ) (presumption of parental custody creates heavy burden on nonparent for conservatorship)

Ray v. Burns, 832 S.W.2d 431 (Tex. App.—Waco 1992, no writ) (grandmother and her employers appointed as JMC's)

Landry v. Nauls, 831 S.W.2d 603 (Tex. App.—Houston [14th Dist.] 1992, no writ) (nonparty grandparent can't be named managing conservator)

May v. May, 829 S.W.2d 373 (Tex. App.—Corpus Christi 1992, writ denied) (grandfather rebuts parental preference, father's claim that drug habit overcome not persuasive)

Neely v. Neely, 698 S.W.2d 758 (Tex. App.—Austin 1985, no writ) (evidence insufficient to rebut presumption that parent prevails over custody claims of step-parent)

Matter of Marriage of Knighton, 685 S.W.2d 719 (Tex. App.—Amarillo 1984), *appeal after remand* 723 S.W.2d 274 ("appropriate" religious training of child not for court to decide)

---

§ 153.131. Presumption That Parent to be Appointed Managing Conservator.

(a) Subject to the prohibition in Section 153.004, unless the court finds that appointment of the parent or parents would not be in the best interest of the child because the appointment would significantly impair the child's physical health or emotional development, a parent shall be appointed sole managing conservator or both parents shall be appointed as joint managing conservators of the child.

(b) It is a rebuttable presumption that the appointment of the parents of a child as joint managing conservators is in the best interest of the child. A finding of a history of family violence involving the parents of a child removes the presumption under this subsection.

Comment

In 1995 this section created a rebuttable presumption that the naming of parents as JMCs is in the best interest of the child. The substantive provisions regulating the appointment of joint managing conservators and the terms of joint conservatorship are not affected in any way by this particular section. The rule regarding the appointment of a parent to furnish the primary residence is continued, § 153.136, *infra*, and the statutory statement that joint managing conservatorship in Texas does not require "equal or nearly equal periods of physical possession" is unchanged, § 153.135, *infra*. Undoubtedly there has been a significant psychological impact on many parents thanks to the legislative declaration that JMC is presumptively in the best interest of the child. Whether that psychological impact has been positive or negative unquestionably has varied greatly from couple to couple. Following the 1995 enactment, considerable discussion ensued about the wisdom—or lack thereof—of the JMC presumption. It seems clear from the lack of discussion about the issue in the 2001 legislative session that Texas Family Law attorneys, their clients, and spokespersons for various interest groups have adjusted to the decision.

CLE/Other Legal Publications

Overcoming presumption in SAPCRs, JMC, SPO and parental presumptions. Sally H. Emerson, 2004 Adv. Fam. L.

Rebutting the Joint Custody Presumption—Child Preferences. Darcy Elizabeth Loveless, 2003 Adv. Fam. L.

Rebutting the JMC presumption. Coye Conner, Jr., 2001 Adv. Fam. L.

How to get even when you already are: equal evidence custody cases. Kevin R. Fuller, 2000 Marriage Dissolution

Leading Cases

Lewelling v. Lewelling, 796 S.W.2d 164 (Tex. 1990) (statutory parental preference creates strong presumption)

In re C.J.F., ___ S.W.3d ___ (Tex. App.—Amarillo 2003, pet. denied) (parental presumption rebutted)

In re P.D.M., 117 S.W.3d 453 (Tex. App.—Fort Worth 2003, pet. denied) (grandmother's suit after death of managing conservator is not original suit subject to father's parental presumption)

In re K.R.P., 80 S.W.3d 669 (Tex. App.—Houston [1st Dist.] 2002, pet. denied) (former step-parent named sole MC over wishes of unfit parents)

Robinson v. Robinson, 16 S.W.3d 451 (Tex. App.—Waco 1999, no pet.) (JMC presumption rebutted, jury's choice of father as sole MC stands)

Doyle v. Doyle, 955 S.W.2d 478 (Tex. App.—Austin 1997, no writ) (presumption of joint managing conservatorship rebutted by evidence of suspicion and hostility)

---

§ 153.132. Rights and Duties of Parent Appointed Sole Managing Conservator.

Unless limited by court order, a parent appointed as sole managing conservator of a child has the rights and duties provided by Subchapter B and the following exclusive rights:

(1) the right to designate the primary residence of the child;

(2) the right to consent to medical, dental, and surgical treatment involving invasive procedures, and to consent to psychiatric and psychological treatment;

(3) the right to receive and give receipt for periodic payments for the support of the child and to hold or disburse these funds for the benefit of the child;

(4) the right to represent the child in legal action and to make other decisions of substantial legal significance concerning the child;

(5) the right to consent to marriage and to enlistment in the armed forces of the United States;

(6) the right to make decisions concerning the child's education;

(7) the right to the services and earnings of the child; and

(8) except when a guardian of the child's estate or a guardian or attorney ad litem has been appointed for the child, the right to act as an agent of the child in relation to the child's estate if the child's action is required by a state, the United States, or a foreign government.

Comment

Throughout the Family Code the right to "establish the primary residence" has been changed to provide the right to "designate" that residence. Apparently moderate or minor change in terminology makes it clear that the person with the right to designate may determine that the child will live with grandma or be sent to a private military school in New Mexico to learn discipline.

Leading Case

Lueg v. Lueg, 976 S.W.2d 308 (Tex. App.—Corpus Christi 1998, pet. denied) (error to order sole MC father to pay child support to PC mother)

---

§ 153.133. Agreement for Joint Managing Conservatorship.

(a) If a written agreement of the parents is filed with the court, the court shall render an order appointing the parents as joint managing conservators only if the agreement:

(1) designates the conservator who has the exclusive right to designate the primary residence of the child and:

(A) establishes, until modified by further order, the geographic area within which the conservator shall maintain the child's primary residence; or

(B) specifies that the conservator may designate the child's primary residence without regard to geographic location;

(2) specifies the rights and duties of each parent regarding the child's physical care, support, and education;

(3) includes provisions to minimize disruption of the child's education, daily routine, and association with friends;

(4) allocates between the parents, independently, jointly, or exclusively, all of the remaining rights and duties of a parent provided by Chapter 151 *[Rights and Duties in Parent–Child Relationship]*;

(5) is voluntarily and knowingly made by each parent and has not been repudiated by either parent at the time the order is rendered; and

(6) is in the best interest of the child.

(b) The agreement may contain an alternative dispute resolution procedure that the parties agree to use before requesting enforcement or modification of the terms and conditions of the joint conservatorship through litigation, except in an emergency.

§ 153.134. Court-Ordered Joint Conservatorship.

(a) If a written agreement of the parents is not filed with the court, the court may render an order appointing the parents joint managing conservators only if the appointment is in the best interest of the child, considering the following factors:

(1) whether the physical, psychological, or emotional needs and development of the child will benefit from the appointment of joint managing conservators;

(2) the ability of the parents to give first priority to the welfare of the child and reach shared decisions in the child's best interest;

(3) whether each parent can encourage and accept a positive relationship between the child and the other parent;

(4) whether both parents participated in child rearing before the filing of the suit;

(5) the geographical proximity of the parents' residences;

(6) if the child is 12 years of age or older, the child's preference, if any, regarding the appointment of joint managing conservators; and

(7) any other relevant factor.

(b) In rendering an order appointing joint managing conservators, the court shall:

(1) designate the conservator who has the exclusive right to determine the primary residence of the child and:

(A) establish, until modified by further order, a geographic area within which the conservator shall maintain the child's primary residence; or

(B) specify that the conservator may determine the child's primary residence without regard to geographic location;

(2) specify the rights and duties of each parent regarding the child's physical care, support, and education;

(3) include provisions to minimize disruption of the child's education, daily routine, and association with friends;

(4) allocate between the parents, independently, jointly, or exclusively, all of the remaining rights and duties of a parent as provided by Chapter 151 *[Rights and Duties in Parent–Child Relationship]*; and

(5) if feasible, recommend that the parties use an alternative dispute resolution method before requesting enforcement or modification of the terms and conditions of the joint conservatorship through litigation, except in an emergency.

Comment

The issue of the right to determine the primary residence of a child by a joint managing conservator has refocused the relocation issue in this context. Recent amendments to this section, and the preceding section dealing with agreements, places the area of conflict exactly where it belongs, between joint conservators. That is, with the same title the real issues are with whom does the child live and which JMC has the right to determine just exactly where that will be? In both the agreement context and the court-ordered JMC contest, this is the crucial issue.

CLE/Other Legal Publications

Rebutting the JMC presumption. Coye Conner, Jr., 2001 ADV. FAM. L.

The dilemma of the child who has chosen: dealing with children's preferences in custody litigation. J. Lindsey Short, Jr., 2001 ADV. FAM. L.

From the mouths of babes: the art of interviewing children in chambers. Judy Parker & Peter A. Sakai, 2001 ADV. FAM. L.

Leading Cases

Phillips v. Beaber, 995 S.W.2d 655 (Tex. 1999), *reversing* 971 S.W.2d 127 (parent with right to establish principle residence is equivalent of sole MC; modification of terms of JMC constitutes a suit to modify custody)

In re Ostrofsky, 112 S.W.3d 925 (Tex. App.—Houston [14th Dist.] 2003, no pet.) (temporary order sending children to boarding school deprived joint managing conservator of right to determine primary residence)

London v. London, 94 S.W.3d 139 (Tex. App.—Houston [14th Dist.] 2002, no pet.) (jury determines residency restriction and father's right to make educational decisions for his children)

Albrecht v. Albrecht, 974 S.W.2d 262 (Tex. App.—San Antonio 1998, no pet.) (jury's decision that father to be primary JMC may not be subverted by trial court's 50/50 time split)

Gray v. Gray, 971 S.W.2d 212 (Tex. App.—Beaumont 1998, no pet.) (modification awarding JMC 50/50 time split affirmed on appeal)

Dennis v. Smith, 962 S.W.2d 67 (Tex. App.—Houston [1st Dist.] 1997, pet. denied) (mother/JMC primary possessory parent, but father/JMC decides where child lives and goes to school)

Wood v. O'Donnell, 894 S.W.2d 555 (Tex. App.—Fort Worth 1995, no writ) (modification of JMC to allow relocation reversed when trial court found move not in child's best interest)

---

§ 153.135. Equal Possession Not Required.

Joint managing conservatorship does not require the award of equal or nearly equal periods of physical possession of and access to the child to each of the joint conservators.

§ 153.136. [~~Court Designation of Primary Physical Residence.~~] [repealed]

§ 153.137. Guidelines for the Possession of Child by Parent Named as Joint Managing Conservator.

The standard possession order provided by Subchapter F constitutes a presumptive minimum amount of time for possession of a child by a parent named as a joint managing conservator who is not awarded the exclusive right to designate the primary residence of the child in a suit.

§ 153.138. Child Support Order Affecting Joint Conservators.

The appointment of joint managing conservators does not impair or limit the authority of the court to order a joint managing conservator to pay child support to another joint managing conservator.

§ 153.139. [repealed]

Subchapter D. Parent Appointed as Possessory Conservator

Introductory Comment

The Texas Legislature has periodically recalibrated the rights of managing conservators and possessory conservators. Generally this process has resulted in significant expansion of the rights of a possessory conservator. But, the importance of this section has been greatly reduced by the specificity now included in the standard possession order, *infra.*

CLE/Other Legal Publication

Keeping the family intact after the pots and pans are divided: negotiating and trying creative possession schedules. Jo Chris G. Lopez, 2002 Adv. Fam. L.

Exceeding or varying from possession guidelines: creative strategies for possession orders and dealing with toddlers and teens. Jan Marie DeLipsey & Barbara D. Nunneley, 2001 Adv. Fam. L.

Visitation: a psychological perspective. Jan Marie DeLipsey, 2001 Adv. Fam. L.

Leading Cases

Ex parte MacCallum, 807 S.W.2d 729 (Tex. 1991) (no clear order to return children from weekend visitation)

Ex parte Brister, 801 S.W.2d 833 (Tex. 1990) (visitation order ambiguous, not enforceable by contempt—irregular work schedule)

Martin v. Martin, 776 S.W.2d 572 (Tex. 1989) (terms of possessory conservatorship within court's discretion; jury denied in modification action)

In re A.P.S., 54 S.W.3d 493 (Tex. App.—Texarkana 2001, no pet.) (order giving father's complete discretion over possessory-conservator mother's access to children error) (in an order appointing a parent as possessory conservator, the trial court must specifically state the times and conditions for possession of or access to the children)

In re Walters, 39 S.W.3d 280 (Tex. App.—Texarkana 2001, no pet.) (because mother appointed PC, error not to provide specific conditions and times for access and possession)

Roosth v. Roosth, 889 S.W.2d 444 (Tex. App.—Houston [14th Dist.] 1994, no writ) (order subjecting father's visitation to mother's approval abuse of discretion)

Hopkins v. Hopkins, 853 S.W.2d 134 (Tex. App.—Corpus Christi 1993, no writ) (if parent awarded visitation, possessory conservatorship must be ordered)

Green v. Green, 850 S.W.2d 809 (Tex. App.—El Paso 1993, writ denied) (father denied possessory conservatorship due to child's wishes and his vulgar and "mean" behavior towards child)

Zetune v. Jafif-Zetune, 774 S.W.2d 387 (Tex. App.—Dallas 1989, writ denied) (visitation provisions did not violate father's religious rights), *cert. denied*, 498 U.S. 813, 112 L. Ed. 2d 26, 111 S.Ct. 51 (1990)

---

§ 153.191. Presumption that Parent to be Appointed Possessory Conservator.

The court shall appoint as a possessory conservator a parent who is not appointed as a sole or joint managing conservator unless it finds that the appointment is not in the best interest of the child and that parental possession or access would endanger the physical or emotional welfare of the child.

§ 153.192. Rights and Duties of Parent Appointed Possessory Conservator.

(a) Unless limited by court order, a parent appointed as possessory conservator of a child has the rights and duties provided by Subchapter B and any other right or duty expressly granted to the possessory conservator in the order.

(b) In ordering the terms and conditions for possession of a child by a parent appointed possessory conservator, the court shall be guided by the guidelines in Subchapter E.

§ 153.193. Minimal Restriction on Parent's Possession or Access.

The terms of an order that denies possession of a child to a parent or imposes restrictions or limitations on a parent's right to possession of or access to a child may not exceed those that are required to protect the best interest of the child.

Subchapter E. Guidelines for the Possession of a Child by a Parent Named as Possessory Conservator

Introductory Comment

These statutory guidelines apply to a parent named as a possessory conservator or to a managing conservator not awarded primary possession; guidelines do not exist for possession of or access to a child by a nonparental possessory conservator. Further, the standard order, *infra*, specifically is applicable only to children three years of age or older; no guidelines exist for a child under three. Very young children, infants through toddlers, must be dealt with individually. However, the standard order is designed to automatically take effect when a child reaches age three. This constitutes legislative approval of a prospective order.

CLE/Other Legal Publications

Overcoming presumption in SAPCRs, JMC, SPO and parental presumptions. Sally H. Emerson, 2004 Adv. Fam. L.

Keeping the family intact after the pots and pans are divided: negotiating and trying creative possession schedules. Jo Chris G. Lopez, 2002 Adv. Fam. L.

Protective/restrictive possession: substance abuse, family violence and other perils. Sally H. Emerson, 2002 Marriage Dissolution

When one size doesn't fit all: unusual issues in structuring possession orders. Marilea W. Lewis, 2002 Marriage Dissolution

Exceeding or varying from possession guidelines: creative strategies for possession orders and dealing with toddlers and teens. Jan Marie DeLipsey & Barbara D. Nunneley, 2001 Adv. Fam. L.

Leading Cases

In re A.P.S., 54 S.W.3d 493 (Tex. App.—Texarkana 2001, no pet.) (mother a danger to two daughters, but award of possessory conservatorship means that access cannot be left to sole discretion of father; in an order appointing a parent as PC, the trial court must specifically state the times and conditions for possession of or access to the children)

In re Lemons, 47 S.W.3d 202 (Tex. App.—Beaumont 2001, no pet.) (absolute discretion over mother's "reasonable visitation" by father in temporary order created lack of enforceability by mother which effectively denied the mother's right to visitation with her child)

---

§ 153.251. Policy and General Application of Guidelines.

(a) The guidelines established in the standard possession order are intended to guide the courts in ordering the terms and conditions for possession of a child by a parent named as a possessory conservator or as the minimum possession for a joint managing conservator.

(b) It is the policy of this state to encourage frequent contact between a child and each parent for periods of possession that optimize the development of a close and continuing relationship between each parent and child.

(c) It is preferable for all children in a family to be together during periods of possession.

(d) The standard possession order is designed to apply to a child three years of age or older.

§ 153.252. Rebuttable Presumption.

In a suit, there is a rebuttable presumption that the standard possession order in Subchapter F:

(1) provides reasonable minimum possession of a child for a parent named as a possessory conservator or joint managing conservator; and

(2) is in the best interest of the child.

§ 153.253. Standard Possession Order Inappropriate or Unworkable.

The court shall render an order that grants periods of possession of the child as similar as possible to those provided by the standard possession order if the work schedule or other special circumstances of the managing conservator, the possessory conservator, or the child, or the year-round school schedule of the child, make the standard order unworkable or inappropriate.

§ 153.254. Child Less Than Three Years of Age.

(a) The court shall render an order appropriate under the circumstances for possession of a child less than three years of age.

(b) The court shall render a prospective order to take effect on the child's third birthday, which presumptively will be the standard possession order.

§ 153.255. Agreement.

The court may render an order for periods of possession of a child that vary from the standard possession order based on the agreement of the parties.

§ 153.256. Factors for Court to Consider.

In ordering the terms of possession of a child under an order other than a standard possession order, the court shall be guided by the guidelines established by the standard possession order and may consider:

(1) the age, developmental status, circumstances, needs, and best interest of the child;

(2) the circumstances of the managing conservator and of the parent named as a possessory conservator; and

(3) any other relevant factor.

§ 153.257. Means of Travel.

In an order providing for the terms and conditions of possession of a child, the court may restrict the means of travel of the child by a legal mode of transportation only after a showing of good cause contained in the record and a finding by the court that the restriction is in the best interest of the child. The court shall specify the duties of the conservators to provide transportation to and from the transportation facilities.

§ 153.258. Request for Findings When Order Varies From Standard Order.

Without regard to Rules 296 through 299, Texas Rules of Civil Procedure, in all cases in which possession of a child by a parent is contested and the possession of the child varies from the standard possession order, on written request made or filed with the court not later than 10 days after the date of the hearing or on oral request made in open court during the hearing, the court shall state in the order the specific reasons for the variance from the standard order.

Texas Family Law Practice Manual

Form 20–7. Request for Findings in Possession Order

Subchapter F. Standard Possession Order

Introductory Comment

The standard possession order contemplates the rendition of a single, uniform order to remain in effect throughout the period of conservatorship. The reality of a child's life does not intrude on the uniformity of the standard order. It is one thing to order regular weekend visitation for a six year old and expect enforcement. It is quite another to expect compliance of an inflexible schedule in dealing with a 16 year old. The order is designed to cover parents who live "close," *i.e.*, 100 miles or less apart, and those who live "far apart," *i.e.,* over 100 miles.

CLE/Other Legal Publication

See annotations to Introductory Comment, Subchapter E, preceding § 153.251, *supra*.

Leading Cases

In re Lemons, 47 S.W.3d 202 (Tex. App.—Beaumont 2001, no pet.) (absolute discretion over mother's "reasonable visitation" by father in temporary order created lack of enforceability by mother which effectively denied the mother's right to visitation with her child)

Jacobs v. Dobrei, 991 S.W.2d 462 (Tex. App.—Dallas 1999, no pet.) (not religious discrimination to award Christmas vacation to mother and Jewish holidays to father)

In re Bertram, 981 S.W.2d 820 (Tex. App.—Texarkana 1998, no pet.) (Texas dad ordered to pick up and return children in Wisconsin is abuse of discretion violating visitation guidelines)

Weldon v. Weldon, 968 S.W.2d 515 (Tex. App.—Texarkana 1998, no pet.) (modification of terms of visitation governed by Chapter 156—Chapter 153 guidelines don't apply)

Wright v. Wright, 867 S.W.2d 807 (Tex. App.—El Paso 1993, writ denied) (variations and alternative arrangements to standard possession order within trial court's discretion)

Voros v. Turnage, 856 S.W.2d 759 (Tex. App.—Houston [1st Dist.] 1993, writ denied) (deviation from standard possession order upheld)

Thompson v. Thompson, 827 S.W.2d 563 (Tex. App.—Corpus Christi 1992, writ denied) (summer-only visitation is an abuse of court's discretion absent sufficient evidence to justify such a restricted schedule)

Texas Family Law Practice Manual

Forms 17–2. Additional Provisions for Long-Distance Access and Visitation; *17–3.* Additional Provisions for Jewish Religious Holidays

---

§ 153.311. Mutual Agreement or Specified Terms for Possession.

The court shall specify in a standard possession order that the parties may have possession of the child at times mutually agreed to in advance by the parties and, in the absence of mutual agreement, shall have possession of the child under the specified terms set out in the standard order.

Comment

This is the most important substantive provision in the standard order. This crucial section provides that the parties may mutually agree to vary the possession of a child at any time, in any mutually acceptable manner, and that the specific terms set out in the standard order take effect only failing such mutual agreement.

---

§ 153.312. Parents Who Reside 100 Miles or Less Apart.

(a) If the possessory conservator resides 100 miles or less from the primary residence of the child, the possessory conservator shall have the right to possession of the child as follows:

(1) on weekends beginning at 6 p.m. on the first, third, and fifth Friday of each month and ending at 6 p.m. on the following Sunday or, at the possessory conservator's election made before or at the time of the rendition of the original or modification order, and as specified in the original or modification order, beginning at the time the child's school is regularly dismissed and ending at 6 p.m. on the following Sunday; and

(2) on **Thursdays** [~~Wednesdays~~] of each week during the regular school term beginning at 6 p.m. and ending at 8 p.m., or, at the possessory conservator's election made before or at the time of the rendition of the original or modification order, and as specified in the original or modification order, beginning at the time the child's school is regularly dismissed and ending at the time the child's school resumes, unless the court finds that visitation under this subdivision is not in the best interest of the child.

(b) The following provisions govern possession of the child for vacations and certain specific holidays and supersede conflicting weekend or Wednesday periods of possession. The possessory conservator and the managing conservator shall have rights of possession of the child as follows:

(1) the possessory conservator shall have possession in even-numbered years, beginning at 6 p.m. on the day the child is dismissed from school for the school's spring

vacation and ending at 6 p.m. on the day before school resumes after that vacation, and the managing conservator shall have possession for the same period in odd-numbered years;

(2) if a possessory conservator:

(A) gives the managing conservator written notice by April 1 of each year specifying an extended period or periods of summer possession, the possessory conservator shall have possession of the child for 30 days beginning not earlier than the day after the child's school is dismissed for the summer vacation and ending not later than seven days before school resumes at the end of the summer vacation, to be exercised in not more than two separate periods of at least seven consecutive days each; or

(B) does not give the managing conservator written notice by April 1 of each year specifying an extended period or periods of summer possession, the possessory conservator shall have possession of the child for 30 consecutive days beginning at 6 p.m. on July 1 and ending at 6 p.m. on July 31;

(3) if the managing conservator gives the possessory conservator written notice by April 15 of each year, the managing conservator shall have possession of the child on any one weekend beginning Friday at 6 p.m. and ending at 6 p.m. on the following Sunday during one period of possession by the possessory conservator under Subdivision (2), provided that the managing conservator picks up the child from the possessory conservator and returns the child to that same place; and

(4) if the managing conservator gives the possessory conservator written notice by April 15 of each year or gives the possessory conservator 14 days' written notice on or after April 16 of each year, the managing conservator may designate one weekend beginning not earlier than the day after the child's school is dismissed for the summer vacation and ending not later than seven days before school resumes at the end of the summer vacation, during which an otherwise scheduled weekend period of possession by the possessory conservator will not take place, provided that the weekend designated does not interfere with the possessory conservator's period or periods of extended summer possession or with Father's Day if the possessory conservator is the father of the child.

History: Amended by 78th Legis., Reg. Sess. (2003), H.B. 913, eff. Sept. 1, 2003, and applies "only to a court order providing for possession of or access to a child rendered on or after that date. A court order rendered before the effective date of this Act is governed by the law in effect on the date the order was rendered, and the former law is continued in effect for that purpose."

Editors' Note: *The legislature failed to amend § 153.312(b) to change the Wednesday period of possession to Thursday to comport with the other changes contained in H.B. 913.*

Comment

The standard possession order has become a way of life for family law practitioners. Basic acceptance of the terms of the standard order by the bench and bar is widely supported (remember when it was the end of Western Civilization as we have known it?).

There has been little real controversy in the basic right of possession to the child for the noncustodial parent who lives within relatively easy driving distance from the custodial parent and child. The first, third and fifth weekends have remained in place since the initiation of the standard order process. The mid-week possession has undergone some significant change since its first adoption, however. Originally, the Wednesday visit was purely a 6:00 p.m. to 8:00 p.m. affair, or to put it more bluntly, a mid-week meal visit. The first major change in this procedure was to provide that at the possessory conservator's election the mid-week meal could be converted into a mid-week overnight visit with the child being returned to the school the following morning. Moreover, the court was directed to approve this process on the request of the possessory conservator unless the court could rule it was "not in the best interest of the child."

In 2003 the second major change to this process occurred. For some time, the advocates for the possessory conservators (read father's groups) have lobbied for substituting Thursday for Wednesday. The rationale for the change is relatively simple. Thursday overnight means that the first, third and fifth weekend will always be a long weekend since the child will arrive Thursday evening and not return to the custodial parent's custody until the following Monday after school. Indeed, on holiday weekends it will be the following Tuesday after school before the child returns.

Identification of a serious dilemma: how long will it be before Luby's Cafeteria has to change its "kid's eat free on Wednesdays" offer to a Thursday program?

---

§ 153.313. Parents Who Reside Over 100 Miles Apart.

If the possessory conservator resides more than 100 miles from the residence of the child, the possessory conservator shall have the right to possession of the child as follows:

(1) either regular weekend possession beginning on the first, third, and fifth Friday as provided under the terms applicable to parents who reside 100 miles or less apart or not more than one weekend per month of the possessory conservator's choice beginning at 6 p.m. on the day school recesses for the weekend and ending at 6 p.m. on the day before school resumes after the weekend, provided that the possessory conservator gives the managing conservator 14 days' written or telephonic notice preceding a designated weekend, and provided that the possessory conservator elects an option for this alternative period of possession by written notice given to the managing conservator within 90 days after the parties begin to reside more than 100 miles apart, as applicable;

(2) each year beginning on the day the child is dismissed from school for the school's spring vacation and ending at 6 p.m. on the day before school resumes after that vacation;

(3) if the possessory conservator:

(A) gives the managing conservator written notice by April 1 of each year specifying an extended period or periods of summer possession, the possessory conservator shall have possession of the child for 42 days beginning not earlier than the day after the child's school is dismissed for the summer vacation and ending not later than seven days before school resumes at the end of the summer vacation, to be exercised in not more than two separate periods of at least seven consecutive days each; or

(B) does not give the managing conservator written notice by April 1 of each year specifying an extended period or periods of summer possession, the possessory conservator shall have possession of the child for 42 consecutive days beginning at 6 p.m. on June 15 and ending at 6 p.m. on July 27;

(4) if the managing conservator gives the possessory conservator written notice by April 15 of each year the managing conservator shall have possession of the child on one weekend beginning Friday at 6 p.m. and ending at 6 p.m. on the following Sunday during one period of possession by the possessory conservator under Subdivision (3), provided that if a period of possession by the possessory conservator exceeds 30 days, the managing conservator may have possession of the child under the terms of this subdivision on two nonconsecutive weekends during that time period, and further provided that the managing conservator picks up the child from the possessory conservator and returns the child to that same place; and

(5) if the managing conservator gives the possessory conservator written notice by April 15 of each year, the managing conservator may designate 21 days beginning not earlier than the day after the child's school is dismissed for the summer vacation and ending not later than seven days before school resumes at the end of the summer vacation, to be exercised in not more than two separate periods of at least seven consecutive days each, during which the possessory conservator may not have possession of the child, provided that the period or periods so designated do not interfere with the possessory conservator's period or periods of extended summer possession or with Father's Day if the possessory conservator is the father of the child.

§ 153.314. Holiday Possession Unaffected by Distance Parents Reside Apart.

The following provisions govern possession of the child for certain specific holidays and supersede conflicting weekend or **Thursday** [~~Wednesdays~~] periods of possession without regard to the distance the parents reside apart. The possessory conservator and the managing conservator shall have rights of possession of the child as follows:

(1) the possessory conservator shall have possession of the child in even-numbered years beginning at 6 p.m. on the day the child is dismissed from school for the Christmas school vacation and ending at noon on December 26, and the managing conservator shall have possession for the same period in odd-numbered years;

(2) the possessory conservator shall have possession of the child in odd-numbered years beginning at noon on December 26 and ending at 6 p.m. on the day before school resumes after that vacation, and the managing conservator shall have possession for the same period in even-numbered years;

(3) the possessory conservator shall have possession of the child in odd-numbered years, beginning at 6 p.m. on the day the child is dismissed from school before Thanksgiving and ending at 6 p.m. on the following Sunday, and the managing conservator shall have possession for the same period in even-numbered years;

(4) the parent not otherwise entitled under this standard order to present possession of a child on the child's birthday shall have possession of the child beginning at 6 p.m. and ending at 8 p.m. on that day, provided that the parent picks up the child from the residence of the conservator entitled to possession and returns the child to that same place;

(5) if a conservator, the father shall have possession of the child beginning at 6 p.m. on the Friday preceding Father's Day and ending on Father's Day at 6 p.m., provided that, if he is not otherwise entitled under this standard order to present possession of the child, he picks up the child from the residence of the conservator entitled to possession and returns the child to that same place; and

(6) if a conservator, the mother shall have possession of the child beginning at 6 p.m. on the Friday preceding Mother's Day and ending on Mother's Day at 6 p.m.,

provided that, if she is not otherwise entitled under this standard order to present possession of the child, she picks up the child from the residence of the conservator entitled to possession and returns the child to that same place.

History: Amended by 78th Legis., Reg. Sess. (2003), H.B. 913, eff. Sept. 1, 2003, and applies "only to a court order providing for possession of or access to a child rendered on or after that date. A court order rendered before the effective date of this Act is governed by the law in effect on the date the order was rendered, and the former law is continued in effect for that purpose."

§ 153.315. Weekend Possession Extended by Holiday.

(a) If a weekend period of possession of the possessory conservator coincides with a school holiday during the regular school term or with a federal, state, or local holiday during the summer months in which school is not in session, the weekend possession shall end at 6 p.m. on a Monday holiday or school holiday or shall begin at 6 p.m. Thursday for a Friday holiday or school holiday, as applicable.

(b) At the possessory conservator's election, made before or at the time of the rendition of the original or modification order, and as specified in the original or modification order, periods of possession extended by a holiday may begin at the time the child's school is regularly dismissed.

§ 153.316. General Terms and Conditions.

The court shall order the following general terms and conditions of possession of a child to apply without regard to the distance between the residence of a parent and the child:

(1) the managing conservator shall surrender the child to the possessory conservator at the beginning of each period of the possessory conservator's possession at the residence of the managing conservator;

(2) if the possessory conservator elects to begin a period of possession at the time the child's school is regularly dismissed, the managing conservator shall surrender the child to the possessory conservator at the beginning of each period of possession at the school in which the child is enrolled;

(3) the possessory conservator shall be ordered to do one of the following:

(A) the possessory conservator shall surrender the child to the managing conservator at the end of each period of possession at the residence of the possessory conservator; or

(B) the possessory conservator shall return the child to the residence of the managing conservator at the end of each period of possession, except that the order shall provide that the possessory conservator shall surrender the child to the managing conservator at the end of each period of possession at the residence of the possessory conservator if:

(i) at the time the original order or a modification of an order establishing terms and conditions of possession or access the possessory conservator and the managing conservator lived in the same county, the possessory conservator's county of residence remains the same after the rendition of the order, and the managing conservator's county of residence changes, effective on the date of the change of residence by the managing conservator; or

(ii) the possessory conservator and managing conservator lived in the same residence at any time during a six-month period preceding the date on which a suit for dissolution of the marriage was filed and the possessory conservator's county of residence remains the same and the managing conservator's county of residence changes after they no longer live in the same residence, effective on the date the order is rendered;

(4) if the possessory conservator elects to end a period of possession at the time the child's school resumes, the possessory conservator shall surrender the child to the managing conservator at the end of each period of possession at the school in which the child is enrolled;

(5) each conservator shall return with the child the personal effects that the child brought at the beginning of the period of possession;

(6) either parent may designate a competent adult to pick up and return the child, as applicable; a parent or a designated competent adult shall be present when the child is picked up or returned;

(7) a parent shall give notice to the person in possession of the child on each occasion that the parent will be unable to exercise that parent's right of possession for a specified period;

(8) written notice shall be deemed to have been timely made if received or postmarked before or at the time that notice is due; and

(9) if a conservator's time of possession of a child ends at the time school resumes and for any reason the child is not or will not be returned to school, the conservator in possession of the child shall immediately notify the school and the other conservator that the child will not be or has not been returned to school.

Comment

Subdivision (1) and (2) set forth the basic rule that the MC is to surrender custody of the child when the PC arrives for pick-up.

Most of the action in this section (and there has been quite a bit) has focused on subdivision (3). The first major change in the manner in which the parties are to conduct themselves altered the pick-up and return process for the noncustodial parent. Now the court is to choose between the pick-up and return process and the pick-up and pick-up process. That is, that each conservator may be required to pick the child up from the residence of the other conservator at the end of these periods of possession. Parenthetically it may be noted that requiring the court to make a choice in the standard order has given no little difficulty to inattentive lawyers or judges. That is, many an order has been signed with neither choice being made, leaving the question open as to how the child is to be returned to the primary managing conservator. A second, even more complicated and convoluted problem provided in (3)(b)(i)-(ii). Those provisions are intended to require a managing conservator who "moved away" to pick up the child at the home of the possessory conservator. The fact situation described automatically switch a pick-up and return into a pick-up and pick-up process. This assumes, of course, that the parents are able to fathom the meaning of relatively opaque statutory language copied into a standard order.

Subdivision (4) merely directs the possessory conservator to return the child as the order directs. Thus, each conservator is "ordered" to obey the order, which seems reasonable.

Subdivisions (5) through (9) constitute the "act in a civilized manner please" provisions. Subdivision (5) says return teddy bears and crisp pinafores when you return the child. Subdivision (6) should be labeled the "competent adult" means "new spouse of conservator." Finally, subdivision (7)-(9) are directed at providing notice as a matter of common courtesy with regard to compliance of the standard order.

---

§ 153.317. Alternative Possession Times.

If a child is enrolled in school and the possessory conservator elects before or at the time of the rendition of the original or modification order, the standard order must expressly provide that the possessory conservator's period of possession shall begin or end, or both, at a different time expressly set in the standard order under and within the range of alternative times provided by one or both of the following subdivisions:

(1) instead of a period of possession by a possessory conservator beginning at 6 p.m. on the day school recesses, the period of possession may be set in the standard possession order to begin at the time the child's school is regularly dismissed or at any time between the time the child's school is regularly dismissed and 6 p.m.; and

(2) except for **Thursday** [~~Wednesdays~~] evening possession, instead of a period of possession by a possessory conservator ending at 6 p.m. on the day before school resumes, the period of possession may be set in the standard order to end at the time school resumes.

History: Amended by 78th Legis., Reg. Sess. (2003), H.B. 913, eff. Sept. 1, 2003, and applies "only to a court order providing for possession of or access to a child rendered on or after that date. A court order rendered before the effective date of this Act is governed by the law in effect on the date the order was rendered, and the former law is continued in effect for that purpose."

Comment

Christmas vacation and Thursday evening possessions are treated in an identical manner to other time periods of possession. More importantly, the judge is mandated to accede to the request of a possessory conservator for an order directing that: (1) Thursday-possession pickups be immediately after school; (2) return be when the next school day begins; or (3) both.

Subchapter G. Appointment of Nonparent as Conservator

Introductory Comment

The parental presumption has always been called "one of the strongest presumptions known." After a statutory amendment to § 153.131, *supra*, as discussed in the *Lewelling* decision below, that presumption is now recognized as such in reality as well as in rhetoric. Nonetheless, there is always a possibility that a nonparent will be named as a sole or joint managing conservator in the best interest of the child. Of course, naming a nonparent as a possessory conservator does not affect the parental preference.

CLE/Other Legal Publications

Standing after Troxel*: grandparents, step-parents and other interlopers.* Linda S. Good, 2004 ADV. FAM. L.

Third party standing. Miriam L. Ackels, 2004 U. TEX. FAM. L. FRONT LINES

The death of abuelita: Troxel's *implications for the border.* Paula L. Thomas, 2004 U. TEX. FAM. L. ON THE BORDER

Nuts and bolts of third party practice—grandparent and non-parent standing. Brian L. Webb & Miriam L. Akers, 2003 ADV. FAM. L., 2003 MARRIAGE DISSOLUTION

Drafting third party actions: three's a crowd—drafting third party actions. Susan Myres & Tara Luedke–Mora, 2002 ADV. FAM. L. DRAFTING

Rights and duties of parents, grandparents and non-parents. Curtis M. Loveless, 2002 ADV. FAM. L.

Who's left standing? Third party standing after Troxel, Aubin *and* Lilley. Linda Sue Good, 2002 MARRIAGE DISSOLUTION

*All those with standing, step forward . . . not so fast, grandma! Post-*Troxel *third-party standing . . . .* Brian L. Webb, 2001 ADV. FAM. L.

Leading Cases

Brook v. Brook, 881 S.W.2d 297 (Tex. 1994) (parental preference not offended when one parent named JMC with a nonparent)

Lewelling v. Lewelling, 796 S.W.2d 164 (Tex. 1990) (statutory parental preference creates strong presumption)

In re C.T.H., 112 S.W.3d 262 (Tex. App.—Beaumont 2003, no pet.) (grandparents have justiciable interest in custody modification after caring for child for over six months)

In re A.J.L., 108 S.W.3d 414 (Tex. App.—Fort Worth 2003, pet. denied) (ex-stepfather lacks standing to obtain visitation with stepkids by modifying his divorce decree of the prior SAPCR order between his ex and kids' father)

Coons-Andersen v. Andersen, 104 S.W.3d 630 (Tex. App.—Dallas 2003, no pet.) (mother's ex-partner lacked standing to seek conservatorship of child born while the two women were still living together)

In re K.R.P., 80 S.W.3d 669 (Tex. App.—Houston [1st Dist.] 2002, pet. denied) (former step-parent named sole MC over wishes of unfit parents)

In re T.J.K., 62 S.W.3d 830 (Tex. App.—Texarkana 2001, no pet.) (father withdraws agreement for maternal grandmother visitation; *Troxel* decision warrants remand to hear modification suit on constitutional claim)

In re C.R.T., 61 S.W.3d 62 (Tex. App.—Amarillo 2001, pet. denied) (aunt named PMC of three of her druggie-sister's children, thereby confirming placement of kids by mom with aunt)

In re J.R.P., 55 S.W.3d 147 (Tex. App.—Corpus Christi 2001, pet. denied) (grandfather denied conservatorship because his home had history of physical and substance abuse)

In re R.D.Y., 51 S.W.3d 314 (Tex. App.—Houston [1st Dist.] 2001, pet. denied) (grant to grandmother of status as primary joint managing conservator of child did not violate the mother's constitutional liberty interest in care, custody and control child)

In re M.A.M., 35 S.W.3d 788 (Tex. App.—Beaumont 2001, no pet.) (grandma wins sole MC over third parties—substantial past contact not required of grandparent for standing in SAPCR)

In re Aubin, 29 S.W.3d 199 (Tex. App.—Beaumont 2000, no pet.) (*Troxel* might be implicated in mother vs. unrelated couple in custody dispute)

E.C. *ex rel.* Gonzales v. Graydon, 28 S.W.3d 825 (Tex. App.—Corpus Christi 2000, no pet.) (stepmother's complaint about only two-hours visit on mother's day rejected)

R.S. v. B.J.J., 883 S.W.2d 711 (Tex. App.—Dallas 1994, no writ) (nonparents prevail in custody battle with parents following their lengthy voluntary relinquishment of possession)

Whitwell v. Whitwell, 878 S.W.2d 221 (Tex. App.—El Paso 1994, no writ) (Australian mother of disabled child prevails in custody battle with paternal grandparents)

Thomas v. Thomas, 852 S.W.2d 31 (Tex. App.—Waco 1993, no writ) (presumption of parental custody creates heavy burden on nonparent for conservatorship)

Ray v. Burns, 832 S.W.2d 431 (Tex. App.—Waco 1992, no writ) (grandmother and her employers appointed as JMC's.)

Landry v. Nauls, 831 S.W.2d 603 (Tex. App.—Houston [14th Dist.] 1992, no writ) (nonparty grandparent can't be named managing conservator)

May v. May, 829 S.W.2d 373 (Tex. App.—Corpus Christi 1992, writ denied) (grandfather rebuts parental preference, father's claim that drug habit overcome not persuasive)

Neely v. Neely, 698 S.W.2d 758 (Tex. App.—Austin 1985, no writ) (evidence insufficient to rebut presumption that parent prevails over custody claims of step-parent)

Texas Family Law Practice Manual

Form 3–51. Petition in Intervention for Conservatorship

§ 153.371. Rights and Duties of Nonparent Appointed as Sole Managing Conservator.

Unless limited by court order or other provisions of this chapter, a nonparent, licensed child-placing agency, or authorized agency appointed as a managing conservator of the child has the following rights and duties:

(1) the right to have physical possession and to direct the moral and religious training of the child;

(2) the duty of care, control, protection, and reasonable discipline of the child;

(3) the duty to provide the child with clothing, food, shelter, education, and medical, psychological, and dental care;

(4) the right to consent for the child to medical, psychiatric, psychological, dental, and surgical treatment and to have access to the child's medical records;

(5) the right to receive and give receipt for payments for the support of the child and to hold or disburse funds for the benefit of the child;

(6) the right to the services and earnings of the child;

(7) the right to consent to marriage and to enlistment in the armed forces of the United States;

(8) the right to represent the child in legal action and to make other decisions of substantial legal significance concerning the child;

(9) except when a guardian of the child's estate or a guardian or attorney ad litem has been appointed for the child, the right to act as an agent of the child in relation to the child's estate if the child's action is required by a state, the United States, or a foreign government;

(10) the right to designate the primary residence of the child and to make decisions regarding the child's education; and

(11) if the parent-child relationship has been terminated with respect to the parents, or only living parent, or if there is no living parent, the right to consent to the adoption of the child and to make any other decision concerning the child that a parent could make.

§ 153.372. Nonparent Appointed as Joint Managing Conservator.

(a) A nonparent, authorized agency, or licensed child-placing agency appointed as a joint managing conservator may serve in that capacity with either another nonparent or with a parent of the child.

(b) The procedural and substantive standards regarding an agreed or court-ordered joint managing conservatorship provided by Subchapter C apply to a nonparent joint managing conservator.

§ 153.3721. Access to Certain Records by Nonparent Joint Managing Conservator.

Unless limited by court order or other provisions of this chapter, a nonparent joint managing conservator has the right of access to the medical records of the child, without regard to whether the right is specified in the order.

§ 153.373. Voluntary Surrender of Possession Rebuts Parental Presumption.

The presumption that a parent should be appointed or retained as managing conservator of the child is rebutted if the court finds that:

(1) the parent has voluntarily relinquished actual care, control, and possession of the child to a nonparent, licensed child-placing agency, or authorized agency for a period of one year or more, a portion of which was within 90 days preceding the date of intervention in or filing of the suit; and

(2) the appointment of the nonparent or agency as managing conservator is in the best interest of the child.

§ 153.374. Designation of Managing Conservator in Affidavit of Relinquishment.

(a) A parent may designate a competent person, authorized agency, or licensed child-placing agency to serve as managing conservator of the child in an unrevoked or irrevocable affidavit of relinquishment of parental rights executed as provided by Chapter 161 *[Termination of the Parent–Child Relationship]*.

(b) The person or agency designated to serve as managing conservator shall be appointed managing conservator unless the court finds that the appointment would not be in the best interest of the child.

§ 153.375. Annual Report by Nonparent Managing Conservator.

(a) A nonparent appointed as a managing conservator of a child shall each 12 months after the appointment file with the court a report of facts concerning the child's welfare, including the child's whereabouts and physical condition.

(b) The report may not be admitted in evidence in a subsequent suit.

§ 153.376. Rights and Duties of Nonparent Possessory Conservator.

(a) Unless limited by court order or other provisions of this chapter, a nonparent, licensed child-placing agency, or authorized agency appointed as a possessory conservator has the following rights and duties during the period of possession:

(1) the duty of care, control, protection, and reasonable discipline of the child;

(2) the duty to provide the child with clothing, food, and shelter; and

(3) the right to consent to medical, dental, and surgical treatment during an emergency involving an immediate danger to the health and safety of the child.

(b) A nonparent possessory conservator has any other right or duty specified in the order.

§ 153.377. Access to Child's Records.

A nonparent possessory conservator has the right of access to medical, dental, psychological, and educational records of the child to the same extent as the managing conservator, without regard to whether the right is specified in the order.

Subchapter H. Rights of Grandparent

Comment

The scope of grandparental visitation under the Family Code is relatively narrow, with access strictly circumscribed to specific fact situations. Most importantly, a grandparent has no right to intervene into an intact nuclear family over the opposition of the biological mother and father. Family autonomy is supreme in that context.

But, once the original family unit is fractured, whether by death, divorce, incarceration, or termination of one parent's rights, the grandparent may seek visitation. One specific fact situation, the creation of a new step-nuclear family, is identified as one in which grandparental visitation may continue over the objection of the marital partners. Only if both parents are terminated and a new family takes over by adoption will the right of grandparental visitation end.

Grandparent visitation has been in the news quite a bit lately. While the Texas statute is quite narrow, other states' laws on this issue vary considerably. The U.S. Supreme Court recently decided that grandparents' rights must be subordinate to the constitutional right of a fit parent to raise his or her child as the parent sees fit without unwarranted interference from the state. The issue is not settled, however. The Court issued six separate opinions, none of which commanded a majority. Moreover, the statute being construed was an extraordinarily liberal law from Washington State that provided anyone could seek visitation with a child and failed to provide any deference to the parents' rights. *See Troxel v. Granville*, 530 U.S. 57, 120 S.Ct. 2054 (2000).

CLE/Other Legal Publications

Standing after Troxel*: grandparents, step-parents and other interlopers.* Linda S. Good, 2004 Adv. Fam. L.

Third party standing. Miriam L. Ackels, 2004 U. Tex. Fam. L. Front Lines

The death of abuelita: Troxel's *implications for the border.* Paula L. Thomas, 2004 U. Tex. Fam. L. on the Border

Nuts and bolts of third party practice—grandparent and non-parent standing. Brian L. Webb & Miriam L. Akers, 2003 Adv. Fam. L., 2003 Marriage Dissolution

Representing extended family and non–family members (parental presumptions, post-Troxel grandparents). Stewart W. Gagnon, 2003 Adv. Fam. L.

Drafting third party actions: three's a crowd—drafting third party actions. Susan Myres & Tara Luedke–Mora, 2002 Adv. Fam. L. Drafting

Rights and duties of parents, grand parents and non-parents. Curtis M. Loveless, 2002 Adv. Fam. L.

Who's left standing? Third party standing after Troxel, Aubin *and* Lilley. Linda Sue Good, 2002 Marriage Dissolution

Leading Cases

Troxel v. Granville, 530 U.S. 57, 120 S.Ct. 2054 (2000) (see comment above)

In re C.T.H., 112 S.W.3d 262 (Tex. App.—Beaumont 2003, no pet.) (grandparents have justiciable interest in custody modification after caring for child for over six months)

In re T.J.K., 62 S.W.3d 830 (Tex. App.—Texarkana 2001, no pet.) (father withdraws agreement for maternal grandmother visitation; *Troxel* decision warrants remand to hear modification suit on constitutional claim)

Lilley v. Lilley, 43 S.W.3d 703 (Tex. App.—Austin 2001, no pet.) (trial court properly considered mother's conflicting views on grandparent visitation in awarding grandfather's visitation)

E.C. *ex rel.* Gonzales v. Graydon, 28 S.W.3d 825 (Tex. App.—Corpus Christi 2000, no pet.) (grandparents erroneously awarded standard order instead of grandparental access) (stepmother's complaint about award of only two hours visit on mother's day rejected)

Smelscer v. Smelscer, 901 S.W.2d 708 (Tex. App.—El Paso 1995, no writ) (grandparents intervention in divorce does not survive death of father)

Ray v. Burns, 832 S.W.2d 431 (Tex. App.—Waco 1992, no writ) (grandmother and her employers appointed as JMC's.)

In re R.N.C., 768 S.W.2d 516 (Tex. App.—Fort Worth 1989, no writ) (terminating grandparental access rights)

Texas Family Law Practice Manual

Chapter 35. Grandparents

Texas Pattern Jury Charges: Family

PJC 216.4. Grandparental Access—Original Suit

---

§ 153.431. Grandparental Appointment as Managing Conservators.

If the parents are deceased, the grandparents may be considered for appointment as managing conservators, but consideration does not alter or diminish the discretionary power of the court.

§ 153.432. Suit for Access.

(a) A biological or adoptive grandparent may request access to a grandchild by filing:

(1) an original suit; or

(2) a suit for modification as provided by Chapter 156 *[Modification]*.

(b) A grandparent may request access to a grandchild in a suit filed for the sole purpose of requesting the relief, without regard to whether the appointment of a managing conservator is an issue in the suit.

§ 153.433. Possession of and Access to Grandchild.

The court shall order reasonable access to a grandchild by a grandparent if:

(1) at the time the relief is requested, at least one biological or adoptive parent of the child has not had that parent's parental rights terminated; and

(2) access is in the best interest of the child, and at least one of the following facts is present:

(A) the grandparent requesting access to the child is a parent of a parent of the child and that parent of the child has been incarcerated in jail or prison during the three-month period preceding the filing of the petition or has been found by a court to be incompetent or is dead;

(B) the parents of the child are divorced or have been living apart for the three-month period preceding the filing of the petition or a suit for the dissolution of the parents' marriage is pending;

(C) the child has been abused or neglected by a parent of the child;

(D) the child has been adjudicated to be a child in need of supervision or a delinquent child under Title 3;

(E) the grandparent requesting access to the child is the parent of a person whose parent-child relationship with the child has been terminated by court order; or

(F) the child has resided with the grandparent requesting access to the child for at least six months within the 24-month period preceding the filing of the petition.

Comment

At first glance, what a difference a word makes. That is, the 1997 elimination of the discretionary "may" and the substitution of an apparently mandatory "shall" regarding grandparental visitation certainly sounds binding. But, because the order continues to depend on whether such access is in the best interest of the child, judicial discretion continues. If grandparental visitation is in the child's interest, it seems obvious that the court should enter the order. By definition, not to do so would be to refuse to do something in the best interest of the child. In short, although the amendment was primarily cosmetic, it does signify a legislative opinion that such orders probably should be granted more frequently than was perceived to have been the case when the legislature last spoke to the matter.

Leading Case

In re Webster, 982 S.W.2d 526 (Tex. App.—Amarillo 1998, no pet.) (the court, not DPRS, must determine appropriate grandparental visitation)

---

§ 153.434. Limitation on Right to Request Access.

A biological or adoptive grandparent may not request possession of or access to a grandchild if:

(1) each of the biological parents of the grandchild has:

(A) died;

(B) had the person's parental rights terminated; or

(C) executed an affidavit of waiver of interest in child or an affidavit of relinquishment of parental rights under Chapter 161 *[Termination of the Parent–Child Relationship]* and the affidavit designates an authorized agency, licensed child-placing agency, or person other than the child's stepparent as the managing conservator of the child; and

(2) the grandchild has been adopted, or is the subject of a pending suit for adoption, by a person other than the child's stepparent.

Comment

A 1997 amendment to this section caused considerable consternation and confusion due to some ambiguous, nonstandard drafting that accidentally slipped through the legislative process. Statutes should never be written in the form of "(1) or (2) and (3)" as this creates an implicit conflict regarding whether the conjunctive between subsections (2) and (3) modifies only subsection (2), or modifies both subsections (1) and (2). As a result, some lawyers incorrectly interpreted the 1997 amendment as totally undercutting grandparental visitation. In fact, grandparental visitation is to be statutorily prohibited only when there is an "out-of-family" adoption, with "family" including a surviving stepparent. The 1999 amendment made this clear.

Leading Case

Raines v. Sugg, 930 S.W.2d 912 (Tex. App.—Fort Worth 1996, no writ) (maternal grandparents entitled to access to grandchild despite child's adoption by father's second wife)

Subchapter I. Prevention of International Parental Child Abduction

> ***Editors' Note:*** *The enactment of Subchapter I, §§ 153.501–153.503, has the following legislative history:*
>
> *History: Enacted by 78th Legis., Reg. Sess. (2003), H.B. 1899, eff. June 20, 2003, and applies "to a suit affecting the parent-child relationship pending in a*

trial court on the effective date of this Act or filed on or after the effective date of this Act."

Introductory Comment

New Subchapter I adds the statutory basis to ensure that courts determine the risk of international parental child abduction in certain cases and order preventive measures based on that risk, if the court deems the risk sufficient to require such an order. The provisions are adapted from a study published by the ABA Center on Children and the Law, and from numerous reports published and disseminated by the U.S. Dept. of State, Office of Children's Issues; the U.S. Dept. of Justice, Office of Juvenile Justice and Delinquency Program; the National Center for Missing and Exploited Children (NCMEC); and other sources. The recommended safeguards have already been successfully utilized in some Texas family court cases to discourage or prevent international parental abduction in high risk cases.

Unfortunately, most Texas family courts remain unaware or underestimate various "red flag" indicators and the need for preventive safeguards. As a result, Texas children continue to remain at high risk for international parental child abduction. When the abduction is to a foreign country, the return of the child very often is extremely difficult, and is impossible in some cases. This warrants more emphasis on preventing such abductions before they occur. Existing federal law implements the provisions of the Hague Convention on the civil aspects of international child abduction, *see* International Child Abduction Remedies Act, 42 U.S.C.A. § 11601, *et seq.* and Hague Convention on the civil aspects of international child abduction, *infra.* Both the federal act and the Hague Convention provide remedies for the wrongful removal or retention of a child in cases of international child abduction, many foreign countries are not parties to the convention. Moreover, even if a country is a signatory, this does not mean that ready compliance may be assured.

Both federal and Texas law prohibit the abduction of a child in violation of the right of custody or access of a person. However, many foreign countries refuse to recognize U.S. custody orders. A large number of parents succeed in abducting children internationally because exits controls in the United States are nonexistent. Some foreign countries (including their embassies and consulates located in the U.S.) issue parents to children they consider to be dual nationals, despite U.S. court orders prohibit such issuance. Many of the foreign abducted national parents are also U.S. citizens or permanent residents who have resided in the United States for many years and have successful jobs or businesses, leading the courts to mistakenly conclude that they do not pose a risk of child abduction. In many foreign countries there are no legal remedies to enable an American parent to secure the return of a child to the U.S., or to gain access to the child in the foreign country. As a result, many American parents have had their children literally stolen, with little or no recourse available under the law. Consequently, the U.S. Dept of Justice, Office of Juvenile Justice and Delinquency Programs (OJJDP) recommends that state legislatures pass this statute to prevent parental abductions. New subchapter I supplements current Texas family law to provide that, in any child custody proceeding in which the court is made aware of evidence indicating a possible risk of international abduction of the child, that the court shall consider certain factors (a.k.a., "red flags") to determine whether safeguards are needed to prevent such an abduction. If the court determines that the need exists, it may take specified measures to discourage or prevent the abduction of the child.

CLE/Other Legal Publications

Concepts and questions of interpretation arising from the Hague Convention on the civil aspects of international child abduction. Adair Dyer, 2004 U. Tex. Fam. L. on the Border

International—unusual child issues Hague, Indian child welfare, UCCJEA, etc. (Workshop) 2003 Adv. Fam. L.

---

§ 153.501. Necessity of Measures to Prevent International Parental Child Abduction.

(a) In a suit, if credible evidence is presented to the court indicating a potential risk of the international abduction of a child by a parent of the child, the court, on its own motion or at the request of a party to the suit, shall determine under this section whether it is necessary for the court to take one or more of the measures described by Section 153.503 to protect the child from the risk of abduction by the parent.

(b) In determining whether to take any of the measures described by Section 153.503, the court shall consider:

(1) the public policies of this state described by Section 153.001(a) and the consideration of the best interest of the child under Section 153.002;

(2) the risk of international abduction of the child by a parent of the child based on the court's evaluation of the risk factors described by Section 153.502;

(3) any obstacles to locating, recovering, and returning the child if the child is abducted to a foreign country; and

(4) the potential physical or psychological harm to the child if the child is abducted to a foreign country.

§ 153.502. Abduction Risk Factors.

(a) To determine whether there is a risk of the international abduction of a child by a parent of the child, the court shall consider evidence that the parent:

(1) has taken, enticed away, kept, withheld, or concealed a child in violation of another person's right of possession of or access to the child, unless the parent presents evidence that the parent believed in good faith that the parent's conduct was necessary to avoid imminent harm to the child;

(2) has previously threatened to take, entice away, keep, withhold, or conceal a child in violation of another person's right of possession of or access to the child;

(3) lacks financial reason to stay in the United States, including evidence that the parent is financially independent, is able to work outside of the United States, or is unemployed;

(4) has recently engaged in planning activities that could facilitate the removal of the child from the United States by the parent, including:

(A) quitting a job;

(B) selling a primary residence;

(C) terminating a lease;

(D) closing bank accounts;

(E) liquidating other assets;

(F) hiding or destroying documents;

(G) applying for a passport or visa for the parent or the child; or

(H) applying to obtain the child's birth certificate or school or medical records;

(5) has a history of domestic violence that the court is required to consider under Section 153.004; or

(6) has a criminal history or a history of violating court orders.

(b) If the court finds that there is credible evidence of a risk of abduction of the child by a parent of the child based on the court's consideration of the factors in Subsection (a), the court shall also consider evidence regarding the following factors to evaluate the risk of international abduction of the child by a parent:

(1) whether the parent has strong familial, emotional, or cultural ties to another country, particularly a country that is not a signatory to or compliant with the Hague Convention on the Civil Aspects of International Child Abduction; and

(2) whether the parent lacks strong ties to the United States, regardless of whether the parent is a citizen or permanent resident of the United States.

(c) If the court finds that there is credible evidence of a risk of abduction of the child by a parent of the child based on the court's consideration of the factors in Subsection (a), the court may also consider evidence regarding the following factors to evaluate the risk of international abduction of the child by a parent:

(1) whether the parent is undergoing a change in status with the United States Immigration and Naturalization Service that would adversely affect that parent's ability to legally remain in the United States;

(2) whether the parent's application for United States citizenship has been denied by the United States Immigration and Naturalization Service;

(3) whether the parent has forged or presented misleading or false evidence to obtain a visa, a passport, a social security card, or any other identification card or has made any misrepresentation to the United States government; or

(4) whether the foreign country to which the parent has ties:

(A) presents obstacles to the recovery and return of a child who is abducted to the country from the United States;

(B) has any legal mechanisms for immediately and effectively enforcing an order regarding the possession of or access to the child issued by this state;

(C) has local laws or practices that would:

(i) enable the parent to prevent the child's other parent from contacting the child without due cause;

(ii) restrict the child's other parent from freely traveling to or exiting from the country because of that parent's gender, nationality, or religion; or

(iii) restrict the child's ability to legally leave the country after the child reaches the age of majority because of the child's gender, nationality, or religion;

(D) is included by the United States Department of State on a list of state sponsors of terrorism;

(E) is a country for which the United States Department of State has issued a travel warning to United States citizens regarding travel to the country;

(F) has an embassy of the United States in the country;

(G) is engaged in any active military action or war, including a civil war;

(H) is a party to and compliant with the Hague Convention on the Civil Aspects of International Child Abduction according to the most recent report on compliance issued by the United States Department of State;

(I) provides for the extradition of a parental abductor and the return of the child to the United States; or

(J) poses a risk that the child's physical health or safety would be endangered in the country because of specific circumstances relating to the child or because of human rights violations committed against children, including arranged marriages, lack of freedom of religion, child labor, lack of child abuse laws, female genital mutilation, and any form of slavery.

§ 153.503. Abduction Prevention Measures.

If the court finds that it is necessary under Section 153.501 to take measures to protect a child from international abduction by a parent of the child, the court may take any of the following actions:

(1) appoint a person other than the parent of the child who presents a risk of abducting the child as the sole managing conservator of the child;

(2) require supervised visitation of the parent by a visitation center or independent organization until the court finds under Section 153.501 that supervised visitation is no longer necessary;

(3) enjoin the parent or any person acting on the parent's behalf from:

(A) disrupting or removing the child from the school or child-care facility in which the child is enrolled; or

(B) approaching the child at any location other than a site designated for supervised visitation;

(4) order passport and travel controls, including controls that:

(A) prohibit the parent and any person acting on the parent's behalf from removing the child from this state or the United States;

(B) require the parent to surrender any passport issued in the child's name, including any passport issued in the name of both the parent and the child; and

(C) prohibit the parent from applying on behalf of the child for a new or replacement passport or international travel visa;

(5) require the parent to provide:

(A) to the United States Department of State's Office of Children's Issues and the relevant foreign consulate or embassy:

(i) written notice of the court-ordered passport and travel restrictions for the child; and

(ii) a properly authenticated copy of the court order detailing the restrictions and documentation of the parent's agreement to the restrictions; and

(B) to the court proof of receipt of the written notice required by Paragraph (A)(i) by the United States Department of State's Office of Children's Issues and the relevant foreign consulate or embassy;

(6) order the parent to execute a bond or deposit security in an amount sufficient to offset the cost of recovering the child if the child is abducted by the parent to a foreign country;

(7) authorize the appropriate law enforcement agencies to take measures to prevent the abduction of the child by the parent; or

(8) include in the court's order provisions:

(A) identifying the United States as the country of habitual residence of the child;

(B) defining the basis for the court's exercise of jurisdiction; and

(C) stating that a party's violation of the order may subject the party to a civil penalty or criminal penalty or to both civil and criminal penalties.

Chapter 154. Child Support.

Subchapter A. Court–Ordered Child Support

Subchapter B. Computing Net Resources Available for Payment of Child Support

Subchapter C. Child Support Guidelines

Subchapter D. Medical Support for Child

Subchapter E. Local Child Support Registry

Subchapter F. Support for a Minor or Adult Disabled Child

> ***Editors' Note:*** *This chapter contains guest commentary by Cynthia Bryant, Deputy Attorney General, and H. Patrick Sullivan, Director of Federal Policy Analysis, all of the Office of the Attorney General Child Support Division, (C.B. & H.P.S.).*

Introductory Comment

Texas child support guidelines apply to the first $6,000 of an obligor's net resources. This coverage has the effect of subjecting the total net resources of well over 95% of all potential obligors to the presumptive application of the guidelines. The child support guidelines also deal with multiple families, thereby resolving a set of problems that had bedeviled Texas courts.

CLE/Other Legal Publications

Child support: maximizing your chances of hitting a home run. Janice L. Green, 2004 Adv. Fam. L.

Deposition strategies for kids and cash. Thomas Albert Greenwald, 2004 ADV. FAM. L.

Child support—setting, modifying, and collecting. Alyssa P. Lemkuil & Dan Lemkuil, 2004 U. TEX. FAM. L. FRONT LINES

International child support cases in Texas. Barry J. Brooks, 2004 U. TEX. FAM. L. ON THE BORDER

Unique and not so unique child support issues. Kim W. Mercier & Christopher M. Lake, 2003 MARRIAGE DISSOLUTION

Child support. Rhonda F. Hunter, 2002 ADV. FAM. L.

Update on state disbursement unit: sending all the child support to San Antonio. Alicia Gray Key, 2002 ADV. FAM. L.

Leading Cases

Bruni v. Bruni, 924 S.W.2d 366 (Tex. 1996) (parents' agreement for obligor to provide support for children until age 21 enforceable as contract; agreement survives the expiration of enforceable decree)

Elfeldt v. Elfeldt, 730 S.W.2d 657 (Tex. 1987) (agreement must specify terms enforceable as contract)

Knight v. Knight, 131 S.W.3d 535 (Tex. App.—El Paso 2004, no pet.) (child support based on husband's income from prior year rather than alleged current income)

In re E.A.S., 123 S.W.3d 565 (Tex. App.—El Paso 2003, pet. denied) (court finds obligor intentionally underemployed with undisclosed financial resources)

In re Knott, 118 S.W.3d 899 (Tex. App.—Texarkana 2003, no pet.) (investment income of new spouse may be community property but to to be included in obligor's net resources; no reason found to deviate from guideline support)

Grayson v. Grayson, 103 S.W.3d 559 (Tex. App.—San Antonio 2003, no pet.) (trial court acted within its discretion in requiring obligor to do more than just make support payments, including providing life insurance and airline tickets)

In re L.R.P., 98 S.W.3d 312 (Tex. App.—Houston [1st Dist.] 2003, pet. dism'd) (monetary gifts from parents and scholarship funds received included in student father's income for net resources)

O'Neal v. O'Neal, 69 S.W.3d 347 (Tex. App.—Eastland 2002, no pet.) (evidence of father's income is necessary to support judgment for child support)

Norris v. Norris, 56 S.W.3d 333 (Tex. App.—El Paso 2001, no pet.) (to reach correct result in computing child support, yearly income swings should be averaged to calculate the most likely future income)

In re J.A.B., 13 S.W.3d 813 (Tex. App.—Fort Worth 2000, no pet.) (child fully enrolled despite multiple unexcused absences)

Crocker v. Attorney General of Texas, 3 S.W.3d 650 (Tex. App.—Austin 1999, no pet.) (modification to continue support past 18 may be valid if child still fully enrolled in high school)

In re A.B., 994 S.W.2d 299 (Tex. App.—Eastland 1999, pet. denied) ("fully enrolled" does not require that post-18 high school student is passing—just trying to pass)

Lueg v. Lueg, 976 S.W.2d 308 (Tex. App.—Corpus Christi 1998, pet. denied) (error to order sole MC father to pay child support to PC mother)

Eubanks v. Eubanks, 892 S.W.2d 181 (Tex. App.—Houston [14th Dist.] 1995, no writ) (percentage of disposable earnings, not gross income, upheld in child support order)

Starck v. Nelson, 878 S.W.2d 302 (Tex. App.—Corpus Christi 1994, no writ) (automatic increases for future child support payments an abuse of discretion)

Varner v. Howe, 860 S.W.2d 458 (Tex. App.—El Paso 1993, no writ) (jury finding advisory regarding child support amount)

Voros v. Turnage, 856 S.W.2d 759 (Tex. App.—Houston [1st Dist.] 1993, writ denied) (reimbursement from obligor to obligee for costs of health insurance approved)

De La Garza v. Salazar, 851 S.W.2d 380 (Tex. App.—San Antonio 1993, no writ) (decree may provide that death does not terminate support obligation)

Kolpack v. Torres, 829 S.W.2d 913 (Tex. App.—Corpus Christi 1992, writ denied) (trust beneficiary must be ordered to pay child support before trustees can be ordered to make such payments)

Baucom v. Crews, 819 S.W.2d 628 (Tex. App.—Waco 1991, no writ) (lump sum child support approved)

Kahn v. Kahn, 813 S.W.2d 708 (Tex. App.—Austin 1991, no writ) (lump sum child support disapproved)

Cross References

Federal IV–D Child Support Program. 42 U.S.C.A. § 651 *et seq.*

Tex. Const. art. XVI, § 28. Garnishment of Wages.

Subchapter A. Court–Ordered Child Support

> ***Editors' Note:*** *This chapter contains guest comments by Cynthia Bryant, Deputy Attorney General, and H. Patrick Sullivan, Director of Federal Policy Analysis, both of the Child Support, Office of the Attorney General Child Support Division, identified as (C.B. & H.P.S.).*

§ 154.001. Support of Child.

(a) The court may order either or both parents to support a child in the manner specified by the order:

(1) until the child is 18 years of age or until graduation from high school, whichever occurs later;

(2) until the child is emancipated through marriage, through removal of the disabilities of minority by court order, or by other operation of law;

(3) until the death of the child; or

(4) if the child is disabled as defined in this chapter, for an indefinite period.

(b) The court may order either or both parents to make periodic payments for the support of a child in a proceeding in which the Department of Protective and Regulatory Services is named temporary managing conservator. In a proceeding in which the Department of Protective and Regulatory Services is named permanent managing conservator of a child whose parents' rights have not been terminated, the court shall order each parent that is financially able to make periodic payments for the support of the child.

(c) In a Title IV–D case, if neither parent has physical possession or conservatorship of the child, the court may render an order providing that a nonparent or agency having physical possession may receive, hold, or disburse child support payments for the benefit of the child.

Comment

Subsection (a) is as simple and straightforward as any provision in the Family Code. It mandates that either or both parents must support their child and, by virtue of the maximum *inclusio unius est exclusio alterius,* only the parents can be ordered to support their child. That means that grandparents and former managing conservators have no obligation to support a child.

Subsection (b) is designed to ensure that DPRS "may" be awarded child support after the department is named temporary managing conservator if the parents are financially able to pay. Note that the phrasing of the statute converts to mandatory "shall order" language when DPRS is named permanent managing conservator.

Subsection (c) states the obvious: if a parent does not have possession of a child or conservatorship the court may redirect payments to a nonparent who has possession of the child, or to an agency. In either case, the payments are for the benefit of the child. Of course, what may be obvious to some was not obvious to the court in *Office of Attorney General v. Carter*, 977 S.W.2d 159 (Tex. App.—Houston [14th Dist.] 1998, no pet.). The trial court refused to reimburse the State of Georgia for AFDC/TANF payments made to the Georgia grandmother of a child. It turned out that the Texas mother had never relinquished legal custody of the child to the grandmother. So the court found that the grandmother's assignment of the right to receive support to the Georgia agency was of no avail and unenforceable insofar as reimbursement of that support to the state from the mother. Inexplicably, the appellate court affirmed. The legislature wasted no time in expressing its dismay at that judicial reasoning by enacting subsection (c) in 1999.

---

§ 154.002. Child Support Through High School Graduation.

(a) **The** [~~If the child is fully enrolled in an accredited secondary school in a program leading toward a high school diploma or enrolled in courses for joint high school and junior college credit pursuant to Section 130.008, Education Code, the~~] court may render an original support order, or modify an existing order, providing child support past the 18th birthday of the child **to be paid only if the child is:**

(1) enrolled:

(A) under Chapter 25, Education Code, in an accredited secondary school in a program leading toward a high school diploma;

(B) under Section 130.008, Education Code, in courses for joint high school and junior college credit; or

(C) on a full-time basis in a private secondary school in a program leading toward a high school diploma; and

(2) complying with:

(A) the minimum attendance requirements of Subchapter C, Chapter 25, Education Code; or

(B) the minimum attendance requirements imposed by the school in which the child is enrolled, if the child is enrolled in a private secondary school.

(b) The request for a support order through high school graduation may be filed before or after the child's 18th birthday.

(c) The order for periodic support may provide that payments continue through the end of the month in which the child graduates.

History: Amended by 78th Legis., Reg. Sess. (2003), H.B. 234, eff. Sept. 1, 2003, and "applies only to a court order or portion of a decree that provides for the support of a child rendered or modified on or after the effective date of this Act. An order or decree rendered or modified before the effective date of this Act is governed by the law in effect on the date the order or decree was rendered or modified, and the former law is continued in effect for that purpose."

Comment

After the passage of the Family Code in 1973, it took the legislature several sessions to realize that the majority of children turn 18 during their senior year in high school. Once that fact was recognized, child support through graduation of high school was quickly adopted. As noted below, a fair amount of litigation has been generated regarding what graduation from high school entails. One thing is clear; graduation must take place prior to the child's 21st birthday before September 1 of any year. The 2003 amendments attempt to resolve as many additional questions as possible to eliminate repeated litigation on the subject.

Leading Cases

In re J.A.B., 13 S.W.3d 813 (Tex. App.—Fort Worth 2000, no pet.) (child fully enrolled despite multiple unexcused absences)

Crocker v. Attorney General of Texas, 3 S.W.3d 650 (Tex. App.—Austin 1999, no pet.) (modification to continue support past 18 may be valid if child still fully enrolled in high school)

In re A.B., 994 S.W.2d 299 (Tex. App.—Eastland 1999, pet. denied) ("fully enrolled" does not require that post–18 high school student is passing—just trying to pass)

Ewing v. Holt, 835 S.W.2d 274 (Tex. App.—Fort Worth 1992, no writ) ("fully enrolled" in high school includes one-credit correspondence course needed to graduate)

In re Frost, 815 S.W.2d 890 (Tex. App.—Amarillo 1991, no writ) (post–18 child enrolled in alternate education program that could lead to high school diploma)

---

§ 154.003. Manner of Payment.

The court may order that child support be paid by:

(1) periodic payments;

(2) a lump-sum payment;

(3) an annuity purchase;

(4) the setting aside of property to be administered for the support of the child as specified in the order; or

(5) any combination of periodic payments, lump-sum payments, annuity purchases, or setting aside of property.

§ 154.004. Place of Payment.

(a) The court shall order the payment of child support to [~~a local registry, the Title IV-D agency, or~~] the state disbursement unit[~~,~~] as provided by Chapter 234[~~, as added by Chapter 911, Acts of the 75th Legislature, Regular Session, 1997~~].

(b) In a Title IV–D case, the court or the Title IV–D agency shall order that income withheld for child support be paid[~~:~~

[~~(1) to the Title IV-D agency through a local registry, which shall forward the payment to the Title IV-D agency;~~

[~~(2) to the Title IV-D agency; or~~

[~~(3)~~] to the state disbursement unit **of this state or, if appropriate, to the state disbursement unit of another state**.

(c) This section does not apply to a child support order that:

(1) was initially rendered by a court before January 1, 1994; and

(2) is not being enforced by the Title IV–D agency.

History: Amended by 78th Legis., Reg. Sess. (2003), S.B. 1805, eff. Sept. 1, 2003, and "applies only to a court order or a portion of a decree that provides for the support of a child that is rendered on or after the effective date of this Act. An order or decree rendered before the effective date of this Act is governed by the law in effect on the date the order or decree was rendered, and the former law is continued in effect for that purpose."

Guest Comment

With the establishment of the state disbursement unit required by federal law, certain child support payments must be directed to that unit as provided by § 234.007(a). These include payments in all cases being enforced by the Title IV–D agency and in all other cases in which the support order was initially issued on or after January 1, 1994, and in which the obligor is subject to income withholding. Subsection (b) enables the court or the IV–D agency to redirect support payments to the disbursement of another state if the obligee has relocated. This conforms to § 159.319(b). (*C.B. & H.P.S.*)

---

§ 154.005. Payments of Support Obligation by Trust.

(a) The court may order the trustees of a spendthrift or other trust to make disbursements for the support of a child to the extent the trustees are required to make payments to a beneficiary who is required to make child support payments as provided by this chapter.

(b) If disbursement of the assets of the trust is discretionary, the court may order child support payments from the income of the trust but not from the principal.

§ 154.006. Termination of Duty of Support.

(a) Unless otherwise agreed in writing or expressly provided in the order or as provided by Subsection (b), the child support order terminates on:

(1) the marriage of the child;

(2) the [~~,~~] removal of the child's disabilities for general purposes;

(3) the [~~, or~~] death of:

(A) the child; or

(B) a parent ordered to pay child support; **or**

(4) a finding by a court that the child:

(A) is 18 years of age or older; and

(B) has failed to comply with the enrollment or attendance requirements described by Section 154.002(a).

(b) Unless a nonparent or agency has been appointed conservator of the child under Chapter 153 *[Conservatorship, Possession, and Access]*, the order for current child support, and any provision relating to conservatorship, possession, or access terminates on the marriage or remarriage of the obligor and obligee to each other.

History: Amended by 78th Legis., Reg. Sess. (2003), H.B. 234, eff. Sept. 1, 2003, and "applies only to a court order or portion of a decree that provides for the support of a child rendered or modified on or after the effective date of this Act. An order or decree rendered or modified before the effective date of this Act is governed by the law in effect on the date the order or decree was rendered or modified, and the former law is continued in effect for that purpose."

Comment

The death of a child will surely end all obligation for child support, but the same is not true with regard to the death of the child-support obligor. Support may continue past the death of a parent if the parties have agreed in writing to that obligation, or if the court has ordered that the estate of the obligor will continue to have support liability. A less complex method of dealing with the financial hardship caused by sudden termination of child support is for the parties to arrange for life insurance coverage on the obligor, the oblige, or both, in order to secure future financial security.

Leading Cases

Deltuva v. Deltuva, 113 S.W.3d 882 (Tex. App.—Dallas 2003, no pet.) (failure to reduce child support as children age-out is reversible error)

Attorney General of Texas v. Stevens, 84 S.W.3d 720 (Tex. App.—Houston [1st Dist.] 2002, no pet.) (disabled obligor not entitled to credit on judgment for child support arrears when dependent receives social security payment for obligor's disability)

In re Allsup, 926 S.W.2d 323 (Tex. App.—Texarkana 1996, no writ) (Social Security dependent benefit offset against retired obligor's child support duty)

Lake v. Lake, 899 S.W.2d 737 (Tex. App.—Dallas 1995, no writ) (credit for social security survivor benefits not allowed towards child support obligation)

§ 154.007. Order to Withhold Child Support From Income.

(a) In a proceeding in which periodic payments of child support are ordered, modified, or enforced, the court or Title IV-D agency shall order that income be withheld from the disposable earnings of the obligor as provided by Chapter 158 *[Withholding from Earnings for Child Support]*.

(b) If the court does not order income withholding, an order for support must contain a provision for income withholding to ensure that withholding may be effected if a delinquency occurs.

(c) A child support order must be construed to contain a withholding provision even if the provision has been omitted from the written order.

(d) If the order was rendered or last modified before January 1, 1987, the order is presumed to contain a provision for income withholding procedures to take effect in the event a delinquency occurs without further amendment to the order or future action by the court.

Comment

The legislature has mandated that an income withholding order be rendered in each and every case, without exception. Note that this does not necessarily mean that an income withholding order will be served on the obligor's employer. *See* § 158.002, *infra*. It does mean that an income withholding order will be available in the courthouse file in every case without requiring a return to court.

§ 154.008. Provision for Medical Support.

The court shall order medical support for the child as provided by Subchapters B and D.

§ 154.009. Retroactive Child Support.

(a) The court may order a parent to pay retroactive child support if the parent:

(1) has not previously been ordered to pay support for the child; and

(2) was not a party to a suit in which support was ordered.

(b) In ordering retroactive child support, the court shall apply the child support guidelines provided by this chapter.

(c) Unless the Title IV–D agency is a party to an agreement concerning support or purporting to settle past, present, or future support obligations by prepayment or otherwise, an agreement between the parties does not reduce or terminate retroactive support that the agency may request.

(d) Notwithstanding Subsection (a), the court may order a parent subject to a previous child support order to pay retroactive child support if:

(1) the previous child support order terminated as a result of the marriage or remarriage of the child's parents;

(2) the child's parents separated after the marriage or remarriage; and

(3) a new child support order is sought after the date of the separation.

(e) In rendering an order under Subsection (d), the court may order retroactive child support back to the date of the separation of the child's parents.

Guest Comment

Subsection (d) provides an exception to the rule that an obligor may not be ordered to pay retroactive support if the obligor had previously been ordered to pay support for the same child. The exception arises where the earlier support order terminated upon the marriage or remarriage of the parties and the parties subsequently separate. When that happens, the court may order the obligor to pay support back to the time of separation. Of course, this scenario could be replayed more than once. (*H.P.S.*)

---

§ 154.010. No Discrimination Based on Marital Status of Parents or Sex.

The amount of support ordered for the benefit of a child shall be determined without regard to:

(1) the sex of the obligor, obligee, or child; or

(2) the marital status of the parents of the child.

Comment

Modeled after the long-time antidiscrimination provision regarding the marital status of the parents of a child, a similar provision applies to the child support obligation. For many years, many judges had a practice of not ordering child support when the obligee was the mother. Although customs die hard, at least statutorily it is absolutely clear that both parents have the obligation to support the child and that obligation is not affected by either the sex or marital status of the parent.

---

§ 154.011. Support Not Conditioned on Possession or Access.

A court may not render an order that conditions the payment of child support on whether a managing conservator allows a possessory conservator to have possession of or access to a child.

Leading Case

In re A.N.H., 70 S.W.3d 918 (Tex. App.—Amarillo 2002, no pet.) (support order conditioned on obligor's right to visitation violates public policy and is void)

---

§ 154.012. Support Paid in Excess of Support Order.

(a) If an obligor is not in arrears and the obligor's child support obligation has terminated, the obligee shall return to the obligor a child support payment made by the obligor that exceeds the amount of support ordered, regardless of whether the payment was made before, on, or after the date the child support obligation terminated.

(b) An obligor may file a suit to recover a child support payment under Subsection (a). If the court finds that the obligee failed to return a child support payment under Subsection (a), the court shall order the obligee to pay to the obligor attorney's fees and all court costs in addition to the amount of support paid after the date the child support order terminated. For good cause shown, the court may waive the requirement that the obligee pay attorney's fees and costs if the court states the reasons supporting that finding.

Guest Comment

Under this section, if a support obligation has terminated and no arrearages are owed, an obligor is due any amounts paid the obligee in excess of the ordered child support amount, no matter when the excess payments may have been made. An obligee who refuses or otherwise fails to return any such amounts to the obligor may be forced to do so by the court, as well as to pay any costs and fees. While this seems and, undoubtedly in most cases, is equitable, there is always the possibility that an obligor may have, for whatever good-hearted reasons, intentionally paid excess support, only to lay claim to such excess payment under this section after a change of heart. *(H.P.S.)*

---

§ 154.013. Continuation of Duty to Pay Support After Death of Obligee.

(a) A child support obligation does not terminate on the death of the obligee but continues as an obligation to the child named in the support order, as required by this section.

(b) Notwithstanding any provision of the Probate Code, a child support payment held by the Title IV-D agency, a local registry, or the state disbursement unit or any uncashed check or warrant representing a child support payment made before, on, or after the date of death of the obligee shall be paid proportionately for the benefit of each surviving child named in the support order and not to the estate of the obligee. The payment is free of any creditor's claim against the deceased obligee's estate and may be disbursed as provided by Subsection (c).

(c) On the death of the obligee, current child support owed by the obligor for the benefit of the child or any amount described by Subsection (b) shall be paid to:

(1) a person, other than a parent, who is appointed as managing conservator of the child;

(2) a person, including the obligor, who has assumed actual care, control, and possession of the child, if a managing conservator or guardian of the child has not been appointed;

(3) the county clerk, as provided by Section 887, Texas Probate Code, in the name of and for the account of the child for whom the support is owed;

(4) a guardian of the child appointed under Chapter XIII, Texas Probate Code, as provided by that code; or

(5) the surviving child, if the child is an adult or has otherwise had the disabilities of minority removed.

(d) On presentation of the obligee's death certificate, the court shall render an order directing payment of child support paid but not disbursed to be made as provided by Subsection (c). A copy of the order shall be provided to:

(1) the obligor;

(2) as appropriate:

(A) the person having actual care, control, and possession of the child;

(B) the county clerk; or

(C) the managing conservator or guardian of the child, if one has been appointed;

(3) the local registry or state disbursement unit and, if appropriate, the Title IV-D agency; and

(4) the child named in the support order, if the child is an adult or has otherwise had the disabilities of minority removed.

(e) The order under Subsection (d) must contain:

(1) a statement that the obligee is deceased and that child support amounts otherwise payable to the obligee shall be paid for the benefit of a surviving child named in the support order as provided by Subsection (c);

(2) the name and age of each child named in the support order; and

(3) the name and mailing address of, as appropriate:

(A) the person having actual care, control, and possession of the child;

(B) the county clerk; or

(C) the managing conservator or guardian of the child, if one has been appointed.

(f) On receipt of the order required under this section, the local registry, state disbursement unit, or Title IV-D agency shall disburse payments as required by the order.

Guest Comment

This section is intended to ensure continuity in the financial support of a child for whom support has been ordered, in the event of the obligee's death. As § 154.006 states, the support obligation ordinarily terminates upon the death of the obligor or the death or legal emancipation of the child. The death of the obligee, however, does not affect the continuing duty of support owed by the obligor to a child named in an order. Under this section, any current support, including amounts that have been collected but not disbursed at the time of an obligee's death, as well as any subsequent support payments, are not to be treated as part of the obligee's estate or subject to any creditor's claims against the estate but are to be paid over for the benefit of each surviving child named in the support order. By court order, payment would be made to the child's caretaker, including through an account administered by the county clerk. Presumably, if the caretaker changed, the court could be petitioned to redirect support payments to the successor caretaker. If the obligor is the new caretaker—as likely will be the case—any undisbursed collections would be returned to the obligor, and no further payments would be made—at least, for as long as the obligor continued to have actual care, control, and possession of the child. If a surviving child is no longer a minor, that child would be entitled to a proportionate share of any collected, but undisbursed support collections at the time of the death of the obligee. The section does not address, however, the more complex issue of support arrearages that may have accrued at the time of the obligee's death, including the question of ownership of those arrearages. (*H.P.S.*)

§ 154.014. Payments in Excess of Court-Ordered Amount.

(a) If a child support agency or local child support registry receives from an obligor who is not in arrears a child support payment in an amount that exceeds the court-ordered amount, the agency or registry, to the extent possible, shall give effect to any expressed intent of the obligor for the application of the amount that exceeds the court-ordered amount.

(b) If the obligor does not express an intent for the application of the amount paid in excess of the court-ordered amount, the agency or registry shall:

(1) credit the excess amount to the obligor's future child support obligation; and

(2) promptly disburse the excess amount to the obligee.

(c) This section does not apply to an obligee who is a recipient of public assistance under Chapter 31, Human Resources Code.

Guest Comment

This renumbered section addresses the situation in which a child support registry receives a support payment exceeding the court-ordered amount. Lacking instruction from the obligor, the registry might treat the overpayment as a gift to the obligee, hold it to be disbursed along with the next periodic support payment, or simply return the excess amount to the obligor. This section directs the registry, in the absence of any expressed intent of the obligor, to credit the excess amount towards future child support payments and promptly to disburse the full amount paid by the obligor to the obligee. (*H.P.S.*)

Texas Family Law Practice Manual

Forms 9–17. Original Petition To Recover Child–Support Payments Made after Child–Support Order Terminated; *9–18.* Order To Recover Child Support Payments Made after Child Support Order Terminated

Subchapter B. Computing Net Resources Available for Payment of Child Support

Leading Case

Norris v. Norris, 56 S.W.3d 333 (Tex. App.—El Paso 2001, no pet.) (to reach correct result in computing child support, yearly income swings should be averaged to calculate the most likely future income)

§ 154.061. Computing Net Monthly Income.

(a) Whenever feasible, gross income should first be computed on an annual basis and then should be recalculated to determine average monthly gross income.

(b) The Title IV–D agency shall annually promulgate tax charts to compute net monthly income, subtracting from gross income social security taxes and federal income tax withholding for a single person claiming one personal exemption and the standard deduction.

Leading Case

Norris v. Norris, 56 S.W.3d 333 (Tex. App.—El Paso 2001, no pet.) (to reach correct result in computing child support, yearly income swings should be averaged to calculate the most likely future income)

§ 154.062. Net Resources.

(a) The court shall calculate net resources for the purpose of determining child support liability as provided by this section.

(b) Resources include:

(1) 100 percent of all wage and salary income and other compensation for personal services (including commissions, overtime pay, tips, and bonuses);

(2) interest, dividends, and royalty income;

(3) self-employment income;

(4) net rental income (defined as rent after deducting operating expenses and mortgage payments, but not including noncash items such as depreciation); and

(5) all other income actually being received, including severance pay, retirement benefits, pensions, trust income, annuities, capital gains, social security benefits, unemployment benefits, disability and workers' compensation benefits, interest income from notes regardless of the source, gifts and prizes, spousal maintenance, and alimony.

(c) Resources do not include:

(1) return of principal or capital;

(2) accounts receivable; or

(3) benefits paid in accordance with aid for families with dependent children.

(d) The court shall deduct the following items from resources to determine the net resources available for child support:

(1) social security taxes;

(2) federal income tax based on the tax rate for a single person claiming one personal exemption and the standard deduction;

(3) state income tax;

(4) union dues; and

(5) expenses for health insurance coverage for the obligor's child.

Comment

It is clear that the "100 percent of all wage and salary income" of subsection (b)(1) includes overtime pay. Obviously, whether the pay is regular or overtime, the court must seek to even out irregularities in wages or salary by taking the long view of the obligor's ability to pay. Considering the past year of employment often will yield a more accurate profile than considering the last paycheck or two.

Leading Cases

Knight v. Knight, 131 S.W.3d 535 (Tex. App.—El Paso 2004, no pet.) (child support based on husband's income from prior year rather than alleged current income)

In re E.A.S., 123 S.W.3d 565 (Tex. App.—El Paso 2003, pet. denied) (court finds obligor intentionally underemployed with undisclosed financial resources)

In re Knott, 118 S.W.3d 899 (Tex. App.—Texarkana 2003, no pet.) (new spouse's income not to be included in parent's net resources; no reason found to deviate from guideline support)

In re L.R.P., 98 S.W.3d 312 (Tex. App.—Houston [1st Dist.] 2003, pet. dism'd) (monetary gifts from parents and scholarship funds received included in student father's income for net resources)

Powell v. Swanson, 893 S.W.2d 161 (Tex. App.—Houston [1st Dist.] 1995, no writ) (trial court's calculations of net resources of self-employed obligor found wanting)

---

§ 154.063. Party to Furnish Information.

The court shall require a party to:

(1) furnish information sufficient to accurately identify that party's net resources and ability to pay child support; and

(2) produce copies of income tax returns for the past two years, a financial statement, and current pay stubs.

§ 154.064. Medical Support for Child Presumptively Provided by Obligor.

The guidelines for support of a child are based on the assumption that the court will order the obligor to provide medical support for the child in addition to the amount of child support calculated in accordance with those guidelines.

§ 154.065. Self-Employment Income.

(a) Income from self-employment, whether positive or negative, includes benefits allocated to an individual from a business or undertaking in the form of a proprietorship, partnership, joint venture, close corporation, agency, or independent contractor, less ordinary and necessary expenses required to produce that income.

(b) In its discretion, the court may exclude from self-employment income amounts allowable under federal income tax law as depreciation, tax credits, or any other business expenses shown by the evidence to be inappropriate in making the determination of income available for the purpose of calculating child support.

§ 154.066. Intentional Unemployment or Underemployment.

If the actual income of the obligor is significantly less than what the obligor could earn because of intentional unemployment or underemployment, the court may apply the support guidelines to the earning potential of the obligor.

Leading Cases

In re E.A.S., 123 S.W.3d 565 (Tex. App.—El Paso 2003, pet. denied) (court finds obligor intentionally underemployed with undisclosed financial resources)

Reyes v. Reyes, 946 S.W.2d 627 (Tex. App.—Waco 1997, no writ) (evidence supported holding obligor underemployed even if incarcerated)

---

§ 154.067. Deemed Income.

(a) When appropriate, in order to determine the net resources available for child support, the court may assign a reasonable amount of deemed income attributable to assets that do not currently produce income. The court shall also consider whether certain property that is not producing income can be liquidated without an unreasonable financial sacrifice because of cyclical or other market conditions. If there is no effective market for the property, the carrying costs of such an investment, including property taxes and note payments, shall be offset against the income attributed to the property.

(b) The court may assign a reasonable amount of deemed income to income-producing assets that a party has voluntarily transferred or on which earnings have intentionally been reduced.

§ 154.068. Wage and Salary Presumption.

In the absence of evidence of the wage and salary income of a party, the court shall presume that the party has wages or salary equal to the federal minimum wage for a 40–hour week.

Comment

This section provides a benchmark for calculating an appropriate child support order in the absence of reliable information about the obligor's financial circumstances, to wit, the federal minimum wage.

Leading Case

In re B.R.G., 48 S.W.3d 812 (Tex. App.—El Paso 2001, no pet.), *see also* 37 S.W.3d 542 (in the absence of proof to the contrary, a trial court is authorized to presume a father earned minimum wage from the time of the birth of his child, even if the father is incarcerated)

§ 154.069. Net Resources of Spouse.

(a) The court may not add any portion of the net resources of a spouse to the net resources of an obligor or obligee in order to calculate the amount of child support to be ordered.

(b) The court may not subtract the needs of a spouse, or of a dependent of a spouse, from the net resources of the obligor or obligee.

Leading Case

In re Knott, 118 S.W.3d 899 (Tex. App.—Texarkana 2003, no pet.) (new spouse's income not to be included in parent's net resources; no reason found to deviate from guideline support)

§ 154.070. Child Support Received by Obligor.

In a situation involving multiple households due child support, child support received by an obligor shall be added to the obligor's net resources to compute the net resources before determining the child support credit or applying the percentages in the multiple household table in this chapter.

Subchapter C. Child Support Guidelines

Introductory Comment

The Texas Legislature has assumed the major role regarding child support guidelines. Undoubtedly, the most significant aspect of the legislatively mandated guidelines is that they are applicable in every case and rebuttably presumed to be in the best interest of the child.

CLE/Other Legal Publications

Child support: maximizing your chances of hitting a home run. Janice L. Green, 2004 ADV. FAM. L.

Deposition strategies for kids and cash. Thomas Albert Greenwald, 2004 ADV. FAM. L.

Child support-setting, modifying, and collecting. Alyssa P. Lemkuil & Dan Lemkuil, 2004 U. TEX. FAM. L. FRONT LINES

Unique and not so unique child support issues. Kim W. Mercier & Christopher M. Lake, 2003 MARRIAGE DISSOLUTION

Child support. Rhonda F. Hunter, 2002 ADV. FAM. L.

Private school, cars and cell phones: strategies for obtaining support outside the guidelines. Janice L. Green, 2001 ADV. FAM. L.

Leading Cases

In re Knott, 118 S.W.3d 899 (Tex. App.—Texarkana 2003, no pet.) (new spouse's income not to be included in parent's net resources; no reason found to deviate from guideline support)

Lide v. Lide, 116 S.W.3d 147 (Tex. App.—El Paso 2003, no pet.) (above guideline support affirmed based on funds available to obligor and children's needs)

Hodson v. Keiser, 81 S.W.3d 363 (Tex. App.—El Paso 2002, no pet.) (above guidelines for violent father justified by increased expenses for counseling children)

Carson v. Hathaway, 997 S.W.2d 760 (Tex. App.—El Paso 1999, no pet.) (reciprocal child support not required between equal JMCs)

Driver v. Driver, 895 S.W.2d 875 (Tex. App.—Texarkana 1995, no writ) (evidence insufficient to show income potential of nonproducing assets)

Powell v. Swanson, 893 S.W.2d 161 (Tex. App.—Houston [1st Dist.] 1995, no writ) ("net resources" is not equivalent to "adjusted gross income" which subtracts depreciation on realty)

Roosth v. Roosth, 889 S.W.2d 445 (Tex. App.—Houston [14th Dist.] 1994, writ denied) (who has the burden to prove up obligor's net resources?)

In re Moss, 887 S.W.2d 186 (Tex. App.—Texarkana 1994, no writ) (no information on obligor's earnings yields minimum wage calculation)

Starck v. Nelson, 878 S.W.2d 302 (Tex. App.—Corpus Christi 1994, no writ) (calculation of net resources allowed to be affected by income of second spouse)

In re Pecht, 874 S.W.2d 797 (Tex. App.—Texarkana 1994, no writ) (special needs of children justify award of child support beyond those of statutory guidelines)

Kish v. Kole, 874 S.W.2d 835 (Tex. App.—Beaumont 1994, no writ) (child support award appropriately based on voluntarily underemployed father's earning potential)

Clark v. Jamison, 874 S.W.2d 312 (Tex. App.—Houston [14th Dist.] 1994, no writ) (child support award in excess of guidelines appropriate based on proven needs of child; reduction denied)

Mai v. Mai, 853 S.W.2d 615 (Tex. App.—Houston [1st Dist.] 1993, no writ) (support in excess of guidelines not supported by evidence)

Giangrosso v. Crosley, 840 S.W.2d 765 (Tex. App.—Houston [1st Dist.] 1992, no writ) (voluntarily unemployed parent with earning potential ordered to pay child support to obligor with rising costs and decreased income)

Edwards v. Edwards, 804 S.W.2d 653 (Tex. App.—Amarillo 1991, no writ) (history of extra payments does not justify deviation from guidelines)

MacCallum v. MacCallum, 801 S.W.2d 579 (Tex. App.—Corpus Christi 1990, writ denied) (guidelines in downward modification motion)

Chamberlain v. Chamberlain, 788 S.W.2d 455 (Tex. App.—Houston [1st Dist.] 1990, writ denied) (trial court's failure to explain deviation from guidelines after request is reversible error)

Laprade v. Laprade, 784 S.W.2d 490 (Tex. App.—Fort Worth 1990, writ denied) (list of factors in guidelines not exclusive; IRS tax credits may be considered)

---

§ 154.121. Guidelines for the Support of a Child.

The child support guidelines in this subchapter are intended to guide the court in determining an equitable amount of child support.

§ 154.122. Application of Guidelines Rebuttably Presumed in Best Interest of Child.

(a) The amount of a periodic child support payment established by the child support guidelines in effect in this state at the time of the hearing is presumed to be reasonable, and an order of support conforming to the guidelines is presumed to be in the best interest of the child.

(b) A court may determine that the application of the guidelines would be unjust or inappropriate under the circumstances.

Comment

The child support guidelines determining the amount of support are explicitly presumed to be in the best interest of the child. The trial court may determine the presumed amount is "unjust or inappropriate," but if that conclusion is reached, the court must have a specific explanation to justify it. *See* § 154.130, *infra*.

---

§ 154.123. Additional Factors for Court to Consider.

(a) The court may order periodic child support payments in an amount other than that established by the guidelines if the evidence rebuts the presumption that application of the guidelines is in the best interest of the child and justifies a variance from the guidelines.

(b) In determining whether application of the guidelines would be unjust or inappropriate under the circumstances, the court shall consider evidence of all relevant factors, including:

(1) the age and needs of the child;

(2) the ability of the parents to contribute to the support of the child;

(3) any financial resources available for the support of the child;

(4) the amount of time of possession of and access to a child;

(5) the amount of the obligee's net resources, including the earning potential of the obligee if the actual income of the obligee is significantly less than what the obligee could earn because the obligee is intentionally unemployed or underemployed and including an increase or decrease in the income of the obligee or income that may be attributed to the property and assets of the obligee;

(6) child care expenses incurred by either party in order to maintain gainful employment;

(7) whether either party has the managing conservatorship or actual physical custody of another child;

(8) the amount of alimony or spousal maintenance actually and currently being paid or received by a party;

(9) the expenses for a son or daughter for education beyond secondary school;

(10) whether the obligor or obligee has an automobile, housing, or other benefits furnished by his or her employer, another person, or a business entity;

(11) the amount of other deductions from the wage or salary income and from other compensation for personal services of the parties;

(12) provision for health care insurance and payment of uninsured medical expenses;

(13) special or extraordinary educational, health care, or other expenses of the parties or of the child;

(14) the cost of travel in order to exercise possession of and access to a child;

(15) positive or negative cash flow from any real and personal property and assets, including a business and investments;

(16) debts or debt service assumed by either party; and

(17) any other reason consistent with the best interest of the child, taking into consideration the circumstances of the parents.

Comment

Deviation from the amount "suggested" by the guidelines is permissible, of course, and may be based on any of the wide variety of factors enumerated.

Leading Cases

Lide v. Lide, 116 S.W.3d 147 (Tex. App.—El Paso 2003, no pet.) (above guideline support affirmed based on funds available to obligor and children's needs)

McGuire v. McGuire, 4 S.W.3d 382 (Tex. App.—Houston [1st Dist.] 1999, no pet.) (obligor successfully obtains reduction in child support after going into business that yields less income—underemployment allegation for trial court to evaluate)

Thomas v. Thomas, 895 S.W.2d 895 (Tex. App.—Waco 1995, writ denied) (expiration of contractual alimony constitutes material change in obligee's financial circumstances warranting modification)

---

§ 154.124. Agreement Concerning Support.

(a) To promote the amicable settlement of disputes between the parties to a suit, the parties may enter into a written agreement containing provisions for support of the child and for modification of the agreement, including variations from the child support guidelines provided by Subchapter C.

(b) If the court finds that the agreement is in the child's best interest, the court shall render an order in accordance with the agreement.

(c) Terms of the agreement **pertaining to child support** in the order may be enforced by all remedies available for enforcement of a judgment, including contempt, but are not enforceable as **a** contract [~~terms unless provided by the agreement~~].

(d) If the court finds the agreement is not in the child's best interest, the court may request the parties to submit a revised agreement or the court may render an order for the support of the child.

History: Amended by 78th Legis., Reg. Sess. (2003), H.B. 889, eff. Sept. 1, 2003, and "applies only to an agreement concerning child support entered into on or after that date. An agreement concerning child support entered into before the effective date of this Act is governed by the law applicable to the agreement before that date, and the former law is continued in effect for that purpose."

Comment

A 1995 amendment to § 153.007, *supra*, specifically banned contractual enforcement of agreements for "support of . . . a child." If, but only if, an agreement reached under this section provides that it is "enforceable as a contract," such a conflict will arise. Assuming that the later enactment of § 153.007 controls, the former anomaly will not prevail. That is, downward modification of the support order would not leave a contractual obligation pending enforceable the pre-modification amount. Obviously, contracts entered before September 1, 1995 remain enforceable. For the next three sessions this section stood as a possible irreconcilable conflict by stating an agreement could be so enforced. In 2003, the Family Law Council sought and obtained a correction to this statutory inconsistency.

Leading Cases

Bruni v. Bruni, 924 S.W.2d 366 (Tex. 1996) (parents' agreement for obligor to provide support for children until age 21 enforceable as contract)

Espeche v Ritzell, 123 S.W.3d 657 (Tex. App.—Houston [14th Dist.] 2003, no pet.) (child's breach of contract suit for agreed-upon support against former stepfather not barred by mother's res judicata)

---

§ 154.125. Application of Guidelines to Net Resources of $6,000 or Less.

(a) The guidelines for the support of a child in this section are specifically designed to apply to situations in which the obligor's monthly net resources are $6,000 or less.

(b) If the obligor's monthly net resources are $6,000 or less, the court shall presumptively apply the following schedule in rendering the child support order:

CHILD SUPPORT GUIDELINES

BASED ON THE MONTHLY NET RESOURCES OF THE OBLIGOR

1 child	20% of Obligor's Net Resources
2 children	25% of Obligor's Net Resources
3 children	30% of Obligor's Net Resources
4 children	35% of Obligor's Net Resources
5 children	40% of Obligor's Net Resources
6+ children	Not less than the amount for 5 children

§ 154.126. Application of Guidelines to Net Resources of More Than $6,000 Monthly.

(a) If the obligor's net resources exceed $6,000 per month, the court shall presumptively apply the percentage guidelines to the first $6,000 of the obligor's net resources. Without further reference to the percentage recommended by these guidelines, the court may order additional amounts of child support as appropriate, depending on the income of the parties and the proven needs of the child.

(b) The proper calculation of a child support order that exceeds the presumptive amount established for the first $6,000 of the obligor's net resources requires that the entire amount of the presumptive award be subtracted from the proven total needs of the child. After the presumptive award is subtracted, the court shall allocate between the parties the responsibility to meet the additional needs of the child according to the circumstances of the parties. However, in no event may the obligor be required to pay more child support than the greater of the presumptive amount or the amount equal to 100 percent of the proven needs of the child.

Leading Cases

Scott v. Younts, 926 S.W.2d 415 (Tex. App.—Corpus Christi 1996, writ denied) (obligor earning $300,000 ordered to pay $2,500 monthly support)

Zajac v. Penkava, 924 S.W.2d 405 (Tex. App.—San Antonio 1996, no writ) (doctor Dad should pay monthly child support of $3,000 on net resources of $13,000 monthly when children's proven needs nearly $8,400)

Panozzo v. Panozzo, 904 S.W.2d 780 (Tex. App.—Corpus Christi 1995, no writ) ($10,000 per month child support is abuse of discretion)

---

§ 154.127. Partial Termination of Support Obligation.

A child support order for more than one child shall provide that, on the termination of support for a child, the level of support for the remaining child or children is in accordance with the child support guidelines.

§ 154.128. Computing Support for Children in More Than One Household.

(a) In applying the child support guidelines for an obligor who has children in more than one household, the court shall apply the percentage guidelines in this subchapter by making the following computation:

(1) determine the amount of child support that would be ordered if all children whom the obligor has the legal duty to support lived in one household by applying the schedule in this subchapter;

(2) compute a child support credit for the obligor's children who are not before the court by dividing the amount determined under Subdivision (1) by the total number of children whom the obligor is obligated to support and multiplying that number by the number of the obligor's children who are not before the court;

(3) determine the adjusted net resources of the obligor by subtracting the child support credit computed under Subdivision (2) from the net resources of the obligor; and

(4) determine the child support amount for the children before the court by applying the percentage guidelines for one household for the number of children of the obligor before the court to the obligor's adjusted net resources.

(b) For the purpose of determining a child support credit, the total number of an obligor's children includes the children before the court for the establishment or modification of a support order and any other children, including children residing with the obligor, whom the obligor has the legal duty of support.

(c) The child support credit with respect to children for whom the obligor is obligated by an order to pay support is computed, regardless of whether the obligor is delinquent in child support payments, without regard to the amount of the order.

Comment

This cleverly devised formula provides a method for computing support for obligors with multiple families, *i.e.,* with children who reside in more than one household. However, sensible practitioners will skip the textual statement for calculating the formula and go directly to the chart provided in the next section.

---

§ 154.129. Alternative Method of Computing Support for Children in More Than One Household.

In lieu of performing the computation under the preceding section, the court may determine the child support amount for the children before the court by applying the percentages in the table below to the obligor's net resources:

MULTIPLE FAMILY ADJUSTED GUIDELINES
(% OF NET RESOURCES)

		Number of children before the court						
		1	2	3	4	5	6	7
Number of	0	20.00	25.00	30.00	35.00	40.00	40.00	40.00
other	1	17.50	22.50	27.38	32.20	37.33	37.71	38.00
children for	2	16.00	20.63	25.20	30.33	35.43	36.00	36.44
whom the	3	14.75	19.00	24.00	29.00	34.00	34.67	35.20
obligor	4	13.60	18.33	23.14	28.00	32.89	33.60	34.18
has a	5	13.33	17.86	22.50	27.22	32.00	32.73	33.33
duty of	6	13.14	17.50	22.00	26.60	31.27	32.00	32.62
support	7	13.00	17.22	21.60	26.09	30.67	31.38	32.00

§ 154.130. Findings in Child Support Order.

(a) Without regard to Rules 296 through 299, Texas Rules of Civil Procedure, in rendering an order of child support, the court shall make the findings required by Subsection (b) if:

(1) a party files a written request with the court not later than 10 days after the date of the hearing;

(2) a party makes an oral request in open court during the hearing; or

(3) the amount of child support ordered by the court varies from the amount computed by applying the percentage guidelines.

(b) If findings are required by this section, the court shall state whether the application of the guidelines would be unjust or inappropriate and shall state the following in the child support order:

"(1) the monthly net resources of the obligor per month are $______;

"(2) the monthly net resources of the obligee per month are $______;

"(3) the percentage applied to the obligor's net resources for child support by the actual order rendered by the court is ______%;

"(4) the amount of child support if the percentage guidelines are applied to the first $6,000 of the obligor's net resources is $______;

"(5) if applicable, the specific reasons that the amount of child support per month ordered by the court varies from the amount stated in Subdivision (4) are: ______; and

"(6) if applicable, the obligor is obligated to support children in more than one household, and:

"(A) the number of children before the court is ______;

"(B) the number of children not before the court residing in the same household with the obligor is ______; and

"(C) the number of children not before the court for whom the obligor is obligated by a court order to pay support, without regard to whether the obligor is delinquent in child support payments, and who are not counted under Paragraph (A) or (B) is ______."

(c) The application of the guidelines under Section 154.129 does not constitute a variance from the child support guidelines requiring specific findings by the court under this section.

Comment

The request for findings in a child support order is specifically placed outside the range of Texas Rules of Civil Procedure 296–299. Response to a request for an explanation is mandatory; failure to justify the deviation from the amount suggested by the guidelines constitutes reversible error. Subsection (b) requires the court to explain its deviation from the guidelines whenever the guidelines would yield an amount different from the sum actually ordered.

Leading Cases

Tenery v. Tenery, 932 S.W.2d 29 (Tex. 1996) (obligor has right to demand findings and conclusions when trial court deviates from child support guidelines)

Haney v. Haney, 834 S.W.2d 490 (Tex. App.—Houston [14th Dist.] 1992, writ denied) (required findings recorded on docket sheet satisfy requirement even though not stated in order)

Hanna v. Hanna, 813 S.W.2d 626 (Tex. App.—Houston [1st Dist.] 1991, no writ) (failure to make requested findings on net resources reversible error)

Chamberlain v. Chamberlain, 788 S.W.2d 455 (Tex. App.—Houston [1st Dist.] 1990, writ denied) (trial court's failure to explain deviation from guidelines after request is reversible error)

Cross References

Tex. R. Civ. P. 296. Requests for Findings of Facts and Conclusions of Law; 297. Time to File Findings of Facts and Conclusions of Law.

Texas Family Law Practice Manual

Forms 20–8. Request for Findings in Child–Support Order.

---

§ 154.131. Retroactive Child Support.

(a) The child support guidelines are intended to guide the court in determining the amount of retroactive child support, if any, to be ordered.

(b) In ordering retroactive child support, the court shall consider the net resources of the obligor during the relevant time period and whether:

(1) the mother of the child had made any previous attempts to notify the obligor of his paternity or probable paternity;

(2) the obligor had knowledge of his paternity or probable paternity;

(3) the order of retroactive child support will impose an undue financial hardship on the obligor or the obligor's family; and

(4) the obligor has provided actual support or other necessaries before the filing of the action.

(c) It is presumed that a court order limiting the amount of retroactive child support to an amount that does not exceed the total amount of support that would have been due for the four years preceding the date the petition seeking support was filed is reasonable and in the best interest of the child.

(d) The presumption created under this section may be rebutted by evidence that the obligor:

(1) knew or should have known that the obligor was the father of the child for whom support is sought; and

(2) sought to avoid the establishment of a support obligation to the child.

(e) An order under this section limiting the amount of retroactive support does not constitute a variance from the guidelines requiring the court to make specific findings under Section 154.130.

Guest Comment

This section provides a method for calculating arrears when a parentage suit determines retroactive support is due. *See* Chapter 160, Uniform Parentage Act, *infra*.

Subsection (c) reflects a concern expressed by public policy groups that large amounts of retroactive support may diminish the ability of many child support obligors to stay current in payment of their support obligations. There was also the sense among lawmakers that an obligor ignorant of having fathered a child—perhaps because of deliberate concealment of the fact by the mother—or an obligor knowing he was the father, but being told by the obligee that his support was not needed or wanted, would be unfairly burdened with a child support obligation reaching back many years. Although the code already clearly provided the court with discretion in determining whether, and how much, retroactive support should be ordered, subsection (c) rebuttably limits retroactive support to an amount not exceeding the amount of support that would have been due under the support guidelines for the four-year period preceding the filing of the petition. In effect, it creates an estoppel by laches defense with the burden of refutation falling upon the obligee or the state, as the case may be. (*H.P.S.*)

Leading Cases

Martinez v. Martinez, 61 S.W.3d 589 (Tex. App.—San Antonio 2001, pet. denied) (order awarding retroactive child support is void without specific notice it is being sought)

Garza v. Blanton, 55 S.W.3d 708 (Tex. App.—Corpus Christi 2001, no pet.) (order for retroactive support in paternity suit discretionary with the court—payments made pre-parentage determination seriously mitigate against such an order)

In re A.P., 46 S.W.3d 347 (Tex. App.—Corpus Christi 2001, no pet.) (court ordered 18 years of retroactive child support for the child before she turned age 20)

§ 154.132. Application of Guidelines to Children of Certain Disabled Obligors.

In applying the child support guidelines for an obligor who has a disability and who is required to pay support for a child who receives benefits as a result of the obligor's disability, the court shall apply the guidelines by determining the amount of child support that would be ordered under the child support guidelines and subtracting from that total the amount of benefits or the value of the benefits paid to or for the child as a result of the obligor's disability.

Comment

Courts have taken different positions as to whether a disabled obligor is entitled to a credit for the amount of payments received by a child as a result of the obligor's disability when the support guidelines are applied. This provision makes it clear that the obligor is entitled to such a credit.

Leading Cases

In re Nichols, 51 S.W.3d 303 (Tex. App.—San Antonio 2000, no pet.) (obligor receives child support credit for V.A. and Social Security payments made on behalf of his children, but not retroactive to time preceding money judgment for arrears)

Reyes v. Gonzales, 22 S.W.3d 516 (Tex. App.—El Paso 1999, pet. denied) (SSI not included in net resources)

In re Rich, 993 S.W.2d 272 (Tex. App.—San Antonio 1999, no pet.) (father entitled to credit against his child support obligation for social security benefits child receives)

In re K.E.T., 974 S.W.2d 760 (Tex. App.—San Antonio 1998, no pet.) (social security disability payments may offset child support, but does not count as credit against claim by the state for assistance paid)

§ 154.133. Application of Guidelines to Children of Obligors Receiving Social Security.

In applying the child support guidelines for an obligor who is receiving social security old age benefits and who is required to pay support for a child who receives benefits as a result of the obligor's receipt of social security old age benefits, the court shall apply the guidelines by determining the amount of child support that would be ordered under the child support guidelines and subtracting from that total the amount of benefits or the value of the benefits paid to or for the child as a result of the obligor's receipt of social security old age benefits.

Guest Comment

The net resources of the obligor to which the court applies the guidelines in determining the child support obligation include any social security benefits, *see* § 154.062, *supra*. Under federal social security law, a minor child or an adult disabled child of an obligor receiving Social Security old age (retirement) benefits is also entitled to receive dependant benefits. This section requires the court to deduct from the amount of child support that would be ordered by the application of the guidelines to the obligor's net resources the amount of dependent benefits received by the child as a result of the obligor's eligibility to social security old age benefits. The provision complements § 154.132, *supra*, which accords the obligor a similar credit with respect to disability benefits. (*H.P.S.*)

OFFICE OF ATTORNEY GENERAL, REVISED 2003 TAX CHARTS

On May 28, 2003, the President signed into law the Jobs and Growth Tax Relief Reconciliation Act of 2003, Pub. L. No. 108–27 (the "Act"). The Act accelerates the phase-in of certain marginal tax rate reductions for individuals that were enacted in the Economic Growth and Tax Relief Reconciliation Act of 2001, Pub. L. No. 107–16. In addition, the Act increases the levels of taxable income subject to the 10% individual tax rate. These provisions of the Act are effective for the 2003 calendar tax year. Accordingly, these provisions of the Act require revisions to the federal income tax information shown in the 2003 Tax Charts previously promulgated by the Office of the Attorney General of Texas.

A line computing net resources for an individual earning the federal minimum wage for a 40 hour week was added to the Employed Persons Tax Chart, and lines showing the gross monthly income corresponding to net resources of $6,000.00 were added to the Employed Persons Tax Chart and to the Self-Employed Persons Tax Chart.

Pursuant to § 154.061(b) of the Texas Family Code, the Office of the Attorney General of Texas, as the Title IV–D agency, has promulgated the following revised tax charts for use during the remainder of 2003 to assist courts in establishing the amount of a child support order. These tax charts are applicable to employed and self-employed persons in computing net monthly income.

INSTRUCTIONS FOR USE

To use these tables, first compute the obligor's annual gross income. Then recompute to determine the obligor's average monthly gross income. These tables provide a method for calculating "monthly net income" for child support purposes, subtracting from monthly gross income the social security taxes and the federal income tax withholding for a single person claiming one personal exemption and the standard deduction.

Thereafter, in many cases the guidelines call for a number of additional steps to complete the necessary calculations. For example, §§ 154.061—154.070 provide for appropriate additions to "income" as that term is defined for federal income tax purposes, and for certain subtractions from monthly net income, in order to arrive at the net resources of the obligor available for child support purposes. If necessary, one m compute an obligee's net resources using similar steps.

EMPLOYED PERSONS*
REVISED 2003 TAX CHART

	Social Security Taxes			
Monthly Gross Wages	Old–Age, Survivors and Disability Insurance Taxes (6.2%)*	Hospital (Medicare) Insurance Taxes (1.45%)	Federal Income Taxes	Net Monthly Income
$100.00	$6.20	$1.45	$0.00	$92.35
$200.00	$12.40	$2.90	$0.00	$184.70
$300.00	$18.60	$4.35	$0.00	$277.05
$400.00	$24.80	$5.80	$0.00	$369.40
$500.00	$31.00	$7.25	$0.00	$461.75
$600.00	$37.20	$8.70	$0.00	$554.10
$700.00	$43.40	$10.15	$5.00	$641.45
$800.00	$49.60	$11.60	$15.00	$723.80
#$892.67	**$55.35**	**$12.94**	**$24.27**	**$800.11**
$900.00	$55.80	$13.05	$25.00	$806.15
$1,000.00	$62.00	$14.50	$35.00	$888.50
$1,100.00	$68.20	$15.95	$45.00	$970.85
$1,200.00	$74.40	$17.40	$55.00	$1,053.20
$1,300.00	$80.60	$18.85	$68.33	$1,132.22
$1,400.00	$86.80	$20.30	$83.33	$1,209.57
$1,500.00	$93.00	$21.75	$98.33	$1,286.92
$1,600.00	$99.20	$23.20	$113.33	$1,364.27
$1,700.00	$105.40	$24.65	$128.33	$1,441.62
$1,800.00	$111.60	$26.10	$143.33	$1,518.97
$1,900.00	$117.80	$27.55	$158.33	$1,596.32
$2,000.00	$124.00	$29.00	$173.33	$1,673.67
$2,100.00	$130.20	$30.45	$188.33	$1,751.02
$2,200.00	$136.40	$31.90	$203.33	$1,828.37
$2,300.00	$142.60	$33.35	$218.33	$1,905.72
$2,400.00	$148.80	$34.80	$233.33	$1,983.07
$2,500.00	$155.00	$36.25	$248.33	$2,060.42
$2,600.00	$161.20	$37.70	$263.33	$2,137.77
$2,700.00	$167.40	$39.15	$278.33	$2,215.12
$2,800.00	$173.60	$40.60	$293.33	$2,292.47
$2,900.00	$179.80	$42.05	$308.33	$2,369.82
$3,000.00	$186.00	$43.50	$323.33	$2,447.17
$3,100.00	$192.20	$44.95	$346.67	$2,516.18
$3,200.00	$198.40	$46.40	$371.67	$2,583.53
$3,300.00	$204.60	$47.85	$396.67	$2,650.88
$3,400.00	$210.80	$49.30	$421.67	$2,718.23
$3,500.00	$217.00	$50.75	$446.67	$2,785.58
$3,600.00	$223.20	$52.20	$471.67	$2,852.93
$3,700.00	$229.40	$53.65	$496.67	$2,920.28
$3,800.00	$235.60	$55.10	$521.67	$2,987.63
$3,900.00	$241.80	$56.55	$546.67	$3,054.98
$4,000.00	$248.00	$58.00	$571.67	$3,122.33
$4,250.00	$263.50	$61.63	$634.17	$3,290.70
$4,500.00	$279.00	$65.25	$696.67	$3,459.08
$4,750.00	$294.50	$68.88	$759.17	$3,627.45
$5,000.00	$310.00	$72.50	$821.67	$3,795.83
$5,250.00	$325.50	$76.13	$884.17	$3,964.20
$5,500.00	$341.00	$79.75	$946.67	$4,132.58
$5,750.00	$356.50	$83.38	$1,009.17	$4,300.95
$6,000.00	$372.00	$87.00	$1,071.67	$4,469.33
$6,250.00	$387.50	$90.63	$1,134.17	$4,637.70
$6,500.00	$403.00	$94.25	$1,200.17	$4,802.58
$6,750.00	$418.50	$97.88	$1,270.17	$4,963.45
$7,000.00	$434.00	$101.50	$1,340.17	$5,124.33
$7,500.00	$449.50	$108.75	$1,480.17	$5,461.58
$8,000.00	$449.50	$116.00	$1,620.17	$5,814.33
##$8,263.17	**$449.50**	**$119.82**	**$1,693.85**	**$6,000.00**

EMPLOYED PERSONS* REVISED 2003 TAX CHART

Monthly Gross Wages	Social Security Taxes: Old–Age, Survivors and Disability Insurance Taxes (6.2%)*	Social Security Taxes: Hospital (Medicare) Insurance Taxes (1.45%)	Federal Income Taxes	Net Monthly Income
$8,500.00	$449.50	$123.25	$1,760.17	$6,167.08
$9,000.00	$449.50	$130.50	$1,900.17	$6,519.83
$9,500.00	$449.50	$137.75	$2,040.17	$6,872.58
$10,000.00	$449.50	$145.00	$2,180.17	$7,225.33
$10,500.00	$449.50	$152.25	$2,320.17	$7,578.08
$11,000.00	$449.50	$159.50	$2,460.17	$7,930.83
$11,500.00	$449.50	$166.75	$2,600.17	$8,283.58
$12,000.00	$449.50	$174.00	$2,743.01	$8,633.49
$12,500.00	$449.50	$181.25	$2,887.28	$8,981.97
$13,000.00	$449.50	$188.50	$3,051.49	$9,310.51
$13,500.00	$449.50	$195.75	$3,219.85	$9,634.90
$14,000.00	$449.50	$203.00	$3,389.88	$9,957.62
$14,500.00	$449.50	$210.25	$3,558.24	$10,282.01
$15,000.00	$449.50	$217.50	$3,728.27	$10,604.73

Footnotes to Employed Persons 2003 Tax Chart:
*For details about the calculations of the Tax Charts, see the website of the Office of the Attorney General, Child Support Division: http://www.oag.state.tx.us/AG_Publications/pdfs/2003taxcharts.pdf

#TEX. FAM. CODE § 154.068 states: "Wage and Salary Presumption. In the absence of evidence of the wage and salary income of a party, the court shall presume that the party has wages or salary equal to the federal minimum wage for a 40–hour week." Based on the federal minimum wage of $5.15 per hour, 40 hours per week for 52 weeks will yield $893.00 monthly gross wages.

##TEX. FAM. CODE § 154.125(a) states: "Application of Guidelines to Net Resources of $6,000 or Less. The guidelines for the support of a child in this section are specifically designed to apply to situations in which the obligor's monthly net resources are $6,000 or less."

SELF-EMPLOYED PERSONS REVISED 2003 TAX CHART*

Monthly Net Earnings From Self-Employment	Social Security Taxes: Old-Age, Survivors and Disability Insurance Taxes (12.4%)	Social Security Taxes: Hospital (Medicare) Insurance Taxes (2.9%)	Federal Income Taxes	Net Monthly Income
$100.00	$11.45	$2.68	$0.00	$85.87
$200.00	$22.90	$5.36	$0.00	$171.74
$300.00	$34.35	$8.03	$0.00	$257.62
$400.00	$45.81	$10.71	$0.00	$343.48
$500.00	$57.26	$13.39	$0.00	$429.35
$600.00	$68.71	$16.07	$0.00	$515.22
$700.00	$80.16	$18.75	$0.05	$601.04
$800.00	$91.61	$21.43	$9.35	$677.61
$900.00	$103.06	$24.10	$18.64	$754.20
$1,000.00	$114.51	$26.78	$27.94	$830.77
$1,100.00	$125.97	$29.46	$37.23	$907.34
$1,200.00	$137.42	$32.14	$46.52	$983.92
$1,300.00	$148.87	$34.82	$55.82	$1,060.49
$1,400.00	$160.32	$37.49	$68.50	$1,133.69
$1,500.00	$171.77	$40.17	$82.44	$1,205.62
$1,600.00	$183.22	$42.85	$96.38	$1,277.55
$1,700.00	$194.67	$45.53	$110.32	$1,349.48
$1,800.00	$206.13	$48.21	$124.26	$1,421.40
$1,900.00	$217.58	$50.88	$138.20	$1,493.34
$2,000.00	$229.03	$53.56	$152.14	$1,565.27
$2,100.00	$240.48	$56.24	$166.08	$1,637.20
$2,200.00	$251.93	$58.92	$180.02	$1,709.13
$2,300.00	$263.38	$61.60	$193.96	$1,781.06
$2,400.00	$274.83	$64.28	$207.90	$1,852.99
$2,500.00	$286.29	$66.95	$221.84	$1,924.92
$2,600.00	$297.74	$69.63	$235.78	$1,996.85

SELF-EMPLOYED PERSONS
REVISED 2003 TAX CHART*

Monthly Net Earnings From Self-Employment	Social Security Taxes: Old-Age, Survivors and Disability Insurance Taxes (12.4%)	Social Security Taxes: Hospital (Medicare) Insurance Taxes (2.9%)	Federal Income Taxes	Net Monthly Income
$2,700.00	$309.19	$72.31	$249.72	$2,068.78
$2,800.00	$320.64	$74.99	$263.66	$2,140.71
$2,900.00	$332.09	$77.67	$277.60	$2,212.64
$3,000.00	$343.54	$80.34	$291.54	$2,284.58
$3,100.00	$354.99	$83.02	$305.48	$2,356.51
$3,200.00	$366.44	$85.70	$319.42	$2,428.44
$3,300.00	$377.90	$88.38	$338.38	$2,495.34
$3,400.00	$389.35	$91.06	$361.62	$2,557.97
$3,500.00	$400.80	$93.74	$384.85	$2,620.61
$3,600.00	$412.25	$96.41	$408.08	$2,683.26
$3,700.00	$423.70	$99.09	$431.32	$2,745.89
$3,800.00	$435.15	$101.77	$454.55	$2,808.53
$3,900.00	$446.60	$104.45	$477.79	$2,871.16
$4,000.00	$458.06	$107.13	$501.02	$2,933.79
$4,250.00	$486.68	$113.82	$559.10	$3,090.40
$4,500.00	$515.31	$120.52	$617.19	$3,246.98
$4,750.00	$543.94	$127.21	$675.27	$3,403.58
$5,000.00	$572.57	$133.91	$733.36	$3,560.16
$5,250.00	$601.20	$140.60	$791.44	$3,716.76
$5,500.00	$629.83	$147.30	$849.53	$3,873.34
$5,750.00	$658.46	$153.99	$907.61	$4,029.94
$6,000.00	$687.08	$160.69	$965.70	$4,186.53
$6,250.00	$715.71	$167.38	$1,023.78	$4,343.13
$6,500.00	$744.34	$174.08	$1,081.86	$4,499.72
$6,750.00	$772.97	$180.78	$1,139.95	$4,656.30
$7,000.00	$801.60	$187.47	$1,201.70	$4,809.23
$7,500.00	$858.86	$200.86	$1,331.81	$5,108.47
$8,000.00	$899.00	$214.25	$1,464.31	$5,422.44
#$8,828.68	**$899.00**	**$236.45**	**$1,693.23**	**$6,000.00**
$8,500.00	$899.00	$227.64	$1,602.44	$5,770.92
$9,000.00	$899.00	$241.03	$1,740.56	$6,119.41
$9,500.00	$899.00	$254.42	$1,878.69	$6,467.89
$10,000.00	$899.00	$267.82	$2,016.81	$6,816.37
$10,500.00	$899.00	$281.21	$2,154.94	$7,164.85
$11,000.00	$899.00	$294.60	$2,293.06	$7,513.34
$11,500.00	$899.00	$307.99	$2,431.19	$7,861.82
$12,000.00	$899.00	$321.38	$2,569.31	$8,210.31
$12,500.00	$899.00	$334.77	$2,710.29	$8,555.94
$13,000.00	$899.00	$348.16	$2,851.26	$8,901.58
$13,500.00	$899.00	$361.55	$3,006.82	$9,232.63
$14,000.00	$899.00	$374.94	$3,174.65	$9,551.41
$14,500.00	$899.00	$388.33	$3,340.79	$9,871.88
$15,000.00	$899.00	$401.72	$3,508.62	$10,190.66

Footnotes to Self–Employed Persons Revised 2003 Tax Chart:
*For details about the calculations of the Tax Charts, see the website of the Office of the Attorney General, Child Support Division: http://www.oag.state.tx.us/AG_Publications/pdfs/2003taxcharts.pdf

#Tex. Fam. Code § 154.125(a) states: "Application of Guidelines to Net Resources of $6,000 or Less. The guidelines for the support of a child in this section are specifically designed to apply to situations in which the obligor's monthly net resources are $6,000 or less."

Subchapter D. Medical Support for Child

Introductory Comment

The trial court has great flexibility to fashion an appropriate order to ensure that health insurance is available to the child. While the cost of health insurance is assumed to be y the obligor, in some circumstances this is impractical or impossible. If the bears the cost of health insurance, a recalculation of the periodic payments of pport is appropriate.

CLE/Other Legal Publications

Ensuring insurance coverage for your client (COBRA, Qualified Medical Support Orders and finding, using and characterizing insurance coverage). Susan Myres, 2001 ADV. FAM. L.

How to get even when you already are: equal evidence custody cases. Kevin R. Fuller, 2000 MARRIAGE DISSOLUTION

Leading Case

State v. Hernandez, 802 S.W.2d 894 (Tex. App.—San Antonio 1991, no writ) (court erred in not ordering health insurance)

Cross References

Continuation of Medical Coverage (COBRA). 29 U.S.C.A. § 1161 *et seq.*

Qualified Medical Child Support Order (QMCSO), 29 U.S.C.A. § 1169.

TEX. INS. CODE ANN. art. 3.51–6. Group and Blanket Accident and Health Insurance.

Texas Family Law Practice Manual

Form 9–1. Medical Child–Support Order

---

§ 154.181. Medical Support Order.

(a) **The** [~~In a suit affecting the parent child relationship or in a proceeding under Chapter 159, the~~] court shall render an order for the medical support of the child as provided by this section and Section 154.182 **in:**

(1) a proceeding in which periodic payments of child support are ordered under this chapter or modified under Chapter 156;

(2) any other suit affecting the parent-child relationship in which the court determines that medical support of the child must be established, modified, or clarified; or

(3) a proceeding under Chapter 159 *[UIFSA]*.

(b) Before a hearing on temporary orders or a final order, if no hearing on temporary orders is held, the court shall require the parties to the proceedings to disclose in a pleading or other statement:

(1) if private health insurance is in effect for the child, the identity of the insurance company providing the coverage, the policy number, which parent is responsible for payment of any insurance premium for the coverage, whether the coverage is provided through a parent's employment, and the cost of the premium; or

(2) if private health insurance is not in effect for the child, whether:

(A) the child is receiving medical assistance under Chapter 32, Human Resources Code;

(B) the child is receiving health benefits coverage under the state child health plan under Chapter 62, Health and Safety Code, and the cost of any premium; and

(C) either parent has access to private health insurance at reasonable cost to that parent.

(c) In rendering temporary orders, the court shall, except for good cause shown, order that any health insurance coverage in effect for the child continue in effect pending the rendition of a final order, except that the court may not require the continuation of any health insurance that is not available to the parent at reasonable cost. If there is no health insurance coverage in effect for the child or if the insurance in effect is not available at a reasonable cost and the child is not receiving medical assistance under Chapter 32, Human Resources Code, or coverage under the state child health plan under Chapter 62, Health and Safety Code, the court shall, except for good cause shown, order health care coverage for the child as provided under Section 154.182.

(d) Except for good cause shown, on rendering a final order the court shall require the parent ordered to provide health care coverage for the child as provided under Section 154.182 to produce evidence to the court's satisfaction that the parent has applied for or secured health insurance or has otherwise taken necessary action to provide for health care coverage for the child, as ordered by the court.

(e) In this section, "reasonable cost" means the cost of a health insurance premium that does not exceed 10 percent of the responsible parent's net income in a month.

History: Amended by 78th Legis., Reg. Sess. (2003), H.B. 1878, eff. Sept. 1, 2003, and applies "only to a suit affecting the parent-child relationship filed on or after the effective date of this Act. A suit affecting the parent-child relationship filed before the effective date of this Act is governed by the law in effect on the date the suit was filed, and the former law is continued in effect for that purpose."

Guest Comment

Subsection (a) clarifies that a new medical support order is not required in every SAPCR, but only in those proceedings which address child support or medical support or in a UIFSA proceeding. Health care coverage of a child is considered an integral part of the child support obligation and must ordinarily be ordered along with financial support. The court, however, must determine how health care coverage will be provided, either by private or government plans. This section lays out a process by which the court is to consider the availability to either parent of affordable coverage for the child. Whereas at one time it was assumed that insurance coverage of a child through a parent's place of employment was available "at reasonable cost," in 2001 the legislature established a new criterion of "reasonable cost" under subsection (e). (*H.P.S.*)

CLE/Other Legal Publications

S.A.P.C.R. solutions. Sydney A. Beckman, 2002 Adv. Fam. L. Drafting

Oh, what a relief it is: TRO's, temporary orders, magistrate's order for emergency protection and other delights. Lisa Beebe, 2001 Adv. Fam. L.

Drafting T.O.s and decrees. Judy Warne, 2001 Adv. Fam. L.

Temporary orders. Wendy S. Burgower, 2001 Marriage Dissolution

---

§ 154.182. Health Insurance.

(a) The court shall consider the cost and quality of health insurance coverage available to the parties and shall give priority to health insurance coverage available through the employment of one of the parties.

(b) In determining the manner in which health insurance for the child is to be ordered, the court shall render its order in accordance with the following priorities, unless a party shows good cause why a particular order would not be in the best interest of the child:

(1) if health insurance is available for the child through the obligor's employment or membership in a union, trade association, or other organization at reasonable cost to the obligor, the court shall order the obligor to include the child in the obligor's health insurance;

(2) if health insurance is not available for the child through the obligor's employment but is available for the child at a reasonable cost through the obligee's employment or membership in a union, trade association, or other organization, the court may order the obligee to provide health insurance for the child, and, in such event, shall order the obligor to pay additional child support to be withheld from earnings under Chapter 158 to the obligee for the actual cost of the health insurance for the child;

(3) if health insurance is not available for the child under Subdivision (1) or (2), the court shall order the obligor to provide health insurance for the child if the court finds that health insurance is available to the obligor for the child from another source and at reasonable cost;

(4) if neither parent has access to private health insurance at a reasonable cost, the court shall order that the custodial parent or, to the extent permitted by law, the noncustodial parent immediately apply on behalf of the child for participation in a medical assistance program under Chapter 32, Human Resources Code, or the state child health plan under Chapter 62, Health and Safety Code, and that the obligor pay additional child support, to be withheld from income under Chapter 158, to the obligee for the actual cost of participation of the child in **the state child health plan** [~~such program~~]; or

(5) if health coverage is not available for the child under Subdivision (1), (2), (3), or (4), the court shall order the obligor to pay the obligee, in addition to any amount ordered under the guidelines for child support, a reasonable amount each month as medical support for the child to be withheld from earnings under Chapter 158.

(c) In this section, "reasonable cost" has the meaning assigned by Section 154.181(e).

History: Amended by 78th Legis., Reg. Sess. (2003), H.B. 1878, eff. Sept. 1, 2003, and applies "only to a suit affecting the parent-child relationship filed on or after the effective date of this Act. A suit affecting the parent-child relationship filed before the effective date of this Act is governed by the law in effect on the date the suit was filed, and the former law is continued in effect for that purpose."

Guest Comment

The guidelines used by the court in determining the amount of child support are based on the assumption that the obligor will be providing the cost of health care coverage for the child, through private insurance available to either the obligor or the obligee at "reasonable cost" or, if affordable private insurance is not available to either party, through government programs, depending upon eligibility requirements. If the obligee is responsible for securing the coverage through a private or a government plan, in addition to court-ordered child support through income withholding the obligor is to reimburse the obligee the cost of any premium—including the cost of participation in the state child health plan. If coverage is not available at "reasonable cost" to either parent through a private or government plan, the obligor is ordered to provide a "reasonable amount" for medical support, to be withheld from the obligor's income in addition to the amount identified under the guidelines for child support. Although "reasonable cost" is statutorily defined (see § 154.181(e), *supra*), "reasonable amount" is left to the court to determine. (*H.P.S.*)

---

§ 154.183. Health Insurance Additional Support Duty of Obligor.

(a) An amount that an obligor is required to pay for health insurance for the child:

(1) is in addition to the amount that the obligor is required to pay for child support under the guidelines for child support;

(2) is a child support obligation; and

(3) may be enforced as a child support obligation.

(b) If the court finds and states in the child support order that the obligee will maintain health insurance coverage for the child at the obligee's expense, the court may increase the amount of child support to be paid by the obligor in an amount not exceeding the total expense to the obligee for maintaining health insurance coverage.

(c) As additional child support, the court shall allocate between the parties, according to their circumstances, the reasonable and necessary health care expenses of a child that are not reimbursed by health insurance.

§ 154.184. Effect of Order.

(a) Receipt of a medical support order requiring that health insurance be provided for a child shall be considered a change in the family circumstances of the employee or member, for health insurance purposes, equivalent to the birth or adoption of a child.

(b) If the employee or member is eligible for dependent health coverage, the employer shall automatically enroll the child for the first 31 days after the receipt of the order or notice of the medical support order under Section 154.186 on the same terms and conditions as apply to any other dependent child.

(c) The employer shall notify the insurer of the automatic enrollment.

(d) During the 31–day period, the employer and insurer shall complete all necessary forms and procedures to make the enrollment permanent or shall report in accordance with this subchapter the reasons the coverage cannot be made permanent.

§ 154.185. Parent to Furnish Information.

(a) The court shall order a parent providing health insurance to furnish to either the obligee, obligor, or child support agency the following information not later than the 30th day after the date the notice of rendition of the order is received:

(1) the social security number of the parent;

(2) the name and address of the parent's employer;

(3) whether the employer is self-insured or has health insurance available;

(4) proof that health insurance has been provided for the child;

(5) if the employer has health insurance available, the name of the health insurance carrier, the number of the policy, a copy of the policy and schedule of benefits, a health insurance membership card, claim forms, and any other information necessary to submit a claim; and

(6) if the employer is self-insured, a copy of the schedule of benefits, a membership card, claim forms, and any other information necessary to submit a claim.

(b) The court shall also order a parent providing health insurance to furnish the obligor, obligee, or child support agency with additional information regarding health insurance coverage not later than the 15th day after the date the information is received by the parent.

§ 154.186. Notice to Employer Concerning Medical Support.

(a) The obligee, obligor, or a child support agency may send to the employer a copy of the order requiring an employee to provide health insurance coverage for a child or may include notice of the medical support order in an order or writ of withholding sent to the employer in accordance with Chapter 158.

(b) In an appropriate Title IV–D case, the Title IV–D agency shall send to the employer the national medical support notice required under Part D, Title IV of the federal Social Security Act (42 U.S.C. Section 651 et seq.), as amended. The notice may be used in any other suit in which an obligor is ordered to provide health insurance coverage for a child.

(c) The Title IV–D agency by rule shall establish procedures consistent with federal law for use of the national medical support notice and may prescribe forms for the efficient use of the notice. The agency shall provide the notice and forms, on request, to obligees, obligors, domestic relations offices, friends of the court, and attorneys.

Guest Comment

Congress has attempted to remove some of the impediments to the attempts of state IV–D agencies to secure and enforce medical coverage for children in IV–D cases (OBRA 1993; Pub. L. 103–66). OBRA contained many improvements that facilitated obtaining and enforcing medical coverage, including the creation of "qualified medical child support orders" (QMCSOs) to obtain coverage for dependent children of employees from group health plans subject to the Employee Retirement Income Security Act of 1974 (ERISA). Despite improved state procedures mandated by federal law for the establishment and enforcement of medical support for children, states continued to experience difficulty in satisfying specific conditions of ERISA, particularly with respect to informational requirements and restrictions against requiring new types or forms of benefits. To more fully address the needs and concerns of sponsors and administrators of group health plans, Congress required the Secretaries of the federal departments of Health and Human Services and Labor to develop and promulgate a federal "national medical support notice" for the enforcement of medical support obligations in IV–D cases, P.L. 105–200. In the 2003 amendment the legislature complied with the federal mandate for IV–D cases and, in addition, authorized, but did not mandate, the use of the federal notice in non-IV–D cases. *(C.B. & H.P.S.)*

§ 154.187. Duties of Employer.

(a) An order or notice under this subchapter to an employer directing that health insurance coverage be provided to a child of an employee or member is binding on a current or subsequent employer on receipt without regard to the date the order was rendered. If the employee or member is eligible for dependent health coverage for the child, the employer shall immediately enroll the child in a health insurance plan regardless of whether the employee is enrolled in the plan. If dependent coverage is not available to the employee or member through the employer's health insurance plan or enrollment cannot be made permanent or if the employer is not responsible or otherwise liable for providing such coverage, the employer shall provide notice to the sender in accordance with Subsection (c).

(b) If additional premiums are incurred as a result of adding the child to the health insurance plan, the employer shall deduct the health insurance premium from the earnings of the employee in accordance with Chapter 158 *[Withholding from Earnings for Child Support]* and apply the amount withheld to payment of the insurance premium.

(c) An employer who has received an order or notice under this subchapter shall provide to the sender, by first class mail not later than the 30th day after the date the employer receives the order or notice, a statement that the child:

(1) has been enrolled in a health insurance plan; or

(2) cannot be enrolled or cannot be enrolled permanently in a health insurance plan and provide the reason why coverage or permanent coverage cannot be provided.

(d) If the employee ceases employment or if the health insurance coverage lapses, the employer shall provide to the sender, by first class mail not later than the 15th day after the date of the termination of employment or the lapse of the coverage, notice of the termination or lapse and of the availability of any conversion privileges.

(e) On request, the employer shall release to the sender information concerning the available health insurance coverage, including the name of the health insurance carrier, the policy number, a copy of the policy and schedule of benefits, a health insurance membership card, and claim forms.

(f) In this section, "sender" means the person sending the order **or notice** under Section 154.186.

(g) An employer who fails to enroll a child, fails to withhold or remit premiums or cash medical support, or discriminates in hiring or employment on the basis of a medical support order **or notice under this subchapter** shall be subject to the penalties and fines in Subchapter C, Chapter 158.

(h) An employer who receives a national medical support notice under Section 154.186 shall comply with the requirements of the notice.

History: Amended by 78th Legis., Reg. Sess. (2003), H.B. 2001, eff. July 1, 2003.

Comment

Medical insurance coverage after divorce is a crucial element in the Texas child support scheme. Subsection (g) puts some teeth in the mandate that employers take steps to ensure such coverage. Subsection (h) requires an employer to comply with the federal notice authorized under § 154.186.

§ 154.188. Failure to Provide or Pay For Required Health Insurance.

A parent ordered to provide health insurance **or to pay the other parent additional child support for the cost of health insurance** who fails to do so is liable for:

(1) necessary medical expenses of the child, without regard to whether the expenses would have been paid if health insurance had been provided; and

(2) the cost of health insurance premiums or contributions, if any, paid on behalf of the child.

History: Amended by 78th Legis., Reg. Sess. (2003), H.B. 1878, eff. Sept. 1, 2003, and applies "only to a suit affecting the parent-child relationship filed on or after the effective date of this Act. A suit affecting the parent-child relationship filed before the effective date of this Act is governed by the law in effect on the date the suit was filed, and the former law is continued in effect for that purpose."

Guest Comment

Under § 154.182(b) an obligor may be ordered to provide health insurance for a child through the obligor's employment or, if such insurance is not available to the obligor at "reasonable cost" but is available to the obligee, to reimburse the obligee the cost of the coverage as additional child support. This section addresses an obligor's liability for failure either to secure ordered coverage for a child or to reimburse the other parent the costs of coverage provided by that parent. The protection afforded the obligee under this section is particularly important in the event the obligor becomes delinquent in payment of support and the obligee faces not only the loss of the additional support to cover health insurance premiums but also medical expenses of the child not covered by health insurance, on top of the unpaid "regular" child support. (*C.B. & H.P.S.*)

§ 154.189. Notice of Termination or Lapse of Insurance Coverage.

(a) An obligor ordered to provide health insurance coverage for a child must notify the obligee and any child support agency enforcing a support obligation against the obligor of the:

(1) termination or lapse of health insurance coverage for the child not later than the 15th day after the date of a termination or lapse; and

(2) availability of additional health insurance to the obligor for the child after a termination or lapse of coverage not later than the 15th day after the date the insurance becomes available.

(b) If termination of coverage results from a change of employers, the obligor, the obligee, or the child support agency may send the new employer a copy of the order requiring the employee to provide health insurance for a child or notice of the medical support order as provided by this subchapter.

§ 154.190. Reenrolling Child for Insurance Coverage.

After health insurance has been terminated or has lapsed, an obligor ordered to provide health insurance coverage for the child must enroll the child in a health insurance plan at the next available enrollment period.

§ 154.191. Remedy Not Exclusive.

(a) This subchapter does not limit the rights of the obligor, obligee, local domestic relations office, or Title IV–D agency to enforce, modify, or clarify the medical support order.

(b) This subchapter does not limit the authority of the court to render or modify a medical support order containing a provision for payment of uninsured health expenses, health care costs, or health insurance premiums that are in addition to and inconsistent with this subchapter.

§ 154.192. Cancellation or Elimination of Insurance Coverage for Child.

(a) Unless the employee or member ceases to be eligible for dependent coverage, or the employer has eliminated dependent health coverage for all of the employer's employees or members, the employer may not cancel or eliminate coverage of a child enrolled under this subchapter until the employer is provided satisfactory written evidence that:

(1) the court order or administrative order requiring the coverage is no longer in effect; or

(2) the child is enrolled in comparable health insurance coverage or will be enrolled in comparable coverage that will take effect not later than the effective date of the cancellation or elimination of the employer's coverage.

§ 154.193. Medical Support Order Not Qualified.

(a) If a plan administrator or other person acting in an equivalent position determines that a medical support order issued under this subchapter does not qualify for enforcement under federal law, the tribunal may, on its own motion or the motion of a party, render an order that qualifies for enforcement under federal law.

(b) The procedure for filing a motion for enforcement of a final order applies to a motion under this section. Service of citation is not required, and a person is not entitled to a jury in a proceeding under this section.

(c) The employer or plan administrator is not a necessary party to a proceeding under this section.

Guest Comment

The provisions of this section are largely superceded by the use of the federal "national medical support notice" under § 154.186. Should a group health plan administrator reject a medical support order as not satisfying the requirements of federal law (ERISA), the IV–D agency or, in non-IV–D cases, an obligee, obligor, friend of the court, domestic relations office or private attorney, may send the federal notice that, by the will of Congress, does satisfy the requirements of federal law. *(C.B. & H.P.S.)*

Subchapter E. Local Child Support Registry

Introductory Comment

The Family Code regulates some aspects of the practices of local child support registries. With the implementation of the state disbursement unit (SDU) under Chapter 234 the scope of operations of the local registries has been significantly changed.

Leading Case

In re Pierre, 50 S.W.3d 554 (Tex. App.—El Paso 2001, no pet.) (without evidence of drug use it is abuse of discretion to require drug and alcohol testing of obligor as supervision officer may direct)

§ 154.241. Local Registry.

(a) A local registry shall receive a court-ordered child support payment or a payment otherwise authorized by law and shall forward the payment, as appropriate, to the Title IV–D agency, local domestic relations office, or obligee within two working days after the date the local registry receives the payment.

(b) A local registry may not require an obligor, obligee, or other party or entity to furnish a certified copy of a court order as a condition of processing child support payments and shall accept as sufficient authority to process the payments a photocopy, facsimile copy, or conformed copy of the court's order.

(c) A local registry shall include with each payment it forwards to the Title IV–D agency the date it received the payment and the withholding date furnished by the employer.

(d) A local registry shall accept child support payments made by personal check, money order, or cashier's check. A local registry may refuse payment by personal check if a pattern of abuse regarding the use of personal checks has been established. Abuse includes checks drawn on insufficient funds, abusive or offensive language written on the check, intentional mutilation of the instrument, or other actions that delay or disrupt the registry's operation.

(e) Subject to Section 154.004, at the request of an obligee, a local registry shall redirect and forward a child support payment to an address and in care of a person or entity designated by the obligee. A local registry may require that the obligee's request be in writing or be made on a form provided by the local registry for that purpose, but may not charge a fee for receiving the request or redirecting the payments as requested.

(f) A local registry may accept child support payments made by credit card, debit card, or automatic teller machine card.

Guest Comment

In 2003 the legislature greatly enhanced both the ability of local registries to process child support payments and the facility of obligors to make such payment by authorizing the use of modern technology under subsection (f), complementing payment by electronic funds transfer under § 154.242). (*C.B. & H.P.S.)*

§ 154.242. Payment or Transfer of Child Support Payments by Electronic Funds Transfer.

(a) A child support payment may be made by electronic funds transfer to:

(1) the Title IV–D agency;

(2) a local registry if the registry agrees to accept electronic payment; or

(3) the state disbursement unit.

(b) A local registry may transmit child support payments to the Title IV–D agency by electronic funds transfer. Unless support payments are required to be made to the state disbursement unit, an obligor may make payments, with the approval of the court entering the order, directly to the bank account of the obligee by electronic transfer and provide verification of the deposit to the local registry. A local registry in a county that makes deposits into personal bank accounts by electronic funds transfer as of April 1, 1995, may transmit a child support payment to an obligee by electronic funds transfer if the obligee maintains a bank account and provides the local registry with the necessary bank account information to complete electronic payment.

§ 154.243. Production of Child Support Payment Record.

The Title IV–D agency, a local registry, or the state disbursement unit may comply with a subpoena or other order directing the production of a child support payment record by sending a certified copy of the record or an affidavit regarding the payment record to the court that directed production of the record.

Subchapter F. Support for a Minor or Adult Disabled Child

Introductory Comment

This subchapter allows a suit seeking post-majority support of a disabled child or a disabled adult to be brought at any time, provided that the disability existed on or before the individual's 18th birthday. The statute does not create a method for the state to be reimbursed by an individual's parents for expenditures incurred on behalf of the institutionalized adult. However, the statute does allow an assignment of the support to the Title IV–D agency.

The support obligor may seek possession of and access to the adult disabled child. Because the person is an adult, however, the possession and access may be refused by the disabled person.

Sections 154.302–.303 have expanded the possibilities for support of an adult disabled child. Heretofore an action would lie only between the two parents, one of whom maintained possession of the adult disabled child and the other of whom could be required to assist by providing financial support. The cause of action has been expanded to allow persons other than a parent to provide the actual care and custody of the adult disabled child and seek support from a parent, or from both the parents. Likely candidates as caretakers are close relatives, such as adult siblings or grandparents, although the statutory coverage is not limited to relatives of the adult disabled child. In fact, the adult child may receive the support directly from the parent if the disability does not impair the adult child's ability to manage his or her financial affairs.

Leading Cases

Worford v. Stamper, 801 S.W.2d 108 (Tex. 1990) (increase in support for disabled child)

In re M.W.T., 12 S.W.3d 598 (Tex. App.—San Antonio 2000, pet. denied) (adult disabled child born out-of-wedlock entitled to post–18 support from father)

Garland v. Garland, 868 S.W.2d 847 (Tex. App.—Dallas 1993, no writ) (guardianship belongs exclusively to probate court; CEJ over support does not preempt probate jurisdiction)

In re Frost, 815 S.W.2d 890 (Tex. App.—Amarillo 1991, no writ) (enrollment of learning disabled student in local college program justifies support beyond age 18)

---

§ 154.301. Definitions.

In this subchapter:

(1) "Adult child" means a child 18 years of age or older.

(2) "Child" means a son or daughter of any age.

§ 154.302. Court-Ordered Support for Disabled Child.

(a) The court may order either or both parents to provide for the support of a child for an indefinite period and may determine the rights and duties of the parents if the court finds that:

(1) the child, whether institutionalized or not, requires substantial care and personal supervision because of a mental or physical disability and will not be capable of self-support; and

(2) the disability exists, or the cause of the disability is known to exist, on or before the 18th birthday of the child.

(b) A court that orders support under this section shall designate a parent of the child or another person having physical custody or guardianship of the child under a court order to receive the support for the child. The court may designate a child who is 18 years of age or older to receive the support directly.

§ 154.303. Standing to Sue.

(a) A suit provided by this subchapter may be filed only by:

(1) a parent of the child or another person having physical custody or guardianship of the child under a court order; or

(2) the child if the child:

(A) is 18 years of age or older;

(B) does not have a mental disability; and

(C) is determined by the court to be capable of managing the child's financial affairs.

(b) The parent, the child, if the child is 18 years of age or older, or other person may not transfer or assign the cause of action to any person, including a governmental or private entity or agency, except for an assignment made to the Title IV-D agency.

§ 154.304. General Procedure.

Except as otherwise provided by this subchapter, the substantive and procedural rights and remedies in a suit affecting the parent-child relationship relating to the establishment, modification, or enforcement of a child support order apply to a suit filed and an order rendered under this subchapter.

§ 154.305. Specific Procedures.

(a) A suit under this subchapter may be filed:

(1) regardless of the age of the child; and

(2) as an independent cause of action or joined with any other claim or remedy provided by this code.

(b) If no court has continuing, exclusive jurisdiction of the child, an action under this subchapter may be filed as an original suit affecting the parent-child relationship.

(c) If there is a court of continuing, exclusive jurisdiction, an action under this subchapter may be filed as a suit for modification as provided by Chapter 156 *[Modification]*.

§ 154.306. Amount of Support After Age 18.

In determining the amount of support to be paid after a child's 18th birthday, the specific terms and conditions of that support, and the rights and duties of both parents with respect to the support of the child, the court shall determine and give special consideration to:

(1) any existing or future needs of the adult child directly related to the adult child's mental or physical disability and the substantial care and personal supervision directly required by or related to that disability;

(2) whether the parent pays for or will pay for the care or supervision of the adult child or provides or will provide substantial care or personal supervision of the adult child;

(3) the financial resources available to both parents for the support, care, and supervision of the adult child; and

(4) any other financial resources or other resources or programs available for the support, care, and supervision of the adult child.

§ 154.307. Modification and Enforcement.

An order provided by this subchapter may contain provisions governing the rights and duties of both parents with respect to the support of the child and may be modified or enforced in the same manner as any other order provided by this title.

§ 154.308. Remedy Not Exclusive.

(a) This subchapter does not affect a parent's:

(1) cause of action for the support of a disabled child under any other law; or

(2) ability to contract for the support of a disabled child.

(b) This subchapter does not affect the substantive or procedural rights or remedies of a person other than a parent, including a governmental or private entity or agency, with respect to the support of a disabled child under any other law.

§ 154.309. Possession of or Access to Adult Disabled Child.

(a) A court may render an order for the possession of or access to an adult disabled child that is appropriate under the circumstances.

(b) Possession of or access to an adult disabled child is enforceable in the manner provided by Chapter 157 *[Enforcement]*. An adult disabled child may refuse possession or access if the adult disabled child is mentally competent.

(c) A court that obtains continuing, exclusive jurisdiction of a suit affecting the parent-child relationship involving a disabled person who is a child retains continuing, exclusive jurisdiction of subsequent proceedings involving the person, including proceedings after the person is an adult.

Comment

Complaint was made to the legislature that after a disabled adult child reaches majority the custodial parent often prevents possession of or access to that child by the other parent. This takes that decision-making out of the custodian's hands, but also provides that a disabled adult child may exercise adult prerogatives.

Chapter 155. Continuing, Exclusive Jurisdiction; Transfer.

Subchapter A. Continuing, Exclusive Jurisdiction

Subchapter B. Identification of Court of Continuing, Exclusive Jurisdiction

Subchapter C. Transfer of Continuing, Exclusive Jurisdiction

Subchapter D. Transfer of Proceedings Within the State When Party or Child Resides Outside the State

---

Subchapter A. Continuing, Exclusive Jurisdiction

Introductory Comment

A major innovation of the Family Code is the principle that the court of original rendition retains continuing, exclusive jurisdiction over all subsequent matters arising out a SAPCR. All further action must begin in that court, even when the fact circumstances dictate that the suit should ultimately be transferred to a more convenient forum. The transferring court is authorized to continue to enforce its temporary orders and to receive and distribute child support payments until the transferee court dockets the case. At that time the transitional period ends, the transferring court loses all jurisdiction, and any further payments received should be forwarded to the transferee court (assuming payments are directed to the court registry).

CLE/Other Legal Publications

Jurisdiction, venue, plea in abatement and the UCCJEA. Douglas R. Woodburn, 2004 MARRIAGE DISSOLUTION

Jurisdiction, venue, transfers, and standing. Brian L. Webb, 2003 ADV. FAM. L.

Leading Cases

Alexander v. Russell, 699 S.W.2d 209 (Tex. 1985) (judge must act in capacity as court of continuing jurisdiction)

Curtis v. Gibbs, 511 S.W.2d 263 (Tex. 1974) (court acquiring dominant jurisdiction prevents another court from asserting jurisdiction)

Chalu v. Shamala, 125 S.W.3d 737 (Tex. App.—Houston [1st Dist.] 2003, no pet.) (no interlocutory appeal from transfer orders)

In re Calderon, 96 S.W.3d 711 (Tex. App.—Tyler 2003, orig. proceeding) (statutory mandatory transfer of SAPCR when child lives in another county for more than six months not overridden by mediated settlement agreement)

In re Powell, 79 S.W.3d 814 (Tex. App.—Fort Worth 2002, no pet.) (transfer of SAPCR CEJ mandatory even when some of six months precedes final decree)

In re G.R.M., 45 S.W.3d 764 (Tex. App.—Fort Worth 2001, no pet.) (Government Code docket equalization trumps Chapter 155, allowing court of continuing, exclusive jurisdiction to transfer, on its own motion, case to another court in same county)

Ramsey v. Ramsey, 19 S.W.3d 548 (Tex. App.—Austin 1999, no pet.) (second SAPCR valid, issued because no notice given court of CEJ of court that issued first SAPCR)

In re Cannon, 993 S.W.2d 354 (Tex. App.—San Antonio 1999, no pet.) (CEJ for child support not affected by moving from Texas more than 10 years earlier)

Hudson v. Markum, 931 S.W.2d 336 (Tex. App.—Dallas 1996, writ denied) (motion to modify support filed during the pendency of appeal of paternity order does not abrogate trial court's continuing, exclusive jurisdiction)

Henry v. Rivera, 783 S.W.2d 766 (Tex. App.—San Antonio 1990, no writ); Hemingway v. Robertson, 778 S.W.2d 199 (Tex. App.—Houston [1st Dist.] 1989, no writ) (court cannot modify managing conservator after child establishes new home state)

Rowland v. Willy, 751 S.W.2d 725 (Tex. App.—Houston [14th Dist.] 1988, no writ) (district court with SAPCR continuing jurisdiction over disabled post-18 child blocks probate court guardianship)

Lewis v. McCoy, 747 S.W.2d 48 (Tex. App.—El Paso 1988, no writ) (death of managing conservator doesn't end continuing jurisdiction)

Hutchings v. Biery, 723 S.W.2d 347 (Tex. App.—San Antonio 1987, no writ) (continuing jurisdiction over visitation portion of decree after child acquires new home state)

Cross Reference

TEX. FAM. CODE ANN. ch. 103. Venue and Transfer of Original Proceedings

Texas Family Law Practice Manual

Chapter 33. Transfer

---

§ 155.001. Acquiring Continuing, Exclusive Jurisdiction.

(a) Except as otherwise provided by this section, a court acquires continuing, exclusive jurisdiction over the matters provided for by this title in connection with a child on the rendition of a final order.

(b) The following final orders do not create continuing, exclusive jurisdiction in a court:

(1) a voluntary or involuntary dismissal of a suit affecting the parent-child relationship;

(2) in a suit to determine parentage, a final order finding that an alleged or presumed father is not the father of the child, except that the jurisdiction of the court is not affected if the child was subject to the jurisdiction of the court or some other court in a suit affecting the parent-child relationship before the commencement of the suit to adjudicate parentage; and

(3) a final order of adoption, after which a subsequent suit affecting the child must be commenced as though the child had not been the subject of a suit for adoption or any other suit affecting the parent-child relationship before the adoption.

(c) If a court of this state has acquired continuing, exclusive jurisdiction, no other court of this state has jurisdiction of a suit with regard to that child except as provided by this chapter or Chapter 262 *[Procedures in Suit by Governmental Entity]*.

(d) Unless a final order has been rendered by a court of continuing, exclusive jurisdiction, a subsequent suit shall be commenced as an original proceeding.

§ 155.002. Retaining Continuing, Exclusive Jurisdiction.

Except as otherwise provided by this subchapter, a court with continuing, exclusive jurisdiction retains jurisdiction of the parties and matters provided by this title.

§ 155.003. Exercise of Continuing, Exclusive Jurisdiction.

(a) Except as otherwise provided by this section, a court with continuing, exclusive jurisdiction may exercise its jurisdiction to modify its order regarding managing conservatorship, possessory conservatorship, possession of and access to the child, and support of the child.

(b) A court of this state may not exercise its continuing, exclusive jurisdiction to modify managing conservatorship if:

(1) the child's home state is other than this state; or

(2) modification is precluded by Chapter 152 *[UCCJEA]*.

(c) A court of this state may not exercise its continuing, exclusive jurisdiction to modify possessory conservatorship or possession of or access to a child if:

(1) the child's home state is other than this state and all parties have established and continue to maintain their principal residence outside this state; or

(2) each individual party has filed written consent with the tribunal of this state for a tribunal of another state to modify the order and assume continuing, exclusive jurisdiction of the suit.

(d) A court of this state may not exercise its continuing, exclusive jurisdiction to modify its child support order if modification is precluded by Chapter 159 *[UIFSA]*.

§ 155.004. Loss of Continuing, Exclusive Jurisdiction.

(a) A court of this state loses its continuing, exclusive jurisdiction to modify its order if:

(1) an order of adoption is rendered after the court acquires continuing, exclusive jurisdiction of the suit;

(2) the parents of the child have remarried each other after the dissolution of a previous marriage between them and file a suit for the dissolution of their subsequent marriage combined with a suit affecting the parent-child relationship as if there had not been a prior court with continuing, exclusive jurisdiction over the child; or

(3) another court assumed jurisdiction over a suit and rendered a final order based on incorrect information received from the bureau of vital statistics that there was no court of continuing, exclusive jurisdiction.

(b) This section does not affect the power of the court to enforce its order for a violation that occurred before the time continuing, exclusive jurisdiction was lost under this section.

§ 155.005. Jurisdiction Pending Transfer.

(a) During the transfer of a suit from a court with continuing, exclusive jurisdiction, the transferring court retains jurisdiction to render temporary orders.

(b) The jurisdiction of the transferring court terminates on the docketing of the case in the transferee court.

Leading Case

Bigham v. Dempster, 901 S.W.2d 424 (Tex. 1995) (case docketed when transferee court receives transfer order and asserts jurisdiction, or when files transferred, whichever is first)

Subchapter B. Identification of Court of Continuing, Exclusive Jurisdiction

Introductory Comment

The request for the identification of the court of continuing jurisdiction is permissive. But, if such a court does exist, it must be identified, because its jurisdiction is not just continuing, it is also exclusive. Failure to properly identify the correct court can result in a voidable decree.

§ 155.101. Request for Identification of Court of Continuing, Exclusive Jurisdiction.

(a) The petitioner or the court shall request from the bureau of vital statistics identification of the court that last had continuing, exclusive jurisdiction of the child in a suit unless:

(1) the petition alleges that no court has continuing, exclusive jurisdiction of the child and the issue is not disputed by the pleadings; or

(2) the petition alleges that the court in which the suit or petition to modify has been filed has acquired and retains continuing, exclusive jurisdiction of the child as the result of a prior proceeding and the issue is not disputed by the pleadings.

(b) The bureau of vital statistics shall, on the written request of the court, an attorney, or a party:

(1) identify the court that last had continuing, exclusive jurisdiction of the child in a suit and give the docket number of the suit; or

(2) state that the child has not been the subject of a suit.

(c) The child shall be identified in the request by name, birthdate, and place of birth.

(d) The bureau of vital statistics shall transmit the information not later than the 10th day after the date on which the request is received.

Cross Reference

TEX. FAM. CODE ANN. § 108.001. Transmittal of Records of Suit by Clerk; § 108.006. Fees

§ 155.102. Dismissal.

If a court in which a suit is filed determines that another court has continuing, exclusive jurisdiction of the child, the court in which the suit is filed shall dismiss the suit without prejudice.

§ 155.103. Reliance on Bureau of Vital Statistics Information.

(a) A court shall have jurisdiction over a suit if it has been, correctly or incorrectly, informed by the bureau of vital statistics that the child has not been the subject of a suit and the petition states that no other court has continuing, exclusive jurisdiction over the child.

(b) If the bureau of vital statistics notifies the court that the bureau has furnished incorrect information regarding the existence of another court with continuing, exclusive jurisdiction before the rendition of a final order, the provisions of this chapter apply.

§ 155.104. Voidable Order.

(a) If a request for information from the bureau of vital statistics relating to the identity of the court having continuing, exclusive jurisdiction of the child has been made under this subchapter, a final order, except an order of dismissal, may not be rendered until the information is filed with the court.

(b) If a final order is rendered in the absence of the filing of the information from the bureau of vital statistics, the order is voidable on a showing that a court other than the court that rendered the order had continuing, exclusive jurisdiction.

Subchapter C. Transfer of Continuing, Exclusive Jurisdiction

Introductory Comment

Transfer in conjunction with the original filing of a SAPCR is appropriate in situations involving improper venue or dominant divorce venue; in such cases the transfer is governed by Chapter 103, *supra*. This subchapter describes the second basic fact situation that calls for a transfer of a SAPCR lawsuit from one Texas court to another Texas court. Note, there is no provision in the Family Code for transfer of a SAPCR to a sister-state court, although a Texas child support order may be enforced out-of-state under UIFSA, *infra*.

Under the provisions of this subchapter, a transfer is required when the child has moved from one county in Texas to another after an original SAPCR decree has established a court of continuing, exclusive jurisdiction, a.k.a. CEJ. Because current information about the circumstances of the child is best obtained in the county where the child makes his home, after a period of six months a transfer becomes mandatory. Almost all of the reported litigation has revolved around this aspect of CEJ. Finally, the transferring court is directed to order the obligor to make payments to the transferee court in order to facilitate the transfer of CEJ to the new court.

CLE/Other Legal Publications

Jurisdiction, venue, transfers, and standing. Brian L. Webb, 2003 ADV. FAM. L.

Jurisdiction and venue. Douglas R. Woodburn, 2000 MARRIAGE DISSOLUTION

Leading Cases

Bigham v. Dempster, 901 S.W.2d 424 (Tex. 1995) (case docketed when transferee court receives transfer order and asserts jurisdiction, or when files transferred, whichever is first)

Tippy v. Walker, 865 S.W.2d 928 (Tex. 1993) (computation of six months residence in county for mandatory transfer begins with actual change of residence, not from signing of order)

Proffer v. Yates, 734 S.W.2d 671 (Tex. 1987) (mandamus issued when court fails to transfer after child resides in new county for six months)

Leonard v. Paxson, 654 S.W.2d 440 (Tex. 1983) (settlement agreement cannot establish venue for SAPCR)

Seay v. Valderas, 643 S.W.2d 395 (Tex. 1982) (after case transferred, transferor court cannot order return of case)

Arias v. Spector, 623 S.W.2d 312 (Tex. 1981) (transfer mandatory)

Ex parte Barnett, 600 S.W.2d 252 (Tex. 1980) (transferee court enforces with full jurisdiction)

Brines v. McIlhaney, 596 S.W.2d 519 (Tex. 1980) (divorce appointing temporary managing conservator doesn't negate mandatory transfer)

Brod v. Baker, 591 S.W.2d 457 (Tex. 1979) (mandatory transfer to county where children reside)

Cassidy v. Fuller, 568 S.W.2d 845 (Tex. 1978) (automatic transfer provisions are enforceable by mandamus)

In re Villareal, 126 S.W.3d 286 (Tex. App.—San Antonio 2003, orig. proceeding) (jurisdiction over mandamus proceeding lost after transfer)

In re T.J.L., 97 S.W.3d 257 (Tex. App.—Houston [14th Dist.] 2002, no pet.) (partial transfer of SAPCR continuing jurisdiction required when one child lives in different county)

In re Calderon, 96 S.W.3d 711 (Tex. App.—Tyler 2003, orig. proceeding) (statutory mandatory transfer of SAPCR when child lives in another county for more than six months not overridden by mediated settlement agreement)

In re Powell, 79 S.W.3d 814 (Tex. App.—Fort Worth 2002, no pet.) (transfer of SAPCR CEJ mandatory even when some of six months precedes final decree)

In re Knotts, 62 S.W.3d 922 (Tex. App.—Texarkana 2001, no pet.) (SAPCR properly transferred) (when a child resides with a parent in a county for more than four years prior to the other parent filing an SAPCR in another county, the SAPCR is properly transferred to the child's county of residence)

In re S.G.S., 53 S.W.3d 848 (Tex. App.—Fort Worth 2001, pet. denied) (father's motion to transfer timely) (responding party to a termination action is required to file his motion to transfer the matter no later than 10:00 a.m. the first Monday after the 20th day after service or notice of suit)

In re Aguilera, 37 S.W.3d 43 (Tex. App.—El Paso 2000, no pet.) (CEJ divorce court replaces SAPCR court)

In re Kramer, 9 S.W.3d 449 (Tex. App.—San Antonio 1999, no pet.) (failure to transfer to county of child's residence promptly and without a hearing improper; pending enforcement motion must be transferred)

In re Simonek, 3 S.W.3d 285 (Tex. App.—Waco 1999, no pet.) (motion to transfer filed incident to motion to modify carries along pending contempt proceeding against movant)

Hathorn v. Sivers, 962 S.W.2d 284 (Tex. App.—Houston [14th Dist.] 1998, no writ) (case properly transferred from district court to county court for more expeditious handling)

Trevino v. Ables, 943 S.W.2d 166 (Tex. App.—San Antonio 1997, no writ) (placement order for foster care not a final order under this chapter)

Bollard v. Berchelmann, 921 S.W.2d 861 (Tex. App.—San Antonio 1996, no writ) (mother, a latecomer to modification SAPCR, filed timely motion to transfer venue)

Fite v. Nelson, 869 S.W.2d 603 (Tex. App.—Houston [14th Dist.] 1994, no writ) (transfer to divorce court not mandatory after final decree in SAPCR)

Martinez v. Flores, 820 S.W.2d 937 (Tex. App.—Corpus Christi 1991, no writ) (if mandatory transfer denied without hearing testimony, correction is by way of mandamus)

Koether v. Morgan, 787 S.W.2d 582 (Tex. App.—Waco 1990, no writ) (children live in different counties)

Mendez v. Atty. Gen. of Texas, 761 S.W.2d 519 (Tex. App.—Corpus Christi 1988, no writ) (untimely filing for transfer)

Botello v. Salazar, 745 S.W.2d 540 (Tex. App.—Houston [14th Dist.] 1988, no writ) (transfer only when proceedings pending)

Cross Reference

TEX. FAM. CODE ANN. ch. 103. Venue and Transfer of Original Proceedings.

§ 155.201. Mandatory Transfer.

(a) On a showing that a suit for dissolution of the marriage of the child's parents has been filed in another court, the court having continuing, exclusive jurisdiction of a suit affecting the parent-child relationship shall transfer the proceedings to the court in which the dissolution of the marriage is pending.

(b) If a suit to modify or a motion to enforce an order is filed in the court having continuing, exclusive jurisdiction of a suit, on the timely motion of a party the court shall transfer the proceeding to another county in this state if the child has resided in the other county for six months or longer.

(c) If a suit to modify or a motion to enforce an order is pending at the time a subsequent suit to modify or motion to enforce is filed, the court may transfer the proceeding as provided by Subsection (b) only if the court could have transferred the proceeding at the time the first motion or suit was filed.

§ 155.202. Discretionary Transfer.

(a) If the basis of a motion to transfer a proceeding under this subchapter is that the child resides in another county, the court may deny the motion if it is shown that the child has resided in that county for less than six months at the time the proceeding is commenced.

(b) For the convenience of the parties and witnesses and in the interest of justice, the court, on the timely motion of a party, may transfer the proceeding to a proper court in another county in the state.

Leading Case

Hathorn v. Sivers, 962 S.W.2d 284 (Tex. App.—Houston [14th Dist.] 1998, no pet.) (intra-county transfer from district court to county court at law upheld)

§ 155.203. Determining County of Child's Residence.

In computing the time during which the child has resided in a county, the court may not require that the period of residence be continuous and uninterrupted but shall look to the child's principal residence during the six-month period preceding the commencement of the suit.

§ 155.204. Procedure for Transfer.

(a) Except as provided by Section 262.203, a motion to transfer by a petitioner or movant is timely if it is made at the time the initial pleadings are filed. A motion to transfer by another party is timely if it is made on or before the first Monday after the 20th day after the date of service of citation or notice of the suit or before the commencement of the hearing, whichever is sooner. If a timely motion to transfer has been filed and no controverting affidavit is filed within the period allowed for its filing, the proceeding shall be transferred promptly without a hearing to the proper court.

(b) On or before the first Monday after the 20th day after the date of notice of a motion to transfer is served, a party desiring to contest the motion must file a controverting affidavit denying that grounds for the transfer exist.

(c) If a controverting affidavit contesting the motion to transfer is filed, each party is entitled to notice not less than 10 days before the date of the hearing on the motion to transfer.

(d) Only evidence pertaining to the transfer may be taken at the hearing.

(e) An order transferring or refusing to transfer the proceeding is not subject to interlocutory appeal.

(f) If a transfer order has been rendered by a court exercising jurisdiction under Chapter 262 *[Procedures in Suit by Governmental Entity]*, a party may file the transfer order with the clerk of the court of continuing, exclusive jurisdiction. On receipt and without a hearing, the clerk of the court of continuing, exclusive jurisdiction shall transfer the files as provided by this subchapter.

§ 155.205. Transfer of Child Support Registry.

(a) On rendition of an order transferring continuing, exclusive jurisdiction to another court, the transferring court shall also order that all future payments of child support be made to the local registry of the transferee court or, if payments have previously been directed to the state disbursement unit, to the state disbursement unit.

(b) The transferring court's local registry or the state disbursement unit shall continue to receive, record, and forward child support payments to the payee until it receives notice that the transferred case has been docketed by the transferee court.

(c) After receiving notice of docketing from the transferee court, the transferring court's local registry shall send a certified copy of the child support payment record to the clerk of the transferee court and shall forward any payments received to the transferee court's local registry or to the state disbursement unit, as appropriate.

§ 155.206. Effect of Transfer.

(a) A court to which a transfer is made becomes the court of continuing, exclusive jurisdiction and all proceedings in the suit are continued as if it were brought there originally.

(b) A judgment or order transferred has the same effect and shall be enforced as if originally rendered in the transferee court.

(c) The transferee court shall enforce a judgment or order of the transferring court by contempt or by any other means by which the transferring court could have enforced its judgment or order. The transferee court shall have the power to punish disobedience of the transferring court's order, whether occurring before or after the transfer, by contempt.

(d) After the transfer, the transferring court does not retain jurisdiction of the child who is the subject of the suit, nor does it have jurisdiction to enforce its order for a violation occurring before or after the transfer of jurisdiction.

§ 155.207. Transfer of Court Files.

(a) On rendition of an order of transfer, the clerk of the court transferring a proceeding shall send to the proper court in the county to which transfer is being made:

(1) the complete files in all matters affecting the child in any pending proceeding;

(2) certified copies of all entries in the minutes;

(3) a certified copy of any order of dissolution of marriage rendered in a suit joined with the suit affecting the parent-child relationship; and

(4) a certified copy of each order rendered.

(b) The clerk of the transferring court shall keep a copy of the transferred files. If the transferring court retains jurisdiction of another child who was the subject of the suit, the clerk shall send a copy of the complete files to the court to which the transfer is made and shall keep the original files.

(c) On receipt of the files, documents, and orders from the transferring court, the clerk of the transferee court shall docket the suit and shall notify all parties, the clerk of the transferring court, and, if appropriate, the transferring court's local registry that the suit has been docketed.

(d) The clerk of the transferring court shall send a certified copy of the order directing payments to the transferee court, to any party or employer affected by that order, and, if appropriate, to the local registry of the transferee court.

Subchapter D. Transfer of Proceedings Within the State When Party or Child Resides Outside the State

§ 155.301. Authority to Transfer.

(a) A court of this state with continuing, exclusive **jurisdiction over a child custody proceeding under Chapter 152 or a** [~~suit or an action for~~] child support **proceeding** under Chapter 159 shall transfer the proceeding to the county of residence of the resident party if one party is a resident of this state and all other parties including the child or all of the children affected by the **proceeding** [~~proceedings~~] reside outside this state.

(b) If one or more of the parties affected by the proceedings reside outside the state and if more than one party or one or more children affected by the proceeding reside in this state in different counties, the court shall transfer the proceeding according to the following priorities:

(1) to the court of continuing, exclusive jurisdiction, if any;

(2) to the county of residence of the child, if applicable, provided that:

(A) Subdivision (1) is inapplicable; or

(B) the court of continuing, exclusive jurisdiction finds that neither a party nor a child affected by the proceeding resides in the county of the court of continuing, exclusive jurisdiction; or

(3) if Subdivisions (1) and (2) are inapplicable, to the county most appropriate to serve the convenience of the resident parties, the witnesses, and the interest of justice.

(c) If a transfer of continuing, exclusive jurisdiction is sought under this section, the procedures for determining and effecting a transfer of proceedings provided by this chapter apply.

History: Amended by 78th Legis., Reg. Sess. (2003), H.B. 913, eff. Sept. 1, 2003, and applies "only to a child custody proceeding under Chapter 152, Family Code [UCCJEA], filed on or after the effective date of this Act. A child custody proceeding under Chapter 152, Family Code, filed before the effective date of this Act is governed by the law in effect on the date that the proceeding was filed, and the former law is continued in effect for that purpose."

Comment

The Uniform Child Custody Jurisdiction and Enforcement Act (Chapter 152, *supra*) and the Uniform Interstate Family Support Act (Chapter 159, *infra*) both incorporate the concept of continuing, exclusive jurisdiction as the touchstone of authority. The enactment of these uniform acts necessitated these conforming provisions to allow for intrastate transfer of UCCJEA and UIFSA proceedings if an original litigant lives in another state and the other litigant continues to reside in Texas, but has moved from the CEJ county in which the custody or support decree was rendered.

Leading Case

In re Casseb, 119 S.W.3d 841 (Tex. App.—San Antonio 2003, no pet.) (transfer of child support proceeding was mandated when child had moved out of state and father had moved counties)

Chapter 156. Modification.

Subchapter A. General Provisions

Subchapter B. Modification of Conservatorship, Possession and Access, or Determination of Residence

Subchapter C. [repealed]

Subchapter D. [repealed]

Subchapter E. Modification of Child Support

Subchapter A. General Provisions

§ 156.001. Orders Subject to Modification.

A court with continuing, exclusive jurisdiction may modify an order that provides for the conservatorship, support, or possession of and access to a child.

§ 156.002. Who can File.

(a) A party affected by an order may file a suit for modification in the court with continuing, exclusive jurisdiction.

(b) A person or entity who, at the time of filing, has standing to sue under Chapter 102 *[Filing Suit]* may file a suit for modification in the court with continuing, exclusive jurisdiction.

CLE/Other Legal Publications

Defending a custody modification without the 3rd prong. JoAl Cannon-Sheridan, 2004 ADV. FAM. L.

Modification in SAPCR's. Sondra Kaighen, 2002 ADV. FAM. L.

Modification issues: custody, child support, possession, terms & conditions. Sydney A. Beckman, 2001 ADV. FAM. L.

Texas Family Law Practice Manual

Chapter 32. Modification of Texas Orders.

Texas Pattern Jury Charges: Family

Chapter 217. Modification of Conservatorship and Support.

---

§ 156.003. Notice.

A party whose rights and duties may be affected by a suit for modification is entitled to receive notice by service of citation.

§ 156.004. Procedure.

The Texas Rules of Civil Procedure applicable to the filing of an original lawsuit apply to a suit for modification under this chapter.

§ 156.005. Frivolous Filing of Suit for Modification.

If the court finds that a suit for modification is filed frivolously or is designed to harass a party, the court shall tax attorney's fees as costs against the offending party.

Leading Case

D.R. v. J.A.R., 894 S.W.2d 91 (Tex. App.—Fort Worth 1995, writ denied) (frivolous modification suit leads to large attorney's fees award)

---

§ 156.006. Temporary Orders.

(a) Except as provided by Subsection (b), the court may render a temporary order in a suit for modification.

(b) While a suit for modification is pending, the court may not render a temporary order that has the effect of changing the designation of the person who has the exclusive right to **designate** [~~determine~~] the primary residence of the child under the final order unless:

(1) the order is necessary because the child's present living environment may endanger the child's physical health or significantly impair the child's emotional development;

(2) the person designated in the final order has voluntarily relinquished the primary care and possession of the child for more than six months and the temporary order is in the best interest of the child; or

(3) the child is 12 years of age or older and has filed with the court in writing the name of the person who is the child's preference to have the exclusive right to **designate** [~~determine~~] the primary residence of the child and the temporary order designating that person is in the best interest of the child.

History: Amended by 78th Legis., Reg. Sess. (2003), H.B. 913, eff. Sept. 1, 2003. "The changes in law made by this Act to Sections 156.101, 156.102(a) and (b), and 156.401(a), Family Code, apply only to an action to modify an order in a suit affecting the parent-child relationship pending on the effective date of this Act or filed on or after that date."

Guest Comment

In 2003 the legislature amended subsection (b) to accord with reality—a party may "designate" the primary residence of the child but only the court may "determine" that residence. *(C.B. & H.P.S.)*

CLE/Other Legal Publications

Oh, what a relief it is: TRO's, temporary orders, magistrate's order for emergency protection and other delights. Lisa Beebe, 2001 ADV. FAM. L.

The dilemma of the child who has chosen: dealing with children's preferences in custody litigation. J. Lindsey Short, Jr., 2001 ADV. FAM. L.

Drafting T.O.s and decrees. Judy Warne, 2001 ADV. FAM. L.

Temporary orders. Wendy S. Burgower, 2001 MARRIAGE DISSOLUTION

Leading Case

In re Ostrofsky, 112 S.W.3d 825 (Tex. App.—Houston [14th] 2003, orig. proceeding) (temporary order in modification suit placing children in boarding school deprives mother of possession of children and her right to determine primary residence)

Subchapter B. Modification of Conservatorship, Possession and Access, or Determination of Residence

Introductory Comment

The 2001 amendments to this chapter are the most dramatic—and far-reaching since the changes promulgated in 1995 and rank in importance with any other changes made in the 27 years plus of the Family Code. First, a brief review.

When the Family Code became effective Jan. 1, 1974, modification of (sole) managing conservatorship (there was no "joint") was measured by a "material and substantial change of circumstances" and "best interest" test. In 1975, the hurdle to modify custody was significantly raised by the addition of a three-prong test. This was perfectly consistent with the thinking of the time that stability for child placement was all important, and that the initial "winner" in a custody battle "retains all the rights, privileges, duties, and powers of a parent to the exclusion of the other parent . . . "[old § 14.02(a), amended in 1993].

Times change. Beginning in 1983, the legislature determined that an order of "reasonable visitation," to a noncustodial parent should be discouraged. All such an order truly meant was that the noncustodial parent had no actual time where possession of the child was his by right. Rather, visitation was at the sufferance of the custodial parent. The initial advisory guidelines for possession suggested were ultimately superceded by a standard order that is presumptively in the client's best interest. The allocation of all rights to the managing conservator has been replaced by a list of rights of conservators; at all times when in possession, and when exclusive rights are appropriate. The nonexistence of joint managing conservatorship was altered, first into JMC by agreement, and then by court order, theoretically even over the objection of the parties, and finally by presumption that JMC is in the child's best interest, § 153.131, *supra*.

Although this subchapter is phrased in terms of "orders subject to modification," reopening of a matter "finally adjudicated" in a prior proceeding more closely resembles the initiation of a new lawsuit than motion practice in ongoing litigation. Modification has long been the most discussed, controversial, and highly litigated aspect of sole and joint managing conservatorships, possessory conservatorships, and child support. Of these, modification from one sole conservator to another was for many years the most highly visible; that winner-take-all formula used a then-familiar three-prong test. But, since 1995 a sole-to-sole action has been governed by a "two prong test," which included "material and significant change," and "positive improvement." In the never ending battle of the sexes waged each legislative session, this amendment is regarded by many as the ultimate triumph for fathers' rights organizations over feminist spokespersons. Many critics claimed that the floodgates of relitigation of custody modification would be open. As is usually the case, such dire predictions have not proven to be accurate. Other complexities included the managing conservator who voluntarily relinquished actual custody, whom the statute placed on a no better than equal footing with the actual custodian after six months. And, of course there was modification of the terms of joint conservatorship, and even modification from JMC to sole MC, which brought the law back to where it started.

All these relatively sophisticated, often excessively subtle, distinctions caused great consternation to attorneys and judges attempting to decipher which standard to apply when modifying a conservatorship. Spurred by the Family Law Council of the State Bar, much of the complexity has been washed away by the 2001 Legislature. Hereafter, this chapter provides a set of uniform standards for modification of all the many varieties of conservatorship. In a sweeping change directed at simplification of the law, Sept. 1, 2001 saw the repeal of provisions relating to voluntary relinquishment, modification from sole managing conservatorship to joint managing conservatorship and vice versa, elimination of statutory definitions of change of circumstance, specific provisions for the modification of joint managing conservatorship and for modification of possession of or access to a child.

In the place of the old is a new, one-section fits all (or at least almost all) of the wide variety of scenarios for modification. Section 156.101 in fact establishes a two-prong test, best interest and one of three "second prongs." The vast majority of modifications will undoubtedly be based on a "best interest" test and a showing of "material and substantial changed circumstances." Note this two-prong test applies to modification of sole managing, joint managing, or possessory conservatorships, and of the terms of any of those.

Two other "two-prong tests are established in § 156.101. First, subsection (2) retains the contentious "choice of child," coupled with best interest. The age for a child to officially register a choice of conservatorships has returned to 12, after a much criticized trial run of age 10. And, subsection (3) continues the "voluntary relinquishment" basis for modification, now tied to the conservator who has the right to provide the primary residence of the child, again coupled with best interest. The same two-prong tests are applicable in situations in which less than one year has elapsed since the order sought to be modified, with the extra affidavit required under the prior law reworded without significant change.

The 2001 amendments also authorize the court to render appropriate orders to allocate increased expenses of a child on a fair and equitable basis. In particular, the court should take note of whether a change in the residence of the child results in increased expenses for the noncustodial parent. Payment of those increased expenses by the party whose residence has changed is rebuttably presumed to be in the best interest of the child, § 156.103, *infra*.

Conviction or deferred adjudication for an offense involving sexual abuse, aggravated sexual abuse, or indecency with a child is sufficient to justify a temporary order and modification of an existing order that provides for the appointment of a conservator or possession of or access to a child. A person who knowingly files a false motion to modify an order or portion of a decree based on the above grounds commits a Class B misdemeanor, § 156.104, *infra*.

The chapter now makes uniform references to a person who has the exclusive right to determine the primary residence of the child in provisions relating to temporary orders, §§ 156.006, 156.101, 156.102, and 156.409.

CLE/Other Legal Publications

See extensive annotations to Introductory Comment preceding § 153.131, supra.

Relocation debate. Kathryn J. Murphy & Mary Johanna McCurley, 2004 ADV. FAM. L.

To move or not to move? That is the question! Barbara D. Nunnelly, 2004 MARRIAGE DISSOLUTION

Relocation. Jan Marie DeLipsey & Barbara D. Nunneley, 2004 U. TEX. FAM. L. FRONT LINES

Relocation—can you pass go? Douglas R. Woodburn, 2003 ADV. FAM. L.

In re V.L.K. v. Troxel: Is the "best interest" standard in a motion to modify the sole managing conservator subject to a due process or due course challenge? David F. Johnson, 34 ST. MARY'S L.J. 623 (2003)

Relocation—where is anyone going? Joan F. Jenkins, 2002 ADV. FAM. L.

Dealing with mobile parents: domicile restrictions and relocation. Jennifer Tull, 2001 ADV. FAM. L.

Leading Cases

Lenz v. Lenz, 79 S.W.3d 10 (Tex. 2002) (evidence presented legally sufficient to support modification of decree to allow mother to relocate to Germany)

In re V.L.K., 24 S.W.3d 338 (Tex. 1999) (parental presumption for custody does not apply in modification litigation)

Martin v. Martin, 776 S.W.2d 572 (Tex. 1989) (modification of terms of possessory conservatorship within court's discretion—jury denied)

In re P.D.M., 117 S.W.3d 453 (Tex. App.—Fort Worth 2003, pet. denied) (grandmother's suit after death of managing conservator is not original suit subject to father's parental presumption)

In re Hood, 113 S.W.3d 525 (Tex. App.—Houston [1st] 2003, orig. proceeding) (death penalty sanctions too sever in custody case, even if recalcitrant movant refuses to comply with court's sanctions so his pleading struck—death penalty too severe in custody battle)

In re C.T.H., 112 S.W.3d 262 (Tex. App.—Beaumont 2003, no pet.) (grandparents have justiciable interest in custody modification after caring for child for over six months)

In re C.R.O., 96 S.W.3d 442 (Tex. App.—Amarillo 2002, pet. denied) (father's request for relocation restriction to county upheld—keeping children from moving to Hawaii found to be in best interest)

In re A.P.P., 74 S.W.3d 570 (Tex. App.—Corpus Christi 2002, no pet.) (default modification decree naming father JMC overturned, objecting mother meets *Craddock* test)

Davis v. Guerrero, 64 S.W.3d 685 (Tex. App.—Austin 2001, no pet.) (court should not entertain motions to alter SAPCR provisions relating to issues covered by an existing guardianship until the guardianship is revoked)

In re T.J.K., 62 S.W.3d 830 (Tex. App.—Texarkana 2001, no pet.) (father free to withdraw consent awarding grandparent's visitation and seek modification of order based on *Troxel*)

Turner v. Turner, 47 S.W.3d 761 (Tex. App.—Houston [1st Dist.] 2001, no pet.) (father modified from P.C. to primary JMC after daughter lives with him for extended period and chooses him first)

Ditraglia v. Romano, 33 S.W.3d 886 (Tex. App.—Austin 2000, no pet.) (older daughter's choice of high school separates siblings—modification of MC of younger daughter rejected)

In re R.R., 26 S.W.3d 569 (Tex. App.—Dallas 2000, no pet.) (error to issue blanket order stopping discovery in conservatorship modification because of pending criminal case alleging sexual abuse)

In re C.Q.T.M., 25 S.W.3d 730 (Tex. App.—Waco 2000, pet. denied) (evidence about conduct and character of new step-parent relevant in modification trial)

Jenkins v. Jenkins, 16 S.W.3d 473 (Tex. App.—El Paso 2000, no pet.) (mom having live-in boyfriend violated terms of JMC; father gets primary residence)

In re Macalik, 13 S.W.3d 43 (Tex. App.—Texarkana 1999, no pet.) (modification of terms of conservatorships subsumed in motion to modify basic sole MC–PC decree)

Enriquez v. Krueck, 887 S.W.2d 497 (Tex. App.—San Antonio 1994, no writ) (mother's behavior not sufficient to prove that retaining her as sole managing conservator would be detrimental to child)

Eason v. Eason, 860 S.W.2d 187 (Tex. App.—Houston [14th Dist.] 1993, no writ) (mother's recalcitrant behavior in litigation justifies modification of her managing conservatorship)

Terry v. Caldwell, 851 S.W.2d 875 (Tex. App.—Houston [14th Dist.] 1993, no writ) (signing agreed order of modification constitutes appearance—no waiver required)

Cheatham v. Rogers, 824 S.W.2d 231 (Tex. App.—Tyler 1992, no writ) (mental health records of court-appointed counselor relevant, and discoverable, in custody modification)

Fair v. Davis, 787 S.W.2d 422 (Tex. App.—Dallas 1990, no writ) (modification of visitation)

Bolden v. Clapp, 751 S.W.2d 674 (Tex. App.—Tyler 1988, no writ) (voluntary relinquishment of possession by managing conservatorship)

Baker v. Ericsson, 689 S.W.2d 492 (Tex. App.—El Paso 1985, no writ) (first prong, "substantial change," clearly established)

---

§ 156.101. Grounds for Modification of Order Establishing Conservatorship or Possession and Access.

The court may modify an order [~~or portion of a decree~~] that provides for the appointment of a conservator of a child, that provides the terms and conditions of conservatorship, or that provides for the possession of or access to a child if modification would be in the best interest of the child and:

(1) the circumstances of the child, a conservator, or other party affected by the order have materially and substantially changed since the **earlier of:**

(A) the date of the rendition of the order; **or**

(B) the date of the signing of a mediated or collaborative law settlement agreement on which the order is based;

(2) the child is at least 12 years of age and has filed with the court, in writing, the name of the **person** [~~conservator~~] who is the child's preference to have the exclusive right to **designate** [~~determine~~] the primary residence of the child; or

(3) the conservator who has the exclusive right to **designate** [~~establish~~] the primary residence of the child has voluntarily relinquished the primary care and possession of the child to another person for at least six months.

History: Amended by 78th Legis., Reg. Sess. (2003), H.B. 913, eff. Sept. 1, 2003. "The changes in law made by this Act to Sections 156.101, 156.102(a) and (b), and 156.401(a), Family Code, apply only to an action to modify an order in a suit affecting the parent-child relationship pending on the effective date of this Act or filed on or after that date."

Comment

The amendment to subsection (2) is significantly less dramatic than the changes mandated by the balance of the statute, as discussed above. A child of 12, rather than 10, may attempt to name his or her preferred managing conservator. If the choice is in the child's best interest, the court may ratify the modification.

CLE/Other Legal Publication

The dilemma of the child who has chosen: dealing with children's preferences in custody litigation. J. Lindsey Short, Jr., 2001 ADV. FAM. L.

Leading Case

Rayburn v. Rayburn, 979 S.W.2d 858 (Tex. App.—Beaumont 1998, no pet.) (neither of the contesting JMC's carried burden of proof to modify terms of conservatorship)

---

§ 156.102. Modification of Exclusive Right to Determine Primary Residence of Child Within One Year of Order.

(a) If a suit seeking to modify the designation of the person having the exclusive right to **designate** [~~determine~~] the primary residence of a child is filed not later than one year after **the earlier of** the date of the rendition of the order **or the date of the signing of a mediated or collaborative law settlement agreement on which the order is based**, the person filing the suit shall execute and attach an affidavit as provided by Subsection (b).

(b) The affidavit must contain, along with supporting facts, at least one of the following allegations:

(1) that the child's present environment may endanger the child's physical health or significantly impair the child's emotional development;

(2) that the person who has the exclusive right to **designate** [~~determine~~] the primary residence of the child is the person seeking or consenting to the modification and the modification is in the best interest of the child; or

(3) that the person who has the exclusive right to **designate** [~~determine~~] the primary residence of the child has voluntarily relinquished the primary care and possession of the child for at least six months and the modification is in the best interest of the child.

(c) The court shall deny the relief sought and refuse to schedule a hearing for modification under this section unless the court determines, on the basis of the affidavit, that facts adequate to support an allegation listed in Subsection (b) are stated in the affidavit. If the court determines that the facts stated are adequate to support an allegation, the court shall set a time and place for the hearing.

History: Amended by 78th Legis., Reg. Sess. (2003), H.B. 913, eff. Sept. 1, 2003. "The changes in law made by this Act to Sections 156.101, 156.102(a) and (b), and 156.401(a), Family Code, apply only to an action to modify an order in a suit affecting the parent-child relationship pending on the effective date of this Act or filed on or after that date."

Leading Case

Burkhart v. Burkhart, 960 S.W.2d 321 (Tex. App.—Houston [1st Dist.] 1997, writ denied) (affidavit failed to allege sufficient facts to justify motion to modify within one year of previous order)

---

§ 156.103. Increased Expenses Because of Change of Residence.

(a) If a change of residence results in increased expenses for a party having possession of or access to a child, the court may render appropriate orders to allocate those increased expenses on a fair and equitable basis, taking into account the cause of the increased expenses and the best interest of the child.

(b) The payment of increased expenses by the party whose residence is changed is rebuttably presumed to be in the best interest of the child.

(c) The court may render an order without regard to whether another change in the terms and conditions for the possession of or access to the child is made.

§ 156.104. Modification of Order on Conviction for Child Abuse; Penalty.

(a) Except as provided by Section 156.1045, the conviction of a conservator, or an order deferring adjudication with regard to the conservator, for an offense involving the abuse of a child under Section 21.11, 22.011, or 22.021, Penal Code, is a material and substantial change of circumstances sufficient to justify a temporary order and modification of an existing court order or portion of a decree that provides for the appointment of a conservator or that sets the terms and conditions of conservatorship or for the possession of or access to a child.

(b) A person commits an offense if the person files a suit to modify an order or portion of a decree based on the grounds permitted under Subsection (a) and the person knows that the person against whom the motion is filed has not been convicted of an offense, or received deferred adjudication for an offense, under Section 21.11, 22.011, or 22.021, Penal Code. An offense under this subsection is a Class B misdemeanor.

§ 156.1045. Modification of Order on Conviction for Family Violence.

(a) The conviction or an order deferring adjudication of a person who is a possessory conservator or a sole or joint managing conservator for an offense involving family violence is a material and substantial change of circumstances sufficient to justify a temporary order and modification of an existing court order or portion of a decree that provides for the appointment of a conservator or that sets the terms and conditions of conservatorship or for the possession of or access to a child to conform the order to the requirements of Section 153.004(d).

(b) A person commits an offense if the person files a suit to modify an order or portion of a decree based on the grounds permitted under Subsection (a) and the person knows that the person against whom the motion is filed has not been convicted of an offense, or received deferred adjudication for an offense, involving family violence. An offense under this subsection is a Class B misdemeanor.

§ 156.105. [repealed]

SUBCHAPTER C. [Repealed]

§§ 156.201 to 156.203. [repealed]

SUBCHAPTER D. [Repealed]

§§ 156.301 to 156.304. [repealed]

Subchapter E. Modification of Child Support

> ***Editors' Note:*** *This subchapter contains guest comments by Cynthia Bryant, Deputy Attorney General, and H. Patrick Sullivan, Director of Federal Policy Analysis, Child Support, Office of the Attorney General, identified as (C.B. & H.P.S.).*

CLE/Other Legal Publications

Child support: maximizing your chances of hitting a home run. Janice L. Green, 2004 ADV. FAM. L.

Child support—setting, modifying, and collecting. Alyssa P. Lemkuil & Dan Lemkuil, 2004 U. TEX. FAM. L. FRONT LINES

Modification of child support—what is the burden and what's a agreement worth? Rhonda F. Hunter, 2003 ADV. FAM. L.

Modification in SAPCR's. Sondra Kaighen, 2002 ADV. FAM. L.

Modification issues: custody, child support, possession, terms & conditions. Sydney A. Beckman, 2001 ADV. FAM. L.

Leading Cases

In re S.A.V., 837 S.W.2d 80 (Tex. 1992) (Texas had minimum contacts to modify child support paid by nonresident)

Royer v. Royer, 98 S.W.3d 284 (Tex. App.—Beaumont 2003, no pet.) (no material change in finances—increased spending at high rate despite an alleged drop in income means no modification of child support)

In re H.S.N., 69 S.W.3d 829 (Tex. App.—Corpus Christi 2002, no pet.) (support order more than three years old and not within 20% or $100 of amount due; review and modification appropriate)

In re B.O.G., 48 S.W.3d 312 (Tex. App.—Waco 2001, pet. denied) (trial court lacked jurisdiction over father's motion to modify child support under UIFSA, § 159.611)

In re Lee Children, 47 S.W.3d 693 (Tex. App.—Waco 2001, no pet.) (trial court cannot modify a final support judgment to add interest obligation not originally included)

In re Davis, 30 S.W.3d 609 (Tex. App.—Texarkana 2000, no pet.) (trial court abused discretion in modifying child support of man on unemployment comp)

Friermood v. Friermood, 25 S.W.3d 758 (Tex. App.—Houston [14th Dist.] 2000, no pet.) (downward mod approved—only one-half of obligor's request, but perhaps far more than guideline's amount)

In re P.J.H., 25 S.W.3d 402 (Tex. App.—Fort Worth 1999, no pet.) (upward modification approved—some tricky maneuvers come to very little)

In re J.G.Z., 963 S.W.2d 114 (Tex. App.—Texarkana 1998, no writ) (increased support modification is retroactive to date of motion to modify, not date of temporary order)

In re S.B.C., 952 S.W.2d 15 (Tex. App.—San Antonio 1997, no writ) (court denied child support reduction by properly considering income of obligor's fiancée)

In re G.J.S., 940 S.W.2d 289 (Tex. App.—San Antonio 1997, no writ) (court properly denied reduction in child support where father had large amount of assets)

Farish v. Farish, 921 S.W.2d 538 (Tex. App.—Beaumont 1996, no writ) (prior child support order not in compliance with guidelines does not automatically establish material and substantial change in circumstances—obligor refused decrease)

Tucker v. Tucker, 908 S.W.2d 530 (Tex. App.—San Antonio 1995, writ denied) (court abused discretion by not reducing support obligation)

Hamer v. Hamer, 906 S.W.2d 263 (Tex. App.—Amarillo 1995, no writ) (father's potential earnings appropriately considered by court)

Hammond v. Hammond, 898 S.W.2d 406 (Tex. App.—Fort Worth 1995, no writ) (material and substantial change in father's circumstances not shown)

Thomas v. Thomas, 895 S.W.2d 895 (Tex. App.—Waco 1995, writ denied) (expiration of contractual alimony constitutes material change in obligee's financial circumstances warranting modification)

Cole v. Cole, 882 S.W.2d 90 (Tex. App.—Houston [14th Dist.] 1994, writ denied) (change in parents' respective expenses supported order directing mother to pay child support)

Holley v. Holley, 864 S.W.2d 703 (Tex. App.—Houston [1st Dist.] 1994, writ denied) (retroactive child support granted in modification pending for almost four years)

Varner v. Howe, 860 S.W.2d 458 (Tex. App.—El Paso 1993, no writ) (jury finding advisory regarding child support amount)

Woodall v. Woodall, 837 S.W.2d 856 (Tex. App.—Houston [14th Dist.] 1992, no writ) (father's decrease in income sustained downward modification of support)

Payne v. Dial, 831 S.W.2d 457 (Tex. App.—Houston [14th Dist.] 1992, no writ) (small changes in net resources do not warrant modification of child support)

Cohen v. Sims, 830 S.W.2d 285 (Tex. App.—Houston [14th Dist.] 1992, writ denied) (child support increased $900 to $2,500 monthly, complaints that more required not sustained)

Ikard v. Ikard, 819 S.W.2d 644 (Tex. App.—El Paso 1991, no writ) (upward modification granted; obligor's net resources exceeded $4,000 per month)

Baucom v. Crews, 819 S.W.2d 628 (Tex. App.—Waco 1991, no writ) (obligor voluntarily underemployed—monthly payments reduced by 50%, but ordered to pay lump sum)

Pettit v. Pettit, 818 S.W.2d 561 (Tex. App.—Beaumont 1991, no writ) (agreement on child support doesn't prevent modification)

MacCallum v. MacCallum, 801 S.W.2d 579 (Tex. App.—Corpus Christi 1990, writ denied) (no modification of visitation or reduction of child support order)

---

§ 156.401. Grounds for Modification of Child Support.

(a) Except as provided by Subsection (b), the court may modify an order that provides for the support of a child if:

(1) the circumstances of the child or a person affected by the order have materially and substantially changed since the **earlier of:**

(A) the date of the order's rendition; or

(B) the date of the signing of a mediated or collaborative law settlement agreement on which the order is based; or

(2) it has been three years since the order was rendered or last modified and the monthly amount of the child support award under the order differs by either 20 percent or $100 from the amount that would be awarded in accordance with the child support guidelines.

(b) A support order may be modified only as to obligations accruing after the earlier of:

(1) the date of service of citation; or

(2) an appearance in the suit to modify.

(c) An order of joint conservatorship, in and of itself, does not constitute grounds for modifying a support order.

(d) Release of a child support obligor from incarceration is a material and substantial change in circumstances for purposes of Subsection (a)(1) if the obligor's child support obligation was abated, reduced, or suspended during the period of the obligor's incarceration.

History: Amended by 78th Legis., Reg. Sess. (2003), H.B. 913, eff. Sept. 1, 2003. "The changes in law made by this Act to Sections 156.101, 156.102(a) and (b), and 156.401(a), Family Code, apply only to an action to modify an order in a suit affecting the parent-child relationship pending on the effective date of this Act or filed on or after that date."

Comment

In 1997 the Legislature mandated that a deviation from the child support guidelines may be sufficient cause to modify child support. Periodic review of the support amount every three years, plus a fixed deviation of relatively narrow scope, authorizes the court to modify support. Note that the required 20% deviation does not equal the flat amount until it reaches $100 per month on a $500 monthly order or more. Any order over $500 requires at least a $100 per month deviation to trigger a modification. Orders for a smaller monthly amount will require a smaller deviation in absolute dollars, *e.g.* a child support order for $250 per month will require only a $50 per month variation from the support guidelines to warrant a modification.

Leading Cases

In re D.S., 76 S.W.3d 512 (Tex. App.—Houston [14th Dist.] 2002, no pet.) (agreed schedule for present and future child support based on anticipated career not modified just because he changed his plans)

In re H.S.N., 69 S.W.3d 829 (Tex. App.—Corpus Christi 2002, no pet.) (support order more than three years old and not within 20% or $100 of amount due; review and modification appropriate)

In re J.G.Z., 963 S.W.2d 144 (Tex. App.—Texarkana 1998, no pet.) (retroactive child support ordered back only to time of motion) (state court lacks authority to award federal tax dependent exemption)

---

§ 156.402. Effect of Guidelines.

(a) The court may consider the child support guidelines for single and multiple families under Chapter 154 *[Child Support]* to determine whether there has been a material or substantial change of circumstances under this chapter that warrants a modification of an existing child support order if the modification is in the best interest of the child.

(b) If the amount of support contained in the order does not substantially conform with the guidelines for single and multiple families under Chapter 154, the court may modify the order to substantially conform with the guidelines if the modification is in the best interest of the child. A court may consider other relevant evidence in addition to the factors listed in the guidelines.

Comment

The child support guidelines may be considered in modifying a prior support order, but the income of a new spouse shall not be considered in calculating the net resources of the obligor or obligee. The guideline formula for multiple family situations applies in a suit for modification.

Leading Case

Lindsey v. Lindsey, 965 S.W.2d 589 (Tex. App.—El Paso 1998, no pet.) (support modified based on fact obligee's income reduced by almost 50%)

---

§ 156.403. Voluntary Additional Support.

A history of support voluntarily provided in excess of the court order does not constitute cause to increase the amount of an existing child support order.

§ 156.404. Net Resources of New Spouse.

(a) The court may not add any portion of the net resources of a new spouse to the net resources of an obligor or obligee in order to calculate the amount of child support to be ordered in a suit for modification.

(b) The court may not subtract the needs of a new spouse, or of a dependent of a new spouse, from the net resources of the obligor or obligee in a suit for modification.

§ 156.405. Change in Lifestyle.

An increase in the needs, standard of living, or lifestyle of the obligee since the rendition of the existing order does not warrant an increase in the obligor's child support obligation.

§ 156.406. Use of Guidelines for Children in More Than One Household.

In applying the child support guidelines in a suit under this subchapter, if the obligor has the duty to support children in more than one household, the court shall apply the percentage guidelines for multiple families under Chapter 154 *[Child Support]*.

§ 156.407. Assignment of Child Support Right.

A notice of assignment filed under Chapter 231 *[Title IV–D Services]* does not constitute a modification of an order to pay child support.

§ 156.408. Modification of Support Order Rendered by Another State.

(a) Unless both parties and the child reside in this state, a court of this state may modify an order of child support rendered by an appropriate tribunal of another state only as provided by Chapter 159.

(b) If both parties and the child reside in this state, a court of this state may modify an order of child support rendered by an appropriate tribunal of another state after registration of the order as provided by Chapter 159.

Guest Comment

A 2001 amendment eliminates a reference in subsection (b) to modification of conservatorship—inasmuch as this subchapter addresses only modification of support—and conforms the subsection to UIFSA jurisdictional principles under § 159.613 for the modification of a child support order by a court of this state where the issuing state has lost exclusive jurisdiction and both parties and the child reside in this state. Nonmodifiable aspects of the controlling order—such as the duration of support—would, however, remain in effect, as required under § 159.611(c). (*H.P.S.*)

---

§ 156.409. Change in Physical Possession. *(first of two)*

(a) If the sole managing conservator of a child or the joint managing conservator who has the exclusive right to determine the primary residence of the child has voluntarily relinquished the primary care and possession of the child to another person for at least six months, the court may modify an order providing for the support of the child to provide that the other person having physical possession of the child shall have the right to receive and give receipt for payments of support for the child and to hold or disburse money for the benefit of the child.

(b) Notice of a motion for modification under this section may be served in the manner for serving a notice under Section 157.065.

§ 156.409. Change in Physical Possession. *(second of two)*

If the sole managing conservator of a child or the joint managing conservator who has the exclusive right to determine the primary residence of the child has voluntarily relinquished the primary care and possession of the child to another person for at least six months, the court may modify an order providing for the support of the child to provide that the other person having physical possession of the child shall have the right to receive and give receipt for payments of support for the child and to hold or disburse money for the benefit of the child.

Guest Comment

The first version of § 156.409 authorizes an exception to the general rule under § 156.003 for service of citation in a suit for modification. Under this version (which is controlling), a notice of a motion for modification may be served by first-class mail under the limited circumstances described in subsection (a). The intent of the exception is to allow the court to move forward with an order directing payment of support to the actual caretaker of the child in cases in which the child has, in effect, been abandoned by the custodial parent. (*H.P.S.*)

---

§ 156.410. Change in Circumstances Resulting From Military Service.

(a) For purposes of Section 156.401(a)(1), the fact that an obligor has been called into active military service in any branch of the United States armed forces is a material and substantial change in circumstances if that active military service:

(1) is for at least 30 consecutive days; and

(2) results in a decrease in the obligor's net resources during the period of service.

(b) A motion for modification under Subsection (a) must be accompanied by the affidavit of the obligor's commanding officer that states:

(1) the date on which the obligor's active military service begins and the date on which that service is expected to end; and

(2) the obligor's anticipated monthly gross income from active military service.

(c) Return of the obligor from the active military service described by Subsection (a) is a material and substantial change in circumstances for purposes of Section 156.401(a)(1) for which an obligee may file a motion for modification of a child support order if the court previously modified the order on the grounds described by Subsection (a).

History: Enacted by 78th Legis., Reg. Sess. (2003), H.B. 674, eff. June 20, 2003, and "applies to a suit for modification of a child support order that is filed on or after the effective date of this Act. A suit for modification that is filed before the effective date of this Act is governed by the law in effect on the date the suit was filed, and the former law is continued in effect for that purpose."

Guest Comment

While § 156.401(a)(1) indeterminately refers to material and substantial changes in circumstances that may occasion a prospective modification of a child support order, this section, added in 2003 and reflecting then current geo-political events, specifically identifies a call-up of a reservist into active military service as a change in circumstances that may warrant modification of a support order. Conversely, an obligor's return to civilian life may lead an obligee to request a modification of a previously modified order. *(C.B. & H.P.S.)*

Chapter 157. Enforcement.

Subchapter A. Pleadings and Defenses

§ 157.001. Motion for Enforcement.
§ 157.002. Contents of Motion.
§ 157.003. Joinder of Claims and Remedies; No Election of Remedies.
§ 157.004. Time Limitations; Enforcement of Possession.
§ 157.005. Time Limitations; Enforcement of Child Support.
§ 157.006. Affirmative Defense to Motion for Enforcement.
§ 157.007. Affirmative Defense to Motion for Enforcement of Possession or Access.
§ 157.008. Affirmative Defense to Motion for Enforcement of Child Support.

Subchapter B. Procedure

§ 157.061. Setting Hearing.
§ 157.062. Notice of Hearing.
§ 157.063. Appearance.
§ 157.064. Special Exception.
§ 157.065. Notice of Hearing, First Class Mail.
§ 157.066. Failure To Appear.

Subchapter C. Failure To Appear; Bond or Security

§ 157.101. Bond or Security for Release of Respondent.
§ 157.102. Capias; Duty of Law Enforcement Officials.
§ 157.103. Capias Fee.
§ 157.104. Conditional Release.
§ 157.105. Release Hearing.
§ 157.106. Cash Bond as Support.
§ 157.107. Appearance Bond or Security Other than Cash Bond as Support.
§ 157.108. Cash Bond as Property of Respondent.
§ 157.109. Security for Compliance with Order.
§ 157.110. Forfeiture of Security for Failure To Comply with Order.
§ 157.111. Forfeiture Not Defense to Contempt.
§ 157.112. Joinder of Forfeiture and Contempt Proceedings.
§ 157.113. Application of Bond Pending Writ.
§ 157.114. Failure To Appear.
§ 157.115. Default Judgment.

Subchapter D. Hearing and Enforcement Order

§ 157.161. Record.
§ 157.162. Proof.
§ 157.163. Appointment of Attorney.
§ 157.164. Payment of Appointed Attorney.
§ 157.165. Probation of Contempt Order.
§ 157.166. Contents of Enforcement Order.
§ 157.167. Respondent To Pay Attorney's Fees and Costs.
§ 157.168. Additional Periods of Possession or Access.

Subchapter E. Community Supervision

Subchapter F. Judgment and Interest

Subchapter G. Child Support Lien

Subchapter H. Habeas Corpus

Subchapter I. Clarification of Orders

Editors' Note: *This chapter contains guest comments by Alicia Gray Key, Executive Director, Office of Court Administration; Cynthia Bryant, Deputy Attorney General; and H. Patrick Sullivan, Director of Federal Policy Analysis, both of the Child Support, Office of the Attorney General Child Support Division, identified as (A.G.K., C.B. & H.P.S.).*

Introductory Comment

In 1983 the only remedies to enforce child support provided in the Family Code were contempt and rendition of a money judgment for arrears. That year, the Texas Legislature provided for a constitutional amendment authorizing wage withholding for child support, which was overwhelmingly approved by the voters. The next major event in the evolutionary process of reforming the enforcement remedies available occurred with the enactment of the federal Child Support Enforcement Amendments of 1984. In the next decade, the legislature enacted as wide an array of remedies as are available in any state. During this same time, Texas moved from a system in which child support orders were wholly within the discretion of the trial court—with the attendant unpredictability—to a highly regulated, predictable system based on child support guidelines rebuttably presumed to be in the child's best interest.

Texas can now claim to be in the first rank of states insofar as the legal remedies available to enforce court-ordered support. The last piece fell into place with the enactment of Chapter 232, Suspension of License for Failure To Pay Child Support, *infra*. Chapters 157 and 158 gather together in one place almost all of the other post-decree enforcement remedies and procedures for SAPCR's.

Subchapters A and B present fourteen detailed statutes, comprising the procedural portion of this chapter. A common structure is established for every motion to enforce an existing final order, whether for child support or for possession of and access to a child.

"Contempt of court" historically has been the chief enforcement remedy. In large part the prior law of contempt has been continued, albeit with the addition of nonsubstantive details lacking in prior statutes which recognize jurisprudential developments in constitutional due process. An important example of innovative thinking is found in §§ 157.006–157.008, modeled after the Penal Code provision for criminal nonsupport, Tex. Pen. Code § 25.05, *infra*. The burden of persuasion regarding "inability to pay" is allocated to the respondent as an affirmative defense.

Civil and coercive contempt is the process by which a court exerts authority to compel obedience to its orders. Punishment for civil contempt may also be characterized as remedial in nature and is generally assessed for the benefit of the movant. Criminal or punitive contempt is designed to punish the contemnor for disobedience of a court order so as to protect the dignity of the judicial system. It is most easily identified by its determinate sentence, *e.g.* "six months in jail as punishment for failure to comply with the court's order." In sum, the contemnor may purge himself of coercive contempt, but not of punitive contempt because the contumacious act has been completed and cannot be undone. To further complicate matters, a finding of contempt may involve elements of contempt both coercive and punitive.

Guest Comment

A 2001 amendment—effective January 1, 2002—changed the interest rate from 12 percent to 6 percent for any child support payment that became due on or after the effective date and for all existing, unconfirmed support arrears. It did not, however, affect the rate—12 percent simple—for existing judgments. A cumulative money judgment under § 157.263, however, rendered on or after the effective date, reduced the 12 percent interest rate to 6 percent on any balance owed under an existing judgment. (*A.G.K. & H.P.S.*)

CLE/Other Legal Publications

Enforcing visitation and child support: writs of habeas corpus, making the teen go, getting the medical expenses reimbursed and more! H.E. Mendez, 2004 ADV. FAM. L.

Enforcement essentials. Jennifer James Robin, 2004 ADV. FAM. L.

Child support—setting, modifying, and collecting. Alyssa P. Lemkuil & Dan Lemkuil, 2004 U. TEX. FAM. L. FRONT LINES

Jurisdiction and enforcement of custody and possession. Brian L. Webb, 2004 U. TEX. FAM. L. ON THE BORDER

Support enforcement: contempt, judgment, withholding, loss of license, contractual, and otherwise. Alyssa P. Lemkuil & Daniel J. Lemkuil, 2003 ADV. FAM. L.

Child support enforcement abroad. Richard S. Orsinger, 2002 ADV. FAM. L.

Enforcement. Victor H. Negron, Jr., 2002 ADV. FAM. L.

Cross References

TEX. FAM. CODE ANN. ch. 232. Suspension of License for Failure To Pay Child Support.

TEX. GOV'T CODE ANN. § 21.002. Contempt of Court.

TEX. PENAL CODE ANN. § 25.05. Criminal Nonsupport.

IV–D Child Support Enforcement. 42 U.S.C.A. § 651 *et seq.*

Family Support Act of 1988, Pub. L. 100–485, 102 Stat. 2343, *see* 5 U.S. Code Cong. & Admin. News 2776 (1988) (last federal legislative action to regulate state enforcement efforts)

Child Support Enforcement Amendments of 1984 [CSEA]. Pub. L. No. 98–378, 98 Stat. 1305, *see* 4 U.S. Code Cong. & Admin. News 2397 (1984) (federal act creating present system), codified at 42 U.S.C.A. § 651 *et seq.* (especially § 666, *see* 45 C.F.R. § 303)

42 U.S.C.A. § § 651–665, P. L. 93–647, 88 Stat. 2351 (first federal intervention in child support enforcement, recoupment of AFDC payments the goal)

Texas Family Law Practice Manual

Chapter 24. Enforcement—Child Support

Chapter 25. Enforcement—Possession and Access

Subchapter A. Pleadings and Defenses

§ 157.001. Motion for Enforcement.

(a) A motion for enforcement as provided in this chapter may be filed to enforce a final order for conservatorship, child support, possession of or access to a child, or other provisions of a final order.

(b) The court may enforce by contempt a final order for possession of and access to a child as provided in this chapter.

(c) The court may enforce a final order for child support as provided in this chapter or Chapter 158.

(d) A motion for enforcement shall be filed in the court of continuing, exclusive jurisdiction.

§ 157.002. Contents of Motion.

(a) A motion for enforcement must, in ordinary and concise language:

(1) identify the provision of the order allegedly violated and sought to be enforced;

(2) state the manner of the respondent's alleged noncompliance;

(3) state the relief requested by the movant; and

(4) contain the signature of the movant or the movant's attorney.

(b) A motion for enforcement of child support:

(1) must include the amount owed as provided in the order, the amount paid, and the amount of arrearages;

(2) if contempt is requested, must include the portion of the order allegedly violated and, for each date of alleged contempt, the amount due and the amount paid, if any;

(3) may include as an attachment a copy of a record of child support payments maintained by the Title IV-D registry or a local registry; and

(4) if the obligor owes arrearages for a child receiving assistance under Part A of Title IV of the federal Social Security Act (42 U.S.C. Section 601 et seq.), may include a request that:

(A) the obligor pay the arrearages in accordance with a plan approved by the court; or

(B) if the obligor is already subject to a plan and is not incapacitated, the obligor participate in work activities, as defined under 42 U.S.C. Section 607(d), that the court determines appropriate.

(c) A motion for enforcement of the terms and conditions of conservatorship or possession of or access to a child must include the date, place, and, if applicable, the time of each occasion of the respondent's failure to comply with the order.

(d) The movant is not required to plead that the underlying order is enforceable by contempt to obtain other appropriate enforcement remedies.

(e) The movant may allege repeated past violations of the order and that future violations of a similar nature may occur before the date of the hearing.

Leading Case

In re Smith, 981 S.W.2d 909 (Tex. App.—Houston [1st Dist.] 1998, no pet.) (criminal [punitive] contempt must be pled in order to be imposed)

---

§ 157.003. Joinder of Claims and Remedies; No Election of Remedies.

(a) A party requesting enforcement may join in the same proceeding any claim and remedy provided for in this chapter, other provisions of this title, or other rules of law.

(b) A motion for enforcement does not constitute an election of remedies that limits or precludes:

(1) the use of any other civil or criminal proceeding to enforce a final order; or

(2) a suit for damages under Chapter 42 *[Civil Liability for Interference with Possessory Interest in Child]*.

§ 157.004. Time Limitations; Enforcement of Possession.

The court retains jurisdiction to render a contempt order for failure to comply with the order of possession and access if the motion for enforcement is filed not later than the sixth month after the date:

(1) the child becomes an adult; or

(2) on which the right of possession and access terminates under the order or by operation of law.

§ 157.005. Time Limitations; Enforcement of Child Support.

(a) The court retains jurisdiction to render a contempt order for failure to comply with the child support order if the motion for enforcement is filed not later than the sixth month after the date:

(1) the child becomes an adult; or

(2) on which the child support obligation terminates under the order or by operation of law.

(b) The court retains jurisdiction to confirm the total amount of child support arrearages and render judgment for past-due child support until the date all current child support and medical support and child support arrearages, including interest and any applicable fees and costs, have been paid.

Comment

An action for confirmation and judgment may be brought for as long as support payments, interest, fees and costs are unpaid.

Leading Cases

In re A.D., 73 S.W.3d 244 (Tex. 2002) (issuance of administrative writ of withholding over 4 years after child turned 18 not violation of constitutional prohibition on retroactive laws)

In re T.L.K., 90 S.W.3d 833 (Tex. App.—San Antonio 2002, no pet.) (limitations defense to revival of money judgment for child support arrears not available in suit brought by A.G.)

In re S.C.S., 48 S.W.3d 831 (Tex. App.—Houston [14th Dist.] 2001, no pet.) (child support arrears collectible until paid since § 157.005 effective on 9/1/99)

---

§ 157.006. Affirmative Defense to Motion for Enforcement.

(a) The issue of the existence of an affirmative defense to a motion for enforcement does not arise unless evidence is admitted supporting the defense.

(b) The respondent must prove the affirmative defense by a preponderance of the evidence.

§ 157.007. Affirmative Defense to Motion for Enforcement of Possession or Access.

(a) The respondent may plead as an affirmative defense to contempt for failure to comply with an order for possession or access to a child that the movant voluntarily relinquished actual possession and control of the child.

(b) The voluntary relinquishment must have been for the time encompassed by the court-ordered periods during which the respondent is alleged to have interfered.

§ 157.008. Affirmative Defense to Motion for Enforcement of Child Support.

(a) An obligor may plead as an affirmative defense in whole or in part to a motion for enforcement of child support that the obligee voluntarily relinquished to the obligor actual possession and control of a child.

(b) The voluntary relinquishment must have been for a time period in excess of any court-ordered periods of possession of and access to the child and actual support must have been supplied by the obligor.

(c) An obligor may plead as an affirmative defense to an allegation of contempt or of the violation of a condition of community service requiring payment of child support that the obligor:

(1) lacked the ability to provide support in the amount ordered;

(2) lacked property that could be sold, mortgaged, or otherwise pledged to raise the funds needed;

(3) attempted unsuccessfully to borrow the funds needed; and

(4) knew of no source from which the money could have been borrowed or legally obtained.

(d) An obligor who has provided actual support to the child during a time subject to an affirmative defense under this section may request reimbursement for that support as a counterclaim or offset against the claim of the obligee.

(e) An action against the obligee for support supplied to a child is limited to the amount of periodic payments previously ordered by the court.

Leading Cases

Ex parte Rojo, 925 S.W.2d 654 (Tex. 1996) (inability to pay valid defense to civil contempt)

Ex parte Dustman, 538 S.W.2d 409 (Tex. 1976) (uncontroverted evidence of contemnor's inability to pay arrearage)

In re A.M., 101 S.W.3d 480 (Tex. App.—Corpus Christi 2002, pet. filed) (obligor supplied support while child in his possession—A.G.'s defense of court—ordered support inappropriate on those facts)

In re Cooper, 38 S.W.3d 715 (Tex. App.—Amarillo 2000, no pet.) (dad's support and medical expenses actually paid for child in his possession more than offset his unpaid support arrears on court-ordered support)

Ex parte Jackson, 911 S.W.2d 230 (Tex. App.—Houston [14th Dist.] 1995, no writ) (habeas denied) (requiring child support obligor to prove inability to pay as affirmative defense upheld as constitutional)

Ex parte Robertson, 880 S.W.2d 803 (Tex. App.—Houston [1st Dist.] 1994, no writ) (inability to pay no defense to criminal contempt)

Ex parte King, 819 S.W.2d 944 (Tex. App.—Houston [14th Dist.] 1991, no writ) (obligor's burden to prove inability to pay not sustained by his affidavit and fact of incarceration)

Subchapter B. Procedure

§ 157.061. Setting Hearing.

(a) On filing a motion for enforcement requesting contempt, the court shall set the date, time, and place of the hearing and order the respondent to personally appear and respond to the motion.

(b) If the motion for enforcement does not request contempt, the court shall set the motion for hearing on the request of a party.

(c) The court shall give preference to a motion for enforcement of child support in setting a hearing date and may not delay the hearing because a suit for modification of the order requested to be enforced has been or may be filed.

§ 157.062. Notice of Hearing.

(a) The notice of hearing must include the date, time, and place of the hearing.

(b) The notice of hearing need not repeat the allegations contained in the motion for enforcement.

(c) Notice of hearing on a motion for enforcement of an existing order providing for child support or possession of or access to a child shall be given to the respondent by personal service of a copy of the motion and notice not later than the 10th day before the date of the hearing.

(d) If a motion for enforcement is joined with another claim:

(1) the hearing may not be held before 10 a.m. on the first Monday after the 20th day after the date of service; and

(2) the provisions of the Texas Rules of Civil Procedure applicable to the filing of an original lawsuit apply.

Leading Cases

In re Digges, 981 S.W.2d 445 (Tex. App.—San Antonio 1998, no pet.) (default judgment taken before time to answer is void)

In re Hathcox, 981 S.W.2d 422 (Tex. App.—Texarkana 1998, no pet.) (new causes of action added to enforcement motion require new answer date before taking default judgment)

---

§ 157.063. Appearance.

A party makes a general appearance for all purposes in an enforcement proceeding if:

(1) the party appears at the hearing or is present when the case is called; and

(2) the party does not object to the court's jurisdiction or the form or manner of the notice of hearing.

§ 157.064. Special Exception.

(a) If a respondent specially excepts to the motion for enforcement or moves to strike, the court shall rule on the exception or the motion to strike before it hears the motion for enforcement.

(b) If an exception is sustained, the court shall give the movant an opportunity to replead and continue the hearing to a designated date and time without the requirement of additional service.

§ 157.065. Notice of Hearing, First Class Mail.

(a) If a party has been ordered under Chapter 105 *[Settings, Hearing, and Orders]* to provide the court and the state case registry with the party's current mailing address, notice of a motion for enforcement may be served by mailing a copy of the notice to the respondent, together with a copy of the motion, by first class mail to the last mailing address of the respondent on file with the court and the registry.

(b) The notice may be sent by the clerk of the court, the movant's attorney, or any person entitled to the address information as provided in Chapter 105 *[Settings, Hearings, and Orders]*.

(c) A person who sends the notice shall file of record a certificate of service showing the date of mailing and the name of the person who sent the notice.

(d) Repealed by Acts 1997, 75th Leg., ch. 911, § 97(a), eff. Sept. 1, 1997.

§ 157.066. Failure to Appear.

If a respondent who has been personally served with notice to appear at a hearing does not appear at the designated time, place, and date to respond to a motion for enforcement of an existing court order, regardless of whether the motion is joined with other claims or remedies, the court may not hold the respondent in contempt but may, on proper proof, grant a default judgment for the relief sought and issue a capias for the arrest of the respondent.

Comment

Personal service of notice is required if the court is to order the issuance of a capias for the arrest of the respondent when the respondent fails to show up as ordered for a hearing. The rule continues that a person may not be adjudicated in contempt in absentia, but other remedies may be invoked by default, and a capias (bench warrant) may issue to bring the no-show physically to the courthouse.

Leading Cases

In re Sheard, 102 S.W.3d 808 (Tex. App.—Beaumont 2003, orig. proceeding) (contempt finding inappropriate when only violation was failure to appear at hearing)

In re White, 45 S.W.3d 787 (Tex. App.—Waco 2001, no pet.) (respondent who fails to personally appear at a hearing regarding enforcement of a previous court support order cannot be held in contempt)

In re Aguilera, 37 S.W.3d 43 (Tex. App.—El Paso 2000, no pet.) (capias valid for arrest of no-show even though show-cause to appear on motion for contempt did not provide 10–day notice)

Subchapter C. Failure to Appear; Bond or Security

Introductory Comment

The capias procedure deals with recalcitrant child support obligors who refuse to appear at hearings. The procedure required for issuance of the capias and after the execution of an arrest has been continued to date with little substantive change. The basic principle is the requirement that a "reasonable" bond be established at the time a capias is issued. There is a statutory presumption that $1,000 is a reasonable amount, but this can be rebutted if the alleged arrearages are in excess of that sum, or if the respondent has a record of prior contempt adjudications.

After an individual is taken into custody on a capias, release may be obtained by posting the "reasonable" bond set at the time the capias was issued. Release on an appearance bond is conditioned on the respondent's promise to appear; this is analogous to criminal law procedure under which it is the duty of the defendant to appear at a scheduled hearing without further official notice of the time and place of that hearing. If the respondent cannot post an appearance bond or other satisfactory security, his release may still be secured by other means, *i.e.*, personal recognizance. An expedited hearing is provided if the respondent cannot be released on his own recognizance and cannot or will not post an appearance bond.

This subchapter also attempts to deal with the dilemma of enforcing child support orders against such disparate obligors as day-laborers and the self-employed. Because withholding from earnings is either impractical or entirely useless in a variety of employment contexts, posting security or a bond to secure ordered periodic payments "may" be required by the court. Unfortunately, only in rare instances is there a possibility that a working class, or sometimes middle class, obligor will be in a financial position to post an adequate bond or other satisfactory security to ensure that support payments will be made.

---

§ 157.101. Bond or Security for Release of Respondent.

(a) When the court orders the issuance of a capias as provided in this chapter, the court shall also set an appearance bond or security, payable to the obligee or to a person designated by the court, in a reasonable amount.

(b) An appearance bond or security in the amount of $1,000 or a cash bond in the amount of $250 is presumed to be reasonable. Evidence that the respondent has attempted to evade service of process, has previously been found guilty of contempt, or has accrued arrearages over $1,000 is sufficient to rebut the presumption. If the presumption is rebutted, the court shall set a reasonable bond.

Leading Case

In re Clark, 977 S.W.2d 152 (Tex. App.—Houston [14th Dist.] 1998, no pet.) (presumption that appearance bond of $1,000 or $250,000 cash bond is reasonable not rebutted)

---

§ 157.102. Capias; Duty of Law Enforcement Officials.

Law enforcement officials shall treat the capias in the same manner as an arrest warrant for a criminal offense and shall enter the capias in the computer records for outstanding warrants maintained by the local police, sheriff, and Department of Public Safety. The capias shall be forwarded to and disseminated by the Texas Crime Information Center and the National Crime Information Center.

§ 157.103. Capias Fees.

(a) The fee for issuing a capias as provided in this chapter is the same as the fee for issuance of a writ of attachment.

(b) The fee for serving a capias is the same as the fee for service of a writ in civil cases generally.

§ 157.104. Conditional Release.

If the respondent is taken into custody and released on bond, the court shall condition the bond on the respondent's promise to appear in court for a hearing as required by the court without the necessity of further personal service of notice on the respondent.

§ 157.105. Release Hearing.

(a) If the respondent is taken into custody and not released on bond, the respondent shall be brought before the court that issued the capias on or before the first working day after the arrest. The court shall determine whether the respondent's appearance in court at a designated time and place can be assured by a method other than by posting the bond or security previously established.

(b) If the respondent is released without posting bond or security, the court shall set a hearing on the alleged contempt at a designated date, time, and place and give the respondent notice of hearing in open court. No other notice to the respondent is required.

(c) If the court is not satisfied that the respondent's appearance in court can be assured and the respondent remains in custody, a hearing on the alleged contempt shall be held as soon as practicable, but not later than the fifth day after the date that the respondent was taken into custody, unless the respondent and the respondent's attorney waive the accelerated hearing.

§ 157.106. Cash Bond as Support.

(a) If the respondent has posted a cash bond and is found to be in arrears in the payment of court-ordered child support, the court shall order that the proceeds of the cash bond be paid to the child support obligee or to a person designated by the court, not to exceed the amount of child support arrearages determined to exist.

(b) This section applies without regard to whether the respondent appears at the hearing.

§ 157.107. Appearance Bond or Security Other Than Cash Bond as Support.

(a) If the respondent fails to appear at the hearing as directed, the court shall order that the appearance bond or security be forfeited and that the proceeds of any judgment on the bond or security, not to exceed the amount of child support arrearages determined to exist, be paid to the obligee or to a person designated by the court.

(b) The obligee may file suit on the bond.

§ 157.108. Cash Bond as Property of Respondent.

A court shall treat a cash bond posted for the benefit of the respondent as the property of the respondent. A person who posts the cash bond does not have recourse in relation to an order regarding the bond other than against the respondent.

§ 157.109. Security for Compliance With Order.

(a) The court may order the respondent to execute a bond or post security if the court finds that the respondent:

(1) has on two or more occasions denied possession of or access to a child who is the subject of the order; or

(2) is employed by an employer not subject to the jurisdiction of the court or for whom income withholding is unworkable or inappropriate.

(b) The court shall set the amount of the bond or security and condition the bond or security on compliance with the court order permitting possession or access or the payment of past-due or future child support.

(c) The court shall order the bond or security payable through the registry of the court:

(1) to the obligee or other person or entity entitled to receive child support payments designated by the court if enforcement of child support is requested; or

(2) to the person who is entitled to possession or access if enforcement of possession or access is requested.

§ 157.110. Forfeiture of Security for Failure to Comply With Order.

(a) On the motion of a person or entity for whose benefit a bond has been executed or security deposited, the court may forfeit all or part of the bond or security deposit on a finding that the person who furnished the bond or security:

(1) has violated the court order for possession of and access to a child; or

(2) failed to make child support payments.

(b) The court shall order the registry to pay the funds from a forfeited bond or security deposit to the obligee or person or entity entitled to receive child support payments in an amount that does not exceed the child support arrearages or, in the case of possession of or access to a child, to the person entitled to possession or access.

(c) The court may order that all or part of the forfeited amount be applied to pay attorney's fees and costs incurred by the person or entity bringing the motion for contempt or motion for forfeiture.

§ 157.111. Forfeiture Not Defense to Contempt.

The forfeiture of bond or security is not a defense in a contempt proceeding.

§ 157.112. Joinder of Forfeiture and Contempt Proceedings.

A motion for enforcement requesting contempt may be joined with a forfeiture proceeding.

§ 157.113. Application of Bond Pending Writ.

If the obligor requests to execute a bond or to post security pending a hearing by an appellate court on a writ, the bond or security on forfeiture shall be payable to the obligee.

§ 157.114. Failure to Appear.

The court may order a capias to be issued for the arrest of the respondent if:

(1) the motion for enforcement requests contempt;

(2) the respondent was personally served; and

(3) the respondent fails to appear.

§ 157.115. Default Judgment.

(a) The court may render a default order for the relief requested if the respondent:

(1) has been personally served, has filed an answer, or has entered an appearance; and

(2) does not appear at the designated time, place, and date to respond to the motion.

(b) If the respondent fails to appear, the court may not hold the respondent in contempt but may order a capias to be issued.

Subchapter D. Hearing and Enforcement Order

Introductory Comment

Two major principles of constitutional due process are codified in this subchapter: (1) the right to remain silent under the 5th Amendment (as applicable in the contempt context); and, (2) the right to appointed counsel of an indigent, alleged contemnor who faces possible incarceration. Note the statute does not specify the length of time of the possible incarceration.

Insofar as the Family Code is concerned, contempt and other remedies apply equally to a violation of an order to pay child support and interference with the noncustodial parent's right of possession of and access to the child. Although a possessory conservator-obligor theoretically has almost identical remedies for violation of court orders to those afforded a managing conservator-obligee, actual practice has not yet caught up with the letter of the law.

CLE/Other Legal Publications

Support enforcement: contempt, judgment, withholding, loss of license, contractual, and otherwise. Alyssa P. Lemkuil & Daniel J. Lemkuil, 2003 ADV. FAM. L.

Enforcement. Victor H. Negron, Jr., 2002 ADV. FAM. L.

Methods of child support enforcement: contempt and non-contempt remedies. Walter P. Mahoney, Jr., 2001 ADV. FAM. L.

Enforcement/Contempt. Daniel J. Lemkuil, 2000 ADV FAM. L.

Leading Cases

Commitment Order

Ex parte Swate, 922 S.W.2d 122 (Tex. 1996) (commitment order increasing punishment imposed by contempt order is void)

Ex parte Jordan, 865 S.W.2d 459 (Tex. 1993) (three days is too long to hold contemnor without written commitment order)

Ex parte Amaya, 748 S.W.2d 224 (Tex. 1988) (contempt commitment order must be signed within reasonable time; over the weekend is too long)

In re Brown, 114 S.W.3d 7 (Tex. App.—Amarillo 2003, orig. proceeding) (next day signing of contempt and commitment order timely)

Ex parte Littleton, 97 S.W.3d 840 (Tex. App.—Texarkana 2003, no pet.) (in absence of both written commitment order and a written contempt order child support contemnor entitled to habeas release)

In re Patillo, 32 S.W.3d 907 (Tex. App.—Corpus Christi 2000, no pet.) (appellate court finds defects in commitment order—reforms errors and keeps child support contemnor in jail)

Ex parte Seligman, 9 S.W.3d 452 (Tex. App.—San Antonio 1999, no pet.) (commitment order signed five days after oral order signed—too long after incarceration)

Ex parte Arnold, 926 S.W.2d 622 (Tex. App.—Beaumont 1996, no writ) (assessment of separate punishments for each contempt violation means void portion of order does not prevent enforcement of remainder of order)

Ex parte Whitehead, 908 S.W.2d 68 (Tex. App.—Houston [1st Dist.] 1995, no writ) (commitment order signed too late to punish contemnor)

Ex parte Morgan, 886 S.W.2d 829 (Tex. App.—Amarillo 1994, no writ) (oral contempt judgment for violation of visitation executed four days later violates mother's due process rights)

Ex parte Coleman, 864 S.W.2d 573 (Tex. App.—Tyler 1993, no writ) (commitment order for contempt must comply with requirements of code)

Ex parte Garcia, 831 S.W.2d 1 (Tex. App.—El Paso 1992, no writ) (coercive contempt order must state action required to purge contempt)

Contempt Order

Ex parte Hernandez, 827 S.W.2d 858 (Tex. 1992) (civil contempt requires both written judgment of contempt and written order of commitment)

Ex parte Strickland, 723 S.W.2d 668 (Tex. 1987) (incarceration requires written judgment of contempt or written order of commitment)

In re Rowe, 113 S.W.3d 749 (Tex. App.—Austin 2003, orig. proceeding) (father's due process rights violated when trial court held him in contempt, without prior notice, for nonpayment of child support)

In re Broussard, 112 S.W.3d 827 (Tex. App.—Houston [14th Dist.] 2003, orig. proceeding) (contempt order found void for ambiguity)

In re Watson, 108 S.W.3d 531 (Tex. App.—Houston [14th Dist.] 2003, orig. proceeding) (criminal contempt order stricken by appellate court as unclear but civil contempt order remains in effect)

In re Nesevitch, 93 S.W.3d 510 (Tex. App.—Houston [14th Dist.] 2002, no pet.) (contempt order insufficient to sustain incarceration—based on exhibit showing payments, not non-payments)

In re Taylor, 28 S.W.3d 240 (Tex. App.—Waco 2000, no pet.) (trial court's refusal to rule on contempt based on alleged violation of conservatorship order elicits mandamus)

Ex parte Chunn, 881 S.W.2d 912 (Tex. App.—Houston [1st Dist.] 1994, no writ) (punishment imposed for contempt cannot be greater than that punishment originally assessed in contempt order)

Ex parte Hightower, 877 S.W.2d 17 (Tex. App.—Dallas 1994, writ dism'd w.o.j.) (attorney's fees incurred in visitation dispute are not enforceable by contempt)

Ex parte Rogers, 820 S.W.2d 35 (Tex. App.—Corpus Christi 1991, no writ) (contempt finding insufficiently specific—the lumping together of all offenses fatal)

Ex parte Balderas, 804 S.W.2d 261 (Tex. App.—Houston [1st Dist.] 1991, no writ) (court cannot increase punishment originally imposed at later compliance hearing)

Due Process Rights

Ex parte Acker, 949 S.W.2d 314 (Tex. 1997) (party must be advised of right to counsel)

Ex parte Keene, 909 S.W.2d 507 (Tex. 1995) (without record or instruction regarding right to counsel, alleged child support contemnor cannot be adjudicated in contempt)

Ex parte Sproull, 815 S.W.2d 250 (Tex. 1991); *Ex parte* Gunther, 758 S.W.2d 226 (Tex. 1988) (alleged contemnor facing "serious punishment," i.e., possible sentence of more than six months incarceration, has right to jury trial)

In re Brown, 114 S.W.3d 7 (Tex. App.—Amarillo 2003, orig. proceeding) (no right to jury trial for petty criminal contempt)

In re Ohiri, 95 S.W.3d 413 (Tex. App.—Houston [1st Dist.] 2002, orig. proceeding) (after compliance hearing, obligor improperly held in contempt and jailed without beign advised of his due process rights)

Ex parte York, 899 S.W.2d 47 (Tex. App.—Waco 1995, no writ) (right to jury trial for serious offense)

Ex parte York, 882 S.W.2d 931 (Tex. App.—Waco 1994, no writ) (civil contempt entitles alleged contemnor to none of the constitutional procedural protections that criminal contempt entails)

Ex parte Howell, 843 S.W.2d 241 (Tex. App.—Houston [1st Dist.] 1993, no writ) (no jury trial for contempt if sentence not more than six months)

Cudd v. Bass, 771 S.W.2d 3 (Tex. App.—Houston [1st Dist.] 1989, no writ) (appointed counsel may pursue writ of habeas corpus and is entitled to compensation)

Fifth Amendment

Ex parte Werblud, 536 S.W.2d 542 (Tex. 1976) (Fifth Amendment privilege in civil case)

In re Baker, 99 S.W.3d 230 (Tex. App.—Eastland 2003, no pet.) (contemnor not informed of right to jury trial when contempt punishment "serious")

Ex parte York, 899 S.W.2d 47 (Tex. App.—Waco 1995, no writ) (in a "serious" contempt case, the court must advise contemnor of his right against self incrimination)

Ex parte Johns, 807 S.W.2d 768 (Tex. App.—Dallas 1991, no writ) (by invoking his Fifth Amendment privilege and not testifying, the contemnor failed to refute former spouse's evidence concerning his ability to pay child support)

Probation

Ex parte Spikes, 909 S.W.2d 245 (Tex. App.—Amarillo 1995, no writ) (probation on contempt finding may not extend beyond five years—revocation thereafter a nullity)

Ex parte Balderas, 804 S.W.2d 261 (Tex. App.—Houston [1st Dist.] 1991, no writ) (court cannot increase punishment originally imposed at later compliance hearing)

Punishment

Rosser v. Squier, 902 S.W.2d 962 (Tex. 1995) ($45,000 fine for contempt summarily reversed)

Ex parte Roosth, 881 S.W.2d 300 (Tex. 1994) (trial court cannot limit the operation of good time behavior credit in punitive contempt sentence)

Ex parte Sproull, 815 S.W.2d 250 (Tex. 1991) (22 year sentence for contempt reversed)

Ex parte Acly, 711 S.W.2d 627 (Tex. 1986) (equal protection requires good time credits for contemnor)

Ex parte Jones, 36 S.W.3d 139 (Tex. App.—Houston [1st Dist.] 2000, pet. refused) (coercive contempt punishment forced return of child, not double jeopardy bar to subsequent penal prosecution for interference with custody)

Ex parte Binse, 932 S.W.2d 619 (Tex. App.—Houston [14th Dist.] 1996, no writ) (incarceration of obligor for failure to pay attorney fees incidental to child support is constitutional)

Reasonable Notice

Ex parte Anderson, 900 S.W.2d 333 (Tex. 1995); *Ex parte* Delcourt, 888 S.W.2d 811 (Tex. 1994) (new commitment order requires notice and hearing)

Rolon v. Rolon, 907 S.W.2d 670 (Tex. App.—Beaumont 1995, no writ) (untimely notice of trial setting given to father's attorney)

Ex parte Friedman, 808 S.W.2d 166 (Tex. App.—El Paso 1991, no writ) (five days notice not sufficient to conduct contempt proceeding)

Release from Contempt

Ex parte Padron, 565 S.W.2d 921 (Tex. 1978) (civil contemnor has the keys to the jailhouse door to purge coercive contempt)

McCoy v. McCoy, 908 S.W.2d 42 (Tex. App.—Houston [1st Dist.] 1995, no writ) (contempt finding not reversible by appeal)

Ex parte Williams, 866 S.W.2d 751 (Tex. App.—Houston [1st Dist.] 1993, no writ) (one little typo and one fee which is not enforceable by contempt does not invalidate basic order of incarceration)

Ex parte Garcia, 831 S.W.2d 1 (Tex. App.—El Paso 1992, no writ) (coercive contempt order must state action required to purge contempt)

Specificity of SAPCR Order

Ex parte Acker, 949 S.W.2d 314 (Tex. 1997) (payments beginning in "June" not specific enough for contempt)

Ex parte MacCallum, 807 S.W.2d 729 (Tex. 1991) (visitation order not sufficiently specific to be enforced by contempt)

Ex parte Brister, 801 S.W.2d 833 (Tex. 1990) (ambiguous visitation order not enforceable by contempt)

Ex parte Garcia, 795 S.W.2d 740 (Tex. 1990); *Ex parte* Holland, 790 S.W.2d 568 (Tex. 1990) (specificity of underlying order required to sustain contempt)

Ex parte Davila, 718 S.W.2d 281 (Tex. 1986) (no incarceration for failure to pay overdue medical expenses)

Ex parte Slavin, 412 S.W.2d 43 (Tex. 1967) (ambiguous decree not enforceable by contempt—probably most cited case on subject)

In re Marriage of Grossnickle, 115 S.W.3d 238 (Tex. App.—Texarkana 2003, no pet.) (trial court's child support order for one-half of private school too vague to be enforced)

Ex parte Sealy, 870 S.W.2d 663 (Tex. App.—Houston [1st Dist.] 1994, no writ) (contempt goes awry by joining two "offenses" and one punishment when one offense not punishable)

Roosth v. Daggett, 869 S.W.2d 634 (Tex. App.—Houston [14th Dist.] 1994, no writ) (contempt not appropriate if attorney's fees labeled as "costs" and not as "child support")

Ex parte Rogers, 820 S.W.2d 35 (Tex. App.—Corpus Christi 1991, no writ) (contempt finding insufficiently specific—lumping together all offenses fatal)

Written Complaint Alleging Specific Violation

Ex parte Barlow, 899 S.W.2d 791 (Tex. App.—Houston [14th Dist.] 1995, no writ) (contempt order based on nonconforming motion to enforce support voids order)

Kawazoe v. Davila, 849 S.W.2d 906 (Tex. App.—San Antonio 1993, no writ) *and* LaRue v. LaRue, 832 S.W.2d 387 (Tex. App.—Tyler 1992, no writ) (holding misrepresentation of termination—stepparent adoption creates estoppel defense)

Goudeau v. Marquez, 830 S.W.2d 681 (Tex. App.—Houston [1st Dist.] 1992, no writ), *and Ex parte* Haynie, 793 S.W.2d 317 (Tex. App.—Houston [14th Dist.] 1990, no writ) (child support contemnors to be ordered to pay attorney's fees unless excused for good cause)

In re Dickinson, 829 S.W.2d 919 (Tex. App.—Amarillo 1992, no writ) (contempt jurisdiction ends six months after duty of support terminates, irrespective of arrears or payback schedule—remedies independent)

Ex parte Bregenzer, 802 S.W.2d 884 (Tex. App.—Houston [1st Dist.] 1991, no writ) (amended motion for contempt filed after child turned 18 approved)

---

§ 157.161. Record.

(a) Except as provided by Subsection (b), a record of the hearing in a motion for enforcement shall be made by a court reporter or as provided by Chapter 201 *[Associate Judge]*.

(b) A record is not required if:

(1) the parties agree to an order; or

(2) the motion does not request incarceration and the parties waive the requirement of a record at the time of hearing, either in writing or in open court, and the court approves waiver.

§ 157.162. Proof.

(a) The movant is not required to prove that the underlying order is enforceable by contempt to obtain other appropriate enforcement remedies.

(b) A finding that the respondent is not in contempt does not preclude the court from ordering any other enforcement remedy, including rendering a money judgment, posting a bond or other security, or withholding income.

(c) A copy of the payment record attached to the motion is evidence of the facts asserted in the payment record and is admissible to show whether payments were made. The respondent may offer controverting evidence.

Leading Case

In re Taylor, 28 S.W.3d 240 (Tex. App.—Waco 2000, no pet.) (trial court's refusal to rule on contempt motion based on mother's alleged violation of conservatorship order elicits mandamus)

---

§ 157.163. Appointment of Attorney.

(a) In a motion for enforcement or motion to revoke community service, the court must first determine whether incarceration of the respondent is a possible result of the proceedings.

(b) If the court determines that incarceration is a possible result of the proceedings, the court shall inform a respondent not represented by an attorney of the right to be represented by an attorney and, if the respondent is indigent, of the right to the appointment of an attorney.

(c) If the court determines that the respondent will not be incarcerated as a result of the proceedings, the court may require a respondent who is indigent to proceed without an attorney.

(d) If the respondent claims indigency and requests the appointment of an attorney, the court shall require the respondent to file an affidavit of indigency. The court may hear evidence to determine the issue of indigency.

(e) Except as provided by Subsection (c), the court shall appoint an attorney to represent the respondent if the court determines that the respondent is indigent.

(f) If the respondent is not in custody, an appointed attorney is entitled to not less than 10 days from the date of the attorney's appointment to respond to the movant's pleadings and prepare for the hearing.

(g) If the respondent is in custody, an appointed attorney is entitled to not less than five days from the date the respondent was taken into custody to respond to the movant's pleadings and prepare for the hearing.

(h) The court may shorten or extend the time for preparation if the respondent and the respondent's attorney sign a waiver of the time limit.

(i) The scope of the court appointment of an attorney to represent the respondent is limited to the allegation of contempt or of violation of community supervision contained in the motion for enforcement or motion to revoke community supervision.

Leading Case

In re Luebe, 983 S.W.2d 889 (Tex. App.—Houston [1st Dist.] 1999, no pet.) (alleged contemnor's ability to borrow money to hire an attorney not a factor to measure claim of indigency)

§ 157.164. Payment of Appointed Attorney.

(a) An attorney appointed to represent an indigent respondent is entitled to a reasonable fee for services within the scope of the appointment in the amount set by the court.

(b) The fee shall be paid from the general funds of the county according to the schedule for the compensation of counsel appointed to defend criminal defendants as provided in the Code of Criminal Procedure.

(c) For purposes of this section, a proceeding in a court of appeals or the Supreme Court of Texas is considered the equivalent of a bona fide appeal to the Texas Court of Criminal Appeals.

§ 157.165. Probation of Contempt Order.

The court may place the respondent on community supervision and suspend commitment if the court finds that the respondent is in contempt of court for failure or refusal to obey an order rendered as provided in this title.

§ 157.166. Contents of Enforcement Order.

(a) An enforcement order must include:

(1) in ordinary and concise language the provisions of the order for which enforcement was requested;

(2) the acts or omissions that are the subject of the order;

(3) the manner of the respondent's noncompliance; and

(4) the relief granted by the court.

(b) If the order imposes incarceration or a fine for criminal contempt, an enforcement order must contain findings identifying, setting out, or incorporating by reference the provisions of the order for which enforcement was requested and the date of each occasion when the respondent's failure to comply with the order was found to constitute criminal contempt.

(c) If the enforcement order imposes incarceration for civil contempt, the order must state the specific conditions on which the respondent may be released from confinement.

§ 157.167. Respondent to Pay Attorney's Fees and Costs.

(a) If the court finds that the respondent has failed to make child support payments, the court shall order the respondent to pay the movant's reasonable attorney's fees and all court costs in addition to the arrearages.

(b) [*H.B. 886*] **If the court finds that the respondent has failed to comply with the terms of an order providing for the possession of or access to a child, the court shall order the respondent to pay the movant's reasonable attorney's fees and all court costs in addition to any other remedy.**

(b) [*H.B. 2588*] **Except as provided by Subsection (d), for** [~~For~~] good cause shown, the court may waive the requirement that the respondent pay attorney's fees and costs if the court states the reasons supporting that finding.

(c) For good cause shown, the court may waive the requirement that the respondent pay attorney's fees and costs if the court states the reasons supporting that finding.

(d) [*H.B. 886*] [~~(c)~~] Fees and costs ordered under **Subsection (a)** [~~this section~~] may be enforced by any means available for the enforcement of child support, including contempt.

(d) [*H.B. 2588*] **If the court finds that the respondent is in contempt of court for failure or refusal to pay child support and that the respondent owes $20,000 or more in child support arrearages, the court may not waive the requirement that the respondent pay attorney's fees and costs unless the court also finds that the respondent:**

(1) is involuntarily unemployed or is disabled; and

(2) lacks the financial resources to pay the attorney's fees and costs.

History: Amended by 78th Legis., Reg. Sess. (2003), H.B. 886, eff. Sept. 1, 2003, and "applies only to an enforcement order rendered on or after that date. An enforcement order rendered before the effective date of this Act is governed by the law in effect on the date the order was rendered, and the former law is continued in effect for that purpose."

History: Amended by 78th Legis., Reg. Sess. (2003), H.B. 2588, eff. Sept. 1, 2003. "The Title IV–D agency may not collect the $25 annual service fee authorized by Section 231.103, Family Code, as amended by this Act, before January 1, 2004. (c) The change in law made by this Act does not by itself constitute a material and substantial change of circumstances under Section 156.401, Family Code, sufficient to warrant modification of a court order or a portion of a decree that provides for the support of a child rendered before the effective date of this Act."

Guest Comment

Prior to amendment of this section in 2003, the court had considerable latitude in finding good cause for not requiring a respondent to pay attorney fees and costs ordered under this section. Subsection (d), added in 2003, abridged the discretion of the court in requiring payment of the fees and costs if the respondent has been found in contempt for failure or refusal to pay support and owes support arrearages of $20,000 or more. Even then, the court may waive the requirement upon finding that the respondent is unable to pay the fees and costs (for reasons similar to the affirmative defense under § 157.008 to a motion for enforcement). *(C.B. & H.P.S.)*

Leading Case

In re Villanueva, 56 S.W.3d 905 (Tex. App.—Houston [1st Dist.] 2001, no pet.) (contempt is one appropriate means to enforce fees and costs in child support case, but trial court abused discretion in setting huge cost bond)

§ 157.168. Additional Periods of Possession or Access.

(a) A court may order additional periods of possession of or access to a child to compensate for the denial of court-ordered possession or access. The additional periods of possession or access:

(1) must be of the same type and duration of the possession or access that was denied;

(2) may include weekend, holiday, and summer possession or access; and

(3) must occur on or before the second anniversary of the date the court finds that court-ordered possession or access has been denied.

(b) The person denied possession or access is entitled to decide the time of the additional possession or access, subject to the provisions of Subsection (a)(1).

Comment

Make-up visitation long has been a goal for noncustodial parents, many of whom have testified to the legislature about unjustified denials of court-ordered possession. Specifying the details of how make-up time is to be computed and exercised seems logical. But keeping track of alleged violations and a make-up schedule will be a daunting task to any court that actually becomes involved in trying to enforce this provision. In short, while this may be a good idea theoretically, absent voluntary compliance by apparently hostile parties it will be very difficult to implement, especially given the costs to enforce.

Subchapter E. Community Supervision

Leading Case

Villañueva v. Office of the Attorney General, 935 S.W.2d 953 (Tex. App.—San Antonio 1996, writ denied) (money judgment for arrearages may be awarded even if underlying order is not enforceable by contempt)

§ 157.211. Conditions of Community Supervision.

If the court places the respondent on community supervision and suspends commitment, the terms and conditions of community supervision may include the requirement that the respondent:

(1) report to the community supervision officer as directed;

(2) permit the community supervision officer to visit the respondent at the respondent's home or elsewhere;

(3) obtain counseling on financial planning, budget management, conflict resolution, parenting skills, alcohol or drug abuse, or other matters causing the respondent to fail to obey the order;

(4) pay required child support and any child support arrearages;

(5) pay court costs and attorney's fees ordered by the court;

(6) seek employment assistance services offered by the Texas Workforce Commission under Section 302.0035, Labor Code, if appropriate; and

(7) participate in mediation or other services to alleviate conditions that prevent the respondent from obeying the court's order.

§ 157.212. Term of Community Supervision.

The community supervision period may not exceed 10 years.

§ 157.213. Community Supervision Fees.

(a) The court may require the respondent to pay a fee to the court in an amount equal to that required of a criminal defendant subject to community supervision.

(b) The court may make payment of the fee a condition of granting or continuing community supervision.

(c) The court shall deposit the fees received under this subchapter as follows:

(1) if the community supervision officer is employed by a community supervision and corrections department, in the special fund of the county treasury provided by the Code of Criminal Procedure to be used for community supervision; or

(2) if the community supervision officer is employed by a domestic relations office, in one of the following funds, as determined by the office's administering entity:

(A) the general fund for the county in which the domestic relations office is located; or

(B) the office fund established by the administering entity for the domestic relations office.

§ 157.214. Motion to Revoke Community Supervision.

A prosecuting attorney, the Title IV-D agency, a domestic relations office, or a party affected by the order may file a verified motion alleging specifically that certain conduct of the respondent constitutes a violation of the terms and conditions of community supervision.

§ 157.215. Arrest for Alleged Violation of Community Supervision.

(a) If the motion to revoke community supervision alleges a prima facie case that the respondent has violated a term or condition of community supervision, the court may order the respondent's arrest by warrant.

(b) The respondent shall be brought promptly before the court ordering the arrest.

§ 157.216. Hearing on Motion to Revoke Community Supervision.

(a) The court shall hold a hearing without a jury on or before the first working day after the date the respondent is arrested under Section 157.215. If the court is unavailable for a hearing on that date, the hearing shall be held not later than the first working day after the date the court becomes available.

(b) The hearing under this section may not be held later than the third working day after the date the respondent is arrested.

(c) After the hearing, the court may continue, modify, or revoke the community supervision.

§ 157.217. Discharge From Community Supervision.

(a) When a community supervision period has been satisfactorily completed, the court on its own motion shall discharge the respondent from community supervision.

(b) The court may discharge the respondent from community supervision on the motion of the respondent if the court finds that the respondent:

(1) has satisfactorily completed one year of community supervision; and

(2) has fully complied with the community supervision order.

Subchapter F. Judgment and Interest

Introductory Comment

Since the Family Code was enacted, a support obligee has had the option to seek a money judgment for delinquent child support. This subchapter continues this remedy with quite a number of alterations to the original version. Most importantly, it is now the duty of a court to render a money judgment for proven arrears; the court does not have the authority to order a retroactive modification of the accrued obligation. This is a nationwide rule: the U.S. Congress directed that child support orders must be final and not retroactively modifiable if a state desires federal financial assistance to enforce child support (and all states want federal subsidies), 42 U.S.C. § 666(a)(9), a.k.a. "the Bradley amendment."

This subchapter adds, or at least clarifies, yet another remedy to the ever-growing arsenal for enforcement of child support orders. In 1993 the complexity of calculating compound interest implicit in the prior statute was removed by providing for 12% simple interest, which was apparently reasonable at the time. But time has proved otherwise. In 2001 the legislature determined that imposing an interest rate on unpaid child support arrears far beyond market rate is counterproductive. That approach leads only to a greater level of noncompliance. Accordingly, the legislature reduced the future interest rate to a more reasonable 6%, *see* § 157.265, *infra.*

CLE/Other Legal Publications

Methods of child support enforcement: contempt and non-contempt remedies, including money judgments, wage withholding, loss of license, and contractual enforcement. Walter P. Mahoney, Jr., 2001 Adv. Fam. L.

Rush and wait? Title IV–D expedited process. Alicia G. Key, Joe Vickers, & Diane Dockery, 2001 Adv. Fam. L.

Sausage on a stick: new legislation affecting the Title IV–D program. Alicia G. Key, 2001 Adv. Fam. L.

Beyond the black hole: the state disbursement unit. John Polk & Judy Anderson, 2001 Adv. Fam. L.

Leading Cases

Williams v. Patton, 821 S.W.2d 141 (Tex. 1991) (settlement of claim for child support arrears must be approved by court)

Huff v. Huff, 648 S.W.2d 286 (Tex. 1983) (pre-statute disapproval of automatic judgments for arrears)

In re W.G.S., 107 S.W.3d 624 (Tex. App.—Corpus Christi 2002, no pet.) (interest on arrears existing on effective date of initial statute (9/1/91) began to run by plain language of statute; pre-1991 interest accrued at statutory rate)

In re A.R.J., 97 S.W. 3d 833 (Tex. App.—Dallas 2003, no pet.) (interest rates on unconfirmed child support arrearages follow patter of 12% through December 31, 2001, 6% after Jan. 1, 2002)

In re M.C.R., 55 S.W.3d 104 (Tex. App.—San Antonio 2001, no pet.) (interest on child support arrears not subject to trial court discretion to increase or decrease)

In re Dryden, 52 S.W.3d 257 (Tex. App.—Corpus Christi 2001, no pet.) (trial court may not preclude obligee from enforcing money judgment for child-support arrears just because obligor complying with payment program)

In re Lee Children, 47 S.W.3d 693 (Tex. App.—Waco 2001, no pet.) (trial court cannot modify a final support judgment to add an interest obligation that was not originally included therein)

Rivera v. Attorney General, 960 S.W.2d 280 (Tex. App.—Houston [1st Dist.] 1997, no writ) (settlement agreement with no order language sufficient for money judgment)

Castle v. Harris, 960 S.W.2d 140 (Tex. App.—Corpus Christi 1997, no writ) (confirmation of arrearages not required for prejudgment interest)

In re Kuykendall, 957 S.W.2d 907 (Tex. App.—Texarkana 1997, no writ) (ten year dormancy on child support judgment does not start until arrearages confirmed)

Eubanks v. Eubanks, 892 S.W.2d 181 (Tex. App.—Houston [14th Dist.] 1995, no writ) (percentage of disposable earnings, not gross income, upheld in child support order)

Vogel v. Vogel, 885 S.W.2d 648 (Tex. App.—Amarillo 1994, writ denied) (percentage of income ordered for child support enforceable by way of money judgment, even if contempt does not lie)

Attorney General v. Wilson, 878 S.W.2d 690 (Tex. App.—Beaumont 1994, no writ) (trial court order not to report or abstract judgment for retroactive child support exceeds court's power)

McConnell v. Attorney General of Texas, 878 S.W.2d 281 (Tex. App.—Corpus Christi 1994, no writ) (child support reduced to money judgment after Florida refuses to enforce RURESA on basis of laches)

Attorney General v. Besaw, 877 S.W.2d 32 (Tex. App.—Beaumont 1994, no writ) (trial court may not reduce or modify arrears owed by father)

In re M.J.Z., 874 S.W.2d 724 (Tex. App.—Houston [1st Dist.] 1994, no writ) (§ 14.41 is jurisdictional in nature, not subject to due diligence analysis)

Buzbee v. Buzbee, 870 S.W.2d 335 (Tex. App.—Waco 1994, no writ) (evidence insufficient to establish offset against child support judgment; arrearages math: an esoteric or arcane science)

Allen v. Blackwell, 866 S.W.2d. 108 (Tex. App.—Waco 1993, writ denied) (time limitations for enforcement of child support are jurisdictional)

Lewis v. Lewis, 853 S.W.2d 850 (Tex. App.—Houston [14th Dist.] 1993, no writ) (offsetting support must correspond to suit for arrears)

Hollander v. Capon, 853 S.W.2d 723 (Tex. App.—Houston [1st Dist.] 1993, writ denied) (four year statute of limitations inapplicable to contract for child support)

Medrano v. Medrano, 810 S.W.2d 426 (Tex. App.—San Antonio 1991, no writ) (prejudgment interest on child support is mandatory)

Gross v. Gross, 808 S.W.2d 215 (Tex. App.—Houston [14th Dist.] 1991, no writ) (order unenforceable by contempt may be enforced by money judgment)

Cross Reference

IV–D Enforcement Procedures. 42 U.S.C.A. § 666(a)(9)

---

§ 157.261. Unpaid Child Support as Judgment.

(a) A child support payment not timely made constitutes a final judgment for the amount due and owing, including interest as provided in this chapter.

(b) For the purposes of this subchapter, interest begins to accrue on the date the judge signs the order for the judgment unless the order contains a statement that the order is rendered on another specific date.

Leading Cases

In re Dryden, 52 S.W.3d 257 (Tex. App.—Corpus Christi 2001, no pet.) (trial court may not preclude obligee from enforcing money judgment for child-support arrears just because obligor complying with payment program)

In re Gonzalez, 981 S.W.2d 313 (Tex. App.—San Antonio 1998, no pet.) (judgment for child support under temporary orders permitted)

---

§ 157.262. Reduction of Arrearages; Abeyance of Enforcement.

(a) Except as provided by this section, in a contempt proceeding or in rendering a money judgment, the court may not reduce or modify the amount of child support arrearages.

(b) In an enforcement action under this chapter, the court may, with the agreement of the Title IV-D agency, hold in abeyance the enforcement of any arrearages, including interest, assigned to the Title IV-D agency under Section 231.104(a) if, for the period of the court's order of abeyance of enforcement, the obligor:

(1) timely and fully pays the obligor's current child support under a court or administrative order; and

(2) is involved in the life of the child for whom support is ordered through the exercise of the obligor's right of possession of or access to the child.

(c) If the court orders an abeyance of enforcement of arrearages under this section, the court may require the obligor to obtain counseling on parenting skills, work skills, job placement, financial planning, conflict resolution, substance abuse, or other matters causing the obligor to fail to obey the child support order.

(d) If the court finds in a subsequent hearing that the obligor has not met the conditions set by the court's order under this section, the court shall terminate the abeyance of enforcement of the arrearages.

(e) On the expiration of the child support order, the court may, with the agreement of the Title IV-D agency, reduce the amount of the arrearages assigned to the Title IV-D agency under Section 231.104(a) if the court finds that the obligor has complied with the conditions set by the court under this section.

(f) The money judgment for arrearages rendered by the court may be subject to a counterclaim or offset as provided by this subchapter.

Guest Comment

Subsection (a) reflects a federal prohibition on retroactive modification of a child support obligation–the so-called "Bradley Amendment" enacted by Congress under the Omnibus Budget Reconciliation Act of 1986 [P.L. 99–509; codified at 42 U.S.C. § 666(a)(9)]. Under § 157.261, "a child support payment not timely made constitutes a final judgment," and under § 157.262(a), the court may not unilaterally "reduce or modify" support arrearages that may accrue under an order. Such retroactive modification, however, must be distinguished from a compromising of arrearages by specific agreement of the parties, just as any money judgment may be compromised or satisfied.

Subsections (b)-(e), authorize the court in a Title IV–D case, with the concurrence of the Title IV–D agency (as the assignee), to reduce support arrearages assigned to the state in cases in which a child of the obligor has received public assistance, *see also* § 231.104(a), *infra*. The court may order an abeyance of enforcement of the arrearages, subject to the obligor's meeting certain conditions specified by the court. If the court subsequently finds that the obligor is failing to meet those conditions, it is directed to terminate the order of abeyance, and the Title IV–D agency will resume enforcement actions. If, however, on the expiration of the order, the court finds that the obligor has satisfied the conditions for abeyance of enforcement, the court may—with the agreement of the Title IV–D agency—reduce, even eliminate, the arrearages assigned to the state. The public policy value of this arrangement relates particularly to situations in which low income obligors struggle to support dependent children—sometimes both inside and outside a marriage—while also being required to pay off public assistance arrearages. This statutory "forgiving" of those arrearages applies only to cases being enforced by the Title IV–D agency and only to arrearages owed the state under an assignment. It does not affect any arrearages that may be owed the custodial parent in a former assistance case. (*A.G.K. & H.P.S.*)

---

§ 157.263. Confirmation of Arrearages.

(a) If a motion for enforcement of child support requests a money judgment for arrearages, the court shall confirm the amount of arrearages and render one cumulative money judgment.

(b) A cumulative money judgment includes:

(1) unpaid child support not previously confirmed;

(2) the balance owed on previously confirmed arrearages or lump sum or retroactive support judgments;

(3) interest on the arrearages; and

(4) a statement that it is a cumulative judgment.

(c) If the amount of arrearages confirmed by the court reflects a credit to the obligor for support arrearages collected from a federal tax refund under 42 U.S.C. Section 664, as amended, and, subsequently, the amount of that credit is reduced because the refund was based on a joint return under which another person was entitled to a share of the refund under 42 U.S.C. Section 664, as amended, the court shall render a new cumulative judgment to include as arrearages an amount equal to the amount by which the credit was reduced.

History: Amended by 78th Legis., Reg. Sess. (2003), H.B. 1878, eff. Sept. 1, 2003. "The change in law made by this Act relating to the modification or enforcement of a child support order rendered before the effective date of this Act applies only to a proceeding for modification or enforcement that is commenced on or after the effective date of this Act. A proceeding for modification or enforcement that is commenced before the effective date of this Act is governed by the law in effect on the date the proceeding was commenced, and the former law is continued in effect for that purpose."

Guest Comment

Subsection (c), added in 2003, relates to the use of an enforcement remedy available only in cases enforced by the IV–D agency; that is, through interception of federal income tax refunds under 42 U.S.C. 664 for payment of past-due child support. The IV–D agency certifies to the Secretary of the Treasury the names of support obligors owing past-due support and the amounts owed. An allegedly delinquent obligor has an opportunity for contest. In turn, Treasury deducts from income tax refunds that are due delinquent obligors amounts equal to the past-due support they owe and forwards those amounts to appropriate state IV–D agencies. If a joint return has been filed, the obligor's innocent spouse is afforded an opportunity to claim an appropriate share of the refund. The obligor may, however, already have received credit under a cumulative money judgment for the full amount of the refund. Should that happen, the court must, upon request, render a new cumulative judgment that does not include any of the refund ultimately paid to the obligor's innocent spouse. (*C.B. & H.P.S.*)

Leading Case

In re Gonzalez, 981 S.W.2d 313 (Tex. App.—San Antonio 1998, no pet.) (obligee entitled to have arrearages reduced to judgment)

---

§ 157.264. Enforcement of Judgment.

(a) A money judgment rendered as provided in this subchapter may be enforced by any means available for the enforcement of a judgment for debts.

(b) The court may render an order requiring:

(1) that income be withheld from the disposable earnings of the obligor in an amount sufficient to discharge the judgment in not more than two years; or

(2) if the obligor is not subject to income withholding, that the obligor make periodic payments to the obligee in an amount sufficient to discharge the judgment within a reasonable time.

Guest Comment

Income withholding is an especially effective enforcement mechanism in the collection of child support arrearages, as well as current support. Not all child support obligors, however, have incomes subject to withholding for child support. This section specifically authorizes the court to order periodic payments on a money judgment for arrearages, even if income withholding is not an available enforcement remedy. Where income withholding is available, the amount ordered must be sufficient to discharge the judgment within two years, the maximum time period allowed under § 158.004 for income withholding if current support is no longer owed. Where income withholding is not available, the court must determine what constitutes "a reasonable time" within which the arrearages are to be discharged. (*A.G.K. & H.P.S.*)

Leading Case

In re M.E.G., 48 S.W.3d 204 (Tex. App.—Corpus Christi 2000, no pet.) (order to pay child support arrears in installments permissible)

---

§ 157.265. Accrual of Interest on Child Support.

(a) Interest accrues on the portion of delinquent child support that is greater than the amount of the monthly periodic support obligation at the rate of six percent simple interest per year from the date the support is delinquent until the date the support is paid or the arrearages are confirmed and reduced to money judgment.

(b) Interest accrues on child support arrearages that have been confirmed and reduced to money judgment as provided in this subchapter at the rate of six percent simple interest per year from the date the order is rendered until the date the judgment is paid.

(c) Interest accrues on a money judgment for retroactive or lump-sum child support at the annual rate of six percent simple interest from the date the order is rendered until the judgment is paid.

Guest Comment

Subsection (a) provides that a full month's child support must be delinquent before interest accrues, regardless of the frequency of support payments over the course of a month (*e.g.*, biweekly). Subsection (c) extends the principle that interest is due on the principal even when acquired by a retroactive lump-sum award.

The reader of this section must pay particular attention to the effective date provision of the 2001 amendment that lowered the rate of interest from 12 percent to 6 percent. The 2001 change in rate affected any child support payment that became due on or after January 1, 2002, as well as amounts of unconfirmed arrearages existing at the time of the effective date. It did not, however, affect any money judgment for arrearages rendered prior to the effective date. Such a judgment would continue to be subject to the former 12 percent simple interest. (*A.G.K. & H.P.S.*)

§ 157.266. Date of Delinquency.

(a) A child support payment is delinquent for the purpose of accrual of interest if the payment is not received before the 31st day after the payment date stated in the order by:

(1) the local registry, Title IV-D registry, or state disbursement unit; or

(2) the obligee or entity specified in the order, if payments are not made through a registry.

(b) If a payment date is not stated in the order, a child support payment is delinquent if payment is not received by the registry or the obligee or entity specified in the order on the date that an amount equal to the support payable for one month becomes past due.

§ 157.267. Interest Enforced as Child Support.

Accrued interest is part of the child support obligation and may be enforced by any means provided for the collection of child support.

§ 157.268. Application of Child Support Payment.

Child support collected shall be applied in the following order of priority:

(1) current child support;

(2) non-delinquent child support owed;

(3) interest on the principal amounts specified in Subdivisions (4) and (5);

(4) the principal amount of child support that has not been confirmed and reduced to money judgment;

(5) the principal amount of child support that has been confirmed and reduced to money judgment; and

(6) the amount of any ordered attorney's fees or costs.

Guest Comment

The purpose of this section is to provide an equitable ordering of priorities in the application of a child support payment. Because the primary intent of a child support payment is to recompense the obligee for the costs of maintaining the child, attorney's fees or costs are last in the application of a payment and will be paid (when collected as part of the child support obligation) only after all amounts due the obligee have been paid. (*A.G.K. & H.P.S.*)

§ 157.269. Retention of Jurisdiction.

A court that renders an order providing for the payment of child support arrearages retains jurisdiction until all current support and medical support and child support arrearages, including interest and any applicable fees and costs, have been paid.

Subchapter G. Child Support Lien

Guest Introductory Comment

Since 1984, federal law has required states to have statutory procedures for imposing liens on the real or personal property of an obligor for past-due child support. The "Personal Responsibility and Work Opportunity Reconciliation Act of 1996" (PRWORA) extended the lien requirements to mandate that liens for child support must arise by operation of law and that liens arising in one state may be enforced in any other state in accordance with the procedural rules of the other state. Also, under PRWORA, state Title IV–D agencies must have the authority to take administrative action to attach and seize assets of an obligor held in financial institutions, to attach public and private retirement funds of an obligor, to impose liens and, in appropriate cases, to force sale of property and distribution of proceeds.

The Texas child support lien statute has undergone a succession of legislative changes. In 2001, the legislature amplified the lien process, adding to it specific procedures for execution and levy on the financial assets of an obligor. Virtually every financial asset of a delinquent obligor may be subject to levy—not just depository accounts, but also proceeds of life insurance policies and retirement accounts owned by the obligor and insurance settlements or awards for negligence, personal injury, or workers' compensation due the obligor. Together, the lien and levy processes constitute a very effective mechanism for the enforcement of past-due child support and, like license suspension, are particularly valuable in cases in which the obligor has income not subject to withholding (*e.g.*, professionals and the self-employed). (*A.G.K. & H.P.S.*)

Leading Case

Dryden v. Dryden, 97 S.W.3d 863 (Tex. App.—Corpus Christi 2003, pet. denied) (exempt protection of certain personal property not applicable to collection of child support; constitutional because "it's not a debt"); see also *In re* S.L.M., 97 S.W.3d 224 (Tex. App.—Amarillo 2002, no pet.)

---

§ 157.311. Definitions.

In this subchapter:

(1) "Account" means:

(A) any type of a demand deposit account, checking or negotiable withdrawal order account, savings account, time deposit account, money market mutual fund account, certificate of deposit, or any other instrument of deposit in which an individual has a beneficial ownership either in its entirety or on a shared or multiple party basis, including any accrued interest and dividends; and

(B) a life insurance policy in which an individual has a beneficial ownership or liability insurance against which an individual has filed a claim or counterclaim[~~, including for workers' compensation~~].

(2) "Claimant" means:

(A) the obligee or a private attorney representing the obligee;

(B) the Title IV-D agency providing child support services;

(C) a domestic relations office or local registry; or

(D) an attorney appointed as a friend of the court.

(3) "Court having continuing jurisdiction" is the court of continuing, exclusive jurisdiction in this state or a tribunal of another state having jurisdiction under the Uniform Interstate Family Support Act or a substantially similar act.

(4) "Financial institution" has the meaning assigned by 42 U.S.C. Section 669a(d)(1) and includes a depository institution, credit union, benefit association, liability or life insurance company, [~~workers' compensation insurer,~~] money market mutual fund, and any similar entity authorized to do business in this state.

(5) "Lien" means a child support lien issued in this or another state.

History: Amended by 78th Legis., Reg. Sess. (2003), H.B. 1878, eff. Sept. 1, 2003. "The change in law made by this Act relating to the modification or enforcement of a child support order rendered before the effective date of this Act applies only to a proceeding for modification or enforcement that is commenced on or after the effective date of this Act. A proceeding for modification or enforcement that is commenced before the effective date of this Act is governed by the law in effect on the date the proceeding was commenced, and the former law is continued in effect for that purpose."

Guest Comment

In 2003, the legislature removed all references to workers' compensation from the definitions under this section and from the balance of this subchapter. As a replacement for lost earned income, workers' compensation benefits are available for child support only through an order or writ of income withholding under Chapter 158, as provided by TEX. LAB. CODE § 408.203(b). *(C.B. & H.P.S.)*

---

§ 157.312. General Provisions.

(a) A claimant may enforce child support by a lien as provided in this subchapter.

(b) The remedies provided by this subchapter do not affect the availability of other remedies provided by law.

(c) The lien is in addition to any other lien provided by law.

(d) A child support lien arises by operation of law against real and personal property of an obligor for all amounts of child support due and owing, including any accrued interest, regardless of whether the amounts have been adjudicated or otherwise determined, subject to the requirements of this subchapter for perfection of the lien.

(e) A child support lien arising in another state may be enforced in the same manner and to the same extent as a lien arising in this state.

(f) A foreclosure action under this subchapter is not required as a prerequisite to levy and execution on a judicial or administrative determination of arrearages as provided by Section 157.327.

(g) A child support lien under this subchapter may not be directed to an employer to attach to the disposable earnings of an obligor paid by the employer.

History: Amended by 78th Legis., Reg. Sess. (2003), H.B. 1878, eff. Sept. 1, 2003. "The change in law made by this Act relating to the modification or enforcement of a child support order rendered before the effective date of this Act applies only to a proceeding for modification or enforcement that is commenced on or after the effective date of this Act. A proceeding for modification or enforcement that is commenced before the effective date of this Act is governed by the law in effect on the date the proceeding was commenced, and the former law is continued in effect for that purpose."

Guest Comment

The lien process is not an exclusive remedy but may be used in concert with other procedures for enforcement of arrearages, including income withholding and license suspension. A specific lien, however, applies not just to the amount of arrearages in existence at the time the lien notice is issued and the lien is perfected, but to all arrearages that accrue up to the time of foreclosure or execution and levy. Moreover, levy and execution may proceed based upon either a judicial or, in Title IV–D cases, an administrative determination of the arrearages, without the requirement of a foreclosure hearing. Subsection (g), added in 2003, clarifies that a child support lien may not be used in place of an order or writ of income withholding. (*A.G.K., C.B. & H.P.S.*)

---

§ 157.313. Contents of Child Support Lien Notice.

(a) Except as provided by Subsection (e), a child support lien notice must contain:

(1) the name and address of the person to whom the notice is being sent;

(2) the style, docket or cause number, and identity of the tribunal of this or another state having continuing jurisdiction of the child support action and, if the case is a Title IV-D case, the case number;

(3) the full name, address, and, if known, the birth date, driver's license number, social security number, and any aliases of the obligor;

(4) the full name and, if known, social security number of the obligee;

(5) the amount of the current or prospective child support obligation, the frequency with which current or prospective child support is ordered to be paid, and the amount of child support arrearages owed by the obligor and the date of the signing of the court order, administrative order, or writ that determined the arrearages or the date and manner in which the arrearages were determined;

(6) the rate of interest specified in the court order, administrative order, or writ or, in the absence of a specified interest rate, the rate provided for by law;

(7) the name and address of the person or agency asserting the lien;

(8) the motor vehicle identification number as shown on the obligor's title if the property is a motor vehicle;

(9) a statement that the lien attaches to all nonexempt real and personal property of the obligor that is located or recorded in the state, including any property specifically identified in the notice;

(10) a statement that any ordered child support not timely paid in the future constitutes a final judgment for the amount due and owing, including interest, and accrues up to an amount that may not exceed the lien amount; and

(11) a statement that the obligor is being provided a copy of the lien notice and that the obligor may dispute the arrearage amount by filing suit under Section 157.323.

(b) A claimant may include any other information that the claimant considers necessary.

(c) The lien notice must be verified.

(d) A claimant must file a notice for each after-acquired motor vehicle.

(e) A notice of a lien for child support under this section may be in the form authorized by federal law or regulation.

Guest Comment

While the lien notice states the amount of arrearages owed at the time the notice is filed or delivered—however that amount may have been determined—it also prospectively engages the possibility of a greater amount of arrearages being owed at the time of foreclosure on the lien or, in the case of financial assets, execution and levy. (*A.G.K. & H.P.S.*)

---

§ 157.314. Filing Lien Notice or Abstract of Judgment; Notice to Obligor.

(a) A child support lien notice or an abstract of judgment for past due child support may be filed by the claimant with the county clerk of:

(1) any county in which the obligor is believed to own nonexempt real or personal property;

(2) the county in which the obligor resides; or

(3) the county in which the court having continuing jurisdiction has venue of the suit affecting the parent-child relationship.

(b) A child support lien notice may be filed with or delivered to the following, as appropriate:

(1) the clerk of the court in which a claim, counterclaim, or suit by, or on behalf of, the obligor, including a claim or potential right to proceeds from an estate as an heir, beneficiary, or creditor, is pending, provided that a copy of the lien is mailed to the attorney of record for the obligor, if any;

(2) an attorney who represents the obligor in a claim or counterclaim that has not been filed with a court;

(3) any other individual or organization believed to be in possession of real or personal property of the obligor; or

(4) any governmental unit or agency that issues or records certificates, titles, or other indicia of property ownership.

(c) Not later than the 21st day after the date of filing or delivering the child support lien notice, the claimant shall provide a copy of the notice to the obligor by first class or certified mail, return receipt requested, addressed to the obligor at the obligor's last known address. If another person is known to have an ownership interest in the property subject to the lien, the claimant shall provide a copy of the lien notice to that person at the time notice is provided to the obligor.

(d) If a child support lien notice is delivered to a financial institution with respect to an account of the obligor, the institution shall immediately:

(1) provide the claimant with the last known address of the obligor; and

(2) notify any other person having an ownership interest in the account that the account has been frozen in an amount not to exceed the amount of the child support arrearage identified in the notice.

Guest Comment

As specified in this section, the filing or delivery of a lien notice has the effect of perfecting the lien. In the case of a financial institution, this means that all assets of the obligor held by that institution are frozen up to the amount stated in the lien notice. This does not mean, however, that a greater amount may not finally be subject to levy. At the time of levy, the amount subject to seizure is the amount determined by the court or the Title IV–D agency to be the arrearages owed at that point—which may be greater or lesser than the amount stated in the lien notice. The claimant is responsible for sending a copy of the lien notice to any known co-owners of the property affected by the lien, as well as to the obligor at a last known address. If the property is an account in a financial institution which may be levied upon, the institution must provide the claimant with the obligor's last known address, in addition to notifying any co-owner of the account. Presumably a financial institution knows who the owners and co-owners of accounts are and has their correct addresses. (*A.G.K. & H.P.S.*)

---

§ 157.3145. Service on Financial Institution.

(a) Service of a child support lien notice on a financial institution relating to property held by the institution in the name of, or in behalf of, an obligor is governed by Section 59.008, Finance Code, if the institution is subject to that law, or may be delivered to the registered agent, the institution's main business office in this state, or another address provided by the institution under Section 231.307.

(b) A financial institution doing business in this state shall comply with the notice of lien and levy under this section regardless of whether the institution's corporate headquarters is located in this state.

History: Amended by 78th Legis., Reg. Sess. (2003), H.B. 1878, eff. Sept. 1, 2003. "The change in law made by this Act relating to the modification or enforcement of a child support order rendered before the effective date of this Act applies only to a proceeding for modification or enforcement that is commenced on or after the effective date of this Act. A proceeding for modification or enforcement that is commenced before the effective date of this Act is governed by the law in effect on the date the proceeding was commenced, and the former law is continued in effect for that purpose."

Guest Comment

This section allows service on a financial institution not just at an in-state location, but also at any out-of-state location designated by the institution, such as a central administrative office maintained by a multi-state institution in another state. Moreover, with respect to compliance with a notice of lien and levy it does not matter that the corporate headquarters of a financial institution doing business in this state are located out-of-state. This section also connects the lien and levy processes under this subchapter with the financial institution data matches—including matches with multi-state institutions—required of the Title IV–D agency under § 231.307. It means, finally, that the Title IV–D agency in particular may go after the financial assets of a delinquent obligor wherever they may be located—at least in the United States. (*A.G.K., C.B., & H.P.S.*)

---

§ 157.315. Recording and Indexing Lien.

(a) On receipt of a child support lien notice, the county clerk shall immediately record the notice in the county judgment records as provided in Chapter 52, Property Code.

(b) The county clerk may not charge the Title IV-D agency, a domestic relations office, a friend of the court, or any other party a fee for recording the notice of a lien. To qualify for this exemption, the lien notice must be styled "Notice of Child Support Lien" or be in the form authorized by federal law or regulation.

(c) The county clerk may not charge the Title IV-D agency, a domestic relations office, or a friend of the court a fee for recording the release of a child support lien. The lien release must be styled "Release of Child Support Lien."

§ 157.316. Perfection of Child Support Lien.

(a) Except as provided by Subsection (b), a child support lien is perfected when an abstract of judgment for past due child support or a child support lien notice is filed or delivered as provided by Section 157.314.

(b) If a lien established under this subchapter attaches to a motor vehicle, the lien must be perfected in the manner provided by Chapter 501, Transportation Code, and the court or Title IV-D agency that rendered the order of child support shall include in the order a requirement that the obligor surrender to the court or Title IV-D agency evidence of the legal ownership of the motor vehicle against which the lien may attach. A lien against a motor vehicle under this subchapter is not perfected until the obligor's title to the vehicle has been surrendered to the court or Title IV-D agency and the Texas Department of Transportation has issued a subsequent title that discloses on its face the fact that the vehicle is subject to a child support lien under this subchapter.

§ 157.317. Property to Which Lien Attaches.

(a) A child support lien attaches to all real and personal property not exempt under the Texas Constitution or other law, including:

(1) an account in a financial institution;

(2)[~~,~~] a retirement plan, including an individual retirement account; **and**

(3)[~~,~~] the proceeds of a life insurance policy, a claim for negligence **or**[~~,~~] personal injury, [~~or workers' compensation,~~] or an insurance settlement or award for the claim, due to or owned by the obligor.

(a–1) A lien attaches on or after the date the lien notice or abstract of judgment is filed with the county clerk of the county in which the property is located, with the court clerk as to property or claims in litigation, or, as to property of the obligor in the possession or control of a third party, from the date the lien notice is filed with that party.

(b) A lien attaches to all nonhomestead real property of the obligor but does not attach to a homestead exempt under the Texas Constitution or the Property Code.

History: Amended by 78th Legis., Reg. Sess. (2003), H.B. 1878, eff. Sept. 1, 2003. "The change in law made by this Act relating to the modification or enforcement of a child support order rendered before the effective date of this Act applies only to a proceeding for modification or enforcement that is commenced on or after the effective date of this Act. A proceeding for modification or enforcement that is commenced before the effective date of this Act is governed by the law in effect on the date the proceeding was commenced, and the former law is continued in effect for that purpose."

Guest Comment

While this section is broadly cast with respect to the property to which a child support lien may attach, the "other law" exception under subsection (a) alludes to the possibility that certain property owned or in the control of an obligor may be exempt from attachment under either state or federal law and, hence, beyond the reach of this enforcement remedy. (*C.B. & H.P.S.*)

---

§ 157.318. Duration and Effect of Child Support Lien.

(a) A lien is effective until all current support and child support arrearages, including interest and any costs and reasonable attorney's fees, have been paid or the lien is otherwise released as provided by this subchapter.

(b) The lien secures payment of all child support arrearages owed by the obligor under the underlying child support order, including arrearages that accrue after the lien notice was filed or delivered as provided by Section 157.314.

(c) The filing of a lien notice or abstract of judgment with the county clerk is a record of the notice and has the same effect as any other lien notice with respect to real property records.

§ 157.319. Effect of Lien Notice.

(a) If a person having actual notice of the lien possesses nonexempt personal property of the obligor that may be subject to the lien, the property may not be paid over, released, sold, transferred, encumbered, or conveyed unless:

(1) a release of lien signed by the claimant is delivered to the person in possession; or

(2) a court, after notice to the claimant and hearing, has ordered the release of the lien because arrearages do not exist.

(b) A person having notice of a child support lien who violates this section may be joined as a party to a foreclosure action under this chapter and is subject to the penalties provided by this subchapter.

(c) This section does not affect the validity or priority of a lien of a health care provider, a lien for attorney's fees, or a lien of a holder of a security interest. This section does not affect the assignment of rights or subrogation of a claim under Title XIX of the federal Social Security Act (42 U.S.C. Section 1396 et seq.), as amended.

§ 157.320. Priority of Lien as to Real Property.

(a) A lien created under this subchapter does not have priority over a lien or conveyance of an interest in the nonexempt real property recorded before the child support lien notice is recorded in the county where the real property is located.

(b) A lien created under this subchapter has priority over any lien or conveyance of an interest in the nonexempt real property recorded after the child support lien notice is recorded in the county clerk's office in the county where the property of the obligor is located.

(c) A conveyance of real property by the obligor after a lien notice has been recorded in the county where the real property is located is subject to the lien and may not impair the enforceability of the lien against the real property.

(d) A lien created under this subchapter is subordinate to a vendor's lien retained in a conveyance to the obligor.

Leading Case

Schumann v. Breedlove & Bensey, 983 S.W.2d 333 (Tex. App.—Houston [1st Dist.] 1998, no pet.) (child support lien does not attach to obligor's former asset filed after obligor assigned asset)

---

§ 157.321. Discretionary Release of Lien.

A child support lien claimant may at any time release a lien on all or part of the property of the obligor or return seized property, without liability, if assurance of payment is considered adequate by the claimant or if the release or return will facilitate the collection of the arrearages. The release or return may not operate to prevent future action to collect from the same or other property owned by the obligor.

§ 157.322. Mandatory Release of Lien.

(a) On payment in full of the amount of child support due, together with any costs and reasonable attorney's fees, the child support lien claimant shall execute and deliver to the obligor or the obligor's attorney a release of the child support lien.

(b) The release of the child support lien is effective when:

(1) filed with the county clerk with whom the lien notice or abstract of judgment was filed; or

(2) delivered to any other individual or organization that may have been served with a lien notice under this subchapter.

§ 157.323. Foreclosure or Suit to Determine Arrearages.

(a) In addition to any other remedy provided by law, an action to foreclose a child support lien, to dispute the amount of arrearages stated in the lien, or to resolve issues of ownership interest with respect to property subject to a child support lien may be brought in:

(1) the court in which the lien notice was filed under Section 157. 314(b)(1);

(2) the district court of the county in which the property is or was located and the lien was filed; or

(3) the court of continuing jurisdiction.

(b) The procedures provided by Subchapter B apply to a foreclosure action under this section, except that a person or organization in possession of the property of the obligor or known to have an ownership interest in property that is subject to the lien may be joined as an additional respondent.

(c) If arrearages are owed by the obligor, the court shall:

(1) render judgment against the obligor for the amount due, plus costs and reasonable attorney's fees;

(2) order any official authorized to levy execution to satisfy the lien, costs, and attorney's fees by selling any property on which a lien is established under this subchapter; or

(3) order an individual or organization in possession of nonexempt personal property or cash owned by the obligor to dispose of the property as the court may direct.

(d) For execution and sale under this section, publication of notice is necessary only for three consecutive weeks in a newspaper published in the county where the property is located or, if there is no newspaper in that county, in the most convenient newspaper in circulation in the county.

§ 157.324. Liability for Failure to Comply With Order or Lien.

A person who knowingly disposes of property subject to a child support lien, who, after a foreclosure hearing, fails to surrender on demand nonexempt personal property as directed by a court or administrative order under this subchapter, or who fails to comply with a notice of levy under this subchapter is liable to the claimant in an amount equal to the arrearages for which the lien, notice of levy, or foreclosure judgment was issued.

§ 157.325. Release of Excess Funds to Debtor or Obligor.

(a) If a person has in the person's possession earnings, deposits, accounts, balances, or other funds or assets of the obligor, including the proceeds of a judgment or other settlement of a claim or counterclaim due to the obligor that are in excess of the amount of arrearages specified in the child support lien, the holder of the nonexempt personal property or the obligor may request that the claimant release any excess amount from the lien. The claimant shall grant the request and discharge any lien on the excess amount unless the security for the arrearages would be impaired.

(b) If the claimant refuses the request, the holder of the personal property or the obligor may file suit under this subchapter for an order determining the amount of arrearages and discharging excess personal property or money from the lien.

§ 157.326. Interest of Obligor's Spouse or Another Person Having Ownership Interest.

(a) A spouse of an obligor or another person having an ownership interest in property that is subject to a child support lien may file suit under Section 157.323 to determine the extent, if any, of the spouse's or other person's interest in real or personal property that is subject to:

(1) a lien perfected under this subchapter; or

(2) an action to foreclose under this subchapter.

(b) After notice to the obligor, the obligor's spouse, any other person alleging an ownership interest, the claimant, and the obligee, the court shall conduct a hearing and determine the extent, if any, of the ownership interest in the property held by the obligor's spouse or other person. If the court finds that:

(1) the property is the separate property of the obligor's spouse or the other person, the court shall order that the lien against the property be released and that any action to foreclose on the property be dismissed;

(2) the property is jointly owned by the obligor and the obligor's spouse, the court shall determine whether the sale of the obligor's interest in the property would result in an unreasonable hardship on the obligor's spouse or family and:

(A) if so, the court shall render an order that the obligor's interest in the property not be sold and that the lien against the property should be released; or

(B) if not, the court shall render an order partitioning the property and directing that the property be sold and the proceeds applied to the child support arrearages; or

(3) the property is owned in part by another person, other than the obligor's spouse, the court shall render an order partitioning the property and directing that the obligor's share of the property be applied to the child support arrearages.

(c) In a proceeding under this section, the spouse or other person claiming an ownership interest in the property has the burden to prove the extent of that ownership interest.

§ 157.327. Execution and Levy on Financial Assets of Obligor.

(a) Notwithstanding any other provision of law, if a judgment or administrative determination of arrearages has been rendered, a claimant may deliver a notice of levy to any financial institution possessing or controlling assets or funds owned by, or owed to, an obligor and subject to a child support lien, including a lien for child support arising in another state.

(b) The notice under this section must:

(1) identify the amount of child support arrearages owing at the time the amount of arrearages was determined; and

(2) direct the financial institution to pay to the claimant, not earlier than the 15th day or later than the 21st day after the date of delivery of the notice, an amount from the assets of the obligor or from funds due to the obligor that are held or controlled by the institution, not to exceed the amount of the child support arrearages identified in the notice, unless:

(A) the institution is notified by the claimant that the obligor has paid the arrearages or made arrangements satisfactory to the claimant for the payment of the arrearages;

(B) the obligor or another person files a suit under Section 157.323 requesting a hearing by the court; or

(C) if the claimant is the Title IV-D agency, the obligor has requested an agency review under Section 157.328.

(c) A financial institution that receives a notice of levy under this section may not close an account in which the obligor has an ownership interest, permit a withdrawal from any account the obligor owns, in whole or in part, or pay funds to the obligor so that any amount remaining in the account is less than the amount of the arrearages identified in the notice, plus any fees due to the institution and any costs of the levy identified by the claimant.

(d) A financial institution that receives a notice of levy under this section shall notify any other person having an ownership interest in an account in which the obligor has an ownership interest that the account has been levied on in an amount not to exceed the amount of the child support arrearages identified in the notice of levy.

(e) The notice of levy may be delivered to a financial institution as provided by Section 59.008, Finance Code, if the institution is subject to that law or may be delivered to the registered agent, the institution's main business office in this state, or another address provided by the institution under Section 231.307.

§ 157.328. Notice of Levy Sent to Obligor.

(a) At the time the notice of levy under Section 157.327 is delivered to a financial institution, the claimant shall serve the obligor with a copy of the notice.

(b) The notice of levy delivered to the obligor must inform the obligor that:

(1) the claimant will not proceed with levy if, not later than the 10th day after the date of receipt of the notice, the obligor pays in full the amount of arrearages identified in the notice or otherwise makes arrangements acceptable to the claimant for the payment of the arrearage amounts; and

(2) the obligor may contest the levy by filing suit under Section 157.323 not later than the 10th day after the date of receipt of the notice.

(c) If the claimant is the Title IV-D agency, the obligor receiving a notice of levy may request review by the agency not later than the 10th day after the date of receipt of the notice to resolve any issue in dispute regarding the existence or amount of the arrearages. The agency shall provide an opportunity for a review, by telephone conference or in person, as appropriate to the circumstances, not later than the fifth business day after the date an oral or written request from the obligor for the review is received. If the review fails to resolve any issue in dispute, the obligor may file suit under Section 157.323 for a hearing by the court not later than the fifth day after the date of the conclusion of the agency review. If the obligor fails to timely file suit, the Title IV-D agency may request the financial institution to release and remit the funds subject to levy.

(d) The notice under this section may be delivered to the last known address of the obligor by first class mail, certified mail, or registered mail.

Guest Comment

The levy process moves rather swiftly. The obligor has to respond with dispatch to the notice, with only ten days within which either to pay the full amount of the arrearages or make arrangements for payment satisfactory to the claimant or to file suit to contest. In a Title IV–D case, however, the obligor may, within 10 days of receipt of the notice, request an administrative review before turning to the court to contest the levy. But even then, from the time of receipt of the notice, the obligor has—at the most—only twenty days within which to put the levy on hold by filing suit. (*A.G.K. & H.P.S.*)

---

§ 157.329. No Liability for Compliance With Notice of Levy.

A financial institution that possesses or has a right to an obligor's assets for which a notice of levy has been delivered and that surrenders the assets or right to assets to a child support lien claimant is not liable to the obligor or any other person for the property or rights surrendered.

§ 157.330. Failure to Comply With Notice of Levy.

A person who possesses or has a right to property that is the subject of a notice of levy delivered to the person and who refuses to surrender the property or right to property to the claimant on demand is liable to the claimant in an amount equal to the value of the property or right to property not surrendered but that does not exceed the amount of the child support arrearages for which the notice of levy has been filed.

§ 157.331. Additional Levy to Satisfy Arrearages.

If the property or right to property on which a notice of levy has been filed does not produce money sufficient to satisfy the amount of child support arrearages identified in the notice of levy, the claimant may proceed to levy on other property of the obligor until the total amount of child support due is paid.

Guest Comment

Delivery of either the notice of lien or notice of levy to a financial institution has the effect of freezing the assets of the obligor in an account held by that institution. Receipt of either notice requires the institution to notify any other person having an ownership interest in the frozen account of the existence of the lien or the impending levy. The difference between the two notices is that the lien notice does not announce, as does the levy notice, that the frozen assets are about to be seized. The lien may encumber the account indefinitely; the levy may exhaust it almost immediately. (*A.G.K. & H.P.S.*)

Subchapter H. Habeas Corpus

Introductory Comment

Before the enactment of the Family Code, the merits of a child custody dispute were often litigated in the context of a habeas corpus proceeding. The Code put an end to that, substituting what has come to be known as "automatic habeas corpus." The sole issue in almost all habeas corpus proceedings is whether the relator is currently entitled to possession of a child by virtue of a valid court order.

For a considerable time trial courts demonstrated great reluctance in accepting this principle, unwillingly yielding considerable judicial discretion. But, thanks to numerous, repeated decisions by the supreme court, the message finally got through to the trial bench. Automatic habeas is now widely accepted in Texas jurisprudence. The primary (theoretical) exception to the summary nature of the writ, the "serious immediate question" of § 157.374 is often argued, but seldom found to exist. Finally, while habeas corpus is not available between parents in the absence of a prior order, the writ has validity when a parent seeks to recover possession of a child from a nonparent.

With the enactment of the Uniform Child Custody Jurisdiction and Enforcement Act in 1999, the remedy of this subchapter has been somewhat upstaged by the so-called "turbo" writ now provided in Ch. 152, Subch. D, *supra*.

Leading Cases

Nature of Writ

Mergerson v. Daggett, 644 S.W.2d 451 (Tex. 1982) (writ improperly granted, custody covered by existing court order)

Gray v. Rankin, 594 S.W.2d 409 (Tex. 1980) (granting of habeas corpus not appealable order)

Strobel v. Thurman, 565 S.W.2d 238 (Tex. 1978) ("grant of the writ should be automatic, immediate, and ministerial . . . upon proof of the bare legal right to possession")

Trader v. Dear, 565 S.W.2d 233 (Tex. 1978) (relator has choice of forums—where child found or in court of continuing jurisdiction)

Lamphere v. Chrisman, 554 S.W.2d 935 (Tex. 1977) (mandamus proper remedy to enforce relator's rights)

Lewelling v. Bosworth, 840 S.W.2d 640 (Tex. App.—Dallas 1992, no writ) (supreme court's mandate did not entitle mother to right of possession of child; time period for automatic habeas began when remand acted upon)

Out-of-State Order

Rush v. Stansbury, 668 S.W.2d 690 (Tex. 1984) (automatic habeas applies to sister state decrees)

Silver v. Storey, 677 S.W.2d 504 (Tex. 1984) (PA order entered without service on respondent establishes that father evaded service)

Perry v. Scoggins, 626 S.W.2d 302 (Tex. 1981) (Missouri custody order entitles father to habeas)

Marshall v. Wilson, 616 S.W.2d 932 (Tex. 1981) (out-of-state custody order enforced by habeas; relator immune from countersuit)

In re Aubin, 29 S.W.3d 199 (Tex. App.—Beaumont 2000, no pet.) (Texas court cannot issue writ of attachment for possession of child residing in another state)

Revey v. Peek, 951 S.W.2d 920 (Tex. App.—Texarkana 1997, no writ) (Arkansas order modifying custody enforced, motion for change of venue denied)

Serious Immediate Question

Schoenfeld v. Onion, 647 S.W.2d 954 (Tex. 1983) (absent dire emergency, habeas automatic, immediate, & ministerial)

Wise v. Yates, 639 S.W.2d 460 (Tex. 1982) (possibility that custodial parent would take children to Taiwan does not present serious immediate danger)

Forbes v. Wettman, 598 S.W.2d 231 (Tex. 1980) (fungus on finger and minor weight loss not serious immediate question)

Parent versus Nonparent

Rodriguez v. McFall, 658 S.W.2d 150 (Tex. 1983) (mother entitled to return of child from paternal grandparents)

Whatley v. Bacon, 649 S.W.2d 297 (Tex. 1983) (surviving father entitled to habeas against maternal grandparents)

Armstrong v. Reiter, 628 S.W.2d 439 (Tex. 1982) (natural mother entitled to recover child from guardian)

Trevino v. Garcia, 627 S.W.2d 147 (Tex. 1982) (habeas overcomes claim of adoption by estoppel)

Saucier v. Pena, 559 S.W.2d 654 (Tex. 1977) (surviving father entitled to return of children from maternal grandparents)

In re Johnston, 957 S.W.2d 945 (Tex. App.—Beaumont 1997, no writ) (noncustodial father entitled to writ for possession of children when mother incarcerated)

Restrictions on Granting Writ

Greene v. Schuble, 654 S.W.2d 436 (Tex. 1983) (automatic habeas means temporary custody issue may not be combined with habeas hearing)

Elliott v. Bradshaw, 587 S.W.2d 108 (Tex. 1978) (temporary order cannot defeat right to habeas corpus)

Standley v. Stewart, 539 S.W.2d 882 (Tex. 1976) (court cannot join hearing to modify conservatorship during habeas proceeding)

Cross Reference

Parental Kidnapping Prevention Act. 28 U.S.C.A. § 1738A.

Texas Family Law Practice Manual

Chapter 27. Physical Possession of Child

---

§ 157.371. Jurisdiction.

(a) The relator may file a petition for a writ of habeas corpus in either the court of continuing, exclusive jurisdiction or in a court with jurisdiction to issue a writ of habeas corpus in the county in which the child is found.

(b) Although a habeas corpus proceeding is not a suit affecting the parent-child relationship, the court may refer to the provisions of this title for definitions and procedures as appropriate.

§ 157.372. Return of Child.

(a) Subject to Chapter 152 *[UCCJEA]* and the Parental Kidnapping Prevention Act (28 U.S.C. Section 1738A), if the right to possession of a child is governed by a court order, the court in a habeas corpus proceeding involving the right to possession of the child shall compel return of the child to the relator only if the court finds that the relator is entitled to possession under the order.

(b) If the court finds that the previous order was granted by a court that did not give the contestants reasonable notice of the proceeding and an opportunity to be heard, the court may not render an order in the habeas corpus proceeding compelling return of the child on the basis of that order.

§ 157.373. Relator Relinquished Possession; Temporary Orders.

(a) If the relator has by consent or acquiescence relinquished actual possession and control of the child for not less than 6 months preceding the date of the filing of the petition for the writ, the court may either compel or refuse to order return of the child.

(b) The court may disregard brief periods of possession and control by the relator during the 6-month period.

(c) In a suit in which the court does not compel return of the child, the court may issue temporary orders under Chapter 105 *[Settings, Hearings, and Orders]* if a suit affecting the parent-child relationship is pending and the parties have received notice of a hearing on temporary orders set for the same time as the habeas corpus proceeding.

CLE/Other Legal Publications

Drafting T.O.s and decrees. Judy Warne, 2001 ADV. FAM. L.

Temporary orders. Wendy S. Burgower, 2001 MARRIAGE DISSOLUTION

---

§ 157.374. Welfare of Child.

Notwithstanding any other provision of this subchapter, the court may render an appropriate temporary order if there is a serious immediate question concerning the welfare of the child.

§ 157.375. Immunity to Civil Process.

(a) While in this state for the sole purpose of compelling the return of a child through a habeas corpus proceeding, the relator is not amenable to civil process and is not subject to the jurisdiction of any civil court except the court in which the writ is pending. The relator is subject to process and jurisdiction in that court only for the purpose of prosecuting the writ.

(b) A request by the relator for costs, attorney's fees, and necessary travel and other expenses under Chapter 106 *[Costs and Attorney's Fees]* or 152 *[UCCJEA]* is not a waiver of immunity to civil process.

§ 157.376. No Existing Order.

(a) If the right to possession of a child is not governed by an order, the court in a habeas corpus proceeding involving the right of possession of the child:

(1) shall compel return of the child to the parent if the right of possession is between a parent and a nonparent and a suit affecting the parent-child relationship has not been filed; or

(2) may either compel return of the child or issue temporary orders under Chapter 105 *[Settings, Hearings, and Orders]* if a suit affecting the parent-child relationship is pending and the parties have received notice of a hearing on temporary orders set for the same time as the habeas corpus proceeding.

(b) The court may not use a habeas corpus proceeding to adjudicate the right of possession of a child between two parents or between two or more nonparents.

Subchapter I. Clarification of Orders

Introductory Comment

These provisions are directly modeled after the clarification procedure found in Title 1, § 9.008 *et seq.* The court of continuing jurisdiction has the opportunity to clarify or rectify errors or ambiguities in an order without reference to the nunc pro tunc test, and without the necessity of meeting the standards for a modification of an original order, *e.g.*, substantial change of circumstances, multi-prong test, etc.

Leading Case

McGehee v. Epley, 661 S.W.2d 924 (Tex. 1983) (clarification order cannot affect substance of original order)

Cross Reference

TEX. R. CIV. P. 316. Correction of Clerical Mistakes in Judgment Record.

Texas Family Law Practice Manual

Forms 24–1. Motion for Clarification of Child Support; *24–2.* Order on Motion for Clarification of Child Support; *25–1.* Motion for Clarification of Possession and Access; *25.2,* Order on Motion for Clarification of Child Support.

---

§ 157.421. Clarifying Nonspecific Order.

(a) A court may clarify an order rendered by the court in a proceeding under this title if the court finds, on the motion of a party or on the court's own motion, that the order is not specific enough to be enforced by contempt.

(b) The court shall clarify the order by rendering an order that is specific enough to be enforced by contempt.

(c) A clarified order does not affect the finality of the order that it clarifies.

§ 157.422. Procedure.

(a) The procedure for filing a motion for enforcement of a final order applies to a motion for clarification.

(b) A person is not entitled to a jury in a proceeding under this subchapter.

§ 157.423. Substantive Change Not Enforceable.

(a) A court may not change the substantive provisions of an order to be clarified under this subchapter.

(b) A substantive change made by a clarification order is not enforceable.

§ 157.424. Relation to Motion for Contempt.

The court may render a clarification order before a motion for contempt is made or heard, in conjunction with a motion for contempt, or after the denial of a motion for contempt.

§ 157.425. Order Not Retroactive.

The court may not provide that a clarification order is retroactive for the purpose of enforcement by contempt.

§ 157.426. Time Allowed to Comply.

(a) In a clarification order, the court shall provide a reasonable time for compliance.

(b) The clarification order may be enforced by contempt after the time for compliance has expired.

Chapter 158. Withholding from Earnings for Child Support.

Subchapter A. Income Withholding Required; General Provisions

Subchapter B. Procedure

Subchapter C. Rights and Duties of Employer

Subchapter D. Judicial Writ of Withholding Issued by Clerk

Subchapter E. Modification, Reduction, or Termination of Withholding

Subchapter F. Administrative Writ of Withholding in Title IV–D Cases

Editors' Note: This chapter contains guest comments by Alicia Gray Key, Executive Director of the Office of Court Administration; and Cynthia Bryant, Deputy Attorney General and H. Patrick Sullivan, Director of Federal Policy Analysis, both of the Office of the Attorney General Child Support Division, identified as (*A.G.K., C.B. & H.P.S.*).

Introductory Comment

Income withholding has become the primary tool for collecting child support and is mandated for all cases. The employer community has quietly accepted the burden of collecting and remitting support without much controversy. Moreover, there has been very little appellate litigation reported on this crucial subject. Federally mandated withholding forms have been implemented to assist employers in processing the paperwork.

CLE/Other Legal Publications

A plainly practical primer on IV–D practice. Steve A. Owen, 2002 ADV. FAM. L.

Update on state disbursement unit: sending all the child support to San Antonio. Alicia Gray Key, 2002 ADV. FAM. L.

Rush and wait? Title IV–D expedited process. Alicia G. Key, Joe Vickers, & Diane Dockery, 2001 ADV. FAM. L.

Sausage on a stick: new legislation affecting the Title IV–D program. Alicia G. Key, 2001 ADV. FAM. L.

Beyond the black hole: the state disbursement unit. John Polk & Judy Anderson, 2001 ADV. FAM. L.

Leading Cases

In re E.D., 102 S.W.3d 859 (Tex. App.—Corpus Christi 2003, no pet.) (no time limitations for A.G. to collect delinquent child support such that administration writ of withholding proper)

Detzler v. Coldwell Banker Island Realtors, 941 S.W.2d 315 (Tex. App.—Corpus Christi 1997, no writ) (real estate office can't be required to withhold support where obligor is paid directly by title company)

Tamez v. Tamez, 822 S.W.2d 688 (Tex. App.—Corpus Christi 1991, writ denied) (wage withholding limited to court-ordered child support—order reformed to eliminate loan repayment and share of retirement benefits)

State v. Nelson, 783 S.W.2d 635 (Tex. App.—Houston [14th Dist.] 1989, writ denied) (trial court has discretion whether to order withholding to recover arrears)

Cross References

Family Support Act of 1988, Pub. L. 100–485, 102 Stat. 2343, *see* 5 U.S. Code Cong. & Admin. News 2776 (1988) (last federal legislative action to regulate state enforcement efforts)

IV–D Child Support Enforcement. 42 U.S.C.A. § 651 *et seq.*

TEX. CONST. ART. XVI, § 28. Garnishment of Wages.

Texas Family Law Practice Manual

Forms 9–2. Request for Issuance of Order/Notice; *9–3.* Order/Notice to Withhold Income for Child Support

---

Subchapter A. Income Withholding Required; General Provisions

§ 158.001. Income Withholding; General Rule.

In a proceeding in which periodic payments of child support are ordered, modified, or enforced, the court or the Title IV-D agency shall order that income be withheld from the disposable earnings of the obligor as provided by this chapter.

§ 158.002. Suspension Of Income Withholding.

Except in a Title IV-D case, the court may provide, for good cause shown or on agreement of the parties, that the order withholding income need not be issued or delivered to an employer until:

(1) the obligor has been in arrears for an amount due for more than 30 days;

(2) the amount of the arrearages is an amount equal to or greater than the amount due for a one-month period; or

(3) any other violation of the child support order has occurred.

Comment

Section 154.007 provides that every SAPCR order involving child support must include an order for income withholding. However, that order need not be delivered to the obligor's employer if good cause for restraint is found by the court. Note, however, that good cause to sit on a withholding order does not exist for a IV–D case. *See* § 158.006, *infra*.

---

§ 158.003. Withholding for Arrearages in Addition to Current Support.

(a) In addition to income withheld for the current support of a child, income shall be withheld from the disposable earnings of the obligor to be applied toward the liquidation of any child support arrearages, including accrued interest as provided in Chapter 157 *[Enforcement]*.

(b) The additional amount to be withheld for arrearages shall be an amount sufficient to discharge those arrearages in not more than two years or an additional 20 percent added to the amount of the current monthly support order, whichever amount will result in the arrearages being discharged in the least amount of time.

§ 158.004. Withholding for Arrearages When no Current Support is Due.

If current support is no longer owed, the court or the Title IV–D agency shall order that income be withheld for arrearages, including accrued interest as provided in Chapter 157 *[Enforcement]*, in an amount sufficient to discharge those arrearages in not more than two years.

§ 158.005. Withholding to Satisfy Judgment for Arrearages.

In rendering a cumulative judgment for arrearages, the court shall order that a reasonable amount of income be withheld from the disposable earnings of the obligor to be applied toward the satisfaction of the judgment.

§ 158.0051. Order for Withholding for Costs and Fees.

(a) In addition to an order for income to be withheld for child support, including child support and child support arrearages, the court may render an order that income be withheld from the disposable earnings of the obligor to be applied towards the satisfaction of any ordered attorney's fees and costs resulting from an action to enforce child support under this title.

(b) An order rendered under this section is subordinate to an order or writ of withholding for child support under this chapter and is subject to the maximum amount allowed to be withheld under Section 158.009.

(c) The court shall order that amounts withheld for fees and costs under this section be remitted directly to the person entitled to the ordered attorney's fees or costs or be paid through a local registry for disbursement to that person.

Guest Comment

Attorney General Opinion (No. JC–0346) (2001), stated that the use of income withholding to collect attorney fees and costs incurred in the enforcement of a child support obligation did not violate the constitutionally authorized garnishment of current wages for personal services for the enforcement of child support. This Opinion confirmed 1999 amendments to § § 158.102–.103, *infra*. This section authorizes the issuance of a specific order or writ for income withholding to satisfy ordered attorney's fees and costs, but it rightly emphasizes the priority of the child support obligation itself, as does the application of payment under § 157.268. (*A.G.K. & H.P.S.*)

§ 158.006. Income Withholding in Title IV-D Suits.

In a Title IV-D case, the court or the Title IV-D agency shall order that income be withheld from the disposable earnings of the obligor and may not suspend, stay, or delay issuance of the order or of a judicial or administrative writ of withholding.

§ 158.007. Extension of Repayment Schedule by Court or Title IV–D Agency; Unreasonable Hardship.

If the court or the Title IV–D agency finds that the schedule for discharging arrearages would cause the obligor, the obligor's family, or children for whom support is due from the obligor to suffer unreasonable hardship, the court or agency may extend the payment period for a reasonable length of time.

Leading Cases

In re Chambers, 5 S.W.3d 341 (Tex. App.—San Antonio 1999, no pet.) (no minimum amount required to withhold to collect arrears—$150 per month to collect nearly $21,000 affirmed)

In re Digges, 981 S.W.2d 445 (Tex. App.—San Antonio 1998, no pet.) (income withholding remedy not limited by time or due process defenses applicable to contempt proceedings)

§ 158.008. Priority of Withholding.

An order or writ of withholding has priority over any garnishment, attachment, execution, or other assignment or order affecting disposable earnings.

§ 158.009. Maximum Amount Withheld From Earnings.

An order or writ of withholding shall direct that any employer of the obligor withhold from the obligor's disposable earnings the amount specified up to a maximum amount of 50 percent of the obligor's disposable earnings.

§ 158.010. Order or Writ Binding on Employer Doing Business in State.

An order or writ of withholding issued under this chapter and delivered to an employer doing business in this state is binding on the employer without regard to whether the obligor resides or works outside this state.

§ 158.011. Voluntary Withholding by Obligor.

(a) An obligor may file with the clerk of the court a notarized or acknowledged request signed by the obligor and the obligee for the issuance and delivery to the obligor's employer of a writ of withholding. A notarized or acknowledged request may be filed under this section regardless of whether a writ or order has been served on any party or of the existence or amount of an arrearage.

(b) On receipt of a request under this section, the clerk shall issue and deliver a writ of withholding in the manner provided by this chapter.

(c) An employer that receives a writ of withholding issued under this section may request a hearing in the same manner and according to the same terms provided by Section 158.205.

(d) An obligor whose employer receives a writ of withholding issued under this section may request a hearing in the manner provided by Section 158.309.

(e) An obligee may contest a writ of withholding issued under this section by requesting, not later than the 180th day after the date on which the obligee discovers that the writ has been issued, a hearing in the manner provided by Section 158.309.

(f) A writ of withholding under this section may not reduce the total amount of child support, including arrearages, owed by the obligor.

Comment

An obligor may wish to have wages withheld to ensure proper payment and to make life less complicated.

Subchapter B. Procedure

§ 158.101. Applicability of Procedure.

Except as otherwise provided in this chapter, the procedure for a motion for enforcement of child support as provided in Chapter 157 *[Enforcement]* applies to an action for income withholding.

§ 158.102. Time Limitations.

An order or writ for income withholding under this chapter may be issued until all current support and child support arrearages, interest, and any applicable fees and costs, including ordered attorney's fees and court costs, have been paid.

Comment

Until a 1999 amendment, § 157.005 imposed a four-year limitation on obtaining a judgment to collect child support after a child became an adult. With the elimination of that limitation, both the judgment remedy and the income withholding remedy for collecting current and past due support, plus interest, continue indefinitely.

Leading Case

In re A.D., 73 S.W.3d 244 (Tex. 2002) (1997 amendment repealing four-year limitation on court's jurisdiction to order withholding for child support constitutional, unlimited time for enforcement not a retroactive law)

§ 158.103. Contents of Order or Writ of Withholding.

An order of withholding or writ of withholding issued under this chapter must contain the information required by the forms prescribed by the Title IV-D agency under Section 158.106.

§ 158.104. Request for Issuance of Order or Judicial Writ of Withholding.

A request for issuance of an order or judicial writ of withholding may be filed with the clerk of the court by the prosecuting attorney, the Title IV–D agency, the friend of the court, a domestic relations office, the obligor, the obligee, or an attorney representing the obligee or obligor.

§ 158.105. Issuance and Delivery of Order or Judicial Writ of Withholding.

(a) On filing a request for issuance of an order or judicial writ of withholding, the clerk of the court shall cause a certified copy of the order or writ to be delivered to the obligor's current employer or to any subsequent employer of the obligor.

(b) The clerk shall issue and mail the certified copy of the order or judicial writ not later than the fourth working day after the date the order is signed or the request is filed, whichever is later.

(c) An order or judicial writ of withholding shall be delivered to the employer by first class mail or, if requested, by certified or registered mail, return receipt requested, electronic transmission, or by service of citation to:

(1) the person authorized to receive service of process for the employer in civil cases generally; or

(2) a person designated by the employer, by written notice to the clerk, to receive orders or writs of withholding.

Guest Comment

The issuance and delivery to an employer of a judicial order or writ of income withholding is a relatively simple ministerial process executed by the clerk, for which the clerk may—and, without exception, does—charge the fee authorized under § 110.004. The original purpose of the fee was, in part, to cover the costs of delivering the order or writ by certified or registered mail. But a 2001 amendment made that mode of delivery dependent upon the specific request of the party requesting issuance. While in general first-class mail may be reliable, that method of delivery provides no way of monitoring whether an employer has actually received the order or writ. Anyone requesting issuance should probably request that this important document be delivered by certified or registered mail. (*A.G.K. & H.P.S.*)

§ 158.106. Forms for Income Withholding.

(a) The Title IV-D agency shall prescribe forms as required by federal law in a standard format entitled order or notice to withhold income for child support.

(b) The Title IV–D agency shall make the appropriate forms available to obligors, obligees, domestic relations offices, friends of the court, and private attorneys.

(c) The Title IV–D agency may prescribe additional forms for the efficient collection of child support and to promote the administration of justice for all parties.

(d) The forms prescribed by the Title IV–D agency under this section may be used to request voluntary withholding under Section 158.011.

§ 158.107. [repealed]

Subchapter C. Rights and Duties of Employer

Leading Case

Casino Magic Corp. v. King, 43 S.W.3d 14 (Tex. App.—Dallas 2001, no pet.) (Louisiana business served with income withholding order escapes money judgment only because no evidence presented to establish liability)

§ 158.201. Order or Writ Binding on Employer.

(a) An employer required to withhold income from earnings is not entitled to notice of the proceedings before the order is rendered or writ of withholding is issued.

(b) An order or writ of withholding is binding on an employer regardless of whether the employer is specifically named in the order or writ.

§ 158.202. Effective Date of and Duration of Withholding.

An employer shall begin to withhold income in accordance with an order or writ of withholding not later than the first pay period following the date on which the order or writ was delivered to the employer and shall continue to withhold income as required by the order or writ as long as the obligor is employed by the employer.

§ 158.203. Remitting Withheld Payments.

(a) The employer shall remit the amount to be withheld to the person or office named in the order or writ on each pay date. The payment must include the date on which the withholding occurred.

(b) For payments made by electronic funds transfer or electronic data interchange, the employer shall transmit the amount withheld not later than the second business day after the pay date.

(c) The employer shall include with each payment transmitted:

(1) the number assigned by the Title IV–D agency, if available, and the county identification number, if available;

(2) the name of the county or the county's federal information processing standard code;

(3) the cause number of the suit under which withholding is required;

(4) the payor's name and social security number; and

(5) the payee's name and, if available, social security number, unless the payment is transmitted by electronic funds transfer.

(d) In a case in which an obligor's income is subject to withholding, the employer shall remit the payment of child support directly to a local registry, the Title IV–D agency, or to the state disbursement unit.

§ 158.204. Employer May Deduct Fee From Earnings.

An employer may deduct an administrative fee of not more than $10 each month from the obligor's disposable earnings in addition to the amount to be withheld as child support.

§ 158.205. Hearing Requested by Employer.

(a) Not later than the 20th day after the date an order or writ of withholding is delivered, the employer may, as appropriate, file a motion with the court or file a request with the Title IV-D agency for a hearing on the applicability of the order or writ to the employer. The Title IV-D agency by rule shall establish procedures for an agency hearing under this section.

(b) The hearing under this section shall be held not later than the 15th day after the date the motion or request was made.

(c) An order or writ of withholding remains binding and payments shall continue to be made pending further order of the court or, in the case of an administrative writ, action of the Title IV-D agency.

§ 158.206. Liability and Obligation of Employer; Workers' Compensation Claims.

(a) An employer receiving an order or a writ of withholding under this chapter, including an order or writ directing that health insurance be provided to a child, who complies with the order or writ is not liable to the obligor for the amount of income withheld and paid as required by the order or writ.

(b) An employer receiving an order or writ of withholding who does not comply with the order or writ is liable:

(1) to the obligee for the amount not paid in compliance with the order or writ, including the amount the obligor is required to pay for health insurance under Chapter 154 *[Child Support]*;

(2) to the obligor for:

(A) the amount withheld and not paid as required by the order or writ; and

(B) an amount equal to the interest that accrues under Section 157.265 on the amount withheld and not paid; and

(3) for reasonable attorney's fees and court costs.

(c) If an obligor has filed a claim for workers' compensation, the obligor's employer shall send a copy of the income withholding order or writ to the insurance carrier with whom the claim has been filed in order to continue the ordered withholding of income.

Guest Comment

State law (V.T.C.A., Labor Code § 408.203) authorizes the garnishment of workers' compensation benefits for child support. Subsection (c) makes the employer responsible for seeing that there is no break in income withholding if an employee files a claim for those benefits . There is no need for the clerk in this instance to issue, deliver, or file a copy of the original writ or order, thereby saving time and expense to the party who originally filed an application for the writ or order. (*A.G.K. & H.P.S.*)

---

§ 158.207. Employer Receiving More Than One Order or Writ.

(a) An employer receiving two or more orders or writs for one obligor shall comply with each order or writ to the extent possible.

(b) If the total amount due under the orders or writs exceeds the maximum amount allowed to be withheld under Section 158.009, the employer shall pay an equal amount towards the current support in each order or writ until the employer has complied fully with each current support obligation and, thereafter, equal amounts on the arrearages until the employer has complied with each order or writ, or until the maximum total amount of allowed withholding is reached, whichever occurs first.

(c) An employer who receives more than one order or writ of withholding that combines withholding for child support and spousal maintenance as provided by Section 8.101 shall withhold income and pay the amount withheld in accordance with Section 8.207.

§ 158.208. Employer may Combine Amounts Withheld.

An employer required to withhold from more than one obligor may combine the amounts withheld and make a single payment to each agency designated if the employer separately identifies the amount of the payment that is attributable to each obligor.

§ 158.209. Employer's Penalty for Discriminatory Hiring or Discharge.

(a) An employer may not use an order or writ of withholding as grounds in whole or part for the termination of employment or for any other disciplinary action against an employee.

(b) An employer may not refuse to hire an employee because of an order or writ of withholding.

(c) If an employer intentionally discharges an employee in violation of this section, the employer continues to be liable to the employee for current wages and other benefits and for reasonable attorney's fees and court costs incurred in enforcing the employee's rights as provided in this section.

(d) An action under this section may be brought by the employee, a friend of the court, the domestic relations office, or the Title IV-D agency.

§ 158.210. Fine for Noncompliance.

(a) In addition to the civil remedies provided by this subchapter or any other remedy provided by law, an employer who knowingly violates the provisions of this chapter may be subject to a fine not to exceed $200 for each occurrence in which the employer fails to:

(1) withhold income for child support as instructed in an order or writ issued under this chapter; or

(2) remit withheld income within the time required by Section 158.203 to the payee identified in the order or writ or to the state disbursement unit.

(b) A fine recovered under this section shall be paid to the county in which the obligee resides and shall be used by the county to improve child support services.

§ 158.211. Notice of Termination of Employment and of New Employment.

(a) If an obligor terminates employment with an employer who has been withholding income, both the obligor and the employer shall notify the court or the Title IV–D agency and the obligee of that fact not later than the seventh day after the date employment terminated and shall provide the obligor's last known address and the name and address of the obligor's new employer, if known.

(b) The obligor has a continuing duty to inform any subsequent employer of the order or writ of withholding after obtaining employment.

§ 158.212. Improper Payment.

An employer who remits a payment to an incorrect office or person shall remit the payment to the agency or person identified in the order of withholding not later than the second business day after the date the employer receives the returned payment.

§ 158.213. Withholding From Workers' Compensation Benefits.

(a) An insurance carrier that receives an order or writ of withholding under Section 158.206 for workers' compensation benefits payable to an obligor shall withhold an amount not to exceed the maximum amount allowed to be withheld from income under Section 158.009 regardless of whether the benefits payable to the obligor for lost income are paid as lump sum amounts or as periodic payments.

(b) An insurance carrier subject to this section shall send the amount withheld for child support to the place of payment designated in the order or writ of withholding.

History: Enacted by 78th Legis., Reg. Sess. (2003), H.B. 1878, eff. Sept. 1, 2003. "The change in law made by this Act relating to the modification or enforcement of a child support order rendered before the effective date of this Act applies only to a proceeding for modification or enforcement that is commenced on or after the effective date of this Act. A proceeding for modification or enforcement that is commenced before the effective date of this Act is governed by the law in effect on the date the proceeding was commenced, and the former law is continued in effect for that purpose."

Guest Comment

Because workers' compensation benefits replace lost earned income, they too are subject to the limits on income withholding for child support prescribed by federal law (42 U.S.C. 666(b)(1)) and § 158.009, *supra*. An order or writ of income withholding sent to a workers' compensation insurance carrier operates just as if sent to an employer. The insurer must comply with the terms of the order or writ and remit withheld benefits to the place of payment designated in the order or writ. *(C.B. & H.P.S.)*

Subchapter D. Judicial Writ of Withholding Issued by Clerk

Introductory Comment

This statute has not been the subject of an authoritative appellate decision. The only attention it has received from the legislature has been by way of technical amendments.

Leading Case

Atty. Gen.'s Office on behalf of State v. Mitchell, 819 S.W.2d 556 (Tex. App.—Dallas 1991, no writ) (time expired to challenge writ of withholding)

Cross Reference

IV–D Child Support and Enforcement. 42 U.S.C.A. § 651 *et seq.*

Texas Family Law Practice Manual

Forms 9–4. Notice of Application for Order/Notice to Withhold Income for Child Support (Judicial Writ of Withholding); *9–5.* Motion to Stay Issuance and Delivery of Order/Notice to Withhold Income for Child Support (Judicial Writ of Withholding); *9–6.* Request for Issuance of Order/Notice to Withhold Income for Child Support (Judicial Writ of Withholding)

---

§ 158.301. Notice of Application for Judicial Writ Of Withholding; Filing.

(a) A notice of application for judicial writ of withholding may be filed if:

(1) a delinquency occurs in child support payments in an amount equal to or greater than the total support due for one month; or

(2) income withholding was not ordered at the time child support was ordered.

(b) The notice of application for judicial writ of withholding may be filed in the court of continuing jurisdiction by:

(1) the Title IV-D agency;

(2) the attorney representing the local domestic relations office;

(3) the attorney appointed a friend of the court as provided in Chapter 202 *[Friend of the Court]*;

(4) the obligor or obligee; or

(5) a private attorney representing the obligor or obligee.

(c) The Title IV-D agency may in a Title IV-D case file a notice of application for judicial writ of withholding on request of the obligor or obligee.

§ 158.302. Contents of Notice of Application for Judicial Writ Of Withholding.

The notice of application for judicial writ of withholding shall be verified and:

(1) state the amount of monthly support due, including medical support, the amount of arrearages or anticipated arrearages, including accrued interest, and the amount of wages that will be withheld in accordance with a judicial writ of withholding;

(2) state that the withholding applies to each current or subsequent employer or period of employment;

(3) state that if the obligor does not contest the withholding within 10 days after the date of receipt of the notice, the obligor's employer will be notified to begin the withholding;

(4) describe the procedures for contesting the issuance and delivery of a writ of withholding;

(5) state that if the obligor contests the withholding, the obligor will be afforded an opportunity for a hearing by the court not later than the 30th day after the date of receipt of the notice of contest;

(6) state that the sole ground for successfully contesting the issuance of a writ of withholding is a dispute concerning the identity of the obligor or the existence or amount of the arrearages, including accrued interest;

(7) describe the actions that may be taken if the obligor contests the notice of application for judicial writ of withholding, including the procedures for suspending issuance of a writ of withholding; and

(8) include with the notice a suggested form for the motion to stay issuance and delivery of the judicial writ of withholding that the obligor may file with the clerk of the appropriate court.

§ 158.303. Interstate Request for Income Withholding.

(a) The registration of a foreign support order as provided in Chapter 159 *[UIFSA]* is sufficient for the filing of a notice of application for judicial writ of withholding.

(b) The notice shall be filed with the clerk of the court having venue as provided in Chapter 159.

(c) Notice of application for judicial writ of withholding may be delivered to the obligor at the same time that an order is filed for registration under Chapter 159.

§ 158.304. Additional Arrearages.

If the notice of application for judicial writ of withholding states that the obligor has repeatedly failed to pay support in accordance with the underlying support order, the judicial writ may include arrearages that accrue between the filing of the notice and the date of the hearing or the issuance of a judicial writ of withholding.

§ 158.305. [repealed]

§ 158.306. Delivery of Notice of Application for Judicial Writ Of Withholding; Time of Delivery.

(a) A notice of application for judicial writ of withholding may be delivered to the obligor by:

(1) hand delivery by a person designated by the Title IV-D agency or local domestic relations office;

(2) first-class or certified mail, return receipt requested, addressed to the obligor's last known address or place of employment; or

(3) by service of citation as in civil cases generally.

(b) If the notice is delivered by mailing or hand delivery, the party who filed the notice shall file with the court a certificate stating the name, address, and date on which the mailing or hand delivery was made.

(c) Notice is considered to have been received by the obligor:

(1) if hand delivered, on the date of delivery;

(2) if mailed by certified mail, on the date of receipt;

(3) if mailed by first-class mail, on the 10th day after the date the notice was mailed; or

(4) if delivered by service of citation, on the date of service.

§ 158.307. Motion to Stay Issuance of Writ of Withholding.

(a) The obligor may stay issuance of a judicial writ of withholding by filing a motion to stay with the clerk of court not later than the 10th day after the date the notice of application for judicial writ of withholding was received.

(b) The grounds for filing a motion to stay issuance are limited to a dispute concerning the identity of the obligor or the existence or the amount of the arrearages.

(c) The obligor shall verify that statements of fact in the motion to stay issuance of the writ are true and correct.

§ 158.308. Effect of Filing Motion to Stay.

The filing of a motion to stay by an obligor in the manner provided by Section 158.307 prohibits the clerk of court from delivering the judicial writ of withholding to any employer of the obligor before a hearing is held.

§ 158.309. Hearing on Motion to Stay.

(a) If a motion to stay is filed in the manner provided by Section 158.307, the court shall set a hearing on the motion and the clerk of court shall notify the obligor, obligee, or their authorized representatives, and the party who filed the application for judicial writ of withholding of the date, time, and place of the hearing.

(b) The court shall hold a hearing on the motion to stay not later than the 30th day after the date the motion was filed, except that a hearing may be held later than the 30th day after filing if both the obligor and obligee agree and waive the right to have the motion heard within 30 days.

(c) Upon hearing, the court shall:

(1) render an order for income withholding that includes a determination of the amount of child support arrearages, including medical support and interest; or

(2) grant the motion to stay.

§ 158.310. Special Exceptions.

(a) A defect in a notice of application for judicial writ of withholding is waived unless the respondent specially excepts in writing and cites with particularity the alleged defect, obscurity, or other ambiguity in the notice.

(b) A special exception under this section must be heard by the court before hearing the motion to stay issuance.

(c) If the court sustains an exception, the court shall provide the party filing the notice an opportunity to refile and the court shall continue the hearing to a date certain without the requirement of additional service.

§ 158.311. Arrearages.

(a) Payment of arrearages after receipt of notice of application for judicial writ of withholding may not be the sole basis for the court to refuse to order withholding.

(b) The court shall order that a reasonable amount of income be withheld to be applied toward the liquidation of arrearages, even though a judgment confirming arrearages has been rendered against the obligor.

§ 158.312. Request for Issuance and Delivery of Writ of Withholding.

(a) If a notice of application for judicial writ of withholding is delivered and a motion to stay is not filed within the time limits provided by Section 158.307, the party who filed the notice shall file with the clerk of the court a request for issuance of the writ of withholding stating the amount of current support, including medical support, the amount of arrearages, and the amount to be withheld from the obligor's income.

(b) The request for issuance may not be filed before the 11th day after the date of receipt of the notice of application for judicial writ of withholding by the obligor.

§ 158.313. Issuance and Delivery of Writ of Withholding.

(a) On the filing of a request for issuance of a writ of withholding, the clerk of the court shall issue the writ.

(b) The writ shall be delivered as provided by Subchapter B.

(c) The clerk shall issue and mail the writ not later than the second working day after the date the request is filed.

§ 158.314. Contents of Writ of Withholding.

The judicial writ of income withholding issued by the clerk must direct that the employer or a subsequent employer withhold from the obligor's disposable income for current child support, including medical support, and child support arrearages an amount that is consistent with the provisions of this chapter regarding orders of withholding.

§ 158.315. Extension of Repayment Schedule by Party; Unreasonable Hardship.

If the party who filed the notice of application for judicial writ of withholding finds that the schedule for repaying arrearages would cause the obligor, the obligor's family, or the children for whom the support is due from the obligor to suffer unreasonable hardship, the party may extend the payment period in the writ.

§ 158.316. Payment of Amount to be Withheld.

The amount to be withheld shall be paid to the person or office named in the writ on each pay date and shall include with the payment the date on which the withholding occurred.

§ 158.317. Failure to Receive Notice of Application for Judicial Writ Of Withholding.

(a) Not later than the 30th day after the date of the first pay period following the date of delivery of the writ of withholding to the obligor's employer, the obligor may file an affidavit with the court that a motion to stay was not timely filed because the notice of application for judicial writ of withholding was not received by the obligor and that grounds exist for a motion to stay.

(b) Concurrently with the filing of the affidavit, the obligor may file a motion to withdraw the writ of withholding and request a hearing on the applicability of the writ.

(c) Income withholding may not be interrupted until after the hearing at which the court renders an order denying or modifying withholding.

§ 158.318. [omitted]

§ 158.319. Issuance and Delivery of Judicial Writ of Withholding to Subsequent Employer.

(a) After the issuance of a judicial writ of withholding by the clerk, a party authorized to file a notice of application for judicial writ of withholding under this subchapter may issue the judicial writ of withholding to a subsequent employer of the obligor by delivering to the employer by certified mail a copy of the writ.

(b) The judicial writ of withholding must include the name, address, and signature of the party and clearly indicate that the writ is being issued to a subsequent employer.

(c) The party shall file a copy of the judicial writ of withholding with the clerk not later than the third working day following delivery of the writ to the subsequent employer. The party shall pay the clerk a fee of $15 at the time the copy of the writ is filed.

(d) The party shall file the postal return receipt from the delivery to the subsequent employer not later than the third working day after the party receives the receipt.

Subchapter E. Modification, Reduction, or Termination of Withholding

Texas Family Law Practice Manual

Forms 9–12. Original Petition To [Terminate/Modify] Order/Notice To Withhold/Writ of Withholding/Order for Withholding; *9–13.* Order [Terminating/Withholding] Order/Notice To Withhold/Writ of Withholding/Order for Withholding.

Leading Cases

In re A.D., 73 S.W.3d 244 (Tex. 2002) (administrative writ proper enforcement tool that removed bar to exercise of court's jurisdiction and therefore is not a retroactive law)

Attorney General v. Redding, 60 S.W.3d 891 (Tex. App.—Dallas 2001, no pet.) (*see In re* A.D., *supra*) (father subject to administrative writ; application of an extended statute of limitations to a claim for support arrears that is not yet barred by limitations does not implicate the vested rights of the obligor)

---

§ 158.401. Modifications to or Termination of Withholding by Title IV–D Agency.

(a) The Title IV–D agency shall establish procedures for the reduction in the amount of or termination of withholding from income on the liquidation of an arrearages or the termination of the obligation of support in Title IV–D cases. The procedures shall provide that the payment of overdue support may not be used as the sole basis for terminating withholding.

(b) At the request of the Title IV-D agency, the clerk of the court shall issue a judicial writ of withholding to the obligor's employer reflecting any modification or changes in the amount to be withheld or the termination of withholding.

§ 158.402. Agreement by Parties Regarding Amount or Duration of Withholding.

(a) An obligor and obligee may agree on a reduction in or termination of income withholding for child support on the occurrence of one of the following contingencies stated in the order:

(1) the child becomes 18 years of age or is graduated from high school, whichever is later;

(2) the child's disabilities of minority are removed by marriage, court order, or other operation of law; or

(3) the child dies.

(b) The obligor and obligee may file a notarized or acknowledged request with the clerk of the court under Section 158.011 for a revised judicial writ of withholding, including the termination of withholding.

(c) The clerk shall issue and deliver to an employer of the obligor a judicial writ of withholding that reflects the agreed revision or termination of withholding.

(d) An agreement by the parties under this section does not modify the terms of a support order.

§ 158.403. Modifications to or Termination of Withholding in Voluntary Withholding Cases.

(a) If an obligor initiates voluntary withholding under Section 158.011, the obligee or an agency providing child support services may file with the clerk of the court a notarized request signed by the obligor and the obligee or agency, as appropriate, for the issuance and delivery to the obligor of a:

(1) modified writ of withholding that reduces the amount of withholding; or

(2) notice of termination of withholding.

(b) On receipt of a request under this section, the clerk shall issue and deliver a modified writ of withholding or notice of termination in the manner provided by Section 158.402.

(c) The clerk may charge a reasonable fee not to exceed $15 for filing the request.

(d) An obligee may contest a modified writ of withholding or notice of termination issued under this section by requesting a hearing in the manner provided by Section 158.309 not later than the 180th day after the date the obligee discovers that the writ or notice has been issued.

§ 158.404. Delivery of Order of Reduction or Termination of Withholding.

If a court has rendered an order that reduces the amount of child support to be withheld or terminates withholding for child support, any person or governmental entity may deliver to the employer a certified copy of the order without the requirement that the clerk of the court deliver the order.

§ 158.405. Liability of Employers.

The provisions of this chapter regarding the liability of employers for withholding apply to an order that reduces or terminates withholding.

Subchapter F. Administrative Writ of Withholding in Title IV–D Cases

Guest Introductory Comment

The federal Personal Responsibility and Work Opportunity Reconciliation Act of 1996 (PRWORA) requires that a state Title IV–D agency have the authority to take certain administrative actions without the necessity of any other judicial or administrative order. Among these actions is the authority to administratively order income withholding for child support. This subchapter implements the federal requirement by providing the Title IV–D agency with the ability to issue a writ of withholding directly, without having to request the issuance of a writ by the clerk as previously required. Once delivered to an employer, however, the administrative writ is filed for the record with the clerk of the court of continuing, exclusive jurisdiction.

The Title IV–D agency's ability to issue an administrative writ directly to an employer should significantly expedite income withholding in IV–D cases. Although an administrative writ may be contested on the same grounds as a writ issued by the clerk, the issuance of an administrative writ, unlike a judicial writ, may not be stayed. As required by PRWORA, the obligor is given notice of the administrative writ only after it has been issued and withholding has commenced. Contest by an obligor to an administrative writ is to be considered first through informal agency proceedings and, then, should any issue remain unresolved, through judicial review. Once all current support, including medical support, and any arrears have been satisfied, the agency may issue a writ terminating withholding. Because the administrative writ process is intended for both intrastate and interstate IV–D cases, the form of the writ will be in a standard format prescribed under federal law by the Secretary of Health and Human Services. *(A.G.K. & H.P.S.)*

---

§ 158.501. Issuance of Administrative Writ of Withholding by Title IV–D Agency.

(a) The Title IV–D agency may initiate income withholding by issuing an administrative writ of withholding for the enforcement of an existing order as authorized by this subchapter.

(b) The Title IV–D agency is the only entity that may issue an administrative writ under this subchapter.

(c) The Title IV-D agency may use the procedures authorized by this subchapter to enforce a support order rendered by a tribunal of another state regardless of whether the order has been registered under Chapter 159 *[UIFSA]*.

Guest Comment

Subsection (c) conforms the use of the administrative writ procedures to UIFSA for administrative enforcement of an interstate order by the Title IV–D agency without initially having to register the order. *See* § 159.507(b), *infra*. (*A.G.K. & H.P.S.*)

---

§ 158.502. When Administrative Writ of Withholding May be Issued.

(a) An administrative writ of withholding under this subchapter may be issued by the Title IV–D agency at any time until all current support, including medical support, and child support arrearages have been paid. The writ issued under this subsection may be based on an obligation in more than one support order.

(b) The Title IV–D agency may issue an administrative writ of withholding that directs that an amount be withheld for an arrearage or adjusts the amount to be withheld for an arrearage. An administrative writ issued under this subsection may be contested as provided by Section 158.506.

(c) The Title IV-D agency may issue an administrative writ of withholding as a reissuance of an existing withholding order on file with the court of continuing jurisdiction or a tribunal of another state. The administrative writ under this subsection is not subject to the contest provisions of Sections 158.505(a)(2) and 158.506.

(d) The Title IV–D agency may issue an administrative writ of withholding to direct child support payments to the state disbursement unit of another state.

History: Amended by 78th Legis., Reg. Sess. (2003), S.B. 1805, eff. Sept. 1, 2003. "Except as provided by Subsection (a) of this section, the changes in law made by this Act apply only to an interstate proceeding to establish, modify, or enforce a support obligation or to determine parentage began on or after the effective date of this Act. A proceeding begun before the effective date is governed by the law in effect on the date the proceeding began, and the former law is continued in effect for that purpose."

Guest Comment

Subsection (d), added in 2003, enables the IV–D agency to redirect income withheld for child support to the disbursement unit of a state to which the obligee has relocated. This conforms to the provisions under § 159.319 (UIFSA) for redirection of support payments in interstate enforcement. (*C.B. & H.P.S.)*

Leading Case

In re A.D., 73 S.W.3d 244 (Tex. 2002) (1997 amendment repealing four-year limitation on court's jurisdiction to order withholding for child support constitutional, unlimited time for enforcement not a retroactive law)

In re A.C.B., 103 S.W.3d 570 (Tex. App.—San Antonio 2003, no pet.) (AG sanctioned for administrative writ of withholding)

---

§ 158.503. Delivery of Administrative Writ to Employer; Filing With Court.

(a) An administrative writ of withholding issued under this subchapter may be delivered to an obligor, obligee, and employer by mail or by electronic transmission.

(b) Not later than the third business day after the date of delivery of the administrative writ of withholding to an employer, the Title IV-D agency shall file a copy of the writ, together with a signed certificate of service, in the court of continuing jurisdiction. The certificate of service may be signed electronically. This subsection does not apply to the enforcement under Section 158.501(c) of a support order rendered by a tribunal of another state.

(c) The copy of the administrative writ of withholding filed with the clerk of court must include:

(1) the name, address, and signature of the authorized attorney or individual that issued the writ;

(2) the name and address of the employer served with the writ; and

(3) a true copy of the information provided to the employer.

(d) The clerk of the court may charge a reasonable fee not to exceed $15 for filing an administrative writ under this section.

§ 158.504. Contents of Administrative Writ of Withholding.

(a) The administrative writ of withholding must be in the form prescribed by the Title IV-D agency as required by this chapter and in a standard format authorized by the United States Department of Health and Human Services.

(b) An administrative writ of withholding issued under this subchapter may contain only the information that is necessary for the employer to withhold income for child support and medical support and shall specify the place where the withheld income is to be paid.

§ 158.505. Notice to Obligor.

(a) On issuance of an administrative writ of withholding, the Title IV-D agency shall send the obligor:

(1) notice that the withholding has commenced, including, if the writ is issued as provided by Section 158.502(b), the amount of the arrearages, including accrued interest;

(2) except as provided by Section 158.502(c), notice of the procedures to follow if the obligor desires to contest withholding on the grounds that the identity of the obligor or the existence or amount of arrearages is incorrect; and

(3) a copy of the administrative writ, including the information concerning income withholding provided to the employer.

(b) The notice required under this section may be sent to the obligor by:

(1) personal delivery by a person designated by the Title IV-D agency;

(2) first-class mail or certified mail, return receipt requested, addressed to the obligor's last known address; or

(3) service of citation as in civil cases generally.

(c) Repealed by Acts 1999, 76th Leg., ch. 556, § 81, eff. Sept. 1, 1999.

§ 158.506. Contest by Obligor to Administrative Writ of Withholding.

(a) Except as provided by Section 158.502(c), an obligor receiving the notice under Section 158.505 may request a review by the Title IV–D agency to resolve any issue in dispute regarding the identity of the obligor or the existence or amount of arrearages. The Title IV–D agency shall provide an opportunity for a review, by telephonic conference or in person, as may be appropriate under the circumstances.

(b) After a review under this section, the Title IV-D agency may issue a new administrative writ of withholding to the employer, including a writ modifying the amount to be withheld or terminating withholding.

(c) If a review under this section fails to resolve any issue in dispute, the obligor is entitled to the remedies provided by Section 158.317 for cases in which a notice of an application for judicial writ of withholding was not received. The obligor may file a motion with the court to withdraw the administrative writ and request a hearing with the court not later than the 30th day after receiving notice of the agency's determination. Income withholding may not be interrupted pending a hearing by the court.

§ 158.507. Administrative Writ Terminating Withholding.

An administrative writ to terminate withholding may be issued and delivered to an employer by the Title IV-D agency when all current support, including medical support, and child support arrearages have been paid.

§ 158.508. [repealed]

Chapter 159. Uniform Interstate Family Support Act

Editors' Note: *Explanation of UIFSA Cross References. To assist bench and bar in construing UIFSA, the "Prefatory Note" and the "Commissioners' Official Comments" regarding provisions of the Act which accompany the official version are reprinted after each section. The section numbers of the uniform act, e.g., UIFSA § 101, correspond to the numbers of the sections in the Family Code, e.g., § 159.101, etc. To avoid confusion for the reader, references in the Commissioners' Official Comments have been edited to reflect the enactment of the Act in Texas.*

All of the extensive amendments to UIFSA were contained in a single bill, and therefore have the following legislative history:

History: Amended by 78th Legis., Reg. Sess. (2003), S.B. 1805, eff. Sept. 1, 2003. (a) The changes in law made by this Act to Section 154.004, Family Code, apply only to a court order or a portion of a decree that provides for the support of a child that is rendered on or after the effective date of this Act. An order or decree rendered before the effective date of this Act is governed by the law in effect on the date the order or decree was rendered, and the former law is continued in effect for that purpose. (b) Except as provided by Subsection (a) of this section, the changes in law made by this Act apply only to an interstate proceeding to establish, modify, or enforce a support obligation or to determine if parentage began on or after the effective date of this Act. A proceeding begun before the effective date is governed by the law in effect on the date the proceeding began, and the former law is continued in effect for that purpose.

Subchapter A. Conflicts Between Provisions

Subchapter B. General Provisions

Subchapter C. Jurisdiction

Subchapter D. Civil Provisions of General Application

Subchapter E. Establishment of Support Order

Subchapter F. Enforcement of Order of Another State Without Registration

Subchapter G. Enforcement and Modification of Support Order After Registration

Subchapter H. Determination of Parentage

Subchapter I. Interstate Rendition

Subchapter J. Miscellaneous Provisions

Authors' Introductory Comment

Effective September 1, 1993, Texas adopted the Uniform Interstate Family Support Act (*UIFSA*) to replace the Revised Uniform Reciprocal Enforcement Act (*RURESA*). In 1996, the National Conference of Commissioners on Uniform State Laws approved a set of amendments to the 1993 act. Also in 1996, Congress enacted the Personal Responsibility and Work Opportunity Reconciliation Act (PRWORA), which mandated enactment of the amended UIFSA by all U.S. jurisdictions by January 1, 1998. Texas passed an amended act in 1997; by May 1, 1998 all states, the District of Columbia, and the U.S. territories had adopted UIFSA.

In August 2001, UIFSA was once again revised by the National Conference of Commissioners on Uniform State Laws. As has occurred in each instance of a UIFSA revision, The Texas Legislature enacted the latest version at the earliest opportunity, *i.e.*, the 2003 session.

CLE/Other Legal Publications

Jurisdiction, special appearance, and conflicts of law. Donn C. Fullenweider, 2004 Adv. Fam. L.

International child support cases in Texas. Barry J. Brooks, 2004 U. Tex. Fam. L. on the Border

Defending Mexican Nationals residing in Mexico in paternity actions in Texas brought under Fam. § 159.201 or the Family Code's long arm statute. Arturo Vazquez, 2004 U. Tex. Fam. L. on the Border

The ABCs of interstate custody and family support jurisdiction. Angela G. Pence, 2003 Adv. Fam. L.

Unique and not so unique child support issues. Kim W. Mercier & Christopher M. Lake, 2003 Marriage Dissolution

Child support. Rhonda F. Hunter, 2002 Adv. Fam. L.

Update on state disbursement unit: sending all the child support to San Antonio. Alicia Gray Key, 2002 Adv. Fam. L.

Interstate alphabet soup. Sally H. Emerson, 2002 ADV. FAM. L.

Jurisdiction and venue. Douglas R. Woodburn, 2000 ADV. FAM. L.

Leading Cases

In re B.C., 52 S.W.3d 926 (Tex. App.—Beaumont 2001, no pet.) (UIFSA determines applicable statute of limitations; in proceeding for arrearages, the statute of limitations of Texas or issuing state, whichever is longer, governs)

In re B.O.G., 48 S.W.3d 312 (Tex. App.—Waco. 2001, pet. denied) (both parents have left Texas, which no longer has jurisdiction to modify child support order)

Attorney General v. Litten, 999 S.W.2d 74 (Tex. App.—Houston [14th Dist.] 1999, no pet.) (application of MO's longer ten-year statute of limitations required by choice of law provision; UIFSA evidence rule permits admission of verified copy of MO law over hearsay objection)

In re Henderson, 982 S.W.2d 566 (Tex. App.—Houston [14th Dist.] 1998, no pet.) (OK obligor not subject to modification or enforcement of OK child support order; fact child lives in TX not controlling)

Cowan v. Moreno, 903 S.W.2d 119 (Tex. App.—Austin 1995, no writ) (UIFSA applies to orders rendered before date of statute)

Texas Family Law Practice Manual

Chapter 34. Interstate Proceedings, Uniform Interstate Family Support Act, Forms *34–3* through *34–13*

COMMISSIONERS' PREFATORY NOTE

I. BACKGROUND INFORMATION

In 1992 the National Conference of Commissioners on Uniform State Laws [hereafter NCCUSL, the Conference, or Uniform Law Commissioners] promulgated the UNIFORM INTERSTATE FAMILY SUPPORT ACT [hereafter UIFSA] as a complete replacement for the two then-existing uniform interstate support acts, the UNIFORM RECIPROCAL ENFORCEMENT OF SUPPORT ACT [URESA] and its revised version [RURESA]. In 1993 two States, Arkansas and Texas, enacted UIFSA. By the summer of 1996, 35 States had adopted the new Uniform Act. That year was a very eventful one in the history of UIFSA. First, a Drafting Committee was convened in Spring 1996 in response to requests from representatives of employer groups for more specific statutory directions regarding interstate child-support withholding orders. Second, the child-support community (primarily the IV–D programs funded by federal subsidies) requested review of the substantive and procedural provisions. As a result, significant amendments to UIFSA were adopted by the Conference in July, 1996.

The Conference promulgated UIFSA in July, 1996. Less than one month later, the U.S. Congress assured that nationwide acceptance of the amended Act was virtually certain. In the "welfare reform" legislation passed in August 1996, officially known as the PERSONAL RESPONSIBILITY AND WORK OPPORTUNITY RECONCILIATION ACT OF 1996 (PRWORA), the enactment of UIFSA, as amended, was mandated as a condition of state eligibility for the federal funding of child support enforcement, as follows:

> Sec. 321. ADOPTION OF UNIFORM STATE LAWS [42 U.S.C. Section 666] is amended by adding at the end the following new subsection:
>
> "(f) Uniform Interstate Family Support Act.—In order to satisfy [42 U.S.C. 654(20)(A)], on and after January 1, 1998, each State must have in effect the Uniform Interstate Family Support Act, as approved by the American Bar Association on February 9, 1993, together with any amendments officially adopted before

January 1, 1998, by the National Conference of Commissioners on Uniform State Laws." P.L. 104–193, Section 321, 110 Stat. 2221.

For a comprehensive history of the events leading up to the replacement of URESA and RURESA by UIFSA, *see* the Prefatory Notes to the 1992 and 1996 versions of the Act found in 9 UNIFORM LAWS ANNOTATED 253, 393 (2000), or John J. Sampson, *Uniform Interstate Family Support Act with Unofficial Annotations*, 27 FAM. L.Q. 91 (1993), and John J. Sampson, *Uniform Interstate Family Support Act (1996), Statutory Text, Prefatory Note, and Commissioners Comments (with More Unofficial Annotations)*, 32 FAM. L.Q. 385 (1998).

In accordance with the congressional mandate, by 1998 all U.S. jurisdictions had enacted UIFSA. Thus, the several states have had between four and eight years of experience with the various iterations of the Act. Moreover, there has been an extraordinary amount of comprehensive training about the Act by the child support enforcement agencies throughout the nation and associated agencies and organizations of those agencies, *e.g.*: U.S. Department of Health and Human Services, Office of Child Support Enforcement (OCSE); National Child Support Enforcement Association (NCSEA); Eastern Regional Interstate Child Support Association (ERICSA); and, Western Interstate Child Support Enforcement Council (WICSEC). As a consequence, the provisions of UIFSA are far more familiar to those who must administer it than ever was true of its predecessor acts, URESA and RURESA.

In 2000 the child-support community again requested that the Act be reviewed and amendments suggested as appropriate. In response to this request, the Conference leadership appointed a new Drafting Committee (the earlier Committee had been disbanded). A single meeting in March 2001 led to significant substantive and procedural amendments that ultimately were approved by the Conference at its Annual Meeting in August, 2001. None of the amendments, however, make a fundamental change in the policies and procedures established in UIFSA 1996. The widespread acceptance of UIFSA is due primarily to the fact that representatives of the child support enforcement community mentioned above participated actively in the drafting of each version of the Act, including the amendments of 2001. In sum, although two sets of amendments have been propounded since the initial 1992 version of UIFSA, its basic principles have remained constant.

II. BASIC PRINCIPLES OF UIFSA

A. In General

1. RECIPROCITY NOT REQUIRED BETWEEN STATES. Reciprocal laws, the hallmark of RURESA and URESA, are not required under UIFSA. Although reciprocity became irrelevant in this country with the universal adoption of UIFSA, reciprocity continues to be an issue with regard to the recognition and enforcement of support orders of foreign countries and their political subdivisions, Sections 102(21), 104, 308. Respect and tolerance for the laws of other states and nations in order to facilitate child support enforcement is another prime goal of the Act. The 2001 amendments continue this perspective by explicitly recognizing that tribunals may extend the principle of comity to foreign support orders, Sections 104 and 210.

2. LONG–ARM JURISDICTION. UIFSA contains a broad provision for asserting long-arm jurisdiction to provide a tribunal in the State of residence of the spouse or a child entitled to support with the maximum possible opportunity to secure personal jurisdiction over an absent respondent, Section 201. This converts what otherwise would be a two-state proceeding into a one-state proceeding. When jurisdiction over a nonresident is obtained, the tribunal may obtain evidence, provide for discovery, and elicit testimony

through use of the same "information route" provided for two-state proceedings, Sections 210, 316–318. Amendments in 2001 to the basic long-arm provision, Section 201, clarified and strengthened the interrelationship between the assertion of such jurisdiction and the continuing nature of personal jurisdiction for enforcement and modification of a support order, Sections 205 and 206.

B. Establishing a Support Order

1. FAMILY SUPPORT. The Act may be used only for proceedings involving the support of a child or spouse of the support obligor; it does not include enforcement of other duties of support found in the statutes of a few states, such as requiring support of an elderly or disabled parent by an adult child, Sections 101(2),(18).

2. LOCAL LAW. UIFSA provides that the procedures and law of the forum apply, with some significant additions or exceptions:

(a) Certain procedures are prescribed for interstate cases even if they are not consistent with local law, i.e.: the contents of interstate petitions, Sections 311 and 602; the nondisclosure of certain sensitive information, Section 312; authority to award fees and costs including attorney's fees, Section 313; elimination of certain testimonial immunities, Section 314; and, limits on the assertion of nonparentage as a defense to support enforcement, Section 315.

(b) Visitation issues cannot be raised in child support proceedings, Section 305(d).

(c) Special rules for the interstate transmission of evidence and discovery are added to help place the maximum amount of information before the deciding tribunal. These procedures are available in cases in which the tribunal asserts jurisdiction over a nonresident, (Sections 210, 316–318), and may have the effect of amending local law in long-arm cases.

(d) The choice-of-law rule for the interpretation of a registered order is that the law of the issuing State governs the underlying terms of the controlling support order. One important exception exists; if the registering and issuing State have different statutes of limitation for enforcement, the longer time limit applies, Section 604.

3. CONTINUING EXCLUSIVE JURISDICTION AND THE ONE–ORDER SYSTEM. Under URESA and RURESA the majority of support proceedings were de novo. Even when an existing order of one State was "registered" in a second State, the registering State often asserted the right to modify the registered order. This meant that multiple support orders could be in effect in several states. As far as is possible, under UIFSA the principle of continuing, exclusive jurisdiction aims to recognize that only one valid support order may be effective at any one time, Sections 205–207. This principle is carried out in Sections 203–211.

4. PRIVATE ATTORNEYS. UIFSA explicitly authorizes parties to retain private legal counsel in support proceedings, Section 309, as well as to use the services of a state support enforcement agency, Section 307(a). The Act expressly takes no position on whether the support enforcement agency's assistance of a supported family establishes an attorney-client relationship with the applicant, Section 307(c).

5. EFFICIENCY. UIFSA streamlines interstate proceedings as follows:

(a) Proceedings may be initiated by or referred to administrative agencies rather than to courts in those states that use those agencies to establish support orders, Section 101(22).

(b) Under the old system, the process began by requiring a local "initiating tribunal" to make a preliminary (and nonbinding) determination of a duty to support, and then forwarding the documents to a "responding tribunal" for a binding decision. Under

UIFSA an individual party or support enforcement agency in the initiating State may file a proceeding directly in a tribunal in the responding State, Section 301. This innovation by UIFSA has proven to be a major contribution to efficient case management. In the unlikely event that some local action is needed, initiation of an interstate case in the initiating State is expressly made ministerial rather than a matter for adjudication or review by a tribunal.

(c) To facilitate efficient interstate establishment, enforcement, and modification of child support orders, forms sanctioned by the federal Office of Child Support Enforcement are available. Although developed in conjunction with the federal IV–D program, private parties and their attorneys who are engaged in an interstate child support case are well advised to use the appropriate forms for transmission of information to the responding State, Section 311(b). The information in those forms is declared to be admissible evidence, Section 316(b).

(d) Authority is provided for the transmission of information and documents through electronic and other modern means of communication, Section 316(e).

(e) Tribunals are directed to permit an out-of-state party or witness to be deposed or to testify by telephone conference, Section 316(f).

(f) Tribunals are required to cooperate in the discovery process for use in a tribunal in another State, Section 318.

(g) A tribunal and a support enforcement agency providing services to a supported family must keep the parties informed about all important developments in a case, Sections 305 and 307.

(h) A registered support order is confirmed and immediately enforceable unless the respondent files an objection in a record within a fixed period of time, almost invariably the 20 days suggested originally, Sections 603 and 607.

6. INTERSTATE PARENTAGE. UIFSA authorizes establishment of parentage in an interstate proceeding, even if not coupled with a proceeding to establish support, Section 701.

C. Enforcing a Support Order

1. DIRECT ENFORCEMENT. UIFSA provides two direct enforcement procedures that do not require assistance from a tribunal. First, a notice may be sent directly to the obligor's employer in another State, Section 501, which triggers income withholding by that employer without the necessity of a hearing unless the employee objects. The Act details the procedure to be followed by the employer in response to an interstate request for direct income withholding, Sections 502–506. Additionally, the Act provides for direct administrative enforcement by the support enforcement agency of the obligor's State, Section 507.

2. REGISTRATION. Enforcement of a support order of another State or nation involving a tribunal of the forum State begins with the registration of the existing support order in a tribunal of the responding State, Sections 601–604. However, the registered order continues to be the order of the issuing State, Sections 605–608. The role of the responding State is limited to enforcing that order except in the very limited circumstances under which modification is permitted, *infra.*

D. Modifying a Support Order

1. REGISTRATION. The first step for a party (whether obligor or obligee) requesting a tribunal of another State to modify an existing child support order is to follow the identical procedure for registration as when enforcement is sought. All modification requests are

subject to strict rules, *infra*, although different sequences are allowable: *i.e.*, registration for enforcement and a later request for modification; or, a request for contemporaneous modification and enforcement.

2. MODIFICATION STATUTORILY RESTRICTED. Under UIFSA, the only tribunal that can modify a support order is one having continuing, exclusive jurisdiction over the support issue. As an initial matter, this is the tribunal that first acquires personal and subject matter jurisdiction over the parties and the support obligation. If modification of the order by the issuing tribunal is no longer appropriate, another tribunal may become vested with the continuing, exclusive jurisdiction necessary to modify the order. Primarily this occurs when neither the individual parties nor the child reside in the issuing State, or when the parties agree in a record that another tribunal may assume modification jurisdiction. Only then may another tribunal with personal jurisdiction over the parties assume continuing, exclusive jurisdiction and have jurisdiction to modify the order, Sections 205, 206, 603(c), 609–612. Further, except for modification by agreement, Section 205 and 207, or when the parties have all moved to the same new State, Section 613, the party petitioning for modification must be a nonresident of the responding State and must submit himself or herself to the forum State, which must have personal jurisdiction over the respondent, Section 611. The vast majority of the time this is the State in which the respondent resides. A colloquial short-hand summary of the principle is that ordinarily the movant for modification of a child support order "must play an away game."

A 2001 amendment adds that even if the parties and child have moved from the issuing State they may agree that the tribunal that issued the controlling order will continue to exercise its continuing, exclusive jurisdiction, Section 205. This recognizes the fact that it may be preferable for the parties to return to a tribunal familiar with the issues rather than to be required to fully inform another tribunal of all the facts and issues that have been previously litigated. This exception may be particularly appropriate if both child-support and spousal-support are involved in the same case; under this Act, jurisdiction to modify the spousal support order is exclusively reserved to the issuing tribunal, regardless of where the parties reside.

Section 613 makes an obvious exception to the nonresident petitioner rule: if the child no longer resides in the issuing State and the parties have moved from the issuing State and by coincidence or design currently reside in the same State, that State has jurisdiction to modify the existing order and assume continuing, exclusive jurisdiction over the child support order.

Section 614 places the duty on the party obtaining a modification to provide notice of the new order to all interested tribunals, and grants the tribunal authority to sanction a party who fails to perform this duty of notice.

To facilitate modification across international borders, another exception to the nonresident petitioner rule was added in 1996 for child support orders issued by foreign jurisdictions. The amendments of 2001 recodified this procedure in a wholly new provision. Section 615 expands on the right of a tribunal of one of the several states to modify a child support order of a foreign country or political subdivision if that jurisdiction is prevented from modifying its order under its local law and the modification would be consistent with standards of due process.

Subchapter A. Conflicts Between Provisions

§ 159.001. Conflicts Between Provisions.

If a provision of this chapter conflicts with a provision of this title or another statute or rule of this state and the conflict cannot be reconciled, this chapter prevails.

Subchapter B. General Provisions

§ 159.101. Short Title.

This chapter may be cited as the Uniform Interstate Family Support Act.

§ 159.102 [~~159.101~~]. Definitions.

In this chapter:

(1) "Child" means an individual, whether over or under the age of majority, who:

(A) is or is alleged to be owed a duty of support by the individual's parent; or

(B) is or is alleged to be the beneficiary of a support order directed to the parent.

(2) "Child support order" means a support order for a child, including a child who has attained the age of majority under the law of the issuing state.

(3) "Duty of support" means an obligation imposed or imposable by law to provide support for a child, spouse, or former spouse, including an unsatisfied obligation to provide support.

(4) "Home state" means the state in which a child lived with a parent or a person acting as parent for at least six consecutive months preceding the time of filing of a petition or a comparable pleading for support and, if a child is less than six months old, the state in which the child lived with a parent or a person acting as parent from the time of birth. A period of temporary absence of any of them is counted as part of the six-month or other period.

(5) "Income" includes earnings or other periodic entitlements to money from any source and any other property subject to withholding for support under the law of this state.

(6) "Income-withholding order" means an order or other legal process directed to an obligor's employer, as provided in Chapter 158, to withhold support from the income of the obligor.

(7) "Initiating state" means a state from which a proceeding is forwarded or in which a proceeding is filed for forwarding to a responding state under this chapter or a law or procedure substantially similar to this chapter[~~, the Uniform Reciprocal Enforcement of Support Act, or the Revised Uniform Reciprocal Enforcement of Support Act~~].

(8) "Initiating tribunal" means the authorized tribunal in an initiating state.

(9) "Issuing state" means the state in which a tribunal issues a support order or renders a judgment determining parentage.

(10) "Issuing tribunal" means the tribunal that issues a support order or renders a judgment determining parentage.

(11) "Law" includes decisional and statutory law and rules and regulations having the force of law.

(12) "Obligee" means:

(A) an individual to whom a duty of support is or is alleged to be owed or in whose favor a support order has been issued or a judgment determining parentage has been rendered;

(B) a state or political subdivision to which the rights under a duty of support or support order have been assigned or that has independent claims based on financial assistance provided to an individual obligee; or

(C) an individual seeking a judgment determining parentage of the individual's child.

(13) "Obligor" means an individual or the estate of a decedent:

(A) who owes or is alleged to owe a duty of support;

(B) who is alleged but has not been adjudicated to be a parent of a child; or

(C) who is liable under a support order.

(14) **"Person" means an individual, corporation, business trust, estate, trust, partnership, limited liability company, association, joint venture, government, governmental subdivision, agency, instrumentality, public corporation, or any other legal or commercial entity.**

(15) "Record" means information that is:

(A) inscribed on a tangible medium or stored in an electronic or other medium; and

(B) retrievable in a perceivable form.

(16) "Register" means to file a support order or judgment determining parentage in the registry of foreign support orders.

(17) [~~(15)~~] "Registering tribunal" means a tribunal in which a support order is registered.

(18) [~~(16)~~] "Responding state" means a state in which a proceeding is filed or to which a proceeding is forwarded for filing from an initiating state under this chapter or a law or procedure substantially similar to this chapter[~~, the Uniform Reciprocal Enforcement of Support Act, or the Revised Uniform Reciprocal Enforcement of Support Act~~].

(19) [~~(17)~~] "Responding tribunal" means the authorized tribunal in a responding state.

(20) [~~(18)~~] "Spousal support order" means a support order for a spouse or former spouse of the obligor.

(21) [~~(19)~~] "State" means a state of the United States, the District of Columbia, Puerto Rico, the United States Virgin Islands, or any territory or insular possession subject to the jurisdiction of the United States. The term includes:

(A) an Indian tribe; and

(B) a foreign **country or political subdivision** [~~jurisdiction~~] that has:

(i) been declared to be a foreign reciprocating country or political subdivision under federal law;

(ii) established a reciprocal arrangement for child support with this state as provided by Section 159.308; or

(iii) enacted a law or established procedures for issuance and enforcement of support orders that are substantially similar to the procedures under this chapter[~~, the Uniform Reciprocal Enforcement of Support Act, or the Revised Uniform Reciprocal Enforcement of Support Act~~].

(22) [~~(20)~~] "Support enforcement agency" means a public official or agency authorized to seek:

(A) enforcement of support orders or laws relating to the duty of support;

(B) establishment or modification of child support;

(C) determination of parentage; [~~or~~]

(D) the location of obligors or their assets; **or**

(E) determination of the controlling child support order.

"Support enforcement agency" does not include a domestic relations office unless that office has entered into a cooperative agreement with the Title IV–D agency to perform duties under this chapter.

(23) [~~(21)~~]"Support order" means a judgment, decree, or order, whether temporary, final, or subject to modification, for the benefit of a child, a spouse, or a former spouse that provides for monetary support, health care, arrearages, or reimbursement and may include related costs and fees, interest, income withholding, attorney's fees, and other relief.

(24) [~~(22)~~]"Tribunal" means a court, administrative agency, or quasi-judicial entity authorized to establish, enforce, or modify support orders or to determine parentage.

Commissioners' Official Comment to UIFSA Section 102

The terms defined in UIFSA have undergone relatively little amendment since its original promulgation in 1992. Two new terms were added in 2003—"person" and "record," found in Subsections (14) and (15), respectively. Other definitions have been amended slightly over the years, but none as significantly as the 2003 amendments to the definition of "State" in Subsection (21).

Many crucial definitions continue to be left to local law. For example, the definitions of "child" and "child-support order" provided by Subsections (1) and (2) refer to "the age of majority" without further elaboration. The exact age at which a child becomes an adult for different purposes is a matter for the law of each State, as is the age at which a parent's duty to furnish child support terminates. Similarly, a wide variety of other terms of art are implicitly left to state law. For example, Subsection (23) refers inter alia to "health care, arrearages, or reimbursement ." All of these terms are subject to individualized definitions on a state-by-state basis.

Subsection (3) defines "duty of support" to mean the legal obligation to provide support, whether or not that duty has been the subject of an order by a tribunal. This broad definition includes both prospective and retrospective obligations to the extent they are imposed by the relevant state law.

For the limited purpose of resolving certain conflicts in the exercise of jurisdiction, Subsection (4) borrows the concept of the "home State of a child" from the UNIFORM CHILD CUSTODY JURISDICTION ACT (UCCJA) and its successor, the UNIFORM CHILD CUSTODY JURISDICTION AND ENFORCEMENT ACT (UCCJEA), versions of which have been adopted in all 50 states, and incorporated into the federal Parental Kidnapping Prevention Act, 42 U.S.C. Section 1738A (PKPA).

Subsection (6) is written broadly to include an "income withholding order" based on "other legal process," as distinguished from "by order of a tribunal." Some states issue such orders administratively, which are entitled to enforcement notwithstanding the fact that no judicial or quasi-judicial process is involved. Federal law requires that, in order to be eligible for federal subsidy monies, each State must provide for income withholding "without the necessity of any application therefor, or for any further action by the court or other entity which issued such order ." 42 U.S.C. Section 666(b)(2). States have complied with this requirement in a variety of ways.

From its beginning UIFSA has permitted direct filing of an interstate proceeding in a responding State without an initial filing in an initiating tribunal. This has become the standard operating procedure for child support enforcement agencies. Thus, a petitioner in one State may seek to establish, enforce, or modify a support order in a second State by either filing in the responding state's tribunal or by directly seeking the assistance of the support enforcement agency in the second State. Although Subsections (7), (8), (18) and (19) supply definitions for "initiating and responding State" and "initiating and responding tribunal," the procedure of "initiation and response" established by the predecessor acts of URESA and RURESA has become an anachronism since the universal enactment of UIFSA.

Until the 2003 amendments, the relationship between UIFSA and the prior uniform acts was captured in the reference to URESA and RURESA as "substantially similar" acts. This phrasing in Subsections (7), (18) and (21), and repeated several times throughout the Act, has been deleted everywhere it appears to avoid confusion that might arise from appearing to incorporate statutes that have been replaced. This is not to suggest in any way that support orders issued under URESA or RURESA are not fully enforceable under UIFSA. Until valid orders issued under those laws expire of their own terms or are replaced by new UIFSA orders, the support orders themselves will continue to have vitality, *see* Sections 201–211, *infra*. In short, UIFSA is specifically designed to function with the earlier acts without conflict. Support orders issued under one of the earlier acts should be honored and enforced in every State. But, despite their common roots, neither URESA nor RURESA can be said to be "substantially similar" with regard to the continuing, exclusive jurisdiction/one-order system established in UIFSA. States are directed to accord full enforcement remedies to support orders issued under the prior acts, but they must apply UIFSA restraint regarding modification. In situations involving multiple orders created under the former system, UIFSA mandates the application of its one-order rules to determine the single order that is entitled to prospective enforcement, *see* Section 207, *infra*.

The term "obligee" in Subsection (12) is defined in a broad manner, which is consistent with common usage. In instances of spousal support, the person owed the duty of support and the person receiving the payments are almost always the same. Use of the term is more complicated in the context of child support. The child is the person to whom the duty of support is owed, and therefore can be viewed as the ultimate obligee. However, "obligee" usually refers to the individual receiving the payments. While this is most commonly the custodial parent or other legal custodian, the "obligee" may be a support enforcement agency that has been assigned the right to receive support payments in order to recoup Temporary Assistance for Needy Families (TANF), 42 U.S.C. Section 601 *et seq.*, formerly known as Aid to Families with Dependent Children (AFDC). Even in the absence of such an assignment, a State may have an independent statutory claim for reimbursement for general assistance provided to a spouse, a former spouse, or a child of an obligor. The Act also uses "obligee" to identify an individual who is asserting a claim for support, not just for a person whose right to support is unquestioned, presumed, or has been established in a legal proceeding.

Subsection (13) provides the correlative definition of an "obligor," which includes an individual who is alleged to owe a duty of support as well as a person whose obligation has previously been determined.

The terms "obligor" and "obligee" inherently contain the legal obligation to pay or receive support, and both terms also implicitly refer to the individuals with a duty to support a child. The one-order system of UIFSA can succeed only if the respective obligations of support are adjusted as the physical possession of a child changes between parents or involves a third party caretaker. This must be accomplished in the context of modification, and not by the creation of multiple orders attempting to reflect each changing custody scenario. Obviously this issue is of concern not only to interstate child-support orders, but applies to intrastate orders as well.

The definition of "record" in new Subsection (14) conforms UIFSA to the Conference standard for legal documentation as established in the UNIFORM ELECTRONIC TRANSACTIONS ACT Section 102(13) [hereafter UETA]. Henceforth, the phrase "in a record" will replace the terminology "in writing" as the appropriate manner to recognize that electronic transmissions and signatures are increasingly appropriate substitutes for more traditional documentation.

The definitions of "responding State" and "responding tribunal" in Subsections (18) and (19) accommodate the direct filing of a petition under UIFSA without the intervention of an initiating tribunal. Both definitions acknowledge the possibility that there may be a responding State and a responding tribunal in a situation where there is no initiating State or initiating tribunal.

Subsection (21) no longer requires reciprocity between the several states, formerly a cornerstone of RURESA and URESA. Public policy favoring enforcement of child support orders is sufficiently strong to warrant waiving any quid pro quo requirement between U.S. jurisdictions. This was true even before the issue was mooted by the enactment of UIFSA by all states by 1998.

The 1996 amendment to Subsection (21) clarified the position that UIFSA, like RURESA before it, does not waive reciprocity in the international context. A major amendment to the text of Subsection (21) was made in 2003 to make clear that a foreign country or political subdivision is defined as a "State" under the Act in three situations. First, a declaration by the U.S. State Department that a foreign jurisdiction is a reciprocating country or political subdivision is controlling for all states. Second, in the absence of such a declaration, each of the several states can make an arrangement with a foreign country or political subdivision for reciprocal enforcement of child support. Finally, a finding may be made that a foreign jurisdiction has a law or procedure substantially similar to UIFSA. That is, a tribunal may consider whether the foreign jurisdiction also has laws and procedures that allow for a U.S. order to be recognized in that foreign jurisdiction independent of a formal reciprocity agreement. The inclusion of foreign political subdivisions is necessary because in some countries the central government will not or cannot bind the subdivisions. For example, reciprocal arrangements with Canada are made on the province level and not with the Canadian federal government.

Although the vast bulk of child support establishment, enforcement, and modification in the United States is performed by the state IV–D agencies, *see* Part IV–D, Social Security Act, 42 U.S.C. Section 651 *et seq.*, Subsection (22) defines the term "support enforcement agency" to include not only those entities, but also any other state or local governmental entities charged with establishing or enforcing support. The 2003 amendment simply adds another key task to the list of powers, that is, determination of the controlling order in multiple order situations.

In 1992 Subsection (24) introduced a completely new term, "tribunal," which replaced the term "court" used in RURESA. With the advent of federally-funded IV–D programs, a number of states have delegated various aspects of child support establishment and enforcement to quasi-judicial bodies and administrative agencies. The term "tribunal" accounts for the breadth of state variations in dealing with support orders. By 2003 the usage has become the standard in the child support enforcement community, although private practitioners who only rarely are involved in such cases may still find the term unfamiliar.

Comment

The second paragraph of § 159.101(20) [UIFSA § 101(20)] relating to the exception of a domestic relations office from the definition of a "support enforcement agency" was added by the Texas Legislature. Local DRO's have a long history of independent operation in this state. Texas domestic relations offices are funded from local fees to enforce child support and visitation; the Texas Legislature was unwilling to impose this additional requirement without some funding source. The variant language is intended to exempt such offices from a duty to provide services in interstate cases unless such services are eligible for federal financial participation through the Title IV–D agency (the attorney general).

---

§ 159.103 [~~159.102~~]. Tribunal of State.

The court is the tribunal of this state.

Commissioners' Official Comment to UIFSA Section 103

The enacting state must identify the court, administrative agency, or the combination of those entities, which constitute the tribunal or tribunals authorized to deal with family support. In a particular state there may be several different such entities authorized to determine family support matters.

---

§ 159.104 [~~159.103~~]. Remedies Cumulative.

(a) Remedies provided in this chapter are cumulative and do not affect the availability of remedies under other law, **including the recognition of a support order of a foreign country or political subdivision on the basis of comity**.

(b) This chapter does not:

(1) provide the exclusive method of establishing or enforcing a support order under the law of this state; or

(2) grant a tribunal of this state jurisdiction to render a judgment or issue an order relating to child custody or visitation in a proceeding under this chapter.

Commissioners' Official Comment to UIFSA Section 104

The existence of procedures for interstate establishment, enforcement, or modification of support or a determination of parentage in UIFSA does not preclude the application of the general law of the forum. Even if the parents live in different states, for example, a petitioner may decide to file an original proceeding for child support (and most likely for other relief as well) directly in the State of residence of the respondent and proceed under that forum's generally applicable support law. In so doing, the petitioner thereby submits to the personal jurisdiction of the forum and foregoes reliance on UIFSA. Once a child support order has been issued, this option is no longer available to interstate parties. Under UIFSA, a State may not permit a party to proceed to obtain a second support order; rather, in further litigation the tribunal must apply the Act's provisions for enforcement of an existing order and limit modification to the strict standards of UIFSA.

The 2003 addition to Subsection (a) specifically recognizes the doctrine of comity as a legitimate function of state law that on a proper showing provides for the recognition of a foreign support order, *see Mississippi Dept. Human Svcs. v. Shelnut*, 772 So.2d 1041 (Miss. 2000). Although the determination by the U.S. State Department that a foreign nation is a reciprocating country is binding on all states, recognition of foreign support orders through comity is dependent on the law of each UIFSA State. The reference to "remedies under other law" is intended to recognize the principle of comity as developed in the forum State by statutory or common law, rather than to create a substantive right independent of that law.

New Subsection (b)(1) gives notice that UIFSA is not the only means for establishing or enforcing a support order with an interstate aspect. Examples abound. A potential child-support obligee may voluntarily submit to the jurisdiction of another State to seek the full range of desired relief under the law of that State using intrastate procedures, rather than resorting to the interstate procedure provided by UIFSA. A nonresident married parent may choose to file a proceeding in the forum State for dissolution of the marriage, including property division and spousal support, and in conjunction seek an order regarding child custody and visitation and child support. A parent may submit to the jurisdiction of another State for a determination of parentage and child support. A support order resulting from each of these scenarios implicates UIFSA. Invariably the issuing tribunal will have continuing, exclusive jurisdiction over its controlling child or spousal support orders as provided by Sections 205, 207, 211, *infra*, with all of the attendant application of the Act to those orders.

On the other hand, Subsection (b)(2) states what is clear under U.S. Supreme Court decisions; the bases of jurisdiction for child custody and visitation orders and the jurisdiction for child-support orders run on separate tracks, compare *May v. Anderson*, 345 U.S. 528 (1953) with *Kulko v. Superior Court*, 436 U.S. 84 (1978). If the child-support order is sought under the authority of UIFSA, the most important aspect of this rule is that a child-support obligee utilizing the provisions of UIFSA to establish child support across State lines submits to jurisdiction for child support only, and does not submit to the jurisdiction of the responding State with regard to child custody or visitation.

Subchapter C. Jurisdiction

Leading Case

Cotton v. Cotton, 57 S.W.3d 506 (Tex. App.—Waco 2001, no pet.) (where there is no basis for in personam jurisdiction of a parent, a trial court lacks the authority to render any judgment or child support payments against the parent)

§ 159.201. Bases for Jurisdiction over Nonresident.

(a) In a proceeding to establish **or**[,] enforce[~~, or modify~~] a support order or to determine parentage, a tribunal of this state may exercise personal jurisdiction over a nonresident individual or the individual's guardian or conservator if:

(1) the individual is personally served with citation in this state;

(2) the individual submits to the jurisdiction of this state by consent, by entering a general appearance, or by filing a responsive document having the effect of waiving any contest to personal jurisdiction;

(3) the individual resided with the child in this state;

(4) the individual resided in this state and provided prenatal expenses or support for the child;

(5) the child resides in this state as a result of the acts or directives of the individual;

(6) the individual engaged in sexual intercourse in this state and the child may have been conceived by that act of intercourse;

(7) the individual asserted parentage in the paternity registry maintained in this state by the bureau of vital statistics; or

(8) there is any other basis consistent with the constitutions of this state and the United States for the exercise of personal jurisdiction.

(b) A tribunal of this state may not use the bases of personal jurisdiction listed in Subsection (a) or in any other law of this state to acquire personal jurisdiction to modify a child support order of another state unless the requirements of Section 159.611 or 159.615 are satisfied.

Commissioners' Official Comment to UIFSA Section 201

Sections 201 and 202 assert what is commonly described as long-arm jurisdiction over a nonresident respondent for purposes of establishing a support order or determining parentage. Inclusion of this long-arm provision in this interstate Act is justified because residents of two separate states are involved in the litigation, both of whom are subject to the personal jurisdiction of the forum. Thus, the case has a clear interstate aspect, despite the fact that only the law of the forum State is applicable. Moreover, this is sufficient to invoke additional UIFSA provisions in an otherwise intrastate proceeding. *See* Sections 202, 316, and 318, *infra*. The intent is to insure that every enacting State has a long-arm statute that is as broad as constitutionally permitted. In situations in which the long-arm statute can be satisfied, the petitioner (either the obligor or the obligee) has two options: (1) utilize the long-arm statute to obtain personal jurisdiction over the respondent; or (2) initiate a two-state proceeding under the succeeding provisions of UIFSA seeking to establish a support order in the respondent's State of residence. Of course, a third option is available that does not implicate UIFSA; a petitioner may file a proceeding in the respondent's State of residence (perhaps to settle all issues between the parties in a single proceeding).

This long-arm statute applies to an order for spousal support as well as an order for child support. However, almost all of the specific provisions relate to child support orders or determinations of parentage. This derives from the fact that the focus of UIFSA is primarily on child support. Only Subsections (1), (2) and (8) are applicable to an action for spousal support asserting long-arm jurisdiction over a nonresident. The first two subsections are wholly noncontroversial insofar as an assertion of personal jurisdiction is concerned. Moreover, assertion of personal jurisdiction under Subsections (1), (2), or (8) will doubtless yield jurisdiction over all matters to be decided between the spouses, including division of property on divorce. Thus, the most obvious possible basis for asserting long-arm jurisdiction over spousal support, *i.e.*, "last matrimonial domicile," is not included in Section 201 to avoid the potential problem of another instance of bifurcated jurisdiction. This restraint avoids a situation in which UIFSA grants long-arm jurisdiction for a spousal support order when the forum State has no correlative statute for property division in divorce.

Under RURESA, multiple support orders affecting the same parties were commonplace. UIFSA creates a *structure* designed to provide for only one support order at a time. The new one-order regime is facilitated and combined with a broad assertion of personal jurisdiction under this long-arm provision. The frequency of a two-state procedure involving the participation of tribunals in both states should be substantially reduced by the introduction of this long-arm statute.

Subsections (1) through (8) are derived from a variety of sources, including the UNIFORM PARENTAGE ACT (1973) Section 8, TEXAS FAMILY CODE Section 102.011, and NEW YORK FAMILY COURT ACT Section 154.

Subsection (1) codifies the holding of *Burnham v. Superior Court*, 495 U.S. 604 (1990), which reaffirms the constitutional validity of asserting personal jurisdiction based on personal service within a State.

Subsection (2) expresses the principle that a nonresident party concedes personal jurisdiction by seeking affirmative relief or by submitting to the jurisdiction by answering or entering an appearance. However, the power to assert jurisdiction over a support issue under the Act does not extend the tribunal's jurisdiction to other matters.

Subsections (3) through (6) identify specific fact situations justifying the assertion of long-arm jurisdiction over a nonresident. Each provides an appropriate affiliating nexus for such an assertion, when judged on a case-by-case basis with an eye on procedural and substantive due process. Further, each subsection does contain a possibility that an overly literal construction of the terms of the statute will overreach due process. For example, Subsection (3) provides that long-arm jurisdiction to establish a support order may be asserted if "the individual resided with the child in this State." The typical scenario contemplated by the statute is that the parties lived as a family unit in the forum State, separated, and one of the parents subsequently moved to another State while the other parent and the child continued to reside in the forum. No time frame is stated for filing a proceeding; this is based on the fact that the absent parent has a support obligation that extends for at least the minority of the child (and often longer in many states).

On the other hand, suppose that the two parents and their child lived in State A for many years, and then decided to move the family to State B to seek better employment opportunities. Those opportunities did not materialize and, after several weeks or a few months of frustration with the situation, one of the parents returned with the child to State A. Under these facts a tribunal of State A may conclude it has long-arm jurisdiction to establish the support obligation of the absent parent. But, suppose that the family's sojourn in State B lasted for many years, and then one parent unilaterally decides to return to State A. It is a reasonable expectation that all tribunals will conclude that assertion of personal jurisdiction over the absent parent immediately after the return based on Subsection (3) would offend due process. The interstate provisions of UIFSA are available to the returning parent to establish child support. Note that State B will have long-arm jurisdiction to establish support under Section 201. *See also* Section 204, *infra*, for the resolution of simultaneous proceedings provided by the Act.

The factual situations catalogued in the first seven subsections are appropriate and constitutionally acceptable grounds upon which to exercise personal jurisdiction over an individual. Subsection (7) is bracketed because not all states maintain putative father registries.

Finally, Subsection (8) tracks the broad, catch-all provisions found in many state statutes, including CALIFORNIA, CIV. P. CODE Section 410.10 (1973); New York, *supra*; and Texas, *supra*. Note, however, that the California provision, standing alone, was found to be inadequate to sustain a child support order under the facts presented in *Kulko v. Superior Court,* 436 U.S. 84 (1978).

When read together, the 2003 amendments to Subsection(a) deleting the term "modify" and the addition of new Subsection (b) are designed to preclude a tribunal of the forum from ignoring the restrictions on modification of child-support orders established by

UIFSA. Some courts broadly construed the former reference to "modify" to justify ignoring the requirement of Section 611 that, absent agreement of the parties, a petitioner for modification of a child-support order of an issuing State when all parties have left that State must be a nonresident of the forum. The 2003 amendments make clear that a tribunal may not apply the long-arm provisions of Subsection (a), or any other law of the forum, and thereby assert that personal jurisdiction over both individual parties to a support order of another State is sufficient to modify that order. The limitations on the exercise of subject matter jurisdiction provided by Sections 611 and 615 must be observed irrespective of the existence of personal jurisdiction over the parties. Long-arm personal jurisdiction over the respondent, standing alone, is not sufficient to grant subject matter jurisdiction over a proposed modification to a tribunal of the State of residence of the petitioner, *see LeTellier v. LeTellier*, 40 S.W.3d 490, 90 A.L.R.5th 707 (Tenn. 2001), *reversing* 1999 WL 732487 (Tenn. App. 1999).

Subsection (b) is intended to cement the principle that modification of an existing order is not subject solely to the usual rules of personal jurisdiction over both parties. Even if a tribunal has personal jurisdiction over both parties, absent agreement of the parties it does not have subject matter jurisdiction to modify a support order of another State if one of the parties or the child reside in the issuing State at the time the modification proceeding is filed, *see* Section 207, *infra*. Even if everyone has moved away from the issuing State, a tribunal having personal jurisdiction over both parties may not modify the order if the petitioner is a resident of the tribunal forum—unless both parties are residents of the forum, *see* Sections 611 and 613, *infra*. Absent an agreement of the parties, in all other cases the movant must be a nonresident, and the tribunal must have personal jurisdiction over the respondent. Almost invariably the respondent will be a resident of the forum.

On rare occasion, however, the required personal jurisdiction over the respondent may be available only by virtue of the long-arm provisions of this section, which explains why Sections 201, 205, 207, 611 and 615 must read in conjunction with one another. An example of such a situation is as follows: the controlling child-support order was issued by a tribunal in State A, which of course had personal jurisdiction over the parties when it issued its order; the obligee and child presently reside in State B (a State the obligor has never even visited); the obligor presently is employed and resides in Nation X, although the obligor's "home base" in the United States can be identified as State C where the headquarters of the obligor's employer is located; and, finally, other than Nation X, the only states that can claim a nexus with the obligor sufficient to assert personal jurisdiction over him are State C and perhaps State A. Under this fact situation, it is necessary to invoke one of the long-arm bases of Section 201 to assert the personal jurisdiction over the obligor necessary to modify the order. Note that the long-arm statute may not be asserted in State B where the movant resides due to the restriction provided in Section 611, even if a basis exists for assertion of long-arm jurisdiction in that State. The employment connection in State C is likely to permit a tribunal in that State to assert jurisdiction to modify the support order based on the catch-all provision, Subsection (a)(8). Further, a tribunal in State A might also find that it has retained jurisdiction to modify the order under Subsection (a)(8) (remember both parties are nonresidents) given the absence or paucity of other U.S. jurisdictions with a nexus to the obligor, *see Phillips v. Phillips*, 826 S.W.2d 746 (Tex. App. 1992). Note, however, that such an action by the original issuing State must be exercised with extreme restraint or the restriction on modification in Section 611 will become a nullity. Concern that long-arm jurisdiction will be asserted in less compelling circumstances than presented in this hypothetical situation is not substantiated by experience with Section 201 in establishment cases filed since the enactment of UIFSA. In fact, overreaching assertions of long-arm jurisdiction have been dealt with satisfactorily on a case-by-case basis using due process constitutional or forum non conveniens grounds. *Rains v. Dept. of Social & Health Serv.*, 989 P.2d 558 (Wash. App. 1998); *Phillips v. Fallen*, 6 S.W.3d 862 (Mo.1999), reversing 1999 WL 50159 (Mo. App. 1999); *Abu-Dalbouh v. Abu-Dalbouh*, 547 N.W.2d 700 (Minn.

Authors' Comment

The Texas Legislature originally omitted Subsection (7) of § 201 of the Uniform Act. However, the 1997 Legislature added a paternity registry to Texas law. *See* Chapter 160 *infra*. Consequently, § 159.201 was amended to recognize this fact.

---

§ 159.202. Duration of Personal Jurisdiction.

Personal [~~A tribunal of this state exercising personal~~] jurisdiction **acquired by a tribunal of this state in a proceeding under this chapter or other law of this state relating to a support order continues as long as the** [~~over a nonresident under Section 159.201 may apply Section 159.316 to receive evidence from another state and Section 159.318 to obtain discovery through a~~] tribunal **has continuing, exclusive jurisdiction to modify its order or continuing jurisdiction to enforce its order under Sections 159.205, 159.206, and 159.211** [~~of another state~~]. [~~In all other respects, Subchapters D-H do not apply and the tribunal shall apply the procedural and substantive law of this state, including the rules on choice of law other than those established by this chapter.~~]

Commissioners' Official Comment to UIFSA Section 202

This section can be said to state a legal truism, albeit a useful one. That is, once a tribunal issues a support order binding on the parties, which must be based on personal jurisdiction by virtue of *Kulko v. Superior Court*, 436 U.S. 84 (1978) and *Vanderbilt v. Vanderbilt*, 354 U.S. 416 (1957), jurisdiction in personam continues absent the statutorily specified reasons for its termination. The rule established by UIFSA is that the personal jurisdiction necessary to sustain enforcement or modification of an order of child support or spousal support persists as long as the order is in force and effect, even as to arrears, *see* Sections 205–207, 211, *infra*. This is true irrespective of the context in which the support order arose, *e.g.*, divorce, UIFSA support establishment, parentage establishment, modification of prior controlling order, etc. Insofar as a child-support order is concerned, depending on specific factual circumstances a distinction is made between continuing, exclusive jurisdiction to modify an order and continuing jurisdiction to enforce an order, *see* Sections 205 and 206, *infra*. Authority to modify a spousal support order is permanently reserved to the issuing tribunal, Section 211, *infra*.

---

§ 159.203. Initiating and Responding Tribunal of State.

Under this chapter, a tribunal of this state may serve as an initiating tribunal to forward proceedings to another state and as a responding tribunal for proceedings initiated in another state.

Commissioners' Official Comment to UIFSA Section 203

This section identifies the various roles a tribunal of the forum may serve; as appropriate, it may act as either an initiating or a responding tribunal. Under UIFSA a tribunal may serve as a responding tribunal even when there is no initiating tribunal in another State.

This accommodates the direct filing of a proceeding in a responding tribunal by a nonresident.

---

§ 159.204. Simultaneous Proceedings.

(a) A tribunal of this state may exercise jurisdiction to establish a support order if the petition or comparable pleading is filed after a pleading is filed in another state only if:

(1) the petition or comparable pleading in this state is filed before the expiration of the time allowed in the other state for filing a responsive pleading challenging the exercise of jurisdiction by the other state;

(2) the contesting party timely challenges the exercise of jurisdiction in the other state; and

(3) if relevant, this state is the home state of the child.

(b) A tribunal of this state may not exercise jurisdiction to establish a support order if the petition or comparable pleading is filed before a petition or comparable pleading is filed in another state if:

(1) the petition or comparable pleading in the other state is filed before the expiration of the time allowed in this state for filing a responsive pleading challenging the exercise of jurisdiction by this state;

(2) the contesting party timely challenges the exercise of jurisdiction in this state; and

(3) if relevant, the other state is the home state of the child.

Commissioners' Official Comment to UIFSA Section 204

Under the one-order system established by UIFSA, it is necessary to provide a new procedure to eliminate the multiple orders so common under RURESA and URESA. This requires cooperation between, and deference by, sister-state tribunals in order to avoid issuance of competing support orders. To this end, tribunals are expected to take an active role in seeking out information about support proceedings in other States concerning the same child. Depending on the circumstances, one or the other of two tribunals considering the same support obligation should decide to defer to the other. In 1992 UIFSA took a significant departure from the approach adopted by the UCCJA ("first filing"), by choosing the "home State of the child" as the primary method for resolving competing jurisdictional disputes, thereby adopting the choice of the federal PARENTAL KIDNAPPING PREVENTION ACT, 28 U.S.C. 1238A Section (C). Given the pre-emptive nature of the PKPA, and the possibility that custody and support will both be involved in some cases, the PKPA/UIFSA choice for resolving disputes between competing jurisdictional assertions was followed in 1997 by the decision of the Conference to replace the UCCJA with the UCCJEA. If the child has no home State, however, "first filing" will continue to control.

---

§ 159.205. Continuing, Exclusive Jurisdiction to Modify Child Support Order.

(a) A tribunal of this state **that has issued** [~~issuing~~] a **child** support order consistent with the law of this state has **and shall exercise** continuing, exclusive jurisdiction **to modify its** [~~over a child support~~] order **if the order is the controlling order and**:

(1) **at the time a request for modification is filed,** [~~as long as~~] this state **is** [~~remains~~] the **state of** residence of the obligor, the individual obligee, or the child for whose benefit the support order is issued; or

(2) [~~until all of~~] the parties **consent in a record or in open court that the** [~~who are individuals have filed written consents with the~~] tribunal of this state **may continue to exercise jurisdiction** [~~for a tribunal of another state~~] to modify **its** [~~the~~] order [~~and assume continuing, exclusive jurisdiction~~].

(b) A tribunal of this state **that has issued** [~~issuing~~] a child support order consistent with the law of this state may not exercise [~~its~~] continuing, **exclusive** jurisdiction to modify the order if:

(1) each party who is an individual files a consent in a record with the tribunal of this state that a tribunal of another state that has jurisdiction over at least one of the parties who is an individual or that is located in the state of residence of the child may modify the order and assume continuing, exclusive jurisdiction; or

(2) the order is not the controlling order [~~the order has been modified by a tribunal of another state under a law substantially similar to this chapter~~].

(c) **A tribunal of this state shall recognize the continuing, exclusive jurisdiction of a tribunal of another state if the** [~~If a child support order of this state is modified by a~~] tribunal of **the other** [~~another~~] state **has issued a child support order that modifies a child support order of a tribunal of this state** under a law substantially similar to this chapter[~~, a tribunal of this state loses its continuing, exclusive jurisdiction with regard to prospective enforcement of the order issued in this state and may only:~~

[~~(1) enforce the order that was modified as to amounts accruing before the modification;~~

[~~(2) enforce nonmodifiable aspects of that order; and~~

[~~(3) provide other appropriate relief for violations of that order that occurred before the effective date of the modification~~].

(d) A tribunal of this state **that does not have** [~~shall recognize the~~] continuing, exclusive jurisdiction **to modify a child support order may serve as an initiating tribunal to request** [~~of~~] a tribunal of another state **to modify a** [~~that issued a child~~] support order **issued in that state** [~~under a law substantially similar to this chapter~~].

(e) A temporary support order issued ex parte or pending resolution of a jurisdictional conflict does not create continuing, exclusive jurisdiction in the issuing tribunal.

(f) Repealed by Acts 2003, 78th Leg., ch. 1247, § 46.

Commissioners' Official Comment to UIFSA Section 205

This section is perhaps the most crucial provision in UIFSA. Drawing on the precedent of the federal Parental Kidnapping Prevention Act, 28 U.S.C. Section 1738A, the issuing tribunal retains continuing, exclusive jurisdiction over a child support order, except in very narrowly defined circumstances. First introduced by UIFSA in 1992, this principle is understood and widely accepted in all jurisdictions. "CEJ," as it is known in the child-support enforcement world, is fundamental to the one-child-support-order-at-a-time principle of UIFSA. At first glance this section appears to have been significantly rewritten; certainly minor adjustments have been made to the substantive rules established. But, with the exception of the addition of and entirely new Subsection (a)(2), the sole intent and effect of the 2003 amendments is to reorganize the statutory language for greater clarity.

The basic concept that the tribunal issuing a support order retains continuing, exclusive jurisdiction to modify that order remains the cornerstone of the Act.

As long as one of the individual parties or the child continues to reside in the issuing State, and as long as the parties do not agree to the contrary, the issuing tribunal has continuing, exclusive jurisdiction over its child-support order—which in practical terms means that it may modify its order. The statute attempts to be even-handed. The identity of the remaining party—obligor or obligee—does not matter. If the individual parties have left the issuing State but the child remains behind, continuing, exclusive jurisdiction [a.k.a. CEJ] remains with the issuing State. Even if all parties and the child no longer reside in the State, the support order continues in existence and is fully enforceable unless and until a modification takes place in accordance with the requirements of Article 6, *infra*. Note, however, that the CEJ of the issuing State over a spousal support order is permanent, *see* Section 211, *infra*.

In 2003 a significant, albeit subtle amendment was made to Subsection (a)(1). The intent was not to make a substantive change, but rather to clarify the original intent of the Drafting Committee. First, the time to measure whether the issuing tribunal has continuing, exclusive jurisdiction to modify its order, or whether all parties and child have left the State, is explicitly stated to be at the time of filing a proceeding to modify the child support order. Second, substitution of the term "is the residence" for the term "remains the residence" makes clear that any interruption of residence of a party between the date of the issuance of the order and the date of filing the request for modification does not affect jurisdiction to modify. Thus, if there is but one order, it is the controlling order in effect and enforceable throughout the United States, notwithstanding the fact that everyone has left the issuing State. If the order is not modified during this time of absence, a return to reside in the issuing State by a party or child will immediately identify the proper forum at the time of filing a proceeding for modification. Although the statute does not speak explicitly to the issue, temporary absence should be treated in a similar fashion. Temporary employment in another State may not forfeit a claim of residence in the issuing State, *State ex rel. Havlin v. Jamison*, 971 S.W.2d 938 (Mo. App. 1998). Of course, residence is a fact question for the trial court, keeping in mind that the question is residence, not domicile.

A substantive change is made by the 2003 amendment that adds entirely new language to Subsection (a)(2). From the beginning of the implementation of the CEJ principle, questions have been raised about why a tribunal may not modify its own order if the parties agree that it should do so even after both parties have left the State. The move of the parties and the child from the State may have been of a very short distance and, although the parties reside outside the issuing State, they may prefer to continue to be governed by the same issuing tribunal because they continue to have a strong affiliation with the issuing tribunal. For example, the child-support order may have been issued by a tribunal of Washington, D.C. Subsequently the obligee and child have moved to Virginia, the obligor now resides in Maryland, and perhaps one or both parties continue to be employed in Washington. The possibility that under such circumstances the parties reasonably may prefer to continue to deal with the issuing tribunal convinced the Drafting Committee to add this exception to the basic principle of CEJ to modify.

The other side of the coin follows logically. Just as Subsection (a) defines the retention of continuing, exclusive jurisdiction, by clear implication the subsection also identifies how jurisdiction to modify may be lost. That is, if all the relevant persons—the obligor, the individual obligee, and the child—have permanently left the issuing State, the issuing State no longer has an appropriate nexus with the parties or child to justify the exercise of jurisdiction to modify its child-support order. *See In re Marriage of Erickson*, Wash. App. Div. 3 2000, 991 P.2d 123, 98 (Wash. App. 2000); *Groseth v. Groseth*, 600 N.W.2d 159

(Neb. 1999). Further, the issuing tribunal has no current information about the factual circumstances of anyone involved, and the taxpayers of that State have no reason to expend public funds on the process. Note, however, that the original order of the issuing tribunal remains valid and enforceable. That order is in effect not only in the issuing State but also in those States in which the order has been registered. It also may be registered and enforced in additional States even after the issuing State has lost its power to modify its order, *see* Sections 601–604, *infra*. The original order remains in effect until it is properly modified in accordance with the narrow terms of Sections 609–612, *infra*.

Subsection (b)(1), reworded in 2003, explicitly states that the issuing State may also lose its continuing, exclusive jurisdiction to modify if the parties consent in a record for another State to assume jurisdiction to modify (even though one of the parties or the child continues to reside in the issuing State). Filing of the record in the issuing State divests the issuing tribunal of its CEJ. *See Peace v. Peace*, 737 A.2d 1164 (N.J. Super. 1999). The Drafting Committee anticipated that such an agreement would seldom occur because of the almost universal desire of each party to prefer his or her local tribunal; but, the Committee also believed that the parties should be allowed to agree upon an alternate forum if they choose to do so. The 2003 rewording of this provision also makes this procedure available in a situation in which all the parties and the child have left the issuing State and are in agreement that a tribunal of the State in which only the movant resides shall assume modification jurisdiction.

Although Subsections (a) and (b) identify the methods for the retention and the loss of continuing, exclusive jurisdiction by the issuing tribunal, this section does not confer jurisdiction to modify on another tribunal. Modification requires that a tribunal have personal jurisdiction over the parties and meet other criteria as provided in Sections 609 through 615, *infra*.

Leading Case

Thompson v. Thompson, 893 S.W.2d 301 (Tex. App.—Houston [1st Dist.] 1995, no writ) (Texas cannot modify URESA support order because Indiana has continuing jurisdiction)

---

§ 159.206. Continuing Jurisdiction to Enforce Child Support Order.

(a) A tribunal of this state **that has issued a child support order consistent with the law of this state** may serve as an initiating tribunal to request a tribunal of another state to enforce:

(1) the order, if the order:

(A) is the controlling order; and

(B) has not been modified by a tribunal of another state that assumed jurisdiction under the Uniform Interstate Family Support Act; or

(2) a money judgment for support arrearages and interest on the order accrued before a determination that an order of another state is the controlling order [~~or modify a support order issued in that state~~].

(b) A tribunal of this state having continuing[~~, exclusive~~] jurisdiction over a support order may act as a responding tribunal to enforce [~~or modify~~] the order. [~~If a party subject to the tribunal's continuing, exclusive jurisdiction no longer resides in the issuing state, in subsequent proceedings the tribunal may apply Section 159.316 to receive evidence from another state and Section 159.318 to obtain discovery through a tribunal of another state.~~

[~~(c) A tribunal of this state that lacks continuing, exclusive jurisdiction over a spousal support order may not serve as a responding tribunal to modify a spousal support order of another state.~~]

Commissioners' Official Comment to UIFSA Section 206

This section is the correlative of the continuing, exclusive jurisdiction asserted in the preceding section. It makes the relatively subtle distinction between the CEJ "to modify a support order" established in Section 205 and the "continuing jurisdiction to enforce" established in this section. A keystone of UIFSA is that the power to enforce the order of the issuing State is not "exclusive" with that State. Rather, on request one or more responding States may also exercise authority to enforce the order of the issuing State. Secondly, under the one-order-at-a-time system, the validity and enforceability of the controlling order continues unabated until it is fully complied with, unless it is replaced by a modified order issued in accordance with the standards established by Sections 609–615. That is, even if the individual parties and the child no longer reside in the issuing State, the controlling order remains in effect and may be enforced by the issuing State or any responding State without regard to the fact that the potential for its modification and replacement exists. The 2003 amendments to Subsection (a) authorize the issuing tribunal to initiate a request for enforcement of its order by a tribunal of another State if its order is controlling, *see* Section 207, or to request reconciliation of the arrears and interest due on its order if another order is controlling.

Subsection (b) reiterates that the issuing State has jurisdiction to serve as a responding State to enforce its own order at the request of another State.

The 2003 amendments moved the second sentence in Subsection (b) to Section 210, *infra*, and moved Subsection (c) to Section 211, *infra*.

---

§ 159.207. Determination of Controlling Child Support Order.

(a) If a proceeding is brought under this chapter and only one tribunal has issued a child support order, the order of that tribunal controls and must be so recognized.

(b) If a proceeding is brought under this chapter and two or more child support orders have been issued by tribunals of this state or another state with regard to the same obligor and **same** child, a tribunal of this state **having personal jurisdiction over both the obligor and individual obligee** shall apply the following rules **to determine by order** [~~in determining~~] which order **controls** [~~to recognize for purposes of continuing, exclusive jurisdiction~~]:

(1) if only one of the tribunals would have continuing, exclusive jurisdiction under this chapter, the order of that tribunal controls and must be so recognized;

(2) if more than one of the tribunals would have continuing, exclusive jurisdiction under this chapter:

(A) [~~,~~] an order issued by a tribunal in the current home state of the child controls **if an order is issued in the current home state of the child; or**

(B) the order most recently issued controls [~~and must be so recognized, but~~] if an order has not been issued in the current home state of the child[~~, the order most recently issued controls and must be so recognized~~]; and

(3) if none of the tribunals would have continuing, exclusive jurisdiction under this chapter, the tribunal of this state [~~having jurisdiction over the parties~~] shall issue a child support order that controls [~~and must be so recognized~~].

(c) If two or more child support orders have been issued for the same obligor and **same** child [~~and if the obligor or the individual obligee resides in this state~~], **on request of** a party **who is an individual or a support enforcement agency**, [~~may request~~] a tribunal of this state **having personal jurisdiction over both the obligor and the obligee who is an individual shall** [~~to~~] determine which order controls [~~and must be so recognized~~] under Subsection (b). The request **may be filed:**

(1) with a registration for enforcement or registration for modification under Subchapter G; or

(2) as a separate proceeding [~~must be accompanied by a certified copy of every support order in effect. The requesting party shall give notice of the request to each party whose rights may be affected by the determination~~].

(d) **A request to determine the controlling order must be accompanied by a copy of each child support order in effect and the applicable record of payments. The requesting party shall give notice of the request to each party whose rights may be affected by the determination.**

(e) The tribunal that issued the controlling order under Subsection (a), (b), or (c) [~~is the tribunal that~~] has continuing[~~, exclusive~~] jurisdiction **to the extent provided** under Section 159.205 **or 159.206**.

(f) [~~(e)~~] A tribunal of this state that determines by order **which order is** [~~the identity of~~] the controlling order under Subsection (b)(1) or (2) **or Subsection (c)** or that issues a new controlling order under Subsection (b)(3) shall state in that order:

(1) the basis upon which the tribunal made its determination;

(2) the amount of prospective child support, if any; and

(3) the total amount of consolidated arrearages and accrued interest, if any, under the orders after all payments are credited under Section 159.209.

(g) [~~(f)~~] Within 30 days after issuance of an order determining **which order is** [~~the identity of~~] the controlling order, the party obtaining the order shall file a certified copy of **the controlling order in** [~~it with~~] each tribunal that issued or registered an earlier order of child support. A party **or support enforcement agency that** [~~who~~] obtains the order and fails to file a certified copy **of the order** is subject to appropriate sanctions by a tribunal in which the issue of failure to file arises. The failure to file does not affect the validity or enforceability of the controlling order.

(h) An order that has been determined to be the controlling order, or a judgment for consolidated support arrearages and interest issued under this section, must be recognized in a proceeding under this chapter.

Commissioners' Official Comment to UIFSA Section 207

Next to the introduction of the concept of continuing exclusive jurisdiction in Section 205, *supra*, the most dramatic founding principle of UIFSA was to establish a system whereby the multiple orders created by URESA and RURESA could be reconciled in the transition from a world with multiple child-support orders to a one-order-at-a-time world. This principle introduced by Section 207 was subsequently incorporated into the requirements of 28 U.S.C. 1738B, Full Faith and Credit for Child Support Orders, a.k.a. FFCCSOA.

Sections 207 and 209–210 are designed to span the gulf between the one-order system created by UIFSA and the multiple-order system previously in place under RURESA and URESA. UIFSA necessarily must provide transitional procedures for the eventual elimination of existing multiple support orders in an expeditious and efficient manner. But, even though all U.S. jurisdictions enacted UIFSA by 1998, many years will pass before its one-order system will be completely in place. Multiple orders covering the same parties and child number in the hundreds of thousands; it can be reasonably anticipated that some of these orders will continue in effect until nearly 2020. To begin the journey toward a one-order system, however, this section provides a relatively simple procedure designed to identify a single viable order that will be entitled to prospective enforcement in every UIFSA State.

Subsection (a) declares that if only one child support order exists, it is to be denominated the controlling order, irrespective of when and where it was issued and whether any of the individual parties or the child continue to reside in the issuing State.

Subsection (b) establishes the priority scheme for recognition and prospective enforcement of a single order among existing multiple orders regarding the same obligor, obligee, and child. The 2003 amendment to Subsection (b) clarifies that a tribunal requested to sort out the multiple orders and determine which one will be prospectively controlling of future payments must have personal jurisdiction over the litigants in order to ensure that its decision is binding on all concerned. For UIFSA to function, one order must be denominated as the controlling order, and its issuing tribunal must be recognized as having continuing, exclusive jurisdiction. In choosing among existing multiple orders, none of which can be distinguished as being in conflict with the principles of UIFSA, Subsection (b)(1) gives first priority to an order issued by the only tribunal that is entitled to continuing, exclusive jurisdiction under the terms of UIFSA, *i.e.,* an individual party or the child continues to reside in that State and no other issuing State meets this criterion. If two or more tribunals would have continuing, exclusive jurisdiction under the Act, Subsection (b)(2) first looks to the tribunal of the child's current home State. If that State has not issued a support order, Subsection (b)(2) looks next to the order most recently issued. Finally, Subsection (b)(3) provides that if none of the existing multiple orders are entitled to be denominated as the controlling order because none of the preceding priorities apply, the forum tribunal is directed to issue a new order, given that it has personal jurisdiction over the obligor and obligee. The new order becomes the controlling order, establishes the continuing, exclusive jurisdiction of the tribunal, and fixes the support obligation and its nonmodifiable aspects, primarily duration of support, *see* Sections 604 and 611(c), *infra.* The rationale for creating a new order to replace existing multiple orders is that there is no valid reason to prefer the terms of any one of the multiple orders over another in the absence of a fact situation described in Subsections (b)(1) or (b)(2).

As originally promulgated, UIFSA did not come to grips with whether existing multiple orders issued by different States might be entitled to full faith and credit without regard to the determination of the controlling order under the Act. The drafters took the position that state law, however uniform, could not interfere with the ultimate interpretation of a constitutional directive. Fortunately, this question has almost certainly been mooted by the 1996 amendment to 28 U.S.C. Section 1738B, Full Faith and Credit for Child Support Orders. Congress incorporated the multiple order recognition provisions of Section 207 of UIFSA into FFCCSOA virtually word for word in the PERSONAL RESPONSIBILITY AND WORK OPPORTUNITY RECONCILIATION ACT OF 1996. Pub. L. 104–193, Aug. 22, 1996, 110 Stat. 2221.

It is not altogether clear whether the terms of UIFSA apply to a strictly intrastate case; that is, a situation in which multiple child support orders have been issued by multiple tribunals of a single State and all parties and the child continue to reside in that State. This is not an uncommon situation, often traceable to the intrastate applicability of RURESA. A literal reading of the statutory language suggests the section applies. Further, FFCCSOA does not make a distinction regarding the tribunals that issued multiple orders. If multiple orders have been issued by different tribunals in the home State of the child, most likely the most recent will be recognized as the controlling order, notwithstanding the fact that UIFSA Section 207(b)(2)(B) and FFCCSOA 42 U.S.C. Section 1738B(f)(3) literally do not apply. At the very least, this section, together with FFCCSOA, provide a template for resolving such conflicts.

Subsection (c), added in 1996, clarifies that any party or a support enforcement agency may request a tribunal of the forum State to identify the controlling order. That party is directed to fully inform the tribunal of all existing child support orders.

The 2003 addition of new Subsection (d) is to assure the tribunal is furnished with all the information needed to make a proper determination of the controlling order as well as the information needed to make a calculation of the consolidated arrears. The party or support enforcement agency requesting the determination of controlling order and determination of consolidated arrears is also required to notify all other parties and entities who may have an interest in either of those determinations. Those with such an interest most likely are support agencies and the obligee.

Relettered Subsection (e) provides that the determination of the controlling order under this section has the effect of establishing the tribunal with continuing, exclusive jurisdiction; only the order of that tribunal is entitled to prospective enforcement by a sister State.

Relettered Subsection (f) directs the forum tribunal to identify the details upon which it makes its determination of the controlling order. In addition, the tribunal is also directed to state specifically the amount of the prospective support, and to reconcile and consolidate the arrears and interest due on all of the multiple orders to the extent possible.

The party obtaining the determination is directed by relettered Subsection (g) to notify all interested tribunals of the decision after the fact. Although tribunals need not be given original notice of the proceeding, all tribunals that have contributed an order to the determination must be informed regarding which order was determined to be controlling, and should also be informed of the consolidated arrears and interest so that the extent of possible subsequent enforcement will be known with regard to each of the orders. The Act does not deal with the resolution of potential conflicting claims regarding arrears; this is left to case-by-case decisions or to federal regulation.

Section 207 presumes that the parties are accorded notice and opportunity to be heard by the tribunal. It also presumes that the tribunal will be fully informed about all existing orders when it is requested to determine which one of the existing multiple child support orders is to be accorded prospective enforcement. If this does not occur and one or more existing orders is not considered by the tribunal, the finality of its decision is likely to turn on principles of estoppel on a case-by-case basis. Finally, new Subsection (h), added in 2003, affirms the concept that when a fully informed tribunal makes a determination of the controlling order for prospective enforcement, or renders a judgment for the amount of the consolidated arrears, the decision is entitled to full faith and credit.

---

§ 159.208. Child Support Orders for Two or More Obligees.

In responding to [~~multiple~~] registrations or petitions for enforcement of two or more child support orders in effect at the same time with regard to the same obligor and different individual obligees, at least one of which was issued by a tribunal of another state, a tribunal of this state shall enforce those orders in the same manner as if the [~~multiple~~] orders had been issued by a tribunal of this state.

Commissioners' Official Comment to UIFSA Section 208

Multiple orders may involve two or more families of the same obligor. Although all such orders are entitled to enforcement, practical difficulties frequently exist. For example, full enforcement of each of the multiple orders may exceed the maximum allowed for income withholding. The federal statute, 42 U.S.C. Section 666(b)(1), requires that to be eligible for the federal funding for enforcement, States must provide a ceiling for child support withholding expressed in a percentage that may not exceed the federal consumer credit code limitations on wage garnishment, 15 U.S.C. Section 1673(b). In order to allocate resources between competing families, UIFSA refers to state law. The basic principle is that one or more foreign orders for the support of an out-of-state family of the obligor, and one or more orders for an in-state family, are all of equal dignity. In allocating payments to different obligees, every child support order should be treated as if it had been issued by a tribunal of the forum State.

---

§ 159.209. Credit for Payments.

A tribunal of this state shall credit amounts [~~Amounts~~] collected [~~and credited~~] for a particular period under a support order [~~issued by a tribunal of another state must be credited~~] against the amounts **owed** [~~accruing or accrued~~] for the same period under **any other child** [~~a~~] support order **for support of the same child** issued by **a** [~~the~~] tribunal of this **or another** state.

Commissioners' Official Comment to UIFSA Section 209

Because of the multiple orders possible under the former reciprocal acts, RURESA and URESA, the predecessor section was nominally concerned with insuring that payments made on a particular order were credited toward the amounts due on all other orders. As a practical matter, however, very little attention was paid to that provision. No mechanism was available to reconcile payments on multiple orders other than the obligor's record keeping, if any.

Quite a different situation is currently in place throughout the nation. The advent and development of IV–D agencies has brought collection of arrears and interest on those arrears to the forefront. Computerized exchange of complex information is now almost instantaneously available in many cases. Thus, deciphering the financial information available to accord credit for payment on one order against other orders is possible to a degree unknown in the days of RURESA. For example, full payment of $300 on an order of State C earns a 100% pro tanto discharge of the current support owed on a $200 order of State A, and a 75% credit against a $400 order of State B. Crediting payments against arrears on multiple orders is more complex, and is subject to different constructions in various states.

Under the one-order system of UIFSA, an obligor ultimately will be ordered to pay only one sum-certain amount for current support, and a sum certain to reduce arrears and interest, if any. Nonetheless, multiple orders will exist for several years into the future. Moreover, even under a one-order system, more than one entity may be engaged in collecting past arrears. Ultimately those collections must be reported to a single entity with final accounting responsibility. Finally, because the nature of human enterprise is such that mistakes are inevitable, at least on occasion multiple orders will continue to be issued in error.

The issuing tribunal is ultimately responsible for the overall control of the enforcement methods employed and for accounting for the payments made on its order from multiple sources. Until that scheme is fully in place, however, it will be necessary to continue to mandate pro tanto credit for actual payments made against all existing orders.

The rewording of this section in 2003 reaffirms the simultaneous accrual and simultaneous credit approach, and provides further substance to the directive in Section 207(f) that a tribunal making a determination of the consolidated arrears must use this approach.

---

§ 159.210. Applicability to Nonresident Subject to Personal Jurisdiction.

(a) Except as provided by Subsection (b), Subchapters D–H do not apply to a tribunal of this state exercising personal jurisdiction over a nonresident in a proceeding under this chapter or under other law of this state relating to a support order or recognizing a support order of a foreign country or political subdivision on the basis of comity. The tribunal shall apply the procedural and substantive law of this state in a proceeding described by this subsection.

(b) Notwithstanding Subsection (a), a tribunal of this state exercising personal jurisdiction over a nonresident in a proceeding under this chapter or under other law of this state relating to a support order or recognizing a support order of a foreign country or political subdivision on the basis of comity may:

(1) receive evidence from another state as provided by Section 159.316;

(2) communicate with a tribunal of another state as provided by Section 159.317; and

(3) obtain discovery through a tribunal of another state as provided by Section 159.318.

Commissioners' Official Comment to UIFSA Section 210

Although this section is a product of the 2003 amendments, in fact it combines provisions formerly found in Sections 202 and 206(b) into a single, comprehensive provision. Section 202 took account of the fact that assertion of long-arm jurisdiction over a nonresident results in a one-state proceeding, notwithstanding the fact that the parties reside in different States. Section 206(b) made a vital contribution to the exercise of continuing, exclusive jurisdiction to modify and continuing jurisdiction to enforce support orders if one of the parties to an original proceeding in the forum State subsequently left the State after the initial support order was issued. Indeed, it is far more common for a support order to be issued in conjunction with a divorce or determination of parentage in which both the obligor and obligee are residents of the forum than to be issued as a result of an assertion of long-arm jurisdiction. Note that either the petitioner or the respondent may be the nonresident party (either of whom may be the obligor or the obligee). And, also note that absent this provision the ordinary intrastate substantive and procedural law of the forum would apply to either fact situation without reference to the fact that one of the parties is a nonresident. In sum, whether the matter at hand involves establishment of an original support order or enforcement or modification of an existing order. If one of the parties resides outside the forum State, the nonresident may avail himself or herself of the special evidentiary and discovery provisions provided by UIFSA.

Except for the three sections specified, the provisions of UIFSA—its title labels it an interstate act—are not applicable to an intrastate proceeding. The first exception allows the tribunal to apply the special rules of evidence and procedure of Section 316 in order to facilitate decision-making when one party resides in another State. The improved interstate exchange of information enables the nonresident to participate as fully as possible in the proceedings without the necessity of personally appearing in the forum State. The same considerations account for authorizing inter-tribunal communications as per Section 317. Finally, the two-state discovery procedures of Section 318 are made applicable in a one-state proceeding when a foreign tribunal can assist in that process. In all other situations, the ordinary substantive and procedural law of the forum State applies to a one-state proceeding. In sum, the parties and the tribunal in a one-state case may utilize those two-state procedures that contribute to economy, efficiency, and fair play.

Finally, the 2003 amendment recognizes and extends the operation of these evidentiary and discovery provisions to a case involving a foreign support order recognized on the basis of comity.

Sec. 159.211. Continuing, Exclusive Jurisdiction to Modify Spousal Support Order.

(a) A tribunal of this state issuing a spousal support order consistent with the law of this state has continuing, exclusive jurisdiction to modify the spousal support order throughout the existence of the support obligation.

(b) A tribunal of this state may not modify a spousal support order issued by a tribunal of another state having continuing, exclusive jurisdiction over that order under the law of that state.

(c) A tribunal of this state that has continuing, exclusive jurisdiction over a spousal support order may serve as:

(1) an initiating tribunal to request a tribunal of another state to enforce the spousal support order issued in this state; or

(2) a responding tribunal to enforce or modify its own spousal support order.

Commissioners' Official Comment to UIFSA Section 211

This is not new language; a 2003 amendment moved former Section 205(f) to this stand-alone section. Complimentary provisions with regard to other aspects of CEJ over a spousal support order are also moved. An order for spousal support is treated differently than an order for child support. The issuing tribunal retains continuing, exclusive jurisdiction over an order of spousal support throughout the entire existence of the support obligation. Sections 205(f) and 206(c) state that the procedures of UIFSA are not available to a responding tribunal to modify the existing spousal support order of the issuing State. This marks a radical departure from RURESA, which treated spousal and child support orders identically. Under UIFSA, "interstate" modification of spousal support is limited to a procedure whereby a proceeding may be initiated outside of the issuing State, but only the tribunal in the original issuing State may modify the order under its law. This approach was expected to have minimal effect on actual practice, a prediction that appears to have been accurate. Interstate modification of pure spousal support was relatively rare under RURESA, and plays almost no part in the activities of support enforcement agencies.

The prohibition of modification of spousal support by a nonissuing state tribunal under UIFSA is consistent with the principle that a tribunal should apply local law to such cases to insure efficient handling and to minimize choice of law problems. Avoiding conflict of law problems is almost impossible if spousal support orders are subject to modification in a second State. For example, States take widely varying views of the effect on a spousal support order of the obligee's remarriage or nonmarital cohabitation. Making a distinction between spousal and child support is further justified because the standards for modification of child support and spousal support are very different. In most jurisdictions a dramatic improvement in the obligor's economic circumstances will have little or no relevance in a proceeding seeking an upward modification of spousal support, while a similar change in an obligor's situation typically is the primary basis for an increase in child support. This disparity is founded on a policy choice that post-divorce success of an obligor-parent should benefit the obligor's child, but not the obligor's ex-spouse.

Finally, UIFSA does not provide for shifting the continuing, exclusive jurisdiction over a spousal-support order by mutual agreement. That procedure is limited to child support under Section 205(b)(1). Note that the Act is silent rather than preclusive on the subject. If the parties wish to enter into such an agreement, it is up to the individual States to decide whether to recognize it. A waiver of continuing, exclusive jurisdiction and subsequent modification of spousal support by a tribunal of another State simply is not authorized by UIFSA, rather than prohibited.

Subchapter D. Civil Provisions of General Application

§ 159.301. Proceedings Under Chapter.

(a) Except as otherwise provided in this chapter, this subchapter applies to all proceedings under this chapter.

(b) Repealed by Acts 2003, 78th Leg., ch. 1247, § 46.

(c) An individual or a support enforcement agency may **initiate** [~~commence~~] a proceeding authorized under this chapter by filing a petition in an initiating tribunal for forwarding to a responding tribunal or by filing a petition or a comparable pleading directly in a tribunal of another state that has or that can obtain personal jurisdiction over the respondent.

Commissioners' Official Comment to UIFSA Section 301

Subsection (a) mandates application of the general provisions of this article to all UIFSA proceedings.

Subsection (b), the once controversial "road map" originally thought by the 1992 Drafting Committee to be required in order to introduce the large number of non-lawyer administrators employed by child support enforcement agencies to the intricacies of UIFSA. Given the extensive training on the Act throughout the nation, the road map no longer can be viewed as necessary.

Subsection (c) continues in a new form the basic two-state procedure long-employed by the former reciprocal acts to establish a support order in the interstate context. Direct filing of a petition in the responding State by an individual or a support enforcement agency without reference to an initiating tribunal State was introduced by UIFSA 1992. Although filing of a petition in an initiating tribunal to be forwarded to a responding tribunal is still recognized as a possible procedure, the direct filing procedure has proven to be one of the most significant improvements in efficient interstate case management. The promulgation and use of the federally mandated forms, Section 311(b), further serves to eliminate any role for the initiating tribunal.

---

§ 159.302. Proceeding by Minor Parent.

A minor parent or a guardian or other legal representative of a minor parent may maintain a proceeding on behalf of or for the benefit of the minor's child.

Commissioners' Official Comment to UIFSA Section 302

A minor parent may maintain a proceeding under UIFSA without the appointment of a guardian ad litem, even if the law of the forum jurisdiction requires a guardian for an in-state case. If a guardian or legal representative has been appointed, he or she may act on behalf of the minor's child in seeking support.

---

§ 159.303. Application of Law of State.

Except as otherwise provided in this chapter, a responding tribunal of this state shall:

(1) apply the procedural and substantive law[~~, including the rules on choice of law,~~] generally applicable to similar proceedings originating in this state and may exercise all powers and provide all remedies available in those proceedings; and

(2) determine the duty of support and the amount payable in accordance with the law and support guidelines of this state.

Commissioners' Official Comment to UIFSA Section 303

Historically States have insisted that forum law be applied to support cases whenever possible. This continues as a key principle of UIFSA. In general, a responding tribunal has the same powers in a proceeding involving interstate parties as it has in an intrastate case. This inevitably means that the Act is not self-contained; rather, it is supplemented by the forum's statutes and procedures governing support orders. To insure the efficient processing of the huge number of interstate support cases, it is vital that decision-makers apply familiar rules of local law to the maximum degree possible. This must be accomplished in a manner consistent with the overriding principle of UIFSA that enforcement is of the issuing tribunal's order, and that the responding State does not make the order its own as a condition of enforcing it.

Prior to the 2003 amendments, choice of law rules of the forum State were specifically invoked in three places; henceforth Section 604 is the sole reference to the issue.

Leading Case

In re B.C., 52 S.W.3d 926 (Tex. App.—Beaumont 2001, no pet.) (in a proceeding for arrearages, the statute of limitations of Texas or the issuing state, whichever is longer, governs)

---

§ 159.304. Duties of Initiating Tribunal.

(a) On the filing of a petition authorized by this chapter, an initiating tribunal of this state shall forward [~~three copies of~~] the petition and its accompanying documents:

(1) to the responding tribunal or appropriate support enforcement agency in the responding state; or

(2) if the identity of the responding tribunal is unknown, to the state information agency of the responding state with a request that they be forwarded to the appropriate tribunal and that receipt be acknowledged.

(b) If **requested by the responding tribunal,** a [~~responding state has not enacted the Uniform Interstate Family Support Act or a law or procedure substantially similar to that Act, a~~] tribunal of this state **shall** [~~may~~] issue a certificate or other document and make findings required by the law of the responding state. If the responding state is a foreign **country or political subdivision** [~~jurisdiction~~], the tribunal **shall** [~~may~~] specify the amount of support sought, **convert that amount into the equivalent amount in the foreign currency under the applicable official or market ex-**

change rate as publicly reported, and provide **any** other documents necessary to satisfy the requirements of the responding state.

Commissioners' Official Comment to UIFSA Section 304

Under UIFSA the role of the initiating tribunal consists of the ministerial function of forwarding the documents to the appropriate entity in the responding State for action. The initiating tribunal has no substantive legal task to perform.

Subsection (b) was designed primarily to facilitate interstate enforcement between UIFSA States and URESA and RURESA States, with some applicability to cases involving foreign jurisdictions. After the nationwide enactment of UIFSA by 1998, *see* Prefatory Note, *supra*, the subsection retains its utility only with regard to support orders of foreign nations. Supplying documentation required by a foreign jurisdiction which is not otherwise required by UIFSA procedure will continue to be appropriate in the international context for the foreseeable future. An initiating tribunal is authorized to cooperate and provide whatever information or documentation is required or requested by a foreign jurisdiction. For example, a statement of the amount of support being requested is required by Canadian provinces before a tribunal will establish a support order. The 2003 amendment adds a duty for the initiating tribunal to state the amount of foreign currency equivalent to that request; there is a corresponding duty of a responding tribunal to convert the foreign currency into dollars if the foreign initiating tribunal does not, Section 305(f).

The reference to "the applicable official or market exchange rate" takes into account the present practices of international money markets. A few countries continue to maintain an official exchange rate for their currency. The vast majority of countries recognize the fact that the value of their currency is subject to daily market fluctuations that are reported on the financial pages of many daily newspapers. Thus, in the example described above, a request for a specific amount of support in U.S. dollars, which is to be translated into Canadian dollars on a specific date, will inevitably have a variable value as the foreign currency rises or falls against the U.S. dollar.

---

§ 159.305. Duties and Powers of Responding Tribunal.

(a) When a responding tribunal of this state receives a petition or comparable pleading from an initiating tribunal or directly under Section 159.301(c), the responding tribunal shall cause the petition or pleading to be filed and notify the petitioner where and when it was filed.

(b) **Except as prohibited by other law, a** [A] responding tribunal of this state[~~, to the extent otherwise authorized by law,~~] may do one or more of the following:

(1) issue or enforce a support order, modify a child support order, **determine the controlling child support order,** or [**render a judgment to**] determine parentage;

(2) order an obligor to comply with a support order and specify the amount and the manner of compliance;

(3) order income withholding;

(4) determine the amount of any arrearages and specify a method of payment;

(5) enforce orders by civil or criminal contempt, or both;

(6) set aside property for satisfaction of the support order;

(7) place liens and order execution on the obligor's property;

(8) order an obligor to keep the tribunal informed of the obligor's current residential address, telephone number, employer, address of employment, and telephone number at the place of employment;

(9) issue a bench warrant or capias for an obligor who has failed after proper notice to appear at a hearing ordered by the tribunal and enter the bench warrant or capias in any local and state computer systems for criminal warrants;

(10) order the obligor to seek appropriate employment by specified methods;

(11) award reasonable attorney's fees and other fees and costs; and

(12) grant any other available remedy.

(c) A responding tribunal of this state shall include in a support order issued under this chapter, or in the documents accompanying the order, the calculations on which the support order is based.

(d) A responding tribunal of this state may not condition the payment of a support order issued under this chapter on compliance by a party with provisions for visitation.

(e) If a responding tribunal of this state issues an order under this chapter, the tribunal shall send a copy of the order to the petitioner and the respondent and to the initiating tribunal, if any.

(f) If requested to enforce a support order, arrearages, or a judgment or to modify a support order stated in a foreign currency, a responding tribunal of this state shall convert the amount stated in the foreign currency to the equivalent amount in dollars under the applicable official or market exchange rate as publicly reported.

Commissioners' Official Comment to UIFSA Section 305

This section establishes a wide variety of duties for a responding tribunal. It contains: ministerial functions, Subsection (a); judicial functions, Subsection (b); and, substantive rules applicable to interstate cases, Subsections (c)-(e). Because a responding tribunal may be an administrative agency rather than a court, the Act explicitly states that a tribunal is not granted powers that it does not otherwise possess under state law. For example, authority to enforce a support order by contempt generally is limited to courts.

Subsection (a) directs the filing of the documents received without regard to whether an initiating tribunal in another State was involved in forwarding the documentation. It also directs that the individual or entity requesting the filing be notified, but leaves the means of that notification to local law. The advent of a variety of swifter, and perhaps even more reliable, forms of notice in the modern era justifies the deletion of a particular form of notice. For example, many States now authorize notice by telephone facsimile (FAX), or by an express delivery service. Already many legal documents are transmitted by electronic mail (email).

Subsection (b) lists duties that, if possessed under state law in connection with in-state cases, are allocated to the responding tribunal in UIFSA cases. Thus, each subdivision purposefully avoids mention of substantive rules. For example, Subsection (b)(7) does not identify the type, nature, or priority of liens that may be issued under UIFSA. As is generally true under the Act, those details will be determined by applicable state law concerning support enforcement remedies of local orders.

Subsection (c) clarifies that the details of calculating the child support order are to be included along with the order. Local law generally requires that variation from the child support guidelines must be explained, *see* 42 U.S.C. Section 667; this requirement is extended to interstate cases.

Subsection (d) states that an interstate support order may not be conditioned on compliance with a visitation order. *Chaisson v. Ragsdale*, 914 S.W.2d 739 (Ark. 1996). While this may be at variance with state law governing intrastate cases, under a UIFSA proceeding the petitioner generally is not present before the tribunal. This distinction justifies prohibiting visitation issues from being litigated in the context of a support proceeding. All States have enacted some version of either the UCCJA or the UCCJEA providing for resolution of visitation issues in interstate cases.

Subsection (e) introduces the policy determination that the petitioner, the respondent, and the initiating tribunal, if any, shall be kept informed about actions taken by the responding tribunal.

Subsection (f) is designed to facilitate enforcement of foreign support orders.

§ 159.306. Inappropriate Tribunal.

If a petition or comparable pleading is received by an inappropriate tribunal of this state, that tribunal shall forward the pleading and accompanying documents to an appropriate tribunal in this state or another state and notify the petitioner where and when the pleading was sent.

Commissioners' Official Comment to UIFSA Section 306

This section directs a tribunal receiving UIFSA documents in error to forward the original documents to their proper destination without undue delay, whether the appropriate tribunal is located in the same State or elsewhere. This section was originally intended to apply both to initiating and responding tribunals receiving such documents, but the practical elimination of the role of initiating tribunals under modern practice now limits the notice requirement to the petitioner, *i.e.*, the individual party or support enforcement agency, that filed (or misfiled) the document directly. For example, if a tribunal is inappropriately designated as the responding tribunal, it shall forward the petition to the appropriate responding tribunal wherever located, if known, and notify the petitioner of its action. Such a procedure is much to be preferred to returning the documents to the petitioner to begin the process anew. Cooperation of this sort will facilitate the ultimate goals of the Act.

§ 159.307. Duties of Support Enforcement Agency.

(a) A support enforcement agency of this state, on request, shall provide services to a petitioner in a proceeding under this chapter.

(b) A support enforcement agency **of this state** that provides services to the petitioner [~~as appropriate~~] shall:

(1) take all steps necessary to enable an appropriate tribunal in this state or another state to obtain jurisdiction over the respondent;

(2) request an appropriate tribunal to set a date, time, and place for a hearing;

(3) make a reasonable effort to obtain all relevant information, including information as to income and property of the parties;

(4) not later than the second day, excluding Saturdays, Sundays, and legal holidays, after the date of receipt of a written notice **in a record** from an initiating, responding, or registering tribunal, send a copy of the notice to the petitioner;

(5) not later than the second day, excluding Saturdays, Sundays, and legal holidays, after the date of receipt of a written communication **in a record** from the respondent or the respondent's attorney, send a copy of the communication to the petitioner; and

(6) notify the petitioner if jurisdiction over the respondent cannot be obtained.

(c) **A support enforcement agency of this state that requests registration of a child support order in this state for enforcement or for modification shall make reasonable efforts to ensure that:**

(1) the order to be registered is the controlling order; or

(2) a request for a determination of which order is the controlling order is made in a tribunal having jurisdiction to make the determination, if two or more child support orders have been issued and a determination of the controlling order has not been made.

(d) A support enforcement agency of this state that requests registration and enforcement of a support order, arrearages, or a judgment stated in a foreign currency shall convert the amount stated in the foreign currency to the equivalent amount in dollars under the applicable official or market exchange rate as publicly reported.

(e) A support enforcement agency of this state shall issue, or request a tribunal of this state to issue, a child support order and an income-withholding order that redirects payment of current support, arrearages, and interest if requested to do so by a support enforcement agency of another state under Section 159.319.

(f) This chapter does not create or negate a relationship of attorney and client or other fiduciary relationship between a support enforcement agency or the attorney for the agency and the individual being assisted by the agency.

Commissioners' Official Comment to UIFSA Section 307

The focus of Subsection (a) is on providing services to a petitioner, and not merely on "representing" the obligee. Care should be exercised in the use of terminology given this substantial alteration of past practice under RURESA. Not only may either the obligee or the obligor request services, but that request may be in the context of the establishment of an initial child-support order, enforcement or review and adjustment of an existing child-support order, or a modification of that order (upward or downward). Note that the Act does not distinguish between child support and spousal support for purposes of providing services. Note also, that the services available may differ significantly; for example, modification of spousal support is limited to the issuing State, *see* Section 205(f), *supra*.

Subsection (b) responds to the past complaints of many petitioners that they were not properly kept informed about the progress of their requests for services.

The 2003 additions of Subsections (c) and (d) are procedural clarifications reflecting actual practice of the support agencies developed after years of experience with the Act. Subsection (c) imposes a duty on all support enforcement agencies to facilitate the UIFSA one-order world by actively searching for cases with multiple orders and obtaining a determination of the controlling order as expeditiously as possible. This agency duty correlates to new Subsection 602(d) regarding the registration process and cases with multiple orders.

Read in conjunction with Section 319, *infra*, new Subsection (e) requires the state support enforcement agency to facilitate redirection of the stream of child support in order that the payments be more efficiently received by the obligee.

Subsection (f) explicitly states that UIFSA neither creates nor rejects the establishment of an attorney-client or fiduciary relationship between the support enforcement agency and a petitioner receiving services from that agency. This highly controversial issue is left to otherwise applicable state law.

---

§ 159.308. Duty of Certain State Officials.

(a) If the attorney general determines that the support enforcement agency is neglecting or refusing to provide services to an individual, the attorney general may order the agency to perform its duties under this chapter or may provide those services directly to the individual.

(b) The governor may determine that a foreign country or political subdivision has established a reciprocal arrangement for child support with this state and take appropriate action for notification of the determination.

Commissioners' Official Comment to UIFSA Section 308

In a carryover from RURESA, Subsection (a) provides that the State Attorney General, or an alternative designated by state law, is given oversight responsibility for the diligent provision of services by the support enforcement agency and the power to seek compliance with the Act.

The 2003 addition of Subsection (b) makes clear that a State has a variety of options in determining the scope of its support enforcement program. In the absence of controlling federal action declaring a foreign jurisdiction to be a reciprocating country or political subdivision, *see* Section 102(21)(B)(i), *supra*, each State may designate an official with authority to make a statewide, binding determination recognizing a foreign country or political subdivision as having a reciprocal arrangement with the that State.

---

§ 159.309. Private Counsel.

An individual may employ private counsel to represent the individual in proceedings authorized by this chapter.

Commissioners' Official Comment to UIFSA Section 309

The right of a party to retain private counsel in a proceeding brought under UIFSA is explicitly recognized. The failure to clearly recognize that power under the prior uniform acts led to confusion and inconsistent decisions.

---

§ 159.310. Duties of State Information Agency.

(a) The Title IV–D agency is the state information agency under this chapter.

(b) The state information agency shall:

(1) compile and maintain a current list, including addresses, of the tribunals in this state that have jurisdiction under this chapter and any support enforcement agencies in this state and send a copy to the state information agency of every other state;

(2) maintain a register of **names and addresses of** tribunals and support enforcement agencies received from other states;

(3) forward to the appropriate tribunal in the **county** [~~place~~] in this state where the [~~individual~~] obligee **who is an individual** or the obligor resides, or where the

obligor's property is believed to be located, all documents concerning a proceeding under this chapter received from an initiating tribunal or the state information agency of the initiating state; and

(4) obtain information concerning the location of the obligor and the obligor's property in this state not exempt from execution, by such means as postal verification and federal or state locator services, examination of telephone directories, requests for the obligor's address from employers, and examination of governmental records, including, to the extent not prohibited by other law, those relating to real property, vital statistics, law enforcement, taxation, motor vehicles, driver's licenses, and social security.

Commissioners' Official Comment to UIFSA Section 310

Subsection (a) identifies the central information agency. Subsection (b) details the duties of that agency insofar as interstate proceedings are concerned. Subsection (b)(4) does not provide independent access to the information sources or to the governmental documents listed. Because States have different requirements and limitations concerning such access based on differing views of the privacy interests of individual citizens, the agency is directed to use all lawful means under the relevant state law to obtain and disseminate information.

---

§ 159.311. Pleadings and Accompanying Documents.

(a) **In a proceeding under this chapter, a** [~~A~~] petitioner seeking to establish [~~or modify~~] a support order, [~~or~~] to determine parentage**, or to register and modify a support order of another state** [~~in a proceeding under this chapter~~] must **file a** [~~verify the~~] petition. Unless otherwise ordered under Section 159.312, the petition or accompanying documents must provide, so far as known, the name, residential address, and social security numbers of the obligor and the obligee **or the parent and alleged parent** and the name, sex, residential address, social security number, and date of birth of each child for **whose benefit** [~~whom~~] support is sought **or whose parentage is to be determined**. **Unless filed at the time of registration, the** [~~The~~] petition must be accompanied by a [~~certified~~] copy of any support order **known to have been issued by another tribunal** [~~in effect~~]. The petition may include any other information that may assist in locating or identifying the respondent.

(b) The petition must specify the relief sought. The petition and accompanying documents must conform substantially with the requirements imposed by the forms mandated by federal law for use in cases filed by a support enforcement agency.

Commissioners' Official Comment to UIFSA Section 311

This section establishes the basic requirements for drafting and filing interstate pleadings. Subsection (a) should be read in conjunction with Section 312, which provides for the confidentiality of certain information if disclosure is likely to result in harm to a party or a child. The 2003 amendments are directed at improving the efficiency of the process. Illustrative of that goal is the requirement that all known support orders be attached to the petition for relief, coupled with the elimination of the requirement that such copies be certified. If a dispute arises over the authenticity of a purported order, the tribunal must, of necessity, sort out conflicting claims at that time. Another improvement is the deletion of the requirement for verified pleadings originated in URESA and carried forward in the original version of UIFSA.

Subsection (b) provides authorization for the use of the federally authorized forms promulgated in connection with the IV–D child support enforcement program and mandates substantial compliance with those forms. Although the use of other forms is not prohibited, standardized documents have resulted in substantial improvement in the efficient processing of UIFSA proceedings.

---

§ 159.312. Nondisclosure of Information in Exceptional Circumstances.

If a party alleges in an affidavit or pleading under oath [~~On a finding, which may be made ex parte,~~] that the health, safety, or liberty of a party or child would be **jeopardized** [~~unreasonably put at risk~~] by [~~the~~] disclosure of **specific** identifying **information regarding the party or the child, the identifying information shall be sealed and may not be disclosed to the other party or to the public. After a hearing in which a tribunal considers the health, safety, or liberty of the party or the child, the** [~~or if an existing order so provides, a~~] tribunal **may** [~~shall~~] order **disclosure of** [~~that the address of the child or party or other identifying~~] information **if the tribunal determines that the disclosure serves the interests of justice** [~~not be disclosed in a pleading or other document filed in a proceeding under this chapter~~].

Commissioners' Official Comment to UIFSA Section 312

Derived from the UNIFORM CHILD CUSTODY JURISDICTION AND ENFORCEMENT ACT, Section 209. Information To Be Submitted to Court. This section is the latest version of the statutory formulation originally developed in UIFSA 1992. Public awareness of and sensitivity to the dangers of domestic violence has significantly increased since interstate enforcement of support originated. This section authorizes confidentiality in instances where there is a serious risk of domestic violence or child abduction. Although local law generally governs the conduct of the forum tribunal, state law may not provide for maintaining secrecy about the exact whereabouts of a litigant or other information ordinarily required to be disclosed under state law, i.e., Social Security number of the parties or the child. If so, this section creates a confidentiality provision that is particularly appropriate in the light of the intractable problems associated with interstate parental kidnapping, *see* the Parental Kidnapping Prevention Act (PKPA), 28 U.S.C. Section 1738A.

---

§ 159.313. Costs and Fees.

(a) The petitioner may not be required to pay a filing fee or other costs.

(b) If an obligee prevails, a responding tribunal may assess against an obligor filing fees, reasonable attorney's fees, other costs, and necessary travel and other reasonable expenses incurred by the obligee and the obligee's witnesses. The tribunal may not assess fees, costs, or expenses against the obligee or the support enforcement agency of either the initiating state or the responding state, except as provided by other law. Attorney's fees may be taxed as costs and may be ordered paid directly to the attorney, who may enforce the order in the attorney's own name. Payment of support owed to the obligee has priority over fees, costs, and expenses.

(c) The tribunal shall order the payment of costs and reasonable attorney's fees if it determines that a hearing was requested primarily for delay. In a proceeding pursuant to Sections 159.601 through 159.608, a hearing is presumed to have been requested primarily for delay if a registered support order is confirmed or enforced without change.

Commissioners' Official Comment to UIFSA Section 313

Under UIFSA either the obligor or the obligee may file a proceeding or seek services from a support enforcement agency, Subsection (a) permits either party to file without payment of a filing fee or other costs. Subsection (b), however, provides that only the support obligor may be assessed the authorized costs and fees.

Subsection (c) provides a sanction to deal with a frivolous contest regarding compliance with an interstate withholding order, registration of a support order, or comparable delaying tactics regarding an appropriate enforcement remedy.

§ 159.314. Limited Immunity of Petitioner.

(a) Participation by a petitioner in a proceeding **under this chapter** before a responding tribunal, whether in person, by private attorney, or through services provided by the support enforcement agency, does not confer personal jurisdiction over the petitioner in another proceeding.

(b) A petitioner is not amenable to service of civil process while physically present in this state to participate in a proceeding under this chapter.

(c) The immunity granted by this section does not extend to civil litigation based on acts unrelated to a proceeding under this chapter committed by a party while present in this state to participate in the proceeding.

Commissioners' Official Comment to UIFSA Section 314

Under Subsection (a), direct or indirect participation in a UIFSA proceeding does not subject a petitioner to an assertion of personal jurisdiction over the petitioner by the forum State in other litigation between the parties. The primary object of this prohibition is to preclude joining disputes over child custody and visitation with the establishment, enforcement, or modification of child support. This prohibition strengthens the ban on visitation litigation established in Section 305(d). A petition for affirmative relief under UIFSA limits the jurisdiction of the tribunal to the boundaries of the support proceeding. In sum, proceedings under UIFSA are not suitable vehicles for the relitigation of all of the issues arising out of a foreign divorce or custody cases. Only enforcement or modification of the support portion of such decrees or orders are relevant. Other issues, such as custody and visitation, or matters relating to other aspect of the divorce decree, are collateral and have no place in a UIFSA proceeding. *Chaisson v. Ragsdale*, 914 S.W.2d 739 (Ark. 1996).

Subsection (b) grants a litigant a variety of limited immunity from service of process during the time that party is physically present in a State for a UIFSA proceeding. The immunity provided is in no way comparable to diplomatic immunity, however, which should be clear from reading Subsection (c) in conjunction with the other subsections.

Subsection (c) does not extend immunity to civil litigation unrelated to the support proceeding which stems from contemporaneous acts committed by a party while present in the State for the support litigation. For example, a petitioner involved in an automobile accident or a contract dispute over the cost of lodging while present in the State does not have immunity from a civil suit on those issues.

§ 159.315. Nonparentage as Defense.

A party whose parentage of a child has been previously determined by or under law may not plead nonparentage as a defense to a proceeding under this chapter.

Commissioners' Official Comment to UIFSA Section 315

Arguably this section does no more than restate the basic principle of *res judicata*. However, there is a great variety of state law regarding presumptions of parentage and available defenses after a prior determination of parentage. As long as a proceeding is brought in an appropriate forum, this section is intended neither to discourage nor encourage collateral attacks in situations in which the law of a foreign jurisdiction is at significant odds with local law. If a collateral attack on a parentage decree is permissible under the law of the issuing jurisdiction, such a proceeding must be pursued in that forum and not in a UIFSA proceeding.

In sum, this section mandates that a parentage decree rendered by another tribunal "pursuant to law" is not subject to collateral attack in a UIFSA proceeding. *State v. Hanson*, 725 So.2d 514 (La. App. 1998). Of course, an attack on an alleged final order based on a fundamental constitutional defect in the parentage decree is permissible in the forum State. For example, a responding tribunal may find that a foreign tribunal acted unconstitutionally by denying a party due process because of a failure of notice and opportunity to be heard or a lack of personal jurisdiction over a party who did not answer or appear. Insofar as the latter ground is concerned, the universal enactment of the long-arm statute asserting personal jurisdiction over a respondent if the child "may have been conceived" in the forum State may greatly reduce successful attacks on a parentage determinations, see Section 201(a)(6), *supra*.

Similarly, the law of the issuing State may provide for a determination of parentage based on certain specific acts of the obligor, such as voluntarily acknowledging parentage as a substitute for a decree. UIFSA also is neutral regarding a collateral attack on such a parentage determination filed in the issuing State. In the meantime, however, the responding tribunal must give effect to such an act of acknowledgment of parentage if it is recognized as determinative in the issuing State. The consistent theme is that a collateral attack on a parentage determination cannot be made in a UIFSA proceeding other than on fundamental due process grounds.

---

§ 159.316. Special Rules of Evidence and Procedure.

(a) The physical presence of **a nonresident party who is an individual** [~~the petitioner~~] in a [~~responding~~] tribunal of this state is not required for the establishment, enforcement, or modification of a support order or the rendition of a judgment determining parentage.

(b) **An** [~~A verified petition,~~] affidavit, **a** document substantially complying with federally mandated forms, **or** [~~and~~] a document incorporated by reference in **an affidavit or document, that would** [~~the petition, affidavit, or document,~~] not **be** [~~excluded~~] under the hearsay rule if given in person, **is** [~~are~~] admissible in evidence if given under **penalty of perjury** [~~oath~~] by a party or witness residing in another state.

(c) A copy of the record of child support payments certified as a true copy of the original by the custodian of the record may be forwarded to a responding tribunal. The copy is evidence of facts asserted in it and is admissible to show whether payments were made.

(d) Copies of bills for testing for parentage and for prenatal and postnatal health care of the mother and child that are furnished to the adverse party not less than 10 days before the date of trial are admissible in evidence to prove the amount of the charges billed and that the charges were reasonable, necessary, and customary.

(e) Documentary evidence **transmitted** [~~sent~~] from another state to a tribunal of this state by telephone, telecopier, or another means that does not provide an original **record** [~~writing~~] may not be excluded from evidence on an objection based on the means of transmission.

(f) In a proceeding under this chapter, a tribunal of this state **shall** [~~may~~] permit a party or witness residing in another state to be deposed or to testify by telephone, audiovisual means, or other electronic means at a designated tribunal or other location in that state. A tribunal of this state shall cooperate with a tribunal of another state in designating an appropriate location for the deposition or testimony.

(g) If a party called to testify at a civil hearing refuses to answer on the ground that the testimony may be self-incriminating, the trier of fact may draw an adverse inference from the refusal.

(h) A privilege against disclosure of communications between spouses does not apply in a proceeding under this chapter.

(i) The defense of immunity based on the relationship of husband and wife or parent and child does not apply in a proceeding under this chapter.

Commissioners' Official Comment to UIFSA Section 316

This section combines many time-tested procedures with additional innovative methods for gathering evidence in interstate cases. The amendment to Subsection (a) ensures that a nonresident petitioner or a nonresident respondent may fully participate in a proceeding under the Act without being required to appear personally. This was always the intent of the provision, but the text was ambiguous in this regard.

Subsections (b) through (f) greatly expand the special rules of evidence originally propounded in RURESA which are designed to take into account the virtually unique nature of the interstate proceedings under this Act. These sections provide exceptions to the otherwise guiding principle of UIFSA, *i.e.*, local procedural and substantive law should apply. Because the out-of-state party, and that party's witnesses, necessarily do not ordinarily appear in person at the hearing, deviation from the ordinary rules of evidence is justified in order to assure that the tribunal will have available to it the maximum amount of information on which to base its decision. The intent throughout these subsections is to eliminate by statute as many potential hearsay problems as possible in interstate litigation, with the goal of providing each party with the means to present evidence, even if not physically present. *See Attorney General v. Litten*, 999 S.W.2d 74 (Tex. App. 1999); *State ex rel. T.L.R. v. R.W.T.*, 737 So.2d 688 (La. 1999).

Subsection (d) provides a simplified means for proving health care expenses related to the birth of a child. Because ordinarily these charges are not in dispute, this is designed to obviate the cost of having health care providers appear in person or of obtaining affidavits of business records from each provider.

Perhaps the most dramatic of the 2003 amendments affecting these special rules of evidence is the change of a single word. The authorization in Subsection (f) of telephonic or audiovisual testimony in depositions and in hearing now substitutes the word "shall" for the word "may." Adoption by the States may herald the day when every relevant court room will be equipped with a speaker phone, at the minimum, if not cameras and audiovisual receivers. This amendment will also eliminate decisions such as *Schwier v. Bernstein*, 734 So.2d 531 (Fla. App. 1999), which construed the use of electronic transmission of testimony to be wholly within the discretion of the tribunal. On a related track, the 2003 amendments to Subsection (b): (1) recognize the pervasive effect of the federal forms promulgated by the Office of Child Support Enforcement, HHS; and (2) replace the necessity of swearing to a document "under oath" with the simpler requirement that the document be provided "under penalty of perjury," as is required by federal income tax form 1040.

Subsections (e) and (f) encourage tribunals and litigants to take advantage of modern methods of communication in interstate support litigation; most dramatically, the out-of-state party is authorized to testify by telephone and supply documents by fax. One of the most useful applications of these subsections has been the combining of (c) and (e) to provide an enforcing tribunal with up-to-date information concerning the amount of arrears.

Subsection (g) codifies the rule in effect in many States that in civil litigation an adverse inference may be drawn from a litigant's silence. If a party refuses to submit to genetic testing, the refusal may be admitted into evidence and the court may resolve the question of paternity against that party on the basis of an inference that the results of the tests would have been unfavorable to the interests of the refusing party.

---

§ 159.317. Communications Between Tribunals.

A tribunal of this state may communicate with a tribunal of another state **or of a foreign country or political subdivision** in **a record** [~~writing~~], by telephone, or by **other** [~~another~~] means, to obtain information concerning the laws [~~of that state~~], the legal effect of a judgment, decree, or order of that tribunal, and the status of a proceeding in the other state**, foreign country, or political subdivision**. A tribunal of this state may furnish similar information by similar means to a tribunal of another state **or of a foreign country or political subdivision**.

Commissioners' Official Comment to UIFSA Section 317

This section authorizes communications between tribunals in order to facilitate decisions. The 2003 amendments extend the coverage of the section to tribunals of foreign nations. Broad cooperation between tribunals is permitted to expedite establishment and enforcement of a support order.

---

§ 159.318. Assistance With Discovery.

A tribunal of this state may:

(1) request a tribunal of another state to assist in obtaining discovery; and

(2) on request, compel a person over whom the tribunal has jurisdiction to respond to a discovery order issued by a tribunal of another state.

Commissioners' Official Comment to UIFSA Section 318

This section takes another logical step to facilitate interstate cooperation by enlisting the power of the forum to assist a tribunal of another State with the discovery process. The grant of authority is quite broad, enabling the tribunal of the enacting State to fashion its remedies to facilitate discovery consistent with local practice.

---

§ 159.319. Receipt and Disbursement of Payments.

(a) A support enforcement agency or tribunal of this state shall disburse promptly any amounts received under a support order, as directed by the order. The agency or tribunal shall furnish to a requesting party or tribunal of another state a certified statement by the custodian of the record of the amounts and dates of all payments received.

(b) If the obligor, the obligee who is an individual, and the child do not reside in this state, on request from the support enforcement agency of this state or another state, the support enforcement agency of this state or a tribunal of this state shall:

(1) direct that the support payment be made to the support enforcement agency in the state in which the obligee is receiving services; and

(2) issue and send to the obligor's employer a conforming income-withholding order or an administrative notice of change of payee reflecting the redirected payments.

(c) The support enforcement agency of this state on receiving redirected payments from another state under a law similar to Subsection (b) shall provide to a requesting party or a tribunal of the other state a certified statement by the custodian of the record of the amount and dates of all payments received.

Commissioners' Official Comment to UIFSA Section 319

The first sentence of Subsection (a) is truly hortatory in nature, although its principle is implemented insofar as support enforcement agencies are concerned by federal regulations promulgated by the Office of Child Support Enforcement. The second sentence confirms the duty of the agency or tribunal to furnish payment information in interstate cases.

The 2003 amendments to Subsections (b) and (c) were inspired by the federal Office of Child Support Enforcement (OCSE), U.S. Department of Health and Human Services. Support enforcement agencies are directed to cooperate in the efficient and expeditious collection and transfer of child support from obligor to obligee. States may choose whether only a tribunal may order redirection of support payments, or whether a support enforcement agency of the State is also authorized to render such an order. Under either approach, the request for such redirection that must be acted upon may only be made by a support enforcement agency in either the issuing State or another State. The basic idea is that redirection of payments will be facilitated, with the proviso that the issuing tribunal be kept informed as to the disposition of the payments made under its order.

Subchapter E. Establishment of Support Order

§ 159.401. Petition to Establish Support Order.

(a) If a support order entitled to recognition under this chapter has not been issued, a responding tribunal of this state may issue a support order if:

(1) the individual seeking the order resides in another state; or

(2) the support enforcement agency seeking the order is located in another state.

(b) The tribunal may issue a temporary child support order if **the tribunal determines that the order is appropriate and the individual ordered to pay is**:

(1) **a presumed father of the child** [~~the respondent has signed a verified statement acknowledging parentage~~];

(2) **a man petitioning to have his paternity adjudicated** [~~the respondent has been determined by or under law to be the parent~~]; [~~or~~]

(3) **a man identified as the father of the child through genetic testing;**

(4) **an alleged father who has declined to submit to genetic testing;**

(5) **a man shown by clear and convincing evidence to be the father of the child;**

(6) **an acknowledged father as provided by applicable state law;**

(7) **the mother of the child;** or

(8) **an individual who has been ordered to pay child support in a previous proceeding and the order has not been reversed or vacated** [~~there is other clear and convincing evidence that the respondent is the child's parent~~].

(c) On finding, after notice and an opportunity to be heard, that an obligor owes a duty of support, the tribunal shall issue a support order directed to the obligor and may issue other orders under Section 159.305.

Commissioners' Official Comment to UIFSA Section 401

This section authorizes a tribunal of the responding State to issue temporary and permanent support orders binding on an obligor over whom the tribunal has personal jurisdiction. UIFSA does not permit such orders to be issued when another support order exists, thereby prohibiting a second tribunal from establishing another support order and the accompanying continuing, exclusive jurisdiction over the matter, *see* Sections 205 and 206.

The 2003 rewording of Subsection (b) conforms the language to the provisions of the UNIFORM PARENTAGE ACT (2000) regarding the individual party who may be ordered to pay temporary support.

Subchapter F. Enforcement of Order of Another State Without Registration

§ 159.501. Employer's Receipt of Income–Withholding Order of Another State.

An income-withholding order issued in another state may be sent **by or on behalf of the obligee or by the support enforcement agency to the person defined as** [~~to~~] the obligor's employer under Chapter 158 without first filing a petition or comparable pleading or registering the order with a tribunal of this state.

Commissioners' Official Comment to UIFSA Section 501

In 1984 Congress mandated that all States adopt procedures for enforcing income-withholding orders of sister States. Direct recognition by the out-of-state obligor's employer of a withholding order issued by another State long was sought by support enforcement associations and other advocacy groups. In 1992 UIFSA recognized such a procedure. The article was extensively amended in 1996, but was the subject only of clarifying amendments in 2003.

Section 501 is deliberately written in the passive voice; the Act does not restrict those who may send an income-withholding order across state lines. Although the sender will ordinarily be a child support enforcement agency or the obligee, the obligor or any other person may supply an employer with the income-withholding order. "Sending a copy" of a withholding order to an employer is clearly distinguishable from "service" of that order on the same employer. Service of an order necessarily intends to invoke a tribunal's authority over an employer doing business in the State. Thus, for there to be valid "service" of a withholding order on an employer in a State, the tribunal must have authority to bind the employer. In most cases, this requires the assertion of the authority of a local responding tribunal in a "registration for enforcement" proceeding. In short, the formality of "service" defeats the whole purpose of direct income withholding across state lines.

In sum, the process contemplated in this article is direct "notification" of an employer in another State of a withholding order without the involvement of initiating or responding tribunals. Therefore, receipt of a copy of a withholding order by facsimile, regular first class mail, registered or certified mail, or any other type of direct notice is sufficient to provide the requisite notice to trigger direct income withholding in the absence of a contest by the employee-obligor.

The 2003 amendments acknowledge that this process is now widely used by not only child support enforcement agencies, but also by private collection agencies or private attorneys acting on behalf of obligees.

---

§ 159.502. Employer's Compliance With Income-Withholding Order of Another State.

(a) On receipt of an income-withholding order, the obligor's employer shall immediately provide a copy of the order to the obligor.

(b) The employer shall treat an income-withholding order issued in another state that appears regular on its face as if the order had been issued by a tribunal of this state.

(c) Except as otherwise provided in Subsection (d) and Section 159.503, the employer shall withhold and distribute the funds as directed in the withholding order by complying with terms of the order that specify:

(1) the duration and amount of periodic payments of current child support, stated as a sum certain;

(2) the person [~~or agency~~] designated to receive payments and the address to which the payments are to be forwarded;

(3) medical support, whether in the form of periodic cash payments, stated as a sum certain, or ordering the obligor to provide health insurance coverage for the child under a policy available through the obligor's employment;

(4) the amount of periodic payments of fees and costs for a support enforcement agency, the issuing tribunal, and the obligee's attorney, stated as sums certain; and

(5) the amount of periodic payments of arrearages and interest on arrearages, stated as sums certain.

(d) An employer shall comply with the law of the state of the obligor's principal place of employment for withholding from income with respect to:

(1) the employer's fee for processing an income-withholding order;

(2) the maximum amount permitted to be withheld from the obligor's income; and

(3) the times within which the employer must implement the withholding order and forward the child support payment.

Commissioners' Official Comment to UIFSA Section 502

In 1996 major employers and national payroll associations urged NCCUSL to supply more detail regarding the rights and duties of an employer on receipt of an income-withholding order from another State. The Conference obliged with amendments to UIFSA establishing a series of steps for employers to track.

When an employer receives an income withholding order from another State, the first step is to notify the employee that an income withholding order has been received naming the employee as the obligor of child support, and that income withholding will begin within the time frame specified by local law. In other words, the employer will initially proceed just as if the withholding order had been received from a tribunal of the employer's State. It is the responsibility of the employee to take whatever protective measures are necessary to prevent the withholding if the employee asserts a defense as provided in Section 506, *infra*.

At this point neither an initiating nor a responding tribunal is directly involved. The withholding order may have been forwarded by the obligee, the obligee's attorney, or the out-of-state IV–D agency. In fact, there is no prohibition against anyone sending a valid copy of an income-withholding order, even a stranger to the litigation, such as the child's grandparent. Subsection (a) does not specify the method for sending this relatively informal notice for direct income withholding, but rather makes the assumption that the employer's communication to the employee regarding receipt of the order will cause an employee-obligor to act to prevent a wrongful invasion of his or her income if it is not owed as current child support or arrears.

Subsection (b) directs an employer of the enacting State to recognize a withholding order of a sister State, subject to the employee's right to contest the validity of the order or its enforcement. Prior to the promulgation of UIFSA, agencies in several States adopted a procedure of sending direct withholding requests to out-of-state employers. A contemporaneous study by the federal General Accounting Office reported that employers in a second State routinely recognized withholding orders of sister States despite an apparent lack of statutory authority to do so. UIFSA marked the first official sanction of this practice. Subsection (b) does not define "regular on its face," but the term should be liberally construed, *see U.S. v. Morton*, 467 U.S. 822 (1984) ("legal process regular on its face"). The rules governing intrastate procedure and defenses for withholding orders will apply to interstate orders.

Subsection (c) answered employers' complaints that insufficient direction for action was given by the original UIFSA. Prior to the 1996 amendments an employer was merely told to "distribute the funds as directed in the withholding order." This section clarifies the terms of the out-of-state order with which the employer must strictly comply. As a general principle, an employer is directed to comply with the specific terms contained in the order, but there are exceptions. Moreover, many income-withholding orders received at that time did not provide the detail necessary for the employer to comply with every directive. Since then, however, the long-anticipated federal forms were promulgated throughout 1997 and 1998, with periodic updates to the present time. Most recently, the text of income withholding orders for child support is fast becoming subject to a nationwide norm. To the extent that an order is silent, the employer is not required to respond to unstated demands of the issuing State. Formerly, employers often were so concerned about ambiguous or incomplete orders that they telephoned child support enforcement agencies in other States to attempt to understand and comply with unstated terms. Employers should not be expected to become investigators or shoulder the responsibility of learning the law of 50 States.

Subsection (c)(1) directs that the amount and duration of periodic payments of current child support must be stated in a sum certain in order to elicit compliance. The duration of the support obligation is fixed by the controlling order and should be stated in the withholding order so that the employer is informed of the date on which the withholding is anticipated to terminate. The "sum certain" requirement is crucial to facilitating the employer's compliance. For example, an order for a "percentage of the obligor's net income," does not satisfy this requirement and is not entitled to compliance from an employer receiving an such an interstate income-withholding order.

Subsection (c)(2) states the obvious: information necessary for compliance must be clearly stated. For example, the destination of the payments must correspond to the destination originally designated or subsequently authorized by the issuing tribunal, such as by the redirection of payments pursuant to Section 319, *supra*. Absent such action by the issuing tribunal, no redirection by any support enforcement agency or other person or entity is authorized by this section.

Subsection (c)(3) provides that medical support for the child must be stated either by a periodic cash payment or, alternatively, by an order directing the employee-obligor to provide health insurance coverage from his employment. In the absence of an order for payment of a sum certain, an order for medical support as child support requires the employer to enroll the obligor's child for coverage if medical insurance is available through the obligor's employment. Failure to enroll the child should elicit, at the least, registration of the order for enforcement in the responding State, to be implemented by an order of a tribunal directing the employer to comply. Because the employer is so directed by the medical support order, enrollment of the child in the health care plan at the employee-obligor's expense is not dependent on the obligor's consent, any more than withholding a sum certain from the obligor's income is subject to a veto. It is up to the employee-obligor to assert any defense to prevent the employer from abiding by the medical support order.

Subsection (c)(4) identifies certain costs and fees incurred in conjunction with the support enforcement that may be added to the withholding order.

Subsection (c)(5) requires that the amount of periodic payments for arrears and interest on arrears also must be stated as a sum certain. If the one-order system is to function properly, the issuing State ultimately must be responsible to account for payments and maintain the record of arrears and interest rate on arrears. Full compliance with the support order will only be achieved when the issuing State determines that the obligation no longer exists.

Subsection (d) identifies those narrow provisions in which the law of the employee's work State applies, rather than the law of the issuing State. A large employer will almost certainly have a number of employees subject to income-withholding orders. From the employer's perspective, the procedural requirements for compliance should be uniform for all of those employees. Certain issues should be matters for the law of the employee's work State, such as the employer's fee for processing, the maximum amount to be withheld, and the time in which to comply. The latter necessarily includes the frequency with which income withholding must occur. This is also consistent with regard to the tax consideration imposed by choice of law considerations. The only element in the list of local laws identified in Subsection (d) which stirred any controversy whatsoever was the fact that the maximum amount permitted to be withheld is to be subject to the law of the employee's work State. Demands of equal treatment for all citizens of the responding State, plus the practical concern that large employers require uniform computer programming mandate this solution.

---

§ 159.503. Employer's Compliance with Two or More Income–Withholding Orders.

If an obligor's employer receives **two or more** [~~multiple~~] income-withholding orders with respect to the earnings of the same obligor, the employer satisfies the terms of the [~~multiple~~] orders if the employer complies with the law of the state of the obligor's principal place of employment to establish the priorities for withholding and allocating income withheld for **two or more** [~~multiple~~] child support obligees.

Commissioners' Official Comment to UIFSA Section 503

Consistent with the Act's general problem-solving approach, the employer is directed to deal with multiple income orders for multiple families in the same manner as required by local law for orders of the forum State.

---

§ 159.504. Immunity From Civil Liability.

An employer who complies with an income-withholding order issued in another state in accordance with this subchapter is not subject to civil liability to an individual or agency with regard to the employer's withholding of child support from the obligor's income.

Commissioners' Official Comment to UIFSA Section 504

Because employer cooperation is a key element in interstate child support enforcement, it is sound policy to state explicitly that an employer who complies with an income-withholding order from another State is immune from civil liability.

---

§ 159.505. Penalties for Noncompliance.

An employer who wilfully fails to comply with an income-withholding order issued by another state and received for enforcement is subject to the same penalties that may be imposed for noncompliance with an order issued by a tribunal of this state.

Commissioners' Official Comment to UIFSA Section 505

Only an employer who willfully fails to comply with an interstate order will be subject to enforcement procedures. Local law is the appropriate source for the applicable sanctions and other remedies available under state law.

---

§ 159.506. Contest by Obligor.

(a) An obligor may contest the validity or enforcement of an income-withholding order issued in another state and received directly by an employer in this state **by registering the order in a tribunal of this state and:**

(1) filing a contest to that order under Subchapter G; or

(2) contesting the order in the same manner as if the order had been issued by a tribunal of this state. [~~Section 159.604 applies to the contest.~~]

(b) The obligor shall give notice of the contest to:

(1) a support enforcement agency providing services to the obligee;

(2) each employer that has directly received an income-withholding order **relating to the obligor**; and

(3) the person [~~or agency~~] designated to receive payments in the income-withholding order or to the obligee, if no person [~~or agency~~] is designated.

Commissioners' Official Comment to UIFSA Section 506

This section incorporates into the interstate context the law regarding defenses an employee-obligor may raise to an intrastate withholding order. Generally, States have accepted the IV–D requirement that the only viable defense is a "mistake of fact." 42 U.S.C. Section 666(b)(4)(A). This apparently includes "errors in the amount of current support owed, errors in the amount of accrued arrearage or mistaken identity of the alleged obligor" while excluding "other grounds, such as the inappropriateness of the amount of support ordered to be paid, changed financial circumstances of the obligor, or lack of visitation." H.R. Rep. No. 98–527, 98th Cong., 1st Sess. 33 (1983). The latter claims must be pursued in a separate proceeding in the appropriate State, not in a UIFSA proceeding.

This procedure is based on the assumption that valid defenses to income withholding for child support are few and far between. Experience has shown that in relatively few cases does an employee-obligor have a complete defense, *e.g.*, the child has died, another contingency ending the support has occurred, the order has been superseded, or there is a case of mistaken identity and the employee is not the obligor. An employee's complaint that "The child support is too high" must be ignored.

However, situations do arise where an employer has received multiple withholding notices regarding the obligor-employee and the same obligee. The notices may even allege conflicting amounts due, especially for payments on arrears. Additionally, many employees claim to have only learned of default orders when the withholding notice Is delivered to the employer; this leads to claims that the order being enforced through income withholding was entered without personal jurisdiction over the obligor-employee.

The 2003 rewording of Subsection (a) affirms that a simple. efficient, and cost-effective method for an employee-alleged obligor to assert a defense is to register the withholding order with a local tribunal and seek protection from that tribunal pending resolution of the contest. This may be accomplished through the obligor's employment of private counsel or by a request for services made to the child support enforcement agency of the responding State. Some States provide administrative procedures for challenging the income withholding that may provide quicker resolution of a dispute than a judicially-based registration and hearing process. In the absence of expeditious action by the employee to assert a defense and contest the direct filing of a notice for withholding, however, the employer must begin income withholding in a timely fashion.

In contrast to the multiple-order system of RURESA, another issue the employee-obligor may raise is that the withholding order received by the employer is not based on the controlling child support order issued by the tribunal with continuing, exclusive jurisdiction, *see* Section 207, *supra*. Such a claim does not constitute a defense to the obligation of child support, but does put at issue the identity of the order to which the employer must respond. Clearly the employer is in no position to make such a decision. When multiple orders involve the same employee-obligor and child, as a practical matter resort to a responding tribunal to resolve a dispute over apportionment almost certainly is necessary.

---

§ 159.507. Administrative Enforcement of Orders.

(a) A party **or support enforcement agency** seeking to enforce a support order or an income-withholding order, or both, issued by a tribunal of another state may send the documents required for registering the order to a support enforcement agency of this state.

(b) On receipt of the documents, the support enforcement agency, without initially seeking to register the order, shall consider and, if appropriate, use any administrative procedure authorized by the law of this state to enforce a support order or an income-withholding order, or both. If the obligor does not contest administrative enforcement, the order need not be registered. If the obligor contests the validity or administrative enforcement of the order, the support enforcement agency shall register the order under this chapter.

Commissioners' Official Comment to UIFSA Section 507

This section authorizes summary enforcement of an interstate child support order through the administrative means available for intrastate orders. Under Subsection (a), an interested party in another State, which necessarily may include a private attorney or a support enforcement agency, may forward a support order or income-withholding order to a support enforcement agency of the responding State. The term "responding State" in this context does not necessarily contemplate resort to a tribunal as an initial step.

Subsection (b) directs the support enforcement agency in the responding State to employ that State's regular administrative procedures to process an out-of-state order. Thus, a local employer accustomed to dealing with the local agency need not change its procedure to comply with an out-of-state order. Similarly, the administrative agency is authorized to apply its ordinary rules equally to both intrastate and interstate orders. For example, if the administrative hearing procedure must be exhausted for an intrastate order before a contesting party may seek relief in a tribunal, the same rule applies to an interstate order received for administrative enforcement.

Subchapter G. Registration, Enforcement, and Modification of Support Order

§ 159.601. Registration of Order for Enforcement.

A support order or income-withholding order issued by a tribunal of another state may be registered in this state for enforcement.

Commissioners' Official Comment to UIFSA Section 601

Sections 601 through 604 establish the basic procedure for the registration of interstate support orders. Formerly, the common practice under RURESA was to initiate a new proceeding for the establishment of a support order, even though there was an existing order for child support. That practice was specifically rejected by UIFSA; the fact that RURESA permitted (really encouraged) initiation of new proceedings under those circumstances led to the multiple support order system that UIFSA is designed to eliminate.

Under the one-order system of UIFSA, only one existing order is to be enforced prospectively. If more than one child-support order exists, Section 207 is designed to resolve the conflict by determining which order is controlling. Registration of an order in a tribunal of the responding State is the first step to enforce a child-support order of another State. Similarly, it is the first step for modification of another State's child-support order and may be the same for identification of the controlling order. Rather than being an optional procedure, as was the case under RURESA, registration under UIFSA is the primary method for interstate enforcement or modification of a child-support order by a tribunal of a responding State. If the prior support order has been validly issued by a tribunal with continuing, exclusive jurisdiction, *see* Section 205, that order is to be prospectively enforced against the obligor in the absence of narrow, strictly-defined fact situations in which an existing order may be modified, *see* Sections 609 through 612. Until that order is modified, however, it is fully enforceable in the responding State.

Although registration that is not accompanied by a request for the affirmative relief of enforcement or modification is not prohibited, the Act does not contemplate registration as serving a purpose in itself.

---

§ 159.602. Procedure to Register Order for Enforcement.

(a) A support order or income-withholding order of another state may be registered in this state by sending to the appropriate tribunal in this state:

(1) a letter of transmittal to the tribunal requesting registration and enforcement;

(2) two copies, including one certified copy, of **the order** [~~all orders~~] to be registered, including any modification of **the** [~~an~~] order;

(3) a sworn statement by the **person requesting** [~~party seeking~~] registration or a certified statement by the custodian of the records showing the amount of any arrearage;

(4) the name of the obligor and, if known:

(A) the obligor's **address and** social security number;

(B) the name and address of the obligor's employer and any other source of income of the obligor; and

(C) a description of and the location of property of the obligor in this state not exempt from execution; and

(5) **except as otherwise provided by Section 159.312,** the name of the obligee and, if applicable, the [~~agency or~~] person to whom support payments are to be remitted.

(b) On receipt of a request for registration, the registering tribunal shall cause the order to be filed as a foreign judgment, together with one copy of the documents and information, regardless of their form.

(c) A petition or comparable pleading seeking a remedy that must be affirmatively sought under other law of this state may be filed at the same time as the request for registration or later. The pleading must specify the grounds for the remedy sought.

(d) If two or more orders are in effect, the person requesting registration shall:

(1) provide to the tribunal a copy of each support order and the documents specified in this section;

(2) identify the order alleged to be the controlling order, if any; and

(3) state the amount of consolidated arrearages, if any.

(e) A request for a determination of which order is the controlling order may be filed separately from or with a request for registration and enforcement or for registration and modification. The person requesting registration shall give notice of the request to each party whose rights may be affected by the determination.

Commissioners' Official Comment to UIFSA Section 602

Subsection (a) outlines the mechanics for registration of an interstate order. Substantial compliance with the requirements is expected, *Twaddell v. Anderson*, 523 S.E.2d 710 (N.C. App. 1999); *In re Chapman*, 973 S.W.2d 346 (Tex. App. 1998).

Subsection (b) confirms that the order being registered is not converted into an order of the responding State, but rather continues to be an order of the issuing State.

Subsection (c) warns that if a particular enforcement remedy must be specifically sought under local law, the same rule of pleading is applicable as in an interstate case. For example, if license suspension or revocation is sought as a remedy for alleged noncompliance with the terms of the order, the substantive and procedural rules of the responding State apply. Whether the range of application of the remedy in the responding State is wider or narrower than that available in the issuing State is irrelevant. The responding tribunal will apply the familiar law of its State, and is neither expected nor authorized to consider the law of the issuing State. In short, the path in enforcing the order of a tribunal of another State is identical to the path followed for enforcing an order of the responding State. The authorization of a later filing to comply with local law contemplates that interstate pleadings may be liberally amended to conform to local practice.

The 2003 amendments adding Subsections (d) and (e) amplify the procedures to be followed when two or more child-support orders exist and registration for enforcement or modification is sought. In such instances, the requester is directed to furnish the tribunal with sufficient information and documentation so that the tribunal may make determinations of the controlling order and of the amount of consolidated arrears and interest as provided by Section 207, *supra*.

Leading Case

In re Chapman, 973 S.W.2d 346 (Tex. App.—Amarillo 1998, no pet.) (missing sworn statement precludes UIFSA registration)

---

§ 159.603. Effect of Registration for Enforcement.

(a) A support order or income-withholding order issued in another state is registered when the order is filed in the registering tribunal of this state.

(b) A registered order issued in another state is enforceable in the same manner and is subject to the same procedures as an order issued by a tribunal of this state.

(c) Except as otherwise provided in this subchapter, a tribunal of this state shall recognize and enforce, but may not modify, a registered order if the issuing tribunal had jurisdiction.

Commissioners' Official Comment to UIFSA Section 603

Until the advent of the 2003 amendments, the registration procedure under UIFSA was nearly identical to that of RURESA. But, the underlying intent of UIFSA registration has always been radically different. Under RURESA, once an order of State A was registered in State B, it became an order of the latter. Under UIFSA, the order continues to be an order of State A, which is to be enforced by a tribunal of State B. The rules of evidence and procedure of State B apply to hearings, except as local law is supplemented or specifically superseded by the Act. The purpose of the 2003 amendments to the registration procedure set forth in Sections 601 through 604 is to confirm and clarify that the order being registered remains a State A order unless and until modification is accomplished.

RURESA specifically subjected a registered order to "proceedings for reopening, vacating, or staying as a support order of this State." These procedures are not authorized under UIFSA. Subsection (b) states that an interstate support order is to be enforced and satisfied in the same manner as if it had been issued by a tribunal of the registering State, although it remains an order of the issuing State. Conceptually, the responding State is enforcing the order of another State, not its own order.

Subsection (c) mandates enforcement of the registered order, *see* also Sections 606 through 608, *infra*. This is at sharp variance with the common interpretation of RURESA, which was generally construed as converting the foreign order into an order of the registering State. Once the registering court concluded that it was enforcing its own order, the next logical step was to issue an order as the court deemed appropriate. Although quite often couched in terms of a "modification," this procedure resulted in yet another order and was a major contributor to the multiple-order system. UIFSA mandates an end to this process. Under UIFSA there will be only one order in existence at any one time. That order is enforceable in a responding State irrespective of whether the order may be modified. In most instances, the support order will be subject to the continuing, exclusive jurisdiction of the issuing State. But sometimes the issuing State will not be able to exercise its authority to modify the order because neither the child nor the parties reside in the issuing State. Nonetheless, the order may be registered and is fully enforceable in a responding State until the potential for modification actually occurs in accordance with the strict terms for such a proceeding, *see* Sections 609–612, *infra*. Thus, the registering tribunal always must bear in mind that the enforcement procedures taken, whether to enforce current support or to assist collecting current and future arrears and interest are made on behalf of the issuing State, and are not to be viewed as modifications of the controlling order.

---

§ 159.604. Choice of Law.

(a) **Except as provided by Subsection (d), the** [~~The~~] law of the issuing state governs:

(1) the nature, extent, amount, and duration of current payments **under a registered support order;**

(2) [~~and other obligations of support and~~] the **computation and** payment of arrearages **and accrual of interest on the arrearages** under the **support** order; **and**

(3) the existence and satisfaction of other obligations under the support order.

(b) In a proceeding for arrearages **under a registered support order**, the statute of limitation [~~under the laws~~] of this state or of the issuing state, whichever [~~statute of limitation~~] is longer, applies.

(c) A responding tribunal in this state shall apply the procedures and remedies of this state to enforce current support and collect arrearages and interest due on a support order of another state registered in this state.

(d) After a tribunal of this or another state determines which order is the controlling order and issues an order consolidating arrearages, if any, the tribunal of this state shall prospectively apply the law of the state issuing the controlling order, including that state's law on interest on arrearages, current and future support, and consolidated arrearages.

Commissioners' Official Comment to UIFSA Section 604

This section identifies situations in which local law is inapplicable. A basic principle of UIFSA is that throughout the process the controlling order remains the order of the issuing State, and that responding States only assist in the enforcement of that order. Absent a loss of continuing, exclusive jurisdiction and a subsequent modification of the order, the order never becomes an "order of the responding State." Ultimate responsibility for enforcement and final resolution of the obligor's compliance with all aspects of the support order belongs to the issuing State. Thus, calculation of whether the obligor has fully complied with the payment of current support, arrears, and interest on arrears is the duty of the issuing State. For example, under Subsection (a) the responding State must recognize and enforce an order of the issuing State for the support of a child until age 21, notwithstanding the fact that the duty of support of a child ends at age 18 under the law of the responding State, *see Robdau v. Commonwealth, Virginia Dept. Social Serv.*, 543 S.E.2d 602 (Va. App. 2001); *State ex rel. Harnes v. Lawrence*, 538 S.E.2d 223 (N.C. App. 2000). Similarly, the law of the issuing State governs whether a payment made for the benefit of a child, such as a Social Security benefit for a child of a disabled obligor, should be credited against the obligor's child support obligation.

The amendments of 2003 to Subsection (a) are intended to clarify the range of subjects that are governed by the choice of law rules established in this section.

Subsection (b) contains another choice of law provision that may diverge from local law. In situations in which the statutes of limitation differ from State to State, the statute with the longer term is to be applied. *Attorney General v. Litten*, 999 S.W.2d 74 (Tex. App. 1999). In interstate cases, arrearages often will have accumulated over a considerable period of time before enforcement is perfected. The rationale for this exception to the general rule is that the obligor should not gain an undue benefit from the choice of residence if the forum State has a shorter statute of limitations for arrearages than does the controlling order State. On the other side of the coin, i.e., the forum has a longer statute of limitations, the obligor will be treated in an identical manner as all other obligors in that State.

Subsection (c) mandates that local law controls with regard to enforcement procedures. For example, if the issuing State has enacted a wide variety of license suspension or revocation statutes, while the responding State has a much narrower list of licenses subject to suspension or revocation, local law prevails.

Subsection (d) may appear to state another truism–the law of the State that issued the controlling order is superior with regard to the terms of the support order itself. However, the last clause in the sentence provides a very important clarifying provision; that is, the law of the issuing State is to be applied to the consolidated arrears, even if the support orders of other States contributed a portion to those arrears.

In sum, the local tribunal applies its own familiar procedures to enforce a support order, but it is clearly enforcing an order of another State and not an order of the forum.

---

§ 159.605. Notice of Registration of Order.

(a) When a support order or income-withholding order issued in another state is registered, the registering tribunal shall notify the nonregistering party. The notice must be accompanied by a copy of the registered order and the documents and relevant information accompanying the order.

(b) **A** [~~The~~] notice **under this section** must inform the nonregistering party:

(1) that a registered order is enforceable as of the date of registration in the same manner as an order issued by a tribunal of this state;

(2) that a hearing to contest the validity or enforcement of the registered order must be requested within 20 days after notice;

(3) that failure to contest the validity or enforcement of the registered order in a timely manner:

(A) will result in confirmation of the order and enforcement of the order and the alleged arrearages; and

(B) precludes further contest of that order with respect to any matter that could have been asserted; and

(4) of the amount of any alleged arrearages.

(c) **If the registering party asserts that two or more orders are in effect, the notice under this section must also:**

(1) identify:

(A) the orders, including which order is alleged by the registering person to be the controlling order; and

(B) the consolidated arrearages, if any;

(2) notify the nonregistering party of the right to a determination of which order is the controlling order;

(3) state that the procedures provided in Subsection (b) apply to the determination of which order is the controlling order; and

(4) state that failure to contest the validity or enforcement of the order alleged to be the controlling order in a timely manner may result in confirmation that the order is the controlling order.

(d) On registration of an income-withholding order for enforcement, the registering tribunal shall notify the obligor's employer under Chapter 158.

Commissioners' Official Comment to UIFSA Section 605

Sections 605–608 provide the procedure for the nonregistering party to contest registration of an order, either because the order is allegedly invalid, superseded, or no longer in effect, or because the enforcement remedy being sought is opposed by the nonregistering party.

Subsections (a) and (b) direct that the nonregistering party be fully informed of the effect of registration. After such notice is given, absent a successful contest by the nonregistering party, the order will be confirmed and future contest will be precluded.

Subsection (c), with new text in 2003, is the correlative to Section 602(d) and (e) regarding the notice to be given to the nonregistering party if a controlling order determination must be made because of the existence of two or more child-support orders. The petitioner requesting this affirmative relief is directed to identify the order alleged to be controlling under Section 207, *supra*. If the nonregistering party does not contest this allegation, either by default or agreement, the order identified as controlling will be confirmed by operation of law by the following section.

Relettered Subsection (d) states the obvious; the obligor's employer must also be notified if income is to be withheld.

---

§ 159.606. Procedure to Contest Validity or Enforcement of Registered Order.

(a) A nonregistering party seeking to contest the validity or enforcement of a registered order in this state shall request a hearing within 20 days after notice of the registration. The nonregistering party may seek under Section 159.607 to:

(1) vacate the registration;

(2) assert any defense to an allegation of noncompliance with the registered order; or

(3) contest the remedies being sought or the amount of any alleged arrearages.

(b) If the nonregistering party fails to contest the validity or enforcement of the registered order in a timely manner, the order is confirmed by operation of law.

(c) If a nonregistering party requests a hearing to contest the validity or enforcement of the registered order, the registering tribunal shall schedule the matter for hearing and give notice to the parties of the date, time, and place of the hearing.

Commissioners' Official Comment to UIFSA Section 606

Subsection (a) directs the "nonregistering party" to contest the registration of a foreign order within a short period of time or forfeit the opportunity to contest. UIFSA provides that either the obligor, the obligee, or a state enforcement agency, may seek to register a foreign support order. In fact, even a stranger to the litigation, for example a grandparent or an employer of an alleged obligor, may register a support order. Thereafter, the nonregistering party is put on notice of the registration and is required to assert any existing defense to the alleged order or forfeit the opportunity. Note that either the obligor or the obligee may have objections to the registered order, although in the vast majority of cases doubtless the obligor will be the nonregistering party. For example, there is a possibility that in multiple order situations either party may register the order most favorable to that party rather than the likely controlling order, thus triggering a contest. However, such chicanery is contrary to Subsection 605(c) and is specifically forbidden for a support enforcement agency, Subsection 307(c).

Subsection (a) is philosophically very different from RURESA which directed that a registered order "shall be treated in the same manner as a support order issued by a court of this State." Under UIFSA a contest of the fundamental provisions of the registered order is not permitted in the responding State. The nonregistering party must return to the issuing State to prosecute such a contest (obviously only as the law of that State permits). The procedure adopted here is akin to the prohibition found in Section 315 against asserting a nonparentage defense in a UIFSA proceeding. In short, raising a collateral issue in a UIFSA proceeding is prohibited, but no attempt is made to preclude the issue from being litigated in another, more appropriate forum if otherwise allowed by that forum.

On the other hand, a nonregistering obligor may assert defenses such as "payment" or "the obligation has terminated" in response to allegations of noncompliance with the registered order. Similarly, a constitutionally-based attack may be asserted, *i.e.*, an alleged lack of personal jurisdiction by the issuing tribunal over a party. There is no defense, however, to registration of a valid foreign support order.

Subsection (b) precludes an untimely contest of a registered support order. As noted above, the nonregistering party is free to seek redress in the issuing State from the tribunal with continuing, exclusive jurisdiction over the support order.

Subsection (c) directs that a hearing be scheduled when the nonregistering party contests some aspect of the registration. At present, federal regulations govern the allowable time frames for contesting income withholding in IV–D cases, see 42 U.S.C. Section 666(b). Additional codification of the procedure process is unwise.

Leading Case

In re Kuykendall, 957 S.W.2d 907 (Tex. App.—Texarkana 1997, no writ) (Kansas decree wording "shall" pay sufficient for monetary judgment in Texas)

---

§ 159.607. Contest of Registration or Enforcement.

(a) A party contesting the validity or enforcement of a registered order or seeking to vacate the registration has the burden of proving one or more of the following defenses:

(1) the issuing tribunal lacked personal jurisdiction over the contesting party;

(2) the order was obtained by fraud;

(3) the order has been vacated, suspended, or modified by a later order;

(4) the issuing tribunal has stayed the order pending appeal;

(5) there is a defense under the law of this state to the remedy sought;

(6) full or partial payment has been made; [~~or~~]

(7) the statute of limitation under Section 159.604 precludes enforcement of some or all of the **alleged** arrearages; **or**

(8) the alleged controlling order is not the controlling order.

(b) If a party presents evidence establishing a full or partial defense under Subsection (a), a tribunal may stay enforcement of the registered order, continue the proceeding to permit production of additional relevant evidence, and issue other appropriate orders. An uncontested portion of the registered order may be enforced by all remedies available under the law of this state.

(c) If the contesting party does not establish a defense under Subsection (a) to the validity or enforcement of the order, the registering tribunal shall issue an order confirming the order.

Commissioners' Official Comment to UIFSA Section 607

Subsection (a) places the burden on the nonregistering party to assert narrowly defined defenses to registration of a support order. The 2003 amendment added an obvious defense that was inadvertently omitted from the original list of defenses. In a multiple order situation, if the nonregistering party contests the allegation regarding the controlling order, either because it allegedly has not been registered or because another order has been misidentified as such, the nonregistering party may defend against enforcement of another order by asserting the existence of a controlling order. Presumably the defense must be substantiated by registration of the other alleged controlling order to be effective.

If the obligor is liable for current support, in the absence of a valid defense under Subsection (b) the registering tribunal must enter an order to enforce that obligation. *State Dept. of Revenue ex rel. Rochell v. Morris*, 736 So. 2d 41 (Fla. App. 1999); *Welsher v. Rager*, 491 S.E.2d 661 (N.C. App. 1997); *Cowan v. Moreno*, 903 S.W.2d 119 (Tex. App.—Austin 1995). Proof of arrearages must result in enforcement; under the Bradley Amendment, 42 U.S.C. Section 666(a)(10), all States are required to treat child support payments as final judgments as they come due (or lose federal funding). Therefore, such arrearages are not subject to retroactive modification.

Subsection (c) provides that failure to successfully contest a registered order requires the tribunal to confirm the validity of the registered order. Although the statute is silent on the subject, it seems likely that *res judicata* requires that both the registering and nonregistering party who fail to register the "true" controlling order will be estopped from subsequently collaterally attacking the confirmed order on the basis that the unmentioned "true order should have been confirmed instead."

---

§ 159.608. Confirmed Order.

Confirmation of a registered order, whether by operation of law or after notice and hearing, precludes further contest of the order with respect to any matter that could have been asserted at the time of registration.

Commissioners' Official Comment to UIFSA Section 608

If the nonregistering party fails to contest, the registered support order is confirmed by operation of law and no tribunal action is necessary. If contested, a registered support order must be confirmed by the forum tribunal if the defense authorized in Section 607 is rejected after a hearing. Either result precludes the nonregistering party from raising any issue that could have been asserted in a hearing. Confirmation of a foreign support order validates both the terms of the order and the asserted arrearages.

---

§ 159.609. Procedure to Register Child Support Order of Another State for Modification.

A party or support enforcement agency seeking to modify or to modify and enforce a child support order issued in another state shall register that order in this state in the same manner provided in Sections 159.601–159.604 if the order has not been registered. A petition for modification may be filed at the same time as a request for registration or later. The pleading must specify the grounds for modification.

Commissioners' Official Comment to UIFSA Section 609

Sections 609 through 615 deal with situations in which it is permissible for a registering State to modify the existing child-support order of another State. A petitioner wishing to register a support order of another State for purposes of modification must conform to the general requirements for pleadings in Section 311 (Pleadings and Accompanying Documents), and follow the procedure for registration set forth in Section 602 (Procedure To Register Order for Enforcement). If the tribunal has the requisite personal jurisdiction over the parties as established in Sections 611, 613, or 615, modification may be sought in conjunction with registration and enforcement, or at a later date after the order has been registered, confirmed, and enforced.

---

§ 159.610. Effect of Registration for Modification.

A tribunal of this state may enforce a child support order of another state registered for purposes of modification in the same manner as if the order had been issued by a tribunal of this state, but the registered order may be modified only if the requirements of Section 159.611**, 159.613, or 159.615** have been met.

Commissioners' Official Comment to UIFSA Section 610

An order registered for purposes of modification may be enforced in the same manner as an order registered for purposes of enforcement. But, the power of the forum tribunal to modify a child-support order of another tribunal is limited by the specific factual preconditions set forth in Sections 611, 613, and 615.

---

§ 159.611. Modification of Child Support Order of Another State.

(a) **Except as provided by Section 159.615, on petition a tribunal of this state may modify** [~~After~~] a child support order issued in another state **and** [~~has been~~] registered in this state[~~, the responding tribunal of this state may modify the order~~] only if Section 159.613 does not apply and after notice and hearing the tribunal finds that:

(1) the following requirements are met:

(A) the child, the [~~individual~~] obligee **who is an individual**, and the obligor do not reside in the issuing state;

(B) a petitioner who is a nonresident of this state seeks modification; and

(C) the respondent is subject to the personal jurisdiction of the tribunal of this state; or

(2) **this state is the state of residence of** the child **and the child**, or a party who is an individual, is subject to the personal jurisdiction of the tribunal of this state and all of the parties who are individuals have filed **in a record** in the issuing tribunal [~~written~~] consents for a tribunal of this state to modify the support order and assume continuing, exclusive jurisdiction [~~over the order; however, for the purposes of this subdivision, if the issuing state is a foreign jurisdiction that has not enacted a law or established procedures substantially similar to the procedures under this chapter, the consent otherwise required of an individual residing in this state is not required for the tribunal to assume jurisdiction to modify the child support order~~].

(b) Modification of a registered child support order is subject to the same requirements, procedures, and defenses that apply to the modification of an order issued by a tribunal of this state, and the order may be enforced and satisfied in the same manner.

(c) **Except as provided by Section 159.615, a** [~~A~~] tribunal of this state may not modify any aspect of a child support order**, including the duration of the obligation of support,** that may not be modified under the law of the issuing state. If two or more tribunals have issued child support orders for the same obligor and **same** child, the order that controls and must be recognized under Section 159.207 establishes the aspects of the support order that are nonmodifiable.

(d) On issuance of an order **by a tribunal of this state** modifying a child support order issued in another state, **the** [~~a~~] tribunal of this state becomes the tribunal of continuing, exclusive jurisdiction.

(e) In a proceeding to modify a child support order, the law of the state that is determined to have issued the initial controlling order governs the duration of the obligation of support. The obligor's fulfillment of the duty of support established by that order precludes imposition of a further obligation of support by a tribunal of this state.

Commissioners' Official Comment to UIFSA Section 611

Under the procedure established by RURESA, after a support order was registered for the purpose of enforcement it was treated as if it had originally been issued by the registering tribunal. Most States interpreted these registration provisions as also authorizing prospective "modification" of the registered order. However, except in circumstances in which both States had the same version of RURESA and the formalities were scrupulously followed, the registering tribunal did not have the legal authority to replace the original order with its own order. In short, most often the purported modification in essence established a new obligation. In sum, by its very terms RURESA contemplated, or even encouraged, the existence of multiple support orders, none of which were directly related to any of the others. Although the issuing tribunal under RURESA retained a version of continuing, exclusive jurisdiction to modify its own order, that power was not exclusive. The typical scenario of those days was that an obligee would seek assistance from a local court, which would determine a duty of support existed and forward a certificate and order and petition to a responding court. The subsequent proceeding in the responding State would bring the obligor before the court. The obligor typically sought modification of the support obligation (which almost always was not being paid) in a forum which presented him with the "hometown advantage." Thus arose the common practice of the issuance of a new, lower child-support order.

Under UIFSA, as long as the issuing State has continuing, exclusive jurisdiction over its child-support order, *see* Section 205(a), *supra*, a registering sister State is precluded from modifying that order. Without doubt, this is the most significant departure from the multiple-order system established by the prior Uniform Act. However, if the issuing State no longer has a sufficient interest in the modification of its order under the factual circumstances described in Section 205(b), *supra*, and restated in this section, after registration the responding State may assume the power to modify the controlling order.

Registration is subdivided into distinct categories: registration for enforcement, for modification, or both. UIFSA is based on recognizing the truism that when an out-of-state support order is registered, the rights and duties of the parties affected have been previously litigated. Because the obligor already has had a day before an appropriate tribunal, an enforcement remedy may be summarily invoked. On the other hand, modification of an existing order presupposes a change in the rights or duties of the parties. The requirements for modification of a child-support order are much more explicit under UIFSA, which allows a tribunal to modify an existing child-support order of another State only if certain quite limited conditions are met. First, the tribunal must have all the prerequisites for the exercise of personal jurisdiction required for rendition of an original support order. Second, one of the restricted fact situations described in Subsection (a) must be present. This section, which is a counterpart to Section 205(a), establishes the conditions under which the continuing, exclusive jurisdiction of the issuing tribunal is released.

Under Subsection (a)(1), before a tribunal in a new forum may modify the controlling order three specific criteria must be satisfied. First, the individual parties affected by the controlling order and the child must no longer reside in the issuing State. Second, the party seeking modification must register the order in a new forum, almost invariably the State of residence of the other party. A colloquial (but easily understood) description of this requirement is that the modification movant must "play an away game on the other party's home field." This rule applies to either obligor or obligee, depending on which of those parties seeks to modify. Proof of the fact that neither individual party nor the child continues to reside in the issuing State may be made directly in the registering State; no purpose would be served by requiring the petitioner to return to the original issuing State for a document to confirm the fact that none of the relevant persons still lives there. Third, the forum must have personal jurisdiction over the parties. This is supplied by the movant submitting to the personal jurisdiction of the forum by seeking affirmative relief, almost always coupled with the fact that the respondent resides in the forum. On rare occasion, the personal jurisdiction over the respondent may be supplied by other factors, *see* Section 201 and the comment thereto, *supra*.

The policies underlying the change affected by Subsection (a)(1) contemplate that the issuing State no longer has an interest in exercising its continuing, exclusive jurisdiction to modify its order. This restriction attempts to achieve a rough justice between the parties in the majority of cases by preventing a litigant from choosing to seek modification in a local tribunal to the marked disadvantage of the other party. For example, an obligor visiting the children at the residence of the obligee cannot be validly served with citation accompanied by a motion to modify the support order. Even though such personal service of the obligor in the obligee's home State is consistent with the jurisdictional requisites of *Burnham v. Superior Court*, 495 U.S. 604 (1990), the motion to modify does not fulfill the requirement of being brought by "a [petitioner] who is a nonresident of this State ." In short, the obligee is required to register the existing order and seek modification of that order in a

State that has personal jurisdiction over the obligor other than the State of the obligee's residence. Again, almost invariably this will be the State of residence of the obligor. Similarly, fairness requires that an obligee seeking to modify or modify and enforce the existing order in the State of residence of the obligor will not be subject to a cross-motion to modify custody or visitation merely because the issuing State has lost its continuing, exclusive jurisdiction over the support order. The same is true of the obligor, who also is required to make a motion to modify support in a State other than that of his or her residence. Yet another benefit is supplied by the procedure mandated in this section. The most typical case is a motion to increase child support by the obligee, the enforcement of which ultimately will primarily, if not exclusively, take place in the obligor's State of residence. Modification and enforcement in the same forum promotes efficiency.

Several arguments sustain the jurisdictional choice made by UIFSA. First, "jurisdiction by ambush" will be avoided. That is, personal service on either the custodial or noncustodial party found within the state borders will not yield jurisdiction to modify. Thus, a parent seeking to exercise rights of visitation, delivering or picking-up the child for such visitation, or engaging in unrelated business activity in the State, will not be involuntarily subjected to protracted litigation in an inconvenient forum. The rule avoids the possible chilling effect on the exercise of parental contact with the child that the possibility of such litigation might have. Second, almost all disputes about whether the tribunal has jurisdiction will be eliminated; submission by the petitioner to the State of residence of the respondent alleviates this issue completely. Finally, because there is an existing order the primary focus will shift to enforcement, thereby curtailing to a degree unnecessary, time-consuming modification efforts. The array of enforcement procedures available administratively to support enforcement agencies may be invoked without resort to action by a tribunal, which had constituted a bottleneck under RURESA and URESA.

There are two exceptions to the rule of Subsection (a)(1) requiring the petitioner to be a nonresident of the forum in which modification is sought. First, under Subsection (a)(2) the parties may agree that a particular forum may serve to modify the order. Second, Section 613, *infra*, applies if all parties have left the original issuing State and now reside in the same new forum State. Subsection (a)(2), which authorizes the parties to terminate the continuing, exclusive jurisdiction of the issuing State by agreement, is based on several implicit assumptions. First, the subsection applies even if the issuing tribunal has continuing, exclusive jurisdiction because one of the parties or the child continues to reside in that State. Subsection (a)(2) also is applicable if the individual parties and the child no longer reside in the issuing State, but agree to submit the modification issue to a tribunal in the petitioner's State of residence. Also implicit in a shift of jurisdiction over the child-support order is that the agreed-upon tribunal must have subject matter jurisdiction and personal jurisdiction over at least one of the parties or the child, and that the other party submits to the personal jurisdiction of that forum. In short, UIFSA does not contemplate that absent parties can agree to confer jurisdiction on a tribunal without a nexus to the parties or the child. But if the other party agrees, either the obligor or the obligee may seek assertion of jurisdiction to modify by a tribunal of the State of residence of either party.

The requirements of Subsection (a) are demonstrated to the tribunal being asked to assume continuing, exclusive jurisdiction. No action to transfer, surrender, or otherwise participate is required or anticipated by the original order-issuing tribunal. The Act does not grant discretion to refuse to yield jurisdiction to the issuing tribunal; nor does it extend discretion to refuse to accept jurisdiction to the assuming tribunal when the statutory requisites are met. However, there is a distinction between the processes involved under Subsection (a)(1) and (a)(2). Once the requirements of (a)(1) or Section 613 have been met for assumption of jurisdiction, the assuming jurisdiction acts on the modification and then notifies the tribunal whose order has been replaced by the order of the assuming tribunal, *see* Section 614, *infra*. In contrast, for a tribunal of another State to assume modification jurisdiction under Subsection (a)(2) it is necessary that the individual parties first agree in a record to submit modification of child support to that tribunal and file their agreement with the issuing tribunal. Thereafter they may then proceed to petition the assuming tribunal to take jurisdiction.

Modification of child support under Subsections (a)(1) and (a)(2) is distinct from custody modification under the federal Parental Kidnapping Prevention Act, 42 U.S.C. Section 1738A, which provides that the court of continuing, exclusive jurisdiction may "decline jurisdiction." Similar provisions are found in the UCCJA, Section 14. In those statutes the methodology for the declination of jurisdiction is not spelled out, but rather is left to the discretion of possibly competing courts for case-by-case determination. The privilege of declining jurisdiction, thereby creating the potential for a vacuum, is not authorized under UIFSA, *see Rosen v. Lantos*, 938 P.2d 729, 734 (N.M. App. 1997). Once a controlling initial child-support order is established under UIFSA, at all times thereafter there is an existing order in effect to be enforced. Even if the issuing tribunal no longer has continuing, exclusive jurisdiction, its order remains fully enforceable until a tribunal with modification jurisdiction issues a new order in conformance with this article.

The degree to which the new standards of one tribunal with continuing, exclusive jurisdiction has been accepted is illustrated by comparing UIFSA to the UNIFORM CHILD CUSTODY JURISDICTION ACT, Sections 12–14, and UNIFORM CHILD CUSTODY JURISDICTION AND ENFORCEMENT ACT Sections 201–202. The UCCJA provides general principles for the judicial determination of an appropriate fact situation for subsequent modification of an existing custody order by another court. In contrast, UIFSA establishes a set of "bright line" rules which must be met before a tribunal may modify an existing child-support order. The intent is to eliminate multiple support orders to the maximum extent possible consistent with the principle of continuing, exclusive jurisdiction that pervades the Act. The UCCJEA borrows heavily, but not identically, from UIFSA. Both UIFSA and UCCJEA seek a world in which there is but one-order-at-a-time for child support and custody and visitation. Both have similar restrictions on the ability of a tribunal to modify the existing order. The major difference between the two acts results from the fact that the basic jurisdictional nexus of each is founded on different consideration. UIFSA has its focus on the personal jurisdiction necessary to bind the obligor to payment of a child-support order. UCCJEA places its focus on the factual circumstances of the child, primarily the "home State" of the child; personal jurisdiction over a parent in order to bind that parent to the custody decree is not required. An example of the disparate consequences of this difference is the fact that a return to the decree State does "not reestablish" continuing jurisdiction under the custody jurisdiction Act, *see* comment to UCCJEA Section 202. But, under UIFSA similar facts permit the issuing State to exercise continuing, exclusive jurisdiction to modify its child-support order if at the time the proceeding is filed the issuing State "is the residence" of one of the individual parties or the child, *see* Section 205(a), *supra*.

Subsection (b) states that when the forum has assumed modification jurisdiction because the issuing State has lost continuing, exclusive jurisdiction, the proceedings will generally follow local law with regard to modification of child-support orders.

The 2003 amendment to Subsection (c) and the addition of Subsection (d) are designed to eliminate scattered attempts to subvert a significant policy decision made when UIFSA was first promulgated. Prior to 1993, American case law was thoroughly in chaos regarding modification of the duration of a child-support obligation when an obligor or obligee moved from one State to another with different ages regarding the duration of the child-support obligation. In those circumstances, whether the obligation ended, extended, or was curtailed was left almost to chance. In a RURESA proceeding, on the obligee's motion some States would increase the duration of the support obligation when the obligor resided in a State with a higher age for the child support obligation. Other States decreased the obligor's duration of child support when the obligor countered with a motion that the new RURESA support order should reflect a shorter duration of the obligation in accordance with local law. Multiple durations of the support obligation, as well as multiple support amounts, were both major problem areas addressed by UIFSA.

From its original promulgation UIFSA determined that the duration of child-support obligation should be fixed by the controlling order, *see Robdau v. Commonwealth, Virginia Dept. Social Serv.*, 543 S.E.2d 602 (Va. App. 2001). If the language was insufficiently specific before the 2003, the amendments should make this decision absolutely clear. The original time frame for support is not modifiable unless the law of the issuing State provides for modification of its duration. Some courts have sought to subvert this policy by holding that completion of the obligation to support a child through age 18 established by the now-completed controlling order does not preclude the imposition of a new obligation thereafter to support the child through age 21 or even to age 23 if the child is enrolled in higher education. Subsection (d) is designed to eliminate these attempts to create multiple, albeit successive, support obligations. Consistent with this principle, if a domestic violence protective order has been entered with a child-support provision that has a duration less than the general child support law of the State that issues the controlling order, the law of that State determines the maximum duration. In sum, absent tribunal error the first child-support order issued under UIFSA will invariably be the initial controlling order. The initial controlling order may be modified and replaced by a new controlling order in accordance with the terms of Sections 609–615, but the duration of the child-support obligation remains constant, even though virtually every other aspect of the original order may be changed. This is also the standard in situations involving multiple valid child-support orders—a problem that will progressively decrease over time as RURESA multiple orders expire or a determination of the initial controlling order is made under Section 207, *supra*. Once a controlling order is identified under these standards, the duration of the support obligation is fixed.

Relettered Subsection (e) provides that upon modification the new order becomes the one order to be recognized by all UIFSA States, and the issuing tribunal acquires continuing, exclusive jurisdiction. Good practice mandates that the tribunal should explicitly state in its order that it is assuming responsibility for the controlling child-support order. Neither the parties nor other tribunals should be required to speculate about the effect of the action taken by the tribunal under this section.

Leading Cases

In re B.O.G., 48 S.W.3d 312 (Tex. App.—Waco 2001, pet. denied) (trial court lacked jurisdiction over father's motion to modify child support—everyone has left Texas)

Link v. Alvarado, 929 S.W.2d 674 (Tex. App.—San Antonio 1996, writ dism'd w.o.j.) (Hawaii's continuing, exclusive jurisdiction over child support order prevents Texas court from modifying child support)

---

§ 159.612. Recognition of Order Modified in Another State.

If a child support order issued by a [A] tribunal of this state **is modified** [~~shall recognize a modification of its earlier child support order~~] by a tribunal of another state that assumed jurisdiction **under the Uniform Interstate Family Support Act, a**

tribunal of this state [~~under a law substantially similar to this chapter and, except as otherwise provided in this chapter, shall on request~~]:

(1) **may** enforce the order that was modified only as to **arrearages and interest** [**amounts**] accruing before the modification;

(2) may [~~enforce only nonmodifiable aspects of the order;~~

[~~(3)~~] provide [~~other~~] appropriate relief [~~only~~] for **violations** [~~a violation~~] of the order that occurred before the effective date of the modification; and

(3) shall [~~(4)~~] recognize the modifying order of the other state, on registration, for the purpose of enforcement.

Commissioners' Official Comment to UIFSA Section 612

A key aspect of UIFSA is the deference to the controlling child-support order of a sister State demanded from a tribunal of the forum State. This applies not just to the original order, but also to a modified child-support order issued by a second State under the standards established by Section 611, 613, and 615. For the Act to function properly, the original issuing State must recognize and accept the modified order as controlling, and must regard its prior order as prospectively inoperative. Because the UIFSA system is based on an interlocking series of state laws, it is fundamental that a modifying tribunal of one State lacks the authority to direct the original issuing State to release its continuing, exclusive jurisdiction. That result is accomplished through the enactment of UIFSA by all States, which empowers a modifying tribunal to assume continuing, exclusive jurisdiction from the original issuing State and requires an issuing State to recognize such an assumption of jurisdiction. This explains why the U.S. Congress took the extraordinary measure in PRWORA of mandating universal passage of UIFSA 1996, as amended, *see* Prefatory Note.

The original issuing tribunal retains authority post-modification to take remedial actions directly connected to its now-modified order.

---

§ 159.613. Jurisdiction to Modify Child Support Order of Another State When Individual Parties Reside in This State.

(a) If all of the parties who are individuals reside in this state and the child does not reside in the issuing state, a tribunal of this state has jurisdiction to enforce and to modify the issuing state's child support order in a proceeding to register that order.

(b) A tribunal of this state exercising jurisdiction under this section shall apply the provisions of Sections 159.101 through 159.209 and 159.601 through 159.614 and the procedural and substantive law of this state to the proceeding for enforcement or modification. Sections 159.301 through 159.507 and 159.701 through 159.802 do not apply.

Commissioners' Official Comment to UIFSA Section 613

A 1996 amendment explicitly dealt with the possibility that the parties and the child subject to a child-support order no longer reside in the issuing State and that the individual parties have moved to the same new State. This section makes it clear that, when the issuing State no longer has continuing, exclusive jurisdiction to modify its order, a tribunal of the State of mutual residence of the individual parties has jurisdiction to modify the child-support order and assume continuing, exclusive jurisdiction. Although the individual parties must reside in the forum State, there is no requirement that the child must also reside in the forum State (although the child must have moved from the issuing State).

Finally, because modification of the child-support order when all parties reside in the forum is essentially an intrastate matter, Subsection (b) withdraws authority to apply most of the substantive and procedural provisions of UIFSA, *i.e.*, those found in the Act other than in Articles 1, 2, and 6. Note, however, that the provision in Section 611(c) forbidding modification of nonmodifiable aspects of the controlling order applies. For example, the duration of the support obligation remains fixed by the original controlling order despite the subsequent residence of all parties in a new State. The fact that the State of the new controlling order has a different duration of for child support is specifically declared to be irrelevant by UIFSA, see Section 611, *supra*. Note that the even-handed approach of the Act is sustained; neither an increase nor a decrease in the duration in the obligation of child support is permitted.

---

§ 159.614. Notice to Issuing Tribunal of Modification.

Within 30 days after issuance of a modified child support order, the party obtaining the modification shall file a certified copy of the order with the issuing tribunal that had continuing, exclusive jurisdiction over the earlier order and in each tribunal in which the party knows the earlier order has been registered. A party who obtains the order and fails to file a certified copy is subject to appropriate sanctions by a tribunal in which the issue of failure to file arises. The failure to file does not affect the validity or enforceability of the modified order of the new tribunal having continuing, exclusive jurisdiction.

Commissioners' Official Comment to UIFSA Section 614

This stand-alone provision is designed to clarify the organization of the Act; it states the crucial proposition that the prevailing party must inform the original issuing tribunal about its loss of continuing, exclusive jurisdiction over its child-support order. Thereafter, the original tribunal may not modify, or review and adjust, the amount of child support. Notice to the issuing tribunal and other affected tribunals that the continuing, exclusive jurisdiction of the former controlling order has been modified is crucial to avoid the confusion and chaos of the multiple-order system UIFSA is designed to replace.

Additionally, the tribunal has authority to impose sanctions on a party who fails to comply with the requirement to give notice of a modification to all interested tribunals. Note, however, that failure to notify a displaced tribunal of a modification of its order does not affect the validity of the modified order.

Sec. 159.615. Jurisdiction to Modify Child Support Order of Foreign Country or Political Subdivision.

(a) If a foreign country or political subdivision that is a state refuses to modify its order or may not under its law modify its order, a tribunal of this state may assume jurisdiction to modify the child support order and bind all individuals subject to the personal jurisdiction of the tribunal regardless of whether:

(1) consent to modification of a child support order has been given under Section 159.611; or

(2) the individual seeking modification is a resident of this state or of the foreign country or political subdivision.

(b) An order issued under this section is the controlling order.

Commissioners' Official Comment to UIFSA Section 615

The amendments of 2003 added Section 615, which expands upon language moved from Section 611 (a)(2). A tribunal of one of the several States may modify a support order of a foreign country or political subdivision when a tribunal of the foreign jurisdiction would have jurisdiction to modify its order under the standards of UIFSA, but under the law or procedure of that foreign jurisdiction the tribunal will not or may not exercise that jurisdiction to modify its order. The standard example cited for the necessity of this special rule involves the conundrum posed to a tribunal of a foreign country having a requirement that the parties be physically present in order to sustain a modification of child support, and lacking the authority to compel a party residing outside of the borders of the country to appear. In such an instance, a tribunal of the forum State may modify the order if it has personal jurisdiction over both parties, including jurisdiction over the absent party who has submitted to the jurisdiction of the forum by making a request for modification of the support order.

Subchapter H. Determination of Parentage

§ 159.701. Proceeding to Determine Parentage.

[~~(a)~~] A **court** [~~tribunal~~] of this state **authorized to determine the parentage of a child** may serve as **a** [~~an initiating or~~] responding tribunal in a proceeding **to determine parentage** brought under this chapter or a law substantially similar to this chapter[~~, the Uniform Reciprocal Enforcement of Support Act, or the Revised Uniform Reciprocal Enforcement of Support Act to determine that the petitioner is a parent of a particular child or to determine that a respondent is a parent of that child~~].

[~~(b) In a proceeding to determine parentage, a responding tribunal of this state shall apply the procedural and substantive law of this state and the rules of this state on choice of law.~~]

Commissioners' Official Comment to UIFSA Section 701

This article authorizes a "pure" parentage action in the interstate context, *i.e.*, an action not joined with a claim for support. Either the mother or a man alleging himself to be the father of a child may bring such an action. Typically, an action to determine parentage across state lines will also seek to establish a support order under the Act, *see* Section 401. An action to establish parentage under UIFSA is to be treated identically to such an action brought in the responding State. Note that in a departure from the rest of this Act, the term "tribunal" is replaced by "court." Although in the several States there are various combinations of judicial and administrative entities that are authorized to establish, enforce, and modify child-support orders, the UNIFORM PARENTAGE ACT (2000) restricts parentage determinations to "a court," *see* UPA (2000) Section 104. The view that only a judicial officer should determine parentage is based on what the Conference believes is sound public policy.

Subchapter I. Interstate Rendition

§ 159.801. Grounds for Rendition.

(a) In this subchapter, "governor" includes an individual performing the functions of governor or the executive authority of a state covered by this chapter.

(b) The governor of this state may:

(1) demand that the governor of another state surrender an individual found in the other state who is charged criminally in this state with having failed to provide for the support of an obligee; or

(2) on the demand **of** [~~by~~] the governor of another state, surrender an individual found in this state who is charged criminally in the other state with having failed to provide for the support of an obligee.

(c) A provision for extradition of individuals not inconsistent with this chapter applies to the demand even if the individual whose surrender is demanded was not in the demanding state when the crime was allegedly committed and has not fled from that state.

Commissioners' Official Comment to UIFSA Section 801

This section has not been amended substantively since 1968. Virtually no controversy has been generated regarding this procedure. Arguably application of Subsection (c) is problematic in situations in which the obligor neither was present in the demanding State at the time of the commission of the crime nor fled from the demanding State. The possibility that an individual may commit a crime in a State without ever being physically present there has elicited considerable discussion and some case law. *See* L. Brilmayer, An Introduction to Jurisdiction in the American Federal System, 329–335 (1986) (discussing minimum contacts theory for criminal jurisdiction); Rotenberg, *Extraterritorial Legislative Jurisdiction and the State Criminal Law*, 38 Tex. L. Rev. 763, 784–87 (1960) (due process requires that the behavior of the defendant must be predictably subject to State's criminal jurisdiction); *cf. Ex parte Boetscher*, 812 S.W.2d 600 (Tex. Crim. App. 1991) (Equal Protection Clause limits disparate treatment of nonresident defendants); *In re King*, 3 Cal.3d 226, 90 Cal. Rptr. 15, 474 P.2d 983 (1970), cert. denied 403 U.S. 931 (enhanced offense for nonresidents impacts constitutional right to travel).

§ 159.802. Conditions of Rendition.

(a) Before making a demand that the governor of another state surrender an individual charged criminally in this state with having failed to provide for the support of an obligee, the governor may require a prosecutor of this state to demonstrate:

(1) that not less than 60 days before the date of the demand, the obligee had initiated proceedings for support under this chapter; or

(2) that initiating the proceeding would be of no avail.

(b) If, under this chapter or a law substantially similar to this chapter, [~~the Uniform Reciprocal Enforcement of Support Act, or the Revised Uniform Reciprocal Enforcement of Support Act,~~] the governor of another state makes a demand that the governor of this state surrender an individual charged criminally in that state with having failed to provide for the support of a child or other individual to whom a duty of support is owed, the governor may require a prosecutor to investigate the demand and report whether a proceeding for support has been initiated or would be effective. If it appears that a proceeding would be effective but has not been initiated, the governor may delay honoring the demand for a reasonable time to permit the initiation of a proceeding.

(c) If a proceeding for support has been initiated and the individual whose rendition is demanded prevails, the governor may decline to honor the demand. If the petitioner prevails and the individual whose rendition is demanded is subject to a support order, the governor may decline to honor the demand if the individual is complying with the support order.

Commissioners' Official Comment to UIFSA Section 802

This section has not undergone significant change since 1968. Interstate rendition remains the last resort for support enforcement, in part because a governor may exercise considerable discretion in deciding whether to honor a demand for rendition of an obligor.

Subchapter J. Miscellaneous Provisions

§ 159.901. Uniformity of Application and Construction.

In applying and construing this chapter, consideration must be given to the need to promote uniformity of [~~This chapter shall be applied and construed to effectuate its general purpose to make uniform~~] the law with respect to the subject **matter** of this chapter among states **that enact a law similar to this chapter** [~~enacting it~~].

§ 159.902. [repealed]

Chapter 160. Uniform Parentage Act

Subchapter A. Application and Construction

Subchapter B. General Provisions

Subchapter C. Parent–Child Relationship

Subchapter D. Voluntary Acknowledgment of Paternity

Subchapter E. Registry of Paternity

Part 1. General Provisions

Part 2. Operation of Registry

Subchapter H. Child of Assisted Reproduction

Subchapter I. Gestational Agreements

Introductory Comment

Texas can rightly claim to have the most progressive parentage legislation of any state. Effective June 14, 2001, Texas adopted the *Uniform Parentage Act (2000)*, replacing former Chapter 160, *Determination of Parentage*. The *Uniform Parentage Act* was approved by the National Conference of Commissioners on Uniform State Laws in 2000 and recommended for approval by all states. Texas was the first state to adopt this uniform act, followed by Washington and Wyoming. Fifteen (15) other states have adopted the original *Uniform Parentage Act (1973)*.

The Act will be familiar to Texas lawyers and judges in many ways. Subchapters C, D and E closely track existing Texas law.

Subchapter F, dealing with genetic testing, moved Texas from an "exclusionary" approach to a "rebuttably identified" approach in paternity proceedings. Testing did not change, but the test results now read differently and places Texas with the majority of other jurisdictions.

Subchapter G brings some change to Texas law, mostly limiting times to challenge presumptions of paternity and clearly defining those individuals who are bound by earlier determinations of paternity. The Texas enactment increases the time from two years for challenge in the uniform act to four years. Existing Texas case law on challenging paternity in the marital context will be of limited significance under amended Chapter 160. On the other hand, the Act eliminates time limitations for children with no presumed father for bringing an action to determine parentage. Section 160.608 introduces paternity by estoppel to Texas statutory law for the first time. Suits for paternity cannot be dismissed with prejudice for want of prosecution.

Subchapter H, dealing with assisted reproduction, is similar to existing Texas law. However, default provisions for an assisted reproduction action after divorce or the death of a spouse are a first in Texas law.

In 2003, Subchapter I dealing with gestational agreements was added. This subchapter was omitted in the original Texas enactment of the Uniform Parentage Act and its addition now completes the Texas' full adoption of the uniform act, subject only to some variations that are noted in the Comments.

CLE/Leading Publications

Parentage: the unsolved mystery. Rhonda F. Hunter, 2004 ADV. FAM. L.

Dad vs. donor: who stays and who pays. Jacqueline Taylor & Ellen A. Yarrell, 2004 U. TEX. FAM. L. FRONT LINES

What the family practitioner should know about the UPA. Lisa Lynne Taylor, 2003 ADV. FAM. L.

Collaborative reproduction. Ellen A. Yarrell, 2003 ADV. FAM. L.

Children inside wedlock/outside wedlock. Janet McCullar, 2003 MARRIAGE DISSOLUTION

Blood will tell: parentage issues in family law litigation. John J. Sampson & Ellen A. Yarrell, 2002 ADV. FAM. L.

Do you think blood will tell? Parentage issues in family law litigation. Ellen A Yarrell, 2002 MARRIAGE DISSOLUTION

The Texas Uniform Parentage Act (2001): establishment of paternity and the nationwide disestablishment controversy. John J. Sampson & Susan Paikin, 2002 MARRIAGE DISSOLUTION

The Uniform Parentage Act: 85% current law; 15% alligator. Charles G. Childress, 2001 ADV. FAM. L. DRAFTING

Uniform Parentage Act (2000) with Official Comments (and Unofficial Annotations by John J. Sampson, Reporter). 35 FAM. L. Q. NO. 1 (Spring 2001)

Who's my mommy / who's my daddy?–a parentage free for all? Ellen A. Yarrell, 2001 ADV. FAM. L.

Leading U.S. Supreme Court Cases

Michael H. v. Gerald D., 491 U.S. 110, 109 S.Ct. 2333, 105 L.Ed.2d 91 (1989) (U.S. Const. does not mandate right of man to establish his paternity of child born to married woman)

Reed v. Campbell, 476 U.S. 852, 90 L.Ed.2d 858, 106 S.Ct. 2234 (1986) (Texas Probate Code held unconstitutional discrimination against illegitimate child)

Lehr v. Robertson, 463 U.S. 248, 77 L.Ed.2d 614, 103 S.Ct. 2985 (1983) (state may restrict claim of biological father to procedure required for paternity registry)

Little v. Streater, 454 U.S. 1, 68 L.Ed.2d 627, 101 S.Ct. 2202 (1981) (indigent respondent has U.S. Const. right to parentage testing in paternity suit brought by state)

Caban v. Mohammed, 441 U.S. 380, 60 L.Ed.2d 297, 99 S.Ct. 1760 (1979) (biological father's actual relationship with child is crucial to determining his rights)

Gomez v. Perez, 409 U.S. 535, 35 L.Ed.2d 56, 93 S.Ct. 872 (1973) (unconstitutional to discriminate between legitimate and illegitimate children regarding father's duty to support)

Stanley v. Illinois, 405 U.S. 645, 31 L.Ed.2d 551, 92 S.Ct. 1208 (1972) (state statute may not presume away father's rights)

Leading Texas Cases

In re R.A.H., 130 S.W.3d 68 (Tex. 2004) (Uniform Parentage Cat's four-year time period for filing paternity contest based on acknowledgment)

In re Z.L.T., 124 S.W.3d 163 (Tex. 2003) (not error to implicitly deny bench warrant to transport prison inmate to paternity trial)

Texas Dept. of Protective & Regulatory Services v. Sherry, 46 S.W.3d 857 (Tex. 2001) (man lacks standing to obtain paternity determination for child who already has adjudicated father)

In re B.I.V., 923 S.W.2d 573 (Tex. 1996) (mother has standing to appeal child support order agreed upon by A.G. and father in connection with paternity suit)

In re J.W.T., 872 S.W.2d 189 (Tex. 1994) (if he acts expeditiously, biological father has Tex. Const. right to establish his paternity over objections of mother and her husband)

Dickson v. Simpson, 807 S.W.2d 726 (Tex. 1991) (nonmarital child must be guaranteed fair opportunity to establish heirship)

In re Baby McLean, 725 S.W.2d 696 (Tex. 1987) (Texas ERA protects rights of biological father in a case where there is no presumed father)

In re Shockley, 123 S.W.3d 642 (Tex. App.—El Paso 2003, no pet.) (mother estopped from requesting parentage testing)

In re J.W., 97 S.W.3d 818 (Tex. App.—Dallas 2003, pet. denied) (child's petition to establish parentage not barred by prior divorce decree)

In re Calderon–Garza, 81 S.W.3d 899 (Tex. App.—El Paso 2002, no pet.) (Texas is home state of child in alleged father's suit to establish parentage)

In re C.S.C., 43 S.W.3d 536 (Tex. App.—Beaumont 2000, no pet.) (man has (Texas) constitutional right to assert his claim of paternity)

Malone v. Thomas, 24 S.W.3d 412 (Tex. App.—Houston [1st Dist.] 1999, no pet.) (deceased's paternity established by his lifetime acts creating presumptions—son is his only heir)

In re J.A.G., 18 S.W.3d 772 (Tex. App.—San Antonio 1999, no pet.) (incarcerated alleged father not entitled to appointed attorney for paternity/child support trial)

Vilely v. Solomon, 16 S.W.3d 106 (Tex. App.—Houston [1st Dist.] 1999, no pet.) (daughter born of marriage unsuccessfully challenges her father's paternity of other out-of-wedlock daughter—DNA test results not explained)

Cross Reference

TEX. PROBATE CODE ANN. § 42. Inheritance Rights of Children.

Texas Family Law Practice Manual

Form 3–38. Parentage Action
Chapter 40. Parentage
Chapter 41. Voluntary Paternity

COMMISSIONERS' PREFATORY NOTE TO UPA

The promulgation of the UNIFORM PARENTAGE ACT in 2000, as amended in 2002, is now the official recommendation of the National Conference of Commissioners on Uniform State Laws on the subject of parentage. This Act relegates to history all of the earlier uniform acts dealing with parentage, to wit, UPA (1973), UPUFA (1988), and USCACA (1988). The amendments of 2002 are the end-result of objections lodged by the American Bar Association Section of Individual Rights and Responsibilities and the ABA Committee on the Unmet Legal Needs of Children, based on the view that in certain respects the 2000 version did not adequately treat a child of unmarried parents equally with a child of married parents. Because equal treatment of nonmarital children was a hallmark of the 1973 Act, the objections caused the drafters of the 2000 version to reconsider certain sections of the Act. Through extended discussion and a meeting of representatives of all the entities involved, a determination was made that the objections had merit. As a result of this process, the amendments shown in this Act were presented by mail ballot to the Commissioners and unanimously approved in November 2002.

In brief outline, UPA (2002) is structured as follows: Subchapter B, General Provisions, adds many new definitions to clarify the participants in determinations of parentage and adapt the Act to recent scientific developments. Subchapter C, Parent–Child Relationship, will look familiar to past users of UPA (1973) because it continues a number of the 1973 provisions with little or no change, while eliminating the ambiguous term "natural" to describe a genetic parent. Subchapter D, Voluntary Acknowledgment of Paternity, is entirely new and is driven by federal mandates that states provide simplified nonjudicial means to establish paternity, especially for newborns and young children. Subchapter E, Registry of Paternity, is entirely new and incorporates a tightly integrated registry law to deal with the rights of a man who is neither an acknowledged, presumed or adjudicated father. A primary goal of this article is to facilitate adoption proceedings. Subchapter F, Genetic Testing, comprehensively covers that subject in ten separate sections (the 1973 Act had one section on the subject). Subchapter G, Proceeding to Adjudicate Parentage, sets forth the parties to, and the procedures for, adjudicating parentage and challenging acknowledgments, presumptions, and judgments. Subchapter H, Child of Assisted Reproduction, recodifies USCACA (1988), but applies its provisions to nonmarital as well as marital children born as a result of assisted reproductive technologies. Subchapter I, Gestational Agreements, is based upon USCACA (1988), but follows only the option that permits enforcement of a gestational agreement. Among the departures from the uniform act, the Texas version is restricted to married couples.

UPA (1973) contained a number of other substantive provisions, including those applicable to child support and custody. These subjects are omitted from UPA (2002) because other state law adequately provides for them.

Finally, Uniform Parentage Act (2002) is consistent with the provisions of two other uniform acts of great significance, namely the Uniform Interstate Family Support Act [UIFSA (1996) and UIFSA (2001)] and the Uniform Child Custody Jurisdiction and Enforcement Act [UCCJEA (1997)].

Editors' Note: *The Texas enactment departs from the uniform version in a few sections; the Commissioners' Commentary has been edited to reflect those changes. The full act, with unedited Commissioners' Commentary, is found at National Conference of Commissioners on Uniform State Laws website: www.nccusl.org.*

Subchapter A. Application and Construction.

§ 160.001. Application and Construction.

This chapter shall be applied and construed to promote the uniformity of the law among the states that enact the Uniform Parentage Act.

§ 160.002. Conflicts Between Provisions.

If a provision of this chapter conflicts with another provision of this title or another state statute or rule and the conflict cannot be reconciled, this chapter prevails.

Authors' Comment

Subchapter A is not an official part of the Uniform Parentage Act but was added by the Legislature to make certain that this chapter prevailed over any inconsistency that may exist elsewhere in the Family Code. Similar provisions are found in Chapter 152, the

Uniform Child Custody Jurisdiction and Enforcement Act, and Chapter 159, the *Uniform Interstate Family Support Act*.

Subchapter B. General Provisions.

§ 160.101. Short Title.

This chapter may be cited as the Uniform Parentage Act.

§ 160.102. Definitions.

In this chapter:

(1) "Adjudicated father" means a man who has been adjudicated by a court to be the father of a child.

(2) "Assisted reproduction" means a method of causing pregnancy other than sexual intercourse. The term includes:

(A) intrauterine insemination;

(B) donation of eggs;

(C) donation of embryos;

(D) in vitro fertilization and transfer of embryos; and

(E) intracytoplasmic sperm injection.

(3) "Child" means an individual of any age whose parentage may be determined under this chapter.

(4) "Commence" means to file the initial pleading seeking an adjudication of parentage in a court of this state.

(5) "Determination of parentage" means the establishment of the parent-child relationship by the signing of a valid acknowledgment of paternity under Subchapter D or by an adjudication by a court.

(6) "Donor" means an individual who produces eggs or sperm used for assisted reproduction, regardless of whether the production is for consideration. The term does not include:

(A) a husband who provides sperm or a wife who provides eggs to be used for assisted reproduction by the wife; or

(B) a woman who gives birth to a child by means of assisted reproduction.

(7) "Ethnic or racial group" means, for purposes of genetic testing, a recognized group that an individual identifies as all or part of the individual's ancestry or that is identified by other information.

(8) "Genetic testing" means an analysis of an individual's genetic markers to exclude or identify a man as the father of a child or a woman as the mother of a child. The term includes an analysis of one or more of the following:

(A) deoxyribonucleic acid; and

(B) blood-group antigens, red-cell antigens, human-leukocyte antigens, serum enzymes, serum proteins, or red-cell enzymes.

(9) "Intended parents" means individuals who enter into an agreement providing that the individuals will be the parents of a child born to a gestational mother by means of assisted reproduction, regardless of whether either individual has a genetic relationship with the child.

(10) "Man" means a male individual of any age.

(11) "Parent" means an individual who has established a parent-child relationship under Section 160.201.

(12) "Paternity index" means the likelihood of paternity determined by calculating the ratio between:

(A) the likelihood that the tested man is the father of the child, based on the genetic markers of the tested man, the mother of the child, and the child, conditioned on the hypothesis that the tested man is the father of the child; and

(B) the likelihood that the tested man is not the father of the child, based on the genetic markers of the tested man, the mother of the child, and the child, conditioned on the hypothesis that the tested man is not the father of the child and that the father of the child is of the same ethnic or racial group as the tested man.

(13) "Presumed father" means a man who, by operation of law under Section 160.204, is recognized as the father of a child until that status is rebutted or confirmed in a judicial proceeding.

(14) "Probability of paternity" means the probability, with respect to the ethnic or racial group to which the alleged father belongs, that the alleged father is the father of the child, compared to a random, unrelated man of the same ethnic or racial group, expressed as a percentage incorporating the paternity index and a prior probability.

(15) "Record" means information that is inscribed on a tangible medium or that is stored in an electronic or other medium and is retrievable in a perceivable form.

(16) "Signatory" means an individual who authenticates a record and is bound by its terms.

(17) "Support enforcement agency" means a public official or public agency authorized to seek:

(A) the enforcement of child support orders or laws relating to the duty of support;

(B) the establishment or modification of child support;

(C) the determination of parentage;

(D) the location of child-support obligors and their income and assets; or

(E) the conservatorship of a child or the termination of parental rights.

Commissioners' Comment to UPA Section 102

Subsection (4) is derived from the UCCJEA (1997) § 102(5).

Subsection (7) defines the "ethnic or racial group" of the individual being tested only for purposes of the genetic testing. The genetic tests themselves do not determine the race or ethnic group of the individual; rather, for the individual who is not excluded, the race or ethnic group provided is used in the paternity calculations. This is done because the use of the race or ethnic group of the tested individual gives the most conservative calculations, that is, those most favoring non-paternity.

Subsection (8) contemplates that the genetic testing used in paternity testing is broad and includes all of the traditional genetic tests, such as blood types and HLA (Human Leukocyte Antigen), as well as newer DNA technologies. In the past the term "blood test" was commonly applied to paternity testing. However, this usage actually referred to the sample collected; in fact, the tests were genetic tests performed on blood samples. The Act uses the scientific term "deoxyribonucleic acid." This is to accommodate the changes in technology used to evaluate the DNA. Early DNA testing involved RFLP technology (Restriction Fragment Length Polymorphism), followed by PCR techniques (Polymerase Chain Reaction); these may be replaced by newer technology, such as SNP (Single

Nucleotide Polymorphisms). The type of DNA technology to be employed is best left to scientific bodies, such as accreditation agencies, *see* Section 503(a), *infra*.

Subsection (10) is derived from the Uniform Putative and Unknown Fathers Act (UPUFA). Defining "man" to include all male humans eliminates the connotation of adulthood, thereby satisfying the obvious need for the Act to cover under-age progenitors as well as adults. Although objection to calling a 14–year-old father a "man" was raised when UPUFA was considered by the Conference, for purposes of procreation such an individual is a man.

Subsection (12) defines a complex concept, the "paternity index." Note that the definition includes statistical measures of the mother and tested man. The tested man may be an alleged father, or any other potential biological father. In fact, under appropriate circumstances Article 5 provides for testing without samples from the mother or the alleged father. In these cases the expert statistically reconstructs the missing potential mother or biological father from genetic testing of samples from their relatives. Therefore the definition is correct even in cases involving a missing parent.

Subsection (15) is derived from the Uniform Electronic Transactions Act § 102(13), which establishes a standard for either paper or electronic record keeping. [TEX. BUS. & COM. CODE ANN. ch. 43]

Authors' Comment to UPA Section 102

UPA (2000) contains definitions for "acknowledged father," "alleged father," and "parent-child relationship," but the Texas Legislative Council, under its drafting guidelines, placed those definitions in Chapter 101, *supra.*

---

§ 160.103. Scope of Chapter; Choice of Law.

(a) This chapter governs every determination of parentage in this state.

(b) The court shall apply the law of this state to adjudicate the parent-child relationship. The applicable law does not depend on:

(1) the place of birth of the child; or

(2) the past or present residence of the child.

(c) This chapter does not create, enlarge, or diminish parental rights or duties under another law of this state.

[~~(d) This chapter does not authorize or prohibit an agreement between a woman and the intended parents of a child in which the woman relinquishes all rights as a parent of a child conceived by means of assisted reproduction and which provides that the intended parents become the parents of the child. If a birth results under a gestational agreement that is unenforceable under the law of this state, the parent child relationship is determined as provided by Subchapter C.~~]

(d) Repealed by Acts 2003, 78th Leg., ch. 457, § 3.

History: Amended by 78th Legis., Reg. Sess. (2003), H.B. 729, eff. Sept. 1, 2003, and "applies to a motion or other request for relief made in a parentage or paternity proceeding that is commenced on or after the effective date of this Act. A motion or other request for relief made in a parentage or paternity proceeding commenced before the effective date of this Act is governed by the law in effect at the time the proceeding was commenced, and the former law is continued in effect for that purpose."

Commissioners' Comment to UPA Section 103

The new UPA conforms to the requirement of 42 U.S.C. § 666(a)(5)(A), that a state must provide that parentage proceedings be available at any time before a child attains 18 years of age or suffer the potential penalty of forfeiture of the federal funds that subsidize child support enforcement by the state.

Subsection (b) is derived from the UIFSA (1996) § 303 and UPA (1973) § 8(b). This section simplifies choice of law principles; the local court is directed to apply local law. If in fact this state is an inappropriate forum, dismissal for forum non-conveniens may be appropriate.

Authors' Comment

In 2003, subsection (d) was repealed as part of the legislation regulating gestational agreements. *See* Subchapter I, Section 160. 751, *et seq.*

§ 160.104. Authorized Courts.

The following courts are authorized to adjudicate parentage under this chapter:

(1) a court with jurisdiction to hear a suit affecting the parent-child relationship under this title; or

(2) a court with jurisdiction to adjudicate parentage under another law of this state.

Commissioners' Comment to UPA Section 104

Source: Uniform Parentage Act (1973) § 8(a).

Although a proceeding to determine parentage is most often associated with an action to establish a child support order, the Act departs from the choice made by the UIFSA (1996) § 102, [Texas Family Code § 159.102] which allows for the establishment of a child support order by an administrative agency. Insofar as establishment of parentage is concerned, UPA (2000) makes the deliberate decision to require a judicial proceeding. This decision is consistent with the practice of most States; in fact, very few States provide for the resolution of disputed paternity through administrative processes. The use of the term "tribunal, as found in UIFSA, was deliberately rejected. Joinder of a parentage proceeding with an action for divorce, annulment, separate maintenance, or child support and custody is left to state law.

§ 160.105. Protection of Participants.

A proceeding under this chapter is subject to the other laws of this state governing the health, safety, privacy, and liberty of a child or any other individual who may be jeopardized by the disclosure of identifying information, including the person's address, telephone number, place of employment, and social security number and the name of the child's day-care facility and school.

Commissioners' Comment to UPA Section 105

Source: UCCJEA (1997) § 209(e). [Texas Family Code § 152.209 (e)]

§ 160.106. Determination of Maternity.

The provisions of this chapter relating to the determination of paternity apply to a determination of maternity.

Commissioners' Comment to UPA Section 106

Source: UPA (1973) § 21.

This section provides for a determination of the mother-child relationship if that issue is in dispute. Except in circumstances involving immigration, cases involving disputed maternity are extraordinarily rare. Therefore, UPA (2000) is otherwise written in terms applicable to the determination of paternity. While certain provisions found in the balance of the Act do not apply in a proceeding to establish maternity, the Act continues the decision made in UPA (1973) not to burden these already complex provisions with unnecessary references to the ascertainment of maternity. Section 160.201(a) is the sole provision in the act specifically relating to the mother-child relationship. In any given case, a judge facing a claim for the determination of the mother-child relationship should have little difficulty deciding which portions of the Act should be applied.

Subchapter C. Parent–Child Relationship.

Authors' Introductory Comment

As part of a social and legal reform in this country during the 70's and 80's, Texas has had laws in place since 1989 forbidding any form of legal discrimination against a child born to unmarried parents.

Leading Cases

Michael H. v. Gerald D., 491 U.S. 110, 105 L.Ed.2d 91, 109 S.Ct. 2333 (1989) (family unity and privacy prevails over any rights biological father may have)

Santosky v. Kramer, 455 U.S. 745, 71 L.Ed.2d 599, 102 S.Ct. 1388 (1982) (constitutional dimension of parent-child relationship)

Wisconsin v. Yoder, 406 U.S. 205, 32 L.Ed.2d 15, 92 S.Ct. 1526 (1972) (state may not compel Amish parents to send children to high school)

In re J.W.T., 872 S.W.2d 189 (Tex. 1994) (if he acts expeditiously, biological father has TEX. CONST. right to establish his paternity over objections of mother and her husband)

In re Baby McLean, 725 S.W.2d 696 (Tex. 1987) (Texas ERA protects rights of biological father in a case where there is no presumed father)

Holick v. Smith, 685 S.W.2d 18 (Tex. 1985), and *In re* G.M., 596 S.W.2d 846 (Tex. 1980) (parenthood is a fundamental, natural, basic civil right)

---

§ 160.201. Establishment of Parent-Child Relationship.

(a) The mother-child relationship is established between a woman and a child by:

(1) the woman giving birth to the child;

(2) an adjudication of the woman's maternity; or

(3) the adoption of the child by the woman.

(b) The father-child relationship is established between a man and a child by:

(1) an unrebutted presumption of the man's paternity of the child under Section 160.204;

(2) an effective acknowledgment of paternity by the man under Subchapter D, unless the acknowledgment has been rescinded or successfully challenged;

(3) an adjudication of the man's paternity;

(4) the adoption of the child by the man; or

(5) the man's consenting to assisted reproduction by his wife under Subchapter H, which resulted in the birth of the child.

Commissioners' Comment to UPA Section 201

Source: UPA (1973), § 4; expanded to include all possible bases of the parent-child relationship.

---

§ 160.202. No Discrimination Based on Marital Status.

A child born to parents who are not married to each other has the same rights under the law as a child born to parents who are married to each other.

Commissioners' Comment to UPA Section 202

Source: UPA (1973) § 2 and Massachusetts Gen. Laws ch. 209C, § 1.

From a legal and social policy perspective, this is one of the most significant substantive provisions of the Act, reaffirming the principle that regardless of the marital status of the parents, children and parents have equal rights with respect to each other. As discussed in the Prefatory Note, U.S. Supreme Court decisions and lower federal and state court decisions require equality of treatment for a child without a presumed father with regard to most areas of substantive law.

The broad statement according equal treatment to a nonmarital child regarding his or her parents is not to be construed as eliminating all possible distinctions in all aspects of the lives of the nonmarital child and parents. For example, UNIFORM PROBATE CODE (1993) § 2–705(b), states that "in construing a dispositive provision of a transferor who is not a natural parent, an individual born to the natural parent is not considered a child of that parent unless the individual while a minor lived as a regular member of the household of that parent or of that parent's parent, brother, sister, spouse, or surviving spouse." In short, the UPC (1993) provides that an individual is presumed not to be included in a class gift from someone other than the child's parent unless that individual lived as a member of the parent's family during childhood. This presumed intent of the donor is rebuttable. Although this provision probably has a disproportionate effect on nonmarital children, the disparity is not based on the circumstances of birth, but rather on post-birth living conditions.

CLE/Leading Publications

Parentage: the unsolved mystery. Rhonda F. Hunter, 2004 ADV. FAM. L.

Dad vs. donor: who stays and who pays. Jacqueline Taylor & Ellen A. Yarrell, 2004 U. TEX. FAM. L. FRONT LINES

Children inside wedlock/outside wedlock. Janet McCullar, 2003 MARRIAGE DISSOLUTION

---

§ 160.203. Consequences of Establishment of Parentage.

Unless parental rights are terminated, a parent-child relationship established under this chapter applies for all purposes, except as otherwise provided by another law of this state.

Commissioners' Comment to UPA Section 203

Source: USCACA (1988) § 10.

This section may seem to state the obvious, but both the statement and the qualifier are necessary because without this explanation a literal reading of §§ 160.201–160.203 could lead to erroneous statutory constructions. The basic purpose of the section is to make clear that a mother, as defined in § 160.201(a), is not a parent once her parental rights have been terminated. Similarly, a man whose paternity has been established by acknowledgment or by court adjudication may subsequently have his parental rights terminated.

The qualifier, "as otherwise provided by another law of this state," is necessary because other statutes may restrict rights of a parent. For example, UPC (1993) § 2-114(c) precludes a parent of a child (and the parent's family) from inheriting from the child by intestate succession "unless that natural parent has openly treated the child as his [or hers] and has not refused to support the child." Similarly, as discussed in the preceding Comment, UPC (1993) § 2-705(b) affects the right of the child to take under class gifts from persons who are not the parents of the child.

---

§ 160.204. Presumption of Paternity.

(a) A man is presumed to be the father of a child if:

(1) he is married to the mother of the child and the child is born during the marriage;

(2) he is married to the mother of the child and the child is born before the 301st day after the date the marriage is terminated by death, annulment, declaration of invalidity, or divorce;

(3) he married the mother of the child before the birth of the child in apparent compliance with law, even if the attempted marriage is or could be declared invalid, and the child is born during the invalid marriage or before the 301st day after the date the marriage is terminated by death, annulment, declaration of invalidity, or divorce; [~~or~~]

(4) he married the mother of the child after the birth of the child in apparent compliance with law, regardless of whether the marriage is or could be declared invalid, he voluntarily asserted his paternity of the child, and:

(A) the assertion is in a record filed with the bureau of vital statistics;

(B) he is voluntarily named as the child's father on the child's birth certificate; or

(C) he promised in a record to support the child as his own; **or**

(5) *[S.B. 1807]* **during the first two years of the child's life, he continuously resided in the household in which the child resided and he represented to others that the child was his own.**

(b) *[H.B. 1878]* A presumption of paternity established under this section may be rebutted only by:

(1) an adjudication under Subchapter G; **or**

(2) the filing of a valid denial of paternity by a presumed father in conjunction with the filing by another person of a valid acknowledgment of paternity as provided by Section 160.305.

History: Amended by 78th Legis., Reg. Sess. (2003), S.B. 1807, eff. Sept. 1, 2003, and "applies only to a suit affecting the parent-child relationship commenced on or after the effective date of this Act. A suit affecting the parent-child relationship commenced before the effective date of this Act is governed by the law in effect on the date the suit was commenced, and the former law is continued in effect for that purpose."

History: Amended by 78th Legis., Reg. Sess. (2003), H.B. 1878, eff. Sept. 1, 2003. "The change in law made by this Act relating to a court order establishing paternity or the obligation to pay child support applies only to a suit affecting the parent-child relationship filed on or after the effective date of this Act. A suit affecting the parent-child relationship filed before the effective date of this Act is governed by the law in effect on the date the suit was filed, and the former law is continued in effect for that purpose."

Commissioners' Comment to UPA Section 204

Source: UPA (1973) § 4.

A network of presumptions was established by UPA (1973) for application to cases in which proof of external circumstances indicate a particular man to be the probable father. The simplest of these is also the best known—birth of a child during the marriage between the mother and a man. When promulgated in 1973, the contemporaneous commentary noted that:

> While perhaps no one state now includes all these presumptions in its law, the presumptions *are* based on existing presumptions of 'legitimacy' in state laws and do not represent a serious departure. Novel is that they have been collected under one roof. All presumptions of paternity are rebuttable in appropriate circumstances. UNIFORM PARENTAGE ACT (1973), Prefatory Note, 9B U.L.A. 379 (2001).

After amendments adopted in 2002, the Uniform Parentage Act retains all but one of the original presumptions of paternity contained in UPA § 4 (1973). Originally the 2000 version of the new Act limited presumptions of paternity to those related to marriage. The objection by the ABA Steering Committee on the Unmet Legal Needs of Children and the Section of Individual Rights and Responsibilities that this could result in differential treatment of children born to unmarried parents resulted in the revision to this section.

Subsection (1) deals with a child born during a marriage; subsection (2) deals with a child conceived during marriage but born after its termination; subsection (3) deals with a child conceived or born during an invalid marriage; and, subsection (4) deals with a child born before a valid or invalid marriage, accompanied by other facts indicating the husband is the father.

Added by amendment in 2002, subsection (5), is a significant revision of UPA § 4(4) (1973), which created a presumption of paternity if a man "receives the child into his home and openly holds out the child as his natural child ...." Because there was no time frame specified in the 1973 act, the language fostered uncertainty about whether the presumption could arise if the receipt of the child into the man's home occurred for a short time or took place long after the child's birth. To more fully serve the goal of treating nonmarital and marital children equally, the "holding out" presumption is restored, subject to an express durational requirement that the man reside with the child for the first two years of the child's life. This mirrors the presumption applied to a married man established by § 607, *infra*. Once this presumption arises, it is subject to attack only under the limited circumstances set forth in § 607 for challenging a marital presumption, and is similarly subject to the estoppel principles of § 608.

One presumption found in UPA (1973) is not repeated in the new Act. Former UPA § 4(5) created a presumption of paternity if the man "acknowledges his paternity of the child in a writing filed with [named agency] [and] ... the mother ... does not dispute the acknowledgment within a reasonable time ...." This presumption was eliminated because it conflicts with Article 3, Voluntary Acknowledgment of Paternity, under which a valid acknowledgment establishes paternity rather than a presumption of paternity.

Finally, subsection (b) is a complete rewrite of UPA (1973) § 4(b). The requirement that a presumption "may be rebutted ... only by clear and convincing evidence" was eliminated from the Act. The same fate was accorded the statement that: "If two or more presumptions arise which conflict with each other, the presumption which on the facts is founded on the weightier considerations of policy and logic controls." Nowadays the existence of modern genetic testing obviates this old approach to the problem of conflicting presumptions when a court is to determine paternity. Nowadays, genetic testing makes it possible in most cases to resolve competing claims to paternity. Moreover, courts may use the estoppel principles in § 608 in appropriate circumstances to deny requests for genetic testing in the interests of preserving a child's ties to the presumed or acknowledged father who openly held himself out as the child's father regardless of whether he is in fact the genetic father.

Authors' Comment

In 2003, subsection (b) was amended to provide that a presumption of paternity may be rebutted by either an adjudication of another man's paternity or by the execution of a valid acknowledgment of paternity. This is a slight variation from the uniform act that provides that only an adjudication can rebut a presumption of paternity. However, an acknowledgment of paternity is deemed to be the legal equivalent of an adjudication. *See* Section 160.305, *infra*.

CLE/Other Legal Publications

Parentage: the unsolved mystery. Rhonda F. Hunter, 2004 ADV. FAM. L.

Dad vs. donor: who stays and who pays. Jacqueline Taylor & Ellen A. Yarrell, 2004 U. TEX. FAM. L. FRONT LINES

Children inside wedlock/outside wedlock. Janet McCullar, 2003 MARRIAGE DISSOLUTION

Predicates, presumptions and privileges. Sherri A. Evans, 2001 ADV. FAM. L.

Leading Cases

In re J.W.T., 872 S.W.2d 189 (Tex. 1994) (if he acts expeditiously, biological father has TEX. CONST. right to establish his paternity over objections of mother and her husband)

In re B.I.V., 870 S.W.2d 12 (Tex. 1994) (failure to join presumed father in paternity proceeding should be challenged by plea in abatement, not by dismissal)

In re S.C.V., 750 S.W.2d 762 (Tex. 1988) (mother rebutted presumption of husband's paternity by blood test exclusion)

Davis v. Davis, 521 S.W.2d 603 (Tex. 1975) (Lord Mansfield's Rule struck down; spouses may testify about nonaccess)

Atty. Gen. of Texas in behalf of Ridge v. Ridge, 773 S.W.2d 645 (Tex. App.—San Antonio 1989, writ denied) (husband obtained finding that he was not the child's father by fraud, bill of review filed on behalf of child)

Espree v. Guillory, 753 S.W.2d 722 (Tex. App.—Houston [1st Dist.] 1988, no writ) (man claiming to be biological father foreclosed by prior SAPCR decree)

Cross Reference

TEX. PROB. CODE ANN. § 42. Inheritance Rights of Children.

Subchapter D. Voluntary Acknowledgment of Paternity.

Commissioners' Prefatory Note to Subchapter D

Voluntary acknowledgment of paternity has long been an alternative to a contested paternity suit. Under UPA (1973) § 4, the inclusion of a man's name on the child's birth certificate created a presumption of paternity, which could be rebutted. A relatively recent enactment of the U.S. Congress has made necessary a fundamental change in the acknowledgment procedure. In the Personal Responsibility and Work Opportunity Reconciliation Act of 1996 (PRWORA, also known as the Welfare Reform Act) Congress conditioned federal child support enforcement funds on a requirement that a state enact laws that greatly strengthen the effect of a man's voluntary acknowledgment of paternity, 42 U.S.C. § 666(a)(5)(C). In brief, a valid, unrescinded, unchallenged acknowledgment of paternity is to be considered equivalent to a judicial determination of paternity.

A comprehensive approach to comply with the congressional mandate is required because the federal act is nonspecific in many respects. Primary among the issues that Congress did not take into account was the fact that a mother who, in cooperation with the actual father of a child, seeks to have that man acknowledge paternity of the child may, in fact, be married to another man. By virtue of parentage laws that are in universal effect, including UPA (2000), the husband of the mother is the presumed father of the child, *see* § 204, *supra*. By ignoring the real possibility that there will be both an acknowledged father and a presumed father, Congress left it to the states to sort out the difficulties inherent in such a fact situation.

Further, PRWORA does not mention that a person acknowledging parentage asserts genetic parentage of the child. Section 301 is designed to prevent circumvention of adoption laws by demanding a sworn assertion of actual parentage of the child through sexual intercourse in support of an acknowledgment under this article.

Sections 302–305 clarify that if a child who is the subject of an acknowledgment also has a presumed father, that man must cooperate by filing a denial of paternity in conjunction with the acknowledgment; if not, the document is void. If the presumed father is unwilling to cooperate, or his whereabouts are unknown, a court proceeding is necessary to resolve the issue of parentage.

Congress also directed that the acknowledgment can be "rescinded" within a particular timeframe, and subsequently can be "challenged"–without stating a timeframe. These procedures are dealt with in Sections 307–309.

---

§ 160.301. Acknowledgment of Paternity.

The mother of a child and a man claiming to be the **biological** father of the child [~~conceived as the result of sexual intercourse with the mother~~] may sign an acknowledgment of paternity with the intent to establish the man's paternity.

History: Amended by 78th Legis., Reg. Sess. (2003), S.B. 1807, eff. Sept. 1, 2003, and "applies only to a suit affecting the parent-child relationship commenced on or after the effective date of this Act. A suit affecting the parent-child relationship commenced before the effective date of this Act is governed by the law in effect on the date the suit was commenced, and the former law is continued in effect for that purpose."

Commissioners' Comment to UPA Section 301

Source: 42 U.S.C. § 666(a)(5)(C)

PRWORA does not explicitly require that a man acknowledging parentage necessarily is asserting his genetic parentage of the child. In order to prevent circumvention of adoption laws, § 301 corrects this omission by requiring a sworn assertion of genetic parentage of the child. A 2002 amendment provides that a man who signs an acknowledgment of paternity declares that he is the genetic father of the child. Thus both the man and the mother acknowledge his paternity, under penalty of perjury, without requiring the parents to spell out the details of their sexual relations. Further, the amended language also takes into account a situation in which a man, who is unable to have sexual intercourse with his partner, may still have contributed to the conception of the child through the use of his own sperm. Henceforth, a man in that situation will be able to recognize legally his paternity through the voluntary acknowledgment procedure.

---

§ 160.302. Execution of Acknowledgment of Paternity.

(a) An acknowledgment of paternity must:

(1) be in a record;

(2) be signed, or otherwise authenticated, under penalty of perjury by the mother and the man seeking to establish paternity;

(3) state that the child whose paternity is being acknowledged:

(A) does not have a presumed father or has a presumed father whose full name is stated; and

(B) does not have another acknowledged or adjudicated father;

(4) state whether there has been genetic testing and, if so, that the acknowledging man's claim of paternity is consistent with the results of the testing; and

(5) state that the signatories understand that the acknowledgment is the equivalent of a judicial adjudication of the paternity of the child and that a challenge to the acknowledgment is permitted only under limited circumstances and is barred after four years.

(b) An acknowledgment of paternity is void if it:

(1) states that another man is a presumed father of the child, unless a denial of paternity signed or otherwise authenticated by the presumed father is filed with the bureau of vital statistics;

(2) states that another man is an acknowledged or adjudicated father of the child; or

(3) falsely denies the existence of a presumed, acknowledged, or adjudicated father of the child.

(c) A presumed father may sign or otherwise authenticate an acknowledgment of paternity.

Commissioners' Comment to UPA Section 302

Source: 42 U.S.C. § 666(a)(5)(C).

The federal statute cited above declares that receipt by a state of the federal subsidy for its child support enforcement program is dependent on state law providing specific procedures for voluntary acknowledgment of paternity. The principle was simple to mandate; but the application is quite complicated.

Problems most notably include fact situations in which the mother of the child is married to someone other than the man who intends to acknowledge his paternity. With an acknowledgment the child would then have both an acknowledged father and a presumed father. To deal with this circumstance, many states have passed laws allowing the presumed father to sign a denial of paternity, which must be filed as part of the acknowledgment. This Act adopts this common sense solution; otherwise the acknowledgment would have no legal consequence because it cannot affect the legal rights of the presumed father.

At least two other provisions of this section warrant special emphasis. Subsection (a)(2) requires that the acknowledgment be "signed, or otherwise authenticated, under penalty of perjury," just as income tax returns and many other government documents require. Clearly, the potential punishment for false swearing is substantial, and the benefits from avoiding the complication of requiring witnesses and a notary are significant in this context. Mandating greater formality would greatly discourage the in-hospital signatures so earnestly desired in 42 U.S.C. § 666(a)(5)(C)(ii).

Similarly, in an attempt to assure full disclosure and avoid false swearing, Subsection (a)(4) requires information regarding whether there has been genetic testing, and if so, confirmation of the fact that the acknowledgment is consistent with the results of that testing. This provision is designed to avoid a possible subversion of the requirements for an adoption. A would-be "father" whose parentage of a child has been excluded by genetic testing may not validly sign an acknowledgment after that fact has been established.

---

§ 160.303. Denial of Paternity.

A presumed father of a child may sign a denial of his paternity. The denial is valid only if:

(1) an acknowledgment of paternity signed or otherwise authenticated by another man is filed under Section 160.305;

(2) the denial is in a record and is signed or otherwise authenticated under penalty of perjury; and

(3) the presumed father has not previously:

(A) acknowledged paternity of the child, unless the previous acknowledgment has been rescinded under Section 160.307 or successfully challenged under Section 160.308; or

(B) been adjudicated to be the father of the child.

§ 160.304. Rules for Acknowledgment and Denial of Paternity.

(a) An acknowledgment of paternity and a denial of paternity may be contained in a single document or in different documents and may be filed separately or simultaneously. If the acknowledgment and denial are both necessary, neither document is valid until both documents are filed.

(b) An acknowledgment of paternity or a denial of paternity may be signed before the birth of the child.

(c) Subject to Subsection (a), an acknowledgment of paternity or denial of paternity takes effect on the date of the birth of the child or the filing of the document with the bureau of vital statistics, whichever occurs later.

(d) An acknowledgment of paternity or denial of paternity signed by a minor is valid if it otherwise complies with this chapter.

Commissioners' Comment to UPA Section 304

Source: 42 U.S.C. § 666(a)(5)(C)(i), requiring a "simple civil process" for voluntary acknowledgment of paternity.

---

§ 160.305. Effect of Acknowledgment or Denial of Paternity.

(a) Except as provided by Sections 160.307 and 160.308, a valid acknowledgment of paternity filed with the bureau of vital statistics is the equivalent of an adjudication of the paternity of a child and confers on the acknowledged father all rights and duties of a parent.

(b) Except as provided by Sections 160.307 and 160.308, a valid denial of paternity filed with the bureau of vital statistics in conjunction with a valid acknowledgment of paternity is the equivalent of an adjudication of the nonpaternity of the presumed father and discharges the presumed father from all rights and duties of a parent.

Commissioners' Comment to UPA Section 305

Source: 42 U.S.C. § 666(a)(5)(D)(ii), requiring that an acknowledgment of paternity be "a legal finding of paternity," and 42 U.S.C. § 666(a)(5)(M), directing that acknowledgments be "filed with the State registry of birth records . . . ".

---

§ 160.306. Filing Fee Not Required.

The bureau of vital statistics may not charge a fee for filing an acknowledgment of paternity or denial of paternity.

§ 160.307. Proceeding for Rescission.

A signatory may rescind an acknowledgment of paternity or denial of paternity by commencing a proceeding to rescind before the earlier of:

(1) the 60th day after the effective date of the acknowledgment or denial, as provided by Section 160.304; or

(2) the date of the first hearing in a proceeding to which the signatory is a party before a court to adjudicate an issue relating to the child, including a proceeding that establishes child support.

Commissioners' Comment to UPA Section 307

This section reflects a decision to require a judicial adjudicatory process to rescind a voluntary acknowledgment of paternity. A federal statute, 42 U.S.C. § 666(a)(5)(c)(D)(ii), mandates that in order to retain the federal child support subsidy, state law must provide signatories with a right of rescission of an acknowledgment of paternity. However, the federal statute does not prescribe the method for the rescission.

---

§ 160.308. Challenge After Expiration of Period for Rescission.

(a) After the period for rescission under Section 160.307 has expired, a signatory of an acknowledgment of paternity or denial of paternity may commence a proceeding to challenge the acknowledgment or denial only on the basis of fraud, duress, or material mistake of fact. The proceeding must be commenced before the fourth anniversary of the date the acknowledgment or denial is filed with the bureau of vital statistics.

(b) A party challenging an acknowledgment of paternity or denial of paternity has the burden of proof.

(c) Notwithstanding any other provision of this chapter, a collateral attack on an acknowledgment of paternity signed under this chapter may not be maintained after the fourth anniversary of the date the acknowledgment of paternity is filed with the bureau of vital statistics.

(d) For purposes of Subsection (a), evidence that, based on genetic testing, the man who is the signatory of an acknowledgement of paternity is not rebuttably identified as the father of a child in accordance with Section 160.505 constitutes a material mistake of fact.

Commissioners' Comment to UPA Section 308

Congress also added a provision for a "challenge" of an acknowledgment of paternity after the period for rescission of a voluntary acknowledgment of paternity has elapsed. Such a collateral attack is to be limited to a challenge based on alleged "fraud, duress, or material mistake of fact," and according to 42 U.S.C. § 666(a)(5)(c)(D)(iii), must be made "in court." Subsection (d) was added to the Texas version to make clear that genetic exclusion is a material mistake of fact.

§ 160.309. Procedure for Rescission or Challenge.

(a) Each signatory to an acknowledgment of paternity and any related denial of paternity must be made a party to a proceeding to rescind or challenge the acknowledgment or denial of paternity.

(b) For purposes of the rescission of or a challenge to an acknowledgment of paternity or denial of paternity, a signatory submits to the personal jurisdiction of this state by signing the acknowledgment or denial. The jurisdiction is effective on the filing of the document with the bureau of vital statistics.

(c) Except for good cause shown, while a proceeding is pending to rescind or challenge an acknowledgment of paternity or a denial of paternity, the court may not suspend the legal responsibilities of a signatory arising from the acknowledgment, including the duty to pay child support.

(d) A proceeding to rescind or to challenge an acknowledgment of paternity or a denial of paternity shall be conducted in the same manner as a proceeding to adjudicate parentage under Subchapter G.

(e) At the conclusion of a proceeding to rescind or challenge an acknowledgment of paternity or a denial of paternity, the court shall order the bureau of vital statistics to amend the birth record of the child, if appropriate.

Commissioners' Comment to UPA Section 309

Although the federal statute does not prescribe the method for "rescission" of an acknowledgment of paternity, it does require a proceeding in court for a subsequent "challenge." Overturning an acknowledgment of paternity is an act of significant legal consequence under either of the prescribed methods allowed. Thus, either method to dispute a prior acknowledgment should require a formal procedure because it may void an otherwise valid legal determination of the child's parentage. A procedure that allows a signatory of an acknowledgment of paternity merely to file a rescission with the state bureau of vital statistics would be an unwise policy choice. Many jurisdictions have come to the same conclusion.

§ 160.310. Ratification Barred.

A court or administrative agency conducting a judicial or administrative proceeding may not ratify an unchallenged acknowledgment of paternity.

Commissioners' Comment to UPA Section 310

Source: 42 U.S.C. § 666(a)(5)(E).

§ 160.311. Full Faith and Credit.

A court of this state shall give full faith and credit to an acknowledgment of paternity or a denial of paternity that is effective in another state if the acknowledgment or denial has been signed and is otherwise in compliance with the law of the other state.

Commissioners' Comment to UPA Section 311

Source: 42 U.S.C. § 666(a)(5)(C)(iv).

PRWORA requires states "to give full faith and credit to such an affidavit [of acknowledgment of paternity] signed in any other state according to its procedures." *Id*. And, Subsection (a)(5)(D)(ii) provides that a "signed voluntary acknowledgment is considered a legal finding of paternity." In sum, federal law requires that an acknowledgment of paternity has the same status as a "judgment," 28 U.S.C. § 1738, a "child custody determination," 28 U.S.C. § 1738A, and a "child support order," 28 U.S.C. § 1738B. This section implements these mandates.

---

§ 160.312. Forms for Acknowledgment and Denial of Paternity.

(a) To facilitate compliance with this subchapter, the bureau of vital statistics shall prescribe forms for the acknowledgment of paternity and the denial of paternity.

(b) A valid acknowledgment of paternity or denial of paternity is not affected by a later modification of the prescribed form.

Commissioners' Comment to UPA Section 312

Source: 42 U.S.C. § 666(a)(5)C)(i),(iv).

The federal Office of Child Support Enforcement has issued an Action Transmittal to all IV–D agencies specifying how to ensure that the forms comply with PRWORA, OCSE–AT–98–02, Required Data Elements for Paternity Acknowledgment Affidavits; *see: http://www.acf.dhhs.gov/programs/cse/ 1998–at.htm*

---

§ 160.313. Release of Information.

The bureau of vital statistics may release information relating to the acknowledgment of paternity or denial of paternity to a signatory of the acknowledgment or denial and to the courts and Title IV-D agency of this or another state.

§ 160.314. Adoption of Rules.

The Title IV-D agency and the bureau of vital statistics may adopt rules to implement this subchapter.

Commissioners' Comment to UPA Section 314

States will implement voluntary acknowledgment of paternity procedures in a variety of ways, depending on local practice. This grant of rulemaking authority to carry out the provisions of this article may include electronic transmission of birth and acknowledgment data to the designated state agency.

---

§ 160.315. Memorandum of Understanding.

(a) The Title IV-D agency and the bureau of vital statistics shall adopt a memorandum of understanding governing the collection and transfer of information for the voluntary acknowledgment of paternity.

(b) The Title IV-D agency and the bureau of vital statistics shall review the memorandum semiannually and renew or modify the memorandum as necessary.

§ 160.316. Suit to Contest Voluntary Statement of Paternity.

(a) A man who executed a voluntary statement of paternity before September 1, 1999, and who, on the basis of that statement, is the subject of a final order declaring him to be a parent of the child who is the subject of the statement may file a suit affecting the parent-child relationship to contest the statement on the basis of fraud, duress, or material mistake of fact in the same manner that a person may contest an acknowledgment of paternity under Sections 160.308 and 160.309. For purposes of this subsection, evidence that, based on genetic testing, the man is not rebuttably identified as the father of a child in accordance with Section 160.505 constitutes a material mistake of fact.

(b) A suit filed under this section to contest a voluntary statement of paternity is not affected by an order with respect to the child that was rendered on the basis of that statement.

(c) The court, on a preliminary finding in a suit under this section that there is credible evidence of fraud, duress, or material mistake of fact regarding the execution of the voluntary statement of paternity, shall order genetic testing as provided by Subchapter F. The person contesting the voluntary statement of paternity shall pay the cost of the testing.

(d) Except as provided by Subsection (e), if the results of the genetic testing do not rebuttably identify the man as the father of the child in accordance with Section 160.505, the court shall set aside:

(1) the final order declaring the man to be a parent of the child; and

(2) any other order with respect to the child that was rendered on the basis of the voluntary statement of paternity.

(e) The court may not set aside under Subsection (d) a final order declaring a man to be a parent of a child if the man who executed the voluntary statement of paternity:

(1) executed the statement knowing that he was not the father of the child; or

(2) subsequently adopted the child.

(f) If the court sets aside a final order as provided by Subsection (d), the court shall order the bureau of vital statistics to amend the birth record of the child. The court may not as a result of the order being set aside:

(1) require an obligee to repay child support paid by the man who executed the voluntary statement of paternity; or

(2) award damages to the man who executed the voluntary statement of paternity.

(g) A suit under this section must be filed before September 1, 2003.

(h) This section expires September 1, 2004.

Authors' Comment to Section 160.316

Section 160.316 is not a uniform provision. Rather, it was added to the Texas version by the legislature to correct an inequality between the former voluntary statement of paternity and the acknowledgment of paternity process established by the uniform act in Subchapter D. In fact, an earlier version of that subchapter was adopted in 1999 as now-repealed §§ 160.201–.216. Because the acknowledgment process provides that a man has four years to challenge his signing of acknowledgment, the legislature determined it is only fair to give those men who signed a voluntary statement of paternity a similar opportunity to challenge a past voluntary statement of paternity. This two year window for filing a challenge expires September 1, 2003, and this section self repeals on September 1, 2004.

Subchapter E. Registry of Paternity.

Commissioners' Prefatory Note to Subchapter E

In *Stanley v. Illinois*, 405 U.S. 645 (1972), the United States Supreme Court held that an unwed father was entitled to a hearing on his fitness as a parent before his children could be taken from him in a dependency proceeding instituted by the state upon the death of the children's mother. That case on its face presented a fairly stable, unwed family situation, although the court did not cite the latter factor as a basis for its decision. The following year, the Conference promulgated the UPA (1973), §§ 24–25 of which dealt with notice of adoption proceedings and proceedings to terminate parental rights in a way that satisfies the *Stanley* requirements.

In *Lehr v. Robertson*, 463 U.S. 248 (1983), the Supreme Court upheld the constitutionality of a New York "putative father registry." The New York statute requires fathers of children born out-of-wedlock to register if they wish to be notified of a termination of parental rights or adoption proceeding. Following a series of well-publicized adoption cases wherein nonmarital fathers had not been given proper notice, legislatures began responding by enacting paternity registries similar to the New York statute. As of May, 2000, at least 28 states had enacted legislation creating paternity registries.

In the view of many commentators, the *Lehr* opinion undercut the rationale of *Stanley* by requiring affirmative action by an alleged father before he would be entitled to notice of a proceeding to terminate his parental rights. The act excepts from registration a man who timely initiates a proceeding for paternity, notwithstanding his failure to register.

> ***Editors' Note:*** *The Texas enactment of UPA (2000) departs from the official text relating to the registry of paternity in two important ways. First the Texas registry is not limited to children under one year of age and applies to children of all ages that might be the subject of a termination proceeding or placed for adoption. Secondly, the registry does not waive service on the alleged father if his whereabouts is known. See* § 160.404, *infra.*

Authors' Introductory Comment

Dealing effectively with the rights of alleged fathers in family law matters has long presented a challenge for attorneys and the courts. Attempting to balance the interests of a biological father to establish a legal relationship with his child while, at the same time, facilitating the adoption of children born outside of marriage to a father who does not take action to establish such a relationship is a daunting task. A number of states, including Texas, have responded by establishing paternity registries. Such registries provide a mechanism for a man alleging himself to be the biological father of a child to take action, independent of the mother of the child, to preserve his right to assert parentage and form a relationship with the child. The Bureau of Vital Statistics (BVS) of the Texas Department of Health is charged with administering the paternity registry.

There remains a question as to the constitutionality of the created registry. The U.S. Supreme Court decision of *Lehr v. Robertson*, 463 U.S. 248 (1983), upheld the right of the State of New York to restrict the claim of a biological father to assert his paternal rights when he failed to register his intent to make such a claim in a state-operated paternity registry. The facts of the case were more than a little outrageous; a man asserting himself to be the father was actually litigating the issue in one court, while a termination and adoption for the child was being sought in another court. The adoption court and the litigants there had full knowledge of the man's pending assertion of paternity in the other court. Notwithstanding the fact that his identity and whereabouts were known, the adoption court proceeded to terminate his rights based on the fact that he had failed to register. According to the Supreme Court, the State of New York had the power to require the registration, and therefore, the man's due process rights were not denied.

Although the New York paternity registry was held not to violate "due process" under the U.S. Constitution, there would be a significant question about the constitutionality of a New York-type registry cutting off all right of a biological father after 30 days for failure to register. Relying on the Texas Constitution's "due course" of law provision, TEX. CONST. Art. I, § 19, the Texas Supreme Court recently dealt with a situation in which a man sought to establish his paternity of a child born to a married woman over the objections of the mother and her husband (the presumed father). The court stated:

> We do not say that our Constitution guarantees a natural father ties with his illegitimate offspring. We do say that one who is arbitrarily prevented from attempting to establish any relationship with his natural child, after making early and unqualified acceptance of parental duties . . . is denied due course of law under section 19 of our Texas Bill of Rights.

In Interest of J.W.T., 872 S.W.2d 189, 198 (Tex. 1994).

In an earlier case, the supreme court held that such rights must extend to a biological father asserting his rights to a child born to an unmarried woman. *In re Baby McLean*, 725 S.W.2d 696 (Tex. 1987). Whether the statutory scheme provided under this subchapter will be deemed to be an arbitrary restriction of the natural father's rights is one that ultimately can only to be resolved in the courts. In this connection, the most objectionable aspects of the New York scheme do not appear in the Texas statute.

Testimony to the Texas legislature indicated that in 1996 some 3,000 men registered with the paternity registry in New York. Also, it was asserted that 17 states have such a registry. The primary value of the registry, of course, is to cut off the rights of biological fathers as soon as possible in order to facilitate adoption. As the bill analysis stated:

> A father may register with the paternity register administered by the Bureau of Vital Statistics by filing a form placed in hospitals, birthing centers, clerk's offices, and other locations. The register protects the parental rights of fathers assuming responsibility for children they may have fathered. The father may not assert any interest in a child if he does not register within 30 days of the child's birth. The mother may contest an alleged father's paternity within 30 days of receipt of a father's paternity registration from the Bureau. Information contained in the registry is confidential and may be released to authorized parties only.

Despite the statement in section 160.258 that a man asserting a paternity claim must register within 30 days of the birth of the child, the "except" proviso eliminates that time limitation for a known father who decides to assert his claim by way of filing a parentage suit before termination of his rights. Further, an alleged father whose identity and whereabouts are known is entitled to service of the petition and citation. The rights of that man may be terminated only by application of the termination provisions of Chapter 161. On the other hand, if a man's identity or whereabouts are unknown, failure to register intent to assert paternity with the Bureau dispenses with the necessity of service of citation by publication. A search of the registry substitutes for that wholly impractical method of notice.

In sum, the Texas version of the paternity registry is primarily a vehicle for terminating the rights of unknown fathers or fathers whose whereabouts cannot be located after the exercise of due diligence.

Cross Reference

TEX. FAM. CODE ANN. § 161.109. Requirement of Paternity Registry Certificate

Part 1. General Provisions

§ 160.401. Establishment of Registry.

A registry of paternity is established in the bureau of vital statistics.

§ 160.402. Registration for Notification.

(a) Except as otherwise provided by Subsection (b), a man who desires to be notified of a proceeding for the adoption of or the termination of parental rights regarding a child that he may have fathered may register with the registry of paternity:

(1) before the birth of the child; or

(2) not later than the 31st day after the date of the birth of the child.

(b) A man is entitled to notice of a proceeding described by Subsection (a) regardless of whether he registers with the registry of paternity if:

(1) a father-child relationship between the man and the child has been established under this chapter or another law; or

(2) the man commences a proceeding to adjudicate his paternity before the court has terminated his parental rights.

(c) A registrant shall promptly notify the registry in a record of any change in the information provided by the registrant. The bureau of vital statistics shall incorporate all new information received into its records but is not required to affirmatively seek to obtain current information for incorporation in the registry.

Commissioners' Comment to UPA Section 402

A registry of paternity protects a claim of paternity from summary termination, but the primary advantage of such a registry is to facilitate infant adoptions through licensed agencies. By registering, a registrant insures that he will receive notice of the possible adoption of a child that he may have fathered if the birth occurs in the state of registration. In this manner, a man may seek to protect his right to assert parentage.

If a state chooses to enact subsection (b)(2), one of the major criticisms of *Lehr v. Robertson, supra,* will be eliminated. In *Lehr*, although the genetic father did not avail himself of the New York putative fathers registry, he had filed a "visitation and paternity" petition in another local court. The trial judge in the adoption proceeding knew the identity of the biological father, where he could be located, and that he was seeking to establish his paternity in another court. Nonetheless, the court granted the adoption and terminated the genetic father's parental rights without notice to him. Subsection (b)(2) exempts an alleged father from the requirement of registration if the man "commences a proceeding to adjudicate his paternity before the court has terminated his parental rights."

The act of registration submits the man to the personal jurisdiction of the tribunals of the state of registration, *see* UIFSA (1996) § 201(7). [Texas Family Code § 159.201(7)]

Authors' Comment

A man who fails to file a notice of intent to claim paternity before the 30th day after the date of birth of the child may not assert an interest in the child except by filing a suit to establish paternity before the man's parental rights have been terminated. Thus, the Texas scheme differs from the procedure enacted by several other states which bars any action to establish paternity by a man claiming to be the child's father despite the fact that no termination action has taken place. Such a rule apparently was rejected by the Texas Legislature as being overly restrictive and perhaps even unconstitutional under the Texas Constitution.

§ 160.403. Notice of Proceeding.

Notice of a proceeding to adopt or to terminate parental rights regarding a child must be given to a registrant who has timely registered with regard to that child. Notice must be given in a manner prescribed for service of process in a civil action.

Commissioners' Comment to UPA Section 403

This section is the logical conclusion to the legal rationale for establishing a paternity registry. In an adoption of a child or termination of parental rights proceeding, the registry provides a clear procedure for resolving whether a nonmarital father intends to assert his rights with regard to the child. If he registers, termination of his rights and adoption of his child may not proceed without notice to him; this affords him the opportunity to assert his paternity and his claims for custody or visitation.

§ 160.404. Termination of Parental Rights: Failure to Register.

The parental rights of a man alleged to be the father of a child may be terminated without notice as provided by Section 161.002 if the man:

(1) did not timely register with the bureau of vital statistics; and

(2) is not entitled to notice under Section 160.402 or 161.002.

Editors' Comment to Section 404

In 1997 a paternity registry was added to Chapter 160, then entitled "Determination of Parentage." In so doing, the Texas Legislature rejected the conclusion of the U.S. Supreme Court in Lehr v. Robertson, 463 U.S. 248 (1983), that it is constitutionally permissible to terminate the parental rights of a genetic father who has failed to register his interest in a child even when his identity and whereabouts are known. Even more egregious was the fact that the putative father was actually seeking to establish his paternity in one trial court at the time that another trial court, with knowledge of that fact, terminated his parental rights for his failure to register in the New York paternity registry.

When the legislature enacted the Uniform Parentage Act in 2001, it chose to continue this policy. Thus, it rejected UPA Sections 404 and 405, as promulgated by NCCUSL, respectively captioned "Termination of Parental Rights: Child Under One Year of Age" and "Termination of Parental Rights: Child at Least One Year of Age." The UPA provides that notice is not required to terminate the parental rights of an alleged father of an infant less than one year old if he has not registered his interest in the child; notice of a proceeding to terminate or adopt to the alleged father is required as in other civil suit if the child is at least one year old.

Section 160.404, a purely-Texas provision, makes the appropriate cross-references to the relevant provisions in this chapter and Chapter 161, "Termination of the Parent-Child Relationship (§§ 160.402, 161.002)." In sum, citation in a SAPCR is required in order to bind an alleged genetic father to a termination decree if his identity and whereabouts are known. If his identity or whereabouts are not known, Section 161.002 permits termination of the alleged father's rights without the necessity of "personal service of citation or citation by publication" if a search of the registry yields a certificate attesting to the fact that he has not filed with the registry.

Part 2. Operation of Registry

§ 160.411. Required Form.

The bureau of vital statistics shall adopt a form for registering with the registry. The form must require the signature of the registrant. The form must state that:

(1) the form is signed under penalty of perjury;

(2) a timely registration entitles the registrant to notice of a proceeding for adoption of the child or for termination of the registrant's parental rights;

(3) a timely registration does not commence a proceeding to establish paternity;

(4) the information disclosed on the form may be used against the registrant to establish paternity;

(5) services to assist in establishing paternity are available to the registrant through the support enforcement agency;

(6) the registrant should also register in another state if the conception or birth of the child occurred in the other state;

(7) information on registries in other states is available from the bureau of vital statistics; and

(8) procedures exist to rescind the registration of a claim of paternity.

§ 160.412. Furnishing of Information; Confidentiality.

(a) The bureau of vital statistics is not required to attempt to locate the mother of a child who is the subject of a registration. The bureau of vital statistics shall send a copy of the notice of the registration to a mother who has provided an address.

(b) Information contained in the registry is confidential and may be released on request only to:

(1) a court or a person designated by the court;

(2) the mother of the child who is the subject of the registration;

(3) an agency authorized by another law to receive the information;

(4) a licensed child-placing agency;

(5) a support enforcement agency;

(6) a party, or the party's attorney of record, to a proceeding under this chapter or a proceeding to adopt or to terminate parental rights regarding a child who is the subject of the registration; and

(7) the registry of paternity in another state.

§ 160.413. Offense: Unauthorized Release of Information.

(a) A person commits an offense if the person intentionally releases information from the registry of paternity to another person, including an agency, that is not authorized to receive the information under Section 160.412.

(b) An offense under this section is a Class A misdemeanor.

§ 160.414. Rescission of Registration.

A registrant may rescind his registration at any time by sending to the registry a rescission in a record or another manner authenticated by him and witnessed or notarized.

§ 160.415. Untimely Registration.

If a man registers later than the 30th day after the date of the birth of the child, the bureau of vital statistics shall notify the registrant that the registration was not timely filed.

§ 160.416. Fees for Registry.

(a) A fee may not be charged for filing a registration or to rescind a registration.

(b) Except as otherwise provided by Subsection (c), the bureau of vital statistics may charge a reasonable fee for making a search of the registry and for furnishing a certificate.

(c) A support enforcement agency is not required to pay a fee authorized by Subsection (b).

Part 3. Search of Registries

§ 160.421. Search of Appropriate Registry.

(a) If a father-child relationship has not been established under this chapter, a petitioner for the adoption of or the termination of parental rights regarding the child must obtain a certificate of the results of a search of the registry.

(b) If the petitioner for the adoption of or the termination of parental rights regarding a child has reason to believe that the conception or birth of the child may have occurred in another state, the petitioner must obtain a certificate of the results of a search of the paternity registry, if any, in the other state.

§ 160.422. Certificate of Search of Registry.

(a) The bureau of vital statistics shall furnish a certificate of the results of a search of the registry on request by an individual, a court, or an agency listed in Section 160.412(b).

(b) The certificate of the results of a search must be signed on behalf of the bureau and state that:

(1) a search has been made of the registry; and

(2) a registration containing the information required to identify the registrant:

(A) has been found and is attached to the certificate; or

(B) has not been found.

(c) A petitioner must file the certificate of the results of a search of the registry with the court before a proceeding for the adoption of or termination of parental rights regarding a child may be concluded.

(d) A search of the registry is not required if the only man alleged to be the father of the child has signed a waiver of interest in, or relinquishment of parental rights with regard to, the child.

§ 160.423. Admissibility of Certificate.

A certificate of the results of a search of the registry in this state or of a paternity registry in another state is admissible in a proceeding for the adoption of or the termination of parental rights regarding a child and, if relevant, in other legal proceedings.

Subchapter F. Genetic Testing.

§ 160.501. Application of Subchapter.

This subchapter governs genetic testing of an individual to determine parentage, regardless of whether the individual:

(1) voluntarily submits to testing; or

(2) is tested under an order of a court or a support enforcement agency.

Commissioners' Comment to UPA Section 501

This section is intended to avoid problems with regard to the admissibility of the result of voluntary genetic testing. Testing is often agreed upon to avoid the cost and delay engendered by requiring a proceeding be filed before the result of genetic testing can be admitted as evidence. If the test excludes the man's paternity, an unnecessary step has been avoided.

---

§ 160.502. Order for Testing.

(a) Except as otherwise provided by this subchapter and by Subchapter G, a court shall order a child and other designated individuals to submit to genetic testing if the request is made by a party to a proceeding to determine parentage.

(b) If a request for genetic testing of a child is made before the birth of the child, the court or support enforcement agency may not order in utero testing.

(c) If two or more men are subject to court-ordered genetic testing, the testing may be ordered concurrently or sequentially.

Commissioners' Comment to UPA Section 502

Source: UPA (1973) § 11; 42 U.S.C. § 666(a)(5)(B)(i) requiring genetic testing in certain cases.

The progress that science has made in understanding molecular genetics since the promulgation of UPA (1973) is phenomenal. Subsection (a) speaks to testing of a "designated individual" other than of the "mother, and alleged or presumed father" to take into account the fact that testing for paternity may proceed without testing the mother. Further, testing may also proceed without testing the alleged father by testing close relatives of that man. Moreover, the right of the court to order testing is not absolute; Sections 607–609 place limitations on genetic testing if the child has a presumed, acknowledged, or adjudicated father.

Subsection (c) is intended to prevent the court from ordering the mother to undergo prenatal testing, such as through amniocentesis or other in utero collection method. These procedures have a measurable risk to the life and health of both the fetus and the mother. If the mother volunteers for such testing, she may undergo prenatal sample collection for parentage determination.

Subsection (d) recognizes that multiple men may be participating in the establishment process. The laboratories prefer to evaluate all persons concurrently, as concurrent testing may prevent multiple sample collections from the child and in rare cases (such as evaluating two non-identical siblings) the laboratory can continue testing until one or both of the tested men are excluded. However, sequential testing is also acceptable.

---

§ 160.503. Requirements for Genetic Testing.

(a) Genetic testing must be of a type reasonably relied on by experts in the field of genetic testing. The testing must be performed in a testing laboratory accredited by:

(1) the American Association of Blood Banks, or a successor to its functions;

(2) the American Society for Histocompatibility and Immunogenetics, or a successor to its functions; or

(3) an accrediting body designated by the federal secretary of health and human services.

(b) A specimen used in genetic testing may consist of one or more samples, or a combination of samples, of blood, buccal cells, bone, hair, or other body tissue or fluid. The specimen used in the testing is not required to be of the same kind for each individual undergoing genetic testing.

(c) Based on the ethnic or racial group of an individual, the testing laboratory shall determine the databases from which to select frequencies for use in the calculation of the probability of paternity of the individual. If there is disagreement as to the testing laboratory's choice:

(1) the objecting individual may require the testing laboratory, not later than the 30th day after the date of receipt of the report of the test, to recalculate the probability of paternity using an ethnic or racial group different from that used by the laboratory;

(2) the individual objecting to the testing laboratory's initial choice shall:

(A) if the frequencies are not available to the testing laboratory for the ethnic or racial group requested, provide the requested frequencies compiled in a manner recognized by accrediting bodies; or

(B) engage another testing laboratory to perform the calculations; and

(3) the testing laboratory may use its own statistical estimate if there is a question regarding which ethnic or racial group is appropriate and, if available, shall calculate the frequencies using statistics for any other ethnic or racial group requested.

(d) If, after recalculation using a different ethnic or racial group, genetic testing does not rebuttably identify a man as the father of a child under Section 160.505, an individual who has been tested may be required to submit to additional genetic testing.

Commissioners' Comment to UPA Section 503

Source: 42 U.S.C. § 666(a)(5)(B)(i)(I)(II) and § 666(a)(5)(F)(i)(I)(II).

As of December 2000, the Secretary of Health and Human Services has not officially designated any accreditation bodies as referenced in subsection (b)(3). But, Information Memorandum O.C.S.E.-IM–97–03, April 10, 1997, from the Deputy Director of the Office of Child Support Enforcement identifies the American Association of Blood Banks and American Society for Histocompatibility and Immunogenetics as meeting this requirement. The accreditation requirement assures that the testing will "be of a type reasonably relied upon by experts in the field of genetic testing."

Subsection (b) clarifies that a "specimen" suitable for genetic testing may be composed from one of a wide variety of constituent elements of "body tissue and fluids." This conforms the statutory language to biological terminology to assure common understanding between the scientific community and the legal profession. In states with statutes employing only the broad terms, bench and bar have evidenced confusion about the fact that blood, buccal cells, bone, hair, etc. are "body tissues."

Subsections (c) and (d) are designed to clarify the use of "race or ethnic group" in the paternity calculations. Generally, the individual tested provides the information regarding the ethnic or racial group to use in the calculations. These sections are designed to avoid last minute changes in the racial designation, a scientific version of "forum shopping", and to easily correct any misunderstanding about which race should be used.

---

§ 160.504. Report of Genetic Testing.

(a) A report of the results of genetic testing must be in a record and signed under penalty of perjury by a designee of the testing laboratory. A report made under the requirements of this subchapter is self-authenticating.

(b) Documentation from the testing laboratory is sufficient to establish a reliable chain of custody that allows the results of genetic testing to be admissible without testimony if the documentation includes:

(1) the name and photograph of each individual whose specimens have been taken;

(2) the name of each individual who collected the specimens;

(3) the places in which the specimens were collected and the date of each collection;

(4) the name of each individual who received the specimens in the testing laboratory; and

(5) the dates the specimens were received.

Commissioners' Comment to UPA Section 504

Source: 42 U.S.C. § 666(a)(5)(F) requiring genetic testing in certain cases.

Subsection (b) is designed to indicate that in civil trials only a minimal showing of reliability of the chain of custody is needed. This avoids evidentiary problems, such as arguments modeled on criminal cases in which the chain of evidence is crucial. If an element of the chain is missing, such a defect may be corrected by affidavit or other testimony as to the reliability of the sample. For example, samples from a deceased individual may be obtained from a coroner's office and a picture of the individual need not be taken. In this case, proof of the chain of custody of the body maintained by the coroner may be provided.

---

§ 160.505. Genetic Testing Results; Rebuttal.

(a) A man is rebuttably identified as the father of a child under this chapter if the genetic testing complies with this subchapter and the results disclose:

(1) that the man has at least a 99 percent probability of paternity, using a prior probability of 0.5, as calculated by using the combined paternity index obtained in the testing; and

(2) a combined paternity index of at least 100 to 1.

(b) A man identified as the father of a child under Subsection (a) may rebut the genetic testing results only by producing other genetic testing satisfying the requirements of this subchapter that:

(1) excludes the man as a genetic father of the child; or

(2) identifies another man as the possible father of the child.

(c) Except as otherwise provided by Section 160.510, if more than one man is identified by genetic testing as the possible father of the child, the court shall order each man to submit to further genetic testing to identify the genetic father.

Commissioners' Comment to UPA Section 505

Source: 42 U.S.C. § 666(a)(5)(G) requiring genetic testing in certain cases.

The selection of a probability of paternity of 99.0% and a combined paternity index of 100 to 1 as the rebuttably identified man as father of the child is consistent with the year 2000 standard of practice in the genetic-testing community. Accrediting agencies require the reporting of both of these numbers. As of December, 2000, 27 states have established a presumption at less than this level. However, for several years the standard of practice in the scientific community has been 99.0%. Therefore, raising the genetic presumption to the 99.0% level should have no impact on those states. This number represents a reasonable level of testing, given the breadth of the Act and potential difficulty of working with some specimens in a probate case. It is not intended as a standard of practice for the laboratories, but as a legal presumption to satisfy the legal standard of proof. Given the rapid progress of science, it is likely that accrediting standards will rise over time. If the standard of practice becomes more strict, the newer standards will be made routine by the requirement that laboratories be accredited in order to perform testing under the Act. But, the legal significance of the genetic presumption stated in this section will be unaffected.

Genetic testing results will usually exceed the statutory minimum. During the drafting of UPA (2000) several statutory presumptions were considered, *i.e.*, 95%, 99%, 99.9% and 99.99%. Genetic testing laboratory representatives presented quite persuasive arguments for a variety of choices. The Drafting Committee ultimately chose to settle on the 99% standard because:

(1) the 99% standard reflects the current standard of the American Association of Blood Banks (STANDARDS FOR PARENTAGE TESTING LABORATORIES, 4th Edition 1999), and the proposed standards (5th Edition, 2001);

(2) the standards promulgated by the various accrediting bodies (American Association of Blood Banks and the American Society for Histocompatibility and Immunogenetics) will, in reality, set the benchmark for genetic testing;

(3) the 99% standard is consistent with the standards of the plurality of American jurisdictions as of December, 2000;

(4) a standard higher than 99% could cause evidentiary problems in probate proceedings because of degraded specimens. Similarly, that problem may arise in cases involving one or more missing individuals, *e.g.*, the mother is not available, but the child and alleged father are available;

(5) the percentage is an evidentiary presumption that the respondent may always challenge by requesting a second test under Section 507; and

(6) a proceeding to adjudicate paternity is a civil action based on a preponderance of the evidence, not a criminal action based on evidence beyond reasonable doubt.

§ 160.506. Costs of Genetic Testing.

(a) Subject to the assessment of costs under Subchapter G, the cost of initial genetic testing must be advanced:

(1) by a support enforcement agency, if the agency is providing services in the proceeding;

(2) by the individual who made the request;

(3) as agreed by the parties; or

(4) as ordered by the court.

(b) In cases in which the cost of genetic testing is advanced by the support enforcement agency, the agency may seek reimbursement from a man who is rebuttably identified as the father.

Commissioners' Comment to UPA Section 506

Source: UPA (1973) § 11; 42 U.S.C. § 666(a)(5)(B)(ii)(I); Little v. Streater, 454 U.S. 1, (1981).

In general, the party seeking relief from a court must bear the cost of the initial genetic testing. The federal law mandates that the support enforcement agency pay the cost of testing, subject to recoupment. Subsection (a)(3) does present the possibility that a court might order a respondent to pay the initial cost.

---

§ 160.507. Additional Genetic Testing.

The court or the support enforcement agency shall order additional genetic testing on the request of a party who contests the result of the original testing. If the previous genetic testing identified a man as the father of the child under Section 160.505, the court or agency may not order additional testing unless the party provides advance payment for the testing.

Commissioners' Comment to UPA Section 507

Source: UPA (1973) § 11; 42 U.S.C. § 666(a)(5)(B)(ii)(II).

Obviously the opportunity for additional testing should be provided if the original testing is contested in good faith. The requirement that the contestant provide advance payment if prior testing has identified a man as the father is intended to discourage spurious contests. This section provides the most important mechanism for determining the accuracy of a paternity test. While extremely rare, even after initial tests indicate a probability of paternity greater than 99.99% it is theoretically possible that additional testing can result in exclusion of the tested man. Likewise, if there is an error in the chain of custody or testing procedures, exclusion is the expected outcome. The only way to reliably determine whether an error occurred is to obtain a second test.

---

§ 160.508. Genetic Testing When All Individuals Not Available.

(a) Subject to Subsection (b), if a genetic testing specimen for good cause and under circumstances the court considers to be just is not available from a man who may be the father of a child, a court may order the following individuals to submit specimens for genetic testing:

(1) the parents of the man;

(2) any brothers or sisters of the man;

(3) any other children of the man and their mothers; and

(4) other relatives of the man necessary to complete genetic testing.

(b) A court may not render an order under this section unless the court finds that the need for genetic testing outweighs the legitimate interests of the individual sought to be tested.

Commissioners' Comment to UPA Section 508

In some cases, the alleged father may be unavailable for testing. Subsection (a) accommodates those cases by providing for testing of the man's relatives to establish his paternity or nonpaternity of a child. Depending on the proceeding, some of the individuals listed for testing in Subsection (a) will be parties to the paternity proceeding and others will not. If an individual does not volunteer to participate in the testing and is not a party, in the absence of this provision the court would be required to decide whether it has the authority to order the testing and whether testing the objecting individual is necessary. This provision resolves the issues. Given the fact that genetic testing in the modern age is not invasive—use of the buccal swab method means that the intrusion into the privacy of the individual is relatively slight compared to the right of the child to have parentage established. Moreover, the alleged parent also has a right to have that fact determined.

Note that no provision is explicitly made for court-ordered testing of maternal relatives because the establishment of paternity by genetic testing is in no way dependent on testing the mother of the child. However, if maternity is at issue, § 106, Determination of Maternity, directs that this section be construed to test the relatives of the mother.

§ 160.509. Deceased Individual.

For good cause shown, the court may order genetic testing of a deceased individual.

Commissioners' Comment to UPA Section 509

In some states, the court with jurisdiction to adjudicate parentage may lack authority to order disinterment of a deceased individual. If so, that authority is provided by this section.

§ 160.510. Identical Brothers.

(a) The court may order genetic testing of a brother of a man identified as the father of a child if the man is commonly believed to have an identical brother and evidence suggests that the brother may be the genetic father of the child.

(b) If each brother satisfies the requirements of Section 160.505 for being the identified father of the child and there is not another identical brother being identified as the father of the child, the court may rely on nongenetic evidence to adjudicate which brother is the father of the child.

Commissioners' Comment to UPA Section 510

This section refers to "identical brothers" rather than "identical twins" to account for the possibility of identical triplets, etc. In some cases, non-identical brothers (and even other related men) will not be excluded after initial genetic testing. This section should not be used to resolve those cases because more sophisticated genetic testing can differentiate between non-identical siblings. If a case occurs in which, after initial testing, two men are not excluded, both men should be ordered to submit to additional testing as provided in Section 505(c) to determine which is the father. In the extremely rare case in which a competent laboratory exhausts all of its in-house testing and still cannot determine which non-identical sibling is excluded, the common practice is to provide the genetic material to another laboratory for more extensive testing to resolve the case.

Contrasting identical brothers with non-identical brothers, identical brothers can never be differentiated by additional genetic testing. This creates a completely different situation for the court. This section resolves the identical-brother conundrum as much as possible, and is designed to prevent the court from simply dismissing the case.

---

§ 160.511. Offense: Unauthorized Release of Specimen.

(a) A person commits an offense if the person intentionally releases an identifiable specimen of another person for any purpose not relevant to the parentage proceeding and without a court order or the written permission of the person who furnished the specimen.

(b) An offense under this section is a Class A misdemeanor.

Commissioners' Comment to UPA Section 511

This section seeks to protect the privacy rights of persons who are tested for a parentage determination. Although the Drafting Committee was not informed of an instance in which a paternity-testing laboratory had released samples or performed unauthorized testing, several states have proposed or passed laws regulating the "genetic privacy" of paternity tests. This section is intended to provide some guidance in this area. The term "identifiable specimen" is included, as there are beneficial uses of samples for anonymous research purposes. For example, the frequency tables used to make calculations are compiled from anonymous data and provide a more precise calculation for all persons involved in paternity testing. On occasion, a court may order the laboratory to release samples. For instance, a man who had been tested in one paternity proceeding and then dies may have his samples utilized in another paternity proceeding if a court orders testing in the second action. Courts have also ordered the release of samples when the tested man has allegedly engaged in criminal conduct. This has occurred when the alleged father has sent an imposter for sample collection. If the state pursues criminal charges, a court might order the laboratory to release the samples to a state crime laboratory for further identification and possible criminal prosecution.

The Drafting Committee was informed that in one case, a grand jury brought indictments for multiple counts of a scheme to defraud, tampering with physical evidence and perjury against the alleged father and the imposter. The results of genetic testing for paternity purposes appear to have no medical or predictive value in any other context. Thus, regulation of the paternity-test results is left to the states. In some states, the records of paternity proceedings are open, thus allowing anyone to obtain the results. A more comprehensive treatment on this subject must necessarily be left to other laws.

The control of the records is left to other state law. In some states paternity records are open to the public, and a fundamental change in handling of the records is beyond the scope of this Act. The accreditation agencies provide guidance on this subject. For example, the American Association of Blood Banks requires that accredited laboratories maintain records for at least five years. Because a laboratory performing testing under this act should be accredited, *see* Section 503(a), *supra*, protection is thus provided to the tested person's records under the accreditation standards.

Subchapter G. Proceeding To Adjudicate Parentage.

Part 1. Nature Of Proceeding

Leading Case

In re Z.L.T., 124 S.W.3d 163 (Tex. 2003) (not error to implicitly deny bench warrant to transport prison inmate to paternity trial)

In re K.M.S., 68 S.W.3d 61 (Tex. App.—Dallas 2001, no pet.) (subsequently adjudicated father failed to give notice or citation to man who alleged himself to be father thereby violating alleged father's constitutional rights—appellate court declines to follow supreme court's definition of "alleged father")

---

§ 160.601. Proceeding Authorized; Rules of Procedure.

(a) A civil proceeding may be maintained to adjudicate the parentage of a child.

(b) The proceeding is governed by the Texas Rules of Civil Procedure.

Commissioners' Comment to UPA Section 601

Source: UPA (1973) § 14.

A determination of paternity is governed by the ordinary rules of civil procedure. The party seeking to establish paternity is entitled to full discovery, to compel the testimony of all witnesses, and to have the case tried by a preponderance of the evidence. "The equipoise of the private interests that are at stake in a paternity proceeding supports the conclusion that the standard of proof normally applied in private litigation is also appropriate for these cases." *Rivera v. Minnich*, 483 U.S. 574, 581 (1987).

A corresponding amendment to UPC § 2–114 was not made until the major revision of 1990 (as further revised in 1993). By that time, it had been recognized as illogical and unjust to impose discriminatory burdens on children born out-of-wedlock who were seeking paternal inheritance. It also had been ruled unconstitutional by application of the intermediate scrutiny test formulated under the 14th Amendment. *Reed v. Campbell*, 476 U.S. 852 (1986). Moreover, by 1990 the preponderance of the evidence standard had been widely applied to determinations of paternity and probate proceedings. Against this background, UPC (1993) abandoned the clear and convincing evidence alternative for determining paternal relationships.

---

§ 160.602. Standing to Maintain Proceeding.

(a) *[S.B. 1807]* Subject to Subchapter D and Sections 160.607 and 160.609 **and except as provided by Subsection (b)**, a proceeding to adjudicate parentage may be maintained by:

(1) the child;

(2) the mother of the child;

(3) a man whose paternity of the child is to be adjudicated;

(4) the support enforcement agency or another government agency authorized by other law;

(5) an authorized adoption agency or licensed child-placing agency;

(6) *[H.B. 729]*a representative authorized by law to act for an individual who would otherwise be entitled to maintain a proceeding but who is deceased, is incapacitated, or is a minor; [~~or~~]

(7) *[H.B. 729]* a person related within the second degree by consanguinity to the mother of the child, if the mother is deceased; **or**

(8) *[H.B. 729]* a person who is an intended parent.

(b) *[S.B. 1807]* After the date a child having no presumed, acknowledged, or adjudicated father becomes an adult, a proceeding to adjudicate the parentage of the adult child may only be maintained by the adult child.

History: Amended by 78th Legis., Reg. Sess. (2003), S.B. 1807, eff. Sept. 1, 2003, and "applies only to a suit affecting the parent-child relationship commenced on or after the effective date of this Act. A suit affecting the parent-child relationship commenced before the effective date of this Act is governed by the law in effect on the date the suit was commenced, and the former law is continued in effect for that purpose."

History: Amended by 78th Legis., Reg. Sess. (2003), H.B. 729, eff. Sept. 1, 2003, and "applies to a motion or other request for relief made in a parentage or paternity proceeding that is commenced on or after the effective date of this Act. A motion or other request for relief made in a parentage or paternity proceeding commenced before the effective date of this Act is governed by the law in effect at the time the proceeding was commenced, and the former law is continued in effect for that purpose."

Commissioners' Comment to UPA Section 602

Source: UPA (1973) § 6.

This section grants standing to a broad range of individuals and agencies to bring a parentage proceeding. But, several limitations on standing to sue are contained within the Act. Subchapter D details the procedures involved in a voluntary acknowledgment of parentage. Sections 607 and 609 establish the ground rules for proceedings involving children with, and without, a presumed father. Subchapter I regulates parentage determinations arising from a gestational agreement.

Authors' Comment

Subsection (b) was added in 2003 as part of the conforming amendment to the 2002 revisions of the Uniform Parentage Act. This limitation prohibits the filing of an intrusive proceeding by an individual claiming to be a parent of an adult child, or by a legal stranger.

---

§ 160.603. Necessary Parties to Proceeding.

The following individuals must be joined as parties in a proceeding to adjudicate parentage:

(1) the mother of the child; and

(2) a man whose paternity of the child is to be adjudicated.

Commissioners' Comment to UPA Section 603

Source: UPA (1973) § 9.

This section partially follows and partially rejects the UPA (1973) requirements regarding who must be named as parties in a parentage proceeding. First, contra to UPA (1973), the child is not a necessary party. Few states require children as necessary parties. Further, with the widespread use of DNA testing, such a requirement has outlived its usefulness. On the other hand, failure to join a child as a party may later result in a child's successful collateral attack on the original determination of paternity to be filed by the child. This subject is discussed more fully in the Commissioners' Comment to Section 637, *infra.*

Second, as far as can be determined, no state requires the children born to a woman during marriage to be named as parties in every divorce proceeding; and, those decrees generally serve as res judicata if a later attack on a earlier determination is mounted. *Id.*

---

§ 160.604. Personal Jurisdiction.

(a) An individual may not be adjudicated to be a parent unless the court has personal jurisdiction over the individual.

(b) A court of this state having jurisdiction to adjudicate parentage may exercise personal jurisdiction over a nonresident individual or the guardian or conservator of the individual if the conditions in Section 159.201 are satisfied.

(c) Lack of jurisdiction over one individual does not preclude the court from making an adjudication of parentage binding on another individual over whom the court has personal jurisdiction.

Commissioners' Comment to UPA Section 604

Source: UPA (1973) § 6(b).

Although custody and visitation proceedings are considered to be status adjudications, and therefore do not require personal jurisdiction over both parents, Subsection (a) confirms the long-standing view that paternity proceedings require personal jurisdiction.

Subsection (b) incorporates the long-arm provision for establishing personal jurisdiction over an absent respondent set forth in UIFSA (1996), which is in effect in every state.

Subsection (c) makes the best of a situation in which an adjudication will almost inevitably be incomplete because not all the necessary parties are subject to the personal jurisdiction of the court. The most likely scenario for this unfortunate circumstance is one in which the mother and alleged father of the child are subject to the court's jurisdiction, but the mother's absent husband is not. Even if the husband's whereabouts are known, if both the forum court and the court of his residence lacks jurisdiction over all three parties, there still is no court with power to bind all of them to a parentage determination.

Subsection (c) takes the common sense approach that a court should not be dissuaded from making a parentage decision, even if it cannot bind all appropriate parties. In the scenario described above, binding the mother and alleged father to a decision of the man's parentage may not technically bind the husband (the presumed father), but more than likely it will end litigation on the subject.

---

§ 160.605. Venue.

Venue for a proceeding to adjudicate parentage is in the county of this state in which:

(1) the child resides or is found;

(2) the respondent resides or is found if the child does not reside in this state; or

(3) a proceeding for probate or administration of the presumed or alleged father's estate has been commenced.

Commissioners' Comment to UPA Section 605

Source: UPA (1973) § 8(c).

The venue provision provides choices proven to be reasonable and convenient since its inclusion in the 1973 Act.

---

§ 160.606. No Time Limitation: Child Having no Presumed, Acknowledged, or Adjudicated Father.

A proceeding to adjudicate the parentage of a child having no presumed, acknowledged, or adjudicated father may be commenced at any time, including after the date:

(1) the child becomes an adult; or

(2) an earlier proceeding to adjudicate paternity has been dismissed based on the application of a statute of limitation then in effect.

Commissioners' Comment to UPA Section 606

Source: UPA (1973) §§ 6, 7.

For a state to retain the federal child support enforcement subsidy, 42 U.S.C. § 666(a)(5)(A)(i) mandates that the states must have laws to "permit the establishment of the paternity of a child at any time before the child attains 18 years of age." States have chosen a wide range of age options: age 18 (20 states), age 19 (6 states), age 20 (2 states), age 21 (10 states), age 22 (2 states), age 23 (2 states), and no limitation (9 states). Several states limit the establishment of parental rights to a shorter period.

The new UPA directs that an individual whose parentage has not been determined has a civil right to determine his or her own parentage, which should not be subject to limitation except when an estate has been closed. Accordingly, if the action is initiated by the child this section allows a proceeding to adjudicate parentage after the child has reached the age of majority. Such a proceeding is the exclusive province of the child, however.

Authors' Comment

Section 160.602(b) was enacted in 2003 to restrict paternity determinations in cases where the child has reached his or her majority. This action can only be maintained by the adult child. This limitation prohibits the filing of an intrusive proceeding by an individual claiming to be a parent of an adult child, or by a legal stranger.

---

§ 160.607. Time Limitation: Child Having Presumed Father.

(a) Except as otherwise provided by Subsection (b), a proceeding brought by a presumed father, the mother, or another individual to adjudicate the parentage of a child having a presumed father shall be commenced not later than the fourth anniversary of the date of the birth of the child.

(b) A proceeding seeking to disprove the father-child relationship between a child and the child's presumed father may be maintained at any time if the court determines that:

(1) the presumed father and the mother of the child did not live together or engage in sexual intercourse with each other during the probable time of conception; and

(2) the presumed father never **represented to others that** [~~openly treated~~] the child **was** [~~as~~] his own.

History: Amended by 78th Legis., Reg. Sess. (2003), S.B. 1807, eff. Sept. 1, 2003, and "applies only to a suit affecting the parent-child relationship commenced on or after the effective date of this Act. A suit affecting the parent-child relationship commenced before the effective date of this Act is governed by the law in effect on the date the suit was commenced, and the former law is continued in effect for that purpose."

Commissioners' Comment to UPA Section 607

Source: UPA (1973) § 6; *cf.* UPC (1993) § 2–114(c).

This section deals with difficult issues. First, it establishes the right of a mother or a presumed marital or nonmarital father to challenge the presumption of his paternity established by § 204. Second, it clarifies the right of a third-party male to claim paternity of a child who has an existing presumed father.

UPA (1973) § 6(a) places a "[five-year] limitation on the time in which a proceeding may be brought for the purpose of declaring the non-existence of the father and child relationship presumed under [the Act]." At that time, the comment noted that:

> "Ten states have denied standing to a man claiming to be the father when the mother was married to another at the time of the child's birth. In some of these states, even though a presumed father may seek to rebut his presumed paternity, a third-party male will be denied standing to raise that same issue."

As of the year 2000, the right of an "outsider" to claim paternity of a child born to a married woman varies considerably among the states. Thirty-three states allow a man alleging himself to be the father of a child with a presumed father to rebut the marital presumption. Some states have granted this right through legislation, while in other states case law has recognized the alleged father's right to rebut the presumption and establish his paternity. In some states, there is both statutory and common law support for the standing of a man alleging himself to be the father to assert his paternity of a child born to a married woman. Not that long ago, some states imposed an absolute bar on a man commencing a proceeding to establish his paternity if state law provides a statutory presumption of the paternity of another man. *See Michael H. v. Gerald D.*, 491 U.S. 110, (1989). It is increasingly clear that those days are coming to an end.

The new UPA attempts to establish a middle ground on these exceedingly complex issues. Subsection (a) establishes a two-year limitation for rebutting the presumption of paternity established under § 204 if the mother and presumed father were cohabiting at the time of conception. The presumption of paternity may be attacked by the mother, the presumed father, or a third-party male during this limited period; thereafter the presumption is immune from attack by any of those individuals except as provided in subsection (b). [The limitations period is four years in Texas]

The reverse fact situation is also clear; a presumption of paternity may be challenged at any time if the mother and the presumed father were not cohabiting and did not engage in sexual intercourse at the probable time of conception and the presumed father never openly held out the child as his own.

Under the fact circumstances described in subsection (b), nonpaternity of the presumed father is generally assumed by all the parties as a practical matter. It is inappropriate for the law to assume a presumption known by all those concerned to be untrue.

In 2003, subsection (b) was amended to conform language to the changes in Section 204 (a) (5).

---

§ 160.608. Authority to Deny Motion for Genetic Testing.

(a) In a proceeding to adjudicate parentage [~~under circumstances described by Section 160.607~~], a court may deny a motion for an order for the genetic testing of the mother, the child, and the presumed father if the court determines that:

(1) the conduct of the mother or the presumed father estops that party from denying parentage; and

(2) it would be inequitable to disprove the father-child relationship between the child and the presumed father.

(b) In determining whether to deny a motion for an order for genetic testing under this section, the court shall consider the best interest of the child, including the following factors:

(1) the length of time between the date of the proceeding to adjudicate parentage and the date the presumed father was placed on notice that he might not be the genetic father;

(2) the length of time during which the presumed father has assumed the role of father of the child;

(3) the facts surrounding the presumed father's discovery of his possible nonpaternity;

(4) the nature of the relationship between the child and the presumed father;

(5) the age of the child;

(6) any harm that may result to the child if presumed paternity is successfully disproved;

(7) the nature of the relationship between the child and the alleged father;

(8) the extent to which the passage of time reduces the chances of establishing the paternity of another man and a child support obligation in favor of the child; and

(9) other factors that may affect the equities arising from the disruption of the father-child relationship between the child and the presumed father or the chance of other harm to the child.

(c) In a proceeding involving the application of this section, a child who is a minor or is incapacitated must be represented by a guardian ad litem.

(d) A denial of a motion for an order for genetic testing must be based on clear and convincing evidence.

(e) If the court denies a motion for an order for genetic testing, the court shall issue an order adjudicating the presumed father to be the father of the child.

(f) This section applies to a proceeding to rescind or challenge an acknowledgment of paternity or a denial of paternity as provided by Section 160.309(d).

History: Amended by 78th Legis., Reg. Sess. (2003), S.B. 1807, eff. Sept. 1, 2003, and "applies only to a suit affecting the parent-child relationship commenced on or after the effective date of this Act. A suit affecting the parent-child relationship commenced before the effective date of this Act is governed by the law in effect on the date the suit was commenced, and the former law is continued in effect for that purpose."

Commissioners' Comment to UPA Section 608

This section incorporates the doctrine of paternity by estoppel, which extends equally to a child with a presumed father or an acknowledged father. In appropriate circumstances, the court may deny genetic testing and find the presumed or acknowledged father to be the father of the child. The most common situation in which estoppel should be applied arises when a man knows that a child is not, or may not be, his genetic child, but the man has affirmatively accepted his role as child's father and both the mother and the child have relied on that acceptance. Similarly, the man may have relied on the mother's acceptance of him as the child's father, and the mother is then estopped to deny the man's presumed parentage.

Subsection (b) delineates the standards for denying genetic testing. Subsection (c) requires the child to be independently represented. Subsection (d) requires an elevated standard of proof before the order for genetic testing can be denied.

Because § 607 places a two-year limitation [four years in Texas] on challenging the presumption of parentage, the application of this section should be applied in those meritorious cases in which the best interest of the child compels the result and the conduct of the mother and presumed or acknowledged father is clear.

In 2003, subsection (f) was added to extend principles of estoppel to children of unmarried parents wherein a proceeding is brought to challenge an acknowledgment of paternity.

§ 160.609. Time Limitation: Child Having Acknowledged or Adjudicated Father.

(a) If a child has an acknowledged father, a signatory to the acknowledgment or denial of paternity may commence a proceeding seeking to rescind the acknowledgment or denial or to challenge the paternity of the child only within the time allowed under Section 160.307 or 160.308.

(b) If a child has an acknowledged father or an adjudicated father, an individual, other than the child, who is not a signatory to the acknowledgment or a party to the adjudication and who seeks an adjudication of paternity of the child must commence a proceeding not later than the fourth anniversary of the effective date of the acknowledgment or adjudication.

Commissioners' Comment to UPA Section 609

A two-year period [four years in Texas] is prescribed in § 307 for a challenge in which the acknowledged or adjudicated father mistakenly believed himself to be the genetic father. A similar limitation is prescribed in § 607(a) for an individual who was not a signatory or a party to the earlier determination.

Leading Cases

In re R.A.H., 130 S.W.3d 68 (Tex. 2004) (putative father not a party in prior suit has 4 years from date adjudication signed to assert his parentage)

Texas Dept. of Protective & Regulatory Services v. Sherry, 46 S.W.3d 857 (Tex. 2001) (purported father of a child lacks standing to bring a paternity action if a prior, final judgment of paternity has been rendered by a court of competent jurisdiction)

Baize v. Baize, 93 S.W.3d 197 (Tex. App.—Houston [14th Dist.] 2002, pet. denied) (mother's post-divorce SAPCR decree denying now ex-husband's paternity of six year-old son came too late)

In re T.S.S., 61 S.W.3d 481 (Tex. App.—San Antonio 2001, pet. denied) (father could have raised issue of parentage at time of divorce such that issue later barred by collateral estoppel)

Wise v. Fryar, 49 S.W.3d 450 (Tex. App.—Eastland 2001, pet. denied) (father did not establish that his failure to pursue paternity during the prior divorce proceedings was without negligence or fault on his part and due to extrinsic fraud; such that he was not entitled to bring a bill of review)

§ 160.610. Joinder of Proceedings.

(a) Except as provided by Subsection (b), a proceeding to adjudicate parentage may be joined with a proceeding for adoption, termination of parental rights, possession of or access to a child, child support, divorce, annulment, or probate or administration of an estate or another appropriate proceeding.

(b) A respondent may not join a proceeding described by Subsection (a) with a proceeding to adjudicate parentage brought under Chapter 159.

Commissioners' Comment to UPA Section 610

Source: UPA (1973) § 8.

Joinder of paternity proceedings with related matters is common, especially when a child support agency seeks to establish paternity and fix child support.

Subsection (b) restricts counterclaims in those instances in which an initiating state sends a paternity suit to the responding state. Because petitioner is "appearing" in the other forum, to permit counterclaims would serve as a major deterrent to bringing such proceedings. This bar does not prevent a separate action for such matters, but there must be independent jurisdiction not arising from the petitioner's appearance in the paternity proceeding.

§ 160.611. Proceedings Before Birth.

(a) A proceeding to determine parentage commenced before the birth of the child may not be concluded until after the birth of the child.

(b) In a proceeding described by Subsection (a), the following actions may be taken before the birth of the child:

(1) service of process;

(2) discovery; and

(3) except as prohibited by Section 160.502, collection of specimens for genetic testing.

Commissioners' Comment to UPA Section 611

This section recognizes that establishing a parental relationship as quickly as possible may be in the best interest of a child. To facilitate that process, some initial steps may be completed prior to the birth of the child.

§ 160.612. Child as Party; Representation.

(a) A minor child is a permissible party, but is not a necessary party to a proceeding under this subchapter.

(b) The court shall appoint an attorney ad litem to represent a child who is a minor or is incapacitated if the child is a party or the court finds that the interests of the child are not adequately represented.

Commissioners' Comment to UPA Section 612

This section rejects UPA (1973) § 9. Consistent with § 603, *supra*, this Act rejects the view that the child necessarily has independent standing in a parentage proceeding. On the other hand, if the court determines that the child in fact does have a position at variance with all the other litigants, an attorney may be appointed to represent that interest.

Part 2. Special Rules for Proceeding to Adjudicate Parentage

§ 160.621. Admissibility of Results of Genetic Testing; Expenses.

(a) Except as otherwise provided by Subsection (c), a report of a genetic testing expert is admissible as evidence of the truth of the facts asserted in the report. The admissibility of the report is not affected by whether the testing was performed:

(1) voluntarily or under an order of the court or a support enforcement agency; or

(2) before or after the date of commencement of the proceeding.

(b) A party objecting to the results of genetic testing may call one or more genetic testing experts to testify in person or by telephone, videoconference, deposition, or another method approved by the court. Unless otherwise ordered by the court, the party offering the testimony bears the expense for the expert testifying.

(c) If a child has a presumed, acknowledged, or adjudicated father, the results of genetic testing are inadmissible to adjudicate parentage unless performed:

(1) with the consent of both the mother and the presumed, acknowledged, or adjudicated father; or

(2) under an order of the court under Section 160.502.

(d) Copies of bills for genetic testing and for prenatal and postnatal health care for the mother and child that are furnished to the adverse party on or before the 10th day before the date of a hearing are admissible to establish:

(1) the amount of the charges billed; and

(2) that the charges were reasonable, necessary, and customary.

Commissioners' Comment to UPA Section 621

Source: 42 U.S.C. § 666(a)(5)(F)(ii); UPA (1973) §§ 10,13.

Justification for additional testing is provided by Subsection (a). If the objecting party can state with specificity the grounds for rejecting a genetic test, and those grounds cannot be clarified under Article 5, retesting should be ordered. For example, if the chain of custody is seriously flawed, or the testing laboratory is not accredited, errors of this sort may be corrected by collecting new specimens and repeating the testing. Unlike the samples collected in a potential criminal proceeding which cannot be replaced, such as a blood alcohol test, the samples in a paternity proceedings remain the same no matter when, or how often, the samples are collected. Any flaw in the original test can be corrected by collection of new samples and additional testing of the individuals.

---

§ 160.622. Consequences of Declining Genetic Testing.

(a) An order for genetic testing is enforceable by contempt.

(b) A court may adjudicate parentage contrary to the position of an individual whose paternity is being determined on the grounds that the individual declines to submit to genetic testing as ordered by the court.

(c) Genetic testing of the mother of a child is not a prerequisite to testing the child and a man whose paternity is being determined. If the mother is unavailable or declines to submit to genetic testing, the court may order the testing of the child and each man whose paternity is being adjudicated.

Commissioners' Comment to UPA Section 622

Source: UPA (1973) § 10.

---

§ 160.623. Admission of Paternity Authorized.

(a) A respondent in a proceeding to adjudicate parentage may admit to the paternity of a child by filing a pleading to that effect or by admitting paternity under penalty of perjury when making an appearance or during a hearing.

(b) If the court finds that the admission of paternity satisfies the requirements of this section and that there is no reason to question the admission, the court shall render an order adjudicating the child to be the child of the man admitting paternity.

Commissioners' Comment to UPA Section 623

Source: 42 U.S.C. 666(a)(5)(D)(i)(II).

---

§ 160.624. Temporary Order.

(a) In a proceeding under this subchapter, the court shall render a temporary order for child support for a child if the order is appropriate and the individual ordered to pay child support:

(1) is a presumed father of the child;

(2) is petitioning to have his paternity adjudicated;

(3) is identified as the father through genetic testing under Section 160.505;

(4) is an alleged father who has declined to submit to genetic testing;

(5) is shown by clear and convincing evidence to be the father of the child; or

(6) is the mother of the child.

(b) A temporary order may include provisions for the possession of or access to the child as provided by other laws of this state.

Commissioners' Comment to UPA Section 624

Source: UIFSA (1996) § 401; 42 U.S.C. 666(a)(5)(J).

CLE/Other Legal Publications

Temporary orders: kids, house, cars, fees & debts—who gets them, who pays and where does the $$ come from? Wendy S. Burgower, 2001 MARRIAGE DISSOLUTION

Part 3. Hearings and Adjudication

§ 160.631. Rules for Adjudication of Paternity.

(a) The court shall apply the rules stated in this section to adjudicate the paternity of a child.

(b) The paternity of a child having a presumed, acknowledged, or adjudicated father may be disproved only by admissible results of genetic testing excluding that man as the father of the child or identifying another man as the father of the child.

(c) Unless the results of genetic testing are admitted to rebut other results of genetic testing, the man identified as the father of a child under Section 160.505 shall be adjudicated as being the father of the child.

(d) Unless the results of genetic testing are admitted to rebut other results of genetic testing, a man excluded as the father of a child by genetic testing shall be adjudicated as not being the father of the child.

(e) If the court finds that genetic testing under Section 160.505 does not identify or exclude a man as the father of a child, the court may not dismiss the proceeding. In that event, the results of genetic testing and other evidence are admissible to adjudicate the issue of paternity.

Commissioners' Comment to UPA Section 631

Source: UPA (1973) § 14.

This section establishes the controlling supremacy of admissible genetic test results in the adjudication of paternity. Other matters such as statute of limitations, equitable estoppel and res judicata may preclude the matter from reaching trial or the court denying genetic testing. However, if test results are admissible, those results control unless other test results create a conflict rebutting the admitted results.

Paragraph (3) is included to ensure that the fact a genetic test does not reach the 99% level decreed in Section 505 will not be perceived as an indicator of an exclusion of paternity. Although test results that do not reach that level do not create a presumption of paternity, the testing should be evaluated as an indicator of paternity along with the other evidence of paternity presented in the proceeding. Presumably expert testimony will be required to provide information about the measure of the weight of a test that does not achieve "at least a 99 percent probability of paternity, using a prior probability of 0.50, as calculated by using the combined paternity index obtained in the testing, and a combined paternity index of at least 100 to 1."

The inclusion of the first clause in paragraph (4) indicates that although a genetic testing exclusion of paternity can be absolute, errors (and sometimes fraud) may occur in testing. Some courts have imposed a rule that a party must first show the test is in error before ordering another test. This imposes an impossible burden because the only accurate method to show that a test is in error is to repeat the testing. Without this clause, some litigants might argue that once an exclusion is obtained it is absolute and no other test can be ordered, even when the first test is shown to be wrong.

---

§ 160.632. Jury Prohibited.

The court shall adjudicate paternity of a child without a jury.

Commissioners' Comment to UPA Section 632

Source: 42 U.S.C. § 666(a)(5)(I), requiring state law to provide that "parties to an action to establish paternity are not entitled to trial by jury. . . . "

UPA (1973) § 14[(d)] prohibited jury trials in parentage proceedings on the basis that "The use of a jury is not desirable in the emotional atmosphere of cases of this nature." Congress agreed when it enacted an effectively identical prohibition in PRWORA (1996).

---

§ 160.633. Hearings; Inspection of Records.

(a) **A** [~~On the request of a party and for good cause shown, the court may order a~~] proceeding under this subchapter **is open** [~~closed~~] to the public **as in other civil cases**.

(b) **Papers** [~~A final order in a proceeding under this subchapter is available for public inspection. Other papers~~] and records **in a proceeding under this subchapter** are available **for public inspection** [~~only with the consent of the parties or on order of the court for good cause~~].

History: Amended by 78th Legis., Reg. Sess. (2003), H.B. 1878, eff. Sept. 1, 2003. "The change in law made by this Act to Section 160.633, Family Code, applies to a suit affecting the parent-child relationship filed before, on, or after the effective date of this Act. A court order rendered before the effective date of this Act providing for the sealing of records in a proceeding is governed by the law in effect on the date the court order was rendered, and the former law is continued in effect for that purpose."

Commissioners' Comment to UPA Section 633

Source: UPA (1973) § 20.

UPA (1973) § 20 was concerned with the privacy of the parties in a paternity proceeding and required closure of the proceedings. The high caseload and the desensitizing of such proceedings, however, lead to the conclusion that mandating closure of the proceedings is no longer appropriate.

Authors' Comment

In 2003, the original provisions of the Uniform Parentage Act 2000 regarding confidentiality of proceedings and records were significantly amended and such proceedings and records are now handled as in other civil cases. Before the amendment, court clerks objected to the requirements of keeping the records under lock and key. In actuality, the amendments merely return Texas law to the manner of handling such records before the adoption of the Uniform Parentage Act.

§ 160.634. Order on Default.

The court shall issue an order adjudicating the paternity of a man who:

(1) after service of process, is in default; and

(2) is found by the court to be the father of a child.

Commissioners' Comment to UPA Section 634

Source: 42 U.S.C. 666(a)(5)(H).

§ 160.635. Dismissal for Want of Prosecution.

The court may issue an order dismissing a proceeding commenced under this chapter for want of prosecution only without prejudice. An order of dismissal for want of prosecution purportedly with prejudice is void and has only the effect of a dismissal without prejudice.

Commissioners' Comment to UPA Section 635

A major principle of UPA (2000)—and its predecessor—is that the child's right to have a determination of paternity is fundamental. This new section confirms this right by declaring that the delinquency of another person in prosecuting such a proceeding may not permanently preclude the ultimate conclusion of that determination.

§ 160.636. Order Adjudicating Parentage; Costs.

(a) The court shall render an order adjudicating whether a man alleged or claiming to be the father is the parent of the child.

(b) An order adjudicating parentage must identify the child by name and date of birth.

(c) Except as otherwise provided by Subsection (d), the court may assess filing fees, reasonable attorney's fees, fees for genetic testing, other costs, and necessary travel and other reasonable expenses incurred in a proceeding under this subchapter. Attorney's fees awarded by the court may be paid directly to the attorney. An attorney who is awarded attorney's fees may enforce the order in the attorney's own name.

(d) The court may not assess fees, costs, or expenses against the support enforcement agency of this state or another state, except as provided by other law.

(e) On request of a party and for good cause shown, the court may order that the name of the child be changed.

(f) If the order of the court is at variance with the child's birth certificate, the court shall order the bureau of vital statistics to issue an amended birth record.

(g) On a finding of parentage, the court may order retroactive child support as provided by Chapter 154 *[Child Support]* and, on a proper showing, order a party to pay an equitable portion of all of the prenatal and postnatal health care expenses of the mother and the child.

(h) In rendering an order for retroactive child support under this section, the court shall use the child support guidelines provided by Chapter 154 *[Child Support]*, together with any relevant factors.

Commissioners' Comment to UPA Section 636

Source: UIFSA (1996) § 313; UPA (1973) §§ 15, 16; 23.

This Act differs from UPA (1973), which attempted to do more than merely establish parentage. For example, UPA (1973) § 15 provided for a wide range of court orders to be made relating to the child's support, custody, guardianship, visitation privileges, as well as to the payment by the father of the mother's expenses of pregnancy and confinement. This Act leaves such matters to other state law. Only in instances where other state law is likely to be inadequate does this Act specify special treatment for litigants, For example, subsections (c) and (d) may be required because ordinary civil litigation probably does not provide for the court to apportion the costs of litigation among the parties.

Leading Cases

Garza v. Blanton, 55 S.W.3d 708 (Tex. App.—Corpus Christi 2001, no pet.) (order for retroactive support in paternity suit discretionary with the court—payments made pre-parentage determination seriously mitigate against such an order)

In re A.P., 46 S.W.3d 347 (Tex. App.—Corpus Christi 2001, no pet.) (once a parent-child relationship is established, it is up to the discretion of the special master to determine whether to award support retroactively to the time of the child's birth)

§ 160.637. Binding Effect of Determination of Parentage.

(a) Except as otherwise provided by Subsection (b) or Section 160.316, a determination of parentage is binding on:

(1) all signatories to an acknowledgment or denial of paternity as provided by Subchapter D; and

(2) all parties to an adjudication by a court acting under circumstances that satisfy the jurisdictional requirements of Section 159.201.

(b) A child is not bound by a determination of parentage under this chapter unless:

(1) the determination was based on an unrescinded acknowledgment of paternity and the acknowledgment is consistent with the results of genetic testing;

(2) the adjudication of parentage was based on a finding consistent with the results of genetic testing and the consistency is declared in the determination or is otherwise shown; or

(3) the child was a party or was represented in the proceeding determining parentage by an attorney ad litem.

(c) In a proceeding to dissolve a marriage, the court is considered to have made an adjudication of the parentage of a child if the court acts under circumstances that satisfy the jurisdictional requirements of Section 159.201, and the final order:

(1) expressly identifies the child as "a child of the marriage" or "issue of the marriage" or uses similar words indicating that the husband is the father of the child; or

(2) provides for the payment of child support for the child by the husband unless paternity is specifically disclaimed in the order.

(d) Except as otherwise provided by Subsection (b), a determination of parentage may be a defense in a subsequent proceeding seeking to adjudicate parentage by an individual who was not a party to the earlier proceeding.

(e) A party to an adjudication of paternity may challenge the adjudication only under the laws of this state relating to appeal, the vacating of judgments, or other judicial review.

Commissioners' Comment to UPA Section 637

A considerable amount of litigation involves exactly who is bound and who is not bound by a final order determining parentage. This section codifies rules regarding the effect of such orders. Subsection (a) provides that, if the order is issued under standards of personal jurisdiction of the UIFSA (1996), the order is binding on all parties to the proceeding. This solves the problem of an order issued without the appropriate jurisdiction, as would be the case of a divorce based on status jurisdiction in which the court lacked the requisite personal jurisdiction over a nonresident party.

Subsection (b) partially resolves the question whether a child is bound by the terms of the order. UPA (1973) required that the child be made a party to a parentage proceeding, and be bound. However, the 1973 Act did not address whether a divorce decree had a legal impact on paternity. A majority of jurisdictions holds that the child is not bound by the divorce decree because the child was not a party to the proceeding. A minority of states holds that the child is bound by the order and that the child is in privity with the parents. In its present formulation, this subsection adopts the majority rule, which does not bind the child during minority unless the parentage order is based on genetic testing or the child was represented by an ad litem.

Subsection (c) resolves whether a divorce decree constitutes a finding of paternity. This subsection provides that a decree is a determination of paternity if the decree states that the child was born of the marriage or grants the husband visitation or custody, or orders support. This is the majority rule in American jurisprudence.

Subsection (d) gives protection to third parties who may claim benefit of an earlier determination of parentage

Finally, the section is silent on whether state IV–D agencies are bound by prior determinations of parentage. This controversial issue is left to other state law. Similarly, issues of collateral attack on final judgments are to be resolved by recourse to other state law, as in civil proceedings generally.

Leading Case

Ince v. Ince, 58 S.W.3d 187 (Tex. App.—Waco 2001, no pet.) (intrinsic fraud regarding adjudication of husband's paternity of child born to wife does not support Bill of Review—dissent argues truth should not be barred by res judicata)

Wise v. Fryar, 49 S.W.3d 450 (Tex. App.—Eastland 2001, pet. denied) (father did not establish that his failure to pursue paternity during the prior divorce proceedings was without negligence or fault on his part and due to extrinsic fraud; such that he was not entitled to bring a bill of review)

Subchapter H. Child of Assisted Reproduction.

Commissioners' Prefatory Note to Subchapter H

Medical science has developed a wide range of assisted reproductive technologies, often referred to as ARTS, which enable childless couples to become parents. Thousands of children are born in the United States each year as the result of ARTS. If a married couple uses their own eggs and sperm to conceive a child born by the wife, the parentage of the child is straightforward. The wife is the mother—by gestation and genetics, the husband is the father—by genetics and presumption, and, insofar as UPA (2000) is concerned, neither fits the definition of a "donor."

If, using assisted reproduction, a wife gives birth to a child conceived using sperm from a man other than her husband, she is the mother and her husband is the presumed father. However, the man providing the sperm might assert his biological paternity, or the husband might seek to rebut the martial presumption of paternity by proving through genetic testing that he is not the genetic father. As was the case in UPA (1973), it is necessary for UPA (2000) to establish the parentage of a child born under these circumstances.

Similarly, assisted reproduction may involve the eggs from a woman other than the wife—perhaps using the husband's sperm, perhaps not. In either event, the Act must clearly exclude the egg donor from claiming maternity. Theoretically, it is even possible that absent legislation the wife could attempt to deny maternity based on her lack of genetic relationship.

Finally, a very common ARTS procedure mixes sperm and eggs to form a pre-zygote that is then frozen for future use. If the couple later divorce or one of them dies, the disposition of these pre-zygotes can be a potential problem on which courts need guidance.

CLE/Leading Publications

Parentage: the unsolved mystery. Rhonda F. Hunter, 2004 Adv. Fam. L.

Dad vs. donor: who stays and who pays. Jacqueline Taylor & Ellen A. Yarrell, 2004 U. Tex. Fam. L. Front Lines

Collaborative reproduction. Ellen A. Yarrell, 2003 Adv. Fam. L.

Leading Case

In re M.C., 65 S.W.3d 188 (Tex. App.—Amarillo 2001, no pet.) (wife entitled to contest husband's claim of ratification of assisted conception of twins born to her during marriage)

---

§ 160.701. Scope of Subchapter.

This subchapter applies only to a child conceived by means of assisted reproduction.

Commissioners' Comment to UPA Section 701

Article 7 applies only to children born as the result of assisted reproduction technologies; a child conceived by sexual intercourse is not covered by this article, irrespective of the alleged intent of the parties. The bracketed clause relates to gestational agreements under Article 8. If a state enacts Article 8, the brackets should be removed. If a state does not enact Article 8, the bracketed subsection should be omitted.

---

§ 160.702. Parental Status of Donor.

A donor is not a parent of a child conceived by means of assisted reproduction.

Commissioners' Comment to UPA Section 702

Source: UPA (1973) § 5(b); USCACA (1988) § 4(a).

If a child is conceived as the result of assisted reproduction, this section clarifies that a donor (whether of sperm or egg) is not a parent of the resulting child. The donor can neither sue to establish parental rights, nor be sued and required to support the resulting child. In sum, donors are eliminated from the parental equation.

UPA (2000) does not deal with many of the complex and serious legal problems raised by the practice of assisted reproduction. Issues such as ownership and disposition of embryos, regulation of the medical procedures, insurance coverage, etc., are left to other statutes or common law. Only the issue of parentage falls within the purview of this Act. This was also the case in UPA (1973), which wholly deferred speaking on the subject except to insure the husband's paternal responsibility when he gave his consent to what was then called "artificial insemination" of his wife (now known in the scientific community as "intrauterine insemination"). The commentary to UPA (1973) stated: "It was thought useful, however, to single out and cover ... at least one fact situation that occurs frequently."

UPA (2000) goes well beyond that narrow view; it governs the parentage issues in all cases in which the birth mother is also the intended mother of the child. It also insures that if the mother is a married woman, her husband will be the father of the child if he gives his consent to assisted reproduction by his wife, no matter which aspect of the technology is utilized. UPA (1973) § 5(b) specified that a male donor would not be considered the father of a child born of artificial insemination if the sperm was provided to a licensed physician for use in artificial insemination of a married woman other than the donor's wife. The Act does not continue the requirement that the donor provide the sperm to a licensed physician.

This section of UPA (2000) further opts not to limit nonparenthood of a donor to situations in which the donor provides sperm for assisted reproduction by a married woman. This requirement is not realistic in light of present practices in the field of assisted reproduction. Instead, donors are to be shielded from parenthood in all situations in which either a married woman or a single woman conceives a child through assisted reproduction. If a married woman bears a child of assisted reproduction using a donor's sperm, the donor will not be the father in any event. Her husband will be the father unless and until the husband's lack of consent to the assisted reproduction is proven within two years of his learning of the birth, *see* § 705, *infra*. This provides certainty of nonparentage for prospective donors. The comment to USCACA § 4(a) states that "nonparenthood is also provided for those donors who provide sperm for assisted reproduction by unmarried women." Under those circumstances—called a "relatively rare situation" in the 1988 comment—"the child would have no legally recognized father." This result is retained in UPA (2000), although the frequency of unmarried women using assisted reproduction appears to have grown significantly since 1988.

The definition of "donor" in Section 102(8), *supra*, includes persons who provide either sperm or eggs for assisted reproduction. Thus, if a woman provides an egg for assisted reproduction that results in another woman bearing the child, the egg donor is not the child's mother. This does not create a burden on the child because § 201(a)(1), *supra*, declares the general rule that the woman who gives birth to a child is that child's mother. It is clear, however, that a wife who provides eggs for her own conception and a husband who provides sperm for use by his wife in assisted reproduction are not "donors" as defined in Section 102(8).

§ 160.703. Husband's Paternity of Child of Assisted Reproduction.

If a husband provides sperm for or consents to assisted reproduction by his wife as provided by Section 160.704, he is the father of a resulting child.

Commissioners' Comment to UPA Section 703

Source: UPA (1973) § 5; USCACA (1988) §§ 1, 3.

The presumptive paternity of the husband of a married woman who bears a child through assisted reproduction reflects a concern for the best interests of the children of assisted reproduction. Of course, a husband who provides sperm for use by his wife in assisted reproduction is the father of any resulting child born to the wife. A similar result is mandated if his sperm is not used when he consents to assisted reproduction by his wife, see § 704, *infra*.

Any uncertainty concerning the identity of the father of such a child ought to be shouldered by the married woman's husband rather than by the child. Thus, the husband (but not someone acting on his behalf, such as a guardian, administrator or executor) has the obligation to file an action aimed at denying paternity through lack of consent to the assisted reproduction rather than the child or mother having an obligation to prove the husband's paternity.

By designating the husband of a woman who bears a child through assisted reproduction as the father, it is intended that he will be considered the father for purposes of any cause of action that arises before the birth of the child. Thus, for example, he would be the father under any state law authorizing a wrongful death action for the death of an unborn child during pregnancy.

§ 160.704. Consent to Assisted Reproduction.

(a) Consent by a married woman to assisted reproduction must be in a record signed by the woman and her husband. This requirement does not apply to the donation of eggs by a married woman for assisted reproduction by another woman.

(b) Failure by the husband to sign a consent required by Subsection (a) before or after the birth of the child does not preclude a finding that the husband is the father of a child born to his wife if the wife and husband openly treated the child as their own.

Commissioners' Comment to UPA Section 704

Source: UPA (1973) § 5; UPC (1993) § 2–114(c).

Subsection (a) continues the requirement that the husband consent to all forms of assisted reproduction. However, the wife is exempted from obtaining her husband's consent if she is acting as an egg donor for another woman.

Subsection (b) provides that even If a husband did not consent to assisted reproduction, he may nonetheless be found to be the father of a child born through that means if he and his wife openly treat the child as their own. This principle is taken from the Uniform Probate Code (1993) section cited above, which provides that neither natural parent (nor that natural parent's kindred) inherit from or through a child unless that natural parent, mother or father, has openly treated the child as his or hers and has not refused to support the child. The latter phrase was not carried forward to subsection (b).

Leading Case

K.B. v. N.B., 811 S.W.2d 634 (Tex. App.—San Antonio 1991, writ denied) (husband's ratification of artificial insemination by conduct substitutes for written consent)

---

§ 160.705. Limitation on Husband's Dispute of Paternity.

(a) Except as otherwise provided by Subsection (b), the husband of a wife who gives birth to a child by means of assisted reproduction may not challenge his paternity of the child unless:

(1) before the fourth anniversary of the date of learning of the birth of the child he commences a proceeding to adjudicate his paternity; and

(2) the court finds that he did not consent to the assisted reproduction before or after the birth of the child.

(b) A proceeding to adjudicate paternity may be maintained at any time if the court determines that:

(1) the husband did not provide sperm for or, before or after the birth of the child, consent to assisted reproduction by his wife;

(2) the husband and the mother of the child have not cohabited since the probable time of assisted reproduction; and

(3) the husband never openly treated the child as his own.

(c) The limitations provided by this section apply to a marriage declared invalid after assisted reproduction.

Commissioners' Comment to UPA Section 705

Source: USCACA (1988) § 3; UPC (1993) § 2–114(c).

Subsection (a) provides for a challenge to a husband's presumed paternity if the conception of the child was through assisted reproduction not consented to by the husband before or after the birth of the child. If a proceeding to establish nonpaternity is timely filed and the husband's lack of consent is demonstrated, the child will be without a legally-recognized father because the sperm donor is not the father under § 702, *supra*. Because the filing of such a nonpaternity proceeding is permitted within two years of the husband's learning of the child's birth, the period of uncertainty concerning the identity of the child's father will be longer than two years in a situation in which an absent husband is not immediately made aware of the child's birth.

Subsection (b) provides an exception to the two-year time limit if the husband's sperm was not used, the couple has not cohabited since the probable time of the use of assisted reproduction, and the husband has never openly treated the child as his own.

---

§ 160.706. Effect of Dissolution of Marriage.

(a) If a marriage is dissolved before the placement of eggs, sperm, or embryos, the former spouse is not a parent of the resulting child unless the former spouse consented in a record that if assisted reproduction were to occur after a divorce the former spouse would be a parent of the child.

(b) The consent of a former spouse to assisted reproduction may be withdrawn by that individual in a record at any time before the placement of eggs, sperm, or embryos.

Commissioners' Comment to UPA Section 706

This section is entirely new, but is derived from the policy stated in Section 707, *infra*. If there is to be no liability for a child conceived after death, then there should be no liability for a child conceived or implanted after divorce. If the wife proceeds with assisted reproduction after a divorce, the former husband is *not the legal parent* of the resulting child unless he has consented in a record to post-divorce assisted reproduction. In such a case, the child will have a legal mother under Section 201(a)(1). The child will have a genetic father, but not a legal father. Intention, rather than biology, is the controlling factor. The section is intended to encourage careful drafting of assisted reproduction agreements. The attorney and the parties themselves should discuss the issue and clarify their intent before a problem arises.

This Act does not attempt to resolve issues as to control of frozen embryos following dissolution of marriage. Those matters are left to other state laws, usually in the context of settlement of divorce and regulation of health care facilities.

---

§ 160.707. Parental Status of Deceased Spouse.

If a spouse dies before the placement of eggs, sperm, or embryos, the deceased spouse is not a parent of the resulting child unless the deceased spouse consented in a record that if assisted reproduction were to occur after death the deceased spouse would be a parent of the child.

Commissioners' Comment to UPA Section 707

Source: USCACA (1988) § 4.

Absent consent in a record, the death of a spouse whose genetic material is subsequently used either in conceiving an embryo or in implanting an already existing embryo into a womb ends the potential parenthood of the deceased. This section is designed primarily to avoid the problems of intestate succession which could arise if the posthumous use of a person's genetic material could lead to the deceased being determined to be a parent. Of course, a spouse who wants to explicitly provide for such children in his or her will may do so.

Subchapter I. Gestational Agreements

Editors' Note: *All of the amendments to Subchapter I have the following legislative history:*

History: Enacted by 78th Legis., Reg. Sess. (2003), H.B. 729, eff. Sept. 1, 2003, and "applies to a motion or other request for relief made in a parentage or paternity proceeding that is commenced on or after the effective date of this Act. A motion or other request for relief made in a parentage or paternity proceeding commenced before the effective date of this Act is governed by the law in effect at the time the proceeding was commenced, and the former law is continued in effect for that purpose."

Commissioners' Prefatory Note to Subchapter I

The longstanding shortage of adoptable children in this country has caused many persons to enlist a gestational mother (previously known as a surrogate) in order to have a child of their own genetic making. Assisted reproduction, as regulated by Subchapter H, involves two people who wish to become parents. In contrast, a gestational agreement (previously known as a surrogacy agreement) involves at least three parties; the couple who wish to become parents (the intended mother and father), and a woman who agrees to bear a child for them through the use of assisted reproduction (the gestational mother). Additional persons may be involved. For example, if the proposed gestational mother is married, her husband must be included in the agreement to dispense with his presumptive paternity of a child born to his wife. An egg donor or a sperm donor, or both, may be involved, although neither will be joined as a party to the agreement. Thus, by definition, a child born pursuant to a gestational agreement needs to have his or her *maternity* as well as *paternity* clarified.

The subject of gestational agreements was last addressed by the National Conference of Commissioners on Uniform State Laws in 1988 with the adoption of USCACA (1988). Because some Commissioners believed that such agreements should be prohibited, while others believed that such agreements should be allowed, but regulated, USCACA offered two alternatives on the subject: to regulate such activities through a judicial review process or to void such contracts. Only two states have adopted either version of the Act; Virginia chose to regulate such agreements, while North Dakota opted to void them. In the twelve years since the promulgation drafting of USCACA, approximately one-half of the states have developed statutory or case law on the issue. Of those, about one-half have recognized such agreements, and the other half has rejected them. In states rejecting such agreements, the legal status of children born pursuant to a gestational agreement is uncertain. Also troubling is the question of whether full faith and credit applies if an agreement was entered into in a state that does recognize such an agreement to be valid. The remaining states do not have adequate laws on the subject.

Voiding or criminalizing gestational agreements will force individuals to find friendly legal forums for the process, which raises a host of legal issues. For example, a couple may return to their home state with a child born as the consequence of a gestational agreement entered into in a state recognizing that agreement. This presents a full faith and credit question if their home state has a statute declaring gestational agreements to be void.

Despite these legal issues, thousands of children are born each year pursuant to gestational agreements. One thing ought to be clear; a child born under these circumstances is entitled to have its status clarified. Nonetheless, in some states, the legislature may feel that it is not yet ready to tackle the issue. For that reason, this article is bracketed: that is, it is optional. For states ready to deal with the issue, the Act provides a model that meets their needs. Those feeling that the issue is still too unsettling may omit this part of UPA(2000) without doing damage to the other provisions.

Despite the lack of acceptance of USCACA, the Conference again finds that the subject is increasingly worthy of legislative attention. Therefore, with some modest modifications, the subject is included in UPA (2000). A relatively minor grammatical change in this version is the elimination of the term "surrogate," which nonetheless has a substantial significance. First, to label a woman who bears a child a "surrogate" does not comply with the dictionary definition of the term under any construction, to wit: "a person appointed to act in the place of another" or "something serving as a substitute." This was especially true when "surrogate" included a woman who supplied both "egg and womb," that is, who is both gestational and genetic mother. The term was eliminated because the assisted reproduction community has generally rejected this pattern to avoid the psychological and legal issues that arise when the "surrogate" changes her mind about the agreement. Further, and of equal importance, the term "surrogate" has acquired a significant negative connotation in American society, which confuses rather than enlightens the discussion.

The single term "gestational mother" is both more accurate and more inclusive, to wit, it covers a woman who, through assisted reproduction, provides the gestational heritage of a child to be raised by the intended parents. A woman who supplies both functions, gestational and genetic, or who only performs the gestational function, is included in the new term. The practice of having a woman perform both functions is generally strongly disfavored by the assisted reproduction community. Experience has shown that the gestational mother's genetic link to the child sometimes creates additional emotional and psychological problems in enforcing a gestational agreement.

UPA (2000) takes the position that entering into a gestational agreement is a significant legal act that should be reviewed by a court, just as an adoption is judicially reviewed. The procedure established generally follows that of the 1988 Act, but departs in several important ways. First, nonvalidated gestational agreements are unenforceable (not void), thereby providing a strong incentive for the participants to seek judicial scrutiny. Second, the restriction under USCACA that at least one of the intended parents would be genetically related to the child born of the gestational agreement has been eliminated. Third, individuals who enter into nonvalidated gestational agreements and later refuse to adopt the resulting child may be liable for support of the child.

Assisted reproduction facilities and numerous other entities are involved in the gestational agreement. Internet sites are omnipresent promoting such agreements. As of December, 2000, states take a variety of approaches to gestational agreements: eleven states allow such agreements by statutes or case law; six states void such agreements by statute; eight states statutorily ban compensation to the gestational mother; and two states have judicially refused to recognize such agreements.

Although legal recognition of gestational agreements is undoubtedly controversial, the plain fact is that medical science has raced ahead of the law without heed to the views of the general public—or legislators. Courts have recently come to acknowledge this reality when forced to render decisions regarding collaborative reproduction, noting that artificial insemination, gestational carriers, cloning and gene splicing are part of the present, as well as of the future. One court predicted that even if all forms of assisted reproduction were outlawed in a particular state, its courts would still be called upon to decide on the identity of the lawful parents of a child resulting from those procedures undertaken in less restrictive states.

The intractable issue remains; who must provide the child with maintenance and support? In its opinion, one court stated:

> Again we must call on the Legislature to sort out the parental rights and responsibilities of those involved in artificial reproduction. No matter what one thinks of artificial insemination, traditional and gestational surrogacy (in all of its permutations) and—as now appears in the not-too-distant future, cloning and even gene splicing—courts are still going to be faced with the problem of determining lawful parentage. A child cannot be ignored. Even if all the means of artificial reproduction were outlawed with draconian criminal penalties visited on the doctors and parties involved, courts would still be called upon to decide who the lawful parents are and who—other than the taxpayers—is obligated to provide maintenance and support for the child. These cases will not go away. Again we must call on the Legislature to sort out the parental rights and responsibilities of those involved in artificial reproduction. . . . Courts can continue to make decisions on an ad hoc basis without necessarily imposing some grand scheme. . . .

> Or, the Legislature can act to impose a broader order which, even though it might not be perfect on a case-by-case basis, would bring some predictability to those who seek to make use of artificial reproductive techniques.

In re Buzzanca, 1998 Cal. App. Lexis 180; 72 Cal. Rptr. 2d 280, 61 Cal. App. 4th 1410 (1998).

Authors' Comment

The Texas adoption of legislation governing gestational agreements is an important advancement for couples desiring to use such methods for having children. The Texas statutes depart in three important ways from the Uniform Parentage Act as amended in 2002. First, Texas restricts the use of validated agreements to married couples. Secondly, the intended mother must demonstrate that she is unable to give birth to a child. Finally, the gestational mother may not contribute her own egg for the embryo, and therefore the gestational mother is not genetically linked to the child. Notwithstanding these differences, this legislation will undoubtedly grow in importance in the future of Texas families.

---

§ 160.751. Definition.

In this subchapter, "gestational mother" means a woman who gives birth to a child conceived under a gestational agreement.

§ 160.752. Scope of Subchapter; Choice of Law.

(a) Notwithstanding any other provision of this chapter or another law, this subchapter authorizes an agreement between a woman and the intended parents of a child in which the woman relinquishes all rights as a parent of a child conceived by means of assisted reproduction and that provides that the intended parents become the parents of the child.

(b) This subchapter controls over any other law with respect to a child conceived under a gestational agreement under this subchapter.

§ 160.753. Establishment of Parent–Child Relationship.

(a) Notwithstanding any other provision of this chapter or another law, the mother-child relationship exists between a woman and a child by an adjudication confirming the woman as a parent of the child born to a gestational mother under a gestational agreement if the gestational agreement is validated under this subchapter or enforceable under other law, regardless of the fact that the gestational mother gave birth to the child.

(b) The father-child relationship exists between a child and a man by an adjudication confirming the man as a parent of the child born to a gestational mother under a gestational agreement if the gestational agreement is validated under this subchapter or enforceable under other law.

§ 160.754. Gestational Agreement Authorized.

(a) A prospective gestational mother, her husband if she is married, each donor, and each intended parent may enter into a written agreement providing that:

(1) the prospective gestational mother agrees to pregnancy by means of assisted reproduction;

(2) the prospective gestational mother, her husband if she is married, and each donor other than the intended parents, if applicable, relinquish all parental rights and duties with respect to a child conceived through assisted reproduction;

(3) the intended parents will be the parents of the child; and

(4) the gestational mother and each intended parent agree to exchange throughout the period covered by the agreement all relevant information regarding the health of the gestational mother and each intended parent.

(b) The intended parents must be married to each other. Each intended parent must be a party to the gestational agreement.

(c) The gestational agreement must require that the eggs used in the assisted reproduction procedure be retrieved from an intended parent or a donor. The gestational mother's eggs may not be used in the assisted reproduction procedure.

(d) The gestational agreement must state that the physician who will perform the assisted reproduction procedure as provided by the agreement has informed the parties to the agreement of:

(1) the rate of successful conceptions and births attributable to the procedure, including the most recent published outcome statistics of the procedure at the facility at which it will be performed;

(2) the potential for and risks associated with the implantation of multiple embryos and consequent multiple births resulting from the procedure;

(3) the nature of and expenses related to the procedure;

(4) the health risks associated with, as applicable, fertility drugs used in the procedure, egg retrieval procedures, and egg or embryo transfer procedures; and

(5) reasonably foreseeable psychological effects resulting from the procedure.

(e) The parties to a gestational agreement must enter into the agreement before the 14th day preceding the date the transfer of eggs, sperm, or embryos to the gestational mother occurs for the purpose of conception or implantation.

(f) A gestational agreement does not apply to the birth of a child conceived by means of sexual intercourse.

(g) A gestational agreement may not limit the right of the gestational mother to make decisions to safeguard her health or the health of an embryo.

Commissioners' Comment to UPA Section 801
[Texas Family Code Section 160.754]

Source: USCACA §§ 1(3), 5, 9.

The previous uniform act on this subject, USCACA, proposed two alternatives, one of which was to declare that gestational agreements were to be void. Subsection (a) rejects that approach. The scientific state of the art and the medical facilities providing the technological capacity to utilize a woman other than the wife as the gestational mother, guarantee that such agreements will continue to be written. Subsection (a) recognizes that certainty and initiates a procedure for its regulation by a judicial officer. All the persons directly involved in the procedure must enter into a written agreement; this includes the intended parents, the gestational mother, and her husband if she is married. In addition, if there are donors involved, they must also sign the agreement. The agreement must provide that the intended parents will be the parents of any child born pursuant to the agreement while all of the others (gestational mother, her husband, if any, and the donors, as appropriate) relinquish all rights and duties of parenthood.

Under subsection (b), a valid gestational agreement requires the participation of two intended parents who are married to each other. Although some Commissioners raised objection to not permitting unmarried persons to agree to be intended parents in an enforceable gestational agreement, this decision continues the proscription initiated in USCACA. Given the controversial nature of these agreements, the most worthy fact circumstances meriting legal recognition is the plight of childless married couples. Note that this section simply authorizes such agreements. It does not give them effect in terms of designating parenthood, etc. In order to become enforceable, subsection (c) demands that the agreement must be validated by the appropriate court under Section 160.756.

Subsection (e) is intended to shield these gestational agreements that include payment of the gestational mother from attack under "baby-selling" statutes that prohibit payment of money to the natural mother in adoptions.

Subsection (f) is intended to acknowledge that the gestational mother, as a pregnant woman, has a constitutionally-recognized right to decide issues regarding her health care and that of the unborn child. In other words, the intended parents have no right to demand that the gestational mother expose herself to undue medical risk.

If the conditions of this section are met, the parties may move forward to a court for approval of their agreement.

Authors' Comment

The 2002 version of the Uniform Parentage Act is not restricted to married couples, but the Texas Legislature chose to adopt the 2000 version of the Act as it pertains to gestational agreements.

---

§ 160.755. Petition to Validate Gestational Agreement.

(a) The intended parents and the prospective gestational mother under a gestational agreement may commence a proceeding to validate the agreement.

(b) A person may maintain a proceeding to validate a gestational agreement only if:

(1) the prospective gestational mother or the intended parents have resided in this state for the 90 days preceding the date the proceeding is commenced;

(2) the prospective gestational mother's husband, if she is married, is joined as a party to the proceeding; and

(3) a copy of the gestational agreement is attached to the petition.

Commissioners' Comment to UPA Section 802 [Texas Family Code Section 160.755]

Source: USCACA § 6(a).

Sections 160.755 and 160.756, the core sections of this subchapter, provide for state involvement, through supervision by a court, of the gestational agreement before, during, and after the assisted reproduction process. The purpose of early involvement is to insure that the parties are appropriate for a gestational agreement, that they understand the consequences of what they are about to do, and that the best interests of a child born of the gestational agreement are considered before the arrangement is authorized. The trigger for state involvement is a petition brought by all the parties to the arrangement (including the gestational mother's husband if she is married) in which the parties seek a judicial order authorizing the assisted reproduction contemplated by their agreement. The agreement itself must be submitted to the court.

To discourage forum shopping, subsection (b)(1) requires that the petition may only be filed to a state in which the intended parents or the gestational mother have been resident for at least 90 days.

---

§ 160.756. Hearing to Validate Gestational Agreement.

(a) A gestational agreement must be validated as provided by this section.

(b) The court may validate a gestational agreement as provided by Subsection (c) only if the court finds that:

(1) the parties have submitted to the jurisdiction of the court under the jurisdictional standards of this chapter;

(2) the medical evidence provided shows that the intended mother is unable to carry a pregnancy to term and give birth to the child or is unable to carry the pregnancy to term and give birth to the child without unreasonable risk to her physical or mental health or to the health of the unborn child;

(3) unless waived by the court, an agency or other person has conducted a home study of the intended parents and has determined that the intended parents meet the standards of fitness applicable to adoptive parents;

(4) each party to the agreement has voluntarily entered into and understands the terms of the agreement;

(5) the prospective gestational mother has had at least one previous pregnancy and delivery and carrying another pregnancy to term and giving birth to another child would not pose an unreasonable risk to the child's health or the physical or mental health of the prospective gestational mother; and

(6) the parties have adequately provided for which party is responsible for all reasonable health care expenses associated with the pregnancy, including providing for who is responsible for those expenses if the agreement is terminated.

(c) If the court finds that the requirements of Subsection (b) are satisfied, the court may render an order validating the gestational agreement and declaring that the intended parents will be the parents of a child born under the agreement.

(d) The court may validate the gestational agreement at the court's discretion. The court's determination of whether to validate the agreement is subject to review only for abuse of discretion.

Commissioners' Comment to UPA Section 803
[Texas Family Code Section 160.756]

Source: USCACA § 6(b).

This pre-conception authorization process for a gestational agreement is roughly analogous to adoption procedures in place in most jurisdictions as of December, 2000.

Just as adoption contemplates the transfer of parentage of a child from the natural to the adoptive parents, a gestational agreement involves the transfer from the gestational mother to the intended parents. UPA (2000) is designed to protect the interests of the child to be born under the gestational agreement as well as the interests of gestational mother and the intended parents. It should be noted that in contrast to USCACA (1988) § 1(3), there is no requirement that at least one of the intended parents be genetically related to the child born of a gestational agreement. Given the state of art in the science, this is an unrealistic provision as of the medical science available in 2000. Similarly, the likelihood that the gestational mother will also be the genetic mother is not directly addressed in UPA (2000), while USCACA (1988) virtually assumed that the fact pattern would be typical. Experience with the intractable problems caused by such a combination has dissuaded the majority of fertility laboratories from following that practice. *See In re Baby M.*, 537 A.2d 1227 (N.J. 1988).

Section 160.756 seeks to protect the interests of the child in several ways. The major protection of the child is the authorization procedure itself. By providing for a court order authorizing the assisted reproduction and the gestational agreement, the Act establishes closely supervised gestational arrangements to guarantee the security and well being of the child. Once a petition has been filed, subsection (a) permits—but does not require—the court to validate a gestational agreement. If validating, the court must declare that the intended parents will be the parents of any child born pursuant to, and during the term of, the agreement.

The court must hold a hearing on the petition. Under subsection (b) the court must make six separate findings before validating the agreement. Subsection (b)(1) requires the court to insure that the 90-day residency requirement of Section 160.755 has been satisfied and that it has jurisdiction over the parties;

The intended parents, who by virtue of subsection (b)(2) are by definition unable to procreate through traditional means, have their interests protected. In addition to the very existence of the court authorization procedure which gives effect to the gestational agreement, help is provided through assurances to them that the gestational mother is capable and is knowingly entering the arrangement. There must be medical evidence that the wife is unable to bear a child or is unable to so without unreasonable risk to her or the child. The clear intent of subsection (b)(2) is to deny validation of a gestational agreement to a couple who are capable of having a child through assisted reproduction or sexual intercourse. This procedure is not created simply to allow a couple to avoid the inconvenience of a pregnancy.

Under subsection(b)(3), the court will be informed of the results of a home study of the intended parents. They must meet the standards imposed upon would-be adoptive parents.

The interests of all the parties are protected by subsection (b)(4), which is designed to protect the individuals involved from the possibility of overreaching or fraud. All must enter into the agreement voluntarily and with full knowledge of the consequences of their actions.

Subsection (b)(5) specifically requires that the court find the gestational mother has had at least one previous pregnancy and delivery. Presumably, such a finding will help insure that she fully understands the nature and experience of pregnancy. Her consent to be the gestational mother is thus with full knowledge of what she has agreed to do, including to relinquish the child born to her to the intended parents. The court must also find the contemplated pregnancy and delivery will not pose unreasonable physical or mental health risks to her. The interest of producing a healthy child is promoted by the additional required finding that the pregnancy will not be unreasonably risky to the child.

The requirement of assurance of health-care expenses until birth imposed by subsection (b)(6) further protects the gestational mother.

Subsection (d) mandates that whether or not to validate the agreement is within the discretion of the court and is subject to review only for abuse of discretion.

Section 160.756, while constructing a detailed set of requirements for the petition and the findings that must be made before an authorizing order can be issued, nowhere states the consequences of violations of the rules. Because of the variety of types of violations that could possibly occur, a bright-line rule concerning the effect of such violations is inappropriate. The question of the consequences of a failure to abide by the rules of Section 160.756 is left to a case-by-case determination. A court should be guided in making such a determination by the narrow purpose of the Act to permit gestational agreements and the equities of a particular situation. Note that Section 160.759 provides a period for termination of the agreement and vacating of the order. The discovery of a failure to abide by the rules of Section 160.756 would certainly provide the occasion for terminating the agreement. On the other hand, if a failure to abide by the rules of Section 160.756 is discovered by a party during a time when Section 160.759 termination would be permissible, failure to terminate might be an appropriate reason to estop the party from later seeking to overturn or ignore the Section 160.756 order.

§ 160.757. Inspection of Records.

The proceedings, records, and identities of the parties to a gestational agreement under this subchapter are subject to inspection under the same standards of confidentiality that apply to an adoption under the laws of this state.

Commissioners' Comment to UPA Section 804 [Texas Family Code Section 160.757]

The procedures involved in this subchapter are exceptionally personal, thereby warranting protection from invasions of privacy. Adoption records provide a suitable model for these records.

§ 160.758. Continuing, Exclusive Jurisdiction.

Subject to Section 152.201, a court that conducts a proceeding under this subchapter has continuing, exclusive jurisdiction of all matters arising out of the gestational agreement until the date a child born to the gestational mother during the period covered by the agreement reaches 180 days of age.

Commissioners' Comment to UPA Section 805 [Texas Family Code 160.758]

Source: USCACA § 6(e).

This section is designed to minimize the possibility of parallel litigation in different states and the consequent risk of childnapping for strategic purposes. The court that validated the gestational agreement will have authority to enforce the gestational agreement until the child is 180 days old. Note that only the parentage issues and enforcement issues are covered; collateral matters, such as custody, visitation, and child support are not contemplated as subject to the strictures of this chapter.

§ 160.759. Termination of Gestational Agreement.

(a) Before a prospective gestational mother becomes pregnant by means of assisted reproduction, the prospective gestational mother, her husband if she is married, or either intended parent may terminate a gestational agreement validated under Section 160.756 by giving written notice of the termination to each other party to the agreement.

(b) A person who terminates a gestational agreement under Subsection (a) shall file notice of the termination with the court. A person having the duty to notify the court who does not notify the court of the termination of the agreement is subject to appropriate sanctions.

(c) On receipt of the notice of termination, the court shall vacate the order rendered under Section 160.756 validating the gestational agreement.

(d) A prospective gestational mother and her husband, if she is married, may not be liable to an intended parent for terminating a gestational agreement if the termination is in accordance with this section.

Commissioners' Comment to UPA Section 806 [Texas Family Code Section 160.759]

Source: USCACA § 7.

Subsection (a) permits a party to terminate a gestational agreement after the authorization order by canceling the arrangement before the pregnancy has been established. This provides for cancellation during a time when the interests of the parties would not be unduly prejudiced by termination. By definition, the procreation process has not begun. The intended parents certainly have an expectation interest during this time, but the nature of this interest is little different from that which they would have while they were attempting to create a pregnancy through traditional means. In contrast to the next subsection, termination of the agreement does not require "good cause."

Under subsection (b) a party who wishes to terminate the agreement must inform the other parties in writing, and must also file notice with the court. The court must then vacate the order validating the agreement. An individual who does not notify the court of his/her termination of the agreement is subject to sanction.

USCACA (1988) provided extensive explanation of termination of an agreement by a gestational mother who has provided the egg for the assisted reproduction. This possibility is not repeated in UPA (2000) because it is a remote likelihood that an agreement for the gestational mother to furnish the egg will be countenanced in 2001. Assisted reproduction, as conducted as of today, does not approve that practice.

Subsection (d) provides that before pregnancy a gestational mother is not liable to the intended parents for terminating the agreement. UPA (2000) does not speak explicitly to termination of the agreement after pregnancy. Several sections deal with the issue, at least under certain described circumstances. Section 160.754 (g) recognizes that the gestational mother has plenary power to decide issues of her health and the health of the fetus. Sections 160.756(a) and 160.760 direct that the intended parents are in fact the parents of the child with an enforceable right to the possession of the child.

---

§ 160.760. Parentage Under Validated Gestational Agreement.

(a) On the birth of a child to a gestational mother under a validated gestational agreement, the intended parents shall file a notice of the birth

with the court not later than the 300th day after the date assisted reproduction occurred.

(b) After receiving notice of the birth, the court shall render an order that:

(1) confirms that the intended parents are the child's parents;

(2) requires the gestational mother to surrender the child to the intended parents, if necessary; and

(3) requires the bureau of vital statistics to issue a birth certificate naming the intended parents as the child's parents.

(c) If a person alleges that a child born to a gestational mother did not result from assisted reproduction, the court shall order that scientifically accepted parentage testing be conducted to determine the child's parentage.

Commissioners' Comment to UPA Section 807 [Texas Family Code Section 160.760]

Source: USCACA § 8.

Under subsection (a), parentage of a child born pursuant to an approved gestational agreement within 300 days of the use of assisted reproduction is vested in the intended parents if the order under Section 160.756 is still in effect. Notice of the birth of the child must be filed by the intended parents. The court, upon receipt of the notice, shall issue an order confirming that the intended parents are the legal parents of the child and direct the issuance of a birth certificate to confirm the court's determination. If necessary, the court may also order the gestational mother to surrender the child to the intended parents.

§ 160.761. Effect of Gestational Mother's Marriage After Validation of Agreement.

If a gestational mother is married after the court renders an order validating a gestational agreement under this subchapter:

(1) the validity of the gestational agreement is not affected;

(2) the gestational mother's husband is not required to consent to the agreement; and

(3) the gestational mother's husband is not a presumed father of the child born under the terms of the agreement.

Commissioners' Comment to UPA Section 808 [Texas Family Code Section 160.761]

Source: USCACA § 9.

If, after the original court order validates the gestational agreement, the gestational mother marries, the gestational agreement continues to be valid and the consent of her new husband is not required. The new husband is neither a party to the original action nor the presumed father of a resulting child, and therefore ought not be burdened with the status of parent unless he is the genetic father or chooses to adopt the child.

§ 160.762. Effect of Gestational Agreement That is Not Validated.

(a) A gestational agreement that is not validated as provided by this subchapter is unenforceable, regardless of whether the agreement is in a record.

(b) The parent-child relationship of a child born under a gestational agreement that is not validated as provided by this subchapter is determined as otherwise provided by this chapter.

(c) A party to a gestational agreement that is not validated as provided by this subchapter who is an intended parent under the agreement may be held liable for the support of a child born under the agreement, even if the agreement is otherwise unenforceable.

(d) The court may assess filing fees, reasonable attorney's fees, fees for genetic testing, other costs, and necessary travel and other reasonable expenses incurred in a proceeding under this section. Attorney's fees awarded by the court may be paid directly to the attorney. An attorney who is awarded attorney's fees may enforce the order in the attorney's own name.

Commissioners' Comment to UPA Section 809
[Texas Family Code Section 160. 762]

Source: USCACA §§ 5(b),10.

This section distinguishes between an unenforceable agreement and a prohibited one. Given the widespread use of assisted reproductive technologies in modern society, the Act attempts only to regularize the parentage aspects of the science, not to regulate the practice of assisted reproduction. If individuals choose to ignore the protections afforded gestational agreements by the Act, parentage questions will remain when a child is born as a result of an nonvalidated gestational agreement. The Act provides no assistance to the intended parents; the gestational mother is denominated the mother irrespective of the source of the eggs. While donors of either eggs or sperm are not parents in this circumstance, subsection (c) permits the court to hold the intended parents to an obligation to support the resulting child, even though the balance of the agreement will not be enforced.

Under USCACA (1988), agreements that were not approved were declared "void." Under UPA(2000), a nonapproved agreement is declared "unenforceable." The result may be virtually the same in some instances. As under the prior Act, the gestational mother is the mother of a child conceived through assisted reproduction if the gestational agreement has not been judicially approved as provided in this article. Her husband, if he is a party to such agreement, is presumed to be the father. If the gestational mother's husband is not a party to the agreement, or if she is unmarried, paternity of the child will be left to existing law, if any. If the mother decides to keep the child, the intended parents have no recourse. If the parties agree that the intended parents will raise the child, the only method whereby they may become parents of the child will be through adoption.

---

§ 160.763. Health Care Facility Reporting Requirement.

(a) The Texas Department of Health by rule shall develop and implement a confidential reporting system that requires each health care facility in this state at which assisted reproduction procedures are performed under gestational agreements to report statistics related to those procedures.

(b) In developing the reporting system, the department shall require each health care facility described by Subsection (a) to annually report:

(1) the number of assisted reproduction procedures under a gestational agreement performed at the facility during the preceding year; and

(2) the number and current status of embryos created through assisted reproduction procedures described by Subdivision (1) that were not transferred for implantation.

Authors' Comment

This section is not a provision of the Uniform Parentage Act. It was added by the Texas Legislature in order to gather reliable information on the number of gestational agreements undertaken in this state.

Chapter 161. Termination of the Parent–Child Relationship

Subchapter A. Grounds

Subchapter B. Procedures

Subchapter C. Hearing and Order

Editors' Note: *This chapter contains guest commentary by Charles G. Childress, Children's Rights Clinic, University of Texas Law School, and former Chief Attorney, Field Operations, Legal Division, Texas Department of Protective and Regulatory Services, identified as (C.G.C.).*

Introductory Comment

The termination of the parent-child relationship might be called the capital punishment of civil law. It constitutes the final, irreversible severance of all legal rights and duties between a parent and child. A termination suit may arise in several very different contexts: (1) a private termination between one parent and the other, usually to facilitate a stepparent adoption; (2) an intrafamily termination in which relatives of the child seek to terminate the rights of allegedly culpable parents; (3) a termination by an adoption agency to facilitate the adoption of an infant, usually a child without a presumed father; and (4) intervention by the state to terminate allegedly culpable parents on grounds of the abuse or neglect of the child, or on another less frequently alleged statutory ground.

CLE/Other Legal Publications

Termination and adoption: the latest news. Ellen A. Yarrell, 2004 ADV. FAM. L.

Termination and adoption: it ain't over till it's over.[two articles] Sandra D. Hachem; Edwin J. (Ted) Terry, Jimmy Vaught, Karl E. Hays & James W. LaRue, 2002 MARRIAGE DISSOLUTION

Grounds for termination of parental rights. Phoebe Knauer, Pamela K. Parker, Lana S. Shadwick, Cathren Page Koehlert & Charles G. Childress, 2002–2 FAM. L. SECT. REP.

Surviving the maze: termination and adoption. Ellen A. Yarrell, Leslie A. Grant & Dianne Bissaillon, 2002 U. TEX. FAM. L. ON FRONT LINES

Overview of issues pertaining to credibility of child sexual abuse allegations and investigations. D. Ross Miller, P. Caren Phelan, 2001 MARRIAGE DISSOLUTION

Leading U.S. Supreme Court Cases

M.L.B. v. S.L.J., 519 U.S. 102, 117 S.Ct. 555 (1996) (appeal of termination of parental rights may not be conditioned on payment for trial transcript by indigent mother)

Santosky v. Kramer, 455 U.S. 745, 71 L.Ed.2d 599, 102 S.Ct. 1388 (1982) (clear and convincing evidence needed to terminate parental rights)

Lassiter v. Department of Social Services., 452 U.S. 18, 68 L.Ed.2d 640, 101 S.Ct. 2153 (1981) (no constitutional right to appointed counsel for parent)

Leading Texas Cases

In re G.M., 596 S.W.2d 846 (Tex. 1980) (must prove termination by clear and convincing evidence)

In re N.R.C., 94 S.W.3d 799 (Tex. App.—Houston [14th Dist.] 2002, pet. denied) (death penalty sanctions against parent how fails to deposit funds to cover attorney ad litem's fees in appropriate in private termination suit)

In re K.L., 91 S.W.3d 1 (Tex. App.—Fort Worth 2002, rule 53.7(f) motion granted) (parents entitled to effective appointed counsel in termination cases as a 14th amendment right)

In re D.S., 82 S.W.3d 743 (Tex. App.—Corpus Christi 2002, no pet.) (summary automatic denial of incarcerated parent's request to be present at termination trial is reversible error)

Lumbis v. Texas Dept. of Protective & Regulatory Services, 65 S.W.3d 844 (Tex. App.—Austin 2002, no pet.) (parents in a termination case are not entitled to the same constitutional guarantee of effective counsel afforded to criminal defendants)

In re L.S.R., 60 S.W.3d 376 (Tex. App.—Fort Worth 2001, no pet.) (termination where parents' mental retardation does not, as a matter of law, negate their ability to knowingly neglect their children)

In re C.W., 65 S.W.3d 353 (Tex. App.—Beaumont 2001, no pet.) (mother's presence via telephone for the entirety of the termination hearing, along with being represented by counsel who was physically present at the hearing, satisfied any and all due process requirements)

Cross Reference

Tex. Penal Code Ann. §§ 25.08. Sale or Purchase of Child; 25.09. Advertising for Placement of Child

Texas Family Law Practice Manual

Chapter 36. Termination
Chapter 38. Combined Termination and Adoption of Stepchild
Chapter 39. Ancillary Forms for Termination and Adoption

Subchapter A. Grounds

§ 161.001. Involuntary Termination of Parent-Child Relationship.

The court may order termination of the parent-child relationship if the court finds by clear and convincing evidence:

(1) that the parent has:

(A) voluntarily left the child alone or in the possession of another not the parent and expressed an intent not to return;

(B) voluntarily left the child alone or in the possession of another not the parent without expressing an intent to return, without providing for the adequate support of the child, and remained away for a period of at least three months;

(C) voluntarily left the child alone or in the possession of another without providing adequate support of the child and remained away for a period of at least six months;

(D) knowingly placed or knowingly allowed the child to remain in conditions or surroundings which endanger the physical or emotional well-being of the child;

(E) engaged in conduct or knowingly placed the child with persons who engaged in conduct which endangers the physical or emotional well-being of the child;

(F) failed to support the child in accordance with the parent's ability during a period of one year ending within six months of the date of the filing of the petition;

(G) abandoned the child without identifying the child or furnishing means of identification, and the child's identity cannot be ascertained by the exercise of reasonable diligence;

(H) voluntarily, and with knowledge of the pregnancy, abandoned the mother of the child beginning at a time during her pregnancy with the child and continuing through the birth, failed to provide adequate support or medical care for the mother during the period of abandonment before the birth of the child, and remained apart from the child or failed to support the child since the birth;

(I) contumaciously refused to submit to a reasonable and lawful order of a court under Subchapter D, Chapter 261 *[Investigation of Report of Child Abuse or Neglect]*;

(J) been the major cause of:

(i) the failure of the child to be enrolled in school as required by the Education Code; or

(ii) the child's absence from the child's home without the consent of the parents or guardian for a substantial length of time or without the intent to return;

(K) executed before or after the suit is filed an unrevoked or irrevocable affidavit of relinquishment of parental rights as provided by this chapter;

(L) been convicted or has been placed on community supervision, including deferred adjudication community supervision, for being criminally responsible for the death or serious injury of a child under the following sections of the Penal Code or adjudicated under Title 3 for conduct that caused the death or serious injury of a child and that would constitute a violation of one of the following Penal Code sections:

(i) Section 19.02 (murder);

(ii) Section 19.03 (capital murder);

(iii) Section 19.04 (manslaughter);

(iv) Section 21.11 (indecency with a child);

(v) Section 22.01 (assault);

(vi) Section 22.011 (sexual assault);

(vii) Section 22.02 (aggravated assault);

(viii) Section 22.021 (aggravated sexual assault);

(ix) Section 22.04 (injury to a child, elderly individual, or disabled individual);

(x) Section 22.041 (abandoning or endangering child);

(xi) Section 25.02 (prohibited sexual conduct);

(xii) Section 43.25 (sexual performance by a child); and

(xiii) Section 43.26 (possession or promotion of child pornography);

(M) had his or her parent-child relationship terminated with respect to another child based on a finding that the parent's conduct was in violation of Paragraph (D) or (E) or substantially equivalent provisions of the law of another state;

(N) constructively abandoned the child who has been in the permanent or temporary managing conservatorship of the Department of Protective and Regulatory Services or an authorized agency for not less than six months, and:

(i) the department or authorized agency has made reasonable efforts to return the child to the parent;

(ii) the parent has not regularly visited or maintained significant contact with the child; and

(iii) the parent has demonstrated an inability to provide the child with a safe environment;

(O) failed to comply with the provisions of a court order that specifically established the actions necessary for the parent to obtain the return of the child who has been in the permanent or temporary managing conservatorship of the Department of Protective and Regulatory Services for not less than nine months as a result of the child's removal from the parent under Chapter 262 *[Procedures in Suit by Governmental Entity]* for the abuse or neglect of the child;

(P) used a controlled substance, as defined by Chapter 481, Health and Safety Code, in a manner that endangered the health or safety of the child, and:

(i) failed to complete a court-ordered substance abuse treatment program; or

(ii) after completion of a court-ordered substance abuse treatment program, continued to abuse a controlled substance;

(Q) knowingly engaged in criminal conduct that has resulted in the parent's:

(i) conviction of an offense; and

(ii) confinement or imprisonment and inability to care for the child for not less than two years from the date of filing the petition;

(R) been the cause of the child being born addicted to alcohol or a controlled substance, other than a controlled substance legally obtained by prescription, as defined by Section 261.001; or

(S) voluntarily delivered the child to a designated emergency infant care provider under Section 262.302 without expressing an intent to return for the child; and

(2) that termination is in the best interest of the child.

Comment

This section provides the laundry list of the culpable conduct grounds that can lead to parental termination. It is a long-standing rule by both statute and constitutionally-based court decisions that the standard of proof in a termination case is "by clear and convincing evidence."

Subsections (1)(A) through (1)(C) involve the abandonment of a child by a parent.

Subsections (1)(D) and (1)(E) are usually referred to as the abuse and neglect grounds, and are commonly pled by the Department of Protective and Regulatory Services (DPRS), in state intervention cases.

Subsection (1)(F) is the nonsupport ground customarily used by one parent to terminate the rights of the other parent, particularly to facilitate a stepparent adoption. The one-year requirement for nonsupport is strictly construed.

Subsections (1)(G) through (1)(J) seldom, if ever, are applied. Subsection (1)(K) allows for termination based on a voluntary affidavit of relinquishment of parental rights, perhaps the most common procedure to accomplish legal termination.

Subsections (1)(L) and (1)(M), significantly change the statutory scheme from above. Conduct neither directed at, nor directly affecting, a child who is the subject of the suit can form the basis for termination. In short, a ground for termination is available if the parent has been guilty in the past of the requisite culpable conduct directed against another child. In 1997 the legislature clarified subsection (1)(L) by identifying the crimes that create a risk of termination of other children. Subsection (1)(M) was expanded to cover termination of parental rights due to substantially equivalent culpable conduct in another state resulting in a termination.

Subsection (1)(N) provides a ground to be used in those situations in which a child has been removed from a home before serious damage to the child has occurred, and before a termination ground exists. Thereafter, a ground for termination may come into existence if the parent does not maintain contact with the child and does not take the steps required to convince the court that the child can be safely returned to the parent. Originally, subsection (1)(N) was narrowly drawn to require at least a year's time to pass before a default in responsible parenting would trigger the ground for termination. Later the time to prove "constructive abandonment" by a parent was shortened to six months and the "contact" that a parent must maintain with the child in DPRS care was required to be "regular and significant." This eliminated irregular or incidental contact with the child as a defense to termination based on this ground.

Several grounds primarily focus on children who end up in the care of DPRS as a result of a report of child abuse or neglect. Subsection (1)(O) is an offshoot of a long-term effort by DPRS to convince the legislature to enact a ground for termination based on a parent's failure to cooperate with the caseworkers and with the plans established for the dysfunctional parents by DPRS. Although the legislature has always refused to accept parental noncooperation as a ground for termination, an analogous ground has been accepted. If the parent fails to obey court orders to take the action necessary to obtain the return of the child, a sufficient ground is created if the child remains in the permanent or temporary managing conservatorship of the department for at least nine months.

Subsection (1)(P) also represents a breakthrough for a long sought after ground for termination, *i.e.*, the use of controlled substances that damage the child. Additionally, the ground applies if a parent fails to complete a court-ordered substance abuse treatment program.

Similarly, there has been a good deal of litigation about the subject matter of subsection (1)(Q), imprisonment as a ground for termination of parental rights. The ground is somewhat ambiguous because it is unclear whether it is the sentence of "not less than two years" or whether the individual must actually be incarcerated for that length of time. For example, if an individual is sentenced to life imprisonment, may termination proceed immediately or must there be a two year delay before the ground is fully met and the termination may proceed?

Subsection (1)(R) expands on subsection (1)(P) by declaring that harm to a child in utero by use of cocaine, crack, or alcohol, which results in significant damage by way of birth defects or addiction by a newborn creates a termination ground.

Subsection (1)(S) is one aspect of the "Baby Moses Law," which encourages a parent (read "mother") not to abandon an infant in an unsafe place. A designated emergency infant care provider may take possession of such an infant, provide care, and deliver the child to DPRS. The parent cannot be detained and is exempt from prosecution under TEX. PEN. CODE § 22.041 (affirmative defense to prosecution for child abandonment when the child has been delivered to an emergency infant care provider). The parent is not exempt from prosecution for injury to the child or from termination of parental rights based on the voluntary abandonment, *see* § 262.301 *et seq.*, *infra*.

In all instances, a two-part procedure is required. That is, subsection (2) requires that whenever culpable parental conduct has been proven, it must be independently shown that termination also is in the best interest of the child. *(C.G.C.)*

Leading Cases

Evidentiary Factors

Holley v. Adams, 544 S.W.2d 367 (Tex. 1976) (list of factors sufficient for court's determination of best interest of child)

Wiley v. Spratlan, 543 S.W.2d 349 (Tex. 1976) (nonsupporting parent's ability to pay must be proven for an entire year to support determination)

In re W.S.M., 107 S.W.3d 772 (Tex. App.—Texarkana 2003, no pet.) (child's love for parents does not preclude termination)

In re C.N.S., 105 S.W.3d 104 (Tex. App.—Waco 2003, no pet.) (termination evidence on (q) grounds not required if (c) grounds proven)

In re D.J., 100 S.W.3d 658 (Tex. App.—Dallas 2003, pet. denied) (termination of father's rights for abuse affirmed but insufficient evidence to establish termination of mother's rights)

In re Caballero, 53 S.W.3d 391 (Tex. App.—Amarillo 2001, pet. denied) (termination of father's parental rights appropriate where the father's criminal conduct resulted in his imprisonment and his inability to care for his child as he failed to show he could "care for the child" through surrogates)

In re A.P., 42 S.W.3d 248 (Tex. App.—Waco 2001, pet. denied) (there was more than sufficient evidence to support the jury's findings by clear and convincing evidence that termination of the burglar father's rights were in the best interest of the children)

In re C.D., 962 S.W.2d 145 (Tex. App.—Fort Worth 1998, no writ) (attorney ad litem entitled to call witness that state may not have been allowed to call)

In re Z.W.C., 856 S.W.2d 281 (Tex. App.—Houston [1st Dist.] 1993, no writ) (must prove ability to pay for each month of statutory one-year period to find termination for failure to support)

Slatton v. Brazoria County Protective Services Unit, 804 S.W.2d 550 (Tex. App.—Texarkana 1991, no writ) (conduct occurring before denial of termination in earlier trial is not admissible in second suit for termination)

Jury Submission

Texas Dept. of Human Services v. E.B., 802 S.W.2d 647 (Tex. 1990) (upholding broad-form submission to jury)

In re B.K.D., 131 S.W.3d 10 (Tex. App.—Fort Worth 2003, pet. denied) (broad form answers based on legally and factually sufficient evidence support termination of parental rights of several fathers and mother)

In re J.R., 123 S.W.3d 669 (Tex. App.—Houston [14th Dist.] 2003, no pet.) (incarcerated father entitled to jury trial in termination upon proper request)

In re J.W., 123 S.W.3d 669 (Tex. App.—Dallas 2003, no pet.) (broad form questions allowed—jurors not required to sort out which of the 46 grounds was the critical straw in the termination evidence)

In re J.C., 108 S.W.3d 914 (Tex. App.—Texarkana 2003, no pet.) (delay in appointing counsel for indigent inmate father tolls period for timely request of jury trial for termination)

In re M.G.D., 108 S.W.3d 508 (Tex. App.—Houston [14th Dist.] 2003, pet. denied) (trial court's N.O.V. of jury's verdict termination mother's rights an abuse of discretion—termination found in children's best interest despite mother's reform)

In re D.L.B., 943 S.W.2d 175 (Tex. App.—San Antonio 1997, no writ) (jury verdict declining termination upheld even though father incarcerated for five years)

Matter of Marriage of Hill, 893 S.W.2d 753 (Tex. App.—Amarillo 1995, writ denied) (instructing jury on alternative grounds for termination acceptable)

Director of Dallas County Child Protective Services v. Bowling, 833 S.W.2d 730 (Tex. App.—Dallas 1992, no writ) (jury question on whether father's rights to be terminated regarding child born after his abuse of older sibling)

Right to Attend/Right to Record

Jones v. Stayman, 747 S.W.2d 369 (Tex. 1987) (right to a free statement of facts following a termination)

In re J.D.S., 111 S.W.3d 324 (Tex. App.—Texarkana 2003, no pet.) (trial court's summary denial of father's request for warrant to attend termination trial in person was an abuse of discretion)

Termination Reversed

In re J.W., 52 S.W.3d 730 (Tex. 2001) (terminated parents have right to amend defective indigency affidavits on appeal)

Holick v. Smith, 685 S.W.2d 18 (Tex. 1985) (mother arranged for adequate support for children)

Richardson v. Green, 677 S.W.2d 497 (Tex. 1984) (child's statement regarding abuse not res gestae)

Schiesser v. State, 544 S.W.2d 373 (Tex. 1976) (termination improper; no evidence mother left children without expressing intent to return)

In re T.H., 131 S.W.3d 598 (Tex. App.—Texarkana 2004, pet. filed) (evidence not sufficient to establish that incarcerated father knowingly allowed child to remain in endangering conditions)

In re J.L., 127 S.W.3d 911 (Tex. App.—Corpus Christi 2004, pet. filed) (meager circumstantial evidence legally insufficient to prove termination grounds by clear and convincing standard)

In re J.D.S., 111 S.W.3d 324 (Tex. App.—Texarkana 2003, no pet.) (summary denial of father's request for warrant to attend termination trial in person was an abuse of discretion)

In re D.P., 96 S.W.3d 333 (Tex. App.—Amarillo 2001, no pet.) (mother's rights should not have been terminated because not established that she was the one who abused child)

In re C.T.E., 95 S.W.3d 462 (Tex. App.—Houston [1st Dist.] 2002, pet. denied) (termination of rights of professional—criminal father does not meet appellate court's understanding of "best interests")

In re J.B., 93 S.W.3d 609 (Tex. App.—Waco 2002, pet. denied) (termination of mother's rights reversed because not given 45 days notice of trial in accordance with T.R.C.P. 245)

Jones v. Tex. Dept. of Protective & Regulatory Services, 85 S.W.3d 483 (Tex. App.—Austin 2002, no pet.) (teenage mother in DPRS care signed parental relinquishment under fact situation warranting her bill of review)

In re D.T., 34 S.W.3d 625 (Tex. App.—Fort Worth 2000, pet. denied) (evidence insufficient to sustain termination of parental rights of bad-check artist)

In re Stevenson, 27 S.W.3d 195 (Tex. App.—San Antonio 2000, pet. denied) (father awarded new trial, jury not instructed he had to "know" child was his before he could neglect it)

In re T.R.R., 986 S.W.2d 931 (Tex. App.—Corpus Christi 1998, no pet.) (defective pleading, lack of lawyer, and failure to appoint ad litem sufficient to support granting a bill of review)

In re D.L.N., 958 S.W.2d 934 (Tex. App.—Waco 1997, writ denied) (mothers visit every few weeks or months with child does not constitute "staying away for six months")

Swinney v. Mosher, 830 S.W.2d 187 (Tex. App.—Fort Worth 1992, writ denied) (revocation of affidavit of relinquishment effective—mother's placement of child for adoption not evidence of abandonment)

Neal v. Texas Dept. of Human Services, 814 S.W.2d 216 (Tex. App.—San Antonio 1991, writ denied) (mother unduly influenced by father to sign affidavit of relinquishment)

Termination Affirmed

In re A.V., 113 S.W.3d 335 (Tex. 2003) (incarceration "for not less than two years" to be applied prospectively—not retroactive statute)

In re C.H., 89 S.W.3d 17 (Tex. 2002) (standard of review for termination is whether evidence is such that fact finder could reasonably form firm belief or conviction about state's allegations)

In re K.R., 63 S.W.3d 796 (Tex. 2001), *reversing and rendering*, 22 S.W.3d 85 (shackling of father at trial harmless error that does not require reversal of jury finding for termination of parental rights)

In re M.C., 917 S.W.2d 268 (Tex. 1996) (neglect that leaves children in potentially dangerous situations sustains termination irrespective of lack of physical abuse)

Texas Dept. of Human Services v. White, 817 S.W.2d 62 (Tex. 1991) (admission in evidence of photo of child with foster family not reversible error)

Texas Dept. of Human Services v. Boyd, 727 S.W.2d 531 (Tex. 1987) (criminal conduct resulting in imprisonment defined as endangering conduct; actual harm not necessary)

Brown v. McLennan County Children's Protective Services, 627 S.W.2d 390 (Tex. 1982) (irrevocable affidavit of relinquishment signed by young mother upheld)

Goffney v. Lowry, 554 S.W.2d 157 (Tex. 1977) (eligibility for pauper's affidavit supports appeal of termination)

In re A.B., 125 S.W.3d 769 (Tex. App.—Texarkana 2003, pet. denied) (sexual abuse endangered children affirming termination)

In re C.A.J., 122 S.W.3d 888 (Tex. App—Fort Worth 2003, no pet.) (child's best interests support termination because of mother's drug addiction and criminal history)

In re A.H., 114 S.W.750 (Tex. App.—Dallas 2003, no pet.) (mediated settlement agreement to terminate parental rights binding on parent)

In re D.S.A., 113 S.W.3d 567 (Tex. App.—Amarillo 2003, no pet.) (prison inmate father constructively abandoned three daughters and was unable to provide them with good environment)

In re Castillo, 101 S.W.3d 174 (Tex. App.—Amarillo 2003, pet. denied) (conviction for murder of one child affirmed as grounds for termination as to other 2 children)

In re J.I.T.P., 99 S.W.3d 841 (Tex. App.—Houston [14th Dist.] 2003, no pet.) (domestic violence endangered child such that violent home unsuitable for infant)

In re C.D.B., 94 S.W.3d 306 (Tex. App.—Corpus Christi 2002, no pet.) (inattentive, non-paying father's rights terminated by jury)

In re E.L.T., 93 S.W.3d 372 (Tex. App.—Houston [14th Dist.] 2002, no pet.) (mother's claim of incompetence not sufficient to warrant continuance or overturn termination decree)

W.B. v. Texas Dept. of Protective and Regulatory Services, 82 S.W.3d 739 (Tex. App.—Corpus Christi 2002, no pet.) (60 year prison sentence sufficient to warrant termination)

In re G.C., 66 S.W.3d 517 (Tex. App.—Fort Worth 2001, no pet.) (six-person jury does not deny equal protection or due process in termination proceeding)

In re M.E.C., 66 S.W.3d 449 (Tex. App.—Waco 2001, no pet.) (trial judge's signature on jury charge from mother's trial admitted in father's termination proceedings, not reversible error)

In re D.M., 58 S.W.3d 801 (Tex. App.—Fort Worth 2001, no pet.) (imprisonment, standing alone, is not endangering conduct, but together with other conduct justifies termination)

In re W.C., 56 S.W.3d 863 (Tex. App.—Houston [14th Dist.] 2001, no pet.) (mother failed to show she did not severely injure her child on multiple occasions or that she was capable of change)

In re J.M.S., 43 S.W.3d 60 (Tex. App.—Houston [1st Dist.] 2001, no pet.) (mother's trial counsel was not ineffective for failing to object to admissible testimony relating to previous termination proceedings)

In re J.M.T., 39 S.W.3d 234 (Tex. App.—Waco 1999, no pet.) (termination for nonsupport sustained on basis that obligor had ability to pay)

In re Tidwell, 35 S.W.3d 115 (Tex. App.—Texarkana 2000, no pet.) (mother need not have "certain knowledge" her child is being sexually abused under circumstances strongly indicating such abuse)

In re S.F., 32 S.W.3d 318 (Tex. App.—San Antonio 2000, no pet.) (termination of rights of criminal-to-the-bone father upheld in what concurring judge labels "frivolous appeal")

In re J.M.C.A., 31 S.W.3d 692 (Tex. App.—Houston [1st Dist.] 2000, no pet.) (mother's tolerance of sexual abuse of her 4–year-old justifies termination of all four of her children—broad form rules)

Green v. Texas Dept. of Protective & Regulatory Services, 25 S.W.3d 213 (Tex. App.—El Paso 2000, no pet.) (mother's rights terminated due to her continued relationship with stepfather/child molester)

In re D.S., 19 S.W.3d 525 (Tex. App.—Fort Worth 2000, no pet.) (doctor's expert opinion regarding immersion burns admissible, as was caseworker's testimony of admission obtained in jail interview)

Cooper v. Bushong, 10 S.W.3d 20 (Tex. App.—Austin 1999, pet. denied) (termination of father's rights based on binding arbitration)

In re B.S.T., 977 S.W.2d 481 (Tex. App.—Houston [14th Dist.] 1998, no pet.) (evidence sufficient to sustain constructive abandonment under subsection (1)(N))

In re Powers, 974 S.W.2d 867 (Tex. App.—Houston [14th Dist.] 1998, no pet.) (unwed teenage mother [age 19] cannot withdraw affidavit of relinquishment)

Avery v. State, 963 S.W.2d 550 (Tex. App.—Houston [1st Dist.] 1997, no writ) (evidence of prior termination 17 years ago not too remote)

In re B.R., 950 S.W.2d 113 (Tex. App.—El Paso 1997, no writ) (conviction for murdering child's mother sufficient for terminating parental rights)

Edwards v. Texas Dept. of Protective & Regulatory Services, 946 S.W.2d 130 (Tex. App.—El Paso 1997, no writ) (stricter review of evidence in appeal of order terminating parental rights)

R.W. v. Texas Dept. of Protective & Regulatory Services, 944 S.W.2d 437 (Tex. App.—Houston [14th Dist.] 1997) (presumed father's culpable neglect of parental duties before adjudication of paternity warrants termination)

In re J.J., 911 S.W.2d 437 (Tex. App.—Texarkana 1995, writ denied) (order terminating parental rights will not be reversed unless contrary to overwhelming weight of evidence)

Dupree v. Texas Dept. of Protective & Regulatory Services, 907 S.W.2d 81 (Tex. App.—Dallas 1995, no writ) (parental rights terminated with regards to cocaine-positive baby)

Spurlock v. Texas Dept. of Protective & Regulatory Services, 904 S.W.2d 152 (Tex. App.—Austin 1995, writ denied) (termination upheld on grounds schizophrenic mother unable to care for children now and in the future)

In re R.D.S., 902 S.W.2d 714 (Tex. App.—Amarillo 1995, no writ) (evidence sufficient to prove leaving of child with no intent to return)

Trevino v. Texas Dept. of Protective & Regulatory Services, 893 S.W.2d 243 (Tex. App.—Austin 1995, no writ) (termination of imprisoned father in best interest of very young children so adoption possible)

D.O. v. Texas Dept. of Human Services, 851 S.W.2d 351 (Tex. App.—Austin 1993, no writ) (father knew of mother's failure to protect children and did nothing)

In re R.R.F., 846 S.W.2d 65 (Tex. App.—Corpus Christi 1992, writ denied) (father's long-term lack of interest, plus kids' attitude, justifies termination)

In re B.R., 822 S.W.2d 103 (Tex. App.—Tyler 1992, writ denied) (mother's rights terminated after failing to protect children against sexual abuse by father)

---

§ 161.002. Termination of the Rights of an Alleged Biological Father.

(a) The procedural and substantive standards for termination of parental rights apply to the termination of the rights of an alleged father.

(b) The rights of an alleged father may be terminated if:

(1) after being served with citation, he does not respond by timely filing an admission of paternity or a counterclaim for paternity under Chapter 160;

(2) he has not registered with the paternity registry under Chapter 160, and after the exercise of due diligence by the petitioner:

(A) his identity and location are unknown; or

(B) his identity is known but he cannot be located; or

(3) he has registered with the paternity registry under Chapter 160, but the petitioner's attempt to personally serve citation at the address provided to the registry and at any other address for the alleged father known by the petitioner has been unsuccessful, despite the due diligence of the petitioner.

(c) The termination of the rights of an alleged father under Subsection (b)(2) rendered on or after January 1, 1998, does not require personal service of citation or citation by publication on the alleged father.

(d) The termination of rights of an alleged father under Subsection (b)(3) does not require service of citation by publication on the alleged father.

(e) The court shall not render an order terminating parental rights under Subsection (b)(2) unless the court, after reviewing the petitioner's sworn affidavit describing the petitioner's effort to identify and locate the alleged father and considering any evidence submitted by the attorney ad litem for the alleged father, has found that the petitioner exercised due diligence in attempting to identify and locate the alleged father. The order shall contain specific findings regarding due diligence of the petitioner.

(f) The court shall not render an order terminating parental rights under Subsection (b)(3) unless the court, after reviewing the petitioner's sworn affidavit describing the petitioner's effort to obtain personal service of citation on the alleged father and considering any evidence submitted by the attorney ad litem for the alleged father, has found that the petitioner exercised due diligence in attempting to obtain service on the alleged father. The order shall contain specific findings regarding the exercise of due diligence of the petitioner.

Comment

Relying on the Texas Equal Rights Amendment, the Texas Supreme Court held that a "father who steps forward, willing and able to shoulder responsibilities of raising a child, should not be required to meet a higher burden of proof solely because he is male." *In re Baby McLean*, 725 S.W.2d 696, 698 (Tex. 1987). This holding greatly strengthened the claims of biological fathers, and, by implication, mandates their involvement in the lawsuit (whether voluntary or not). Subsequently, the supreme court extended this right to a man alleging himself to be the biological father of a child with a presumed father, provided the action is taken expeditiously. *See In re J.W.T.,* 872 S.W.2d 189, 198 (Tex. 1994).

The two supreme court decisions inspired statutory clarification to the indefinite concept of a man "timely filing" his paternity claim. However, this section actually was written to deal with the far more likely scenario of an alleged biological father who wants nothing more than to escape all responsibility for the child. If so, a default by the alleged father creates an independent ground for termination. That is, failure to answer after service of citation, and no admission of, or counterclaim for, paternity gives rise to a ground for termination. Note that this constitutes a legislative determination that "doing nothing" in this factual context is sufficient culpable conduct to warrant termination of potential parental rights.

Subsection (b)(2) provides that the parental rights of an alleged father who fails to register with the paternity registry established by Subchapter D, Chapter 160, may be terminated if the petitioner exercised due diligence to ascertain the identity and location of the alleged father. Note that under § 161.002(c) personal service or citation by publication is not required for termination of such a man's rights after January 1, 1998. When terminating parental rights under this provision, subsection (e) directs the court to make an inquiry as to whether the petitioner has exercised due diligence in attempting to locate the alleged father.

Subsection (b)(3) permits termination of the parental rights of an alleged father who claims paternity by registering but cannot be personally served at the address provided to the registry, provided that the court determines that petitioner has exercised due diligence to locate him.

As of Sept. 1, 2001, if there is a presumed father a timely claim is defined by the Texas Uniform Parentage Act as a suit brought within four years after the birth of the child. *See* § 160.607, *supra*. This is a substantial increase in the time allowed to file suit in many instances. Former law required that such a claim be asserted within two years of the child's birth, or within two years after a presumption arose of that paternity of another man.

A father who fails to claim possible paternity of a child after being served with citation, or fails to either register with, or maintain a good address in the paternity registry may have his parental rights terminated without the need to otherwise prove his unfitness as a parent. To discourage fraud or overreaching by the petitioner, this section requires that the petitioner exercise due diligence in identifying, locating and serving the father, even if the man has failed to register with the paternity registry. Citation by publication is not required on an alleged father who cannot be identified or located and fails to avail himself of the paternity registry. However, appointment of an attorney ad litem for the absent alleged father and an inquiry into the petitioner's diligence in attempting to locate him are required.

A father who is personally served and simply ignores the suit may find his parental rights terminated under this section. He is not entitled to an appointed attorney ad litem or to a "due diligence" inquiry. A default order may be rendered after the answer date on proof that the alleged father was served and that the termination is in the best interest of the child. On the other hand, a man who appears and is adjudicated to be the father of the child has the same rights as any other parent. His parental rights can be involuntarily terminated only if grounds for the termination are established under this chapter.

This section is intended to encourage the entry of timely default judgments, and to discourage the practice of carrying a defaulting party along with the case until the final trial, which frequently results in a last-minute appearance with its inherent complications.

Leading Cases

O'Connell v. Kirchner, 513 U.S. 1138, 115 S.Ct. 1084, 130 L.Ed.2d 873 (1995) (stay denied in "Baby Richard" case: Illinois adoption invalid, biological father's parental rights not properly terminated, *see In re* Petition of Doe, 638 N.E.2d 181 (1994))

Michael H. v. Gerald D., 491 U.S. 110, 105 L.Ed.2d 91, 109 S.Ct. 2333, (1989) (U.S. Const. does not mandate right of man to establish his paternity of child born to married woman)

In re J.W.T., 872 S.W.2d 189 (Tex. 1994) (under certain factual circumstances, biological father has Tex. Const. right to establish his paternity over objections of mother and her husband)

In re Unnamed Baby McLean, 725 S.W.2d 696 (Tex. 1987) (equal rights for biological fathers)

---

§ 161.003. Involuntary Termination: Inability to Care for Child.

(a) The court may order termination of the parent-child relationship in a suit filed by the Department of Protective and Regulatory Services if the court finds that:

(1) the parent has a mental or emotional illness or a mental deficiency that renders the parent unable to provide for the physical, emotional, and mental needs of the child;

(2) the illness or deficiency, in all reasonable probability, proved by clear and convincing evidence, will continue to render the parent unable to provide for the child's needs until the 18th birthday of the child;

(3) the department has been the temporary or sole managing conservator of the child of the parent for at least six months preceding the date of the hearing on the termination held in accordance with Subsection (c);

(4) the department has made reasonable efforts to return the child to the parent; and

(5) the termination is in the best interest of the child.

(b) Immediately after the filing of a suit under this section, the court shall appoint an attorney ad litem to represent the interests of the parent against whom the suit is brought.

(c) A hearing on the termination may not be held earlier than 180 days after the date on which the suit was filed.

(d) An attorney appointed under Subsection (b) shall represent the parent for the duration of the suit unless the parent, with the permission of the court, retains another attorney.

Comment

This section does not require culpable conduct on the part of a parent who is unable to meet the child's needs due to a persistent mental disability, whether by reason of mental illness or retardation. A parent who is permanently institutionalized, or a parent living in the community who, to the degree that medical science can predict, will not be able to care for the child, may have his or her rights terminated without regard to actual wrongdoing by the parent directed at the child. The protection of parental rights has been strengthened by a requirement that the court must find that DPRS has made reasonable efforts to return the child to the parent.

Subsection (c) prohibits the court from holding a termination hearing sooner than 180 days after the suit is filed. Formerly, subsection (a)(3) also required that the department have managing conservatorship for six months before filing the petition. Taken together, at a minimum these subsections required two consecutive six-month periods from the filing of the original petition before the case could be heard on the merits. This result was inconsistent with the twelve-month deadline mandated by § 263.401 in order to minimize the time children spend in foster care. Presently, the statute continues to require: (1) the immediate appointment of an attorney for the allegedly disabled parent; (2) the department to prove that reasonable efforts have been made to return the child; and, (3) the child has been in foster care for at least six months preceding trial on the merits. In balancing the competing interests involved, the legislature rationally came down on the side of the innocent child to the theoretical disadvantage of the innocent, but incompetent, parent.

CLE/Other Legal Publications

Mental deficiency: parent's mental deficiency as factor in termination of parental rights—modern status. 1 A.L.R.5th 469 (1992)

Leading Cases

In re B.L.M., 114 S.W.3d 641 (Tex. App.—Fort Worth 2003, no pet.) (father's paranoid schizophrenia justified termination as the mental illness rendered him incapable to care for children)

In re J.O.C., 47 S.W.3d 108 (Tex. App.—Waco 2001, no pet.) (mother's lack of parenting skills, her failure to learn to care for her developmentally delayed child, and the lack of bond between the mother and child is sufficient for termination of her parental rights)

Spurlock v. Texas Dept. of Protective & Regulatory Services, 904 S.W.2d 152 (Tex. App.—Austin 1995, writ denied) *and In re* Carroll, 819 S.W.2d 591 (Tex. App.—Tyler, 1991, no writ) (mother's inability to care for children due to mental illness; statute held constitutional as applied).

§ 161.004. Termination of Parental Rights After Denial of Prior Petition to Terminate.

(a) The court may terminate the parent-child relationship after rendition of an order that previously denied termination of the parent-child relationship if:

(1) the petition under this section is filed after the date the order denying termination was rendered;

(2) the circumstances of the child, parent, sole managing conservator, possessory conservator, or other party affected by the order denying termination have materially and substantially changed since the date that the order was rendered;

(3) the parent committed an act listed under Section 161.001 before the date the order denying termination was rendered; and

(4) termination is in the best interest of the child.

(b) At a hearing under this section, the court may consider evidence presented at a previous hearing in a suit for termination of the parent-child relationship of the parent with respect to the same child.

Comment

This section attempts to codify (and clarify—albeit in a confusing manner) problems encountered when there has been a prior action by which the court determined that termination was not warranted, whether for reason of a failure of proof of sufficient culpable conduct by the parent or because termination was not in the child's best interest at that time. Subsection (b) makes clear that evidence from a prior proceeding is admissible in a successive action brought seeking to terminate parental rights.

Leading Case

In re T.V., 27 S.W.3d 622 (Tex. App.—Waco 2000, no pet.) (first termination hearing did not yield final decree—second hearing produced pre-first hearing evidence led to termination—concurrence cites § 161.004, a first)

---

§ 161.005. Termination When Parent is Petitioner.

(a) A parent may file a suit for termination of the petitioner's parent-child relationship. The court may order termination if termination is in the best interest of the child.

(b) If the petition designates the Department of Protective and Regulatory Services as managing conservator, the department shall be given service of citation. The court shall notify the department if the court appoints the department as the managing conservator of the child.

Comment

Although in theory a parent can terminate his or her own rights, in practice, the courts do not favor such an action, especially if the underlying purpose is to avoid the child support obligation.

---

§ 161.006. Termination After Abortion.

(a) A petition requesting termination of the parent-child relationship with respect to a parent who is not the petitioner may be granted if the child was born alive as the result of an abortion.

(b) In this code, "abortion" means an intentional expulsion of a human fetus from the body of a woman induced by any means for the purpose of causing the death of the fetus.

(c) The court or the jury may not terminate the parent-child relationship under this section with respect to a parent who:

(1) had no knowledge of the abortion; or

(2) participated in or consented to the abortion for the sole purpose of preventing the death of the mother.

§ 161.007. Termination When Pregnancy Results From Criminal Act.

The court may order the termination of the parent-child relationship of a parent and a child if the court finds that:

(1) the parent has been convicted of an offense committed under Section 22.011, 22.021, or 25.02, Penal Code;

(2) as a direct result of the commission of the offense by the parent, the victim of the offense became pregnant with the parent's child; and

(3) termination is in the best interest of the child.

Comment

This section permits a court to terminate the parental rights of a parent who has committed the offense of sexual assault, aggravated sexual assault or prohibited sexual conduct, thereby causing the victim to become pregnant. Termination of the wrongdoer's parental rights must be in the resulting child's best interest, of course.

Leading Case

In re A.L.H.C., 49 S.W.3d 911 (Tex. App.—Dallas 2001, pet. denied) (mom ran away with child after countersued for termination—she's not entitled to bill of review)

Subchapter B. Procedures

§ 161.101. Petition Allegations.

A petition for the termination of the parent-child relationship is sufficient without the necessity of specifying the underlying facts if the petition alleges in the statutory language the ground for the termination and that termination is in the best interest of the child.

§ 161.102. Filing Suit for Termination Before Birth.

(a) A suit for termination may be filed before the birth of the child.

(b) If the suit is filed before the birth of the child, the petition shall be styled "In the Interest of an Unborn Child." After the birth, the clerk shall change the style of the case to conform to the requirements of Section 102.008.

Comment

This section is primarily intended to facilitate the placement of newborn infants for adoption by authorized agencies.

---

§ 161.103. Affidavit of Voluntary Relinquishment of Parental Rights.

(a) An affidavit for voluntary relinquishment of parental rights must be:

(1) signed after the birth of the child, but not before 48 hours after the birth of the child, by the parent, whether or not a minor, whose parental rights are to be relinquished;

(2) witnessed by two credible persons; and

(3) verified before a person authorized to take oaths.

(b) The affidavit must contain:

(1) the name, address, and age of the parent whose parental rights are being relinquished;

(2) the name, age, and birth date of the child;

(3) the names and addresses of the guardians of the person and estate of the child, if any;

(4) a statement that the affiant is or is not presently obligated by court order to make payments for the support of the child;

(5) a full description and statement of value of all property owned or possessed by the child;

(6) an allegation that termination of the parent-child relationship is in the best interest of the child;

(7) one of the following, as applicable:

(A) the name and address of the other parent;

(B) a statement that the parental rights of the other parent have been terminated by death or court order; or

(C) a statement that the child has no presumed father and that an affidavit of status of the child has been executed as provided by this chapter;

(8) a statement that the parent has been informed of parental rights and duties;

(9) a statement that the relinquishment is revocable, that the relinquishment is irrevocable, or that the relinquishment is irrevocable for a stated period of time;

(10) if the relinquishment is revocable, a statement in boldfaced type concerning the right of the parent signing the affidavit to revoke the relinquishment only if the revocation is made before the 11th day after the date the affidavit is executed;

(11) if the relinquishment is revocable, the name and address of a person to whom the revocation is to be delivered; and

(12) the designation of a prospective adoptive parent, the Department of Protective and Regulatory Services, if the department has consented in writing to the designation, or a licensed child-placing agency to serve as managing conservator of the child and the address of the person or agency.

(c) The affidavit may contain:

(1) a waiver of process in a suit to terminate the parent-child relationship filed under this chapter or in a suit to terminate joined with a petition for adoption; and

(2) a consent to the placement of the child for adoption by the Department of Protective and Regulatory Services or by a licensed child-placing agency.

(d) A copy of the affidavit shall be provided to the parent at the time the parent signs the affidavit.

(e) The relinquishment in an affidavit that designates the Department of Protective and Regulatory Services or a licensed child-placing agency to serve as the managing conservator is irrevocable. A relinquishment in any other affidavit of relinquishment is revocable unless it expressly provides that it is irrevocable for a stated period of time not to exceed 60 days after the date of its execution.

(f) A relinquishment in an affidavit of relinquishment of parental rights that fails to state that the relinquishment is irrevocable for a stated time is revocable as provided by Section 161.1035.

(g) To revoke a relinquishment under Subsection (e) the parent must sign a statement witnessed by two credible persons and verified before a person authorized to take oaths. A copy of the revocation shall be delivered to the person designated in the affidavit. If a parent attempting to revoke a relinquishment under this subsection has knowledge that a suit for termination of the parent-child relationship has been filed based on the parent's affidavit of relinquishment of parental rights, the parent shall file a copy of the revocation with the clerk of the court.

(h) The affidavit may not contain terms for limited post-termination contact between the child and the parent whose parental rights are to be relinquished as a condition of the relinquishment of parental rights.

History: Amended by 78th Legis., Reg. Sess. (2003), H.B. 1536, eff. Sept. 1, 2003, and "applies only to a suit affecting the parent-child relationship pending in a trial court or filed on or after that date. A suit affecting the parent-child relationship in which a final order is rendered before the effective date of this Act is governed by the law in effect on the date the order was rendered."

Comment

An affidavit of relinquishment is commonly employed as the ground for termination in cases involving a state intervention in the family when a parent ultimately decides to concede the issue. Such affidavits are virtually universal in infant adoptions pursued by an authorized agency, at least insofar as the mother's rights are concerned. The key fact is that an affidavit is irrevocable when given to the state or to an authorized agency, but may be made irrevocable only for a 60–day period when executed in a private case.

A parent (read "mother") may not validly sign an affidavit of relinquishment until at least 48 hours after the birth of a child. This is designed to assure that she has given a knowing, voluntary relinquishment of her parental rights. The statute is primarily designed to foreclose a claim by the mother that the document was signed while she was under the influence of drugs or other medication used in the delivery of the infant.

This restriction was opposed by some agencies because it allegedly would cause problems given the fact that under the then-current hospital practice a new mother often was discharged in less than 48 hours. In response to this insensitive, and sometimes dangerous, cost-cutting procedure, federal and state legislation has intervened to modify this practice by hospitals. Texas Insurance Code, art. 21.53F establishes "required coverage for minimum inpatient stay following birth" for a health benefit plan that provides maternity benefits at "48 hours following an uncomplicated vaginal delivery; and 96 hours following an uncomplicated delivery by caesarean (sic) section."

Subsections (b)-(e) provide additional details about the procedure and contents of an affidavit of relinquishment. Subsections (f) and (g) prescribe a formal method for revoking affidavits that are revocable. If an affidavit fails to state that the relinquishment is irrevocable, revocation is required within a window lasting eleven days. *See* § 161.1035, *infra*.

CLE/Other Legal Publication

Validity of birth parent's "blanket" consent to adoption which fails to identify adoptive parents. 15 A.L.R.5th 1 (1993)

Leading Cases

Brown v. McLennan County Children's Protective Services, 627 S.W.2d 390 (Tex. 1982) (irrevocable affidavit signed by young mother is constitutional—waiver of process and notice also irrevocable—signing of affidavit is evidence of best interest)

Rogers v. Searle, 544 S.W.2d 114 (Tex. 1976) (extrinsic fraud regarding affidavit of relinquishment)

Mosley v. Dallas Co. Child Protective Services, 110 S.W.3d 658 (Tex. App.—Dallas 2003, pet. denied) (because mother voluntarily signed affidavits of relinquishment, bill of review fails)

Jones v. Tex. Dept. of Protective & Regulatory Services, 85 S.W.3d 483 (Tex. App.—Austin 2002, no pet.) (teenage mother in DPRS care signed parental relinquishment under fact situation warranting her bill of review)

Terrell v. Chambers, 630 S.W.2d 800 (Tex. App.—Tyler 1982, writ ref'd n. r. e.) (affidavit of relinquishment plus best interest required in private termination)

S.A.S. v. Catholic Family Services, Inc., 613 S.W.2d 540 (Tex. Civ. App.—Amarillo 1981, no writ) (minor may validly relinquish parental rights)

---

§ 161.1035. Revocability of Certain Affidavits.

An affidavit of relinquishment of parental rights or affidavit of waiver of interest in a child that fails to state that the relinquishment or waiver is irrevocable for a stated time is:

(1) revocable only if the revocation is made before the 11th day after the date the affidavit is executed; and

(2) irrevocable on or after the 11th day after the date the affidavit is executed.

Comment

This section provides that an affidavit of relinquishment or affidavit of waiver of interest that fails to state that it is irrevocable for a stated time is revocable. The revocation must be made before the 11th day after execution, after which an unrevoked affidavit becomes irrevocable.

§ 161.104. Rights of Designated Managing Conservator Pending Court Appointment.

A person, licensed child-placing agency, or authorized agency designated managing conservator of a child in an irrevocable or unrevoked affidavit of relinquishment has a right to possession of the child superior to the right of the person executing the affidavit, the right to consent to medical, surgical, dental, and psychological treatment of the child, and the rights and duties given by Chapter 153 *[Conservatorship. Possession, and Access]* to a possessory conservator until such time as these rights and duties are modified or terminated by court order.

§ 161.105. Affidavit of Status of Child.

(a) If the child has no presumed father, an affidavit shall be:

(1) signed by the mother, whether or not a minor;

(2) witnessed by two credible persons; and

(3) verified before a person authorized to take oaths.

(b) The affidavit must:

(1) state that the mother is not and has not been married to the alleged father of the child;

(2) state that the mother and alleged father have not attempted to marry under the laws of this state or another state or nation;

(3) state that paternity has not been established under the laws of any state or nation; and

(4) contain one of the following, as applicable:

(A) the name and whereabouts of a man alleged to be the father;

(B) the name of an alleged father and a statement that the affiant does not know the whereabouts of the father;

(C) a statement that an alleged father has executed an acknowledgment of paternity under Chapter 160 *[Uniform Parentage Act]* and an affidavit of relinquishment of parental rights under this chapter and that both affidavits have been filed with the court; or

(D) a statement that the name of an alleged father is unknown.

(c) The affidavit of status of child may be executed at any time after the first trimester of the pregnancy of the mother.

Comment

This section provides a mechanism for identifying the biological father when the mother wishes to relinquish her parental rights.

§ 161.106. Affidavit of Waiver of Interest in Child.

(a) A man may sign an affidavit disclaiming any interest in a child and waiving notice or the service of citation in any suit filed or to be filed affecting the parent-child relationship with respect to the child.

(b) The affidavit may be signed before the birth of the child.

(c) The affidavit shall be:

(1) signed by the man, whether or not a minor;

(2) witnessed by two credible persons; and

(3) verified before a person authorized to take oaths.

(d) The affidavit may contain a statement that the affiant does not admit being the father of the child or having had a sexual relationship with the mother of the child.

(e) An affidavit of waiver of interest in a child may be used in a suit in which the affiant attempts to establish an interest in the child. The affidavit may not be used in a suit brought by another person, licensed child-placing agency, or authorized agency to establish the affiant's paternity of the child.

(f) A waiver in an affidavit under this section that designates the Department of Protective and Regulatory Services or a licensed child-placing agency to serve as the managing conservator is irrevocable. A waiver in any other affidavit under this section is revocable unless it expressly provides that it is irrevocable for a stated period not to exceed 60 days after the date of execution.

(g) A waiver in an affidavit under this section that fails to state that the waiver is irrevocable for a stated time is revocable as provided by Section 161.1035.

(h) An affidavit under this section that contains a waiver that is revocable must contain:

(1) a statement in boldfaced type concerning the right of the person who executed the affidavit to revoke the affidavit only if the revocation is made before the 11th day after the date the affidavit is executed; and

(2) the name and address of the person to whom the revocation is to be delivered.

(i) A copy of the affidavit shall be provided to the person who executed the affidavit at the time the person signs the affidavit.

(j) To revoke a waiver, the person who executed the affidavit must sign a statement witnessed by two credible persons and verified before a person authorized to take oaths. A copy of the revocation shall be delivered to the person designated in the affidavit of waiver of interest in a child. If a person attempting to revoke an affidavit under this subsection has knowledge that a suit for termination of the parent-child relationship based on the person's waiver of interest in a child has been filed, the person shall file a copy of the revocation with the clerk of the court.

Comment

This section is designed to give an alleged or probable father an easy out; he may relinquish all of his rights, if any, without acknowledging paternity (or even that he ever met the mother). Subsection (f) clarifies that a waiver of interest in favor of DPRS or a licensed child-placing agency is irrevocable.

Subsection (g) provides that an affidavit of waiver of interest that fails to state that the waiver is irrevocable for a stated period of time is revocable. Subsection (h) mandates the contents of the affidavit, and subsection (j) details the procedure for revoking it.

§ 161.107. Missing Parent or Relative.

(a) In this section:

(1) "Parent" means a parent whose parent-child relationship with a child has not been terminated.

(2) "Relative" means a parent, grandparent, or adult sibling or child.

(b) If a parent of the child has not been personally served in a suit in which the Department of Protective and Regulatory Services seeks termination, the department must make a diligent effort to locate that parent.

(c) If a parent has not been personally served and cannot be located, the department shall make a diligent effort to locate a relative of the missing parent to give the relative an opportunity to request appointment as the child's managing conservator.

(d) If the department is not able to locate a missing parent or a relative of that parent and sufficient information is available concerning the physical whereabouts of the parent or relative, the department shall request the state agency designated to administer a statewide plan for child support to use the parental locator service established under 42 U.S.C. Section 653 to determine the location of the missing parent or relative.

(e) The department shall be required to provide evidence to the court to show what actions were taken by the department in making a diligent effort to locate the missing parent and relative of the missing parent.

Comment

This statute was enacted in response to public criticism of DPRS for failing to diligently search for absent parents and for extended family members before terminating parental rights. By definition the section applies only when the rights of one parent are being terminated. If the rights of the "other parent" are also being terminated, a diligent search is required to serve citation, whether personally or constructively. In point of fact, DPRS must seek to serve an absent parent with citation by its own regulations, by statutory requirement of § 263.202, and to meet constitutional due process. At least in theory, DPRS may not be appointed managing conservator without a clear showing that the agency made diligent efforts to locate the absent parent and the relatives of that parent.

Cross Reference

Federal Parent Locator Service. 42 U.S.C.A. § 65.

---

§ 161.108. Release of Child From Hospital or Birthing Center.

(a) Before or at the time an affidavit of relinquishment of parental rights under Section 161.103 is executed, the mother of a newborn child may authorize the release of the child from the hospital or birthing center to a licensed child-placing agency, the Department of Protective and Regulatory Services, or another designated person.

(b) A release under this section must be:

(1) executed in writing;

(2) witnessed by two credible adults; and

(3) verified before a person authorized to take oaths.

(c) A hospital or birthing center shall comply with the terms of a release executed under this section without requiring a court order.

§ 161.109. Requirement of Paternity Registry Certificate.

(a) If an affidavit of status of child as provided by this chapter states that the father of the child is unknown and no probable father is known, a certificate from the bureau of vital statistics signed by the registrar that a diligent search has been made of the paternity registry maintained by the bureau and that a registration has not been found pertaining to the father of the child in question must be filed with the court before a trial on the merits in the suit for termination may be held.

(b) In a proceeding to terminate parental rights in which the alleged or probable father has not been personally served with citation or signed an affidavit of relinquishment or an affidavit of waiver of interest, the court may not terminate the parental rights of the alleged or probable father, whether known or unknown, unless a certificate from the bureau of vital statistics signed by the registrar states that a diligent search has been made of the paternity registry maintained by the bureau and that a filing or registration has not been found pertaining to the father of the child in question.

Comment

Subsection (a) requires that when an affidavit of status states the father is unknown and no probable father is known, a certificate from the paternity registry must be filed with the court prior to a trial on the merits on termination. In most instances, undoubtedly the certificate will show that a search of the registry has been made and that BVS did not find anyone who had registered claiming to be the father of the child in question. Some attorneys specializing in the representation of child-placing (adoption) agencies have suggested that even if a particular man is named in an affidavit of status and he has executed an affidavit of waiver of interest in the child, the safest practice may be to obtain a certificate from BVS to ensure that no one else has claimed an interest in the child. In those extremely rare instances in which the certificate discloses that a man has registered a claim of paternity, the petitioner is required to serve him as provided by § 102.009(a)(9).

Cross Reference

TEX. FAM. CODE ch. 160. Uniform Parentage Act; Subchapter E, Registry of Paternity.

Subchapter C. Hearing and Order

§ 161.201. [repealed]

§ 161.2011. Continuance; Access to Child.

(a) A parent whose rights are subject to termination in a suit affecting the parent-child relationship and against whom criminal charges are filed that directly relate to the grounds for which termination is sought may file a motion requesting a continuance of the final trial in the suit until the criminal charges are resolved. The court may grant the motion only if the court finds that a continuance is in the best interest of the child. Notwithstanding any continuance granted, the court shall conduct status and permanency hearings with respect to the child as required by Chapter 263 *[Review of Placement of Children]* and shall comply with the dismissal date under Section 263.401.

(b) Nothing in this section precludes the court from issuing appropriate temporary orders as authorized in this code.

(c) The court in which a suit to terminate the parent-child relationship is pending may render an order denying a parent access to a child if the parent is indicted for criminal activity that constitutes a ground for terminating the parent-child relationship under Section 161.001. The denial of access under this section shall continue until the date the criminal charges for which the parent was indicted are resolved and the court renders an order providing for access to the child by the parent.

Comment

Chapter 263 mandates that the termination suit be resolved within one year. It has been unclear what effect the "criminal continuance" provided in this section was intended to have on the permanency timeframes in Child Protective Services cases. Prior to a 2001 amendment to subsection (a), the statute mandated that the trial court "shall not proceed to final trial in a suit to terminate the parent-child relationship" while related criminal charges were pending. There was a loophole; the court could deny the continuance in the termination suit if proceeding to trial was in the best interest of the child. But, many courts were reluctant to make such a finding. On the other hand, some courts viewed the continuance as a stay of the Chapter 263 deadlines, thus allowing the child to remain in foster care for indefinite periods of time. Subsection (a) now makes clear that a continuance may be granted only if: (1) requested by a parent; and, (2) the delay is in the best interest of the child. It also makes clear that the Chapter 263 deadlines remain in place. Thus, the continuance under this section cannot have the effect of delaying the final termination trial beyond 18 months.

Under subsection (c) a court may limit access to the child by the parent facing criminal charges when a termination suit and criminal charges related to the termination suit are pending. In effect, the child could become a stranger to the parent, compounding the harm if the ultimate decision were to result in a return of the child to the parent. It seems unlikely such a fact situation will occur with any frequency, if ever.

Leading Case

In re Texas Department of Protective Regulatory Services, 71 S.W.3d 446 (Tex. App.—Fort Worth 2002, orig. proceeding) (amendment to § 161.2011 applied to case pending on its effective date; mandamus granted to require trial court to "set the cases for final disposition before [dismissal date]").

---

§ 161.202. Preferential Setting.

In a termination suit, after a hearing, the court shall grant a motion for a preferential setting for a final hearing on the merits filed by a party to the suit or by the attorney or guardian ad litem for the child and shall give precedence to that hearing over other civil cases if:

(1) termination would make the child eligible for adoption; and

(2) discovery has been completed or sufficient time has elapsed since the filing of the suit for the completion of all necessary and reasonable discovery if diligently pursued.

§ 161.203. Dismissal of Petition.

A suit to terminate may not be dismissed nor may a nonsuit be taken unless the dismissal or nonsuit is approved by the court. The dismissal or nonsuit approved by the court is without prejudice.

Comment

This section is intended to prevent collusion between parents or other parties which has the effect of hiding relevant facts regarding a danger to the child. Whether the court will ferret out those facts when presented with an agreed order for dismissal is problematic. The intent is to make clear that a dismissal without trial of a suit to terminate does not have res judicata effect.

---

§ 161.204. Termination Based on Affidavit of Waiver of Interest.

In a suit for termination, the court may render an order terminating the parent-child relationship between a child and a man who has signed an affidavit of waiver of interest in the child, if the termination is in the best interest of the child.

Guest Comment

This section is intended to prevent the waste of resources inherent in the formerly common practice of serving process by publication on other "possible fathers" when the alleged father has signed an affidavit of waiver of interest. The waiver of interest has been likened to a quit-claim deed because the man is required to admit paternity to sign the waiver. However, like a quit-claim deed, it makes no sense to obtain a waiver of interest from man who is not thought to be the genetic father of the child. The court should only render a termination order if the evidence shows there is a parent-child relationship to be terminated. If the evidence fails to show that the man is genetically related to the child, the court should render an order under Chapter 160 adjudicating the man not to be the father of the child. *(C.G.C.)*

---

§ 161.205. Order Denying Termination.

If the court does not order termination of the parent-child relationship, the court shall:

(1) deny the petition; or

(2) render any order in the best interest of the child.

Guest Comment

If the finder of fact does not find for termination, the court may either dismiss the petition or may render an order, inter alia, which awards permanent managing conservatorship to DPRS. In short, the state may lose a suit for termination and still prevail in fact.

The statute clearly distinguishes between dismissal and a final order after trial. Denial of a termination petition has res judicata effect, but a dismissal of a petition does not. The trial court may still render further orders, including an order granting permanent managing conservatorship to the department or to another person if the parental preference under § 153.131 has been rebutted. *(C.G.C.)*

---

§ 161.206. Order Terminating Parental Rights.

(a) If the court finds by clear and convincing evidence grounds for termination of the parent-child relationship, it shall render an order terminating the parent-child relationship.

(b) **Except as provided by Section 161.2061, an** [~~An~~] order terminating the parent-child relationship divests the parent and the child of all legal rights and duties with respect to each other, except that the child retains the right to inherit from and through the parent unless the court otherwise provides.

(c) Nothing in this chapter precludes or affects the rights of a biological or adoptive maternal or paternal grandparent to reasonable access under Chapter 153 *[Conservatorship, Possession, and Access]*.

History: Amended by 78th Legis., Reg. Sess. (2003), H.B. 1536, eff. Sept. 1, 2003, and "applies only to a suit affecting the parent-child relationship pending in a trial court or filed on or after that date. A suit affecting the parent-child relationship in which a final order is rendered before the effective date of this Act is governed by the law in effect on the date the order was rendered."

Comment

If the court or jury determines that both a culpable ground and best interest exist, termination results. The decree means exactly what it says—a final irrevocable end of the parent-child relationship.

Leading Cases

Texas Dept. of Human Services v. E.B., 802 S.W.2d 647 (Tex. 1990) (broad-form submission to jury upheld)

Texas Dept. of Human Services v. Boyd, 727 S.W.2d 531 (Tex. 1987) (criminal conduct resulting in imprisonment defined as endangering conduct; actual harm to child not required)

In re Baby McLean, 725 S.W.2d 696 (Tex. 1987) (equal rights for biological fathers)

Durham v. Barrow, 600 S.W.2d 756 (Tex. 1980) (biological parent has no standing to attack an adoption after termination)

---

§ 161.2061. Terms Regarding Limited Post–termination Contact.

(a) If the court finds it to be in the best interest of the child, the court may provide in an order terminating the parent-child relationship that the biological parent who filed an affidavit of voluntary relinquishment of parental rights under Section 161.103 shall have limited post-termination contact with the child as provided by Subsection (b) on the agreement of the biological parent and the Department of Protective and Regulatory Services.

(b) The order of termination may include terms that allow the biological parent to:

(1) receive specified information regarding the child;

(2) provide written communications to the child; and

(3) have limited access to the child.

(c) The terms of an order of termination regarding limited post-termination contact may be enforced only if the party seeking enforcement pleads and proves that, before filing the motion for enforcement, the party attempted in good faith to resolve the disputed matters through mediation.

(d) The terms of an order of termination under this section are not enforceable by contempt.

(e) The terms of an order of termination regarding limited post-termination contact may not be modified.

(f) An order under this section does not:

(1) affect the finality of a termination order; or

(2) grant standing to a parent whose parental rights have been terminated to file any action under this title other than a motion to enforce the terms regarding limited post-termination contact until the court renders a subsequent adoption order with respect to the child.

History: Enacted by 78th Legis., Reg. Sess. (2003), H.B. 1536, eff. Sept. 1, 2003, and "applies only to a suit affecting the parent-child relationship pending in a trial court or filed on or after that date. A suit affecting the parent-child relationship in which a final order is rendered before the effective date of this Act is governed by the law in effect on the date the order was rendered."

Leading Case

In re R.J.A.H., 101 S.W.3d 762 (Tex. App.—Houston [1st Dist.] 2003, no pet.) (post-termination visitation provisions found void for vagueness)

---

§ 161.2062. Provision for Limited Contact Between Biological Parent and Child.

(a) An order terminating the parent-child relationship may not require that a subsequent adoption order include terms regarding limited post-termination contact between the child and a biological parent.

(b) The inclusion of a requirement for post-termination contact described by Subsection (a) in a termination order does not:

(1) affect the finality of a termination or subsequent adoption order; or

(2) grant standing to a parent whose parental rights have been terminated to file any action under this title after the court renders a subsequent adoption order with respect to the child.

History: Enacted by 78th Legis., Reg. Sess. (2003), H.B. 1536, eff. Sept. 1, 2003, and "applies only to a suit affecting the parent-child relationship pending in a trial court or filed on or after that date. A suit affecting the parent-child relationship in which a final order is rendered before the effective date of this Act is governed by the law in effect on the date the order was rendered."

§ 161.207. Appointment of Managing Conservator on Termination.

(a) If the court terminates the parent-child relationship with respect to both parents or to the only living parent, the court shall appoint a suitable, competent adult, the Department of Protective and Regulatory Services, a licensed child-placing agency, or an authorized agency as managing conservator of the child. An agency designated managing conservator in an unrevoked or irrevocable affidavit of relinquishment shall be appointed managing conservator.

(b) The order of appointment may refer to the docket number of the suit and need not refer to the parties nor be accompanied by any other papers in the record.

§ 161.208. Appointment of Department of Protective and Regulatory Services as Managing Conservator.

If a parent of the child has not been personally served in a suit in which the Department of Protective and Regulatory Services seeks termination, the court that terminates a parent-child relationship may not appoint the Department of Protective and Regulatory Services as permanent managing conservator of the child unless the court determines that:

(1) the department has made a diligent effort to locate a missing parent who has not been personally served and a relative of that parent; and

(2) a relative located by the department has had a reasonable opportunity to request appointment as managing conservator of the child or the department has not been able to locate the missing parent or a relative of the missing parent.

§ 161.209. Copy of Order of Termination.

A copy of an order of termination rendered under Section 161.206 is not required to be mailed to parties as provided by Rules 119a and 239a, Texas Rules of Civil Procedure.

§ 161.210. Sealing of File.

The court, on the motion of a party or on the court's own motion, may order the sealing of the file, the minutes of the court, or both, in a suit for termination.

§ 161.211. Direct or Collateral Attack on Termination Order.

(a) Notwithstanding Rule 329, Texas Rules of Civil Procedure, the validity of an order terminating the parental rights of a person who has been personally served or who has executed an affidavit of relinquishment of parental rights or an affidavit of waiver of interest in a child or whose rights have been terminated under Section 161.002(b) is not subject to collateral or direct attack after the sixth month after the date the order was signed.

(b) Notwithstanding Rule 329, Texas Rules of Civil Procedure, the validity of an order terminating the parental rights of a person who is served by citation by publication is not subject to collateral or direct attack after the sixth month after the date the order was signed.

(c) A direct or collateral attack on an order terminating parental rights based on an unrevoked affidavit of relinquishment of parental rights or affidavit of waiver of interest in a child is limited to issues relating to fraud, duress, or coercion in the execution of the affidavit.

Chapter 162. Adoption.

Subchapter A. Adoption of a Child

Subchapter B. Interstate Compact on the Placement of Children

Subchapter C. Interstate Compact on Adoption and Medical Assistance

Subchapter D. Adoption Services by the Department of Protective and Regulatory Services

Subchapter E. Voluntary Adoption Registries

Subchapter F. Adoption of an Adult

Subchapter G. Miscellaneous Provisions

Introductory Comment

Adoption replaces the biological parents of a child with adoptive legal parents. All connection with the biological parents must first be severed, either by the death of the natural parents or by termination of their parental rights. An adoption case may be instituted as a one-step procedure by joining the termination and adoption causes of action, or by a two-step procedure in which a separate adoption lawsuit follows a termination.

CLE/Other Legal Publications

Termination and adoption: the latest news. Ellen A. Yarrell, 2004 ADV. FAM. L.

Adoption and orphan issues. Barbara Hines, 2004 U. TEX. FAM. L. ON THE BORDER

Requirements for adoption of a Mexican minor by an U.S. citizen. Javier Alonso Martinez Gonzalez, 2004 U. TEX. FAM. L. ON THE BORDER

Adoption update. Heidi Bruegel Cox, 2002 ADV. FAM. L.

Adoption of foreign children. Cynthia Rucker Allen, 2002 ADV. FAM. L.

Termination and adoption: it ain't over till it's over. [Two articles] Sandra D. Hachem; Edwin J. (Ted) Terry, Jimmy Vaught, Karl E. Hays & James W. LaRue, 2002 MARRIAGE DISSOLUTION

Leading Cases

Green v. Remling, 608 S.W.2d 905 (Tex. 1980), *on remand*, 610 S.W.2d 817 (Tex. Civ. App.—Houston [1st Dist.] 1980, no writ) (social study properly considered by trial court in adoption controversy)

Durham v. Barrow, 600 S.W.2d 756 (Tex. 1980) (adoption based on faulty termination attacked by bill of review)

Vela v. Marywood, 17 S.W.3d 750 (Tex. App.—Austin 2000, pet. denied per curiam, 2001 WL 459170) (false or misleading representations violated the adoption agency's duty to fully disclose legal effect of open-adoption on biological mother's rights.)

In re M.L.P.J., 16 S.W.3d 45 (Tex. App.—Eastland 2000, pet. denied) (equitable adoption will not sustain child support order; doctrine inapplicable to SAPCRs)

Spiers v. Maples, 970 S.W.2d 166 (Tex. App.—Fort Worth 1998, no pet.) (adoption by estoppel shown)

Luna v. Estate of Rodriguez, 906 S.W.2d 576 (Tex. App.—Austin 1995, no writ) (necessary proof for equitable adoption)

Cross References

Indian Child Welfare Act. 25 U.S.C.A. §§ 1901–1923.

TEX. HEALTH & SAFETY CODE ANN. ch. 192. Birth Records.

TEX. HUM. RES. CODE ANN. ch. 42. Regulation of Child–Care Facilities.

TEX. PENAL CODE ANN. § 25.02. Prohibited Sexual Contact; § 25.08. Sale or Purchase of Child; § 25.09. Advertising for Placement of Child.

Subchapter A. Adoption of a Child

§ 162.001. Who May Adopt and be Adopted.

(a) Subject to the requirements for standing to sue in Chapter 102 *[Filing Suit]*, an adult may petition to adopt a child who may be adopted.

(b) A child residing in this state may be adopted if:

(1) the parent-child relationship as to each living parent of the child has been terminated or a suit for termination is joined with the suit for adoption;

(2) the parent whose rights have not been terminated is presently the spouse of the petitioner and the proceeding is for a stepparent adoption;

(3) the child is at least two years old, the parent-child relationship has been terminated with respect to one parent, the person seeking the adoption [~~is the child's former stepparent and~~] has been a managing conservator or has had actual care, possession, and control of the child for a period of six months preceding the adoption **or is the child's former stepparent**, and the nonterminated parent consents to the adoption; or

(4) the child is at least two years old, the parent-child relationship has been terminated with respect to one parent, and the person seeking the adoption is the child's former stepparent and has been a managing conservator or has had actual care, possession, and control of the child for a period of one year preceding the adoption.

(c) If an affidavit of relinquishment of parental rights contains a consent for the Department of Protective and Regulatory Services or a licensed child-placing agency to place the child for adoption and appoints the department or agency managing conservator of the child, further consent by the parent is not required and the adoption order shall terminate all rights of the parent without further termination proceedings.

History: Amended by 78th Legis., Reg. Sess. (2003), H.B. 980, eff. Sept. 1, 2003, and "applies only to a suit for adoption filed on or after the effective date of this Act. A suit for adoption filed before the effective date of this Act is governed by the law in effect on the date the suit was filed, and the former law is continued in effect for that purpose."

Comment

Texas law provides adoption agencies with the widest possible range for adoptive placements; any single or married adult is eligible to adopt a child available for adoption.

Subsections (b)(3)-(4) alter the general rule that a child is not eligible for adoption until after the termination of parental rights or death of both parents, or the death or termination of the rights of one parent for a stepparent adoption. Subsection (b)(3) provides that a child may be adopted by a former stepparent if parental rights of one parent have been terminated. The former stepparent must have had actual care, possession, and control of the child for a period of six months if the nonterminated parent consents to the adoption, or for one year if the nonterminated parent does not consent. Compliance with the ICPC (Interstate Compact on Placement of Children) is also necessary. *See* Subchapter B, *infra*.

Leading Cases

In re W.E.R., 669 S.W.2d 716 (Tex. 1984) (single male adoption denied, apparently on best interest test)

In re Hughes, 770 S.W.2d 635 (Tex. App.—Houston [1st Dist.] 1989, no writ) (mother who voluntarily relinquished rights has no vested right to sue for adoption of her natural child)

§ 162.002. Prerequisites to Petition.

(a) If a petitioner is married, both spouses must join in the petition for adoption.

(b) A petition in a suit for adoption or a suit for appointment of a nonparent managing conservator with authority to consent to adoption of a child must include:

(1) a verified allegation that there has been compliance with Subchapter B ; or

(2) if there has not been compliance with Subchapter B, a verified statement of the particular reasons for noncompliance.

§ 162.0025. [repealed]

§ 162.003. Pre–adoptive Home Screening and Post–placement Report.

In a suit for adoption, a pre-adoptive home screening and post-placement report must be conducted as provided in Chapter 107 *[Costs and Attorney's Fees]*.

§ 162.004. [repealed]

§ 162.0045. Preferential Setting.

The court shall grant a motion for a preferential setting for a final hearing on an adoption and shall give precedence to that hearing over all other civil cases not given preference by other law if the social study has been filed and the criminal history for the person seeking to adopt the child has been obtained.

§ 162.005. Preparation of Health, Social, Educational, and Genetic History Report.

(a) This section does not apply to an adoption by the child's:

(1) grandparent;

(2) aunt or uncle by birth, marriage, or prior adoption; or

(3) stepparent.

(b) Before placing a child for adoption, the Department of Protective and Regulatory Services, a licensed child-placing agency, or the child's parent or guardian shall compile a report on the available health, social, educational, and genetic history of the child to be adopted.

(c) The report shall include a history of physical, sexual, or emotional abuse suffered by the child, if any.

(d) If the child has been placed for adoption by a person or entity other than the department, a licensed child-placing agency, or the child's parent or guardian, it is the duty of the person or entity who places the child for adoption to prepare the report.

(e) The person or entity who places the child for adoption shall provide the prospective adoptive parents a copy of the report as early as practicable before the first meeting of the adoptive parents with the child. The copy of the report shall be edited to protect the identity of birth parents and their families.

(f) The department, licensed child-placing agency, parent, guardian, person, or entity who prepares and files the original report is required to furnish supplemental medical, psychological, and psychiatric information to the adoptive parents if that information becomes available and to file the supplemental information where the original report is filed. The supplemental information shall be retained for as long as the original report is required to be retained.

§ 162.006. Right to Examine Records.

(a) The department, licensed child-placing agency, person, or entity placing a child for adoption shall inform the prospective adoptive parents of their right to examine the records and other information relating to the history of the child. The person or entity placing the child for adoption shall edit the records and information to protect the identity of the biological parents and any other person whose identity is confidential.

(b) The department, licensed child-placing agency, or court retaining a copy of the report shall provide a copy of the report that has been edited to protect the identity of the birth parents and any other person whose identity is confidential to the following persons on request:

(1) an adoptive parent of the adopted child;

(2) the managing conservator, guardian of the person, or legal custodian of the adopted child;

(3) the adopted child, after the child is an adult;

(4) the surviving spouse of the adopted child if the adopted child is dead and the spouse is the parent or guardian of a child of the deceased adopted child; or

(5) a progeny of the adopted child if the adopted child is dead and the progeny is an adult.

(c) A copy of the report may not be furnished to a person who cannot furnish satisfactory proof of identity and legal entitlement to receive a copy.

(d) A person requesting a copy of the report shall pay the actual and reasonable costs of providing a copy and verifying entitlement to the copy.

(e) The report shall be retained for 99 years from the date of the adoption by the department or licensed child-placing agency placing the child for adoption. If the agency ceases to function as a child-placing agency, the agency shall transfer all the reports to the department or, after giving notice to the department, to a transferee agency that is assuming responsibility for the preservation of the agency's adoption records. If the child has not been placed for adoption by the department or a licensed child-placing agency and if the child is being adopted by a person other than the child's stepparent, grandparent, aunt, or uncle by birth, marriage, or prior adoption, the person or entity who places the child for adoption shall file the report with the department, which shall retain the copies for 99 years from the date of the adoption.

§ 162.0065. Editing Adoption Records in Department Placement.

Notwithstanding any other provision of this chapter, in an adoption in which a child is placed for adoption by the Department of Protective and Regulatory Services, the department is not required to edit records to protect the identity of birth parents and other persons whose identity is confidential if the department determines that information is already known to the adoptive parents or is readily available through other sources, including the court records of a suit to terminate the parent-child relationship under Chapter 161.

History: Enacted by 78th Legis., Reg. Sess. (2003), S.B. 579, eff. Sept. 1, 2003, and "applies only to the records of a child who is placed for adoption by the Department of Protective and Regulatory Services on or after the effective date of this Act. The records of a child who is placed for adoption by the Department of Protective and Regulatory Services before the effective date of this Act are governed by the law in effect on the date the child was placed for adoption, and the former law is continued in effect for that purpose."

§ 162.007. Contents of Health, Social, Educational, and Genetic History Report.

(a) The health history of the child must include information about:

(1) the child's health status at the time of placement;

(2) the child's birth, neonatal, and other medical, psychological, psychiatric, and dental history information;

(3) a record of immunizations for the child; and

(4) the available results of medical, psychological, psychiatric, and dental examinations of the child.

(b) The social history of the child must include information, to the extent known, about past and existing relationships between the child and the child's siblings, parents by birth, extended family, and other persons who have had physical possession of or legal access to the child.

(c) The educational history of the child must include, to the extent known, information about:

(1) the enrollment and performance of the child in educational institutions;

(2) results of educational testing and standardized tests for the child; and

(3) special educational needs, if any, of the child.

(d) The genetic history of the child must include a description of the child's parents by birth and their parents, any other child born to either of the child's parents, and extended family members and must include, to the extent the information is available, information about:

(1) their health and medical history, including any genetic diseases and disorders;

(2) their health status at the time of placement;

(3) the cause of and their age at death;

(4) their height, weight, and eye and hair color;

(5) their nationality and ethnic background;

(6) their general levels of educational and professional achievements, if any;

(7) their religious backgrounds, if any;

(8) any psychological, psychiatric, or social evaluations, including the date of the evaluation, any diagnosis, and a summary of any findings;

(9) any criminal conviction records relating to a misdemeanor or felony classified as an offense against the person or family or public indecency or a felony violation of a statute intended to control the possession or distribution of a substance included in Chapter 481, Health and Safety Code; and

(10) any information necessary to determine whether the child is entitled to or otherwise eligible for state or federal financial, medical, or other assistance.

§ 162.008. Filing of Health, Social, Educational, and Genetic History Report.

(a) This section does not apply to an adoption by the child's:

(1) grandparent;

(2) aunt or uncle by birth, marriage, or prior adoption; or

(3) stepparent.

(b) A petition for adoption may not be granted until the following documents have been filed:

(1) a copy of the health, social, educational, and genetic history report signed by the child's adoptive parents; and

(2) if the report is required to be submitted to the bureau of vital statistics under Section 162.006(e), a certificate from the bureau acknowledging receipt of the report.

(c) A court having jurisdiction of a suit affecting the parent-child relationship may by order waive the making and filing of a report under this section if the child's biological parents cannot be located and their absence results in insufficient information being available to compile the report.

§ 162.0085. Criminal History Report Required.

(a) In a suit affecting the parent-child relationship in which an adoption is sought, the court shall order each person seeking to adopt the child to obtain that person's own criminal history record information. The court shall accept under this section a person's criminal history record information that is provided by the Department of Protective and Regulatory Services or by a licensed child-placing agency that received the information from the department if the information was obtained not more than one year before the date the court ordered the history to be obtained.

(b) A person required to obtain information under Subsection (a) shall obtain the information in the manner provided by Section 411.128, Government Code.

Cross Reference

TEX. GOV'T CODE ANN. § 411.128. Access to Criminal History Record Information: Person Seeking To Adopt Child.

---

§ 162.009. Residence With Petitioner.

(a) The court may not grant an adoption until the child has resided with the petitioner for not less than six months.

(b) On request of the petitioner, the court may waive the residence requirement if the waiver is in the best interest of the child.

Comment

Waiver of the six months residence of the child with the prospective adoptive parents is commonplace. Moreover, quite often the requisite time period has been met before the adoption petition is filed.

---

§ 162.010. Consent Required.

(a) Unless the managing conservator is the petitioner, the written consent of a managing conservator to the adoption must be filed. The court may waive the requirement of consent by the managing conservator if the court finds that the consent is being refused or has been revoked without good cause. A hearing on the issue of consent shall be conducted by the court without a jury.

(b) If a parent of the child is presently the spouse of the petitioner, that parent must join in the petition for adoption and further consent of that parent is not required.

(c) A child 12 years of age or older must consent to the adoption in writing or in court. The court may waive this requirement if it would serve the child's best interest.

Leading Case

In re M.T., 21 S.W.3d 925 (Tex. App.—Beaumont 2000, no pet.) (DPRS refusal to consent to foster parent adoption withheld without good cause)

---

§ 162.011. Revocation of Consent.

At any time before an order granting the adoption of the child is rendered, a consent required by Section 162.010 may be revoked by filing a signed revocation.

§ 162.012. Direct or Collateral Attack.

(a) Notwithstanding Rule 329, Texas Rules of Civil Procedure, the validity of an adoption order is not subject to attack after six months after the date the order was signed.

(b) The validity of a final adoption order is not subject to attack because a health, social, educational, and genetic history was not filed.

Comment

Subsection (a) shortens the time to attack directly or collaterally an adoption order, similar to the change made in termination matters, § 161.211, *infra*. The reference to Rule 329, Texas Rules of Civil Procedure ensures that the six month time frame also applies to actions based on citation by publication.

---

§ 162.013. Abatement or Dismissal.

(a) If the sole petitioner dies or the joint petitioners die, the court shall dismiss the suit for adoption.

(b) If one of the joint petitioners dies, the proceeding shall continue uninterrupted.

(c) If the joint petitioners divorce, the court shall abate the suit for adoption. The court shall dismiss the petition unless the petition is amended to request adoption by one of the original petitioners.

Comment

Given the automatic abatement and potential dismissal, and given the waiting time and expense of an infant adoption, prospective adoptive parents who decide to divorce may wish to delay filing that action until after an adoption is complete. Whether that is fair to the child is problematic.

Leading Case

Hopper v. Brittain, 612 S.W.2d 636 (Tex. Civ. App.—Houston [14th Dist.] 1981, no writ) (divorced wife and new husband adopt child after she and her former husband originally had custody)

---

§ 162.014. Attendance at Hearing Required.

(a) If the joint petitioners are husband and wife and it would be unduly difficult for one of the petitioners to appear at the hearing, the court may waive the attendance of that petitioner if the other spouse is present.

(b) A child to be adopted who is 12 years of age or older shall attend the hearing. The court may waive this requirement in the best interest of the child.

§ 162.015. Race or Ethnicity.

(a) In determining the best interest of the child, the court may not deny or delay the adoption or otherwise discriminate on the basis of race or ethnicity of the child or the prospective adoptive parents.

(b) This section does not apply to a person, entity, tribe, organization, or child custody proceeding subject to the Indian Child Welfare Act of 1978 (25 U.S.C. Section 1901 et seq.). In this subsection "child custody proceeding" has the meaning provided by 25 U.S.C. Section 1903.

Comment

This section makes certain that race or ethnicity is not considered in the placement of a child for adoption.

CLE/Other Legal Publications

Two parents are better than none: whether two single, African–American adults, who are not in a traditional marriage or a romantic or sexual relationship with each other, should be allowed to jointly adopt and co-parent African American children. Angela Mae Kupenda, 35 J. FAM. L. 703 (1996–97)

---

§ 162.016. Adoption Order.

(a) If a petition requesting termination has been joined with a petition requesting adoption, the court shall also terminate the parent-child relationship at the same time the adoption order is rendered. The court must make separate findings that the termination is in the best interest of the child and that the adoption is in the best interest of the child.

(b) If the court finds that the requirements for adoption have been met and the adoption is in the best interest of the child, the court shall grant the adoption.

(c) The name of the child may be changed in the order if requested.

Comment

Not only must all procedural requirements be met, but the court must also find that adoption is in the child's best interest.

---

§ 162.017. Effect of Adoption.

(a) An order of adoption creates the parent-child relationship between the adoptive parent and the child for all purposes.

(b) An adopted child is entitled to inherit from and through the child's adoptive parents as though the child were the biological child of the parents.

(c) The terms "child," "descendant," "issue," and other terms indicating the relationship of parent and child include an adopted child unless the context or express language clearly indicates otherwise.

(d) Nothing in this chapter precludes or affects the rights of a biological or adoptive maternal or paternal grandparent to reasonable access, as provided in Chapter 153 *[Conservatorship, Possession, and Access]*.

Comment

The adoptive parents are legally substituted in toto for the biological parents. This includes inheritance rights from the adoptive parents and the collateral relatives. Note however, under Section 161.206(b), *supra*, the child retains the right to inherit from his or her biological parents "unless the court otherwise provides."

---

§ 162.018. Access to Information.

(a) The adoptive parents are entitled to receive copies of the records and other information relating to the history of the child maintained by the department, licensed child-placing agency, person, or entity placing the child for adoption.

(b) The adoptive parents and the adopted child, after the child is an adult, are entitled to receive copies of the records that have been edited to protect the identity of the biological parents and any other person whose identity is confidential and other information relating to the history of the child maintained by the department, licensed child-placing agency, person, or entity placing the child for adoption.

(c) It is the duty of the person or entity placing the child for adoption to edit the records and information to protect the identity of the biological parents and any other person whose identity is confidential.

(d) At the time an adoption order is rendered, the court shall provide to the parents of an adopted child information provided by the bureau of vital statistics that describes the functions of the voluntary adoption registry under Subchapter E. The licensed child-placing agency shall provide to each of the child's biological parents known to the agency, the information when the parent signs an affidavit of relinquishment of parental rights, affidavit of status of child, or affidavit of waiver of interest in a child. The information shall include the right of the child or biological parent to refuse to participate in the registry. If the adopted child is 14 years old or older the court shall provide the information to the child.

§ 162.019. Copy of Order.

A copy of the adoption order is not required to be mailed to the parties as provided in Rules 119a and 239a, Texas Rules of Civil Procedure.

§ 162.020. Withdrawal or Denial of Petition.

If a petition requesting adoption is withdrawn or denied, the court may order the removal of the child from the proposed adoptive home if removal is in the child's best interest and may enter any order necessary for the welfare of the child.

§ 162.021. Sealing File.

(a) The court, on the motion of a party or on the court's own motion, may order the sealing of the file and the minutes of the court, or both, in a suit requesting an adoption.

(b) Rendition of the order does not relieve the clerk from the duty to send information regarding adoption to the bureau of vital statistics as required by this subchapter and Chapter 108 *[Central Record File; Vital Statistics]*.

§ 162.022. Confidentiality Maintained by Clerk.

The records concerning a child maintained by the district clerk after entry of an order of adoption are confidential. No person is entitled to access to the records or may obtain information from the records except for good cause under an order of the court that issued the order.

§ 162.023. Adoption Order From Foreign Country.

(a) Except as otherwise provided by law, an adoption order rendered to a resident of this state that is made by a foreign country shall be accorded full faith and credit by the courts of this state and enforced as if the order were rendered by a court in this state unless the adoption law or process of the foreign country violates the fundamental principles of human rights or the laws or public policy of this state.

(b) A person who adopts a child in a foreign country may register the order in this state. A petition for registration of a foreign adoption order may be combined with a petition for a name change. If the court finds that the foreign adoption order meets the requirements of Subsection (a), the court shall order the state registrar to:

(1) register the order under Chapter 192, Health and Safety Code; and

(2) file a certificate of birth for the child under Section 192.006, Health and Safety Code.

§ 162.024. [repealed]

§ 162.025. Placement by Unauthorized Person; Offense.

(a) A person who is not the natural or adoptive parent of the child, the legal guardian of the child, or a child-placing agency licensed under Chapter 42, Human Resources Code, commits an offense if the person:

(1) serves as an intermediary between a prospective adoptive parent and an expectant parent or parent of a minor child to identify the parties to each other; or

(2) places a child for adoption.

(b) It is not an offense under this section if a professional provides legal or medical services to:

(1) a parent who identifies the prospective adoptive parent and places the child for adoption without the assistance of the professional; or

(2) a prospective adoptive parent who identifies a parent and receives placement of a child for adoption without the assistance of the professional.

(c) An offense under this section is a Class B misdemeanor.

Comment

This section addresses concerns about the brokering of Texas children for adoption. Under its provisions children may be placed for adoption only by a parent (natural or adoptive), legal guardian, or licensed child-placing agency (including DPRS). Any other person who places a child for adoption commits a criminal offense. Additionally, except for licensed agencies, serving as an intermediary between a biological and prospective adoptive parent is illegal. Providing medical or legal services to a parent or adoptive parent does not violate the law, provided that the doctor or lawyer does not bring the parties together.

Lawyers handling adoptions should also review § 25.09, Penal Code, *infra.* Unless the advertiser is a licensed agency, advertising is prohibited in the public media, including the Internet, for the placement of a child or to obtain a child for adoption,. Additionally, § 162.107 establishes a criminal offense for violating the provisions of the Interstate Compact on the Placement of Children. The ICPC is mandatory reading for lawyers who choose to handle adoption matters.

Subchapter B. Interstate Compact on the Placement of Children

Introductory Comment

Issues regarding this compact between states, commonly referred to as the ICPC, arise frequently in litigation involving an allegedly abused and neglected child. For example, placement of the child with relatives residing in another state triggers an ICPC inquiry—at least, it is supposed to do so. Interestingly, a Westlaw search identifies exactly five cases involving the ICPC; two were unreported and one was not subject to Texas jurisdiction.

Leading Cases

Rodriguez v. Lutheran Social Services of Texas, 814 S.W.2d 153 (Tex. App.—San Antonio 1991, writ denied) (testimony did not convincingly show that ICPC not involved)

Broyles v. Ashworth, 782 S.W.2d 31 (Tex. App.—Fort Worth 1989, no writ) (mother's revocation of relinquishment did not entitle her, as "sending agency" to custody of children placed with TMC's)

---

§ 162.101. Definitions.

In this subchapter:

(1) "Appropriate public authorities," with reference to this state, means the executive director.

(2) "Appropriate authority in the receiving state," with reference to this state, means the executive director.

(3) "Compact" means the Interstate Compact on the Placement of Children.

(4) "Executive head," with reference to this state, means the governor.

§ 162.102. Adoption of Compact; Text.

The Interstate Compact on the Placement of Children is adopted by this state and entered into with all other jurisdictions in form substantially as provided by this subchapter.

INTERSTATE COMPACT ON THE PLACEMENT OF CHILDREN

ARTICLE I. PURPOSE AND POLICY

It is the purpose and policy of the party states to cooperate with each other in the interstate placement of children to the end that:

(a) Each child requiring placement shall receive the maximum opportunity to be placed in a suitable environment and with persons or institutions having appropriate qualifications and facilities to provide a necessary and desirable degree and type of care.

(b) The appropriate authorities in a state where a child is to be placed may have full opportunity to ascertain the circumstances of the proposed placement, thereby promoting full compliance with applicable requirements for the protection of the child.

(c) The proper authorities of the state from which the placement is made may obtain the most complete information on the basis on which to evaluate a projected placement before it is made.

(d) Appropriate jurisdictional arrangements for the care of children will be promoted.

ARTICLE II. DEFINITIONS

As used in this compact:

(a) "Child" means a person who, by reason of minority, is legally subject to parental, guardianship, or similar control.

(b) "Sending agency" means a party state, officer, or employee thereof; a subdivision of a party state, or officer or employee thereof; a court of a party state; a person, corporation, association, charitable agency, or other entity which sends, brings, or causes to be sent or brought any child to another party state.

(c) "Receiving state" means the state to which a child is sent, brought, or caused to be sent or brought, whether by public authorities or private persons or agencies, and whether for placement with state or local public authorities or for placement with private agencies or persons.

(d) "Placement" means the arrangement for the care of a child in a family free or boarding home or in a child-caring agency or institution but does not include any institution caring for the mentally ill, mentally defective, or epileptic or any institution primarily educational in character, and any hospital or other medical facility.

ARTICLE III. CONDITIONS FOR PLACEMENT

(a) No sending agency shall send, bring, or cause to be sent or brought into any other party state any child for placement in foster care or as a preliminary to a possible adoption unless the sending agency shall comply with each and every requirement set forth in this article and with the applicable laws of the receiving state governing the placement of children therein.

(b) Prior to sending, bringing, or causing any child to be sent or brought into a receiving state for placement in foster care or as a preliminary to a possible adoption, the sending agency shall furnish the appropriate public authorities in the receiving state written notice of the intention to send, bring, or place the child in the receiving state. The notice shall contain:

(1) the name, date, and place of birth of the child;

(2) the identity and address or addresses of the parents or legal guardian;

(3) the name and address of the person, agency, or institution to or with which the sending agency proposes to send, bring, or place the child;

(4) a full statement of the reasons for such proposed action and evidence of the authority pursuant to which the placement is proposed to be made.

(c) Any public officer or agency in a receiving state which is in receipt of a notice pursuant to Paragraph (b) of this article may request of the sending agency, or any other appropriate officer or agency of or in the sending agency's state, and shall be entitled to receive therefrom, such supporting or additional information as it may deem necessary under the circumstances to carry out the purpose and policy of this compact.

(d) The child shall not be sent, brought, or caused to be sent or brought into the receiving state until the appropriate public authorities in the receiving state shall notify the sending agency, in writing, to the effect that the proposed placement does not appear to be contrary to the interests of the child.

ARTICLE IV. PENALTY FOR ILLEGAL PLACEMENT

The sending, bringing, or causing to be sent or brought into any receiving state of a child in violation of the terms of this compact shall constitute a violation of the laws respecting the placement of children of both the state in which the sending agency is located or from which it sends or brings the child and of the receiving state. Such violation may be punished or subjected to penalty in either jurisdiction in accordance with its laws. In addition to liability for any such punishment or penalty, any such violation shall constitute full and sufficient grounds for the suspension or revocation of any license, permit, or other legal authorization held by the sending agency which empowers or allows it to place or care for children.

ARTICLE V. RETENTION OF JURISDICTION

(a) The sending agency shall retain jurisdiction over the child sufficient to determine all matters in relation to the custody, supervision, care, treatment, and disposition of the child which it would have had if the child had remained in the sending agency's state, until the child is adopted, reaches majority, becomes self-supporting, or is discharged with the concurrence of the appropriate authority in the receiving state. Such jurisdiction shall also include the power to effect or cause the return of the child or its transfer to another location and custody pursuant to law. The sending agency shall continue to have financial responsibility for support and maintenance of the child during the period of the placement. Nothing contained herein shall defeat a claim of jurisdiction by a receiving state sufficient to deal with an act of delinquency or crime committed therein.

(b) When the sending agency is a public agency, it may enter into an agreement with an authorized public or private agency in the receiving state providing for the performance of one or more services in respect of such case by the latter as agent for the sending agency.

(c) Nothing in this compact shall be construed to prevent a private charitable agency authorized to place children in the receiving state from performing services or acting as agent in that state for a private charitable agency of the sending state; nor to prevent the agency in the receiving state from discharging financial responsibility for the support and maintenance of a child who has been placed on behalf of the sending agency without relieving the responsibility set forth in Paragraph (a) hereof.

ARTICLE VI. INSTITUTIONAL CARE OF DELINQUENT CHILDREN

A child adjudicated delinquent may be placed in an institution in another party jurisdiction pursuant to this compact but no such placement shall be made unless the child is given a court hearing on notice to the parent or guardian with opportunity to be heard, prior to his being sent to such other party jurisdiction for institutional care and the court finds that:

(1) equivalent facilities for the child are not available in the sending agency's jurisdiction; and

(2) institutional care in the other jurisdiction is in the best interest of the child and will not produce undue hardship.

ARTICLE VII. COMPACT ADMINISTRATOR

The executive head of each jurisdiction party to this compact shall designate an officer who shall be general coordinator of activities under this compact in his jurisdiction and who, acting jointly with like officers of other party jurisdictions, shall have power to promulgate rules and regulations to carry out more effectively the terms and provisions of this compact.

ARTICLE VIII. LIMITATIONS

This compact shall not apply to:

(a) the sending or bringing of a child into a receiving state by his parent, stepparent, grandparent, adult brother or sister, adult uncle or aunt, or his guardian and leaving the child with any such relative or nonagency guardian in the receiving state; or

(b) any placement, sending, or bringing of a child into a receiving state pursuant to any other interstate compact to which both the state from which the child is sent or brought and the receiving state are party, or to any other agreement between said states which has the force of law.

ARTICLE IX. ENACTMENT AND WITHDRAWAL

This compact shall be open to joinder by any state, territory, or possession of the United States, the District of Columbia, the Commonwealth of Puerto Rico, and, with the consent of congress, the government of Canada or any province thereof. It shall become effective with respect to any such jurisdiction when such jurisdiction has enacted the same into law. Withdrawal from this compact shall be by the enactment of a statute repealing the same, but shall not take effect until two years after the effective date of such statute and until written notice of the withdrawal has been given by the withdrawing state to the governor of each other party jurisdiction. Withdrawal of a party state shall not affect the rights, duties, and obligations under this compact of any sending agency therein with respect to a placement made prior to the effective date of withdrawal.

ARTICLE X. CONSTRUCTION AND SEVERABILITY

The provisions of this compact shall be liberally construed to effectuate the purposes thereof. The provisions of this compact shall be severable and if any phrase, clause, sentence, or provision of this compact is declared to be contrary to the constitution of any party state or of the United States or the applicability thereof to any government, agency, person, or circumstance is held invalid, the validity of the remainder of this compact and the applicability thereof to any government, agency, person, or circumstance shall not be affected thereby. If this compact shall be held contrary to the constitution of any state party thereto, the compact shall remain in full force and effect as to the remaining states and in full force and effect as to the state affected as to all severable matters.

§ 162.103. Financial Responsibility for Child.

(a) Financial responsibility for a child placed as provided in the compact is determined, in the first instance, as provided in Article V of the compact. After partial or complete default of performance under the provisions of Article V assigning financial responsibility, the executive director may bring suit under Chapter 154 *[Child Support]* and may file a complaint with the appropriate prosecuting attorney, claiming a violation of Section 25.05, Penal Code.

(b) After default, if the executive director determines that financial responsibility is unlikely to be assumed by the sending agency or the child's parents, the executive director may cause the child to be returned to the sending agency.

(c) After default, the department shall assume financial responsibility for the child until it is assumed by the child's parents or until the child is safely returned to the sending agency.

§ 162.104. Approval of Placement.

The executive director may not approve the placement of a child in this state without the concurrence of the individuals with whom the child is proposed to be placed or the head of an institution with which the child is proposed to be placed.

§ 162.105. Placement in Another State.

A juvenile court may place a delinquent child in an institution in another state as provided by Article VI of the compact. After placement in another state, the court retains jurisdiction of the child as provided by Article V of the compact.

§ 162.106. Compact Authority.

(a) The governor shall appoint the executive director of the Department of Protective and Regulatory Services as compact administrator.

(b) The executive director shall designate a deputy compact administrator and staff necessary to execute the terms of the compact in this state.

§ 162.107. Offenses; Penalties.

(a) An individual, agency, corporation, or child-care facility that violates a provision of the compact commits an offense. An offense under this subsection is a Class B misdemeanor.

(b) An individual, agency, corporation, child-care facility, or child-care institution in this state that violates Article IV of the compact commits an offense. An offense under this subsection is a Class B misdemeanor. On conviction, the court shall revoke any license to operate as a child-care facility or child-care institution issued by the department to the entity convicted and shall revoke any license or certification of the individual, agency, or corporation necessary to practice in the state.

Subchapter C. Interstate Compact on Adoption and Medical Assistance

§ 162.201. Adoption of Compact; Text.

The Interstate Compact on Adoption and Medical Assistance is adopted by this state and entered into with all other jurisdictions joining in the compact in form substantially as provided under this subchapter.

INTERSTATE COMPACT ON ADOPTION AND MEDICAL ASSISTANCE

ARTICLE I. FINDINGS

The legislature finds that:

(a) Finding adoptive families for children for whom state assistance is desirable, under Subchapter D, Chapter 162 *[Adoption]*, and assuring the protection of the interest of the children affected during the entire assistance period require special measures when the adoptive parents move to other states or are residents of another state.

(b) The provision of medical and other necessary services for children, with state assistance, encounters special difficulties when the provision of services takes place in other states.

ARTICLE II. PURPOSES

The purposes of the compact are to:

(a) authorize the Department of Protective and Regulatory Services, with the concurrence of the Health and Human Services Commission, to enter into interstate agreements with agencies of other states for the protection of children on behalf of whom adoption assistance is being provided by the Department of Protective and Regulatory Services; and

(b) provide procedures for interstate children's adoption assistance payments, including medical payments.

ARTICLE III. DEFINITIONS

In this compact:

(a) "Adoption assistance state" means the state that signs an adoption assistance agreement in a particular case.

(b) "Residence state" means the state in which the child resides by virtue of the residence of the adoptive parents.

(c) "State" means a state of the United States, the District of Columbia, the Commonwealth of Puerto Rico, the Virgin Islands, Guam, the Commonwealth of the Northern Mariana Islands, or a territory or possession of or a territory or possession administered by the United States.

ARTICLE IV. COMPACTS AUTHORIZED

The Department of Protective and Regulatory Services, through its executive director, is authorized to develop, participate in the development of, negotiate, and enter into one or more interstate compacts on behalf of this state with other states to implement one or more of the purposes of this compact. An interstate compact authorized by this article has the force and effect of law.

ARTICLE V. CONTENTS OF COMPACTS

A compact entered into under the authority conferred by this compact shall contain:

(1) a provision making the compact available for joinder by all states;

(2) a provision for withdrawal from the compact on written notice to the parties, with a period of one year between the date of the notice and the effective date of the withdrawal;

(3) a requirement that protections under the compact continue for the duration of the adoption assistance and apply to all children and their adoptive parents who on the effective date of the withdrawal are receiving adoption assistance from a party state other than the one in which they reside and have their principal place of abode;

(4) a requirement that each case of adoption assistance to which the compact applies be covered by a written adoption assistance agreement between the adoptive parents and the state child welfare agency of the state that provides the adoption assistance and that the agreement be expressly for the benefit of the adopted child and enforceable by the adoptive parents and the state agency providing the adoption assistance; and

(5) other provisions that are appropriate for the proper administration of the compact.

ARTICLE VI. OPTIONAL CONTENTS OF COMPACTS

A compact entered into under the authority conferred by this compact may contain the following provisions, in addition to those required under Article V of this compact:

(1) provisions establishing procedures and entitlement to medical, developmental, child-care, or other social services for the child in accordance with applicable laws, even if the child and the adoptive parents are in a state other than the one responsible for or providing the services or the funds to defray part or all of the costs thereof; and

(2) other provisions that are appropriate or incidental to the proper administration of the compact.

ARTICLE VII. MEDICAL ASSISTANCE

(a) A child with special needs who resides in this state and who is the subject of an adoption assistance agreement with another state is entitled to receive a medical assistance identification from this state on the filing in the state medical assistance agency of a certified copy of the adoption assistance agreement obtained from the adoption assistance state. In accordance with rules of the state medical assistance agency, the adoptive parents, at least annually, shall show that the agreement is still in effect or has been renewed.

(b) The state medical assistance agency shall consider the holder of a medical assistance identification under this article as any other holder of a medical assistance identification under the laws of this state and shall process and make payment on claims on the holder's account in the same manner and under the same conditions and procedures as for other recipients of medical assistance.

(c) The state medical assistance agency shall provide coverage and benefits for a child who is in another state and who is covered by an adoption assistance agreement made by the Department of Protective and Regulatory Services for the coverage or benefits, if any, not provided by the residence state. The adoptive parents acting for the child may submit evidence of payment for services or benefit amounts not payable in the residence state and shall be reimbursed for those amounts. Services or benefit amounts covered under any insurance or other third-party medical contract or arrangement held by the child or the adoptive parents may not be reimbursed. The state medical assistance agency shall adopt rules implementing this subsection. The additional coverage and benefit amounts provided under this subsection are for services for which there is no federal contribution or services that, if federally aided, are not provided by the residence state. The rules shall include procedures for obtaining prior approval for services in cases in which prior approval is required for the assistance.

(d) The submission of a false, misleading, or fraudulent claim for payment or reimbursement for services or benefits under this article or the making of a false, misleading, or fraudulent statement in connection with the claim is an offense under this subsection if the person submitting the claim or making the statement knows or should know that the claim or statement is false, misleading, or fraudulent. A person who commits an offense under this subsection may be liable for a fine not to exceed $10,000 or imprisonment for not more than two years, or both the fine and the imprisonment. An offense under this subsection that also constitutes an offense under other law may be punished under either this subsection or the other applicable law.

(e) This article applies only to medical assistance for children under adoption assistance agreements with states that have entered into a compact with this state under which the other state provides medical assistance to children with special needs under adoption assistance agreements made by this state. All other children entitled to medical assistance under adoption assistance agreements entered into by this state are eligible to receive the medical assistance in accordance with the laws and procedures that apply to the agreement.

ARTICLE VIII. FEDERAL PARTICIPATION

Consistent with federal law, the Department of Protective and Regulatory Services and the Health and Human Services Commission, in connection with the administration of this compact or a compact authorized by this compact, shall include the provision of adoption assistance and medical assistance for which the federal government pays some or all of the cost in any state plan made under the Adoption Assistance and Child Welfare Act of 1980 (Pub. L. No. 96–272), Titles IV-E and XIX of the Social Security Act, and other applicable federal laws. The Department of Protective and Regulatory Services and the Health and Human Services Commission shall apply for and administer all relevant federal aid in accordance with law.

§ 162.202. Authority of Department of Protective and Regulatory Services.

The Department of Protective and Regulatory Services, with the concurrence of the Health and Human Services Commission, may develop, participate in the development of, negotiate, and enter into one or more interstate compacts on behalf of this state with other states to implement one or more of the purposes of this subchapter. An interstate compact authorized by this article has the force and effect of law.

§ 162.203. Compact Administration.

The executive director of the Department of Protective and Regulatory Services shall serve as the compact administrator. The administrator shall cooperate with all departments, agencies, and officers of this state and its subdivisions in facilitating the proper administration of the compact and any supplemental agreements entered into by this state. The executive director and the commissioner of human services shall designate deputy compact administrators to represent adoption assistance services and medical assistance services provided under Title XIX of the Social Security Act.

§ 162.204. Supplementary Agreements.

The compact administrator may enter into supplementary agreements with appropriate officials of other states under the compact. If a supplementary agreement requires or authorizes the use of any institution or facility of this state or requires or authorizes the provision of a service by this state, the supplementary agreement does not take effect until approved by the head of the department or agency under whose jurisdiction the institution or facility is operated or whose department or agency will be charged with rendering the service.

§ 162.205. Payments by State.

The compact administrator, subject to the approval of the chief state fiscal officer, may make or arrange for payments necessary to discharge financial obligations imposed on this state by the compact or by a supplementary agreement entered into under the compact.

§ 162.206. Penalties.

A person who, under a compact entered into under this subchapter, knowingly obtains or attempts to obtain or aids or abets any person in obtaining, by means of a wilfully false statement or representation or by impersonation or other fraudulent device, any assistance on behalf of a child or other person to which the child or other person is not entitled, or assistance in an amount greater than that to which the child or other person is entitled, commits an offense. An offense under this section is a Class B misdemeanor. An offense under this section that also constitutes an offense under other law may be punished under either this section or the other applicable law.

Subchapter D. Adoption Services by the Department of Protective and Regulatory Services

§ 162.301. Definitions.

In this subchapter:

(1) "Adoption assistance agreement" means a written agreement, binding on the parties to the agreement, between the department and the prospective adoptive parents that specifies the nature and amount of any payment, services, or assistance to be provided under the agreement and stipulates that the agreement will remain in effect without regard to the state in which the prospective adoptive parents reside at any particular time.

(2) "Child" means a child who cannot be placed for adoption with appropriate adoptive parents without the provision of adoption assistance because of factors including ethnic background, age, membership in a minority or sibling group, the presence of a medical condition, or a physical, mental, or emotional disability.

(3) "Department" means the Department of Protective and Regulatory Services.

§ 162.302. Adoption Assistance Program.

(a) The department shall administer a program designed to promote the adoption of children by providing information to prospective adoptive parents concerning the availability and needs of the children, assisting the parents in completing the adoption process, and providing adoption assistance necessary for the parents to adopt the children.

(b) The legislature intends that the program benefit children residing in foster homes at state or county expense by providing them with the stability and security of permanent homes and that the costs paid by the state and counties for foster home care for the children be reduced.

(c) The program shall be carried out by licensed child-placing agencies or county child-care or welfare units under rules adopted by the department.

(d) The department shall keep records necessary to evaluate the program's effectiveness in encouraging and promoting the adoption of children.

(e) It is the intent of the legislature that the department in providing adoption services, when it is in the children's best interest, keep siblings together and whenever possible place siblings in the same adoptive home.

§ 162.303. Dissemination of Information.

The department, county child-care or welfare units, and licensed child-placing agencies shall disseminate information to prospective adoptive parents concerning the availability and needs of children for adoption and the existence of adoption assistance for parents who adopt them. Special effort shall be made to disseminate the information to families that have lower income levels or that belong to disadvantaged groups.

§ 162.304. Financial and Medical Assistance.

(a) The department shall enter into adoption assistance agreements with the adoptive parents of a child as authorized by Part E of Title IV of the federal Social Security Act, as amended (42 U.S.C. Section 673).

(b) The adoption of a child may be subsidized by the department. The need for and amount of the subsidy shall be determined by the department under its rules.

(c) In addition to the subsidy under Subsection (b), the department may subsidize the cost of medical care for a child. The department shall determine the amount and need for the subsidy.

(d) The county may pay a subsidy under Subsection (b) or (c) if the county is responsible for the child's foster care at the time of the child's adoptive placement.

(e) If the child is receiving supplemental security income from the federal government, the state may pay the subsidy regardless of whether the state is the managing conservator for the child.

§ 162.3041. Continuation of Assistance After Child's 18th Birthday.

(a) The department shall, in accordance with department rules, offer adoption assistance after a child's 18th birthday to the child's adoptive parents under an existing adoption assistance agreement entered into under Section 162.304 until:

(1) the first day of the month of the child's 21st birthday if the department determines, as provided by department rules, that:

(A) the child has a mental or physical disability that warrants the continuation of that assistance;

(B) the child, or the child's adoptive parent on behalf of the child, has applied for federal benefits under the supplemental security income program (42 U.S.C. Section 1381 et seq.), as amended; and

(C) the child's adoptive parents are providing the child's financial support; or

(2) if the child does not meet the requirements of Subdivision (1), the earlier of:

(A) the date the child ceases to regularly attend high school or a vocational or technical program;

(B) the date the child obtains a high school diploma or high school equivalency certificate;

(C) the date the child's adoptive parents stop providing financial support to the child; or

(D) the first day of the month of the child's 19th birthday.

(b) In determining whether a child meets the requirements of Subdivision (a)(1), the department may conduct an assessment of the child's mental or physical disability or may contract for the assessment to be conducted.

(c) The department and any person with whom the department contracts to conduct an assessment under Subsection (b) shall:

(1) inform the adoptive parents of the child for whom the assessment is conducted of the application requirement under Subsection (a)(1)(B) for federal benefits for the child under the supplemental security income program (42 U.S.C. Section 1381 et seq.), as amended;

(2) provide assistance to the adoptive parents and the child in preparing an application for benefits under that program; and

(3) provide ongoing consultation and guidance to the adoptive parents and the child throughout the eligibility determination process for benefits under that program.

(d) If the legislature does not appropriate sufficient money to provide adoption assistance to the adoptive parents of all children described by Subsection (a), the department shall provide adoption assistance only to the adoptive parents of children described by Subsection (a)(1).

Comment

Because the 2001 legislature did not appropriate additional money to provide the extended adoption assistance described in this new section, the enabling clause took that possibility into account. Therefore, DPRS "may, but is not required to, implement this Act using other appropriations available for the purpose."

§ 162.305. Funds.

The department and other state agencies shall actively seek and use federal funds available for the purposes of this subchapter.

§ 162.306. Postadoption Services.

(a) The department may provide services after adoption to adoptees and adoptive families for whom the department provided services before the adoption.

(b) The department may provide services under this section directly or through contract.

(c) The services may include financial assistance, respite care, placement services, parenting programs, support groups, counseling services, crisis intervention, and medical aid.

§ 162.307. [repealed]

§ 162.308. Race or Ethnicity.

(a) The department, a county child-care or welfare unit, or a licensed child-placing agency may not make an adoption placement decision on the presumption that placing a child in a family of the same race or ethnicity as the race or ethnicity of the child is in the best interest of the child.

(b) Unless an independent psychological evaluation specific to a child indicates that placement with a family of a particular race or ethnicity would be detrimental to the child, the department, county child-care or welfare unit, or licensed child-placing agency may not deny, delay, or prohibit the adoption of a child because the department, county, or agency is attempting to locate a family of a particular race or ethnicity.

(c) This section does not prevent or limit the recruitment of minority families as adoptive families, but the recruitment of minority families may not be a reason to delay placement of a child with an available family of a race or ethnicity different from that of the child.

(d) A state or county employee who violates this section is subject to immediate dismissal. A licensed child-placing agency that violates this section is subject to action by the licensing agency as a ground for revocation or suspension of the agency's license.

(e) A district court, on the application for an injunction or the filing of a petition complaining of a violation of this section by any person residing in the county in which the court has jurisdiction, shall enforce this section by issuing appropriate orders. An action for an injunction is in addition to any other action, proceeding, or remedy authorized by law. An applicant or petitioner who is granted an injunction or given other appropriate relief under this section is entitled to the costs of the suit, including reasonable attorney's fees.

§ 162.309. Advisory Committee on Promoting Adoption of Minority Children.

(a) An advisory committee on promoting the adoption of and provision of services to minority children is established within the department.

(b) The committee is composed of 12 members appointed by the board of the Department of Protective and Regulatory Services. The board shall appoint to the committee individuals who in the aggregate have knowledge of and experience in community education, cultural relations, family support, counseling, and parenting skills and education. At least six members must be ordained members of the clergy.

(c) A committee member serves for a two-year term and may be appointed for additional terms.

(d) A member of the committee receives no compensation but is entitled to reimbursement for actual and necessary expenses incurred in performing the member's duties under this section.

(e) The committee shall elect one member to serve as presiding officer. The presiding officer serves for a two-year term and may be elected for additional terms.

(f) The department shall set the time and place of the first committee meeting. The committee shall meet at least quarterly.

(g) The department shall pay the expenses of the committee and shall supply necessary personnel and supplies.

(h) To promote the adoption of and provision of services to minority children, the committee shall:

(1) study, develop, and evaluate programs and projects relating to community awareness and education, family support, counseling, parenting skills and education, and reform of the child welfare system;

(2) consult with churches and other cultural and civic organizations; and

(3) report to the department at least annually the committee's recommendations for department programs and projects that will promote the adoption of and provision of services to minority children.

(i) On receiving the committee's recommendations, the department may adopt rules to implement a program or project recommended under this section. The department may solicit, accept, and use gifts and donations to implement a program or project recommended by the committee.

(j) The department shall report to the legislature not later than November 1 of each even-numbered year following the first year in which it receives recommendations under this section regarding committee recommendations and action taken by the department under this section.

(k) The recruitment of minority families may not be a reason to delay placement of a child with an available family of a race or ethnicity different from that of the child.

Subchapter E. Voluntary Adoption Registries

§ 162.401. Purpose.

The purpose of this subchapter is to provide for the establishment of mutual consent voluntary adoption registries through which adoptees, birth parents, and biological siblings may voluntarily locate each other. It is not the purpose of this subchapter to inhibit or prohibit persons from locating each other through other legal means or to inhibit or affect in any way the provision of postadoptive services and education, by adoption agencies or others, that go further than the procedures set out for registries established under this subchapter.

§ 162.402. Definitions.

In this subchapter:

(1) "Administrator" means the administrator of a mutual consent voluntary adoption registry established under this subchapter.

(2) "Adoptee" means a person 18 years of age or older who has been legally adopted in this state or another state or country.

(3) "Adoption" means the act of creating the legal relationship of parent and child between a person and a child who is not the biological child of that person. The term does not include the act of establishing the legal relationship of parent and child between a man and a child through proof of paternity or voluntary legitimation proceedings.

(4) "Adoption agency" means a person, other than a natural parent or guardian of a child, who plans for the placement of or places a child in the home of a prospective adoptive parent.

(5) "Adoptive parent" means an adult who is a parent of an adoptee through a legal process of adoption.

(6) "Alleged father" means a man who is not deemed by law to be or who has not been adjudicated to be the biological father of an adoptee and who claims or is alleged to be the adoptee's biological father.

(7) "Authorized agency" means a public agency authorized to care for or to place children for adoption or a private entity approved for that purpose by the department through a license, certification, or other means. The term includes a licensed child-placing agency or a previously licensed child-placing agency that has ceased operations and has transferred its adoption records to the bureau or an agency authorized by the department to place children for adoption and a licensed child-placing agency that has been acquired by, merged with, or otherwise succeeded by an agency authorized by the department to place children for adoption.

(8) "Biological parent" means a man or woman who is the father or mother of genetic origin of a child.

(9) "Biological siblings" means persons who share a common birth parent.

(10) "Birth parent" means:

(A) the biological mother of an adoptee;

(B) the man adjudicated or presumed under Chapter 151 *[Rights and Duties in Parent–Child Relationship]* to be the biological father of an adoptee; and

(C) a man who has signed a consent to adoption, affidavit of relinquishment, affidavit of waiver of interest in child, or other written instrument releasing the adoptee for adoption, unless the consent, affidavit, or other instrument includes a sworn refusal to admit or a denial of paternity. The term includes a birth mother and birth father but does not include a person adjudicated by a court of competent jurisdiction as not being the biological parent of an adoptee.

(11) "Central registry" means the mutual consent voluntary adoption registry established and maintained by the bureau under this subchapter.

(12) "Department" means the Department of Protective and Regulatory Services.

(13) "Registry" means a mutual consent voluntary adoption registry established under this subchapter.

(14) "Bureau" means the bureau of vital statistics.

> ***Editors' Note:*** *Subsection 10(B) above contains an incorrect reference to chapter 151 regarding presumptions of paternity. Those provisions are now found in the Uniform Parentage Act, § 160.204.*

§ 162.403. Establishment of Voluntary Adoption Registries.

(a) The bureau shall establish and maintain a mutual consent voluntary adoption registry.

(b) Except as provided by Subsection (c), an agency authorized by the department to place children for adoption and an association comprised exclusively of those agencies may establish a mutual consent voluntary adoption registry. An agency may contract with any other agency authorized by the department to place children for adoption or with an association comprised exclusively of those agencies to perform registry services on its behalf.

(c) An authorized agency that did not directly or by contract provide registry services as required by this subchapter on January 1, 1984, may not provide its own registry service. The bureau shall operate through the central registry those services for agencies not permitted to provide a registry under this section.

§ 162.404. Requirement to Send Information to Central Registry.

An authorized agency that is permitted to provide a registry under this subchapter or that participates in a mutual consent voluntary adoption registry with an association of authorized agencies shall send to the central registry a duplicate of all information the registry maintains in the agency's registry or sends to the registry in which the agency participates.

§ 162.405. Determination of Appropriate Registry.

(a) The administrator of the central registry shall determine the appropriate registry to which an applicant is entitled to apply.

(b) On receiving an inquiry by an adoptee, birth parent, or sibling who has provided satisfactory proof of age and identity and paid all required inquiry fees, the administrator of the central registry shall review the information on file in the central index and consult with the administrators of other registries in the state to determine the identity of any appropriate registry through which the adoptee, birth parent, or sibling may register.

(c) Each administrator shall, not later than the 30th day after the date of receiving an inquiry from the administrator of the central registry, respond in writing to the inquiry that the registrant was not placed for adoption by an agency served by that registry or that the registrant was placed for adoption by an agency served by that registry. If the registrant was placed for adoption by an agency served by the registry, the administrator shall file a report with the administrator of the central registry including:

(1) the name of the adopted child as shown in the final adoption decree;

(2) the birth date of the adopted child;

(3) the docket number of the adoption suit;

(4) the identity of the court that granted the adoption;

(5) the date of the final adoption decree;

(6) the identity of the agency, if any, through which the adopted child was placed; and

(7) the identity, address, and telephone number of the registry through which the adopted child may register as an adoptee.

(d) After completing the investigation, the administrator of the central registry shall issue an official certificate stating:

(1) the identity of the registry through which the adoptee, birth parent, or biological sibling may apply for registration, if known; or

(2) if the administrator cannot make a conclusive determination, that the adoptee, birth parent, or biological sibling is entitled to apply for registration through the central registry.

§ 162.406. Registration Eligibility.

(a) An adoptee who is 18 years of age or older may apply to a registry for information about the adoptee's birth parents and biological siblings.

(b) A birth parent who is 18 years of age or older may apply to a registry for information about an adoptee who is a child by birth of the birth parent.

(c) An alleged father who is 18 years of age or older and who acknowledges paternity but is not, at the time of application, a birth father may register as a birth father but may not otherwise be recognized as a birth father for the purposes of this subchapter unless:

(1) the adoptee's birth mother in her application identifies him as the adoptee's biological father; and

(2) additional information concerning the adoptee obtained from other sources is not inconsistent with his claim of paternity.

(d) A biological sibling who is 18 years of age or older may apply to a registry for information about the person's adopted biological siblings.

(e) Only birth parents, adoptees, and biological siblings may apply for information through a registry.

(f) A person, including an authorized agency, may not apply for information through a registry as an agent, attorney, or representative of an adoptee, birth parent, or biological sibling.

§ 162.407. Registration.

(a) The administrator shall require each registration applicant to sign a written application.

(b) An adoptee adopted or placed through an authorized agency may register through the registry maintained by that agency or the registry to which the agency has delegated registry services or through the central registry maintained by the bureau.

(c) Birth parents and biological siblings shall register through:

(1) the registry of the authorized agency through which the adoptee was adopted or placed; or

(2) the central registry.

(d) The administrator may not accept an application for registration unless the applicant:

(1) provides proof of identity as provided by Section 162.408;

(2) establishes the applicant's eligibility to register; and

(3) pays all required registration fees.

(e) A registration remains in effect until the 99th anniversary of the date the registration is accepted unless a shorter period is specified by the applicant or the registration is withdrawn before that time.

(f) A registrant may withdraw the registrant's registration in writing without charge at any time.

(g) After a registration is withdrawn or expires, the registrant shall be treated as if the person has not previously registered.

(h) A completed registry application must be accepted or rejected before the 46th day after the date the application is received. If an application is rejected, the administrator shall provide the applicant with a written statement of the reason for the rejection.

§ 162.408. Proof of Identity.

The rules and minimum standards of the Texas Board of Health for the bureau must provide for proof of identity in order to facilitate the purposes of this subchapter and to protect the privacy rights of adoptees, adoptive parents, birth parents, biological siblings, and their families.

§ 162.409. Application.

(a) An application must contain:

(1) the name, address, and telephone number of the applicant;

(2) any other name or alias by which the applicant has been known;

(3) the age, date of birth, and place of birth of the applicant;

(4) the original name of the adoptee, if known;

(5) the adoptive name of the adoptee, if known;

(6) a statement that the applicant is willing to allow the applicant's identity to be disclosed to a registrant who is eligible to learn the applicant's identity;

(7) the name, address, and telephone number of the agency or other entity, organization, or person placing the adoptee for adoption, if known, or, if not known, a statement that the applicant does not know that information;

(8) an authorization to the administrator and the administrator's designees to inspect all vital statistics records, court records, and agency records, including confidential records, relating to the birth, adoption, marriage, and divorce of the applicant or to the birth and death of any child or sibling by birth or adoption of the applicant;

(9) the specific address to which the applicant wishes notice of a successful match to be mailed;

(10) a statement that the applicant either does or does not consent to disclosure of identifying information about the applicant after the applicant's death;

(11) a statement that the registration is to be effective for 99 years or for a stated shorter period selected by the applicant; and

(12) a statement that the adoptee applicant either does or does not desire to be informed that registry records indicate that the applicant has a biological sibling who has registered under this subchapter.

(b) The application may contain the applicant's social security number if the applicant, after being advised of the right not to supply the number, voluntarily furnishes it.

(c) The application of a birth parent must include:

(1) the original name and date of birth or approximate date of birth of each adoptee with respect to whom the parent is registering;

(2) the names of all other birth children, including maiden names, aliases, dates and places of birth, and names of the birth parents;

(3) each name known or thought by the applicant to have been used by the adoptee's other birth parent;

(4) the last known address of the adoptee's other birth parent; and

(5) other available information through which the other birth parent may be identified.

(d) The application of a biological sibling must include:

(1) a statement explaining the applicant's basis for believing that the applicant has one or more biological siblings;

(2) the names, including maiden and married names, and aliases of all the applicant's siblings by birth and adoption and their dates and places of birth, if known;

(3) the names of the applicant's legal parents;

(4) the names of the applicant's birth parents, if known; and

(5) any other information known to the applicant through which the existence and identity of the applicant's biological siblings can be confirmed.

(e) An application may also contain additional information through which the applicant's identity and eligibility to register may be ascertained.

(f) The administrator shall assist the applicant in filling out the application if the applicant is unable to complete the application without assistance, but the administrator may not furnish the applicant with any substantive information necessary to complete the application.

§ 162.410. [repealed]

§ 162.411. Fees.

(a) The costs of establishing, operating, and maintaining a registry may be recovered in whole or in part through users' fees charged to applicants and registrants.

(b) Each registry shall establish a schedule of fees for services provided by the registry. The fees shall be reasonably related to the direct and indirect costs of establishing, operating, and maintaining the registry.

(c) A fee may not be charged for withdrawing a registration.

(d) The fees collected by the bureau shall be deposited in a special fund in the general revenue fund. Funds in the special fund may be appropriated only for the administration of the central registry.

(e) The administrator may waive users' fees in whole or in part if the applicant provides satisfactory proof of financial inability to pay the fees.

§ 162.412. Supplemental Information.

(a) A registrant may amend the registrant's registration and submit additional information to the administrator. A registrant shall notify the administrator of any change in the registrant's name or address that occurs after acceptance of the application.

(b) The administrator does not have a duty to search for a registrant who fails to register a change of name or address.

§ 162.413. Counseling.

The applicant must participate in counseling for not less than one hour with a social worker or mental health professional with expertise in postadoption counseling after the administrator has accepted the application for registration and before the release of confidential information.

§ 162.414. Matching Procedures.

(a) The administrator shall process each registration in an attempt to match the adoptee and the adoptee's birth parents or the adoptee and the adoptee's biological siblings.

(b) The administrator shall determine that there is a match if the adult adoptee and the birth mother or the birth father have registered or if a biological sibling has registered.

(c) To establish or corroborate a match, the administrator shall request confirmation of a possible match from the bureau. If the agency operating the registry has in its own records sufficient information through which the match may be confirmed, the administrator may, but is not required to, request confirmation from the bureau. The bureau may confirm or deny the match without breaching the duty of confidentiality to the adoptee, adoptive parents, birth parents, or biological siblings and without a court order.

(d) To establish a match, the administrator may also request confirmation of a possible match from the agency, if any, that has possession of records concerning the adoption of an adoptee or from the court that granted the adoption, the hospital where the adoptee or any biological sibling was born, the physician who delivered the adoptee or biological sibling, or any other person who has knowledge of the relevant facts. The agency, court, hospital, physician, or person with knowledge may confirm or deny the match without breaching any duty of confidentiality to the adoptee, adoptive parents, birth parents, or biological siblings.

(e) If a match is denied by a source contacted under Subsection (d), the administrator shall make a full and complete investigation into the reliability of the denial. If the match is corroborated by other reliable sources and the administrator is satisfied that the denial is erroneous, the administrator may make disclosures but shall report to the adoptee, birth parents, and biological siblings involved that the match was not confirmed by all information sources.

§ 162.415. [repealed]

§ 162.416. Disclosure of Identifying Information.

(a) When a match has been made and confirmed to the administrator's satisfaction, the administrator shall mail to each registrant, at the registrant's last known address, by fax or registered or certified mail, return receipt requested, delivery restricted to addressee only, a written notice:

(1) informing the registrant that a match has been made and confirmed;

(2) reminding the registrant that the registrant may withdraw the registration before disclosures are made, if desired; and

(3) notifying the registrant that before any identifying disclosures are made, the registrant must:

(A) sign a written consent to disclosure that allows the disclosure of identifying information about the other registrants to the registrant and allows the disclosure of identifying information about the registrant to other registrants;

(B) participate in counseling for not less than one hour with a social worker or mental health professional who has expertise in postadoption counseling; and

(C) provide the administrator with written certification that the counseling required under Subdivision (B) has been completed.

(b) Identifying information about a registrant shall be released without the registrant's having consented after the match to disclosure if the registrant is dead, the registrant's registration was valid at the time of death, and the registrant had in writing specifically authorized the postdeath disclosure in the registrant's application or in a supplemental statement filed with the administrator.

(c) Identifying information about a deceased birth parent may not be released until each surviving child of the deceased birth parent is an adult or until each child's surviving parent, guardian, managing conservator, or legal custodian consents in writing to the disclosure.

(d) The administrator shall prepare and release written disclosure statements identifying information about each of the registrants if the registrants complied with Subsection (a) and, before the 60th day after the date notification of match was mailed, the registrant or registrants have not withdrawn their registrations.

(e) If the administrator establishes that a match cannot be made because of the death of an adoptee, birth parent, or biological sibling, the administrator shall promptly notify the affected registrant. The administrator shall disclose the reason why a match cannot be made and may disclose nonidentifying information concerning the circumstances of the person's death.

§ 162.417, [repealed]

§ 162.418. [repealed]

§ 162.419. Registry Records Confidential.

(a) All applications, registrations, records, and other information submitted to, obtained by, or otherwise acquired by a registry are confidential and may not be disclosed to any person or entity except in the manner authorized by this subchapter.

(b) Information acquired by a registry may not be disclosed under freedom of information or sunshine legislation, rules, or practice.

(c) A person may not file or prosecute a class action litigation to force a registry to disclose identifying information.

§ 162.420. Rulemaking.

(a) The Texas Board of Health shall make rules and adopt minimum standards for the bureau to:

(1) administer the provisions of this subchapter; and

(2) ensure that each registry respects the right to privacy and confidentiality of an adoptee, birth parent, and biological sibling who does not desire to disclose the person's identity.

(b) The bureau shall conduct a comprehensive review of all rules and standards adopted under this subchapter not less than every six years.

(c) In order to provide the administrators an opportunity to review proposed rules and standards and send written suggestions to the Texas Board of Health, the board shall, before adopting rules and minimum standards, send a copy of the proposed rules and standards not less than 60 days before the date they take effect to:

(1) the administrator of each registry established under this subchapter; and

(2) the administrator of each agency authorized by the department to place children for adoption.

§ 162.421. Prohibited Acts; Criminal Penalties.

(a) This subchapter does not prevent the bureau from making known to the public, by appropriate means, the existence of voluntary adoption registries.

(b) Information received by or in connection with the operation of a registry may not be stored in a data bank used for any purpose other than operation of the registry.

(c) A person commits an offense if the person knowingly or recklessly discloses information from a registry application, registration, record, or other information submitted to, obtained by, or otherwise acquired by a registry in violation of this subchapter. This subsection may not be construed to penalize the disclosure of information from adoption agency records. An offense under this subsection is a felony of the second degree.

(d) A person commits an offense if the person with criminal negligence causes or permits the disclosure of information from a registry application, registration, record, or other information submitted to, obtained by, or otherwise acquired by a registry in violation of this subchapter. This subsection may not be construed to penalize the disclosure of information from adoption agency records. An offense under this subsection is a Class A misdemeanor.

(e) A person commits an offense if the person impersonates an adoptee, birth parent, or biological sibling with the intent to secure confidential information from a registry established under this subchapter. An offense under this subsection is a felony of the second degree.

(f) A person commits an offense if the person impersonates an administrator, agent, or employee of a registry with the intent to secure confidential information from a registry established under this subchapter. An offense under this subsection is a felony of the second degree.

(g) A person commits an offense if the person, with intent to deceive and with knowledge of the statement's meaning, makes a false statement under oath in connection with the operation of a registry. An offense under this subsection is a felony of the third degree.

§ 162.422. Immunity From Liability.

(a) The bureau or authorized agency establishing or operating a registry is not liable to any person for obtaining or disclosing identifying information about a birth parent, adoptee, or biological sibling within the scope of this subchapter and under its provisions.

(b) An employee or agent of the bureau or of an authorized agency establishing or operating a registry under this subchapter is not liable to any person for obtaining or disclosing identifying information about a birth parent, adoptee, or biological sibling within the scope of this subchapter and under its provisions.

(c) A person or entity furnishing information to the administrator or an employee or agent of a registry is not liable to any person for disclosing information about a birth parent, adoptee, or biological sibling within the scope of this subchapter and under its provisions.

(d) A person or entity is not immune from liability for performing an act prohibited by Section 162.421.

Subchapter F. Adoption of an Adult

§ 162.501. Adoption of Adult.

The court may grant the petition of an adult residing in this state to adopt another adult according to this subchapter.

Comment

An adoption of one adult by another is almost invariably intended to affect inheritance rights. The only duty of the court is to confirm that all adults involved have agreed to the adoption. The adult adoption process is now used by same-sex couples to cross-adopt each other and thereby give standing to a partner if the other partner is a parent of a child.

Leading Cases

Lehman v. Corpus Christi Nat'l Bank, 668 S.W.2d 687 (Tex. 1984) (adult adoptees have same inheritance rights as child adoptees)

Hagman v. Hagman, 886 S.W.2d 398 (Tex. App.—Dallas 1994, writ denied) (person adopted as an adult qualifies as "bodily issue" under will)

---

§ 162.502. Jurisdiction.

The petitioner shall file a suit to adopt an adult in the district court or a statutory county court granted jurisdiction in family law cases and proceedings by Chapter 25, Government Code, in the county of the petitioner's residence.

§ 162.503. Requirements of Petition.

(a) A petition to adopt an adult shall be entitled "In the Interest of __________, An Adult."

(b) If the petitioner is married, both spouses must join in the petition for adoption.

§ 162.504. Consent.

A court may not grant an adoption unless the adult consents in writing to be adopted by the petitioner.

§ 162.505. Attendance Required.

The petitioner and the adult to be adopted must attend the hearing. For good cause shown, the court may waive this requirement, by written order, if the petitioner or adult to be adopted is unable to attend.

§ 162.506. Adoption Order.

(a) The court shall grant the adoption if the court finds that the requirements for adoption of an adult are met.

(b) Notwithstanding that both spouses have joined in a petition for the adoption of an adult as required by Section 162.503(b), the court may grant the adoption of the adult to both spouses or, on request of the spouses, to only one spouse.

§ 162.507. Effect of Adoption.

(a) The adopted adult is the son or daughter of the adoptive parents for all purposes.

(b) The adopted adult is entitled to inherit from and through the adopted adult's adoptive parents as though the adopted adult were the biological child of the adoptive parents.

(c) The adopted adult retains the right to inherit from the adult's biological parents. However, a biological parent may not inherit from or through an adopted adult.

Subchapter G. Miscellaneous Provisions

§ 162.601. Incentives for Licensed Child-Placing Agencies.

(a) Subject to the availability of funds, the Department of Protective and Regulatory Services shall pay, in addition to any other amounts due, a monetary incentive to a licensed child-placing agency for the completion of an adoption:

(1) of a child, as defined by Section 162.301, receiving or entitled to receive foster care at department expense; and

(2) arranged with the assistance of the agency.

(b) The incentive may not exceed 25 percent of the amount the department would have spent to provide one year of foster care for the child, determined according to the child's level of care at the time the adoption is completed.

(c) For purposes of this section, an adoption is completed on the date on which the court issues the adoption order.

§ 162.602. Documentation to Accompany Petition for Adoption or Annulment or Revocation of Adoption.

At the time a petition for adoption or annulment or revocation of adoption is filed, the petitioner shall also file completed documentation that may be used by the clerk of the court, at the time the petition is granted, to comply with Section 192.009, Health and Safety Code, and Section 108.003.

History: Enacted by 78th Legis., Reg. Sess. (2003), H.B. 2886, eff. Sept. 1, 2003, and "applies only to a certificate or report that the bureau of vital statistics of the Texas Department of Health determines requires correction on or after that date."

Subtitle C. Judicial Resources and Services

★★★

Chapter 201. Associate Judge

Subchapter A. Associate Judge

Subchapter B. Associate Judge for Title IV–D Cases

Subchapter C. Associate Judge for Child Protection Cases

Editors' Note: *This chapter contains guest commentary by: Charles G. Childress, Children's Rights Clinic, University of Texas Law School, and former Chief Attorney, Field Operations, Legal Division, Texas Department of Protective and Regulatory Services; Alicia Gray Key, Director, Office of Court Administration, and H. Patrick Sullivan, Director of Federal Policy Analysis, Child Support Division, Office of the Attorney General of Texas; and J. Andrew Hathcock, Associate Judge, Child Protection Court of Central Texas; respectively identified as (C.G.C., A.G.K. & H.P.S., or J.A.H.).*

Subchapter A. Associate Judge

Introductory Comment

As the population of Texas exploded over the last two decades of the 20th Century, the legislature did not adequately respond to increasing demand vis-à-vis the creation of new district courts or provision for additional county courts-at-law to exercise family law jurisdiction. Instead, the legislature enacted statutes that authorized counties to employ associate judges to assist with an ever expanding family law caseload. The elected judges were given both appointment authority and the duty of supervision. What began as a simple program of adding a judge or two to assist in crowded metropolitan counties has grown exponentially into a comprehensive, statewide judicial system with three separate categories of associate judges.

Interestingly, the three types of associate judges have similar, but not identical powers to decide cases that come before them. For example, general jurisdiction associate judges (Subchapter A) may render temporary orders and agreed or default orders but all other orders recommended and signed by an associate judge must be ratified by the referring court. An associate judge for child protection cases (Subchapter C) may render and sign any order except a final order after a trial on the merits. Further, a final order recommended by an associate judge takes effect without ratification by the referring court if a *de novo* appeal is not requested. Finally, very few of the actions of associate judges handling Title IV–D child support cases (Subchapter B, formerly known as a child support masters) require ratification by a district judge.

§ 201.001. Appointment.

(a) A judge of a court having jurisdiction of a suit under this title or Title 1 or 4 may appoint a full-time or part-time associate judge to perform the duties authorized by this chapter if the commissioners court of a county in which the court has jurisdiction authorizes the employment of an associate judge.

(b) If a court has jurisdiction in more than one county, an associate judge appointed by that court may serve only in a county in which the commissioners court has authorized the associate judge's appointment.

(c) If more than one court in a county has jurisdiction of a suit under this title or Title 1 or 4 the commissioners court may authorize the appointment of an associate judge for each court or may authorize one or more associate judges to share service with two or more courts.

(d) If an associate judge serves more than one court, the associate judge's appointment must be made with the unanimous approval of all the judges under whom the associate judge serves.

(e) This section does not apply to an associate judge appointed under Subchapter B or C.

§ 201.002. Qualifications.

To be eligible for appointment as an associate judge, a person must meet the requirements and qualifications to serve as a judge of the court or courts for which the associate judge is appointed.

§ 201.003. Compensation.

(a) An associate judge shall be paid a salary determined by the commissioners court of the county in which the associate judge serves.

(b) If an associate judge serves in more than one county, the associate judge shall be paid a salary as determined by agreement of the commissioners courts of the counties in which the associate judge serves.

(c) The associate judge's salary is paid from the county fund available for payment of officers' salaries.

(d) This section does not apply to an associate judge appointed under Subchapter B or C.

§ 201.004. Termination of Associate Judge.

(a) An associate judge who serves a single court serves at the will of the judge of that court.

(b) The employment of an associate judge who serves more than two courts may only be terminated by a majority vote of all the judges of the courts which the associate judge serves.

(c) The employment of an associate judge who serves two courts may be terminated by either of the judges of the courts which the associate judge serves.

(d) This section does not apply to an associate judge appointed under Subchapter B or C.

§ 201.005. Cases That May Be Referred.

(a) Except as provided by this section, a judge of a court may refer to an associate judge any aspect of a suit over which the court has jurisdiction under this title or Title 1 or 4 including any matter ancillary to the suit.

(b) Unless a party files a written objection to the associate judge hearing a trial on the merits, the judge may refer the trial to the associate judge. A trial on the merits is any final adjudication from which an appeal may be taken to a court of appeals.

(c) A party must file an objection to an associate judge hearing a trial on the merits or presiding at a jury trial not later than the 10th day after the date the party receives notice that the associate judge will hear the trial. If an objection is filed, the referring court shall hear the trial on the merits or preside at a jury trial.

(d) The requirements of Subsections (b) and (c) shall apply whenever a judge has authority to refer the trial of a suit under this title, Title 1, or Title 4 to an associate judge, master, or other assistant judge regardless of whether the assistant judge is appointed under this subchapter.

Comment

An associate judge may preside at a jury trial, including a trial for termination of parental rights, unless a party objects or the referring court determines that the associate judge should not handle the case. *(C.G.C.)*

---

§ 201.006. Order of Referral.

(a) In referring a case to an associate judge, the judge of the referring court shall render:

(1) an individual order of referral; or

(2) a general order of referral specifying the class and type of cases to be heard by the associate judge.

(b) The order of referral may limit the power or duties of an associate judge.

§ 201.007. Powers of Associate Judge.

(a) Except as limited by an order of referral, an associate judge may:

(1) conduct a hearing;

(2) hear evidence;

(3) compel production of relevant evidence;

(4) rule on the admissibility of evidence;

(5) issue a summons for the appearance of witnesses;

(6) examine a witness;

(7) swear a witness for a hearing;

(8) make findings of fact on evidence;

(9) formulate conclusions of law;

(10) recommend an order to be rendered in a case;

(11) regulate all proceedings in a hearing before the associate judge;

(12) order the attachment of a witness or party who fails to obey a subpoena;

(13) order the detention of a witness or party found guilty of contempt, pending approval by the referring court as provided by Section 201.013;

(14) render and sign:

(A) a final order agreed to in writing as to both form and substance by all parties; or

(B) a final default order; and

(15) take action as necessary and proper for the efficient performance of the associate judge's duties.

(b) An associate judge may, in the interest of justice, refer a case back to the referring court regardless of whether a timely objection to the associate judge hearing the trial on the merits or presiding at a jury trial has been made by any party.

(c) An agreed order or a default order rendered and signed by an associate judge under Subsection (a) constitutes an order of the referring court.

Comment

The legislature has conferred broad powers on associate judges. Subsection (b) permits the associate judge to refer a case back to the presiding court "in the interest of justice" even if no party objects. For example, if it is clear that an appeal to the referring court is inevitable no matter how the associate judge may rule, justice, or at least judicial economy, may best be served by having the case tried by the district judge.

An agreed order or a default order signed by the associate judge will no longer require the approval of the referring court, but this provision combined with a change to § 201.016, *infra*, makes the appellate timetable start from the date the agreed order or default order is signed by the associate judge.

The legislature added to the powers of an associate judge by granting authority to render final judgment on agreed orders and defaults in subsection (a)(14). Normally the findings and recommendations of an associate judge become an order of the referring court only when the referring court signs an order conforming to the associate judge's report. The 2003 amendments eliminated that fundamentally unnecessary step with respect to agreed and default orders, thereby providing some relief to the workload of the referring court and expediting the enforcement of these specific orders.

Presumably, a de novo appeal to the presiding judge is still available if filed within three days. However, this section, combined with the change to § 201.016(c), *infra*, establishes that the date an agreed order or default order is signed by the associate judge starts the appellate timetables running. Any other order recommended and signed by an associate judge must be ratified by the referring court. *See* § 201.013(b), *infra*. Compare with the powers of an associate judge for child protection cases, who may render and sign any order except a final order after a trial on the merits. *See* § 201.204, *infra*. *(C.G.C.; J.A.H.; A.G.K. & H.P.S.)*

Leading Case

In re A.J.L., 108 S.W.3d 414 (Tex. App.—Fort Worth 2003, pet. denied) (former stepfather's standing to pursue modification of biological parents' custody order within power of associate judge to decide)

---

§ 201.008. Attendance of Bailiff.

A bailiff may attend a hearing by an associate judge if directed by the referring court.

§ 201.009. Court Reporter.

(a) A court reporter may be provided during a hearing held by an associate judge appointed under this chapter. A court reporter is required to be provided when the associate judge presides over a jury trial or a final termination hearing.

(b) A party, the associate judge, or the referring court may provide for a reporter during the hearing, if one is not otherwise provided.

(c) The record may be preserved in the absence of a court reporter by any other means approved by the associate judge.

(d) The referring court or associate judge may tax the expense of preserving the record under Subsection (c) as costs.

(e) On appeal of the associate judge's report or proposed order, the referring court may consider testimony or other evidence in the record, if the record is taken by a court reporter, in addition to witnesses or other matters presented under Section 201.015.

Comment

If the referring court and the associate judge exercise the authority for the associate judge to preside at termination or jury trials, a court reporter must be provided for the trial. Although appeal to the referring court is still available with the "de novo" standard of review, the referring court may consider the record made at the hearing before the associate judge, along with any additional evidence presented by the parties, as evidence to support the proposed judgment. *(C.G.C.)*

---

§ 201.010. Witness.

(a) A witness appearing before an associate judge is subject to the penalties for perjury provided by law.

(b) A referring court may fine or imprison a witness who:

(1) failed to appear before an associate judge after being summoned; or

(2) improperly refused to answer questions if the refusal has been certified to the court by the associate judge.

§ 201.011. Report.

(a) The associate judge's report may contain the associate judge's findings, conclusions, or recommendations, including a proposed order. The associate judge's report must be in writing in the form directed by the referring court. The form may be a notation on the referring court's docket sheet.

(b) After a hearing, the associate judge shall provide the parties participating in the hearing notice of the substance of the associate judge's report. The notice may be given in the form of a proposed order.

(c) Notice may be given to the parties:

(1) in open court, by an oral statement or a copy of the associate judge's written report, including any proposed order;

(2) by certified mail, return receipt requested; or

(3) by facsimile transmission.

(d) The associate judge shall certify the date of mailing of notice by certified mail or the date of the facsimile transmission. There is a rebuttable presumption that notice is received on the date stated on:

(1) the signed return receipt, if notice was provided by certified mail; or

(2) the confirmation page produced by the facsimile machine, if notice was provided by facsimile transmission.

(e) After a hearing conducted by an associate judge, the associate judge shall send the associate judge's signed and dated report, including any proposed order, and all other papers relating to the case to the referring court.

Comment

Associate judges routinely provide a proposed order to parties, rather than a separate "recommendation." This approach is an acceptable method of providing the necessary "report" to the parties and the referring court. After September 1, 2003, certified mail will not be presumed delivered in three days. Unanswered is how to deal with individuals that simply refuse to sign for the mail. *(C.G.C.)*

Leading Case

Robles v. Robles, 965 S.W.2d 605 (Tex. App.—Houston [1st Dist.] 1998, no writ) (associate judge adequately provided parties with notice of substance of report)

---

§ 201.012. Notice of Right to Appeal.

(a) Notice of the right of appeal to the judge of the referring court shall be given to all parties.

(b) The notice may be given:

(1) by oral statement in open court;

(2) by posting inside or outside the courtroom of the referring court; or

(3) as otherwise directed by the referring court.

§ 201.013. Order of Court.

(a) Pending appeal of the associate judge's report, including any proposed order, to the referring court, the decisions and recommendations of the associate judge are in full force and effect and are enforceable as an order of the referring court, except for orders providing for the appointment of a receiver.

(b) Except as provided by Section 201.007(c), if an appeal to the referring court is not filed or the right to an appeal to the referring court is waived, the findings and recommendations of the associate judge become the order of the referring court only on the referring court's signing an order conforming to the associate judge's report.

(c) An order by an associate judge for the temporary detention or incarceration of a witness or party shall be presented to the referring court on the day the witness or party is detained or incarcerated. The referring court, without prejudice to the right of appeal provided by Section 201.015, may approve the temporary detention or incarceration or may order the release of the party or witness, with or without bond, pending appeal. If the referring court is not immediately available, the associate judge may order the release of the party or witness, with or without bond, pending appeal or may continue the person's detention or incarceration for not more than 72 hours.

Comment

An agreed order or a default judgment signed by the associate judge may "become the order of the referring court" without the signature of the referring court under section

201.007(c). The language in Subsection (c) permits temporary detention, or release on bond, of a person found guilty of contempt of court pending an appeal to the referring court. Before adoption of this provision, some associate judges ordered a contemnor to report for jail on a specific date after the referring court would have time to sign the commitment order. Not surprisingly, many of those so ordered failed to return. Other associate judges immediately transferred the contemnor to the referring court for "approval" of the order, thus denying the contemnor three days to consider whether to request a de novo appeal. *(C.G.C.)*

Leading Case

Kennedy v. Kennedy, 125 S.W.3d 14 (Tex. App.—Austin, 2003, no pet.) (trial court could not adopt and approve entirety of associate judge's order before hearing former wife's de novo appeal—conditional approval required within 72 hours only to continue incarceration)

---

§ 201.014. Judicial Action on Associate Judge's Report.

Unless a party files a written notice of appeal, the referring court may:

(1) adopt, modify, or reject the associate judge's report, including any proposed order;

(2) hear further evidence; or

(3) recommit the matter to the associate judge for further proceedings.

§ 201.015. Appeal to Referring Court.

(a) A party may appeal an associate judge's report by filing notice of appeal not later than the third day after the date the party receives notice of the substance of the associate judge's report as provided by Section 201.011.

(b) An appeal to the referring court must be in writing specifying the findings and conclusions of the associate judge to which the party objects. The appeal is limited to the specified findings and conclusions.

(c) On appeal to the referring court, the parties may present witnesses as in a hearing de novo on the issues raised in the appeal. The court may also consider the record from the hearing before the associate judge, including the charge to and verdict returned by a jury, if the record was taken by a court reporter.

(d) Notice of an appeal to the referring court shall be given to the opposing attorney under Rule 21a, Texas Rules of Civil Procedure.

(e) If an appeal to the referring court is filed by a party, any other party may file an appeal to the referring court not later than the seventh day after the date the initial appeal was filed.

(f) The referring court, after notice to the parties, shall hold a hearing on all appeals not later than the 30th day after the date on which the initial appeal was filed with the referring court.

(g) Before the start of a hearing by an associate judge, the parties may waive the right of appeal to the referring court in writing or on the record.

(h) Denial of an appeal under this section or waiver of the right to appeal to the referring court does not affect the right of a party to file a motion for new trial, motion for judgment notwithstanding the verdict, or other post-trial motion.

(i) A party may not demand a second jury on appeal of an associate judge's report, including any proposed order, resulting from a jury trial.

Comment

Any party may appeal the associate judge's order by filing a notice of appeal within three days after receiving notice of the order or of the substance of the recommendation. The hearing before the presiding judge is de novo, but if a court reporter's record is available that record and any jury charge and verdict may be considered as part of the de novo review. A party may file a motion for new trial or other post-trial motions when an associate judge has presided, but if the presiding judge's signature is not required because the order was agreed or by default, the time to file such motions or a notice of appeal runs from the date the order was signed by the associate judge. *See* § 201.016, *infra*.

Subsection (i) prohibits parties from requesting a second jury on appeal from an associate judge's order based on a jury verdict. *(C.G.C.)*

Leading Cases

State ex rel. Latty v. Owens, 907 S.W.2d 484 (Tex. 1995) (although de novo hearing not held as required, district court's inadvertent adoption of master's recommendation is final appealable order)

In re D.J.M., 114 S.W.3d 637 (Tex. App.—Fort Worth 2003, pet. denied) (waiving record before associate judge means record absent of needed information for sufficiency of evidence review)

In re N.R.C., 94 S.W.3d 799 (Tex. App.—Houston [14th Dist.] 2002, pet. denied) (appeal of associate judge's ruling to presiding judge not required to preserve appeal to court of appeals)

In re E.M., 54 S.W.3d 849 (Tex. App.—Corpus Christi 2001, no pet.) (to be entitled to a de novo hearing on appeal of an associate judge's recommendations to the referring court, a party must timely file a written notice of appeal containing the associate judge's findings and conclusions to which the party objects)

Fountain v. Knebel, 45 S.W.3d 736 (Tex. App.—Dallas 2001, no pet.) (requiring referring court to hold hearing on appeal within thirty days designed to require prompt resolution of appeal from associate judge's rulings—right is to de novo hearing, not to mediation by trial judge)

Attorney General v. Orr, 989 S.W.2d 464 (Tex. App.—Austin 1999, no pet.) (notice of appeal requires de novo hearing by district court—which is new and independent action with all attributes of original civil action)

Harrell v. Harrell, 986 S.W.2d 629 (Tex. App.—El Paso 1998, no pet.) (requirement of de novo hearing within 30 days not jurisdictional—enforceable against referring court only)

Peacock v. Humble, 933 S.W.2d 341 (Tex. App.—Austin 1996, no writ) (to count 3–day period for appeal, include Saturday & Sunday unless Sunday is the third day; Tex. R. Civ. P. 4 inapplicable)

---

§ 201.016. Appellate Review.

(a) Failure to appeal to the referring court, by waiver or otherwise, the approval by the referring court of an associate judge's report does not deprive a party of the right to appeal to or request other relief from a court of appeals or the supreme court.

(b) Except as provided by Subsection (c), the date an order or judgment by the referring court is signed is the controlling date for the purposes of appeal to or request for other relief from a court of appeals or the supreme court.

(c) The date an agreed order or a default order is signed by an associate judge is the controlling date for the purpose of an appeal to, or a request for other relief relating to the order from, a court of appeals or the supreme court.

Comment

Because an agreed order or default order rendered and signed by an associate judge constitutes an order of the referring court (§ 201.007, *supra*), the date on which an associate judge signs such an order is the controlling date in an appeal to an appellate court (skipping the de novo step). *(A.G.K. & H.P.S.)*

Leading Cases

In re W.G.S., 2002 WL 31953452 (Tex. App.—Corpus Christi 2002) (failure to appeal to referring court resulting in approval of associate judge's report does not deprive party of right to appeal)

In re N.R.C., 94 S.W.3d 799 (Tex. App.—Houston [14th Dist.] 2002, no pet.) (failure to appeal associate judge's sanctions to trial court doesn't preclude appeal to Court of Appeals)

---

§ 201.017. Immunity.

An associate judge appointed under this subchapter has the judicial immunity of a district judge. All existing immunity granted an associate judge by law, express or implied, continues in full force and effect.

§ 201.018. Visiting Associate Judge.

(a) If an associate judge appointed under this subchapter is temporarily unable to perform the judge's official duties because of absence or illness, injury, or other disability, a judge of a court having jurisdiction of a suit under this title or Title 1 or 4 may appoint a visiting associate judge to perform the duties of the associate judge during the period of the associate judge's absence or disability if the commissioners court of a county in which the court has jurisdiction authorizes the employment of a visiting associate judge.

(b) To be eligible for appointment under this section, a person must have served as an associate judge for at least two years.

(c) Sections 201.001 through 201.017 apply to a visiting associate judge appointed under this section.

(d) This section does not apply to an associate judge appointed under Subchapter B.

Subchapter B. Associate Judge for Title IV–D Cases

Introductory Comment

Heretofore the corps of judicial officers who specialize in establishing, enforcing, and modifying child support orders were known as "child support masters." Effective Sept. 1, 2003, the legislature has remedied the psychological imbalance between these judges and other appointed judges by renaming the function as one performed by an "associate judge for Title IV–D cases." The intent of the change was to achieve uniformity of nomenclature in this chapter with respect to the judicial officers who hear cases upon referral from a court. The term "child support master" had been used in Texas family law since 1987 when the state instituted a system of child support masters in response to a federal mandate under the Family Support Act of 1986 that states use administrative or quasi-judicial process for expeditiously handing cases being enforced by their Title IV–D child support enforcement agencies. The use of "Master" was derived from the "Masters in Chancery" provided under Rule 171, Texas Rules of Civil Procedure who may be appointed "for good cause" by a court to conduct hearings, take evidence, and make a report of findings to the referring court "in exceptional cases."

The now "associate judges for Title IV–D cases" preside over all cases prosecuted by the Attorney General of Texas, as the state's designated Title IV–D agency (Chapter 231 *infra*). While in many ways child support masters resembled administrative hearing officers, they clearly belonged to the judicial branch of government. The child support A.J.'s, together with the "cluster-court" associate judges described in the following subchapter, are unique in Texas jurisprudence because: (1) their caseloads are extremely specialized; (2) they are appointed by the presiding judges of the administrative judicial regions; and, (3) they may be appointed to serve in more than one court. Although in many ways child support associate judges resemble administrative hearing officers, they clearly belong to the judicial branch of government. While in most respects the powers and duties of an associate judge specializing in child support mirror those of an associate judge with general family law jurisdiction as described in Subchapter A, significantly fewer actions taken by a child support associate judge require ratification by a referring court. *(A.G.K. & H.P.S.)*

CLE/Other Legal Publications

A plainly practical primer on IV–D practice. Steve A. Owen, 2002 Adv. Fam. L.

Representing clients in Title IV–D. Hon. Michael Sinha & Steven A. Owen, 2000 Adv. Fam. L.

Cross References

IV–D Child Support Enforcement. 42 U.S.C.A. § 651 *et seq.*, § 666(a)(2) (expedited processes); *see* 45 C.F.R. § 303.101

---

§ 201.101. Authority of Presiding Judge.

(a) The presiding judge of each administrative judicial region, after conferring with the judges of courts in the region having jurisdiction of Title IV–D cases, shall determine which courts require the appointment of a full-time or part-time associate judge to complete each Title IV–D case within the time specified in this subchapter.

(b) The presiding judge may limit the appointment to a specified time period and may terminate an appointment at any time.

(c) An associate judge appointed under this subchapter may be appointed to serve more than one court. Two or more judges of administrative judicial regions may jointly appoint one or more associate judges to serve the regions.

(d) If the presiding judge determines that a court requires an associate judge for Title IV–D cases, the presiding judge shall appoint an associate judge for that purpose. Except as provided under Subsection (e), if an associate judge is appointed for a court under this subchapter, all Title IV–D cases shall be referred to the associate judge by a general order for each county issued by the judge of the court for which the associate judge is appointed, or, in the absence of that order, by a general order issued by the presiding judge who appointed the associate judge. Referral of Title IV–D cases may not be made for individual cases or case by case.

(e) If a county has entered into a contract with the Title IV–D agency under Section 231.0011, enforcement services may be directly provided by county personnel as provided under Section 231.0011(d), including judges and associate judges of the courts of the county.

Comment

Normally all IV–D cases are referred to the associate judge under a general order of the referring court. Subsection (e), however, carves out an exception for courts in those counties in which, by local rule and a contract with the Title IV–D agency, all new support orders are automatically subject to IV–D services unless the obligee in a case specifically declines the services. This exception enables judges to retain in their courts such cases as they choose, while turning the others over to the associate judge for Title IV–D cases. *(A.G.K. & H.P.S.)*

§ 201.102. Application of Law Governing Associate Judges.

(a) Subchapter A applies to an associate judge appointed under this subchapter, except that, to the extent of any conflict between this subchapter and Subchapter A, this subchapter prevails.

(b) An associate judge appointed under this subchapter may reside anywhere within the administrative judicial region in which the court to which the associate judge is appointed is located. An associate judge appointed to serve in two or more administrative judicial regions may reside anywhere within the regions.

§ 201.103. Designation of Host County.

(a) The presiding judges of the administrative judicial regions by majority vote shall determine the host county of an associate judge appointed under this subchapter.

(b) The host county shall provide an adequate courtroom and quarters, including furniture, necessary utilities, and telephone equipment and service, for the associate judge and other personnel assisting the associate judge.

(c) An associate judge is not required to reside in the host county.

§ 201.104. Powers of Associate Judge.

(a) On the motion of a party or the associate judge, an associate judge may refer a complex case back to the judge for final disposition after the associate judge has recommended temporary support.

(b) An associate judge may render and sign any order that is not a final order on the merits of the case.

(c) An associate judge may recommend to the referring court any order after a trial on the merits.

(d) Only the referring court may hear and render an order on a motion for post-judgment relief, including a motion for a new trial or to vacate, correct, or reform a judgment.

(e) Notwithstanding Subsection (d) and subject to Section 201.1042(g), an associate judge may hear and render an order on:

(1) a suit to modify or clarify an existing child support order;

(2) a motion to enforce a child support order or revoke a respondent's community supervision and suspension of commitment; or

(3) a respondent's compliance with the conditions provided in the associate judge's report for suspension of the respondent's commitment.

Comment

Subsection (b) provides that a pre-trial or temporary order rendered by the associate judge need not be ratified by the referring court. It is unclear whether a party has the right to appeal such an order to the referring court, because only "recommendations" may be appealed under § 201.1042, *infra*. Subsection (d) clarifies that only the referring court may hear and act on post-judgment motions for a new trial or to vacate, correct, or reform a judgment. This limitation, however, does not prevent an associate judge from hearing post-judgment motions for contempt or modification of final child support orders, as provided under subsection (e). *(A.G.K. & H.P.S.)*

---

§ 201.1041. Judicial Action on Associate Judge's Report.

(a) If an appeal to the referring court is not filed or the right to appeal is waived, a recommendation of the associate judge, other than a recommendation of enforcement by contempt or a recommendation of the immediate incarceration of a party, shall become an order of the referring court by operation of law without ratification by the referring court.

(b) An associate judge's report that recommends enforcement by contempt or the immediate incarceration of a party becomes an order of the referring court only if:

(1) the referring court signs an order adopting the associate judge's recommendation; and

(2) the order meets the requirements of Section 157.166.

(c) Except as provided by Subsection (b), the decisions and recommendations of the associate judge have full force and effect and are enforceable as an order of the referring court during an appeal of the associate judge's report to the referring court.

Comment

Most recommendations of the associate judge, including those to establish paternity, establish or modify support, or to reduce unpaid child support to judgment, may be appealed to the referring court. If not timely appealed, or if the right to appeal has been waived, such recommendations become enforceable court orders without the necessity of ratification by the referring court. An associate judge's recommendation of contempt or immediate enforcement, however, must be ratified by the referring court. *(A.G.K. & H.P.S.)*

---

§ 201.1042. Appeal to Referring Court.

(a) Except as provided by this section, Section 201.015 applies to an appeal of the associate judge's recommendations.

(b) The party appealing an associate judge's recommendation shall file notice with the referring court and the clerk of the court.

(c) A respondent who timely files an appeal of an associate judge's report recommending incarceration after a finding of contempt shall be brought before the referring court not later than the first working day after the date on which the respondent files the appeal. The referring court shall determine whether the respondent should be released on bond or whether the respondent's appearance in court at a designated time and place can be otherwise assured.

(d) If the respondent under Subsection (c) is released on bond or other security, the referring court shall condition the bond or other security on the respondent's promise to appear in court for a hearing on the appeal at a designated date, time, and place, and the referring court shall give the respondent notice of the hearing in open court. No other notice to the respondent is required.

(e) If the respondent under Subsection (c) is released without posting bond or security, the court shall set a hearing on the appeal at a designated date, time, and place and give the respondent notice of the hearing in open court. No other notice to the respondent is required.

(f) If the referring court is not satisfied that the respondent's appearance in court can be assured and the respondent remains incarcerated, a hearing on the appeal shall be held as soon as practicable, but not later than the fifth day after the date the respondent's notice of appeal was filed, unless the respondent and, if represented, the respondent's attorney waive the accelerated hearing.

(g) Until a hearing is held on a timely filed appeal under this section or the referring court has rendered an order on a timely filed motion for new trial or a motion to vacate, correct, or reform a judgment, an associate judge may not hold a hearing on the respondent's compliance with conditions in the associate judge's report for suspension of commitment or on a motion to revoke the respondent's community supervision and suspension of commitment.

Comment

The caption to this section does not describe the entirety of its contents. Subsections (a) and (b) are innocuous enough, merely providing for appeal and notice. But the remaining subsections are designed to implement the associate judge's recommendation for contempt and incarceration. Read together, subsections (c) and (f) rather clearly indicate that an associate judge may order a respondent to be held in custody until the next working day, at which time the respondent must be "brought before the referring court" for a hearing on whether he "should be released." *(C.G.C.)*

An obligor who is incarcerated by the associate judge cannot obtain immediate release by filing an appeal of the associate judge's recommendation. This procedure follows the § 157.105 release hearing that the court conducts after an obligor is arrested on a capias for failure to appear. Under subsection (g), the associate judge may not hold a hearing on a respondent's compliance with conditions in the associate judge's report for suspension of commitment or on a motion to revoke community supervision and suspension of commitment if a timely filed appeal of the associate judge's report is pending or if the referring court has rendered an order for a new trial or post-judgment relief. The intent is to achieve an orderly process and to avoid conflicting actions by the associate judge on the one hand and the referring court on the other. *(A.G.K. & H.P.S.)*

Leading Cases

Phagan v. Aleman, 29 S.W.3d 632 (Tex. App.—Houston [1st Dist.] 2000, no pet.) (appeal from child-support master's recommended order absolutely entitled to de novo hearing)

Attorney General v. Orr, 989 S.W.2d 464 (Tex. App.—Austin 1999, no pet.) (notice of appeal requires de novo hearing by district court—which is new and independent action with all attributes of original civil action)

§ 201.105. Compensation of Associate Judge.

(a) An associate judge appointed under this subchapter is entitled to a salary to be determined by a majority vote of the presiding judges of the administrative judicial regions. The salary may not exceed 90 percent of the salary paid to a district judge as set by the General Appropriations Act.

(b) The associate judge's salary shall be paid from county funds available for payment of officers' salaries or from funds available from the state and federal government as provided by this subchapter.

§ 201.106. Child Support Court Monitor and Other Personnel.

(a) The presiding judge of an administrative judicial region or the presiding judges of the administrative judicial regions, by majority vote, may appoint other personnel, including a child support court monitor for each associate judge appointed under this subchapter, as needed to implement and administer the provisions of this subchapter.

(b) The salaries of the personnel and court monitors shall be paid from county funds available for payment of officers' salaries or from funds available from the state and federal government as provided by this subchapter.

§ 201.1065. Duties of Child Support Court Monitor.

(a) A child support court monitor appointed under this subchapter shall monitor child support cases in which the obligor is placed on probation for failure to comply with the requirements of a child support order.

(b) In monitoring a child support case, a court monitor shall:

(1) conduct an intake assessment of the needs of an obligor that, if addressed, would enable the obligor to comply with a child support order;

(2) refer an obligor to employment services offered by the employment assistance program under Section 302.0035, Labor Code, if appropriate;

(3) provide mediation services or referrals to services, if appropriate;

(4) schedule periodic contacts with an obligor to assess compliance with the child support order and whether additional support services are required;

(5) monitor the amount and timeliness of child support payments owed and paid by an obligor; and

(6) if appropriate, recommend that the court:

(A) discharge an obligor from or modify the terms of the obligor's community supervision; or

(B) revoke an obligor's community supervision.

Comment

A 2003 amendment to this section significantly expanded the duties of the court monitor to include recommending, in appropriate cases, discharge from, or the modification of, the terms and conditions of community supervision or even revocation of community supervision. *(A.G.K. & H.P.S.)*

---

§ 201.1066. Supervision of Associate Judges.

The office of court administration shall assist the presiding judges in:

(1) monitoring the associate judges' compliance with job performance standards and federal and state laws and policies;

(2) addressing the training needs and resource requirements of the associate judges;

(3) conducting annual performance evaluations for the associate judges and other personnel appointed under this subchapter based on written personnel performance standards adopted by the presiding judges; and

(4) receiving, investigating, and resolving complaints about particular associate judges or the associate judge program under this subchapter based on a uniform process adopted by the presiding judges.

§ 201.107. State and Federal Funds.

(a) The office of court administration may contract with the Title IV–D agency for available state and federal funds under Title IV–D and may employ personnel needed to implement and administer this subchapter. An associate judge, a court monitor for each associate judge, and other personnel appointed under this subchapter are state employees for all purposes, including accrual of leave time, insurance benefits, retirement benefits, and travel regulations.

(b) The presiding judges of the administrative judicial regions, state agencies, and counties may contract with the Title IV–D agency for available federal funds under Title IV–D to reimburse costs and salaries associated with associate judges, court monitors, and personnel appointed under this subchapter and may also use available state funds and public or private grants.

(c) The presiding judges and the Title IV–D agency shall act and are authorized to take any action necessary to maximize the amount of federal funds available under the Title IV–D program.

§ 201.108. [repealed]

§ 201.1085. [repealed]

§ 201.109. [repealed]

§ 201.110. Time for Disposition of Title IV–D Cases.

(a) Title IV–D cases must be completed from the time of successful service to the time of disposition within the following time:

(1) 75 percent within six months; and

(2) 90 percent within one year.

(b) Title IV–D cases shall be given priority over other cases.

(c) A clerk or judge may not restrict the number of Title IV–D cases that are filed or heard in the courts.

Comment

This section reflects the requirements of federal law for the expedited processing of Title IV–D cases, as provided by 42 U.S.C. 666(a)(2), 45 CFR 303.101). *(A.G.K. & H.P.S.)*

§ 201.111. Time to Act on Associate Judge's Report that Includes Finding of Contempt.

(a) Not later than the 10th day after the date an associate judge's report recommending a finding of contempt is filed, the referring court shall:

(1) adopt, approve, or reject the report;

(2) hear further evidence; or

(3) recommit the matter for further proceedings.

(b) The time limit in Subsection (a) does not apply if a party has filed a written notice of appeal to the referring court.

§ 201.112. Limitation on Law Practice by Certain Associate Judges.

A full-time associate judge appointed under this subchapter may not engage in the private practice of law.

§ 201.113. Visiting Associate Judge.

(a) If an associate judge appointed under this subchapter is temporarily unable to perform the associate judge's official duties because of absence resulting from family circumstances, illness, injury, disability, or military service, or if there is a vacancy in the position of associate judge, the presiding judge of the administrative judicial region in which the associate judge serves or the vacancy occurs may appoint a visiting associate judge for Title IV–D cases to perform the duties of the associate judge during the period the associate judge is unable to perform the associate judge's duties or until another associate judge is appointed to fill the vacancy.

(b) A person is not eligible for appointment under this section unless the person has served as a child support master or associate judge for at least two years before the date of appointment.

(c) A visiting associate judge appointed under this section is subject to each provision of this chapter that applies to an associate judge serving under a regular appointment under this subchapter. A visiting associate judge appointed under this section is entitled to compensation to be determined by a majority vote of the presiding judges of the administrative judicial regions through use of funds under this subchapter. A visiting associate judge is not considered to be a state employee for any purpose.

Subchapter C. Associate Judge for Child Protection Cases

Introductory Comment

This subchapter establishes a system parallel to the associate judges who specialize in Title IV–D child support cases; here the goal is to establish and fund associate judges to handle child protection cases filed by the Department of Protective and Regulatory Services, a.k.a. DPRS or CPS in its local guise. These courts were started with Federal grant funds through the Court Improvement Project. The pilot projects were called Cluster Courts because they clustered the child protection cases in several counties into one docket, and are called Specialized Foster Care Courts in the appropriations legislation. Tex. Code Crim. Proc. Ann. art. 56.54 permits the legislature to use money from the victims of crime fund to administer the associate judge program under this subchapter. The associate judges created under this subchapter are state employees appointed and supervised by the presiding judges of the administrative judicial regions (similar to the IV–D associate judges, *supra*). There are fifteen of these specialized courts serving 125 counties. Ten of the fifteen employ associate judges, and the other five use visiting judges. (*J.A.H.*)

---

§ 201.201. Authority of Presiding Judge.

(a) The presiding judge of each administrative judicial region, after conferring with the judges of courts in the region having family law jurisdiction and a child protection caseload, shall determine which courts require the appointment of a full-time or part-time associate judge to complete each case within the times specified in Chapters 262 and 263.

(b) The presiding judge may limit the appointment to a specified period and may terminate an appointment at any time.

(c) An associate judge appointed under this subchapter may be appointed to serve more than one court. Two or more judges of administrative judicial regions may jointly appoint one or more associate judges to serve the regions.

(d) If the presiding judge determines that a court requires an associate judge, the presiding judge shall appoint an associate judge. If an associate judge is appointed for a court, all child protection cases shall be referred to the associate judge by a general order for each county issued by the judge of the court for which the associate judge is appointed or, in the absence of that order, by a general order issued by the presiding judge who appointed the associate judge.

(e) This section does not limit the jurisdiction of a court to issue orders under Chapter 262 or 263.

§ 201.202. Application of Law Governing Associate Judges.

(a) Except as provided by this subchapter, Subchapter A applies to an associate judge appointed under this subchapter.

(b) An associate judge may reside anywhere in the administrative judicial region in which the court to which the associate judge is appointed is located. An associate judge appointed to serve in two or more administrative judicial regions may reside anywhere in the regions.

§ 201.203. Designation of Host County.

(a) Subject to the approval of the commissioners court of the proposed host county, the presiding judges of the administrative judicial regions by majority vote shall determine the host county of an associate judge appointed under this subchapter.

(b) The host county shall provide an adequate courtroom and quarters, including furniture, necessary utilities, and telephone equipment and service, for the associate judge and other personnel assisting the associate judge.

(c) An associate judge is not required to reside in the host county.

§ 201.204. General Powers of Associate Judge.

(a) On the motion of a party or the associate judge, an associate judge may refer a complex case back to the referring court for final disposition after recommending temporary orders for the protection of a child.

(b) An associate judge may render and sign any pretrial order.

(c) An associate judge may recommend to the referring court any order after a trial on the merits.

Comment

Until recently, associate judges did not have the power to render judgment. Associate judges for child protection cases may now render and sign any order except for an order after a trial on the merits, and may recommend any order after a trial on the merits. An order recommended by an associate judge takes effect without ratification by the referring court if a *de novo* appeal is not requested. *See* § 201.2041, below. This should simplify life in the rural areas served by associate judges for child protection cases in which a District Judge is not always readily available to countersign orders. (*J.A.H.*)

---

§ 201.2041. Judicial Action on Associate Judge's Report.

If an appeal to the referring court is not filed or the right to appeal is waived, a recommendation of the associate judge becomes an order of the referring court by operation of law without ratification by the referring court.

Comment

A final agreed or default order is effective for purposes of post-judgment motions and the appellate timetable on the date signed by the associate judge. *See* § 201.016(c)above. Temporary orders in a SCLS case become orders of the referring court by operation of law without ratification under this section. The statute is silent on exactly when the appellate timetable begins to run in a contested case in which the referring court's signature is not required. Despite the precedent of § 201.016 which starts the appellate clock on the associate judge's signature on an agreed or default order, the more logical time for that to occur in this situation may be at the expiration of the three-day de novo period. *See* §§ 201.007, 201.013. *(C.G.C.)*

---

§ 201.2042. Appeal to Referring Court.

(a) Except as provided by this section, Section 201.015 applies to an appeal of the associate judge's recommendations.

(b) The party appealing an associate judge's recommendation shall file notice with the referring court and the clerk of the court.

Comment

Section 201.015 requires that notice of appeal must be given to the opposing attorney, but does not specify that the notice must be filed with the referring court or the clerk. Now the notice must be filed with both the referring court and the clerk of the court, in CPS cases. Supposedly there are some things that go without saying; apparently this is not one of them. *(C.G.C.)*

§ 201.205. Compensation of Associate Judge.

(a) An associate judge appointed under this subchapter is entitled to a salary as determined by a majority vote of the presiding judges of the administrative judicial regions. The salary may not exceed 90 percent of the salary paid to a district judge as set by the state General Appropriations Act.

(b) The associate judge's salary shall be paid from county funds available for payment of officers' salaries subject to the approval of the commissioners court or from funds available from the state and federal governments as provided by this subchapter.

§ 201.206. Personnel.

(a) The presiding judge of an administrative judicial region or the presiding judges of the administrative judicial regions, by majority vote, may appoint personnel as needed to implement and administer the provisions of this subchapter.

(b) The salaries of the personnel shall be paid from county funds available for payment of officers' salaries subject to the approval of the commissioners court or from funds available from the state and federal governments as provided by this subchapter.

§ 201.2061. Supervision of Associate Judges.

The office of court administration shall assist the presiding judges in:

(1) monitoring the associate judges' compliance with any applicable job performance standards, uniform practices adopted by the presiding judges, and federal and state laws and policies;

(2) addressing the training needs and resource requirements of the associate judges;

(3) conducting annual performance evaluations for the associate judges and other personnel appointed under this subchapter based on written personnel performance standards adopted by the presiding judges; and

(4) receiving, investigating, and resolving complaints about particular associate judges or the associate judge program under this subchapter based on a uniform process adopted by the presiding judges.

§ 201.207. State and Federal Funds; Personnel.

(a) The office of court administration may contract for available state and federal funds from any source and may employ personnel needed to implement and administer this subchapter. An associate judge and other personnel appointed under this subsection are state employees for all purposes, including accrual of leave time, insurance benefits, retirement benefits, and travel regulations.

(b) The presiding judges of the administrative judicial regions, state agencies, and counties may contract for available federal funds from any source to reimburse costs and salaries associated with associate judges and personnel appointed under this section and may also use available state funds and public or private grants.

(c) The presiding judges and the office of court administration in cooperation with other agencies shall take action necessary to maximize the amount of federal money available to fund the use of associate judges under this subchapter.

§ 201.208. Assignment of Judges and Appointment of Visiting Associate Judges.

(a) This chapter does not limit the authority of a presiding judge to assign a judge eligible for assignment under Chapter 74, Government Code, to assist in processing cases in a reasonable time.

(b) If an associate judge appointed under this subchapter is temporarily unable to perform the associate judge's official duties because of absence resulting from family circumstances, illness, injury, disability, or military service, or if there is a vacancy in the position of associate judge, the presiding judge of the administrative judicial region in which the associate judge serves or the vacancy occurs may appoint a visiting associate judge to perform the duties of the associate judge during the period the associate judge is unable to perform the associate judge's duties or until another associate judge is appointed to fill the vacancy.

(c) A person is not eligible for appointment under this section unless the person has served as an associate judge for at least two years before the date of appointment.

(d) A visiting associate judge appointed under this section is subject to each provision of this chapter that applies to an associate judge serving under a regular appointment under this subchapter. A visiting associate judge appointed under this section is entitled to compensation, to be determined by a majority vote of the presiding judges of the administrative judicial regions, through use of funds under this subchapter. A visiting associate judge is not considered to be a state employee for any purpose.

§ 201.209. Limitation on Law Practice by Associate Judge.

An associate judge appointed under this subchapter may not engage in the private practice of law.

Chapter 202. Friend of the Court.

Introductory Comment

This chapter authorizes county governments and trial courts to initiate voluntary "friend of the court" programs. The concept is derived from the system for enforcing child support and visitation employed in Michigan. The basic principle is that the attorney (or the domestic relations office appointed to act in that capacity) does not represent any of the parties, nor represent the child. Rather, a duty is owed to the court to ensure that all aspects of its orders are enforced and appropriate under the existing circumstances. Generally, both child support and visitation are subject to enforcement motions filed by the friend of the court. Similarly, a petition to modify support or possession may seek an increase or decrease in the support order, or to modify the terms of visitation in an appropriate manner (as viewed by the friend of the court). Texas courts have embraced the program in a wide variety of ways, ranging from a case-by-case appointment of an attorney to enforce support to a general appointment of an individual with a courthouse office and staff to perform that function.

---

§ 202.001. Appointment.

(a) After an order for child support or possession of or access to a child has been rendered, a court may appoint a friend of the court on:

(1) the request of a person alleging that the order has been violated; or

(2) its own motion.

(b) A court may appoint a friend of the court in a proceeding under Part D of Title IV of the federal Social Security Act (42 U.S.C. Section 651 et seq.) only if the Title IV–D agency agrees in writing to the appointment.

(c) The duration of the appointment of a friend of the court is as determined by the court.

(d) In the appointment of a friend of the court, the court shall give preference to:

(1) a local domestic relations office;

(2) a local child support collection office;

(3) the local court official designated to enforce actions as provided in Chapter 159 *[UIFSA]*; or

(4) an attorney in good standing with the State Bar of Texas.

(e) In the execution of a friend of the court's duties under this subchapter, a friend of the court shall represent the court to ensure compliance with the court's order.

Comment

Subsection (e) makes clear that the duty of the friend of the court is to represent the court and not one of the parties or the child.

---

§ 202.002. Authority and Duties.

(a) A friend of the court may coordinate nonjudicial efforts to improve compliance with a court order relating to child support or possession of or access to a child by use of:

(1) telephone communication;

(2) written communication;

(3) one or more volunteer advocates under Chapter 107 *[Special Appointments and Social Studies]*;

(4) informal pretrial consultation;

(5) one or more of the alternate dispute resolution methods under Chapter 154, Civil Practice and Remedies Code;

(6) a licensed social worker;

(7) a family mediator; and

(8) employment agencies, retraining programs, and any similar resources to ensure that both parents can meet their financial obligations to the child.

(b) A friend of the court, not later than the 15th day of the month following the reporting month:

(1) shall report to the court or monitor reports made to the court on:

(A) the amount of child support collected as a percentage of the amount ordered; and

(B) efforts to ensure compliance with orders relating to possession of or access to a child; and

(2) may file an action to enforce, clarify, or modify a court order relating to child support or possession of or access to a child.

(c) A friend of the court may file a notice of delinquency and a request for a writ of income withholding under Chapter 158 *[Withholding from Earnings for Child Support]* in order to enforce a child support order.

Comment

The friend of the court is implicitly directed to engage in a wide range of nonjudicial activities in an effort to settle a case prior to seeking enforcement by more conventional means. Subsection (b) is the key, authorizing the friend of court to keep track of compliance by monitoring payments, in cooperation with whomever serves as the court's registry, and to take action independently when compliance falls below 100 percent (a lofty goal).

---

§ 202.003. Duty of Local Offices and Officials to Report.

A local domestic relations office, a local registry, or a court official designated to receive child support under a court order shall, if ordered by the court, report to the court or a friend of the court on a monthly basis:

(1) any delinquency and arrearage in child support payments; and

(2) any violation of an order relating to possession of or access to a child.

§ 202.004. Access to Information.

A friend of the court may arrange access to child support payment records by electronic means if the records are computerized.

§ 202.005. Compensation.

(a) A friend of the court is entitled to compensation for services rendered and for expenses incurred in rendering the services.

(b) The court may assess the amount that the friend of the court receives in compensation against a party to the suit in the same manner as the court awards costs under Chapter 106 *[Costs and Attorney's Fees]*.

(c) A friend of the court or a person who acts as the court's custodian of child support records, including the clerk of a court, may apply for and receive funds from the child support and court management account under Section 21.007, Government Code.

(d) A friend of the court who receives funds under Subsection (c) shall use the funds to reimburse any compensation the friend of the court received under Subsection (b).

Chapter 203. Domestic Relations Office.

---

§ 203.001. Definitions.

In this chapter:

(1) "Administering entity" means a commissioners court, juvenile board, or other entity responsible for administering a domestic relations office under this chapter.

(2) "Domestic relations office" means a county office that serves families, county departments, and courts to ensure effective implementation of this title.

§ 203.002. Establishment of Domestic Relations Office.

A commissioners court may establish a domestic relations office.

§ 203.003. Administration.

(a) A domestic relations office shall be administered:

(1) as provided by the commissioners court; or

(2) if the commissioners court does not otherwise provide for the administration of the office, by the juvenile board that serves the county in which the domestic relations office is located.

(b) The administering entity shall appoint and assign the duties of a director who shall be responsible for the day-to-day administration of the office. A director serves at the pleasure of the administering entity.

(c) The administering entity shall determine the amount of money needed to operate the office.

(d) A commissioners court that establishes a domestic relations office under this chapter may execute a bond for the office. A bond under this subsection must be:

(1) executed with a solvent surety company authorized to do business in the state; and

(2) conditioned on the faithful performance of the duties of the office.

(e) The administering entity shall establish procedures for the acceptance and use of a grant or donation to the office.

§ 203.004. Powers and Duties.

(a) A domestic relations office may:

(1) collect and disburse child support payments that are ordered by a court to be paid through a domestic relations registry;

(2) maintain records of payments and disbursements made under Subdivision (1);

(3) file a suit, including a suit to:

(A) establish paternity;

(B) enforce a court order for child support or for possession of and access to a child; and

(C) modify or clarify an existing child support order;

(4) provide an informal forum in which:

(A) mediation is used to resolve disputes in an action under Subdivision (3); or

(B) an agreed repayment schedule for delinquent child support is negotiated as an alternative to filing a suit to enforce a court order for child support under Subdivision (3);

(5) prepare a court-ordered social study;

(6) represent a child as guardian ad litem in a suit in which:

(A) termination of the parent-child relationship is sought; or

(B) conservatorship of or access to a child is contested;

(7) serve as a friend of the court;

(8) provide predivorce counseling ordered by a court;

(9) provide community supervision services under Chapter 157;

(10) provide information to assist a party in understanding, complying with, or enforcing the party's duties and obligations under Subdivision (3); and

(11) provide, directly or through a contract, visitation services, including supervision of court-ordered visitation, visitation exchange, or other similar services.

(b) A court having jurisdiction in a proceeding under this title, Title 3, or Section 25.05, Penal Code, may order that child support payments be made through a domestic relations office.

(c) A domestic relations office may:

(1) hire or contract for the services of attorneys to assist the office in providing services under this chapter; and

(2) employ community supervision officers or court monitors.

§ 203.005. Fees and Charges.

(a) The administering entity may authorize a domestic relations office to assess and collect:

(1) an initial operations fee not to exceed $15 to be paid to the domestic relations office on the filing of a suit;

(2) in a county that has a child support enforcement cooperative agreement with the Title IV–D agency, an initial child support service fee not to exceed $36 to be paid to the domestic relations office on the filing of a suit;

(3) a reasonable application fee to be paid by an applicant requesting services from the office;

(4) a reasonable attorney's fee and court costs incurred or ordered by the court;

(5) a monthly service fee not to exceed $3 to be paid annually in advance by a managing conservator and possessory conservator for whom the domestic relations office provides child support services;

(6) community supervision fees as provided by Chapter 157 if community supervision officers are employed by the domestic relations office;

(7) a reasonable fee for preparation of a court-ordered social study; and

(8) in a county that provides visitation services under Sections 153.014 and 203.004 a reasonable fee to be paid to the domestic relations office at the time the visitation services are provided.

(b) The first payment of a fee under Subsection (a)(4) is due on the date that the person required to pay support is ordered to begin child support, alimony, or separate maintenance payments. Subsequent payments of the fee are due annually and in advance.

(c) The director of a domestic relations office shall attempt to collect all fees in an efficient manner.

(d) The administering entity may provide for an exemption from the payment of a fee authorized under this section if payment of the fee is not practical or in the interest of justice. Fees that may be exempted under this subsection include fees related to:

(1) spousal and child support payments made under an interstate pact;

(2) a suit brought by the Texas Department of Human Services;

(3) activities performed by the Department of Protective and Regulatory Services or another governmental agency, a private adoption agency, or a charitable organization; and

(4) services for a person who has applied for or who receives public assistance under the laws of this state.

(e) A fee authorized by this section for providing child support services is part of the child support obligation and may be enforced against both an obligor and obligee by any method available for the enforcement of child support, including contempt.

§ 203.006. Fund.

(a) As determined by the administering entity, fees collected or received by a domestic relations office shall be deposited in:

(1) the general fund for the county in which the domestic relations office is located; or

(2) the office fund established for the domestic relations office.

(b) The administering entity shall use the domestic relations office fund to provide money for services authorized by this chapter.

(c) A domestic relations office fund may be supplemented as necessary from the county's general fund or from other money available from the county.

§ 203.007. Access to Records; Offense.

(a) A domestic relations office may obtain the records described by Subsections (b), (c), (d), and (e) that relate to a person who has:

(1) been ordered to pay child support;

(2) been designated as a possessory conservator or managing conservator of a child;

(3) been designated to be the father of a child; or

(4) executed an acknowledgment of paternity.

(b) A domestic relations office is entitled to obtain from the Department of Public Safety records that relate to:

(1) a person's date of birth;

(2) a person's most recent address;

(3) a person's current driver's license status;

(4) motor vehicle accidents involving a person; and

(5) reported traffic-law violations of which a person has been convicted.

(c) A domestic relations office is entitled to obtain from the Texas Workforce Commission records that relate to:

(1) a person's address;

(2) a person's employment status and earnings;

(3) the name and address of a person's current or former employer; and

(4) unemployment compensation benefits received by a person.

(d) To the extent permitted by federal law, a domestic relations office is entitled to obtain from the national directory of new hires established under 42 U.S.C. Section 653(i), as amended, records that relate to a person described by Subsection (a), including records that relate to:

(1) the name, telephone number, and address of the person's employer;

(2) information provided by the person on a W-4 form; and

(3) information provided by the person's employer on a Title IV-D form.

(e) To the extent permitted by federal law, a domestic relations office is entitled to obtain from the state case registry records that relate to a person described by Subsection (a), including records that relate to:

(1) the street and mailing address and the social security number of the person;

(2) the name, telephone number, and address of the person's employer;

(3) the location and value of real and personal property owned by the person; and

(4) the name and address of each financial institution in which the person maintains an account and the account number for each account.

(f) An agency required to provide records under this section may charge a domestic relations office a fee for providing the records in an amount that does not exceed the amount paid for those records by the agency responsible for Title IV-D cases.

(g) The Department of Public Safety, the Texas Workforce Commission, or the office of the secretary of state may charge a domestic relations office a fee not to exceed the charge paid by the Title IV-D agency for furnishing records under this section.

(h) Information obtained by a domestic relations office under this section that is confidential under a constitution, statute, judicial decision, or rule is privileged and may be used only by that office.

(i) A person commits an offense if the person releases or discloses confidential information obtained under this section without the consent of the person to whom the information relates. An offense under this subsection is a Class C misdemeanor.

(j) A domestic relations office is entitled to obtain from the office of the secretary of state the following information about a registered voter to the extent that the information is available:

(1) complete name;

(2) current and former street and mailing address;

(3) sex;

(4) date of birth;

(5) social security number; and

(6) telephone number.

Chapter 204. Child Support Collection by Private Entity

§ 204.001. Applicability.

This chapter applies only to a county that did not have the authority to contract with a private entity to receive, disburse, and record payments or restitution of child support on January 1, 1997.

§ 204.002. Authority to Contract.

A county, acting through its commissioners court or domestic relations office, may contract with a private entity to:

(1) enforce, collect, receive, and disburse:

(A) child support payments;

(B) other amounts due under a court order containing an order to pay child support; and

(C) fees, including fees provided by this chapter;

(2) maintain appropriate records, including records of child support and other amounts and fees that are due, past due, paid, or delinquent;

(3) locate absent parents;

(4) furnish statements to parents accounting for payments that are due, past due, paid, or delinquent;

(5) send billings and other appropriate notices to parents;

(6) perform any duty or function that a local registry is authorized to perform;

(7) perform any duty or function in connection with the state case registry; or

(8) provide another child support or visitation enforcement service authorized by the commissioners court, including mediation of disputes related to child support or visitation.

§ 204.003. Terms and Conditions of Contract.

The commissioners court or domestic relations office shall include all appropriate terms and conditions in the contract that it determines are reasonable to secure the services of a private entity as provided by this chapter, including:

(1) provisions specifying the services to be provided by the entity;

(2) the method, conditions, and amount of compensation for the entity;

(3) provisions for the security of funds collected as child support, fees, or other amounts under the contract or that otherwise provide reasonable assurance to the county of the entity's full and faithful performance of the contract;

(4) provisions specifying the records to be kept by the entity, including any records necessary to fully account for all funds received and disbursed as child support, fees, or other amounts;

(5) requirements governing the inspection, verification, audit, or explanation of the entity's accounting or other records;

(6) the county's right to terminate the contract on 30 days' notice to the private entity if the private entity engages in an ongoing pattern of child support enforcement that constitutes wilful and gross misconduct subjecting delinquent obligors to unconscionable duress, abuse, or harassment;

(7) provisions permitting an obligor and obligee to jointly waive the monitoring procedure, if not required by law, by written request approved by order of the court having jurisdiction of the suit in which the child support order was issued; and

(8) provisions for the disclosure or nondisclosure of information or records maintained or known to the entity as a result of contract performance, including a requirement for the private entity to:

(A) disclose to any child support obligor that the private entity is attempting to enforce the obligor's child support obligation; and

(B) make no disclosure of the information or records other than in furtherance of the effort to enforce the child support order.

§ 204.004. Funding.

(a) To provide or recover the costs of providing services authorized by this chapter, a commissioners court, on its behalf or on behalf of the domestic relations office, may:

(1) provide by order for the assessment and collection of a reasonable fee at the time a party files a suit affecting the parent-child relationship;

(2) provide by order for the assessment and collection of a fee of $3 per month at a time specified for payment of child support;

(3) provide by order for the assessment and collection of a late payment fee of $4 per month to be imposed if an obligor does not make a payment of child support in full when due;

(4) accept or receive funds from public grants or private sources available for providing services authorized by this chapter; or

(5) use any combination of funding sources specified by this subsection.

(b) The commissioners court, on its behalf or on behalf of the domestic relations office, may:

(1) provide by order for reasonable exemptions from the collection of fees authorized by Subsection (a); and

(2) require payment of a fee authorized by Subsection (a)(2) annually and in advance.

(c) The commissioners court may not charge a fee under Subsection (a)(2) if the amount of child support ordered to be paid is less than the equivalent of $100 per month.

(d) The fees established under Subsection (a) may be collected by any means provided for the collection of child support. The commissioners court may provide by order, on its behalf or on behalf of the domestic relations office, for the manner of collection of fees and the apportionment of payments received to meet fee obligations.

§ 204.005. Cumulative Effect of Chapter.

A power or duty conferred on a county, county official, or county instrumentality by this chapter is cumulative of the powers and duties created or conferred by other law.

Subtitle D. Administrative Services

★★★

Chapter 231. Title IV–D Services.

Subchapter A. Administration of Title IV–D Program

Subchapter B. Services Provided by Title IV–D Program

Subchapter C. Payment of Fees and Costs

Subchapter D. Location of Parents and Resources

Editors' Note: *This chapter contains guest commentary by Cynthia Bryant, Deputy Attorney General, and H. Patrick Sullivan, Director of Federal Policy Analysis, both of the Child Support Division, Office of the Attorney General of*

Texas; and, Alicia Gray Key, Director, Office of Court Administration; respectively identified as (C.B. & H.P.S., A.G.K.).

Introductory Comment

Under the Child Support Enforcement Amendments of 1984, Congress required states to adopt expedited procedures for child support enforcement, whether by judicial or administrative processes or some combination of the two, in order to meet new federal time frames for establishing and enforcing support obligations in cases enforced by state Title IV–D agencies. Moreover, the 1984 Act imposed a number of "statutorily prescribed procedures" (for example, mandatory income withholding for support) which all states had to institute as a condition for receiving federal matching funds for the operation of their IV–D child support enforcement programs. The federal Family Support Act of 1986 extended the use of expedited processes to paternity establishment, added new state law requirements, and mandated the development of automated systems for data management and case processing by state Title IV–D agencies. The child support enforcement provisions of the Personal Responsibility and Work Opportunity Act of 1996 (PRWORA) enlarged the authority of state Title IV–D agencies through the use of expedited administrative procedures, expanded the role of automated systems in support enforcement, and compelled greater uniformity of family law and legal processes among the states. *(A.G.K. & H.P.S.)*

CLE/Other Legal Publications

A plainly practical primer on IV–D practice. Steve A. Owen, 2002 ADV. FAM. L.

Representing clients in Title IV–D. Hon. Michael K. Sinha & Steven A. Owen, 2000 ADV. FAM. L.

Leading Cases

Blessing v. Freestone, 520 U.S. 329, 117 S.Ct. 1353 (1997) (applicants for child support enforcement do not have cause of action against IV–D agency for inadequate services)

Office of Attorney General v. Lee, 92 S.W.3d 526 (Tex. 2002) (A.G. not required to pay any portion of appellate filing fee)

In re A.C.B., 103 S.W.3d 559 (Tex. App.—San Antonio 2003, no pet.) (AG sanctioned for administrative writ of withholding)

In re E.D., 102 S.W.3d 859 (Tex. App.—Corpus Christi 2003, no pet.) (revival of dormant judgment by administrative writ of withholding not barred)

In re A.M., 101 S.W.3d 480 (Tex. App.—Corpus Christi 2003, pet. filed) (as assignee to collect child support arrearages, A.G. subject to obligor's cross-motion for reimbursement of support he furnished during periods he had possession of children—A.G. lacked standing to defend mother's interests or represent her)

In re A.M.E., 71 S.W.3d 401 (Tex. App.—San Antonio 2001, no pet.) (A.G., not grandmother, entitled to receive payments on arrearage judgment)

In re M.E.G., 48 S.W.3d 204 (Tex. App.—Corpus Christi 2001, no pet.) (A.G. gave adequate notice to enforce support, proved its standing, and entitle to judgment and deferred distribution of entire arrearage)

Rivera v. Attorney General, 960 S.W.2d 280 (Tex. App.—Houston [1st Dist.] 1997, no writ) (child's emancipation does not prevent A.G. from bringing action for support judgment)

Attorney General v. Wilson, 878 S.W.2d 690 (Tex. App.—Beaumont 1994, no writ) (trial court may not order A.G. not to abstract or report judgment)

Blake v. Blake, 878 S.W.2d 209 (Tex. App.—Corpus Christi 1994, writ denied), *cert. denied*, 115 S.Ct. 648, 130 L.Ed.2d 553 (1994) (retroactive support obtained by A.G. relying on residual limitations) (allegedly indigent father not denied due process by failure to appoint counsel)

Attorney General v. Cartwright, 874 S.W.2d 210 (Tex. App.—Houston [14th Dist.] 1994, writ denied) (attorney general subject to sanctions for groundless suit for collection of arrearages)

Attorney General v. Allred, 871 S.W.2d 298 (Tex. App.—Fort Worth 1994, no writ) (res judicata does not preclude A.G.'s action, although prior suit by D.A. dismissed with prejudice for failure to prosecute)

Reyna v. Attorney General, 863 S.W.2d 558 (Tex. App.—Fort Worth 1993, no writ) (alleged father cannot assert laches defense in action brought by A.G. to determine paternity, collect child support and recoup public funds)

Subchapter A. Administration of Title IV–D Program

§ 231.001. Designation of Title IV–D Agency.

The office of the attorney general is designated as the state's Title IV–D agency.

§ 231.0011. Development of Statewide Integrated System for Child Support and Medical Support Enforcement.

(a) The Title IV–D agency shall have final approval authority on any contract or proposal for delivery of Title IV–D services under this section and in coordination with the Texas Judicial Council, the Office of Court Administration of the Texas Judicial System, the federal Office of Child Support Enforcement, and state, county, and local officials, shall develop and implement a statewide integrated system for child support and medical support enforcement, employing federal, state, local, and private resources to:

(1) unify child support registry functions;

(2) record and track all child support orders entered in the state;

(3) establish an automated enforcement process which will use delinquency monitoring, billing, and other enforcement techniques to ensure the payment of current support;

(4) incorporate existing enforcement resources into the system to obtain maximum benefit from state and federal funding; and

(5) ensure accountability for all participants in the process, including state, county, and local officials, private contractors, and the judiciary.

(b) Counties and other providers of child support services shall be required, as a condition of participation in the unified system, to enter into a contract with the Title IV–D agency, to comply with all federal requirements for the Title IV–D program, and to maintain at least the current level of funding for activities which are proposed to be included in the integrated child support system.

(c) The Title IV–D agency may contract with any county meeting technical system requirements necessary to comply with federal law for provision of Title IV–D services in that county. All new cases in which support orders are entered in such county after the effective date of a monitoring contract shall be Title IV–D cases. Any other case in the county, subject to federal requirements and the agreement of the county and the Title IV–D agency, may be included as a Title IV–D case. Any obligee under a support order may refuse Title IV–D enforcement services unless required to accept such services pursuant to other law.

(d) Counties participating in the unified enforcement system shall monitor all child support registry cases and on delinquency may, subject to the approval of the Title IV–D agency, provide enforcement services through:

(1) direct provision of services by county personnel;

(2) subcontracting all or portions of the services to private entities or attorneys; or

(3) such other methods as may be approved by the Title IV–D agency.

(e) The Title IV–D agency may phase in the integrated child support registry and enforcement system, and the requirement to implement the system shall be contingent on the receipt of locally generated funds and federal reimbursement. Locally generated funds include but are not limited to funds contributed by counties and cities.

(f) The Title IV–D agency shall adopt rules to implement this section.

(g) Participation in the statewide integrated system for child support and medical support enforcement by a county is voluntary, and nothing in this section shall be construed to mandate participation.

(h) This section does not limit the ability of the Title IV–D agency to enter into an agreement with a county for the provision of services as authorized under Section 231.002.

§ 231.0012. Child Support Enforcement Management.

The person appointed by the attorney general as the person responsible for managing the Title IV-D agency's child support enforcement duties shall report directly to the attorney general.

§ 231.0013. Dedication of Funds.

Appropriations made to the Title IV-D agency for child support enforcement may be expended only for the purposes for which the money was appropriated.

§ 231.002. Powers and Duties.

(a) The Title IV–D agency may:

(1) accept, transfer, and expend funds, subject to the General Appropriations Act, made available by the federal or state government or by another public or private source for the purpose of carrying out this chapter;

(2) adopt rules for the provision of child support services;

(3) initiate legal actions needed to implement this chapter; and

(4) enter into contracts or agreements necessary to administer this chapter.

(b) The Title IV–D agency may perform the duties and functions necessary for locating children under agreements with the federal government as provided by 42 U.S.C. Section 663.

(c) The Title IV–D agency may enter into agreements or contracts with federal, state, or other public or private agencies or individuals for the purpose of carrying out the agency's responsibilities under federal or state law. The agreements or contracts between the agency and other state agencies or political subdivisions of this or another state, including a consortia of multiple states, and agreements or contracts with vendors for the delivery of program services are not subject to Chapter 771 or 783, Government Code.

(d) Consistent with federal law and any international treaty or convention to which the United States is a party and that has been ratified by the United States Congress, the Title IV–D agency may:

(1) on approval by and in cooperation with the governor, pursue negotiations and enter into reciprocal arrangements with the federal government, another state, or a

foreign country or a political subdivision of the federal government, state, or foreign country to:

(A) establish and enforce child support obligations; and

(B) establish mechanisms to enforce an order providing for possession of or access to a child rendered under Chapter 153 *[Conservatorship, Possession, and Access]*;

(2) spend money appropriated to the agency for child support enforcement to engage in international child support enforcement; and

(3) spend other money appropriated to the agency necessary for the agency to conduct the agency's activities under Subdivision (1).

(e) The Title IV–D agency may take the following administrative actions with respect to the location of a parent, the determination of parentage, and the establishment, modification, and enforcement of child support and medical support orders required by 42 U.S.C. Section 666(c), without obtaining an order from any other judicial or administrative tribunal:

(1) issue an administrative subpoena, as provided by Section 231.303, to obtain financial or other information;

(2) order genetic testing for parentage determination, as provided by Chapter 233 *[Child Support Review Process]*;

(3) order income withholding, as provided by Chapter 233, and issue an administrative writ of withholding, as provided by Chapter 158; and

(4) take any action with respect to execution, collection, and release of a judgment or lien for child support necessary to satisfy the judgment or lien, as provided by Chapter 157 *[Enforcement]*.

(f) The Title IV–D agency shall recognize and enforce the authority of the Title IV–D agency of another state to take actions similar to the actions listed in this section.

(g) The Title IV–D agency shall develop and use procedures for the administrative enforcement of interstate cases meeting the requirements of 42 U.S.C. Section 666(a)(14) under which the agency:

(1) shall promptly respond to a request made by another state for assistance in a Title IV–D case; and

(2) may, by electronic or other means, transmit to another state a request for assistance in a Title IV–D case.

(h) In each Title IV–D case in which the total amount of a child support obligor's child support delinquency is at least $5,000 and the obligor owns property in the state or resides in the state, the Title IV–D agency shall enforce the child support obligation by filing a child support lien under Subchapter G, Chapter 157. This subsection does not prohibit the Title IV–D agency from filing a child support lien in any other case in which a lien may be filed under Subchapter G, Chapter 157.

(i) The Title IV–D agency may provide a release or satisfaction of a judgment for all or part of the amount of the arrearages assigned to the Title IV–D agency under Section 231.104(a).

Comment

PRWORA required states to have laws providing the IV–D agency with authority to take specific administrative actions without the necessity of any other judicial or administrative order. This section lists those administrative actions, as well as other federal mandates relating to administrative enforcement of interstate cases and authorizes the IV–D agency to enter into multi-state consortia for interstate enforcement. It also includes specific provisions for international enforcement of child support and custody orders.

Federal law does not require the IV–D agency to enforce custody and access rights and, therefore, does not authorize federal matching funds for any enforcement actions relating to custody and access. This section authorizes the attorney general to pursue the establishment of reciprocal arrangements with foreign nations for the enforcement of both child support and custody and access rights to the extent that federal law and international treaties allow and specific funds are appropriated.

The IV–D agency provides child support enforcement services upon the request of any foreign country which the secretaries of the U.S. Departments of State and of Health and Human Services "declare" to be a reciprocating country for enforcement purposes. States on their own may enter into reciprocal agreements for support enforcement with foreign countries that are not the subject of a declaration. The IV–D agency must treat any request from a foreign reciprocating country in the same manner as an interstate request and may not charge a requesting country or foreign obligee any fee for services, although the agency may attempt to recover fees from the obligor.

Subsection (d) is quite unusual in its scope. The agency is authorized to negotiate and recognize foreign nations or their political subdivisions for reciprocal enforcement of child support orders. Texas has done so with a large number of Canadian provinces and European nations, including (as of June 1, 2003) Australia, Czech Republic, Ireland, Netherlands, Norway, Poland, Portugal, Slovak Republic, Switzerland, and the Canadian Provinces of Alberta, British Columbia, Manitoba, Newfoundland/Labrador, Nova Scotia, and Ontario. (*A.G.K. & H.P.S.*)

Subsection (i) codifies under this section's enumeration of the powers and duties of the IV–D agency the authority of the agency, identified under § 157.272, *supra*, to "forgive" support arrearages assigned to the state (§ 231.104 *infra*). The agency may not, of course, compromise or release a judgment of support arrearages owed a custodial parent. *(C.B. & H.P.S.)*

---

§ 231.003. Forms and Procedures.

The Title IV–D agency shall by rule promulgate any forms and procedures necessary to comply fully with the intent of this chapter.

§ 231.004. [repealed]

§ 231.005. Biennial Report Required.

(a) The Title IV–D agency shall report to the legislature each biennium on:

(1) the effectiveness of the agency's child support enforcement activity in reducing the state's public assistance obligations;

(2) the use and effectiveness of all enforcement tools authorized by state or federal law or otherwise available to the agency; and

(3) the progress and impact of the Title IV–D agency's efforts to use private contractors to perform Title IV–D program functions.

(b) The agency shall develop a method for estimating the costs and benefits of the child support enforcement program and the effect of the program on appropriations for public assistance.

§ 231.006. Ineligibility to Receive State Grants or Loans or Receive Payment on State Contracts.

(a) A child support obligor who is more than 30 days delinquent in paying child support and a business entity in which the obligor is a sole proprietor, partner, shareholder, or owner with an ownership interest of at least 25 percent is not eligible to:

(1) receive payments from state funds under a contract to provide property, materials, or services; or

(2) receive a state-funded grant or loan.

(a–1) *[H.B. 529]* **A child support obligor who is more than six months delinquent in paying child support is not eligible to receive student financial assistance paid directly to the obligor by the comptroller. This subsection does not apply to an obligor who submits to the comptroller:**

(1) a sworn affidavit from the obligor or obligee stating that the obligor is current on the obligor's child support payments; and

(2) a written statement from the obligor that the obligor has made a request to the Title IV–D agency to correct the errors in the obligor's payment record.

(b) *[H.B. 529]* A child support obligor or business entity ineligible to receive payments under Subsection (a) **or a child support obligor ineligible to receive payments under Subsection (a–1)** remains ineligible until:

(1) all arrearages have been paid; [~~or~~]

(2) the obligor is in compliance with a written repayment agreement or court order as to any existing delinquency; **or**

(b) *[H.B. 518]* A child support obligor or business entity ineligible to receive payments under Subsection (a) remains ineligible until:

(1) all arrearages have been paid; [~~or~~]

(2) the obligor is in compliance with a written repayment agreement or court order as to any existing delinquency; **or**

(3) the court of continuing jurisdiction over the child support order has granted the obligor an exemption from Subsection (a) as part of a court-supervised effort to improve earnings and child support payments.

(c) A bid or an application for a contract, grant, or loan paid from state funds must include the name and social security number of the individual or sole proprietor and each partner, shareholder, or owner with an ownership interest of at least 25 percent of the business entity submitting the bid or application.

(d) A contract, bid, or application subject to the requirements of this section must include the following statement:

"Under Section 231.006, Family Code, the vendor or applicant certifies that the individual or business entity named in this contract, bid, or application is not ineligible to receive the specified grant, loan, or payment and acknowledges that this contract may be terminated and payment may be withheld if this certification is inaccurate."

(e) If a state agency determines that an individual or business entity holding a state contract is ineligible to receive payment under Subsection (a), the contract may be terminated.

(f) If the certificate required under Subsection (d) is shown to be false, the vendor is liable to the state for attorney's fees, the costs necessary to complete the contract, including the cost of advertising and awarding a second contract, and any other damages provided by law or contract.

(g) This section does not create a cause of action to contest a bid or award of a state grant, loan, or contract. This section does not impose a duty on the Title IV-D agency to collect information to send to the comptroller to withhold a payment to a business entity. The Title IV-D agency and other affected agencies are encouraged to develop a system by which the Title IV-D agency may identify a business entity that is ineligible to receive a state payment under Subsection (a) and to ensure that a state payment to the entity is not made. This system should be implemented using existing funds and only if the Title IV-D agency, comptroller, and other affected agencies determine that it will be cost-effective.

(h) This section does not apply to a contract between governmental entities.

(i) The Title IV-D agency may adopt rules or prescribe forms to implement any provision of this section.

(j) A state agency may accept a bid that does not include the information required under Subsection (c) if the state agency collects the information before the contract, grant, or loan is executed.

History: Amended by 78th Legis., Reg. Sess. (2003), H.B. 529, eff. Sept. 1, 2003, and "applies only to student financial assistance paid on or after the effective date of this Act."

History: Amended by 78th Legis., Reg. Sess. (2003), H.B. 518, eff. Sept. 1, 2003, and "applies only to a suit affecting the parent-child relationship filed on or after that date. A suit affecting the parent-child relationship filed before the effective date of this Act is governed by the law in effect on the date that the suit was filed, and the former law is continued in effect for that purpose."

Comment

This section casts a broad net to constrain delinquent child support obligors who might otherwise be eligible to apply for or receive state funds from contracts, loans, grants, and even student aid programs (*e.g.,* state university scholarships, student loans, and work-assistance grants). Subsection (a–1), added in 2003, seeks to distinguish "student assistance" from other forms of state grants or loans and applies a different term of support delinquency (six months instead of 30 days) as the condition for ineligibility for financial assistance. Presumably recipients of "student assistance" could lose the means through state-funded aid to complete a degree or certificate program that might enable them to earn a living and pay child support. Relief, however, is provided those who fall under subsection (a) through an exemption from the court, under subsection (b)(3), "as part of a court-supervised effort to improve earnings and child support payments." Students appear not to be so fortunate. *(C.B. & H.P.S.)*

§ 231.007. Debts to State.

(a) A person obligated to pay child support in a case in which the Title IV-D agency is providing services under this chapter who does not pay the required support is indebted to the state for the purposes of Section 403.055, Government Code, if the Title IV-D agency has reported the person to the comptroller under that section properly.

(b) The amount of a person's indebtedness to the state under Subsection (a) is equal to the sum of:

(1) the amount of the required child support that has not been paid; and

(2) any interest, fees, court costs, or other amounts owed by the person because the person has not paid the support.

(c) The Title IV-D agency is the sole assignee of all payments, including payments of compensation, by the state to a person indebted to the state under Subsection (a).

(d) On request of the Title IV-D agency:

(1) the comptroller shall make payable and deliver to the agency any payments for which the agency is the assignee under Subsection (c), if the comptroller is responsible for issuing warrants or initiating electronic funds transfers to make those payments; and

(2) a state agency shall make payable and deliver to the Title IV-D agency any payments for which the Title IV-D agency is the assignee under Subsection (c) if the comptroller is not responsible for issuing warrants or initiating electronic funds transfers to make those payments.

(e) A person indebted to the state under Subsection (a) may eliminate the debt by:

(1) paying the entire amount of the debt; or

(2) resolving the debt in a manner acceptable to the Title IV-D agency.

(f) The comptroller or a state agency may rely on a representation by the Title IV-D agency that:

(1) a person is indebted to the state under Subsection (a); or

(2) a person who was indebted to the state under Subsection (a) has eliminated the debt.

(g) Except as provided by Subsection (h), the payment of workers' compensation benefits to a person indebted to the state under Subsection (a) is the same for the purposes of this section as any other payment made to the person by the state. Notwithstanding Section 408.203, Labor Code, an order or writ to withhold income from workers' compensation benefits is not required before the benefits are withheld or assigned under this section.

(h) The amount of weekly workers' compensation benefits that may be withheld or assigned under this section may not exceed 50 percent of the person's weekly compensation benefits. The comptroller or a state agency may rely on a representation by the Title IV–D agency that a withholding or assignment under this section would not violate this subsection.

(i) Section 403.055(d), Government Code, does not authorize the comptroller to issue a warrant or initiate an electronic funds transfer to pay the compensation or remuneration of an individual who is indebted to the state under Subsection (a).

(j) Section 2107.008(h), Government Code, does not authorize a state agency to pay the compensation or remuneration of an individual who is indebted to the state under Subsection (a).

(k) In this section, "compensation," "state agency," and "state officer or employee" have the meanings assigned by Section 403.055, Government Code.

§ 231.008. Disposition of Funds.

(a) The Title IV–D agency shall deposit money received under assignments or as fees in a special fund in the state treasury. The agency may spend money in the fund for the administration of this chapter, subject to the General Appropriations Act.

(b) All other money received under this chapter shall be deposited in a special fund in the state treasury.

(c) Sections 403.094 and 403.095, Government Code, do not apply to a fund described by this section.

§ 231.009. Payment of Penalties.

From funds appropriated for the Title IV–D agency, the agency shall reimburse the Texas Department of Human Services for any penalty assessed under Title IV–A of the federal Social Security Act (42 U.S.C. Section 651 et seq.) that is assessed because of the agency's administration of this chapter.

§ 231.010. Cooperation With Department of Protective and Regulatory Services.

(a) In this section, "department" means the Department of Protective and Regulatory Services.

(b) To the extent possible, the Title IV-D agency shall:

(1) provide to the department access to all of the Title IV-D agency's available child support locating resources;

(2) allow the department to use the Title IV-D agency's child support enforcement system to track child support payments and to have access to the agency's management reports that show payments made;

(3) make reports on Title IV-E, Social Security Act (42 U.S.C. Section 670 et seq.), foster care collections available to the department in a timely manner; and

(4) work with the department to obtain child support payments for protective services cases in which the department is responsible for providing care for children under temporary and final orders.

§ 231.011. Interagency Work Group.

(a) The Title IV–D agency shall convene a standing work group to develop and maintain an interagency partnership strategy. The director of the Title IV–D agency shall lead the work group.

(b) The work group shall consist of representatives from the Department of Protective and Regulatory Services, the Texas Department of Human Services, the Texas Department of Health, the Texas Workforce Commission, and the office of the comptroller. The executive head of each agency shall appoint the agency's representative. If the work group addresses an issue that is under the authority of the Health and Human Services Commission, the work group shall include a representative from that commission when addressing that issue.

(c) The interagency partnership strategy shall:

(1) identify methods to improve the exchange of data between the agencies represented in the work group;

(2) develop procedures to coordinate the child support efforts of each agency in the work group;

(3) identify the benefits of contracts under which a state agency provides child support services related to the agency's core competency to the Title IV–D agency;

(4) identify ways to improve client intake and client referral;

(5) develop methods to enhance foster care child support collections;

(6) increase the recovery of Medicaid for the Title IV–D agency and the Texas Department of Health; and

(7) examine the benefits of contracts under which the comptroller or a private entity provides services regarding the receipt and payment of child support.

(d) Each agency represented on the work group shall identify specific child support services that are related to the agency's areas of core competence and may be provided by the agency under a contract. The work group shall develop strategies to obtain child support services from the agencies.

§ 231.012. County Advisory Work Group.

(a) The director of the Title IV–D agency shall establish a county advisory work group to assist the Title IV–D agency in developing and changing child support programs that affect counties. The work group shall consist of at least one of each of the following:

(1) county judge;

(2) county commissioner;

(3) district clerk;

(4) domestic relations officer;

(5) associate judge for Title IV–D cases; and

(6) district court judge.

(b) The director of the Title IV–D agency shall appoint the members of the work group after consulting with the relevant professional or trade associations of the professions that are represented on the work group. The director of the Title IV–D agency shall determine the number of members of the work group and shall designate the presiding officer of the group.

(c) The work group shall:

(1) advise the director of the Title IV–D agency of the impact on counties that a proposed child support program or a change in a program may have;

(2) establish a state-county child support improvement plan;

(3) advise the Title IV–D agency on the operation of the state disbursement unit;

(4) plan for monetary incentives for county partnership programs;

(5) expand the number of agreements with counties for enforcement services; and

(6) work with relevant statewide associations on a model partnership agreement.

(d) A work group member or the member's designee may not receive compensation but is entitled to reimbursement for actual and necessary expenses incurred in performing the member's duties under this section.

(e) The work group is not an advisory committee as defined by Section 2110.001, Government Code. Chapter 2110, Government Code, does not apply to the work group.

§ 231.013. Information Resources Steering Committee.

(a) The Title IV–D agency shall create an information resources steering committee to:

(1) oversee information resource project development for the Title IV–D agency;

(2) make strategic prioritization recommendations;

(3) facilitate development of accurate information for the director of the Title IV–D agency; and

(4) perform other functions as determined by the director of the Title IV–D agency.

(b) The steering committee must include a senior management executive representing each significant function of the Title IV–D agency. The steering committee may include a person representing:

(1) counties; or

(2) a vendor contracting with the Title IV–D agency.

(c) The director of the Title IV–D agency shall appoint the members of the steering committee after consulting with the Department of Information Resources.

§ 231.014. Personnel.

The director of the Title IV–D agency shall provide to the employees of the Title IV–D agency, as often as necessary, information regarding the requirements for employment under this title, including information regarding a person's responsibilities under applicable laws relating to standards of conduct for state employees.

§ 231.015. Insurance Reporting Pilot Program.

(a) In consultation with the Texas Department of Insurance and representatives of the insurance industry in this state, including insurance trade associations, the Title IV-D agency by rule shall establish a pilot program to improve the use of child support liens under Chapter 157. The pilot program shall develop processes under which insurance companies may voluntarily cooperate with the Title IV-D agency in identifying obligors who are subject to liens for child support arrearages to intercept certain liability insurance settlements or awards for claims in satisfaction of the arrearage amounts.

(b) An insurance company that provides information or otherwise responds to a notice of child support lien or levy under Subchapter G, Chapter 157, or acts in good faith to comply with procedures established in the pilot program under this section is not liable for those acts under any law to any person.

Subchapter B. Services Provided by Title IV–D Program

§ 231.101. Title IV–D Child Support Services.

(a) The Title IV–D agency may provide all services required or authorized to be provided by Part D of Title IV of the federal Social Security Act (42 U.S.C. Section 651 et seq.), including:

(1) parent locator services;

(2) paternity determination;

(3) child support and medical support establishment;

(4) review and adjustment of child support orders;

(5) enforcement of child support and medical support orders; and

(6) collection and distribution of child support payments.

(b) At the request of either the obligee or obligor, the Title IV-D agency shall review a child support order once every three years and, if appropriate, adjust the support amount to meet the requirements of the child support guidelines under Chapter 154 *[Child Support]*.

(c) Except as notice is included in the child support order, a party subject to a support order shall be provided notice not less than once every three years of the party's right to request that the Title IV-D agency review and, if appropriate, adjust the amount of ordered support.

(d) The Title IV-D agency may review a support order at any time on a showing of a material and substantial change in circumstances, taking into consideration the best interests of the child.

(e) The Title IV-D agency shall distribute a child support payment received by the agency from an employer within two working days after the date the agency receives the payment.

Comment

The federal Family Support Act of 1988 required states, on pain of loss of federal matching funds for their IV–D programs, to have procedures for the periodic review and, as needed, adjustment of child support amounts in orders being enforced by the IV–D agency in order to ensure that the support amounts remain consistent with state child support guidelines. This section incorporates the federal review and adjustment requirements, as amended by PRWORA. Reviews are conducted on a three-year cycle, but only at the request of either the obligee or obligor or, in the case of public assistance cases, the IV–D agency itself. This automatic review process does not preclude, however, a review at any time on a showing of a material and substantial change of circumstances, subject to the best interests of the child. *(A.G.K. & H.P.S.)*

§ 231.102. Eligibility for Child Support Services.

The Title IV–D agency on application or as otherwise authorized by law may provide services for the benefit of a child without regard to whether the child has received public assistance.

§ 231.103. Application and Service Fees.

(a) The Title IV–D agency may:

(1) charge a reasonable application fee;

(2) charge a $25 annual service fee; and

(3) to the extent permitted by federal law, recover costs for the services provided in a Title IV–D case.

(b) An application fee may not be charged in a case in which the Title IV–D agency provides services because the family receives public assistance.

(c) An application fee may not exceed a maximum amount established by federal law.

(d) The Title IV–D agency may only charge an annual service fee in a Title IV–D case if the recipient of Title IV–D services has never received public assistance under Part A of Title IV of the federal Social Security Act (42 U.S.C. Section 601 et seq.) and the recipient receives more than $500 in support payments in a year. The annual service fee may only be deducted from support payments that exceed $500 annually.

(e) The Title IV–D agency may impose and collect a fee as authorized by federal law for each request for parent locator services under Section 231.101(a).

(f) The state disbursement unit established and operated by the Title IV–D agency under Chapter 234 may collect a monthly service fee of $3 deducted from support payments in a case for which the Title IV–D agency is not providing services.

(g) The Title IV–D agency by rule shall establish procedures for the imposition of fees and recovery of costs authorized under this section.

(h) The attorney general child support application and service fee account is an account in the general revenue fund in the state treasury. The account consists of all fees and costs collected under this section. The Title IV–D agency may only use the money in the account for agency program expenditures.

Comment

Federal law (42 U.S.C. 654(6)) requires a state's IV–D agency to charge an application fee for services in cases in which the applicant is not a recipient of public assistance, and it authorizes the agency to charge other appropriate fees and to recover administrative costs for providing services in these cases. In 2003, the legislature specifically identified under this section a set of fees that the agency may levy. Although under the federal funding scheme any fees and costs recovered by the IV–D must be shared with the federal government, under subsection (h) the amounts retained by the state must be reinvested in the IV–D program, thereby producing additional federal matching funds for the operation of the program. *(C.B. & H.P.S.)*

---

§ 231.104. Assignment of Right To Support.

(a) To the extent authorized by federal law, the approval of an application for or the receipt of financial assistance as provided by Chapter 31, Human Resources Code, constitutes an assignment to the Title IV-D agency of any rights to support from any other person that the applicant or recipient may have personally or for a child for whom the applicant or recipient is claiming assistance.

(b) An application for child support services is an assignment of support rights to enable the Title IV–D agency to establish and enforce child support and medical support obligations, but an assignment is not a condition of eligibility for services.

§ 231.105. Notice of Change of Payee.

(a) Child support payments for the benefit of a child whose support rights have been assigned to the Title IV-D agency under Section 231.104 shall be made payable to the Title IV-D agency and transmitted to the state disbursement unit as provided by Chapter 234.

(b) If a court has ordered support payments to be made to an applicant for or recipient of financial assistance or to an applicant for or recipient of Title IV-D services, the Title IV-D agency shall, on providing notice to the obligee and the obligor, direct the obligor or other payor to make support payments payable to the Title IV-D agency and to transmit the payments to the state disbursement unit. The Title IV-D agency shall file a copy of the notice with the court ordering the payments and with the child support registry. The notice must include:

(1) a statement that the child is an applicant for or recipient of financial assistance, or a child other than a recipient child for whom Title IV-D services are provided;

(2) the name of the child and the caretaker for whom support has been ordered by the court;

(3) the style and cause number of the case in which support was ordered; and

(4) instructions for the payment of ordered support to the agency.

(c) On receipt of a copy of the notice under Subsection (b), the clerk of the court shall file the notice in the appropriate case file.

Comment

Under federal law, an application for, or receipt of, public assistance constitutes an assignment to the state of rights to child support. Similarly, under state law an approved application for IV–D services in non-public assistance cases constitutes an assignment of support rights. Where there is such an assignment in a IV–D case, a court order has been needed in order to redirect support payments to the IV–D agency. Under PRWORA, the agency itself must have the authority, without the requirement of a court order, to effect a change of payee if there is an assignment of support or if support payments (as in the case of all income withholding) are required to be made to the new state disbursement unit under Chapter 234. Using the administrative procedures, the agency itself may direct any payor of support to send payments directly to the agency and notify the court ordering the support and the local support registry of this change. *(A.G.K. & H.P.S.)*

---

§ 231.106. Notice of Termination of Assignment.

(a) On termination of support rights to the Title IV-D agency, the Title IV-D agency shall, after providing notice to the obligee and the obligor, send a notice of termination of assignment to the obligor or other payor, which may direct that all or a portion of the payments be made payable to the agency and to other persons who are entitled to receive the payments.

(b) The Title IV–D agency shall send a copy of the notice of termination of assignment to the court ordering the support and to the child support registry, and on receipt of the notice the clerk of the court shall file the notice in the appropriate case file. The clerk may not require an order of the court to terminate the assignment and direct support payments to the person entitled to receive the payment.

Comment

The IV–D agency must send notice of any termination of assignment of support rights to the obligee, the obligor, and to the appropriate court and local registry. The notice may redirect support payments to a payee other than the agency, although in most instances it will not because of the PRWORA requirement that, with limited exceptions, income withholding be made through the state disbursement unit. *(A.G.K. & H.P.S.)*

---

§ 231.107. Certificate of Assignment or of Termination of Assignment.

If an abstract of judgment or a child support lien on support amounts assigned to the Title IV-D agency under this chapter has previously been filed of record, the agency shall file for recordation, with the county clerk of each county in which such abstract or lien has been filed, a certificate that a notice of change of payee or a notice of termination of assignment has been issued by the agency.

Comment

A lien for child support under Chapter 157 attaches when a lien notice or abstract of judgment is filed with the clerk of a county in which the obligor resides, has nonexempt real or personal property, or in which the court having continuing jurisdiction is located. The certification of an assignment of support rights to the state protects that assignment in the event of foreclosure of the lien or an action to release the lien. *(A.G.K. & H.P.S.)*

---

§ 231.108. Confidentiality of Records and Privileged Communications.

(a) Except as provided by Subsection (c), all files and records of services provided under this chapter, including information concerning a custodial parent, noncustodial parent, child, and an alleged or presumed father, are confidential.

(b) Except as provided by Subsection (c), all communications made by a recipient of financial assistance under Chapter 31, Human Resources Code, or an applicant for or recipient of services under this chapter are privileged.

(c) The Title IV–D agency may use or release information from the files and records, including information that results from a communication made by a recipient of financial assistance under Chapter 31, Human Resources Code, or by an applicant for or recipient of services under this chapter, for purposes directly connected with the administration of the child support, paternity determination, parent locator, or aid to families with dependent children programs. The Title IV–D agency may release information from the files and records to a consumer reporting agency in accordance with Section 231.114.

(d) The Title IV–D agency by rule may provide for the release of information to public officials.

(e) The Title IV-D agency may not release information on the physical location of a person if:

(1) a protective order has been entered with respect to the person; or

(2) there is reason to believe that the release of information may result in physical or emotional harm to the person.

(f) The Title IV–D agency, by rule, may provide for the release of information to persons for purposes not prohibited by federal law.

(g) The final order in a suit adjudicating parentage is available for public inspection as provided by Section 160.633.

History: Amended by 78th Legis., Reg. Sess. (2003), H.B. 1878, eff. Sept. 1, 2003. "The change in law made by this Act relating to a court order establishing paternity or the obligation to pay child support applies only to a suit affecting the parent-child relationship filed on or after the effective date of this Act. A suit affecting the parent-child relationship filed before the effective date of this Act is governed by the law in effect on the date the suit was filed, and the former law is continued in effect for that purpose."

Comments

For the most part the provisions of this section reflect the confidentiality requirements of federal law with respect to the operation of state IV–D programs. (*See* 42 U.S.C. § 654(26).) *(C.B. & H.P.S.)*

---

§ 231.109. Attorneys Representing State.

(a) Attorneys employed by the Title IV–D agency may represent this state or another state in an action brought under the authority of federal law or this chapter.

(b) The Title IV–D agency may contract with private attorneys, other private entities, or political subdivisions of the state to provide services in Title IV–D cases.

(c) The Title IV–D agency shall provide copies of all contracts entered into under this section to the Legislative Budget Board and the Governor's Office of Budget and Planning, along with a written justification of the need for each contract, within 60 days after the execution of the contract.

(d) An attorney employed to provide Title IV-D services represents the interest of the state and not the interest of any other party. The provision of services by an attorney under this chapter does not create an attorney-client relationship between the attorney and any other party. The agency shall, at the time an application for child support services is made, inform the applicant that neither the Title IV–D agency nor any attorney who provides services under this chapter is the applicant's attorney and that the attorney providing services under this chapter does not provide legal representation to the applicant.

(e) An attorney employed by the Title IV–D agency or as otherwise provided by this chapter may not be appointed or act as a guardian ad litem or attorney ad litem for a child or another party.

§ 231.110. Authorization of Service.

The provision of services by the Title IV–D agency under this chapter or Part D of Title IV of the federal Social Security Act (42 U.S.C. Section 651 et seq.) does not authorize service on the agency of any legal notice that is required to be served on any party other than the agency.

§ 231.111. Disqualification of Agency.

A court shall not disqualify the Title IV–D agency in a legal action filed under this chapter or Part D of Title IV of the federal Social Security Act (42 U.S.C. Section 651 et seq.) on the basis that the agency has previously provided services to a party whose interests may now be adverse to the relief requested.

§ 231.112. Information on Paternity Establishment.

On notification by the state registrar under Section 192.005(d), Health and Safety Code, that the items relating to the child's father are not completed on a birth certificate filed with the state registrar, the Title IV–D agency may provide to:

(1) the child's mother and, if possible, the man claiming to be the child's biological father written information necessary for the man to complete an acknowledgment of paternity as provided by Chapter 160; and

(2) the child's mother written information:

(A) explaining the benefits of having the child's paternity established; and

(B) regarding the availability of paternity establishment and child support enforcement services.

§ 231.113. Enforcement of Support Obligations in Public Assistance Cases.

To the extent possible, the Title IV–D agency shall enforce a child support obligation in a case involving a child who receives financial assistance under Chapter 31, Human Resources Code, not later than the first anniversary of the date the agency receives from the Texas Department of Human Services the information the department is required to provide to assist in the enforcement of that obligation.

§ 231.114. Reports of Child Support Payments to Consumer Reporting Agencies.

(a) The Title IV–D agency shall make information available in accordance with this section to a consumer reporting agency regarding the amount of child support owed and the amount paid by an obligor in a Title IV–D case.

(b) Before disclosing the information to consumer reporting agencies, the Title IV–D agency shall send the obligor a notice by mail to the obligor's last known address. The notice must include:

(1) the information to be released, including the amount of the obligor's child support obligation and delinquency, if any, that will be reported;

(2) the procedure available for the obligor to contest the accuracy of the information; and

(3) a statement that the information will be released if the obligor fails to contest the disclosure before the 30th day after the date of mailing of the notice.

(c) If the obligor does not contest the disclosure within the period specified by Subsection (b), the Title IV–D agency shall make the information available to the consumer reporting agency.

(d) The Title IV–D agency shall regularly update the information released to a consumer reporting agency under this section to ensure the accuracy of the released information.

(e) The Title IV–D agency may charge a consumer reporting agency a reasonable fee for making information available under this section, including all applicable mailing costs.

(f) In this section:

(1) "Consumer reporting agency" means any person that regularly engages in whole or in part in the practice of assembling or evaluating consumer credit information or other information on consumers for monetary fees, for dues, or on a cooperative nonprofit basis, to furnish consumer reports to third parties.

(2) "Obligor" means any person required to make payments under the terms of a support order for a child.

(3) "Title IV–D case" means a case in which services are being provided by the Title IV–D agency under Part D of Title IV of the federal Social Security Act (42 U.S.C. Section 651 et seq.) seeking to locate an absent parent, determine parentage, or establish, modify, enforce, or monitor a child support obligation.

§ 231.115. Noncooperation by Recipient of Public Assistance.

(a) The failure by a person who is a recipient of public assistance under Chapter 31, Human Resources Code, to provide accurate information as required by Section 31.0315, Human Resources Code, shall serve as the basis for a determination by the Title IV–D agency that the person did not cooperate with the Title IV–D agency.

(b) The Title IV–D agency shall:

(1) identify the actions or failures to act by a recipient of public assistance that constitute noncooperation with the Title IV–D agency;

(2) adopt rules governing noncompliance; and

(3) send noncompliance determinations to the Texas Department of Human Services for immediate imposition of sanctions.

(c) In adopting rules under this section that establish the basis for determining that a person has failed to cooperate with the Title IV–D agency, the Title IV–D agency shall consider whether:

(1) good cause exists for the failure to cooperate;

(2) the person has failed to disclose the name and location of an alleged or probable parent of the child, if known by the person, at the time of applying for public assistance or at a subsequent time; and

(3) the person named a man as the alleged father and the man was subsequently excluded by parentage testing as being the father if the person has previously named another man as the child's father.

§ 231.116. Information on Internet.

The Title IV-D agency shall place on the Internet for public access child support information to assist the public in child support matters, including application forms, child support collection in other states, and profiles of certain obligors who are in arrears in paying child support.

Comment

The intent of this provision is to advertise the availability of IV–D services, as well as to identify delinquent obligors to be reported for an award; § 231.309, *infra*, authorizes the agency to make an offer for such information. *(A.G.K. & H.P.S.)*

---

§ 231.1165. Information on Service of Citation.

The Title IV-D agency shall update the agency's child support automated system to inform the parties in a suit of the service of citation in the suit not later than the first business day after the date the agency receives notice that citation has been served. The information required by this section must be available by telephone and on the Internet.

Comment

The intent of this section is to save an obligee in a IV–D case from being required to make special arrangements to attend a child support hearing, or from making an unnecessary trip to the courthouse only to learn that the obligor has not been successfully served a citation requiring appearance. Unfortunately, often the IV–D agency itself does not learn of an unsuccessful attempt at service until its attorneys arrive for a hearing. *(A.G.K. & H.P.S.)*

---

§ 231.117. Unemployed and Underemployed Obligors.

(a) The Title IV-D agency shall refer to appropriate state and local entities that provide employment services any unemployed or underemployed obligor who is in arrears in court-ordered child support payments.

(b) A referral under Subsection (a) may include:

(1) skills training and job placement through:

(A) the Texas Workforce Commission; or

(B) the agency responsible for the food stamp employment and training program (7 U.S.C. Section 2015(d));

(2) referrals to education and literacy classes; and

(3) counseling regarding:

(A) substance abuse;

(B) parenting skills;

(C) life skills; and

(D) mediation techniques.

(c) The Title IV-D agency may require an unemployed or underemployed obligor to complete the training, classes, or counseling to which the obligor is referred under this section. The agency shall suspend under Chapter 232 the license of an obligor who fails to comply with the requirements of this subsection.

(d) A court or the Title IV–D agency may issue an order that requires the parent to either work, have a plan to pay overdue child support, or participate in work activities appropriate to pay the overdue support.

§ 231.118. Service of Citation.

(a) The Title IV–D agency may contract with private process servers to serve a citation, a subpoena, an order, or any other document required or appropriate under law to be served a party.

(b) For the purposes of Rule 103 of the Texas Rules of Civil Procedure, a person who serves a citation or any other document under this section is authorized to serve the document without a written court order authorizing the service.

(c) Issuance and return of the process shall be made in accordance with law and shall be verified by the person serving the document.

§ 231.119. Ombudsman Program.

(a) The Title IV–D agency shall establish an ombudsman program to process and track complaints against the Title IV–D agency. The director of the Title IV–D agency shall:

(1) designate an employee to serve as chief ombudsman to manage the ombudsman program; and

(2) designate an employee in each field office to act as the ombudsman for the office.

(b) The Title IV–D agency shall develop and implement a uniform process for receiving and resolving complaints against the Title IV–D agency throughout the state. The process shall include statewide procedures to inform the public and recipients of Title IV–D services of the right to file a complaint against the Title IV–D agency, including the mailing addresses and telephone numbers of appropriate Title IV–D agency personnel responsible for receiving complaints and providing related assistance.

(c) The ombudsman in each field office shall ensure that an employee in the field office responds to and attempts to resolve each complaint that is filed with the field office. If a complaint cannot be resolved at the field office level, the ombudsman in the field office shall refer the complaint to the chief ombudsman.

(d) The Title IV–D agency shall maintain a file on each written complaint filed with the Title IV–D agency. The file must include:

(1) the name of the person who filed the complaint;

(2) the date the complaint is received by the Title IV–D agency;

(3) the subject matter of the complaint;

(4) the name of each person contacted in relation to the complaint;

(5) a summary of the results of the review or investigation of the complaint; and

(6) an explanation of the reason the file was closed, if the agency closed the file without taking action other than to investigate the complaint.

(e) The Title IV–D agency, at least quarterly until final disposition of the complaint, shall notify the person filing the complaint and each person who is a subject of the complaint of the status of the investigation of the complaint unless the notice would jeopardize an undercover investigation.

(f) The Title IV–D agency shall provide to the person filing the complaint and to each person who is a subject of the complaint a copy of the Title IV–D agency's policies and procedures relating to complaint investigation and resolution.

§ 231.120. Toll-free Telephone Number for Employers.

The Title IV–D agency shall maintain a toll-free telephone number at which personnel are available during normal business hours to answer questions from employers responsible for withholding child support. The Title IV–D agency shall inform employers about the toll-free telephone number.

§ 231.121. Availability of Brochures.

The Title IV-D agency shall ensure that all Title IV-D brochures published by the agency are available to the public at courthouses where family law cases are heard in the state.

Comment

Federal law already requires the IV–D agency to publicize agency services available to the public. This section prescribes a specific way of publicizing such services on the apparent assumption that parties in family law cases will have either the time for, or interest in, browsing brochures in a courthouse hallway. *(A.G.K. & H.P.S.)*

Subchapter C. Payment of Fees and Costs

§ 231.201. Definitions.

In this subchapter:

(1) "Federal share" means the portion of allowable expenses for fees and other costs that will be reimbursed by the federal government under federal law and regulations regarding the administration of the Title IV–D program.

(2) "State share" means the portion of allowable expenses for fees and other costs that remain after receipt of the federal share of reimbursement and that is to be reimbursed by the state or may be contributed by certified public expenditure by a county.

§ 231.202. Authorized Costs and Fees in Title Iv–d Cases.

In a Title IV–D case filed under this title, the Title IV–D agency shall pay:

(1) filing fees and fees for issuance and service of process as provided by Chapter 110 of this code and by Sections 51.317, 51.318(b)(2), and 51.319(2), Government Code;

(2) fees for transfer as provided by Chapter 110;

(3) fees for the issuance and delivery of orders and writs of income withholding in the amounts provided by Chapter 110;

(4) **the** [a] fee **that sheriffs and constables are authorized to charge for serving process under Section 118.131, Local Government Code,** [~~of $45~~] for each item of process to each individual on whom service is required, including service by certified or registered mail, to be paid to a sheriff, constable, or clerk whenever service of process is required; and

(5) the fee for filing an administrative writ of withholding under Section 158.503(d).

History: Amended by 78th Legis., Reg. Sess. (2003), S.B. 1165, eff. Sept. 1, 2003, and "applies only to a service of process made on or after that date. A service of process made before the effective date of this Act is governed by the law in effect on the date the service of process is made, and the former law is continued in effect for that purpose."

Comment

In 1991 the legislature authorized payment to the counties of the filing costs and service fees in cases enforced by the IV–D agency. Since that enactment, federal funds (equal to 66 percent of total costs and fees) have been passed through to counties, with the balance to be paid either by the counties or through specific appropriation made to the attorney general for that purpose. Subsequent amendments to the Family Code have expanded the categories of fees and costs in IV–D cases eligible for reimbursement. Section 158.503(d) authorizes a fee for filing an administrative writ of withholding issued by the IV–D agency, thereby providing counties with further income for a ministerial act of little consequence. *(A.G.K. & H.P.S.)*

---

§ 231.2025. Contingency Fees.

The Title IV-D agency may pay a contingency fee in a contract or agreement between the agency and a private agency or individual authorized under Section 231.002(c).

§ 231.203. State Exemption From Bond Not Affected.

This subchapter does not affect, nor is this subchapter affected by, the exemption from bond provided by Section 6.001, Civil Practice and Remedies Code.

§ 231.204. Prohibited Fees in Title IV-D Cases.

Except as provided by this subchapter, an appellate court, a clerk of an appellate court, a district or county clerk, sheriff, constable, or other government officer or employee may not charge the Title IV-D agency or a private attorney or political subdivision that has entered into a contract to provide Title IV-D services any fees or other amounts otherwise imposed by law for services rendered in, or in connection with, a Title IV-D case, including:

(1) a fee payable to a district clerk for:

(A) performing services related to the estates of deceased persons or minors;

(B) certifying copies; or

(C) comparing copies to originals;

(2) a court reporter fee, except as provided by Section 231.209;

(3) a judicial fund fee;

(4) a fee for a child support registry, enforcement office, or domestic relations office;

(5) a fee for alternative dispute resolution services; and

(6) a filing fee or other costs payable to a clerk of an appellate court.

Comment

The services for which the IV–D agency may be charged fees are enumerated under § 231.202, *supra*. The list of services under this section for which the agency may not be charged fees is, of course, not intended to be exclusive or limiting. Even if it is not identified in this list, a fee not specifically required elsewhere in law to be paid by the IV–D agency may not be assessed against the agency. *(A.G.K. & H.P.S.)*

---

§ 231.205. Limitations on Liability of Attorney General for Authorized Fees and Costs.

(a) The Title IV–D agency is liable for a fee or cost under this subchapter only to the extent that an express, specific appropriation is made to the agency exclusively for that purpose. To the extent that state funds are not available, the amount of costs and fees that are not reimbursed by the federal government and that represent the state share shall be paid by certified public expenditure by the county through the clerk of the court, sheriff, or constable. This section does not prohibit the agency from spending other funds appropriated for child support enforcement to provide the initial expenditures necessary to qualify for the federal share.

(b) The Title IV–D agency is liable for the payment of the federal share of reimbursement for fees and costs under this subchapter only to the extent that the federal share is received, and if an amount is paid by the agency and that amount is disallowed by the federal government or the federal share is not otherwise received, the clerk of the court, sheriff, or constable to whom the payment was made shall return the amount to the agency not later than the 30th day after the date on which notice is given by the agency.

§ 231.206. Restriction on Fees for Child Support or Registry Services in Title IV–D Cases.

A district clerk, a county child support registry or enforcement office, or a domestic relations office may not assess or collect fees for processing child support payments or for child support services from the Title IV–D agency, a managing conservator, or a possessory conservator in a Title IV–D case, except as provided by this subchapter.

§ 231.207. Method of Billing for Allowable Fees.

(a) To be entitled to reimbursement under this subchapter, the clerk of the court, sheriff, or constable must submit one monthly billing to the Title IV–D agency.

(b) The monthly billing must be in the form and manner prescribed by the Title IV–D agency and be approved by the clerk, sheriff, or constable.

§ 231.208. Agreements for Reimbursement in Lieu of Fees.

(a) The Title IV–D agency and a qualified county may enter into a written agreement under which reimbursement for salaries and certain other actual costs incurred by the clerk, sheriff, or constable in Title IV–D cases is provided to the county.

(b) A county may not enter into an agreement for reimbursement under this section unless the clerk, sheriff, or constable providing service has at least two full-time employees each devoted exclusively to providing services in Title IV–D cases.

(c) Reimbursement made under this section is in lieu of all costs and fees provided by this subchapter.

§ 231.209. Payment for Services Not Affected by This Subchapter.

Without regard to this subchapter and specifically Section 231.205, the Title IV–D agency may pay the costs for:

(1) the services of an official court reporter for the preparation of statements of facts;

(2) the costs for the publication of citation served by publication; and

(3) mileage or other reasonable travel costs incurred by a sheriff or constable when traveling out of the county to execute an outstanding warrant or capias, to be reimbursed at a rate not to exceed the rate provided for mileage or other costs incurred by state employees in the General Appropriations Act.

§ 231.210. Authority to Pay Litigation Expenses.

(a) The Title IV–D agency may pay all fees, expenses, costs, and bills necessary to secure evidence and to take the testimony of a witness, including advance payments or purchases for transportation, lodging, meals, and incidental expenses of custodians of evidence or witnesses whose transportation is necessary and proper for the production of evidence or the taking of testimony in a Title IV–D case.

(b) In making payments under this section, the Title IV–D agency shall present vouchers to the comptroller that have been sworn to by the custodian or witness and approved by the agency. The voucher shall be sufficient to authorize payment without the necessity of a written contract.

(c) The Title IV–D agency may directly pay a commercial transportation company or commercial lodging establishment for the expense of transportation or lodging of a custodian or witness.

§ 231.211. Award of Cost Against Nonprevailing Party in Title IV–D Case.

(a) At the conclusion of a Title IV–D case, the court may assess attorney's fees and all court costs as authorized by law against the nonprevailing party, except that the court may not assess those amounts against the Title IV–D agency or a private attorney or political subdivision that has entered into a contract under this chapter or any party to whom the agency has provided services under this chapter. Such fees and costs may not exceed reasonable and necessary costs as determined by the court.

(b) The clerk of the court may take any action necessary to collect any fees or costs assessed under this section.

Comment

The trial court is authorized to award fees and costs in IV–D cases against the nonprevailing party—meaning the obligor. One litigant, the attorney general, a.k.a. the State of Texas, is exempt from the payment of those fees even if the government fails to prevail (thereby saving the taxpayers cash at the expense of the private party, which is what sovereign immunity is all about).

Subchapter D. Location of Parents and Resources

§ 231.301. Title IV–D Parent Locator Services.

(a) The parent locator service conducted by the Title IV–D agency shall be used to obtain information for:

(1) child support establishment and enforcement purposes regarding the identity, social security number, location, employer and employment benefits, income, and assets or debts of any individual under an obligation to pay child or medical support or to whom a support obligation is owed; or

(2) the establishment of paternity.

(b) As authorized by federal law, the following persons may receive information under this section:

(1) a person or entity that contracts with the Title IV–D agency to provide services authorized under Title IV–D or an employee of the Title IV–D agency;

(2) an attorney who has the duty or authority, by law, to enforce an order for possession of or access to a child;

(3) a court, or an agent of the court, having jurisdiction to render or enforce an order for possession of or access to a child;

(4) the resident parent, legal guardian, attorney, or agent of a child who is not receiving public assistance; and

(5) a state agency that administers a program operated under a state plan as provided by 42 U.S.C. Section 653(c).

§ 231.302. Information to Assist in Location of Persons or Property.

(a) The Title IV-D agency of this or another state may request and obtain information relating to the identity, location, employment, compensation, benefits, income, and property holdings or other assets of any person from a state or local government agency, private company, institution, or other entity as necessary to establish, modify, or enforce a support order.

(b) A government agency, private company, institution, or other entity shall provide the information requested under Subsection (a) directly to the Title IV-D agency, without the requirement of payment of a fee for the information, and shall, subject to safeguards on privacy and information security, provide the information in the most efficient and expeditious manner available, including electronic or automated transfer and interface. Any individual or entity disclosing information under this section in response to a request from a Title IV-D agency may not be held liable in any civil action or proceeding to any person for the disclosure of information under this subsection.

(c) To assist in the administration of laws relating to child support enforcement under Parts A and D of Title IV of the federal Social Security Act (42 U.S.C. Sections 601–617 and 651–669):

(1) each licensing authority shall request and each applicant for a license shall provide the applicant's social security number;

(2) each agency administering a contract that provides for a payment of state funds shall request and each individual or entity bidding on a state contract shall provide the individual's or entity's social security number as required by Section 231.006, Family Code; and

(3) each agency administering a state-funded grant or loan program shall request and each applicant for a grant or loan shall provide the applicant's social security number as required by Section 231.006, Family Code.

(d) This section does not limit the right of an agency or licensing authority to collect and use a social security number under another provision of law.

(e) Except as provided by Subsection (d), a social security number provided under this section is confidential and may be disclosed only for the purposes of responding to a request for information from an agency operating under the provisions of Part A or D of Title IV of the federal Social Security Act (42 U.S.C. Sections 601 et seq. and 651 et seq).

(f) Information collected by the Title IV-D agency under this section may be used only for child support purposes.

(g) In this section, "licensing authority" has the meaning assigned by Section 232.001.

Comment

In 1996 PRWORA significantly expanded the access of state IV–D agencies to various kinds of information useful in child support enforcement. As part of the certification requirements under the Family Support Act of 1988, the IV–D agency's automated system must electronically interface with, among other information sources, the state agencies responsible for administering public assistance and unemployment and workers' compensation programs, the state agencies maintaining property records, vital records, corrections records, and motor vehicle records, and consumer credit reporting bureaus. Under PRWORA, without the necessity of any other court or administrative order and preferably by automated means, the IV–D agency of this or another state must be able to access information from any state or local agency, private company, institution, or any other entity possessing information needed for support enforcement purposes. This includes information from public or private employers about employment, compensation, and benefits and, by administrative subpoena, information appearing in customer records of public utilities and cable companies and information on the assets and liabilities of obligees and obligors maintained in records of financial institutions. Although access to, and release of, information must be subject to appropriate security safeguards and privacy protections, the greatly expanded disclosure of confidential or otherwise sensitive information, particularly through automated data exchanges, increases opportunities for the inappropriate or unauthorized use of the information, not to mention data error.

PRWORA also mandated that states have laws and procedures for the recordation of social security numbers on applications for driver's, professional, recreational, and marriage licenses, on records relating to divorce decrees, support orders, and paternity acknowledgments, and on death certificates. *(A.G.K. & H.P.S.)*

---

§ 231.303. Title IV–D Administrative Subpoena.

(a) The Title IV-D agency of this state or another state may issue an administrative subpoena to any individual or private or public entity in this state to furnish information necessary to carry out the purposes of child support enforcement under 42 U.S.C. Section 651 et seq. or this chapter.

(b) An individual or entity receiving an administrative subpoena under this section shall comply with the subpoena. The Title IV-D agency may impose a fine in an amount not to exceed $500 on an individual or entity that fails without good cause to comply with an administrative subpoena. An alleged or presumed father or a parent who fails to comply with a subpoena without good cause may also be subject to license suspension under Chapter 232.

(c) A court may compel compliance with an administrative subpoena and with any administrative fine for failure to comply with the subpoena and may award attorney's fees and costs to the Title IV-D agency in enforcing an administrative subpoena on proof that an individual or organization failed without good cause to comply with the subpoena.

(d) An individual or organization may not be liable in a civil action or proceeding for disclosing financial or other information to a Title IV-D agency under this section. The Title IV-D agency may disclose information in a financial record obtained from a financial institution only to the extent necessary:

(1) to establish, modify, or enforce a child support obligation; or

(2) to comply with Section 233.001, as added by Chapter 420, Acts of the 75th Legislature, Regular Session, 1997.

Comment

This section complies with the requirement of PRWORA that the IV–D agency have the authority to issue an administrative subpoena and to impose sanctions for failure to comply with a subpoena. Under this section, the real authority for compelling compliance lies with the court, although on its own the agency, following procedures under Chapter 232, may suspend a license of a presumed or alleged father or a parent who fails to comply with an administrative subpoena. The agency's subpoena power may be particularly valuable in gaining access to information on the location and assets of absent parents. *(A.G.K. & H.P.S.)*

---

§ 231.304. [repealed]

§ 231.305. Memorandum of Understanding on Child Support for Children Receiving Public Assistance.

(a) The Title IV–D agency and the Texas Department of Human Services by rule shall adopt a memorandum of understanding governing the establishment and enforcement of court-ordered child support in cases involving children who receive financial assistance under Chapter 31, Human Resources Code. The memorandum shall require the agency and the department to:

(1) develop procedures to ensure that the information the department is required to collect to establish and enforce child support:

(A) is collected from the person applying to receive the financial assistance at the time the application is filed;

(B) is accurate and complete when the department forwards the information to the agency;

(C) is not information previously reported to the agency; and

(D) is forwarded to the agency in an expeditious manner;

(2) develop procedures to ensure that the agency does not duplicate the efforts of the department in gathering necessary information;

(3) clarify each agency's responsibilities in the establishment and enforcement of child support;

(4) develop guidelines for use by eligibility workers and child support enforcement officers in obtaining from an applicant the information required to establish and enforce child support for that child;

(5) develop training programs for appropriate department personnel to enhance the collection of information for child support enforcement;

(6) develop a standard time, not to exceed 30 days, for the department to initiate a sanction on request from the agency;

(7) develop procedures for agency participation in department appeal hearings relating to noncompliance sanctions;

(8) develop performance measures regarding the timeliness and the number of sanctions resulting from agency requests for noncompliance sanctions; and

(9) prescribe:

(A) the time in which the department is required to forward information under Subdivision (1)(D); and

(B) what constitutes complete information under Subdivision (1)(B).

(b) The Title IV–D agency and the Texas Department of Human Services shall review and renew or modify the memorandum not later than January 1 of each even-numbered year.

§ 231.306. Maximizing Medical Support Establishment and Collection by the Title IV–D Agency.

(a) On the installation of an automated child support enforcement system, the Title IV–D agency is strongly encouraged to:

(1) maximize the collection of medical support; and

(2) establish cash medical support orders for children eligible for medical assistance under the state Medicaid program for whom private insurance coverage is not available.

(b) In this section, "medical support" has the meaning assigned by Section 101.020.

§ 231.307. Financial Institution Data Matches.

(a) The Title IV-D agency shall develop a system meeting the requirements of federal law (42 U.S.C. Sections 666(a)(4) and (17)) for the exchange of data with financial institutions doing business in the state to identify an account of an obligor owing past-due child support and to enforce support obligations against the obligor, including the imposition of a lien and a levy and execution on an obligor's assets held in financial institutions as required by federal law (42 U.S.C. Section 666(c)(1)(G)).

(b) The Title IV-D agency by rule shall establish procedures for data matches authorized under this section.

(c) The Title IV–D agency may enter into an agreement with one or more states to create a consortium for data matches authorized under this section. The Title IV–D agency may contract with a vendor selected by the consortium to perform data matches with financial institutions.

(d) A financial institution providing information or responding to a notice of child support lien provided under Subchapter G, Chapter 157, or otherwise acting in good faith to comply with the Title IV–D agency's procedures under this section may not be liable under any federal or state law for any damages that arise from those acts.

(e) In this section:

(1) "Financial institution" has the meaning assigned by Section 157.311; and

(2) "Account" has the meaning assigned by Section 157.311.

(f) A financial institution participating in data matches authorized by this section may provide the Title IV-D agency an address for the purpose of service of notices or process required in actions under this section or Subchapter G, Chapter 157 *[Enforcement]*.

Comment

PRWORA requires the IV–D agency to establish a system, using automatic processes to the extent possible, under which financial institutions doing business in the state provide the agency each quarter with information on obligors who have accounts in the institutions and whom the agency has identified as being delinquent in support payments. Although at the time only one state has had any experience in executing such data matches, Congress mandated the process as a support enforcement "tool" for all states. Presumably once the assets of a delinquent obligor have been located, the IV–D agency will be able to move quickly to impose and execute a child support lien on those assets up to the amount of support arrearages. On receiving a lien notice, the institution is not to be held liable for encumbering and surrendering assets in complying with a lien. To meet the federal mandate fully, however, the IV–D agency must enter into agreements with not only all banks in the state, but also with all credit unions, benefit associations, insurance companies, safe deposit companies, mutual funds, and any other entity that offers a financial "account." Because this is an intrastate system, accounts which an obligor might maintain outside the state will not necessarily be detected. States can, however, expand their search through multi-state consortia. Moreover, the federal Office of Child Support Enforcement provides a mechanism through the Federal Parent Locator Service for matching state data on delinquent child support obligors with account information in multi-state financial institutions. *(A.G.K. & H.P.S.)*

---

§ 231.308. Public Identification of Certain Obligors.

(a) The Title IV-D agency shall develop a program to identify publicly certain child support obligors who are delinquent in the payment of child support. The program shall include the displaying of photographs and profiles of obligors in public and private locations. The Title IV-D agency shall use posters, the news media, and other cost-effective methods to display photographs and profiles of certain obligors who are in arrears in paying child support. The Title IV-D agency shall divide the state into at least six regions for local identification of certain child support obligors who are delinquent in the payment of child support.

(b) The Title IV-D agency may not disclose information under this section that is by law required to remain confidential.

Comment

The use of a "most wanted" program not only serves to highlight the problem of nonsupport; it also results in the arrest of obligors who have sought to evade their child support responsibilities. *(C.B. & H.P.S.)*

---

§ 231.309. Rewards for Information.

(a) The Title IV-D agency may offer a reward to an individual who provides information to the agency that leads to the collection of child support owed by an obligor who is delinquent in paying support.

(b) The Title IV-D agency shall adopt rules providing for the amounts of rewards offered under this section and the circumstances under which an individual providing information described in Subsection (a) is entitled to receive a reward.

(c) A reward paid under this section shall be paid from the child support retained collections account.

Comment

If the IV–D agency exercises the reward option, it must balance the size of the rewards it may be able to offer against other operating costs; both rewards and ongoing agency expenses come from the same account. *(C.B. & H.P.S.)*

---

§ 231.310. Interagency Work Group.

(a) The Title IV-D agency shall establish a work group to facilitate the sharing of data and resources to locate parents and relatives of children served by the Title IV-D agency and other health and human services agencies.

(b) The work group shall consist of representatives from the Title IV-D agency, the Department of Protective and Regulatory Services, the Texas Department of Human Services, the Texas Department of Health, the Texas Workforce Commission, the Texas

Department of Public Safety, the Texas Rehabilitation Commission, and the Texas Department of Criminal Justice.

(c) The commissioner of human services or the commissioner's designee shall serve as the work group's presiding officer.

(d) The work group shall evaluate the procedures used by each agency in the work group to locate parents and relatives of children served by the agencies and develop a mechanism to ensure that each agency in the work group, or any private contractor performing location functions for an agency, is able to access information in the database of each other agency without paying a fee.

(e) The work group shall evaluate opportunities for using outside contracting and coordinating efforts with other community resources.

(f) To the extent possible, the Department of Protective and Regulatory Services and the Title IV-D agency shall use outside contractors and community resources to locate parents in child protection and child support cases.

Chapter 232. Suspension of License

Editors' Note: *This chapter contains guest commentary by Howard G. Baldwin, Jr., former First Assistant, Cynthia Bryant, Deputy Attorney General, and H. Patrick Sullivan, Director of Federal Policy Analysis, Child Support Division, Office of the Attorney General of Texas; and, Alicia Gray Key, Director, Office of Court Administration; identified respectively as (H.G.B., C.B. & H.P.S., A.G.K.).*

Introductory Comment

As a child support enforcement remedy, this chapter provides for the suspension of a business, occupational, professional, recreational, or driver's license of an obligor who: (1) is in arrears in an amount equal to, or greater than, the total support due for 90 days; (2) has been provided an opportunity to make payments towards the arrears under an agreed or court-ordered repayment plan; and, (3) has failed to comply with the plan. The purpose of the statute is not to suspend licenses, but to compel compliance with child support orders—perhaps after other means of compliance have been attempted and exhausted. Just the threat of license suspension, however, may be enough to get a recalcitrant obligor to make timely and full payments or, where there are arrearages, to agree to, and comply with, a repayment plan. The effect of the statute is similar to that of coercive civil contempt; the penalty of license suspension is contingent on failure to comply either with the agreed or court-ordered repayment of the support arrearages.

The Texas statute is designed to provide both an administrative and a judicial process. In non-IV–D cases, a petition for license suspension is filed with the court of continuing jurisdiction or the court in which a child support order has been registered. In IV–D cases, the IV–D agency may handle cases through hearings conducted by an administrative law judge or through the judicial process as provided in non-IV–D cases. Either way, the determination of whether or not to suspend a license is left with the tribunal, not with the licensing agency. Only after an order suspending a license has been rendered is the licensing authority required to act. This means that a new license may not be denied for failure to pay child support, but, once issued, a license may be suspended.

While the federal requirement with respect to the license suspension applies only to child support enforcement, the use of this enforcement mechanism has been expanded to include the enforcement of a court order pertaining to the possession of, or access to, a child. *(A.G.K., H.P.S., & H.G.B.)*

Leading Case

In re M.E.G., 48 S.W.3d 204 (Tex. App.—2001, no pet.) (A.G. authorized to suspend obligor's licenses if he failed to pay the arrearage)

CLE/Other Legal Publications

See annotations, Chapter 157, Enforcement, *supra*.

---

§ 232.001. Definitions.

In this chapter:

(1) "License" means a license, certificate, registration, permit, or other authorization that:

(A) is issued by a licensing authority;

(B) is subject before expiration to suspension, revocation, forfeiture, or termination by the issuing licensing authority; and

(C) a person must obtain to:

(i) practice or engage in a particular business, occupation, or profession;

(ii) operate a motor vehicle; or

(iii) engage in any other regulated activity, including hunting, fishing, or other recreational activity for which a license or permit is required.

(2) "Licensing authority" means a department, commission, board, office, or other agency of the state or a political subdivision of the state that issues a license.

(3) "Order suspending license" means an order issued by the Title IV-D agency or a court directing a licensing authority to suspend a license.

(4) "Subpoena" means a judicial or administrative subpoena issued in a parentage determination or child support proceeding under this title.

§ 232.002. Licensing Authorities Subject to Chapter.

The following are licensing authorities subject to this chapter:

(1) Department of Agriculture;

(2) Texas Commission on Alcohol and Drug Abuse;

(3) Texas Alcoholic Beverage Commission;

(4) Texas Appraiser Licensing and Certification Board;

(5) Texas Board of Architectural Examiners;

(6) State Board of Barber Examiners;

(7) Texas Board of Chiropractic Examiners;

(8) Comptroller of Public Accounts;

(9) Texas Cosmetology Commission;

(10) Court Reporters Certification Board;

(11) State Board of Dental Examiners;

(12) Texas State Board of Examiners of Dietitians;

(13) Texas Funeral Service Commission;

(14) Texas Department of Health;

(15) Texas Department of Human Services;

(16) Texas Board of Professional Land Surveying;

(17) Texas Department of Licensing and Regulation;

(18) Texas State Board of Examiners of Marriage and Family Therapists;

(19) Texas State Board of Medical Examiners;

(20) Midwifery Board;

(21) Texas Commission on Environmental Quality;

(22) Board of Nurse Examiners;

(23) Texas Board of Occupational Therapy Examiners;

(24) Texas Optometry Board;

(25) Parks and Wildlife Department;

(26) Texas State Board of Examiners of Perfusionists;

(27) Texas State Board of Pharmacy;

(28) Texas Board of Physical Therapy Examiners;

(29) Texas State Board of Plumbing Examiners;

(30) Texas State Board of Podiatric Medical Examiners;

(31) Polygraph Examiners Board;

(32) Texas Commission on Private Security;

(33) Texas State Board of Examiners of Professional Counselors;

(34) Texas Board of Professional Engineers;

(35) Department of Protective and Regulatory Services;

(36) Texas State Board of Examiners of Psychologists;

(37) Texas State Board of Public Accountancy;

(38) Department of Public Safety of the State of Texas;

(39) Public Utility Commission of Texas;

(40) Railroad Commission of Texas;

(41) Texas Real Estate Commission;

(42) State Bar of Texas;

(43) Texas State Board of Social Worker Examiners;

(44) State Board of Examiners for Speech–Language Pathology and Audiology;

(45) Texas Structural Pest Control Board;

(46) Board of Tax Professional Examiners;

(47) Secretary of State;

(48) Supreme Court of Texas;

(49) Texas Transportation Commission;

(50) State Board of Veterinary Medical Examiners;

(51) Texas Ethics Commission;

(52) Advisory Board of Athletic Trainers;

(53) State Committee of Examiners in the Fitting and Dispensing of Hearing Instruments;

(54) Texas Board of Licensure for Professional Medical Physicists;

(55) Texas Department of Insurance;

(56) Texas Board of Orthotics and Prosthetics;
(57) savings and loan commissioner;
(58) Texas Juvenile Probation Commission; and
(59) Texas Lottery Commission under Chapter 466, Government Code.

§ 232.0021. Application of Chapter to Texas Lottery Commission.

With respect to the Texas Lottery Commission, this chapter applies only to a lottery ticket sales agent license issued under Chapter 466, Government Code.

§ 232.003. Suspension of License.

(a) A court or the Title IV-D agency may issue an order suspending a license as provided by this chapter if an individual who is an obligor:

(1) owes overdue child support in an amount equal to or greater than the total support due for three months under a support order;

(2) has been provided an opportunity to make payments toward the overdue child support under a court-ordered or agreed repayment schedule; and

(3) has failed to comply with the repayment schedule.

(b) A court or the Title IV-D agency may issue an order suspending a license as provided by this chapter if a parent or alleged parent has failed, after receiving appropriate notice, to comply with a subpoena.

(c) A court may issue an order suspending license as provided by this chapter for an individual for whom a court has rendered an enforcement order under Chapter 157 finding that the individual has failed to comply with the terms of a court order providing for the possession of or access to a child.

Comment

The order suspending a license with respect to a support arrearage may be rendered only if the obligor has had an opportunity to meet a repayment plan and has failed to do so. The plan itself need not have been ordered or agreed to prior to the filing of a petition for license suspension. With respect to suspending a license for failure to comply with a subpoena, the only requirement is that a subpoena was duly served.

While originally intended as an enforcement remedy in child support cases, subsection (c) extends license suspension to the enforcement of a court order providing for the possession of, or access to, a child. Amending language in other sections of the chapter to extend the use of license suspension might incorrectly suggest that the IV–D agency may enforce rights of possession or access. This, however, is not an activity for which the agency receives a subsidy under federal law. So, for the purposes of this chapter, only the court will enforce visitation and custody rights through license suspension. *(A.G.K. & H.P.S.)*

---

§ 232.004. Petition for Suspension of License.

(a) A child support agency or obligee may file a petition to suspend, as provided by this chapter, a license of an obligor who has an arrearage equal to or greater than the total support due for 90 days under a support order.

(b) In a Title IV–D case, the petition shall be filed with the Title IV–D agency, the court of continuing jurisdiction, or the tribunal in which a child support order has been registered under Chapter 159 *[UIFSA]*. The tribunal in which the petition is filed obtains jurisdiction over the matter.

(c) In a case other than a Title IV-D case, the petition shall be filed in the court of continuing jurisdiction or the court in which a child support order has been registered under Chapter 159 *[UIFSA]*.

(d) A proceeding in a case filed with the Title IV-D agency under this chapter is governed by the contested case provisions of Chapter 2001, Government Code, except that Section 2001.054 does not apply to the proceeding. The director of the Title IV-D agency or the director's designee may render a final decision in a contested case proceeding under this chapter.

Comment

License suspension is a remedy available to private as well as public child support enforcement agencies. The only requirement for filing a petition with respect to child support is that there be an arrearage equal to an amount due for 90 or more days; there is no need for a repayment plan to be in existence at the time of filing. Although this section does not specifically identity failure to comply with a subpoena as a basis for filing a petition, that may be inferred from other sections of the statute. *(A.G.K. & H.P.S.)*

§ 232.005. Contents of Petition.

(a) A petition under this chapter must state that license suspension is required under Section 232.003 and allege:

(1) the name and, if known, social security number of the individual;

(2) with regard to each license, the type, and if known, number of any license the individual is believed to hold and the name of the licensing authority that issued the license; and

(3) the amount of arrearages owed under the child support order or the facts associated with the individual's failure to comply with:

(A) a subpoena; or

(B) the terms of a court order providing for the possession of or access to a child.

(b) A petition under this chapter may include as an attachment a copy of:

(1) the record of child support payments maintained by the Title IV-D registry or local registry;

(2) the subpoena with which the individual has failed to comply, together with proof of service of the subpoena; or

(3) with respect to a petition for suspension under Section 232.003(c):

(A) the enforcement order rendered under Chapter 157 describing the manner in which the individual was found to have not complied with the terms of a court order providing for the possession of or access to a child; and

(B) the court order containing the provisions that the individual was found to have violated.

Comment

Although the contents of the petition may identify a single type of license issued by a licensing authority, the effect of a final order is the suspension of any type of license issued by the licensing authority that may be available to the delinquent obligor. *See* § 232.001(i), *supra*. *(A.G.K. & H.P.S.)*

§ 232.006. Notice.

(a) On the filing of a petition under Section 232.004, the clerk of the court or the Title IV-D agency shall deliver to the individual:

(1) notice of the individual's right to a hearing before the court or agency;

(2) notice of the deadline for requesting a hearing; and

(3) a hearing request form if the proceeding is in a Title IV-D case.

(b) Notice under this section may be served as in civil cases generally.

(c) The notice must contain the following prominently displayed statement in boldfaced type, capital letters, or underlined:

"AN ACTION TO SUSPEND ONE OR MORE LICENSES ISSUED TO YOU HAS BEEN FILED. YOU MAY EMPLOY AN ATTORNEY TO REPRESENT YOU IN THIS ACTION. IF YOU OR YOUR ATTORNEY DO NOT REQUEST A HEARING BEFORE THE 21ST DAY AFTER THE DATE OF SERVICE OF THIS NOTICE, AN ORDER OF LICENSE SUSPENSION MAY BE RENDERED."

§ 232.007. Hearing on Petition to Suspend License.

(a) A request for a hearing and motion to stay suspension must be filed with the court or Title IV-D agency by the individual not later than the 20th day after the date of service of the notice under Section 232.006.

(b) If a request for a hearing is filed, the court or Title IV-D agency shall:

(1) promptly schedule a hearing;

(2) notify each party of the date, time, and location of the hearing; and

(3) stay suspension pending the hearing.

(c) In a case involving support arrearages, a record of child support payments made by the Title IV-D agency or a local registry is evidence of whether the payments were made. A copy of the record appearing regular on its face shall be admitted as evidence at a hearing under this chapter, including a hearing on a motion to revoke a stay. Either party may offer controverting evidence.

(d) In a case in which an individual has failed to comply with a subpoena, proof of service is evidence of delivery of the subpoena.

§ 232.008. Order Suspending License for Failure to Pay Child Support.

(a) On making the findings required by Section 232.003, the court or Title IV-D agency shall render an order suspending the license unless the individual:

(1) proves that all arrearages and the current month's support have been paid;

(2) shows good cause for failure to comply with the subpoena or the terms of the court order providing for the possession of or access to a child; or

(3) establishes an affirmative defense as provided by Section 157.008(c).

(b) The court or Title IV-D agency may stay an order suspending a license conditioned on the individual's compliance with:

(1) a reasonable repayment schedule that is incorporated in the order;

(2) the requirements of a reissued and delivered subpoena; or

(3) the requirements of any court order pertaining to the possession of or access to a child.

(c) An order suspending a license with a stay of the suspension may not be served on the licensing authority unless the stay is revoked as provided by this chapter.

(d) A final order suspending license rendered by a court or the Title IV-D agency shall be forwarded to the appropriate licensing authority by the clerk of the court or Title IV-D agency. The clerk shall collect from an obligor a fee of $5 for each order mailed.

(e) If the court or Title IV-D agency renders an order suspending license, the individual may also be ordered not to engage in the licensed activity.

(f) If the court or Title IV-D agency finds that the petition for suspension should be denied, the petition shall be dismissed without prejudice, and an order suspending license may not be rendered.

Comment

Although the caption states the subject is the order suspending a license, that is true only for the first clause of Subsection (a). In fact, the primary focus of the section is on the means whereby a suspension order may be stayed. Subsections (a) and (b) provide five different reasons for a stay, including full payment and the obligor's compliance with a repayment plan in the case of a support arrearage, or compliance with a reissued subpoena in the case of noncompliance with a subpoena. Subsequent failure to comply with either a repayment plan or a new subpoena may result in a revocation of the stay under § 232.012.

Subsection (a) provides that an obligor is not subject to license suspension if the obligor establishes as an affirmative defense that he was incapable of complying with the order because he lacked the ability to pay the court-ordered support, he has no property that could be sold or otherwise used to pay the support, and that he unsuccessfully attempted to borrow to pay the support and knows of no other means to legally borrow or otherwise obtain the amount needed to pay. *(H.G.B., A.G.K. & H.P.S.)*

---

§ 232.009. Default Order.

The court or Title IV-D agency shall consider the allegations of the petition for suspension to be admitted and shall render an order suspending the license of an obligor without the requirement of a hearing if the court or Title IV-D agency determines that the individual failed to respond to a notice issued under Section 232.006 by:

(1) requesting a hearing; or

(2) appearing at a scheduled hearing.

Comment

License suspension is virtually automatic if an individual fails to respond to notice of a suspension action by timely requesting a hearing or appearing at a requested hearing. *(A.G.K. & H.P.S.)*

---

§ 232.010. Review of Final Administrative Order.

An order issued by a Title IV-D agency under this chapter is a final agency decision and is subject to review under the substantial evidence rule as provided by Chapter 2001, Government Code.

Comment

In reviewing an agency decision with respect to the suspension of a license the reviewing court must determine whether a reasonable basis exists in the record for that decision, not whether it was the correct decision. *(A.G.K. & H.P.S.)*

---

§ 232.011. Action by Licensing Authority.

(a) On receipt of a final order suspending license, the licensing authority shall immediately determine if the authority has issued a license to the individual named on the order and, if a license has been issued:

(1) record the suspension of the license in the licensing authority's records;

(2) report the suspension as appropriate; and

(3) demand surrender of the suspended license if required by law for other cases in which a license is suspended.

(b) A licensing authority shall implement the terms of a final order suspending license without additional review or hearing. The authority may provide notice as appropriate to the license holder or to others concerned with the license.

(c) A licensing authority may not modify, remand, reverse, vacate, or stay an order suspending license issued under this chapter and may not review, vacate, or reconsider the terms of a final order suspending license.

(d) An individual who is the subject of a final order suspending license is not entitled to a refund for any fee or deposit paid to the licensing authority.

(e) An individual who continues to engage in the business, occupation, profession, or other licensed activity after the implementation of the order suspending license by the licensing authority is liable for the same civil and criminal penalties provided for engaging in the licensed activity without a license or while a license is suspended that apply to any other license holder of that licensing authority.

(f) A licensing authority is exempt from liability to a license holder for any act authorized under this chapter performed by the authority.

(g) Except as provided by this chapter, an order suspending license or dismissing a petition for the suspension of a license does not affect the power of a licensing authority to grant, deny, suspend, revoke, terminate, or renew a license.

(h) The denial or suspension of a driver's license under this chapter is governed by this chapter and not by the general licensing provisions of Chapter 521, Transportation Code.

(i) An order issued under this chapter to suspend a license applies to each license issued by the licensing authority subject to the order for which the obligor is eligible. The licensing authority may not issue or renew any other license for the obligor until the court or the Title IV-D agency renders an order vacating or staying an order suspending license.

Comment

Some licensing authorities issue more than one type of license. Subsection (i) clarifies that the ordered suspension of license applies to any type of license that the licensing authority may issue to the obligor. *(A.G.K. & H.P.S.)*

---

§ 232.012. Motion to Revoke Stay.

(a) The obligee, support enforcement agency, court, or Title IV-D agency may file a motion to revoke the stay of an order suspending license if the individual who is subject of an order suspending license does not comply with:

(1) the terms of a reasonable repayment plan entered into by the individual;

(2) the requirements of a reissued subpoena; or

(3) the terms of any court order pertaining to the possession of or access to a child.

(b) Notice to the individual of a motion to revoke stay under this section may be given by personal service or by mail to the address provided by the individual, if any, in the order suspending license. The notice must include a notice of hearing. The notice must be provided to the individual not less than 10 days before the date of the hearing.

(c) A motion to revoke stay must allege the manner in which the individual failed to comply with the repayment plan, the reissued subpoena, or the court order pertaining to possession of or access to a child.

(d) If the court or Title IV-D agency finds that the individual is not in compliance with the terms of the repayment plan, reissued subpoena, or court order pertaining to possession of or access to a child, the court or agency shall revoke the stay of the order suspending license and render a final order suspending license.

Comment

The second chance given an individual through the opportunity, provided under § 232.008, to comply with a repayment plan for support arrearages or a reissued subpoena is voided if the individual fails to comply with the plan or reissued subpoena. *(A.G.K. & H.P.S.)*

---

§ 232.013. Vacating or Staying Order Suspending License.

(a) The court or Title IV–D agency may render an order vacating or staying an order suspending an individual's license if:

(1) the individual has:

(A) paid all delinquent child support or has established a satisfactory payment record;

(B) complied with the requirements of a reissued subpoena; or

(C) complied with the terms of any court order providing for the possession of or access to a child; or

(2) the court or Title IV–D agency determines that good cause exists for vacating or staying the order.

(b) The clerk of the court or Title IV–D agency shall promptly deliver an order vacating or staying an order suspending license to the appropriate licensing authority. The clerk shall collect from an obligor a fee of $5 for each order mailed.

(c) On receipt of an order vacating or staying an order suspending license, the licensing authority shall promptly issue the affected license to the individual if the individual is otherwise qualified for the license.

(d) An order rendered under this section does not affect the right of the child support agency or obligee to any other remedy provided by law, including the right to seek relief under this chapter. An order rendered under this section does not affect the power of a licensing authority to grant, deny, suspend, revoke, terminate, or renew a license as otherwise provided by law.

Comment

With respect to child support enforcement, the purpose of license suspension is to compel compliance with the support obligation by requiring the obligor to pay all delinquent support or to submit to a repayment plan before the suspension is lifted. There may, however, be circumstances in which the suspension order should be stayed or vacated (*e.g.*, the parties have reunited). Subsection (a)(2), added in 2003, allows the court or IV–D agency to make a "good cause" determination in any case. *(C.B. & H.P.S.)*

---

§ 232.014. Fee by Licensing Authority.

A licensing authority may charge a fee to an individual who is the subject of an order suspending license in an amount sufficient to recover the administrative costs incurred by the authority under this chapter.

§ 232.015. Cooperation Between Licensing Authorities and Title IV–D Agency.

(a) The Title IV-D agency may request from each licensing authority the name, address, social security number, license renewal date, and other identifying information for each individual who holds, applies for, or renews a license issued by the authority.

(b) A licensing authority shall provide the requested information in the form and manner identified by the Title IV-D agency.

(c) The Title IV-D agency may enter into a cooperative agreement with a licensing authority to administer this chapter in a cost-effective manner.

(d) The Title IV-D agency may adopt a reasonable implementation schedule for the requirements of this section.

(e) The Title IV-D agency, the comptroller, and the Texas Alcoholic Beverage Commission shall by rule specify additional prerequisites for the suspension of licenses relating to state taxes collected under Title 2, Tax Code. The joint rules must be adopted not later than March 1, 1996.

§ 232.016. Rules, Forms, and Procedures.

The Title IV-D agency by rule shall prescribe forms and procedures for the implementation of this chapter.

Chapter 233. Child Support Review Process to Establish or Enforce Support Obligations.

Editors' Note: *This chapter contains guest commentary by Howard G. Baldwin, Jr., former First Assistant; Cynthia Bryant, Deputy Attorney General; Alicia Gray Key, former General Counsel; and H. Patrick Sullivan, Director of Federal Policy Analysis, all of the Child Support Division, Office of the Texas Attorney General, identified respectively as (H.G.B., C.B., A.G.K. & H.P.S.).*

Introductory Comment

This chapter provides an administrative method to deal with child support matters. The process has been amended many times since it was first authorized in 1991. Originally, the legislature created a quasi-administrative "expedited agreed order" process for use by child support agencies, including county domestic relations offices and the Office of the Attorney General as the IV–D agency. The purpose was to encourage agreed orders that could be ratified by the court without the necessity of a hearing. In 1993, a more elaborate "child support review process" was instituted, requiring negotiation conferences in the agency's office to attempt informal resolution of the issues. That process gave the child support agency the authority to issue child support review orders with or without the agreement of the parties. Amendments since that time have streamlined the process and improved its effectiveness. New administrative procedures, including administrative parentage testing orders and administrative subpoenas, were added in 1997 in response to requirements of PRWORA. The use of the child support review process was specifically restricted to the IV–D agency.

Successive legislative revisions of the process have removed some of the earlier mandatory forms and procedures, resulting in greater flexibility in agreed cases. Detailed financial affidavits and mandatory negotiation conferences, for example, are no longer required. The process continues to allow for judicial review of an agency decision, requires the agency to petition the court for confirmation of the review order, and permits the parties to request a court hearing on any issue raised in the review order. *(A.G.K. & H.P.S.)*

CLE/Other Legal Publications

A plainly practical primer on IV–D practice. Steve A. Owen, 2002 ADV. FAM. L.

Representing clients in Title IV–D. Hon. Michael K. Sinha & Steven A. Owen, 2000 Adv. Fam. L.

---

§ 233.001. Purpose.

(a) The purpose of the procedures specified in the child support review process authorized by this chapter is to enable the Title IV-D agency to take expedited administrative actions to establish, modify, and enforce child support and medical support obligations, to determine parentage, or to take any other action authorized or required under Part D, Title IV, of the federal Social Security Act (42 U.S.C. Section 651 et seq.), and Chapter 231 *[Title IV–D Services]*.

(b) A child support review order issued under this chapter and confirmed by a court constitutes an order of the court and is enforceable by any means available for the enforcement of child support obligations under this code, including withholding income, filing a child support lien, and suspending a license under Chapter 232 *[Suspension of License]*.

Comment

Once the review order is confirmed by a court, it is the operative order of the court and is enforceable by any means, including contempt. *(A.G.K. & H.P.S.)*

---

§ 233.002. Agreements Encouraged.

To the extent permitted by this chapter, the Title IV-D agency shall encourage agreement of the parties.

§ 233.003. Bilingual Forms Required.

A notice or other form used to implement administrative procedures under this chapter shall be printed in both Spanish and English.

§ 233.004. Interpreter Required.

If a party participating in an administrative proceeding under this chapter does not speak English or is hearing impaired, the Title IV-D agency shall provide for interpreter services at no charge to the party.

§ 233.005. Initiating Administrative Actions.

An administrative action under this chapter may be initiated by issuing a notice of child support review under Section 233.006 or a notice of proposed child support review order under Section 233.009 or 233.0095 to each party entitled to notice.

§ 233.006. Contents of Notice of Child Support Review.

(a) The notice of child support review issued by the Title IV-D agency must:

(1) describe the procedure for a child support review, including the procedures for requesting a negotiation conference;

(2) inform the recipient that the recipient may be represented by legal counsel during the review process or at a court hearing; and

(3) inform the recipient that the recipient may refuse to participate or cease participation in the child support review process, but that the refusal by the recipient to participate will not prevent the completion of the process or the filing of a child support review order.

(b) In addition to the information required by Subsection (a), the notice of child support review may inform the recipient that:

(1) an affidavit of financial resources included with the notice must be executed by the recipient and returned to the Title IV-D agency not later than the 15th day after the date the notice is received or delivered; and

(2) if the requested affidavit of financial resources is not returned as required, the agency may:

(A) proceed with the review using the information that is available to the agency; and

(B) file a legal action without further notice to the recipient, except as otherwise required by law.

Comment

The process begins when the agency notifies the parties, either by personal service or first class mail, that a review will take place. The agency has the option, rather than the mandate, to include a financial affidavit to be completed by the parties with the notice. *(A.G.K. & H.P.S.)*

§ 233.007. Service of Notice.

(a) A notice required in an administrative action under this chapter may be delivered by personal service or first class mail on each party entitled to citation or notice as provided by Chapter 102 *[Filing Suit]*.

(b) This section does not apply to notice required on filing of a child support review order or to later judicial actions.

§ 233.008. Administrative Subpoena in Child Support Review.

In a child support review under this chapter, the Title IV-D agency may issue an administrative subpoena authorized under Chapter 231 to any individual or organization believed to have financial or other information needed to establish, modify, or enforce a support order.

§ 233.009. Notice of Proposed Child Support Review Order; Negotiation Conference.

(a) After an investigation and assessment of financial resources, the Title IV-D agency may serve on the parties a notice of proposed child support review order in enforcing or modifying an existing order.

(b) The notice of proposed child support review order shall state:

(1) the amount of periodic payment of child support due, the amount of any overdue support that is owed as an arrearage as of the date of the notice, and the amounts that are to be paid by the obligor for current support due and in payment on the arrearage owed;

(2) that the person identified in the notice as the party responsible for payment of the support amounts may contest the notice order on the grounds that:

(A) the respondent is not the responsible party;

(B) the dependent child is no longer entitled to child support; or

(C) the amount of monthly support or arrearage is incorrectly stated; and

(3) that, if the person identified in the notice as the party responsible for payment of the support amounts does not contest the notice in writing or request a negotiation conference to discuss the notice not later than the 15th day after the date the notice was delivered, the Title IV-D agency may file a child support review order for child support and for medical support for the child as provided by Chapter 154 *[Child Support]* according to the information available to the agency.

(c) The Title IV-D agency may schedule a negotiation conference without a request from a party.

(d) The Title IV-D agency shall schedule a negotiation conference on the timely request of a party.

(e) The agency may conduct a negotiation conference, or any part of a negotiation conference, by telephone conference call, by video conference, as well as in person and may adjourn the conference for a reasonable time to permit mediation of issues that cannot be resolved by the parties and the agency.

(f) Notwithstanding any other provision of this chapter, if the parties have agreed to the terms of a proposed child support review order and each party has signed the order, including a waiver of the right to service of process as provided by Section 233.018, the Title IV-D agency may immediately present the order and waiver to the court for confirmation without conducting a negotiation conference or requiring the production of financial information.

Comment

If a child support obligation already exists, the agency may have sufficient information in its files to calculate a judgment for arrears or a modification of the current support amount. In such a case, the proposed order is mailed to begin the review process. Although procedures exist for scheduling and conducting formal negotiation conferences, the conference may be omitted in agreed cases. *(A.G.K. & H.P.S.)*

§ 233.0095. Notice of Proposed Child Support Review Order in Cases of Acknowledged Paternity.

(a) If an individual has signed the acknowledgment of paternity as the father of the child or executed a statement of paternity, the Title IV–D agency may serve on the parties a notice of proposed child support review order.

(b) The notice of proposed child support review order shall state:

(1) the amount of periodic payment of child support due;

(2) that the person identified in the notice as the party responsible for payment of the support amounts may only contest the amount of monthly support; and

(3) that, if the person identified in the notice as the party responsible for payment of the support amounts does not contest the notice in writing or request a negotiation conference to discuss the notice not later than the 15th day after the date the notice was delivered, the Title IV–D agency may file the child support order for child support and for medical support for the child as provided by Chapter 154 according to the information available to the agency.

(c) The Title IV–D agency may schedule a negotiation conference without a request from a party.

(d) The Title IV–D agency shall schedule a negotiation conference on the timely request of a party.

(e) The Title IV–D agency may conduct a negotiation conference, or any part of a negotiation conference, by telephone conference call, by video conference, or in person and may adjourn the conference for a reasonable time to permit mediation of issues that cannot be resolved by the parties and the agency.

(f) Notwithstanding any other provision of this chapter, if paternity has been acknowledged, the parties have agreed to the terms of a proposed child support review order, and each party has signed the order, including a waiver of the right to service of process as provided by Section 233.018, the Title IV-D agency may immediately present the order and waiver to the court for confirmation without conducting a negotiation conference or requiring the production of financial information.

Comment

This section expressly permits the use of the child support review process if paternity has been acknowledged. *See* Chapter 160 [*Uniform Parentage Act*], *supra.* In such a case, the process may be employed as an expeditious way to obtain a court order for support, possession or access, and conservatorship. In agreed cases, the formalities of the negotiation conference and the production of financial records may be omitted. *(A.G.K. & H.P.S.)*

---

§ 233.010. Notice of Negotiation Conference; Failure to Attend Conference.

(a) The Title IV-D agency shall notify all parties entitled to notice of the negotiation conference of the date, time, and place of the conference not later than the 10th day before the date of the conference.

(b) If a party fails to attend the scheduled conference, the agency may proceed with the review and file a child support review order according to the information available to the agency.

§ 233.011. Rescheduling Negotiation Conference; Notice Required.

(a) The Title IV-D agency may reschedule or adjourn a negotiation conference on the request of any party.

(b) The Title IV-D agency shall give all parties notice of a rescheduled conference not later than the third day before the date of the rescheduled conference.

§ 233.012. Information Required to be Provided at Negotiation Conference.

At the beginning of the negotiation conference, the child support review officer shall review with the parties participating in the conference information provided in the notice of child support review and inform the parties that:

(1) the purpose of the negotiation conference is to provide an opportunity to reach an agreement on a child support order;

(2) if the parties reach an agreement, the review officer will prepare an agreed review order to be effective immediately on being confirmed by the court, as provided by Section 233.024;

(3) a party does not have to sign a review order prepared by the child support review officer but that the Title IV-D agency may file a review order without the agreement of the parties;

(4) the parties may sign a waiver of the right to service of process;

(5) a party may request a court hearing on a nonagreed order at any time before the 20th day after the date a petition for confirmation of the order is filed; and

(6) a party may file a motion for a new trial at any time before the 30th day after an order is confirmed by the court.

Comment

If the parties reach an agreement, they may also sign a waiver of the right to service of the subsequent petition to confirm the order. The order is then presented to the court, and becomes effective immediately upon being confirmed. Any party who does not agree or who does not attend the conference is entitled to personal service of the petition to confirm and a copy of the order, and may request a court hearing within 20 days. *(A.G.K. & H.P.S.)*

---

§ 233.013. Determining Support Amount; Modification.

(a) The Title IV-D agency may use any information obtained by the agency from the parties or any other source and shall apply the child support guidelines provided by this code to determine the appropriate amount of child support.

(b) If it has been three years since a child support order was rendered or last modified and the amount of the child support award under the order differs by either 20 percent or $100 from the amount that would be awarded under the child support guidelines, the Title IV-D agency shall file an appropriate child support review order, including an order that has the effect of modifying an existing court or administrative order for child support without the necessity of filing a motion to modify.

§ 233.014. Record of Proceedings.

(a) For the purposes of this chapter, documentary evidence relied on by the child support review officer, including an affidavit of a party, together with the child support review order is a sufficient record of the proceedings.

(b) The Title IV-D agency is not required to make any other record or transcript of the negotiation conference.

§ 233.015. Issuance of Child Support Review Order or Finding That No Order Should be Issued; Effect.

(a) If a negotiation conference does not result in agreement by all parties to the child support review order, the Title IV-D agency shall render a final decision in the form of a child support review order or a determination that the agency should not issue a child support review order not later than the fifth day after the date of the negotiation conference.

(b) If the Title IV-D agency determines that the agency should not issue a child support order, the agency shall immediately provide each party with notice of the determination by personal delivery or by first class mail.

(c) A determination that a child support order should not be issued must include a statement of the reasons that an order is not being issued and a statement that the agency's determination does not affect the right of the Title IV-D agency or a party to request any other remedy provided by law.

Comment

The child support review process is designed to handle routine cases. If a review officer becomes aware of domestic violence or some other complicating factor, the officer may decide that no order should be issued. The agency would still have the right to petition the court for any appropriate remedy in the case. *(A.G.K. & H.P.S.)*

§ 233.016. Vacating Child Support Review Order.

(a) The Title IV-D agency may vacate a child support review order at any time before the order is filed with the court.

(b) A new negotiation conference, with notice to all parties, may be scheduled or the Title IV-D agency may make a determination that a child support review order should not be issued and give notice of that determination as provided by this chapter.

§ 233.017. Contents of Child Support Review Order.

(a) An order issued under this chapter must be reviewed and signed by an attorney of the Title IV-D agency and must contain all provisions that are appropriate for an order under this title, including current child support, medical support, a determination of any arrearages or retroactive support, and, if not otherwise ordered, income withholding.

(b) A child support review order providing for the enforcement of an order may not contain a provision that imposes incarceration or a fine or contains a finding of contempt.

(c) A child support review order that establishes or modifies an amount of previously ordered support must include the findings required by Section 154.130.

(d) A child support review order that is not agreed to by all the parties may specify and reserve for the court at the confirmation hearing unresolved issues relating to conservatorship or possession of a child.

Comment

Although the order, once confirmed, thereafter is enforceable by contempt, the child support review order itself may not include a finding of contempt or a provision for a fine or incarceration. *(A.G.K. & H.P.S.)*

§ 233.018. Additional Contents of Agreed Child Support Review Order.

(a) If a negotiation conference results in an agreement of the parties, each party must sign the child support review order and the order must contain as to each party:

(1) a waiver by the party of the right to service of process and a court hearing [~~and the making of a record on the petition for confirmation~~];

(2) the mailing address of the party; and

(3) the following statement printed on the order in boldfaced type, in capital letters, or underlined:

"I ACKNOWLEDGE THAT I HAVE READ AND UNDERSTAND THIS CHILD SUPPORT REVIEW ORDER. I UNDERSTAND THAT IF I SIGN THIS ORDER, IT WILL BE CONFIRMED BY THE COURT WITHOUT FURTHER NOTICE TO ME. I KNOW THAT I HAVE A RIGHT TO REQUEST THAT A COURT RECONSIDER THE ORDER BY FILING A MOTION FOR A NEW TRIAL AT ANY TIME BEFORE THE 30TH DAY AFTER THE DATE OF THE CONFIRMATION OF THE ORDER BY THE COURT. I KNOW THAT IF I DO NOT OBEY THE TERMS OF THIS ORDER I MAY BE HELD IN CONTEMPT OF COURT."

(b) If a negotiation conference results in an agreement on some but not all issues in the case, the parties may sign a waiver of service along with an agreement to appear in court at a specified date and time for a determination by the court of all unresolved issues. Notice of the hearing is not required.

History: Amended by 78th Legis., Reg. Sess. (2003), H.B. 1878, eff. Sept. 1, 2003. The change in law made by this Act relating to the modification or enforcement of a child support order rendered before the effective date of this Act applies only to a proceeding for modification or enforcement that is commenced on or after the effective date of this Act. A proceeding for modification or enforcement that is commenced before the effective date of this Act is governed by the law in effect on the date the proceeding was commenced, and the former law is continued in effect for that purpose.

§ 233.019. Filing of Agreed Review Order.

(a) The Title IV-D agency shall file an agreed child support review order and a waiver of service signed by the parties with the clerk of the court having continuing jurisdiction of the child who is the subject of the order.

(b) If there is not a court of continuing jurisdiction, the Title IV-D agency shall file the agreed review order with the clerk of a court having jurisdiction under this title.

(c) If applicable, an acknowledgment of paternity or a written report of a parentage testing expert and any documentary evidence relied upon by the agency shall be filed with the agreed review order as an exhibit to the order.

§ 233.020. Contents of Petition for Confirmation of Nonagreed Order.

(a) A petition for confirmation of a child support review order not agreed to by the parties:

(1) must include the final review order as an attachment to the petition; and

(2) may include a waiver of service executed under Section 233.018(b) and an agreement to appear in court for a hearing.

(b) Documentary evidence relied on by the Title IV–D agency, including, if applicable, an acknowledgment of paternity or a written report of a parentage testing expert, shall be filed with the clerk as exhibits to the petition, but are not required to be served on the parties. The petition must identify the exhibits that are filed with the clerk.

§ 233.021. Duties of Clerk of Court.

(a) On the filing of an agreed child support review order or of a petition for confirmation of a nonagreed order issued by the Title IV-D agency, the clerk of court shall endorse on the order or petition the date and time the order or petition is filed.

(b) In an original action, the clerk shall endorse the appropriate court and cause number on the agreed review order or on the petition for confirmation of a nonagreed order.

(c) The clerk shall deliver by personal service a copy of the petition for confirmation of a nonagreed review order and a copy of the order, to each party entitled to service who has not waived service.

(d) A clerk of a district court is entitled to collect in a child support review case the fees authorized in a Title IV-D case by Chapter 231 *[Title IV–D Services].*

§ 233.022. Form to Request a Court Hearing on Nonagreed Order.

(a) A court shall consider any responsive pleading that is intended as an objection to confirmation of a child support review order not agreed to by the parties, including a general denial, as a request for a court hearing.

(b) The Title IV-D agency shall:

(1) make available to each clerk of court copies of the form to request a court hearing on a nonagreed review order; and

(2) provide the form to request a court hearing to a party to the child support review proceeding on request of the party.

(c) The clerk shall furnish the form to a party to the child support review proceeding on the request of the party.

§ 233.023. Time to Request a Court Hearing.

A party may file a request for a court hearing not later than the 20th day after the date the petition for confirmation of a nonagreed child support review order is delivered to the party.

§ 233.024. Confirmation of Agreed Order.

(a) **On the filing of an agreed child support review order signed by all parties, together with** [~~If the court finds that all parties have appropriately agreed to a child support review order and that there is~~] waiver of service, the court shall sign the order not later than the third day after the filing of the order. The court may sign the order before filing the order, but the signed order shall immediately be filed.

(b) On confirmation by the court, the Title IV-D agency shall immediately deliver to each party a copy of the signed agreed review order.

History: Amended by 78th Legis., Reg. Sess. (2003), H.B. 1878, eff. Sept. 1, 2003. The change in law made by this Act relating to the modification or enforcement of a child support order rendered before the effective date of this Act applies only to a proceeding for modification or enforcement that is commenced on or after the effective date of this Act. A proceeding for modification or enforcement that is commenced before the effective date of this Act is governed by the law in effect on the date the proceeding was commenced, and the former law is continued in effect for that purpose.

Comment

The ratification by the court of an agreed child support review order is intended to be a simple process. If the all parties have signed the order and waived service, the court is to confirm the order, without the necessity of hearing or any other action by the court, "not later than the third day after the filing of the order." *(C.B. & H.P.S.)*

---

§ 233.025. Effect of Request for Hearing on Nonagreed Order; Pleading.

(a) A request for hearing or an order setting a hearing on confirmation of a nonagreed child support review order stays confirmation of the order pending the hearing.

(b) At a hearing on confirmation, any issues in dispute shall be heard in a trial de novo.

(c) The petition for confirmation and the child support review order constitute a sufficient pleading by the Title IV-D agency for relief on any issue addressed in the petition and order.

(d) The request for hearing may limit the scope of the de novo hearing by specifying the issues that are in dispute.

§ 233.026. Time for Court Hearing.

(a) When a timely request for a court hearing has been filed as provided by Section 233.023, the [~~A~~] court shall hold a hearing on the confirmation of a child support review order that has not been agreed to by the parties not later than the 30th day after the date the [~~last party to be served files a timely~~] request **was filed** [~~for a court hearing~~].

(b) A court may not hold a hearing on the confirmation of a nonagreed child support review order if a party does not timely request a hearing as provided by Section 233.023.

(c) If the court resets the time of the hearing, the reset hearing shall be held not later than the 30th day after the date set for the initial hearing.

History: Amended by 78th Legis., Reg. Sess. (2003), H.B. 1878, eff. Sept. 1, 2003. The change in law made by this Act relating to the modification or enforcement of a child support order rendered before the effective date of this Act applies only to a proceeding for modification or enforcement that is commenced on or after the effective date of this Act. A proceeding for modification or enforcement that is commenced before the effective date of this Act is governed by the law in effect on the date the proceeding was commenced, and the former law is continued in effect for that purpose.

Comment

A hearing on the confirmation of a nonagreed child support review order is contingent upon a timely request being made by a party. If no such request has been received by the court, the court may not on its own hold a hearing on the order but must sign the review order as an order of the court "not later than the 30th day after the date the petition for confirmation was delivered to the last party entitled to service" (§ 233.0271, *infra*). *(C.B. & H.P.S.)*

---

§ 233.027. Order After Hearing; Effect of Confirmation Order.

(a) After the hearing on the confirmation of a nonagreed child support review order, the court shall:

(1) if the court finds that the order should be confirmed, immediately sign a confirmation order and enter the order as an order of the court;

(2) if the court finds that the relief granted in the child support review order is inappropriate, sign an appropriate order at the conclusion of the hearing or as soon

after the conclusion of the hearing as is practical and enter the order as an order of the court; or

(3) if the court finds that all relief should be denied, enter an order that denies relief and includes specific findings explaining the reasons that relief is denied.

(b) On the signing of a confirmation order by the judge of the court, the child support review order becomes a final order of the court.

(c) If the party who requested the hearing fails to appear at the hearing, the court shall sign a confirmation order and enter the order as an order of the court.

History: Amended by 78th Legis., Reg. Sess. (2003), H.B. 1878, eff. Sept. 1, 2003. The change in law made by this Act relating to the modification or enforcement of a child support order rendered before the effective date of this Act applies only to a proceeding for modification or enforcement that is commenced on or after the effective date of this Act. A proceeding for modification or enforcement that is commenced before the effective date of this Act is governed by the law in effect on the date the proceeding was commenced, and the former law is continued in effect for that purpose.

Comment

If a party who has not agreed to the review order timely requests a court hearing, the court conducts a trial de novo on any issue in dispute. The court has wide discretion to confirm the proposed order, enter a different order, or deny all relief. The failure of the requesting party to appear at the hearing results in an automatic confirmation of the nonagreed order by the court. *(C.B., A.G.K. & H.P.S.)*

§ 233.0271. Confirmation of Nonagreed Order Without Hearing.

(a) If a request for hearing has not been timely received, the court shall confirm and sign a nonagreed child support review order not later than the 30th day after the date the petition for confirmation was delivered to the last party entitled to service.

(b) The Title IV-D agency shall immediately deliver a copy of the confirmed nonagreed review order to each party, together with notice of right to file a motion for a new trial not later than the 30th day after the date the order was confirmed by the court.

§ 233.028. Special Child Support Review Procedures Relating to Establishment of Parentage.

(a) If the parentage of a child has not been established, the notice of child support review delivered to the parties must include an allegation that the recipient is a biological parent of the child. The notice shall inform the parties that:

(1) not later than the 15th day after the date of delivery of the notice, the alleged parent of the child shall either sign a statement of paternity or an acknowledgment of paternity or deny in writing that the alleged parent is the biological parent of the child;

(2) either party may request that scientifically accepted parentage testing be conducted to assist in determining the identities of the child's parents;

(3) if the alleged parent timely denies parentage of the child, the Title IV-D agency shall order parentage testing; and

(4) if the alleged parent does not deny parentage of the child, the Title IV-D agency may conduct a negotiation conference.

(b) If all parties agree to the child's parentage, the agency may file an agreed child support review order as provided by this chapter.

(c) If a party denies parentage, the Title IV-D agency shall order parentage testing and give each party notice of the time and place of testing. If either party fails or refuses to participate in administrative parentage testing, the Title IV-D agency may file a child support review order resolving the question of parentage against that party. The court shall confirm the child support review order as a temporary or final order of the court only after an opportunity for parentage testing has been provided.

(d) If genetic testing identifies the alleged parent as the parent of the child and the results of a verified written report of a genetic testing expert meet the requirements of Chapter 160 *[Uniform Parentage Act]* for issuing a temporary order, the Title IV-D agency may conduct a negotiation conference to resolve any issues of support and file with the court a child support review order.

(e) If the results of parentage testing exclude an alleged parent from being the biological parent of the child, the Title IV-D agency shall issue and provide to each party a child support review order that declares that the excluded person is not a parent of the child.

(f) Any party may file a petition for confirmation of a child support review order issued under this section.

Comment

This section authorizes the IV–D agency to order parentage testing. The alleged father is first given the opportunity to sign an acknowledgment of paternity, or to request testing. Testing is scheduled and paid for by the agency, but in the event of a "positive" result, an order establishing parentage will likely include an order that the father reimburse the state for the cost of testing. The alleged father who fails to submit to testing is subject to the entry of a default order resolving the issue. *(A.G.K. & H.P.S.)*

§ 233.029. Administrative Procedure Law Not Applicable.

The child support review process under this chapter is not governed by Chapter 2001, Government Code.

Chapter 234. State Case Registry, Disbursement Unit, and Directory of New Hires.

Subchapter A. Unified State Case Registry and Disbursement Unit

Subchapter B. State Directory of New Hires

> ***Editors' Note:*** *This chapter contains guest commentary by Howard G. Baldwin, Jr., former First Assistant; Cynthia Bryant, Deputy Attorney General; Alicia Gray Key, former General Counsel; and H. Patrick Sullivan, Director of Federal Policy Analysis, all of the Child Support Division, Office of the Texas Attorney General, identified respectively as (H.G.B., C.B., A.G.K. & H.P.S.).*

Introductory Comment

Among the major child support enforcement mandates of the federal "Personal Responsibility and Work Opportunity Reconciliation Act of 1996" (PRWORA) are requirements for the establishment and operation of a state case registry of support orders, a state disbursement unit for support collection and distribution, and a state directory of new hires. All three of these operations are related to the automated system of the IV–D agency, the Office of the Texas Attorney General, Child Support Division.

The IV–D agency is specifically required under PRWORA to establish, as an integrated component of its automated system, a case registry containing records of all child support orders being enforced by the agency and all other orders rendered or modified in the state on or after October 1, 1998. The system must also be capable of electronic data exchanges with other state and federal data bases.

The state case registry required by PRWORA must maintain not only full records in all IV–D cases, but also house abstracts of support orders in non-IV–D cases, using standardized data elements prescribed by the federal Department of Health and Human

Services. Information in the case registry must be shared with a national case registry within the Federal Parent Locator Service, as well as with other state agencies and the registries of other states. Information in the case registry must be shared with a national case registry within the Federal Parent Locator Service, as well as with other state agencies and the registries of other states.

Under PRWORA, there must be a centralized state unit responsible for collecting and disbursing support in all IV–D cases and in all other cases subject to income withholding. This State Disbursement Unit provides a central, single location to which employers in the state shall remit income withheld for child support. As a result of the implementation of the State Disbursement Unit, the work of local registries will be significantly reduced once the unit is fully operational. Although the federal law originally required full implementation by October, 1999, many states, including Texas, took much longer to convert payment processing in existing cases to the unit. To the extent possible, the disbursement unit must use automated procedures, electronic processes, and computer technology to receive and identify payments, disburse collections, and provide information to a parent, upon request, on the status of payments. In IV–D cases, the agency's automated system must be used to assist in the disbursement of support collections, transmitting income withholding notices and orders to employers or other income sources, monitoring payments for the identification of any delinquencies, and taking appropriate enforcement actions when payment delinquencies occur. Under § 234.007, when the State Disbursement Unit was implemented, local courts were notified to include in orders for income withholding that payments should be directed to the unit. A notice of place of payment will be filed by the IV–D agency to redirect payments from the local registry (district clerk or domestic relations office) to the State Disbursement Unit and this notice will be sent to the obligor, obligee, employer and court.

The state directory of new hires required under PRWORA contains information on all new hires reported by all public and private employers doing business in the state and may be operated either within or outside the Title IV–D agency's automated system, although the directory must interface with the state case registry within the IV–D automated system. Using the W–4 or equivalent form, employers are required to report to the directory certain information on each new employee within 20 days of hiring. This information may be transmitted by mail, electronically, or magnetically, and multi state employers may designate one state to which to report all new hire information. Federal employers must report directly to a national new hire directory within the federal Parent Locator Service. Within 7 days of receipt, information in the state directory must be automatically matched with records in the state case registry to identify obligors for whom income withholding orders or notices need to be issued and to issue those orders or notices. Information in the state directory is also transmitted to the national directory to be compared with data in the national case registry and is made available to the IV–D agency for its purposes, as well as to the state-operated Income and Eligibility and Verification System (IEVS) and the state employment security agency (SESA) for the purpose of verifying eligibility for public assistance benefits (including cash welfare, Medicaid, and food stamps) and unemployment compensation benefits.

Together, these three databases are at the core of what PRWORA envisions as a complex, fully interactive, intrastate and interstate automated information network through which rapid data matches will take place between the state IV–D agency and other state agencies, among the case registries and locator services of all states, and between state databases and federal sources in and through the expanded Federal Parent Locator Service. Successful performance of the mandates for child support enforcement that PRWORA places upon the states is predicated upon the expansion of both state and federal computer systems to create a continuous loop of information concerning not just IV–D cases, but all child support cases, within the state and nationwide. *(A.G.K., H.P.S. & H.G.B.)*

CLE/Other Legal Publications

Update on SDU: Sending All the Child Support to San Antonio. Alicia G. Key, 2002 Adv. Fam. L.

Subchapter A. Unified State Case Registry and Disbursement Unit

§ 234.001. Establishment and Operation of State Case Registry and State Disbursement Unit.

(a) The Title IV-D agency shall establish and operate a state case registry and state disbursement unit meeting the requirements of 42 U.S.C. Sections 654a(e) and 654b and this subchapter.

(b) The state case registry shall maintain records of child support orders in Title IV–D cases and in other cases in which a child support order has been established or modified in this state on or after October 1, 1998.

(c) The state disbursement unit shall:

(1) receive, maintain, and furnish records of child support payments in Title IV-D cases and other cases as authorized by law;

(2) forward child support payments as authorized by law;

(3) maintain child support payment records made through the state disbursement unit; and

(4) make available to a local registry each day in a manner determined by the Title IV-D agency with the assistance of the work group established under Section 234.003 the following information:

(A) the cause number of the suit under which withholding is required;

(B) the payor's name and social security number;

(C) the payee's name and, if available, social security number;

(D) the date the disbursement unit received the payment;

(E) the amount of the payment; and

(F) the instrument identification information.

(d) A certified child support payment record produced by the state disbursement unit is admissible as evidence of the truth of the information contained in the record and does not require further authentication or verification.

Comment

This section authorizes the state IV–D agency to establish and operate the federally mandated state case registry and state disbursement unit without articulating procedural details which will be left to agency rules. Under this section, the disbursement unit and case registry are, to the extent possible, a unified enterprise, located within the IV–D agency's statewide system. *(A.G.K. & H.P.S.)*

---

§ 234.002. Integrated System for Child Support and Medical Support Enforcement.

The statewide integrated system for child support and medical support enforcement under Chapter 231 shall be part of the state case registry and state disbursement unit authorized by this subchapter.

Comment

This section authorizes the establishment of a "statewide integrated system for child support and medical support enforcement" (ICSS) in which counties may voluntarily participate under a contract with the attorney general as the state IV–D agency. The purpose of the ICSS project is to bring local child support registry and IV–D registry functions together in a unified child support registry system using automated processes for recording and tracking child support orders, monitoring compliance with those orders, and initiating enforcement actions when support delinquencies occur. Because of a federal waiver, absent a refusal of services by the custodial parent, all support orders established or modified in the courts of the participating counties are deemed IV–D cases without the requirement of an application for IV–D services. This significant pre-PRWORA project constitutes a core component of the state case registry required under PRWORA. *(A.G.K. & H.P.S.)*

---

§ 234.003. [expired]

§ 234.004. Contracts and Cooperative Agreements.

(a) The Title IV-D agency may enter into contracts and cooperative agreements as necessary to establish and operate the state case registry and state disbursement unit authorized under this subchapter.

(b) To the extent funds are available for this purpose, the Title IV-D agency may enter into contracts or cooperative agreements to process through the state disbursement unit child support collections in cases not otherwise eligible under 42 U.S.C. Section 654b.

§ 234.005. [expired]

§ 234.006. Effective Date and Procedures.

The Title IV-D agency, in cooperation with the work group established under Section 234.003, may adopt rules in compliance with federal law for the operation of the state case registry and the state disbursement unit.

§ 234.007. Notice of Place of Payment.

(a) The Title IV–D agency shall notify the courts that the state disbursement unit has been established. After receiving notice of the establishment of the state disbursement unit, a court that orders income to be withheld for child support shall order that all income withheld for child support be paid to the state disbursement unit.

(b) In order to redirect payments from a local registry to the state disbursement unit after the date of the establishment of the state disbursement unit, the Title IV–D agency shall issue a notice of place of payment informing the obligor, obligee, and employer that income withheld for child support is to be paid to the state disbursement unit.

(c) A copy of the notice under Subsection (b) shall be filed with the court of continuing jurisdiction and with the local child support registry.

(d) The notice under Subsection (b) must include:

(1) the name of the child for whom support is ordered and of the person to whom support is ordered by the court to be paid;

(2) the style and cause number of the case in which support is ordered; and

(3) instructions for the payment of ordered support to the state disbursement unit.

(e) On receipt of a copy of the notice under Subsection (b), the clerk of the court shall file the notice in the appropriate case file.

(f) The notice under Subsection (b) may be used by the Title IV–D agency to redirect child support payments from the state disbursement unit of this state to the state disbursement unit of another state.

History: Amended by 78th Legis., Reg. Sess. (2003), H.B. 1805, eff. Sept. 1, 2003, and applies "only to an interstate proceeding to establish, modify, or enforce a support obligation or to determine parentage began on or after the effective date of this Act. A proceeding begun before the effective date is governed by the law in effect on the date the proceeding began, and the former law is continued in effect for that purpose."

Comment

Subsection (f), added in 2003, conforms to an important 2001 amendment to the Uniform Interstate Family State Support Act (UIFSA) for the redirection of support payments to an obligee who has moved from this to another state. *See* § 159.319(b), *supra*. The notice of place of payment required under this section may be used by the IV–D agency to ensure that support payments paid to the Texas state disbursement unit are promptly redirected to the disbursement unit of the state to which the obligee has relocated. *(C.B. & H.P.S.)*

---

§ 234.008. Deposit, Distribution, and Issuance of Payments.

(a) Except as provided by Subsection (c), not later than the second business day after the date the state disbursement unit receives a child support payment, the state disbursement unit shall distribute the payment to the Title IV–D agency or the obligee.

(b) The state disbursement unit shall deposit daily all child support payments in a trust fund with the state comptroller. Subject to the agreement of the comptroller, the state disbursement unit may issue checks from the trust fund.

(c) In a case in which a service fee is authorized under Section 231.103(d), the state disbursement unit shall deduct the amount of the fee from the support payment before the payment is disbursed to the obligee.

Comment

In 2003 the legislature authorized the IV–D agency to charge a monthly service fee of $3.00 for the processing by the disbursement unit of support payments in cases not receiving IV–D full enforcement services at the time a support collection is made, § 231.103(d). The purpose of the fee is to help offset costs incurred by the disbursement unit in processing income withholding and other support payments in non-IV–D cases that receive only registry services. The fee is retained by the disbursement unit from monthly collections that exceed the amount of the fee itself and is separate from, and in addition to, any fee that may be charged in non-IV–D cases handled by a domestic relations office. *See* § 203.005, *supra.* *(C.B. & H.P.S.)*

---

§ 234.009. Official Child Support Payment Record.

(a) The record of child support payments maintained by a local registry is the official record of a payment received directly by the local registry.

(b) The record of child support payments maintained by the state disbursement unit is the official record of a payment received directly by the unit.

(c) After the date child support payments formerly received by a local registry are redirected to the state disbursement unit, a local registry may accept a record of payments furnished by the state disbursement unit and may add the payments to the record of payments maintained by the local registry so that a complete payment record is available for use by the court.

(d) If the local registry does not add payments received by the state disbursement unit to the record maintained by the registry as provided by Subsection (c), the official record of child support payments consists of the record maintained by the local registry for payments received directly by the registry and the record maintained by the state disbursement unit for payments received directly by the unit.

§ 234.0091. Administrative Review of Child Support Payment Record.

(a) On request, the state disbursement unit shall provide to an obligor or obligee a copy of the record of child support payments maintained by the unit. The record must include the amounts and dates of all payments received from or on behalf of the obligor and disbursed to the obligee.

(b) An obligor or obligee may request that the Title IV–D agency investigate an alleged discrepancy between the child support payment record provided by the state disbursement unit under Subsection (a) and the payment records maintained by the obligor or obligee. The obligor or obligee making the request must provide to the Title IV–D agency documentation of the alleged discrepancy, including a canceled check or other evidence of a payment or disbursement at issue.

(c) The Title IV–D agency shall respond to a request under Subsection (b) not later than the 20th day after the date the agency receives the request. If, after an investigation, the agency determines that the child support payment record maintained by the state disbursement unit should be amended, the state disbursement unit shall immediately make the required amendment to the record and notify the obligor or obligee who made the request under Subsection (b) of that amendment.

Comment

Under federal law, one of the "required procedures" of the state disbursement unit is to provide an obligor or obligee, upon request, with "timely information on the current status of support payments" processed through the unit, 42 U.S.C. 654B(b)(4). This section goes beyond the federal requirement by enabling an obligor or obligee to challenge any discrepancy between the official payment record produced by the disbursement unit and the record of the obligor or obligee with respect to payment or receipt of support processed through the unit. Inasmuch as the IV–D agency is responsible for the operation of the disbursement unit, it must, under this section, promptly investigate an alleged discrepancy upon receipt of supporting evidence from the obligor or obligee and, if warranted, immediately make appropriate changes in the payment record. *(C.B. & H.P.S.)*

---

§ 234.010. Direct Deposit of Child Support Payments.

(a) The state disbursement unit authorized under this chapter may transmit a child support payment to an obligee by electronic funds transfer if the obligee maintains an account with a financial institution.

(b) The work group convened under this subchapter may develop a plan to assist an obligee who does not have an account with a financial institution to obtain an account.

(c) The work group may determine whether it is feasible and cost-effective for the state to administer an electronic benefits transfer system for child support obligees and may recommend implementation of such a system to the Title IV-D agency.

(d) After receiving any recommendations by the work group under Subsection (c), the Title IV-D agency or the vendor selected by the Title IV-D agency to operate the state disbursement unit may provide for electronic benefits transfer, if the request for proposals issued by the Title IV-D agency and any contract resulting from the selection of a vendor to provide the services specified in the request for proposals provides for electronic benefits transfer.

(e) The work group may recommend and the Title IV-D agency may establish procedures to implement this section.

(f) The Title IV-D agency, after receiving the recommendation of the work group, may require an obligee to receive payments by direct deposit to the obligee's bank account or by electronic benefits transfer to an account established by the Title IV-D agency or the state disbursement unit if the account is established at no cost to the obligee.

§ 234.011. Use of Electronic Benefits Transfer for Child Support Payments.

The Title IV-D agency, in coordination with the Texas Department of Human Services and the comptroller of public accounts, shall study the use of an existing electronic benefits transfer system to determine the advisability of and method for implementation of a debit card child support system. If it is determined that such a system is feasible and cost-effective, these agencies shall begin implementation of such a system. These agencies must report their findings and progress to the legislature by December 1, 2000.

Subchapter B. State Directory of New Hires.

Introductory Comment

This section authorized the IV–D agency to develop and operate the new hires directory in cooperation with the Texas Workforce Commission, although other state agencies will necessarily be involved because of the electronic interfaces the directory must have with entities administering public welfare and workers' compensation programs. Federal law does not require the IV–D agency to house the directory, although the sort of linkage the directory must have with the case registry and the national directory of new hires within the Federal Parent Locator Services argued for the agency's custodianship of the directory. Because of the complexity of federal statutory requirements and the paucity of federal regulatory guidance, procedural details for the operation of the directory are left to the IV–D agency's rulemaking authority. *(A.G.K. & H.P.S.)*

---

§ 234.101. Definitions.

In this subchapter:

(1) "Employee" means an individual who is an employee within the meaning of Chapter 24 of the Internal Revenue Code of 1986 (26 U.S.C. Section 3401(c)). The term does not include an employee of a state agency performing intelligence or counterintelligence functions if the head of the agency has determined that reporting employee information under this subchapter could endanger the safety of the employee or compromise an ongoing investigation or intelligence activity.

(2) "Employer" has the meaning given that term by Section 3401(d) of the Internal Revenue Code of 1986 (26 U.S.C. Section 3401(d)) and includes a governmental entity and a labor organization, as that term is identified in Section 2(5) of the National Labor Relations Act (29 U.S.C. Section 152(5)), including an entity, also known as a "hiring hall," used by the labor organization and an employer to carry out requirements of an agreement between the organization and an employer described in Section 8(f)(3) of that Act (29 U.S.C. Section 158(f)(3)).

§ 234.102. Operation of New Hire Directory.

In cooperation with the Texas Workforce Commission, the Title IV-D agency shall develop and operate a state directory to which employers in the state shall report each newly hired or rehired employee in accordance with the requirements of 42 U.S.C. Section 653a.

§ 234.103. Contracts and Cooperative Agreements.

The Title IV-D agency may enter into cooperative agreements and contracts as necessary to create and operate the directory authorized under this subchapter.

§ 234.104. Procedures.

The Title IV-D agency by rule shall establish procedures for reporting employee information and for operating a state directory of new hires meeting the requirements of federal law.

Chapter 235. Sharing Information in State Case Registry.

§ 235.001. Request for Information.

(a) The state case registry shall provide information under this chapter on the written request of a custodial parent whose case:

(1) is included in the state case registry established under 42 U.S.C. Section 654a and for whom the Title IV-D agency is not providing enforcement services; or

(2) would otherwise not be required to be included in the state case registry under 42 U.S.C. Section 654a but who has applied for inclusion under Section 235.002.

(b) The state case registry shall provide to a custodial parent under Subsection (a) who makes a request for information or, to the extent provided by federal law, to an attorney, friend of the court, guardian ad litem, or domestic relations office designated by the parent any information in the registry required by 42 U.S.C. Section 654a(e) concerning the parent's case.

(c) To the extent permitted by federal law, the state case registry shall provide the information described by Subsection (b) to a domestic relations office or friend of the court that requests information regarding a case described by Subsection (a).

§ 235.002. Request to Include Case in Registry.

The case of a custodial parent whose case would otherwise not be included in the state case registry under 42 U.S.C. Section 654a may be included in the state case registry by making a written request to the registry either directly or through an attorney, friend of the court, guardian ad litem, or domestic relations office designated by the custodial parent. The request must be accompanied by a certified copy of the court order requiring the payment of child support.

§ 235.003. Application for Services Not Required.

The Title IV-D agency may not require an application for services as a condition for:

(1) releasing information under Section 235.001; or

(2) including a case in the state case registry under Section 235.002.

§ 235.004. Fees.

(a) The state case registry may charge a fee for:

(1) including in the registry a child support case entered in the registry under Section 235.002; and

(2) providing information concerning a case as authorized by Section 235.001.

(b) The amount of a fee under this section may not exceed the actual costs incurred by the state case registry in providing the services.

Chapter 236. Competitive Bidding for Child Support Collection Services.

Introductory Comment

States are increasingly looking to the private sector for cost-effective ways to deliver some of the services offered by the IV–D agencies, particularly the collection of child support. These provisions authorize the State Council on Competitive Government, under GOV'T CODE ch. 2162, to explore with the IV–D agency possibilities for contracting out appropriate agency services and for recovering from the parties in non-public assistance cases the costs of providing services. The demands of growing caseloads and increasing fiscal constraints are making both the use of private contractors and the recovery of administrative expenditures attractive options to state IV–D programs, but both have their drawbacks. Because of the complexity of federal regulations governing the IV–D program, state agencies have found that they must closely monitor the performance of private contractors to ensure that federal standards and time frames are met. Still, states are finding that certain child support enforcement services can be delivered more efficiently and with increased cost-effectiveness by private contractors than by the public agency because of the private sector's greater flexibility in acquiring and using resources and freedom from bureaucratic procedures. With respect to the recovery of costs, few states have elected either to charge administrative costs against obligees who usually rely on every dollar of collected support or to attempt to recover these costs from obligors who usually do very well just to pay current support fully and timely. Nonetheless, financial exigencies are compelling state IV–D agencies to re-examine their funding mechanisms and to consider equitable ways of charging fees for services in appropriate cases. *(A.G.K. & H.P.S.)*

---

§ 236.001. Definition.

In this chapter, "council" means the State Council on Competitive Government.

§ 236.002. Powers and Duties of Council.

(a) The council shall:

(1) establish an initiative called "Kids Can't Wait" to increase child support enforcement;

(2) identify child support enforcement functions performed by the Title IV-D agency that may be competitively bid;

(3) establish guidelines for referral of child support enforcement cases to a contractor;

(4) after consulting with the Title IV-D agency, make recommendations regarding competitive bidding of child support enforcement functions that are identified under Subdivision (2);

(5) consider the benefits of the state's participation in an electronic parent locator network or a similar national service designed to locate parents who owe child support;

(6) study the feasibility of cost recovery options in child support collection actions for children who do not receive public assistance; and

(7) engage in other activities necessary for the administration of this chapter.

(b) The Title IV-D agency shall coordinate with the council regarding competitive bidding of child support enforcement functions identified under this section.

(c) A member of the council may designate an employee of the state agency represented by the member to perform any of the member's powers or duties under this section.

(d) The Title IV-D agency shall cooperate with the council if requested by the council.

(e) The council and the Title IV-D agency shall report not later than October 1, 1998, to the presiding officer of each house of the legislature the results of the council's efforts under this section.

Comment

The State Council on Competitive Government is mandated to explore ways to enhance the delivery of state agency services through competitive bidding among agencies and between state agencies and private vendors. This section brings IV–D child support enforcement services into the arena of competitive bidding under the direction of the council. *(A.G.K. & H.P.S.)*

§ 236.003. Child Support Collection Agreement.

The Title IV-D agency or a contractor awarded a contract under this chapter to collect child support may enter into an agreement with a person liable for the payment of child support. The agreement may relate to any matter that may be adjudicated by a court, including:

(1) the determination of paternity;

(2) the determination of the amount of child support due;

(3) the method of making child support payments;

(4) the imposition of income garnishment or withholding;

(5) the payment of fees;

(6) the reimbursement of costs; and

(7) other child support enforcement matters permitted by state or federal law.

Comment

The intent of this section is unclear. Under Chapter 233, the IV–D agency may already enter into agreements relating "to any matter that may be adjudicated by a court." But such an agreement would involve both the obligor and obligee and, in the form of an agreed order, would have to be confirmed by the court. This provision suggests that a private child support collection agency could work out agreements with just the obligor (or a presumed or alleged father) concerning matters well beyond, say, a plan to repay arrearages as a condition for avoiding suspension of a license under Chapter 232. The questionable usefulness of this section is matched only by its unintelligibility. *(A.G.K. & H.P.S.)*

Subtitle E. Protection of the Child

Chapter

***

Chapter 261. Investigation of Report of Child Abuse or Neglect.

Subchapter A. General Provisions

Subchapter B. Report of Abuse or Neglect; Immunities

Subchapter C. Confidentiality and Privileged Communication

Subchapter D. Investigations

Subchapter E. Investigations of Abuse, Neglect, or Exploitation in Certain Facilities

Editors' Note: *This chapter contains guest commentary by Charles G. Childress, Children's Rights Clinic, University of Texas Law School, and former Chief Attorney, Field Operations, Legal Division, Texas Department of Protective and Regulatory Services, identified as (C.G.C.).*

CLE/Other Legal Publications

The duty to report child abuse. Camile Glasscock Dubose, 2004 ADV. FAM. L.

Overview of abuse, neglect and intra-family violence. Oscar Gabaldon, 2004 U. TEX. FAM. L. ON THE BORDER

Reporting child abuse—ethical and practical considerations. Coye Conner, Jr., 2002 ADV. FAM. L.

Who ya' gonna call when CPS comes a knockin'? Ann E. Coover, 2000 ADV. FAM. L.

Leading Cases

Perry v. S.N., 973 S.W.2d 301 (Tex. 1998) (failure to report child abuse does not create a new tort)

B.K. v. Cox, 116 S.W.3d 351 (Tex. App.—Houston [14th Dist.] 2003, no pet.) (doctor performing court-ordered psychological exams entitled to claim derived judicial immunity in mother's suit for failure to report abuse)

Walker v. Pollock, 981 S.W.2d 226 (Tex. App.—Houston [1st Dist.] 1998, no pet.) (doctor who misdiagnosed child's medical status protected from civil liability—child abuse allegation was trigger for examination)

Blum v. Julian, 977 S.W.2d 819 (Tex. App.—Fort Worth 1998, no pet.) (licensed counselor report of suspected sexual abuse privileged in absence of bad faith or malice)

Subchapter A. General Provisions

§ 261.001. Definitions.

In this chapter:

(1) "Abuse" includes the following acts or omissions by a person:

(A) mental or emotional injury to a child that results in an observable and material impairment in the child's growth, development, or psychological functioning;

(B) causing or permitting the child to be in a situation in which the child sustains a mental or emotional injury that results in an observable and material impairment in the child's growth, development, or psychological functioning;

(C) physical injury that results in substantial harm to the child, or the genuine threat of substantial harm from physical injury to the child, including an injury that is at variance with the history or explanation given and excluding an accident or reasonable discipline by a parent, guardian, or managing or possessory conservator that does not expose the child to a substantial risk of harm;

(D) failure to make a reasonable effort to prevent an action by another person that results in physical injury that results in substantial harm to the child;

(E) sexual conduct harmful to a child's mental, emotional, or physical welfare, including conduct that constitutes the offense of indecency with a child under Section 21.11, Penal Code, sexual assault under Section 22.011, Penal Code, or aggravated sexual assault under Section 22.021, Penal Code;

(F) failure to make a reasonable effort to prevent sexual conduct harmful to a child;

(G) compelling or encouraging the child to engage in sexual conduct as defined by Section 43.01, Penal Code;

(H) causing, permitting, encouraging, engaging in, or allowing the photographing, filming, or depicting of the child if the person knew or should have known that the resulting photograph, film, or depiction of the child is obscene as defined by Section 43.21, Penal Code, or pornographic;

(I) the current use by a person of a controlled substance as defined by Chapter 481, Health and Safety Code, in a manner or to the extent that the use results in physical, mental, or emotional injury to a child;

(J) causing, expressly permitting, or encouraging a child to use a controlled substance as defined by Chapter 481, Health and Safety Code; or

(K) causing, permitting, encouraging, engaging in, or allowing a sexual performance by a child as defined by Section 43.25, Penal Code.

(2) "Department" means the Department of Protective and Regulatory Services.

(3) "Designated agency" means the agency designated by the court as responsible for the protection of children.

(4) "Neglect" includes:

(A) the leaving of a child in a situation where the child would be exposed to a substantial risk of physical or mental harm, without arranging for necessary care for the child, and the demonstration of an intent not to return by a parent, guardian, or managing or possessory conservator of the child;

(B) the following acts or omissions by a person:

(i) placing a child in or failing to remove a child from a situation that a reasonable person would realize requires judgment or actions beyond the child's level of maturity, physical condition, or mental abilities and that results in bodily injury or a substantial risk of immediate harm to the child;

(ii) failing to seek, obtain, or follow through with medical care for a child, with the failure resulting in or presenting a substantial risk of death, disfigurement, or bodily injury or with the failure resulting in an observable and material impairment to the growth, development, or functioning of the child;

(iii) the failure to provide a child with food, clothing, or shelter necessary to sustain the life or health of the child, excluding failure caused primarily by financial inability unless relief services had been offered and refused; or

(iv) placing a child in or failing to remove the child from a situation in which the child would be exposed to a substantial risk of sexual conduct harmful to the child; or

(C) the failure by the person responsible for a child's care, custody, or welfare to permit the child to return to the child's home without arranging for the necessary care for the child after the child has been absent from the home for any reason, including having been in residential placement or having run away.

(5) "Person responsible for a child's care, custody, or welfare" means a person who traditionally is responsible for a child's care, custody, or welfare, including:

(A) a parent, guardian, managing or possessory conservator, or foster parent of the child;

(B) a member of the child's family or household as defined by Chapter 71;

(C) a person with whom the child's parent cohabits;

(D) school personnel or a volunteer at the child's school; or

(E) personnel or a volunteer at a public or private child-care facility that provides services for the child or at a public or private residential institution or facility where the child resides.

(6) "Report" means a report that alleged or suspected abuse or neglect of a child has occurred or may occur.

(7) "Board" means the Board of Protective and Regulatory Services.

(8) "Born addicted to alcohol or a controlled substance" means a child:

(A) who is born to a mother who during the pregnancy used a controlled substance, as defined by Chapter 481, Health and Safety Code, other than a controlled substance legally obtained by prescription, or alcohol; and

(B) who, after birth as a result of the mother's use of the controlled substance or alcohol:

(i) experiences observable withdrawal from the alcohol or controlled substance;

(ii) exhibits observable or harmful effects in the child's physical appearance or functioning; or

(iii) exhibits the demonstrable presence of alcohol or a controlled substance in the child's bodily fluids.

§ 261.002. Central Registry.

(a) The department shall establish and maintain in Austin a central registry of reported cases of child abuse or neglect.

(b) The department may adopt rules necessary to carry out this section. The rules shall provide for cooperation with local child service agencies, including hospitals, clinics, and schools, and cooperation with other states in exchanging reports to effect a national registration system.

§ 261.003. Application to Students in School for Deaf or School for Blind and Visually Impaired.

This chapter applies to the investigation of a report of abuse or neglect of a student, without regard to the age of the student, in the Texas School for the Deaf or the Texas School for the Blind and Visually Impaired.

§ 261.004. Statistics of Abuse and Neglect of Children.

(a) The department shall prepare and disseminate statistics by county relating to the department's activities under this subtitle and include the information specified in Subsection (b) in an annual report available to the public.

(b) The department shall report the following information:

(1) the number of initial phone calls received by the department alleging abuse and neglect;

(2) the number of children reported to the department as having been abused and neglected;

(3) the number of reports received by the department alleging abuse or neglect and assigned by the department for investigation;

(4) of the children to whom Subdivision (2) applies:

(A) the number for whom the report was substantiated;

(B) the number for whom the report was unsubstantiated;

(C) the number for whom the report was determined to be false;

(D) the number who did not receive services from the department under a state or federal program;

(E) the number who received services, including preventative services, from the department under a state or federal program; and

(F) the number who were removed from the child's home during the preceding year;

(5) the number of families in which the child was not removed, but the child or family received services from the department;

(6) the number of children who died during the preceding year as a result of child abuse or neglect;

(7) of the children to whom Subdivision (6) applies, the number who were in foster care at the time of death;

(8) the number of child protective services workers responsible for report intake, assessment, or investigation;

(9) the response time by the department with respect to conducting an initial investigation of a report of child abuse or neglect;

(10) the response time by the department with respect to commencing services to families and children for whom an allegation of abuse or neglect has been made;

(11) the number of children who were returned to their families or who received family preservation services and who, before the fifth anniversary of the date of return or receipt, were the victims of substantiated reports of child abuse or neglect, including abuse or neglect resulting in the death of the child;

(12) the number of cases pursued by the department in each stage of the judicial process, including civil and criminal proceedings and the results of each proceeding; and

(13) the number of children for whom a person was appointed by the court to represent the best interests of the child and the average number of out-of-court contacts between the person and the child.

(c) The department shall compile the information specified in Subsection (b) for the preceding year in a report to be submitted to the legislature and the general public not later than February 1 of each year.

Subchapter B. Report of Abuse or Neglect; Immunities

Introductory Comment

This subchapter is primarily hortatory. Although it imposes a duty on ordinary citizens to report suspected child abuse or neglect under penalty of criminal prosecution for failure to do so, in fact prosecutions are extremely rare (but not unique).

CLE/Other Legal Publications

Reporting child abuse—ethical and practical considerations. Coye Conner, Jr., 2002 ADV. FAM. L.

Who ya' gonna call when CPS comes a knockin'? Ann E. Coover, 2000 ADV. FAM. L.

Where are the reasonable efforts to enforce the reasonable efforts requirement? Monitoring state compliance under the Adoption Assistance and Child Welfare Act of 1980. Shawn L. Raymond, 77 TEX. L. REV. 1235 (1999)

Leading Cases

DeShaney v. Winnebago County Dept. Social Services, 489 U.S. 189, 103 L.Ed.2d 249, 109 S.Ct. 998 (1989) (U.S. Const. does not mandate tort liability of caseworkers who fail to rescue abused child after report)

Perry v. S.N., 973 S.W.2d 301(Tex. 1998) (statutory duty to report child abuse does not create cause of action based on negligence per se)

Mattix–Hill v. Reck, 923 S.W.2d 596 (Tex. 1996) (DHS caseworker doesn't inflict intentional emotional distress on parent)

Scott v. Butcher, 906 S.W.2d 14 (Tex. 1995) (failure to report suspected child sexual abuse not negligence per se, but fact question of duty arises)

B.K. v. Cox, 116 S.W.3d 351 (Tex. App.—Houston [14th Dist.] 2003, no pet.) (doctor performing court-ordered psychological exams entitled to claim derived judicial immunity in mother's suit for failure to report abuse)

Walker v. Pollock, 981 S.W.2d 226 (Tex. App.—Houston [1st Dist.] 1998, no pet.) (doctor who misdiagnosed child's medical status protected from civil liability—child abuse allegation was trigger for examination)

Blum v. Julian, 977 S.W.2d 819 (Tex. App.—Fort Worth 1998, no pet.) (licensed counselor report of suspected sexual abuse privileged in absence of bad faith or malice)

Marshall v. Sackett, 907 S.W.2d 925 (Tex. App.—Houston [1st Dist.] 1995, no writ) (CPS program director immune when makes good faith investigation of alleged medical neglect even if refusal of treatment based on religious beliefs)

Gonzalez v. Avalos, 866 S.W.2d 346 (Tex. App.—El Paso 1993, writ dism'd w.o.j., 907 S.W.2d 443 (Tex. 1995)) (DPRS supervisor not entitled to immunity when failed to investigate abuse allegations)

---

§ 261.101. Persons Required to Report; Time to Report.

(a) A person having cause to believe that a child's physical or mental health or welfare has been adversely affected by abuse or neglect by any person shall immediately make a report as provided by this subchapter.

(b) If a professional has cause to believe that a child has been abused or neglected or may be abused or neglected, or that a child is a victim of an offense under Section 21.11, Penal Code, and the professional has cause to believe that the child has been abused as defined by Section 261.001, the professional shall make a report not later than the 48th hour after the hour the professional first suspects that the child has been or may be abused or neglected or is a victim of an offense under Section 21.11, Penal Code. A professional may not delegate to or rely on another person to make the report. In this subsection, "professional" means an individual who is licensed or certified by the state or who is an employee of a facility licensed, certified, or operated by the state and who, in the normal course of official duties or duties for which a license or certification is required, has direct contact with children. The term includes teachers, nurses, doctors, day-care employees, employees of a clinic or health care facility that provides reproductive services, juvenile probation officers, and juvenile detention or correctional officers.

(c) The requirement to report under this section applies without exception to an individual whose personal communications may otherwise be privileged, including an attorney, a member of the clergy, a medical practitioner, a social worker, a mental health professional, and an employee of a clinic or health care facility that provides reproductive services.

(d) Unless waived in writing by the person making the report, the identity of an individual making a report under this chapter is confidential and may be disclosed only:

(1) as provided by Section 261.201; or

(2) to a law enforcement officer for the purposes of conducting a criminal investigation of the report.

Comment

Texas imposes a broad duty to report child abuse or neglect on all citizens, including professionals. Professionals include juvenile probation, juvenile detention and correctional officers, and the employees of a clinic or other health care facility providing "reproductive services." Note that the attorney-client privilege does not exempt a lawyer who learns of abuse from the duty to report, although an attorney who reports abuse may not be required to testify about communications with a client. This requirement has been broadly applied by an Attorney General's Opinion, DM–458, and the legislature has rejected all efforts to soften or limit the requirement.

The identity of the person making the report is strictly protected. In some cases this has forced the department to black-out (redact) this information from the documents even though the identity of the reporter was known and had no concern about his or her identity being known to the alleged perpetrator.

Subsection (d) permits a person reporting abuse to waive confidentiality. *(C.G.C.)*

Leading Case

Boardman v. State, 56 S.W.3d 63 (Tex. App.—Houston [14th Dist.] 2001, pet. refused) (defendant may not rely on a clergy communication privilege to exclude confession that he sexually assaulted his three children)

---

§ 261.102. Matters to be Reported.

A report should reflect the reporter's belief that a child has been or may be abused or neglected or has died of abuse or neglect.

§ 261.103. Report Made to Appropriate Agency.

(a) Except as provided by Subsection (b) and Section 261.405, a report shall be made to:

(1) any local or state law enforcement agency;

(2) the department if the alleged or suspected abuse involves a person responsible for the care, custody, or welfare of the child;

(3) the state agency that operates, licenses, certifies, or registers the facility in which the alleged abuse or neglect occurred; or

(4) the agency designated by the court to be responsible for the protection of children.

(b) A report may be made to the Texas Youth Commission instead of the entities listed under Subsection (a) if the report is based on information provided by a child while under the supervision of the commission concerning the child's alleged abuse of another child.

Comment

A person wishing to report child abuse or neglect may report to law enforcement officers, other state agencies, or the Department of Protective and Regulatory Services [DPRS] on a 24–hour toll-free number, ***1–800–252–5400***. The reporter is not required to determine whether the abuser is "responsible for the care, custody, or welfare of the child" before making the report. Other provisions in this chapter require that the department refer cases to law enforcement or the appropriate agency if it is determined that the alleged perpetrator is not a caretaker. The Texas Youth Commission is the primary investigative agency when the alleged perpetrator is a child in TYC custody. *(C.G.C.)*

---

§ 261.104. Contents of Report.

The person making a report shall identify, if known:

(1) the name and address of the child;

(2) the name and address of the person responsible for the care, custody, or welfare of the child; and

(3) any other pertinent information concerning the alleged or suspected abuse or neglect.

§ 261.105. Referral of Report by Department or Law Enforcement.

(a) All reports received by a local or state law enforcement agency that allege abuse or neglect by a person responsible for a child's care, custody, or welfare shall be referred immediately to the department or the designated agency.

(b) The department or designated agency shall immediately notify the appropriate state or local law enforcement agency of any report it receives, other than a report from a law enforcement agency, that concerns the suspected abuse or neglect of a child or death of a child from abuse or neglect.

(c) In addition to notifying a law enforcement agency, if the report relates to a child in a facility operated, licensed, certified, or registered by a state agency, the department shall refer the report to the agency for investigation.

(d) If the department initiates an investigation and determines that the abuse or neglect does not involve a person responsible for the child's care, custody, or welfare, the department shall refer the report to a law enforcement agency for further investigation. If the department determines that the abuse or neglect involves an employee of a public primary or secondary school, and that the child is a student at the school, the department shall orally notify the superintendent of the school district in which the employee is employed about the investigation.

(e) In cooperation with the department, the Texas Youth Commission by rule shall adopt guidelines for identifying a report made to the commission under Section 261.103(b) that is appropriate to refer to the department or a law enforcement agency for investigation. Guidelines adopted under this subsection must require the commission to consider the severity and immediacy of the alleged abuse or neglect of the child victim.

Comment

This section requires cooperation among law enforcement agencies, the department and licensing agencies to ensure that reports of child abuse are properly investigated. As part of treatment programs in TYC, children in custody are encouraged to report and discuss past delinquent conduct. Some of these reports may lead to information concerning caretaker abuse or failure to protect, or may be serious enough to require some follow-up contact with the apparent victim; others may be too remote or vague to merit further investigation. Subsection (e) requires TYC, in cooperation with the department, to develop rules to guide the referral process. *(C.G.C.)*

§ 261.1055. Notification of District Attorneys.

(a) A district attorney may inform the department or designated agency that the district attorney wishes to receive notification of some or all reports of suspected abuse or neglect of children who were in the county at the time the report was made or who were in the county at the time of the alleged abuse or neglect.

(b) If the district attorney makes the notification under this section, the department or designated agency shall, on receipt of a report of suspected abuse or neglect, immediately notify the district attorney as requested and the department or designated agency shall forward a copy of the reports to the district attorney on request.

§ 261.106. Immunities.

(a) A person acting in good faith who reports or assists in the investigation of a report of alleged child abuse or neglect or who testifies or otherwise participates in a judicial proceeding arising from a report, petition, or investigation of alleged child abuse or neglect is immune from civil or criminal liability that might otherwise be incurred or imposed.

(b) Immunity from civil and criminal liability extends to an authorized volunteer of the department or a law enforcement officer who participates at the request of the department in an investigation of alleged or suspected abuse or neglect or in an action arising from an investigation if the person was acting in good faith and in the scope of the person's responsibilities.

(c) A person who reports the person's own abuse or neglect of a child or who acts in bad faith or with malicious purpose in reporting alleged child abuse or neglect is not immune from civil or criminal liability.

Leading Cases

Chaney v. Corona, 103 S.W.3d 608 (Tex. App.—San Antonio 2003, pet. denied) (school principal had reasonable basis for reporting teacher for suspected child abuse committed on student; immunity statute applies)

State v. Harrod, 81 S.W.3d 904 (Tex. App.—Dallas 2002, pet. refused) (mother failed to immediately report sexual abuse of her daughters, criminal immunity statute doesn't apply)

§ 261.107. False Report; Penalty.

(a) A person commits an offense if the person knowingly or intentionally makes a report as provided in this chapter that the person knows is false or lacks factual foundation. An offense under this section is a Class A misdemeanor unless it is shown on the trial of the offense that the person has previously been convicted under this section, in which case the offense is a state jail felony.

(b) A finding by a court in a suit affecting the parent-child relationship that a report made under this chapter before or during the suit was false or lacking factual foundation may be grounds for the court to modify an order providing for possession of or access to the child who was the subject of the report by restricting further access to the child by the person who made the report.

(c) The appropriate county prosecuting attorney shall be responsible for the prosecution of an offense under this section.

Comment

The criminal penalties provided by this section for a false report, or for failure to report under § 261.109, are seldom enforced. Subsection (b) permits the making of a false report to be used as a ground for restricting access by the accuser to the child. A party contemplating making a claim of a false report must also consider the risk that a court may award damages to the reporter if the claim of false report is determined to be frivolous under § 261.108, *infra*. The net effect of these conflicting provisions may discourage litigation on either side of the issue. *(C.G.C.)*

§ 261.108. Frivolous Claims Against Person Reporting.

(a) In this section:

(1) "Claim" means an action or claim by a party, including a plaintiff, counterclaimant, cross-claimant, or third-party plaintiff, requesting recovery of damages.

(2) "Defendant" means a party against whom a claim is made.

(b) A court shall award a defendant reasonable attorney's fees and other expenses related to the defense of a claim filed against the defendant for damages or other relief arising from reporting or assisting in the investigation of a report under this chapter or participating in a judicial proceeding resulting from the report if:

(1) the court finds that the claim is frivolous, unreasonable, or without foundation because the defendant is immune from liability under Section 261.106; and

(2) the claim is dismissed or judgment is rendered for the defendant.

(c) To recover under this section, the defendant must, at any time after the filing of a claim, file a written motion stating that:

(1) the claim is frivolous, unreasonable, or without foundation because the defendant is immune from liability under Section 261.106; and

(2) the defendant requests the court to award reasonable attorney's fees and other expenses related to the defense of the claim.

§ 261.109. Failure to Report; Penalty.

(a) A person commits an offense if the person has cause to believe that a child's physical or mental health or welfare has been or may be adversely affected by abuse or neglect and knowingly fails to report as provided in this chapter.

(b) An offense under this section is a Class B misdemeanor.

Leading Cases

Porter v. State, 121 S.W.3d 404 (Tex. App.—Amarillo 2003, pet. refused) (day care operator failed to report child abuse when her employees inadvertently left small child alone in van for over an hour)

State v. Harrod, 81 S.W.3d 904 (Tex. App.—Dallas 2002, pet. refused) (mother failed to immediately report sexual abuse of her daughters, criminal immunity statute doesn't apply)

White v. State, 50 S.W.3d 31 (Tex. App.—Waco 2001, pet. refused) (ex-wife convicted for failure to report abuse of her former step-daughter by her ex-husband)

§ 261.110. Employer Retaliation Prohibited.

(a) In this section, "professional" has the meaning assigned by Section 261.101(b).

(b) An employer may not suspend or terminate the employment of, or otherwise discriminate against, a person who is a professional and who in good faith:

(1) reports child abuse or neglect to:

(A) the person's supervisor;

(B) an administrator of the facility where the person is employed;

(C) a state regulatory agency; or

(D) a law enforcement agency; or

(2) initiates or cooperates with an investigation or proceeding by a governmental entity relating to an allegation of child abuse or neglect.

(c) A person whose employment is suspended or terminated or who is otherwise discriminated against in violation of this section may sue for injunctive relief, damages, or both.

(d) A plaintiff who prevails in a suit under this section may recover:

(1) actual damages, including damages for mental anguish even if an injury other than mental anguish is not shown;

(2) exemplary damages under Chapter 41, Civil Practice and Remedies Code, if the employer is a private employer;

(3) court costs; and

(4) reasonable attorney's fees.

(e) In addition to amounts recovered under Subsection (d), a plaintiff who prevails in a suit under this section is entitled to:

(1) reinstatement to the person's former position or a position that is comparable in terms of compensation, benefits, and other conditions of employment;

(2) reinstatement of any fringe benefits and seniority rights lost because of the suspension, termination, or discrimination; and

(3) compensation for wages lost during the period of suspension or termination.

(f) A public employee who alleges a violation of this section may sue the employing state or local governmental entity for the relief provided for by this section. Sovereign immunity is waived and abolished to the extent of liability created by this section. A person having a claim under this section may sue a governmental unit for damages allowed by this section.

(g) In a suit under this section against an employing state or local governmental entity, a plaintiff may not recover compensatory damages for future pecuniary losses, emotional pain, suffering, inconvenience, mental anguish, loss of enjoyment of life, and other nonpecuniary losses in an amount that exceeds:

(1) $50,000, if the employing state or local governmental entity has fewer than 101 employees in each of 20 or more calendar weeks in the calendar year in which the suit is filed or in the preceding year;

(2) $100,000, if the employing state or local governmental entity has more than 100 and fewer than 201 employees in each of 20 or more calendar weeks in the calendar year in which the suit is filed or in the preceding year;

(3) $200,000, if the employing state or local governmental entity has more than 200 and fewer than 501 employees in each of 20 or more calendar weeks in the calendar year in which the suit is filed or in the preceding year; and

(4) $250,000, if the employing state or local governmental entity has more than 500 employees in each of 20 or more calendar weeks in the calendar year in which the suit is filed or in the preceding year.

(h) If more than one subdivision of Subsection (g) applies to an employing state or local governmental entity, the amount of monetary damages that may be recovered from the entity in a suit brought under this section is governed by the applicable provision that provides the highest damage award.

(i) A plaintiff suing under this section has the burden of proof, except that there is a rebuttable presumption that the plaintiff's employment was suspended or terminated or that the plaintiff was otherwise discriminated against for reporting abuse or neglect if the suspension, termination, or discrimination occurs before the 61st day after the date on which the person made a report in good faith.

(j) A suit under this section may be brought in a district or county court of the county in which:

(1) the plaintiff was employed by the defendant; or

(2) the defendant conducts business.

(k) It is an affirmative defense to a suit under Subsection (b) that an employer would have taken the action against the employee that forms the basis of the suit based solely on information, observation, or evidence that is not related to the fact that the employee reported child abuse or neglect or initiated or cooperated with an investigation or proceeding relating to an allegation of child abuse or neglect.

(l) A public employee who has a cause of action under Chapter 554, Government Code, based on conduct described by Subsection (b) may not bring an action based on that conduct under this section.

(m) This section does not apply to a person who reports the person's own abuse or neglect of a child or who initiates or cooperates with an investigation or proceeding by a governmental entity relating to an allegation of the person's own abuse or neglect of a child.

Comment

Virtually everyone having cause to believe that a child is being abused or neglected has a duty to report the abuse and cooperate with an investigation. However, there has been no specific protection for teachers, day-care employees or others from retaliation by an employer for making a report or for cooperating with an investigation. This section prohibits employer retaliation against an employee who in good faith reports child abuse or neglect or cooperates with an investigation of such a report. *(C.G.C.)*

§ 261.111. Refusal of Psychiatric or Psychological Treatment of Child.

(a) In this section, "psychotropic drug" means a substance that is:

(1) used in the diagnosis, treatment, or prevention of a disease or as a component of a medication; and

(2) intended to have an altering effect on perception, emotion, or behavior.

(b) The refusal of a parent, guardian, or managing or possessory conservator of a child to administer or consent to the administration of a psychotropic drug to the child, or to consent to any other psychiatric or psychological treatment of the child, does not by itself constitute neglect of the child unless the refusal to consent:

(1) presents a substantial risk of death, disfigurement, or bodily injury to the child; or

(2) has resulted in an observable and material impairment to the growth, development, or functioning of the child.

Subchapter C. Confidentiality and Privileged Communication

Introductory Comment

The only privileged communications recognized by this chapter are those between an attorney and client. This testimonial privilege protects confidential communications; it is not a blanket privilege that immunizes an attorney from responsibility to report injury to a child caused by abuse or neglect.

Leading Case

TDHS v. Benson, 893 S.W.2d 236 (Tex. App.—Austin 1995, writ denied) (child abuse report is confidential; court voids agency policy regarding second reports and professionals, but governmental immunity applies to agency)

§ 261.201. Confidentiality and Disclosure of Information.

(a) The following information is confidential, is not subject to public release under Chapter 552, Government Code, and may be disclosed only for purposes consistent with this code and applicable federal or state law or under rules adopted by an investigating agency:

(1) a report of alleged or suspected abuse or neglect made under this chapter and the identity of the person making the report; and

(2) except as otherwise provided in this section, the files, reports, records, communications, audiotapes, videotapes, and working papers used or developed in an investigation under this chapter or in providing services as a result of an investigation.

(b) A court may order the disclosure of information that is confidential under this section if:

(1) a motion has been filed with the court requesting the release of the information;

(2) a notice of hearing has been served on the investigating agency and all other interested parties; and

(3) after hearing and an in camera review of the requested information, the court determines that the disclosure of the requested information is:

(A) essential to the administration of justice; and

(B) not likely to endanger the life or safety of:

(i) a child who is the subject of the report of alleged or suspected abuse or neglect;

(ii) a person who makes a report of alleged or suspected abuse or neglect; or

(iii) any other person who participates in an investigation of reported abuse or neglect or who provides care for the child.

(c) In addition to Subsection (b), a court, on its own motion, may order disclosure of information that is confidential under this section if:

(1) the order is rendered at a hearing for which all parties have been given notice;

(2) the court finds that disclosure of the information is:

(A) essential to the administration of justice; and

(B) not likely to endanger the life or safety of:

(i) a child who is the subject of the report of alleged or suspected abuse or neglect;

(ii) a person who makes a report of alleged or suspected abuse or neglect; or

(iii) any other person who participates in an investigation of reported abuse or neglect or who provides care for the child; and

(3) the order is reduced to writing or made on the record in open court.

(d) The adoptive parents of a child who was the subject of an investigation and an adult who was the subject of an investigation as a child are entitled to examine and make copies of any report, record, working paper, or other information in the possession, custody, or control of the state that pertains to the history of the child. The department may edit the documents to protect the identity of the biological parents and any other person whose identity is confidential, **unless this information is already known to the adoptive parents or is readily available through other sources, including the court records of a suit to terminate the parent-child relationship under Chapter 161**.

(e) Before placing a child who was the subject of an investigation, the department shall notify the prospective adoptive parents of their right to examine any report, record, working paper, or other information in the possession, custody, or control of the state that pertains to the history of the child.

(f) The department shall provide prospective adoptive parents an opportunity to examine information under this section as early as practicable before placing a child.

(g) Notwithstanding Subsection (b), the department, on request and subject to department rule, shall provide to the parent, managing conservator, or other legal representative of a child who is the subject of reported abuse or neglect information concerning the reported abuse or neglect that would otherwise be confidential under this section if the department has edited the information to protect the confidentiality of the identity of the person who made the report and any other person whose life or safety may be endangered by the disclosure.

(h) This section does not apply to an investigation of child abuse or neglect in a home or facility regulated under Chapter 42, Human Resources Code.

History: Amended by 78th Legis., Reg. Sess. (2003), S.B. 579, eff. Sept. 1, 2003, and "applies only to the records of a child who is placed for adoption by the Department of Protective and Regulatory Services on or after the effective date of this Act. The records of a child who is placed for adoption by the Department of Protective and Regulatory Services before the effective date of this Act are governed by the law in effect on the date the child was placed for adoption, and the former law is continued in effect for that purpose."

Comment

The Open Records Act does not apply to files or records of the department relating to an investigation or to services provided as a result of that investigation. The specific provisions of this section also limit the discretion of the department to respond to certain kinds of discovery, because a court order is required for release of unredacted records. Protection for the confidentiality of caretakers, such as foster parents, when the release of information could endanger their lives or safety is provided. Subsection (h) clarifies that this provision does not apply to licensing investigations, which are controlled by federal and state confidentiality provisions under Tex. Hum. Res. Code Ann. chs. 40 and 48. *(C.G.C.)*

---

§ 261.202. Privileged Communication.

In a proceeding regarding the abuse or neglect of a child, evidence may not be excluded on the ground of privileged communication except in the case of communications between an attorney and client.

Leading Case

Boardman v. State, 56 S.W.3d 63 (Tex. App.—Houston [14th Dist.] 2001, pet. refused) (defendant may not rely on a clergy communication privilege to exclude confession that he sexually assaulted his three children)

Subchapter D. Investigations

§ 261.301. Investigation of Report.

(a) With assistance from the appropriate state or local law enforcement agency, the department or designated agency shall make a prompt and thorough investigation of a report of child abuse or neglect allegedly committed by a person responsible for a child's care, custody, or welfare. The investigation shall be conducted without regard to any pending suit affecting the parent-child relationship.

(b) A state agency shall investigate a report that alleges abuse or neglect occurred in a facility operated, licensed, certified, or registered by that agency as provided by Subchapter E. In conducting an investigation for a facility operated, licensed, certified, registered, or listed by the department, the department shall perform the investigation as provided by:

(1) Subchapter E; and

(2) the Human Resources Code.

(c) The department is not required to investigate a report that alleges child abuse or neglect by a person other than a person responsible for a child's care, custody, or welfare. The appropriate state or local law enforcement agency shall investigate that report if the agency determines an investigation should be conducted.

(d) The department may by rule assign priorities and prescribe investigative procedures for investigations based on the severity and immediacy of the alleged harm to the child. The primary purpose of the investigation shall be the protection of the child.

(e) As necessary to provide for the protection of the child, the department or designated agency shall determine:

(1) the nature, extent, and cause of the abuse or neglect;

(2) the identity of the person responsible for the abuse or neglect;

(3) the names and conditions of the other children in the home;

(4) an evaluation of the parents or persons responsible for the care of the child;

(5) the adequacy of the home environment;

(6) the relationship of the child to the persons responsible for the care, custody, or welfare of the child; and

(7) all other pertinent data.

(f) An investigation of a report to the department **that is assigned the highest priority in accordance with department rules adopted under Subsection (d) and that alleges an immediate risk** of [~~serious~~] physical or sexual abuse of a child **that could result in the death of or serious harm to the child** shall be conducted jointly by **a peace officer, as defined by Article 2.12, Code of Criminal Procedure,** [~~an investigator~~] from the appropriate local law enforcement agency and the department or **the** agency responsible for conducting an investigation under Subchapter E.

(g) The inability or unwillingness of a local law enforcement agency to conduct a joint investigation under Subsection (f) does not constitute grounds to prevent or prohibit the department from performing its duties under this subtitle. The department shall document any instance in which a law enforcement agency is unable or unwilling to conduct a joint investigation under Subsection (f).

(h) The department and the appropriate local law enforcement agency shall conduct an investigation, other than an investigation under Subchapter E, as provided by this section and Article 2.27, Code of Criminal Procedure, if the investigation is of a report of child abuse or neglect that is assigned the highest priority in accordance with department rules adopted under Subsection (d) and that alleges an immediate risk of physical or sexual abuse of a child that could result in the death of or serious harm to the child. Immediately on receipt of a report described by this subsection, the department shall notify the appropriate local law enforcement agency of the report.

History: Amended by 78th Legis., Reg. Sess. (2003), S.B. 669, eff. Sept. 1, 2003, and "applies only to the investigation of a report of child abuse or neglect made on or after that date. The investigation of a report of child abuse or neglect made before the effective date of this Act is governed by the law in effect on the date the report was made, and the former law is continued in effect for that purpose."

Comment

This section requires cooperation between the department and law enforcement agencies in serious abuse cases. The primary purpose of a DPRS investigation is to protect the child, not to develop a criminal case against the perpetrator. Subsection (b) provides that licensing investigations are conducted under provisions of the TEX. HUM. REX. CODE ANN., as well as Chapter 261, Subchapter E, *infra*. Required standards of care are different; for example, corporal punishment may be "reasonable discipline" when administered by a parent, but is not permitted in licensed child care facilities. *(C.G.C.)*

Leading Cases

DeShaney v. Winnebago County Dept. Social Services, 489 U.S. 189, 103 L.Ed.2d 249, 109 S. Ct. 998 (1989) (U.S. Const. does not mandate tort liability of caseworkers who fail to rescue abused child after report)

Department of Protective and Regulatory Services v. Schutz, 101 S.W.3d 512 (Tex. App.—Houston [1st Dist.] 2002, no pet.) (parents operating foster home could not seek relief from neglect finding in district court prior to exhausting administrative remedies)

---

§ 261.3015. Flexible Response System.

(a) In assigning priorities and prescribing investigative procedures based on the severity and immediacy of the alleged harm to a child under Section 261.301(d), the board by rule shall establish a flexible response system to allow the department to allocate resources by investigating serious cases of abuse and neglect and providing assessment and family preservation services in less serious cases.

(b) The classification under the flexible response system of a case may be changed as warranted by the circumstances.

(c) The department may implement the flexible response system by establishing a pilot program in a single department service region. The department shall study the results of the system in the region in determining the method by which to implement the system statewide.

§ 261.3019. [expired]

§ 261.302. Conduct of Investigation.

(a) The investigation may include:

(1) a visit to the child's home, unless the alleged abuse or neglect can be confirmed or clearly ruled out without a home visit; and

(2) an interview with and examination of the subject child, which may include a medical, psychological, or psychiatric examination.

(b) The interview with and examination of the child may:

(1) be conducted at any reasonable time and place, including the child's home or the child's school;

(2) include the presence of persons the department or designated agency determines are necessary; and

(3) include transporting the child for purposes relating to the interview or investigation.

(c) The investigation may include an interview with the child's parents and an interview with and medical, psychological, or psychiatric examination of any child in the home.

(d) If, before an investigation is completed, the investigating agency believes that the immediate removal of a child from the child's home is necessary to protect the child from further abuse or neglect, the investigating agency shall file a petition or take other action under Chapter 262 to provide for the temporary care and protection of the child.

(e) An interview with a child alleged to be a victim of physical abuse or sexual abuse shall be audiotaped or videotaped unless the investigating agency determines that good cause exists for not audiotaping or videotaping the interview in accordance with rules of the agency. Good cause may include, but is not limited to, such considerations as the age of the child and the nature and seriousness of the allegations under investigation. Nothing in this subsection shall be construed as prohibiting the investigating agency from audiotaping or videotaping an interview of a child on any case for which such audiotaping or videotaping is not required under this subsection. The fact that the investigating agency failed to audiotape or videotape an interview is admissible at the trial of the offense that is the subject of the interview.

Comment

The investigative agency has broad authority to contact the child and collect information under this section. The mandate for recording the interview with a child has drawn some opposition from Children's Advocacy Centers; as a result, recording is not routinely performed in all centers. The only stated penalty for failing to record the interview is that the defendant may introduce evidence about the failure to record "at the trial of the offense that is the subject of the interview." Yet to be decided is whether the use of the word "offense" restricts the admissibility of this fact to criminal cases. The Attorney General may address the issue of compliance with this requirement in setting standards for Children's Advocacy Centers under Chapter 264, Subchapter E. *(C.G.C.)*

§ 261.303. Interference With Investigation; Court Order.

(a) A person may not interfere with an investigation of a report of child abuse or neglect conducted by the department or designated agency.

(b) If admission to the home, school, or any place where the child may be cannot be obtained, then for good cause shown the court having family law jurisdiction shall order the parent, the person responsible for the care of the children, or the person in charge of any place where the child may be to allow entrance for the interview, examination, and investigation.

(c) If a parent or person responsible for the child's care does not consent to release of the child's prior medical, psychological, or psychiatric records or to a medical, psychological, or psychiatric examination of the child that is requested by the department or designated agency, the court having family law jurisdiction shall, for good cause shown, order the records to be released or the examination to be made at the times and places designated by the court.

(d) A person, including a medical facility, that makes a report under Subchapter B shall release to the department or designated agency, as part of the required report under Section 261.103, records that directly relate to the suspected abuse or neglect without requiring parental consent or a court order.

Comment

This section permits the department or agency investigating child abuse allegations to gather necessary information concerning the child. Subsection (c) provides that a court may order release of relevant records as well as examination of a child reported to have been abused.

Subsection (d) makes clear that records immediately related to the report may be released as part of the report without a court order. Both the Medical Practices Act [art. 4495b, Sec. 5.08 (h)(1)] and the TEX. HEALTH & SAFETY CODE ANN. [§ 241.153(9)] provide that medical records may be released to governmental agencies as authorized or required by law. It had been unclear whether "any other pertinent information" under § 261.104 included medical records related to the report. The amendment makes clear that a doctor who reports a spiral bone fracture may show the x-ray picture to an investigator without waiting for a court order or consent of the apparently abusive parents. *(C.G.C.)*

§ 261.304. Investigation of Anonymous Report.

(a) If the department receives an anonymous report of child abuse or neglect by a person responsible for a child's care, custody, or welfare, the department shall conduct a preliminary investigation to determine whether there is any evidence to corroborate the report.

(b) An investigation under this section may include a visit to the child's home and an interview with and examination of the child and an interview with the child's parents. In addition, the department may interview any other person the department believes may have relevant information.

(c) Unless the department determines that there is some evidence to corroborate the report of abuse, the department may not conduct the thorough investigation required by this chapter or take any action against the person accused of abuse.

§ 261.305. Access to Mental Health Records.

(a) An investigation may include an inquiry into the possibility that a parent or a person responsible for the care of a child who is the subject of a report under Subchapter B has a history of medical or mental illness.

(b) If the parent or person does not consent to an examination or allow the department or designated agency to have access to medical or mental health records requested by the department or agency, the court having family law jurisdiction, for good cause shown, shall order the examination to be made or that the department or agency be permitted to have access to the records under terms and conditions prescribed by the court.

(c) If the court determines that the parent or person is indigent, the court shall appoint an attorney to represent the parent or person at the hearing. The fees for the appointed attorney shall be paid as provided by Chapter 107.

(d) A parent or person responsible for the child's care is entitled to notice and a hearing when the department or designated agency seeks a court order to allow a medical, psychological, or psychiatric examination or access to medical or mental health records.

(e) This access does not constitute a waiver of confidentiality.

Comment

This section applies only to parents or caretakers of a child reported to have been abused or neglected. The court may, prior to the filing of a SAPCR, order access to the medical records of the parent or caretaker to determine if there is a history of medical or mental illness that may bear upon the probability of abuse or neglect. Note that subsection (c) mandates that if the parent or caretaker is indigent, an attorney must be appointed for that person. *(C.G.C.)*

---

§ 261.306. Removal of Child From State.

(a) If the department or designated agency has reason to believe that a person responsible for the care, custody, or welfare of the child may remove the child from the state before the investigation is completed, the department or designated agency may file an application for a temporary restraining order in a district court without regard to continuing jurisdiction of the child as provided in Chapter 155.

(b) The court may render a temporary restraining order prohibiting the person from removing the child from the state pending completion of the investigation if the court:

(1) finds that the department or designated agency has probable cause to conduct the investigation; and

(2) has reason to believe that the person may remove the child from the state.

§ 261.307. Information Relating to Investigation Procedure.

As soon as possible after initiating an investigation of a parent or other person having legal custody of a child, the department shall provide to the person a brief and easily understood summary of:

(1) the department's procedures for conducting an investigation of alleged child abuse or neglect, including:

(A) a description of the circumstances under which the department would request to remove the child from the home through the judicial system; and

(B) an explanation that the law requires the department to refer all reports of alleged child abuse or neglect to a law enforcement agency for a separate determination of whether a criminal violation occurred;

(2) the person's right to file a complaint with the department or to request a review of the findings made by the department in the investigation;

(3) the person's right to review all records of the investigation unless the review would jeopardize an ongoing criminal investigation;

(4) the person's right to seek legal counsel;

(5) references to the statutory and regulatory provisions governing child abuse and neglect and how the person may obtain copies of those provisions; and

(6) the process the person may use to acquire access to the child if the child is removed from the home.

§ 261.308. Submission of Investigation Report.

(a) The department or designated agency shall make a complete written report of the investigation.

(b) If sufficient grounds for filing a suit exist, the department or designated agency shall submit the report, together with recommendations, to the court, the district attorney, and the appropriate law enforcement agency.

(c) On receipt of the report and recommendations, the court may direct the department or designated agency to file a petition requesting appropriate relief as provided in this title.

§ 261.309. Review of Department Investigations.

(a) The department shall by rule establish policies and procedures to resolve complaints relating to and conduct reviews of child abuse or neglect investigations conducted by the department.

(b) If a person under investigation for allegedly abusing or neglecting a child requests clarification of the status of the person's case or files a complaint relating to the conduct of the department's staff or to department policy, the department shall conduct an informal review to clarify the person's status or resolve the complaint. The immediate supervisor of the employee who conducted the child abuse or neglect investigation or against whom the complaint was filed shall conduct the informal review as soon as possible but not later than the 14th day after the date the request or complaint is received.

(c) If, after the department's investigation, the person who is alleged to have abused or neglected a child disputes the department's determination of whether child abuse or neglect occurred, the person may request an administrative review of the findings. A department employee in administration who was not involved in or did not directly supervise the investigation shall conduct the review. The review must sustain, alter, or reverse the department's original findings in the investigation.

(d) Unless a civil or criminal court proceeding or an ongoing criminal investigation relating to the alleged abuse or neglect investigated by the department is pending, the department employee shall conduct the review prescribed by Subsection (c) as soon as possible but not later than the 45th day after the date the department receives the request. If a civil or criminal court proceeding or an ongoing criminal investigation is pending, the department may postpone the review until the court proceeding is completed.

(e) A person is not required to exhaust the remedies provided by this section before pursuing a judicial remedy provided by law.

(f) This section does not provide for a review of an order rendered by a court.

§ 261.310. Investigation Standards.

(a) The department shall by rule develop and adopt voluntary standards for persons who investigate suspected child abuse or neglect at the state or local level. The standards shall encourage professionalism and consistency in the investigation of suspected child abuse or neglect.

(b) The standards must provide for a minimum number of hours of annual professional training for interviewers and investigators of suspected child abuse or neglect.

(c) The professional training curriculum developed under this section shall include information concerning:

(1) physical abuse and neglect, including distinguishing physical abuse from ordinary childhood injuries;

(2) psychological abuse and neglect;

(3) available treatment resources; and

(4) the incidence and types of reports of child abuse and neglect that are received by the investigating agencies, including information concerning false reports.

(d) The standards shall recommend:

(1) that videotaped and audiotaped interviews with a suspected victim be uninterrupted;

(2) a maximum number of interviews with and examinations of a suspected victim;

(3) procedures to preserve evidence, including the original notes, videotapes, and audiotapes; and

(4) that an investigator of suspected child abuse or neglect make a reasonable effort to locate and inform each parent of a child of any report of abuse or neglect relating to the child.

§ 261.311. Notice of Report.

(a) When during an investigation of a report of suspected child abuse or neglect a representative of the department or the designated agency conducts an interview with or an examination of a child, the department or designated agency shall make a reasonable effort before 24 hours after the time of the interview or examination to notify each parent of the child and the child's legal guardian, if one has been appointed, of the nature of the allegation and of the fact that the interview or examination was conducted.

(b) If a report of suspected child abuse or neglect is administratively closed by the department or designated agency as a result of a preliminary investigation that did not include an interview or examination of the child, the department or designated agency shall make a reasonable effort before the expiration of 24 hours after the time the investigation is closed to notify each parent and legal guardian of the child of the disposition of the investigation.

(c) The notice required by Subsection (a) or (b) is not required if the department or agency determines that the notice is likely to endanger the safety of the child who is the subject of the report, the person who made the report, or any other person who participates in the investigation of the report.

(d) The notice required by Subsection (a) or (b) may be delayed at the request of a law enforcement agency if notification during the required time would interfere with an ongoing criminal investigation.

§ 261.312. Review Teams; Offense.

(a) The department shall establish review teams to evaluate department casework and decision-making related to investigations by the department of child abuse or neglect. The department may create one or more review teams for each region of the department for child protective services. A review team is a citizen review panel or a similar entity for the purposes of federal law relating to a state's child protection standards.

(b) A review team consists of five members who serve staggered two-year terms. Review team members are appointed by the director of the department and consist of community representatives and private citizens who live in the region for which the team is established. Each member must be a parent who has not been convicted of or indicted for an offense involving child abuse or neglect, has not been determined by the department to have engaged in child abuse or neglect, or is not under investigation by the department for child abuse or neglect. A member of a review team is a department volunteer for the purposes of Section 411.114, Government Code.

(c) A review team conducting a review of an investigation may conduct the review by examining the facts of the case as outlined by the department caseworker and law enforcement personnel. A review team member acting in the member's official capacity may receive information made confidential under Section 40.005, Human Resources Code, or Section 261.201.

(d) A review team shall report to the department the results of the team's review of an investigation. The review team's report may not include confidential information. The findings contained in a review team's report are subject to disclosure under Chapter

552, Government Code. This section does not require a law enforcement agency to divulge information to a review team that the agency believes would compromise an ongoing criminal case, investigation, or proceeding.

(e) A member of a review team commits an offense if the member discloses confidential information. An offense under this subsection is a Class C misdemeanor.

§ 261.3125. Investigations Coordinator.

(a) The department shall employ in each region of the department for child protective services at least one child protective services investigations coordinator. The job responsibilities of the investigations coordinator must focus only on child abuse and neglect investigation issues, including reports of child abuse required by Section 261.101, to achieve a greater compliance with that section, and on assessing and improving the effectiveness of the department in providing for the protection of children in the region.

(b) The duties of a child protective services investigations coordinator must include the duty to:

(1) conduct staff reviews and evaluations of cases determined to involve a high risk to the health or safety of a child, including cases of abuse reported under Section 261.101;

(2) monitor cases in which there have been multiple referrals to the department of child abuse or neglect involving the same family, child, or person alleged to have committed the abuse or neglect; and

(3) approve decisions and assessments related to investigations of cases of child abuse or neglect that involve a high risk to the health or safety of a child.

§ 261.313. [omitted]

§ 261.314. Testing.

(a) The department shall provide testing as necessary for the welfare of a child who the department believes, after an investigation under this chapter, has been sexually abused, including human immunodeficiency virus (HIV) testing of a child who was abused in a manner by which HIV may be transmitted.

(b) Except as provided by Subsection (c), the results of a test under this section are confidential.

(c) If requested, the department shall report the results of a test under this section to:

(1) a court having jurisdiction of a proceeding involving the child or a proceeding involving a person suspected of abusing the child;

(2) a person responsible for the care and custody of the child as a foster parent; and

(3) a person seeking to adopt the child.

§ 261.315. Removal of Certain Investigation Information From Records.

(a) At the conclusion of an investigation in which the department determines that the person alleged to have abused or neglected a child did not commit abuse or neglect, the department shall notify the person of the person's right to request the department to remove information about the person's alleged role in the abuse or neglect report from the department's records.

(b) On request under Subsection (a) by a person whom the department has determined did not commit abuse or neglect, the department shall remove information from the department's records concerning the person's alleged role in the abuse or neglect report.

(c) The board shall adopt rules necessary to administer this section.

§ 261.316. Exemption From Fees for Medical Records.

The department is exempt from the payment of a fee otherwise required or authorized by law to obtain a medical record from a hospital or health care provider if the request for a record is made in the course of an investigation by the department.

Subchapter E. Investigations of Abuse, Neglect, or Exploitation in Certain Facilities

§ 261.401. Agency Investigation.

(a) Notwithstanding Section 261.001, in this section:

(1) "Abuse" means an intentional, knowing, or reckless act or omission by an employee, volunteer, or other individual working under the auspices of a facility that causes or may cause emotional harm or physical injury to, or the death of, a child served by the facility as further described by rule or policy.

(2) "Exploitation" means the illegal or improper use of a child or of the resources of a child for monetary or personal benefit, profit, or gain by an employee, volunteer, or other individual working under the auspices of a facility as further described by rule or policy.

(3) "Neglect" means a negligent act or omission by an employee, volunteer, or other individual working under the auspices of a facility, including failure to comply with an individual treatment plan, plan of care, or individualized service plan, that causes or may cause substantial emotional harm or physical injury to, or the death of, a child served by the facility as further described by rule or policy.

(b) A state agency that operates, licenses, certifies, or registers a facility in which children are located shall make a prompt, thorough investigation of a report that a child has been or may be abused, neglected, or exploited in the facility. The primary purpose of the investigation shall be the protection of the child.

(c) A state agency shall adopt rules relating to the investigation and resolution of reports received as provided by this subchapter. The Health and Human Services Commission shall review and approve the rules of agencies other than the Texas Department of Criminal Justice, Texas Youth Commission, or Texas Juvenile Probation Commission to ensure that those agencies implement appropriate standards for the conduct of investigations and that uniformity exists among agencies in the investigation and resolution of reports.

(d) The Texas School for the Blind and Visually Impaired and the Texas School for the Deaf shall adopt policies relating to the investigation and resolution of reports received as provided by this subchapter. The Health and Human Services Commission shall review and approve the policies to ensure that the Texas School for the Blind and Visually Impaired and the Texas School for the Deaf adopt those policies in a manner consistent with the minimum standards adopted by the Health and Human Services Commission under Section 261.407.

Comment

Children in institutional settings are not only dependent on staff for personal care and protection, they are vulnerable to financial exploitation as well. In addition to abuse and neglect, "exploitation" of a child is part of the prohibited conduct that must be investigated. The definitions of "abuse," "exploitation," and "neglect" conform to those used by the affected agencies. *(C.G.C.)*

---

§ 261.402. Investigative Reports.

(a) A state agency shall prepare and keep on file a complete written report of each investigation conducted by the agency under this subchapter.

(b) A state agency shall immediately notify the appropriate state or local law enforcement agency of any report the agency receives, other than a report from a law enforcement agency, that concerns the suspected abuse, neglect, or exploitation of a child or the death of a child from abuse or neglect. If the state agency finds evidence indicating that a child may have been abused, neglected, or exploited, the agency shall report the evidence to the appropriate law enforcement agency.

(c) A state agency that licenses, certifies, or registers a facility in which children are located shall compile, maintain, and make available statistics on the incidence of child abuse, neglect, and exploitation in the facility.

(d) A state agency shall compile, maintain, and make available statistics on the incidence of child abuse, neglect, and exploitation in a facility operated by the state agency.

§ 261.403. Complaints.

(a) If a state agency receives a complaint relating to an investigation conducted by the agency concerning a facility operated by that agency in which children are located, the agency shall refer the complaint to the agency's board.

(b) The board of a state agency that operates a facility in which children are located shall ensure that the procedure for investigating abuse, neglect, and exploitation allegations and inquiries in the agency's facility is periodically reviewed under the agency's internal audit program required by Chapter 2102, Government Code.

§ 261.404. Investigations in Facilities Under Department of Mental Health and Mental Retardation.

(a) The department shall investigate a report of abuse, neglect, or exploitation of a child receiving services:

(1) in a facility operated by the Texas Department of Mental Health and Mental Retardation;

(2) in or from a community center, a local mental health authority, or a local mental retardation authority; or

(3) through a program providing services to that child by contract with a facility operated by the Texas Department of Mental Health and Mental Retardation, a community center, a local mental health authority, or a local mental retardation authority.

(b) The department shall investigate the report under rules developed jointly between the department and the Texas Department of Mental Health and Mental Retardation.

(c) The definitions of "abuse" and "neglect" prescribed by Section 261.001 do not apply to an investigation under this section.

(d) In this section, "community center," "local mental health authority," and "local mental retardation authority" have the meanings assigned by Section 531.002, Health and Safety Code.

§ 261.405. Investigations in Juvenile Justice Programs and Facilities.

(a) In this section:

(1) "Juvenile justice facility" means a facility operated wholly or partly by the juvenile board or by a private vendor under a contract with the juvenile board or county that serves juveniles under juvenile court jurisdiction. The term includes:

(A) a public or private juvenile pre-adjudication secure detention facility, including a holdover facility;

(B) a public or private juvenile post-adjudication secure correctional facility except for a facility operated solely for children committed to the Texas Youth Commission; and

(C) a public or private non-secure juvenile post-adjudication residential treatment facility that is not licensed by the Department of Protective and Regulatory Services or the Texas Commission on Alcohol and Drug Abuse.

(2) "Juvenile justice program" means a program operated wholly or partly by the juvenile board or by a private vendor under a contract with a juvenile board that serves juveniles under juvenile court jurisdiction. The term includes:

(A) a juvenile justice alternative education program; and

(B) a non-residential program that serves juvenile offenders under the jurisdiction of the juvenile court.

(b) A report of alleged abuse, neglect, or exploitation in any juvenile justice program or facility shall be made to the Texas Juvenile Probation Commission and a local law enforcement agency for investigation.

(c) The Texas Juvenile Probation Commission shall conduct an investigation as provided by this chapter if the commission receives a report of alleged abuse, neglect, or exploitation in any juvenile justice program or facility.

(d) In an investigation required under this section, the investigating agency shall have access to medical and mental health records as provided by Subchapter D.

Comment

This section designates TJPC as the primary investigative agency in facilities operated by a juvenile probation department or contractor. TJPC is also given access to medical and mental health records on the same terms as the department. *(C.G.C.)*

§ 261.406. Investigations in Schools.

(a) On receipt of a report of alleged or suspected abuse or neglect of a child in a public or private school under the jurisdiction of the Texas Education Agency, the department shall perform an investigation as provided by this chapter.

(b) The department shall send a written report of the department's investigation, as appropriate, to the Texas Education Agency, the agency responsible for teacher certification, the local school board or the school's governing body, and the school principal or director, unless the principal or director is alleged to have committed the abuse or neglect, for appropriate action. On request, the department shall provide a copy of the report of investigation to the parent, managing conservator, or legal guardian of a child who is the subject of the investigation and to the person alleged to have committed the abuse or neglect. The report of investigation shall be edited to protect the identity of the persons who made the report of abuse or neglect. Section 261.201(b) applies to the release of confidential information relating to the investigation of a report of abuse or neglect under this section and to the identity of the person who made the report of abuse or neglect.

(c) Nothing in this section may prevent a law enforcement agency from conducting an investigation of a report made under this section.

(d) The Board of Protective and Regulatory Services shall adopt rules necessary to implement this section.

Comment

The department is required to investigate allegations of abuse or neglect in schools. The provision for confidentiality has been limited to the reporter, as with all other investigations. The requirement to redact from the reports all individuals who "provided information" for the report has not, in practice, been followed because it would be impossible to write a report without identifying any of the informants. *(C.G.C.)*

§ 261.407. Minimum Standards.

(a) The Health and Human Services Commission by rule shall adopt minimum standards for the investigation under Section 261.401 of suspected child abuse, neglect, or exploitation in a facility.

(b) A rule or policy adopted by a state agency or institution under Section 261.401 must be consistent with the minimum standards adopted by the Health and Human Services Commission.

(c) This section does not apply to a facility under the jurisdiction of the Texas Department of Criminal Justice, Texas Youth Commission, or Texas Juvenile Probation Commission.

§ 261.408. Information Collection.

(a) The Health and Human Services Commission by rule shall adopt uniform procedures for collecting information under Section 261.401, including procedures for collecting information on deaths that occur in facilities.

(b) The department shall receive and compile information on investigations in facilities. An agency submitting information to the department is responsible for ensuring the timeliness, accuracy, completeness, and retention of the agency's reports.

(c) This section does not apply to a facility under the jurisdiction of the Texas Department of Criminal Justice, Texas Youth Commission, or Texas Juvenile Probation Commission.

§ 261.409. Investigations in Facilities Under Texas Youth Commission Jurisdiction.

The board of the Texas Youth Commission by rule shall adopt standards for:

(1) the investigation under Section 261.401 of suspected child abuse, neglect, or exploitation in a facility under the jurisdiction of the Texas Youth Commission; and

(2) compiling information on those investigations.

Chapter 262. Procedures in Suit by Governmental Entity to Protect Health and Safety of Child.

Subchapter A. General Provisions

Subchapter B. Taking Possession of Child

Subchapter C. Adversary Hearing

Subchapter D. Emergency Possession of Certain Abandoned Children

Editors' Note: *This chapter contains guest commentary by Cynthia Bryant, Deputy Attorney General of Child Support Enforcement; and Charles G. Childress, Children's Rights Clinic, University of Texas Law School, and former Chief Attorney, Field Operations, Legal Division, Texas Department of Protective and Regulatory Services, identified as (C.B. & C.G.C.).*

Introductory Comment

This chapter authorizes police, juvenile probation officers, and caseworkers from DPRS to take possession of a child in an emergency. This may be done with either the prior approval of a judicial officer, or without such an order if the situation warrants immediate state intervention to rescue a child from dangerous circumstances. Because actions taken under Chapter 262 are all temporary in nature, virtually no case law has developed. It appears that the practices and procedures in place in the various counties vary considerably, but to an unknown degree. Since a substantial part of the foster care funding for children taken into the care of DPRS under this chapter comes from the federal government, many of the provisions in this chapter have been updated over the years to comply with changing federal mandates and interpretations, most notably the requirements of the Adoption and Safe Families Act of 1997, 42 U.S.C.A. 678 *et seq.* This chapter also contains substantive and procedural guidance for cases in which prior notice to the parent or caretaker and a hearing before removal may be provided without undue danger to the child. *(C.B. & C.G.C.)*

CLE/Other Legal Publications

The duty to report child abuse. Camile Glasscock Dubose, 2004 Adv. Fam. L.

Ineffective assistance of Counsel in the CPS case. Sandra D. Hachem, 2004 Adv. Fam. L.

Overview of abuse, neglect and intra-family violence. Oscar Gabaldon, 2004 U. Tex. Fam. L. on the Border

Reporting child abuse—ethical and practical considerations. Coye Conner, Jr., 2002 Adv. Fam. L.

Overview of issues pertaining to credibility of child sexual abuse allegations and investigations. D. Ross Miller, P. Caren Phelan, 2001 Marriage Dissolution

Who ya' gonna call when CPS comes a knockin'? Ann E. Coover, 2000 Adv. Fam. L.

Where are the reasonable efforts to enforce the reasonable efforts requirement? Monitoring state compliance under the Adoption Assistance and Child Welfare Act of 1980. Shawn L. Raymond, 77 Tex. L. Rev. 1235 (1999)

Leading Cases

Baltimore City Dept. Social Serv. v. Bouknight, 493 U.S. 54, 110 S.Ct. 900, 107 L.Ed.2d 992 (1990) (a custodial parent ordered by the court to produce the child may not claim the Fifth Amendment privilege against self incrimination to resist the order)

Moore v. Sims, 442 U.S. 415, 60 L.Ed.2d 994, 99 S.Ct. 2371 (1979), *reversing* Sims v. State Dept. of Public Welfare, 438 F. Supp. 1179 (S. D. Tex. 1977), *rev'd*, 442 U.S. 415, 60 L.Ed.2d 994, 99 S.Ct. 2371 (1979) (Texas emergency procedures found unconstitutional by three-judge panel, reversed on *Younger* grounds)

Black v. Dallas County Child Welfare Unit, 835 S.W.2d 626 (Tex. 1992) (award of attorney's fees against governmental unit for its frivolous and unreasonable actions)

In re M.C.M., 57 S.W.3d 27 (Tex. App.—Houston [1st Dist.] 2001, no pet.) (without considering the time during which the case is stayed, a termination suit must be resolved within the time remaining on the 18 month statutory deadline)

Albright v. Texas Department of Human Services, 859 S.W.2d 575 (Tex. App.—Houston [1st Dist.] 1993, no writ) (social worker acting in good faith with reasonable cause to investigate abuse allegation is immune from personal liability)

Cross Reference

Adoption Assistance and Child Welfare Act of 1980. 42 U.S.C.A. §§ 671–675

Subchapter A. General Provisions

§ 262.001. Authorized Actions by Governmental Entity.

(a) A governmental entity with an interest in the child may file a suit affecting the parent-child relationship requesting an order or take possession of a child without a court order as provided by this chapter.

(b) In determining the reasonable efforts that are required to be made with respect to preventing or eliminating the need to remove a child from the child's home or to make it possible to return a child to the child's home, the child's health and safety is the paramount concern.

Comment

The state, acting through DPRS or its various law enforcement agencies, has the authority and the power to rescue a child and to file a SAPCR seeking managing or possessory conservatorship or a termination of parental rights. Subsection (b) reflects a shift of emphasis away from decreeing that rehabilitation of a dysfunctional family is the primary goal in dealing with abuse and neglect cases. That goal must give way if it creates a realistic danger to a child's health and safety. The Adoption and Safe Families Act of 1997 (ASFA), 42 U.S.C.A. 678 *et. seq.* altered that position which was apparently held by Congress prior to its enactment. Henceforth, the paramount concern in protective services cases is to be the child's health and safety. *(C.G.C.)*

---

§ 262.002. Jurisdiction.

A suit brought by a governmental entity requesting an order under this chapter may be filed in a court with jurisdiction to hear the suit in the county in which the child is found.

§ 262.003. Civil Liability.

A person who takes possession of a child without a court order is immune from civil liability if, at the time possession is taken, there is reasonable cause to believe there is an immediate danger to the physical health or safety of the child.

Comment

The immunity from civil liability seems to require an objective standard of reasonableness rather than subjective good faith by the actor.

Leading Cases

DeShaney v. Winnebago County Dept. Social Services, 489 U.S. 189, 103 L.Ed.2d 249, 109 S.Ct. 998 (1989) (U.S. Const. does not mandate tort liability of caseworkers who fail to rescue abused child after report)

Gonzalez v. Avalos, 866 S.W.2d 346 (Tex. App.—El Paso 1993), writ dism'd w.o.j., 907 S.W.2d 443 (Tex. 1995) (DPRS supervisor not entitled to immunity when failed to investigate abuse allegations)

Albright v. Texas Department of Human Services, 859 S.W.2d 575 (Tex. App.—Houston [1st Dist.] 1993, no writ) (social worker acting in good faith with reasonable cause to investigate abuse allegation is immune from personal liability)

---

§ 262.004. Accepting Voluntary Delivery of Possession of Child.

A law enforcement officer or a juvenile probation officer may take possession of a child without a court order on the voluntary delivery of the child by the parent, managing conservator, possessory conservator, guardian, caretaker, or custodian who is presently entitled to possession of the child.

§ 262.005. Filing Petition After Accepting Voluntary Delivery of Possession of Child.

When possession of the child has been acquired through voluntary delivery of the child to a law enforcement officer or juvenile probation officer, the law enforcement officer or juvenile probation officer taking the child into possession shall cause a suit to be filed not later than the 60th day after the date the child is taken into possession.

§ 262.006. Living Child After Abortion.

(a) An authorized representative of the Department of Protective and Regulatory Services may assume the care, control, and custody of a child born alive as the result of an abortion as defined by Chapter 161.

(b) The department shall file a suit and request an emergency order under this chapter.

(c) A child for whom possession is assumed under this section need not be delivered to the court except on the order of the court.

§ 262.007. Possession and Delivery of Missing Child.

(a) A law enforcement officer who, during a criminal investigation relating to a child's custody, discovers that a child is a missing child and believes that a person may flee with or conceal the child shall take possession of the child and provide for the delivery of the child as provided by Subsection (b).

(b) An officer who takes possession of a child under Subsection (a) shall deliver or arrange for the delivery of the child to a person entitled to possession of the child.

(c) If a person entitled to possession of the child is not immediately available to take possession of the child, the law enforcement officer shall deliver the child to the Department of Protective and Regulatory Services. Until a person entitled to possession of the child takes possession of the child, the department may, without a court order, retain possession of the child not longer than five days after the date the child is delivered to the department. While the department retains possession of a child under this subsection, the department may place the child in foster home care. If a parent or other person entitled to possession of the child does not take possession of the child before the sixth day after the date the child is delivered to the department, the department shall proceed under this chapter as if the law enforcement officer took possession of the child under Section 262.104.

Comment

A law enforcement officer investigating a criminal offense related to child custody must take possession of the child if the officer believes that a person may flee with or conceal the child, and must deliver the child to a person entitled to possession or to DPRS. The department has five days to locate and deliver the child to a caretaker. If no caretaker can be found within that time, a court order must be obtained giving the department conservatorship. Neither state nor federal foster care payments are available for the cost of care of a child unless a legal proceeding is filed. This change, and a parallel change to § 262.110, reduce county exposure for these costs. *(C.G.C.)*

---

§ 262.008. Abandoned Children.

(a) An authorized representative of the Department of Protective and Regulatory Services may assume the care, control, and custody of a child:

(1) who is abandoned without identification or a means for identifying the child; and

(2) whose identity cannot be ascertained by the exercise of reasonable diligence.

(b) The department shall immediately file a suit to terminate the parent-child relationship of a child under Subsection (a).

(c) A child for whom possession is assumed under this section need not be delivered to the court except on the order of the court.

§ 262.009. Temporary Care of Child Taken Into Possession.

An employee of or volunteer with a law enforcement agency who successfully completes a background and criminal history check approved by the law enforcement agency may assist a law enforcement officer or juvenile probation officer with the temporary care of a child who is taken into possession by a governmental entity without a court order under this chapter until further arrangements regarding the custody of the child can be made.

Subchapter B. Taking Possession of Child

§ 262.101. Filing Petition Before Taking Possession of Child.

An original suit filed by a governmental entity that requests permission to take possession of a child without prior notice and a hearing must be supported by an affidavit sworn to by a person with personal knowledge and stating facts sufficient to satisfy a person of ordinary prudence and caution that:

(1) there is an immediate danger to the physical health or safety of the child or the child has been a victim of neglect or sexual abuse and that continuation in the home would be contrary to the child's welfare;

(2) there is no time, consistent with the physical health or safety of the child, for a full adversary hearing under Subchapter C; and

(3) reasonable efforts, consistent with the circumstances and providing for the safety of the child, were made to prevent or eliminate the need for the removal of the child.

Comment

This provision provides both the substantive and pleading requirements when removal of a child is to be made pursuant to court order, but without prior notice to the parents and opportunity for hearing. Recent federal legislation and policy interpretations called into question the prior wording of the Texas emergency removal provisions, which asserted that there was "no time" to make "reasonable efforts" to prevent or eliminate the need for removal of the child. While minimal efforts—such as simply asking about relatives or other safe temporary placements—may be "reasonable" under the circumstances, there is always "time" to consider such options. If such minimal efforts have been made consistent with the circumstances and the immediate need to protect the child, the federal requirement of a "reasonable effort to prevent removal" has been satisfied. In the unlikely event that the federal authorities would find that there were not "reasonable efforts" by DPRS in its activities to prevent or eliminate the need for removal at the time of removal, it would lose eligibility to receive federal foster care payments during a child's subsequent time in substitute care. In all cases, an affidavit is required "sufficient to satisfy a person of ordinary prudence and caution" that removal of the child is necessary. *(C.G.C.)*

§ 262.1015. Removal of Alleged Perpetrator; Offense.

(a) If the department determines after an investigation that child abuse has occurred and that the child would be protected in the child's home by the removal of the alleged perpetrator of the abuse, the department shall file a petition for the removal of the alleged perpetrator from the residence of the child rather than attempt to remove the child from the residence.

(b) A court may issue a temporary restraining order in a suit by the department for the removal of an alleged perpetrator under Subsection (a) if the department's petition states facts sufficient to satisfy the court that:

(1) there is an immediate danger to the physical health or safety of the child or the child has been a victim of sexual abuse;

(2) there is no time, consistent with the physical health or safety of the child, for an adversary hearing;

(3) the child is not in danger of abuse from a parent or other adult with whom the child will continue to reside in the residence of the child; and

(4) the issuance of the order is in the best interest of the child.

(c) The order shall be served on the alleged perpetrator and on the parent or other adult with whom the child will continue to reside.

(d) A temporary restraining order under this section expires not later than the 14th day after the date the order was rendered.

(e) A temporary restraining order under this section and any other order requiring the removal of an alleged perpetrator from the residence of a child shall require that the parent or other adult with whom the child will continue to reside in the child's home make a reasonable effort to monitor the residence and report to the department and the appropriate law enforcement agency any attempt by the alleged perpetrator to return to the residence.

(f) The court shall order the removal of an alleged perpetrator if the court finds that the child is not in danger of abuse from a parent or other adult with whom the child will continue to reside in the child's residence and that:

(1) the presence of the alleged perpetrator in the child's residence constitutes a continuing danger to the physical health or safety of the child; or

(2) the child has been the victim of sexual abuse and there is a substantial risk that the child will be the victim of sexual abuse in the future if the alleged perpetrator remains in the residence.

(g) A person commits an offense if the person is a parent or other person with whom a child resides, the person is served with an order containing the requirement specified by Subsection (e), and the person fails to make a reasonable effort to monitor the residence of the child or to report to the department and the appropriate law enforcement agency an attempt by the alleged perpetrator to return to the residence. An offense under this section is a Class A misdemeanor.

(h) A person commits an offense if, in violation of a court order under this section, the person returns to the residence of the child the person is alleged to have abused. An offense under this subsection is a Class A misdemeanor, except that the offense is a felony of the third degree if the person has previously been convicted under this subsection.

Comment

DPRS may seek an order removing an alleged perpetrator of child abuse from the home if the agency "determines" that the child can be protected in the home by a parent or other adult. Finding a fact situation in which the alleged perpetrator is ordered to leave will probably continue to be "a good idea" honored in theory, but avoided in practice. After all, what if he doesn't stay away as ordered and the child is re-abused? How will that read in the newspapers?

---

§ 262.102. Emergency Order Authorizing Possession of Child.

(a) Before a court may, without prior notice and a hearing, issue a temporary restraining order or attachment of a child in a suit brought by a governmental entity, the court must find that:

(1) there is an immediate danger to the physical health or safety of the child or the child has been a victim of neglect or sexual abuse and that continuation in the home would be contrary to the child's welfare;

(2) there is no time, consistent with the physical health or safety of the child and the nature of the emergency, for a full adversary hearing under Subchapter C; and

(3) reasonable efforts, consistent with the circumstances and providing for the safety of the child, were made to prevent or eliminate the need for removal of the child.

(b) In determining whether there is an immediate danger to the physical health or safety of a child, the court may consider whether the child's household includes a person who has:

(1) abused or neglected another child in a manner that caused serious injury to or the death of the other child; or

(2) sexually abused another child.

(c) If, based on the recommendation of or a request by the department, the court finds that child abuse or neglect has occurred and that the child requires protection from family violence by a member of the child's family or household, the court shall render a temporary order under Chapter 71 for the protection of the child. In this subsection, "family violence" has the meaning assigned by Section 71.004.

Comment

Before issuing an ex parte order for removal of a child the court must find that the specific requirements of subsection (a) have been met. If these prerequisites are not met, the court may order notice and set an adversary hearing under this chapter without granting ex parte relief. On rare occasion that may actually happen in some counties.

Chapter 262 provides three options for intervention by DPRS into a family: (1) emergency removal prior to obtaining a court order; (2) removal after obtaining an ex parte order; or, (3) removal after notice and hearing. Because the procedure for obtaining a court order is listed first, it may be presumed that prior judicial approval is the first option that should be considered. The department's affidavit must show facts sufficient to "satisfy a person of ordinary prudence and caution that there is an immediate danger to the physical health or safety of the child or the child has been a victim of sexual abuse." Some commentators have likened this standard to the "probable cause" requirement for a search warrant in a criminal law context. That in fact is true, but the language used here is unique to avoid the implication of a criminal law standard. No matter whether the court orders removal before or after a hearing, in order to qualify the child for federal foster care funding the court must find that DPRS made reasonable efforts under the circumstances to prevent removal. Supposedly the court may make the "reasonable efforts to prevent removal" finding after, but not more than 60 days after, the initial removal. In fact, it is usually made in a basically pro forma manner at the earliest opportunity. Failure of the court to make the required finding could result in loss of all eligibility for foster care funding for the entire time the child spends in substitute care. Federal law also requires that a court confirm, either by a pre-removal order or at the first hearing after the child is taken into care, that continuing in the home would be "contrary to the welfare" of the child. Failure to meet this requirement also could result in the loss of all federal funding for the child's substitute care. In short, DPRS is careful to ensure that its temporary orders contain a recitation of the appropriate findings. *(C.G.C.)*

---

§ 262.103. Duration of Temporary Restraining Order and Attachment.

A temporary restraining order or attachment of the child issued under this chapter expires not later than 14 days after the date it is issued unless it is extended as provided by the Texas Rules of Civil Procedure.

§ 262.104. Taking Possession of a Child in Emergency Without a Court Order.

If there is no time to obtain a temporary restraining order or attachment before taking possession of a child consistent with the health and safety of that child, an authorized representative of the Department of Protective and Regulatory Services, a law enforcement officer, or a juvenile probation officer may take possession of a child without a court order under the following conditions, only:

(1) on personal knowledge of facts that would lead a person of ordinary prudence and caution to believe that there is an immediate danger to the physical health or safety of the child;

(2) on information furnished by another that has been corroborated by personal knowledge of facts and all of which taken together would lead a person of ordinary prudence and caution to believe that there is an immediate danger to the physical health or safety of the child;

(3) on personal knowledge of facts that would lead a person of ordinary prudence and caution to believe that the child has been the victim of sexual abuse;

(4) on information furnished by another that has been corroborated by personal knowledge of facts and all of which taken together would lead a person of ordinary prudence and caution to believe that the child has been the victim of sexual abuse; or

(5) on information furnished by another that has been corroborated by personal knowledge of facts and all of which taken together would lead a person of ordinary prudence and caution to believe that the parent or person who has possession of the child is currently using a controlled substance as defined by Chapter 481, Health and Safety Code, and the use constitutes an immediate danger to the physical health or safety of the child.

Comment

If prior judicial approval is not feasible, this section provides that a CPS caseworker, a juvenile probation officer, or a law enforcement officer may take immediate possession of a child in danger, subject to a prompt—almost invariably ex parte—judicial hearing. Although the statute seems to clearly discourage "emergency rescue" if prior notice and hearing, or at least a prior ex-parte order, is feasible without endangering the child, the exact nature of the emergency is determined by the worker or officer at the scene. According to the DPRS Child Protection Services Handbook, a caseworker should consider emergency removal only if other options for protecting the child are ruled out. But, official policy and actual practice are not always congruent.

If a child is "rescued" without prior judicial approval, a post-pickup hearing is required "no later than the first working day after the child is taken into possession." Under supposedly extraordinary circumstances the time for the ex parte hearing may be extended to three days. By permitting this hearing to be ex parte, the statute allows the common practice of eliciting the requisite judicial approval without notice to the parents. The statute requires that the ex parte order be based upon a review of a sworn petition or affidavit; most courts seldom require sworn testimony. Although theoretically the burden of proof is on the state, it is very difficult for the court, in the absence of the parent or other caretaker, to choose to do anything other than continue possession of the child with the state until a full adversary hearing can be held as required by § 202.201, *supra*. *(C.B. & C.G.C.)*

§ 262.105. Filing Petition After Taking Possession of Child in Emergency.

(a) When a child is taken into possession without a court order, the person taking the child into possession, without unnecessary delay, shall:

(1) file a suit affecting the parent-child relationship;

(2) request the court to appoint an attorney ad litem for the child; and

(3) request an initial hearing to be held by no later than the first working day after the date the child is taken into possession.

(b) If the Department of Protective and Regulatory Services files a suit affecting the parent-child relationship required under Subsection (a)(1) seeking termination of the parent-child relationship, the department shall file the suit not later than the 45th day after the date the department assumes the care, control, and custody of a child under Section 262.303.

§ 262.106. Initial Hearing After Taking Possession of Child in Emergency Without Court Order.

(a) The court in which a suit has been filed after a child has been taken into possession without a court order by a governmental entity shall hold an initial hearing on or before the first working day after the date the child is taken into possession. The court shall render orders that are necessary to protect the physical health and safety of the child. If the court is unavailable for a hearing on the first working day, then, and only in that event, the hearing shall be held no later than the first working day after the court becomes available, provided that the hearing is held no later than the third working day after the child is taken into possession.

(b) The initial hearing may be ex parte and proof may be by sworn petition or affidavit if a full adversary hearing is not practicable.

(c) If the initial hearing is not held within the time required, the child shall be returned to the parent, managing conservator, possessory conservator, guardian, caretaker, or custodian who is presently entitled to possession of the child.

(d) For the purpose of determining under Subsection (a) the first working day after the date the child is taken into possession, the child is considered to have been taken into possession by the Department of Protective and Regulatory Services on the expiration of the five-day period permitted under Section 262.007(c) or 262.110(b), as appropriate.

Comment

An initial hearing generally must be held on the first working day after a child is taken into the possession of the department under § 262.104. If the child is taken into possession with intent to return home, the hearing must be held on the day after expiration of the five days allowed for locating parents or custodians. *(C.G.C.)*

---

§ 262.107. Standard for Decision at Initial Hearing After Taking Possession of Child Without a Court Order in Emergency.

(a) The court shall order the return of the child at the initial hearing regarding a child taken in possession without a court order by a governmental entity unless the court is satisfied that:

(1) there is a continuing danger to the physical health or safety of the child if the child is returned to the parent, managing conservator, possessory conservator, guardian, caretaker, or custodian who is presently entitled to possession of the child or the evidence shows that the child has been the victim of sexual abuse on one or more occasions and that there is a substantial risk that the child will be the victim of sexual abuse in the future;

(2) continuation of the child in the home would be contrary to the child's welfare; and

(3) reasonable efforts, consistent with the circumstances and providing for the safety of the child, were made to prevent or eliminate the need for removal of the child.

(b) In determining whether there is a continuing danger to the physical health or safety of a child, the court may consider whether the household to which the child would be returned includes a person who has:

(1) abused or neglected another child in a manner that caused serious injury to or the death of the other child; or

(2) sexually abused another child.

Comment

To qualify the child for federal foster care funding, the court must find that the current conditions in the home are such that continuation of the child in the home would be contrary to the child's welfare, as well as that reasonable efforts were made to prevent or eliminate the need for removal of the child. *(C.G.C.)*

---

§ 262.108. Unacceptable Facilities for Housing Child.

When a child is taken into possession under this chapter, that child may not be held in isolation or in a jail, juvenile detention facility, or other secure detention facility.

§ 262.109. Notice to Parent, Conservator, or Guardian.

(a) The department or other agency must give written notice as prescribed by this section to each parent of the child or to the child's conservator or legal guardian when a representative of the Department of Protective and Regulatory Services or other agency takes possession of a child under this chapter.

(b) The written notice must be given as soon as practicable, but in any event not later than the first working day after the date the child is taken into possession.

(c) The written notice must include:

(1) the reasons why the department or agency is taking possession of the child and the facts that led the department to believe that the child should be taken into custody;

(2) the name of the person at the department or agency that the parent, conservator, or other custodian may contact for information relating to the child or a legal proceeding relating to the child;

(3) a summary of legal rights of a parent, conservator, guardian, or other custodian under this chapter and an explanation of the probable legal procedures relating to the child; and

(4) a statement that the parent, conservator, or other custodian has the right to hire an attorney.

(d) The written notice may be waived by the court at the initial hearing:

(1) on a showing that:

(A) the parents, conservators, or other custodians of the child could not be located; or

(B) the department took possession of the child under Subchapter D; or

(2) for other good cause.

Comment

This section requires DPRS to provide a notice of removal to the parent or caretaker when it takes physical custody of a child under Chapter 262. The legislative necessity of enacting a statutory directive on this matter does not represent a high point of bureaucratic sensitivity. In the agency's defense, however, it has developed a comprehensive form to give the required notice to what may be a frantic parent who has arrived home only to find a left-alone child missing.

The court may, but is not required to, waive the required written notice under special circumstances, such as: (1) the inability to locate the parent or caretaker; (2) the child is an abandoned infant delivered to an emergency care provider under Subchapter D; or, (3) for other "good cause." Removal of the child takes place after a court hearing at which the requisite information was provided by the court to the parents or their attorney. By its terms, this section requires the written notice to be given by law enforcement officers, juvenile probation officers, and "designated emergency infant care providers," all of whom are authorized to take possession of a child under this chapter. *(C.G.C.)*

---

§ 262.110. Taking Possession of Child in Emergency With Intent to Return Home.

(a) An authorized representative of the Department of Protective and Regulatory Services, a law enforcement officer, or a juvenile probation officer may take temporary possession of a child without a court order on discovery of a child in a situation of danger to the child's physical health or safety when the sole purpose is to deliver the child without unnecessary delay to the parent, managing conservator, possessory conservator, guardian, caretaker, or custodian who is presently entitled to possession of the child.

(b) Until a parent or other person entitled to possession of the child takes possession of the child, the department may retain possession of the child without a court order for not more than five days. On the expiration of the fifth day, if a parent or other person entitled to possession does not take possession of the child, the department shall take action under this chapter as if the department took possession of the child under Section 262.104.

§ 262.111. [repealed]

§ 262.112. Expedited Hearing and Appeal.

(a) The Department of Protective and Regulatory Services is entitled to an expedited hearing under this chapter in any proceeding in which a hearing is required if the department determines that a child should be removed from the child's home because of an immediate danger to the physical health or safety of the child.

(b) In any proceeding in which an expedited hearing is held under Subsection (a), the department, parent, guardian, or other party to the proceeding is entitled to an expedited appeal on a ruling by a court that the child may not be removed from the child's home.

(c) If a child is returned to the child's home after a removal in which the department was entitled to an expedited hearing under this section and the child is the subject of a subsequent allegation of abuse or neglect, the department or any other interested party is entitled to an expedited hearing on the removal of the child from the child's home in the manner provided by Subsection (a) and to an expedited appeal in the manner provided by Subsection (b).

Comment

If the trial court is not willing or able to hear a petition for emergency removal under § 262.102, the department or law officer may be able to take action under § 262.104. The trial court is required by § 262.106 to hear the matter on the next working day after the removal. It is therefore difficult to conceive of a circumstance under which the department would have a complaint about denial of an expedited hearing under this section. There does not appear to be a reported case in which an interlocutory appeal of an order denying removal has been filed by DPRS. *(C.G.C.)*

§ 262.113. Filing Suit Without Taking Possession of Child.

An original suit filed by a governmental entity that requests to take possession of a child after notice and a hearing must be supported by an affidavit sworn to by a person with personal knowledge and stating facts sufficient to satisfy a person of ordinary prudence and caution that:

(1) reasonable efforts have been made to prevent or eliminate the need to remove the child from the child's home; and

(2) allowing the child to remain in the home would be contrary to the child's welfare.

Comment

This section specifies pleading requirements when it is not necessary to remove a child prior to notice and hearing, but family preservation efforts have failed and continuation in the home would be contrary to the child's welfare. The "reasonable efforts" and "contrary to welfare" provisions track federal foster care standards, and must be established for federal financial participation in the cost of foster care. *(C.G.C.)*

Subchapter C. Adversary Hearing

§ 262.201. Full Adversary Hearing; Findings of the Court.

(a) Unless the child has already been returned to the parent, managing conservator, possessory conservator, guardian, caretaker, or custodian entitled to possession and the temporary order, if any, has been dissolved, a full adversary hearing shall be held not later than the 14th day after the date the child was taken into possession by the governmental entity.

(b) At the conclusion of the full adversary hearing, the court shall order the return of the child to the parent, managing conservator, possessory conservator, guardian, caretaker, or custodian entitled to possession unless the court finds sufficient evidence to satisfy a person of ordinary prudence and caution that:

(1) there was a danger to the physical health or safety of the child which was caused by an act or failure to act of the person entitled to possession and for the child to remain in the home is contrary to the welfare of the child;

(2) the urgent need for protection required the immediate removal of the child and reasonable efforts, consistent with the circumstances and providing for the safety of the child, were made to eliminate or prevent the child's removal; and

(3) reasonable efforts have been made to enable the child to return home, but there is a substantial risk of a continuing danger if the child is returned home.

(c) If the court finds sufficient evidence to satisfy a person of ordinary prudence and caution that there is a continuing danger to the physical health or safety of the child and for the child to remain in the home is contrary to the welfare of the child, the court shall issue an appropriate temporary order under Chapter 105. The court shall require each parent, alleged father, or relative of the child before the court to provide the Department of Protective and Regulatory Services with information necessary to locate any other absent parent, alleged father, or relative of the child. The court shall inform each parent in open court that parental and custodial rights and duties may be subject to restriction or to termination unless the parent or parents are willing and able to provide the child with a safe environment. If the court finds that the child requires protection from family violence by a member of the child's family or household, the court shall render a protective order under Title 4 for the child. In this subsection, "family violence" has the meaning assigned by Section 71.004.

(d) In determining whether there is a continuing danger to the physical health or safety of the child, the court may consider whether the household to which the child would be returned includes a person who:

(1) has abused or neglected another child in a manner that caused serious injury to or the death of the other child; or

(2) has sexually abused another child.

(e) The court shall place a child removed from the child's custodial parent with the child's noncustodial parent or with a relative of the child if placement with the noncustodial parent is inappropriate, unless placement with the noncustodial parent or a relative is not in the best interest of the child.

(f) When citation by publication is needed for a parent or alleged or probable father in an action brought under this chapter because the location of the parent, alleged father, or probable father is unknown, the court may render a temporary order without delay at any time after the filing of the action without regard to whether notice of the citation by publication has been published.

(g) For the purpose of determining under Subsection (a) the 14th day after the date the child is taken into possession, a child is considered to have been taken into possession by the department on the expiration of the five-day period permitted under Section 262.007(c) or 262.110(b), as appropriate.

Comment

The "full adversary hearing" terminology appears nowhere else in the Family Code, nor anywhere else in Texas statutes for that matter. Details regarding the exact nature of a "full adversary hearing" are left to local practice (almost certainly with considerable variation). In any event, the state has the burden of proving its right to retain possession of a child because of a continuing danger. Again the test is "satisfy a person of ordinary prudence and caution." In this section, the decision-maker is a judge rather than a caseworker, law enforcement officer, or juvenile probation officer as was the case when the child was taken into protection. Findings that "reasonable efforts" were made to allow the child to return home are also required to assure federal foster care funding. Obviously, such efforts would be of no avail if the court finds that there is a substantial risk of a continuing danger if the child is returned home.

The term "full adversary hearing" is intended to contrast with the *ex parte* hearings described earlier in this chapter in which "proof may be by sworn petition if a full adversary hearing is not practicable." Practitioners sometimes refer to this as the "fourteen day" hearing, as it is mandated to be held within 14 days after the child is taken into possession. Sometimes, the mandate is delayed and the full adversary hearing must be continued thanks to difficulties with achieving service on respondent parents or the natural delay caused by the appointment of counsel for indigent parents.

Subsection (c) provides parents their first warning to reform their ways or risk losing their kids, and requires the parents or other parties to provide information necessary to locate an alleged father, absent parent or relative.

The term "full adversary hearing" is in contrast to the "hearings" on removal described in earlier sections of this chapter, which are generally *ex parte* hearings. This hearing must be held within 14 days after the child is taken into possession either as a result of an *ex parte* order or without an order. If the court has previously granted the department temporary managing conservatorship [hereafter TMC], the time lines for hearings and the deadline for reaching permanency under Chapter 263 run from the date of the TMC order. If the TMC appointment is made at this hearing, the time period begins to run then. *(C.B. & C.G.C.)*

Leading Case

In re E.D.L., 105 S.W.3d 679 (Tex. App.—Ft. Worth 2003, pet. filed) (14–day deadline for holding "full adversary hearing" is not jurisdictional, but is enforceable by mandamus)

---

§ 262.2015. Aggravated Circumstances.

(a) The court may waive the requirement of a service plan and the requirement to make reasonable efforts to return the child to a parent and may accelerate the trial schedule to result in a final order for a child under the care of the department at an earlier date than provided by Subchapter D, Chapter 263, if the court finds that the parent has subjected the child to aggravated circumstances.

(b) The court may find under Subsection (a) that a parent has subjected the child to aggravated circumstances if:

(1) the parent abandoned the child without identification or a means for identifying the child;

(2) the child is a victim of serious bodily injury or sexual abuse inflicted by the parent or by another person with the parent's consent;

(3) the parent has engaged in conduct against the child that would constitute an offense under the following provisions of the Penal Code:

(A) Section 19.02 (murder);

(B) Section 19.03 (capital murder);

(C) Section 19.04 (manslaughter);

(D) Section 21.11 (indecency with a child);

(E) Section 22.011 (sexual assault);

(F) Section 22.02 (aggravated assault);

(G) Section 22.021 (aggravated sexual assault);

(H) Section 22.04 (injury to a child, elderly individual, or disabled individual);

(I) Section 22.041 (abandoning or endangering child);

(J) Section 25.02 (prohibited sexual conduct);

(K) Section 43.25 (sexual performance by a child); or

(L) Section 43.26 (possession or promotion of child pornography);

(4) the parent voluntarily left the child alone or in the possession of another person not the parent of the child for at least six months without expressing an intent to return and without providing adequate support for the child;

(5) the parent's parental rights with regard to another child have been involuntarily terminated based on a finding that the parent's conduct violated Section 161.001(1)(D) or (E) or a substantially equivalent provision of another state's law; or

(6) the parent has been convicted for:

(A) the murder of another child of the parent and the offense would have been an offense under 18 U.S.C. Section 1111(a) if the offense had occurred in the special maritime or territorial jurisdiction of the United States;

(B) the voluntary manslaughter of another child of the parent and the offense would have been an offense under 18 U.S.C. Section 1112(a) if the offense had occurred in the special maritime or territorial jurisdiction of the United States;

(C) aiding or abetting, attempting, conspiring, or soliciting an offense under Subdivision (A) or (B); or

(D) the felony assault of the child or another child of the parent that resulted in serious bodily injury to the child or another child of the parent.

(c) On finding that reasonable efforts to make it possible for the child to safely return to the child's home are not required, the court shall at any time before the 30th day after the date of the finding, conduct an initial permanency hearing under Subchapter D, Chapter 263. Separate notice of the permanency plan is not required but may be given with a notice of a hearing under this section.

(d) The Department of Protective and Regulatory Services shall make reasonable efforts to finalize the permanent placement of a child for whom the court has made the finding described by Subsection (c). The court shall set the suit for trial on the merits as required by Subchapter D, Chapter 263, in order to facilitate final placement of the child.

Comment

As required by the Adoption and Safe Families Act, 42 U.S.C.A. 678 *et seq.*, this section provides a definition of the "aggravated circumstances" which will justify a waiver of the general directive to the department to preserve the family and return the child to it. If such efforts are waived, the case must be put on a fast track to permanency. *(C.G.C.)*

§ 262.202. Identification of Court of Continuing, Exclusive Jurisdiction.

If at the conclusion of the full adversary hearing the court renders a temporary order, the governmental entity shall request identification of a court of continuing, exclusive jurisdiction as provided by Chapter 155.

§ 262.203. Transfer of Suit.

(a) On the motion of a party or the court's own motion, if applicable, the court that rendered the temporary order shall in accordance with procedures provided by Chapter 155:

(1) transfer the suit to the court of continuing, exclusive jurisdiction, if any;

(2) if grounds exist for mandatory transfer from the court of continuing, exclusive jurisdiction under Section 155.201, order transfer of the suit from that court; or

(3) if grounds exist for transfer based on improper venue, order transfer of the suit to the court having venue of the suit under Chapter 103.

(b) Notwithstanding Section 155.204, a motion to transfer relating to a suit filed under this chapter may be filed separately from the petition and is timely if filed while the case is pending.

(c) Notwithstanding Sections 6.407 and 103.002, a court exercising jurisdiction under this chapter is not required to transfer the suit to a court in which a parent has filed a suit for dissolution of marriage before a final order for the protection of the child has been rendered under Subchapter E, Chapter 263.

Comment

The court with jurisdiction under Chapter 262 may hear and decide mandatory transfer cases. If the facts establish that the child has resided for six months or longer in the county in which the suit for protection of the child has been filed, it is not necessary to return to the former court of continuing jurisdiction for a hearing. The Chapter 262 court may also transfer the case to the court of continuing jurisdiction or to a court with venue. A motion to transfer may be filed separately from the petition at any time before final judgment.

Subsection (c) prevents a parent from filing for divorce in a different county as a tactic to delay or derail a child protection case. The suit affecting the parent child relationship will not be transferred until a final order for the protection of the child has been entered. *(C.G.C.)*

---

§ 262.204. Temporary Order in Effect Until Superseded.

(a) A temporary order rendered under this chapter is valid and enforceable until properly superseded by a court with jurisdiction to do so.

(b) A court to which the suit has been transferred may enforce by contempt or otherwise a temporary order properly issued under this chapter.

Comment

Any Texas court with jurisdiction to hear a SAPCR has authority to render an order under Chapter 262 for the protection of a child. Such orders continue in force until superseded by the court with proper venue or continuing jurisdiction, if that should prove to be a court other than one taking the emergency action.

---

§ 262.205. Hearing When Child Not in Possession of Governmental Entity.

(a) In a suit requesting possession of a child after notice and hearing, the court may render a temporary restraining order as provided by Section 105.001. The suit shall be promptly set for hearing.

(b) After the hearing, the court may grant the request to remove the child from the parent, managing conservator, possessory conservator, guardian, caretaker, or custodian entitled to possession of the child if the court finds sufficient evidence to satisfy a person of ordinary prudence and caution that:

(1) reasonable efforts have been made to prevent or eliminate the need to remove the child from the child's home; and

(2) allowing the child to remain in the home would be contrary to the child's welfare.

(c) If the court orders removal of the child from the child's home, the court shall:

(1) issue an appropriate temporary order under Chapter 105; and

(2) inform each parent in open court that parental and custodial rights and duties may be subject to restriction or termination unless the parent is willing and able to provide a safe environment for the child.

(d) If citation by publication is required for a parent or alleged or probable father in an action under this chapter because the location of the person is unknown, the court may render a temporary order without regard to whether notice of the citation has been published.

(e) Unless it is not in the best interest of the child, the court shall place a child who has been removed under this section with:

(1) the child's noncustodial parent; or

(2) another relative of the child if placement with the noncustodial parent is inappropriate.

(f) If the court finds that the child requires protection from family violence by a member of the child's family or household, the court shall render a protective order for the child under Title 4.

Comment

This section provides a framework for an adversary hearing when prior removal of the child has not been necessary. The court may enjoin the parents from removing the child from the jurisdiction of the court, or render other appropriate restraining orders short of placing the child in the possession of the department. Upon hearing, the court must determine whether reasonable efforts have been made to prevent or eliminate the need to remove the child from the child's home, and whether allowing the child to remain in the home would be contrary to the child's welfare. These standards mirror federal requirements for foster care payments. If the court grants temporary managing conservatorship to the department, the case must be resolved within one year in accordance with the case processing time frames for reaching permanency under Chapter 263. *(C.G.C.)*

Subchapter D. Emergency Possession of Certain Abandoned Children.

Introductory Comment

The provisions of this subchapter and the related Penal Code statute are commonly known as the "Baby Moses Law" (abandonment in bull rushes optional). The intent of this subchapter is to encourage parents not to abandon infants in unsafe places by establishing "designated emergency infant care providers" that may take possession of the infant, provide care, and deliver the child to DPRS. The parent cannot be detained and is exempt from prosecution under Tex. Pen. Code § 22.041 (affirmative defense to prosecution for child abandonment when the child has been delivered to an emergency medical services provider). The parent is not exempt from prosecution for injury to the child or from termination of parental rights based on the voluntary abandonment, *see* § 161.001(S), *supra*. (C.G.C.)

---

§ 262.301. Definitions.

In this chapter:

(1) "Designated emergency infant care provider" means:

(A) an emergency medical services provider;

(B) a hospital; or

(C) a child-placing agency licensed by the Department of Protective and Regulatory Services under Chapter 42, Human Resources Code, that:

(i) agrees to act as a designated emergency infant care provider under this subchapter; and

(ii) has on staff a person who is licensed as a registered nurse under Chapter 301, Occupations Code, or who provides emergency medical services under Chapter 773, Health and Safety Code, and who will examine and provide emergency medical services to a child taken into possession by the agency under this subchapter.

(2) "Emergency medical services provider" has the meaning assigned that term by Section 773.003, Health and Safety Code.

§ 262.302. Accepting Possession of Certain Abandoned Children.

(a) A designated emergency infant care provider shall, without a court order, take possession of a child who appears to be 60 days old or younger if the child is voluntarily delivered to the provider by the child's parent and the parent did not express an intent to return for the child.

(b) A designated emergency infant care provider who takes possession of a child under this section has no legal duty to detain or pursue the parent and may not do so unless the child appears to have been abused or neglected. The designated emergency infant care provider has no legal duty to ascertain the parent's identity and the parent may remain anonymous. However, the parent may be given a form for voluntary disclosure of the child's medical facts and history.

(c) A designated emergency infant care provider who takes possession of a child under this section shall perform any act necessary to protect the physical health or safety of the child. The designated emergency infant care provider is not liable for damages related to the provider's taking possession of, examining, or treating the child, except for damages related to the provider's negligence.

§ 262.303. Notification of Possession of Abandoned Child.

(a) Not later than the close of the first business day after the date on which a designated emergency infant care provider takes possession of a child under Section 262.302, the provider shall notify the Department of Protective and Regulatory Services that the provider has taken possession of the child.

(b) The department shall assume the care, control, and custody of the child immediately on receipt of notice under Subsection (a).

§ 262.304. Filing Petition after Accepting Possession of Abandoned Child.

A child for whom the Department of Protective and Regulatory Services assumes care, control, and custody under Section 262.303 shall be treated as a child taken into possession without a court order, and the department shall take action as required by Section 262.105 with regard to the child.

§ 262.305. Report to Law Enforcement Agency; Investigation.

(a) Immediately after assuming care, control, and custody of a child under Section 262.303, the Department of Protective and Regulatory Services shall report the child to appropriate state and local law enforcement agencies as a potential missing child.

(b) A law enforcement agency that receives a report under Subsection (a) shall investigate whether the child is reported as missing.

§ 262.306. Notice.

Each designated emergency infant care provider shall post in a conspicuous location a notice stating that the provider is a designated emergency infant care provider location and will accept possession of a child in accordance with this subchapter.

§ 262.307. Reimbursement for Care of Abandoned Child.

The department shall reimburse a designated emergency infant care provider that takes possession of a child under Section 262.302 for the cost to the provider of assuming the care, control, and custody of the child.

Chapter 263. Review of Placement of Children Under Care of Department of Protective and Regulatory Services.

Subchapter A. General Provisions

Subchapter B. Service Plan

Subchapter C. Status Hearing

Subchapter D. Permanency Hearings

Subchapter E. Final Order for Child Under Department Care

Subchapter F. Placement Review Hearings

Editors' Note: *This chapter contains guest commentary by Cynthia Bryant, Deputy Attorney General of Child Support Enforcement, and Charles G. Childress, Children's Rights Clinic, University of Texas Law School, and former Chief Attorney, Field Operations, Legal Division, Texas Department of Protective and Regulatory Services, respectively identified as (C.B. & C.G.C.).*

Introductory Comment

This chapter provides for judicial review of the circumstances of children under the care of the Texas Department of Protective and Regulatory Services [DPRS] to prevent children from being "lost in the welfare system."

Landmark legislation mandating a basic one-year deadline for lawsuits in which the state intervenes in a family was enacted in a attempt to accelerate placement of children and not to allow them to languish in an unresolved status. In termination or conservatorship suits filed by DPRS, the clock starts ticking on the date the court makes its temporary order appointing DPRS as the child's temporary managing conservator. The court has until the first Monday after the first anniversary of that temporary order to resolve the case by rendering a final order. If there is no final order by the one-year deadline, or by 18 months if the court grants a one-time extension of not longer than six-months, the DPRS suit must be dismissed.

The court must schedule a status hearing at 60 days and permanency hearings at 120 day intervals thereafter. The hearings must address not only the needs of the child and the progress toward achieving a permanent placement for the child, but the progress of the parties toward resolving the case with a final order rendered before the one-year deadline. The court must set a final hearing sufficiently in advance of the dismissal date to allow for rendition of a final order before the deadline.

Even after the final judgment is rendered, the statute seeks to move the child to permanency outside the foster care system. An appeal, if one is filed, must be accelerated, *see* § 263.405, *infra*. The court must continue to monitor progress toward adoption, if that is the goal, even after a termination decree has become final. *(C.B. & C.G.C.)*

Leading Cases

In re Bishop, 8 S.W.3d 412 (Tex. App.—Waco 1999, no pet.) (case must be dismissed and children returned to parents after 1–year time limit to resolve termination suit passes without 180–day extension)

In re A.B.B., 785 S.W.2d 828 (Tex. App.—Amarillo 1990, no writ) (return of child to mother as result of review hearing [now permanency hearing] upheld)

Cross References

Adoption Assistance and Child Welfare Act of 1980. 42 U.S.C.A. §§ 421, 472, 475, 671–675.

Subchapter A. General Provisions

§ 263.001. Definitions.

(a) In this chapter:

(1) "Department" means the Department of Protective and Regulatory Services.

(2) "Child's home" means the place of residence of at least one of the child's parents.

(3) "Household" means a unit composed of persons living together in the same dwelling, without regard to whether they are related to each other.

(4) "Substitute care" means the placement of a child who is in the conservatorship of the department or an authorized agency in care outside the child's home. The term includes foster care, institutional care, adoption, or placement with a relative of the child.

(b) In the preparation and review of a service plan under this chapter, a reference to the parents of the child includes both parents of the child unless the child has only one parent or unless, after due diligence by the department in attempting to locate a parent, only one parent is located, in which case the reference is to the remaining parent.

§ 263.002. Review of Placements by Court.

In a suit affecting the parent-child relationship in which the department or an authorized agency has been appointed by the court or designated in an affidavit of relinquishment of parental rights as the temporary or permanent managing conservator of a child, the court shall hold a hearing to review the conservatorship appointment and substitute care.

§ 263.003 [repealed]

§ 263.004 [repealed]

§ 263.005. Enforcement of Family Service Plan.

The department shall designate existing department personnel to ensure that the parties to a family service plan comply with the plan.

§ 263.006. Warning to Parents.

At the status hearing under Subchapter C and at each permanency hearing under Subchapter D held after the court has rendered a temporary order appointing the department as temporary managing conservator, the court shall inform each parent in open court that parental and custodial rights and duties may be subject to restriction or to termination unless the parent or parents are willing and able to provide the child with a safe environment.

Comment

The warning to parents required by this section is a critical aspect of the permanency statute. Even if the current expectation of the department is reunification of the family, there is almost always a concurrent alternative possibility for termination or permanent managing conservatorship if the parents cannot or will not provide the child with a safe home. The court is responsible for reminding the parents and all parties of this fact in open court at each review hearing. *(C.B. & C.G.C.)*

Subchapter B. Service Plan

§ 263.101. Department to File Service Plan.

Not later than the 45th day after the date the court renders a temporary order appointing the department as temporary managing conservator of a child under Chapter 262, the department or other agency appointed as the managing conservator of a child shall file a service plan.

Comment

The requirement that DPRS present a comprehensive service plan to the court within 45 days of its appointment as temporary managing conservator is intended to expedite the processing of cases and speed final determinations by focusing the department's attention on long-range planning for the children at an early stage. *(C.G.C.)*

---

§ 263.1015. Service Plan Not Required.

A service plan is not required under this subchapter in a suit brought by the department for the termination of the parent-child relationship for a child who has been abandoned without identification and whose identity cannot be determined.

Comment

Developing a plan of services for parents who abandon an unidentified or unidentifiable child would truly be a pointless act. *(C.B.)*

---

§ 263.102. Service Plan; Contents.

(a) The service plan must:

(1) be specific;

(2) be in writing;

(3) be prepared by the department or other agency in conference with the child's parents;

(4) state appropriate deadlines;

(5) state whether the goal of the plan is:

(A) return of the child to the child's parents;

(B) termination of parental rights and placement of the child for adoption; or

(C) because of the child's special needs or exceptional circumstances, continuation of the child's care out of the child's home;

(6) state steps that are necessary to:

(A) return the child to the child's home if the placement is in foster care;

(B) enable the child to remain in the child's home with the assistance of a service plan if the placement is in the home under the department's or other agency's supervision; or

(C) otherwise provide a permanent safe placement for the child;

(7) state the actions and responsibilities that are necessary for the child's parents to take to achieve the plan goal during the period of the service plan and the assistance to be provided to the parents by the department or other authorized agency toward meeting that goal;

(8) state the name of the person with the department or other agency whom the child's parents may contact for information relating to the child if other than the person preparing the plan; and

(9) prescribe any other term or condition that the department or other agency determines to be necessary to the service plan's success.

(b) The service plan shall include the following statement:

TO THE PARENT: THIS IS A VERY IMPORTANT DOCUMENT. ITS PURPOSE IS TO HELP YOU PROVIDE YOUR CHILD WITH A SAFE ENVIRONMENT WITHIN THE REASONABLE PERIOD SPECIFIED IN THE PLAN. IF YOU ARE UNWILLING OR UNABLE TO PROVIDE YOUR CHILD WITH A SAFE ENVIRONMENT, YOUR PARENTAL AND CUSTODIAL DUTIES AND RIGHTS MAY BE RESTRICTED OR TERMINATED OR YOUR CHILD MAY NOT BE RETURNED TO YOU. THERE WILL BE A COURT HEARING AT WHICH A JUDGE WILL REVIEW THIS SERVICE PLAN.

(c) If both parents are available but do not live in the same household and do not agree to cooperate with one another in the development of a service plan for the child, the department in preparing the service plan may provide for the care of the child in the home of either parent or the homes of both parents as the best interest of the child requires.

§ 263.103. Service Plan: Signing and Taking Effect.

(a) Before the service plan is signed, the child's parents and the representative of the department or other agency shall discuss each term and condition of the plan.

(b) The child's parents and the person preparing the service plan shall sign the plan, and the department shall give each parent a copy of the service plan.

(c) If the department or other authorized agency determines that the child's parents are unable or unwilling to sign the service plan, the department may file the plan without the parents' signatures.

(d) The plan takes effect when:

(1) the child's parents and the appropriate representative of the department or other authorized agency sign the plan; or

(2) the department or other authorized agency files the plan without the parents' signatures.

(e) The service plan is in effect until amended by the court.

§ 263.104. Amended Service Plan.

(a) The service plan may be amended at any time.

(b) The amended service plan supersedes the previously filed service plan and takes effect when:

(1) the child's parents and the appropriate representative of the department or other authorized agency sign the plan; or

(2) the department or other authorized agency determines that the child's parents are unable or unwilling to sign the amended plan and files it without the parents' signatures.

(c) The amended service plan remains in effect until amended by the court.

§ 263.105. Review of Service Plan.

(a) The service plan currently in effect shall be filed with the court.

(b) The court shall review the plan at the next required hearing under this chapter after the plan is filed.

§ 263.106. Court Implementation of Service Plan.

The court may render appropriate orders to implement or require compliance with an original or amended service plan.

Subchapter C. Status Hearing

§ 263.201. Status Hearing; Time.

(a) Not later than the 60th day after the date the court renders a temporary order appointing the department as temporary managing conservator of a child, the court shall hold a status hearing to review the child's status and the service plan developed for the child.

(b) A status hearing is not required if the court holds an initial permanency hearing under Section 262.2015 before the date a status hearing is required by this section.

Comment

The status review hearing must be held not later than 60 days after the appointment of DPRS as temporary managing conservator of the child. If a status hearing is not held because the parents have been found guilty of subjecting the child to "aggravated circumstances," the case will be on an even faster track. The court has only 30 days after the order under § 262.2015 to hold the initial permanency hearing. *(C.G.C.)*

---

§ 263.202. Status Hearing; Findings.

(a) If all parties entitled to citation and notice under this chapter were not served, the court shall make findings as to whether:

(1) the department or other agency has exercised due diligence to locate all necessary persons; and

(2) each custodial parent, alleged father, or relative of the child before the court has furnished to the department all available information necessary to locate another absent parent, alleged father, or relative of the child through exercise of due diligence.

(b) A status hearing shall be limited to matters related to the contents and execution of the service plan filed with the court. The court shall review the service plan that the department or other agency filed under this chapter for reasonableness, accuracy, and compliance with requirements of court orders and make findings as to whether:

(1) a plan that has the goal of returning the child to the child's parents adequately ensures that reasonable efforts are made to enable the child's parents to provide a safe environment for the child; and

(2) the child's parents have reviewed and understand the service plan and have been advised that unless the parents are willing and able to provide the child with a safe environment, even with the assistance of a service plan, within the reasonable period of time specified in the plan, the parents' parental and custodial duties and rights may be subject to restriction or to termination under this code or the child may not be returned to the parents.

(c) The court shall advise the parties that progress under the service plan will be reviewed at all subsequent hearings.

(d) If a service plan with respect to a parent has not been filed with the court, the court shall consider whether to waive the service plan under Section 262.2015.

Comment

This section requires the court to inquire at the status hearing whether parents or other parties have provided information necessary to locate an alleged father, an absent parent, or a relative of the child. The first sentence of Subsection (b) makes clear that the parties may not use the status hearing to relitigate the issues that the court determined at the full adversary hearing, *i.e.,* the removal of the child from the home. Rather, the court is directed to review the service plan that will be used as a yardstick in determining when, or whether, the child can be returned to the parent.

Subsection (d) permits the judge to consider whether "aggravated circumstances" exist if the department does not file a service plan. *(C.G.C.)*

Subchapter D. Permanency Hearings

Introductory Comment

Review hearings held during the time that DPRS has placed the child in temporary foster care are named "permanency" hearings to distinguish them from "placement review" hearings, which are held after a final judgment is rendered. *(C.B. & C.G.C.)*

§ 263.301. Notice.

(a) Notice of a permanency hearing shall be given as provided by Rule 21a, Texas Rules of Civil Procedure, to all persons entitled to notice of the hearing.

(b) The following persons are entitled to at least 10 days' notice of a permanency hearing and are entitled to present evidence and be heard at the hearing:

(1) the department;

(2) the foster parent, preadoptive parent, relative of the child providing care, or director of the group home or institution where the child is residing;

(3) each parent of the child;

(4) the managing conservator or guardian of the child;

(5) an attorney ad litem appointed for the child under Chapter 107;

(6) a volunteer advocate appointed for the child under Chapter 107; and

(7) any other person or agency named by the court to have an interest in the child's welfare.

(c) If a person entitled to notice under Chapter 102 or this section has not been served, the court shall review the department's or other agency's efforts at attempting to locate all necessary persons and requesting service of citation and the assistance of a parent in providing information necessary to locate an absent parent.

§ 263.302. Child's Attendance at Hearing.

The child shall attend each permanency hearing unless the court specifically excuses the child's attendance. Failure by the child to attend a hearing does not affect the validity of an order rendered at the hearing.

Comment

Mandating the child's attendance unless excused states the obverse of the former statute that allowed the court to "dispense with the attendance of the child." The child is, after all, the focus of these permanency plans and hearings. Although the court controls the extent of the child's participation, his or her presence puts a human face on what might otherwise appear bureaucratic or perfunctory. While the child's absence won't invalidate the results of the hearing, the sense of the statute is that ordinarily the child should attend. *(C.B.)*

---

§ 263.3025. Permanency Plan.

(a) The department shall prepare a permanency plan for a child for whom the department has been appointed temporary managing conservator. The department shall give a copy of the plan to each person entitled to notice under Section 263.301(b) not later than the 10th day before the date of the child's first permanency hearing.

(b) In addition to the requirements of the department rules governing permanency planning, the permanency plan must contain the information required to be included in a permanency progress report under Section 263.303.

(c) The department shall modify the permanency plan for a child as required by the circumstances and needs of the child.

(d) In preparing the permanency plan for a child taken into possession under Subchapter D, Chapter 262, the department is not required to conduct a search for or give preference to the child's relatives for purposes of permanent placement if the department does not have information concerning the child's identity or the identities of the child's parents.

§ 263.303. Permanency Progress Report.

(a) Not later than the 10th day before the date set for each permanency hearing other than the first permanency hearing, the department or other authorized agency shall file with the court and provide to each party, the child's attorney ad litem, and the child's volunteer advocate a permanency progress report unless the court orders a different period for providing the report.

(b) The permanency progress report must:

(1) recommend that the suit be dismissed; or

(2) recommend that the suit continue, and:

(A) identify the date for dismissal of the suit under this chapter;

(B) provide:

(i) the name of any person entitled to notice under Chapter 102 who has not been served;

(ii) a description of the efforts by the department or another agency to locate and request service of citation; and

(iii) a description of each parent's assistance in providing information necessary to locate an unserved party;

(C) evaluate the parties' compliance with temporary orders and with the service plan;

(D) evaluate whether the child's placement in substitute care meets the child's needs and recommend other plans or services to meet the child's special needs or circumstances;

(E) describe the permanency plan for the child and recommend actions necessary to ensure that a final order consistent with that permanency plan is rendered before the date for dismissal of the suit under this chapter; and

(F) with respect to a child 16 years of age or older, identify the services needed to assist the child in the transition to adult life.

(c) A parent whose parental rights are the subject of a suit affecting the parent-child relationship, the attorney for that parent, or the child's attorney ad litem or guardian ad litem may file a response to the department's or other agency's report filed under Subsection (b). A response must be filed not later than the third day before the date of the hearing.

Comment

In its permanency progress report DPRS must recommend either that its suit be dismissed, *i.e.,* that the child be returned home, or that the suit continue. In addition to a focus on the child's needs and possible family services, DPRS must provide its calculation of the dismissal date and information about barriers, such as service and locate problems, to achieve a final order before the dismissal date. All parties and the child's advocates are entitled to a copy of the report 10 days prior to the hearing, and may file a written responses to correct or challenge the report. The responses, if filed, should be filed at least three days before the hearing. In actual practice. The 10–day deadline is often missed, which ordinarily has little consequence beyond a justified complaint being lodged without eliciting a sanction. *(C.B. & C.G.C.)*

§ 263.304. Initial Permanency Hearing; Time.

(a) Not later than the 180th day after the date the court renders a temporary order appointing the department as temporary managing conservator of a child, the court shall hold a permanency hearing to review the status of, and permanency plan for, the child to ensure that a final order consistent with that permanency plan is rendered before the date for dismissal of the suit under this chapter.

(b) The court shall set a final hearing under this chapter on a date that allows the court to render a final order before the date for dismissal of the suit under this chapter. Any party to the suit or an attorney ad litem for the child may seek a writ of mandamus to compel the court to comply with the duties imposed by this subsection.

Comment

Consistent with the one-year deadline for temporary foster care, the first permanency hearing is to be held within 180 days after the appointment of DPRS as temporary managing conservator. Subsection (b) gives the department, the parents, and the child an enforceable right to obtain a timely trial setting in order to dispose of the case within the required time-frames. *(C.B. & C.G.C.)*

§ 263.305. Subsequent Permanency Hearings.

A subsequent permanency hearing before entry of a final order shall be held not later than the 120th day after the date of the last permanency hearing in the suit. For good cause shown or on the court's own motion, the court may order more frequent hearings.

Comment

Consistent with the one-year deadline for temporary foster care, the permanency hearings are timed to bring the case to the attention of the court several times before the absolute dismissal date deadline. Except when the "monitored return to parent" provision, § 263.403, comes into play, the deadline for any case for the first permanency hearing is about 180 days before the "Monday next" one-year deadline in the case. On this schedule, the second permanency hearing will be about 120 days later, which will be approximately 60 days prior to the one-year deadline. If an extension is granted, there will be a hearing at 420 days. If there is to be yet another permanency hearing, it must be held before the 540–day mark, which is the drop-dead deadline of 18 months. *(C.G.C.)*

Leading Case

In re N.V.D., 102 S.W.3d 268 (Tex. App.—Beaumont 2003, no pet.) (failure to conduct permanency review hearing within 120 days of prior permanency review harmless error; mother partially responsible)

---

§ 263.306. Permanency Hearings: Procedure.

(a) At each permanency hearing the court shall:

(1) identify all persons or parties present at the hearing or those given notice but failing to appear;

(2) review the efforts of the department or another agency in:

(A) attempting to locate all necessary persons;

(B) requesting service of citation; and

(C) obtaining the assistance of a parent in providing information necessary to locate an absent parent, alleged father, or relative of the child;

(3) review the efforts of each custodial parent, alleged father, or relative of the child before the court in providing information necessary to locate another absent parent, alleged father, or relative of the child;

(4) return the child to the parent or parents if the child's parent or parents are willing and able to provide the child with a safe environment and the return of the child is in the child's best interest;

(5) place the child with a person or entity, other than a parent, entitled to service under Chapter 102 if the person or entity is willing and able to provide the child with a safe environment and the placement of the child is in the child's best interest;

(6) evaluate the department's efforts to identify relatives who could provide the child with a safe environment, if the child is not returned to a parent or another person or entity entitled to service under Chapter 102;

(7) evaluate the parties' compliance with temporary orders and the service plan;

(8) determine whether:

(A) the child continues to need substitute care;

(B) the child's current placement is appropriate for meeting the child's needs, including with respect to a child who has been placed outside of the state, whether that placement continues to be in the best interest of the child; and

(C) other plans or services are needed to meet the child's special needs or circumstances;

(9) if the child is placed in institutional care, determine whether efforts have been made to ensure placement of the child in the least restrictive environment consistent with the best interest and special needs of the child;

(10) if the child is 16 years of age or older, order services that are needed to assist the child in making the transition from substitute care to independent living if the services are available in the community;

(11) determine plans, services, and further temporary orders necessary to ensure that a final order is rendered before the date for dismissal of the suit under this chapter; and

(12) determine the date for dismissal of the suit under this chapter and give notice in open court to all parties of:

(A) the dismissal date;

(B) the date of the next permanency hearing; and

(C) the date the suit is set for trial.

(b) The court shall also review the service plan, permanency report, and other information submitted at the hearing to:

(1) determine:

(A) the safety of the child;

(B) the continuing necessity and appropriateness of the placement;

(C) the extent of compliance with the case plan; and

(D) the extent of progress that has been made toward alleviating or mitigating the causes necessitating the placement of the child in foster care; and

(E) whether the department has made reasonable efforts to finalize the permanency plan that is in effect for the child; and

(2) project a likely date by which the child may be returned to and safely maintained in the child's home, placed for adoption, or placed in permanent managing conservatorship.

Comment

Procedures for permanency hearings focus on the one-year time limit for temporary foster care, as well as on the child's current placement and prospects for being placed in a safe and permanent home. The court evaluates the efforts of the department and other parties to locate and serve necessary parties (a potential barrier to meeting the deadline), and to identify relatives who might care for the child. The court may remove the child from foster care and place the child with a parent or nonparent who can provide a safe environment consistent with the child's best interests. However, unless the department is removed as temporary managing conservator, placement outside foster care does not stop the clock on the permanency deadline.

A monitored placement with the parent under § 263.403, with the department maintaining temporary managing conservatorship, can toll the running of the time limit for up to six months. But, the monitored placement order must be carefully drafted in exact compliance with the statute. *See In re* Neal, 4 S.W.3d 443 (Tex. App.—Houston [1st Dist.] 1999, orig. proceeding). If the child remains in foster care with the clock still ticking, the court must determine what else needs to be done to ensure that the time limit is met. And, just to make sure that all parties get the message that there is a deadline coming up, the court must warn the parents that their rights may be terminated as required by § 263.006 and give all parties notice of the upcoming dismissal date, the next permanency hearing, and the setting of a trial on the merits.

Subsection (b) conforms to 42 U.S.C.A. § 675(5)(B), to ensure that all federal permanency review requirements of the Adoption and Safe Families Act of 1997 are brought to the attention of the court and addressed. *(C.B. & C.G.C.)*

---

§ 263.307. Factors in Determining Best Interest of Child.

(a) In considering the factors established by this section, the prompt and permanent placement of the child in a safe environment is presumed to be in the child's best interest.

(b) The following factors should be considered by the court, the department, and other authorized agencies in determining whether the child's parents are willing and able to provide the child with a safe environment:

(1) the child's age and physical and mental vulnerabilities;

(2) the frequency and nature of out-of-home placements;

(3) the magnitude, frequency, and circumstances of the harm to the child;

(4) whether the child has been the victim of repeated harm after the initial report and intervention by the department or other agency;

(5) whether the child is fearful of living in or returning to the child's home;

(6) the results of psychiatric, psychological, or developmental evaluations of the child, the child's parents, other family members, or others who have access to the child's home;

(7) whether there is a history of abusive or assaultive conduct by the child's family or others who have access to the child's home;

(8) whether there is a history of substance abuse by the child's family or others who have access to the child's home;

(9) whether the perpetrator of the harm to the child is identified;

(10) the willingness and ability of the child's family to seek out, accept, and complete counseling services and to cooperate with and facilitate an appropriate agency's close supervision;

(11) the willingness and ability of the child's family to effect positive environmental and personal changes within a reasonable period of time;

(12) whether the child's family demonstrates adequate parenting skills, including providing the child and other children under the family's care with:

(A) minimally adequate health and nutritional care;

(B) care, nurturance, and appropriate discipline consistent with the child's physical and psychological development;

(C) guidance and supervision consistent with the child's safety;

(D) a safe physical home environment;

(E) protection from repeated exposure to violence even though the violence may not be directed at the child; and

(F) an understanding of the child's needs and capabilities; and

(13) whether an adequate social support system consisting of an extended family and friends is available to the child.

(c) In the case of a child 16 years of age or older, the following guidelines should be considered by the court in determining whether to adopt the permanency plan submitted by the department:

(1) whether the permanency plan submitted to the court includes the services planned for the child to make the transition from foster care to independent living; and

(2) whether this transition is in the best interest of the child.

§ 263.308 [repealed]

§ 263.309. [repealed]

Subchapter E. Final Order For Child Under Department Care.

§ 263.401. Dismissal After One Year; Extension.

(a) Unless the court has rendered a final order or granted an extension under Subsection (b), on the first Monday after the first anniversary of the date the court rendered a temporary order appointing the department as temporary managing conservator, the court shall dismiss the suit affecting the parent-child relationship filed by the department that requests termination of the parent-child relationship or requests that the department be named conservator of the child.

(b) The court may retain the suit on the court's docket for a period not to exceed 180 days after the time described by Subsection (a), if the court finds that continuing the appointment of the department as temporary managing conservator is in the best interest of the child. If the court retains the suit on the court's docket, the court shall render an order in which the court:

(1) schedules the new date for dismissal of the suit not later than the 180th day after the time described by Subsection (a);

(2) makes further temporary orders for the safety and welfare of the child as necessary to avoid further delay in resolving the suit; and

(3) sets a final hearing on a date that allows the court to render a final order before the required date for dismissal of the suit under this subsection.

(c) If the court grants an extension but does not render a final order or dismiss the suit on or before the required date for dismissal under Subsection (b), the court shall dismiss the suit. The court may not grant an additional extension that extends the suit beyond the required date for dismissal under Subsection (b).

(d) For purposes of this section, a final order is an order that:

(1) requires that a child be returned to the child's parent;

(2) names a relative of the child or another person as the child's managing conservator;

(3) without terminating the parent-child relationship, appoints the department as the managing conservator of the child; or

(4) terminates the parent-child relationship and appoints a relative of the child, another suitable person, or the department as managing conservator of the child.

Comment

Texas children can no longer be kept in temporary foster care indefinitely. The threat of mandatory dismissal of the department's suit has forced DPRS to accelerate its own assessment process and to push the courts for final resolution of the cases.

Subsections (b) and (c) reinforce the trial court's duty to set the trial date early enough to permit the rendition of a final order before the new dismissal date. A trial court that still fails to set a final hearing on the merits in a timely manner may face a petition for mandamus under § 263.304. *(C.B. & C.G.C.)*

Leading Cases

In re C.V.G., 1112 S.W.3d 180 (Tex. App.—Houston [1st Dist.] 2003, no pet.) (TDRPS found to have missed extension of one-year dismissal date but foster parent's intervention authorized termination decree)

In re U.P., 105 S.W.3d 222 (Tex. App.—Houston [14th Dist.] 2003, pet. denied) (father waived claim that statute has expired when he failed to raise it with trial court)

In re B.W., 99 S.W.3d 757 (Tex. App.—Houston [1st Dist.] 2003, no pet.) (agreeing to consolidate original case with newborns case and reset trial date constituted agreement to extension past original statutory dismissal date)

In re L.J.S., 96 S.W.3d 692 (Tex. App.—Amarillo 2003, pet. denied) (DPRS may file second termination petition after time has expired when new facts warranting termination alleged)

In re L.L., 65 S.W.3d 194 (Tex. App.—Amarillo 2001, no pet.) (statutory "shall dismiss" mandatory when time expires, notwithstanding parties made separate agreement extending dismissal date pursuant to Tex. R. Civ. P.)

In re Bishop, 8 S.W.3d 412 (Tex. App.—Waco 1999, no pet.) (case must be dismissed and children returned to parents on 180th day following extension order; extension order issued within one year from TMC of youngest child valid)

---

§ 263.402. Limit on Extension; Waiver.

(a) The parties to a suit under this chapter may not extend the deadlines set by the court under this subchapter by agreement or otherwise.

(b) A party to a suit under this chapter who fails to make a timely motion to dismiss the suit or to make a motion requesting the court to render a final order before the deadline for dismissal under this subchapter waives the right to object to the court's failure to dismiss the suit. A motion to dismiss under this subsection is timely if the motion is made before the department has introduced all of the department's evidence, other than rebuttal evidence, at the trial on the merits.

Comment

The parties may not extend the statutory deadlines set by the court by agreement. In addition, a party may not lie behind a log and jump out crying "dismissal" after the department has presented its case-in-chief at trial. Because either party may compel the court to set the case for trial in time to complete the trial before the deadline, a party that fails to seek dismissal before the department completes its case during trial waives the mandatory dismissal provision. This addition aims to overturn appellate decisions that have affirmed dismissal of a termination lawsuit after a case had been submitted to the jury simply because the judgment on the jury verdict was not rendered before the dismissal date. *(C.G.C.)*

Leading Cases

In re J.B.W., 99 S.W.3d 218 (Tex. App.—Fort Worth 2003, pet. filed) (parents waived right to object on appeal to trial court's failure to dismiss termination after statutory time expired—new "remedial" statute applied retroactively)

In re Bishop, 8 S.W.3d 412 (Tex. App.—Waco 1999, mand. denied) (order following permanency hearing constituted extension order)

---

§ 263.403. Monitored Return of Child to Parent.

(a) Notwithstanding Section 263.401, the court may retain jurisdiction and not dismiss the suit or render a final order as required by that section if the court renders a temporary order that:

(1) finds that retaining jurisdiction under this section is in the best interest of the child;

(2) orders the department to return the child to the child's parent;

(3) orders the department to continue to serve as temporary managing conservator of the child; and

(4) orders the department to monitor the child's placement to ensure that the child is in a safe environment.

(b) If the court renders an order under this section, the court shall:

(1) include in the order specific findings regarding the grounds for the order; and

(2) schedule a new date, not later than the 180th day after the date the temporary order is rendered, for dismissal of the suit.

(c) If a child placed with a parent under this section must be moved from that home by the department before the dismissal of the suit or the rendering of a final order, the court shall, at the time of the move, schedule a new date for dismissal of the suit. The new dismissal date may not be later than the original dismissal date established under Section 263.401 or the 180th day after the date the child is moved under this subsection, whichever date is later.

(d) If the court renders an order under this section, the court must include in the order specific findings regarding the grounds for the order.

Comment

The permanency clock keeps running as long as the child is out of the home in the temporary conservatorship of DPRS, whether the substitute care is paid foster care or an unpaid relative placement. The only exception to this rule is provided by this section, which permits a monitored placement back with the parents for up to 180 days. If the placement breaks down and the child must be returned to substitute care, the court has until 180 days after the removal or the original dismissal date, whichever is later, to render a final order. If the placement back in the home extends beyond 180 days, both state and federal law require a new removal order meeting the requirements of Chapter 262. Not only is the suit subject to dismissal, but federal foster care funding is not available if the child is removed from the home after 180 days of "monitoring" in the absence of a new removal order. *(C.B. & C.G.C.)*

§ 263.404. Final Order Appointing Department as Managing Conservator Without Terminating Parental Rights.

(a) The court may render a final order appointing the department as managing conservator of the child without terminating the rights of the parent of the child if the court finds that:

(1) appointment of a parent as managing conservator would not be in the best interest of the child because the appointment would significantly impair the child's physical health or emotional development; and

(2) it would not be in the best interest of the child to appoint a relative of the child or another person as managing conservator.

(b) In determining whether the department should be appointed as managing conservator of the child without terminating the rights of a parent of the child, the court shall take the following factors into consideration:

(1) that the child will reach 18 years of age in not less than three years;

(2) that the child is 12 years of age or older and has expressed a strong desire against termination or being adopted;

(3) that the child has special medical or behavioral needs that make adoption of the child unlikely; and

(4) the needs and desires of the child.

Comment

Permanent foster care is a poor option for any child. Even a "committed foster parent" cannot guarantee a child the stability that a relative or adoptive family can provide. Thus, the legislature has restated the parental presumption from § 153.131(a), and added a requirement that relative placement be considered before placement with DPRS. Permanent managing conservatorship of a child with the state should clearly be the last option considered. *(C.G.C.)*

---

§ 263.405. Appeal of Final Order.

(a) An appeal of a final order rendered under this subchapter is governed by the rules of the supreme court for accelerated appeals in civil cases and the procedures provided by this section. The appellate court shall render its final order or judgment with the least possible delay.

(b) Not later than the 15th day after the date a final order is signed by the trial judge, a party intending to appeal the order must file with the trial court a statement of the point or points on which the party intends to appeal. The statement may be combined with a motion for a new trial.

(c) A motion for a new trial, a request for findings of fact and conclusions of law, or any other post-trial motion in the trial court does not extend the deadline for filing a notice of appeal under Rule 26.1(b), Texas Rules of Appellate Procedure, or the deadline for filing an affidavit of indigence under Rule 20, Texas Rules of Appellate Procedure.

(d) The trial court shall hold a hearing not later than the 30th day after the date the final order is signed to determine whether:

(1) a new trial should be granted;

(2) a party's claim of indigence, if any, should be sustained; and

(3) the appeal is frivolous as provided by Section 13.003(b), Civil Practice and Remedies Code.

(e) If a party claims indigency and requests the appointment of an attorney, the court shall require the person to file an affidavit of indigency and shall hear evidence to determine the issue of indigency. If the court does not render a written order denying the claim of indigence or requiring the person to pay partial costs before the 36th day after the date the final order being appealed is signed, the court shall consider the person to be indigent and shall appoint counsel to represent the person.

(f) The appellate record must be filed in the appellate court not later than the 60th day after the date the final order is signed by the trial judge, unless the trial court, after a hearing, grants a new trial or denies a request for a trial court record at no cost.

(g) The appellant may appeal the court's order denying the appellant's claim of indigence or the court's finding that the appeal is frivolous by filing with the appellate court the reporter's record and clerk's record of the hearing held under this section, both of which shall be provided without advance payment, not later than the 10th day after the date the court makes the decision. The appellate court shall review the records and may require the parties to file appellate briefs on the issues presented, but may not hear oral argument on the issues. The appellate court shall render appropriate orders after reviewing the records and appellate briefs, if any.

(h) Except on a showing of good cause, the appellate court may not extend the time for filing a record or appellate brief.

Comment

This section establishes specific post-trial procedures for prompt resolution of child protection cases. These cases are now clearly subject to accelerated appeals under the Texas Rules of Appellate Procedure, as provided by this section and by amendments to § 109.002. A notice of appeal must be filed within 20 days after the judgment is signed. The party seeking to appeal must reveal the points for appeal within 15 days after the judgment is signed. The trial court must hold a hearing within 30 days after the judgment is signed to determine whether: (1) a new trial should be granted; (2) the appellant is indigent; and, (3) the appeal is frivolous. If the court does not sign an order denying the claim of indigence by the 36th day after the final judgment is signed, the party is deemed to be indigent. Because the records in these cases are often voluminous, the clerk and court reporter have 60 days to file the record. If the court denies the appeal because the points raised are frivolous, the appellant is entitled to a prompt interlocutory review of that decision under Subsection (g). No extension of filing or briefing deadlines is allowed except upon a showing of good cause and order of the appellate court. *(C.G.C.)*

Leading Case

In re C.S., 132 S.W.3d 499 (Tex. App.—Houston [14th Dist.] 2004, no pet.) (appeal not filed timely in case where DRPS named managing conservator)

In re B.G., 104 S.W.3d 565 (Tex. App.—Waco 2202, no pet.) (would-be appellant of termination allowed to file appeal even after missing deadline for accelerated appeal)

In re M.G.D., 108 S.W.3d 508 (Tex. App.—Houston [14th Dist.] 2003, pet. denied) (appellate counsel appointed without affidavit of indigency, but respondent's testimony proved inability to hire lawyer)

In re J.A.G., 92 S.W.3d 539 (Tex. App.—Amarillo 2002, no pet.) (appellate court has no jurisdiction to consider appeal if notice of appeal not filed within 20 days after judgment signed and motion to extend time not filed before 35th day after judgment signed)

In re D.R.L.M., 84 S.W.3d 281 (Tex. App.—Fort Worth 2002, pet. denied) (failure to file statement of error points within 15 days does not deprive appellate court of jurisdiction).

In re H.R., 87 S.W.3d 691 (Tex. App.—San Antonio 2002, no pet.) (indigent mother entitled to appointed counsel on appeal).

---

§ 263.406. Court Information System.

The Office of Court Administration of the Texas Judicial System shall consult with the courts presiding over cases brought by the department for the protection of children to develop an information system to track compliance with the requirements of this subchapter for the timely disposition of those cases.

§ 263.407. Final Order Appointing Department as Managing Conservator of Certain Abandoned Children; Termination of Parental Rights.

(a) In a suit to terminate the parent-child relationship, there is a rebuttable presumption that a parent who delivers a child to a designated emergency infant care provider in accordance with Subchapter D, Chapter 262, consents to the termination of parental rights with regard to the child.

(b) If a person claims to be the parent of a child taken into possession under Subchapter D, Chapter 262, before the court renders a final order terminating the parental rights of the child's parents, the court shall order genetic testing for parentage determination unless parentage has previously been established. The court shall hold the petition for termination of the parent-child relationship in abeyance for a period not to exceed 60 days pending the results of the genetic testing.

Comment

Proof that the parent has voluntarily delivered the child to a designated emergency infant care provider under § 262.302 is a ground for termination. This section provides a further presumption of consent to that termination. If an alleged father or mother appears, any necessary genetic testing must be done within 60 days. *(C.G.C.)*

Subchapter F. Placement Review Hearings

Introductory Comment

Section 153.375 requires a non-parent managing conservator other than DPRS to file an annual report of the child's welfare with the court. DPRS, however, must provide detailed information to the court for review of the child's situation every six months. *(C.G.C.)*

§ 263.501. Placement Review After Final Order.

(a) If the department has been named as a child's managing conservator in a final order that does not include termination of parental rights, the court shall conduct a placement review hearing at least once every six months until the child becomes an adult.

(b) If the department has been named as a child's managing conservator in a final order that terminates a parent's parental rights, the court shall conduct a placement review hearing at least once every six months until the date the child is adopted or the child becomes an adult.

(c) Notice of a placement review hearing shall be given as provided by Rule 21a, Texas Rules of Civil Procedure, to each person entitled to notice of the hearing.

(d) The following are entitled to not less than 10 days' notice of a placement review hearing:

(1) the department;

(2) the foster parent, preadoptive parent, relative of the child providing care, or director of the group home or institution in which the child is residing;

(3) each parent of the child;

(4) each possessory conservator or guardian of the child;

(5) the child's attorney ad litem and volunteer advocate, if the appointments were not dismissed in the final order; and

(6) any other person or agency named by the court as having an interest in the child's welfare.

(e) The court may dispense with the requirement that the child attend a placement review hearing.

Comment

The court must hold a placement review hearing at least every six months until the child is adopted, the final order is modified and the child placed in the permanent managing conservatorship of someone other than the department, or the child becomes an adult. Federal law requires these reviews be held at least once per year as a condition of federal funding for the substitute care. To ensure that the department is not the only potential source of information for the court, notice of the hearing must be given at least 10 days in advance to adults having regular contact or ongoing relationships with the child. *(C.G.C.)*

---

§ 263.502. Placement Review Report.

(a) Not later than the 10th day before the date set for a placement review hearing, the department or other authorized agency shall file a placement review report with the court and provide a copy to each person entitled to notice under Section 263.501(d).

(b) For good cause shown, the court may order a different time for filing the placement review report or may order that a report is not required for a specific hearing.

(c) The placement review report must:

(1) evaluate whether the child's current placement is appropriate for meeting the child's needs;

(2) evaluate whether efforts have been made to ensure placement of the child in the least restrictive environment consistent with the best interest and special needs of the child if the child is placed in institutional care;

(3) identify the services that are needed to assist a child who is at least 16 years of age in making the transition from substitute care to independent living if the services are available in the community;

(4) identify other plans or services that are needed to meet the child's special needs or circumstances; and

(5) describe the efforts of the department or authorized agency to place the child for adoption if parental rights to the child have been terminated and the child is eligible for adoption.

Comment

In preparation for the placement review hearing, the department reports on the child's needs and placement and, if parental rights have been terminated, its efforts to locate an adoptive home. *(C.B.)*

---

§ 263.503. Placement Review Hearings; Procedure.

At each placement review hearing, the court shall determine whether:

(1) the child's current placement is necessary, safe, and appropriate for meeting the child's needs, including with respect to a child placed outside of the state, whether the placement continues to be appropriate and in the best interest of the child;

(2) efforts have been made to ensure placement of the child in the least restrictive environment consistent with the best interest and special needs of the child if the child is placed in institutional care;

(3) the services that are needed to assist a child who is at least 16 years of age in making the transition from substitute care to independent living are available in the community;

(4) other plans or services are needed to meet the child's special needs or circumstances;

(5) the department or authorized agency has exercised due diligence in attempting to place the child for adoption if parental rights to the child have been terminated and the child is eligible for adoption; and

(6) the department or authorized agency has made reasonable efforts to finalize the permanency plan that is in effect for the child.

Comment

Both state and federal law recognize long term foster care is a poor solution for the child. Federal statutes and regulations refer to these continuing hearings as permanency hearings. The department must assess, and the court must review at each hearing, whether the current placement is the best available and whether the department has made reasonable efforts to finalize the permanency plan that is in effect for the child (*i.e.,* achieve a stable and permanent placement). A final order does not close the door on efforts to locate an adoptive home for a child eligible for adoption, nor on efforts to seek a stable permanent placement for every child in foster care. *(C.G.C.)*

Chapter 264. Child Welfare Services.

Subchapter A. General Provisions

Subchapter B. Foster Care

Subchapter C. Child and Family Services

Subchapter D. Services to At–Risk Youth

§ 264.301. Services for At–Risk Youth.
§ 264.302. Early Youth Intervention Services.
§ 264.303. Commencement of Civil Action for Determination of at-Risk Children.
§ 264.304. Hearing; Determination of At–Risk Child.
§ 264.305. Court Order for Services.
§ 264.306. Sanctions.

Subchapter E. Children's Advocacy Centers

§ 264.401. Definition.
§ 264.402. Establishment of Children's Advocacy Center. **[amended]**
§ 264.403. Interagency Memorandum of Understanding.
§ 264.404. Board Representation. **[amended]**
§ 264.405. Duties.
§ 264.406. Multidisciplinary Team. **[amended]**
§ 264.407. Liability.
§ 264.408. Use of Information and Records; Confidentiality and Ownership.
§ 264.409. Administrative Contracts.
§ 264.410. Contracts with Children's Advocacy Centers.
§ 264.411. Eligibility for Contracts. **[amended]**

Subchapter F. Child Fatality Review and Investigation

§ 264.501. Definitions.
§ 264.502. Committee.
§ 264.503. Purpose and Duties of Committee and Specified State Agencies.
§ 264.504. Meetings of Committee.
§ 264.505. Establishment of Review Team.
§ 264.506. Purpose and Duties of Review Team.
§ 264.507. Duties of Presiding Officer.
§ 264.508. Review Procedure.
§ 264.509. Access to Information.
§ 264.510. Meeting of Review Team.
§ 264.511. Use of Information and Records; Confidentiality.
§ 264.512. Governmental Units.
§ 264.513. Report of Death of Child.
§ 264.514. Procedure in the Event of Reportable Death.
§ 264.515. Investigation.

Subchapter G. Court–Appointed Volunteer Advocate Programs

§ 264.601. Definitions.
§ 264.602. Contracts with Advocate Programs.
§ 264.603. Administrative Contracts.
§ 264.604. Eligibility for Contracts.
§ 264.605. Contract Form.
§ 264.606. Criteria for Award of Contracts.
§ 264.607. Contract Requirements.
§ 264.608. Report to the Legislature.
§ 264.609. Rule–Making Authority.

Subchapter H. Child Abuse Program Evaluation

Subchapter I. Communities in Schools Program [transferred to Tex. Educ. Code]

Editors' Note: *Subchapter I, Chapter 264, Family Code, was transferred to Chapter 33, Education Code, and redesignated as Subchapter E, Chapter 33, Education Code by the 78th Legis. Reg. Sess. (2003), H.B. 2292, eff. Sept. 1, 2003. For reference to the statutory text, see previous editions of SAMPSON & TINDALL.*

Editors' Note: *This chapter contains guest commentary by Howard G. Baldwin, Jr., Former First Assistant, Office of the Attorney General; and Charles G. Childress, Children's Rights Clinic, University of Texas Law School, and former Chief Attorney, Legal Division, Texas Department of Protective and Regulatory Services, respectively identified as (H.G.B.) and (C.G.C.).*

Introductory Comment

The provisions of this chapter are undoubtedly of limited utility to the practicing attorney. It contains the restrictions and mandated actions for DPRS to follow in carrying out its duties as the designated agency for child protection.

Subchapter A. General Provisions

§ 264.001. Definition.

In this chapter, "department" means the Department of Protective and Regulatory Services.

§ 264.002. Duties of Department.

(a) The department shall:

(1) promote the enforcement of all laws for the protection of abused and neglected children; and

(2) take the initiative in all matters involving the interests of children where adequate provision has not already been made.

(b) The department shall give special attention to the dissemination of information through bulletins and visits, where practical, to all agencies operating under a provision of law affecting the welfare of children.

(c) Through the county child welfare boards, the department shall work in conjunction with the commissioners courts, juvenile boards, and all other officers and agencies involved in the protection of children. The department may use and allot funds for the establishment and maintenance of homes, schools, and institutions for the care, protection, education, and training of children in conjunction with a juvenile board, a county or city board, or any other agency.

(d) The department shall visit and study the conditions in state-supported eleemosynary institutions for children and shall make actions for the management and operation of the institutions that ensure that the children receive the best possible training in contemplation of their earliest discharge from the institutions.

(e) The department may not spend state funds to accomplish the purposes of this chapter unless the funds have been specifically appropriated for those purposes.

§ 264.003. [repealed]

§ 264.004. Allocation of State Funds.

(a) The department shall establish a method of allocating state funds for children's protective services programs that encourages and rewards the contribution of funds or services from all persons, including local governmental entities.

(b) Except as provided by this subsection, if a contribution of funds or services is made to support a children's protective services program in a particular county, the department shall use the contribution to benefit that program. The department may use the contribution for another purpose only if the commissioners court of the county gives the department written permission.

(c) The department may use state and federal funds to provide benefits or services to children and families who are otherwise eligible for the benefits or services, including foster care, adoption assistance, medical assistance, family reunification services, and other child protective services and related benefits without regard to the immigration status of the child or the child's family.

§ 264.005. County Child Welfare Boards.

(a) The commissioners court of a county may appoint a child welfare board for the county. The commissioners court and the department shall determine the size of the board and the qualifications of its members. However, a board must have not less than seven and not more than 15 members, and the members must be residents of the county. The members shall serve at the pleasure of the commissioners court and may be removed by the court for just cause. The members serve without compensation.

(b) With the approval of the department, two or more counties may establish a joint child welfare board if that action is found to be more practical in accomplishing the purposes of this chapter. A board representing more than one county has the same powers as a board representing a single county and is subject to the same conditions and liabilities.

(c) The members of a county child welfare board shall select a presiding officer and shall perform the duties required by the commissioners court and the department to accomplish the purposes of this chapter.

(d) A county child welfare board is an entity of the department for purposes of providing coordinated state and local public welfare services for children and their families and for the coordinated use of federal, state, and local funds for these services. The child welfare board shall work with the commissioners court.

(e) A county child welfare board is a governmental unit for the purposes of Chapter 101, Civil Practice and Remedies Code.

(f) A county child protective services board member may receive information that is confidential under Section 40.005, Human Resources Code, or Section 261.201 when the board member is acting in the member's official capacity.

(g) A child welfare board may conduct a closed meeting under Section 551.101, Government Code, to discuss, consider, or act on a matter that is confidential under Section 40.005, Human Resources Code, or Section 261.201.

§ 264.006. County Funds.

The commissioners court of a county may appropriate funds from its general fund or any other fund for the administration of its county child welfare board. The court may provide for services to and support of children in need of protection and care without regard to the immigration status of the child or the child's family.

§ 264.007. Cooperation With Department of Health and Human Services.

The department is the state agency designated to cooperate with the United States Department of Health and Human Services in:

(1) establishing, extending, and strengthening public welfare services for the protection and care of abused or neglected children;

(2) developing state services for the encouragement and assistance of adequate methods of community child welfare organizations and paying part of the cost of district, county, or other local child welfare services in rural areas and in other areas of special need; and

(3) developing necessary plans to implement the services contemplated in this section and to comply with the rules of the United States Department of Health and Human Services under the federal Social Security Act (42 U.S.C. Section 651 et seq.).

§ 264.008. Child Welfare Service Fund.

The child welfare service fund is a special fund in the state treasury. The fund shall be used to administer the child welfare services provided by the department.

§ 264.009. Legal Representation of Department.

(a) Except as provided by Subsection (b), (c), or (f), in any action under this code, the department shall be represented in court by the county attorney of the county where the action is brought, unless the district attorney or criminal district attorney of the county elects to provide representation.

(b) If the county attorney, district attorney, or criminal district attorney is unable to represent the department in an action under this code because of a conflict of interest or because special circumstances exist, the attorney general shall represent the department in the action.

(c) If the attorney general is unable to represent the department in an action under this code, the attorney general shall deputize an attorney who has contracted with the department under Subsection (d) or an attorney employed by the department under Subsection (e) to represent the department in the action.

(d) Subject to the approval of the attorney general, the department may contract with a private attorney to represent the department in an action under this code.

(e) The department may employ attorneys to represent the department in an action under this code.

(f) In a county with a population of 2.8 million or more, in an action under this code, the department shall be represented in court by the attorney who represents the state in civil cases in the district or county court of the county where the action is brought. If such attorney is unable to represent the department in an action under this code because of a conflict of interest or because special circumstances exist, the attorney general shall represent the department in the action.

Comment

Assigning child abuse and neglect cases to the local criminal prosecutor occasionally may create an awkward situation because the same office will be handling cases on both the civil and criminal sides of the docket. District attorneys don't seem to be bothered, however, by this potential conflict of interest between their assistant D.A.'s.

---

§ 264.010. Child Abuse Plan; Limitation on Expenditure of Funds.

(a) Funds appropriated for protective services, child and family services, and the purchased service system for the department may only be spent on or after March 1, 1996, in a county that provides the department with a child abuse prevention and protection plan. If a plan is not submitted to the department under this section, the department shall document the county's failure to submit a plan and may spend appropriated funds in the county to carry out the department's duties under this subtitle.

(b) A child abuse prevention and protection plan may be submitted by the governing body of a county or of a regional council of governments in which the county is an active participant.

(c) The department may not require a child abuse prevention and protection plan to exceed five double-spaced letter-size pages. The county or council of governments may voluntarily provide a longer plan.

(d) A child abuse prevention and protection plan must:

(1) specify the manner of communication between entities who are parties to the plan, including the department, the Texas Department of Human Services, local law enforcement agencies, the county and district attorneys, members of the medical and social service community, foster parents, and child advocacy groups; and

(2) provide other information concerning the prevention and investigation of child abuse in the area for which the plan is adopted.

§ 264.011. Local Accounts.

(a) The department may establish and maintain local bank or savings accounts for a child who is under the managing conservatorship of the department as necessary to administer funds received in trust for or on behalf of the child.

(b) Funds maintained in an account under this section may be used by the department to support the child, including for the payment of foster care expenses, or may be paid to a person providing care for the child.

§ 264.0111. Money Earned by Child.

(a) A child for whom the department has been appointed managing conservator and who has been placed by the department in a foster home or child-care institution as defined by Chapter 42, Human Resources Code, is entitled to keep any money earned by the child during the time of the child's placement.

(b) The child may deposit the money earned by the child in a bank or savings account subject to the sole management and control of the child as provided by Section 34.305, Finance Code. The child is the sole and absolute owner of the deposit account.

(c) If a child earns money as described by this section and is returned to the child's parent or guardian, the child's parent or guardian may not interfere with the child's authority to control, transfer, draft on, or make a withdrawal from the account.

(d) In this section, a reference to money earned by a child includes any interest that accrues on the money.

(e) The department may adopt rules to implement this section.

Comment

Children in the care of residential treatment centers are commonly encouraged to earn and manage their own money in order to improve their self-esteem and sense of responsibility. But when these children leave the care of the state and return home, parents or caretakers may undermine those efforts by exercising their parental rights to the child's earnings, *i.e.,* closing the account and spending the money.

This new section eliminates the ownership and managerial rights of parents to the accumulated earnings of a child who has been returned home after earning money and establishing a bank account while in state custody. *(C.G.C.)*

§ 264.012. Burial Expenses for Child in Foster Care.

(a) The department shall request that the parents pay reasonable and necessary burial expenses for a child for whom the department has been appointed managing conservator and who dies in foster care, including a request that if the parents have an insurance policy or a bank account for the child, that the parents spend the proceeds from the policy or money in the account on the burial expenses. If the parents cannot pay all or part of the burial expenses, the department shall spend funds appropriated for the child protective services program to pay reasonable and necessary burial expenses for the child.

(b) The department may accept donations, gifts, or in-kind contributions to cover the costs of any burial expenses for children for whom the department has been appointed managing conservator.

(c) This section does not apply to a foster parent.

Subchapter B. Foster Care

§ 264.101. Foster Care Payments.

(a) The department may pay the cost of foster care for a child:

(1) for whom the department has initiated a suit and has been named managing conservator under an order rendered under this title,

who is a resident of the state, and who has been placed by the department in a foster home or child-care institution, as defined by Chapter 42, Human Resources Code; or

(2) who is under the placement and care of a state agency or political subdivision with which the department has entered into an agreement to reimburse the cost of care and supervision of the child.

(b) The department may not pay the cost of protective foster care for a child for whom the department has been named managing conservator under an order rendered solely under Section 161.001(1)(J).

(c) The payment of foster care, including medical care, for a child as authorized under this subchapter shall be made without regard to the child's eligibility for federally funded care.

(d) The Board of Protective and Regulatory Services may adopt rules that establish criteria and guidelines for the payment of foster care, including medical care, for a child and for providing care for a child after the child becomes 18 years of age if the child is regularly attending high school, an institution of higher education, or a vocational or technical program.

(e) The department may accept and spend funds available from any source to pay for foster care, including medical care, for a child in the department's care.

(f) In this section, "child" means a person who:

(1) is under 22 years of age and for whom the department has been appointed managing conservator of the child before the date the child became 18 years of age; or

(2) is the responsibility of an agency with which the department has entered into an agreement to provide care and supervision of the child.

§ 264.1015. Liability of Child's Estate for Foster Care.

(a) The cost of foster care provided for a child, including medical care, is an obligation of the estate of the child and the estate is liable to the department for the cost of the care.

(b) The department may take action to recover from the estate of the child the cost of foster care for the child.

§ 264.102. County Contracts.

(a) The department may contract with a county commissioners court to administer the funds authorized by this subchapter for eligible children in the county and may require county participation.

(b) The payments provided by this subchapter do not abrogate the responsibility of a county to provide child welfare services.

§ 264.103. Direct Payments.

The department may make direct payments for foster care to a foster parent residing in a county with which the department does not have a contract authorized by Section 264.102.

§ 264.104. Parent or Guardian Liability.

(a) The parent or guardian of a child is liable to the state or to the county for a payment made by the state or county for foster care of a child under this subchapter.

(b) The cost of foster care for a child, including medical care, is a legal obligation of the child's parents, and the estate of a parent of the child is liable to the department for payment of the costs.

(c) The funds collected by the state under this section shall be used by the department for child welfare services.

§ 264.105. Medical Services Payments.

The department shall attempt to maximize the use of federal funding to provide medical care payments authorized by Section 264.101(c) for children for whom the department has been named managing conservator.

§ 264.106. Contracts for Substitute Care Services.

(a) The department shall:

(1) assess the need for substitute care services throughout the state; and

(2) contract with substitute care providers only to the extent necessary to meet the need for those services.

(b) Before contracting with a substitute care provider, the department shall determine whether:

(1) community resources are available to support children placed under the provider's care; and

(2) the appropriate public school district has sufficient resources to support children placed under the provider's care if the children will attend public school.

(c) In addition to the requirements of Section 40.058(b), Human Resources Code, a contract with a substitute care provider must include provisions that:

(1) enable the department to monitor the effectiveness of the provider's services; and

(2) authorize the department to terminate the contract or impose sanctions for a violation of a provision of the contract that specifies performance criteria.

(d) In determining whether to contract with a substitute care provider, the department shall consider the provider's performance under any previous contract for substitute care services between the department and the provider.

(e) In this section, "substitute care provider" means a person who provides residential care for children for 24 hours a day, including:

(1) a child-care institution, as defined by Section 42.002, Human Resources Code;

(2) a child-placing agency, as defined by Section 42.002, Human Resources Code;

(3) a foster group home or foster family home, as defined by Section 42.002, Human Resources Code; and

(4) an agency group home or agency home, as defined by Section 42.002, Human Resources Code, other than an agency group home, agency home, or a foster home verified or certified by the department.

§ 264.1061. Foster Parent Performance.

The department shall monitor the performance of a foster parent who has been verified by the department in the department's capacity as a child-placing agency. The method under which performance is monitored must include the use of objective criteria by which the foster parent's performance may be assessed. The department shall include references to the criteria in a written agreement between the department and the foster parent concerning the foster parent's services.

§ 264.107. Placement of Children.

(a) The department shall use a system for the placement of children in contract residential care, including foster care, that conforms to the levels of care adopted and maintained by the Health and Human Services Commission.

(b) The department shall use the standard application for the placement of children in contract residential care as adopted and maintained by the Health and Human Services Commission.

§ 264.1075. Use of Assessment Services.

Before placing a child in substitute care, the department shall use assessment services provided by a child-care facility or child-placing agency in accordance with Section 42.0425, Human Resources Code, to determine the appropriate substitute care for the child.

§ 264.108. Race or Ethnicity.

(a) The department may not make a foster care placement decision on the presumption that placing a child in a family of the same race or ethnicity as the race or ethnicity of the child is in the best interest of the child.

(b) Unless an independent psychological evaluation specific to a child indicates that placement or continued living with a family of a particular race or ethnicity would be detrimental to the child, the department may not:

(1) deny, delay, or prohibit placement of a child in foster care because the department is attempting to locate a family of a particular race or ethnicity; or

(2) remove a child from foster care with a family that is of a race or ethnicity different from that of the child.

(c) The department may not remove a child from foster care with a family that is of a race or ethnicity different from that of the child for the sole reason that continued foster care with that family may:

(1) strengthen the emotional ties between the child and the family; or

(2) increase the potential of the family's desire to adopt the child because of the amount of time the child and the family are together.

(d) This section does not prevent or limit the department's recruitment of minority families as foster care families, but the recruitment of minority families may not be a reason to delay placement of a child in foster care with an available family of a race or ethnicity different from that of the child.

(e) An employee who violates this section is subject to immediate dismissal.

(f) The department by rule shall define what constitutes a delay under Subsections (b) and (d).

(g) A district court, on the application for an injunction or the filing of a petition complaining of a violation of this section by any person residing in the county in which the court has jurisdiction, shall enforce this section by issuing appropriate orders. An action for an injunction is in addition to any other action, proceeding, or remedy authorized by law. An applicant or petitioner who is granted an injunction or given other appropriate relief under this section is entitled to the costs of the suit, including reasonable attorney's fees.

Comment

This companion to § 162.308, *supra*, applies to placements in foster care rather than to placements for adoption. *See also* § 162.015, *supra*.

---

§ 264.109. Assignment of Support Rights in Substitute Care Cases.

(a) The placement of a child in substitute care by the department constitutes an assignment to the state of any support rights attributable to the child as of the date the child is placed in substitute care.

(b) If a child placed by the department in substitute care is entitled under federal law to Title IV-D child support enforcement services without the requirement of an application for services, the department shall immediately refer the case to the Title IV-D agency. If an application for Title IV-D services is required and the department has been named managing conservator of the child, then an authorized representative of the department shall be the designated individual entitled to apply for services on behalf of the child and shall promptly apply for the services.

(c) The department and the Title IV-D agency shall execute a memorandum of understanding for the implementation of the provisions of this section and for the allocation between the department and the agency, consistent with federal laws and regulations, of any child support funds recovered by the Title IV-D agency in substitute care cases. All child support funds recovered under this section and retained by the department or the Title IV-D agency and any federal matching or incentive funds resulting from child support collection efforts in substitute care cases shall be in excess of amounts otherwise appropriated to either the department or the Title IV-D agency by the legislature.

§ 264.110. Adoptive Parent Registry.

(a) The department shall establish a registry of persons who are willing to accept foster care placement of a child in the care of the department. The child may be placed temporarily with a person registered under this section pending termination of the parent-child relationship.

(b) A person registered under this section must satisfy requirements adopted by rule by the department.

(c) The department shall maintain a list of persons registered under this section and shall make a reasonable effort to place a child with the first available qualified person on the list if a qualified extended family member is not available for the child.

(d) Before a child may be placed with a person under this section, the person must sign a written statement in which the person agrees to the immediate removal of the child by the department under circumstances determined by the department.

(e) A person registered under this section is not entitled to compensation during the time the child is placed in the person's home but may receive support services provided for the child by the department.

(f) A person registered under this section has the right to be considered first for the adoption of a child placed in the person's home if the parent-child relationship is terminated with regard to the child.

(g) The department may refuse to place a child with a person registered under this section only for a reason permitted under criteria adopted by department rule.

(h) The department shall make the public aware of the existence and benefits of the adoptive parent registry through appropriate existing department communication methods.

§ 264.111. Adoption and Substitute Information.

(a) The department shall maintain in the department's central database information concerning children placed in the department's custody, including:

(1) for each formal adoption of a child in this state:

(A) the length of time between the date of the permanency plan decision of adoption and the date of the actual placement of the child with an adoptive family;

(B) the length of time between the date of the placement of the child for adoption and the date a final order of adoption was rendered;

(C) if the child returned to the department's custody after the date a final order of adoption was rendered for the child, the time between the date the final adoption order was rendered and the date the child returned to the department's custody; and

(D) for the adoptive family of a child under Paragraph (C), whether the family used postadoption program services before the date the child returned to the department's custody; and

(2) for each placement of a child in substitute care:

(A) the level of care the child was determined to require;

(B) whether the child was placed in an appropriate setting based on the level of care determined for the child;

(C) the number of moves for the child in substitute care and the reasons for moving the child;

(D) the length of stay in substitute care for the child from the date of initial placement to the date of approval of a permanency plan for the child;

(E) the length of time between the date of approval of a permanency plan for the child and the date of achieving the plan;

(F) whether the child's permanency plan was long-term substitute care;

(G) whether the child's achieved permanency plan was placement with an appropriate relative or another person, other than a foster parent, having standing; and

(H) whether the child was adopted by the child's foster parents.

(b) In addition to the information required in Subsection (a), the department shall compile information on:

(1) the number of families that used postadoption program services to assist in maintaining adoptive placements;

(2) the number of children returned to the department's custody after placement with an adoptive family but before a final adoption order was rendered;

(3) the number of children returned to the department's custody after the date a final order of adoption was rendered for the child;

(4) the number of adoptive families who used postadoption program services before the date a child placed with the family returned to the department's custody;

(5) the percentage of children who were placed in an appropriate setting based on the level of care determined for the child;

(6) the percentage of children placed in a department foster home;

(7) the percentage of children placed in a private child-placing agency;

(8) the number of children whose permanency plan was long-term substitute care;

(9) the number of children whose achieved permanency plan was placement with an appropriate relative or another person, other than a foster parent, having standing;

(10) the number of children adopted by the child's foster parents; and

(11) the number of children whose achieved permanency plan was removal of the disabilities of minority.

(c) The department shall make the information maintained under this section, other than information that is required by law to be confidential, available to the public by computer.

§ 264.112. Report on Children in Substitute Care.

(a) The department shall report the status for children in substitute care to the Board of Protective and Regulatory Services at least once every 12 months.

(b) The report shall analyze the length of time each child has been in substitute care and the barriers to placing the child for adoption or returning the child to the child's parent or parents.

§ 264.113. Returning Child to School. *[first of two]*

(a) If the department takes possession of a child under Chapter 262 during the school year, the department shall ensure that the child returns to school not later than the third school day after the date an order is rendered providing for possession of the child by the department, unless the child has a physical or mental condition of a temporary and remediable nature that makes the child's attendance infeasible.

(b) If a child has a physical or mental condition of a temporary and remediable nature that makes the child's attendance in school infeasible, the department shall notify the school in writing that the child is unable to attend school. If the child's physical or mental condition improves so that the child's attendance in school is feasible, the department shall ensure that the child immediately returns to school.

§ 264.113. Foster Parent Recruitment. *[second of two]*

(a) In this section, " faith-based organization" means a religious or denominational institution or organization, including an organization operated for religious, educational, or charitable purposes and operated, supervised, or controlled, in whole or in part, by or in connection with a religious organization.

(b) The department shall develop a program to recruit and retain foster parents from faith-based organizations. As part of the program, the department shall:

(1) collaborate with faith-based organizations to inform prospective foster parents about the department's need for foster parents, the requirements for becoming a foster parent, and any other aspect of the foster care program that is necessary to recruit foster parents;

(2) provide training for prospective foster parents recruited under this section; and

(3) identify and recommend ways in which faith-based organizations may support persons as they are recruited, are trained, and serve as foster parents.

History: Enacted by 78th Legis., Reg. Sess. (2003), S.B. 1489, eff. June 20, 2003, and "applies only to a cause of action that accrues on or after the effective date of this Act. A cause of action that accrues before the effective date of this Act is governed by the law in effect immediately before the effective date of this Act, and the former law is continued in effect for that purpose."

§ 264.114. Immunity From Liability.

(a) A faith-based organization, including the organization's employees and volunteers, that participates in a program under this chapter is subject to civil liability as provided by Chapter 84, Civil Practice and Remedies Code.

(b) A faith-based organization that provides financial or other assistance to a foster parent or to a member of the foster parent's household is not liable

for damages arising out of the conduct of the foster parent or a member of the foster parent's household.

History: Enacted by 78th Legis., Reg. Sess. (2003), S.B. 1489, eff. June 20, 2003, and "applies only to a cause of action that accrues on or after the effective date of this Act. A cause of action that accrues before the effective date of this Act is governed by the law in effect immediately before the effective date of this Act, and the former law is continued in effect for that purpose."

Subchapter C. Child and Family Services

§ 264.201. Services by Department.

(a) When the department provides services directly or by contract to an abused or neglected child and the child's family, the services shall be designed to:

(1) prevent further abuse;

(2) alleviate the effects of the abuse suffered;

(3) prevent removal of the child from the home; and

(4) provide reunification services when appropriate for the return of the child to the home.

(b) The department shall emphasize ameliorative services for sexually abused children.

(c) The department shall provide or contract for necessary services to an abused or neglected child and the child's family without regard to whether the child remains in or is removed from the family home. If parental rights have been terminated, services may be provided only to the child.

(d) The services may include in-home programs, parenting skills training, youth coping skills, and individual and family counseling.

(e) The department may not provide and a court may not order the department to provide supervision for visitation in a child custody matter unless the department is a petitioner or intervener in the underlying suit.

Comment

Subsection (e) prohibits use of DPRS employees to provide visitation supervision in private cases. The temptation to turn to the child abuse professionals for this service has proven almost irresistible to some trial judges. However, the legislature has never appropriated funds for this service. The limited resources of the department must be devoted to more pressing duties relating to serious child abuse and neglect. *(C.G.C.)*

§ 264.202. Standards and Effectiveness.

(a) The department, with assistance from national organizations with expertise in child protective services, shall define a minimal baseline of in-home and foster care services for abused or neglected children that meets the professionally recognized standards for those services. The department shall attempt to provide services at a standard not lower than the minimal baseline standard.

(b) The department, with assistance from national organizations with expertise in child protective services, shall develop outcome measures to track and monitor the effectiveness of in-home and foster care services.

§ 264.203. Required Participation.

(a) Except as provided by Subsection (d), the court on request of the department may order the parent, managing conservator, guardian, or other member of the abused or neglected child's household to participate in the services the department provides or purchases for alleviating the effects of the abuse or neglect and to permit the child and any siblings of the child to receive the services.

(b) The department may request the court to order the parent, managing conservator, guardian, or other member of the child's household to participate in the services whether the child resides in the home or has been removed from the home.

(c) If the person ordered to participate in the services fails to follow the court's order, the court may impose community service as a sanction for contempt.

(d) If the court does not order the person to participate, the court in writing shall specify the reasons for not ordering participation.

§ 264.204. [repealed]

§ 264.205. Swift Adoption Teams.

(a) The department shall develop swift adoption teams to expedite the process of placing a child under the jurisdiction of the department for adoption. Swift adoption teams developed under this section shall, in performing their duties, attempt to place a child for adoption with an appropriate relative of the child.

(b) A swift adoption team shall consist of department personnel who shall operate under policies adopted by rule by the department. The department shall set priorities for the allocation of department resources to enable a swift adoption team to operate successfully under the policies adopted under this subsection.

(c) The department shall, using a system of measurement developed by the department, report to the legislature on the success of swift adoption teams in expediting the administrative procedures and the length of time in placing children for adoption. The report shall include recommendations by the department concerning legislation that would enable the department to further improve adoption placements. The department shall report under this section on or before December 1 of each even-numbered year.

§ 264.206. Search for Adoptive Parents.

(a) The department shall begin its efforts to locate qualified persons to adopt a child, including persons registered with the adoptive parent registry under Subchapter B, at the time the department's permanency plan for the child becomes the termination of the parent-child relationship and adoption of the child.

(b) The department shall report to the court in which the department petitions for termination of the parent-child relationship on the child's adoptability and the department's search for prospective adoptive parents for the child, including information relating to the department's efforts to work with licensed child-placing agencies.

§ 264.207. Department Planning and Accountability.

(a) The department shall adopt policies that provide for the improvement of the department's services for children and families, including policies that provide for conducting a home study within four months after the date an applicant is approved for an adoption and documenting the results of the home study within 30 days after the date the study is completed. The policies adopted under this section must:

(1) be designed to increase the accountability of the department to individuals who receive services and to the public; and

(2) assure consistency of services provided by the department in the different regions of the state.

(b) To accomplish the goals stated in Subsection (a), the department shall:

(1) establish time frames for the initial screening of families seeking to adopt children;

(2) provide for the evaluation of the effectiveness of the department's management-level employees in expeditiously making permanent placements for children;

(3) establish, as feasible, comprehensive assessment services in various locations in the state to determine the needs of children and families served by the department;

(4) emphasize and centralize the monitoring and promoting of the permanent placement of children receiving department services;

(5) establish goals and performance measures in the permanent placement of children;

(6) seek private licensed child-placing agencies to place a child in the department's managing conservatorship who has been available for permanent placement for more than 90 days;

(7) provide information to private licensed child-placing agencies concerning children under Subdivision (6);

(8) provide incentives for a private licensed child-placing agency that places a child, as defined by Section 162.301, under Subdivision (6);

(9) encourage foster parents to be approved by the department as both foster parents and adoptive parents;

(10) address failures by the department's service regions in making permanent placements for children in a reasonable time; and

(11) require the department's service regions to participate in the Texas Adoption Resources Exchange.

§ 264.208. Location of Parents.

(a) The department shall create a division staffed by personnel trained in locating parents and relatives of children throughout the state.

(b) The department shall use outside contractors and volunteer resources to the extent feasible to perform its responsibilities under this section.

Comment

This section requires the department to establish a "locate" division in order to speed the process to reach a final order and find permanent placements for abused or neglected children. *(C.G.C.)*

Subchapter D. Services to At–Risk Youth

§ 264.301. Services for At–Risk Youth.

(a) The department shall operate a program to provide services for children in at-risk situations and for the families of those children.

(b) The services under this section may include:

(1) crisis family intervention;

(2) emergency short-term residential care;

(3) family counseling;

(4) parenting skills training;

(5) youth coping skills training;

(6) mentoring; and

(7) advocacy training.

§ 264.302. Early Youth Intervention Services.

(a) This section applies to a child who:

(1) is seven years of age or older and under 17 years of age; and

(2) has not had the disabilities of minority for general purposes removed under Chapter 31.

(b) The department shall operate a program under this section to provide services for children in at-risk situations and for the families of those children.

(c) The department may not provide services under this section to a child who has:

(1) at any time been referred to juvenile court for engaging in conduct that violates a penal law of this state of the grade of felony other than a state jail felony; or

(2) been found to have engaged in delinquent conduct under Title 3.

(d) The department may provide services under this section to a child who engages in conduct for which the child may be found by a court to be an at-risk child, without regard to whether the conduct violates a penal law of this state of the grade of felony other than a state jail felony, if the child was younger than 10 years of age at the time the child engaged in the conduct.

(e) The department shall provide services for a child and the child's family if a contract to provide services under this section is available in the county and the child is referred to the department as an at-risk child by:

(1) a court under Section 264.304;

(2) a juvenile court or probation department as part of a progressive sanctions program under Chapter 59;

(3) a law enforcement officer or agency under Section 52.03; or

(4) a justice or municipal court under Article 45.057, Code of Criminal Procedure.

(f) The services under this section may include:

(1) crisis family intervention;

(2) emergency short-term residential care for children 10 years of age or older;

(3) family counseling;

(4) parenting skills training;

(5) youth coping skills training;

(6) advocacy training; and

(7) mentoring.

Comment

Texas DPRS is authorized to provide services to "at-risk" youth, age 7 to 17, as an option to juvenile proceedings under Title 3.

Subsection (e) lists those who may refer the child and the child's family to DPRS for services. DPRS may not provide services to a child over 10 years of age who has previously been referred to the juvenile court for delinquent conduct that would be a felony offense. *(H.G.B.)*

---

§ 264.303. Commencement of Civil Action for Determination of At-Risk Children.

(a) The department may file a civil action to request any district court or county court, other than a juvenile court, to determine that a child is an at-risk child. A person with whom the department contracts to provide services under Section 264.302 may file an action under this section if the department has approved the filing.

(b) Notice of the action must be provided to:

(1) the child;

(2) the parent, managing conservator, or guardian of the child; and

(3) any other member of the child's household who may be affected by an order of the court if the court finds that the child is an at-risk child.

(c) A person served with notice of the action may, but is not required, to file a written answer. Any answer must be filed before the hearing on the action begins.

§ 264.304. Hearing; Determination of At-Risk Child.

(a) Unless a later date is requested by the department, the court shall set a date and time for the hearing not later than 30 days after the date the action is filed.

(b) The court is the trier of fact at the hearing.

(c) The court shall determine that the child is an at-risk child if the court finds that the child has engaged in the following conduct:

(1) conduct, other than a traffic offense and except as provided by Subsection (d), that violates:

(A) the penal laws of this state; or

(B) the penal ordinances of any political subdivision of this state;

(2) the unexcused voluntary absence of the child on 10 or more days or parts of days within a six-month period or three or more days or parts of days within a four-week period from school without the consent of the child's parent, managing conservator, or guardian;

(3) the voluntary absence of the child from the child's home without the consent of the child's parent, managing conservator, or guardian for a substantial length of time or without intent to return;

(4) conduct that violates the laws of this state prohibiting driving while intoxicated or under the influence of intoxicating liquor (first or second offense) or driving while under the influence of any narcotic drug or of any other drug to a degree that renders the child incapable of safely driving a vehicle (first or second offense); or

(5) conduct that evidences a clear and substantial intent to engage in any behavior described by Subdivisions (1)–(4).

(d) The court may not determine that a child is an at-risk child if the court finds that the child engaged in conduct violating the penal laws of this state of the grade of felony other than a state jail felony when the child was 10 years of age or older.

§ 264.305. Court Order for Services.

(a) Except as provided by Subsection (b), if the court finds that the child is an at-risk child under Section 264.304, the court may order the child, the child's parent, managing conservator, or guardian or any other member of the child's household to participate in services provided by the department under Section 264.302 and contained in a plan approved by the court.

(b) The court may order an at-risk child to participate in services involving emergency short-term residential care only if the court finds that the child engaged in conduct described by Section 264.304(c)(1), (2), (3), or (4).

(c) An order rendered by a court under this section expires not later than six months after the date the order was rendered.

Comment

This section authorizes a court to declare a child to be an "at-risk" child and to order the child, the child's parents, managing conservator, or guardian to participate in services provided by DPRS. *(H.G.B.)*

§ 264.306. Sanctions.

(a) A child who violates a court order under Section 264.305 by failing to participate in services provided by the department engages in conduct indicating a need for supervision and the department shall refer the child to an appropriate juvenile authority for proceedings under Title 3 for that conduct.

(b) A parent, managing conservator, guardian, or other member of the child's household who violates a court order under Section 264.305 by failing to participate in services provided by the department is subject to contempt of court. The court may under its contempt powers impose a community service requirement.

Comment

A child who fails to participate in the services ordered under § 264.305 may be referred by the court for proceedings under Title 3. Additionally, a court has the power to hold in contempt a parent, managing conservator or guardian who fails to participate in such services as ordered by the court. *(H.G.B.)*

Subchapter E. Children's Advocacy Centers

§ 264.401. Definition.

In this subchapter, "center" means a children's advocacy center.

§ 264.402. Establishment of Children's Advocacy Center.

On the execution of a memorandum of understanding under Section 264.403, a children's advocacy center may be established by community members and the participating entities described by Section 264.403(a) to serve a county or two or more contiguous counties.

§ 264.403. Interagency Memorandum of Understanding.

(a) Before a center may be established under Section 264.402, a memorandum of understanding regarding participation in operation of the center must be executed among:

(1) the division of the department responsible for child abuse investigations;

(2) representatives of county and municipal law enforcement agencies that investigate child abuse in the area to be served by the center;

(3) the county or district attorney who routinely prosecutes child abuse cases in the area to be served by the center; and

(4) a representative of any other governmental entity that participates in child abuse investigations or offers services to child abuse victims that desires to participate in the operation of the center.

(b) A memorandum of understanding executed under this section shall include the agreement of each participating entity to cooperate in:

(1) developing a cooperative, team approach to investigating child abuse;

(2) reducing, to the greatest extent possible, the number of interviews required of a victim of child abuse to minimize the negative impact of the investigation on the child; and

(3) developing, maintaining, and supporting, through the center, an environment that emphasizes the best interests of children and that provides investigatory and rehabilitative services.

(c) A memorandum of understanding executed under this section may include the agreement of one or more participating entities to provide office space and administrative services necessary for the center's operation.

§ 264.404. Board Representation.

(a) In addition to any other persons appointed or elected to serve on the governing board of a children's advocacy center, the governing board must include an executive officer of, or an employee selected by an executive officer of:

(1) a law enforcement agency that investigates child abuse in the area served by the center;

(2) the child protective services division of the department; and

(3) the county or district attorney's office involved in the prosecution of child abuse cases in the area served by the center.

(b) Service on a center's board by an executive officer or employee under Subsection (a) is an additional duty of the person's office or employment.

§ 264.405. Duties.

A center shall:

(1) assess victims of child abuse and their families to determine their need for services relating to the investigation of child abuse;

(2) provide services determined to be needed under Subdivision (1);

(3) provide a facility at which a multidisciplinary team appointed under Section 264.406 can meet to facilitate the efficient and appropriate disposition of child abuse cases through the civil and criminal justice systems; and

(4) coordinate the activities of governmental entities relating to child abuse investigations and delivery of services to child abuse victims and their families.

§ 264.406. Multidisciplinary Team.

(a) A center's multidisciplinary team must include employees of the participating agencies who are professionals involved in the investigation or prosecution of child abuse cases.

(b) A center's multidisciplinary team may also include professionals involved in the delivery of services, including medical and mental health services, to child abuse victims and the victims' families.

(c) A multidisciplinary team shall meet at regularly scheduled intervals to:

(1) review child abuse cases determined to be appropriate for review by the multidisciplinary team; and

(2) coordinate the actions of the entities involved in the investigation and prosecution of the cases and the delivery of services to the child abuse victims and the victims' families.

(d) A multidisciplinary team may review a child abuse case in which the alleged perpetrator does not have custodial control or supervision of the child or is not responsible for the child's welfare or care.

(e) When acting in the member's official capacity, a multidisciplinary team member is authorized to receive information made confidential by Section 40.005, Human Resources Code, or Section 261.201 or 264.408.

§ 264.407. Liability.

(a) A person is not liable for civil damages for a recommendation made or an opinion rendered in good faith while acting in the official scope of the person's duties as a member of a multidisciplinary team or as a board member, staff member, or volunteer of a center.

(b) The limitation on civil liability of Subsection (a) does not apply if a person's actions constitute gross negligence.

§ 264.408. Use of Information and Records; Confidentiality and Ownership.

(a) The files, reports, records, communications, and working papers used or developed in providing services under this chapter are confidential and not subject to public release under Chapter 552, Government Code, and may only be disclosed for purposes consistent with this chapter. Disclosure may be to:

(1) the department, department employees, law enforcement agencies, prosecuting attorneys, medical professionals, and other state agencies that provide services to children and families; and

(2) the attorney for the child who is the subject of the records and a court-appointed volunteer advocate appointed for the child under Section 107.031.

(b) Information related to the investigation of a report of abuse or neglect under Chapter 261 and services provided as a result of the investigation is confidential as provided by Section 261.201.

(c) The department, a law enforcement agency, and a prosecuting attorney may share with a center information that is confidential under Section 261.201 as needed to provide services under this chapter. Confidential information shared with or provided to a center remains the property of the agency that shared or provided the information to the center.

(d) A videotaped interview of a child made at a center is the property of the prosecuting attorney involved in the criminal prosecution of the case involving the child.

If no criminal prosecution occurs, the videotaped interview is the property of the attorney involved in representing the department in a civil action alleging child abuse or neglect. If the matter involving the child is not prosecuted, the videotape is the property of the department if the matter is an investigation by the department of abuse or neglect. If the department is not investigating or has not investigated the matter, the videotape is the property of the agency that referred the matter to the center. If the center employs a custodian of records for videotaped interviews of children, the center is responsible for the custody of the videotape. A videotaped interview may be shared with other agencies under a written agreement.

(e) The department shall be allowed access to a center's videotaped interviews of children.

§ 264.409. Administrative Contracts.

(a) The department or the office of the attorney general may contract with a statewide organization of individuals or groups of individuals who have expertise in the establishment and operation of children's advocacy center programs. The statewide organization shall provide training, technical assistance, and evaluation services for local children's advocacy center programs.

(b) If the office of the attorney general enters into a contract under this section, the contract must provide that the statewide organization may not spend annually for administrative purposes more than 12 percent of the annual amount appropriated to the office of the attorney general for purposes of this section.

Comment

This provision places the Children's Advocacy Center program with the Attorney General's office. The Attorney General is already the umbrella agency for Court Appointed Volunteer Advocate Programs under Subchapter G. *(C.G.C.)*

---

§ 264.410. Contracts With Children's Advocacy Centers.

(a) The statewide organization with which the department or the office of the attorney general contracts under Section 264.409 shall contract for services with eligible centers to enhance the existing services of the programs.

(b) The contract under this section may not result in reducing the financial support a local center receives from another source.

(c) If the attorney general enters into a contract with a statewide organization under Section 264.409, the attorney general by rule shall adopt standards for eligible local centers. The statewide organization shall assist the attorney general in developing the standards.

§ 264.411. Eligibility for Contracts.

(a) A public entity **that operated as a center under this subchapter before November 1, 1995,** or **a** nonprofit entity is eligible for a contract under Section 264.410 if the entity:

(1) has a signed memorandum of understanding as provided by Section 264.403;

(2) operates under the authority of a governing board as provided by Section 264.404;

(3) has a multidisciplinary team of persons involved in the investigation or prosecution of child abuse cases or the delivery of services as provided by Section 264.406;

(4) holds regularly scheduled case reviews as provided by Section 264.406;

(5) operates in a neutral and physically separate space from the day-to-day operations of any public agency partner;

(6) has developed a method of statistical information gathering on children receiving services through the center and shares such statistical information with the statewide organization, the department, and the office of the attorney general when requested;

(7) has an in-house volunteer program;

(8) employs an executive director who is answerable to the board of directors of the entity and who is not the exclusive salaried employee of any public agency partner; and

(9) operates under a working protocol that includes a statement of:

(A) the center's mission;

(B) each agency's role and commitment to the center;

(C) the type of cases to be handled by the center; [~~and~~]

(D) **the center's procedures** [~~procedure~~] for **conducting** case reviews **and forensic interviews and for ensuring access to specialized medical and mental health services; and**

(E) the center's policies regarding confidentiality and conflict resolution.

(b) The statewide organization may waive the requirements specified in Subsection (a) if it determines that the waiver will not adversely affect the center's ability to carry out its duties under Section 264.405. Any waiver that is granted must be identified in the written contract with the center.

History: Amended by 78th Legis., Reg. Sess. (2003), H.B. 263, eff. Sept. 1, 2003. The change in law made by this Act to Section 264.411(a), Family Code, applies only to a contract entered into under Section 264.410, Family Code, on or after the effective date of this Act. A contract entered into before the effective date of this Act is governed by the law in effect on the date the contract was entered into, and the former law is continued in effect for that purpose.''

Subchapter F. Child Fatality Review and Investigation

§ 264.501. Definitions.

In this subchapter:

(1) ''Autopsy'' and ''inquest'' have the meanings assigned by Article 49.01, Code of Criminal Procedure.

(2) ''Bureau of vital statistics'' means the bureau of vital statistics of the Texas Department of Health.

(3) ''Child'' means a person younger than 18 years of age.

(4) ''Committee'' means the child fatality review team committee.

(5) ''Department'' means the Department of Protective and Regulatory Services.

(6) ''Health care provider'' means any health care practitioner or facility that provides medical evaluation or treatment, including dental and mental health evaluation or treatment.

(7) ''Meeting'' means an in-person meeting or a meeting held by telephone or other electronic medium.

(8) "Preventable death" means a death that may have been prevented by reasonable medical, social, legal, psychological, or educational intervention. The term includes the death of a child from:

(A) intentional or unintentional injuries;

(B) medical neglect;

(C) lack of access to medical care;

(D) neglect and reckless conduct, including failure to supervise and failure to seek medical care; and

(E) premature birth associated with any factor described by Paragraphs (A) through (D).

(9) "Review" means a reexamination of information regarding a deceased child from relevant agencies, professionals, and health care providers.

(10) "Review team" means a child fatality review team established under this subchapter.

(11) "Unexpected death" includes a death of a child that, before investigation:

(A) appears to have occurred without anticipation or forewarning; and

(B) was caused by trauma, suspicious or obscure circumstances, sudden infant death syndrome, abuse or neglect, or an unknown cause.

§ 264.502. Committee.

(a) The child fatality review team committee is composed of:

(1) a person appointed by and representing the state registrar for the bureau of vital statistics;

(2) a person appointed by and representing the director of protective services for families and children of the department;

(3) a person appointed by and representing the director of the bureau of epidemiology of the Texas Department of Health; and

(4) individuals selected under Subsection (b).

(b) The members of the committee who serve under Subsections (a)(1) through (3) shall select the following additional committee members:

(1) a criminal prosecutor involved in prosecuting crimes against children;

(2) a sheriff;

(3) a justice of the peace;

(4) a medical examiner;

(5) a police chief;

(6) a pediatrician experienced in diagnosing and treating child abuse and neglect;

(7) a child educator;

(8) a child mental health provider;

(9) a public health professional;

(10) a child protective services specialist;

(11) a sudden infant death syndrome family service provider;

(12) a neonatologist;

(13) a child advocate; and

(14) a chief juvenile probation officer.

(c) Members of the committee selected under Subsection (b) serve two-year terms that expire on February 1 of each even-numbered year.

(d) Members selected under Subsection (b) must reflect the geographical, cultural, racial, and ethnic diversity of the state.

(e) An appointment to a vacancy on the committee shall be made in the same manner as the original appointment.

(f) Members of the committee shall select a presiding officer from the members of the committee.

(g) The presiding officer of the committee shall call the meetings of the committee, which shall be held at least quarterly.

(h) A member of the committee is not entitled to compensation for serving on the committee but is entitled to reimbursement for the member's travel expenses as provided in the General Appropriations Act. Reimbursement under this subsection for a person serving on the committee under Subsection (a)(1) or (3) shall be paid from funds appropriated to the Texas Department of Health. Reimbursement for other persons serving on the committee shall be paid from funds appropriated to the department.

§ 264.503. Purpose and Duties of Committee and Specified State Agencies.

(a) The purpose of the committee is to:

(1) develop an understanding of the causes and incidence of child deaths in this state;

(2) identify procedures within the agencies represented on the committee to reduce the number of preventable child deaths; and

(3) promote public awareness and make recommendations to the governor and the legislature for changes in law, policy, and practice to reduce the number of preventable child deaths.

(b) To ensure that the committee achieves its purpose, the department and the Texas Department of Health shall perform the duties specified by this section.

(c) The department shall:

(1) recognize the creation and participation of review teams;

(2) promote and coordinate training to assist the review teams in carrying out their duties;

(3) assist the committee in developing model protocols for:

(A) the reporting and investigating of child fatalities for law enforcement agencies, child protective services, justices of the peace and medical examiners, and other professionals involved in the investigations of child deaths;

(B) the collection of data regarding child deaths; and

(C) the operation of the review teams; and

(4) develop and implement procedures necessary for the operation of the committee.

(d) The department shall promote education of the public regarding the incidence and causes of child deaths, the public role in preventing child deaths, and specific steps the public can undertake to prevent child deaths. The committee shall enlist the support and assistance of civic, philanthropic, and public service organizations in the performance of the duties imposed under this subsection.

(e) The Texas Department of Health shall:

(1) collect data under this subchapter and coordinate the collection of data under this subchapter with other data collection activities; and

(2) perform annual statistical studies of the incidence and causes of child fatalities using the data collected under this subchapter.

(f) The committee shall issue annual reports on the committee's activities, including findings and recommendations relating to each purpose and duty of the committee described by this section. Not later than December 1 of each even-numbered year, the committee shall publish the report and submit a copy of the report to the governor, lieutenant governor, and speaker of the house of representatives.

§ 264.504. Meetings of Committee.

(a) Except as provided by Subsections (b), (c), and (d), meetings of the committee are subject to the open meetings law, Chapter 551, Government Code, as if the committee were a governmental body under that chapter.

(b) Any portion of a meeting of the committee during which the committee discusses an individual child's death is closed to the public and is not subject to the open meetings law, Chapter 551, Government Code.

(c) Information identifying a deceased child, a member of the child's family, a guardian or caretaker of the child, or an alleged or suspected perpetrator of abuse or neglect of the child may not be disclosed during a public meeting.

(d) Information regarding the involvement of a state or local agency with the deceased child or another person described by Subsection (c) may not be disclosed during a public meeting.

(e) The committee may conduct an open or closed meeting by telephone conference call or other electronic medium. A meeting held under this subsection is subject to the notice requirements applicable to other meetings. The notice of the meeting must specify as the location of the meeting the location where meetings of the committee are usually held. Each part of the meeting by telephone conference call that is required to be open to the public shall be audible to the public at the location specified in the notice of the meeting as the location of the meeting and shall be tape-recorded. The tape recording shall be made available to the public.

(f) This section does not prohibit the committee from requesting the attendance at a closed meeting of a person who is not a member of the committee and who has information regarding a deceased child.

§ 264.505. Establishment of Review Team.

(a) A multidisciplinary and multiagency child fatality review team may be established for a county to review child deaths in that county. A review team for a county with a population of less than 50,000 may join with an adjacent county or counties to establish a combined review team.

(b) Any person who may be a member of a review team under Subsection (c) may initiate the establishment of a review team and call the first organizational meeting of the team.

(c) A review team may include:

(1) a criminal prosecutor involved in prosecuting crimes against children;

(2) a sheriff;

(3) a justice of the peace or medical examiner;

(4) a police chief;

(5) a pediatrician experienced in diagnosing and treating child abuse and neglect;

(6) a child educator;

(7) a child mental health provider;

(8) a public health professional;

(9) a child protective services specialist;

(10) a sudden infant death syndrome family service provider;

(11) a neonatologist;

(12) a child advocate; and

(13) a chief juvenile probation officer.

(d) Members of a review team may select additional team members according to community resources and needs.

(e) A review team shall select a presiding officer from its members.

§ 264.506. Purpose and Duties of Review Team.

(a) The purpose of a review team is to decrease the incidence of preventable child deaths by:

(1) providing assistance, direction, and coordination to investigations of child deaths;

(2) promoting cooperation, communication, and coordination among agencies involved in responding to child fatalities;

(3) developing an understanding of the causes and incidence of child deaths in the county or counties in which the review team is located;

(4) recommending changes to agencies, through the agency's representative member, that will reduce the number of preventable child deaths; and

(5) advising the committee on changes to law, policy, or practice that will assist the team and the agencies represented on the team in fulfilling their duties.

(b) To achieve its purpose, a review team shall:

(1) adapt and implement, according to local needs and resources, the model protocols developed by the department and the committee;

(2) meet on a regular basis to review child fatality cases and recommend methods to improve coordination of services and investigations between agencies that are represented on the team;

(3) collect and maintain data as required by the committee; and

(4) submit to the bureau of vital statistics data reports on deaths reviewed as specified by the committee.

(c) A review team shall initiate prevention measures as indicated by the review team's findings.

§ 264.507. Duties of Presiding Officer.

The presiding officer of a review team shall:

(1) send notices to the review team members of a meeting to review a child fatality;

(2) provide a list to the review team members of each child fatality to be reviewed at the meeting;

(3) submit data reports to the bureau of vital statistics not later than the 30th day after the date on which the review took place; and

(4) ensure that the review team operates according to the protocols developed by the department and the committee, as adapted by the review team.

§ 264.508. Review Procedure.

(a) The review team of the county in which the injury, illness, or event that was the cause of the death of the child occurred, as stated on the child's death certificate, shall review the death.

(b) On receipt of the list of child fatalities under Section 264.507, each review team member shall review the member's records and the records of the member's agency for information regarding each listed child.

§ 264.509. Access to Information.

(a) A review team may request information and records regarding a deceased child as necessary to carry out the review team's purpose and duties. Records and information that may be requested under this section include:

(1) medical, dental, and mental health care information; and

(2) information and records maintained by any state or local government agency, including:

(A) a birth certificate;

(B) law enforcement investigative data;

(C) medical examiner investigative data;

(D) juvenile court records;

(E) parole and probation information and records; and

(F) child protective services information and records.

(b) On request of the presiding officer of a review team, the custodian of the relevant information and records relating to a deceased child shall provide those records to the review team.

(c) This subsection does not authorize the release of the original or copies of the mental health or medical records of any member of the child's family or the guardian or caretaker of the child or an alleged or suspected perpetrator of abuse or neglect of the child which are in the possession of any state or local government agency as provided in Subsection (a)(2). Information relating to the mental health or medical condition of a member of of the child's family or the guardian or caretaker of the child or the alleged or suspected perpetrator of abuse or neglect of the child acquired as part of an investigation by a state or local government agency as provided in Subsection (a)(2) may be provided to the review team.

§ 264.510. Meeting of Review Team.

(a) A meeting of a review team is closed to the public and not subject to the open meetings law, Chapter 551, Government Code.

(b) This section does not prohibit a review team from requesting the attendance at a closed meeting of a person who is not a member of the review team and who has information regarding a deceased child.

(c) Except as necessary to carry out a review team's purpose and duties, members of a review team and persons attending a review team meeting may not disclose what occurred at the meeting.

(d) A member of a review team participating in the review of a child death is immune from civil or criminal liability arising from information presented in or opinions formed as a result of a meeting.

§ 264.511. Use of Information and Records; Confidentiality.

(a) Information and records acquired by the committee or by a review team in the exercise of its purpose and duties under this subchapter are confidential and exempt from disclosure under the open records law, Chapter 552, Government Code, and may only be disclosed as necessary to carry out the committee's or review team's purpose and duties.

(b) A report of the committee or of a review team or a statistical compilation of data reports is a public record subject to the open records law, Chapter 552, Government Code, as if the committee or review team were a governmental body under that chapter, if the report or statistical compilation does not contain any information that would permit the identification of an individual.

(c) A member of a review team may not disclose any information that is confidential under this section.

(d) Information, documents, and records of the committee or of a review team that are confidential under this section are not subject to subpoena or discovery and may not be introduced into evidence in any civil or criminal proceeding, except that information, documents, and records otherwise available from other sources are not immune from subpoena, discovery, or introduction into evidence solely because they were presented during proceedings of the committee or a review team or are maintained by the committee or a review team.

§ 264.512. Governmental Units.

The committee and a review team are governmental units for purposes of Chapter 101, Civil Practice and Remedies Code. A review team is a unit of local government under that chapter.

§ 264.513. Report of Death of Child.

(a) A person who knows of the death of a child younger than six years of age shall immediately report the death to the medical examiner of the county in which the death occurs or, if the death occurs in a county that does not have a medical examiner's office or that is not part of a medical examiner's district, to a justice of the peace in that county.

(b) The requirement of this section is in addition to any other reporting requirement imposed by law, including any requirement that a person report child abuse or neglect under this code.

(c) A person is not required to report a death under this section that is the result of a motor vehicle accident. This subsection does not affect a duty imposed by another law to report a death that is the result of a motor vehicle accident.

§ 264.514. Procedure in the Event of Reportable Death.

(a) A medical examiner or justice of the peace notified of a death of a child under Section 264.513 shall hold an inquest under Chapter 49, Code of Criminal Procedure, to determine whether the death is unexpected or the result of abuse or neglect. An inquest is not required under this subchapter if the child's death is expected and is due to a congenital or neoplastic disease. A death caused by an infectious disease may be considered an expected death if:

(1) the disease was not acquired as a result of trauma or poisoning;

(2) the infectious organism is identified using standard medical procedures; and

(3) the death is not reportable to the Texas Department of Health under Chapter 81, Health and Safety Code.

(b) The medical examiner or justice of the peace shall immediately notify an appropriate local law enforcement agency if the medical examiner or justice of the peace determines that the death is unexpected or the result of abuse or neglect, and that agency shall investigate the child's death.

(c) In this section, the terms "abuse" and "neglect" have the meaning assigned those terms by Section 261.001.

Comment

Subsection (b) makes clear that even an "expected" death resulting from child abuse or neglect must be reported to law enforcement by the medical examiner or justice of the peace. Tex. Health and Safety Code Ann. § 673.002 requires an autopsy for all unexplained deaths of children 12 months old or younger and requires the Department of Health to develop rules defining Sudden Infant Death Syndrome (SIDS) and to provide reimbursement for required autopsies. *(C.G.C.)*

§ 264.515. Investigation.

(a) The investigation required by Section 264.514 must include:

(1) an autopsy, unless an autopsy was conducted as part of the inquest;

(2) an inquiry into the circumstances of the death, including an investigation of the scene of the death and interviews with the parents of the child, any guardian or caretaker of the child, and the person who reported the child's death; and

(3) a review of relevant information regarding the child from an agency, professional, or health care provider.

(b) The review required by Subsection (a)(3) must include a review of any applicable medical record, child protective services record, record maintained by an emergency medical services provider, and law enforcement report.

(c) The committee shall develop a protocol relating to investigation of an unexpected death of a child under this section. In developing the protocol, the committee shall consult with individuals and organizations that have knowledge and experience in the issues of child abuse and child deaths.

Subchapter G. Court–Appointed Volunteer Advocate Programs

§ 264.601. Definitions.

In this subchapter:

(1) "Abused or neglected child" means a child who is:

(A) the subject of a suit affecting the parent-child relationship filed by a governmental entity; and

(B) under the control or supervision of the department.

(2) "Volunteer advocate program" means a volunteer-based, nonprofit program that provides advocacy services to abused or neglected children with the goal of obtaining a permanent placement for a child that is in the child's best interest.

§ 264.602. Contracts With Advocate Programs.

(a) The statewide organization with which the attorney general contracts under Section 264.603 shall contract for services with eligible volunteer advocate programs to expand the existing services of the programs.

(b) The contract under this section may not result in reducing the financial support a volunteer advocate program receives from another source.

(c) The attorney general shall develop a scale of state financial support for volunteer advocate programs that declines over a six-year period beginning on the date each individual contract takes effect. After the end of the six-year period, the attorney general may not provide more than 50 percent of the volunteer advocate program's funding.

(d) The attorney general by rule shall adopt standards for a local volunteer advocate program. The statewide organization shall assist the attorney general in developing the standards.

§ 264.603. Administrative Contracts.

(a) The attorney general shall contract with one statewide organization of individuals or groups of individuals who have expertise in the dynamics of child abuse and neglect and experience in operating volunteer advocate programs to provide training, technical assistance, and evaluation services for the benefit of local volunteer advocate programs. The contract shall require measurable goals and objectives for expanding local volunteer child advocate programs to areas of the state in which those programs do not exist.

(b) The contract under this section shall provide that not more than 12 percent of the annual legislative appropriation to implement this subchapter may be spent for administrative purposes by the statewide organization with which the attorney general contracts under this section.

§ 264.604. Eligibility for Contracts.

(a) A person is eligible for a contract under Section 264.602 only if the person is a public or private nonprofit entity that operates a volunteer advocate program that:

(1) uses individuals appointed as volunteer advocates or guardians ad litem by the court to provide for the needs of abused or neglected children;

(2) has provided court-appointed advocacy services for at least two years;

(3) provides court-appointed advocacy services for at least 10 children each month; and

(4) has demonstrated that the program has local judicial support.

(b) The statewide organization with which the attorney general contracts under Section 264.603 may not contract with a person that is not eligible under this section. However, the statewide organization may waive the requirement in Subsection (a)(3) for an established program in a rural area or under other special circumstances.

§ 264.605. Contract Form.

A person shall apply for a contract under Section 264.602 on a form provided by the attorney general.

§ 264.606. Criteria for Award of Contracts.

The statewide organization with which the attorney general contracts under Section 264.603 shall consider the following in awarding a contract under Section 264.602:

(1) the volunteer advocate program's eligibility for and use of funds from local, state, or federal governmental sources, philanthropic organizations, and other sources;

(2) community support for the volunteer advocate program as indicated by financial contributions from civic organizations, individuals, and other community resources;

(3) whether the volunteer advocate program provides services that encourage the permanent placement of children through reunification with their families or timely placement with an adoptive family; and

(4) whether the volunteer advocate program has the endorsement and cooperation of the local juvenile court system.

§ 264.607. Contract Requirements.

(a) The attorney general shall require that a contract under Section 264.602 require the volunteer advocate program to:

(1) make quarterly and annual financial reports on a form provided by the attorney general;

(2) cooperate with inspections and audits that the attorney general makes to ensure service standards and fiscal responsibility; and

(3) provide as a minimum:

(A) independent and factual information in writing to the court and to counsel for the parties involved regarding the child;

(B) advocacy through the courts for permanent home placement and rehabilitation services for the child;

(C) monitoring of the child to ensure the safety of the child and to prevent unnecessary movement of the child to multiple temporary placements;

(D) reports in writing to the presiding judge and to counsel for the parties involved;

(E) community education relating to child abuse and neglect;

(F) referral services to existing community services;

(G) a volunteer recruitment and training program, including adequate screening procedures for volunteers;

(H) procedures to assure the confidentiality of records or information relating to the child; and

(I) compliance with the standards adopted under Section 264.602.

(b) The statewide organization with which the attorney general contracts under Section 264.603 may require that a contract under Section 264.602 require the volunteer advocate program to use forms provided by the attorney general.

(c) The attorney general shall develop forms in consultation with a statewide organization of individuals or groups of individuals who have expertise in the dynamics of child abuse and neglect and experience in operating volunteer advocate programs.

§ 264.608. Report to the Legislature.

(a) Before each regular session of the legislature, the attorney general shall publish a report that:

(1) summarizes reports from volunteer advocate programs under contract with the attorney general;

(2) analyzes the effectiveness of the contracts made by the attorney general under this chapter; and

(3) provides information on:

(A) the expenditure of funds under this chapter;

(B) services provided and the number of children for whom the services were provided; and

(C) any other information relating to the services provided by the volunteer advocate programs under this chapter.

(b) The attorney general shall submit copies of the report to the governor, lieutenant governor, speaker of the house of representatives, the Legislative Budget Board, and members of the legislature.

§ 264.609. Rule-Making Authority.

The attorney general may adopt rules necessary to implement this chapter.

§ 264.610. Confidentiality.

The attorney general may not disclose information gained through reports, collected case data, or inspections that would identify a person working at or receiving services from a volunteer advocate program.

§ 264.611. Consultations.

In implementing this chapter, the attorney general shall consult with individuals or groups of individuals who have expertise in the dynamics of child abuse and neglect and experience in operating volunteer advocate programs.

§ 264.612. Funding.

(a) The attorney general may solicit and receive grants or money from either private or public sources, including by appropriation by the legislature from the general revenue fund, to implement this chapter.

(b) The need for and importance of the implementation of this chapter by the attorney general requires priority and preferential consideration for appropriation.

(c) Repealed by Acts 1995, 74th Leg., ch. 751, § 128, eff. Sept. 1, 1995.

§ 264.613. Use of Information and Records; Confidentiality.

(a) The files, reports, records, communications, and working papers used or developed in providing services under this subchapter are confidential and not subject to disclosure under Chapter 552, Government Code, and may only be disclosed for purposes consistent with this subchapter.

(b) Information described by Subsection (a) may be disclosed to:

(1) the department, department employees, law enforcement agencies, prosecuting attorneys, medical professionals, and other state agencies that provide services to children and families;

(2) the attorney for the child who is the subject of the information; and

(3) eligible children's advocacy centers.

(c) Information related to the investigation of a report of abuse or neglect of a child under Chapter 261 and services provided as a result of the investigation are confidential as provided by Section 261.201.

Subchapter H. Child Abuse Program Evaluation

§ 264.701. Child Abuse Program Evaluation Committee.

(a) The Child Abuse Program Evaluation Committee is established within the Department of Protective and Regulatory Services.

(b) The committee is appointed by the Board of Protective and Regulatory Services and is composed of the following 15 members:

(1) an officer or employee of the Texas Education Agency;

(2) two officers or employees of the Department of Protective and Regulatory Services;

(3) an officer or employee of the Texas Juvenile Probation Commission;

(4) an officer or employee of the Texas Department of Mental Health and Mental Retardation;

(5) an officer or employee of the Health and Human Services Commission;

(6) three members of the public who have knowledge of and experience in the area of delivery of services relating to child abuse and neglect;

(7) three members of the public who have knowledge of and experience in the area of evaluation of programs relating to the prevention and treatment of child abuse and neglect; and

(8) three members of the public who are or have been recipients of services relating to the prevention or treatment of child abuse or neglect.

(c) In appointing members to the committee under Subsection (b)(8), the board shall consider appointing:

(1) an adult who as a child was a recipient of services relating to the prevention or treatment of child abuse or neglect; and

(2) a custodial and a noncustodial parent of a child who is or was a recipient of services relating to the prevention or treatment of child abuse or neglect.

(d) A committee member appointed to represent a state agency or entity serves at the pleasure of the board or until termination of the person's employment or membership with the agency or entity. The public members serve staggered six-year terms, with the terms of three public members expiring on September 1 of each even-numbered year.

(e) A member of the committee serves without compensation. A public member is entitled to reimbursement for travel expenses and per diem as provided by the General Appropriations Act.

(f) The committee shall elect from its members a presiding officer and any other officers considered necessary.

(g) Appointments to the committee shall be made without regard to the race, color, handicap, sex, religion, age, or national origin of an appointee.

(h) The committee shall:

(1) develop and adopt policies and procedures governing the system each state agency uses to evaluate the effectiveness of programs to prevent or treat child abuse or neglect with which the agency contracts;

(2) develop and adopt standard definitions of "child abuse treatment" and "child abuse prevention" to be used in implementing and administering the evaluation system created under this subchapter;

(3) develop and adopt standard models and guidelines for prevention and treatment of child abuse to be used in implementing and administering the evaluation system created under this subchapter;

(4) develop and adopt, in cooperation with each affected state agency, a schedule for each agency's adoption and implementation of the committee's evaluation system that considers each agency's budget cycle;

(5) develop and adopt a standard report form and a reporting schedule for the affected agencies;

(6) develop and adopt objective criteria by which the performance of child abuse programs may be measured after reports under this subchapter are submitted and evaluated; and

(7) report annually to the Board of Protective and Regulatory Services, governor, lieutenant governor, and speaker of the house of representatives on the results of the committee's evaluation process.

(i) In adopting an evaluation system under this subchapter, the committee shall allow the affected agencies as much latitude as possible in:

(1) the methods used to collect the required data; and

(2) the timetable for full implementation of the system, allowing for gradual implementation of the system according to classes of program providers.

(j) Each agency that contracts with a public or private entity for services relating to a program for the prevention or treatment of child abuse or neglect shall adopt and implement the committee's evaluation system and shall report to the committee as required by this subchapter.

Added by Acts 1991, 72nd Leg., 1st C.S., ch. 14, § 5.02(a), eff. Nov. 12, 1991. Amended by Acts 1995, 74th Leg., ch. 76, § 8.128, eff. Sept. 1, 1995. Renumbered from V.T.C.A., Government Code § 772.007 and amended by Acts 1995, 74th Leg., ch. 943, § 12, eff. Sept. 1, 1995. Amended by Acts 1997, 75th Leg., ch. 165, § 6.10, eff. Sept. 1, 1997; Acts 2001, 77th Leg., ch. 957, § 5, eff. Sept. 1, 2001.

Subchapter I. Communities in Schools Program

Editors' Note: *Subchapter I, Chapter 264, Family Code, was transferred to Chapter 33, Education Code, and redesignated as Subchapter E, Chapter 33, Education Code by the 78th Legis. Reg. Sess. (2003), H.B. 2292, eff. Sept. 1, 2003.*

Chapter 265. Prevention and Early Intervention Services.

Introductory Comment

This chapter establishes a division in DPRS to coordinate prevention and early intervention programs. The department is responsible for managing the Services to At–Risk Youth program under Chapter 264, Subchapter D. Three other prevention and early intervention programs, the "Communities in Schools" program, the "Parents as Teachers" program, and the "Buffalo Soldier Heritage Program" are all under the direction of the DPRS. The division is also intended to maximize the impact of funding, develop accountability systems and ensure that the State of Texas obtains its share of federal funding. DPRS is given a broad grant of authority to consolidate prevention and early intervention services that already exist within the agency and to add services to the extent existing resources allow.

---

§ 265.001. Definitions.

In this chapter:

(1) "Department" means the Department of Protective and Regulatory Services.

(2) "Division" means the prevention and early intervention services division within the department.

(3) "Prevention and early intervention services" means programs intended to provide early intervention or prevent at-risk behaviors that lead to child abuse, delinquency, running away, truancy, and dropping out of school.

§ 265.002. Prevention and Early Intervention Services Division.

The department shall operate a division to provide services for children in at-risk situations and for the families of those children and to achieve the consolidation of prevention and early intervention services within the jurisdiction of a single agency in order to avoid fragmentation and duplication of services and to increase the accountability for the delivery and administration of these services. The division shall be called the prevention and early intervention services division and shall have the following duties:

(1) to plan, develop, and administer a comprehensive and unified delivery system of prevention and early intervention services to children and their families in at-risk situations;

(2) to improve the responsiveness of services for at-risk children and their families by facilitating greater coordination and flexibility in the use of funds by state and local service providers;

(3) to provide greater accountability for prevention and early intervention services in order to demonstrate the impact or public benefit of a program by adopting outcome measures; and

(4) to assist local communities in the coordination and development of prevention and early intervention services in order to maximize federal, state, and local resources.

§ 265.003. Consolidation of Programs.

(a) In order to implement the duties provided in Section 265.002, the department shall consolidate into the division programs with the goal of providing early intervention or prevention of at-risk behavior that leads to child abuse, delinquency, running away, truancy, and dropping out of school.

(b) The division may provide additional prevention and early intervention services in accordance with Section 265.002.

Texas Constitution and Related Texas Law

As amended through the 78th Legislature, Fourth Called Session (2004)

Texas Constitution of 1876

Article 1. Bill of Rights

§ 3a. Equality Under the Law.

Article 16. General Provisions

§ 15. Separate and Community Property of Husband and Wife.
§ 28. Garnishment of Wages.
§ 50. Homestead: Protection From Forced Sale; Mortgages, Trust Deeds and Liens.
§ 51. Amount of Homestead; Uses.

Texas Civil Practice and Remedies Code

Chapter 154. Alternative Dispute Resolution Procedures.

Subchapter A. General Provisions

§ 154.001. Definitions.
§ 154.002. Policy.
§ 154.003. Responsibility of Courts and Court Administrators.

Subchapter B. Alternative Dispute Resolution Procedures

§ 154.021. Referral of Pending Disputes for Alternative Dispute Resolution Procedure.
§ 154.022. Notification and Objection.
§ 154.023. Mediation.
§ 154.024. Mini–Trial.
§ 154.025. Moderated Settlement Conference.
§ 154.026. Summary Jury Trial.
§ 154.027. Arbitration.

Subchapter C. Impartial Third Parties

§ 154.051. Appointment of Impartial Third Parties.
§ 154.052. Qualifications of Impartial Third Party.
§ 154.053. Standards and Duties of Impartial Third Parties.
§ 154.054. Compensation of Impartial Third Parties.
§ 154.055. Qualified Immunity of Impartial Third Parties.

Subchapter C. Termination of Interest in Public Retirement System

§ 804.101. Termination of Interest in Public Retirement System.

Texas Penal Code

Chapter 12. Punishments [Selected sections summarized].

Chapter 22. Assaultive Offenses [Selected sections summarized].

Chapter 25. Offenses Against the Family.

§ 25.01. Bigamy.
§ 25.02. Prohibited Sexual Conduct.
§ 25.03. Interference with Child Custody.
§ 25.031. Agreement To Abduct from Custody.
§ 25.04. Enticing a Child.
§ 25.05. Criminal Nonsupport.
§ 25.06. Harboring Runaway Child.
§ 25.07. Violation of Protective Order or Magistrate's Order.
§ 25.071. Violation of Protective Order Preventing Offense Caused by Bias or Prejudice.
§ 25.08. Sale or Purchase of Child.
§ 25.09. Advertising for Placement of Child.
§ 25.10. Interference with Rights of Guardian of the Person.

Chapter 38. Obstructing Governmental Operation [Selected section summarized].

Chapter 42. Offenses Against Public Order and Decency [Selected sections in full].

§ 42.07. Harassment.
§ 42.072. Stalking.

Chapter 46. Weapons [Selected sections summarized].

Texas Property Code

Chapter 41. Interests in Land.

§ 41.001. Interests in Land Exempt from Seizure.
§ 41.002. Definition of Homestead.
§ 41.003. Temporary Renting of a Homestead.
§ 41.004. Abandonment of a Homestead.
§ 41.005. Voluntary Designation of Homestead.
§ 41.006. Certain Sales of Homestead.
§ 41.007. Home Improvement Contract.
§ 41.008. Conflict with Federal Law.
§ 41.021. Notice To Designate.
§ 41.022. Designation by Homestead Claimant.

Chapter 42. Personal Property.

★★★

Texas Constitution Of 1876

Article 1. Bill of Rights
Article 16. General Provisions

★★★

Article 1. Bill Of Rights

§ 3a. Equality Under the Law.

Equality under the law shall not be denied or abridged because of sex, race, color, creed, or national origin. This amendment is self-operative.

Comment

Predictions of a flood of litigation revolving around the passage of the Texas Equal Rights Amendment thus far have not been borne out by experience. Over thirty years have passed without the ERA making a truly significant impact on the practice of family law.

CLE/Other Legal Publications

Framing a Texas Bill of Rights argument. James C. Harrington, 24 St. Mary's L.J. 399 (1993)

The Equal Rights Amendment: governmental action and individual liberty. William W. Kilgarlin & Banks Tarver, 68 Tex. L. Rev. 1545 (1990)

Leading Cases

Board of Trustees of Bastrop I.S.D. v. Toungate, 958 S.W.2d 365 (Tex. 1997) (school district, not parents, entitled to determine length of boy's hair)

In re J.W.T., 872 S.W.2d 189 (Tex. 1994) (under certain factual circumstances, biological father has Tex. Const. right to establish his paternity over objections of mother and her husband)

In re Unnamed Baby McLean, 725 S.W.2d 696 (Tex. 1987) (constitutional analysis applicable to construing Texas ERA)

In re Guthrie, 45 S.W.3d 719 (Tex. App.—Dallas 2001, pet. denied) (Texas ERA mandates parents of child-without-presumed-father have equal right to choose surname—best interests test yields surname of biological father here)

Parvin v. Dean, 7 S.W.3d 264 (Tex. App.—Fort Worth 1999, no pet.) (denial of father's cause of action for mental anguish from negligently caused loss of his viable fetus violated Texas ERA)

Dennis v. Smith, 962 S.W.2d 67 (Tex. App.—Houston [1st Dist.] 1997, writ denied) (1960's caselaw giving preference to mother in custody dispute is now considered illegal sex discrimination under Texas ERA)

Lens Express, Inc. v. Ewald, 907 S.W.2d 64 (Tex. App.—Austin 1995, no writ); Maloy v. City of Lewisville, 848 S.W.2d 380 (Tex. App.—Fort Worth 1993, no writ) (ERA elevates sex to suspect classification, due strict scrutiny protection yielding only to compelling state interest)

Messina v. State, 904 S.W.2d 178 (Tex. App.—Dallas 1995, no writ) (ERA allows sex-based distinction if required by physical characteristics)

Article XVI. General Provisions

§ 15. Separate and Community Property of Husband and Wife.

All property, both real and personal, of a spouse owned or claimed before marriage, and that acquired afterward by gift, devise or descent, shall be the separate property of that spouse; and laws shall be passed more clearly defining the rights of the spouses, in relation to separate and community property; provided that persons about to marry and spouses, without the intention to defraud pre-existing creditors, may by written instrument from time to time partition between themselves all or part of their property, then existing or to be acquired, or exchange between themselves the community interest of one spouse or future spouse in any property for the community interest of the other spouse or future spouse in other community property then existing or to be acquired, whereupon the portion or interest set aside to each spouse shall be and constitute a part of the separate property and estate of such spouse or future spouse; spouses also may from time to time, by written instrument, agree between themselves that the income or property from all or part of the separate property then owned or which thereafter might be acquired by only one of them, shall be the separate property of that spouse; if one spouse makes a gift of property to the other that gift is presumed to include all the income or property which might arise from that gift of property; spouses may agree in writing that all or part of their community property becomes the property of the surviving spouse on the death of a spouse; and spouses may agree in writing that all or part of the separate property owned by either or both of them shall be the spouses' community property.

Comment

Since 1980 three amendments to the constitutional framework for our community property regime were overwhelmingly passed by Texas voters. The 1980 amendment authorized antenuptial and postnuptial agreements under which the spouses or persons about to marry could opt out of the system partially or entirely. The 1987 amendment validated survivorship agreements between the spouses regarding community property. Finally, in 1999 Texans voted to allow spouses to convert separate property into community property by written agreement. The pattern is clear. Given a choice, Texans opt for the right to control and manage their property without paternalistic protection from courts applying rigid rules based on construction of a 19th Century view of property rights.

CLE/Other Legal Publications

See annotations to TEX. FAM. CODE ANN. ch. 4, *supra*.

Changing the rules by agreement: the new era in characterization, management, and liability of marital property. Thomas M. Featherston, Jr. and Amy E. Douthitt, 49 BAYLOR L. REV. 271 (1997)

Leading Cases

Beck v. Beck, 814 S.W.2d 745 (Tex. 1991), *cert. denied*, 117 L.Ed.2d 494, 112 S.Ct. 1266 (1992) (under doctrine of implied ratification, a premarital agreement signed in 1978 was made valid by the 1980 amendment to the Texas Constitution)

Hilley v. Hilley, 342 S.W.2d 565 (Tex. 1961) (community property with right of survivorship prohibited; decision overturned by 1987 amendment)

Arnold v. Leonard, 273 S.W. 799 (Tex. 1925) (Texas Constitution defines separate property, cannot be altered by statute)

McElwee v. McElwee, 911 S.W.2d 182 (Tex. App.—Houston [1st Dist.] 1995, writ denied) (constitutional definition of "separate property" exclusive, may not be enlarged by legislative action or by what is just and right)

Haynes v. Stripling, 812 S.W.2d 397 (Tex. App.—Eastland 1991, no writ) (CPWROS created by 1987 constitutional amendment applies to defective JTWROS accounts opened before passage)

Cross Reference

TEX. FAM. CODE chs. 3–5, *supra*.

---

§ 28. Garnishment of Wages.

No current wages for personal service shall ever be subject to garnishment, except for the enforcement of court-ordered:

(1) child support payments; or

(2) spousal maintenance.

Comment

In 1985 this section was amended by an overwhelming majority of voter to allow for wage withholding to collect periodic child support payments, see Chapter 158, *infra*, to see the sweep of that amendment. After spousal maintenance was enacted in 1995, two sessions later (1999), In 1999, the voters authorized an exception to the constitutional prohibition against wage garnishment in order to collect past-due spousal maintenance. In 2001, the legislature set forth the method and procedures for withholding spousal maintenance from the income of the obligor. See §§ 8.101–8.305, *supra*.

Cross Reference

TEX. FAM. CODE ANN. ch. 8. Spousal Maintenance; ch. 154. Child Support; ch. 158. Wage Withholding.

---

§ 50. Homestead; Protection From Forced Sale; Mortgages, Trust Deeds and Liens.

(a) The homestead of a family, or of a single adult person, shall be, and is hereby protected from forced sale, for the payment of all debts except for:

(1) the purchase money thereof, or a part of such purchase money;

(2) the taxes due thereon;

(3) an owelty of partition imposed against the entirety of the property by a court order or by a written agreement of the parties to the partition, including a debt of one spouse in favor of the other spouse resulting from a division or an award of a family homestead in a divorce proceeding;

(4) the refinance of a lien against a homestead, including a federal tax lien resulting from the tax debt of both spouses, if the homestead is a family homestead, or from the tax debt of the owner;

(5) work and material used in constructing new improvements thereon, if contracted for in writing, or work and material used to repair or renovate existing improvements thereon if:

(A) the work and material are contracted for in writing, with the consent of both spouses, in the case of a family homestead, given in the same manner as is required in making a sale and conveyance of the homestead;

(B) the contract for the work and material is not executed by the owner or the owner's spouse before the fifth day after the owner makes written application for any extension of credit for the work and material, unless the work and material are necessary to complete immediate repairs to conditions on the homestead property that materially affect the health or safety of the owner or person residing in the homestead and the owner of the homestead acknowledges such in writing;

(C) the contract for the work and material expressly provides that the owner may rescind the contract without penalty or charge within three days after the execution of the contract by all parties, unless the work and material are necessary to complete immediate repairs to conditions on the homestead property that materially affect the health or safety of the owner or person residing in the homestead and the owner of the homestead acknowledges such in writing; and

(D) the contract for the work and material is executed by the owner and the owner's spouse only at the office of a third-party lender making an extension of credit for the work and material, an attorney at law, or a title company;

(6) an extension of credit that:

> ***Editors' Note:*** *The balance of Subsection (a)(6)—several pages of text—is omitted to conserve space. For that text, see the 1999 edition of* Sampson & Tindall's Texas Fam. Code Ann. *or the current* Vernon's Tex. Const. Ann. *An additional constitutional amendment to subsection (a)(6) was ratified by Texas voters on September 13, 2003.*

(7) a reverse mortgage; or

(8) the conversion and refinance of a personal property lien secured by a manufactured home to a lien on real property, including the refinance of the purchase price of the manufactured home, the cost of installing the manufactured home on the real property, and the refinance of the purchase price of the real property.

(b) An owner or claimant of the property claimed as homestead may not sell or abandon the homestead without the consent of each owner and the spouse of each owner, given in such manner as may be prescribed by law.

(c) No mortgage, trust deed, or other lien on the homestead shall ever be valid unless it secures a debt described by this section, whether such mortgage, trust deed, or other lien, shall have been created by the owner alone, or together with his or her spouse, in case the owner is married. All pretended sales of the homestead involving any condition of defeasance shall be void.

(d) A purchaser or lender for value without actual knowledge may conclusively rely on an affidavit that designates other property as the homestead of the affiant and that states that the property to be conveyed or encumbered is not the homestead of the affiant.

(e) A refinance of debt secured by a homestead and described by any subsection under Subsections (a)(1)–(a)(5) that includes the advance of additional funds may not be secured by a valid lien against the homestead unless:

(1) the refinance of the debt is an extension of credit described by Subsection (a)(6) of this section; or

(2) the advance of all the additional funds is for reasonable costs necessary to refinance such debt or for a purpose described by Subsection (a)(2), (a)(3), or (a)(5) of this section.

(f) A refinance of debt secured by the homestead, any portion of which is an extension of credit described by Subsection (a)(6) of this section, may not be secured by a valid lien against the homestead unless the refinance of the debt is an extension of credit described by Subsection (a)(6) or (a)(7) of this section.

(g) An extension of credit described by Subsection (a)(6) of this section may be secured by a valid lien against homestead property if the extension of credit is not closed before the 12th day after the lender provides the owner with the following written notice on a separate instrument:

> **Editors' Note:** *The text of the six-pages of the constitutional regulation of "home equity loans" and "reverse mortgages" is omitted, to wit, the balance of Subsection (g) and Subsections (h)-(s). For that text, see the 1999 edition of* SAMPSON & TINDALL'S TEXAS FAM. CODE ANN. *or the current* VERNON'S TEX. CONST. ANN.

Comment

From the early days of the Texas Republic, homesteads have been nearly sanctified, including protection from creditors and a prohibition on the use of the homestead as collateral. In 1997, the voters of Texas took the opportunity to re-examine the prohibition on home equity loans when they overwhelmingly approved an amendment to Texas Constitution art. XVI, § 50. The amendment permits two new encumbrances to be fixed on a homestead for certain extensions of credit beyond those that have been traditionally allowed (*e.g.*, purchase money liens; tax liens; owelty liens; refinance liens; and materialmen's liens). The amendments allow general extensions of credit and reverse mortgages to be secured by a lien on the homestead.

Specifically, the amendment limits the principal amount of any general extension of credit secured by the homestead to an amount that, when added to the principal balances of all other liens against the property, is less than 80 percent of the fair market value of the homestead. Furthermore, the loans may be foreclosed only by court order. The loans also require a twelve day "cooling off" period, beginning at either the time the application is made or at the time the borrower receives a statutory statement of rights under a home equity loan, whichever is later. Only then may the closing documents for the loan be signed. Furthermore, the borrower may, without penalty or charge, rescind the loan within 3 days after closing. Only one home equity loan may be secured by the homestead at any one time. Moreover, the loan cannot be for an open-ended account "that may be debited from time to time or under which credit may be extended from time to time."

The reverse mortgage provisions allow borrowers age 62 or older to receive advances based on the equity in the homestead. No payment on the principal or interest on the advances or loans is due until the homestead property is sold or otherwise transferred, or the property is no longer used as a residence by the borrower for a period of more than 180 consecutive days.

In 2001 Texas voters approved a relatively minor amendment to this section that (1) provides a shorter time period (from 12 to 5 days) for a homestead owner to consider whether to enter into a contract that imposes a lien on the homestead for work and material used in the construction, repair, or renovation of improvements on residential homestead property; and (2) includes the conversion and refinance of a personal property lien secured by a manufactured home to a lien on real property as a debt on homestead property subject to a forced sale. The amendment took effect January 1, 2002. As noted above, Texas voters will be deciding the fate of two additional constitutional amendments on September 13, 2003, both of which will be to liberalize the making of such loans.

CLE/Other Legal Publications

Homestead—what you need to know in the 21st Century. Barbara D. Nunneley, 2003 MARRIAGE DISSOLUTION

Home equity loans in Texas: maintaining the Texas tradition of homestead protection. Julia Patterson Forrester, 55 SMU L. REV. 157 (2002)

Taking Texas home equity for a walk, but keeping it on a short leash! Charles C. Boettcher, 30 TEX. TECH L. REV. 197 (1999)

A call for bankruptcy reform: the Fifth Circuit limits the Texas homestead exemption and further complicates the exemption controversy. Michael Denham, 30 TEX. TECH L. REV. 269 (1999)

Leading Cases

Lot 39, Section C, Northern Hills v. State, 85 S.W.3d 429 (Tex. App.—Eastland 2002, pet. denied) (homestead exemption inapplicable to forfeiture for criminal conduct on premises)

Duran v. Henderson, 71 S.W.3d 833 (Tex. App.—Texarkana 2002, pet. denied) (debtor, adult daughter and her son are "family" for purposes of homestead exemption)

Montague v. National Loan Investors, 70 S.W.3d 242 (Tex. App.—San Antonio 2002, rev. denied) (wife (and husband's estate) can claim ranch pledged as security as homestead—jury finding of no estoppel based on disclaimer to obtain loan prevails)

---

§ 51. Amount of Homestead; Uses.

The homestead, not in a town or city, shall consist of not more than two hundred acres of land, which may be in one or more parcels, with the improvements thereon; the homestead in a city, town or village, shall consist of lot or contiguous lots amounting to not more than 10 acres of land, together with any improvements on the land; provided, that the homestead in a city, town or village shall be used for the purposes of a home, or as both an urban home and a place to exercise a calling or business, of the homestead claimant, whether a single adult person, or the head of a family; provided also, that any temporary renting of the homestead shall not change the character of the same, when no other homestead has been acquired; provided further that a release or refinance of an existing lien against a homestead as to a part of the homestead does not create an additional burden on the part of the homestead property that is unreleased or subject to the refinance, and a new lien is not invalid only for that reason.

Comment

The expansion of an allowable urban homestead from one acre to ten acres might seem to some to be a bit excessive. The apparent triggering event for the proposal was the expansion of at least one city into a rural area containing a number of ten-acre "ranchettes." A subsequent major raise in appraised value left the ranchette owners without the homestead protection they had when they originally settled in the formerly rural area. On the other hand, ten acres in downtown Dallas or River Oaks in Houston is a whole lot of homestead protection.

Texas Civil Practice and Remedies Code

Chapter 154. Alternative Dispute Resolution Procedures

Subchapter A. General Provisions

Subchapter B. Alternative Dispute Resolution Procedures

Subchapter C. Impartial Third Parties

Subchapter D. Miscellaneous Provisions

Comment

Please refer to the comments and annotations to Tex. Fam. Code Ann. §§ 6.601–.602, and § 153.071, *supra*.

CLE/Legal Publications

Those other Texas codes—things the family lawyer needs to know about codifications outside the Family Code. Richard R. Orsinger, 2004 Adv. Fam. L.

"Speaking in codes": what every family lawyer should know about the Civil Practices & Remedies Code, Property Code, and Business & Commerce Code. Thomas P. Goranson, 2003, 2001 Adv. Fam. L.

Subchapter A. General Provisions

Leading Case

Cooper v. Bushong, 10 S.W.3d 20 (Tex. App.—Austin 1999, pet. denied) (agreement to binding arbitration in paternity suit basically means neither party nor the trial court may second-guess arbitrator's decision)

---

§ 154.001. Definitions.

In this chapter:

(1) "Court" includes an appellate court, district court, constitutional county court, statutory county court, family law court, probate court, municipal court, or justice of the peace court.

(2) "Dispute resolution organization" means a private profit or nonprofit corporation, political subdivision, or public corporation, or a combination of these, that offers alternative dispute resolution services to the public.

§ 154.002. Policy.

It is the policy of this state to encourage the peaceable resolution of disputes, with special consideration given to disputes involving the parent-child relationship, including the mediation of issues involving conservatorship, possession, and support of children, and the early settlement of pending litigation through voluntary settlement procedures.

§ 154.003. Responsibility of Courts and Court Administrators.

It is the responsibility of all trial and appellate courts and their court administrators to carry out the policy under Section 154.002.

Subchapter B. Alternative Dispute Resolution Procedures

Leading Cases

See also Annotations for Family Code chapter 6, subchapter G and §§ 153.0071–.0072, *supra.*

In re Cartwright, 104 S.W.3d 706, (Tex. App.—Houston [1 Dist.] 2002, no pet.) (AID calls for arbitration of property issue; appointment of judge who mediated child custody dispute instead of arbitrator named in AID is abuse of discretion)

§ 154.021. Referral of Pending Disputes for Alternative Dispute Resolution Procedure.

(a) A court may, on its own motion or the motion of a party, refer a pending dispute for resolution by an alternative dispute resolution procedure including:

(1) an alternative dispute resolution system established under Chapter 26, Acts of the 68th Legislature, Regular Session, 1983 (Article 2372aa, Vernon's Texas Civil Statutes);

(2) a dispute resolution organization; or

(3) a nonjudicial and informally conducted forum for the voluntary settlement of citizens' disputes through the intervention of an impartial third party, including those alternative dispute resolution procedures described under this subchapter.

(b) The court shall confer with the parties in the determination of the most appropriate alternative dispute resolution procedure.

§ 154.022. Notification and Objection.

(a) If a court determines that a pending dispute is appropriate for referral under Section 154.021, the court shall notify the parties of its determination.

(b) Any party may, within 10 days after receiving the notice under Subsection (a), file a written objection to the referral.

(c) If the court finds that there is a reasonable basis for an objection filed under Subsection (b), the court may not refer the dispute under Section 154.021.

§ 154.023. Mediation.

(a) Mediation is a forum in which an impartial person, the mediator, facilitates communication between parties to promote reconciliation, settlement, or understanding among them.

(b) A mediator may not impose his own judgment on the issues for that of the parties.

(c) Mediation includes victim-offender mediation by the Texas Department of Criminal Justice described in Article 56.13, Code of Criminal Procedure.

§ 154.024. Mini–Trial.

(a) A mini-trial is conducted under an agreement of the parties.

(b) Each party and counsel for the party present the position of the party, either before selected representatives for each party or before an impartial third party, to define the issues and develop a basis for realistic settlement negotiations.

(c) The impartial third party may issue an advisory opinion regarding the merits of the case.

(d) The advisory opinion is not binding on the parties unless the parties agree that it is binding and enter into a written settlement agreement.

§ 154.025. Moderated Settlement Conference.

(a) A moderated settlement conference is a forum for case evaluation and realistic settlement negotiations.

(b) Each party and counsel for the party present the position of the party before a panel of impartial third parties.

(c) The panel may issue an advisory opinion regarding the liability or damages of the parties or both.

(d) The advisory opinion is not binding on the parties.

§ 154.026. Summary Jury Trial.

(a) A summary jury trial is a forum for early case evaluation and development of realistic settlement negotiations.

(b) Each party and counsel for the party present the position of the party before a panel of jurors.

(c) The number of jurors on the panel is six unless the parties agree otherwise.

(d) The panel may issue an advisory opinion regarding the liability or damages of the parties or both.

(e) The advisory opinion is not binding on the parties.

§ 154.027. Arbitration.

(a) Nonbinding arbitration is a forum in which each party and counsel for the party present the position of the party before an impartial third party, who renders a specific award.

(b) If the parties stipulate in advance, the award is binding and is enforceable in the same manner as any contract obligation. If the parties do not stipulate in advance that the award is binding, the award is not binding and serves only as a basis for the parties' further settlement negotiations.

Subchapter C. Impartial Third Parties

§ 154.051. Appointment of Impartial Third Parties.

(a) If a court refers a pending dispute for resolution by an alternative dispute resolution procedure under Section 154.021, the court may appoint an impartial third party to facilitate the procedure.

(b) The court may appoint a third party who is agreed on by the parties if the person qualifies for appointment under this subchapter.

(c) The court may appoint more than one third party under this section.

§ 154.052. Qualifications of Impartial Third Party.

(a) Except as provided by Subsections (b) and (c), to qualify for an appointment as an impartial third party under this subchapter a person must have completed a minimum of 40 classroom hours of training in dispute resolution techniques in a course conducted by an alternative dispute resolution system or other dispute resolution organization approved by the court making the appointment.

(b) To qualify for an appointment as an impartial third party under this subchapter in a dispute relating to the parent-child relationship, a person must complete the training required by Subsection (a) and an additional 24 hours of training in the fields of family dynamics, child development, and family law.

(c) In appropriate circumstances, a court may in its discretion appoint a person as an impartial third party who does not qualify under Subsection (a) or (b) if the court bases its appointment on legal or other professional training or experience in particular dispute resolution processes.

§ 154.053. Standards and Duties of Impartial Third Parties.

(a) A person appointed to facilitate an alternative dispute resolution procedure under this subchapter shall encourage and assist the parties in reaching a settlement of their dispute but may not compel or coerce the parties to enter into a settlement agreement.

(b) Unless expressly authorized by the disclosing party, the impartial third party may not disclose to either party information given in confidence by the other and shall at all times maintain confidentiality with respect to communications relating to the subject matter of the dispute.

(c) Unless the parties agree otherwise, all matters, including the conduct and demeanor of the parties and their counsel during the settlement process, are confidential and may never be disclosed to anyone, including the appointing court.

(d) Each participant, including the impartial third party, to an alternative dispute resolution procedure is subject to the requirements of Subchapter B, Chapter 261, Family Code *[Investigation of Report of Child Abuse or Neglect]*, and Subchapter C, Chapter 48, Human Resources Code.

Comment

Under subsection (d), child abuse must be reported to the appropriate authorities even when discovered in what would otherwise be a confidential alternative dispute resolution session.

---

§ 154.054. Compensation of Impartial Third Parties.

(a) The court may set a reasonable fee for the services of an impartial third party appointed under this subchapter.

(b) Unless the parties agree to a method of payment, the court shall tax the fee for the services of an impartial third party as other costs of suit.

§ 154.055. Qualified Immunity of Impartial Third Parties.

(a) A person appointed to facilitate an alternative dispute resolution procedure under this subchapter or under Chapter 152 relating to an alternative dispute resolution system established by counties, or appointed by the parties whether before or after the institution of formal judicial proceedings, who is a volunteer and who does not act with wanton and wilful disregard of the rights, safety, or property of another, is immune from civil liability for any act or omission within the course and scope of his or her duties or functions as an impartial third party. For purposes of this section, a volunteer impartial third party is a person who does not receive compensation in excess of reimbursement for expenses incurred or a stipend intended as reimbursement for expenses incurred.

(b) This section neither applies to nor is it intended to enlarge or diminish any rights or immunities enjoyed by an arbitrator participating in a binding arbitration pursuant to any applicable statute or treaty.

Subchapter D. Miscellaneous Provisions

§ 154.071. Effect of Written Settlement Agreement.

(a) If the parties reach a settlement and execute a written agreement disposing of the dispute, the agreement is enforceable in the same manner as any other written contract.

(b) The court in its discretion may incorporate the terms of the agreement in the court's final decree disposing of the case.

(c) A settlement agreement does not affect an outstanding court order unless the terms of the agreement are incorporated into a subsequent decree.

§ 154.072. Statistical Information on Disputes Referred.

The Texas Supreme Court shall determine the need and method for statistical reporting of disputes referred by the courts to alternative dispute resolution procedures.

§ 154.073. Confidentiality of Certain Records And Communications.

(a) Except as provided by Subsections (c), (d), (e), and (f), a communication relating to the subject matter of any civil or criminal dispute made by a participant in an alternative dispute resolution procedure, whether before or after the institution of formal judicial proceedings, is confidential, is not subject to disclosure, and may not be used as evidence against the participant in any judicial or administrative proceeding.

(b) Any record made at an alternative dispute resolution procedure is confidential, and the participants or the third party facilitating the procedure may not be required to testify in any proceedings relating to or arising out of the matter in dispute or be subject to process requiring disclosure of confidential information or data relating to or arising out of the matter in dispute.

(c) An oral communication or written material used in or made a part of an alternative dispute resolution procedure is admissible or discoverable if it is admissible or discoverable independent of the procedure.

(d) A final written agreement to which a governmental body, as defined by Section 552.003, Government Code, is a signatory that is reached as a result of a dispute resolution procedure conducted under this chapter is subject to or excepted from required disclosure in accordance with Chapter 552, Government Code.

(e) If this section conflicts with other legal requirements for disclosure of communications, records, or materials, the issue of confidentiality may be presented to the court having jurisdiction of the proceedings to determine, in camera, whether the facts, circumstances, and context of the communications or materials sought to be disclosed warrant a protective order of the court or whether the communications or materials are subject to disclosure.

(f) This section does not affect the duty to report abuse or neglect under Subchapter B, Chapter 261, Family Code, and abuse, exploitation, or neglect under Subchapter C, Chapter 48, Human Resources Code.

(g) This section applies to a victim-offender mediation by the Texas Department of Criminal Justice as described in Article 56.13, Code of Criminal Procedure.

Leading Case

In re M.S., 46 Tex.S.Ct.J. 999 (July 3, 2003) (agreement detailing what action mother agreed to take to have children returned to her care admissible as a public record in termination proceeding)

Texas Code of Criminal Procedure

Editors' Note: *Family law practitioners regularly encounter issues of "family violence" and find it necessary to make reference to Title 4 of the Family Code. Many fact situations also implicate related sections of the Texas Code of Criminal Procedure and the Texas Penal Code. These statutes are often not a part of the practice of our readership and are unfamiliar to them. In this chapter we intend to provide a quick reference to some of the relevant provisions without going into excessive detail. To this end, most of the statutory citations are briefly summarized, rather than being set forth in full text. Provisions of special significance are provided in full.*

Throughout this chapter guest commentary is provided by Bree Buchanan, Children's Rights Clinic, University of Texas School of Law, and former Public Policy Director, Texas Council on Family Violence, 1998–2002, identified as (B.B.).

Chapter 5. Family Violence Prevention Act [Selected articles summarized].

Chapter 7A. Protective Order for Victim of Sexual Assault [Chapter summarized].

Chapter 14. Arrest Without Warrant [Selected article summarized].

Chapter 17. Bail [Selected articles in full or summarized].

Chapter 42. Judgment and Sentence [Selected article summarized].

Chapter 56. Rights of Crime Victims [Selected articles summarized].

CLE/Other Legal Publications

Criminal law concerns in family law cases. Joe Marr Wilson, 2003 ADV. FAM. L.

Criminal law and the family practice. Barbara D. Nunneley & J.C. Ball, 2002 ADV. FAM. L.

Online Resources: Domestic and Sexual Violence

National Center for Victims of Crime http://www.ncvc.org
National Domestic Violence Hotline http://www.ndvh.org
National Sexual Violence Resource Center http://www.nsvrc.org
Texas Association Against Sexual Assault http://www.taasa.org
Texas Council on Family Violence http://www.tcfv.org
Texas Office of Attorney: General Sexual Assault Prevention and Crisis Services http://www.oag.state.tx.us/victims/sapcs

U.S. Department of Justice Office on Violence Against Women http://www.ojp.usdoj.gov/ovc
Violence Against Women Online http://www.vaw.umn.edu
Women's Advocacy Project http://www.women-law.org

Chapter 5. Family Violence Prevention Act.

Art. 5.01. Legislative Statement.

Summary: Family violence is a serious danger and threat to society and its members. Victims are entitled to maximum protection. Law enforcement and judicial officers shall protect the victim, without regard to the relationship between the alleged offender and victim. *(B.B.)*

Art. 5.03. Family or Household Relationship Does Not Create an Exception to Official Duties.

Summary: The family or household relationship between an alleged violator and the victim of family violence is not relevant to the duties of officers which is to prevent the commission of criminal offenses. *(B.B.)*

Art. 5.04. Duties of Peace Officers.

Summary: Primary duties are to protect any potential victim of family violence, enforce the law of this state, enforce a protective order from another jurisdiction as provided by Chapter 88, Family Code, and make lawful arrests of violators. The officer shall also advise any adult victim of all reasonable means to prevent further family violence, including giving written notice of the victim's legal rights and remedies and availability of shelter or other community services for family violence victims. The officer must also advise the victim of the right to request a magistrate's order for emergency protection, and that the victim need not be present when the order is issued. *(B.B.)*

Art. 5.045. Standby Assistance: Liability.

Summary: At the discretion of a peace officer, the officer may stay with a victim of family violence to protect the victim and allow the victim to take the personal property of the victim or of a child in the care of the victim to a place of safety in an orderly manner. A peace officer who provides this assistance cannot be held civilly liable for any act that occurs because of the assistance, or any act that occurs because the officer chose not to provide the assistance. *(B.B.)*

Art. 5.05. Reports and Records.

Summary: A peace officer who investigates a family violence incident or who responds to a disturbance call that may involve family violence shall make a written report (Family Violence Incident Report) and each agency shall establish a departmental code for identifying and retrieving such reports as well as establishing procedures to inform their officers of protective orders. A certified copy of a protective order is valid as proof of the protective order. *(B.B.)*

Art. 5.06. Duties of Prosecuting Attorneys and Courts.

Summary: Prosecuting attorneys and courts are prohibited from dismissing or delaying any family violence criminal proceeding because a civil proceeding is pending and from requiring proof that a party is involved in a suit affecting the parent-child relationship or a dissolution of a marriage prior to proceeding with the case. A prosecutor's decision to file a protective order should be made without regard to whether a criminal complaint has been filed. *(B.B.)*

Art. 5.07. Venue for Protective Order Offenses.

Summary: A criminal violation of a protective order can be prosecuted in either the county where the order was violated or the county where the order was issued. *(B.B.)*

Art. 5.08. Mediation in Family Violence Cases.

Summary: In a criminal prosecution arising from family violence, as defined by Family Code § 71.004, a court shall not refer or order the victim or the defendant involved to mediation, dispute resolution, arbitration, or other similar procedures. *(B.B.)*

Chapter 7A. Protective Order for Victim of Sexual Assault.

Summary: In 2003 the legislature expanded access to protective orders to include individuals who have been sexually assaulted but who do not meet the relationship requirements of consanguinity, marriage, dating or household currently required under Title 4, Family Code protective orders. The application may be filed: (1) by the victim, or a prosecutor on the victim's behalf; (2) in a district court, juvenile court having the jurisdiction of a district court, statutory county-court-at-law or in the constitutional county court. (Art. 7A.01)

If there is a "clear and present danger of sexual assault or other harm to the applicant" the court may enter a temporary ex parte order for the applicant and anyone in the applicant's family or household. (Art. 7A.02)

After a hearing on the application, the court must find whether there are reasonable grounds to believe that the applicant is a victim of sexual assault and the subject of a threat that reasonably placed the applicant in fear of further harm from the alleged offender. Upon making these findings, the court must issue a protective that includes a statement of the required findings. (Art. 7A.03)

The conditions that a court may impose on the perpetrator, the statutorily mandated warning language, and enforcement mechanisms track those authorized in a protective order under Title 4, Family Code. (Art. 7A.04–06) Violation of a condition of the sexual assault protective order is a Class A misdemeanor. § 38.112(c) Tex. Pen. Code.

Chapter 14. Arrest Without Warrant

Art. 14.03(a)(3). Authority of Peace Officer.

Summary: Even if the violation is not committed in the officer's view, an arrest without warrant may be made if the officer has probable cause to believe:

- a violation of protective order has occurred;
- an assault resulting in bodily injury to a member of a person's family or household has been committed;
- the offender has prevented or interfered with an individual's ability to place a telephone call in an emergency. *(B.B.)*

Chapter 17. Bail.

Art. 17.29. Accused Liberated.

Summary: Before an arrested family violence or stalking perpetrator can be released on bail, the agency holding the offender shall make a "reasonable attempt" to notify the victim or a designee of the impending release. At the time of arrest, the arresting officer shall collect the victim's address and telephone number (or a person designated by the victim), and pass this information along to the agency holding the perpetrator. *(B.B.)*

Art. 17.291. Further detention of certain persons.

(a) In this article:

(1) "family violence" has the meaning assigned to that phrase by Section 71.004, Family Code; and

(2) "magistrate" has the meaning assigned to it by Article 2.09 of this code.

(b) Article 17.29 does not apply when a person has been arrested or held without a warrant in the prevention of family violence if there is probable cause to believe the violence will continue if the person is immediately released. The head of the agency arresting or holding such a person may hold the person for a period of not more than four hours after bond has been posted. This detention period may be extended for an additional period not to exceed 48 hours, but only if authorized in a writing directed to the person having custody of the detained person by a magistrate who concludes that:

(1) the violence would continue if the person is released; and

(2) if the additional period exceeds 24 hours, probable cause exists to believe that the person committed the instant offense and that, during the 10-year period preceding the date of the instant offense, the person has been arrested:

(A) on more than one occasion for an offense involving family violence; or

(B) for any other offense, if a deadly weapon, as defined by Section 1.07, Penal Code, was used or exhibited during commission of the offense or during immediate flight after commission of the offense.

Comment

Immediate release of an accused is not mandated even after a bond has been posted if there is probable cause to believe that violence will continue on that immediate release. The arresting agency may hold such person for up to four additional hours after bond is posted. The defendant may be detained for up to 24 hours if a magistrate concludes that the violence would continue if the person is released immediately. As prescribed in subsection (b), that period can be extended up to 48 hours if one of two additional specified, albeit relatively complex, criteria is found to exist by the magistrate. *(B.B.)*

Art. 17.292. Magistrate's Order for Emergency Protection.

(a) At a defendant's appearance before a magistrate after arrest for an offense involving family violence or an offense under Section 42.072, Penal Code, the magistrate may issue an order for emergency protection on the magistrate's own motion or on the request of:

(1) the victim of the offense;

(2) the guardian of the victim;

(3) a peace officer; or

(4) the attorney representing the state.

(b) At a defendant's appearance before a magistrate after arrest for an offense involving family violence, the magistrate shall issue an order for emergency protection if the arrest is for an offense that also involves:

(1) serious bodily injury to the victim; or

(2) the use or exhibition of a deadly weapon during the commission of an assault.

(c) The magistrate in the order for emergency protection may prohibit the arrested party from:

(1) committing:

(A) family violence or an assault on the person protected under the order; or

(B) an act in furtherance of an offense under Section 42.072, Penal Code;

(2) communicating:

(A) directly with a member of the family or household or with the person protected under the order in a threatening or harassing manner; or

(B) a threat through any person to a member of the family or household or to the person protected under the order;

(3) going to or near:

(A) the residence, place of employment, or business of a member of the family or household or of the person protected under the order; or

(B) the residence, child care facility, or school where a child protected under the order resides or attends; or

(4) possessing a firearm, unless the person is a peace officer, as defined by Section 1.07, Penal Code, actively engaged in employment as a sworn, full-time paid employee of a state agency or political subdivision.

(d) The victim of the offense need not be present in court when the order for emergency protection is issued.

(e) In the order for emergency protection the magistrate shall specifically describe the prohibited locations and the minimum distances, if any, that the party must maintain, unless the magistrate determines for the safety of the person or persons protected by the order that specific descriptions of the locations should be omitted.

(f) To the extent that a condition imposed by an order for emergency protection issued under this article conflicts with an existing court order granting possession of or access to a child, the condition imposed under this article prevails for the duration of the order for emergency protection.

(f-1) To the extent that a condition imposed by an order issued under this article conflicts with a condition imposed by an order subsequently issued under Chapter 85, Subtitle B, Title 4, Family Code, or under Title 1 or Title 5, Family Code, the condition imposed by the order issued under the Family Code prevails.

(f-2) To the extent that a condition imposed by an order issued under this article conflicts with a condition imposed by an order subsequently issued under Chapter 83, Subtitle B, Title 4, Family Code, the condition imposed by the order issued under this article prevails unless the court issuing the order under Chapter 83, Family Code:

(1) is informed of the existence of the order issued under this article; and

(2) makes a finding in the order issued under Chapter 83, Family Code, that the court is superseding the order issued under this article.

(g) An order for emergency protection issued under this article must contain the following statements printed in bold-face type or in capital letters:

"A VIOLATION OF THIS ORDER BY COMMISSION OF AN ACT PROHIBITED BY THE ORDER MAY BE PUNISHABLE BY A FINE OF AS MUCH AS $4,000 OR BY CONFINEMENT IN JAIL FOR AS LONG AS ONE YEAR OR BY BOTH. AN ACT THAT RESULTS IN FAMILY VIOLENCE OR A STALKING OFFENSE MAY BE PROSECUTED AS A SEPARATE MISDEMEANOR OR FELONY OFFENSE. IF THE ACT IS PROSECUTED AS A SEPARATE FELONY OFFENSE, IT IS PUNISHABLE BY CONFINEMENT IN PRISON FOR AT LEAST TWO YEARS. THE POSSESSION OF A FIREARM BY A PERSON, OTHER THAN A PEACE OFFICER, AS DEFINED BY SECTION 1.07, PENAL CODE, ACTIVELY ENGAGED IN EMPLOYMENT AS A SWORN, FULL-TIME PAID EMPLOYEE OF A STATE AGENCY OR POLITICAL SUBDIVISION, WHO IS SUBJECT TO THIS ORDER MAY BE PROSECUTED AS A SEPARATE OFFENSE PUNISHABLE BY CONFINEMENT OR IMPRISONMENT.

"NO PERSON, INCLUDING A PERSON WHO IS PROTECTED BY THIS ORDER, MAY GIVE PERMISSION TO ANYONE TO IGNORE OR VIOLATE ANY PROVISION OF THIS ORDER. DURING THE TIME IN WHICH THIS ORDER IS VALID, EVERY PROVISION OF THIS ORDER IS IN FULL FORCE AND EFFECT UNLESS A COURT CHANGES THE ORDER."

(h) The magistrate issuing an order for emergency protection under this article shall send a copy of the order to the chief of police in the municipality where the member of the family or household or individual protected by the order resides, if the person resides in a municipality, or to the sheriff of the county where the person resides, if the person does not reside in a municipality. If the victim of the offense is not present when the order is issued, the magistrate issuing the order shall order an appropriate peace officer to make a good faith effort to notify, within 24 hours, the victim that the order has been issued by calling the victim's residence and place of employment. The clerk of the court shall send a copy of the order to the victim.

(i) If an order for emergency protection issued under this article prohibits a person from going to or near a child care facility or school, the magistrate shall send a copy of the order to the child care facility or school.

(j) An order for emergency protection issued under this article is effective on issuance, and the defendant shall be served a copy of the order in open court. An order for emergency protection issued under this article remains in effect up to the 61st day but not less than 31 days after the date of issuance. **After notice to each affected party**

and a hearing, the issuing court may modify all or part of an order issued under this article if the court finds that:

(1) the order as originally issued is unworkable;

(2) the modification will not place the victim of the offense at greater risk than did the original order; and

(3) the modification will not in any way endanger a person protected under the order.

(k) To ensure that an officer responding to a call is aware of the existence and terms of an order for emergency protection issued under this article, each municipal police department and sheriff shall establish a procedure within the department or office to provide adequate information or access to information for peace officers of the names of persons protected by an order for emergency protection issued under this article and of persons to whom the order is directed. The police department or sheriff may enter an order for emergency protection issued under this article in the department's or office's record of outstanding warrants as notice that the order has been issued and is in effect.

(l) In the order for emergency protection, the magistrate may suspend a license to carry a concealed handgun issued under Section 411.177, Government Code, that is held by the defendant.

(m) In this article:

(1) "Family," "family violence," and "household" have the meanings assigned by Chapter 71, Family Code.

(2) "Firearm" has the meaning assigned by Chapter 46, Penal Code.

(n) On motion, notice, and hearing, or on agreement of the parties, an order for emergency protection issued under this article may be transferred to the court assuming jurisdiction over the criminal act giving rise to the issuance of the emergency order for protection. On transfer, the criminal court may modify all or part of an order issued under this subsection in the same manner and under the same standards as the issuing court under Subsection (j).

History: Amended by 78th Legis., Reg. Sess. (2003), H.B. 297, eff. Sept. 1, 2003, and "applies only to an order for emergency protection issued under Article 17.292, Code of Criminal Procedure, as amended by this Act, on or after that date."

Comment

In 1995 a new "protective order" was created to deal with emergency situations. It was specifically designed to provide a summary order at a defendant's appearance before a magistrate after arrest for a family violence offense of stalking. The Magistrate's Order is criminally enforceable similar to the Title 4 protective order, but originally it was valid for only 31 days. Both the 1997 and 1999 sessions saw amendments to strengthen and clarify the statute. It is now clear that the statute applies to both family relationships and victims of stalking, for which a family relationship is not required. Further, the emergency protection may be extended to 61 days.

CLE/Other Legal Publications

Family violence. (Workshop) 2003 Adv. Fam. L.

In the crossfire: protective orders, what happens when federal law collides with family law (VAWA and Brady) and how magistrate orders impact family law litigation. Lorraine Wilson, 2001 Adv. Fam. L.

Leading Case

In re Salgado, 53 S.W.3d 752 (Tex. App.—El Paso 2001, no pet.) (in realm of family violence magistrate's protective order supersedes any other orders for conservatorship or possession of child for duration of order)

Cross Reference

Tex. Pen. Code Ann. §§ 42.07. Harassment; 42.072. Stalking, *infra*.

Art. 17.293. Delivery of Order for Emergency Protection to Other Persons.

The magistrate or the clerk of the magistrate's court issuing an order for emergency protection under Article 17.292 that suspends a license to carry a concealed handgun shall immediately send a copy of the order to the appropriate division of the Department of Public Safety at its Austin headquarters. On receipt of the order suspending the license, the department shall:

(1) record the suspension of the license in the records of the department;

(2) report the suspension to local law enforcement agencies, as appropriate; and

(3) demand surrender of the suspended license from the license holder.

Chapter 42. Judgment and Sentence.

Art. 42.23. Notification of Court of Family Violence Conviction.

Summary: If a prosecutor learns that a defendant is subject to the jurisdiction of another court relating to an order that provides for conservatorship, possession or access to a child, the prosecutor must notify the court in which the defendant is being tried of the existence of the order and court of continuing jurisdiction. The criminal court must notify the court of continuing jurisdiction of a conviction or entry of an order deferring adjudication. *(B.B.)*

Chapter 56. Rights of Crime Victims.

Art. 56.11. Notification to Victim of Release or Escape of Defendant.

Summary: The Texas Department of Criminal Justice or the sheriff must give notice to the victim and local law enforcement of the release or escape of a defendant convicted of an offense involving family violence, stalking, or violation of a protective order or magistrate's order. *(B.B.)*

Art. 56.42. Payment of Relocation Expenses for Victim.

Summary: A victim of family violence or sexual assault occurring at the victim's place of residence may receive a single assistance payment in an amount not to $2,000 to be used for relocation expenses; including expenses for rental deposit, utility connections, expenses relating to the moving of belongings, motor vehicle mileage expenses, and for out-of-state moves, transportation, lodging, and meals; and $1,800 to be used for housing rental expenses. *(B.B.)*

Texas Government Code

Title 2. Judicial Branch

Chapter 74. Court Administration Act

§ 74.053. Objection to Judge Assigned to a Trial Court.

(a) When a judge is assigned **to a trial court** under this chapter:

(1) the order of assignment must state whether the judge is an active, former, retired, or senior judge; and

(2) the presiding judge shall, if it is reasonable and practicable and if time permits, give notice of the assignment to each attorney representing a party to the case that is to be heard in whole or part by the assigned judge.

(b) If a party to a civil case files a timely objection to the assignment, the judge shall not hear the case. Except as provided by Subsection (d), each party to the case is only entitled to one objection under this section for that case.

(c) An objection under this section must be filed **not later than the seventh day after the date the party receives actual notice of the assignment or** before the **date the** first hearing or trial, including pretrial hearings, **commences, whichever date occurs earlier. The presiding judge may extend the time to file an objection under this section on written motion by a party who demonstrates good cause** [~~over which the assigned judge is to preside~~].

(d) **An assigned** [~~A former~~] judge or justice who was **defeated in the last primary or general election for which the judge or justice was a candidate for the judicial office held by the judge or justice** [~~not a retired judge~~] may not sit in a case if either party objects to the judge or justice.

(e) An active judge assigned under this chapter is not subject to an objection.

(f) For purposes of this section, notice of an assignment may be given and an objection to an assignment may be filed by electronic mail.

(g) In this section, "party" includes multiple parties aligned in a case as determined by the presiding judge.

History: Amended by 78th Legis., Reg. Sess. (2003), H.B. 3306, eff. June 18, 2003, and "applies only to a case that is pending or commences on or after the effective date of this Act."

CLE/Other Legal Publications

Those other Texas codes—things the family lawyer needs to know about codifications outside the Family Code. Richard R. Orsinger, 2004 ADV. FAM. L.

Object—recuse—disqualify: I want a new judge. William W. Harris, 2002 ADV. FAM. L.

Leading Cases

In re Naylor, 120 S.W.3d 498 (Tex. App.—Texarkana 2003) (judge has discretionary right to recuse himself in absence of statutory duty to do so; untimely objection to assigned judge irrelevant)

In re Canales, 52 S.W.3d 698 (Tex. 2001) (plaintiff required to object to visiting judge's appointment before he presided over any pretrial hearings, without regard to terms of particular order under which judge was assigned)

Dunn v. Street, 938 S.W.2d 33 (Tex. 1997) (visiting judge abused discretion by issuing show cause order after sustaining timely objection to his sitting)

Flores v. Banner, 932 S.W.2d 500 (Tex. 1996) (visiting judge abused discretion by refusing to disqualify himself after timely objection to any "former judge")

In re Flores, 53 S.W.3d 428 (Tex. App.—San Antonio 2001, no pet.) (presiding judge who receives plaintiff's motion for recusal of trial judge not "assigned" judge subject to recusal)

Bourgeois v. Collier, 959 S.W.2d 241 (Tex. App.—Dallas 1997, no writ) (recusal mandatory; visiting judge who presided by general assignment over contempt proceeding lacked authority, without special assignment, to preside over merits trial)

Mercer v. Driver, 923 S.W.2d 656 (Tex. App.—Houston [1st Dist.] 1995, orig. proceeding) (disqualification of visiting judge assigned to hear motion to recuse another judge from custody proceeding mandatory)

Wolfe v. Wolfe, 918 S.W.2d 533 (Tex. App.—El Paso 1996, writ denied); Morris v. Short, 902 S.W.2d 566 (Tex. App.—Houston [1st Dist.] 1995, writ denied) (objection to visiting judge untimely, not first matter presented for ruling—motion for continuance previously ruled on)

Kellogg v. Martin, 810 S.W.2d 302 (Tex. App.—Texarkana 1991, no writ) (grandparents with standing in [DPRS] termination suit had standing to object to judge assignment)

Ex parte Holland, 807 S.W.2d 827(Tex. App.—Dallas 1991, dism. w.o.j.) (assignment of visiting judge to hear modification of child support expired with final order—new assignment to preside over contempt motion subject of proper objection)

Title 8. Public Retirement Systems

Chapter 804. Domestic Relations Orders and Spousal Consent

Subchapter A. Qualified Domestic Relations Orders

Subchapter B. Spousal Consent Requirements

Subchapter C. Termination of Interest in Public Retirement System

CLE/Other Legal Publications

See the annotations to Tex. Fam. Code Ann. § 7.003, *supra.*

Those other Texas codes—things the family lawyer needs to know about codifications outside the Family Code. Richard R. Orsinger, 2004 Adv. Fam. L.

Handling the state retirement plans: teacher retirement, county and district retirement, and state employment retirement, including survivor benefits. Curtis M. Loveless, 2001 Adv. Fam. L.

Leading Cases

Kunin v. Feofanov, 69 F.3d 59 (5th Cir. 1995) (Texas statute terminating nonemployee spouse's interest in public pension at death did not violate prohibition against transforming community property into separate property)

Sanderlin v. Sanderlin, 929 S.W.2d 121 (Tex. App.—San Antonio 1996, pet. denied) (divorce decree provision stating wife "divested of all right, title, interest and claim" to the benefits extinguished any rights she may have had under prior beneficiary designation)

Conti v. Conti, 866 S.W.2d 671 (Tex. App.—Houston [14th Dist.] 1993, writ denied) (court properly clarified and enforced divorce decree to meet requirements for QDRO)

Irving Fireman's Relief and Retirement Fund v. Sears, 803 S.W.2d 747 (Tex. App.—Dallas 1990, no writ) (public retirement funds not exempt from divorce court order requiring direct payment of benefits to member's former wife—fund can be sued directly if trustees chose not to elect coverage under this chapter)

Subchapter A. Qualified Domestic Relations Orders

§ 804.001. Definitions.

In this chapter:

(1) "Alternate payee" means a spouse, former spouse, child, or other dependent of a member or retiree who is recognized by a domestic relations order as having a right to receive all or a portion of the benefits payable by a public retirement system with respect to such member or retiree.

(2) "Domestic relations order" means any judgment, decree, or order, including approval of a property settlement agreement, which relates to the provision of child support, alimony payments, or marital property rights to a spouse, former spouse, child, or other dependent of a member or retiree, and is made pursuant to a domestic relations law, including a community property law of the State of Texas or of another state.

(3) "Public retirement system" means the Employees Retirement System of Texas, the Judicial Retirement System of Texas Plan One, the Judicial Retirement System of Texas Plan Two, the Teacher Retirement System of Texas, the Texas County and District Retirement System, the Texas Municipal Retirement System, and any other continuing, organized program of service retirement, disability retirement, or death benefits for officers or employees of the state or a political subdivision or of an agency or instrumentality of the state or a political subdivision and includes the optional retirement program governed by Chapter 830. Public retirement system does not include:

(A) a program, other than the optional retirement program, for which benefits are administered by a life insurance company;

(B) a program providing only workers' compensation benefits;

(C) a program administered by the federal government;

(D) an individual retirement account or individual retirement annuity within the meaning of Section 408, or a retirement bond within the meaning of Section 409, of the Internal Revenue Code of 1986;

(E) a plan described by Subsection (d) of Section 401 of the Internal Revenue Code of 1986;

(F) a group or an individual account plan consisting of an annuity contract described by Subsection (b) of Section 403 of the Internal Revenue Code of 1986, other than a 403(b) contract or plan under the optional retirement program;

(G) an eligible state deferred compensation plan described by Subsection (b) of Section 457 of the Internal Revenue Code of 1986; or

(H) the program established by Chapter 615.

(4) "Qualified domestic relations order" means a domestic relations order which creates or recognizes the existence of an alternate payee's right or assigns to an alternate payee the right to receive all or a portion of the benefits payable with respect to a member or retiree under a public retirement system, which directs the public retirement system to disburse benefits to the alternate payee, and which meets the requirements of Section 804.003.

(5) "Statewide retirement system" means the Employees Retirement System of Texas, the Judicial Retirement System of Texas Plan One, the Judicial Retirement System of Texas Plan Two, the Teacher Retirement System of Texas, the Texas County and District Retirement System, or the Texas Municipal Retirement System.

§ 804.002. Application of Chapters.

This subchapter and Subchapter C apply to each statewide retirement system and to the optional retirement program governed by Chapter 830. This subchapter and Subchapter C also apply to each other public retirement system for which the board of trustees of the system elects to adopt the provisions of this subchapter and Subchapter C. An election under this section must be by order or resolution and need not set out the text of this subchapter or Subchapter C. A board of trustees may not elect to adopt only this subchapter or Subchapter C.

§ 804.003. Qualified Domestic Relations Orders.

(a) Sections 811.005, 821.005, 831.004, 836.004, 841.006, and 851.006 and any similar antialienation provisions contained in any other public retirement system shall apply to the creation, assignment, recognition, or enforcement of a right to any benefit payable with respect to a member or retiree of a public retirement system to which the section applies pursuant to a domestic relations order unless the order is determined to be a qualified domestic relations order.

(b) Except as provided in Subsection (d), the administrative head of a public retirement system to which this chapter applies and to which a domestic relations order is submitted or his designee has exclusive authority to determine whether a domestic relations order is a qualified domestic relations order. A determination by the administrative head or his designee under this section may be appealed only to the board of trustees of the public retirement system. An appeal to the board of trustees of a statewide retirement system is a contested case under Chapter 2001. However, the board of a statewide retirement system by rule may waive the requirement of an appeal to the board. On appeal of a decision made by the board of trustees or by the administrative head if there is no appeal to the board under this section, the standard of review is by substantial evidence.

(c) Except as provided in Subsection (d), a court does not have jurisdiction over a public retirement system to which this chapter applies with respect to a divorce or other domestic relations action in which an alternate payee's right to receive all or a portion of the benefits payable to a member or retiree under the public retirement system is created or established. A party to such an action who attempts to make a public retirement system a party to the action contrary to the provision of this subsection shall be liable to the public retirement system for its costs and attorney's fees.

(d) Under the optional retirement program, applicable carriers shall determine whether a domestic relations order is a qualified domestic relations order. If a dispute arises over the determination of whether a domestic relations order is a qualified domestic relations order which cannot be resolved by the procedure described in Subsection (g), the court which issued the order or which otherwise has jurisdiction over the matter shall resolve the dispute with respect to a divorce or other domestic relations action in which an alternate payee's right to receive all or a portion of the benefits payable to a member or retiree under the optional retirement program is created or established.

(e) For the purposes of this section, benefits payable with respect to a member or retiree under the retirement system include the types of benefits payable by a public retirement system and a withdrawal of contributions from a public retirement system.

(f) A domestic relations order is a qualified domestic relations order only if such order:

(1) clearly specifies the name, social security number, and last known mailing address, if any, of the member or retiree and the name, social security number, and mailing address of each alternate payee covered by the order;

(2) clearly specifies the amount or percentage of the member's or retiree's benefits to be paid by a public retirement system to each such alternate payee or the manner in which such amount or percentage is to be determined;

(3) clearly specifies the number of payments or the period to which such order applies;

(4) clearly specifies that such order applies to a designated public retirement system;

(5) does not require the public retirement system to provide any type or form of benefit or any option not otherwise provided under the plan;

(6) does not require the public retirement system to provide increased benefits determined on the basis of actuarial value;

(7) does not require the payment of benefits to an alternate payee which are required to be paid to another alternate payee under another order previously determined to be a qualified domestic relations order; and

(8) does not require the payment of benefits to an alternate payee before the retirement of a member, the distribution of a withdrawal of contributions to a member, or other distribution to a member required by law.

(g) A public retirement system may reject a domestic relations order as a qualified domestic relations order unless the order:

(1) provides for a proportional reduction of the amount awarded to an alternate payee in the event of the retirement of the member before normal retirement age;

(2) does not purport to require the designation of a particular person as the recipient of benefits in the event of a member's or annuitant's death;

(3) does not purport to require the selection of a particular benefit payment plan or option;

(4) provides clearly for each possible benefit distribution under plan provisions;

(5) does not require any action on the part of the retirement system contrary to its governing statutes or plan provision other than the direct payment of the benefit awarded to an alternate payee;

(6) does not make the award of an interest contingent on any condition other than those conditions resulting in the liability of a retirement system for payments under its plan provisions;

(7) does not purport to award any future benefit increases that are provided or required by the legislature; and

(8) provides for a proportional reduction of the amount awarded to an alternate payee in the event that benefits available to the retiree or member are reduced by law.

(h) The administrative head of a public retirement system to which this chapter applies or his designee (or applicable carrier, if under the optional retirement program), upon receipt of a certified copy of a domestic relations order, shall determine whether such order is a qualified domestic relations order and shall notify the member or retiree and each alternate payee of such determination. If the order is determined to be a qualified domestic relations order, the public retirement system (or applicable carrier, if under the optional retirement program), shall pay benefits in accordance with the order. If the order is determined not to be a qualified domestic relations order, the member or retiree or any alternate payee named in the order may appeal the administrative head's determination in the manner specified in Subsection (b) or the optional retirement program carrier's determination in the manner specified in Subsection (d) and may petition the court which issued the order to amend the order so that it will be qualified. The court which issued the order or which would otherwise have jurisdiction over the matter has jurisdiction to amend the order so that it will be qualified even though all other matters incident to the action or proceeding have been fully and finally adjudicated.

(i) During any period in which the issue of whether a domestic relations order is a qualified domestic relations order is being determined by the agency administrative head, his designee, the board of trustees, a court of competent jurisdiction, optional retirement program carrier, or otherwise, the public retirement system shall separately account for the amounts, in this section referred to as the "segregated amounts," which would have been payable to the alternate payee during such period if the order had been determined to be a qualified domestic relations order.

(j) If a domestic relations order is determined to be a qualified domestic relations order, then the public retirement system (or applicable carrier, if under the optional retirement program) shall pay the segregated amounts without interest to the person or persons entitled thereto and shall thereafter pay benefits pursuant to the order.

(k) If a domestic relations order is determined not to be a qualified domestic relations order or if within 18 months of the date a domestic relations order is received by the public retirement system (or applicable carrier, if under the optional retirement program) the issue as to whether such order is a qualified domestic relations order is not resolved, then the public retirement system (or applicable carrier, if under the optional retirement program) shall pay the segregated amounts without interest and shall thereafter pay benefits to the person or persons who would have been entitled to such amounts if there had been no order. This subsection shall not be construed to limit or otherwise affect any liability, responsibility, or duty of a party with respect to any other party to the action out of which the order arose.

(l) Any determination that an order is a qualified domestic relations order which is made after the close of the 18-month period shall be applied prospectively only.

(m) The public retirement system, the board of trustees, and officers and employees of the public retirement system (or applicable carrier, if under the optional retirement program) shall not be liable to any person for making payments of any benefits in accordance with a domestic relations order in a cause in which a member or a retiree was a party or for making payments in accordance with Subsection (k).

(n) The board of trustees of a public retirement system may promulgate rules it deems necessary to implement the provisions of this section.

(o) Except as specifically provided in this subtitle or by any other statute, public employment does not confer special privileges or immunities on a public employee. An ownership or beneficial interest in any retirement, pension, or other financial plan not included in the definition of "public retirement system" as set forth in Section 804.001 held in whole or in part by an officer or employee of the state or a political subdivision or of an agency or an instrumentality of either, whether obtained in connection with that employment or otherwise, shall be subject to the requirements of the federal laws governing qualified domestic relations orders.

§ 804.004. Life Annuity or Lump-Sum Payment in Lieu of Benefits Awarded by a Qualified Domestic Relations Order.

(a) The board of trustees of a public retirement system to which this chapter applies may by rule provide that, in lieu of paying an alternate beneficiary the interest awarded by a qualified domestic relations order, the system may pay the alternate beneficiary an amount that is the actuarial equivalent of such interest in the form of:

(1) an annuity payable in equal monthly installments for the life of the alternate payee; or

(2) a lump sum.

(b) The determination of whether to pay an amount authorized by this section in lieu of the interest awarded by the qualified domestic relations order shall be at the sole discretion of the public retirement system.

(c) If a public retirement system elects to pay the alternate payee pursuant to this section, the benefit payable by the system to the member, retiree, or beneficiary shall be reduced by the interest in the benefit awarded to the alternate payee by the qualified domestic relations order.

(d) If the public retirement system pays the alternate payee pursuant to this section, the retirement system shall be entitled to rely on a beneficiary designation or benefit option selection made or changed pursuant to its plan without regard to any domestic relations order.

§ 804.005. Payment in Certain Circumstances in Lieu of Benefits Awarded by Qualified Domestic Relations Order.

(a) This section applies only to the Employees Retirement System of Texas and the Teacher Retirement System of Texas.

(b) A public retirement system to which this section applies shall pay an alternate payee of a member of the retirement system who is described by Subsection (c), if the alternate payee so elects and in lieu of the interest awarded by a qualified domestic relations order on or after January 1, 1985, an amount that is the alternate payee's portion of the actuarial equivalent of the accrued retirement benefit of the member of the retirement system, determined as if the member retired on the date of the alternate payee's election. The amount becomes payable at the time the actuarial equivalent is determined, and the amount is payable in the form of an annuity payable in equal monthly installments for the life of the alternate payee.

(c) A member whose benefits are subject to partial payment under this section is one who has not retired from the retirement system, has attained the greater of the age of

62 or normal retirement age and the service requirements for service retirement, and retains credit and contributions in the retirement system attributable to that service.

(d) If an alternate payee elects to be paid under this section, the retirement system shall reduce the benefit payable by the system to the member or the member's beneficiary by the alternate payee's portion of the actuarial equivalent determined under Subsection (b).

(e) In determining under Subsection (b) the actuarial equivalent of an accrued retirement benefit, the system shall consider the member's benefit as a normal age standard service retirement annuity, without regard to any optional annuity chosen or beneficiary designated by the member.

(f) The beginning of monthly payments under this section terminates any interest that the alternate payee who receives the payment might otherwise have in benefits that accrue to the account of the member after the date the initial payment to the alternate payee is made.

(g) A public retirement system may adopt rules for administration of this section.

Subchapter B. Spousal Consent Requirements

§ 804.051. Authority to Require Spousal Consent.

A public retirement system may adopt rules to require spousal consent for the selection of a service retirement annuity other than a joint and survivor annuity that pays benefits to the member's spouse on the death of the member or for the selection of a death benefits plan that pays benefits in the form of an annuity to a person other than the member's spouse on the death of the member.

Subchapter C. Termination of Interest in Public Retirement System

§ 804.101. Termination of Interest in Public Retirement System.

The death of an alternate payee as defined in Section 804.001 or the death of a spouse of a member or retiree of a public retirement system to which this chapter applies shall terminate the interest of the alternate payee or spouse in that public retirement system. This section shall not affect an interest in a public retirement system accrued to an individual as a member of the public retirement system.

Texas Penal Code

★★★

Editors' Note: *Family law practitioners regularly encounter issues of "family violence" and find it necessary to make reference to Title 4 of the Family Code. Many fact situations also implicate related sections of the Texas Code of Criminal Procedure and the Texas Penal Code. These statutes are often not a part of the practice of our readership and are unfamiliar to them. In this chapter we intend to provide a quick reference to some of the relevant provisions without going into excessive detail. To this end, most of the statutory citations are briefly summarized, rather than being set forth in full text. Provisions of special significance are provided in full.*

Throughout this chapter guest commentary is provided by Bree Buchanan, Children's Rights Clinic, University of Texas School of Law, and former Public Policy Director, Texas Council on Family Violence, 1998–2002, identified as (B.B.).

CLE/Other Legal Publications

Crime and immigration. Lee J. Ter?n, 2004 U. TEX. FAM. L. ON THE BORDER

The impact of criminal law on Texas family law practice. Joe Marr Wilson, 2003 ADV. FAM. L.

Criminal law and the family practice. Barbara D. Nunneley & J.C. Ball, 2002 ADV. FAM. L.

In the Crossfire: protective orders, what happens when federal law collides with family law (VAWA and Brady) and how magistrate orders impact family law litigation. Lorraine Wilson, 2001 ADV. FAM. L.

What every family law lawyer needs to know about criminal law. E. Lee Gabriel & Margaret E. Barnes, 2000 MARRIAGE DISSOLUTION

Chapter 12. Punishments

§ 12.23. Class C Misdemeanor.

Summary: Punishment is a maximum fine of $500. *(B.B.)*

---

§ 12.22. Class B Misdemeanor.

Summary: Punishment is a maximum of 180 days in jail and/or a maximum $2,000 fine. *(B.B.)*

---

§ 12.21. Class A Misdemeanor.

Summary: Punishment is a maximum of one year in jail and/or maximum $4,000 fine. If previously convicted of a Class A misdemeanor (§ 12.43), punishment is confinement in jail for 90 days up to one year, and/or a maximum fine of $4,000. *(B.B.)*

---

§ 12.35. State Jail Felony.

Summary: Punishment is 180 days to a maximum of two years in a state jail and/or a maximum $10,000 fine. *(B.B.)*

---

§ 12.34. Third Degree Felony.

Summary: Punishment is confinement in a community correctional facility for maximum of one year, or confinement in a state prison for 2–10 years, and a potential maximum fine of $10,000. *(B.B.)*

---

§ 12.33. Second Degree Felony.

Summary: Punishment is confinement in a state prison for 2–20 years and a potential maximum fine of $10,000. *(B.B.)*

---

§ 12.32. First Degree Felony.

Summary: Punishment is confinement in a state prison for 5–99 years, or for life, and a potential maximum fine of $10,000. *(B.B.)*

---

§ 12.42. Penalties for Repeat and Habitual Felony Offenders.

Summary: 1997 amendments deleted the sex offender "three strikes" language added in 1995 and replaced it with a "two strikes" provision.

A defendant convicted of sexual assault, aggravated sexual assault, aggravated kidnapping with intent to sexually abuse, or burglary with intent to commit a sex offense, shall be punished with life in prison if that defendant has one prior conviction for sexual performance by a child, child pornography, indecency with a child, sexual assault, aggravated sexual assault, prohibited sexual conduct, aggravated kidnapping with intent to sexually abuse, burglary with intent to commit a sex offense, or for any offense under the laws of another state with elements substantially similar to those listed here. Under this "two strikes" provision, a community supervision or deferred adjudication counts as a prior conviction for enhancement purposes. *(B.B.)*

Chapter 22. Assaultive Offenses

§ 22.01. Assault.

Summary: A person commits an offense if the person.

- intentionally, knowingly, or recklessly causes bodily injury to another, including the person's spouse;
- intentionally or knowingly threatens another with imminent bodily injury, including the person's spouse; or
- intentionally or knowingly causes physical contact with another when the person knows or should reasonably believe that the other will regard the contact as offensive or provocative.

An offense under Subsection (a)(1) is a Class A misdemeanor.

Beginning in 1999, an assault is punishable as a felony of the third degree if the offense was committed against a family member and the defendant has been previously convicted of an offense against a member of the defendant's family or household. Deferred adjudication counts as the first offense. Previously the third conviction was only a state jail felony. *(B.B.)*

---

§ 22.011. Sexual Assault of Adults and Children.

Summary: The 78th Legislature clarified that sexual assault of males, as well as females, is punishable under this section. An offense under this section is a second-degree felony. Sexual assault of a child includes the actor causing the mouth of a child to contact the anus or sexual organ of another person, including the actor. *(B.B.)*

---

§ 22.02. Aggravated Assault.

Summary: This section defines aggravated assault as an assault that causes serious bodily injury to another or where a deadly weapon is used or exhibited during an assault. An offense under this section is a second-degree felony, and it becomes a first-degree felony if the offense is committed in retaliation against a witness, prospective witness, informant, public servant or person who has reported the occurrence of a crime. *(B.B.)*

---

§ 22.021. Aggravated Sexual Assault of Adults.

Summary: An aggravated sexual assault is a sexual assault in which the following also occurs: serious bodily injury or an attempt to cause death which places the victim in fear that death, serious bodily injury, or kidnapping of any person will occur; or in which a deadly weapon is exhibited during the same criminal episode. An offense under this section is a first-degree felony.

For aggravated sexual assault of a child, only contact with the actor's anus or sexual organ is required, along with the above aggravated circumstances. *(B.B.)*

---

§ 22.07. Terroristic Threat.

Summary: In 2003 the legislature enhanced the offense of terroristic threat from a Class B misdemeanor to a Class A if the offense is committed against a member of the person's family or household or otherwise constitutes family violence. *(B.B.)*

Chapter 25. Offenses Against the Family

§ 25.01. Bigamy.

(a) An individual commits an offense if:

(1) he is legally married and he:

(A) purports to marry or does marry a person other than his spouse in this state, or any other state or foreign country, under circumstances that would, but for the actor's prior marriage, constitute a marriage; or

(B) lives with a person other than his spouse in this state under the appearance of being married; or

(2) he knows that a married person other than his spouse is married and he:

(A) purports to marry or does marry that person in this state, or any other state or foreign country, under circumstances that would, but for the person's prior marriage, constitute a marriage; or

(B) lives with that person in this state under the appearance of being married.

(b) For purposes of this section, "under the appearance of being married" means holding out that the parties are married with cohabitation and an intent to be married by either party.

(c) It is a defense to prosecution under Subsection (a)(1) that the actor reasonably believed that his marriage was void or had been dissolved by death, divorce, or annulment.

(d) For the purposes of this section, the lawful wife or husband of the actor may testify both for or against the actor concerning proof of the original marriage.

(e) An offense under this section is a Class A misdemeanor.

§ 25.02. Prohibited Sexual Conduct.

(a) An individual commits an offense if he engages in sexual intercourse or deviate sexual intercourse with a person he knows to be, without regard to legitimacy:

(1) his ancestor or descendant by blood or adoption;

(2) his stepchild or stepparent, while the marriage creating that relationship exists;

(3) his parent's brother or sister of the whole or half blood;

(4) his brother or sister of the whole or half blood or by adoption; or

(5) the children of his brother or sister of the whole or half blood or by adoption.

(b) For purposes of this section:

(1) "Deviate sexual intercourse" means any contact between the genitals of one person and the mouth or anus of another person with intent to arouse or gratify the sexual desire of any person.

(2) "Sexual intercourse" means any penetration of the female sex organ by the male sex organ.

(c) An offense under this section is a felony of the third degree.

§ 25.03. Interference With Child Custody.

(a) A person commits an offense if the person takes or retains a child younger than 18 years when the person:

(1) knows that the person's taking or retention violates the express terms of a judgment or order of a court disposing of the child's custody; or

(2) has not been awarded custody of the child by a court of competent jurisdiction, knows that a suit for divorce or a civil suit or application for habeas corpus to dispose of the child's custody has been filed, and takes the child out of the geographic area of the counties composing the judicial district if the court is a district court or the county if the court is a statutory county court, without the permission of the court and with the intent to deprive the court of authority over the child.

(b) A noncustodial parent commits an offense if, with the intent to interfere with the lawful custody of a child younger than 18 years, the noncustodial parent knowingly entices or persuades the child to leave the custody of the custodial parent, guardian, or person standing in the stead of the custodial parent or guardian of the child.

(c) It is a defense to prosecution under Subsection (a)(2) that the actor returned the child to the geographic area of the counties composing the judicial district if the court is a district court or the county if the court is a statutory county court, within three days after the date of the commission of the offense.

(d) An offense under this section is a state jail felony.

Leading Cases

Ex parte Rhodes, 974 S.W.2d 735 (Tex. Crim. App. 1998) (double jeopardy clause barred prosecution interference with child custody due to previous criminal contempt conviction based on same conduct)

Roberts v. State, 619 S.W.2d 161 (Tex. Crim. App. 1981) (retaining child outside Texas in violation of valid court order gives Texas jurisdiction to prosecute under statute)

Schier v. State, 60 S.W.3d 340 (Tex. App.—Houston [14th Dist.] 2001, pet. ref'd) (evidence of negative conditions in mother's home failed to establish father's "necessity defense" because he did not show child threatened with imminent harm)

Ex parte Jones, 36 S.W.3d 139 (Tex. App.—Houston [1st Dist.] 2000, pet. ref'd) (successful coercive contempt punishment that forced return of child is not double jeopardy bar to subsequent prosecution for interference with custody)

Smith v. State, 874 S.W.2d 269 (Tex. App.—Houston [14th Dist.] 1994, pet. denied) (necessity defense refuted—no justification to keep children out of U.S. for over seven years regardless of what danger they were in before abduction)

Briggs v. State, 807 S.W.2d 648 (Tex. App.—Houston [1st Dist.] 1991, pet. ref'd) (parent and stepparent knew they were violating temporary order when they removed child from shelter)

Perry v. State, 727 S.W.2d 781 (Tex. App.—Austin 1987, pet. ref'd) (mother knowingly retained custody after visitation ended; allegedly ambiguous order regarding transportation costs not sufficient excuse)

---

§ 25.031. Agreement to Abduct From Custody.

(a) A person commits an offense if the person agrees, for remuneration or the promise of remuneration, to abduct a child younger than 18 years of age by force, threat of force, misrepresentation, stealth, or unlawful entry, knowing that the child is under the care and control of a person having custody or physical possession of the child under a court order or under the care and control of another person who is exercising care and control with the consent of a person having custody or physical possession under a court order.

(b) An offense under this section is a state jail felony.

§ 25.04. Enticing a Child.

(a) A person commits an offense if, with the intent to interfere with the lawful custody of a child younger than 18 years, he knowingly entices, persuades, or takes the child from the custody of the parent or guardian or person standing in the stead of the parent or guardian of such child.

(b) An offense under this section is a Class B misdemeanor, unless it is shown on the trial of the offense that the actor intended to commit a felony against the child, in which event an offense under this section is a felony of the third degree.

Leading Case

Davis v. State, 736 S.W.2d 217 (Tex. App.—Corpus Christi 1987, no writ) (child's adoptive father convicted for enticing, nothing in legislative history indicates intent to exclude custody or visitation disputes from application of statute)

---

§ 25.05. Criminal Nonsupport.

(a) An individual commits an offense if the individual intentionally or knowingly fails to provide support for the individual's child younger than 18 years of age, or for the individual's child who is the subject of a court order requiring the individual to support the child.

(b) For purposes of this section, "child" includes a child born out of wedlock whose paternity has either been acknowledged by the actor or has been established in a civil suit under the Family Code or the law of another state.

(c) Under this section, a conviction may be had on the uncorroborated testimony of a party to the offense.

(d) It is an affirmative defense to prosecution under this section that the actor could not provide support for the actor's child.

(e) The pendency of a prosecution under this section does not affect the power of a court to enter an order for child support under the Family Code.

(f) An offense under this section is a state jail felony.

Comment

Before the Office of the Attorney General became the state's IV–D agency, local prosecutors were an integral part of the child support establishment and enforcement system in Texas. One remedy to combat nonpayment was this statute, which was often filed and sometimes pursued. It remains on the books, but is now employed very infrequently.

Leading Cases

Williams v. State, 114 S.W.3d 920 (Tex. Crim. App. 2003) (parent could be sentenced for two years; stipulated failure to pay child support committed when offense state jail felony)

State v. Paiz, 817 S.W.2d 84 (Tex. Crim. App. 1991) (Texas has jurisdiction over defendant in criminal support case who has never been in state)

Williams v. State, 71 S.W.3d 862 (Tex. App.—Texarkana 2002, pet. granted) (imprisonment for criminal nonpayment of child support not unconstitutional imprisonment for nonpayment of debt)

Harvill v. State, 13 S.W.3d 478 (Tex. App.—Corpus Christi 2000, no pet.) (sentence imposed unauthorized under applicable version of criminal nonsupport statute

Belcher v. State, 962 S.W.2d 653 (Tex. App.—Austin 1998, no writ) (jury verdict stands—its failure to find affirmative defense of inability to pay not manifestly unjust)

State v. Johnson, 948 S.W.2d 39 (Tex. App.—Houston [14th Dist.] 1997, no writ) (prior contempt proceedings did not present double jeopardy bar to prosecution for criminal nonsupport)

Lyons v. State, 834 S.W.2d 715 (Tex. App.—Texarkana 1992, no writ) (inability to pay is affirmative defense, not an element of offense of criminal nonsupport)

---

§ 25.06. Harboring Runaway Child.

(a) A person commits an offense if he knowingly harbors a child and he is criminally negligent about whether the child:

(1) is younger than 18 years; and

(2) has escaped from the custody of a peace officer, a probation officer, the Texas Youth Council, or a detention facility for children, or is voluntarily absent from the child's home without the consent of the child's parent or guardian for a substantial length of time or without the intent to return.

(b) It is a defense to prosecution under this section that the actor was related to the child within the second degree by consanguinity or affinity, as determined under Chapter 573, Government Code.

(c) It is a defense to prosecution under this section that the actor notified:

(1) the person or agency from which the child escaped or a law enforcement agency of the presence of the child within 24 hours after discovering that the child had escaped from custody; or

(2) a law enforcement agency or a person at the child's home of the presence of the child within 24 hours after discovering that the child was voluntarily absent from home without the consent of the child's parent or guardian.

(d) An offense under this section is a Class A misdemeanor.

(e) On the receipt of a report from a peace officer, probation officer, the Texas Youth Council, a foster home, or a detention facility for children that a child has escaped its custody or upon receipt of a report from a parent, guardian, conservator, or legal custodian that a child is missing, a law enforcement agency shall immediately enter a record of the child into the National Crime Information Center.

§ 25.07. Violation of Protective Order or Magistrate's Order.

(a) A person commits an offense if, in violation of an order issued under Section 6.504 or Chapter 85, Family Code, under Article 17.292, Code of Criminal Procedure, or by another jurisdiction as provided by Chapter 88, Family Code, the person knowingly or intentionally:

(1) commits family violence or an act in furtherance of an offense under Section 42.072;

(2) communicates:

(A) directly with a protected individual or a member of the family or household in a threatening or harassing manner;

(B) a threat through any person to a protected individual or a member of the family or household; **or** [and]

(C) in any manner with the protected individual or a member of the family or household except through the person's attorney or a person appointed by the court, if the order prohibits any communication with a protected individual or a member of the family or household;

(3) goes to or near any of the following places as specifically described in the order:

(A) the residence or place of employment or business of a protected individual or a member of the family or household; or

(B) any child care facility, residence, or school where a child protected by the order normally resides or attends; or

(4) possesses a firearm.

(b) For the purposes of this section:

(1) "Family violence," " family," "household," and "member of a household" have the meanings assigned by Chapter 71 [*Definitions*], Family Code.

(2) "Firearm" has the meaning assigned by Chapter 46.

(c) If conduct constituting an offense under this section also constitutes an offense under another section of this code, the actor may be prosecuted under either section or under both sections.

(d) Reconciliatory actions or agreements made by persons affected by an order do not affect the validity of the order or the duty of a peace officer to enforce this section.

(e) A peace officer investigating conduct that may constitute an offense under this section for a violation of an order may not arrest a person protected by that order for a violation of that order.

(f) It is not a defense to prosecution under this section that certain information has been excluded, as provided by Section 85.007, Family Code, or Article 17.292, Code of Criminal Procedure, from an order to which this section applies.

(g) An offense under this section is a Class A misdemeanor unless it is shown on the trial of the offense that the defendant has previously been convicted under this section two or more times or has violated the protective order by committing an assault or the offense of stalking, in which event the offense is a third degree felony.

History: Amended by 78th Legis., Reg. Sess. (2003), S.B. 317, eff. Sept. 1, 2003, and "applies only to an offense committed on or after the effective date of this Act. An offense committed before the effective date of this Act is covered by the law in effect when the offense was committed, and the former law is continued in effect for that purpose. For purposes of this subsection, an offense was committed before the effective date of this Act if any element of the offense was committed before that date."

Comment

Anti-family-violence advocates regard the enforceability of Title 4 protective orders by law enforcement officers as perhaps the crucial element in protecting victims of domestic violence. This milestone was first reached in 1983 (four years after the original Title 4 first came into being). It has been amended each and every legislative session since that beginning. In 1995 the criminalization of a violation was extended the Magistrate's Order for Emergency Protection, *infra*.

In 2003 the legislature corrected a longstanding point of confusion in this statute by substituting "or" for "and." This simple amendments clarifies that only one of the three prohibited types of communication, as described in § 25.07(a)(2)(A–C), must be proven instead of all three (direct threat, threat through a third party OR any manner of communication if expressly prohibited in the protective order).

An offense under this section is a Class A misdemeanor unless it is shown at trial that the defendant has been convicted under this section two or more times or has violated the protective order by committing an assault or the offense of stalking in which case it becomes a 3d degree felony. It is the duty of a peace officer to enforce the order by arresting the violator, even if persons affected by the order have made reconciliatory actions or agreements. *(B.B.)*

CLE/Other Legal Publications

Criminal law concerns in family law cases. Joe Marr Wilson, 2003 Adv. Fam. L.

Criminal law and the family practice. Barbara D. Nunneley & J.C. Ball, 2002 Adv. Fam. L.

In the crossfire: protective orders, what happens when federal law collides with family law (VAWA and Brady) and how magistrate orders impact family law litigation. Lorraine Wilson, 2001 Adv. Fam. L.

Leading Cases

Gharbi v. State, 131 S.W.3d 481 (Tex. Crim. App. 2003) (defendant's ex-wife a "protected individual" under protective order issued in favor of defendant's daughter)

Lee v. State, 799 S.W.2d 750 (Tex. Crim. App. 1990) (written agreement by parties in protective order suit enforceable by criminal sanctions; required warnings provided adequate notice of possible criminal charges)

Sisk v. State, 74 S.W.3d 893 (Tex. App.—Fort Worth 2002, no pet.) (on more than one occasion defendant intentionally followed alleged victim knowing she would regard his conduct as threatening bodily injury)

Ex parte Pool, 71 S.W.3d 462 (Tex. App.—Tyler 2002, no pet.) (defendant pled guilty to violation of protective order to avoid burglary charge stemming from the same incident—not double jeopardy)

Collins v. State, 955 S.W.2d 464 (Tex. App.—Fort Worth 1997, no pet.) (protective order need not be sufficiently specific to sustain contempt, order need only be specific enough to allege culpable conduct) (prohibition wife's residence not inherent conflict with right to pick up son there on Father's Day and birthday)

Small v. State, 809 S.W.2d 253 (Tex. App.—San Antonio 1991, pet. refused) (knowledge of order essential; "knowing, intentional" violation must be proven beyond a reasonable doubt)

Cross Reference

Tex. Crim. Proc. Code Ann. § 17.292. Magistrate's Order for Emergency Protection, *supra*.

§ 25.071. Violation of Protective Order Preventing Offense Caused by Bias or Prejudice.

(a) A person commits an offense if, in violation of an order issued under Article 6.08, Code of Criminal Procedure, the person knowingly or intentionally:

(1) commits an offense under Title 5[1] or Section 28.02, 28.03, or 28.08 and commits the offense because of bias or prejudice as described by Article 42.014, Code of Criminal Procedure;

(2) communicates:

(A) directly with a protected individual in a threatening or harassing manner;

(B) a threat through any person to a protected individual; or

(C) in any manner with the protected individual, if the order prohibits any communication with a protected individual; or

(3) goes to or near the residence or place of employment or business of a protected individual.

(b) If conduct constituting an offense under this section also constitutes an offense under another section of this code, the actor may be prosecuted under either section or under both sections.

(c) A peace officer investigating conduct that may constitute an offense under this section for a violation of an order may not arrest a person protected by that order for a violation of that order.

(d) An offense under this section is a Class A misdemeanor unless it is shown on the trial of the offense that the defendant has previously been convicted under this section two or more times or has violated the protective order by committing an assault, in which event the offense is a third degree felony.

§ 25.08. Sale or Purchase of Child.

(a) A person commits an offense if he:

(1) possesses a child younger than 18 years of age or has the custody, conservatorship, or guardianship of a child younger than 18 years of age, whether or not he has actual possession of the child, and he offers to accept, agrees to accept, or accepts a thing of value for the delivery of the child to another or for the possession of the child by another for purposes of adoption; or

(2) offers to give, agrees to give, or gives a thing of value to another for acquiring or maintaining the possession of a child for the purpose of adoption.

(b) It is an exception to the application of this section that the thing of value is:

(1) a fee or reimbursement paid to a child-placing agency as authorized by law;

(2) a fee paid to an attorney, social worker, mental health professional, or physician for services rendered in the usual course of legal or medical practice or in providing adoption counseling;

(3) a reimbursement of legal or medical expenses incurred by a person for the benefit of the child; or

(4) a necessary pregnancy-related expense paid by a child-placing agency for the benefit of the child's parent during the pregnancy or after the birth of the child as permitted by the minimum standards for child-placing agencies and Department of Protective and Regulatory Services rules.

(c) An offense under this section is a felony of the third degree**, except that the offense is a felony of the second degree if the actor commits the offense with intent to commit an offense under Section 43.25**.

History: Amended by 78th Legis., Reg. Sess. (2003), H.B. 236, eff. Sept. 1, 2003, and "applies only to an offense committed on or after the effective date of this Act. For purposes of this section, an offense is committed before the effective date of this Act if any element of the offense occurs before the effective date. An offense committed before the effective date of this Act is covered by the law in effect when the offense was committed, and the former law is continued in effect for that purpose."

Leading Cases

Thacker v. State, 889 S.W.2d 380 (Tex. App.—Houston [14th Dist.] 1994, pet. denied) (lump sum payments to birth mother by sole proprietor of adoption agency not for medical or legal services)

DeJesus v. State, 889 S.W.2d 373 (Tex. App.—Houston [14 Dist.] 1994, no pet.) (statute violated if person has actual possession or legal custody of child, and offers to accept, agrees to accept or accepts thing of value for delivery or for possession of child for adoption)

Kingsley v. State, 744 S.W.2d 191 (Tex. App.—Dallas 1987, pet. dism'd) (statute not unconstitutionally vague; adoption attorney's payments to mother clearly not legal or medical expenses)

Botello v. State, 720 S.W.2d 838 (Tex. App.—San Antonio 1986, pet. refused) (statute gives reasonable notice of acts constituting sale of child, does not violate due process)

---

§ 25.09. Advertising for Placement of Child.

(a) A person commits an offense if the person advertises in the public media that the person will place a child for adoption or will provide or obtain a child for adoption.

(b) This section does not apply to a licensed child-placing agency that is identified in the advertisement as a licensed child-placing agency.

(c) An offense under this section is a Class A misdemeanor unless the person has been convicted previously under this section, in which event the offense is a felony of the third degree.

(d) In this section:

(1) "Child" has the meaning assigned by Section 101.003, Family Code.

(2) "Public media" has the meaning assigned by Section 38.01. The term also includes communications through the use of the Internet or another public computer network.

§ 25.10. Interference with Rights of Guardian of the Person.

(a) In this section:

(1) "Possessory right" means the right of a guardian of the person to have physical possession of a ward and to establish the ward's legal domicile, as provided by Section 767(1), Texas Probate Code.

(2) "Ward" has the meaning assigned by Section 601, Texas Probate Code.

(b) A person commits an offense if the person takes, retains, or conceals a ward when the person knows that the person's taking, retention, or concealment interferes with a possessory right with respect to the ward.

(c) An offense under this section is a state jail felony.

(d) This section does not apply to a governmental entity where the taking, retention, or concealment of the ward was authorized by Subtitle E, Title 5, Family Code, or Chapter 48, Human Resources Code.

Chapter 38. Obstructing Governmental Operation

§ 38.112. Violation of Protective Order Issued on Basis of Sexual Assault.

Summary: If a protective order has been issued under TEX. PENAL CODE ch 7A, *supra*, a person commits an Class A misdemeanor offense if the person knowingly communicates with the applicant or a member of the family or household, goes to or near a prohibited location, or possesses a firearm. *(B.B.)*

Chapter 42. Disorderly Conduct and Related Offenses

§ 42.062. Interference with Emergency Telephone Call.

Summary: An individual commits an offense if the individual knowingly prevents or interferes with another's ability to place an emergency telephone call or recklessly renders unusable a telephone that would otherwise be used to place an emergency telephone call. Violation of this offense is a Class A misdemeanor. In 2003 the legislature changed the definition of emergency in this section from "imminent danger of serious bodily injury" to "fear of imminent assault." *(B.B.)*

---

§ 42.07. Harassment

(a) A person commits an offense if, with intent to harass, annoy, alarm, abuse, torment, or embarrass another, he:

(1) initiates communication by telephone, in writing, or by electronic communication and in the course of the communication makes a comment, request, suggestion, or proposal that is obscene;

(2) threatens, by telephone, in writing, or by electronic communication, in a manner reasonably likely to alarm the person receiving the threat, to inflict bodily injury on the person or to commit a felony against the person, a member of his family or household, or his property;

(3) conveys, in a manner reasonably likely to alarm the person receiving the report, a false report, which is known by the conveyor to be false, that another person has suffered death or serious bodily injury;

(4) causes the telephone of another to ring repeatedly or makes repeated telephone communications anonymously or in a manner reasonably likely to harass, annoy, alarm, abuse, torment, embarrass, or offend another;

(5) makes a telephone call and intentionally fails to hang up or disengage the connection;

(6) knowingly permits a telephone under the person's control to be used by another to commit an offense under this section; or

(7) sends repeated electronic communications in a manner reasonably likely to harass, annoy, alarm, abuse, torment, embarrass, or offend another.

(b) In this section:

(1) "Electronic communication" means a transfer of signs, signals, writing, images, sounds, data, or intelligence of any nature transmitted in whole or in part by a wire, radio, electromagnetic, photoelectronic, or photo-optical system. The term includes:

(A) a communication initiated by electronic mail, instant message, network call, or facsimile machine; and

(B) a communication made to a pager.

(2) "Family" and "household" have the meaning assigned by Chapter 71, Family Code.

(3) "Obscene" means containing a patently offensive description of or a solicitation to commit an ultimate sex act, including sexual intercourse, masturbation, cunnilingus, fellatio, or anilingus, or a description of an excretory function.

(c) An offense under this section is a Class B misdemeanor, except that the offense is a Class A misdemeanor if the actor has previously been convicted under this section.

Leading Cases

Barrera v. State, 978 S.W.2d 665 (Tex. App.—Corpus Christi 1998, pet. ref'd) (notes victim made of caller's remarks not hearsay, admissible evidence of intended harassment)

Blount v. State, 961 S.W.2d 282 (Tex. App.—Houston [1st Dist.] 1997, pet. ref'd) (conviction for telephone harassment proven by four repeated calls, request to cease, obscene name-calling with intent to harass and annoy)

DeWillis v. State, 951 S.W.2d 212 (Tex. App.—Houston 1997, no pet.) (telephone harassment statute not unconstitutionally vague as applied; repeatedly ringing or calling anonymously violates "reasonable person" standard)

§ 42.072. Stalking.

(a) A person commits an offense if the person, on more than one occasion and pursuant to the same scheme or course of conduct that is directed specifically at another person, knowingly engages in conduct, including following the other person, that:

(1) the actor knows or reasonably believes the other person will regard as threatening:

(A) bodily injury or death for the other person;

(B) bodily injury or death for a member of the other person's family or household; or

(C) that an offense will be committed against the other person's property;

(2) causes the other person or a member of the other person's family or household to be placed in fear of bodily injury or death or fear that an offense will be committed against the other person's property; and

(3) would cause a reasonable person to fear:

(A) bodily injury or death for himself or herself;

(B) bodily injury or death for a member of the person's family or household; or

(C) that an offense will be committed against the person's property.

(b) An offense under this section is a felony of the third degree, except that the offense is a felony of the second degree if the actor has previously been convicted under this section.

(c) In this section, "family," "household," and "member of a household" have the meanings assigned by Chapter 71, Family Code.

Comment

Other stalking laws are related to victim notification and civil liability of stalkers. TEX. CODE CRIM. PROC. art. 17.29, *supra*, provides that before an arrested stalker can be released on bail, the agency holding the offender must make a reasonable attempt to notify the victim or her designee of the impending release. TEX. CIV. PRAC. & REM. CODE ch. 85, *Civil Liability of Stalkers*, allows a victim of stalking to sue the stalker in civil court to recover "actual and exemplary" financial compensation for the crime. The victim must show that the stalking occurred on more than one occasion. *(B.B.)*

Leading Cases

Davis v. State, 125 S.W.3d 734 (Tex. App.—Texarkana 2003) (sentence of eight years not disproportionate—extensive harassment, assaults, property damage, and threats of bodily injury or death by disassembling body parts)

Sisk v. State, 74 S.W.3d 893 (Tex. App.—Fort Worth 2002, no pet.) (on more than one occasion defendant intentionally followed alleged victim knowing she would regard his conduct as threatening bodily injury)

State v. Newsom, 64 S.W.3d 478 (Tex. App.—El Paso 2002, no pet.) (prior conviction must be final to enhance repeat stalking offense from misdemeanor to felony)

Ex parte Reese, 23 S.W.3d 54 (Tex. App.—Austin 2000, pet. refused) (prior conviction for contempt did not bar subsequent prosecution for stalking on double jeopardy grounds)

Clements v. State, 19 S.W.3d 442 (Tex. App.—Houston [1st Dist.] 2000, no pet.) (statute not unconstitutionally vague; specifies prohibited conduct, *e.g.,* conduct known or reasonably believed will be regarded as threatening bodily injury or death)

Cross Reference

Tex. Crim. Proc. Code Ann. art. 17.292. Magistrate's Order for Emergency Protection, *supra*.

Chapter 46. Weapons

§ 46.06. Unlawful Possession of Firearm.

Summary: A person convicted of a Class A misdemeanor family violence assault commits an offense by possessing a firearm during the 5-year period after the person's release from confinement or community supervision following conviction.

A person subject to a final protective order, a magistrate's order of emergency protection, or a valid foreign protective order commits an offense by possessing a firearm while subject to the order. As with the corresponding federal law, peace officers engaged in active duty are exempt from the protective order firearms prohibition.

These sections mirror the existing federal ban on possession of firearms by family violence offenders. 18 U.S.C. 922(g)(8), (9). A violation of these offenses is a Class A misdemeanor. *(B.B.)*

§ 46.06. Unlawful Transfer of Certain Weapons.

Summary: A person commits an offense if the person knowingly purchases, rents, leases, or receives as a loan or gift from another a handgun while an active protective order is directed to the actor. *(B.B.)*

Texas Property Code

★★★

Chapter 41. Interests in Land

CLE/Other Legal Publications

See annotations to Tex. Fam. Code ch. 5, *supra*, and Tex. Prop. Code ch. 42, *infra*.

Those other Texas codes—things the family lawyer needs to know about codifications outside the Family Code. Richard R. Orsinger, 2004 Adv. Fam. L.

---

§ 41.001. Interests in Land Exempt from Seizure.

(a) A homestead and one or more lots used for a place of burial of the dead are exempt from seizure for the claims of creditors except for encumbrances properly fixed on homestead property.

(b) Encumbrances may be properly fixed on homestead property for:

(1) purchase money;

(2) taxes on the property;

(3) work and material used in constructing improvements on the property if contracted for in writing as provided by Sections 53.254(a), (b), and (c);

(4) an owelty of partition imposed against the entirety of the property by a court order or by a written agreement of the parties to the partition, including a debt of one spouse in favor of the other spouse resulting from a division or an award of a family homestead in a divorce proceeding;

(5) the refinance of a lien against a homestead, including a federal tax lien resulting from the tax debt of both spouses, if the homestead is a family homestead, or from the tax debt of the owner;

(6) an extension of credit that meets the requirements of Section 50(a)(6), Article XVI, Texas Constitution; or

(7) a reverse mortgage that meets the requirements of Sections 50(k)–(p), Article XVI, Texas Constitution.

(c) The homestead claimant's proceeds of a sale of a homestead are not subject to seizure for a creditor's claim for six months after the date of sale.

§ 41.002. Definition of Homestead.

(a) If used for the purposes of an urban home or as both an urban home and a place to exercise a calling or business, the homestead of a family or a single, adult person, not otherwise entitled to a homestead, shall consist of not more than 10 acres of land which may be in one or more contiguous lots, together with any improvements thereon.

(b) If used for the purposes of a rural home, the homestead shall consist of:

(1) for a family, not more than 200 acres, which may be in one or more parcels, with the improvements thereon; or

(2) for a single, adult person, not otherwise entitled to a homestead, not more than 100 acres, which may be in one or more parcels, with the improvements thereon.

(c) A homestead is considered to be urban if, at the time the designation is made, the property is:

(1) located within the limits of a municipality or its extraterritorial jurisdiction or a platted subdivision; and

(2) served by police protection, paid or volunteer fire protection, and at least three of the following services provided by a municipality or under contract to a municipality:

(A) electric;

(B) natural gas;

(C) sewer;

(D) storm sewer; and

(E) water.

(d) The definition of a homestead as provided in this section applies to all homesteads in this state whenever created.

CLE/Other Legal Publications

Homestead—what you need to know in the 21st century. Barbara Nunneley, 2003 Marriage Dissolution

Home equity loans in Texas: maintaining the Texas tradition of homestead protection. Julia Patterson Forrester, 55 SMU L. Rev. 157 (2002)

Taking Texas home equity for a walk, but keeping it on a short leash! Charles C. Boettcher, 30 Tex. Tech L. Rev. 197 (1999)

A call for bankruptcy reform: the Fifth Circuit limits the Texas homestead exemption and further complicates the exemption controversy. Michael Denham, 30 Tex. Tech L. Rev. 269 (1999)

Leading Case

Duran v. Henderson, 71 S.W.3d 833 (Tex. App.—Texarkana 2002, pet. denied) (debtor, adult daughter and her son are "family" for purposes of homestead exemption)

---

§ 41.003. Temporary Renting of a Homestead.

Temporary renting of a homestead does not change its homestead character if the homestead claimant has not acquired another homestead.

§ 41.004. Abandonment of a Homestead.

If a homestead claimant is married, a homestead cannot be abandoned without the consent of the claimant's spouse.

Leading Cases

Exocet, Inc. v. Cordes, 815 S.W.2d 350 (Tex. App.—Austin 1991, no writ) (judgment creditor must prove abandonment of homestead)

Buckner v. Buckner, 815 S.W.2d 877 (Tex. App.—Tyler 1991, no writ) (special relationship between husband and wife includes expressions of legal opinions)

---

§ 41.005. Voluntary Designation of Homestead.

(a) If a rural homestead of a family is part of one or more parcels containing a total of more than 200 acres, the head of the family and, if married, that person's spouse may voluntarily designate not more than 200 acres of the property as the homestead. If a rural homestead of a single adult person, not otherwise entitled to a homestead, is part of one or more parcels containing a total of more than 100 acres, the person may voluntarily designate not more than 100 acres of the property as the homestead.

(b) If an urban homestead of a family, or an urban homestead of a single adult person not otherwise entitled to a homestead, is part of one or more contiguous lots containing a total of more than 10 acres, the head of the family and, if married, that person's spouse or the single adult person, as applicable, may voluntarily designate not more than 10 acres of the property as the homestead.

(c) Except as provided by Subsection (e) or Subchapter B, to designate property as a homestead, a person or persons, as applicable, must make the designation in an instrument that is signed and acknowledged or proved in the manner required for the recording of other instruments. The person or persons must file the designation with the county clerk of the county in which all or part of the property is located. The clerk shall record the designation in the county deed records. The designation must contain:

(1) a description sufficient to identify the property designated;

(2) a statement by the person or persons who executed the instrument that the property is designated as the homestead of the person's family or as the homestead of a single adult person not otherwise entitled to a homestead;

(3) the name of the current record title holder of the property; and

(4) for a rural homestead, the number of acres designated and, if there is more than one survey, the number of acres in each.

(d) A person or persons, as applicable, may change the boundaries of a homestead designated under Subsection (c) by executing and recording an instrument in the manner required for a voluntary designation under that subsection. A change under this subsection does not impair rights acquired by a party before the change.

(e) Except as otherwise provided by this subsection, property on which a person receives an exemption from taxation under Section 11.43, Tax Code, is considered to have been designated as the person's homestead for purposes of this subchapter if the property is listed as the person's residence homestead on the most recent appraisal roll for the appraisal district established for the county in which the property is located. If a person designates property as a homestead under Subsection (c) or Subchapter B and a different property is considered to have been designated as the person's homestead under this subsection, the designation under Subsection (c) or Subchapter B, as applicable, prevails for purposes of this chapter.

(f) If a person or persons, as applicable, have not made a voluntary designation of a homestead under this section as of the time a writ of execution is issued against the person, any designation of the person's or persons' homestead must be made in accordance with Subchapter B.

(g) An instrument that made a voluntary designation of a homestead in accordance with prior law and that is on file with the county clerk on September 1, 1987, is considered a voluntary designation of a homestead under this section.

§ 41.006. Certain Sales of Homestead.

(a) Except as provided by Subsection (c), any sale or purported sale in whole or in part of a homestead at a fixed purchase price that is less than the appraised fair market value of the property at the time of the sale or purported sale, and in connection with which the buyer of the property executes a lease of the property to the seller at lease payments that exceed the fair rental value of the property, is considered to be a loan with all payments made from the seller to the buyer in excess of the sales price considered to be interest subject to Title 4, Finance Code.

(b) The taking of any deed in connection with a transaction described by this section is a deceptive trade practice under Subchapter E, Chapter 17, Business & Commerce Code, and the deed is void and no lien attaches to the homestead property as a result of the purported sale.

(c) This section does not apply to the sale of a family homestead to a parent, stepparent, grandparent, child, stepchild, brother, half brother, sister, half sister, or grandchild of an adult member of the family.

§ 41.007. Home Improvement Contract.

(a) A contract described by Section 41.001(b)(3) must contain the following warning conspicuously printed, stamped, or typed in a size equal to at least 10-point bold type or computer equivalent, next to the owner's signature line on the contract:

"IMPORTANT NOTICE: You and your contractor are responsible for meeting the terms and conditions of this contract. If you sign this contract and you fail to meet the terms and conditions of this contract, you may lose your legal ownership rights in your home. KNOW YOUR RIGHTS AND DUTIES UNDER THE LAW."

(b) A violation of Subsection (a) of this section is a false, misleading, or deceptive act or practice within the meaning of Section 17.46, Business & Commerce Code, and is actionable in a public or private suit brought under the provisions of the Deceptive Trade Practices-Consumer Protection Act (Subchapter E, Chapter 17, Business & Commerce Code).

§ 41.008. Conflict With Federal Law.

To the extent of any conflict between this subchapter and any federal law that imposes an upper limit on the amount, including the monetary amount or acreage amount, of homestead property a person may exempt from seizure, this subchapter prevails to the extent allowed under federal law.

§ 41.021. Notice to Designate.

If an execution is issued against a holder of an interest in land of which a homestead may be a part and the judgment debtor has not made a voluntary designation of a homestead under Section 41.005, the judgment creditor may give the judgment debtor notice to designate the homestead as defined in Section 41.002. The notice shall state that if the judgment debtor fails to designate the homestead within the time allowed by Section 41.022, the court will appoint a commissioner to make the designation at the expense of the judgment debtor.

§ 41.022. Designation by Homestead Claimant.

At any time before 10 a.m. on the Monday next after the expiration of 20 days after the date of service of the notice to designate, the judgment debtor may designate the homestead as defined in Section 41.002 by filing a written designation, signed by the judgment debtor, with the justice or clerk of the court from which the writ of execution was issued, together with a plat of the area designated.

§ 41.023. Designation by Commissioner.

(a) If a judgment debtor who has not made a voluntary designation of a homestead under Section 41.005 does not designate a homestead as provided in Section 41.022, on motion of the judgment creditor, filed within 90 days after the issuance of the writ of execution, the court from which the writ of execution issued shall appoint a commissioner to designate the judgment debtor's homestead. The court may appoint a surveyor and others as may be necessary to assist the commissioner. The commissioner shall file his designation of the judgment debtor's homestead in a written report, together with a plat of the area designated, with the justice or clerk of the court not more than 60 days after the order of appointment is signed or within such time as the court may allow.

(b) Within 10 days after the commissioner's report is filed, the judgment debtor or the judgment creditor may request a hearing on the issue of whether the report should be confirmed, rejected, or modified as may be deemed appropriate in the particular circumstances of the case. The commissioner's report may be contradicted by evidence from either party, when exceptions to it or any item thereof have been filed before the hearing, but not otherwise. After the hearing, or if there is no hearing requested, the court shall designate the homestead as deemed appropriate and order sale of the excess.

(c) The commissioner, a surveyor, and others appointed to assist the commissioner are entitled to such fees and expenses as are deemed reasonable by the court. The court shall tax these fees and expenses against the judgment debtor as part of the costs of execution.

§ 41.024. Sale of Excess.

An officer holding an execution sale of property of a judgment debtor whose homestead has been designated under this chapter may sell the excess of the judgment debtor's interest in land not included in the homestead.

Chapter 42. Personal Property

CLE/Other Legal Publications

See annotations to TEX. FAM. CODE ANN. ch. 5, *supra*.

Bankruptcy. Joseph A. Friedman, 2003 ADV. FAM. L.

"Speaking in codes": what every family lawyer should know about the Civil Practices & Remedies Code, Property Code, and Business & Commerce Code. Thomas P. Goranson, 2003, 2001 ADV. FAM. L.

Family law and bankruptcy. Diana S. Friedman & Joseph A. Friedman, 2000 ADV. FAM. L.; 1998 ADV. FAM. L.

A call for bankruptcy reform: the Fifth Circuit limits the Texas homestead exemption and further complicates the exemption controversy. 30 TEX. TECH L. REV. 269 (1999)

Leading Cases

Dryden v. Dryden, 97 S.W.3d 863 (Tex. App.—Corpus Christi 2003) (child support obligors distinguishable from protections afforded debtors exempting certain property; that obligation not a debt)

Leibman v. Grand, 981 S.W.2d 426 (Tex. App.—El Paso 1998, no pet.) (judgment debtor made payments to purchase annuity with intent to defraud judgment creditor, annuity subject to turnover)

Lozano v. Lozano, 975 S.W.2d 63 (Tex. App.—Houston [14 Dist.] 1998, pet. denied) (trial court had authority to order turnover of property located in Mexico, but not to order turnover of property directly to judgment creditor)

Burns v. Miller, Hiersche, Martens & Hayward, P.C., 948 S.W.2d 317 (Tex. App.—Dallas 1997, pet. denied) (spendthrift trust assets "exempt" from turnover—and, even though not exempt after distribution, remain not subject to turnover)

---

§ 42.001. Personal Property Exemption.

(a) Personal property, as described in Section 42.002, is exempt from garnishment, attachment, execution, or other seizure if:

(1) the property is provided for a family and has an aggregate fair market value of not more than $60,000, exclusive of the amount of any liens, security interests, or other charges encumbering the property; or

(2) the property is owned by a single adult, who is not a member of a family, and has an aggregate fair market value of not more than $30,000, exclusive of the amount of any liens, security interests, or other charges encumbering the property.

(b) The following personal property is exempt from seizure and is not included in the aggregate limitations prescribed by Subsection (a):

(1) current wages for personal services, except for the enforcement of court-ordered child support payments;

(2) professionally prescribed health aids of a debtor or a dependent of a debtor; and

(3) alimony, support, or separate maintenance received or to be received by the debtor for the support of the debtor or a dependent of the debtor.

(c) This section does not prevent seizure by a secured creditor with a contractual landlord's lien or other security in the property to be seized.

(d) Unpaid commissions for personal services not to exceed 25 percent of the aggregate limitations prescribed by Subsection (a) are exempt from seizure and are included in the aggregate.

§ 42.002. Personal Property.

(a) The following personal property is exempt under Section 42.001(a):

(1) home furnishings, including family heirlooms;

(2) provisions for consumption;

(3) farming or ranching vehicles and implements;

(4) tools, equipment, books, and apparatus, including boats and motor vehicles used in a trade or profession;

(5) wearing apparel;

(6) jewelry not to exceed 25 percent of the aggregate limitations prescribed by Section 42.001(a);

(7) two firearms;

(8) athletic and sporting equipment, including bicycles;

(9) a two-wheeled, three-wheeled, or four-wheeled motor vehicle for each member of a family or single adult who holds a driver's license or who does not hold a driver's license but who relies on another person to operate the vehicle for the benefit of the nonlicensed person;

(10) the following animals and forage on hand for their consumption:

(A) two horses, mules, or donkeys and a saddle, blanket, and bridle for each;

(B) 12 head of cattle;

(C) 60 head of other types of livestock; and

(D) 120 fowl; and

(11) household pets.

(b) *[first of two]* Personal property, unless precluded from being encumbered by other law, may be encumbered by a security interest under Section 9.203, Business & Commerce Code, or Subchapter F, Chapter 501, Transportation Code, or by a lien fixed by other law, and the security interest or lien may not be avoided on the ground that the property is exempt under this chapter.

(b) *[second of two]* Personal property, unless precluded from being encumbered by other law, may be encumbered by a security interest under Subchapter B, Chapter 9, Business & Commerce Code, or Subchapter F, Chapter 501, Transportation Code, or by a lien fixed by other law, and the security interest or lien may not be avoided on the ground that the property is exempt under this chapter.

§ 42.0021. Additional Exemption for Retirement Plan.

(a) In addition to the exemption prescribed by Section 42.001, a person's right to the assets held in or to receive payments, whether vested or not, under any stock bonus, pension, profit-sharing, or similar plan, including a retirement plan for self-employed individuals, and under any annuity or similar contract purchased with assets distributed from that type of plan, and under any retirement annuity or account described by Section 403(b) or 408A of the Internal Revenue Code of 1986, and under any individual retirement account or any individual retirement annuity, including a simplified employee pension plan, is exempt from attachment, execution, and seizure for the satisfaction of debts unless the plan, contract, or account does not qualify under the applicable provisions of the Internal Revenue Code of 1986. A person's right to the assets held in or to receive payments, whether vested or not, under a government or church plan or contract is also exempt unless the plan or contract does not qualify under the definition of a government or church plan under the applicable provisions of the federal Employee Retirement Income Security Act of 1974. If this subsection is held invalid or preempted by federal law in whole or in part or in certain circumstances, the subsection remains in effect in all other respects to the maximum extent permitted by law.

(b) Contributions to an individual retirement account, other than contributions to a Roth IRA described in Section 408A, Internal Revenue Code of 1986, or annuity that exceed the amounts deductible under the applicable provisions of the Internal Revenue Code of 1986 and any accrued earnings on such contributions are not exempt under this section unless otherwise exempt by law. Amounts qualifying as nontaxable rollover contributions under Section 402(a)(5), 403(a)(4), 403(b)(8), or 408(d)(3) of the Internal Revenue Code of 1986 before January 1, 1993, are treated as exempt amounts under Subsection (a). Amounts treated as qualified rollover contributions under Section 408A, Internal Revenue Code of 1986, are treated as exempt amounts under Subsection (a). In addition, amounts qualifying as nontaxable rollover contributions under Section 402(c), 402(e)(6), 402(f), 403(a)(4), 403(a)(5), 403(b)(8), 403(b)(10), 408(d)(3), or 408A of the Internal Revenue Code of 1986 on or after January 1, 1993, are treated as exempt amounts under Subsection (a).

(c) Amounts distributed from a plan or contract entitled to the exemption under Subsection (a) are not subject to seizure for a creditor's claim for 60 days after the date of distribution if the amounts qualify as a nontaxable rollover contribution under Subsection (b).

(d) A participant or beneficiary of a stock bonus, pension, profit-sharing, retirement plan, or government plan is not prohibited from granting a valid and enforceable security interest in the participant's or beneficiary's right to the assets held in or to receive payments under the plan to secure a loan to the participant or beneficiary from the plan, and the right to the assets held in or to receive payments from the plan is subject to attachment, execution, and seizure for the satisfaction of the security interest or lien granted by the participant or beneficiary to secure the loan.

(e) If Subsection (a) is declared invalid or preempted by federal law, in whole or in part or in certain circumstances, as applied to a person who has not brought a proceeding under Title 11, United States Code, the subsection remains in effect, to the maximum extent permitted by law, as to any person who has filed that type of proceeding.

(f) A reference in this section to a specific provision of the Internal Revenue Code of 1986 includes a subsequent amendment of the substance of that provision.

§ 42.0022. Exemption for College Savings Plans.

(a) In addition to the exemption prescribed by Section 42.001, a person's right to the assets held in or to receive payments or benefits under any of the

following is exempt from attachment, execution, and seizure for the satisfaction of debts:

(1) any fund or plan established under Subchapter F, Chapter 54, Education Code, including the person's interest in a prepaid tuition contract;

(2) any fund or plan established under Subchapter G, Chapter 54, Education Code, including the person's interest in a savings trust account; or

(3) any qualified tuition program of any state that meets the requirements of Section 529, Internal Revenue Code of 1986, as amended.

(b) If any portion of this section is held to be invalid or preempted by federal law in whole or in part or in certain circumstances, this section remains in effect in all other respects to the maximum extent permitted by law.

History: Enacted by 78th Legis., Reg. Sess. (2003), S.B. 1588, eff. Sept. 1, 2003, and "applies to a person's right to the assets held in or to receive payments or benefits under any fund, plan or program described by Section 42.0022, Property Code, as added by this Act, on and after the effective date of this Act without regard to whether any money and other property was contributed to or paid in connection with the fund, plan or program to establish the person's right to those assets, payments, or benefits before, on, or after the effective date of this Act."

§ 42.003. Designation of Exempt Property.

(a) If the number or amount of a type of personal property owned by a debtor exceeds the exemption allowed by Section 42.002 and the debtor can be found in the county where the property is located, the officer making a levy on the property shall ask the debtor to designate the personal property to be levied on. If the debtor cannot be found in the county or the debtor fails to make a designation within a reasonable time after the officer's request, the officer shall make the designation.

(b) If the aggregate value of a debtor's personal property exceeds the amount exempt from seizure under Section 42.001(a), the debtor may designate the portion of the property to be levied on. If, after a court's request, the debtor fails to make a designation within a reasonable time or if for any reason a creditor contests that the property is exempt, the court shall make the designation.

§ 42.004. Transfer of Nonexempt Property.

(a) If a person uses the property not exempt under this chapter to acquire, obtain an interest in, make improvement to, or pay an indebtedness on personal property which would be exempt under this chapter with the intent to defraud, delay, or hinder an interested person from obtaining that to which the interested person is or may be entitled, the property, interest, or improvement acquired is not exempt from seizure for the satisfaction of liabilities. If the property, interest, or improvement is acquired by discharging an encumbrance held by a third person, a person defrauded, delayed, or hindered is subrogated to the rights of the third person.

(b) A creditor may not assert a claim under this section more than two years after the transaction from which the claim arises. A person with a claim that is unliquidated or contingent at the time of the transaction may not assert a claim under this section more than one year after the claim is reduced to judgment.

(c) It is a defense to a claim under this section that the transfer was made in the ordinary course of business by the person making the transfer.

§ 42.005. Child Support Liens.

Sections 42.001, 42.002, and 42.0021 of this code do not apply to a child support lien established under Subchapter G, Chapter 157 *[Enforcement]*, Family Code.

Cross Reference

TEX. FAM. CODE ANN. § 157.311 *et seq.* (child support liens), *supra.*

---

§ 42.0051. Disclaimer Required.

(a) A person may not deliver a written advertisement offering, for a fee, to designate property as a homestead as provided by Section 41.005 unless there is a disclaimer on the advertisement that is conspicuous and printed in 14–point boldface type or 14–point uppercase typewritten letters that makes the following statement or a substantially similar statement:

THIS DOCUMENT IS AN ADVERTISEMENT OF SERVICES. IT IS NOT AN OFFICIAL DOCUMENT OF THE STATE OF TEXAS.

(b) A person's failure to provide a disclaimer on an advertisement as required by Subsection (a) is considered a false, misleading, or deceptive act or practice for purposes of Section 17.46(a), Business & Commerce Code, and is subject to action by the consumer protection division of the attorney general's office as provided by Section 17.46(a), Business & Commerce Code.

Related Federal Law

Selected Statutory, Regulatory and Treaty Provisions

As amended through the Second Session of the 108th Congress, Public Law 108–261 (approved June 25, 2004)

Federal Criminal Law

U.S.C.A. Title 18: Crimes and Criminal Procedure

Indian Child Welfare Act

U.S.C.A. Title 25: Indians

Federal Income Tax

U.S.C.A. Title 26: Internal Revenue Code

§ 66. Treatment of Community Income.
§ 71. Alimony and Separate Maintenance Payments.

Regulations [26 C.F.R.]

§ 1.71–1. Alimony and Separate Maintenance Payments; Income to Wife or Former Wife.
§ 1.71–1T. Alimony and Separate Maintenance Payments (temporary).

§ 121. Exclusion of Gain from Sale of Principal Residence.
§ 152. Dependent Defined.

Regulations [26 C.F.R.]

§ 1.152.–4T. Dependency Exemption in the Case of a Child of Divorced Parent, etc. (temporary).

§ 215. Alimony, etc., Payments.

Regulations [26 C.F.R.]

§ 1.215–1. Periodic Alimony Payments.
§ 1.215–1T. Alimony, etc., Payments (temporary).

§ 1041. Transfers of Property Between Spouses or Incident to Divorce.

Regulations [26 C.F.R.]

§ 1.1041–1T. Treatment of Transfer of Property Between Spouses or Incident to Divorce (temporary).

§ 6015. Relief From Joint and Several Liability on Joint Return.

Full Faith and Credit

U.S.C.A. Title 28: Judiciary and Judicial Procedure

§ 1738A. Full Faith and Credit Given to Child Custody Determinations. (*Parental Kidnapping Prevention Act)*
§ 1738B. Full Faith and Credit for Child Support Orders.
§ 1738C. Certain Acts, Records, and Proceedings and the Effect Thereof. (*Defense of Marriage Act*)

International Child Abduction Remedies Act

U.S.C.A. Title 42: The Public Health and Welfare

§ 11601. Findings and Declarations.
§ 11602. Definitions.
§ 11603. Judicial Remedies.
§ 11604. Provisional Remedies.
§ 11605. Admissibility of Documents.
§ 11606. United States Central Authority.
§ 11607. Costs and Fees.
§ 11608. Collection, Maintenance, and Dissemination of Information.
§ 11608a. Office of Children's Issues.
§ 11609. Interagency Coordinating Group.
§ 11610. Authorization of Appropriations.

Hague Convention on the Civil Aspects of International Child Abduction

Servicemembers Civil Relief Act

U.S.C.A. Title 50. Appendix: War and National Defense

§ 511. Definitions.
§ 512. Jurisdiction and applicability of Act.
§ 513. Protection of persons secondarily liable.
§ 514. Extension of protections to citizens serving with allied forces.
§ 516. Extension of rights and protections to reserves ordered to report for military service and to persons ordered to report for induction.
§ 517. Waiver of rights pursuant to written agreement.
§ 518. Exercise of rights under Act not to affect certain future financial transactions.
§ 519. Legal representatives.
§ 521. Protection of servicemembers against default judgments.
§ 522. Stay of proceedings when servicemember has notice.
§ 523. Fines and penalties under contracts.
§ 524. Stay or vacation of execution of judgments, attachments, and garnishments.
§ 525. Duration and term of stays; codefendants not in service.
§ 526. Statute of limitations.
§ 527. Maximum rate of interest on debts incurred before military service.
§ 581. Inappropriate use of Act.
§ 582. Certificates of service; persons reported missing.
§ 583. Interlocutory orders.
§ 591. Anticipatory relief.
§ 592. Power of attorney.
§ 593. Professional liability protection.

★★★

Federal Criminal Law

U.S.C.A. Title 18: Crimes and Criminal Procedure

§ 228. Failure To Pay Legal Child Support Obligations.
§ 1204. International Parental Kidnapping.
§ 2265. Full Faith and Credit Given to Protection Orders.
§ 2266. Definitions.

Child Support Recovery Act *(CSRA)*

Chapter 11A—Child Support

§ 228. Failure To Pay Legal Child Support Obligations.

(a) Offense. Any person who—

(1) willfully fails to pay a support obligation with respect to a child who resides in another State, if such obligation has remained unpaid for a period longer than 1 year, or is greater than $5,000;

(2) travels in interstate or foreign commerce with the intent to evade a support obligation, if such obligation has remained unpaid for a period longer than 1 year, or is greater than $5,000; or

(3) willfully fails to pay a support obligation with respect to a child who resides in another State, if such obligation has remained unpaid for a period longer than 2 years, or is greater than $10,000; shall be punished as provided in subsection (c).

(b) Presumption. The existence of a support obligation that was in effect for the time period charged in the indictment or information creates a rebuttable presumption that the obligor has the ability to pay the support obligation for that time period.

(c) Punishment. The punishment for an offense under this section is—

(1) in the case of a first offense under subsection (a)(1), a fine under this title, imprisonment for not more than 6 months, or both; and

(2) in the case of an offense under paragraph (2) or (3) of subsection (a), or a second or subsequent offense under subsection (a)(1), a fine under this title, imprisonment for not more than 2 years, or both.

(d) Mandatory restitution. Upon a conviction under this section, the court shall order restitution under section 3663A in an amount equal to the total unpaid support obligation as it exists at the time of sentencing.

(e) Venue. With respect to an offense under this section, an action may be inquired of and prosecuted in a district court of the United States for—

(1) the district in which the child who is the subject of the support obligation involved resided during a period during which a person described in subsection (a) (referred to in this subsection as an "obliger") failed to meet that support obligation;

(2) the district in which the obliger resided during a period described in paragraph (1); or

(3) any other district with jurisdiction otherwise provided for by law.

(f) Definitions. As used in this section—

(1) the term "Indian tribe" has the meaning given that term in section 102 of the Federally Recognized Indian Tribe List Act of 1994 (25 U.S.C. 479a);

(2) the term "State" includes any State of the United States, the District of Columbia, and any commonwealth, territory, or possession of the United States; and

(3) the term "support obligation" means any amount determined under a court order or an order of an administrative process pursuant to the law of a State or of an Indian tribe to be due from a person for the support and maintenance of a child or of a child and the parent with whom the child is living.

Comment

At the urging of the U.S. Commission on Interstate Child Support and numerous advocacy groups, in 1992 Congress made it a federal crime to avoid payment of child support by leaving a state. In 1998, Congress passed the "Deadbeat Parents Punishment Act of 1998" revising this section and adding new provisions for restitution and venue.

CLE/Other Legal Publications

See annotations to TEX. FAM. CODE ANN. Ch. 157, supra

Sausage on a stick: new legislation affecting the Title IV–D program. Alicia G. Key, 2001 ADV. FAM. L.

Leading Cases

U.S. v. Hill, 279 F.3d 731 (9th Cir. 2002) (extraterritorial jurisdiction asserted over wife who harbored husband in Mexico; his alleged evasion of child support had obvious detrimental effects in U.S.)

U.S. v. Molak, 276 F.3d 45 (1st Cir. 2002) ("child" not limited to persons under age 18, can include adult children)

U.S. v. Gill, 264 F.3d 929 (9th Cir. 2002) (restitution for willful failure to pay child support includes accrued interest on arrears if interest mandatorily imposed by state law)

U.S. v. Ballek, 170 F.3d 871 (9th Cir. 1999) (Alaska) ("willful" failure to pay child support can mean having money and refusing to provide it or not having money because of failure to obtain it by available means)

U.S. v. Russell, 186 F.3d 883 (8th Cir. 1999) (S.D.) (nonpayment of child support obligation did not violate ex post facto clause; mere accrual of arrearage not criminalized, but willful failure to pay is post-enactment occurrence)

U.S. v. Mussari, 152 F.3d 1156 (9th Cir. 1998) (Ariz.) (subjecting parent to federal criminal penalties for failure to pay support without differentiating nonpayments before and after effective date of statute is unconstitutional ex post facto enforcement)

U.S. v. Bailey, 115 F.3d 1222 (5th Cir. 1997) (Tex.), *cert. denied*, 118 S.Ct. 866 (CSRA does not offend principles of federalism and comity; prosecution turns only on violation of state court order)

U.S. v. Hampshire, 95 F.3d 999 (10th Cir. 1996) (Kan.), *cert. denied*, 519 U.S. 1084, 117 S.Ct. 753 (CSRA does not violate commerce clause; activities substantially relate to and substantially affect interstate commerce)

The International Parental Kidnapping Crime Act of 1993

Chapter 55—Kidnapping

§ 1204. International Parental Kidnapping.

(a) Whoever removes a child from the United States, or attempts to do so, or retains a child (who has been in the United States) outside the United States with intent to obstruct the lawful exercise of parental rights shall be fined under this title or imprisoned not more than 3 years, or both.

(b) As used in this section—

(1) the term "child" means a person who has not attained the age of 16 years; and

(2) the term "parental rights", with respect to a child, means the right to physical custody of the child—

(A) whether joint or sole (and includes visiting rights); and

(B) whether arising by operation of law, court order, or legally binding agreement of the parties.

(c) It shall be an affirmative defense under this section that—

(1) the defendant acted within the provisions of a valid court order granting the defendant legal custody or visitation rights and that order was obtained pursuant to the Uniform Child Custody Jurisdiction Act or the Uniform Child Custody Jurisdiction and Enforcement Act and was in effect at the time of the offense;

(2) the defendant was fleeing an incidence or pattern of domestic violence; or

(3) the defendant had physical custody of the child pursuant to a court order granting legal custody or visitation rights and failed to return the child as a result of circumstances beyond the defendant's control, and the defendant notified or made reasonable attempts to notify the other parent or lawful custodian of the child of such circumstances within 24 hours after the visitation period had expired and returned the child as soon as possible.

(d) This section does not detract from The Hague Convention on the Civil Aspects of International Parental Child Abduction, done at The Hague on October 25, 1980.

Comment

The International Parental Kidnapping Crime Act of 1993 (IPKCA) makes international child abduction a federal felony. Intent to obstruct the lawful exercise of parental rights by removing or retaining outside of the United States a child who has been in the United States is a crime. Three affirmative defenses are available, *i.e.*, that the defendant:

(1) acted pursuant to a lawful court order under the Uniform Child Custody Jurisdiction and Enforcement Act (UCCJEA);

(2) was fleeing an incident of domestic violence; or,

(3) was unable to return the child for circumstances beyond the defendant's control and tried to notify the person entitled to custody and did return the child as quickly as possible.

In enacting the statute, Congress clearly indicated a preference for resort to the civil remedies under the Hague Convention rather than the criminal remedy provided here.

CLE/Other Legal Publications

Jurisdiction, special appearance, and conflicts of law. Donn C. Fullenweider, 2004 ADV. FAM. L.

Immigration and its effect on relocation, jurisdiction and divorce. J. Joseph Reina, 2004 ADV. FAM. L.

Jurisdiction, venue, plea in abatement and the UCCJEA. Douglas R. Woodburn, 2004 MARRIAGE DISSOLUTION

Jurisdiction and enforcement of custody and possession. Brian L. Webb, 2004 U. TEX. FAM. L. ON THE BORDER

The ABCs of interstate conservatorship and family support jurisdiction. Angela G. Pence, 2003 ADV. FAM. L.

International and unusual child issues. (Workshop) 2003 ADV. FAM. L.

Jurisdiction over foreign litigants: dissolution, property division, spousal support, child support. Bill De La Garza & Jo Ann Carter, 2002 ADV. FAM. L.

Interstate alphabet soup. Sally H. Emerson, 2002 ADV. FAM. L.

International and cross border issues. (Workshop) 2002 ADV. FAM. L.

Extraterritorial custody issues: the UCCJEA, PKPA, and the Hague Convention. Lynn Kamin, 2001 ADV. FAM. L.

Construction and application of International Child Abduction Remedies Act. (42 U.S.C.A. § 11601 *et seq.*). 125 A.L.R. Fed 217

Leading Cases

U.S. v. Amer, 110 F.3d 873 (2d Cir. 1997), *cert. denied*, 118 S.Ct. 258 (1997) (IPKCA conviction does not violate defendant's free exercise rights notwithstanding allegation that children's removal from U.S. was for religious reasons)

U.S. v. Alahmad, 28 F.Supp.2d 1273, 996 F.Supp. 1055 (D. Colo. 1998) (state court visitation order vests maternal grandmother with "parental rights"; out-of-wedlock father's continued retention of child outside U.S. obstructs her exercise of those rights and subjects him to IPKCA)

Cross References

Missing Children Act of 1982, 28 U.S.C.A. § 534(a)

Missing Children's Assistance Act of 1984, 42 U.S.C.A. § 5771, *et seq.*

National Child Search Assistance Act of 1990, 42 U.S.C.A. § 5779–80

Parental Kidnapping Prevention Act (PKPA), 28 U.S.C.A. § 1738A

Violence Against Women Act *(VAWA)*

Chapter 110A—Domestic Violence and Stalking

§ 2265. Full Faith and Credit Given to Protection Orders.

(a) Full faith and credit. Any protection order issued that is consistent with subsection (b) of this section by the court of one State or Indian tribe (the issuing State or Indian tribe) shall be accorded full faith and credit by the court of another State or Indian tribe (the enforcing State or Indian tribe) and enforced as if it were the order of the enforcing State or tribe.

(b) Protection order. A protection order issued by a State or tribal court is consistent with this subsection if—

(1) such court has jurisdiction over the parties and matter under the law of such State or Indian tribe; and

(2) reasonable notice and opportunity to be heard is given to the person against whom the order is sought sufficient to protect that person's right to due process. In the case of ex parte orders, notice and opportunity to be heard must be provided within the time required by State or tribal law, and in any event within a reasonable time after the order is issued, sufficient to protect the respondent's due process rights.

(c) Cross or counter petition. A protection order issued by a State or tribal court against one who has petitioned, filed a complaint, or otherwise filed a written pleading for protection against abuse by a spouse or intimate partner is not entitled to full faith and credit if—

(1) no cross or counter petition, complaint, or other written pleading was filed seeking such a protection order; or

(2) a cross or counter petition has been filed and the court did not make specific findings that each party was entitled to such an order.

(d) Notification and registration.

(1) Notification. A State or Indian tribe according full faith and credit to an order by a court of another State or Indian tribe shall not notify or require notification of the party against whom a protection order has been issued that the protection order has been registered or filed in that enforcing State or tribal jurisdiction unless requested to do so by the party protected under such order.

(2) No prior registration or filing as prerequisite for enforcement. Any protection order that is otherwise consistent with this section shall be accorded full faith and credit, notwithstanding failure to comply with any requirement that the order be registered or filed in the enforcing State or tribal jurisdiction.

(e) Tribal court jurisdiction. For purposes of this section, a tribal court shall have full civil jurisdiction to enforce protection orders, including authority to enforce any orders through civil contempt proceedings, exclusion of violators from Indian lands, and other appropriate mechanisms, in matters arising within the authority of the tribe.

§ 2266. Definitions.

In this chapter:

(1) Bodily injury. The term "bodily injury" means any act, except one done in self-defense, that results in physical injury or sexual abuse.

(2) Course of conduct. The term "course of conduct" means a pattern of conduct composed of 2 or more acts, evidencing a continuity of purpose.

(3) Enter or leave Indian country. The term "enter or leave Indian country" includes leaving the jurisdiction of 1 tribal government and entering the jurisdiction of another tribal government.

(4) Indian country. The term "Indian country" has the meaning stated in section 1151 of this title.

(5) Protection order. The term "protection order" includes any injunction or other order issued for the purpose of preventing violent or threatening acts or harassment against, or contact or communication with or physical proximity to, another person, including any temporary or final order issued by a civil and criminal court (other than a support or child custody order issued pursuant to State divorce and child custody laws, except to the extent that such an order is entitled to full faith and credit under other Federal law) whether obtained by filing an independent action or as a pendente lite order in another proceeding so long as any civil order was issued in response to a complaint, petition, or motion filed by or on behalf of a person seeking protection.

(6) Serious bodily injury. The term "serious bodily injury" has the meaning stated in section 2119(2).

(7) Spouse or intimate partner. The term "spouse or intimate partner" includes—

(A) for purposes of—

(i) sections other than 2261A, a spouse or former spouse of the abuser, a person who shares a child in common with the abuser, and a person who cohabits or has cohabited as a spouse with the abuser; and

(ii) section 2261A, a spouse or former spouse of the target of the stalking, a person who shares a child in common with the target of the stalking, and a person who cohabits or has cohabited as a spouse with the target of the stalking; and

(B) any other person similarly situated to a spouse who is protected by the domestic or family violence laws of the State or tribal jurisdiction in which the injury occurred or where the victim resides.

(8) State. The term "State" includes a State of the United States, the District of Columbia, and a commonwealth, territory, or possession of the United States.

(9) Travel in interstate or foreign commerce. The term "travel in interstate or foreign commerce" does not include travel from 1 State to another by an individual who is a member of an Indian tribe and who remains at all times in the territory of the Indian tribe of which the individual is a member.

Comment

Although the federal cause of action under 42 U.S.C.A. 13981 was struck down by the U.S. Supreme Court in U.S. v. Morrison, below, the requirement of this statute for states to give Full Faith and Credit to protective orders of other states is not affected by that decision.

Leading Case

U.S. v. Morrison, 529 U.S. 598, 120 S.Ct. 1740, 146 L.Ed.2d 658 (2000) (VAWA's federal civil remedy for victims of gender-motivated violence, 42 U.S.C.A. § 13981, exceeds Congress' constitutional authority)

CLE/Other Legal Publications

Domestic violence: including protective orders and the psychology of abuse. Judy L. Warne, 2004 Adv. Fam. L.

What's love got to do with it? how a finding of family violence directly affects your family law case. Kathleen A. Hamilton, 2004 Marriage Dissolution

Overview of abuse, neglect and intra-family violence. Oscar Gabaldon, 2004 U. Tex. Fam. L. on the Border

When domestic violence and child abuse collide: Tension within the family violence field. Bree Buchanan, 2003 Adv. Fam. L.

In the crossfire: protective orders, what happens when federal law collides with family law (VAWA and Brady) and how magistrate orders impact family law litigation. Lorraine Wilson, 2001 Adv. Fam. L.

Indian Child Welfare Act of 1978

U.S.C.A. Title 25: Indians

Chapter 21—Indian Child Welfare

Comment

In 1978 Congress determined that in a custody dispute anywhere in the United States which involves a child with Indian (Native American) blood, the proper jurisdiction of that dispute is with the child's tribe. Reading the statement of Congressional policy will explain the reasons for this preemptive determination.

CLE/Other Legal Publications

THE INDIAN CHILD WELFARE ACT HANDBOOK: A LEGAL GUIDE TO THE CUSTODY AND ADOPTION OF NATIVE AMERICAN CHILDREN. B.J. Jones, (ABA Family Law Section), http://www.abanet.org/store/order.html

When the family is Native American. Sheila Corbine & Wendy Helgemo, 23 FAM. ADVOCATE No. 4 at 45 (2001)

Internet Resources

Native American Indian Child Welfare Resources on the Internet:
www.nicwa.org; or
www.nal.usda.gov/ric/ruralres/nativeam.htm

Indian Child Welfare Bibliography:
http://www.nicwa.org/library/icwabib.htm

Leading Cases

Mississippi Band of Choctaw Indians v. Holyfield, 490 U.S. 109, 104 L.Ed. 2d 29, 109 S.Ct. 1597 (1989) (tribal court has jurisdiction over child of unmarried Indian mother who never lived on reservation)

Navajo Nation v. Superior Court of State of Wash., 47 F.Supp.2d 1233 (E.D. Wash. 1999) (no private cause of action for alleged violation of ICWA preferences for adoptive placement of Indian child)

Comanche Nation v. Fox, 128 S.W.3d 745 (Tex. App.—Austin 2004, no pet.) (mother and Indian tribe entitled to new trial in conservatorship proceedings even though ICWA found not to apply to child custody modification proceeding)

In re W.D.H., 43 S.W.3d 30 (Tex. App.—Houston [14th Dist.] 2001, pet. denied) (ICWA obviously preempts Family Code when termination of parental rights affects child as enrolled member of tribe)

Doty–Jabbaar v. Dallas County Child Protective Services, 19 S.W.3d 870 (Tex. App.—Dallas 2000, pet. denied) (termination of mother's parental rights reversed; ICWA provisions require remedial services be provided and shown to be unsuccessful)

Yavapai–Apache Tribe v. Mejia, 906 S.W.2d 152 (Tex. App.—Houston [14th Dist.] 1995, mand. motion overrul.) (mother's tribe motion to transfer jurisdiction to tribal court correctly denied)

★★★

§ 1901. Congressional Findings.

Recognizing the special relationship between the United States and the Indian tribes and their members and the Federal responsibility to Indian people, the Congress finds—

(1) that clause 3, section 8, article I of the United States Constitution provides that "The Congress shall have Power * * * To regulate Commerce * * * with Indian tribes [1]" and, through this and other constitutional authority, Congress has plenary power over Indian affairs;

(2) that Congress, through statutes, treaties, and the general course of dealing with Indian tribes, has assumed the responsibility for the protection and preservation of Indian tribes and their resources;

(3) that there is no resource that is more vital to the continued existence and integrity of Indian tribes than their children and that the United States has a direct interest, as trustee, in protecting Indian children who are members of or are eligible for membership in an Indian tribe;

(4) that an alarmingly high percentage of Indian families are broken up by the removal, often unwarranted, of their children from them by nontribal public and private agencies and that an alarmingly high percentage of such children are placed in non-Indian foster and adoptive homes and institutions; and

(5) that the States, exercising their recognized jurisdiction over Indian child custody proceedings through administrative and judicial bodies, have often failed to recognize the essential tribal relations of Indian people and the cultural and social standards prevailing in Indian communities and families.

§ 1902. Congressional Declaration of Policy.

The Congress hereby declares that it is the policy of this Nation to protect the best interests of Indian children and to promote the stability and security of Indian tribes and families by the establishment of minimum Federal standards for the removal of Indian children from their families and the placement of such children in foster or adoptive homes which will reflect the unique values of Indian culture, and by providing for assistance to Indian tribes in the operation of child and family service programs.

§ 1903. Definitions.

For the purposes of this chapter, except as may be specifically provided otherwise, the term—

(1) "child custody proceeding" shall mean and include—

(i) "foster care placement" which shall mean any action removing an Indian child from its parent or Indian custodian for temporary placement in a foster home or institution or the home of a guardian or conservator where the parent or Indian custodian cannot have the child returned upon demand, but where parental rights have not been terminated;

(ii) "termination of parental rights" which shall mean any action resulting in the termination of the parent-child relationship;

(iii) "preadoptive placement" which shall mean the temporary placement of an Indian child in a foster home or institution after the termination of parental rights, but prior to or in lieu of adoptive placement; and

(iv) "adoptive placement" which shall mean the permanent placement of an Indian child for adoption, including any action resulting in a final decree of adoption.

Such term or terms shall not include a placement based upon an act which, if committed by an adult, would be deemed a crime or upon an award, in a divorce proceeding, of custody to one of the parents.

(2) "extended family member" shall be as defined by the law or custom of the Indian child's tribe or, in the absence of such law or custom, shall be a person who has reached the age of eighteen and who is the Indian child's grandparent, aunt or uncle, brother or sister, brother-in-law or sister-in-law, niece or nephew, first or second cousin, or stepparent;

(3) "Indian" means any person who is a member of an Indian tribe, or who is an Alaska Native and a member of a Regional Corporation as defined in section 1606 of Title 43;

(4) "Indian child" means any unmarried person who is under age eighteen and is either (a) a member of an Indian tribe or (b) is eligible for membership in an Indian tribe and is the biological child of a member of an Indian tribe;

(5) "Indian child's tribe" means (a) the Indian tribe in which an Indian child is a member or eligible for membership or (b), in the case of an Indian child who is a member of or eligible for membership in more than one tribe, the Indian tribe with which the Indian child has the more significant contacts;

(6) "Indian custodian" means any Indian person who has legal custody of an Indian child under tribal law or custom or under State law or to whom temporary physical care, custody, and control has been transferred by the parent of such child;

(7) "Indian organization" means any group, association, partnership, corporation, or other legal entity owned or controlled by Indians, or a majority of whose members are Indians;

(8) "Indian tribe" means any Indian tribe, band, nation, or other organized group or community of Indians recognized as eligible for the services provided to Indians by the Secretary because of their status as Indians, including any Alaska Native village as defined in section 1602(c) of Title 43;

(9) "parent" means any biological parent or parents of an Indian child or any Indian person who has lawfully adopted an Indian child, including adoptions under

tribal law or custom. It does not include the unwed father where paternity has not been acknowledged or established;

(10) "reservation" means Indian country as defined in section 1151 of Title 18 and any lands, not covered under such section, title to which is either held by the United States in trust for the benefit of any Indian tribe or individual or held by any Indian tribe or individual subject to a restriction by the United States against alienation;

(11) "Secretary" means the Secretary of the Interior; and

(12) "tribal court" means a court with jurisdiction over child custody proceedings and which is either a Court of Indian Offenses, a court established and operated under the code or custom of an Indian tribe, or any other administrative body of a tribe which is vested with authority over child custody proceedings.

§ 1911. Indian Tribe Jurisdiction Over Indian Child Custody Proceedings.

(a) Exclusive jurisdiction.

An Indian tribe shall have jurisdiction exclusive as to any State over any child custody proceeding involving an Indian child who resides or is domiciled within the reservation of such tribe, except where such jurisdiction is otherwise vested in the State by existing Federal law. Where an Indian child is a ward of a tribal court, the Indian tribe shall retain exclusive jurisdiction, notwithstanding the residence or domicile of the child.

(b) Transfer of proceedings; declination by tribal court.

In any State court proceeding for the foster care placement of, or termination of parental rights to, an Indian child not domiciled or residing within the reservation of the Indian child's tribe, the court, in the absence of good cause to the contrary, shall transfer such proceeding to the jurisdiction of the tribe, absent objection by either parent, upon the petition of either parent or the Indian custodian or the Indian child's tribe: *Provided*, That such transfer shall be subject to declination by the tribal court of such tribe.

(c) State court proceedings; intervention.

In any State court proceeding for the foster care placement of, or termination of parental rights to, an Indian child, the Indian custodian of the child and the Indian child's tribe shall have a right to intervene at any point in the proceeding.

(d) Full faith and credit to public acts, records, and judicial proceedings of Indian tribes.

The United States, every State, every territory or possession of the United States, and every Indian tribe shall give full faith and credit to the public acts, records, and judicial proceedings of any Indian tribe applicable to Indian child custody proceedings to the same extent that such entities give full faith and credit to the public acts, records, and judicial proceedings of any other entity.

§ 1912. Pending Court Proceedings.

(a) Notice; time for commencement of proceedings; additional time for preparation.

In any involuntary proceeding in a State court, where the court knows or has reason to know that an Indian child is involved, the party seeking the foster care placement of, or termination of parental rights to, an Indian child shall notify the parent or Indian custodian and the Indian child's tribe, by registered mail with return receipt requested, of the pending proceedings and of their right of intervention. If the identity or location of the parent or Indian custodian and the tribe cannot be determined, such notice shall be given to the Secretary in like manner, who shall have fifteen days after receipt to provide the requisite notice to the parent or Indian custodian and the tribe. No foster care placement or termination of parental rights proceeding shall be held until at least ten days after receipt of notice by the parent or Indian custodian and the tribe or the Secretary: *Provided*, That the parent or Indian custodian or the tribe shall, upon request, be granted up to twenty additional days to prepare for such proceeding.

(b) Appointment of counsel.

In any case in which the court determines indigency, the parent or Indian custodian shall have the right to court-appointed counsel in any removal, placement, or termination proceeding. The court may, in its discretion, appoint counsel for the child upon a finding that such appointment is in the best interest of the child. Where State law makes no provision for appointment of counsel in such proceedings, the court shall promptly notify the Secretary upon appointment of counsel, and the Secretary, upon certification of the presiding judge, shall pay reasonable fees and expenses out of funds which may be appropriated pursuant to section 13 of this title.

(c) Examination of reports or other documents.

Each party to a foster care placement or termination of parental rights proceeding under State law involving an Indian child shall have the right to examine all reports or other documents filed with the court upon which any decision with respect to such action may be based.

(d) Remedial services and rehabilitative programs; preventive measures.

Any party seeking to effect a foster care placement of, or termination of parental rights to, an Indian child under State law shall satisfy the court that active efforts have been made to provide remedial services and rehabilitative programs designed to prevent the breakup of the Indian family and that these efforts have proved unsuccessful.

(e) Foster care placement orders; evidence; determination of damage to child.

No foster care placement may be ordered in such proceeding in the absence of a determination, supported by clear and convincing evidence, including testimony of qualified expert witnesses, that the continued custody of the child by the parent or Indian custodian is likely to result in serious emotional or physical damage to the child.

(f) Parental rights termination orders; evidence; determination of damage to child.

No termination of parental rights may be ordered in such proceeding in the absence of a determination, supported by evidence beyond a reasonable doubt, including testimony of qualified expert witnesses, that the continued custody of the child by the parent or Indian custodian is likely to result in serious emotional or physical damage to the child.

§ 1913. Parental Rights; Voluntary Termination.

(a) Consent; record; certification matters; invalid consents.

Where any parent or Indian custodian voluntarily consents to a foster care placement or to termination of parental rights, such consent shall not be valid unless executed in writing and recorded before a judge of a court of competent jurisdiction and accompanied by the presiding judge's certificate that the terms and consequences of the consent were fully explained in detail and were fully understood by the parent or Indian custodian. The court shall also certify that either the parent or Indian custodian fully understood the explanation in English or that it was interpreted into a language that the parent or Indian custodian understood. Any consent given prior to, or within ten days after, birth of the Indian child shall not be valid.

(b) Foster care placement; withdrawal of consent.

Any parent or Indian custodian may withdraw consent to a foster care placement under State law at any time and, upon such withdrawal, the child shall be returned to the parent or Indian custodian.

(c) Voluntary termination of parental rights or adoptive placement; withdrawal of consent; return of custody.

In any voluntary proceeding for termination of parental rights to, or adoptive placement of, an Indian child, the consent of the parent may be withdrawn for any reason at any time prior to the entry of a final decree of termination or adoption, as the case may be, and the child shall be returned to the parent.

(d) Collateral attack; vacation of decree and return of custody; limitations.

After the entry of a final decree of adoption of an Indian child in any State court, the parent may withdraw consent thereto upon the grounds that consent was obtained through fraud or duress and may petition the court to vacate such decree. Upon a finding that such consent was obtained through fraud or duress, the court shall vacate such decree and return the child to the parent. No adoption which has been effective for at least two years may be invalidated under the provisions of this subsection unless otherwise permitted under State law.

§ 1914. Petition to Court of Competent Jurisdiction To Invalidate Action upon Showing of Certain Violations.

Any Indian child who is the subject of any action for foster care placement or termination of parental rights under State law, any parent or Indian custodian from whose custody such child was removed, and the Indian child's tribe may petition any court of competent jurisdiction to invalidate such action upon a showing that such action violated any provision of sections 1911, 1912, and 1913 of this title.

§ 1915. Placement of Indian Children.

(a) Adoptive placements; preferences.

In any adoptive placement of an Indian child under State law, a preference shall be given, in the absence of good cause to the contrary, to a placement with (1) a member of the child's extended family; (2) other members of the Indian child's tribe; or (3) other Indian families.

(b) Foster care or preadoptive placements; criteria; preferences.

Any child accepted for foster care or preadoptive placement shall be placed in the least restrictive setting which most approximates a family and in which his special needs, if any, may be met. The child shall also be placed within reasonable proximity to his or her home, taking into account any special needs of the child. In any foster care or preadoptive placement, a preference shall be given, in the absence of good cause to the contrary, to a placement with—

(i) a member of the Indian child's extended family;

(ii) a foster home licensed, approved, or specified by the Indian child's tribe;

(iii) an Indian foster home licensed or approved by an authorized non-Indian licensing authority; or

(iv) an institution for children approved by an Indian tribe or operated by an Indian organization which has a program suitable to meet the Indian child's needs.

(c) Tribal resolution for different order of preference; personal preference considered; anonymity in application of preferences.

In the case of a placement under subsection (a) or (b) of this section, if the Indian child's tribe shall establish a different order of preference by resolution, the agency or court effecting the placement shall follow such order so long as the placement is the least restrictive setting appropriate to the particular needs of the child, as provided in subsection (b) of this section. Where appropriate, the preference of the Indian child or parent shall be considered: *Provided*, That where a consenting parent evidences a desire for anonymity, the court or agency shall give weight to such desire in applying the preferences.

(d) Social and cultural standards applicable.

The standards to be applied in meeting the preference requirements of this section shall be the prevailing social and cultural standards of the Indian community in which the parent or extended family resides or with which the parent or extended family members maintain social and cultural ties.

(e) Record of placement; availability.

A record of each such placement, under State law, of an Indian child shall be maintained by the State in which the placement was made, evidencing the efforts to comply with the order of preference specified in this section. Such record shall be made available at any time upon the request of the Secretary or the Indian child's tribe.

§ 1916. Return of Custody.

(a) Petition; best interests of child.

Notwithstanding State law to the contrary, whenever a final decree of adoption of an Indian child has been vacated or set aside or the adoptive parents voluntarily consent to the termination of their parental rights to the child, a biological parent or prior Indian custodian may petition for return of custody and the court shall grant such petition unless there is a showing, in a proceeding subject to the provisions of section 1912 of this title, that such return of custody is not in the best interests of the child.

(b) Removal from foster care home; placement procedure.

Whenever an Indian child is removed from a foster care home or institution for the purpose of further foster care, preadoptive, or adoptive placement, such placement shall be in accordance with the provisions of this chapter, except in the case where an Indian child is being returned to the parent or Indian custodian from whose custody the child was originally removed.

§ 1917. Tribal Affiliation Information and Other Information of Protection of Rights from Tribal Relationship; Application of Subject of Adoptive Placement; Disclosure by Court.

Upon application by an Indian individual who has reached the age of eighteen and who was the subject of an adoptive placement, the court which entered the final decree shall inform such individual of the tribal affiliation, if any, of the individual's biological parents and provide such other information as may be necessary to protect any rights flowing from the individual's tribal relationship.

§ 1918. Reassumption of Jurisdiction over Child Custody Proceedings.

(a) Petition; suitable plan; approval by Secretary.

Any Indian tribe which became subject to State jurisdiction pursuant to the provisions of the Act of August 15, 1953 (67 Stat. 588), as amended by Title IV of the Act of April 11, 1968 (82 Stat. 73, 78), or pursuant to any other Federal law, may reassume jurisdiction over child custody proceedings. Before any Indian tribe may reassume jurisdiction over Indian child custody proceedings, such tribe shall present to the Secretary for approval a petition to reassume such jurisdiction which includes a suitable plan to exercise such jurisdiction.

(b) Criteria applicable to consideration by Secretary; partial retrocession.

(1) In considering the petition and feasibility of the plan of a tribe under subsection (a) of this section, the Secretary may consider, among other things:

(i) whether or not the tribe maintains a membership roll or alternative provision for clearly identifying the persons who will be affected by the reassumption of jurisdiction by the tribe;

(ii) the size of the reservation or former reservation area which will be affected by retrocession and reassumption of jurisdiction by the tribe;

(iii) the population base of the tribe, or distribution of the population in homogeneous communities or geographic areas; and

(iv) the feasibility of the plan in cases of multitribal occupation of a single reservation or geographic area.

(2) In those cases where the Secretary determines that the jurisdictional provisions of section 1911(a) of this title are not feasible, he is authorized to accept partial retrocession which will enable tribes to exercise referral jurisdiction as provided in section 1911(b) of this title, or, where appropriate, will allow them to exercise exclusive jurisdiction as provided in section 1911(a) of this title over limited community or geographic areas without regard for the reservation status of the area affected.

(c) Approval of petition; publication in Federal Register; notice; reassumption period; correction of causes for disapproval.

If the Secretary approves any petition under subsection (a) of this section, the Secretary shall publish notice of such approval in the Federal Register and shall notify the affected State or States of such approval. The Indian tribe concerned shall reassume jurisdiction sixty days after publication in the Federal Register of notice of approval. If the Secretary disapproves any petition under subsection (a) of this section, the Secretary shall provide such technical assistance as may be necessary to enable the tribe to correct any deficiency which the Secretary identified as a cause for disapproval.

(d) Pending actions or proceedings unaffected.

Assumption of jurisdiction under this section shall not affect any action or proceeding over which a court has already assumed jurisdiction, except as may be provided pursuant to any agreement under section 1919 of this title.

§ 1919. Agreements Between States and Indian Tribes.

(a) Subject coverage.

States and Indian tribes are authorized to enter into agreements with each other respecting care and custody of Indian children and jurisdiction over child custody proceedings, including agreements which may provide for orderly transfer of jurisdiction on a case-by-case basis and agreements which provide for concurrent jurisdiction between States and Indian tribes.

(b) Revocation; notice; actions or proceedings unaffected.

Such agreements may be revoked by either party upon one hundred and eighty days' written notice to the other party. Such revocation shall not affect any action or proceeding over which a court has already assumed jurisdiction, unless the agreement provides otherwise.

§ 1920. Improper Removal of Child from Custody; Declination of Jurisdiction; Forthwith Return of Child: Danger Exception.

Where any petitioner in an Indian child custody proceeding before a State court has improperly removed the child from custody of the parent or Indian custodian or has improperly retained custody after a visit or other temporary relinquishment of custody, the court shall decline jurisdiction over such petition and shall forthwith return the child to his parent or Indian custodian unless returning the child to his parent or custodian would subject the child to a substantial and immediate danger or threat of such danger.

§ 1921. Higher State or Federal Standard Applicable To Protect Rights of Parent or Indian Custodian of Indian Child.

In any case where State or Federal law applicable to a child custody proceeding under State or Federal law provides a higher standard of protection to the rights of the parent or Indian custodian of an Indian child than the rights provided under this subchapter, the State or Federal court shall apply the State or Federal standard.

§ 1922. Emergency Removal or Placement of Child; Termination; Appropriate Action.

Nothing in this subchapter shall be construed to prevent the emergency removal of an Indian child who is a resident of or is domiciled on a reservation, but temporarily located off the reservation, from his parent or Indian custodian or the emergency placement of such child in a foster home or institution, under applicable State law, in order to prevent imminent physical damage or harm to the child. The State authority, official, or agency involved shall insure that the emergency removal or placement terminates immediately when such removal or placement is no longer necessary to prevent imminent physical damage or harm to the child and shall expeditiously initiate a child custody proceeding subject to the provisions of this subchapter, transfer the child to the jurisdiction of the appropriate Indian tribe, or restore the child to the parent or Indian custodian, as may be appropriate.

§ 1923. Effective Date.

None of the provisions of this subchapter, except sections 1911(a), 1918, and 1919 of this title, shall affect a proceeding under State law for foster care placement, termination of parental rights, preadoptive placement, or adoptive placement which was initiated or completed prior to one hundred and eighty days after November 8, 1978, but shall apply to any subsequent proceeding in the same matter or subsequent proceedings affecting the custody or placement of the same child.

Federal Income Tax

U.S.C.A. Title 26: Internal Revenue Code

Introductory Comment

The federal tax statutes included in this publication are not individually annotated. The articles, books, and cases listed below should accomplish this task. Many are written with a Texas point of view, and all should be readily available to Texas practitioners.

Major Resource Materials

Melvyn B. Frumkes, Frumkes on Divorce Taxation (James Publishing 2003), (714) 755–5450, www.jamespublishing.com

2003 U.S. Master Tax Guide (CCH Inc.), 1–800–248–3248, www.cch.com

Jack Zuckerman and William F. Wolf, Understanding Business Tax Returns: A Lawyer's Handbook (ABA Family Law Section 1998); www.abanet.org/family/home

BNA Family Law Reporter: Reference File and Tax Guide, *www.bna.com*

CLE/Other Legal Publications

Dissecting the complex tax return. Randall B. Wilhite, 2004 Adv. Fam. L.

Alimony and maintenance: enforceability, contractual agreements, creative uses and new tax traps. Patricia A. Wicoff, 2004 Adv. Fam. L.

Top 10 tax issues everyone should understand. Geoffrey S. Poll, 2004 Adv. Fam. L.

Divorce and taxes. Geoffrey Poll, 2004 U. Tex. Fam. L. Front Lines

Family law tax issues. Edwin W. Davis, 2003 Adv. Fam. L.

Tax issues. (Workshop) 2003 Adv. Fam. L.

Demystifying tax returns. Patrice L. Ferguson, 2003 Marriage Dissolution

Tax. Geoffrey S. Poll, 2002 Adv. Fam. L.

Hidden jewels in the tax return. Glenn David Villafranca, 2002 Marriage Dissolution

Through the past darkly: reviewing tax returns. Kathleen Anderson & Robert D. Cocanower, 2001 ADV. FAM. L.

Basic tax—tax brackets, dependency exemptions, year-of-divorce taxes, tax sheltered plans, alimony, and tax law violations. Panel, 2001 ADV. FAM. L.

Complex tax issues. Panel, 2001 ADV. FAM. L.

Top 10 taxation issues in divorces. Bryan C. Rice & James C. Penn, 2001 MARRIAGE DISSOLUTION

Family law and the IRS. Edwin W. Davis, 2000 ADV. FAM. L.

Drafting tax motivated provisions—Stock option, alimony, and business buyouts. Randall B. Wilhite, 2000 ADV. FAM. L. DRAFTING

Leading Cases

United States v. Mitchell, 403 U.S. 190, 29 L.Ed. 2d 406, 91 S.Ct. 1763 (1971) (state law controls whether income is separate or community)

Francis v. Francis, 412 S.W.2d 29 (Tex. 1967) (contractual alimony enforceable under Texas law of contracts)

Kimsey v. Kimsey, 965 S.W.2d 690 (Tex. App.—El Paso 1998, no pet.) (divorce decree must specify whether parties were to file joint or separate tax returns for years of marriage in which no returns were filed)

In re C.C.N.S., 955 S.W.2d 448 (Tex. App.—Fort Worth 1997, no writ) (trial court not authorized to rotate dependency exemption between parents)

Brooks v. Brooks, 515 S.W.2d 730 (Tex. Civ. App.—Eastland 1974, writ ref. n.r.e.) (order to pay "community debts" does not include obligation to pay taxes)

---

§ 66. Treatment of Community Income.

(a) Treatment of community income where spouses live apart. If—

(1) 2 individuals are married to each other at any time during a calendar year;

(2) such individuals—

(A) live apart at all times during the calendar year, and

(B) do not file a joint return under section 6013 with each other for a taxable year beginning or ending in the calendar year;

(3) one or both of such individuals have earned income for the calendar year which is community income; and

(4) no portion of such earned income is transferred (directly or indirectly) between such individuals before the close of the calendar year,

then, for purposes of this title, any community income of such individuals for the calendar year shall be treated in accordance with the rules provided by section 879(a).

(b) Secretary may disregard community property laws where spouse not notified of community income. The Secretary may disallow the benefits of any community property law to any taxpayer with respect to any income if such taxpayer acted as if solely entitled to such income and failed to notify the taxpayer's spouse before the due date (including extensions) for filing the return for the taxable year in which the income was derived of the nature and amount of such income.

(c) Spouse relieved of liability in certain other cases. Under regulations prescribed by the Secretary, if—

(1) an individual does not file a joint return for any taxable year,

(2) such individual does not include in gross income for such taxable year an item of community income properly includible therein which, in accordance with the rules contained in section 879(a), would be treated as the income of the other spouse,

(3) the individual establishes that he or she did not know of, and had no reason to know of, such item of community income, and

(4) taking into account all facts and circumstances, it is inequitable to include such item of community income in such individual's gross income,

then, for purposes of this title, such item of community income shall be included in the gross income of the other spouse (and not in the gross income of the individual). Under procedures prescribed by the Secretary, if, taking into account all the facts and circumstances, it is inequitable to hold the individual liable for any unpaid tax or any deficiency (or any portion of either) attributable to any item for which relief is not available under the preceding sentence, the Secretary may relieve such individual of such liability.

(d) Definitions. For purposes of this section—

(1) Earned income. The term "earned income" has the meaning given to such term by section 911(d)(2).

(2) Community income. The term "community income" means income which, under applicable community property laws, is treated as community income.

(3) Community property laws. The term "community property laws" means the community property laws of a State, a foreign country, or a possession of the United States.

§ 71. Alimony and Separate Maintenance Payments.

(a) General rule. Gross income includes amounts received as alimony or separate maintenance payments.

(b) Alimony or separate maintenance payments defined. For purposes of this section—

(1) In general. The term "alimony or separate maintenance payment" means any payment in cash if—

(A) such payment is received by (or on behalf of) a spouse under a divorce or separation instrument,

(B) the divorce or separation instrument does not designate such payment as a payment which is not includible in gross income under this section and not allowable as a deduction under section 215,

(C) in the case of an individual legally separated from his spouse under a decree of divorce or of separate maintenance, the payee spouse and the payor spouse are not members of the same household at the time such payment is made, and

(D) there is no liability to make any such payment for any period after the death of the payee spouse and there is no liability to make any payment (in cash or property) as a substitute for such payments after the death of the payee spouse.

(2) Divorce or separation instrument. The term "divorce or separation instrument" means—

(A) a decree of divorce or separate maintenance or a written instrument incident to such a decree,

(B) a written separation agreement, or

(C) a decree (not described in subparagraph (A)) requiring a spouse to make payments for the support or maintenance of the other spouse.

(c) Payments to support children.

(1) In general. Subsection (a) shall not apply to that part of any payment which the terms of the divorce or separation instrument fix (in terms of an amount of money or a part of the payment) as a sum which is payable for the support of children of the payor spouse.

(2) Treatment of certain reductions related to contingencies involving child. For purposes of paragraph (1), if any amount specified in the instrument will be reduced—

(A) on the happening of a contingency specified in the instrument relating to a child (such as attaining a specified age, marrying, dying, leaving school, or a similar contingency), or

(B) at a time which can clearly be associated with a contingency of a kind specified in subparagraph (A),

an amount equal to the amount of such reduction will be treated as an amount fixed as payable for the support of children of the payor spouse.

(3) Special rule where payment is less than amount specified in instrument. For purposes of this subsection, if any payment is less than the amount specified in the instrument, then so much of such payment as does not exceed the sum payable for support shall be considered a payment for such support.

(d) Spouse. For purposes of this section, the term "spouse" includes a former spouse.

(e) Exception for joint returns. This section and section 215 shall not apply if the spouses make a joint return with each other.

(f) Recomputation where excess front-loading of alimony payments.—

(1) In general. If there are excess alimony payments—

(A) the payor spouse shall include the amount of such excess payments in gross income for the payor spouse's taxable year beginning in the 3rd post-separation year, and

(B) the payee spouse shall be allowed a deduction in computing adjusted gross income for the amount of such excess payments for the payee's taxable year beginning in the 3rd post-separation year.

(2) Excess alimony payments. For purposes of this subsection, the term "excess alimony payments" mean the sum of—

(A) the excess payments for the 1st post-separation year, and

(B) the excess payments for the 2nd post-separation year.

(3) Excess payments for 1st post-separation year. For purposes of this subsection, the amount of the excess payments for the 1st post-separation year is the excess (if any) of—

(A) the amount of the alimony or separate maintenance payments paid by the payor spouse during the 1st post-separation year, over

(B) the sum of—

(i) the average of—

(I) the alimony or separate maintenance payments paid by the payor spouse during the 2nd post-separation year, reduced by the excess payments for the 2nd post-separation year, and

(II) the alimony or separate maintenance payments paid by the payor spouse during the 3rd post-separation year, plus

(ii) $15,000.

(4) Excess payments for 2nd post-separation year. For purposes of this subsection, the amount of the excess payments for the 2nd post-separation year is the excess (if any) of—

(A) the amount of the alimony or separate maintenance payments paid by the payor spouse during the 2nd post-separation year, over

(B) the sum of—

(i) the amount of the alimony or separate maintenance payments paid by the payor spouse during the 3rd post-separation year, plus

(ii) $15,000.

(5) Exceptions.—

(A) Where payment ceases by reason of death or remarriage. Paragraph (1) shall not apply if—

(i) either spouse dies before the close of the 3rd post-separation year, or the payee spouse remarries before the close of the 3rd post-separation year, and

(ii) the alimony or separate maintenance payments cease by reason of such death or remarriage.

(B) Support payments. For purposes of this subsection, the term "alimony or separate maintenance payment" shall not include any payment received under a decree described in subsection (b)(2)(C).

(C) Fluctuating payments not within control of payor spouse. For purposes of this subsection, the term "alimony or separate maintenance payment" shall not include any payment to the extent it is made pursuant to a continuing liability (over a period of not less than 3 years) to pay a fixed portion or portions of the income from a business or property or from compensation for employment or self-employment.

(6) Post-separation years. For purposes of this subsection, the term "1st post-separation years" means the 1st calendar year in which the payor spouse paid to the payee spouse alimony or separate maintenance payments to which this section applies. The 2nd and 3rd post-separation years shall be the 1st and 2nd succeeding calendar years, respectively.

(g) Cross references.—

(1) For deduction of alimony or separate maintenance payments, see section 215.

(2) For taxable status of income of an estate or trust in the case of divorce, etc., see section 682.

History: Amended by P.L. 99514 and P.L. 98–369.

REGULATIONS [26 C.F.R.]

Editors' Note: *To date the IRS has not replaced its "official" regulations, § 1.71–1, even though the "temporary regulations" which responded to the Deficit Reduction Act of 1984 were promulgated that same year. Indeed, as noted below, some of the Q/A and other portions of § 1.71–1T have been out-of-date since enactment of the Tax Reform Act of 1986. Although it can be argued that there can be no justification for such delay in confirming (and updating) regulations, even a cursory examination of the Internal Revenue Code will convince any reasonable person that there can be no justification for the complexity of the Code itself.*

§ 1.71–1T. Alimony and Separate Maintenance Payments (temporary).

(a) In general.

Q–1 What is the income tax treatment of alimony or separate maintenance payments?

A–1 Alimony or separate maintenance payments are, under section 71, included in the gross income of the payee spouse and, under section 215, allowed as a deduction from the gross income of the payor spouse.

> ***Editors' Note:*** *Q/A 2 does not reflect P.L. 99–515 (1986).*

Q–2 What is an alimony or separate maintenance payment?

A–2 An alimony or separate maintenance payment is any payment received by or on behalf of a spouse (which for this purpose includes a former spouse) of the payor under a divorce or separation instrument that meets all of the following requirements:

(a) The payment is in cash (see A–5).

(b) The payment is not designated as a payment which is excludible from the gross income of the payee and nondeductible by the payor (see A–8).

(c) In the case of spouses legally separated under a decree of divorce or separate maintenance, the spouses are not members of the same household at the time the payment is made (see A–9).

(d) The payor has no liability to continue to make any payment after the death of the payee (or to make any payment as a substitute for such payment) and the divorce or separation instrument states that there is no such liability (see A–10).

(e) The payment is not treated as child support (see A–15).

(f) To the extent that one or more annual payments exceed $10,000 during any of the 6–post-separation years, the payor is obligated to make annual payments in each of the post-separation years (see A–19).

Q–3 In order to be treated as alimony or separate maintenance payments, must the payments be "periodic" as that term was defined prior to enactment of the Tax Reform Act of 1984 or be made in discharge of a legal obligation of the payor to support the payee arising out of a marital or family relationship?

A–3 No. The Tax Reform Act of 1984 replaces the old requirements with the requirements described in A–2 above. Thus, the requirements that alimony or separate maintenance payments be "periodic" and be made in discharge of a legal obligation to support arising out of a marital or family relationship have been eliminated.

Q–4 Are the instruments described in section 71(a) of prior law the same as divorce or separation instruments described in section 71, as amended by the Tax Reform Act of 1984?

A–4 Yes.

(b) Specific requirements.

Q–5 May alimony or separate maintenance payments be made in a form other than cash?

A–5 No. Only cash payments (including checks and money orders payable on demand) qualify as alimony or separate maintenance payments. Transfers of services or property (including a debt instrument of a third party or an annuity contract), execution of a debt instrument by the payor, or the use of property of the payor do not qualify as alimony or separate maintenance payments.

Q–6 May payments of cash to a third party on behalf of a spouse qualify as alimony or separate maintenance payments if the payments are pursuant to the terms of a divorce or separation instrument?

A–6 Yes. Assuming all other requirements are satisfied, a payment of cash by the payor spouse to a third party under the terms of the divorce or separation instrument will qualify as a payment of cash which is received "on behalf of a spouse." For example, cash payments of rent, mortgage, tax, or tuition liabilities of the payee spouse made under the terms of the divorce or separation instrument will qualify as alimony or separate maintenance payments. Any payments to maintain property owned by the payor spouse and used by the payee spouse (including mortgage payments, real estate taxes and insurance premiums) are not payments on behalf of a spouse even if those payments are made pursuant to the terms of the divorce or separation instrument. Premiums paid by the payor spouse for term or whole life insurance on the payor's life made under the terms of the divorce or separation instrument will qualify as payments on behalf of the payee spouse to the extent that the payee spouse is the owner of the policy.

Q–7 May payments of cash to a third party on behalf of a spouse qualify as alimony or separate maintenance payments if the payments are made to the third party at the written request of the payee spouse?

A–7 Yes. For example, instead of making an alimony or separate maintenance payment directly to the payee, the payor spouse may make a cash payment to a charitable organization if such payment is pursuant to the written request, consent or ratification of the payee spouse. Such request, consent or ratification must state that the parties intend the payment to be treated as an alimony or separate maintenance payment to the payee spouse subject to the rules of section 71, and must be received by the payor spouse prior to the date of filing of the payor's first return of tax for the taxable year in which the payment was made.

Q–8 How may spouses designate that payments otherwise qualifying as alimony or separate maintenance payments shall be excludible from the gross income of the payee and nondeductible by the payor?

A–8 The spouses may designate that payments otherwise qualifying as alimony or separate maintenance payments shall be nondeductible by the payor and excludible from gross income by the payee by so providing in a divorce or separation instrument (as defined in section 71(b)(2)). If the spouses have executed a written separation agreement (as described in section 71(b)(2)(B)), any writing signed by both spouses which designates otherwise qualifying alimony or separate maintenance payments as nondeductible and excludible and which refers to the written separation agreement will be treated as a written separation agreement (and thus a divorce or separation instrument) for purposes of the preceding sentence. If the spouses are subject to temporary support orders (as described in section 71(b)(2)(C)), the designation of otherwise qualifying alimony or separate payments as nondeductible and excludible must be made in the original or a subsequent temporary support order. A copy of the instrument containing the designation of payments as not alimony or separate maintenance payments must be attached to the payee's first filed return of tax (Form 1040) for each year in which the designation applies.

Q–9 What are the consequences if, at the time a payment is made, the payor and payee spouses are members of the same household?

A–9 Generally, a payment made at the time when the payor and payee spouses are members of the same household cannot qualify as an alimony or separate maintenance payment if the spouses are legally separated under a decree of divorce or of separate maintenance. For purposes of the preceding sentence, a dwelling unit formerly shared by both spouses shall not be considered two separate households even if the spouses physically separate themselves within the dwelling unit. The spouses will not be treated as members of the same household if one spouse is preparing to depart from the household of the other spouse, and does depart not more than one month after the date the payment is made. If the spouses are not legally separated under a decree of divorce or separate maintenance, a payment under a written separation agreement or a decree described in section 71(b)(2)(C) may qualify as an alimony or separate maintenance payment notwithstanding that the payor and payee are members of the same household at the time the payment is made.

Q–10 Assuming all other requirements relating to the qualification of certain payments as alimony or separate maintenance payments are met, what are the consequences if the payor spouse is required to continue to make the payments after the death of the payee spouse?

A–10 None of the payments before (or after) the death of the payee spouse qualify as alimony or separate maintenance payments.

Editors' Note: *Q/A 11 and 12 do not reflect P.L. 99–515 (1986).*

Q–11 What are the consequences if the divorce or separation instrument fails to state that there is no liability for any period after the death of the payee spouse to continue to make any payments which would otherwise qualify as alimony or separate maintenance payments?

A–11 If the instrument fails to include such a statement, none of the payments, whether made before or after the death of the payee spouse, will qualify as alimony or separate maintenance payments.

Example (1). A is to pay B $10,000 in cash each year for a period of 10 years under a divorce or separation instrument which does not state that the payments will terminate upon the death of B. None of the payments will qualify as alimony or separate maintenance payments.

Example (2). A is to pay B $10,000 in cash each year for a period of 10 years under a divorce or separation instrument which states that the payments will terminate upon the death of B. In addition, under the instrument, A is to pay B or B's estate $20,000 in cash each year for a period of 10 years. Because the $20,000 annual payments will not terminate upon the death of B, these payments will not qualify as alimony or separate maintenance payments. However, the separate $10,000 annual payments will qualify as alimony or separate maintenance payments.

Q–12 Will a divorce or separation instrument be treated as stating that there is no liability to make payments after the death of the payee spouse if the liability to make such payments terminates pursuant to applicable local law or oral agreement?

A–12 No. Termination of the liability to make payments must be stated in the terms of the divorce or separation instrument.

Q–13 What are the consequences if the payor spouse is required to make one or more payments (in cash or property) after the death of the payee spouse as a substitute for the continuation of pre-death payments which would otherwise qualify as alimony or separate maintenance payments?

A–13 If the payor spouse is required to make any such substitute payments, none of the otherwise qualifying payments will qualify as alimony or separate maintenance payments. The divorce or separation instrument need not state, however, that there is no liability to make any such substitute payment.

Q–14 Under what circumstances will one or more payments (in cash or property) which are to occur after the death of the payee spouse be treated as a substitute for the continuation of payments which would otherwise qualify as alimony or separate maintenance payments?

A–14 To the extent that one or more payments are to begin to be made, increase in amount, or become accelerated in time as a result of the death of the payee spouse, such payments may be treated as a substitute for the continuation of payments terminating on the death of the payee spouse which would otherwise qualify as alimony or separate maintenance payments. The determination of whether or not such payments are a substitute for the continuation of payments which would otherwise qualify as alimony or separate maintenance payments, and of the amount of the otherwise qualifying alimony or separate maintenance payments for which any such payments are a substitute, will depend on all of the facts and circumstances.

Example (1). Under the terms of a divorce decree, A is obligated to make annual alimony payments to B of $30,000, terminating on the earlier of the expiration of 6 years or the death of B. B maintains custody of the minor children of A and B. The decree provides that at the death of B, if there are minor children of A and B remaining, A will be obligated to make annual payments of $10,000 to a trust, the income and corpus of which are to be used for the benefit of the children until the youngest child attains the age of majority. These facts indicate that A's liability to make annual $10,000 payments in trust for the benefit of his minor children upon the death of B is a substitute for $10,000 of the $30,000 annual payments to B. Accordingly, $10,000 of each of the $30,000 annual *payments to B will not qualify as alimony or separate maintenance payments.*

Example (2). Under the terms of a divorce decree, A is obligated to make annual alimony payments to B of $30,000, terminating on the earlier of the expiration of 15 years or the death of B. The divorce decree provides that if B dies before the expiration of the 15 year period, A will pay to B's estate the difference between the total amount that A would have paid had B survived, minus the amount actually paid. For example, if B dies at the end of the 10th year in which payments are made, A will pay to B's estate $150,000 ($450,000$300,000). These facts indicate that A's liability to make a lump sum payment to B's estate upon the death of B is a substitute for the full amount of each of the annual $30,000 payments to B. Accordingly, none of the annual $30,000 payments to B will qualify as alimony or separate maintenance payments. The result would be the same if the lump sum payable at B's death were discounted by an appropriate interest factor to account for the prepayment.

(c) Child support payments.

Q–15 What are the consequences of a payment which the terms of the divorce or separation instrument fix as payable for the support of a child of the payor spouse?

A–15 A payment which under the terms of the divorce or separation instrument is fixed (or treated as fixed) as payable for the support of a child of the payor spouse does not qualify as an alimony or separate maintenance payment. Thus, such a payment is not deductible by the payor spouse or includible in the income of the payee spouse.

Q–16 When is a payment fixed (or treated as fixed) as payable for the support of a child of the payor spouse?

A–16 A payment is fixed as payable for the support of a child of the payor spouse if the divorce or separation instrument specifically designates some sum or portion (which sum or portion may fluctuate) as payable for the support of a child of the payor spouse. A payment will be treated as fixed as payable for the support of a child of the payor spouse if the payment is reduced (a) on the happening of a contingency relating to a child of the payor, or (b) at a time which can clearly be associated with such a contingency. A payment may be treated as fixed as payable for the support of a child of the payor spouse even if other separate payments specifically are designated as payable for the support of a child of the payor spouse.

Q–17 When does a contingency relate to a child of the payor?

A–17 For this purpose, a contingency relates to a child of the payor if it depends on any event relating to that child, regardless of whether such event is certain or likely to occur. Events that relate to a child of the payor include the following: the child's attaining a specified age or income level, dying, marrying, leaving school, leaving the spouse's household, or gaining employment.

Q–18 When will a payment be treated as to be reduced at a time which can clearly be associated with the happening of a contingency relating to a child of the payor?

A–18 There are two situations, described below, in which payments which would otherwise qualify as alimony or separate maintenance payments will be presumed to be reduced at a time clearly associated with the happening of a contingency relating to a child of the payor. In all other situations, reductions in payments will not be treated as clearly associated with the happening of a contingency relating to a child of the payor.

The first situation referred to above is where the payments are to be reduced not more than 6 months before or after the date the child is to attain the age of 18, 21, or local age of majority. The second situation is where the payments are to be reduced on two or more occasions which occur not more than one year before or after a different child of the payor spouse attains a certain age between the ages of 18 and 24, inclusive. The certain age referred to in the preceding sentence must be the same for each such child, but need not be a whole number of years.

The presumption in the two situations described above that payments are to be reduced at a time clearly associated with the happening of a contingency relating to a child of the payor may be rebutted (either by the Service or by taxpayers) by showing that the time at which the payments are to be reduced was determined independently of any contingencies relating to the children of the payor. The presumption in the first situation will be rebutted conclusively if the reduction is a complete cessation of alimony or separate maintenance payments during the sixth post-separation year (described in A–21) or upon the expiration of a 72–month period. The presumption may also be rebutted in other circumstances, for example, by showing that alimony payments are to be made for a period customarily provided in the local jurisdiction, such as a period equal to one-half the duration of the marriage.

Example: A and B are divorced on July 1, 1985, when their children, C (born July 15, 1970) and D (born September 23, 1972), are 14 and 12, respectively. Under the divorce decree, A is to make alimony payments to B of $2,000 per month. Such payments are to be reduced to $1,500 per month on January 1, 1991 and to $1,000 per month on January 1, 1995. On January 1, 1991, the date of the first reduction in payments, C will be 20 years 5 months and 17 days old. On January 1, 1995, the date of the second reduction in payments, D will be 22 years 3 months and 9 days old. Each of the reductions in payments is to occur not more than one year before or after a different child of A attains the age of 21 years and 4 months. (Actually, the reductions are to occur not more than one year before or after C and D attain any of the ages 21 years 3 months and 9 days through 21 years 5 months and 17 days.) Accordingly, the reductions will be presumed to clearly be associated with the happening of a contingency relating to C and D. Unless this presumption is rebutted, payments under the divorce decree equal to the sum of the reduction ($1,000 per month) will be treated as fixed for the support of the children of A and therefore will not qualify as alimony or separate maintenance payments.

> ***Editors' Note:*** *Temporary Reg. § 1.71–1T does not reflect P.L. 99–515 (1986).*

(d) Excess front-loading rules.

Q–19 What are the excess front-loading rules?

A–19 The excess front-loading rules are two special rules which may apply to the extent that payments in any calendar year exceed $10,000. The first rule is a minimum term rule, which must be met in order for any annual payment, to the extent in excess of $10,000, to qualify as an alimony or separate maintenance payment (see A–2(f)). This rule requires that alimony or separate maintenance payments be called for, at a minimum, during the 6 "post-separation years". The second rule is a recapture rule which characterizes payments retrospectively by requiring a recalculation and inclusion in income by the payor and deduction by the payee of previously paid alimony or separate maintenance payments to the extent that the amount of such payments during any of the 6 "post-separation years" falls short of the amount of payments during a prior year by more than $10,000.

Q–20 Do the excess front-loading rules apply to payments to the extent that annual payments never exceed $10,000?

A–20 No. For example, A is to make a single $10,000 payment to B. Provided that the other requirements of section 71 are met, the payment will qualify as an alimony or separate maintenance payment. If A were to make a single $15,000 payment to B, $10,000 of the payment would qualify as an alimony or separate maintenance payment and $5,000 of the payment would be disqualified under the minimum term rule because payments were not to be made for the minimum period.

Q–21 Do the excess front-loading rules apply to payments received under a decree described in section 71(b)(2)(C)?

A–21 No. Payments under decrees described in section 71(b)(2)(C) are to be disregarded entirely for purposes of applying the excess front-loading rules.

Q–22 Both the minimum term rule and the recapture rule refer to 6 "post-separation years". What are the 6 "post separation years"?

A–22 The 6 "post-separation years" are the 6 consecutive calendar years beginning with the first calendar year in which the payor pays to the payee an alimony or separate maintenance payment (except a payment made under a decree described in section 71(b)(2)(C)). Each year within this period is referred to as a "post-separation year". The 6–year period need not commence with the year in which the spouses separate or divorce, or with the year in which payments under the divorce or separation instrument are made, if no payments during such year qualify as alimony or separate maintenance payments. For example, a decree for the divorce of A and B is entered in October, 1985. The decree requires A to make monthly payments to B commencing November 1, 1985, but A and B are members of the same household until February 15, 1986 (and as a result, the payments prior to January 16, 1986, do not qualify as alimony payments). For purposes of applying the excess front-loading rules to payments from A to B, the 6 calendar years 1986 through 1991 are post-separation years. If a spouse has been making payments pursuant to a divorce or separation instrument described in section

71(b)(2)(A) or (B), a modification of the instrument or the substitution of a new instrument (for example, the substitution of a divorce decree for a written separation agreement) will not result in the creation of additional post-separation years. However, if a spouse has been making payments pursuant to a divorce or separation instrument described in section 71(b)(2)(C), the 6–year period does not begin until the first calendar year in which alimony or separate maintenance payments are made under a divorce or separation instrument described in section 71(b)(2)(A) or (B).

Q–23 How does the minimum term rule operate?

A–23 The minimum term rule operates in the following manner. To the extent payments are made in excess of $10,000, a payment will qualify as an alimony or separate maintenance payment only if alimony or separate maintenance payments are to be made in each of the 6 post-separation years. For example, pursuant to a divorce decree, A is to make alimony payments to B of $20,000 in each of the 5 calendar years 1985 through 1989. A is to make no payment in 1990. Under the minimum term rule, only $10,000 will qualify as an alimony payment in each of the calendar years 1985 through 1989. If the divorce decree also required A to make a $1 payment in 1990, the minimum term rule would be satisfied and $20,000 would be treated as an alimony payment in each of the calendar years 1985 through 1989. The recapture rule would, however, apply for 1990. For purposes of determining whether alimony or separate maintenance payments are to be made in any year, the possible termination of such payments upon the happening of a contingency (other than the passage of time) which has not yet occurred is ignored (unless such contingency may cause all or a portion of the payment to be treated as a child support payment).

Q–24 How does the recapture rule operate?

A–24 The recapture rule operates in the following manner. If the amount of alimony or separate maintenance payments paid in any post-separation year (referred to as the "computation year") falls short of the amount of alimony or separate maintenance payments paid in any prior post-separation year by more than $10,000, the payor must compute an "excess amount" for the computation year. The excess amount for any computation year is the sum of excess amounts determined with respect to each prior post-separation year. The excess amount determined with respect to a prior post-separation year is the excess of (1) the amount of alimony or separate maintenance payments paid by the payor spouse during such prior post-separation year, over (2) the amount of the alimony or separate maintenance payments paid by the payor spouse during the computation year plus $10,000. For purposes of this calculation, the amount of alimony or separate maintenance payments made by the payor spouse during any post-separation year preceding the computation year is reduced by any excess amount previously determined with respect to such year. The rules set forth above may be illustrated by the following example. A makes alimony payments to B of $25,000 in 1985 and $12,000 in 1986. The excess amount with respect to 1985 that is recaptured in 1986 is $3,000 ($25,000–($12,000 + $10,000)). For purposes of subsequent computation years, the amount deemed paid in 1985 is $22,000. If A makes alimony payments to B of $1,000 in 1987, the excess amount that is recaptured in 1987 will be $12,000. This is the sum of an $11,000 excess amount with respect to 1985 ($22,000—$1,000 + $10,000)) and a $1,000 excess amount with respect to 1986 ($12,000–($1,000 + $10,000)). If, prior to the end of 1990, payments decline further, additional recapture will occur. The payor spouse must include the excess amount in gross income for his/her taxable year beginning with or in the computation year. The payee spouse is allowed a deduction for the excess amount in computing adjusted gross income for his/her taxable year beginning with or in the computation year. However, the payee spouse must compute the excess amount by reference to the date when payments were made and not when payments were received.

Q–25 What are the exceptions to the recapture rule?

A–25 Apart from the $10,000 threshold for application of the recapture rule, there are three exceptions to the recapture rule. The first exception is for payments received under temporary support orders described in section 71(b)(2)(C) (see A–21). The second exception is for any payment made pursuant to a continuing liability over the period of the post-separation years to pay a fixed portion of the payor's income from a business or property or from compensation for employment or self-employment. The third exception is where the alimony or separate maintenance payments in any post-separation year cease by reason of the death of the payor or payee or the remarriage (as defined under applicable local law) of the payee before the close of the computation year. For example, pursuant to a divorce decree, A is to make cash payments to B of $30,000 in each of the calendar years 1985 through 1990. A makes cash payments of $30,000 in 1985 and $15,000 in 1986, in which year B remarries and A's alimony payments cease. The recapture rule does not apply for 1986 or any subsequent year. If alimony or separate maintenance payments made by A decline or cease during a post-separation year for any other reason (including a failure by the payor to make timely payments, a modification of the divorce or separation instrument, a reduction in the support needs of the payee, or a reduction in the ability of the payor to provide support) excess amounts with respect to prior post-separation years will be subject to recapture.

(e) Effective dates.

Q–26 When does section 71, as amended by the Tax Reform Act of 1984, become effective?

A–26 Generally, section 71, as amended, is effective with respect to divorce or separation instruments (as defined in section 71(b)(2)) executed after December 31, 1984. If a decree of divorce or separate maintenance executed after December 31, 1984, incorporates or adopts without change the terms of the alimony or separate maintenance payments under a divorce or separation instrument executed before January 1, 1985, such decree will be treated as executed before January 1, 1985. A change in the amount of alimony or separate maintenance payments or the time period over which such payments are to continue, or the addition or deletion of any contingencies or conditions relating to such payments is a change in the terms of the alimony or separate maintenance payments. For example, in November 1984, A and B executed a written separation agreement. In February 1985, a decree of divorce is entered in substitution for the written separation agreement. The decree of divorce does not change the terms of the alimony A pays to B. The decree of divorce will be treated as executed before January 1, 1985 and hence alimony payments under the decree will be subject to the rules of section 71 prior to amendment by the Tax Reform Act of 1984. If the amount or time period of the alimony or separate maintenance payments are not specified in the pre–1985 separation agreement or if the decree of divorce changes the amount or term of such payments, the decree of divorce will not be treated as executed before January 1, 1985, and alimony payments under the decree will be subject to the rules of section 71, as amended by the Tax Reform Act of 1984.

Section 71, as amended, also applies to any divorce or separation instrument executed (or treated as executed) before January 1, 1985 that has been modified on or after January 1, 1985, if such modification expressly provides that section 71, as amended by the Tax Reform Act of 1984, shall apply to the instrument as modified. In this case, section 71, as amended, is effective with respect to payments made after the date the instrument is modified.

---

§ 121. Exclusion of Gain from Sale of Principal Residence.

(a) Exclusion. Gross income shall not include gain from the sale or exchange of property if, during the 5–year period ending on the date of the sale or exchange, such property has been owned and used by the taxpayer as the taxpayer's principal residence for periods aggregating 2 years or more.

(b) Limitations.—

(1) In general. The amount of gain excluded from gross income under subsection (a) with respect to any sale or exchange shall not exceed $250,000.

(2) Special rules for joint returns. In the case of a husband and wife who make a joint return for the taxable year of the sale or exchange of the property—

(A) $500,000 limitation for certain joint returns. Paragraph (1) shall be applied by substituting "$500,000" for "$250,000" if.—

(i) either spouse meets the ownership requirements of subsection (a) with respect to such property;

(ii) both spouses meet the use requirements of subsection (a) with respect to such property; and

(iii) neither spouse is ineligible for the benefits of subsection (a) with respect to such property by reason of paragraph (3).

(B) Other joint returns. If such spouses do not meet the requirements of subparagraph (A), the limitation under paragraph (1) shall be the sum of the limitations under paragraph (1) to which each spouse would be entitled if such spouses had not been married. For purposes of the preceding sentence, each spouse shall be treated as owning the property during the period that either spouse owned the property.

(3) Application to only 1 sale or exchange every 2 years.—

(A) In general. Subsection (a) shall not apply to any sale or exchange by the taxpayer if, during the 2–year period ending on the date of such sale or exchange, there was any other sale or exchange by the taxpayer to which subsection (a) applied.

(B) Pre-May 7, 1997, sales not taken into account. Subparagraph (A) shall be applied without regard to any sale or exchange before May 7, 1997.

(c) Exclusion for taxpayers failing to meet certain requirements.—

(1) In general. In the case of a sale or exchange to which this subsection applies, the ownership and use requirements of subsection (a), and subsection (b)(3), shall not apply; but the dollar limitation under paragraph (1) or (2) of subsection (b), whichever is applicable, shall be equal to—

(A) the amount which bears the same ratio to such limitation (determined without regard to this paragraph) as

(B)(i) the shorter of—

(I) the aggregate periods, during the 5–year period ending on the date of such sale or exchange, such property has been owned and used by the taxpayer as the taxpayer's principal residence; or

(II) the period after the date of the most recent prior sale or exchange by the taxpayer to which subsection (a) applied and before the date of such sale or exchange, bears to

(ii) 2 years.

(2) Sales and exchanges to which subsection applies. **This subsection shall apply to any sale or exchange if—**

(A) **subsection (a) would not (but for this subsection) apply to such sale or exchange by reason of—**

(i) a failure to meet the ownership and use requirements of subsection (a), or

(ii) subsection (b)(3), and

(B) such sale or exchange is by reason of a change in place of employment, health, or, to the extent provided in regulations, unforeseen circumstances.

(d) Special rules.—

(1) Joint returns. If a husband and wife make a joint return for the taxable year of the sale or exchange of the property, subsections (a) and (c) shall apply if either spouse meets the ownership and use requirements of subsection (a) with respect to such property.

(2) Property of deceased spouse. For purposes of this section, in the case of an unmarried individual whose spouse is deceased on the date of the sale or exchange of property, the period such unmarried individual owned and used such property shall include the period such deceased spouse owned and used such property before death.

(3) Property owned by spouse or former spouse. For purposes of this section—

(A) Property transferred to individual from spouse or former spouse. In the case of an individual holding property transferred to such individual in a transaction described in section 1041(a), the period such individual owns such property shall include the period the transferor owned the property.

(B) Property used by former spouse pursuant to divorce decree, etc. Solely for purposes of this section, an individual shall be treated as using property as such individual's principal residence during any period of ownership while such individual's spouse or former spouse is granted use of the property under a divorce or separation instrument (as defined in section 71(b)(2)).

(4) Tenant-stockholder in cooperative housing corporation. For purposes of this section, if the taxpayer holds stock as a tenant-stockholder (as defined in section 216) in a cooperative housing corporation (as defined in such section), then—

(A) the holding requirements of subsection (a) shall be applied to the holding of such stock, and

(B) the use requirements of subsection (a) shall be applied to the house or apartment which the taxpayer was entitled to occupy as such stockholder.

(5) Involuntary conversions.—

(A) In general. For purposes of this section, the destruction, theft, seizure, requisition, or condemnation of property shall be treated as the sale of such property.

(B) Application of section 1033. In applying section 1033 (relating to involuntary conversions), the amount realized from the sale or exchange of property shall be treated as being the amount determined without regard to this section, reduced by the amount of gain not included in gross income pursuant to this section.

(C) Property acquired after involuntary conversion. If the basis of the property sold or exchanged is determined (in whole or in part) under section 1033(b) (relating to basis of property acquired through involuntary conversion), then the holding and use by the taxpayer of the converted property shall be treated as holding and use by the taxpayer of the property sold or exchanged.

(6) Recognition of gain attributable to depreciation. Subsection (a) shall not apply to so much of the gain from the sale of any property as does not exceed the portion of the depreciation adjustments (as defined in section 1250(b)(3)) attributable to periods after May 6, 1997, in respect of such property.

(7) Determination of use during periods of out-of-residence care. In the case of a taxpayer who—

(A) becomes physically or mentally incapable of selfcare, and

(B) owns property and uses such property as the taxpayer's principal residence during the 5–year period described in subsection (a) for periods aggregating at least 1 year,

then the taxpayer shall be treated as using such property as the taxpayer's principal residence during any time during such 5–year period in which the taxpayer owns the property and resides in any facility (including a nursing home) licensed by a State or political subdivision to care for an individual in the taxpayer's condition.

(8) Sales of remainder interests. For purposes of this section—

(A) In general. At the election of the taxpayer, this section shall not fail to apply to the sale or exchange of an interest in a principal residence by reason of such interest being a remainder interest in such residence, but this section shall not apply to any other interest in such residence which is sold or exchanged separately.

(B) Exception for sales to related parties. Subparagraph (A) shall not apply to any sale to, or exchange with, any person who bears a relationship to the taxpayer which is described in section 267(b) or 707(b).

(9) Members of uniformed services and foreign service.

(A) In general. At the election of an individual with respect to a property, the running of the 5–year period described in subsections (a) and (c)(1)(B) and paragraph (7) of this subsection with respect to such property shall be suspended during any period that such individual or such individual's spouse is serving on qualified official extended duty as a member of the uniformed services or of the Foreign Service of the United States.

(B) Maximum period of suspension. The 5–year period described in subsection (a) shall not be extended more than 10 years by reason of subparagraph (A).

(C) Qualified official extended duty. For purposes of this paragraph—

(i) In general.—The term "qualified official extended duty" means any extended duty while serving at a duty station which is at least 50 miles from such property or while residing under Government orders in Government quarters.

(ii) Uniformed services.—The term "uniformed services" has the meaning given such term by section 101(a)(5) of title 10, United States Code, as in effect on the date of the enactment of this paragraph.

(iii) Foreign service of the United States.—The term "member of the Foreign Service of the United States" has the meaning given the term " member of the Service" by paragraph (1), (2), (3), (4), or (5) of section 103 of the Foreign Service Act of 1980, as in effect on the date of the enactment of this paragraph.

(iv) Extended duty.—The term "extended duty" means any period of active duty pursuant to a call or order to such duty for a period in excess of 90 days or for an indefinite period.

(D) Special rules relating to election.

(i) Election limited to 1 property at a time.—An election under subparagraph (A) with respect to any property may not be made if such an election is in effect with respect to any other property.

(ii) Revocation of election.—An election under subparagraph (A) may be revoked at any time.

(e) Denial of exclusion for expatriates. This section shall not apply to any sale or exchange by an individual if the treatment provided by section 877(a)(1) applies to such individual.

(f) Election to have section not apply. This section shall not apply to any sale or exchange with respect to which the taxpayer elects not to have this section apply.

(g) Residences acquired in rollovers under section 1034. For purposes of this section, in the case of property the acquisition of which by the taxpayer resulted under section 1034 (as in effect on the day before the date of the enactment of this section) in the nonrecognition of any part of the gain realized on the sale or exchange of another residence, in determining the period for which the taxpayer has owned and used such property as the taxpayer's principal residence, there shall be included the aggregate periods for which such other residence (and each prior residence taken into account under section 1223(7) in determining the holding period of such property) had been so owned and used.

§ 152. Dependent Defined.

(a) General definition. For purposes of this subtitle, the term "dependent" means any of the following individuals over half of whose support, for the calendar year in which the taxable year of the taxpayer begins, was received from the taxpayer (or is treated under subsection (c) or (e) as received from the taxpayer):

(1) A son or daughter of the taxpayer, or a descendant of either,

(2) A stepson or stepdaughter of the taxpayer,

(3) A brother, sister, stepbrother, or stepsister of the taxpayer,

(4) The father or mother of the taxpayer, or an ancestor of either,

(5) A stepfather or stepmother of the taxpayer,

(6) A son or daughter of a brother or sister of the taxpayer,

(7) A brother or sister of the father or mother of the taxpayer,

(8) A son-in-law, daughter-in-law, father-in-law, mother-in-law, brother-in-law, or sister-in-law of the taxpayer, or

(9) An individual (other than an individual who at any time during the taxable year was the spouse, determined without regard to section 7703, of the taxpayer) who, for the taxable year of the taxpayer, has as his principal place of abode the home of the taxpayer and is a member of the taxpayer's household.

(b) Rules relating to general definition. For purposes of this section—

(1) The terms "brother" and "sister" include a brother or sister by the halfblood.

(2) In determining whether any of the relationships specified in subsection (a) or paragraph (1) of this subsection exists, a legally adopted child of an individual (and a child who is a member of an individual's household, if placed with such individual by an authorized placement agency for legal adoption by such individual), or a foster

child of an individual (if such child satisfies the requirements of subsection (a)(9) with respect to such individual), shall be treated as a child of such individual by blood.

(3) The term "dependent" does not include any individual who is not a citizen or national of the United States unless such individual is a resident of the United States or of a country contiguous to the United States. The preceding sentence shall not exclude from the definition of "dependent" any child of the taxpayer legally adopted by him, if, for the taxable year of the taxpayer, the child has as his principal place of abode the home of the taxpayer and is a member of the taxpayer's household, and if the taxpayer is a citizen or national of the United States.

(4) A payment to a wife which is includible in the gross income of the wife under section 71 or 682 shall not be treated as a payment by her husband for the support of any dependent.

(5) An individual is not a member of the taxpayer's household if at any time during the taxable year of the taxpayer the relationship between such individual and the taxpayer is in violation of local law.

(c) Multiple support agreements. For purposes of subsection (a), over half of the support of an individual for a calendar year shall be treated as received from the taxpayer if—

(1) no one person contributed over half of such support;

(2) over half of such support was received from persons each of whom, but for the fact that he did not contribute over half of such support, would have been entitled to claim such individual as a dependent for a taxable year beginning in such calendar year;

(3) the taxpayer contributed over 10 percent of such support; and

(4) each person described in paragraph (2) (other than the taxpayer) who contributed over 10 percent of such support files a written declaration (in such manner and form as the Secretary may by regulations prescribe) that he will not claim such individual as a dependent for any taxable year beginning in such calendar year.

(d) Special support test in case of students. For purposes of subsection (a), in the case of any individual who is—

(1) a son, stepson, daughter, or stepdaughter of the taxpayer (within the meaning of this section), and

(2) a student (within the meaning of section 151(c)(4)),

amounts received as scholarships for study at an educational organization described in section 170(b)(1)(A)(ii) shall not be taken into account in determining whether such individual received more than half of his support from the taxpayer.

(e) Support test in case of child of divorced parents, etc.—

(1) Custodial parent gets exemption. Except as otherwise provided in this subsection, if—

(A) a child (as defined in section 151(c)(3)) receives over half of his support during the calendar year from his parents—

(i) who are divorced or legally separated under a decree of divorce or separate maintenance,

(ii) who are separated under a written separation agreement, or

(iii) who live apart at all times during the last 6 months of the calendar year, and

(B) such child is in the custody of one or both of his parents for more than one-half of the calendar year, such child shall be treated, for purposes of subsection (a), as receiving over half of his support during the calendar year from the parent having custody for a greater portion of the calendar year (hereinafter in this subsection referred to as the "custodial parent").

(2) Exception where custodial parent releases claim to exemption for the year. A child of parents described in paragraph (1) shall be treated as having received over half of his support during a calendar year from the noncustodial parent if—

(A) the custodial parent signs a written declaration (in such manner and form as the Secretary may by regulations prescribe) that such custodial parent will not claim such child as a dependent for any taxable year beginning in such calendar year, and

(B) the noncustodial parent attaches such written declaration to the noncustodial parent's return for the taxable year beginning during such calendar year.

For purposes of this subsection, the term "noncustodial parent" means the parent who is not the custodial parent.

(3) Exception for multiple-support agreement. This subsection shall not apply in any case where over half of the support of the child is treated as having been received from a taxpayer under the provisions of subsection (c).

(4) Exception for certain pre–1985 instruments.—

(A) In general. A child of parents described in paragraph (1) shall be treated as having received over half his support during a calendar year from the noncustodial parent if—

(i) a qualified pre–1985 instrument between the parents applicable to the taxable year beginning in such calendar year provides that the noncustodial parent shall be entitled to any deduction allowable under section 151 for such child, and

(ii) the noncustodial parent provides at least $600 for the support of such child during such calendar year.

For purposes of this subparagraph, amounts expended for the support of a child or children shall be treated as received from the noncustodial parent to the extent that such parent provided amounts for such support.

(B) Qualified pre–1985 instrument. For purposes of this paragraph, the term "qualified pre–1985 instrument" means any decree of divorce or separate maintenance or written agreement—

(i) which is executed before January 1, 1985,

(ii) which on such date contains the provision described in subparagraph (A)(i), and

(iii) which is not modified on or after such date in a modification which expressly provides that this paragraph shall not apply to such decree or agreement.

(5) Special rule for support received from new spouse of parent. For purposes of this subsection, in the case of the remarriage of a parent, support of a child received from the parent's spouse shall be treated as received from the parent.

(6) Cross reference.—

For provision treating child as dependent of both parents for purposes of medical expense deduction, see section 213(d)(5).

Leading Case

Lystad v. Lystad, 916 S.W.2d 617 (Tex. App.—Fort Worth 1996, no writ) (trial court lacks power to award federal income tax exemption for child to noncustodial parent over custodian's objection)

REGULATIONS [26 C.F.R.]

§ 1.152–4T. Dependency Exemption in the Case of a Child of Divorced Parent, etc. (temporary).

(a) In general.

Q–1 Which parent may claim the dependency exemption in the case of a child of divorced or separated parents?

A–1 Provided the parents together would have been entitled to the dependency exemption had they been married and filing a joint return, the parent having custody of a child for the greater portion of the year (the custodial parent) will generally be entitled to the dependency exemption. This rule applies to parents not living together during the last 6 months of the calendar year, as well as those divorced or separated under a separation agreement.

Q–2 Are there any exceptions to the general rule in A–1?

A–2 Yes, there are three exceptions. The general rule does not apply (i) if a multiple support agreement is in effect (see section 152(c)), (ii) if a decree or agreement executed prior to January 1, 1985 provides that the custodial parent has agreed to release his or her claim to the dependency exemption to the noncustodial parent and the noncustodial parent provides at least $600 of support to the child (see section 152(e)(4)), or (iii) if the custodial parent relinquishes the exemption in the manner described in A–3.

Q–3 How may the exemption for a dependent child be claimed by a noncustodial parent?

A–3 A noncustodial parent may claim the exemption for a dependent child only if the noncustodial parent attaches to his/her income tax return for the year of the exemption a written declaration from the custodial parent stating that he/she will not claim the child as a dependent for the taxable year beginning in such calendar year. The written declaration may be made on a form to be provided by the Service for this purpose. Once the Service has released the form, any declaration made other than on the official form shall conform to the substance of such form.

Q–4 For what period may a custodial parent release to the noncustodial parent a claim to the exemption for a dependent child?

A–4 The exemption may be released for a single year, for a number of specified years (for example, alternate years), or for all future years, as specified in the declaration. If the exemption is released for more than one year, the original release must be attached to the return of the noncustodial spouse and a copy of such release must be attached to his/her return for each succeeding taxable year for which he/she claims the dependency exemption.

Q–5 May only the custodial parent claim a deduction under section 213(d) for medical expenses paid by the parent or an income exclusion under section 105(b) for medical expenses paid by an employer for a dependent child?

A–5 No. Under the new rules, if a child receives over half of his support during the calendar year from his parents who are divorced or legally separated under a decree of divorce or separate maintenance, or who are separated under a written separation agreement, that child will be treated as a dependent of both parents for purposes of sections 105(b) and 213(d). Thus, a parent can deduct medical expenses paid by that parent for a child even though a dependency exemption for the child is claimed by the other parent. The special rule of sections 105(b) and 213(d) does not apply where over half of the support of a child is treated as having been received from a person under the provisions of section 152(c) (relating to multiple support agreements).

Q–6 When does section 152(e), as amended by the Tax Reform Act of 1984, become effective?

A–6 Section 152(e), as amended, is effective with respect to dependency exemptions for taxable years beginning after December 31, 1984.

---

§ 215. Alimony, etc., Payments.

(a) General rule. In the case of an individual, there shall be allowed as a deduction an amount equal to the alimony or separate maintenance payments paid during such individual's taxable year.

(b) Alimony or separate maintenance payments defined. For purposes of this section, the term "alimony or separate maintenance payment" means any alimony or separate maintenance payment (as defined in section 71(b)) which is includible in the gross income of the recipient under section 71.

(c) Requirement of identification number. The Secretary may prescribe regulations under which—

(1) any individual receiving alimony or separate maintenance payments is required to furnish such individual's taxpayer identification number to the individual making such payments, and

(2) the individual making such payments is required to include such taxpayer identification number on such individual's return for the taxable year in which such payments are made.

(d) Coordination with section 682. No deduction shall be allowed under this section with respect to any payment if, by reason of section 682 (relating to income of alimony trusts), the amount thereof is not includible in such individual's gross income.

REGULATIONS [26 C.F.R.]

§ 1.215–1. Periodic Alimony, etc., Payments.

(a) A deduction is allowable under section 215 with respect to periodic payments in the nature of, or in lieu of, alimony or an allowance for support actually paid by the taxpayer during his taxable year and required to be included in the income of the payee wife or former wife, as the case may be, under section 71. As to the amounts required to be included in the income of such wife or former wife, see section 71 and the regulations thereunder. For definition of "husband" and "wife" see section 7701(a) (17).

(b) The deduction under section 215 is allowed only to the obligor spouse. It is not allowed to an estate, trust, corporation, or any other person who may pay the alimony obligation of such obligor spouse. The obligor spouse, however, is not allowed a deduction for any periodic payment includible under section 71 in the income of the wife or former wife, which payment is attributable to property transferred in discharge of his obligation and which, under section 71(d) or section 682, is not includible in his gross income.

(c) The following examples, in which both H and W file their income tax returns on the basis of a calendar year, illustrate cases in which a deduction is or is not allowed under section 215:

Example 1. Pursuant to the terms of a decree of divorce, H, in 1956, transferred securities valued at $100,000 in trust for the benefit of W, which fully discharged all his obligations to W. The periodic payments made by the trust to W are required to be included in W's income under section 71. Such payments are stated in section 71(d) not to be includible in H's income and, therefore, under section 215 are not deductible from his income.

Example 2. A decree of divorce obtained by W from H incorporated a previous agreement of H to establish a trust, the trustees of which were instructed to pay W $5,000 a year for the remainder of her life. The court retained jurisdiction to order H to provide further payments if necessary for the support of W. In 1956 the trustee paid to W $4,000 from the income of the trust and $1,000 from the corpus of the trust. Under the provisions of sections 71 and 682(b), W would include $5,000 in her income for 1956. H would not include any part of the $5,000 in his income nor take a deduction therefor. If H had paid the $1,000 to W pursuant to court order rather than allowing the trustees to pay it out of corpus, he would have been entitled to a deduction of $1,000 under the provisions of section 215.

(d) For other examples, see sections 71 and 682 and the regulations thereunder.

§ 1.215–1T. Alimony, etc., Payments (temporary).

Q–1 What information is required by the Internal Revenue Service when an alimony or separate maintenance payment is claimed as a deduction by a payor?

A–1 The payor spouse must include on his/her first filed return of tax (Form 1040) for the taxable year in which the payment is made the payee's social security number, which the payee is required to furnish to the payor. For penalties applicable to a payor spouse who fails to include such information on his/her return of tax or to a payee spouse who fails to furnish his/her social security number to the payor spouse, see section 6676.

---

§ 1041. Transfers of Property Between Spouses or Incident to Divorce.

(a) General rule. No gain or loss shall be recognized on a transfer of property from an individual to (or in trust for the benefit of)—

(1) a spouse, or

(2) a former spouse, but only if the transfer is incident to the divorce.

(b) Transfer treated as gift; transferee has transferor's basis. In the case of any transfer of property described in subsection (a)—

(1) for purposes of this subtitle, the property shall be treated as acquired by the transferee by gift, and

(2) the basis of the transferee in the property shall be the adjusted basis of the transferor.

(c) Incident to divorce. For purposes of subsection (a)(2), a transfer of property is incident to the divorce if such transfer—

(1) occurs within 1 year after the date on which the marriage ceases, or

(2) is related to the cessation of the marriage.

(d) Special rule where spouse is nonresident alien. Subsection (a) shall not apply if the spouse (or former spouse) of the individual making the transfer is a nonresident alien.

(e) Transfers in trust where liability exceeds basis. Subsection (a) shall not apply to the transfer of property in trust to the extent that—

(1) the sum of the amount of the liabilities assumed, plus the amount of the liabilities to which the property is subject, exceeds

(2) the total of the adjusted basis of the property transferred.

Proper adjustment shall be made under subsection (b) in the basis of the transferee in such property to take into account gain recognized by reason of the preceding sentence.

REGULATIONS [26 C.F.R.]

> ***Editors' Note:*** *To date the IRS has not replaced its "official" regulations, § 1.1041–1, even though the "temporary regulations" which responded to the Deficit Reduction Act of 1984 were promulgated that same year. Indeed, as noted below, some of § 1.1041–1T are now out-of-date.*

§ 1.1041–1T. Treatment of Transfer of Property Between Spouses or Incident To Divorce (Temporary).

Q–1 How is the transfer of property between spouses treated under section 1041?

A–1 Generally, no gain or loss is recognized on a transfer of property from an individual to (or in trust for the benefit of) a spouse or, if the transfer is incident to a divorce, a former spouse. The following questions and answers describe more fully the scope, tax consequences and other rules which apply to transfers of property under section 1041.

(a) Scope of section 1041 in general.

Q–2 Does section 1041 apply only to transfers of property incident to divorce?

A–2 No. Section 1041 is not limited to transfers of property incident to divorce. Section 1041 applies to any transfer of property between spouses regardless of whether the transfer is a gift or is a sale or exchange between spouses acting at arm's length (including a transfer in exchange for the relinquishment of property or marital rights or an exchange otherwise governed by another nonrecognition provision of the Code). A divorce or legal separation need not be contemplated between the spouses at the time of the transfer nor must a divorce or legal separation ever occur.

Example (1). A and B are married and file a joint return. A is the sole owner of a condominium unit. A sale or gift of the condominium from A to B is a transfer which is subject to the rules of section 1041.

Example (2). A and B are married and file separate returns. A is the owner of an independent sole proprietorship, X Company. In the ordinary course of business, X Company makes a sale of property to B. This sale is a transfer of property between spouses and is subject to the rules of section 1041.

Example (3). Assume the same facts as in example (2), except that X Company is a corporation wholly owned by A. This sale is not a sale between spouses subject to the rules of section 1041. However, in appropriate circumstances, general tax principles, including the step-transaction doctrine, may be applicable in recharacterizing the transaction.

Q–3 Do the rules of section 1041 apply to a transfer between spouses if the transferee spouse is a nonresident alien?

A–3 No. Gain or loss (if any) is recognized (assuming no other nonrecognition provision applies) at the time of a transfer of property if the property is transferred to a spouse who is a nonresident alien.

Q–4 What kinds of transfers are governed by section 1041?

A–4 Only transfers of property (whether real or personal, tangible or intangible) are governed by section 1041. Transfers of services are not subject to the rules of section 1041.

Q–5 Must the property transferred to a former spouse have been owned by the transferor spouse during the marriage?

A–5 No. A transfer of property acquired after the marriage ceases may be governed by section 1041.

(b) Transfer incident to the divorce.

Q–6 When is a transfer of property "incident to the divorce"?

A–6 A transfer of property is "incident to the divorce" in either of the following 2 circumstances

(1) The transfer occurs not more than one year after the date on which the marriage ceases, or

(2) The transfer is related to the cessation of the marriage. Thus, a transfer of property occurring not more than one year after the date on which the marriage ceases need not be related to the cessation of the marriage to qualify for section 1041 treatment. (See A–7 for transfers occurring more than one year after the cessation of the marriage.)

Q–7 When is a transfer of property "related to the cessation of the marriage?"

A–7 A transfer of property is treated as related to the cessation of the marriage if the transfer is pursuant to a divorce or separation instrument, as defined in section 71(b)(2), and the transfer occurs not more than 6 years after the date on which the marriage ceases. A divorce or separation instrument includes a modification or amendment to such decree or instrument. Any transfer not pursuant to a divorce or separation instrument and any transfer occurring more than 6 years after the cessation of the marriage is presumed to be not related to the cessation of the marriage. This presumption may be rebutted only by showing that the transfer was made to effect the division of property owned by the former spouses at the time of the cessation of the marriage. For example, the presumption may be rebutted by showing that (a) the transfer was not made within the one-and six-year periods described above because of factors which hampered an earlier transfer of the property, such as legal or business impediments to transfer or disputes concerning the value of the property owned at the time of the cessation of the marriage, and (b) the transfer is effected promptly after the impediment to transfer is removed.

Q–8 Do annulments and the cessations of marriages that are void ab initio due to violations of state law constitute divorces for purposes of section 1041?

A–8 Yes.

(c) Transfers on behalf of a spouse.

Q–9 May transfers of property to third parties on behalf of a spouse (or former spouse) qualify under section 1041?

A–9 Yes. There are three situations in which a transfer of property to a third party on behalf of a spouse (or former spouse) will qualify under section 1041, provided all other requirements of the section are satisfied. The first situation is where the transfer to the third party is required by a divorce or separation instrument. The second situation is where the transfer to the third party is pursuant to the written request of the other spouse (or former spouse). The third situation is where the transferor receives from the other spouse (or former spouse) a written consent or ratification of the transfer to the third party. Such consent or ratification must state that the parties intend the transfer to be treated as a transfer to the nontransferring spouse (or former spouse) subject to the rules of section 1041 and must be received by the transferor prior to the date of filing of the transferor's first return of tax for the taxable year in which the transfer was made. In the three situations described above, the transfer of property will be treated as made directly to the nontransferring spouse (or former spouse) and the nontransferring spouse will be treated as immediately transferring the property to the third party. The deemed transfer from the nontransferring spouse (or former spouse) to the third party is not a transaction that qualifies for nonrecognition of gain under section 1041. This A–9 shall not apply to transfers to which § 1.1041–2 applies.

(d) Tax consequences of transfers subject to section 1041.

Q–10 How is the transferor of property under section 1041 treated for income tax purposes?

A–10 The transferor of property under section 1041 recognizes no gain or loss on the transfer even if the transfer was in exchange for the release of marital rights or other consideration. This rule applies regardless of whether the transfer is of property separately owned by the transferor or is a division (equal or unequal) of community property. Thus, the result under section 1041 differs from the result in United States v. Davis, 370 U.S. 65 (1962).

Q–11 How is the transferee of property under section 1041 treated for income tax purposes?

A–11 The transferee of property under section 1041 recognizes no gain or loss upon receipt of the transferred property. In all cases, the basis of the transferred property in the hands of the transferee is the adjusted basis of such property in the hands of the transferor immediately before the transfer. Even if the transfer is a bona fide sale, the transferee does not acquire a basis in the transferred property equal to the transferee's cost (the fair market value). This carryover basis rule applies whether the adjusted basis of the transferred property is less than, equal to, or greater than its fair market value at the time of transfer (or the value of any consideration provided by the transferee) and applies for purposes of determining loss as well as gain upon the subsequent disposition of the property by the transferee. Thus, this rule is different from the rule applied in section 1015(a) for determining the basis of property acquired by gift.

Q–12 Do the rules described in A–10 and A–11 apply even if the transferred property is subject to liabilities which exceed the adjusted basis of the property?

A–12 Yes. For example, assume A owns property having a fair market value of $10,000 and an adjusted basis of $1,000. In contemplation of making a transfer of this property incident to a divorce from B, A borrows $5,000 from a bank, using the property as security for the borrowing. A then transfers the property to B and B assumes, or takes the property subject to, the liability to pay the $5,000 debt. Under section 1041, A recognizes no gain or loss upon the transfer of the property, and the adjusted basis of the property in the hands of B is $1,000.

Q–13 Will a transfer under section 1041 result in a recapture of investment tax credits with respect to the property transferred?

A–13 In general, no. Property transferred under section 1041 will not be treated as being disposed of by, or ceasing to be section 38 property with respect to, the transferor. However, the transferee will be subject to investment tax credit recapture if, upon or after the transfer, the property is disposed of by, or ceases to be section 38 property with respect to, the transferee. For example, as part of a divorce property settlement, B receives a car from A that has been used in A's business for two years and for which an investment tax credit was taken by A. No part of A's business is transferred to B and B's use of the car is solely personal. B is subject to recapture of the investment tax credit previously taken by A.

(e) Notice and recordkeeping requirement with respect to transactions under section 1041.

Q–14 Does the transferor of property in a transaction described in section 1041 have to supply, at the time of the transfer, the transferee with records sufficient to determine the adjusted basis and holding period of the property at the time of the transfer and (if applicable) with notice that the property transferred under section 1041 is potentially subject to recapture of the investment tax credit?

A–14 Yes. A transferor of property under section 1041 must, at the time of the transfer, supply the transferee with records sufficient to determine the adjusted basis and holding period of the property as of the date of the transfer. In addition, in the case of a transfer of property which carries with it a potential liability for investment tax credit recapture, the transferor must, at the time of the transfer, supply the transferee with records sufficient to determine the amount and period of such potential liability. Such records must be preserved and kept accessible by the transferee.

(f) Property settlements, effective dates, transitional periods and elections.

Q–15 When does section 1041 become effective?

A–15 Generally, section 1041 applies to all transfers after July 18, 1984. However, it does not apply to transfers after July 18, 1984 pursuant to instruments in effect on or before July 18, 1984. (See A–16 with respect to exceptions to the general rule.)

Q–16 Are there any exceptions to the general rule stated in A–15 above?

A–16 Yes. Two transitional rules provide exceptions to the general rule stated in A–15. First, section 1041 will apply to transfers after July 18, 1984 under instruments that were in effect on or before July 18, 1984 if both spouses (or former spouses) elect to have section 1041 apply to such transfers. Second, section 1041 will apply to all transfers after December 31, 1983 (including transfers under instruments in effect on or before July 18, 1984) if both spouses (or former spouses) elect to have section 1041 apply. (See A–18 relating to the time and manner of making the elections under the first or second transitional rule.)

Q–17 Can an election be made to have section 1041 apply to some, but not all, transfers made after December 31, 1983, or some but not all, transfers made after July 18, 1984 under instruments in effect on or before July 18, 1984?

A–17 No. Partial elections are not allowed. An election under either of the two elective transitional rules applies to all transfers governed by that election whether before or after the election is made, and is irrevocable.

(g) Property settlements—time and manner of making the elections under section 1041.

Q–18 How do spouses (or former spouses) elect to have section 1041 apply to transfers after December 31, 1983, or to transfers after July 18, 1984 under instruments in effect on or before July 18, 1984?

A–18 In order to make an election under section 1041 for property transfers after December 31, 1983, or property transfers under instruments that were in effect on or before July 18, 1984, both spouses (or former spouses) must elect the application of the rules of section 1041 by attaching to the transferor's first filed income tax return for the taxable year in which the first transfer occurs, a statement signed by both spouses (or former spouses) which includes each spouse's social security number and is in substantially the form set forth at the end of this answer.

In addition, the transferor must attach a copy of such statement to his or her return for each subsequent taxable year in which a transfer is made that is governed by the transitional election. A copy of the signed statement must be kept by both parties. The election statements shall be in substantially the following form:

In the case of an election regarding transfers after 1983:

Section 1041 Election

The undersigned hereby elect to have the provisions of section 1041 of the Internal Revenue Code apply to all qualifying transfers of property after December 31, 1983. The undersigned understand that section 1041 applies to all property transferred between spouses, or former spouses incident to divorce. The parties further understand that the effects for Federal income tax purposes of having section 1041 apply are that (1) no gain or loss is recognized by the transferor spouse or former spouse as a result of this transfer; and (2) the basis of the transferred property in the hands of the transferee is the adjusted basis of the property in the hands of the transferor immediately before the transfer, whether or not the adjusted basis of the transferred property is less than, equal to, or greater than its fair market value at the time of the transfer. The undersigned understand that if the transferee spouse or former spouse disposes of the property in a transaction in which gain is recognized, the amount of gain which is taxable may be larger than it would have been if this election had not been made.

In the case of an election regarding preexisting decrees:

Section 1041 Election

The undersigned hereby elect to have the provisions of section 1041 of the Internal Revenue Code apply to all qualifying transfers of property after July 18, 1984 under any instrument in effect on or before July 18, 1984. The undersigned understand that section 1041 applies to all property transferred between spouses, or former spouses incident to the divorce. The parties further understand that the effects for Federal income tax purposes of having section 1041 apply are that (1) no gain or loss is recognized by the transferor spouse or former spouse as a result of this transfer; and (2) the basis of the transferred property in the hands of the transferee is the adjusted basis of the property in the hands of the transferor immediately before the transfer, whether or not the adjusted basis of the transferred property is less than, equal to, or greater than its fair market value at the time of the transfer. The undersigned understand that if the transferee spouse or former spouse disposes of the property in a transaction in which gain is recognized, the amount of gain which is taxable may be larger than it would have been if this election had not been made.

---

§ 6015. Relief From Joint and Several Liability on Joint Return.

(a) In general. Notwithstanding section 6013(d)(3)—

(1 an individual who has made a joint return may elect to seek relief under the procedures prescribed under subsection (b); and

(2) if such individual is eligible to elect the application of subsection (c), such individual may, in addition to any election under paragraph (1), elect to limit such individual's liability for any deficiency with respect to such joint return in the manner prescribed under subsection (c).

Any determination under this section shall be made without regard to community property laws.

(b) Procedures for relief from liability applicable to all joint filers.—

(1) In general. Under procedures prescribed by the Secretary, if—

(A) a joint return has been made for a taxable year;

(B) on such return there is an understatement of tax attributable to erroneous items of one individual filing the joint return;

(C) the other individual filing the joint return establishes that in signing the return he or she did not know, and had no reason to know, that there was such understatement;

(D) taking into account all the facts and circumstances, it is inequitable to hold the other individual liable for the deficiency in tax for such taxable year attributable to such understatement; and

(E) the other individual elects (in such form as the Secretary may prescribe) the benefits of this subsection not later than the date which is 2 years after the date the Secretary has begun collection activities with respect to the individual making the election,

then the other individual shall be relieved of liability for tax (including interest, penalties, and other amounts) for such taxable year to the extent such liability is attributable to such understatement.

(2) Apportionment of relief. If an individual who, but for paragraph (1)(C), would be relieved of liability under paragraph (1), establishes that in signing the return such individual did not know, and had no reason to know, the extent of such understatement, then such individual shall be relieved of liability for tax (including interest, penalties, and other amounts) for such taxable year to the extent that such liability is attributable to the portion of such understatement of which such individual did not know and had no reason to know.

(3) Understatement. For purposes of this subsection, the term "understatement" has the meaning given to such term by section 6662(d)(2)(A).

(c) Procedures to limit liability for taxpayers no longer married or taxpayers legally separated or not living together.—

(1) In general. Except as provided in this subsection, if an individual who has made a joint return for any taxable year elects the application of this subsection, the individual's liability for any deficiency which is assessed with respect to the return shall not exceed the portion of such deficiency properly allocable to the individual under subsection (d).

(2) Burden of proof. Except as provided in subparagraph (A)(ii) or (C) of paragraph (3), each individual who elects the application of this subsection shall have the burden of proof with respect to establishing the portion of any deficiency allocable to such individual.

(3) Election.—

(A) Individuals eligible to make election.—

(i) In general. An individual shall only be eligible to elect the application of this subsection if—

(I) at the time such election is filed, such individual is no longer married to, or is legally separated from, the individual with whom such individual filed the joint return to which the election relates; or

(II) such individual was not a member of the same household as the individual with whom such joint return was filed at any time during the 12–month period ending on the date such election is filed.

(ii) Certain taxpayers ineligible to elect. If the Secretary demonstrates that assets were transferred between individuals filing a joint return as part of a fraudulent scheme by such individuals, an election under this subsection by either individual shall be invalid (and section 6013(d)(3) shall apply to the joint return).

(B) Time for election. An election under this subsection for any taxable year may be made at any time after a deficiency for such year is asserted but not later than 2 years after the date on which the Secretary has begun collection activities with respect to the individual making the election.

(C) Election not valid with respect to certain deficiencies. If the Secretary demonstrates that an individual making an election under this subsection had actual knowledge, at the time such individual signed the return, of any item giving rise to a deficiency (or portion thereof) which is not allocable to such individual under subsection (d), such election shall not apply to such deficiency (or portion). This subparagraph shall not apply where the individual with actual knowledge establishes that such individual signed the return under duress.

(4) Liability increased by reason of transfers of property to avoid tax—

(A) In general. Notwithstanding any other provision of this subsection, the portion of the deficiency for which the individual electing the application of this subsection is liable (without regard to this paragraph) shall be increased by the value of any disqualified asset transferred to the individual.

(B) Disqualified asset. For purposes of this paragraph—

(i) In general. The term "disqualified asset" means any property or right to property transferred to an individual making the election under this subsection with respect to a joint return by the other individual filing such joint return if the principal purpose of the transfer was the avoidance of tax or payment of tax.

(ii) Presumption.—

(I) In general. For purposes of clause (i), except as provided in subclause (II), any transfer which is made after the date which is 1 year before the date on which the first letter of proposed deficiency which allows the taxpayer an opportunity for administrative review in the Internal Revenue Service Office of Appeals is sent shall be presumed to have as its principal purpose the avoidance of tax or payment of tax.

(II) Exceptions. Subclause (I) shall not apply to any transfer pursuant to a decree of divorce or separate maintenance or a written instrument incident to such a decree or to any transfer which an individual establishes did not have as its principal purpose the avoidance of tax or payment of tax.

(d) Allocation of deficiency. For purposes of subsection (c).—

(1) In general. The portion of any deficiency on a joint return allocated to an individual shall be the amount which bears the same ratio to such deficiency as the net amount of items taken into account in computing the deficiency and allocable to the individual under paragraph (3) bears to the net amount of all items taken into account in computing the deficiency.

(2) Separate treatment of certain items. If a deficiency (or portion thereof) is attributable to—

(A) the disallowance of a credit; or

(B) any tax (other than tax imposed by section 1 or 55) required to be included with the joint return;

and such item is allocated to one individual under paragraph (3), such deficiency (or portion) shall be allocated to such individual. Any such item shall not be taken into account under paragraph (1).

(3) Allocation of items giving rise to the deficiency. For purposes of this subsection—

(A) In general. Except as provided in paragraphs (4) and (5), any item giving rise to a deficiency on a joint return shall be allocated to individuals filing the return in the same manner as it would have been allocated if the individuals had filed separate returns for the taxable year.

(B) Exception where other spouse benefits. Under rules prescribed by the Secretary, an item otherwise allocable to an individual under subparagraph (A) shall be allocated to the other individual filing the joint return to the extent the item gave rise to a tax benefit on the joint return to the other individual.

(C) Exception for fraud. The Secretary may provide for an allocation of any item in a manner not prescribed by subparagraph (A) if the Secretary establishes that such allocation is appropriate due to fraud of one or both individuals.

(4) Limitations on separate returns disregarded. If an item of deduction or credit is disallowed in its entirety solely because a separate return is filed, such disallowance shall be disregarded and the item shall be computed as if a joint return had been filed and then allocated between the spouses appropriately. A similar rule shall apply for purposes of section 86.

(5) Child's liability. If the liability of a child of a taxpayer is included on a joint return, such liability shall be disregarded in computing the separate liability of either spouse and such liability shall be allocated appropriately between the spouses.

(e) Petition for review by Tax Court.—

(1) In general. In the case of an individual against whom a deficiency has been asserted and who elects to have subsection (b) or (c) apply—

(A) In general. In addition to any other remedy provided by law, the individual may petition the Tax Court (and the Tax Court shall have jurisdiction) to determine the appropriate relief available to the individual under this section if such petition is filed—

(i) at any time after the earlier of—

(I) the date the Secretary mails, by certified or registered mail to the taxpayer's last known address, notice of the Secretary's final determination of relief available to the individual, or

(II) the date which is 6 months after the date such election is filed with the Secretary, and

(ii) not later than the close of the 90th day after the date described in clause (i)(I).

(B) Restrictions applicable to collection of assessment.—

(i) In general. Except as otherwise provided in section 6851 or 6861, no levy or proceeding in court shall be made, begun, or prosecuted against the individual making an election under subsection (b) or (c) for collection of any assessment to which such election relates until the close of the 90th day referred to in subparagraph (A)(ii), or, if a petition has been filed with the Tax Court under subparagraph (A), until the decision of the Tax Court has become final. Rules similar to the rules of section 7485 shall apply with respect to the collection of such assessment.

(ii) Authority to enjoin collection actions. Notwithstanding the provisions of section 7421(a), the beginning of such levy or proceeding during the time the prohibition under clause (i) is in force may be enjoined by a proceeding in the proper court, including the Tax Court. The Tax Court shall have no jurisdiction under this subparagraph to enjoin any action or proceeding unless a timely petition has been filed under subparagraph (A) and then only in respect of the amount of the assessment to which the election under subsection (b) or (c) relates.

(2) Suspension of running of period of limitations. The running of the period of limitations in section 6502 on the collection of the assessment to which the petition under paragraph (1)(A) relates shall be suspended—

(A) for the period during which the Secretary is prohibited by paragraph (1)(B) from collecting by levy or a proceeding in court and for 60 days thereafter, and

(B) if a waiver under paragraph (5) is made, from the date the claim for relief was filed until 60 days after the waiver is filed with the Secretary.

(3) Limitation on tax court jurisdiction. If a suit for refund is begun by either individual filing the joint return pursuant to section 6532—

(A) the Tax Court shall lose jurisdiction of the individual's action under this section to whatever extent jurisdiction is acquired by the district court or the United States Court of Federal Claims over the taxable years that are the subject of the suit for refund, and

(B) the court acquiring jurisdiction shall have jurisdiction over the petition filed under this subsection.

(4) Notice to other spouse. The Tax Court shall establish rules which provide the individual filing a joint return but not making the election under subsection (b) or (c) with adequate notice and an opportunity to become a party to a proceeding under either such subsection.

(5) Waiver. An individual who elects the application of subsection (b) or (c) (and who agrees with the Secretary's determination of relief) may waive in writing at any time the restrictions in paragraph (1)(B) with respect to collection of the outstanding assessment (whether or not a notice of the Secretary's final determination of relief has been mailed).

(f) Equitable relief. Under procedures prescribed by the Secretary, if—

(1) taking into account all the facts and circumstances, it is inequitable to hold the individual liable for any unpaid tax or any deficiency (or any portion of either); and

(2) relief is not available to such individual under subsection (b) or (c),

the Secretary may relieve such individual of such liability.

(g) Credits and refunds.

(1) In general. Except as provided in paragraphs (2) and (3), notwithstanding any other law or rule of law (other than section 6511, 6512(b) , 7121, or 7122), credit or refund shall be allowed or made to the extent attributable to the application of this section.

(2) Res judicata. In the case of any election under subsection (b) or (c), if a decision of a court in any prior proceeding for the same taxable year has become final, such decision shall be conclusive except with respect to the qualification of the individual for relief which was not an issue in such proceeding. The exception contained in the preceding sentence shall not apply if the court determines that the individual participated meaningfully in such prior proceeding.

(3) Credit and refund not allowed under subsection (c). No credit or refund shall be allowed as a result of an election under subsection (c).

(h) Regulations. The Secretary shall prescribe such regulations as are necessary to carry out the provisions of this section, including—

(1) regulations providing methods for allocation of items other than the methods under subsection (d)(3); and

(2) regulations providing the opportunity for an individual to have notice of, and an opportunity to participate in, any administrative proceeding with respect to an election made under subsection (b) or (c) by the other individual filing the joint return.

Full Faith and Credit

U.S.C.A. Title 28: Judiciary and Judicial Procedure

★★★

Parental Kidnapping Prevention Act *(PKPA)*

§ 1738A. Full Faith and Credit Given to Child Custody Determinations.

(a) The appropriate authorities of every State shall enforce according to its terms, and shall not modify except as provided in subsections (f), (g), and (h) of this section, any custody determination or visitation determination made consistently with the provisions of this section by a court of another State.

(b) As used in this section, the term—

(1) "child" means a person under the age of eighteen;

(2) "contestant" means a person, including a parent or grandparent, who claims a right to custody or visitation of a child;

(3) "custody determination" means a judgment, decree, or other order of a court providing for the custody of a child, and includes permanent and temporary orders, and initial orders and modifications;

(4) "home State" means the State in which, immediately preceding the time involved, the child lived with his parents, a parent, or a person acting as parent, for at least six consecutive months, and in the case of a child less than six months old, the State in which the child lived from birth with any of such persons. Periods of temporary absence of any of such persons are counted as part of the six-month or other period;

(5) "modification" and "modify" refer to a custody or visitation determination which modifies, replaces, supersedes, or otherwise is made subsequent to, a prior custody or visitation determination concerning the same child, whether made by the same court or not;

(6) "person acting as a parent" means a person, other than a parent, who has physical custody of a child and who has either been awarded custody by a court or claims a right to custody;

(7) "physical custody" means actual possession and control of a child;

(8) "State" means a State of the United States, the District of Columbia, the Commonwealth of Puerto Rico, or a territory or possession of the United States; and

(9) "visitation determination" means a judgment, decree, or other order of a court providing for the visitation of a child and includes permanent and temporary orders and initial orders and modifications.

(c) A child custody or visitation determination made by a court of a State is consistent with the provisions of this section only if—

(1) such court has jurisdiction under the law of such State; and

(2) one of the following conditions is met:

(A) such State (i) is the home State of the child on the date of the commencement of the proceeding, or (ii) had been the child's home State within six months before the date of the commencement of the proceeding and the child is absent from such State because of his removal or retention by a contestant or for other reasons, and a contestant continues to live in such State;

(B) (i) it appears that no other State would have jurisdiction under subparagraph (A), and (ii) it is in the best interest of the child that a court of such State assume jurisdiction because (I) the child and his parents, or the child and at least one contestant, have a significant connection with such State other than mere physical presence in such State, and (II) there is available in such State substantial evidence concerning the child's present or future care, protection, training, and personal relationships;

(C) the child is physically present in such State and (i) the child has been abandoned, or (ii) it is necessary in an emergency to protect the child because the child, a sibling, or parent of the child has been subjected to or threatened with mistreatment or abuse;

(D) (i) it appears that no other State would have jurisdiction under subparagraph (A), (B), (C), or (E), or another State has declined to exercise jurisdiction on the ground that the State whose jurisdiction is in issue is the more appropriate forum to determine the custody or visitation of the child, and (ii) it is in the best interest of the child that such court assume jurisdiction; or

(E) the court has continuing jurisdiction pursuant to subsection (d) of this section.

(d) The jurisdiction of a court of a State which has made a child custody or visitation determination consistently with the provisions of this section continues as long as the requirement of subsection (c)(1) of this section continues to be met and such State remains the residence of the child or of any contestant.

(e) Before a child custody or visitation determination is made, reasonable notice and opportunity to be heard shall be given to the contestants, any parent whose parental rights have not been previously terminated and any person who has physical custody of a child.

(f) A court of a State may modify a determination of the custody of the same child made by a court of another State, if—

(1) it has jurisdiction to make such a child custody determination; and

(2) the court of the other State no longer has jurisdiction, or it has declined to exercise such jurisdiction to modify such determination.

(g) A court of a State shall not exercise jurisdiction in any proceeding for a custody or visitation determination commenced during the pendency of a proceeding in a court of another State where such court of that other State is exercising jurisdiction consistently with the provisions of this section to make a custody or visitation determination.

(h) A court of a State may not modify a visitation determination made by a court of another State unless the court of the other State no longer has jurisdiction to modify such determination or has declined to exercise jurisdiction to modify such determination.

Historical Note

Congressional Findings and Declaration of Purposes for Parental Kidnapping Prevention Act of 1980. Section 7 of Pub. L. 96–611 provided that:

(a) The Congress finds that—

(1) there is a large and growing number of cases annually involving disputes between persons claiming rights of custody and visitation of children under the laws, and in the courts, of different States, the District of Columbia, the Commonwealth of Puerto Rico, and the territories and possessions of the United States;

(2) the laws and practices by which the courts of those jurisdictions determine their jurisdiction to decide such disputes, and the effect to be given the decisions of such disputes by the courts of other jurisdictions, are often inconsistent and conflicting;

(3) those characteristics of the law and practice in such cases, along with the limits imposed by a Federal system on the authority of each such jurisdiction to conduct investigations and take other actions outside its own boundaries, contribute to a tendency of parties involved in such disputes to frequently resort to the seizure, restraint, concealment, and interstate transportation of children, the disregard of court orders, excessive relitigation of cases, obtaining of conflicting orders by the courts of various jurisdictions, and interstate travel and communication that is so expensive and time consuming as to disrupt their occupations and commercial activities; and

(4) among the results of those conditions and activities are the failure of the courts of such jurisdictions to give full faith and credit to the judicial proceedings of the other jurisdictions, the deprivation of rights of liberty and property without due process of law, burdens on commerce among such jurisdictions and with foreign nations, and harm to the welfare of children and their parents and other custodians.

(b) For those reasons it is necessary to establish a national system for locating parents and children who travel from one such jurisdiction to another and are concealed in connection with such disputes, and to establish national standards under which the courts of such jurisdictions will determine their jurisdiction to decide such disputes and the effect to be given by each such jurisdiction to such decisions by the courts of other such jurisdictions.

(c) The general purposes of sections 6 to 10 of this Act [enacting this section and sections 654(17) and 663 of Title 42 U.S.C.A., The Public Health and Welfare, amending section 655(a) of Title 42, and enacting provisions set out as notes under this section and sections 663 of Title 42 and 1073 of Title 18 U.S.C.A., Crimes and Criminal Procedure] are to—

(1) promote cooperation between State courts to the end that a determination of custody and visitation is rendered in the State which can best decide the case in the interest of the child;

(2) promote and expand the exchange of information and other forms of mutual assistance between States which are concerned with the same child;

(3) facilitate the enforcement of custody and visitation decrees of sister States;

(4) discourage continuing interstate controversies over child custody in the interest of greater stability of home environment and of secure family relationships for the child;

(5) avoid jurisdictional competition and conflict between State courts in matters of child custody and visitation which have in the past resulted in the shifting of children from State to State with harmful effects on their well-being; and

(6) deter interstate abductions and other unilateral removals of children undertaken to obtain custody and visitation awards.

State Court Proceedings for Custody Determinations; Priority Treatment; Fees, Costs, and Other Expenses. Section 8(c) of Pub. L. 96–611 provided that:

In furtherance of the purposes of section 1738A of title 28, United States Code [this section], as added by subsection (a) of this section, State courts are encouraged to—

(1) afford priority to proceedings for custody determinations; and

(2) award to the person entitled to custody or visitation pursuant to a custody determination which is consistent with the provisions of such section 1738A [this section], necessary travel expenses, attorneys' fees, costs of private investigations, witness fees or expenses, and other expenses incurred in connection with such custody determination in any case in which—

(A) a contestant has, without the consent of the person entitled to custody or visitation pursuant to a custody determination which is consistent with the provisions of such section 1738A [this section],

(i) wrongfully removed the child from the physical custody of such person, or

(ii) wrongfully retained the child after a visit or other temporary relinquishment of physical custody; or

(B) the court determines it is appropriate.

Comment

Nationwide the law of child custody jurisdiction was badly out of alignment between 1980, when the Parental Kidnapping Prevention Act (PKPA) was passed by Congress, and the time when the Uniform Child Custody Jurisdiction and Enforcement Act (UCCJEA) was promulgated in 1997 to replace the UCCJA, a 1968 uniform act. A disparity existed for nearly two decades between the terms of the federal act for according Full Faith and Credit for Child Custody Orders, and the provisions of the laws of the several states. Incidentally, the Texas version of the UCCJA was in compliance with the PKPA. The enactment of the Uniform Child Custody Jurisdiction and Enforcement Act [FAM. CODE ch. 152] in 1999 maintains our statutory compliance with the PKPA (and brings the others into compliance). The states that have enacted the UCCJEA as of July 9, 2004 are Alabama, Alaska, Arizona, Arkansas, California, Colorado, Connecticut, Delaware, District of Columbia, Florida, Georgia, Hawaii, Idaho, Illinois, Iowa, Kansas, Kentucky, Maine, Maryland, Michigan, Minnesota, Mississippi, Montana, Nebraska, Nevada, New Mexico, New York, North Carolina, North Dakota, Oklahoma, Oregon, Rhode Island, Tennessee, Texas, Utah, Virginia, Washington, and West Virginia.

CLE/Other Legal Publications

See annotations to Tex. Fam. Code Ann. Ch. 152, UCCJEA, *supra*

An intricate maze of child-snatching statutes. Richard E. Crouch, 23 FAM. ADVOCATE No. 4 at 29 (2001)

> ***Editors' Note:*** *the following citations must be read with caution insofar as they discuss the relationship between the UCCJA and the PKPA. Since Sept. 1, 1999 Texas law is the UCCJEA, Chapter 152, supra.*

Leading Cases

See annotations to TEX. FAM. CODE ANN. CH. 152, UCCJEA, *supra*

Thompson v. Thompson, 484 U.S. 174, 98 L.Ed. 2d 512, 108 S.Ct. 513 (1988) (PKPA does not create federal jurisdiction in district courts)

In re S.A.V., 837 S.W.2d 80 (Tex. 1992) (although Texas and Minnesota had concurrent custody jurisdiction under UCCJA, Minnesota declined to exercise its continuing jurisdiction under PKPA)

Rush v. Stansbury, 668 S.W.2d 690 (Tex. 1984) (Tennessee decree must be honored per PKPA)

In re McCormick, 87 S.W.3d 746 (Tex. App.—Amarillo 2002, no pet.) (Texas retains UCCJEA modification jurisdiction over father and son now living in Kansas)

In re Calderon–Garza, 81 S.W.3d 899 (Tex. App.—El Paso 2002, no pet.) (Texas was two-month-old infant's home state under UCCJEA when alleged father filed paternity suit)

In re E.K.N., 24 S.W.3d 586 (Tex. App.—Fort Worth 2000, no pet.) (California does not have continuing, exclusive jurisdiction under PKPA because no custody determination was made)

Welborn–Hosler v. Hosler, 870 S.W.2d 323 (Tex. App.—Houston [14th Dist.] 1994, no writ) (PKPA designed to prevent jurisdictional conflicts over child custody, takes precedence over any state law)

White v. Blake, 859 S.W.2d 551 (Tex. App.—Tyler 1993, no writ) (Texas has jurisdiction over termination proceeding against non-resident parent, but UCCJA and PKPA dictate Alabama is primary forum)

Reppond v. Blake, 822 S.W.2d 759 (Tex. App.—Tyler 1992, no writ) (PKPA doesn't give jurisdiction to modify custody to TX court which no longer may exercise continuing jurisdiction)

Bolger v. Bolger, 678 S.W.2d 194 (Tex. App.—Corpus Christi 1984, ref. n.r.e.) (meaning of NY "custody determination" established through exhibits offered into evidence)

Cross Reference

TEX. FAM. CODE ch. 152. Uniform Child Custody Jurisdiction and Enforcement Act.

Full Faith and Credit for Child Support Orders *(FFCCSOA)*

§ 1738B. Full Faith and Credit for Child Support Orders.

(a) General rule. The appropriate authorities of each State—

(1) shall enforce according to its terms a child support order made consistently with this section by a court of another State; and

(2) shall not seek or make a modification of such an order except in accordance with subsections (e), (f), and (i).

(b) Definitions. In this section:

"child" means—

(A) a person under 18 years of age; and

(B) a person 18 or more years of age with respect to whom a child support order has been issued pursuant to the laws of a State.

"child's State" means the State in which a child resides.

"child's home State" means the State in which a child lived with a parent or a person acting as parent for at least 6 consecutive months immediately preceding the time of filing of a petition or comparable pleading for support and, if a child is less than 6 months old, the State in which the child lived from birth with any of them. A period of temporary absence of any of them is counted as part of the 6–month period.

"child support" means a payment of money, continuing support, or arrearages or the provision of a benefit (including payment of health insurance, child care, and educational expenses) for the support of a child.

"child support order"—

(A) means a judgment, decree, or order of a court requiring the payment of child support in periodic amounts or in a lump sum; and

(B) includes—

(i) a permanent or temporary order; and

(ii) an initial order or a modification of an order.

"contestant" means—

(A) a person (including a parent) who—

(i) claims a right to receive child support;

(ii) is a party to a proceeding that may result in the issuance of a child support order; or

(iii) is under a child support order; and

(B) a State or political subdivision of a State to which the right to obtain child support has been assigned.

"court" means a court or administrative agency of a State that is authorized by State law to establish the amount of child support payable by a contestant or make a modification of a child support order.

"modification" means a change in a child support order that affects the amount, scope, or duration of the order and modifies, replaces, supersedes, or otherwise is made subsequent to the child support order.

"State" means a State of the United States, the District of Columbia, the Commonwealth of Puerto Rico, the territories and possessions of the United States, and Indian country (as defined in section 1151 of title 18).

(c) Requirements of child support orders. A child support order made by a court of a State is made consistently with this section if—

(1) a court that makes the order, pursuant to the laws of the State in which the court is located and subsections (e), (f), and (g)—

(A) has subject matter jurisdiction to hear the matter and enter such an order; and

(B) has personal jurisdiction over the contestants; and

(2) reasonable notice and opportunity to be heard is given to the contestants.

(d) Continuing jurisdiction. A court of a State that has made a child support order consistently with this section has continuing, exclusive jurisdiction over the order if the State is the child's State or the residence of any individual contestant unless the court of another State, acting in accordance with subsections (e) and (f), has made a modification of the order.

(e) Authority to modify orders. A court of a State may modify a child support order issued by a court of another State if—

(1) the court has jurisdiction to make such a child support order pursuant to subsection (i); and

(2)(A) the court of the other State no longer has continuing, exclusive jurisdiction of the child support order because that State no longer is the child's State or the residence of any individual contestant; or

(B) each individual contestant has filed written consent with the State of continuing, exclusive jurisdiction for a court of another State to modify the order and assume continuing, exclusive jurisdiction over the order.

(f) Recognition of child support orders. If 1 or more child support orders have been issued with regard to an obligor and a child, a court shall apply the following rules in determining which order to recognize for purposes of continuing, exclusive jurisdiction and enforcement:

(1) If only 1 court has issued a child support order, the order of that court must be recognized.

(2) If 2 or more courts have issued child support orders for the same obligor and child, and only 1 of the courts would have continuing, exclusive jurisdiction under this section, the order of that court must be recognized.

(3) If 2 or more courts have issued child support orders for the same obligor and child, and more than 1 of the courts would have continuing, exclusive jurisdiction under this section, an order issued by a court in the current home State of the child must be recognized, but if an order has not been issued in the current home State of the child, the order most recently issued must be recognized.

(4) If 2 or more courts have issued child support orders for the same obligor and child, and none of the courts would have continuing, exclusive jurisdiction under this section, a court having jurisdiction over the parties shall issue a child support order, which must be recognized.

(5) The court that has issued an order recognized under this subsection is the court having continuing, exclusive jurisdiction under subsection (d).

(g) Enforcement of modified orders. A court of a State that no longer has continuing, exclusive jurisdiction of a child support order may enforce the order with respect to nonmodifiable obligations and unsatisfied obligations that accrued before the date on which a modification of the order is made under subsections (e) and (f).

(h) Choice of law.—

(1) In general. In a proceeding to establish, modify, or enforce a child support order, the forum State's law shall apply except as provided in paragraphs (2) and (3).

(2) Law of State of issuance of order. In interpreting a child support order including the duration of current payments and other obligations of support, a court shall apply the law of the State of the court that issued the order.

(3) Period of limitation. In an action to enforce arrears under a child support order, a court shall apply the statute of limitation of the forum State or the State of the court that issued the order, whichever statute provides the longer period of limitation.

(i) Registration for modification. If there is no individual contestant or child residing in the issuing State, the party or support enforcement agency seeking to modify, or to modify and enforce, a child support order issued in another State shall register that order in a State with jurisdiction over the nonmovant for the purpose of modification.

Historical Note

Congressional Findings and Declaration of Purposes. **(Pub. L. 103–383 § 2)**

(a) Findings.—The Congress finds that—

(1) there is a large and growing number of child support cases annually involving disputes between parents who reside in different States;

(2) the laws by which the courts of different jurisdictions determine their authority to establish child support orders are not uniform;

(3) those laws, along with the limits imposed by the Federal system on the authority of each State to take certain actions outside its own boundaries—

(A) encourage noncustodial parents to relocate outside the States where their children and the custodial parents reside to avoid the jurisdiction of the courts of such States, resulting in an increase in the amount of interstate travel and communication required to establish and collect child support orders and a burden on custodial parents that is expensive, time consuming, and disruptive of occupations and commercial activity;

(B) contribute to the pressing problem of relatively low levels of child support payments in interstate cases and to inequities in child support payments levels that are based solely on the noncustodial parent's choice of residence;

(C) encourage a disregard of court orders resulting in massive arrearages nationwide;

(D) allow noncustodial parents to avoid the payment of regularly scheduled child support payments for extensive periods of time, resulting in substantial hardship for the children for whom support is due and for their custodians; and

(E) lead to the excessive relitigation of cases and to the establishment of conflicting orders by the courts of various jurisdictions, resulting in confusion, waste of judicial resources, disrespect for the courts, and a diminution of public confidence in the rule of law; and

(4) among the results of the conditions described in this subsection are—

(A) the failure of the courts of the State to give full faith and credit to the judicial proceedings of the other States;

(B) the deprivation of rights of liberty and property without due process of law;

(C) burdens on commerce among the States; and

(D) harm to the welfare of children and their parents and other custodians.

(b) Statements of policy. In view of the findings made in subsection (a), it is necessary to establish national standards under which the courts of the various States shall determine their jurisdiction to issue a child support order and the effect to be given by each State to child support orders issued by the courts of other States.

(c) Purposes. The purposes of this Act [enacting this section and a provision set out as a note under section 1 of this title] are—

(1) to facilitate the enforcement of child support orders among the States;

(2) to discourage continuing interstate controversies over child support in the interest of greater financial stability and secure family relationships for the child; and

(3) to avoid jurisdictional competition and conflict among State courts in the establishment of child support orders.

Introductory Comment

In the early 1990s, the U.S. Congress and the National Conference of Commissioners on Uniform State Laws (NCCUSL) were on parallel tracks aiming at a common destination—improving child support enforcement in the United States. Congress had appointed a National Commission on Interstate Child Support Enforcement to recommend changes. At the same time NCCUSL had appointed a drafting committee to revise, and ultimately to replace, URESA and RURESA. In the summer of 1992, the federal commission and NCCUSL both acted, the former to report to Congress and the latter to promulgate the Uniform Interstate Family Support Act (UIFSA) and urge all states to adopt it. The end product was the result of a cooperative effort between the federal commission and the Conference, with considerable input from the federal commissioners. In 1994 Congress enacted the Full Faith and Credit for Child Support Orders Act (FFCCSOA, pronounced fak-so-ah). The uniform act and the federal act were very similar, but not identical. By 1996, 34 states had enacted UIFSA, and of course all were bound by FFCCSOA. But there were some slight differences.

In 1996 the two relevant bodies, NCCUSL and Congress, acted again almost simultaneously. Corrective amendments were made to UIFSA and FFCCSOA was amended to reflect UIFSA language. Indeed, the acts became virtually identical. The key to all this was that Congress mandated that all U.S. jurisdictions enact UIFSA, as amended in 1996 by January 1, 1998. In the opinion of the authors, the amendments to FFCCSOA, and the directive to all states to enact UIFSA, eliminate any possibility of argument that the two acts are inconsistent. To argue otherwise would be to presume that Congress had acted illogically—a presumption that courts to not indulge in the ordinary course of statutory construction. As the caselaw following indicates, all constitutional attacks on FFCCSOA have failed and, with very little exception, the new acts have been found to be reciprocally complementary.

CLE/Other Legal Publications

See annotations to Tex. Fam. Code Ann. Ch. 154. Child Support, and Tex. Fam. Code Ann. Ch. 159. Uniform Interstate Family Support Act, *supra*

A federal hand in child support. Laura W. Morgan, 23 Fam. Advocate No. 4 at 10 (2001)

Recognition and enforcement of judgments and child support obligations in United States and Canadian courts. Russell J. Weintraub, 34 Tex. Int'l L.J. 361 (1999)

Leading Cases

See annotations to Tex. Fam. Code Ann. Ch. 159. UIFSA, *supra*

Cowan v. Moreno, 903 S.W.2d 119 (Tex. App.—Austin 1995, no writ) (facially valid support order creates a prima facie case for proponent of order—party challenging registration bears burden to prove order invalid)

Cross References

Tex. Fam. Code Ann. ch. 159, Uniform Interstate Family Support Act, *supra*

Child Support Recovery Act of 1992, 18 U.S.C.A. § 228, *supra*

Defense of Marriage Act *(DOMA)*

§ 1738C. Certain Acts, Records, and Proceedings and the Effect Thereof.

No State, territory, or possession of the United States, or Indian tribe, shall be required to give effect to any public act, record, or judicial proceeding of any other State, territory, possession, or tribe respecting a relationship between persons of the same sex that is treated as a marriage under the laws of such other State, territory, possession, or tribe, or a right or claim arising from such relationship.

Historical Note

House Report No. 104–664, July 9, 1996; see 1996 U.S. Code Cong. and Adm. News, p. 2905, 1996 WL 391835 (Excerpt)

PURPOSE AND SUMMARY

H.R. 3396, the Defense of Marriage Act, has two primary purposes. The first is to defend the institution of traditional heterosexual marriage. The second is to protect the right of the States to formulate their own public policy regarding the legal recognition of same-sex unions, free from any federal constitutional implications that might attend the recognition by one State of the right for homosexual couples to acquire marriage licenses.

To achieve these purposes, H.R. 3396 has two operative provisions. Section 2, entitled "Powers Reserved to the States," provides that no State shall be required to accord full faith and credit to a marriage license issued by another State if it relates to a relationship between persons of the same sex. And Section 3 defines the terms "marriage" and "spouse," for purposes of federal law only, to reaffirm that they refer exclusively to relationships between persons of the opposite sex.

BACKGROUND AND NEED FOR LEGISLATION

H.R. 3396 is a response to a very particular development in the State of Hawaii. As will be explained in greater detail below, the state courts in Hawaii appear to be on the verge of requiring that State to issue marriage licenses to same-sex couples. The prospect of permitting homosexual couples to "marry" in Hawaii threatens to have very real consequences both on federal law and on the laws (especially the marriage laws) of the various States.

More specifically, if Hawaii (or some other State) recognizes same-sex marriages, other States that do not permit homosexuals to marry would be confronted with the complicated issue of whether they are nonetheless obligated under the Full Faith and Credit Clause of the United States Constitution to give binding legal effect to such unions. With regard to federal law, a decision by one State to authorize same-sex marriage would raise the issue of whether such couples are entitled to federal benefits that depend on marital status. H.R. 3396 anticipates these complicated questions by laying down clear rules to guide their resolution, and it does so in a manner that preserves each State's ability to decide the underlying policy issue however it chooses.

In 2003, the Texas Legislature joined at least 36 other states by enacting TEX. FAM. CODE § 6.204, Recognition of Same–Sex Marriage or Civil Union, *supra*. The caption may be somewhat misleading, given the fact that the statute decrees that such relationships are against the public policy of Texas and will not be recognized.

Comment

Almost no contemporary subject has been more discussed in legal publications and less litigated in courts than same-sex marriage or a variant thereof, such as a legally recognized relationship involving a same sex couple. Surprisingly, American corporate culture is often more tolerant on the issue than society at large. For example, many corporate medical insurance plans allow employees to extend coverage to a same-sex significant other.

The dearth of litigation may soon end. Vermont enacted a "civil union statute," effective April 26, 2000. The statute grants lesbian and gay couples most of the same rights and benefits available to married couples under state law. The statute directs town clerks to issue licenses for civil unions that will entitle couples to more than 300 specific benefits. Earlier, the Vermont Supreme Court ruled that same-sex couples must be offered the same "benefits" and "protections" given married heterosexual couples, but left it up to the Legislature to decide whether to accomplish this goal through traditional marriage or an alternate institution. *Baker v. State, infra.* New York Law School Professor Arthur S. Leonard provides analysis of the specific provisions of the Vermont civil union measure at: *http://www.lgny.com/issue_129/pages_129/news3_129.html*

Leading Cases

Shahar v. Bowers, 114 F.3d 1097 (11th Cir. 1997) (Ga.) (AG did not violate employee's First Amendment right of free association by withdrawing job offer based on the employee's same-sex marriage; public service interest of GA outweighed employee's personal association interests; GA policy on same-sex marriage inferred from statute prohibiting such a union and GA delegation support of DOMA)

Baker v. Vermont, 744 A.2d 864 (Vt. 1999) (persons of the same sex constitutionally may not be deprived of statutory benefits and protections afforded persons of opposite sex who choose to marry)

Littleton v. Prange, 9 S.W.3d 223 (Tex. App.—San Antonio 1999, pet. denied) (transsexual who brought medical malpractice action in capacity as surviving spouse of male patient denied recovery; "she" was born male—dicta court notes that same-sex marriage not recognized in Texas and DOMA would allow Texas to refuse to give effect to such a union even if it is recognized in another state)

Baehr v. Miike, 1996 WL 694235 (Hawaii Cir. Ct. 1997) (the fact that Congress enacted the Defense of Marriage Act does not prove that same-sex marriage will result in harm to an important public interest, even though the consequences of other states' recognition or non-recognition of a Hawaii same-sex marriage is an "important issue")

> ***Editors' Note:*** *There are literally hundreds of articles in legal publications on this subject, a large proportion of which discuss same-sex couples in connection with DOMA. A selection is provided below.*

Legal Publications

Informal marriages and marriages in other states. Laura D. Dale, Susan Myres & Ellen A. Yarrell, 2004 Marriage Dissolution

Choice of law problems arising when unmarried cohabitants change domiciles. William A. Reppy, Jr., 55 SMU L. Rev. 273 (2002)

Evaluating the sex discrimination argument for lesbian and gay rights. Edward Stein, 49 UCLA L. Rev. 471 (2001)

Symposium, same-sex marriage: the debate in Hawaii and the nation. 22 Haw. L. Rev. 1 (2000)

Same-sex marriage, choice of law, and public policy. Andrew Koppelman, 76 Tex. L. Rev. 921 (1998) (assumes valid same-sex marriage in State A, constitutionality of State B DOMA statute; choice of law and public policy decisions regarding nonresident same-sex litigants)

Cross Reference

Tex. Fam. Code Ann. § 6.204. Recognition of Same–Sex Marriage or Civil Union, *supra*

International Child Abduction

U.S.C.A. Title 42. The Public Health And Welfare

Chapter 121—International Child Abduction Remedies

★★★

Comment

The Convention on the Civil aspects of International Child Abduction (hereafter "Hague Convention"), *infra*, was established at The Hague on October 25, 1980. The United States ratified the Convention on April 29, 1988, and became a "Contracting State" effective July 1, 1988, Executive Order No. 12648, 53 Fed. Reg. 30637 (1988). Ratification moved the United States into the mainstream of Western nations on this subject. Although only a minority of members of the United Nations have ratified the Convention, most of the nations with which U.S. citizens have regular contact are covered. Congress deemed that under our legal system it was also necessary to implement the Convention, enacting the International Child Abduction Remedies Act on April 29, 1988 (hereafter "ICARA"), *see* 51 Fed. Reg. 10494–10516 (1986) (includes the U.S. State Department's legal analysis of the Convention).

Legislative History

Except as otherwise specifically noted, all of the statutory text in this chapter was enacted by Pub. L. 100–300, § 12, Apr. 29, 1988, 102 Stat. 442, 1988 Acts. House Report No. 100–525, see 1988 U.S. Code Cong. and Adm. News, p. 386.

Legal Publications

See comprehensive list of Legal Publications cited under Hague Convention, *infra*.

Construction and application of International Child Abduction Remedies Act, 125 ALR Fed 217

Leading Cases

Access to child:

Fernandez v. Yeager, 121 F.Supp.2d 1118 (W.D. Mich. 2000) *and* Bromley v. Bromley, 30 F.Supp.2d 857 (E.D. Pa. 1998) (federal courts lack jurisdiction to resolve suits seeking access to child)

Acquiescence in removal or retention of child:

Friedrich v. Friedrich, 78 F.3d 1060 (6th Cir. 1996) (father did not acquiesce in wrongful removal)

In re Robinson, 983 F.Supp. 1339 (D. Colo. 1997) (voluntary, court-approved "undertaking" to obey U.K. restraining order did not compel finding that father no longer had right to custody)

Currier v. Currier, 845 F.Supp. 916 (D. N.H. 1994) (German mother did not consent to or acquiesce in father's removal of children from Germany by signing private custody agreement; subsequently rescinded)

Wanninger v. Wanninger, 850 F.Supp. 78 (D. Mass. 1994) (even assuming father consented to mother's initial removal of children to U.S. for limited period, his subsequent actions only showed attempts to reconcile)

Burden of proof:

Lops v. Lops, 140 F.3d 927 (11th Cir. 1998) (affirmative defense to wrongful removal must establish asserted exception by preponderance of evidence)

In re Prevot, 59 F.3d 556 (6th Cir. 1995) (petitioning parent exercising custodial rights at time children were removed from habitual residence; responding parent must establish exception to return requirement by clear and convincing evidence)

Nunez–Escudero v. Tice–Menley, 58 F.3d 374 (8th Cir. 1995) (petitioner must initially prove child was removed from "habitual residence" by preponderance; if burden met, parent who removed child must show by clear and convincing evidence applicability of exception)

Friedrich v. Friedrich, 983 F.2d 1396, 125 A.L.R. Fed. 703 (6th Cir. 1993) (if preponderance of evidence shows child's removal was wrongful from "habitual residence," burden shifts to show exceptions); *accord* Steffen F. v. Severina P., 966 F.Supp. 922 (D. Ariz. 1997)

Steffen F. v. Severina P., 966 F.Supp. 922 (D. Ariz. 1997) (respondent mother had burden to establish by clear and convincing evidence affirmative defense of grave risk of harm to child)

Application of Ponath, 829 F.Supp. 363 (D. Utah 1993) (respondent had burden to establish by preponderance of the evidence any of the exceptions to return the child)

Comity [not Full Faith and Credit]:

Diorinou v. Mezitis, 237 F.3d 133 (2d Cir. 2001) (comity principles, not FF & C, yield deference to Greek decision)

Morton v. Morton, 982 F.Supp. 675 (D. Neb. 1997) (federal district court required to give preclusive and dispositive weight to decisions of Utah state court and German court requiring child's return from Germany)

Construction:

Rydder v. Rydder, 49 F.3d 369 (8th Cir. 1995) (Hague Convention and ICARA do not require ad hoc determination of underlying merits or balancing of equities, or allow adjudicate of merits of underlying custody claim)

Wojcik v. Wojcik, 959 F.Supp. 413 (E.D. Mich. 1997) (exceptions that would preclude return of child do not include American court's belief that it can better or more quickly resolve dispute)

Zajaczkowski v. Zajaczkowska, 932 F.Supp. 128 (D. Md. 1996) (only issue is whether child has been abducted from country of habitual residence or wrongfully retained outside that country; hearing on merits of custody dispute not contemplated)

Journe v. Journe, 911 F.Supp. 43 (D. Puerto Rico 1995) (purpose of Hague Convention, implemented by ICARA, is to return children to their country of habitual residence for resolution of any custody dispute)

Duquette v. Tahan, 600 A.2d 472 (N.J. Super. A.D. 1991) (if petitioner establishes prerequisites invoking Hague Convention, application is mandatory and child must be returned, subject only to its specific exceptions)

Continual exercise of rights:

Freier v. Freier, 969 F.Supp. 436 (E.D. Mich. 1996) (father continuously exercised his custodial rights under Israeli law while he, mother, and child lived there)

Costs and Fees:

Rydder v. Rydder, 49 F.3d 369 (8th Cir. 1995) (award of fees and costs was "clearly inappropriate" because of mother's straitened financial circumstances)

Distler v. Distler, 26 F.Supp.2d 723 (D. N.J. 1998) (mother could recover variety of expenses, including Israeli counsel fees)

Freier v. Freier, 985 F.Supp. 710 (E.D. Mich. 1997) (attorney fees are reasonable) (plaintiff entitled to transportation costs to return child to Israel) (fees were not recoverable for: office overhead; law clerk's services; copy expenses; interpreters' services not court appointed)

Berendsen v. Nichols, 938 F.Supp. 737 (D. Kan. 1996) ($125 per hour commensurate with usual rates) (reimbursement of costs for telephone calls, facsimile transmissions, witness fees, certified mail and postage, service fees, copying, filing fees, mileage, motel costs, rental car expenses, and gas) (costs and attorney fees reduced by 15% because of father's financial status and child support)

Viragh v. Foldes, 612 N.E.2d 241, 415 Mass. 96 (Mass. 1993) (noncustodial parent not entitled to attorney's fees; enforced right of visitation, but failed to have children returned to Hungary)

Roszkowski v. Roszkowska, 644 A.2d 1150, 274 N.J. Super. 620 (N.J.Super.Ch. 1993) (court may require party to pay legal and travel expenses and costs incurred in locating child as sanction for wrongful removal)

Fugitive Disentitlement:

In re Prevot, 59 F.3d 556 (6th Cir. 1995) (father fled U.S. after criminal conviction; as fugitive, he was disentitled from pursuing ICARA petition)

Grave Risk of Harm:

Silverman v. Silverman, 2002 WL 971808 (D.Minn. 2002) (as of 2002 Israel is "war zone" justifying denial of return under "grave risk" exception)

Blondin v. Dubois, 189 F.3d 240 (2d Cir. 1999) (grave risk of harm found, but on remand trial court to consider range of remedies allowing for return to home country while protecting children pending custody award by French court)

Friedrich v. Friedrich, 78 F.3d 1060 (6th Cir. 1996) (affirmative defense of grave risk of psychological harm to child not shown; just usual adjustment problems with relocation of a child)

Nunez–Escudero v. Tice–Menley, 58 F.3d 374 (8th Cir. 1995) (insufficient evidence of grave risk to child; allegations that removing mother was physically, sexually, and mentally abused by father too general)

Rydder v. Rydder, 49 F.3d 369 (8th Cir. 1995) (allegation that separation of primary caretaker from child creates risk of psychological harm unsubstantiated in absence of specific evidence)

Janakakis–Kostun v. Janakakis, 6 S.W.2d 843 (Ky. Ct. App. 1999) (grave risk not established, mother required to return child to Greece; fact father intemperate, often unkind, slapped and spanked children did not justify refusing return)

Rodriguez v. Rodriguez, 33 F.Supp.2d 456 (D. Md. 1999) (return denied; father physically abused children, mother and children suffering from Post Traumatic Stress Syndrome)

In re Walsh, 31 F.Supp.2d 200 (D. Mass. 1998) (mother alleged domestic violence; no evidence of immediate harm to children or that Irish authorities would not deal with problems)

Steffen F. v. Severina P., 966 F.Supp. 922 (D. Ariz. 1997) (proof child attached and bonded with parent and would become detached and unbonded in event of removal may constitute grave risk of harm)

Freier v. Freier, 969 F.Supp. 436 (E.D. Mich. 1996) (no clear and convincing evidence daughter would be in grave risk of physical or psychological harm if returned to Israel)

In re Prevot, 855 F.Supp. 915, *reversed*, 59 F.3d 556 (W.D. Tenn. 1994) (clinical psychologist's testimony that return of four-year-old to France would cause grave psychological harm insufficient)

Currier v. Currier, 845 F.Supp. 916 (D. N.H. 1994) (no credible evidence raising serious doubt about safety, propriety or nurturing character of German environment)

In re Coffield, 644 N.E.2d 662 (Ohio App. 1994) (evidence concerning mother's lifestyle and care for child prior to abduction not relevant to whether child at "grave risk" if returned to Australia)

Tahan v. Duquette, 613 A.2d 486, 259 N.J. Super. 328 (N.J. Super. A.D. 1992) (grave risk of harm exception not intended for consideration in plenary custody proceeding)

Sheikh v. Cahill, 546 N.Y.S.2d 517, 145 Misc.2d 171 (N.Y. Sup. 1989) (no substantiation of grave risk; stated preference of nine-year old to stay with father result of being "wooed" during visitation)

Habitual Residence:

Mozes v. Mozes, 239 F.3d 1067 (9th Cir. 2001) (criteria established for deciding when "temporary visit" supplants habitual residence)

Miller v. Miller, 240 F.3d 392 (4th Cir. 2001) and Diorinou v. Mezitis, 237 F.3d 133 (2d Cir. 2001) (parent cannot create habitual residence by sequestering child)

Lops v. Lops, 140 F.3d 927 (11th Cir. 1998) (habitual residence of minor children was Germany at time of removal, even though mother lived with children in Belgium for four months prior to removal)

Nunez–Escudero v. Tice–Menley, 58 F.3d 374 (8th Cir. 1995) (ruling that Mexico was not child's "habitual residence" erroneous; child born in and lived in Mexico until removed by mother)

Rydder v. Rydder, 49 F.3d 369 (8th Cir. 1995) (child returned to Poland, children's habitual residence, where father was temporarily employed)

Friedrich v. Friedrich, 983 F.2d 1396 (6th Cir. 1993) (habitual residence of child is Germany; born there to German father and American mother, lived there exclusively except for few short vacations)

In re Morris, 55 F.Supp.2d 1156 (D. Colo. 1999) (habitual residence not affected if family intends to stay in another country for defined period of less than one year)

Freier v. Freier, 969 F.Supp. 436 (E.D. Mich. 1996) (despite annual visits of four-year-old to Michigan, habitual residence Israel where both parents had lived continuously prior to birth)

In re Prevot, 855 F.Supp. 915, reversed 59 F.3d 556 (W.D. Tenn. 1994) (although children were born in U.S., parents lived in France for two years before mother returned them to U.S.)

Wanninger v. Wanninger, 850 F.Supp. 78 (D. Mass. 1994) (father entitled to joint legal custody under German law; children born there, lived and attended school there before mother's wrongful removal)

Application of Ponath, 829 F.Supp. 363 (D. Utah 1993) (Utah habitual residence; child was born there, taken for a voluntary extended visit to the father's family in Germany where mother and child were detained by means of verbal, emotional, and physical abuse)

Levesque v. Levesque, 816 F.Supp. 662 (D. Kan. 1993) (habitual residence Germany, where child resided with mother as agreed by parents)

Meredith v. Meredith, 759 F.Supp. 1432 (D. Ariz. 1991) (habitual residence Arizona where child was born and lived until she accompanied mother on purported "temporary holiday visit" to France)

Janakakis–Kostun v. Janakakis, 6 S.W.3d 843 (Ky. Ct. App. 1999) (habitual residence requires fact-specific focus on child's ordinary residence and whether residence is settled from child's point of view)

Flores v. Contreras, 981 S.W.2d 246 (Tex. App.—San Antonio 1998, pet. denied) (son returned to Mexican mother as habitual residence)

Harsacky v. Harsacky, 930 S.W.2d 410 (Ky. App. 1996) (children not returned because Finland not children's habitual residence)

Ciotola v. Fiocca, 684 N.E.2d 763 (Ohio Com. Pleas 1997) (return to child's habitual residence means return to Italy rather return than to father)

Jurisdiction:

Lops v. Lops, 140 F.3d 927 (11th Cir. 1998) (court has jurisdiction to decide merits only of the wrongful removal claim, not of underlying custody dispute)

Friedrich v. Friedrich, 78 F.3d 1060 (6th Cir. 1996) (seminal decision on topic—whether parent exercised custody rights well or badly goes to merits of custody dispute, which is beyond subject matter jurisdiction of federal courts)

Feder v. Evans–Feder, 63 F.3d 217 (3d Cir. 1995), *vacating* 866 F.Supp. 860 (federal district court erroneously held child's habitual residence not Australia; remanded to decide if an exception applies despite Australian court's finding of mother's wrongful retention of child in U.S.)

Morton v. Morton, 982 F.Supp. 675 (D. Neb. 1997) (Utah state court had jurisdiction to decide "wrongfulness" of former wife's removal of child to Germany; Utah maintains jurisdiction to modify its own custody decree)

Currier v. Currier, 845 F.Supp. 916 (D. N.H. 1994) (federal district court may determine which contracting state has jurisdiction to determine custody of abducted children, but cannot resolve underlying custody dispute)

Falls v. Downie, 871 F.Supp. 100 (D. Mass. 1994) (21–month-old not habitual resident of Germany at time of alleged wrongful retention; court lacked subject matter jurisdiction over child who lived in U.S. for 8 months with mother's agreement)

Brown v. Brown, 83 Cal. Rptr.2d 716, 71 Cal. App.4th 358 (1999) (suit to change custody and visitation properly dismissed; court lacked jurisdiction to modify Austrian court orders)

Matter of Cohen, 602 N.Y.S.2d 994, 158 Misc.2d 1018 (N.Y. Sup. 1993) (parents didn't agree to relocate children to Israel, so father could not invoke Hague Convention)

Tyszka v. Tyszka, 503 N.W.2d 726, *appeal denied*, 511 N.W.2d 683 (Mich. App. 1993) (after determining that children had been wrongfully retained in U.S. and should be returned to France, divorce court should have left issue of custody to French tribunal)

Sheikh v. Cahill, 546 N.Y.S.2d 517 (N.Y. Sup. 1989) (father cannot challenge validity of foreign court order in state court proceeding to enforce prior state custody decree)

Nonsignatory Nation:

In re David B. v. Helen O., 625 N.Y.S.2d 436 (N.Y. Fam. Ct. 1995) (children not habitual residents of the United Kingdom as alleged; rather, habitual residents of Nigeria—a nonsignatory nation precluding relief under Hague)

Matter of Mohsen, 715 F.Supp. 1063 (D. Wyo. 1989) (child in exclusive custody of mother could not seek redress under Hague Convention, child last habitually resident in nonsignatory nation)

Notice:

Brooke v. Willis, 907 F.Supp. 57 (S.D. N.Y. 1995) (mother received actual notice by telephone of father's wrongful abduction claim and attempts to personally serve her)

Settled in Environment:

Lops v. Lops, 140 F.3d 927 (11th Cir. 1998) (children removed from Germany to U.S. not "well-settled" due to grandmother's more active involvement with children rather than father)

Friedrich v. Friedrich, 78 F.3d 1060 (6th Cir. 1996), Wojcik v. Wojcik, 959 F.Supp. 413 (E.D. Mich. 1997) ("settled in their environment" exception to wrongful retention applicable, mother did not hide children; immediately telephoned French father to notify him of location of children)

Zuker v. Andrews, 2 F.Supp.2d 134 (D. Mass. 1998) (if petition for return of child filed more than year after the retention, respondent must show child is settled in new environment; inferentially return would be disruptive with likely harmful effects)

In re Robinson, 983 F.Supp. 1339 (D. Colo. 1997) (objection of ten-year-old to returning to his father in United Kingdom product of undue influence; accorded no weight)

Temporary Orders:

Application of McCullough on Behalf of McCullough, 4 F.Supp.2d 411 (W.D. Pa. 1998) (reasonable probability of eventual success on merits sustains TRO; possibility mother might flee prior to transfer of physical custody to father would result in irreparable harm)

Freier v. Freier, 969 F.Supp. 436 (E.D. Mich. 1996) (injunction prohibiting mother from leaving Israel until custody proceedings settled does not establish return of child from Michigan would violate fundamental freedom to travel; due process available in Israel)

Zajaczkowski v. Zajaczkowska, 932 F.Supp. 128 (D. Md. 1996) (unless it is plainly apparent that petitioner not entitled to relief, court should order respondent to appear and produce the child via habeas corpus)

Klam v. Klam, 797 F.Supp. 202 (E.D. N.Y. 1992) (German citizen not entitled to a "warrant" in lieu of a writ of habeas corpus to bring his children before the court for proceedings)

In re Lewin, ____ S.W.3d ____, 2004 WL 1193951 (Tex. App.—Austin 2004, no pet. hist.) (court should have ordered return of child to Canada and not issue temporary orders keeping child in Texas)

Voluntary Dismissal:

Ohlander v. Larson, 114 F.3d 1531 (10th Cir. 1997) (mother should have been allowed to dismiss Hague Convention petition after she took child to Sweden and father filed his own Hague petition there)

Waiver:

Lops v. Lops, 140 F.3d 927 (11th Cir. 1998) (parties' consent to transfer ICARA petition from Georgia court to South Carolina court waived right to complain)

Journe v. Journe, 911 F.Supp. 43 (D. Puerto Rico 1995) (father not entitled to return of children to habitual residence of France, waived remedy by obtaining dismissal of custody action in French court)

Wrongful Removal or Retention:

Toren v. Toren, 191 F.3d 23 (1st Cir. 1999) (mother has custody of children in U.S. pursuant to agreement until July 2000; no wrongful retention simply because father believes she will not return children)

Ohlander v. Larson, 114 F.3d 1531, *cert. denied* 118 S.Ct. 702 (10th Cir. 1997) (federal district court should not have considered removal of child from U.S. to Sweden in violation of court order, father had not filed cross-petition)

In re Prevot, 59 F.3d 556 (6th Cir. 1995) (wrongful removal occurs when child is removed from habitual residence when custody rights actually being exercised)

Friedrich v. Friedrich, 983 F.2d 1396, 125 A.L.R. Fed. 703 (6th Cir. 1993) (wrongful removal to be strictly defined; ad hoc determination or balancing of equities contrary to primary purpose of Hague to preserve status quo and to deter parents from crossing international boundaries in search of sympathetic court)

Zuker v. Andrews, 2 F.Supp.2d 134 (D. Mass. 1998) (no wrongful retention; mother and Argentinian father tacitly agreed that mother and child would remain in U.S.)

Steffen F. v. Severina P., 966 F.Supp. 922 (D. Ariz. 1997) (20–month-old habitual resident of country in which he was born and from which wrongfully taken by mother, notwithstanding she had joint custody of child)

Wojcik v. Wojcik, 959 F.Supp. 413 (E.D. Mich. 1997) (joint custody presumed under French law; father exercised his parental rights after living together with children immediately before removal)

Falls v. Downie, 871 F.Supp. 100 (D. Mass. 1994) (21–month-old not habitual resident of Germany at time of alleged wrongful retention by father in Massachusetts)

Currier v. Currier, 845 F.Supp. 916 (D. N.H. 1994) (German mother exercising valid custody rights under German law at time father removed children)

Sampson v. Sampson, 975 P.2d 1211 (Kan. 1999) (father was exercising rights of custody through regular visitation; mother's taking them from birthplace to U.S. wrongful, children returned to Israel; father exercising his custodial rights at time of removal)

Crall–Shaffer v. Shaffer, 663 N.E.2d 1346 (Ohio App. 1995) (father residing in France with custodial order of French court entitled to return of child)

Roszkowski v. Roszkowska, 644 A.2d 1150, 274 N.J. Super. 620 (N.J.Super.Ch. 1993) (wrongful removal or retention of child occurs when action violates custody rights of individual who was exercising those rights)

Viragh v. Foldes, 612 N.E.2d 241, 415 Mass. 96 (Mass. 1993) (custodial parent's retention of children in the U.S. not wrongful in view of ruling of Hungarian court that custodial parent should retain custody)

L.H. v. Youth Welfare Office of Wiesbaden, Germany, 568 N.Y.S.2d 852, 150 Misc.2d 490 (N.Y. Fam. Ct. 1991) (Hague Convention has no bearing on child custody proceeding without wrongful removal or retention)

In re Vernor, 94 S.W.3d 201 (Tex. App.—Austin 2002, orig. proceeding) (removal to Australia not wrongful where father's had no custodial rights at the time of removal)

Cross References

Tex. Fam. Code Ann. ch. 152, Uniform Interstate Child Custody Jurisdiction Act, *supra.*

International Parental Kidnapping Act of 1993, 18 U.S.C.A. § 1204, *supra*

Missing Children Act of 1982, 28 U.S.C.A. § 534(a)

Missing Children's Assistance Act of 1984, 42 U.S.C.A. § 5771, *et seq.*

National Child Search Assistance Act of 1990, 42 U.S.C.A. § 5779–80

Parental Kidnapping Prevention Act (PKPA), 28 U.S.C.A. § 1738A, *supra*

IV–D Child Support Enforcement, Parent Locator Service made available to Central Authority, 42 U.S.C.A. § 663.

---

§ 11601. Findings and Declarations.

(a) Findings

The Congress makes the following findings:

(1) The international abduction or wrongful retention of children is harmful to their well-being.

(2) Persons should not be permitted to obtain custody of children by virtue of their wrongful removal or retention.

(3) International abductions and retentions of children are increasing, and only concerted cooperation pursuant to an international agreement can effectively combat this problem.

(4) The Convention on the Civil Aspects of International Child Abduction, done at The Hague on October 25, 1980, establishes legal rights and procedures for the prompt return of children who have been wrongfully removed or retained, as well as for securing the exercise of visitation rights. Children who are wrongfully removed or retained within the meaning of the Convention are to be promptly returned unless one of the narrow exceptions set forth in the Convention applies. The Convention provides a sound treaty framework to help resolve the problem of international abduction and retention of children and will deter such wrongful removals and retentions.

(b) Declarations

The Congress makes the following declarations:

(1) It is the purpose of this chapter to establish procedures for the implementation of the Convention in the United States.

(2) The provisions of this chapter are in addition to and not in lieu of the provisions of the Convention.

(3) In enacting this chapter the Congress recognizes—

(A) the international character of the Convention; and

(B) the need for uniform international interpretation of the Convention.

(4) The Convention and this chapter empower courts in the United States to determine only rights under the Convention and not the merits of any underlying child custody claims.

§ 11602. Definitions.

For the purposes of this chapter—

(1) the term "applicant" means any person who, pursuant to the Convention, files an application with the United States Central Authority or a Central Authority of any other party to the Convention for the return of a child alleged to have been wrongfully removed or retained or for arrangements for organizing or securing the effective exercise of rights of access pursuant to the Convention;

(2) the term "Convention" means the Convention on the Civil Aspects of International Child Abduction, done at The Hague on October 25, 1980;

(3) the term "Parent Locator Service" means the service established by the Secretary of Health and Human Services under section 653 of this title;

(4) the term "petitioner" means any person who, in accordance with this chapter, files a petition in court seeking relief under the Convention;

(5) the term "person" includes any individual, institution, or other legal entity or body;

(6) the term "respondent" means any person against whose interests a petition is filed in court, in accordance with this chapter, which seeks relief under the Convention;

(7) the term "rights of access" means visitation rights;

(8) the term "State" means any of the several States, the District of Columbia, and any commonwealth, territory, or possession of the United States; and

(9) the term "United States Central Authority" means the agency of the Federal Government designated by the President under section 11606(a) of this title.

§ 11603. Judicial Remedies.

(a) Jurisdiction of courts.

The courts of the States and the United States district courts shall have concurrent original jurisdiction of actions arising under the Convention.

(b) Petitions.

Any person seeking to initiate judicial proceedings under the Convention for the return of a child or for arrangements for organizing or securing the effective exercise of rights of access to a child may do so by commencing a civil action by filing a petition for the relief sought in any court which has jurisdiction of such action and which is authorized to exercise its jurisdiction in the place where the child is located at the time the petition is filed.

(c) Notice.

Notice of an action brought under subsection (b) of this section shall be given in accordance with the applicable law governing notice in interstate child custody proceedings.

(d) Determination of case.

The court in which an action is brought under subsection (b) of this section shall decide the case in accordance with the Convention.

(e) Burdens of proof.

(1) A petitioner in an action brought under subsection (b) of this section shall establish by a preponderance of the evidence—

(A) in the case of an action for the return of a child, that the child has been wrongfully removed or retained within the meaning of the Convention; and

(B) in the case of an action for arrangements for organizing or securing the effective exercise of rights of access, that the petitioner has such rights.

(2) In the case of an action for the return of a child, a respondent who opposes the return of the child has the burden of establishing—

(A) by clear and convincing evidence that one of the exceptions set forth in article 13b or 20 of the Convention applies; and

(B) by a preponderance of the evidence that any other exception set forth in article 12 or 13 of the Convention applies.

(f) Application of Convention.

For purposes of any action brought under this chapter—

(1) the term "authorities", as used in article 15 of the Convention to refer to the authorities of the state of the habitual residence of a child, includes courts and appropriate government agencies;

(2) the terms "wrongful removal or retention" and "wrongfully removed or retained", as used in the Convention, include a removal or retention of a child before the entry of a custody order regarding that child; and

(3) the term "commencement of proceedings", as used in article 12 of the Convention, means, with respect to the return of a child located in the United States, the filing of a petition in accordance with subsection (b) of this section.

(g) Full faith and credit.

Full faith and credit shall be accorded by the courts of the States and the courts of the United States to the judgment of any other such court ordering or denying the return of a child, pursuant to the Convention, in an action brought under this chapter.

(h) Remedies under Convention not exclusive.

The remedies established by the Convention and this chapter shall be in addition to remedies available under other laws or international agreements.

§ 11604. Provisional Remedies.

(a) Authority of courts.

In furtherance of the objectives of article 7(b) and other provisions of the Convention, and subject to the provisions of subsection (b) of this section, any court exercising jurisdiction of an action brought under section 11603(b) of this title may take or cause to be taken measures under Federal or State law, as appropriate, to protect the well-being of the child involved or to prevent the child's further removal or concealment before the final disposition of the petition.

(b) Limitation on authority.

No court exercising jurisdiction of an action brought under section 11603(b) of this title may, under subsection (a) of this section, order a child removed from a person having physical control of the child unless the applicable requirements of State law are satisfied.

§ 11605. Admissibility of Documents.

With respect to any application to the United States Central Authority, or any petition to a court under section 11603 of this title, which seeks relief under the Convention, or any other documents or information included with such application or petition or provided after such submission which relates to the application or petition, as the case may be, no authentication of such application, petition, document, or information shall be required in order for the application, petition, document, or information to be admissible in court.

§ 11606. United States Central Authority.

(a) Designation.

The President shall designate a Federal agency to serve as the Central Authority for the United States under the Convention.

(b) Functions.

The functions of the United States Central Authority are those ascribed to the Central Authority by the Convention and this chapter.

(c) Regulatory authority.

The United States Central Authority is authorized to issue such regulations as may be necessary to carry out its functions under the Convention and this chapter.

(d) Obtaining information from Parent Locator Service.

The United States Central Authority may, to the extent authorized by the Social Security Act [42 U.S.C.A. § 301 et seq.], obtain information from the Parent Locator Service.

(e) Grant Authority.

The United States Central Authority is authorized to make grants to, or enter into contracts or agreements with, any individual, corporation, other Federal, State, or local agency, or private entity or organization in the United States for purposes of accomplishing its responsibilities under the Convention and this chapter.

Comment

The Department of State was designated as the Central Authority of the United States under the Hague Convention by Executive Order No. 12648, dated August 11, 1988. *See* 53 Fed. Reg. 30637.

---

§ 11607. Costs and Fees.

(a) Administrative costs

No department, agency, or instrumentality of the Federal Government or of any State or local government may impose on an applicant any fee in relation to the administrative processing of applications submitted under the Convention.

(b) Costs incurred in civil actions

(1) Petitioners may be required to bear the costs of legal counsel or advisors, court costs incurred in connection with their petitions, and travel costs for the return of the child involved and any accompanying persons, except as provided in paragraphs (2) and (3).

(2) Subject to paragraph (3), legal fees or court costs incurred in connection with an action brought under section 11603 of this title shall be borne by the petitioner unless they are covered by payments from Federal, State, or local legal assistance or other programs.

(3) Any court ordering the return of a child pursuant to an action brought under section 11603 of this title shall order the respondent to pay necessary expenses incurred

by or on behalf of the petitioner, including court costs, legal fees, foster home or other care during the course of proceedings in the action, and transportation costs related to the return of the child, unless the respondent establishes that such order would be clearly inappropriate.

§ 11608. Collection, maintenance, and dissemination of information.

(a) In general

In performing its functions under the Convention, the United States Central Authority may, under such conditions as the Central Authority prescribes by regulation, but subject to subsection (c) of this section, receive from or transmit to any department, agency, or instrumentality of the Federal Government or of any State or foreign government, and receive from or transmit to any applicant, petitioner, or respondent, information necessary to locate a child or for the purpose of otherwise implementing the Convention with respect to a child, except that the United States Central Authority—

(1) may receive such information from a Federal or State department, agency, or instrumentality only pursuant to applicable Federal and State statutes; and

(2) may transmit any information received under this subsection notwithstanding any provision of law other than this chapter.

(b) Requests for information

Requests for information under this section shall be submitted in such manner and form as the United States Central Authority may prescribe by regulation and shall be accompanied or supported by such documents as the United States Central Authority may require.

(c) Responsibility of government entities

Whenever any department, agency, or instrumentality of the United States or of any State receives a request from the United States Central Authority for information authorized to be provided to such Central Authority under subsection (a) of this section, the head of such department, agency, or instrumentality shall promptly cause a search to be made of the files and records maintained by such department, agency, or instrumentality in order to determine whether the information requested is contained in any such files or records. If such search discloses the information requested, the head of such department, agency, or instrumentality shall immediately transmit such information to the United States Central Authority, except that any such information the disclosure of which—

(1) would adversely affect the national security interests of the United States or the law enforcement interests of the United States or of any State; or

(2) would be prohibited by section 9 of Title 13;

shall not be transmitted to the Central Authority. The head of such department, agency, or instrumentality shall, immediately upon completion of the requested search, notify the Central Authority of the results of the search, and whether an exception set forth in paragraph (1) or (2) applies. In the event that the United States Central Authority receives information and the appropriate Federal or State department, agency, or instrumentality thereafter notifies the Central Authority that an exception set forth in paragraph (1) or (2) applies to that information, the Central Authority may not disclose that information under subsection (a) of this section.

(d) Information available from Parent Locator Service

To the extent that information which the United States Central Authority is authorized to obtain under the provisions of subsection (c) of this section can be obtained through the Parent Locator Service, the United States Central Authority shall first seek to obtain such information from the Parent Locator Service, before requesting such information directly under the provisions of subsection (c) of this section.

(e) Recordkeeping

The United States Central Authority shall maintain appropriate records concerning its activities and the disposition of cases brought to its attention.

§ 11608a. Office of Children's Issues.

(a) Director requirements

The Secretary of State shall fill the position of Director of the Office of Children's Issues of the Department of State (in this section referred to as the "Office") with an individual of senior rank who can ensure long-term continuity in the management and policy matters of the Office and has a strong background in consular affairs.

(b) Case officer staffing

Effective April 1, 2000, there shall be assigned to the Office of Children's Issues of the Department of State a sufficient number of case officers to ensure that the average caseload for each officer does not exceed 75.

(c) Embassy contact

The Secretary of State shall designate in each United States diplomatic mission an employee who shall serve as the point of contact for matters relating to international abductions of children by parents. The Director of the Office shall regularly inform the designated employee of children of United States citizens abducted by parents to that country.

(d) Reports to parents

(1) In general

Except as provided in paragraph (2), beginning 6 months after November 29, 1999, and at least once every 6 months thereafter, the Secretary of State shall report to each parent who has requested assistance regarding an abducted child overseas. Each such report shall include information on the current status of the abducted child's case and the efforts by the Department of State to resolve the case.

(2) Exception

The requirement in paragraph (1) shall not apply in a case of an abducted child if—

(A) the case has been closed and the Secretary of State has reported the reason the case was closed to the parent who requested assistance; or

(B) the parent seeking assistance requests that such reports not be provided.

History: Pub. L. 106–113, Nov. 29, 1999, 113 Stat. 1501. "This section was . . . enacted . . . not as part of the International Child Abduction Remedies Act, which otherwise comprises this chapter."

§ 11609. Interagency Coordinating Group.

The Secretary of State, the Secretary of Health and Human Services, and the Attorney General shall designate Federal employees and may, from time to time, designate private citizens to serve on an interagency coordinating group to monitor the operation of the Convention and to provide advice on its implementation to the United States Central Authority and other Federal agencies. This group shall meet from time to time at the request of the United States Central Authority. The agency in which the United States Central Authority is located is authorized to reimburse such private citizens for travel and other expenses incurred in participating at meetings of the interagency coordinating group at rates not to exceed those authorized under subchapter I of chapter 57 of Title 5 for employees of agencies.

§ 11610. Authorization of Appropriations.

There are authorized to be appropriated for each fiscal year such sums as may be necessary to carry out the purposes of the Convention and this chapter.

Hague Convention on the Civil Aspects of International Child Abduction.

On July 1, 1988 the Hague Convention entered into force in the United States. A total of 37 counties have ratified this multi-national commitment to stamp out international child snatching. In addition, a nonmember nation may "accede" to the Convention with a member nation. This means that the Convention can be in full effect between Nations A and B even though A is a signatory and B is not. Although B is not bound to recognize custody decrees from all signatories, the terms of the Convention are in effect to bind the actions of the relevant authorities of the two nations. Note: The Convention does not apply to abductions that took place before a nation ratified the Convention or before two nations acceded to the Convention with respect to each other.

Nations which have ratified or acceded to the Convention with respect to the United States as of July 1, 2003 are:

Argentina (June 1, 1991)
Australia (July 1, 1988)
Austria (Oct. 1, 1988)
Bahamas (Jan. 1, 1994)
Belgium (May 1, 1999)
Belize (Nov. 1, 1989)
Bosnia & Herzegovina (Dec. 1, 1991)
Brazil (Dec. 1, 2003)
Burkina Faso (Nov. 1, 1992)
Canada (July 1, 1988)
Chile (July 1, 1994)
China
  only Hong Kong Admin. Region (Sept. 1, 1997)
  and Macau (March 1, 1999)
Colombia (June 1, 1996)
Croatia (Dec. 1, 1991)
Cyprus (March 1, 1995)
Czech Republic (March 1, 1998)
Denmark (July 1, 1991)
Ecuador (April 1, 1992)
Finland (Aug. 1, 1994)
France (July 1, 1988)
Germany (Dec. 1, 1990)
Greece (June 1, 1993)
Honduras (June 1, 1994)
Hungary (July 1, 1988)
Iceland (Dec. 1, 1996)
Ireland (Oct. 1, 1991)
Israel (Dec. 1, 1991)
Italy (May 1, 1995)
Luxembourg (July 1, 1988)
Former Yugoslav Republic of Macedonia (Dec. 1, 1991)
Malta (Feb. 1, 2003)
Mauritius (Oct. 1, 1993)
Mexico (Oct. 1, 1991)
Monaco (June 1, 1993)
Netherlands (Sept. 1, 1990)
New Zealand (Nov. 1, 1992)
Norway (April 1, 1989)
Panama (June 1, 1994)
Poland (Nov. 1, 1992)
Portugal (July 1, 1988)
Romania (June 1, 1993)
St. Kitts and Nevis (June 1, 1995)
Slovak Republic (Feb. 1, 2001)
Slovenia (April 1, 1995)
South Africa (Nov. 1, 1997)
Spain (July 1, 1988)
Sweden (June 1, 1989)
Switzerland (July 1, 1988)
Turkey (Aug. 1, 2000)
United Kingdom (July 1, 1988)
  Bermuda (March 1, 1999)
  Cayman Islands (Aug. 1, 1998)
  Falkland Islands (June 1, 1998)
  Isle of Man (Sept. 1, 1991)
  Montserrat (March 1, 1999)
Venezuela (Jan. 1, 1997)
Yugoslavia, Federal Republic of (Dec. 1, 1991)
Zimbabwe (Aug. 1, 1995)

Major information and Research Resources

Your first stop should be to present your questions regarding the Convention to the Office of Children's Issues, U.S. Department of State, 2201 C Street N.W., Room 4800, Washington D.C., 20520 (telephone: (202) 647–2688, fax: (202) 647–2835); website, at *http://travel.state.gov/children'sissues.html/ica*. Of particular use is the 29 page booklet published by the State Department available on line at *http://travel.state.gov/int'lchildabduction.html*

For other questions (or if you are visiting The Hague), you might contact the Permanent Bureau of the Hague Conference on Private International Law, 6 Scheveningseweg, 2517 KT The Hague, Netherlands. Telephone: 31/70–363.33.03; Telex: 33383; Telefax: 31/70–360.48.67; e-mail, *info@hcch.net*; website, *http://www.hcch.net*

INTERNATIONAL CHILD ABDUCTIONS, SECOND EDITION: A GUIDE TO APPLYING THE 1988 HAGUE CONVENTION, WITH FORMS, GLORIA F. DEHART, EDITOR, (1993). Published by the ABA Family Law Section This manual provides most of the basic information you need to invoke and apply the Hague Convention—with the forms necessary for its use. It also includes the history of the development of the convention; legislative history in the U.S. and of the implementing legislation; text of the convention and a legal analysis; conclusions of the special committee on the operation of the convention; instructions for using the Hilton computer system of cases and information. The paperback book is 190 pages, 8 1/2 x 11. PRICE: $24.95 for ABA Family Law Section Members; $29.95 for nonmembers. To order telephone 1–800–285–2221 or contact *http://www.abanet.org/family/pubs/5130056.html*

Finally, every lawyer or judge handling family-related child abduction cases should visit the website of William M. Hilton, an attorney in private practice in Santa Clara, CA. The site has approximately hundreds of files covering issues and cases related to the Hague Convention on the Civil Aspects of International Child Abduction, the U.S. implementing legislation (ICARA), the UCCJA and UCCJEA, and the federal Parental Kidnapping Prevention Act (PKPA). The site is loaded with the texts of judicial decisions related to the Hague Convention, articles about the Convention, etc. There are also links to other Web sites with information on international child abduction. Files are regularly added, usually one or two a week. A brief description, with key words, of all of these files is given in the File Description sub-file. These files are made available to anyone who wishes to use them, at no charge. William M. Hilton, Box 269, Santa Clara, CA 95052–0269. Telephone: 408–246–8511; FAX: 408–246–0114; e-mail: *hilton34@hiltonhouse.com; http://www.hiltonhouse.com*

Legal Publications

Concepts and questions of interpretation arising from the Hague Convention on the civil aspects of international child abduction. Adair Dyer, 2004 U. TEX. FAM. L. ON THE BORDER

Prevention of international parental child abduction—keeping the horses (or in this case the minor children) in the barn instead of chasing them down after they've escaped. Kathleen C. Anderson, 2004 U. TEX. FAM. L. ON THE BORDER

The ABCs of interstate conservatorship and family support jurisdiction. Angela G. Pence, 2003 ADV. FAM. L.

International and cross border issues. (Workshop) 2003, 2002 ADV. FAM. L.

Jurisdiction over foreign litigants: dissolution, property division, spousal support, child support. Bill De La Garza & Jo Ann Carter, 2002 ADV. FAM. L.

Interstate alphabet soup. Sally H. Emerson, 2002 ADV. FAM. L.

Leading Cases

See Leading Cases listed under ICARA, 42 U.S.C.A. §§ 11601–11610, *supra*.

Cross References

See Cross References listed under ICARA, *supra*.

HAGUE CONVENTION ON THE CIVIL ASPECTS OF INTERNATIONAL CHILD ABDUCTION

The States signatory to the present Convention, Firmly convinced that the interests of children are of paramount importance in matters relating to their custody, Desiring to protect children internationally from the harmful effects of their wrongful removal or retention and to establish procedures to ensure their prompt return to the State of their habitual residence, as well as to secure protection for rights of access, Have resolved to conclude a Convention to this effect, and have agreed upon the following provisions—

CHAPTER I—SCOPE OF THE CONVENTION

Article 1

The objects of the present Convention are—

(a) to secure the prompt return of children wrongfully removed to or retained in any Contracting State; and

(b) to ensure that rights of custody and of access under the law of one Contracting State are effectively respected in the Other Contracting States.

Article 2

Contracting States shall take all appropriate measures to secure within their territories the implementation of the objects of the Convention. For this purpose they shall use the most expeditious procedures available.

Article 3

The removal or the retention of a child is to be considered wrongful where—

(a) it is in breach of rights of custody attributed to a person, an institution or any other body, either jointly or alone, under the law of the State in which the child was habitually resident immediately before the removal or retention; and

(b) at the time of removal or retention those rights were actually exercised, either jointly or alone, or would have been so exercised but for the removal or retention. The rights of custody mentioned in sub-paragraph (a) above, may arise in particular by operation of law or by reason of a judicial or administrative decision, or by reason of an agreement having legal effect under the law of that State.

Article 4

The Convention shall apply to any child who was habitually resident in a Contracting State immediately before any breach of custody or access rights. The Convention shall cease to apply when the child attains the age of 16 years.

Article 5

For the purposes of this Convention—

(a) "rights of custody" shall include rights relating to the care of the person of the child and, in particular, the right to determine the child's place of residence;

(b) "rights of access" shall include the right to take a child for a limited period of time to a place other than the child's habitual residence.

CHAPTER II—CENTRAL AUTHORITIES

Article 6

A Contracting State shall designate a Central Authority to discharge the duties which are imposed by the Convention upon such authorities.

Federal States, States with more than one system of law or States having autonomous territorial organizations shall be free to appoint more than one Central Authority and to specify the territorial extent of their powers. Where a State has appointed more than one Central Authority, it shall designate the Central Authority to which applications may be addressed for transmission to the appropriate Central Authority within that State.

Article 7

Central Authorities shall cooperate with each other and promote cooperation amongst the competent authorities in their respective States to secure the prompt return of children and to achieve the other objects of this Convention. In particular, either directly or through any intermediary, they shall take all appropriate measures—

(a) to discover the whereabouts of a child who has been wrongfully removed or retained;

(b) to prevent further harm to the child or prejudice to interested parties by taking or causing to be taken provisional measures;

(c) to secure the voluntary return of the child or to bring about an amicable resolution of the issues;

(d) to exchange, where desirable, information relating to the social background of the child;

(e) to provide information of a general character as to the law of their State in connection with the application of the Convention;

(f) to initiate or facilitate the institution of judicial or administrative proceedings with a view to obtaining the return of the child and, in a proper case, to make arrangements for organizing or securing the effective exercise of rights of access;

(g) where the circumstances so require, to provide or facilitate the provision of legal aid and advice, including the participation of legal counsel and advisers;

(h) to provide such administrative arrangements as may be necessary and appropriate to secure the safe return of the child;

(i) to keep each other informed with respect to the operation of this Convention and, as far as possible, to eliminate any obstacles to its application.

CHAPTER III—RETURN OF CHILDREN

Article 8

Any person, institution or other body claiming that a child has been removed or retained in breach of custody rights may apply either to the Central Authority of the child's habitual residence or to the Central Authority of any other Contracting State for assistance in securing the return of the child. The application shall contain—

(a) information concerning the identity of the applicant, of the child and of the person alleged to have removed or retained the child;

(b) where available, the date of birth of the child;

(c) the grounds on which the applicant's claim for return of the child is based;

(d) all available information relating to the whereabouts of the child and the identity of the person with whom the child is presumed to be. The application may be accompanied or supplemented by—

(e) an authenticated copy of any relevant decision or agreement;

(f) a certificate or an affidavit emanating from a Central Authority, or other competent authority of the State of the child's habitual residence, or from a qualified person, concerning the relevant law of that State;

(g) any other relevant document.

Article 9

If the Central Authority which receives an application referred to in Article 8 has reason to believe that the child is in another Contracting State, it shall directly and without delay transmit the application to the Central Authority of that Contracting State and inform the requesting Central Authority, or the applicant, as the case may be.

Article 10

The Central Authority of the State where the child is shall take or cause to be taken all appropriate measures in order to obtain the voluntary return of the child.

Article 11

The judicial or administrative authorities of Contracting States shall act expeditiously in proceedings for the return of children. If the judicial or administrative authority concerned has not reached a decision within six weeks from the date of commencement of the proceedings, the applicant or the Central Authority of the requested State, on its own initiative or if asked by the Central Authority of the requesting State, shall have the right to request a statement of the reasons for the delay. If a reply is received by the Central Authority of the requested State, that Authority shall transmit the reply to the Central Authority of the requesting State, or to the applicant, as the case may be.

Article 12

Where a child has been wrongfully removed or retained in terms of Article 3 and, at the date of the commencement of the proceedings before the judicial or administrative authority of the Contracting State where the child is, a period of less than one year has elapsed from the date of the wrongful removal or retention, the authority concerned shall order the return of the child forthwith.

The judicial or administrative authority, even where the proceedings have been commenced after the expiration of the period of one year referred to in the preceding paragraph, shall also order the return of the child, unless it is demonstrated that the child is now settled in its new environment.

Where the judicial or administrative authority in the requested State has reason to believe that the child has been taken to another State, it may stay the proceedings or dismiss the application for the return of the child.

Article 13

Notwithstanding the provisions of the preceding Article, the judicial or administrative authority of the requested State is not bound to order the return of the child if the person, institution or other body which opposes its return establishes that—

(a) the person, institution or other body having the care of the person of the child was not actually exercising the custody rights at the time of removal or retention, or had consented to or subsequently acquiesced in the removal or retention; or

(b) there is a grave risk that his or her return would expose the child to physical or psychological harm or otherwise place the child in an intolerable situation.

The judicial or administrative authority may also refuse to order the return of the child if it finds that the child objects to being returned and has attained an age and degree of maturity at which it is appropriate to take account of its views.

In considering the circumstances referred to in this Article, the judicial and administrative authorities shall take into account the information relating to the social background of the child provided by the Central Authority or other competent authority of the child's habitual residence.

Article 14

In ascertaining whether there has been a wrongful removal or retention within the meaning of Article 3, the judicial or administrative authorities of the requested State may take notice directly of the law of, and of judicial or administrative decisions, formally recognized or not in the State of the habitual residence of the child, without recourse to the specific procedures for the proof of that law or for the recognition of foreign decisions which would otherwise be applicable.

Article 15

The judicial or administrative authorities of a Contracting State may, prior to the making of an order for the return of the child, request that the applicant obtain from the authorities of the State of the habitual residence of the child a decision or other determination that the removal or retention was wrongful within the meaning of Article 3 of the Convention, where such a decision or determination may be obtained in that State. The Central Authorities of the Contracting States shall so far as practicable assist applicants to obtain such a decision or determination.

Article 16

After receiving notice of a wrongful removal or retention of a child in the sense of Article 3, the judicial or administrative authorities of the Contracting State to which the child has been removed or in which it has been retained shall not decide on the merits of rights of custody until it has been determined that the child is not to be returned under this Convention or unless an application under this Convention is not lodged within a reasonable time following receipt of the notice.

Article 17

The sole fact that a decision relating to custody has been given in or is entitled to recognition in the requested State shall not be a ground for refusing to return a child under this Convention, but the judicial or administrative authorities of the requested State may take account of the reasons for that decision in applying this Convention.

Article 18

The provisions of this Chapter do not limit the power of a judicial or administrative authority to order the return of the child at any time.

Article 19

A decision under this Convention concerning the return of the child shall not be taken to be a determination on the merits of any custody issue.

Article 20

The return of the child under the provisions of Article 12 may be refused if this would not be permitted by the fundamental principles of the requested State relating to the protection of human rights and fundamental freedoms.

CHAPTER IV—RIGHTS OF ACCESS

Article 21

An application to make arrangements for organizing or securing the effective exercise of rights of access may be presented to the Central Authorities of the Contracting States in the same way as an application for the return of a child.

The Central Authorities are bound by the obligations of cooperation which are set forth in Article 7 to promote the peaceful enjoyment of access rights and the fulfillment of any conditions to which the exercise of those rights may be subject.

The Central Authorities shall take steps to remove, as far as possible, all obstacles to the exercise of such rights. The Central Authorities, either directly or through intermediaries, may initiate or assist in the institution of proceedings with a view to organizing or protecting these rights and securing respect for the conditions to which the exercise of these rights may be subject.

CHAPTER V—GENERAL PROVISIONS

Article 22

No security, bond or deposit, however described, shall be required to guarantee the payment of costs and expenses in the judicial or administrative proceedings falling within the scope of this Convention.

Article 23

No legalization or similar formality may be required in the context of this Convention.

Article 24

Any application, communication or other document sent to the Central Authority of the requested State shall be in the original language, and shall be accompanied by a translation into the official language or one of the official languages of the requested State or, where that is not feasible, a translation into French or English.

However, a Contracting State may, by making a reservation in accordance with Article 42, object to the use of either French or English, but not both, in any application, communication or other document sent to its Central Authority.

Article 25

Nationals of the Contracting States and persons who are habitually resident within those States shall be entitled in matters concerned with the application of this Convention to legal aid and advice in any other Contracting State on the same conditions as if they themselves were nationals of and habitually resident in that State.

Article 26

Each Central Authority shall bear its own costs in applying this Convention.

Central Authorities and other public services of Contracting States shall not impose any charges in relation to applications submitted under this Convention. In particular, they may not require any payment from the applicant towards the costs and expenses of the proceedings or, where applicable, those arising from the participation of legal counsel or advisers. However, they may require the payment of the expenses incurred or to be incurred in implementing the return of the child.

However, a Contracting State may, by making a reservation in accordance with Article 42, declare that it shall not be bound to assume any costs referred to in the preceding paragraph resulting from the participation of legal counsel or advisers or from court proceedings, except insofar as those costs may be covered by its system of legal aid and advice.

Upon ordering the return of a child or issuing an order concerning rights of access under this Convention, the judicial or administrative authorities may, where appropriate, direct the person who removed or retained the child, or who prevented the exercise of rights of access, to pay necessary expenses incurred by or on behalf of the applicant, including travel expenses, any costs incurred or payments made for locating the child, the costs of legal representation of the applicant, and those of returning the child.

Article 27

When it is manifest that the requirements of this Convention are not fulfilled or that the application is otherwise not well founded, a Central Authority is not bound to accept the application. In that case, the Central Authority shall forthwith inform the applicant or the Central Authority through which the application was submitted, as the case may be, of its reasons.

Article 28

A Central Authority may require that the application be accompanied by a written authorization empowering it to act on behalf of the applicant, or to designate a representative so to act.

Article 29

This Convention shall not preclude any person, institution or body who claims that there has been a breach of custody or access rights within the meaning of Article 3 or 21 from applying directly to the judicial or administrative authorities of a Contracting State, whether or not under the provisions of this Convention.

Article 30

Any application submitted to the Central Authorities or directly to the judicial or administrative authorities of a Contracting State in accordance with the terms of this Convention, together with documents and any other information appended thereto or provided by a Central Authority, shall be admissible in the courts or administrative authorities of the Contracting States.

Article 31

In relation to a State which in matters of custody of children has two or more systems of law applicable in different territorial units—

(a) any reference to habitual residence in that State shall be construed as referring to habitual residence in a territorial unit of that State;

(b) any reference to the law of the State of habitual residence shall be construed as referring to the law of the territorial unit in that State where the child habitually resides.

Article 32

In relation to a State which in matters of custody of children has two or more systems of law applicable to different categories of persons, any reference to the law of that State shall be construed as referring to the legal system specified by the law of that State.

Article 33

A State within which different territorial units have their own rules of law in respect of custody of children shall not be bound to apply this Convention where a State with a unified system of law would not be bound to do so.

Article 34

This Convention shall take priority in matters within its scope over the Convention of October 5, 1961 concerning the powers of authorities and the law applicable in respect of the protection of minors, as between Parties to both Conventions. Otherwise the present Convention shall not restrict the application of an international instrument in force between the State of origin and the State addressed or other law of the State addressed for the purposes of obtaining the return of a child who has been wrongfully removed or retained or of organizing access rights.

Article 35

This Convention shall apply as between Contracting States only to wrongful removals or retentions occurring after its entry into force in those States. Where a declaration has been made under Article 39 or 40, the reference in the preceding paragraph to a Contracting State shall be taken to refer to the territorial unit or units in relation to which this Convention applies.

Article 36

Nothing in this Convention shall prevent two or more Contracting States, in order to limit the restrictions to which the return of the child may be subject, from agreeing among themselves to derogate from any provisions of this Convention which may imply such a restriction.

CHAPTER VI—FINAL CLAUSES

Article 37

The Convention shall be open for signature by the States which were Members of the Hague Conference on Private International Law at the time of its Fourteenth Session.

It shall be ratified, accepted or approved and the instruments of ratification, acceptance or approval shall be deposited with the Ministry of Foreign Affairs of the Kingdom of the Netherlands.

Article 38

Any other State may accede to the Convention. The instrument of accession shall be deposited with the Ministry of Foreign Affairs of the Kingdom of the Netherlands.

The Convention shall enter into force for a state acceding to it on the first day of the third calendar month after the deposit of its instrument of accession. The accession will have effect only as regards the relations between the acceding State and such Contracting States as will have declared their acceptance of the accession. Such a declaration will also have to be made by any Member State ratifying, accepting or approving the Convention after an accession. Such declaration shall be deposited at the Ministry of Foreign Affairs of the Kingdom of the Netherlands; this Ministry shall forward, through diplomatic channels, a certified copy to each of the Contracting States.

The Convention will enter into force as between the acceding State and the State that has declared its acceptance of the accession on the first day of the third calendar month after the deposit of the declaration of acceptance.

Article 39

Any State may, at the time of signature, ratification, acceptance, approval or accession, declare that the Convention shall extend to all the territories for the international relations of which it is responsible, or to one or more of them. Such a declaration shall take effect at the time the Convention enters into force for that State. Such declaration, as well as any subsequent extension, shall be notified to the Ministry of Foreign Affairs of the Kingdom of the Netherlands.

Article 40

If a Contracting State has two or more territorial units in which different systems of law are applicable in relation to matters dealt with in this Convention, it may at the time of signature, ratification, acceptance, approval or accession declare that this Convention shall extend to all its territorial units or only to one or more of them and may modify this declaration by submitting another declaration at any time.

Any such declaration shall be notified to the Ministry of Foreign Affairs of the Kingdom of the Netherlands and shall state expressly the territorial units to which the Convention applies.

Article 41

Where a Contracting State has a system of government under which executive, judicial and legislative powers are distributed between central and other authorities within that State, its signature or ratification, acceptance or approval of, or accession to this Convention, or its making of any declaration in terms of Article 40 shall carry no implication as to the internal distribution of powers within that State.

Article 42

Any State may, not later than the time of ratification, acceptance, approval or accession, or at the time of making a declaration in terms of Article 39 or 40, make one or both of the reservations provided for in Article 24 and Article 26, third paragraph. No other reservation shall be permitted. Any State may at any time withdraw a reservation it has made. The withdrawal shall be notified to the Ministry of Foreign Affairs of the Kingdom of the Netherlands. The reservation shall cease to have effect on the first day of the third calendar month after the notification referred to in the preceding paragraph.

Article 43

The Convention shall enter into force on the first day of the third calendar month after the deposit of the third instrument of ratification, acceptance, approval or accession referred to in Articles 37 and 38. Thereafter the Convention shall enter into force—

(1) for each State ratifying, accepting, approving or acceding to it subsequently, on the first day of the third calendar month after the deposit of its instrument of ratification, acceptance, approval or accession;

(2) for any territory or territorial unit to which the Convention has been extended in conformity with Article 39 or 40, on the first day of the third calendar month after the notification referred to in that Article.

Article 44

The Convention shall remain in force for five years from the date of its entry into force in accordance with the first paragraph of Article 43 even for States which subsequently have ratified, accepted, approved it or acceded to it. If there has been no denunciation, it shall be renewed tacitly every five years.

Any denunciation shall be notified to the Ministry of Foreign Affairs of the Kingdom of the Netherlands at least six months before the expire of the five year period. It may be limited to certain of the territories or territorial units to which the Convention applies.

The denunciation shall have effect only as regards the State which has notified it. The Convention shall remain in force for the other Contracting States.

Article 45

The Ministry of Foreign Affairs of the Kingdom of the Netherlands shall notify the States Members of the Conference, and the States which have acceded in accordance with Article 38, of the following—

(1) the signatures and ratifications, acceptances and approvals referred to in Article 37;

(2) the accessions referred to in Article 38;

(3) the date on which the Convention enters into force in accordance with Article 43;

(4) the extensions referred to in Article 39;

(5) the declarations referred to in Articles 38 and 40;

(6) the reservations referred to in Article 24 and Article 26, third paragraph, and the withdrawals referred to in Article 42;

(7) the denunciations referred to in Article 44. In witness whereof the undersigned, being duly authorized thereto, have signed this Convention.

Done at The Hague, on the 25th day of October, 1980 in the English and French languages, both texts being equally authentic, in a single copy which shall be deposited in the archives of the Government of the Kingdom of the Netherlands, and of which a certified copy shall be sent, through diplomatic channels, to each to the States Members of the Hague Conference on Private International Law at the date of its Fourteenth Session.

Servicemembers Civil Relief Act

U.S.C.A. Title 50. Appendix: War and National Defense

★★★

Editors' Note*: This chapter contains guest commentary by David D. Farr, the associate judge of the 257th District Court, Harris County, Texas, and a Major, Chief, Legal Assistance, 49th AD, Texas Army National Guard, identified as (D.D.F.).*

Introductory Comment

The Soldiers' and Sailors' Civil Relief Act (50 U.S.C. app. Sections 501–594 (2000)) has provided the cornerstone for the blanket of protections afforded to military servicemembers in regard to judicial stays of proceedings and consumer protections since its enactment in 1918. On December 19, 2003, President George W. Bush signed Public Law Number 108–189 constituting the first major amendment to the act since its last major revision in 1940. The newly titled, Servicemembers Civil Relief Act, attempts to account for almost sixty-four years of judicial interpretation and to, in the words of the new act, "restate, clarify, and revise the Soldiers' and Sailors' Civil Relief Act of 1940". In addition, the new act simplifies and clarifies the old law in an attempt to make it more "user-friendly" for the general practitioner. Lastly, the new act updates the provisions to account for changes in daily life since 1940 and the modern practices of the judicial system across the nation. *(D.D.F.)*

§ 511. Definitions.

For the purposes of this Act [sections 501 to 596 of this Appendix]:

(1) Servicemember.

The term "servicemember" means a member of the uniformed services, as that term is defined in section 101(a)(5) of title 10, United States Code.

(2) Military service.

The term "military service" means—

(A) in the case of a servicemember who is a member of the Army, Navy, Air Force, Marine Corps, or Coast Guard—

(i) active duty, as defined in section 101(d)(1) of title 10, United States Code, and

(ii) in the case of a member of the National Guard, includes service under a call to active service authorized by the President or the Secretary of Defense for a period of more than 30 consecutive days under section 502(f) of title 32, United States Code, for purposes of responding to a national emergency declared by the President and supported by Federal funds;

(B) in the case of a servicemember who is a commissioned officer of the Public Health Service or the National Oceanic and Atmospheric Administration, active service; and

(C) any period during which a servicemember is absent from duty on account of sickness, wounds, leave, or other lawful cause.

(3) Period of military service.

The term "period of military service" means the period beginning on the date on which a servicemember enters military service and ending on the date on which the servicemember is released from military service or dies while in military service.

(4) Dependent.

The term "dependent", with respect to a servicemember, means—

(A) the servicemember's spouse;

(B) the servicemember's child (as defined in section 101(4) of title 38, United States Code); or

(C) an individual for whom the servicemember provided more than one-half of the individual's support for 180 days immediately preceding an application for relief under this Act [sections 501 to 596 of this Appendix].

(5) Court.

The term "court" means a court or an administrative agency of the United States or of any State (including any political subdivision of a State), whether or not a court or administrative agency of record.

(6) State.

The term "State" includes—

(A) a commonwealth, territory, or possession of the United States; and

(B) the District of Columbia.

(7) Secretary concerned.

The term "Secretary concerned"—

(A) with respect to a member of the armed forces, has the meaning given that term in section 101(a)(9) of title 10, United States Code;

(B) with respect to a commissioned officer of the Public Health Service, means the Secretary of Health and Human Services; and

(C) with respect to a commissioned officer of the National Oceanic and Atmospheric Administration, means the Secretary of Commerce.

(8) Motor vehicle.

The term "motor vehicle" has the meaning given that term in section 30102(a)(6) of title 49, United States Code.

§ 512. Jurisdiction and Applicability of Act.

(a) Jurisdiction.

This Act [sections 501 to 596 of this Appendix] applies to—

(1) the United States;

(2) each of the States, including the political subdivisions thereof; and

(3) all territory subject to the jurisdiction of the United States.

(b) Applicability to proceedings.

This Act [sections 501 to 596 of this Appendix] applies to any judicial or administrative proceeding commenced in any court or agency in any jurisdiction subject to this Act [said sections]. This Act [said sections] does not apply to criminal proceedings.

(c) Court in which application may be made.

When under this Act [sections 501 to 596 of this Appendix] any application is required to be made to a court in which no proceeding has already been commenced with respect to the matter, such application may be made to any court which would otherwise have jurisdiction over the matter.

§ 513. Protection of Persons Secondarily Liable.

(a) Extension of protection when actions stayed, postponed, or suspended.

Whenever pursuant to this Act [sections 501 to 596 of this Appendix] a court stays, postpones, or suspends (1) the enforcement of an obligation or liability, (2) the prosecution of a suit or proceeding, (3) the entry or enforcement of an order, writ, judgment, or decree, or (4) the performance of any other act, the court may likewise grant such a stay, postponement, or suspension to a surety, guarantor, endorser, accommodation maker, comaker, or other person who is or may be primarily or secondarily subject to the obligation or liability the performance or enforcement of which is stayed, postponed, or suspended.

(b) Vacation or set-aside of judgments.

When a judgment or decree is vacated or set aside, in whole or in part, pursuant to this Act [sections 501 to 596 of this Appendix], the court may also set aside or vacate, as the case may be, the judgment or decree as to a surety, guarantor, endorser, accommodation maker, comaker, or other person who is or may be primarily or secondarily liable on the contract or liability for the enforcement of the judgment or decree.

(c) Bail bond not to be enforced during period of military service.

A court may not enforce a bail bond during the period of military service of the principal on the bond when military service prevents the surety from obtaining the attendance of the principal. The court may discharge the surety and exonerate the bail, in accordance with principles of equity and justice, during or after the period of military service of the principal.

(d) Waiver of rights.

(1) Waivers not precluded.

This Act [sections 501 to 596 of this Appendix] does not prevent a waiver in writing by a surety, guarantor, endorser, accommodation maker, comaker, or other person (whether primarily or secondarily liable on an obligation or liability) of the protections provided under subsections (a) and (b). Any such waiver is effective only if it is executed as an instrument separate from the obligation or liability with respect to which it applies.

(2) Waiver invalidated upon entrance to military service.

If a waiver under paragraph (1) is executed by an individual who after the execution of the waiver enters military service, or by a dependent of an individual who after the execution of the waiver enters military service, the waiver is not valid after the beginning of the period of such military service unless the waiver was executed by such individual or dependent during the period specified in section 106 [section 516 of this Appendix].

§ 514. Extension of Protections to Citizens Serving with Allied Forces.

A citizen of the United States who is serving with the forces of a nation with which the United States is allied in the prosecution of a war or military action is entitled to the relief and protections provided under this Act [sections 501 to 596 of this Appendix] if that service with the allied force is similar to military service as defined in this Act [sections 501 to 596 of this Appendix]. The relief and protections provided to such citizen shall terminate on the date of discharge or release from such service.

§ 516. Extension of Rights and Protections to Reserves Ordered to Report for Military Service and to Persons Ordered to Report for Induction.

(a) Reserves ordered to report for military service.

A member of a reserve component who is ordered to report for military service is entitled to the rights and protections of this title and titles II and III [of this Appendix] during the period beginning on the date of the member's receipt of the order and ending on the date on which the member reports for military service (or, if the order is revoked before the member so reports, or the date on which the order is revoked).

(b) Persons ordered to report for induction.

A person who has been ordered to report for induction under the Military Selective Service Act (50 U.S.C. App. 451 et seq.) is entitled to the rights and protections provided a servicemember under this title and titles II and III [of this Appendix] during the period beginning on the date of receipt of the order for induction and ending on the date on which the person reports for induction (or, if the order to report for induction is revoked before the date on which the person reports for induction, on the date on which the order is revoked).

§ 517. Waiver of Rights Pursuant to Written Agreement.

(a) In general.

A servicemember may waive any of the rights and protections provided by this Act [sections 501 to 596 of this Appendix]. In the case of a waiver that permits an action described in subsection (b), the waiver is effective only if made pursuant to a written agreement of the parties that is executed during or after the servicemember's period of military service. The written agreement shall specify the legal instrument to which the waiver applies and, if the servicemember is not a party to that instrument, the servicemember concerned.

(b) Actions requiring waivers in writing.

The requirement in subsection (a) for a written waiver applies to the following:

(1) The modification, termination, or cancellation of—

(A) a contract, lease, or bailment; or

(B) an obligation secured by a mortgage, trust, deed, lien, or other security in the nature of a mortgage.

(2) The repossession, retention, foreclosure, sale, forfeiture, or taking possession of property that—

(A) is security for any obligation; or

(B) was purchased or received under a contract, lease, or bailment.

(c) Coverage of periods after orders received.

For the purposes of this section—

(1) a person to whom section 106 [section 516 of this Appendix] applies shall be considered to be a servicemember; and

(2) the period with respect to such a person specified in subsection (a) or (b), as the case may be, of section 106 [section 516 of this Appendix] shall be considered to be a period of military service.

§ 518. Exercise of Rights Under act not to Affect Certain Future Financial Transactions.

Application by a servicemember for, or receipt by a servicemember of, a stay, postponement, or suspension pursuant to this Act [sections 501 to 596 of this Appendix] in the payment of a tax, fine, penalty, insurance premium, or other civil obligation or liability of that servicemember shall not itself (without regard to other considerations) provide the basis for any of the following:

(1) A determination by a lender or other person that the servicemember is unable to pay the civil obligation or liability in accordance with its terms.

(2) With respect to a credit transaction between a creditor and the servicemember—

(A) a denial or revocation of credit by the creditor;

(B) a change by the creditor in the terms of an existing credit arrangement; or

(C) a refusal by the creditor to grant credit to the servicemember in substantially the amount or on substantially the terms requested.

(3) An adverse report relating to the creditworthiness of the servicemember by or to a person engaged in the practice of assembling or evaluating consumer credit information.

(4) A refusal by an insurer to insure the servicemember.

(5) An annotation in a servicemember's record by a creditor or a person engaged in the practice of assembling or evaluating consumer credit information, identifying the servicemember as a member of the National Guard or a reserve component.

(6) A change in the terms offered or conditions required for the issuance of insurance.

§ 519. Legal Representatives.

(a) Representative

A legal representative of a servicemember for purposes of this Act [sections 501 to 596 of this Appendix] is either of the following:

(1) An attorney acting on the behalf of a servicemember.

(2) An individual possessing a power of attorney.

(b) Application

Whenever the term "servicemember" is used in this Act [sections 501 to 596 of this Appendix], such term shall be treated as including a reference to a legal representative of the servicemember.

§ 521. Protection of Servicemembers Against Default Judgments.

(a) Applicability of section

This section applies to any civil action or proceeding in which the defendant does not make an appearance.

(b) Affidavit requirement

(1) Plaintiff to file affidavit

In any action or proceeding covered by this section, the court, before entering judgment for the plaintiff, shall require the plaintiff to file with the court an affidavit—

(A) stating whether or not the defendant is in military service and showing necessary facts to support the affidavit; or

(B) if the plaintiff is unable to determine whether or not the defendant is in military service, stating that the plaintiff is unable to determine whether or not the defendant is in military service.

(2) Appointment of attorney to represent defendant in military service

If in an action covered by this section it appears that the defendant is in military service, the court may not enter a judgment until after the court appoints an attorney to represent the defendant. If an attorney appointed under this section to represent a servicemember cannot locate the servicemember, actions by the attorney in the case shall not waive any defense of the servicemember or otherwise bind the servicemember.

(3) Defendant's military status not ascertained by affidavit

If based upon the affidavits filed in such an action, the court is unable to determine whether the defendant is in military service, the court, before entering judgment, may require the plaintiff to file a bond in an amount approved by the court. If the defendant is later found to be in military service, the bond shall be available to indemnify the defendant against any loss or damage the defendant may suffer by reason of any judgment for the plaintiff against the defendant, should the judgment be set aside in whole or in part. The bond shall remain in effect until expiration of the time for appeal and setting aside of a judgment under applicable Federal or State law or regulation or under any applicable ordinance of a political subdivision of a State. The court may issue such orders or enter such judgments as the court determines necessary to protect the rights of the defendant under this Act [sections 501 to 596 of this Appendix].

(4) Satisfaction of requirement for affidavit

The requirement for an affidavit under paragraph (1) may be satisfied by a statement, declaration, verification, or certificate, in writing, subscribed and certified or declared to be true under penalty of perjury.

(c) Penalty for making or using false affidavit

A person who makes or uses an affidavit permitted under subsection (b) (or a statement, declaration, verification, or certificate as authorized under subsection (b)(4)) knowing it to be false, shall be fined as provided in title 18, United States Code, or imprisoned for not more than one year, or both.

(d) Stay of proceedings

In an action covered by this section in which the defendant is in military service, the court shall grant a stay of proceedings for a minimum period of 90 days under this subsection upon application of counsel, or on the court's own motion, if the court determines that—

(1) there may be a defense to the action and a defense cannot be presented without the presence of the defendant; or

(2) after due diligence, counsel has been unable to contact the defendant or otherwise determine if a meritorious defense exists.

(e) Inapplicability of section 202 procedures

A stay of proceedings under subsection (d) shall not be controlled by procedures or requirements under section 202 [section 522 of this Appendix].

(f) Section 202 protection

If a servicemember who is a defendant in an action covered by this section receives actual notice of the action, the servicemember may request a stay of proceeding under section 202 [section 522 of this Appendix].

(g) Vacation or setting aside of default judgments

(1) Authority for court to vacate or set aside judgment

If a default judgment is entered in an action covered by this section against a servicemember during the servicemember's period of military service (or within 60 days after termination of or release from such military service), the court entering the judgment shall, upon application by or on behalf of the servicemember, reopen the judgment for the purpose of allowing the servicemember to defend the action if it appears that—

(A) the servicemember was materially affected by reason of that military service in making a defense to the action; and

(B) the servicemember has a meritorious or legal defense to the action or some part of it.

(2) Time for filing application

An application under this subsection must be filed not later than 90 days after the date of the termination of or release from military service.

(h) Protection of bona fide purchaser

If a court vacates, sets aside, or reverses a default judgment against a servicemember and the vacating, setting aside, or reversing is because of a provision of this Act [sections 501 to 596 of this Appendix], that action shall not impair a right or title acquired by a bona fide purchaser for value under the default judgment.

§ 522. Stay of Proceedings when Servicemember Has Notice.

(a) Applicability of section

This section applies to any civil action or proceeding in which the defendant at the time of filing an application under this section—

(1) is in military service or is within 90 days after termination of or release from military service; and

(2) has received notice of the action or proceeding.

(b) Stay of proceedings

(1) Authority for stay

At any stage before final judgment in a civil action or proceeding in which a servicemember described in subsection (a) is a party, the court may on its own motion and shall, upon application by the servicemember, stay the action for a period of not less than 90 days, if the conditions in paragraph (2) are met.

(2) Conditions for stay

An application for a stay under paragraph (1) shall include the following:

(A) A letter or other communication setting forth facts stating the manner in which current military duty requirements materially affect the servicemember's ability to appear and stating a date when the servicemember will be available to appear.

(B) A letter or other communication from the servicemember's commanding officer stating that the servicemember's current military duty prevents appearance and that military leave is not authorized for the servicemember at the time of the letter.

(c) Application not a waiver of defenses

An application for a stay under this section does not constitute an appearance for jurisdictional purposes and does not constitute a waiver of any substantive or procedural defense (including a defense relating to lack of personal jurisdiction).

(d) Additional stay

(1) Application

A servicemember who is granted a stay of a civil action or proceeding under subsection (b) may apply for an additional stay based on continuing material affect of military duty on the servicemember's ability to appear. Such an application may be made by the servicemember at the time of the initial application under subsection (b) or when it appears that the servicemember is unavailable to prosecute or defend the action. The same information required under subsection (b)(2) shall be included in an application under this subsection.

(2) Appointment of counsel when additional stay refused

If the court refuses to grant an additional stay of proceedings under paragraph (1), the court shall appoint counsel to represent the servicemember in the action or proceeding.

(e) Coordination with section 201 [section 521 of this Appendix]

A servicemember who applies for a stay under this section and is unsuccessful may not seek the protections afforded by section 201 [section 521 of this Appendix].

(f) Inapplicability to section 301 [section 531 of this Appendix]

The protections of this section do not apply to section 301 [section 531 of this Appendix].

§ 523. Fines and Penalties under Contracts.

(a) Prohibition of penalties

When an action for compliance with the terms of a contract is stayed pursuant to this Act [sections 501 to 596 of this Appendix], a penalty shall not accrue for failure to comply with the terms of the contract during the period of the stay.

(b) Reduction or waiver of fines or penalties

If a servicemember fails to perform an obligation arising under a contract and a penalty is incurred arising from that nonperformance, a court may reduce or waive the fine or penalty if—

(1) the servicemember was in military service at the time the fine or penalty was incurred; and

(2) the ability of the servicemember to perform the obligation was materially affected by such military service.

§ 524. Stay or Vacation of Execution of Judgments, Attachments, and Garnishments.

(a) Court action upon material affect determination

If a servicemember, in the opinion of the court, is materially affected by reason of military service in complying with a court judgment or order, the court may on its own motion and shall on application by the servicemember—

(1) stay the execution of any judgment or order entered against the servicemember; and

(2) vacate or stay an attachment or garnishment of property, money, or debts in the possession of the servicemember or a third party, whether before or after judgment.

(b) Applicability

This section applies to an action or proceeding commenced in a court against a servicemember before or during the period of the servicemember's military service or within 90 days after such service terminates.

§ 525. Duration and Term of Stays; Codefendants Not in Service.

(a) Period of stay

A stay of an action, proceeding, attachment, or execution made pursuant to the provisions of this Act [sections 501 to 596 of this Appendix] by a court may be ordered for the period of military service and 90 days thereafter, or for any part of that period. The court may set the terms and amounts for such installment payments as is considered reasonable by the court.

(b) Codefendants

If the servicemember is a codefendant with others who are not in military service and who are not entitled to the relief and protections provided under this Act [sections 501 to 596 of this Appendix], the plaintiff may proceed against those other defendants with the approval of the court.

(c) Inapplicability of section

This section does not apply to sections 202 and 701 [sections 522 and 591 of this Appendix].

§ 526. Statute of Limitations.

(a) Tolling of statutes of limitation during military service

The period of a servicemember's military service may not be included in computing any period limited by law, regulation, or order for the bringing of any action or proceeding in a court, or in any board, bureau, commission, department, or other agency of a State (or political subdivision of a State) or the United States by or against the servicemember or the servicemember's heirs, executors, administrators, or assigns.

(b) Redemption of real property

A period of military service may not be included in computing any period provided by law for the redemption of real property sold or forfeited to enforce an obligation, tax, or assessment.

(c) Inapplicability to internal revenue laws

This section does not apply to any period of limitation prescribed by or under the internal revenue laws of the United States.

§ 527. Maximum Rate of Interest on Debts Incurred Before Military Service.

(a) Interest rate limitation

(1) Limitation to 6 percent

An obligation or liability bearing interest at a rate in excess of 6 percent per year that is incurred by a servicemember, or the servicemember and the servicemember's spouse jointly, before the servicemember enters military service shall not bear interest at a rate in excess of 6 percent per year during the period of military service.

(2) Forgiveness of interest in excess of 6 percent

Interest at a rate in excess of 6 percent per year that would otherwise be incurred but for the prohibition in paragraph (1) is forgiven.

(3) Prevention of acceleration of principal

The amount of any periodic payment due from a servicemember under the terms of the instrument that created an obligation or liability covered by this section shall be reduced by the amount of the interest forgiven under paragraph (2) that is allocable to the period for which such payment is made.

(b) Implementation of limitation

(1) Written notice to creditor

In order for an obligation or liability of a servicemember to be subject to the interest rate limitation in subsection (a), the servicemember shall provide to the creditor written notice and a copy of the military orders calling the servicemember to military service and any orders further extending military service, not later than 180 days after the date of the servicemember's termination or release from military service.

(2) Limitation effective as of date of order to active duty

Upon receipt of written notice and a copy of orders calling a servicemember to military service, the creditor shall treat the debt in accordance with subsection (a), effective as of the date on which the servicemember is called to military service.

(c) Creditor protection

A court may grant a creditor relief from the limitations of this section if, in the opinion of the court, the ability of the servicemember to pay interest upon the obligation or liability at a rate in excess of 6 percent per year is not materially affected by reason of the servicemember's military service.

(d) Interest

As used in this section, the term "interest" includes service charges, renewal charges, fees, or any other charges (except bona fide insurance) with respect to an obligation or liability.

§ 581. Inappropriate Use of Act.

If a court determines, in any proceeding to enforce a civil right, that any interest, property, or contract has been transferred or acquired with the intent to delay the just enforcement of such right by taking advantage of this Act [sections 501 to 596 of this Appendix], the court shall enter such judgment or make such order as might lawfully be entered or made concerning such transfer or acquisition.

§ 582. Certificates of Service; Persons Reported Missing.

(a) Prima facie evidence

In any proceeding under this Act [sections 501 to 596 of this Appendix], a certificate signed by the Secretary concerned is prima facie evidence as to any of the following facts stated in the certificate:

(1) That a person named is, is not, has been, or has not been in military service.

(2) The time and the place the person entered military service.

(3) The person's residence at the time the person entered military service.

(4) The rank, branch, and unit of military service of the person upon entry.

(5) The inclusive dates of the person's military service.

(6) The monthly pay received by the person at the date of the certificate's issuance.

(7) The time and place of the person's termination of or release from military service, or the person's death during military service.

(b) Certificates

The Secretary concerned shall furnish a certificate under subsection (a) upon receipt of an application for such a certificate. A certificate appearing to be signed by the Secretary concerned is prima facie evidence of its contents and of the signer's authority to issue it.

(c) Treatment of servicemembers in missing status

A servicemember who has been reported missing is presumed to continue in service until accounted for. A requirement under this Act [sections 501 to 596 of this Appendix] that begins or ends with the death of a servicemember does not begin or end until the servicemember's death is reported to, or determined by, the Secretary concerned or by a court of competent jurisdiction.

§ 583. Interlocutory Orders.

An interlocutory order issued by a court under this Act [sections 501 to 596 of this Appendix] may be revoked, modified, or extended by that court upon its own motion or otherwise, upon notification to affected parties as required by the court.

§ 591. Anticipatory Relief.

(a) Application for relief

A servicemember may, during military service or within 180 days of termination of or release from military service, apply to a court for relief—

(1) from any obligation or liability incurred by the servicemember before the servicemember's military service; or

(2) from a tax or assessment falling due before or during the servicemember's military service.

(b) Tax liability or assessment

In a case covered by subsection (a), the court may, if the ability of the servicemember to comply with the terms of such obligation or liability or pay such tax or assessment has been materially affected by reason of military service, after appropriate notice and hearing, grant the following relief:

(1) Stay of enforcement of real estate contracts

(A) In the case of an obligation payable in installments under a contract for the purchase of real estate, or secured by a mortgage or other instrument in the nature of a mortgage upon real estate, the court may grant a stay of the enforcement of the obligation—

(i) during the servicemember's period of military service; and

(ii) from the date of termination of or release from military service, or from the date of application if made after termination of or release from military service.

(B) Any stay under this paragraph shall be—

(i) for a period equal to the remaining life of the installment contract or other instrument, plus a period of time equal to the period of military service of the servicemember, or any part of such combined period; and

(ii) subject to payment of the balance of the principal and accumulated interest due and unpaid at the date of termination or release from the applicant's military service or from the date of application in equal installments during the combined period at the rate of interest on the unpaid balance prescribed in the contract or other instrument evidencing the obligation, and subject to other terms as may be equitable.

(2) Stay of enforcement of other contracts

(A) In the case of any other obligation, liability, tax, or assessment, the court may grant a stay of enforcement—

(i) during the servicemember's military service; and

(ii) from the date of termination of or release from military service, or from the date of application if made after termination or release from military service.

(B) Any stay under this paragraph shall be—

(i) for a period of time equal to the period of the servicemember's military service or any part of such period; and

(ii) subject to payment of the balance of principal and accumulated interest due and unpaid at the date of termination or release from military service, or the date of application, in equal periodic installments during this extended period at the rate of interest as may be prescribed for this obligation, liability, tax, or assessment, if paid when due, and subject to other terms as may be equitable.

(c) Affect of stay on fine or penalty

When a court grants a stay under this section, a fine or penalty shall not accrue on the obligation, liability, tax, or assessment for the period of compliance with the terms and conditions of the stay.

§ 592. Power of Attorney.

(a) Automatic extension

A power of attorney of a servicemember shall be automatically extended for the period the servicemember is in a missing status (as defined in section 551(2) of title 37, United States Code) if the power of attorney—

(1) was duly executed by the servicemember—

(A) while in military service; or

(B) before entry into military service but after the servicemember—

(i) received a call or order to report for military service; or

(ii) was notified by an official of the Department of Defense that the person could receive a call or order to report for military service;

(2) designates the servicemember's spouse, parent, or other named relative as the servicemember's attorney in fact for certain, specified, or all purposes; and

(3) expires by its terms after the servicemember entered a missing status.

(b) Limitation on power of attorney extension

A power of attorney executed by a servicemember may not be extended under subsection (a) if the document by its terms clearly indicates that the power granted expires on the date specified even though the servicemember, after the date of execution of the document, enters a missing status.

§ 593. Professional Liability Protection.

(a) Applicability

This section applies to a servicemember who—

(1) after July 31, 1990, is ordered to active duty (other than for training) pursuant to sections 688, 12301(a), 12301(g), 12302, 12304, 12306, or 12307 of title 10, United States Code, or who is ordered to active duty under section 12301(d) of such title during a period when members are on active duty pursuant to any of the preceding sections; and

(2) immediately before receiving the order to active duty—

(A) was engaged in the furnishing of health-care or legal services or other services determined by the Secretary of Defense to be professional services; and

(B) had in effect a professional liability insurance policy that does not continue to cover claims filed with respect to the servicemember during the period of the servicemember's active duty unless the premiums are paid for such coverage for such period.

(b) Suspension of coverage

(1) Suspension

Coverage of a servicemember referred to in subsection (a) by a professional liability insurance policy shall be suspended by the insurance carrier in accordance with this subsection upon receipt of a written request from the servicemember by the insurance carrier.

(2) Premiums for suspended contracts

A professional liability insurance carrier—

(A) may not require that premiums be paid by or on behalf of a servicemember for any professional liability insurance coverage suspended pursuant to paragraph (1); and

(B) shall refund any amount paid for coverage for the period of such suspension or, upon the election of such servicemember, apply such amount for the payment of any premium becoming due upon the reinstatement of such coverage.

(3) Nonliability of carrier during suspension

A professional liability insurance carrier shall not be liable with respect to any claim that is based on professional conduct (including any failure to take any action in a professional capacity) of a servicemember that occurs during a period of suspension of that servicemember's professional liability insurance under this subsection.

(4) Certain claims considered to arise before suspension

For the purposes of paragraph (3), a claim based upon the failure of a professional to make adequate provision for a patient, client, or other person to receive professional services or other assistance during the period of the professional's active duty service shall be considered to be based on an action or failure to take action before the beginning of the period of the suspension of professional liability insurance under this subsection, except in a case in which professional services were provided after the date of the beginning of such period.

(c) Reinstatement of coverage

(1) Reinstatement required

Professional liability insurance coverage suspended in the case of any servicemember pursuant to subsection (b) shall be reinstated by the insurance carrier on the date on which that servicemember transmits to the insurance carrier a written request for reinstatement.

(2) Time and premium for reinstatement

The request of a servicemember for reinstatement shall be effective only if the servicemember transmits the request to the insurance carrier within 30 days after the date on which the servicemember is released from active duty. The insurance carrier shall notify the servicemember of the due date for payment of the premium of such insurance. Such premium shall be paid by the servicemember within 30 days after receipt of that notice.

(3) Period of reinstated coverage

The period for which professional liability insurance coverage shall be reinstated for a servicemember under this subsection may not be less than the balance of the period for which coverage would have continued under the insurance policy if the coverage had not been suspended.

(d) Increase in premium

(1) Limitation on premium increases

An insurance carrier may not increase the amount of the premium charged for professional liability insurance coverage of any servicemember for the minimum period of the reinstatement of such coverage required under subsection (c)(3) to an amount greater than the amount chargeable for such coverage for such period before the suspension.

(2) Exception

Paragraph (1) does not prevent an increase in premium to the extent of any general increase in the premiums charged by that carrier for the same professional liability coverage for persons similarly covered by such insurance during the period of the suspension.

(e) Continuation of coverage of unaffected persons

This section does not—

(1) require a suspension of professional liability insurance protection for any person who is not a person referred to in subsection (a) and who is covered by the same professional liability insurance as a person referred to in such subsection; or

(2) relieve any person of the obligation to pay premiums for the coverage not required to be suspended.

(f) Stay of civil or administrative actions

(1) Stay of actions

A civil or administrative action for damages on the basis of the alleged professional negligence or other professional liability of a servicemember whose professional liability insurance coverage has been suspended under subsection (b) shall be stayed until the end of the period of the suspension if—

(A) the action was commenced during the period of the suspension;

(B) the action is based on an act or omission that occurred before the date on which the suspension became effective; and

(C) the suspended professional liability insurance would, except for the suspension, on its face cover the alleged professional negligence or other professional liability negligence or other professional liability of the servicemember.

(2) Date of commencement of action

Whenever a civil or administrative action for damages is stayed under paragraph (1) in the case of any servicemember, the action shall have been deemed to have been filed on the date on which the professional liability insurance coverage of the servicemember is reinstated under subsection (c).

(g) Effect of suspension upon limitations period

In the case of a civil or administrative action for which a stay could have been granted under subsection (f) by reason of the suspension of professional liability insurance coverage of the defendant under this section, the period of the suspension of the coverage shall be excluded from the computation of any statutory period of limitation on the commencement of such action.

(h) Death during period of suspension

If a servicemember whose professional liability insurance coverage is suspended under subsection (b) dies during the period of the suspension—

(1) the requirement for the grant or continuance of a stay in any civil or administrative action against such servicemember under subsection (f)(1) shall terminate on the date of the death of such servicemember; and

(2) the carrier of the professional liability insurance so suspended shall be liable for any claim for damages for professional negligence or other professional liability of the deceased servicemember in the same manner and to the same extent as such carrier would be liable if the servicemember had died while covered by such insurance but before the claim was filed.

(i) Definitions

For purposes of this section:

(1) Active duty

The term "active duty" has the meaning given that term in section 101(d)(1) of title 10, United States Code.

(2) Profession

The term "profession" includes occupation.

(3) Professional

The term "professional" includes occupational.

General Index

Section numbers refer to the Texas Family Code unless otherwise noted.

> ***Editors' Note:*** *If you cannot find a subject covered in the index, please notify John J. Sampson at jsampson@mail.law.utexas.edu, or Harry L. Tindall at htindall@tindallfoster.com. Our goal is to provide a user-friendly index. For example, a lawyer called to observe that the "emancipation" statutes were not listed in the index. The addition of that term to the index with a cross reference to ch. 42, Removal of Disabilities of Minority, cured the problem.*

†